A

DICTIONARY OF LAW,

CONSISTING OF

JUDICIAL DEFINITIONS AND EXPLANATIONS

OF

WORDS, PHRASES, AND MAXIMS,

AND AN

EXPOSITION OF THE PRINCIPLES OF LAW:

COMPRISING A

DICTIONARY AND COMPENDIUM OF AMERICAN
AND ENGLISH URISPRUDENCE.

BY

WILLIAM C. ANDERSON,

OF THE PENNSYLVANIA BAR.

CHICAGO:

T. H. FLOOD AND COMPANY,

LAW PUBLISHERS.

1889.

INTRODUCTION.

The title Dictionary of Law has been chosen for this book because it seeks to define and otherwise explain law terms and expressions, to show the application of legal principles, and to present judicial interpretations of common words and phrases.

Similar productions, heretofore issued, are marked, in the opinion of the writer, by the following imperfections:

1. Absence of judicial matter, especially of judicial definitions or interpretations and reasoning; also, dearth of non-technical terms as cross-references.

2. Neglect or omission of important subjects, and needless repetition of matter under different heads.

3. Inattention to pronunciation, and lack of discrimination in selecting words for etymological explanation.

4. Omission of the names of the parties to important cases, and of the dates when decisions were rendered.

5. The presence of thousands of obsolete Anglo-Saxon, Old English, Scotch, Spanish, French, and civil law words and phrases, antiquated Norman and Latin expressions, and matters of a purely non-legal character,— a mass of material of no use to student or practitioner, of interest to the legal antiquarian alone.

In the preparation of this work care has been taken not to follow in the "beaten path" of law dictionaries. Under the following heads its plan is set forth:

1. The different spellings of terms are noted, the preferred spelling being placed first, with comment where pertinent.

2. The correct pronunciation of words often mispronounced is indicated, according to Webster's Dictionary.

3. As to etymology, while the aim has been to discriminate between terms whose origin is of no importance or interest and such as contain in their ancient form somewhat of their present signification, the supposed origin of all technical terms is stated.

4. The definitions are printed in the larger type, except where incorporated in a paragraph along with explanatory matter.

The endeavor has been to find definitions framed by the courts, the highest tribunals of this country receiving the preference. Some by text-writers also are given. Where a court explains rather than defines a term (as, in a charge to a jury), such explanation has generally been condensed. Definitions thought to be too narrow or too broad in statement have been modified with a view to greater fullness and clearness.

But all changes in the phraseology of definitions are indicated. A single bracket [denotes that a slight or immaterial change has been made; a double bracket [ ] that the substance only is given — that the definition is recast, or that a definition is constructed out of the language employed by the authority cited, or is formed upon partial or incomplete definitions found in the accompanying citations.

The absence of a bracket denotes that no change has been made in the language of the court. This last class of definitions makes up the body of the DICTIONARY portion of the book, and constitutes one of the special features mentioned — its large number of *judicially* framed definitions.

The word "whence," which will be noticed in the text immediately after some definitions, does not necessarily mean that the word or words which follow it are derived from the title word, but that they are derivatives from the same root word,— the latter being sometimes included in the appended list. This is done to avoid repetitions under different forms of the same word.

Expressions having the same initial word are placed under that word, arranged alphabetically with reference to the second word. Thus, *A mensa* will be found under A, and not between Amends and Amerce.

For typographical reasons, general cross-references have been advanced to the beginning of a few articles, and some common words, not originally intended for definition, have been defined.

5. Synonyms are treated under the leading word of the group. For positives and negatives — words beginning with *dis-*, *il-*, *in-*, *non-*, *re-*, *un-*, reference should be had to the simple word, except where the negative itself is the word most used. Examples, Dishonor, Insolvency, and Insanity.

6. The Latin and Norman-French law terms now in use have been collected, and such maxims and phrases as student and practitioner alike meet in the books they consult. The selection also includes important terms found in treatises on Roman law, mention of the primitive meaning of terms current under new applications, and explanation of a few terms in ancient law long obsolete but occasionally referred to as of historical interest.

Each Latin maxim or phrase is entered, in whole or in part, as a title or subtitle under its initial word; but if that word is unimportant, like the particles *a*, *ab*, *con*, *de*, *in*, *nam*, *pro*, *qui*, *quod*, *ut*, or is an adjective, a cross-reference is made from such word to the principal word, under which the expression is explained at length.

7. Having given the origin of a term, and the senses in which it is used, where the importance of the subject warrants it, the value of the idea or the extent of its application in the affairs of society is stated — by comment, more or less extended, or by reference to a related topic under which such information may be found. These remarks, which are printed in the smaller type and compose the COMMENTARY portion of the work, consist, in brief, of matters pertaining, it is believed, to every recognized branch of the law, and set forth the "reasoning of the law" itself.

For English common law antedating the adoption of the Constitution, I have relied chiefly upon the commentaries of Blackstone, making my own abridgment of that invaluable treatise, and citing it in all cases. Many statements of principles have been taken from the commentaries and decisions of Chancellor Kent, more from the works and decisions of Judge Story, and not a few paragraphs from other and later standard writers.

Under appropriate heads have been embodied the various provisions of the Constitution of the United States, and many from the constitutions of the States. When the former is given *verbatim* its original orthography and punctuation have been restored.

Quotations are made from English statutes followed in this country.

Still more frequently acts of Congress, from the earliest to the latest date, have been drawn upon — very important recent ones being reprinted entire; also, enactments in the several States, including sections from codes.

There are also presented decisions of the courts on the foregoing subjects, explanatory of questions of general and sometimes of local importance, and, for the most part, of permanent interest. To this end, all the decisions of the United States Supreme Court have been read, and thousands of the decisions rendered in the States — indeed, entire series of State reports.

8. In the cross-references a subject may be found to be not the title word, but its shortest form.

English words are referred to foreign words, and *vice versa*, wherever there is likeness or sameness of sense between them, and a perusal of both will contribute to an understanding of the general subject.

Sub-titles referred to under the title word are italicised.

Having treated each word where it will be soonest comprehended in its own meaning or meanings and as related to other subjects, references to it, under heads where it might be incidentally treated, are entered.

Specific terms are *fully* defined only under the generic head with which they are associated. Thus under "Express" the reader will not find "express contract:" he will there find "express" explained, generically and specifically, but it is only under "Contract" that he will learn anything substantial about "express contract." Not so, with local or isolated expressions, such as "Baby Act," and "Lynch Law."

9. In the selection of cases, preference is given, upon all subjects, to the decisions of the Supreme Court and the circuit courts of the United States, and, next, to those of the highest courts of the States.

Decisions reviewing or collecting earlier cases have also been preferred.

In a very few instances the dates of decisions are not given because not known. In collections of leading cases, where the annotations are the important matter, the year of the title case may not be stated.

From 108 to 128 United States Supreme Court Reports (October, 1882, to January, 1889), the year when an opinion was rendered is given; prior to 108 U. S., the reporters noted only the year of the term to which the writ of error or the appeal was taken.

Cases without the names of the parties are such as follow a text-book quoted; or they occur where it was not thought necessary to make copious reference to definitions on common technical terms; or where a later quotes an earlier authority already given in full; or they are so added in order not to take up space on a point already supported by cases cited at length; or they establish a principle universally accepted; or they concern incidental or illustrative matters; or they show where a term or maxim was applied. Cited to a common word, they will sometimes be found to contain that word without suggestion as to its general meaning or use.

The word "cases," printed at the end of a citation, imports that the court examined previous decisions which will be found discussed or referred to in the decision itself. This device, while saving space, directs the reader to *other cases* on the same subject.

The abbreviation *id.* refers to another volume in the same set or series; *ib.*, to the volume last mentioned. Unless otherwise indicated, *new series* is meant, where there is also an "old series." "R." stands for Railroad or Railway. "Constitution" means Constitution of the United States; while "constitution" refers to the similar instrument belonging to a particular State. "Supreme Court" means the Supreme Court of the United States; in a few instances, for purposes of distinction, the names of the other Federal courts begin with capital letters. "State" refers to one of the United States; "state" to a nation; "R. S." to the Revised Statutes of the United States; "Government" to the National government.

The first descriptive word in the names of corporations has been sought for. Some reports furnish nothing more than "Insurance Co." or "Railroad Co."

Unless otherwise noted, the original or star pages are intended.

10. I have received valuable information from other dictionaries. For original extracts taken from them due credit has been given. Definitions from these books, adopted by the courts, are noted. Where a court has approved a definition of a common word as found in a vernacular dictionary, or in a cyclopædia, the title of such work is placed after the particular case, separated from it by a colon; so, also, with matter from other sources.

11. References are made to useful articles in the law periodicals, especially to such as discuss cases, and to a few articles in lay publications.

12. A knowledge of the chief events in the lives of Sir William Blackstone, James Kent, and Joseph Story, the most widely read of law-writers,— in particular, the circumstances under which their works were composed, with information as to different editions,— being useful to all students of the law, and those works having been largely quoted throughout this book — brief biographies are inserted under the names of those distinguished jurists.

Hoping that the volume will in some degree lighten the labors of student and practitioner, it is submitted to the kindly consideration of the profession.

PITTSBURGH, PA., March 1, 1889.   W. C. ANDERSON.

DICTIONARY OF LAW.

A.

A, or **a,** the first letter of the alphabet, is used in legal, legislative, and judicial writings as a numerical character, as an abbreviation, and as a word:

1. The capital serves for marking — (1) the first division, chapter, or other large portion of a legal treatise or digest; (2) the first appendix in a report: of cases, or of a commission or committee; (3) the first schedule to a constitution or a statute; (4) the first series of an issue of corporate or governmental bonds; (5) the first distinct portion of any other tabulated statement.

The small letter designates — (1) in old law-books, the first page of a leaf or folio (*b* designating the second page); (2) in modern works, the first paragraph of new matter inserted in the body of a volume: as, of a new section printed between older sections; (3) the first foot-note to a page in the first edition of a book: in enlarged editions, especially those prepared by annotators, a note subjoined to such foot-note is designated as a^1, or $(a)^1$, a^2, etc.

The other letters, capital and small (in the language of printers, upper case and lower case), are used in the same manner.

2. Indicates the first of a number of documents or other proofs: as, Exhibit "A," or "A 1," "A 2," etc.

The other letters, in their order, are similarly employed. See further EXHIBIT, 2.

In the old States, volumes containing recorded instruments were formerly, and perhaps are still, designated by letters, or by letters and numbers: as, A, or A 1; B, or B 1; A 2, B 2; AA, BB. To avoid errors and confusion in copying references, some of the letters, as J, K, N, U, V, Y, were not used.[1]

3. As an abbreviation, usually denotes American, *anno*, appeal, article, assistant, associate, attorney.

Has been used for *al* in the expression *et al.*[1] See ALIUS.

Formerly stood for *adversus* (*versus*); as, Cockle *a.* Underwood.[2]

Among the Puritans, a convicted adultress wore an A upon the front of her dress, in Plymouth colony by law of 1658, or earlier, and in Vermont as late as 1785.

A. D. *Anno Domini*, in the year of our Lord. See YEAR.

A. G. Attorney-general.

A. J. Assistant, or associate, judge or justice. *A. JJ.* Associate judges or justices. *A. L. J.* Associate law judge or justice. See JUDGE.

A. R. *Anno regni*, in the year of the reign.

A 1. Of the highest class.

Originated with underwriters in rating vessels: the A denoted that the hull of a particular ship was well built and seaworthy for a voyage of any length; the 1 the efficient state of her tackle, sails, apparel, and other appurtenances. B, C, and other letters, indicated lower conditions of seaworthiness; 2, 3, and perhaps other numerals, inferior or insufficient appurtenances.[3]

4. The indefinite article *a* or *an*.

Often used in the sense of *any*, and then applies to more than one individual object.[4]

---

in the office of the recorder of deeds for Philadelphia county, Pa., it continued from 1683 to 1799; in the county court of Augusta, Va., from 1745 to 1879; in the office of recorder of deeds for Allegheny county, Pa., from 1788 to 1849. In the last county there is a deed book N 5, or volume 86. In the department of internal affairs at Harrisburg, Pa., the patent books (early numbers of which contain the grants from William Penn) are designated as A 1 to 20, AA 1 to 16, P 1 to 65, H 1 to 74; and there is also in use a second series of account books designated as AA, BB, etc., to HH 4, which last is in use in 1888.

[1] 58 N. H. 3, 4, 6, 7, *et seq.*

[2] 1 Abb. Pr. R. o. s. 1; *id.*, vols. I–XIX.

[3] See Webster's Dict., p. 1782; Chambers' Ency., tit. A.

[4] Nat. Union Bank *v.* Copeland, 141 Mass. 266 (1886).

---

[1] In the superior court of Baltimore city, Md., this practice, which was begun in 1651, continued to 1797;

Where directors are empowered to issue a note or accept a bill of exchange, they may give several notes or bills, equal to the sum specified.[1] See ANY; THE.

5. The Latin preposition: from, away from, by, in, on. Compare AB.

A fortiori. With stronger (reason); with more right; much more.

A private person, and a *fortiori* a peace-officer, present when a felony is committed, is bound to arrest the felon.[2]

A *multo fortiori*. By far the stronger — reason, right, equity.[3, 4]

A gratia. Out of favor; from mere indulgence, and not of right. See GRACE.

A latere. By the side: collaterally.

Said of succession to property; but now of rare occurrence.

A mensa et thoro (*toro*). From table and bed: from bed and board. **A vinculo matrimonii.** From the bond of matrimony.

The former describes a "partial" divorce: separation of the parties by law, with all rights preserved; the latter, a "total" divorce: complete dissolution of the marriage relation with all incidental rights. See further DIVORCE.

A nativitate. From birth, from infancy.

The legal settlement of an idiot a *nativitate* is that of his father.[5]

A posteriori. From what comes after — the effect. **A priori.** From what goes before — the cause.

Reasoning from an effect back to its supposed cause is described as a *posteriori;* reasoning or argument from an assumed cause to the result it may or must produce is termed a *priori*.[4]

A prendre. F. See PROFIT, A prendre.

A quo. From which.

As, the court a *quo* a cause has been removed, by an appeal or a writ of error. Correlative *ad quem*, to which. See further QUI, QUO.

A retro. In arrear, *q. v.*

A sociis. From its associates; from its surroundings; from the context. See further NOSCITUR.

A teneris annis. From tender years; by reason of youth. See NEGLIGENCE.

A verbis legis. See LEX, A verbis, etc.

---

[1] Thompson *v.* Wesleyan Association, 65 E. C. L. 849 (1849). See also Sharff *v.* Commonwealth, 2 Binn. *516, 519 (1810).

[2] 4 Bl. Com. 292.

[3] 100 U. S. 633.

[4] Although strictly terms in logic, these expressions are so common in law language that they may be considered *quasi* legal.

[5] Shippen *v.* Gaines, 17 Pa. 42 (1851).

A vinculo. See *A mensa, etc.*

AB. L. From.

Takes the place of a before a vowel sound. See A, 5; ABS.

Ab assuetis. See INJURIA, Ab assuetis.

Ab inconvenienti. From hardship, *q. v.*

Ab initio. From the beginning; from inception.

A contract is said to be illegal, a writ, an action, or a service, irregular or void, *ab initio*. See TRESPASS, Ab initio.

Ab intestato. From an intestate (owner).

Ab invito. By one unwilling: unwillingly. See INVITUS.

Ab irato. By one in anger — displeased.

A gift, bequest or devise, adverse to the interest of any heir is sometimes said to be made *ab irato*.

ABANDON.[1] To relinquish, surrender, disclaim, desert, forsake, give up wholly. Whence abandonment, non-abandonment, and (though rare) abandoner, abandonee.

As, to abandon property, a relation, a proceeding — any species of right.

"Abandon" includes the intention and the external act by which it is carried into effect.[2]

To constitute an abandonment of a right, there must be an unequivocal and decisive act of the party showing a determination not to have the benefit designed.[3] See ESTOPPEL.

For example, a homestead is abandoned by an act which shows an intention wholly to relinquish it; not by temporary absence.[4]

A statute may require that this intention be proven by a declaration duly executed and recorded.[5]

There is a difference between "abandoning" and "surrendering" a right or thing; between giving it up because regarded as useless, and assigning or transferring it to another as valuable. When one surrenders a thing by solemn agreement in writing, he certainly does not "abandon" it in the sense in which that word is generally understood.[6]

1. **Property.** An object of property remains the owner's till such time as he does some act which shows an intention to abandon it; then it becomes *publici juris* once

---

[1] F. *a*, to; *ban-*, to proscribe, give up. See BAN.

[2] Livermore *v.* White, 74 Me. 455 (1883), Appleton, C. J.

[3] [Dawson *v.* Daniel, 2 Flip. 309 (1878), Hammond, J.

[4] Hurt *v.* Hollingsworth, 100 U. S. 104 (1879); 29 Minn. 20.

[5] Tipton *v.* Martin, 71 Cal. 328 (1886); Cal. Civ. Code, §§ 1243-44.

[6] [Hagan *v.* Gaskill, 42 N. J. E. 217 (1886), Bird, V. C.

more, liable to appropriation by the next occupant.[1]

"If a man be dissatisfied with his immovable estate and abandon it, immediately he departs from it corporally, with the intention that it shall no longer be his; and it will become the property of him who first enters thereon."[2] See DERELICTION, 2.

Property is abandoned when it is thrown away, or its possession is voluntarily forsaken by the owner,— in which case it will become the property of the first occupant; or, when it is voluntarily lost or left without the hope or expectation of again acquiring it,— then it becomes the property of the finder, subject to the superior claim of the owner; except that in salvage cases, by the admiralty law, the finder may hold possession until he is paid his compensation or till the property is submitted to legal jurisdiction for ascertainment of the compensation.[3] See FIND, 1.

To an abandonment of "land" there must be a concurrence of the act of leaving the premises vacant, so that they may be appropriated by the next comer, with an intention of not returning.[4] See VACANT.

No rule of law, applicable to all cases, can be laid down, as to what change of a "station" will constitute an abandonment or relocation. Every relocation involves, in one sense, an abandonment of the old station.[5]

The abandonment of an "easement" imports a non-user of it. All acts of enjoyment must have totally ceased for the same length of time that was necessary to create the original presumption.[6] See EASEMENT.

A person may abandon an "invention" in two senses: (1) When he gives up his idea, abandons it in the popular sense, relinquishes the intention of perfecting it, so that another person may take up the same thing and become the original and first inventor; (2) when, having made an invention, he allows the public to use it without objection.[7] See PATENT, 2.

In the law of marine insurance, abandonment is the act of cession, by which in cases where the loss or destruction of the property, though not absolute, is highly imminent, or its recovery is too expensive to be worth the attempt, the assured, on condition of receiving at once the whole amount of the insurance, relinquishes to the underwriters all his property and interest in the thing insured, as far as it is covered by the policy, with all the claims that may ensue from its ownership, and all profits that may arise from its recovery.[1]

The yielding up or surrendering to the insurer by the insured of his interest in the property.[2]

Usually made by the owner of the property when informed of the peril or loss. He gives the insurer notice of the abandonment, the effect of which is to place the insurer in his position to the extent of the interest insured.[2]

To be made within reasonable time; which is a question of fact and of law. No particular form is necessary, nor need it be in writing; but it should be explicit, and not left to be inferred from equivocal acts. The insured must yield up all his interest in the subject. Regularly made, operates as a transfer of the property to the underwriter.[3]

"The right of abandonment does not depend upon the certainty, but on the high probability, of a total loss, either of the property or of the voyage, or both. The insured is to act, not upon certainties, but upon probabilities, and if the facts present a case of extreme hazard, and of probable expense exceeding half the value of the ship, the insured may abandon; though it should happen that she was afterward recovered at less expense." If the abandonment, when made, is good, the rights of the parties are definitely fixed, and do not become changed by subsequent events; if not good, subsequent circumstances will not impart validity to it.[4]

Where the interest insured is that of a part owner, or when the entire owner insures some definite part, the abandonment is limited to a cession of the insured interest; but, when the insurance reaches every part of the ownership indiscriminately, the abandonment extends to the entire property, though its value exceeds the amount of the insurance. For the protection of the underwriter, the abandonment relates back to the date of the loss.[5] See DERELICTION, 3; Loss, 2.

The doctrine is not applicable to fire insurance.[6]

---

[1] [1 Bl. Com. 9-10.

[2] Partidas, 3, Tit. 4, law 50; Sideck v. Duran, 67 Tex. 262 (1887), cases.

[3] Eads v. Brazelton, 22 Ark. 509 (1861), cases, Fairchild, J.

[4] Judson v. Malloy, 40 Cal. 810 (1870), Rhodes, C. J.

[5] Attorney-General v. Eastern R. Co., 137 Mass. 48 (1884).

See also 64 Ill. 238; 49 N. Y. 346; 2 Johns. 98; 9 Pa. 273; 21 W. Va. 286; 40 Am. Dec. 464, n.; 2 Washb. Real Prop. 370.

[6] Corning v. Gould, 16 Wend. 535-36 (1837), cases; 3 Mas. 275.

[7] [American, &c. Dressing Machine Co. v. American Tool Co., 4 Fish. P. C. 299 (1870). And see Planing-Machine Co. v. Keith, 101 U. S. 485 (1879); Bump, Patents, 246.

[1] 2 Arnould, Mar. Ins. 912.

[2] [Merchants', &c. Mar. Ins. Co. v. Duffield, 2 Handy, 127 (Ohio, 1855).

[3] Chesapeake Ins. Co. v. Stark, 6 Cranch, C. C. 272 (1810), Marshall, C. J.; Patapsco Ins. Co. v. Southgate, 5 Pet. 621 (1831); The City of Norwich, 118 U. S. 492, 506 (1886); 4 Pet. 144; 4 B. Mon. 544; 6 Ohio St. 203; 12 Mo. Ap. 250-51; 32 E. C. L. 110-20; 2 Arn. Mar. Ins. 912-942; 2 Pars. Mar. Ins. 111-200.

[4] Bradlie v. Maryland Ins. Co., 12 Pet. 397 (1838), Story, J., quoting 3 Kent, 321; Marshall v. Delaware Ins. Co., 4 Cranch, 206 (1808). Same cases approved, Orient Mut. Ins. Co. v. Adams, 123 U. S. 67 (1887), Harlan, J.

[5] The Manitoba, 30 F. R. 129 (1887).

[6] May, Ins. § 421a.

2. **Relation or Duty.** The relation of husband and wife, of parent and child, or of master and servant.

(1) The act of a husband in voluntarily leaving his wife with an intention to forsake her entirely, — never to return to her, and never to resume his marital duties toward her or to claim his marital rights.[1]

Such neglect as either leaves the wife destitute of the common necessaries of life, or would leave her destitute but for the charity of others.[2]

Exists when a man fails to supply his wife with such necessaries and comforts of life as are within his reach, and by cruelty compels her to quit him and seek shelter and protection elsewhere.[3] See further CAUSE, 1 (2), Reasonable; DESERTION, 1; DIVORCE.

(2) The act of a parent in exposing an infant of tender years (usually under seven) in any place, with intent wholly to desert it.[4] See DISPOSE, 2.

(3) For an apprentice, a sailor, or a soldier, to quit his service, intending not to return to it. See DESERTION, 2, 3.

3. **Of Legal Proceedings.** *Voluntary*, when of the plaintiff's own accord; *involuntary*, when the defendant compels him either to abandon or to continue the action. See NONSUIT; RETRAXIT.

ABATE.[5] To quash, beat down, destroy.[6]

"Abating" is used in three senses. The first and primitive sense is that of beating down a nuisance; the second, that of abating a writ or action — its overthrow or defeat by some fatal exception to it; in the third denotes that the rightful possession or freehold of an heir or devisee is overthrown by the rude intervention of a stranger.[7]

In such expressions as to abate a demand, duties, rents, taxes, the word has no distinctly technical meaning. Compare REBATE.

Abater; abator. He who actually removes a nuisance; also, he who abates a freehold. See 1, *infra*.

Abatement. Demolition, destruction, diminution, removal, suspension.

In equity practice, a suspension of proceedings in a suit from want of parties capable of proceeding therein.[1]

1. **Abatement of a freehold; of an estate.** Where a person dies seized of an inheritance, and, before the heir or devisee enters, a stranger, who has no right, makes entry and gets possession of the freehold.[2] Compare AMOTION, 1.

2. **Abatement of a legacy.** The reduction of a legacy, in case of insufficiency of assets to pay all debts and other legacies.

First, general legacies, and then specific legacies, abate proportionately.

The rule is that where bequests are made in the form of a general legacy, and are pure bounty, and there is no expression in or inference to be drawn from the will manifesting an intention to give them priority, in case of a deficiency of funds to pay them in full, they abate ratably: on the principle that equality is equity.[3] See LEGACY.

3. **Abatement of a nuisance.** The removal of a nuisance.

Whatever unlawfully annoys or doeth damage to another may be abated, *i. e.*, taken away or removed by the party aggrieved thereby, he committing no riot.[4]

An injunction may prevent, and a verdict for damages may punish, but neither will "abate" a nuisance.[5] See further NUISANCE.

4. **Abatement of a writ.** Quashing or setting it aside on account of some fatal defect in it.[6]

A plea in abatement is one mode. Sometimes it is the duty of the court to abate a writ *ex officio*. Where the writ is a nullity, so that judgment thereon would be incurably erroneous, it is *de facto* abated.[7]

Plea in abatement. Matter of defense which defeats an action for the present, because of a defect in the writ or declaration.[8]

Such plea is: (1) *of the writ* — for an irregularity, defect, or informality, in its terms, form, issue, service or return, or for want of jurisdiction in the court; (2) *to the action* — as misconceived, or because the right has not yet accrued, or because another action is pending;[1] (3) *to the declaration*, on account of — (a)

---

[1] [Moore v. Stevenson, 27 Conn. 25 (1858), Ellsworth, J. A *feme-sole* trader law.

[2] [Washburn v. Washburn, 9 Cal. 476 (1858), Field, J. A divorce case.

[3] Levering v. Levering, 16 Md. 219 (1860), Bartol, J. A divorce case.

[4] See State v. Davis, 70 Mo. 468 (1869); 4 Bl. Com. 198.

[5] F. *abattre*: L. *ab-batuere*, to beat down, prostrate.

[6] Case v. Humphrey, 6 Conn. 140 (1826).

[7] [3 Bl. Com. 168.

[1] See Story, Eq. Pl. §§ 20, n, 354.

[2] 3 Bl. Com. 168.

[3] Titus v. Titus, 26 N. J. E. 114, 117-19 (1875), cases, Runyon, Ch.; Brown v. Brown, 79 Va. 650 (1884), cases.

[4] [3 Bl. Com. 5, 168.

[5] Ruff v. Phillips, 50 Ga. 132 (1873).

[6] [3 Bl. Com. 168, 302.]

[7] Case v. Humphrey, 6 Conn. 140 (1826).

[8] [3 Bl. Com. 302. See also Steph. Plead. 47; Gould Plead. 235.

the misnomer of a party; (b) the disability of a party:[2] alienage, infancy, coverture, lunacy, imprisonment, non-existence of a corporation; (c) a privilege (q. v.) in the defendant; (d) non-joinder or mis-joinder of parties; (e) a departure as between the writ and the declaration; (f) a variance between the writ and the instrument sued upon.

If the action be such as survives (q. v.), the representative of a deceased party may be substituted.[3]

Pleadable to an indictment, but chiefly for misnomer.[2][1]

Because they are dilatory, pleas in abatement are not favored. Each plea must give a better writ, i. e., show how the writ may be amended. Each must also precede a plea to the merits,[2][1] and a plea in bar;[4] and be verified by affidavit.

Judgment upon a plea is, for the plaintiff — respondeat ouster, that the defendant answer anew; for the defendant — quod billa cassetur, that the writ be made void or abated.[5]

See AMENDMENT, 1; QUASH; PLEA; PLEADING; REVIVE, 1. Compare BAR, 3, Plea in.

ABBREVIATIONS.
A judge may, without proof, determine the meaning of the customary abbreviations of Christian names,[6] names of offices,[7] names of places,[8] and common words.[9] See AMBIGUITY; NAME, 1.

See, in this book, particular words, and the collections of abbreviations at the beginning of each letter.

In declaring upon an instrument containing abbreviated terms, extrinsic averments may be used to make them intelligible; and evidence of the sense in which the parties were in the habit of using the abbreviations, and of their conventional meaning, is admissible, but not to show the intention of one party in using them.[10]

Generally, in indictments, common words are to be used as descriptive of the matter. Abbreviations of terms employed by men of science or in the arts will not answer, without full explanation of their meaning in common language. The use of A. D., year of our Lord, because of its universality, constitutes an exception. Arabic figures and Roman letters have also become indicative of numbers as fully as words written out could be. Their general use makes them known to all men. But unexplained initials, as, for example, initials referring to public land surveys, may not be employed in an indictment.[1]

ABDUCTION.[2]
Taking away a wife, child, or ward, by fraud and persuasion, or open violence.[3]

In private or civil law, the act of taking away a man's wife by violence or persuasion.[4]

In criminal law, the act of taking away or detaining a woman either against her own will, or, in the case of a minor, against the will of her parents or other person having the lawful charge of her.[5]

Any unlawful seizure or detention of a female.[6]

The taking may be accomplished by solicitations or inducements, as well as by force. This, at least, is the intention of the California statute which punishes abductions for purposes of prostitution.[7] In New York, also, it must be proved that there was persuasive inducement on the part of the accused, for the purposes of prostitution; mere permission or allowance to follow such a life is not enough. And proof must be given, aside from the testimony of the alleged abducted female, of the taking and the specific intent.[8]

Harboring against the will is abduction. Not, protection against abuse, nor shelter given after the parent or guardian has relinquished the right of control. Every abduction includes a false imprisonment. The remedies are trespass vi et armis for damages, and indictment for the assault and battery.[9] See KIDNAPING; SERVITUDE, 1.

ABET.[10]
To aid, encourage, promote the commission of an offense; to incite a person to commit a crime. Whence abettor, abetment. See ACCESSARY; AID, 1.

If men who are present at a quarrel encourage a battery, they thereby assume the consequences of the act, equally with the party who does the beating; often, indeed, they are more culpable. It is not necessary that encouragement should consist of appeals. It is enough that they sanction what is being done, and

---

[1] Cook v. Burnley, 11 Wall. 668 (1867).

[2] Society for Propagation of the Gospel v. Town of Pawlet, 4 Pet. 501 (1830).

[3] 4 Bl. Com. 334.

[4] Baltimore, &c. R. Co. v. Harris, 12 Wall. 84 (1870); Pointer v. State, 89 Ind. 257 (1883).

[5] 3 Bl. Com. 302-3. See generally Gould, Plead. 235-78; Stephen, Plead. 47-51.

[6] Gordon's Lessee v. Holiday, 1 Wash. 289 (1805); Weaver v. McElhenon, 13 Mo. 90 (1850); Stephen v. State, 11 Ga. 241 (1852).

[7] Moseley's " Adm'r " v. Mastin, 37 Ala. 221 (1861).

[8] Ellis v. Park, 8 Tex. 205 (1852); Russell v. Martin, 15 id. 238 (1855).

[9] Jaqua v. Witham, &c. Co., 106 Ind. 547-48 (1886); Dana v. Fiedler, 12 N. Y. 40, 46 (1854); 1 Greenl. Ev. § 282; 2 Whart. Ev. § 1003; Best, Ev. 232, 262.

[10] Jaqua v. Witham, &c. Co., 106 Ind. 547-48 (1886), cases; Robinson v. Kanawha Bank, 44 Ohio St. 441 (1886).

[1] United States v. Reichert, 32 F. R. 147 (1887), Field, J. See Bish. Contr. § 377

[2] L. ab-ducere, to lead away.

[3] See 3 Bl. Com. 139; Carpenter v. People, 8 Barb. 606 (1850); State v. George, 93 N. C. 570 (1885).

[4] 3 Stephen, Com. 437.

[5] [Sweet's Law Dict.

[6] See 1 Russell, Crimes, 9 Am. ed., 940; 5 Strob. (S. Car.) 1.

[7] People v. Marshall, 59 Cal. 388 (1881).

[8] People v. Plath, 100 N. Y. 590 (1885), cases, Ruger, C. J.; Penal Code, § 282; Laws 1884, c. 46, § 2; amended, Laws 1886, c. 31.

[9] 3 Bl. Com. 139-41. As to place, see 6 Cr. L. M. 357-60 (1884), cases.

[10] F. a-beter, to bait, lure on.

manifest this by demonstrations of resistance to any who might desire to interfere to prevent it; or by words, gestures or acts, indicating approval.[1]

ABEYANCE.[2] In expectation, remembrance, and contemplation of law; in suspense.[3]

Subsisting in contemplation of law.[4]

In abeyance: undetermined.

Said of a fee or a freehold when there is no person *in esse* in whom it can vest and abide: though the law considers it as always potentially existing, and ready to vest when a proper owner appears.[5]

Thus, in a grant to A for life and then to the heirs of B, the fee is not in A or B, nor can it vest in the "heirs" of B till after his death: it therefore remains in waiting or abeyance, during the life of B.[5]

It is a maxim of the common law that a fee cannot be in abeyance. The maxim rests upon reasons that have now no existence, and it is not now of universal application. Even where it still applies, being a common-law maxim, it must yield to a statutory provision inconsistent with it — as, the Confiscation Act of 1862.[6]

The franchise of a corporation may be in abeyance;[7] so may a grant of land to a charity.[8] In this category, also, are all property rights of a bankrupt until final adjudication;[9] and, a capture until a prize court has passed upon it.[10]

ABIDE. To await; as, in saying that costs abide the event of the suit.

Abide by. To conform to, obey.

"To abide by an award" is to stand by the determination of the arbitrators, and take the consequences of the award; to await the award without revoking the submission; not, necessarily, to acquiesce in, or not to dispute the award.[11]

The language employed in arbitration bonds, "to abide by the award," is to prevent the revocation or breaking of the contract of submission, rather than to apply to the actual finding of the arbitrators.[12]

In a bond "to appear and abide the order of the court," means to perform, to execute, to conform to, such order. An obligation to appear and abide the final order and judgment (in force through the entire

proceedings), although it does not oblige the defendant to attend court personally and consecutively, yet it does require him to take notice, by himself or his representative, of each step in the proceeding, and to attend personally when by law necessary.[1]

"To abide and satisfy" a judgment or order is to perform, execute, conform to, and to satisfy it; that is, to carry it into complete effect.[2]

Abiding conviction. Of guilt — a settled and fixed conviction, a conviction which may follow a careful examination of the whole evidence in the case.[3]

ABILITY. See CAPACITY; DISABILITY; PECUNIARY; REHABILITATE; RESPONSIBLE.

ABLEGATUS. See MINISTER, 3.

ABODE. The place where a person dwells.

Prescribed as the criterion of the residence required to constitute a legal voter, nothing more than a domicil, a house, which the party is at liberty to leave, as interest or whim may dictate, but without any present intention to change it.[4]

The place where a college is situated may or may not be a student's permanent abode. To such as are free from parental control, and regard the place as their home, having no other place to which to return in case of sickness or affliction, it is, *pro hac vice*, their home, their permanent abode.[4]

A college student may be both a voter and a student; and if he in good faith elects to make the place his home, to the exclusion of all other places, he may acquire a legal residence, although he may intend to remove from such place at some fixed time, or at some indefinite period in the future.[5] See DOMICIL.

ABORTION.[6] The act of miscarrying, or producing young before the natural time, or before the foetus is perfectly formed; also, the foetus itself so brought forth.[7]

"Miscarriage" means bringing forth the foetus before it is perfectly formed and capable of living. The word "abortion" is equivalent to miscarriage in its primary meaning; but it has a secondary meaning, in which it is used to denote the off-spring.[8]

At common law an indictment will not lie for an attempt to procure an abortion with the consent of the

[1] Frantz *v.* Lenhart, 56 Pa. 367 (1867). See 50 Conn. 101, 92.

[2] F. *abeiance*, suspension, waiting: *abayer*, to expect.

[3] 2 Bl. Com. 107, 216, 318.

[4] 4 Kent, 260.

[5] 2 Bl. Com. 107.

[6] Wallach *v.* Van Riswick, 92 U. S. 212 (1875).

[7] Dartmouth College *v.* Woodward, 4 Wheat. 691 (1819).

[8] Town of Pawlet *v.* Clark, 9 Cranch, 332 (1815).

[9] Bank *v.* Sherman, 101 U. S. 406 (1879).

[10] 1 Kent, 102. See also 5 Mass. 555; 15 *id.* 464.

[11] Shaw *v.* Hatch, 6 N. H. 163 (1833).

[12] Marshall *v.* Reed, 48 N. H. 40 (1868); 17 *id.* 461; 35 *id.* 198.

[1] Hodge *v.* Hodgdon, 8 Cush. 297 (1851), Shaw, C. J.; 108 Mass. 585; 30 Kan. 88; 13 R. I. 125; 7 Tex. Ap. 38.

[2] Erickson *v.* Elder, 34 Minn. 371 (1885), Berry, J.

[3] [Hopt *v.* Utah, 120 U. S. 439 (1887), Field, J.

[4] Dale *v.* Irwin, 78 Ill. 181 (1875): Ill. R. S. 1874. See Fry's Election Case, 71 Pa. 302 (1872); McCrary, Elections, § 34.

[5] Pedigo *v.* Grimes, Ind. Sup. Ct. (Nov. 1887), cases; Sanders *v.* Getchell, 76 Me. 165 (1884); Vanderpoel *v.* O'Hanlon, 53 Iowa, 249 (1880), cases.

[6] L. *abortio*, untimely birth.

[7] [Butler *v.* Wood, 10 How. Pr. 224 (1854).

[8] Mills *v.* Commonwealth, 13 Pa. 633 (1850), Coulter, J.

mother, until she is "quick with child." It was considered that the child had an independent existence only when the embryo had advanced to the degree of maturity designated by that phrase, although, in reference to civil rights, an infant *in ventre sa mere* was regarded as a person in being.[1] See QUICKENING.

It is a flagrant crime at common law to attempt to procure a miscarriage or an abortion. By that law it is not the murder of a living child which constitutes the offense, but the destruction of gestation by wicked means and against nature.[2]

Notwithstanding an infant *in ventre* is treated by the law, for some purposes, as born, or as a human being, yet it is otherwise with reference to making the act of causing its miscarriage murder, unless so declared by statute. When the infant is born it becomes a human being, within the meaning of the law; and if it should die by reason of potions or bruises received in the womb, it would be murder in the person who administered or gave them, with a view of causing a miscarriage.[2] See MALICE, Constructive.

Abortion, as a crime, is found only in modern statutes and treatises. No mention is made of it in the ancient common-law writers.[4]

The intent not being specifically to take life, some States have made the offense a statutory felony, and punish any unlawful attempt to procure a miscarriage.[5]

The woman cannot be indicted as an accomplice.[6]

Abortionists' articles are non-mailable,[7] and non-importable.[8] See ATTEMPT; DECOY.

ABOUT. 1. Carrying weapons concealed "about" the person means: near, in close proximity, within convenient control and easy reach.[9]

2. In close proximity to; closely approximating.

An agreement to furnish "about 1000 tons" of metal per month will not allow the shipment of a quantity materially less than that number of tons.[1]

"About forty acres" implies that the actual quantity is a near approximation to forty acres.[2] See ESTIMATE; MORE OR LESS.

3. Imports not only nearness of time, quality, or degree, but, also, making preparation to do a thing, or being actually engaged in doing it.[3]

A man is about to convert his property into money when he is near doing it, is making preparations to do it, is actually about to dispose of the property.[4] See ABSCOND.

ABOVE. Upper, higher; superior.

"Above all incumbrances" means in excess of such incumbrances.[4]

Court above. The court to which a cause is removed.

Defendant above. The party who is defendant before an appellate court. **Plaintiff above.** The plaintiff in an appellate court.

Opposed — court, plaintiff, and defendant *below*. See BAIL Above. Compare SUPRA.

ABRIDGE.[5] 1. To shorten, condense; to epitomize, reduce, contract.

A reasonable abridgment of a copyrighted publication is permitted as a new production, involving in its preparation intellectual labor. Not so as to a mere colorable reduction, which is not real nor fair and does not require invention and judgment. What constitutes a fair and reasonable abridgment is a question difficult to answer. But a mere selection, or different arrangement of parts, so as to bring the work into a smaller compass, is not such abridgment. There must be real, substantial condensation of the materials, and intellectual labor and judgment bestowed thereon; and not merely the facile use of scissors, or extracts of the essential parts.[6]

A "compilation" consists of selected extracts from different authors; an "abridgment" is a condensation of the views of one author.[7]

The former cannot be extended so as to convey the same knowledge as the original work; the latter con-

---

[1] Commonwealth *v.* Parker, 9 Metc. 266 (1845), Shaw, C. J.

[2] Mills *v.* Commonwealth, *ante.* Commented on in cases below, especially in Mitchell *v.* Commonwealth, 78 Ky. 206-7 (1879).

[3] Abrams *v.* Foshee, 3 Iowa, 278-79 (1856). To same effect, State *v.* Cooper, 22 N. J. L. 53-58 (1849), cases; Smith *v.* State, 33 Me. 54-55 (1851), cases; State *v.* Moore, 25 Iowa, 131-37 (1868), cases; Evans *v.* People, 49 N. Y. 88 (1872); State *v.* Dickinson, 41 Wis. 309 (1877), cases; Mitchell *v.* Commonwealth, 78 Ky. 204 (1879); State *v.* Slagle, 82 N. C. 653 (1880). And see 10 Cent. L. J. 338; 4 Bl. Com. 201; 2 Whart. Cr. L. § 1220.

[4] State *v.* Cooper, 22 N. J. L. 55, 53-58 (1849), cases; 3 Coke, Inst. 50; 1 Bl. Com. 129.

[5] See Commonwealth *v.* Wood, 11 Gray, 85 (1858); Commonwealth *v.* Boynton, 116 Mass. 343 (1874); Commonwealth *v.* Felch, 132 *id.* 22 (1882); Commonwealth *v.* Taylor, *ib.* 261 (1882); State *v.* Watson, 30 Kan. 281 (1883); Commonwealth *v.* Railing, 113 Pa. 37 (1886); 2 Whart. Cr. L. §§ 1220-28.

[6] People *v.* Vedder, 98 N. Y. 630, 632 (1885), cases.

[7] Act 3 March, 1879; 1 Sup. R. S. p. 229.

[8] R. S. §§ 2491-92; Act 3 March, 1883, 22 St. L. 489, 490.

[9] State *v.* McManus, 89 N. C. 558 (1883).

[1] Norrington *v.* Wright, 115 U. S. 204 (1885). And see Brawley *v.* United States, 96 *id.* 171-72 (1877).

[2] Stevens *v.* McKnight, 40 Ohio St. 341 (1883). See also Baltimore Land Society *v.* Smith, 54 Md. 208 (1880); 16 C. B. 36; 44 L. T. R. 152.

[3] [Hockspringer *v.* Ballenburg, 16 Ohio, 308, 312 (1847): 59 Tex. 285. See also Von Lingen *v.* Davidson, 4 F. R. 350 (1880); s. c. 11 Rep. 5.

[4] Williams *v.* McDonald, 42 N. J. E. 395 (1886).

[5] F. *abreger*, to shorten.

[6] Folsom *v.* Marsh, 2 Story, 107, 115 (1841), Story, J. Concerned letters reprinted from "Sparks' Life of Washington."

[7] Story's Executors *v.* Holcombe, 4 McLean, 308-14 (1847), McLean, J. Concerned an abridgment of "Story's Commentaries on Equity Jurisprudence."

tains an epitome of the work abridged, and, consequently, conveys substantially the same knowledge. The former cannot adopt the arrangement of the works cited, the latter must adopt the arrangement of the work abridged. The former infringes the copyright if the matter transcribed, when published, impairs the value of the original work; but a fair abridgment, though it injures the original, is lawful. To "abridge" is to epitomize, to reduce, to contract. To copy certain passages from a book, omitting others, is in no sense an abridgment: the judgment is not exercised in condensing the author's views; his language is copied, not condensed. To "abridge" is to preserve the substance, the essence of the work, in language suited to such purpose.[1]

An abridgment of an original work, where intellectual labor and judgment are involved, made and condensed by another person, without the consent of the author, is not an infringement of a copyright on the original, especially as to histories, translations, and abridgments not of a character to supersede the original.[2] See further COMPILE; PIRACY, 2.

2. "Abridgment" has also been used to describe a book in which the substance of reports, or of the rules of law to be deduced from them, are concisely and more or less systematically stated.[3] Compare DIGEST.

3. To subtract, diminish, limit, curtail, restrict, discriminate against.

"No State shall make . . . laws which shall abridge the privileges or immunities of citizens of the United States."[4]

The exercise of any right may be regulated by law. The right to pursue a lawful employment is not "abridged," within the Fourteenth Amendment, by an ordinance which merely prescribes the reasonable conditions under which such business may be carried on.[5] See CITIZEN.

ABROAD. In English chancery law, beyond the seas. See DEPOSITION; SEA.

ABROGATE. See REPEAL; RESCIND.

ABS. The form of *a* or *ab* (from) in composition. See A, 5.

ABSCOND.[6] To hide, conceal or absent one's self clandestinely, with intent to avoid legal process.[7]

In an attachment-of-debtor law, may not apply to an act about to be done.[7] See ABOUT, 3.

---

[1] Story's Executors v. Holcombe, 4 McLean, 308-14 (1847), *ante*.

[2] Lawrence v. Dana, 4 Cliff. 79-86 (1869), cases, Clifford, J. Concerned an infringement of the copyright of "Wheaton's Elements of International Law."

[3] See 1 Bl. Com. 72; 1 Kent, 507; Story's Misc. Writ. 79; North Am. Rev., July, 1826, pp. 8-13.

[4] Constitution, Amd. XIV.

[5] Re Bickerstaff, 70 Cal. 38-40 (1886), cases.

[6] L. *abs*, away; *condere*, to hide.

[7] Bennett v. Avant, 2 Sneed, 153 (1854).

An absent and absconding debtor is one who lives without the State, or intentionally conceals himself from his creditors, or withdraws himself from the reach of their suits, with intent to frustrate their demands.[1]

If a debtor departs from his usual residence, or remains absent therefrom, or conceals himself in his house, so that he cannot be served with process, with intent unlawfully to delay or defraud his creditors, he is an absconding debtor.[1] See ABSENT.

ABSENT. Being away: away, not present; not at one's domicil or usual place of business; out of the jurisdiction. Compare PRESENCE.

Absentee. A person who has resided in the State and has departed without leaving any one to represent him; also, a person who was never domiciliated in the State and resides abroad.[2]

Absence does not necessarily mean out of the State; it may refer to cases of default without service of process. Where the presence of a defendant is not secured by appearance or service of summons to appear, a judgment rendered upon his involuntary default is rendered "in his absence."[3] See ABSCOND.

Notice by publication (*q. v.*) is often given to absent defendants.

Brief or temporary absence from a dwelling-house, in the law of arson, burglary, and insurance (*qq. v.*), does not, as a rule, affect the owner's rights.

ABSOLUTE.[4] Exclusive; without condition or incumbrance; complete; perfect; final; opposed to conditional, qualified, relative: as,

Absolute or an absolute — acceptance, alienation, allegiance, bail, bond, confirmation, conveyance, decree, delivery, divorce, estate, fee, guaranty, nullity, ownership, possession, privilege, property, right, rule, sale, waiver, warranty, *qq. v.*

Absolute means complete, unconditional, not relative, not limited, independent of anything extraneous. In the sense of "complete, not limited," distinguishes an estate in fee from an estate in remainder. In the sense of "unconditional," describes a bond, a conveyance, or an estate without condition. In the sense of "not relative," describes the rights of a man in a state of nature, as contradistinguished from those which pertain to him in his social relations. Characterizes a pure estate, unmixed and unconnected with any peculiarities or qualifications; a naked estate, freed from every qualification and restriction, in the donee. Thus, it may describe an estate given to a married

---

[1] Fitch v. Waite, 5 Conn. 121 (1823).

[2] Morris v. Bienvenu, 30 La. An. 880 (1878): Civ. Code, art. 3556.

[3] James v. Townsend, 104 Mass. 371-73, 369 (1870).

[4] L. *ab-solvere*, to free from, set free.

woman, without the exclusion of the husband, in distinction from an estate qualified with that exclusion. The most usual acceptation, when used of estates, is, not independent, but the opposite of partial or conditional.[1]

Absolute is often used as the opposite of "conditional" and in the same sense as "perfect." It signifies without any condition or incumbrance.[2]

That is an absolute interest in property which is so completely vested in the individual that he can by no contingency be deprived of it without his own consent. "Absolute" may be used synonymously with "vested," and as contradistinguished from contingent or conditional; as in speaking of the absolute property of an assured.[3]

ABSQUE. L. Without; except.

Absque hoc. Without this. **Absque tali causa.** Without such cause.

Technical words of denial at common law. The former introduces the negative part of a special traverse and follows the affirmative part or inducement. The latter denies the matter of a plea by which defendant seeks to excuse a tortious act. See further, TRAVERSE.

ABSTRACT.[4] 1, v. To take or withdraw from; to remove or take away.

Under § 5209, Rev. St., an officer of a national bank may be guilty of "abstracting" funds, money, and credits, without any *animus furandi*. The statute may be satisfied with an intent to injure or defraud some company, body politic or corporate, or individual person, other than the banking association whose property is abstracted, or merely to deceive some other officer of the association, or an agent appointed to examine its affairs.[5]

To abstract a public record for the purpose of destroying or mutilating it has been generally made a criminal offense.

2, n. That which is drawn off: an epitome, a summary.

Referring to records, ordinarily a brief, not a copy, of that from which it is taken.[6]

But may be used in the sense of "copy."[7]

Abstract of title. A concise statement of the record evidence of one's title or interest in realty. Frequently spoken of as an "abstract."

In conveyancing, an abstract or summary of the most important parts of the deeds and other instruments composing the evidences of a title to real estate, arranged usually in chronological order, and intended to show the origin, course and incidents of the title, without the necessity of referring to the deeds themselves. It also contains a statement of all charges, incumbrances, and liabilities to which the property may be subjected, and of which it is in any way material for purchasers to be apprised.[1]

The person preparing a perfect abstract must fully understand all the laws on the subject of conveyancing, descents, uses, trusts, devises,— every branch of the law that can affect real estate in its mutations from owner to owner.[2]

ABUNDANS. See CAUTELA.

ABUSE.[3] 1. An improper use; a custom or practice contrary to the intendment of law or to good morals.

Common expressions are: the abuse of authority, of discretion, of a thing bailed, of process, of a distress, of a prisoner; of the liberty of free speech; of a witness, *qq. v.*

2. The synonym of injure; in its largest sense, ill-use or improper treatment of another person or of a dumb animal. Compare CRUELTY.

In a statute punishing the deflowering of a female child, is limited by the words with which it is connected referring to the same subject-matter. The term itself includes physical injury, which is also included in the words "carnally knew." Our statutes, following the English, describe the offense by the words "unlawfully and carnally know and abuse any woman child under the age of ten years."[4] See SEDUCTION.

ABUT. To touch or meet. Compare ADJOINING.

Abutment. The part of a bridge which touches the land. See BRIDGE.

Abuttal. The point at which tracts of land meet; the butting or bounding of lands.

Abutting. Usually, although not necessarily, imports "in contact" with.[5]

Properties *abut* upon a street; and their owners are *abutting* owners. See further STREET.

AC. See AD.

ACADEMY. See ABODE; CADET; COLLEGE, 2; SCHOOL, Public.

---

[1] Johnson's Adm. v. Johnson, 32 Ala. 640-42 (1858), cases, Walker, J.

[2] Converse v. Kellogg, 7 Barb. 597 (1850); 2 N. Y. 357.

[3] Hough v. City Fire Ins. Co., 29 Conn. 20 (1860), Sanford, J.; Williams v. Buffalo German Ins. Co., 17 F. R. 65 (1883), cases.

[4] L. *abs-trahere*, to draw away or off.

[5] United States v. Northway (President Second Nat. Bank of Jefferson, Ohio), 120 U. S. 327, 334-36 (1887), Matthews, J.

[6] [Dickinson v. Railroad Co., 7 W. Va. 413 (1874).

[7] Wilhite v. Barr, 67 Mo. 286 (1878).

[1] Burrill's Law Dict.; Warvelle, Abstr. Title, § 2.

[2] Banker v. Caldwell, 3 Minn. 101 (1859); 7 W. Va. 413.

[3] L. *ab*, amiss; *uti*, to use.

[4] Dawkins v. State, 58 Ala. 379, 378 (1877), Brickell, C. J. See generally Commonwealth v. Roosnell, 143 Mass. 32 (1887).

[5] Cohen v. Cleveland, 43 Ohio St. 197 (1885).

ACCELERATE. To shorten the period after which an interest or estate is to vest in possession or enjoyment.

ACCEPTANCE.[1] A receiving — with approval, or conformably to the purpose of a tender or offer; receiving with intention to retain.

Whence acceptor, non-acceptance.

A person is said to accept the service of a notice, an offer, a bid, the terms of a contract, a guaranty, a charter, rent, goods delivered, a bill of exchange.

1. At common law, a sale of goods, wares, or merchandise was complete upon acceptance of the offer to sell. The Statute of Frauds requires that before an action can be maintained there must have been both a delivery and an acceptance of the article by the purchaser or by his duly authorized agent. In determining, in a particular case, whether there was a binding acceptance, the courts consider the intention of the parties and the nature of the property.[2]

It is a question for the jury whether, under all the circumstances, the acts which the buyer does or forbears to do amount to a receipt and acceptance. But where the facts are not in dispute it is for the court to determine their legal effect; also when the facts are not such as can in law warrant finding an acceptance. To take the contract out of the operation of the statute, there must be " acts of such a character as to place the property unequivocally within the power and under the exclusive dominion of the buyer as absolute owner, discharged of all liens for the price." [3] See FRAUDS, Statute of; OFFER, 1.

2. Acceptance of a bill of exchange is an assent or agreement to comply with the request or order contained in the bill, or, in other words, an assent or agreement to pay the bill according to the tenor of the acceptance, when due.[4]

An engagement to pay the bill according to the tenor of the acceptance; a general acceptance being an engagement to pay according to the tenor of the bill.[5]

"Accepted," on a bill of exchange, is an engagement to pay the bill in money when due. Indorsed

---

[1] L. *accipere*, to receive.

[2] See Bullock v. Tschergi, 13 F. R. 345 (1882); Mahan v. United States, 16 Wall. 146 (1872); 1 Reed, St. Fr. §§ 258-303, cases; 28 Minn. 354; 2 Kent, 494; 3 Pars. Contr. 39; 2 Bl. Com. 447.

[3] Hinchman v. Lincoln, 124 U. S. 38 (1888), cases, Matthews, J., quoting Marsh v. Rouse, 44 N. Y. 647 (1871), cases. See also Shindler v. Houston, 1 *id.* 265 (1848); 49 Am. Dec. 325-40 (1883), cases; Remick v. Sandford, 120 Mass. 316 (1876), cases; Baldey v. Parker, 2 Barn. & C. *40 (1823); Benj. Sales, § 187; Browne, Stat. Fr. § 317 a.

[4] Gallagher v. Nichols, 60 N. Y. 445 (1875), Miller, J.; 12 Barb. 669; 1 Pars. N. & B. 281.

[5] Cox v. Nat. Bank of New York, 100 U. S. 712 (1879), Clifford, J.

---

upon non-negotiable paper, would not import a consideration.[1]

The bill itself, after acceptance, is also called " an acceptance."

Acceptor. He who accepts a bill of exchange, — usually the drawee.

An acceptance is commonly made by writing "accepted" upon the face of the bill and signing thereunder the acceptor's name; but there is no particular place, and no uniform formula, observed.

Acceptances are: express, and implied; verbal, and written; prior to drawing the bill; before or after maturity; for accommodation; after protest; absolute, qualified, conditional; by all the drawees, by one or more of them, by a person not a drawee for the honor of the drawer or of an indorser. They are "complete," when in exact conformity with the tenor of the bill; " qualified," when the engagement is to pay at a different time, place, or manner, from the tenor; and " conditional," when the obligation to pay is to commence on the happening of some event or circumstance.[2]

Every act giving credit to a bill amounts to an acceptance; and this, once fairly and fully made and consummated, cannot be revoked. But the drawee has a reasonable time in which to obtain desired and pertinent information.[3]

Unless forbidden by statute, a promise to accept an existing bill is an acceptance whether the promise is in writing or by parol.

The acceptor is to the drawer as the maker of a promissory note is to the payee, *i. e.*, he is the principal debtor, and the drawer is his surety. His liability is governed by the terms of the acceptance.[4]

Acceptors of a bill of exchange by the act of acceptance admit the genuineness of the signatures of the drawees, and the competency of the drawers to assume that responsibility. Such an act imports an engagement, on the part of the acceptor, with the payee or other lawful holder of the bill, to pay the same if duly presented, when it becomes due according to the tenor of the acceptance. He engages to pay the holder, whether payee or indorsee, the full amount of the bill at maturity, and if he does not, the holder has a right of action against him, and he may also have one against the drawee. Drawers of bills of exchange, however, are not liable to the holder, under such circumstances, until it appears that the bill was duly presented, and that the acceptor refused or neglected to pay according to the tenor of the instrument; their liability is contingent and subject to those conditions

---

[1] Cowan v. Halleck, 9 Col. 578 (1886), cases.

[2] See 1 Pars. Contr. 267; 2 Pars. N. & B. 281; 1 Daniel, Neg. Inst. § 496; 64 Ala. 28-33; 109 Mass. 414.

[3] 3 Kent, 82-88.

[4] Scudder v. Union Nat. Bank, 91 U. S. 413-14 (1875), cases; Cox v. Nat. Bank of New York, 100 *id.* 713, 712-18 (1879), cases.

precedent.[1] See CHECK; EXCHANGE, 2, Bill of; PLACE, 1, Of payment; PROTEST, 2.

ACCESS.[2] Going to or with: approach, intercourse, or opportunity therefor. Opposed, **non-access.**

In a special sense, refers to sexual intercourse between a husband and wife, and imports its occurrence or opportunity of communicating for that purpose.

The presumption that children born in lawful wedlock are legitimate, may be rebutted by evidence showing that there could have been no intercourse. Where there were opportunities for intercourse, evidence to establish impotency is generally not admitted. Non-access is not presumed from the mere fact that the parties lived apart in the same country.[3]

A parent will not be permitted to prove non-access for the purpose of bastardizing issue born in wedlock. The admission of such testimony would be unseemly and scandalous; it would reveal immoral conduct in the parents, and the child, who is in no fault, would be the chief sufferer. Modern statutes allowing parties to testify in their own behalf have not changed this rule of law.[4]

ACCESSARY.[5] He who is not the chief actor in an offense, nor present at its performance, but is in some way concerned therein, either before or after the fact committed.[6]

If a person does no more than procure, advise or assist, he is only an accessary; but if he is present, consenting, aiding, procuring, advising, or assisting, he is a "principal."[7]

Accessary before the fact. One who, being absent at the time of the crime committed, doth yet procure, counsel, or command another to commit the crime.[8]

Accessary at the fact. An aider and abetter was formerly defined to be an "accessary *at* the fact." He is now spoken of as a principal in the first or second degree.[9]

Accessary after the fact. One who, knowing a felony to have been committed,

receives, relieves, comforts, or assists the felon.[1]

In treason and misdemeanors, all participants are principals. The nearest relatives dare not aid or receive one another. Mere presence makes an accessary before the fact a principal in the second degree. An accessary before the fact is liable for all that ensues from the unlawful act. The manner of executing his command is simply a collateral circumstance. Any assistance given a felon to hinder his being apprehended, tried, or punished, makes the assister an accessary after the fact. A person acquitted as a principal may be indicted as an accessary after the fact; and one may be indicted as an accessary both before and after the fact.[2]

Whatever will make a party an accessary before the fact in felony will make him a principal in misdemeanor, if properly charged as such. . The acts, conduct, and declarations of each confederate, made during the pendency of the enterprise, are evidence, as part of the *res gestæ*, against all concerned; but a confession made subsequently to the crime affects only him who makes it. . . . Where the accessary is tried with the principal, the confession of the latter is admissible to prove his own guilt, and where he confesses by pleading guilty and retiring, the record of such conviction is *prima facie* evidence of his guilt at the trial of other defendants. Evidence of the confession of an accessary, to prove the guilt of the principal, cannot be admitted under an indictment against the accessary, unless the guilt or conviction of the principal is alleged in the indictment. The rule at common law was that the accessary could not be convicted until the guilt of the principal was established; so that the principal was first to be convicted or both indicted and tried together. . . . When the accessary is indicted before the principal has been convicted, the indictment, whether separate or joint, must allege the guilt of the principal, as the offense of the accessary depends upon the principal's guilt and is never to be regarded as complete unless the chief offense was actually committed. When principal and accessary are indicted together, the regular course is to introduce all substantive evidence against all the parties before they are required to state their defense. Then the jury are instructed to consider the case of the principal defendant in the first place, and, if they find him not guilty, that it is their duty also to acquit the accessary; but if they find him guilty, they are to proceed to examine the charge against the accessary, and declare whether it is sustained.[3]

Every accessary after the fact to murder, robbery, or piracy, shall be imprisoned not more than three years, and fined not more than five hundred dollars. Every accessary after the fact to any robbery of the carrier, agent, or other person intrusted with the mail, of such mail or of any part thereof, shall be fined not

---

[1] Hoffman v. Bank of Milwaukee, 12 Wall. 186, 193 (1870), Clifford, J.

[2] Ac-cess', or ac'-cess,— Webster.

[3] 2 Greenl. Ev. §§ 150–51; 1 *id.* § 28; 1 Whart. Ev. § 608; 2 *id.* § 1298; 1 Bl. Com. 457.

[4] Tioga County v. South Creek Township, 75 Pa. 436–37 (1874); Boykin v. Boykin, 70 N. C. 263–64 (1874), cases; Melvin v. Melvin, 58 N. H. 570 (1879), cases; King v. Inhab. Sourton, 31 E. C. L. 315–16 (1836), cases.

[5] Ac-ces'-sary,— Webster. L. *accessorius,* q. v. Also spelled -ory, but -ary is preferred. See ACCESSORY.

[6] 4 Bl. Com. 35; 3 Cliff. 227.

[7] United States v. Wilson, Baldw. 103 (1830). See also Speer v. Hiles, 67 Wis. 363 (1886), cases.

[8] 4 Bl. Com. 37: 1 Hale, P. C. 615.

[9] United States v. Hartwell, 3 Cliff. 226 (1869).

[1] 4 Bl. Com. 37; 14 R. I. 283.

[2] 4 Bl. Com. 36–40. See also State v. Davis, 14 R. I. 283 (1883).

[3] United States v. Hartwell, 3 Cliff. 226–31 (1869), cases, Clifford, J. See also 2 Steph. Hist. Cr. L. Eng. 229.

more than two thousand dollars, and be imprisoned at hard labor not more than two years;[1] and for stealing any letter, or other mail matter, or inclosure therein, not more than five years imprisonment and one thousand dollars fine.[2] Accessaries to murder, robbery or other piracy upon the seas, shall suffer death.[3]

" An accessary is he who stands by, and aids, abets, or assists, or who, not being present, aiding, abetting, or assisting, hath advised, encouraged, aided or abetted the perpetration of the crime. He who thus aids, abets, assists, advises or encourages shall be considered as principal and punished accordingly. Every such accessary, when a crime is committed within or without this State by his aid or procurement in this State, may be indicted and convicted at the same time as the principal, or before, or after his conviction, and whether the principal is convicted or amenable to justice, or not, and punished as principal."[4]

See ABET; ACCOMPLICE; AID, 1; ANARCHISTS' CASE; DECOY; HUSBAND; PRESENCE; PRINCIPAL, 5.

ACCESSIO. L. Increase; accession, *q. v.*

Accessio cedit principali. Increase goes with the principal.

Any addition belongs to the owner of the principal object. See ACCESSORIUM.

ACCESSION. Addition, increase; augmentation. See ACCESSIO.

Specifically, the right to all that which one's own property produces, whether that property be movable or immovable, and the right to that which is united to it, either naturally or artificially.[5]

The fruits of the earth, produced naturally or by human industry, the increase of animals, new species of articles made by one person out of the materials of another, and increments to land, are embraced within the definition.[6]

The doctrine of property arising from accession is grounded on the right of occupancy. By the Roman law, if any corporeal substance received an accession by natural or artificial means, the original owner of the thing, by virtue of his right of possession, was entitled to the thing in its improved state; but if the thing itself became changed into a different species, as by making wine out of another's grapes, it belonged to the new operator, who was only to make satisfaction to the former proprietor for the materials so converted. These doctrines have since been confirmed by the courts.[6]

The rule is that the accession goes with the principal thing.[7]

See ACCESSORIUM; ACCESSORY; ACCRETION; INCIDENT; PARTUS. Compare CONFUSION, Of goods.

ACCESSORIUM. L. An accessory thing; the incident.

Accessorium sequitur principale, or principalem, or naturam sui principalis. The accessory follows the principal thing, or the principal, or the nature of the principal.

The incident follows the principal. The more worthy draws to itself the less worthy.[1] See ACCESSION.

ACCESSORIUS. L. An accessary; an assistant.

Accessorius sequitur naturam sui principalis. An assistant follows the character of his chief.

An accessary follows the nature of his principal — in treason and misdemeanors: he cannot he guilty of a higher degree of crime.[2] See further ACCESSARY.

ACCESSORY.[3] 1. Accompanying; incidental; subservient; appurtenant: as, an accessory contract or obligation, *qq. v.*

2. Whatever is connected as an incident or subordinate thing to another as the principal. See ACCESSION.

3. An accessary, *q. v.*

Accessorial. Going with some other as the chief or more important thing: as, an offense of an accessorial nature,[4] an accessorial service.[5]

ACCIDENT. See ACCIDERE.

An event or occurrence which happens unexpectedly, from the uncontrollable operations of nature alone, and without human agency; or an event resulting undesignedly and unexpectedly from human agency alone, or from the joint operation of both.[6]

An event from an unknown cause, or an unusual and unexpected event from a known cause; chance, casualty.[7]

In equity, includes not only inevitable casualties and such as are caused by the act of God, but also those that arise from unforeseen occurrences, misfortunes, losses, and acts or omissions of other persons, without the fault, negligence, or misconduct of the party.[8] See MISTAKE; RELIEF, 2.

---

[1] R. S. §§ 5533, 5472.

[2] R. S. §§ 5535, 5467, 5469, 5471.

[3] R. S. §§ 5323–24.

[4] Ill. Rev. St., Cothran's ed., p. 506, cases. On casual connection, see 20 Cent. Law J. 3–6 (1885), cases.

[5] [3 Kent, 360.

[6] 2 Bl. Com. 405.

[7] 2 Kent, 360.

---

[1] See 2 Bl. Com. 11, 36, 176; Broom, Max. 497.

[2] See 3 Inst. 139; 4 Bl. Com. 36; Broom, Max. 497.

[3] Ac-ces′-sory,— Webster.

[4] 12 Wheat. 476; 1 Greenl. Ev. § 294.

[5] 2 F. R. 478.

[6] Morris *v.* Platt, 32 Conn. 85 (1864), Butler, J.

[7] Crutchfield *v.* Richmond, &c. R. Co., 76 N. C. 322 (1877), Reade, J.

[8] Bostwick *v.* Stiles, 35 Conn. 198 (1868), Park, J.;

Avoidable, unavoidable, and **inevitable accident.** Accidents are: (1) Such as are "inevitable" or absolutely unavoidable, because effected or influenced by the uncontrollable operations of nature. (2) Such as result from human agency alone, but are "unavoidable" under the circumstances. (3) Such as are "avoidable," because, in a given case, the act was not called for by any duty or necessity, and the injury resulted from the want of that extraordinary care which the law reasonably requires of one doing such a lawful act, or because the accident was the result of actual negligence or folly, and might, with reasonable care adapted to the emergency, have been avoided.

"Unavoidable accident" does not mean an accident which it is physically impossible in the nature of the things to prevent; but an accident not occasioned in any degree, remotely or directly, by the want of such care or skill as the law holds every man bound to exercise.[1]

No one is responsible for that which is merely the act of God or "inevitable accident." But when human agency is combined with it and neglect occurs in the employment of such agency, a liability for damages results from the neglect.[2]

In maritime law, "inevitable accident" is a relative term, to be construed not absolutely, but reasonably with regard to the circumstances of each case. In that light it signifies an occurrence which the party charged with the collision could not possibly prevent by the exercise of ordinary care, caution, and maritime skill; as, a collision resulting from the darkness of the night.[3]

"Unavoidable accidents or dangers," in a bill of lading, mean such accidents as are unavoidable by the carrier. To avail himself of such as an exception to his liability he must prove their existence, and clearly show that there was no default on his part.[4]

Where a collision occurs exclusively from natural causes, the loss must rest where it falls, on the principle that no one is responsible for such an accident. . . . It is only where a disaster happens from natural causes, and without negligence or fault on either side, that "inevitable accident" as a defense can be admitted — a collision which occurs where both parties have endeavored, by every means in their power, with due care and caution, and a proper display of nautical skill, to prevent the occurrence of the accident.[1]

"Inevitable accident," within the meaning of the maritime law, is where a vessel is pursuing a lawful avocation in a lawful manner, using proper precaution against danger, and an accident occurs.[2]

When a casualty occurs, which might have been prevented by the use of known and proper means, it is not "inevitable."[3] See further ACT, Of God; COLLISION, 2.

Accidents in insurance law. In a policy insuring a person "against death or injury by accident" it is difficult to define "accident" so as to draw with perfect accuracy a line between injury or death from accident, and from natural causes. But in the term, thus used, some violence, casualty, or *vis major*, is necessarily involved.[4]

Disease produced by the action of a known cause cannot be considered as "accidental" — unless, for example, exposure is brought about by circumstances which may give it the character of accident. In one sense, disease or death through the direct effect of a known natural cause may be said to be accidental, inasmuch as it is uncertain beforehand whether the effect will ensue in any particular case. Yet diseases arising from malaria or infection have always been considered, not as accidental, but as proceeding from natural causes. Sunstroke arises from a natural cause, although it implies exposure to the sun.[4]

A large proportion of the events called accidents happen through some carelessness of the party injured. Thus, men are injured by the careless use of fire-arms, of explosives, of machinery, etc., where a little greater care on their part would have prevented it. Yet such injuries, having been unexpected, and not caused intentionally, are always called accidents, and properly so. . . . An accident may happen from an unknown, or be an unusual result of a known cause, and therefore unexpected; as where a person is injured in passing from the platform of a railway depot to a car in motion.[5]

Death by accident means death from any unexpected event which happens as by

---

1 Story, Eq. § 78; Bisp. Eq. § 174; Pom. Eq. § 823; 17 F. R. 616.

¹ [Dygert v. Bradley, 8 Wend. 473 (1832).

² Chidester v. Consolidated Ditch Co., 59 Cal. 202 (1881), cases.

³ The Morning Light, 2 Wall. 560–61 (1864), cases, Clifford, J.

⁴ Hays v. Kennedy, 41 Pa. 378–86 (1861), cases, Lowrie, C. J.

¹ Union Steamship Co. v. N. Y. & Va. Steamship Co., 24 How. 313 (1860), cases, Clifford, J.

² The Grace Girdler, 7 Wall. 203 (1868), cases, Swayne, J. See also Stewart v. Ship Austria, 7 Saw. 437 (1882); s. c. 14 F. R. 300.

³ Ladd v. Foster, 31 F. R. 827 (1887).

⁴ Sinclair v. Maritime Passengers Assur. Co., 107 E. C. L. 484 (1861), Cockburn, C. J.

⁵ Schneider v. Provident Life Ins. Co., 24 Wis. 29–31 (1869), Paine, J.

chance, or which does not take place according to the usual course of things.[1]

When the object of a company is to insure against bodily injuries produced by external, violent, and accidental means, all combined, there can be no recovery where an assured innocently drank poison.[2]

Within a policy against injury or death from "external, violent, and accidental means," excepting injury or death from "poison," a recovery was had for death from poison *absorbed* into the system by handling hides.[3] See POISON.

A policy against "bodily injuries, effected through external, accidental, and violent means," occasioning death or complete disability to do business, providing that "this insurance shall not extend to death or disability caused by bodily infirmities or disease, by suicide, or self-inflicted injuries,"—covers a death by hanging one's self while insane.[4] See SUICIDE.

The burden of proof rests upon the insurer to show that the assured did not use the required degree of 'diligence for his personal safety.' . . . The use of the word "accidental" will not prevent recovery for injuries to which the negligence of the assured contributed.[5]

Within the meaning of the rules of a beneficial society, an "accident" has its usual signification of an event that takes place without one's foresight or expectation.[6]

In this sense it includes an injury received by one in a common affray, when no fault on his part is shown.[6]

A "railway accident" is any accident having its essence in the peculiarities or properties of railway traveling;[7] an accident attributable to the fact that the injured party is a passenger on the railway, and arising out of an act immediately connected with his being such a passenger.[8]

See CASUALTY; CAUSE, 1, Proximate; CONVEYANCE, 1; INJURY; NEGLIGENCE; RES, Perit, etc.

---

[1] North American Life, &c. Ins. Co. *v.* Burroughs, 69 Pa. 51 (1871), Williams, J. Approved, Bacon *v.* Accident Association, 44 Hun, 607, *infra.*

[2] Pollock *v.* United States Mut. Accident Association, 102 Pa. 234 (1883).

[3] Bacon *v.* United States Mut. Accident Association, 44 Hun, 599 (1887), cases.

[4] Accident Ins. Co. *v.* Crandal, 120 U. S. 527, 531-32 (1887), cases, Gray, J.

[5] Freeman *v.* Travelers' Ins. Co., 144 Mass. 575 (1887), cases; s. c., 36 Alb. Law J. 127. As to "total disability," see Saveland *v.* Fidelity & Casualty Ins. Co., 67 Wis. 176 (1886).

[6] Supreme Council of Chosen Friends *v.* Garrigus, 104 Ind. 140 (1884), Zollars, J.

[7] Theobald *v.* Railway Passenger Assur. Co., 26 E. L. & Eq. 437 (1854), Alderson, B.

[8] *Ibid.* 440, Pollock, C. B.

That accidents are not crimes, see 21 Cent. Law J. 264-70 (1885), cases.

ACCIDERE. L. To fall upon: to come to, arrive at; to come to hand; to fall out, come to pass, happen.

Quando acciderint. When they (assets) come to hand.

Where an executor or an administrator pleads *plene administravit,* the plaintiff may pray judgment of assets *quando acciderint,* or traverse the plea.[1]

ACCOMMODATION. Convenience, favor, benefit. An engagement made as a favor to another, and without consideration; something done to oblige another; as, a loan of money or credit.

Accommodation paper. A loan of the maker's credit, without restriction as to the manner of its use, by means of a bill of exchange or a promissory note, and by making, accepting, or indorsing the same, as the case may be.

A payee may use such instrument, as the name imports, for his own benefit, in any manner he may judge best calculated to advance his interests. Thus, he may pay an existing debt with it, sell or discount it, or pledge it as collateral security.

A holder for value may recover, though he knew that no consideration passed between the parties to the paper; if otherwise, the purpose of the paper would be defeated. But the want of a consideration is a good defense as against the party accommodated.[2]

Being out of the regular course of business, a partner, unauthorized, may not thus loan the name of his firm.[3] See ACCOMMODATUM.

ACCOMMODATUM. L. A loan for use without pay, the thing to be restored *in specie.*

A species of bailment, *q. v.* The same as *commodatum.*[4]

ACCOMPLICE.[5] One who is in some way concerned in the commission of a crime, whether as principal or as an accessary. . . . One of many equally concerned in a felony, the term being applied to those who are admitted to give evidence against their fellow criminals for the furtherance of justice.[6]

---

[1] See 1 Pet. C. C. 442, n; 67 Ga. 49; 19 S. C. 251.

[2] Appleton *v.* Donaldson, 3 Pa. 386 (1846); Lord *v.* Ocean Bank, 20 *id.* 386 (1853), Black, C. J.; Moore *v.* Baird, 30 *id.* 139 (1858); Dunn *v.* Weston, 71 Me. 283 (1880), Appleton, C. J.; 109 U. S. 667; 55 Pa. 75; 3 Kent, 42, 86; Byles, Bills, 131-32, note by Sharswood.

[3] 1 Daniel, Neg. Inst. 272; 1 Pars. N. & B. 259; 1 Bates, Partn. § 349, cases.

[4] 2 Kent, 573.

[5] F. *accomplic, complice,* a confederate: L. *complicem,* folded with, interwoven; involved.

[6] Cross *v.* People, 47 Ill. 158 (1868), Breese, C. J. And see People *v.* Smith, 28 Hun, 627 (1883), Daniels, J.; Cook *v.* State, 14 Tex. Ap. 101 (1883), White, P. J.; *ib.* 591.

One who in any manner participates in the criminality of an act, either as a principal or an accessary.[1]

One who knowingly, voluntarily, and with common intent with the principal offender unites in the commission of a crime.[2]

Whether to allow an accomplice, who has turned state's evidence, a separate trial, or to enter a *nolle prosequi* and admit him as a witness, is discretionary with the court. He is serviceable as a witness until sentenced. To bring the chief offender to justice justifies the practice. Accomplices never corroborate each other; but an informer is not subject to this rule;[3] and the rule is not applicable to civil issues.[4]

The corroboration ought to be as to some fact the truth or falsehood of which goes to prove or disprove the charge.[5] But the testimony of a feigned accomplice does not need corroboration. Whether or not one is a feigned accomplice is for the jury.[6]

Accomplices, not previously convicted of an infamous crime, when separately tried, are competent witnesses for or against each other; and the universal usage is that such a party, if called and examined by the public prosecutor on the trial of his associates in guilt, will not be prosecuted for the same offense, provided it appears that he acted in good faith and that he testified fully and fairly. But it is equally clear that he cannot plead such fact in bar of an indictment against him, nor avail himself of it upon his trial, for it is merely an equitable title to the mercy of the executive, subject to the conditions stated, and can only come before the court by way of application to put off the trial in order to give the prisoner time to apply to the executive for that purpose. Some of the elements of the usage had their origin in the ancient practice of approvement. . . It is regarded as the province of the public prosecutor to determine whether or not the accomplice shall be examined for the state. In order to acquire the information necessary to determine the question, the prosecutor will grant the accomplice an interview, with the understanding that any communication he may make will be strictly confidential. Interviews are for mutual explanation, and so do not absolutely commit either party; but if the accomplice is subsequently called and examined, he is entitled to a recommendation for executive clemency. The accomplice may be pardoned prior to conviction, or the public prosecutor may *nol. pros.* the indictment, or advise the prisoner to plead guilty with the right to retract and plead to the merits if his application for pardon shall be un-successful. Where attempt is made to put him to trial in spite of his equitable right to a pardon, the prisoner may move that the trial be postponed, supporting his motion by his own affidavit, when the court may insist to be informed of all the circumstances; or the court may order that he be acquitted at the trial.[1]

See ACCESSARY; APPROVE, 5; PARDON; PARTICEPS.

ACCORD.[2] Agreement; satisfaction.

A satisfaction agreed upon between the party injuring and the party injured.[3]

An agreement, in the case of a contract, where the creditor agrees to accept some other thing in lieu of that which is contracted or promised to be done.[4]

Used in the plea " accord *and* satisfaction."

When performed, constitutes a bar to all actions.

The money or property must be offered in satisfaction of the claim, and upon the condition that if accepted it is a satisfaction, and the claimant must be made to understand that he takes it subject to such condition.[5]

The bar rests on the agreement and not on the mere reception of property; for whatever amount may have been received, the right of action will not be extinguished, unless it was agreed that the property should be received in satisfaction of the injury. An accord by parol, or by writing not under seal, cannot be set up as a bar to an action of debt founded on a record, or to a judgment in the nature of a record, nor to a debt by specialty, where the debt arises upon the deed; but it may be interposed as a bar to a claim for damages founded upon the breach of a specialty.[6]

Furthermore, an accord must be legal, reasonable, advantageous to the creditor, certain, complete, and be made by the debtor. It may proceed from a partner or a joint wrong-doer for him and his associates, and may be accepted by one co-plaintiff. When a definite sum of money is agreed upon, a less sum is not considered a satisfaction, unless there is an additional benefit.[7]

The technical rule, that an unsealed agreement to accept a smaller sum than the entire debt does not bind the creditor, has been falling into disfavor. It is now held that where a new element enters into the

---

[1] Polk v. State, 36 Ark. 126 (1880), Eakin, J. See too Russ. Crimes, 26; 4 Bl. Com. 34, 331.

[2] People v. Bolanger, 71 Cal. 20 (1886): Whart. Cr. Ev. § 440.

[3] 1 Greenl. Ev. § 379.

[4] Kalckhoff v. Zoehrlaut, 43 Wis. 379 (1877). See 71 N. Y. 137.

[5] State v. Miller, 97 N. C. 488 (1887); Commonwealth v. Bosworth, 22 Pick. 399 (1839), cases; State v. Maney, 54 Conn. 190 (1886); People v. Flath, 100 N. Y. 593 (1886).

[6] People v. Bolanger, 71 Cal. 19–20 (1886); 30 *id.* 316.

[1] Whiskey Cases (United States v. Ford), 99 U. S. 595, 599–606 (1878), cases, Clifford, J. See also Rex v. Rudd, 1 Cowp. 336 (1775), Mansfield, C. J.; Commonwealth v. Knapp, 10 Pick. 492–94 (1830); Commonwealth v. Holmes, 127 Mass. 429–45 (1879), cases, Gray, C. J.; State v. Graham, 41 N. J. L. 16–22 (1879), cases; Oliver v. Commonwealth, 77 Va. 590 (1883); 66 Ga. 346; 133 Mass. 402.

[2] F. *accorder*, to agree.

[3] 3 Bl. Com. 15–16.

[4] Way v. Russell, 33 F. R. 7 (1887): 1 Swift's Dig. 499 24 Conn. 613; 75 N. Y. 574.

[5] Preston v. Grant, 34 Vt. 203 (1861); Bull v. Bull, 43 Conn. 462 (1876).

[6] Mitchell v. Hawley, 4 Denio, 417–18 (1847).

[7] See Cumber v. Wane, 1 Sm. L. C. 604 [*445], cases; 20 Wall. 309; 40 Ark. 184; 6 Col. 162; 44 Conn. 541; 87 Ind. 256; 88 *id.* 45; 29 Minn. 254–55; 38 Pa. 147; 1 Wash. T. 328; 2 Pars. Contr. 193; 1 Greenl. Ev. § 28.

agreement of compromise, the entire debt is satisfied; as, for example, a promise to pay at an earlier day, at a different place, in a different thing, or a promise by a new party.[1]

ACCORDING. Compare BY, 3; SECUNDUM.

Where a mortgage is conditioned for the payment of money "according to" the tenor of a note, to secure which the mortgage is given, the terms of the note are viewed as imported into the mortgage.[2] See VERBUM, Verba illata, etc.

According to law. After the ending of a life estate, land was to go to the male heir nearest the testator "according to law." Held, that the estate was to descend as the law would have given it to the heir.[3]

Since, after a verdict and judgment, a reasonable intendment will be made, on error, in favor of a complaint which shows a substantial cause of action, an averment that an affidavit was made "according to law" will be held to mean that it was made in the time required by law.[4]

In 1809 a testator devised land to his son for life, and then to his children "according to law." The testator died in 1812, and the son in 1860 leaving children. Held, that the children were to take equally as the law stood in 1860, when the distribution was to be made.[5]

Where, in an appeal from the judgment of a justice of the peace, the docket entry showed that bail had been given "according to the act of assembly," the recognizance was held to be sufficient.[6]

A bond conditioned for the faithful discharge of the duties of an office "according to law," embraces duties required by laws in force during the term of the officer, whether enacted before or after the execution of the bond.[7]

An administrator is to administer "according to law," that is, to fulfil his functions, to perform all his duties.[8]

See DULY; LAWFUL; VALID; VOID.

ACCOUNT.[9] 1. The primary idea is, some matter of debt and credit, or demand in the nature of debt and credit, between parties. It implies that one is responsible to another for moneys or other things, either on the score of contract or of some fiduciary relation, of a public or private nature, created by law or otherwise.[10]

Some matter of debt and credit, or of a demand in the nature of debt and credit, between parties, arising out of contract, or of a fiduciary relation, or some duty imposed by law.[1]

Current or running account. An account to which items are being added at intervals; an account open to further charges.

First account; partial account; final account. Designate the number or completeness of accounts presented to a court for confirmation.

Mutual accounts. Those having original charges by persons against each other; accounts kept between merchants.

Open account. An account with one or more items unsettled; also, an account with dealings still continuing.

Account rendered. An account exhibiting the creditor's demand delivered to the debtor — as a basis for settlement.

Account stated. An account rendered by the creditor and assented to by the debtor.

An account to be "continuous" must be without break or interruption. "Open" means not closed; "current," running, passing, a connected series. A "continuous, open, current account" is an account which is not interrupted or broken, not closed by settlement or otherwise; a running, connected series of transactions.[2]

Death "closes" accounts in one sense, that is, there can be no further additions on either side, but they still remain "open" for adjustment and set-off, which is not the case with an account "stated;" for that supposes a rendering of the account by the party who is the creditor, with a balance struck, and assent to that balance, expressed or implied.[3]

In the statute of limitations, the exception in favor of "merchants' accounts" applies to actions of assumpsit as well as of account. It extends to all accounts "current" which concern the trade of merchandise between merchant and merchant. An account "closed" by the cessation of dealings is not an account "stated."[4]

An "account concerning the trade of merchandise between merchant and merchant" is not barred by the statute of limitations, though none of the items are within six years after the action was brought.

---

[1] Seymour v. Goodrich, 80 Va. 304–5 (1885), cases; Bish. Contr. § 50, cases. On paying a part for the whole debt, see 24 Cent. Law J. 175 (1887).

[2] Scheibe v. Kennedy, 64 Wis. 569 (1885).

[3] McIntyre v. Ramsey, 23 Pa. 319 (1854).

[4] McElhaney v. Gilleland, 30 Ala. 183, 188 (1857).

[5] Van Tilburgh v. Hollingshead, 14 N. J. E. 32 (1861).

[6] Harvey v. Beach, 38 Pa. 500 (1861).

[7] Dawson v. State, 38 Ohio St. 3 (1882). See also 18 N. Y. 115; 32 Minn. 162.

[8] Balch v. Hooper, 32 Minn. 162 (1884).

[9] F. aconter, acompter; L. ad-con-putare, to reckon up together. See COMPUTARE.

[10] Whitwell v. Willard, 1 Metc. 217 (1840), Shaw, C. J.

Approved, Stringham v. Supervisors, 24 Wis. 598 (1869); McWilliams v. Allan, 45 Mo. 574 (1870); McCamant v. Batsell, 59 Tex. 367 (1883).

[1] Nelson v. Posey County, 105 Ind. 288 (1885), Mitchell, J.; Watson v. Penn, 108 id. 25 (1886).

[2] Tucker v. Quimby, 37 Iowa, 19 (1873), Miller, J.

[3] Bass v. Bass, 8 Pick. 192 (1829), Parker, C. J.; Volkening v. DeGraaf, 81 N. Y. 270–71 (1880); McCamant v. Batsell, 59 Tex. 368–69 (1883).

[4] Mandeville v. Wilson, 5 Cranch, 18 (1809), Marshall, C. J.

Whether an account concerns " the trade of merchandise " is a fact for the jury. Such accounts include accounts for merchandise bought and sold, and demands for money growing out of the trade of merchandise.[1]

Accounts are "mutual" where each party makes charges against the other in his books, for property sold, services rendered, money advanced, etc., as, for rent due.[2]

The term " mutual accounts " is used in statutes of limitations, declaring that, when suit is founded upon any such account, the time for suing may be reckoned from the last item proved. To constitute such account there must have been reciprocal demands between the parties. An account where there are no credits except payments is not such a mutual account.[3]

In Massachusetts, to a " mutual and open account current " there must be a mutual agreement, express or implied, that the items of the account upon one side and the other are to be set against each other. There must be one account upon which the items upon either side belong, and upon which they operate to extinguish each other *pro tanto*, so that the balance upon either side is the debt between the parties.[4]

A "mutual account" is one based on a course of dealing wherein each party has given credit to the other, on the faith of indebtedness to him. If the items on one side are mere payments on the indebtedness to the other, the account is not mutual. Whether or not an account is a mutual account is a question of fact. The doctrine that the statute of limitations does not begin to run against either party until the last just item is obtained on either side, does not rest on the notion that every credit in favor of one is an admission by him of indebtedness to the other, or a new promise to pay, but upon a mutual understanding, either express or implied from the conduct of the parties, that they will continue to credit each other until, at least, one desires to terminate the course of confidential dealing, and that the balance will then be ascertained, become then due, and be paid by the one finally indebted. Either party may terminate the mutual understanding at any time by actual payment of the balance, by stating the account for that purpose, by demanding a settlement privately, by suit, or by any other act which evinces his determination to deal no longer that way. Without proof of its termination, the law presumes that such a mutual understanding, once proved or admitted, runs through all the dealings of the parties until the complete bar of the statute has attached.[5]

A " partial account " implies that nothing is settled

by it, but the matters constituting the items in question in the statement of it.[1]

An "account rendered " and not objected to within a reasonable time is to be regarded as admitted, by the party charged, to be *prima facie* correct. If certain items are objected to, within reasonable time, and others not, the latter are to be regarded as covered by such an admission. When the facts are clear, what is a reasonable time is a matter of law; where the proofs are conflicting, it is a mixed one of law and fact. Between merchants at home, an account presented, and remaining unobjected to after the lapse of several posts, is, ordinarily, by acquiescence, a stated account. The principle is that the silence of a party to whom an account is sent, warrants the inference of an admission of its correctness. This inference is more or less strong according to circumstances. It may be repelled by showing facts which are inconsistent with it, as that the party was absent from home, suffering from illness, or expected shortly to see the other party, and preferred and intended to make his objections in person.[2]

Unless objected to within a reasonable time an account rendered becomes an account stated, and cannot be impeached except for fraud or mistake. What constitutes reasonable time is a question of law.[3]

A " running account " refers to cases of reciprocity and mutuality of dealings between parties, and not to cases where the items are all on one side.[4]

That an account is " settled " is only *prima facie* evidence of its correctness. It may be impeached by proof of unfairness, or mistake, in law or in fact; and if it be confined to particular items it concludes nothing in relation to other items not stated.[5]

Merely rendering an account does not make it "stated." If the other party receives the account, admits the correctness of the items, claims the balance, or offers to pay it, it becomes a stated account.[6]

In stating an account two things are necessary: That there be a mutual examination of each other's items; and, that there be a mutual agreement as to the correctness of the allowance and disallowance of the respective claims, and of the balance, on final adjustment. Yet it is not necessary to show such examination and agreement: these may be implied from circumstances. An omission to object to the account rendered, raises merely an inference that the party is satisfied with it. Any circumstances rebutting such inference, or calculated to raise a counter inference, are competent evidence as to the actual intention of the parties.[7]

[1] Bass v. Bass, 8 Pick. 192 (1829), Parker, C. J.; Volkening v. DeGraaf, 81 N. Y. 270-71 (1880); McCamant v. Batsell, 59 Tex. 368-69 (1883).

[2] Edmonstone v. Thomson, 15 Wend. 556 (1836), Savage, C. J.; Ross v. Ross, 6 Hun, 81 (1875), cases; Prenatt v. Runyon, 12 Ind. 177 (1859).

[3] Fraylor v. Sonora Mining Co., 17 Cal. 596 (1861); *ib.* 344; 35 *id.* 122; 1 Ga. 228; 12 Ind. 174; 51 Me. 104; 8 Pars. Contr. 86.

[4] Eldridge v. Smith, 144 Mass. 36 (1887), Morton, C. J.; Pub. Sts. *c.* 197, § 8.

[5] Gunn v. Gunn, 74 Ga. 555, 557-68 (1885), cases, Clarke, J.

[1] Leslie's Appeal, 63 Pa. 386 (1869); 39 *id.* 186.

[2] Wiggins v. Burkham, 10 Wall. 131 (1869), Swayne, J. See also 1 Story, Eq. §§ 526, 520; 18 N. Y. 289.

[3] Standard Oil Co. v. Van Etten, 107 U. S. 334 (1882), cases.

[4] Leonard v. United States, 18 Ct. Cl. 385 (1883).

[5] Perkins v. Hart, 11 Wheat. 256 (1826), Washington, J.; Hager v. Thomson, 1 Black, 93 (1861).

[6] Toland v. Sprague, 12 Pet. 335 (1838), Barbour, J.; Zacarino v. Pallotti, 49 Conn. 38 (1881).

[7] Lockwood v. Thorne, 18 N. Y. 288, 298 (1858); 1 Story, Eq. §§ 526-28; 13 Bradw. 43; 58 N. H. 250; 59 Tex. 118, 369.

Without impugning the rule that an account rendered which has become an account stated is open to correction for fraud or mistake, other principles come into operation, where a party to a stated account, who is under a duty, from the usages of business or otherwise, to examine it within a reasonable time after having an opportunity to do so, and give timely notice of his objections thereto, neglects to make such examination, or to have it made, in good faith, by another; by reason of which negligence, the other party, relying upon the account as having been acquiesced in or approved, has failed to take steps for his protection which he could and would have taken had such notice been given. In other words, parties to a stated account may be estopped by their conduct from questioning its conclusiveness.[1]

A complex and intricate account is an unfit subject for examination in court, and ought always to be referred to a commissioner for report, with a view to the entry of a final decree by the court.[2]

It is the difficulty of properly adjusting accounts which confers jurisdiction in equity upon them, without much regard to their singleness or mutuality.[3]

A mistake in one item of an account may be corrected without opening up the whole account, unless the plaintiff can show error or fraud in the settlement as to other items.[4]

Accountable. Liable to demand for the exhibition of an account; under obligation to disclose fully the circumstances of a transaction involving the investment or expenditure of trust funds.

Accountable receipt. A written acknowledgment of the receipt, by the maker of it, of money or other personal property, coupled with a promise or obligation to account for or pay to some person the whole or some part thereof.[5]

Such receipt for money may be in legal effect, though not in form, a promissory note.[6]

Accountant. One who states in writing the nature, condition, and value of trust property committed to his charge; also, one skilled in stating accounts.

Account-render. An action at law, in fiduciary matters, wherein a jury settles disputed items.

If no account has been made, the remedy is by writ of account *de computo:* commanding the defendant to render a just account to the plaintiff, or show cause *contra.* In this there are two judgments for the plaintiff: that the defendant do account (*quod computet*) before an auditor; and, then, that he pay the plaintiff whatever he is found in arrears. . . . The most ready and effectual way to settle matters of account is by a bill in a court of equity, where a discovery may be had on the defendant's oath. Wherefore, actions of account, to compel a man to bring in and settle his account, are now seldom used; though, when an account is once stated, nothing is more common than an action upon the implied *assumpsit* to pay the balance. . . . For want of discovery at law, the courts of equity have acquired a concurrent jurisdiction with other courts in all matters of account. As incident to accounts, they take concurrent cognizance of the administration of personal assets, and consequently of debts, legacies, the distribution of the residue, and the conduct of executors and administrators. They also take concurrent jurisdiction of all dealings in partnership, and many other mercantile transactions; also of bailiffs, receivers, agents, etc,[1]

The action of account-render is founded upon contract, and the engagement between partners that each shall account to every other for himself, and not for his copartner. It is a several liability; no two are responsible to another jointly.[2]

Where mutual accounts are intricate, a bill in equity is preferable.[3] Compare *Account, Action of.*

Account-book; book-account. See BOOK, Account.

Action of account. Action of account-render, *q. v.*

Proceeds upon the ground that the defendant rightfully had money for some purpose; and he cannot be in default until he has refused or neglected to account after being called upon. The judgments are: that the defendant account with the plaintiff; after accounting, that he pay him the balance found due.[4]

Place to our account. An order [superfluous] on a bill or draft, that the drawee charge the maker with the amount, after payment.[5]

See further AUDIT; BALANCE; CHARGE; DEMAND; REST, 2; SETTLE, 3; VOUCHER; ADMINISTRATOR; AGENT;

---

[1] Leather Manufacturers' Bank v. Morgan, 117 U. S. 107 (1886), Harlan, J. A depositor in the bank sent his check-book to be written up and received it back with entries of credits and debits and his paid checks as vouchers, but, from delay in examining the book and checks, failed to discover that his confidential clerk had raised certain checks to the amount of $10,000, in time to enable the bank to indemnify itself. See also Swayze v. Swayze, 37 N. J. E. 190 (1883), cases.

See generally, as to account stated, 22 Cent. Law J. 76 (1886), cases.

[2] Dubourg v. United States, 7 Pet. 626 (1833); Tillar v. Cook, 77 Va. 479-81 (1883); 13 Bradw. 120; 37 N. J. E. 157, 564, 571; 94 N. Y. 80-81; 17 F. R. 19, 21, cases.

[3] State v. Churchill, 48 Ark. 433-36 (1886), cases.

[4] Carpenter v. Kent, 101 N. Y. 594 (1886); 2 Barb. 586.

[5] State v. Riebe, 27 Minn. 317 (1880), Gilfillan, C. J.; Gen. St. Minn. 1878, c. 96, § 1. And see Mason v. Aldrich, 36 id. 284 (1886), cases; Commonwealth v. Talbot, 2 Allen, 161 (1861); Commonwealth v. Lawless, 101 Mass. 32 (1869).

[1] 3 Bl. Com. 164, 437. See 1 Story, Eq. §§ 442-59.

[2] Portsmouth v. Donaldson, 32 Pa. 204 (1858), Strong, J.

[3] Dubourg v. United States, 7 Pet. 625 (1833).

[4] Travers v. Dyer, 16 Blatch. 181 (1879); 3 Bl. Com. 164; 2 Bates, Partn. § 899, cases.

[5] Byles, Bills, 91.

ASSIGNEE; EXECUTOR; GUARDIAN; PARTNERSHIP; PASS; RECEIPT; MISTAKE; PAYMENT; SALE; TRUST, 1.

2. The claim, demand, or right of action, for such balance as may be found to be due upon an account current or closed; as, an account in bank, to assign an account.

3. Interest, benefit, behalf: as, in saying that an agent (*q. v.*) acts upon account of his principal; a policy issued upon account of whom it may concern (*q. v.*); a collection (*q. v.*) made for the account of another person.

4. Reason, ground, consideration. See CONDITION.

ACCRESCERE. L. To grow to, come by increase, add to: to accrue, attach. See ACTIO, Non accrevit; JUS, Accrescendi.

ACCRETION. A mode of acquiring title to realty, where portions of the soil are added by gradual deposit, through the operation of natural causes, to that already in possession of the owner.[1] See ACCRESCERE.

The deposit itself is ordinarily called alluvion, *q. v.* Compare AVULSION.

At common law, imperceptible increase to land on the bank of a river by alluvial formations, occasioned by the washing up of the sand or earth, or by dereliction, as where the river shrinks back below the usual watermark.[2]

When by addition, it should be so gradual that no one can see how much is added each moment of time.[2]

Until new land is made or emerges, there can be no "accretion" to or increase of the land of which it shall constitute a part. The term, importing an addition of what possesses the characteristics of land, cannot, therefore, be construed to include oysters planted opposite to land.[3]

The rule governing additions made to land bounded by a river, lake, or sea, has been much discussed and variously settled by usage and positive law. Almost all jurists and legislators, however, have agreed that the owner of the land, thus bounded, is entitled to these additions. By some, the rule has been vindicated on the principle of natural justice that he who sustains the burden of losses and of repairs, imposed by the contiguity of waters, ought to receive whatever benefits they may bring by accretion; by others, it is derived from the principle of public policy, that it is the interest of the community that all land should have an owner, and most convenient, that insensible additions to the shore should follow the title to the shore itself.[4]

It is generally conceded that the riparian title attaches to subsequent accretions to the land affected by the gradual and imperceptible operations of natural causes. But whether it attaches to land reclaimed by artificial means from the bed of the river, or to sudden accretions produced by unusual floods, is a question each State decides for itself. By the common law, such additions to the land on tide or navigable waters belong to the crown.[1]

An aerolite belongs to the owner of the fee of the land upon which it falls. Therefore, a pedestrian upon a highway who first discovers such stone cannot claim title to it, the highway being a mere easement for travel.[2]

ACCROACH.[3] To attempt, or assume, to exercise royal power.[4]

ACCRUE.[5] 1. To be or become added to; to fall due.

Accrued. Due and payable.

Accruing. Falling due; becoming but not yet due.

As, accrued or accruing — dividend, interest, pension, rent.

Accruing costs are such costs as become due and are created after judgment; as, the costs of an execution.[6]

2. To attach, arise, come into existence, commence, enure.

Benefits, and a right or cause of action, are said to accrue at a certain time.[7] See LIMITATION, 3.

Accruer, clause of. A clause in a gift to tenants in common, that upon the death of one tenant his share shall go to the survivor.

Extends only to the original, not to accrued shares, unless (as is ordinarily the case) it is otherwise expressly stated.

ACCUMULATION.[8] A gathering in quantity; also, the sums or other things so gathered.

Accumulative. Heaping up; additional; cumulative, *q. v.*

At common law, the utmost length of time allowed for the contingency of an executory devise to happen in was that of a life or lives in being and one-and-twenty years afterward.[9]

Under this rule, one Peter Thelluson, in 1796, de-

---

[1] [3 Washb. R. P. 451. See also 4 Kent, 428; 34 La. An. 838.

[2] [Lammers *v.* Nissen, 4 Neb. 250 (1876), Gantt, J.

[3] Hess *v.* Muir, 65 Md. 597 (1886), Ritchie, J.

[4] Banks *v.* Ogden, 2 Wall. 67 (1864), Chase, C. J. See

also New Orleans *v.* United States, 10 Pet. 717 (1836); Jones *v.* Johnston, 18 How. 156 (1855); 2 Bl. Com. 261–62.

[1] Barney *v.* Keokuk, 94 U. S. 337 (1876), Bradley, J.; Steers *v.* City of Brooklyn, 101 N. Y. 56 (1885), cases.

[2] Maas *v.* Amana Society, Ill. (1877): 16 Alb. L. J. 76; 13 Irish Law T. 381.

[3] F. *accrocher,* to draw to one's self: *croc,* a hook.

[4] See 4 Bl. Com. 76; 2 Steph. Hist. Cr. L. Eng. 246.

[5] F. *accreu:* L. *accrescere,* q. v.

[6] 87 Ind. 254; 91 Ill. 95.

[7] 98 U. S. 476; 17 F. R. 872; 1 Story, Eq. § 212.

[8] L. *ad-cumulare,* to amass: *cumulus,* a heap.

[9] 2 Bl. Com. 174; 2 Kent, 353.

vised his fortune to trustees, for accumulation during the lives of three sons and of their sons, *and* during the life of the survivor. At the death of this last survivor the fund was to be divided into three shares — one share for the eldest male lineal descendant of each of his three sons; upon failure of such descendant, the share to go to the descendants of the other sons. The testator left three sons and four grandsons living, and twin sons born soon after his death. It was found that at the death of these nine persons the fund would exceed nineteen million pounds; and, upon the supposition of only one person to take and a majority of ten years, that the sum would exceed thirty-two million pounds. The will was upheld, as within the limits of the common-law rule, by the court of chancery in 1798, and by the House of Lords in 1805.[1]

By statute of 39 & 40 Geo. III (1799), c. 98, known as the Thellusson Act or the Statute of Accumulations, accumulation was forbidden beyond the life of the grantor (or testator), twenty-one years from his death, and during the minority of any person living or in *ventre sa mere* at his death, or during the minority of any person who, under deed or will, would, if of full age, be entitled to the income.[2]

And such also is the law in most of the States: so that directions for accumulation beyond those limitations are void.[3] See ALIENATIO, Rei; DEVISE, Executory; PERPETUITY.

ACCUSARE. L. To lay to one's charge; to accuse, *q. v.*

Accusare nemo se debet. No one is obliged to accuse himself.

Nemo tenetur seipsum accusare. No one is bound to accuse himself.

Nemo tenetur seipsum prodere. No one is bound to betray or expose himself.

It is the privilege of a witness not to answer a question where there is real, not imaginary, danger that the answer may criminate himself.

The rule is intended to preserve the witness from temptation to commit perjury.

A husband cannot testify against his wife, or *vice versa*.[4] But a bankrupt must answer fully as to the disposition of his property.[5] And a member of a public corporation may be compelled to testify against the corporation.[6]

The rule has been relaxed, and a difference made between private crimes or those arising out of commerce or the private relations of society, and public crimes or those relating strictly to the general welfare of the state.[7]

See CRIMINATE; STULTIFY; TURPITUDE.

ACCUSE. To charge with violation of law; specifically, to charge with criminal misconduct. See ACCUSARE.

Accusation. A charge that one has committed a misdemeanor or crime; also, the act of preferring such a charge.

"To accuse" is to bring a charge against one before some court or officer; and the person thus charged is "the accused."[1]

A threat to accuse of a crime does not refer to accusing by way of railing, or slander, or bearing false witness under a separate accusation made by others, but the institution or participation in the institution of a criminal charge before some one held out as competent to entertain such a charge in lawful course.[5]

See CRIME; EXAMINATION, 2; INDICTMENT; STATEMENT, 1.

ACCUSTOMED. See CUSTOM; HABIT.

Where a deed conveyed a water privilege with the power and appurtenances as they then existed, and with the right to rebuild a dam, and to pass and repass in the use of the same over the "accustomed way," it was held that the right of way must be regarded as limited to the last accustomed way.[2]

ACKNOWLEDGMENT. Owning to; avowal, admission.

1. A statement by a debtor that a claim, barred by the statute of limitations, is still a valid obligation.

Takes the case out of the statute, and revives the original cause of action.

An acknowledgment which will revive the original cause of action must be unqualified and unconditional. It must show positively that the debt is due in whole or in part. If connected with circumstances which affect the claim, or if conditional, it may amount to a new *assumpsit* for which the old debt is a sufficient consideration; or if it be construed to revive the original debt, that revival is conditional, and the performance of the condition, or a readiness to perform it, must be shown.[3]

A new promise, as a new cause of action, ought to be proved in a clear and explicit manner, and be in its terms unequivocal and determinate; and, if any conditions are annexed, they ought to be shown to be performed. If there be no express promise, but a promise to be raised by implication of law from the acknowledgment of the party, such acknowledgment ought to contain an unqualified and direct admission of a subsisting debt, which the party is liable and willing to pay. If there be accompanying circumstances which repel the presumption of a promise or intention to pay; if the expressions be equivocal, vague, and indeterminate, leading to no certain conclusion, but at best to probable inferences, which may affect different minds

---

[1] Thellusson *v.* Woodford, 4 Ves. 227–343; 11 *id.* 112–50.

[2] 4 Kent, 284; Will. R. P. 306.

[3] 4 Kent, 346, 271; Pray *v.* Hegeman, 92 N. Y. 514–15 (1883); Scott *v.* West, 63 Wis. 574–82 (1885), cases.

[4] 1 Greenl. Ev. §§ 330, 340.

[5] 3 Pars. Contr. 519.

[6] 1 Greenl. Ev. § 331. See 1 Bl. Com. 443; 4 *id.* 296; 107 Mass. 181; 10 N. Y. 10, 33.

[7] Whart. Max. 23; Broom, Max. 968, 970; 17 Am. Law Rev. 793.

---

[1] People *v.* Braman, 30 Mich. 468–70 (1874), cases, Graves, C. J. See also Commonwealth *v.* Andrews, 132 Mass. 264 (1882).

[2] Ferriss *v.* Knowles, 41 Conn. 308 (1874).

[3] Wetzell *v.* Bussard, 11 Wheat. 315, 311–16 (1826), cases, Marshall, C. J.

in different ways, they ought not to go to a jury as evidence of a new promise to revive the cause of action. Any other course would open up all the mischiefs against which the statute was intended to guard innocent persons, and expose them to the dangers of being entrapped in careless conversations, and betrayed by prejudices. It may be that in this manner an honest debt may sometimes be lost, but many unfounded recoveries will be prevented.[1]

No case has gone the length of saying that there must be an express promise to pay in terms. A clear, distinct, unequivocal acknowledgment of a debt as an existing obligation, identifying it so that there can be no mistake as to what it refers to, made to a creditor or his agent, takes a case out of the statute.[2]

"I will pay the debt as soon as possible," constitutes a new and sufficient acknowledgment.[3]

Acknowledgment does not necessarily imply words.[4] See further PROMISE, New.

2. The act of a grantor in going before a competent officer and declaring that the instrument he produces is his act and deed.[5]

Also, the official certificate that such declaration was made.

The acknowledgment or the proof which may authorize the admission of a deed to record, and the recording thereof, are provisions for the security of creditors and purchasers. They are essential to the validity of the deed as to those persons, not as to the grantor.[6]

An acknowledgment, regular on its face, makes the instrument evidence, without further proof, and fits it for being recorded. The exact words of the statute need not be followed: it is sufficient if the meaning be clearly and fully expressed.[7]

In the case of a wife, the certificate must show that she was examined separate and apart from her husband; that she was of full age; that the contents of the deed were first made known to her; and that she acted of her own free will. Otherwise, although recorded, her acknowledgment constitutes neither a record nor notice.[8]

Conveyance of the estates of married women by deed, with separate examination and acknowledgment, has taken the place of the alienation of such estates by "fine" in a court of record under the law of England. For fraud in levying a fine, the court of chancery would grant relief, as in the case of any other conveyance. And so now, her deed of conveyance does not bind her if her acknowledgment was obtained by fraud or duress, or if, by reason of infancy or insanity, she was not competent to make the contract. Statute of 18 Edw. I. (1290) enacted that if a *feme covert* should be a party to a fine, she was first to be examined by certain justices; and if she dissented, the fine was not to be levied. This was held to mean that the fine ought not to be received without her examination and consent; but that if it was received, neither she nor her heirs could be permitted to deny that she was examined and freely consented; for this would be contradicting the record, and tend to weaken the assurances of real property.

The object of statutes requiring the separate examination of the wife to be taken by an officer, to be certified by him in a particular form, and to be recorded in the public registry, is not only to protect her by making it the duty of such officer to ascertain and to certify that she has not executed the deed by compulsion or in ignorance of its contents, but to facilitate the conveyance of the estates of married women, and to secure and perpetuate evidence, upon which transferees may rely, that the requirements of the law have been complied with. The duty of the officer involves the exercise of judgment and discretion, and so is a judicial or *quasi* judicial act. The conclusion is that, except in case of fraud, his certificate, made and recorded as the statute requires, is the sole and conclusive evidence of the separate examination and acknowledgment, and that, except where fraud in procuring her execution is alleged, extrinsic evidence of the manner in which the examination was conducted is inadmissible.[1]

Whenever substance is found in a certificate, obvious clerical errors and all technical defects will be disregarded, and, in order to uphold it, the certificate will be read in connection with the instrument and in the light of surrounding circumstances.[2] See EXAMINATION, 5; NOTICE, 1.

3. Admission of a fact; confession of guilt. See CONFESSION, 2.

---

[1] Bell v. Morrison, 1 Pet. 362 (1828), Story, J. See also Moore v. Bank of Columbia, 6 id. 91-94 (1832); Fort Scott v. Hickman, 112 U. S. 163 (1884); Green v. Coos Bay Wagon Co., 23 F. R. 67 (1885), cases; Curtis v. Sacramento, 70 Cal. 414-15 (1886); Chidsey v. Powell, 91 Mo. 626 (1887).

[2] Jones v. Lantz, 63 Pa. 326 (1869), Sharswood, J.; Wolfensburger v. Young, 47 id. 517 (1864); Shaefer v. Hoffman, 113 id. 5 (1886); 114 id. 358; 23 Alb. Law J. 104-5 (1881), cases.

[3] Norton v. Shepard, 48 Conn. 141 (1880), cases.

[4] Bailey v. Boyd, 59 Ind. 298 (1877).

[5] [Short v. Coulee, 28 Ill. 228 (1862), Breese, J.

[6] Lessee of Sicard v. Davis, 6 Pet. 136 (1832).

[7] Wickersham v. Reeves, 1 Iowa, 417 (1855); Owen v. Norris, 5 Blackf. 481 (1840); Becker v. Anderson, 11 Neb. 497 (1881); Spitznagle v. Vanhessch, 13 id. 338 (1882).

[8] See Paxton v. Marshall, 18 F. R. 361, 364-68 (1883), cases; Young v. Duvall, 109 U. S. 577 (1883); McMullen v. Eagan, 21 W. Va. 244-45 (1882), cases; Watson v.

Michael, id. 571-73 (1883), cases; Langton v. Marshall, 59 Tex. 298 (1883); Schley v. Pullman's Palace Car Co., 120 U. S. 575 (1887), citing Ill. cases; 1 Bl. Com. 444.

[1] Hitz v. Jenks, 123 U. S. 301-3 (1887), cases, Gray, J. In this case a notary had taken the acknowledgment in the statutory form, and the wife admitted that the signature was hers, but did not recollect executing the deed, and denied that it was explained to her. *Held*, there being no proof of fraud or duress, evidence to impeach the certificate was properly rejected. See also Davey v. Turner, 1 Dallas, *13 (1765); Lloyd v. Taylor, ib. *17 (1768); Cox v. Gill, 83 Ky. 669 (1886); Davis v. Agnew, 67 Tex. 210 (1886); Cover v. Manaway, 115 Pa. 345 (1887).

[2] King v. Merritt, Sup. Ct. Mich. (Oct. 13, 1887), cases

ACQUAINTED. Implies a mutual acquaintance; as where one swears that he is "well acquainted" with an applicant for naturalization.[1]

Having a substantial knowledge of the subject-matter; as of the paper to which a certificate is affixed.[2]

ACQUETS. See PURCHASE, 3.

ACQUIESCENCE.[3] A keeping quiet: consent inferred from silence or from failure to object, the person to be charged having knowledge of the essential facts. Tacit encouragement to an act done; assent.

Imports mere submission, not approbation; as when it is said that the board of trustees of a college acquiesced in legislation affecting their charter.[4]

Implies such knowledge of facts as will enable the party to take effectual action. One may not then rest until the rights of third persons are involved and the situation of the wrong-doer is materially changed.[5]

Where a person tacitly encourages an act to be done, he cannot afterward exercise his legal right in opposition to such consent, if this encouragement induced the other party to change his position, so that he will be pecuniarily prejudiced by the assertion of such adversary claim.[6]

See further AFFIRM, 2; ESTOPPEL; SILENCE; STALE; WAIVER.

ACQUIRE.[7] To obtain, procure: as, to acquire property, a domicil. Compare HOLD, 6.

Acquired. "In the law of descent, includes lands that come to a person in any other way than by gift, devise, or descent, from an ancestor."[8]

After-acquired. Obtained after some event or transaction: as, property acquired after an adjudication in bankruptcy, or after a judgment has been entered.

Acquisition. Procuring a thing — specifically, property; also, the property itself. See INHERIT; PURCHASE, 2, 3.

Original acquisition. When, at the moment, the thing is not another's, *i. e.*, is acquired by first occupancy — by accession, intellectual labor, etc. *Derivative acquisi-*

tion. When the thing is obtained from another by his act or the act of the law; as in cases of gift, sale, forfeiture, succession, marriage, judgment, insolvency, intestacy.[1]

The property that a bankrupt acquires, after he has devoted all his possessions to the payment of his debts, is his individually.[2]

Where one makes a deed of land as owner and subsequently acquires an outstanding title, the acquisition enures to the grantee by estoppel.[3] See under COVENANT, 1.

A judgment may not be a lien upon after-acquired land, unless specially made so, as by a *scire facias* or some analogous proceeding.[4]

ACQUIT. F. Exonerated, acquitted, cleared.

Autrefois acquit. Formerly acquitted. Opposed, *autrefois convict.* A plea in bar, that the accused has already been cleared of the charge.[5] See ACQUITTAL, Former.

ACQUITTAL. Setting free; deliverance from a charge or suspicion of guilt; the act or action of a jury in finding that a person accused of a crime is not guilty.

Acquitted. "Set free or judicially discharged from an accusation; released from a debt, duty, obligation, charge, or suspicion of guilt."[6]

Refers to both civil and criminal prosecutions.[6]

Acquittal in fact. A verdict of not guilty. **Acquittal in law.** A discharge by operation of law; as, where one is held as an accessary and the principal is acquitted.[7]

Former acquittal. An acquittal in a former prosecution.

When the facts constitute but one offense, though divisible into parts, a final judgment on a charge of one part bars a prosecution for another part. When the facts constitute two or more offenses wherein the lesser is necessarily involved in the greater, and the facts necessary to convict on a second prosecution would necessarily have convicted on the first, then the first judgment bars another prosecution.[8]

The greater includes the lesser crime.[9] Compare CONVICTION, Former.

---

[1] United States v. Jones, 14 Blatch. 90 (1877).

[2] Bohan v. Casey, 5 Mo. Ap. 106-7 (1878).

[3] L. *acquiescere*, to rest in or upon: *quies*, quiet.

[4] Allen v. McKean, 1 Sumn. 314 (1833), Story, J.

[5] Pence v. Langdon, 99 U. S. 581 (1878), Swayne, J. See also Matthews v. Murchison, 17 F. R. 766 (1883); Ramsden v. Dyson, L. R., 1 H. L. 129 (1865).

[6] Swain v. Seamans, 9 Wall. 254, 267, 274 (1869), Clifford, J.

[7] L. *acquirere*, to get, obtain: *quaerere*, to seek.

[8] *Re* Millars' Wills, 2 Lea, 61 (1878); Donahue's Estate, 36 Cal. 332 (1868).

[1] [2 Kent, 355, 386.]

[2] Allen v. Ferguson, 18 Wall. 4 (1873).

[3] Irvine v. Irvine, 9 Wall. 625 (1869).

[4] See Loomis v. Davenport, &c. R. Co., 17 F. R. 305 (1882); 1 Jones, Mortg. § 157. See generally Babcock v. Jones, 15 Kan. 301 (1875), cases; 21 Cent. L. J. 500-3 (1885), cases.

[5] See 4 Bl. Com. 335.

[6] Dolloway v. Turrill, 26 Wend. 400 (1841): Webster.

[7] [2 Coke Inst. 364.]

[8] State v. Elder, 65 Ind. 285-86 (1879), cases; 58 N. H. 257; 4 Cr. L. M. 411.

[9] 18 Cent. Law J. 392-94 (1884), cases.

ACQUITTANCE. A written discharge from the performance of a duty; also, the writing itself.

Includes a common receipt for money paid.[1]

A receipt for damages may operate as an acquittance, when not a release.[2]

An acquittance under seal is a "release," *q. v.*

ACRE. Formerly, in discussing the law of real estate, for brevity, "black acre" and "white acre" were used to distinguish parcels. See ESTIMATE; MORE OR LESS.

ACT. 1. A thing done or performed; the exercise of power; an effect produced by power exerted.[3] See ACTUM.

. "'Act" and "intention" may mean the same as "act" alone, for act implies intention, as in the expression "death by his own act or intention."[4]

A service running through several days, as, inventorying attached goods, may be treated as one act.[5]

The law deals with the acts of men as members of society under a contract *honeste vivere, alterum non laedere, suum cuique tribuere:* to live honorably, hurt nobody, and give to every one his due.[6]

Acts are spoken of as unintentional and as intentional, wanton, malicious, and criminal; as of omission and of commission; as reasonable; as of diligence, and of negligence; as of ownership, of sufferance, of trespass; as of concealment and of fraud; as overt; as judicial, and as ministerial, *qq. v.*

What ought to be done is readily presumed. What ought not to be done, when done, may be valid. Equity treats that as done which ought to be done. He who can and ought to forbid, commands, if he does not forbid. He who fails to prevent what he can prevent, does the act himself. When anything is prohibited, everything by which it may be done is also prohibited. When more is done than ought to be done, that which it was proper to do, is accepted as rightly done. What cannot be done directly cannot be done indirectly. Every act involves its usual consequences, *q. v.* See also ESTOPPEL; RELATION, 1; VALID.

Act of bankruptcy. An act which exposes a debtor to proceedings in a court of bankruptcy, *q. v.*

Act of God. Such inevitable accident as cannot be prevented by human care, skill or foresight; but results from natural causes, such as lightning and tempest, floods and inundation.[7]

Something superhuman, or something in opposition to the act of man.[1]

Every "act of God" is an "inevitable accident," because no human agency can resist it; but it does not follow that every inevitable accident is an act of God. Damage done by lightning is an inevitable accident, and also an act of God, but the collision of two vessels, in the dark, is an inevitable accident, and not an act of God.[2]

That may be an "inevitable accident" which no human foresight or precaution can prevent; while "act of God" denotes a natural accident which could not happen by the intervention of man. The latter expression excludes all human agency. Moreover, to excuse a carrier, the act of God must also be the immediate, not the remote, cause of the loss.[3]

Courts and writers have differed as to whether "unavoidable accident" in a bill of lading is exactly equivalent to the exception of the common law "act of God or of the public enemies." Some treat "inevitable accident," "perils of the sea," "of navigation," "of the road," as equivalent to the "act of God" as this phrase is used by judges and lawyers; and others treat them as expressing different ideas. Others again view them as identical for the purpose of making "inevitable accident" mean "act of God," in the sense of a sudden and violent act of nature; while others make them equivalent in order to make "act of God" mean any accident which the carrier cannot, by proper care, foresight, and skill, avoid. Many cases overlook the common custom of merchants (the law in such matters) that all bills of lading contain an exception against losses by inevitable accident, perils of the sea, etc. If a man signs a bill containing the technical phrase "act of God" he will be held according to the usual custom of commerce.

The maxim *actus Dei nemini facit injuriam* does not appear to be different from *lex non cogit ad impossibilia, impotentia excusat legem, impossibilium nulla obligatio est,* and other maxims of the Roman law.

"Act of God" no more excludes human agency than do such terms as *Deo volente, Deo juvante, ex visitatione Dei,* Providential dispensation, or the Roman terms *fataliter, divinitus, casus fortuitus, damnum fatale,* all which originally referred to the intervention of the gods, in the sense that the appropriate human agency was powerless.

When rights depend upon the life of a man, they end with his death, which is called an "act of God," whether from nature, accident, carelessness, or suicide.[4]

---

[1] State *v.* Shelters, 51 Vt. 104 (1878), cases.

[2] Mitchell *v.* Pratt, Taney, 448 (1841).

[3] See Chumasero *v.* Potts, 2 Monta. 284–85 (1875).

[4] Chapman *v.* Republic Life Ins. Co., 6 Biss. 240 (1874).

[5] Bishop *v.* Warner, 19 Conn. 467 (1849).

[6] 1 Bl. Com. 40: Justinian.

[7] McHenry *v.* Philadelphia, &c. R. Co., 4 Harr., Del., 449 (1846), Booth, C. J.

[1] Chicago, &c. R. Co. *v.* Sawyer, 69 Ill. 289 (1873), cases, McAllister, J.

[2] Fergusson *v.* Brent, 12 Md. 33 (1857), Le Grand, C. J. See also The Charlotte, 9 Bened. 6–16 (1877), cases; 10 id. 310, 312, 320.

[3] Merritt *v.* Earle, 29 N. Y. 117–18 (1864), Wright, J.; Michaels *v.* N. Y. Central R. Co., 30 id. 571 (1864), cases.

[4] Hays *v.* Kennedy, 41 Pa. 379–80, 381, 382 (1861), cases, Lowrie, C. J. Dissenting opinion by Thompson, J., 3 Grant, 357–64, cases: "An opinion characterized

The law was first established by the courts of England with reference to carriers by land, on whom the Roman law imposed no liability beyond that of other bailees for reward. Nor did the Roman law make a distinction between inevitable accident arising from what in English law is termed "the act of God," and inevitable accident arising from other causes, but, on the contrary, afforded immunity to the carrier, without distinction, whenever the loss resulted from "*casus fortuitus*," "*damnum fatale*," or "*vis major*"—unforeseen and unavoidable accident.

It is not under all circumstances that inevitable accident arising from the so-called act of God will, any more than inevitable accident in general by the Roman and continental law, afford immunity to the carrier. This must depend upon his ability to avert the effects of the *vis major*, and the degree of diligence which he is bound to apply to that end.

All causes of inevitable accident may be divided into two classes: those which are occasioned by the elementary forces of nature unconnected with the agency of man or other cause; and those which have their origin, in whole or in part, in the agency of man, whether in acts of commission or omission, of nonfeasance or mis-feasance, or in any other cause independent of the agency of natural forces.

It is not because an accident is occasioned by the agency of nature, and therefore by what may be termed the "act of God," that it necessarily follows that the carrier is entitled to immunity. The carrier is bound to do his utmost to protect the goods from loss or damage, and if he fails herein he becomes liable from the nature of his contract. If by his default in omitting to take the necessary care, loss or damage ensues, he remains responsible, though the so-called act of God may have been the immediate cause of the mischief.

What Story says of "perils of the seas" applies equally to such perils coming within the designation of "acts of God." That is, all that can be required of the carrier is that he shall do all that is reasonably and practically possible to insure the safety of the goods. If he uses all the known means to which prudent and experienced carriers ordinarily have recourse he does all that can be reasonably required of him; and if, under such circumstances, he is overpowered by storm or other natural agency, he is within the rule which gives immunity from the effects of such *vis major* as the act of God. It is, therefore, erroneous to say that the *vis major* must be such as "no amount of human care or skill could have resisted" or the injury such as "no human ability could have prevented."[1]

Where, in an action for the loss of goods, the defense is "an act of God" [an unusual flood], the burden of showing that the negligence of the carrier co-operated to produce the loss is on the shipper. Such defense may be shown under a general denial.[1]

Where a duty is imposed upon a person by law he will not be absolved from liability for non-performance occasioned by an act of God, unless he has expressly stipulated for exemption.[2]

See further ACCIDENT; CARRIER; CONDITION; POSSIBILITY.

Act of honor. Acceptance or indorsement of protested paper, to save the credit of a name thereon. See HONOR, 1.

Act of the law. The operation of legal rules upon a fact or facts; operation of law.[3]

A common expression is "act and operation of law."

Succession to property, surrender of leases, and some divorces are said to be created by act of the law.[4]

An act of the law exonerates from liability.[5]

2. A formal written statement that something has been done; as, that an instrument is the maker's act and deed. See ACKNOWLEDGMENT, 2.

3. A law made by a legislative body.

Used abstractly, or with reference to a particular statute: as, an act of Assembly, of Congress, of legislation, or of the legislature; the Civil Rights Act, the Confiscation Acts, the Factor's Act, the Inter-State Commerce Act, the Legal Tender Act, Recording Acts, the Riot Act, Tenterden's Act, the Tenure of Office Act, qq. v.

Enact. To establish in the form of positive law, or by written law. Whence enactment.

Enacting clause. The section of a bill or statute which establishes the whole document as a law. Commonly begins "Be it enacted, etc.," that is, by the Senate and House of Representatives (or the People) of a State, or of the United States.

The section of a statute which defines an offense is not the enacting clause.[6]

"Act of Congress" is as strong and unequivocal as "statute of Congress."[7]

The legislature, in exercising a power conferred,

---

by fine discrimination, and by accurate research," 1 Smith's Lead. Cases, 413, where extended quotation is made from it.

[1] Nugent v. Smith, L. R., 1 C. P. D. 429–30, 435–36 (1876), cases, Cockburn, C. J.; 1 Story, Bailm. § 512 (a). The defendant received a mare to be carried by him as a common carrier by sea. The jury found that her death was caused partly by very rough weather and partly from struggling due to fright, and that the defendant had not been negligent. The Court of Appeals reversed the lower court, holding that the defendant was not liable for the value of the animal.

[1] Davis v. Wabash, &c. R. Co., 89 Mo. 349–53 (1886), cases, Ray, J. Same case, 25 Am. Law Reg. 650 (1885); ib. 658–60, cases.

[2] Central Trust Co. v. Wabash, &c. R. Co., 31 F. R. 441 (1887).

[3] 17 Wall. 373, 376.

[4] See 1 Bl. Com. 123; 15 Wend. 400; 2 Barb. 180; 2 Whart. Ev. §§ 858–62.

[5] Taylor v. Taintor, 16 Wall. 376 (1872).

[6] United States v. Cook, 17 Wall. 176 (1876).

[7] United States v. Smith, 2 Mas. 151 (1820), Story, J.

enacts laws, and a law is called a statute or an "act." . . . All legislative acts are laws; if not laws, then they are not acts of legislation.[1]

A proposed law is embodied in a *bill.* When this bill is duly passed by the legislative body it becomes an act of that body. When the executive department signs or approves such a bill it becomes a law.[2]

General or **public act.** A statute which binds the community at large. **Private** or **special act.** Such act as operates only upon particular persons and private concerns.

Special or private acts are to be formally shown and pleaded, else the judges are not bound to notice them.[3]

There is no statute fixing the time when acts of Congress shall take effect, but it is settled that where no time is prescribed, they take effect from their date. Where the language employed is "from and after the passage of this act," the same result follows. The act becomes effectual from the day of its date. In such cases it is operative from the first moment of that day, fractions of the day not being recognized.[4]

A thing is done in pursuance of an act when the person who does it is acting honestly, under the powers which the act gives, or in discharge of the duties which it imposes.[5]

See further LAW; LEGISLATE; STATUTE.

ACTA. See ACTUM.

ACTING. Performing; serving; attending to the duties of an office; as, the acting — executor, partner, commissioner of patents, reporter of decisions.

Attached to an officer's title, designates not an appointed incumbent, but merely a *locum tenens* who is performing the duties of an office to which he does not himself claim title.[6]

ACTIO. L. A doing, performing: an action, or right of action.

Actio non accrevit infra sex annos. The action has not accrued within six years: the right of action has not arisen, etc.

The Latin form of the plea of the statute of limitations. In strictness, appropriate only when the action has accrued subsequently to the promise. To an action on the promise, the plea is *non assumpsit infra sex annos.*[7] See ACCRUE, 2.

Actio personalis moritur cum persona. A personal action dies with the person.

Applies to actions merely personal, arising *ex delicto,* for wrongs actually done by the defendant, such as trespass, battery, slander: in which the action cannot be revived by or against any representative. But actions arising *ex contractu,* by breach of promise, in which the right descends to the representative, may be revived: being actions against the property rather than against the person.[1]

Expresses the rule at common law with regard to the surviving of personal actions arising *ex delicto,* for injuries to the person, personalty, or realty. By 4 Edw. III (1331), c. 7, the rule was so modified as to give an action in favor of a personal representative for injuries to personalty; by 3 and 4 Will. IV (1833), c. 42, an action was given against personal representatives for injuries to personalty or realty;[2] and by 9 and 10 Vict. (1846), c. 93, known as Lord Campbell's Act, a right of action for damages for the death of the person injured by the wrongful act, neglect, or default of another, is given to near relatives — husband, wife, parent, child. These statutes have been followed in this country.

At common law actions on penal statutes do not survive. Congress has not changed the rule with respect to actions on the penal statutes of the United States.[3] See further DAMAGES.

Non oritur actio. A right of action does not arise — *ex dolo malo,* out of a fraud; — *ex nudo pacto,* out of an engagement without a consideration; — *ex pacto illicito,* upon an unlawful agreement; — *ex turpi causa* or *contractu,* out of an immoral cause or contract.

Whenever illegality appears, whether the evidence comes from one side or the other, the disclosure is fatal to the case. Consent cannot neutralize its effect.[4] Whatever the contamination reaches it destroys. See further DELICTUM, In pari, etc.

ACTION. 1. Doing a thing, the exercise of power, physical or legal; the thing itself as done; an act, *q. v.:* as, legislative, judicial, executive action, *qq. v.* See CAUSE, 1 (1).

2. "The lawful demand of one's right"[5] — in a court of justice.[6]

An abstract legal right in one person to prosecute another in a court of justice; a "suit" is the actual prosecution of that right.[7]

An action or suit is any proceeding for the

---

[1] People *v.* Tiphaine, 13 How. Pr. 76–77 (1856).

[2] Chumasero *v.* Potts, 2 Monta. 284–85 (1875).

[3] 1 Bl. Com. 86; Unity Township *v.* Burrage, 103 U. S. 454 (1880).

[4] Lapeyre *v.* United States, 17 Wall. 198 (1872), Swayne, J. See also 7 Wheat. 211; 1 Gall. 62; 20 Vt. 653; 21 *id.* 619; 1 Kent, 457.

[5] Smith *v.* Shaw, 21 E. C. L. 126 (1829).

[6] Fraser *v.* United States, 16 Ct. Cl. 514 (1880).

[7] 3 Bl. Com. 308.

---

[1] 3 Bl. Com. 302.

[2] Russell *v.* Sunbury, 37 Ohio St. 374 (1881). See also Henshaw *v.* Miller, 17 How. 219 (1854); Mitchell *v.* Hotchkiss, 48 Conn. 16 (1880); Tufts *v.* Matthews, 10 F. R. 610–11 (1882), cases; 55 Mich. 338; 143 Mass. 305.

[3] Schreiber *v.* Sharpless, 110 U. S. 80 (1884).

[4] Coppell *v.* Hall, 7 Wall. 555–59 (1868), cases; Ewell *v.* Daggs, 108 U. S. 149 (1883), cases; 107 Mass. 440; 92 N. Y. 85; Broom, Max. 297, 729.

[5] 3 Bl. Com. 116.

[6] McBride's Appeal, 72 Pa. 483 (1873).

[7] Hunter's Will, 6 Ohio, 501 (1854).

purpose of obtaining such remedy as the law allows.[1]

In any legal sense, action, suit, and cause are convertible terms.[2]

The "cause" of this lawful demand, or the reason why the plaintiff can make such demand, is some wrong act committed by the defendant, *and* some damage sustained by the plaintiff in consequence thereof: the two elements must unite.[3] See further CAUSE, 2.

Since all wrongs may be considered as merely a privation of right, the plain, natural remedy for every species of wrong is the being put in possession of the right again. This may be effected by a specific delivery or restoration of the subject-matter to the legal owner, or, where that is not possible or at least not adequate, by making a pecuniary satisfaction in damages. The instruments whereby this remedy is obtained are a diversity of actions or suits. The Greeks and Romans had set forms of actions for the redress of distinct injuries. Our actions are founded upon original writs, and these are alterable by legislation only. The several suits, or remedial instruments of justice, are actions personal, real, and mixed.[4]

Whether a writ of error, a *quo warranto*, a *mandamus*, a *scire facias*, a suit in partition, a suit in equity, a summary proceeding — in some of which the court is the actor, — are actions, in the strict sense, has been variously decided.

Action in personam. An action against the person (of the defendant). **Action in rem.** An action against a thing — an inanimate object out of which satisfaction is sought. See RES, 2.

Action of contract or **ex contractu.** An action for the recovery of damages upon a broken contract. In form: *assumpsit*, *debt*, or *covenant* (*qq. v.*) — all founded on promises. **Action of tort** or **ex delicto.** An action for the recovery of personalty withheld, or damages for a wrong not a breach of contract. In form: *trespass*, *case*, *trover*, *replevin*, or *detinue* (*qq. v.*) — all founded on torts or wrongs.[5]

Action on the case. See CASE, 3.

Actionable. That for which an action may be maintained; opposed to *non-actionable*: as, actionable — fraud, defamation.

Words are "actionable *per se*" when the natural consequence of what they impute is damage.[6] See LIBEL, 5; SLANDER.

Amicable action. An action entered of record by agreement and without the service of process, to obtain the judgment of the court in a matter of common interest. Opposed, *adversary* action.

Civil action. Recovers a private right or compensation for deprivation thereof. **Criminal action.** Is instituted by the state for an offense to the community or to society.

Civil actions include actions at law, suits in chancery, proceedings in admiralty, and all other judicial controversies in which rights of property are involved.[1]

Civil action is used in contradistinction to criminal action; as, in the act of July 2, 1864, relating to parties as witnesses.[2]

Common-law action. An action maintainable at common law. **Statutory action.** Such form of action as is given by legislative enactment. See REMEDY, Cumulative.

Cross action. An action brought by the defendant in a suit against the plaintiff upon the same subject-matter, the particular cause of action not being available as set-off in the first suit. See SET-OFF.

Equitable action. An action for money had and received is sometimes so called.

Yet, in the absence of special circumstances, courts of equity refuse jurisdiction, because the remedy at law is complete.[3] See ASSUMPSIT, Implied.

Fictitious action. A suit upon a wager, and under pretense of a controversy, to obtain a judicial opinion upon a question of law. See FICTITIOUS, 1; ISSUE, 3, Feigned.

In action. That for which a suit will lie or is pending. See CHOSE.

Joint action. A suit in which all persons obligated or interested on one side of a controversy appear as co-plaintiffs, and all obligated or interested on the other side are made co-defendants. **Joint and several action.** A suit by either one or all persons on one side as plaintiff or co-plaintiffs, and against either one or all on the other side as defendant or co-defendants. **Separate action.** Such action as each person must

---

[1] Harris *v.* Insurance Co., 35 Conn. 312, 311 (1868); Magill *v.* Parsons, 4 *id.* 322 (1822).

[2] *Exp.* Milligan, 4 Wall. 112 (1866), Davis, J.; 2 McCrary, 180; 18 Blatch. 447; 60 Wis. 478.

[3] Foot *v.* Edwards, 3 Blatch. 313 (1855), Nelson, J.

[4] 3 Bl. Com. 116-17.

[5] See 3 Bl. Com. 117; 13 F. R. 537.

[6] Pollard *v.* Lyon, 91 U. S. 226-38 (1875), cases.

[1] United States *v.* Ten Thousand Cigars, 1 Woolw. 125 (1867).

[2] Green *v.* United States, 9 Wall. 658 (1869). And see 1 Dill. 184; 28 Conn. 580; 69 Ga. 647; 104 Ind. 6, 18; 2 Monta. 70; 51 N. H. 383; 1 Barb. 15; 14 Abb. Pr. 353; 44 Pa. 130; 43 Vt. 297.

[3] Wallis *v.* Shelly, 30 F. R. 748 (1887); Gaines *v.* Miller, 111 U. S. 397-98 (1884), cases.

bring when several complainants cannot pursue a joint remedy. See further JOINT.

Local action. A suit maintainable in some one jurisdiction exclusively. **Transitory action.** A suit maintainable wherever the defendant can be found.

In "local actions," where the possession of land or damages for an actual trespass or waste, etc., affecting land, is to be recovered, the plaintiff must declare his injury to have happened in the very place where it happened; but in "transitory actions," for an injury that might have happened anywhere, as in debt, detinue, slander, the plaintiff may declare in what county he pleases. . . Transitory actions follow the person of the defendant; territorial suits must be discussed in the territorial tribunal.[1]

Actions are deemed "transitory" when the transactions on which they are founded might have taken place anywhere; and "local," when their cause is, in its nature, necessarily local.[2]

Actions which do not seek the recovery of land may be "local" by common law because they arise out of some local subject or from the violation of some local right or interest; as, waste, trespass *quare clausum*, actions on the case for nuisances to houses, for disturbance of a right of way, for the diversion of a water-course, and the like; also, replevin. These actions are personal and local.[3]

When the action by which a remedy is to be enforced is personal and transitory the defendant may be held liable in any court to whose jurisdiction he can be subjected by personal process or by voluntary appearance. Thus, as an action in the nature of trespass to the person is transitory, the venue is immaterial.[4] See ACTOR, 1, Sequitur, etc.

Penal action. A suit brought by an officer of government to recover a penalty imposed by statute. **Popular action.** An action also for a penalty, maintainable by any person. Compare *Qui tam action.* See FORFEITURE; PENALTY.

Qui tam action. *Qui tam:* who as well. The emphatic words in the Latin form of a declaration in an action by an informer for a penalty.

Civil in form, but designed to recover a penalty imposed by a penal statute; therefore, partially at least, criminal in nature.[5]

Sometimes one part of a forfeiture, for which a popular action will lie, is given to the king, to the poor, or to some public use, and the other part to the informer or prosecutor: and then the suit is called a *qui tam* action, because brought by a person "*qui tam pro domino rege, quam pro se ipso*"—as much for his lord the king, as for his own self.

If the king commences the suit he has the whole forfeiture. If any one has begun such action, no other person then can pursue it; and the verdict in the first suit bars other actions. This caused offenders to induce their friends to begin suit, in order to forestall and prevent other actions: which practice is prevented by 4 Hen. VII (1488), c. 20, enacting that no recovery, otherwise than by verdict, obtained by collusion, shall be a bar to any other action prosecuted *bona fide*.[1] That being the law in England in 1776, such action cannot be prosecuted in the name of an informer unless the right is distinctly given by statute.[2]

Real action. An action whereby the plaintiff claims title to lands or tenements, rents, commons, or other hereditaments, in fee-simple, fee-tail, or for term of life. **Personal action.** Such action whereby a man claims a debt, or a personal duty or damages in lieu thereof, or damages for some injury to his person or property. **Mixed action.** Partakes of the nature of both of the former — by it real property is demanded, with personal damages for a wrong sustained.[3]

A "real action" is brought for the specific recovery of lands, tenements, or hereditaments. It includes every form of action where the judgment is for the title and possession of the land demanded; as, ejectment. A "mixed action" is brought for the specific recovery of land, as in a real action, but has joined with this claim one for damages in respect to such property; as, actions of waste and dower. A "personal action" is brought for the specific recovery of chattels, or for damages or other redress for breach of contract and other injuries of every description, the specific recovery of lands and tenements only excepted.[4] See ACTIO, Personalis, etc.

Right of action. Right to bring a suit; such right as will sustain a suit; in particular, a right of remedy or recovery at law.[5]

See ACTIO; BOOK-ACCOUNT, Action of; CIRCUITY; COMMENCE; CONSOLIDATE; DISCONTINUANCE: FORM, 2; GIST; ISSUE, 3; MULTIPLICITY; PARTY, 2; PEND; PROCEEDING; PROCESS, 1; RES, 2.

ACTIVE. 1. Produced by exertion; resulting from intentional action; opposed to passive: as, active — deceit, waste, *qq. v.*

2. Requiring intelligent direction, personal

[1] [3 Bl. Com. 294, 384.

[2] Livingston v. Jefferson, 1 Brock. 209 (1811), Marshall, C. J.

[3] Hall v. Decker, 48 Me. 256-57 (1860).

[4] Dennick v. Central R. Co. of New Jersey, 103 U. S. 17-18, 21 (1880), cases; Livingston v. Jefferson, 4 Hughes, 611-13 (1811), Marshall, C. J.; Oliver v. Loye, 59 Miss. 321-23 (1881), cases; R. S. §§ 739-45, cases.

[5] State v. Kansas City, &c. R. Co., 32 F. R. 726 (1887), Brewer, J.; R. S. Mo. § 1709.

[1] 3 Bl. Com. 161-62.

[2] O'Kelly v. Athens Manuf. Co. 36 Ga. 52 (1867).

[3] [3 Bl. Com. 117-18.

[4] [Hall v. Decker, 48 Me. 255-56 (1860).

[5] As to premature actions, see 21 Cent. Law J. 401-12 (1885), cases.

exertion; opposed to passive: as, an active —
trust, use, *qq. v.*

ACTOR. 1. Lat. A doer; a plaintiff.
See CAVEAT, Actor.

Actor sequitur forum rei. The plaintiff follows the forum of the thing — the
thing in suit, or the residence of the defendant.[1]

Personal actions are to be brought before the tribunal of the defendant's domicil. Actions for collisions
between vessels may be brought where neither party
resides: on the ground that a quasi-contract arises on
the part of the wrong-doer to pay the damage he has
caused, and that the place of performance is taken to
be the port at which the injured vessel first arrives.[2]
See ACTION, 2, Local.

Actori incumbit probatio. On the
plaintiff rests the proving — the "burden of
proof," *q. v.*

2. Eng. (1) A doer, a performer: as, the
chief actor in a crime.[3] See PRINCIPAL, 5.

He who institutes a suit; a plaintiff,[4] *q. v.*

He who avers a matter as a fact or law.

(2) A stage-player. See REVIEW, 3.

ACTUAL. Existing in act; really acted;
real, at present time; as a matter of fact.
Opposed, *constructive:* speculative, implied,
legal.

An assault with "actual" violence is with physical
force put in action, exerted upon the person assailed.[5]

It is common to speak of an actual or the
actual — annexation of a fixture, appropriation of a thing, attachment, battery, breaking, close or curtilage, cost, costs, damage,
delivery, escape, eviction, fraud, knowledge,
levy, loss, malice, notice, occupation, payment, possession, presence, seizure, use,
value, violence, *qq. v.*

ACTUM; ACTUS. L. A thing done:
an act; action.

**Acta exteriora indicant interiora se-
creta.** Outward acts evince the inward purpose. See OVERT; WILL, 1.

Actus curiæ neminem gravabit. An
act of the court shall oppress no one.

A court will not suffer a party to be prejudiced by
its own action, as, by delay. On this principle orders
are sometimes entered *nunc pro tunc,*[6] q. v.

---

[1] 2 Kent, 462.
[2] Thomassen *v.* Whitwell, 9 Bened. 115 (1877).
[3] See 4 Bl. Com. 34.
[4] See 3 Bl. Com. 25.
[5] State *v.* Wells, 31 Conn. 213 (1862). See 16 Op. Att-
Gen. 447, 445.
[6] See Cumber *v.* Wane, 1 Sm. L. C. *444–45; 103 U. S.
65; 119 *id.* 596; 3 Col. 236; Broom, Max. 122.

Actus Dei nemini facit injuriam. An
act of God does wrong to no one.

No one is responsible in damages for the result of
an inevitable accident, *q. v.*

Actus legis nemini facit injuriam.
An act of the law wrongs no man.

An act of the law is to be so limited in its operation
that no right shall be prejudiced.[1]

**Actus non facit reum, nisi mens sit
rea.** An act does not make a man a criminal, unless his intention be criminal.

To constitute a crime the intent and the act must
concur: a mere overt act, without wrongful intention,
does not make guilt.[2] See CONSEQUENCES; MALICE.

AD. L. At, to, for; according to; on account of.

In compounds assimilates with the consonant following, becoming ac-, af-, ag-, al-, an-, ap-, ar-, as-, at-.

Ad colligendum. For collecting (the
goods). See under ADMINISTER, 4.

Ad damnum. To the loss. See DAM-
NUM.

Ad diem. On the (very) day. See DIES.

Ad filum. To the line. See FILUM.

Ad hoc. On this (subject).

Ad idem. To the same (thing or effect).
See ASSENT.

Ad interim. In the meantime; temporarily.

Said of one, as an *assignee,* who serves in the place
of another; also, of a *receipt* for a premium paid,
pending the approval of a risk in insurance against
fire. See INTERIM.

Ad litem. For the suit. See GUARDIAN, 2.

Ad majorem cautelam. For the sake
of caution. See CAUTELA.

Ad medium filum. To the middle line.
See FILUM.

Ad pios usus. For religious purposes.
See USUS.

Ad quæstionem. See QUÆSTIO.

Ad quem. To which. See A, 5, A quo.

Ad quod damnum. To the loss which.
See DAMNUM.

Ad sectam. At the suit of. See SUIT, 1.

Ad valorem. According to valuation.
See DUTY, 2.

ADDITION.[3] 1. Under a statute allowing a mechanic's lien upon an "addition
to a former building," the new structure
must be a lateral addition. It must occupy

---

[1] 2 Bl. Com. 123; 69 Ga. 400; Broom, Max. 127, 409.
[2] 4 Bl. Com. 2, 21; 4 N. Y. 159, 163, 195; Broom, Max.
307.
[3] L. *ad-dare,* to add to.

ground beyond the limits of the original building.[1]

A change in a building by adding to its height, or depth, or to the extent of its interior accommodations, is an "alteration," not an addition.[1]

Additional. Given with, or joined to, some other: as, an additional — building, legacy, security.

Embraces the idea of joining or uniting one thing to another so as to form an aggregate.[2]

"Additional security" is that which, united with or joined to the former security, is deemed to make the aggregate sufficient as a security from the beginning.[2]

2. A word or title added to the name of a person to help identify him.

Addition of estate (*status*): yeoman, gentleman, esquire. Addition of degree: knight, earl, marquess, duke — names of dignity. Addition of domicil: place of residence. Addition of mystery or trade: scrivener, laborer, etc.[3]

By 1 Hen. V. (1413), c. 5, an indictment must set forth the Christian name, surname, and the addition of degree, mystery, place, etc.[4] See NAME, 1.

ADDRESS. 1. The part of a bill in equity which describes the court.[5]

2. The name and residence of the drawee in a bill of exchange. See PROTEST, 2.

ADEMPTION.[6] The act by which a testator pays to his legatee, in his life-time, a general legacy which by his will he had proposed to give him at his death; also, the act by which a specific legacy has become inoperative on account of the testator having parted with the subject.[7] Whence adeem, adeemed.

When a parent gives a legacy as a portion, and, afterward, advances in the same nature, the latter presumably satisfies the former.[8]

The ademption of a legacy of personalty is not usually called a "revocation." When ademption is not used the act is called "satisfaction," "payment," "performance," "execution." But these terms, so used, have not their ordinary sense; for their primary relation is to some debt, duty, or obligation resting absolutely upon a party; whereas a will, having no effect in the maker's life-time, does not bind him to anything. "Ademption" is the most significant.[9] See REVOKE.

If a horse, specifically bequeathed, die during the testator's life-time, or be disposed of by him, the legacy will be lost or adeemed, because there will be nothing on which the bequest can operate. The only question, in such case, is, whether the specific thing remains after the death of the testator.

ADEQUATE.[2] Equal, proportionate, fully sufficient, complete. Opposed to inadequate.

1. If a consideration has some value it need not be adequate. Inadequacy is regarded only when gross and when imposition is apparent; but it may prevent specific performance, and justify small damages for a breach of contract.[3]

The immediate parties to a bargain are the judges of the benefits derivable therefrom. To avoid a bargain for inadequate consideration the inadequacy must be so great and manifest as to shock the conscience and confound the judgment of common sense.[4] See BID.

Gross inadequacy alone does not constitute a sufficient reason to impeach the genuineness of a sale made by a trustee. The inadequacy must be such as to shock the conscience or raise a presumption of fraud or unfairness.[5]

Where gross inadequacy of price is coupled with accident, mistake, or misapprehension, caused by a purchaser or other person interested in a public sale, or by the officer conducting the sale, a court of equity will set the sale aside.[6] See INFLUENCE.

2. Where there is an adequate remedy at law for the redress of an injury, resort may not be had to a court of equity. This means a remedy vested in the complainant to which he may at all times resort at his own option, fully and freely, without let or hindrance.[7]

The remedy at law must be plain, adequate, and complete, and as practical and efficient to the ends of justice and to its prompt administration as the remedy in equity. In that case the adverse party has a right to a trial by a jury.[8]

But a judgment and a fruitless execution at law are not necessary.[9]

The absence of a plain and adequate remedy at law affords the only test of equity jurisdiction; the application of the principle to a particular case must de-

---

Denio, C. J.; Same v. Same, 3 Duer, 541 (1854); Beck v. McGillis, 9 Barb. 56 (1850).

  [1] Ford v. Ford, 23 N. H. 215–17 (1851), cases, Gilchrist, C. J.

  [2] L. *adæquatus*, made equal.

  [3] 1 Pars. Contr. 436, 492, cases.

  [4] 1 Story, Eq. §§ 244–47; Lawrence v. McCalmont, 2 How. 452 (1844).

  [5] Clark v. Freedman's Sav. & Trust Co., 100 U. S. 152 (1879), cases; Cleere v. Cleere, 82 Ala. 588 (1886); Carden v. Lane, 48 Ark. 219 (1886), cases.

  [6] Cole County v. Madden, 91 Mo. 614 (1887), cases; 20 Cent. Law J. 350 (1888), cases.

  [7] Wheeler v. Bedford, 54 Conn. 249 (1886), Park, C. J.

  [8] Morgan v. City of Beloit, 7 Wall. 618 (1868), cases.

  [9] Case v. Beauregard, 101 U. S. 690 (1879).

---

  [1] [Updike v. Skillman, 27 N. J. L. 132 (1858), Green, C. J.

  [2] State v. Hull, 53 Miss. 645 (1876); 139 Mass. 356.

  [3] [Termes de la Ley.

  [4] 4 Bl. Com. 306; 1 *id.* 407; 10 Cush. 402; 1 Metc., Mass., 151.

  [5] See Story, Eq. Pl. § 26.

  [6] L. *adimere*, to take away.

  [7] See 3 Will. Exec. 1320.

  [8] Strother v. Mitchell, 80 Va. 154 (1885); Trimmer v. Bayne, 7 Ves. *515 (1802).

  [9] Langdon v. Astor's Executors, 16 N. Y. 39–40 (1857),

pend altogether upon the character of the case as disclosed by the pleadings.[1] See further EQUITY.

ADHERING. See TREASON.

ADIT. A horizontal entry to a mine.

A statute which provides that "an adit at least ten feet in, along the lode, from the point of discovery, shall be equivalent to a discovery shaft," contemplates that the ten feet may be wholly or in part open or under cover, dependent upon the nature of the ground.[2]

ADJACENT.[3] Near, but not touching. Applied to lots, is synonymous with "contiguous." In another relation it might have a more extended meaning.[4] See ADJOINING; CONTIGUOUS; VICINITY.

Certain acts of Congress authorized the defendant to take from public lands "adjacent" to its road materials necessary for the construction and repair of its railway. *Held*, that the reference was to such materials as could be conveniently reached by ordinary transportation by wagons, and that the privilege did not include the right to transport timber to distant parts of the road.[5]

Where the "adjacent" ends and the non-adjacent begins may be difficult to determine. On the theory that the material is taken on account of the benefit resulting to the land from the construction of the road, the term ought not to be construed to include any land save such as by its proximity to the line of the road is directly and materially benefited by its construction.[6]

ADJOINING.[7] Touching or contiguous, as distinguished from lying near or adjacent; in contact with.[8]

In popular use seems to have no fixed meaning. Frequently expresses nearness.[9]

What is "adjacent" may be separated by the intervention of a third object. What is "adjoining" must touch in some part. What is "contiguous," strictly speaking, should touch along one side.[9]

Towns contiguous at their corners are adjoining.[10]

The whole yard of a house of correction, though divided by a street, from which it is fenced off, is adjoining or appurtenant to the house.[11]

Compare ABUT; ADJACENT; APPERTAIN.

[1] Watson *v.* Sutherland, 5 Wall. 79 (1866).

[2] Electro-Magnetic Mining, &c. Co. *v.* Van Auken, 9 Col. 207 (1886); Gray *v.* Truby, 6 *id.* 278 (1882); Gen. Laws Col. 630, § 7.

[3] L. *adjacere*, to lie near.

[4] Municipality No. Two, 7 La. An. 79 (1852), Eustis, C. J. See Continental Improv. Co. *v.* Phelps, 47 Mich. 299 (1882).

[5] United States *v.* Denver, &c. R. Co. 31 F. R. 886, 889 (1887), Hallett, J.

[6] United States *v.* Chaplin, 31 F. R. 890, 896 (1887), Deady, J.

[7] F. *adjoinder:* L. *ad-jungere*, to join to.

[8] *Re* Ward, 52 N. Y. 397 (1873); Miller *v.* Mann, 55 Vt. 479 (1882); Akers *v.* United R. Co., 43 N. J. L. 110 (1881).

[9] Peverelly *v.* People, 3 Park. Cr. R. 69, 72 (1855); Crabbe, Syn.

[10] Holmes *v.* Carley, 31 N. Y. 289, 293 (1865).

[11] Commonwealth *v.* Curley, 101 Mass. 25 (1869).

ADJOURN.[1] To put off, or defer to another day specified; also, to suspend for a time, to defer, delay.[2]

Referring to a sale or a judicial proceeding, may include fixing the time to which the postponement is made.[2]

Adjournment. Putting off until another time and place.[3]

A continuation of a previous term of court.[4]

A continuance of a session from one day to another.[5] See VACATION.

ADJUDGE. To decide judicially; to adjudicate; sometimes, to declare or deem, but not implying any judgment of a judicial tribunal.

As in a statute declaring that "all lotteries are hereby adjudged to be common nuisances."[6] Compare DEEM.

ADJUDICATA. See ADJUDICATUS.

ADJUDICATE. To determine in the exercise of judicial power; to pronounce judgment in a case.

Adjudicated. Judicially determined: as, an adjudicated — case, bankrupt.

Adjudication. Determination by judicial authority.

Former adjudication. Judicial determination of a matter previously in litigation.

When the judgment, rendered in the former trial between the same parties, is used as a technical estoppel, or is relied upon by way of evidence as conclusive *per se*, it must appear, by the record of the prior suit, that the particular controversy sought to be concluded was necessarily tried and determined — that is, if the record of the former trial shows that the verdict could not have been rendered without deciding the particular matter, it will be considered as having settled that matter as between the parties; and where the record does not show that the matter was necessarily and directly found by the jury, evidence *aliunde* consistent with the record may be received to prove the fact; but, even where it appears extrinsically that the matter was properly within the issue controverted in the former suit, if it be not shown that the verdict and judgment necessarily involved its determination, it will not be concluded.[7]

The former adjudication is a finality, concluding

[1] F. *adjorner*, to put off to another day.

[2] La Farge *v.* Van Wagenen, 14 How. Pr. 58 (1857).

[3] Wilson *v.* Lott, 5 Fla. 305 (1853).

[4] Van Dyke *v.* State, 22 Ala. 60 (1853); 6 Wheat. 109.

[5] Trammell *v.* Bradley, 37 Ark. 379 (1881); 1 Bl. Com. 187.

[6] State *v.* Price, 11 N. J. L. 218 (1830); Blaufus *v.* People, 69 N. Y. 111 (1877).

[7] Packet Company *v.* Sickles, 5 Wall. 592 (1866), cases, Nelson, J.; Aurora City *v.* West, 7 *id.* 102–3 (1868), cases; Goodenow *v.* Litchfield, 59 Iowa, 231 (1882); *ib.* 549.

parties and privies, as to every matter received to sustain or to defeat the claim, and as to what might have been offered for that purpose. But where the second action is upon a different demand, the former judgment is an estoppel only as to the matters in issue upon the determination of which the finding was rendered.[1]

A judgment of a court of competent jurisdiction, upon a question directly involved in one suit, is conclusive as to that question in another suit between the same parties. But to this operation of the judgment it must appear, from the face of the record or be shown by extrinsic evidence, that the precise question was raised and determined in the former suit. If there be any uncertainty on this head in the record,—as, for example, if it appears that several distinct matters may have been litigated, upon one or more of which the judgment may have passed, without indicating which of them was litigated and upon which the judgment was rendered,—the whole subject-matter of the action will be at large, and open to new contention, unless this uncertainty be removed by extrinsic evidence showing the precise point involved and determined. To apply the judgment and give effect to the adjudication actually made, when the record leaves the matter in doubt, such evidence is admissible.[2]

When the second suit involves other matter as well as the matters in issue in the former action, the former judgment operates as an estoppel as to those things which were in issue there, and upon the determination of which the first verdict was rendered. Extrinsic evidence, when not inconsistent with the record and not impugning its verity, is admissible to show that a former action involved matters in issue in the suit on trial, and were necessarily determined by the first verdict.[3]

If a former adjudication is not pleaded as an estoppel evidence may be received to show the truth.[4]

It cannot be said that a case is not an authority on one point because, although that point was properly presented and decided, something else was found in the end which disposed of the whole matter.[5] See ADJUDICATUS, Res, etc.

ADJUDICATUS. L. Decided, settled, adjudged, adjudicated, *q. v.*

Res adjudicata, or **res judicata.** A thing adjudicated; a case decided; a matter settled. Plural, *res adjudicatæ* or *judicatæ.*

To make a matter *res judicata* there must be concurrence of four conditions: identity — in the thing sued for, of the cause of action, of the parties to the action, and of the quality in the persons.[1]

Transit in rem judicatam. It passes into a thing adjudicated; it becomes a judgment.

Applies to a contract upon which a judgment has been obtained.[2]

ADJUST.[3] To determine what is due; to settle; to ascertain: as, to adjust a claim, a demand, a right.

Adjuster. He who determines the amount of a claim; as, a claim against an insurance company.

Adjustment. Settlement of the relative rights of parties, of a demand or cross-demands of any nature; in particular, the settlement of the claim of an insured party after a loss.[4]

Unadjusted. Applied to a demand — that the amount is uncertain, not agreed upon.[5]

ADMEASUREMENT. Ascertainment; apportionment.

A writ which lay against one who usurped more than his share; as, of pasture, dower or other right.[6]

ADMINICULAR.[7] Supporting; aiding; strengthening.

Describes testimony adduced to explain or complete other testimony.[8]

ADMINISTER. 1. To dispense, supply, furnish, give: as, to administer poison, or a stupefying mixture.

Not simply to prescribe or give a drug, but to direct and cause it to be taken.[9]

That offense is not to be confined to the manual administering of poison. So construed, the law would be substantially without effect, and would not reach the large class of offenders at whom it is aimed. "Administer" has a far more extended meaning — to furnish or cause to be furnished and taken, to give or cause to be taken, by any mode.[10]

Etymologically, applicable to anything that can be done by the hand to or for another. Neither fraud

[1] Cromwell v. County of Sac, 94 U. S. 251–58 (1876), cases, Field, J.; *ib.* 364–66, cases; Lumber Company v. Buchtel, 101 *id.* 639 (1879); Litchfield v. Goodenow, 123 *id.* 550–51 (1887): 1 Greenl. Ev. § 523; Gilmer v. Morris, 30 F. R. 459 (1887), cases.

[2] Russell v. Place, 94 U. S. 608 (1876), cases, Field, J.; Corcoran v. Chesapeake, &c. Canal Co., *ib.* 745 (1876). See also Foye v. Patch, 132 Mass. 109–11 (1882), cases; McCalley v. Robinson, 70 Ala. 433 (1881); Moore v. City of Albany, 98 N. Y. 410 (1885); Withers v. Sims, 80 Va. 651 (1885); Bennitt v. Star Mining Co., 119 Ill. 14–15 (1886), cases.

[3] Wilson's Executor v. Deen, 121 U. S. 525, 533 (1887).

[4] Meiss v. Gill, 44 Ohio St. 258–60 (1886), cases.

[5] Railroad Companies v. Schutte, 103 U. S. 143 (1880).

[1] Atchison, &c. R. Co. v. Commissioners, 12 Kan. 135 (1873).

[2] See 11 Pet. 100; 2 Sumn. 436; 15 F. R. 300; 28 Minn. 179, 180; 76 Mo. 38; 85 N. C. 456; 42 N. J. L. 117; 18 Johns. 463; 19 S. C. 156.

[3] L. *ad-justus*, according to right.

[4] See 3 Kent, 240, 335; 2 Phillips, Ins. §§ 1814–15.

[5] Richardson v. Woodbury, 43 Me. 214 (1857).

[6] 3 Bl. Com. 183, 238; 3 Kent, 418.

[7] L. *adminiculum*, a prop.

[8] See 1 Greenl. Ev. § 606.

[9] [Robbins v. State, 8 Ohio St. 165 (1857).

[10] [La Beau v. People, 34 N. Y. 232–33 (1866).

nor deception is a necessary ingredient in the act of administering poison. To force poison into the stomach of another; to compel another by threats of violence to swallow poison; to furnish poison to another for the purpose and with the intention that the person shall commit suicide therewith, and which poison is accordingly taken for that purpose; or to be present at the taking of poison by a suicide, participating in the taking by assistance, persuasion, or otherwise, although the party intends and agrees himself also to commit suicide,— each is a mode of "administering" poison. The word does not then always imply service.[1] See ATTEMPT; NOXIOUS.

2. To dispense, direct the application of: as, to administer the law, justice.[2]

Administrable. Capable of being administered or rendered effective: as, an administrable decree or law.

3. To propound the form of; to give, tender: as, to administer an oath.

4. To manage, to settle: as, to administer the estate of an intestate or of a testator who has no executor.

Administered. Applied to legal ends or uses; opposed to **unadministered**: as, the administered or unadministered effects of a decedent.[3]

Administrator. A man appointed by a competent court to settle the affairs of a decedent's estate. **Administratrix.** A woman charged with that duty.

The former word is generally used, in statutes and decisions, to designate the officer.

Administration. The service rendered, or the charge or duty assumed, in the settlement of a decedent's estate.[4]

While administrator designates a representative named by the court, in opposition to an executor, who is designated by will, administration may mean the management of an estate by either an executor or an administrator. See REPRESENTATIVE, (1).

Maladministration; misadministration. In law-books, in which they are often interchanged, these words mean wrong administration.[5]

Waste and embezzlement are examples.[3]

Administration ad colligendum. For collecting — and preserving perishable goods.[6]

Administration cæterorum. Of the rest —

of the goods which cannot be administered under the limited power already granted.[1]

Administration cum testamento annexo. With the will attached — to the letters.

The Latin words are abbreviated *c. t. a.*

Obtains either when no executor is named or when he who is named will not or cannot serve.

The incumbent follows the statute of distributions, unless otherwise directed by the will.

The administrator, in such case, succeeds to all the ordinary powers of the executor. When the will expressly constitutes the executor a trustee for some special purpose, or vests in him a discretionary power in reference to some matter outside of the ordinary powers and duties of an executor, or charges him with some duty indicating a special confidence reposed in him, such duty or power does not pass to an ordinary administrator.[2]

Administration de bonis non. Concerning goods not — already disposed of.

The Latin words are abbreviated *d. b. n.* Occurs where another administrator has died, or been discharged, leaving a part of the estate unsettled.

Administration de bonis non, cum testamento annexo. Upon goods not administered, and with the will annexed to the letters.

The Latin words are abbreviated *d. b. n., c. t. a.* Occurs where an executor has died, or been discharged, leaving a part of the estate yet to be settled.

An administrator *de bonis non* cannot sue the former administrator or his representative for a *devastavit* or for delinquencies in office, because the latter is liable directly to creditors and the next of kin. The former has to do only with the goods of the intestate unadministered. If any such remain in the hands of the discharged administrator or his representative, *in specie*, he may sue for them either directly or on the bond. Regularly, a decree against the administrator for an amount due, and an order for leave to prosecute his bond, are prerequisites to the maintenance of a suit thereon.[2] But otherwise, under statutes.

The preceding administration must have become vacant by resignation, removal, or death.[4]

Administration durante absentia. During absence — when the absence of the proponent of a will or of the executor delays or imperils settlement of the estate.[5]

Administration durante minori ætate. During minority — while the executor named is under lawful age; at common law seventeen.

---

[1] Blackburn v. State, 23 Ohio St. 162-64 (1872); 11 Fla. 256; 4 Car. & P. 868.

[2] See 3 Bl. Com. 72.

[3] See United States v. Walker, 109 U. S. 263-64 (1883).

[4] See 2 Bl. Com. 490; 92 N. Y. 74; 18 S. C. 351.

[5] Minkler v. State, 14 Neb. 183 (1883); Martin v. Ellerbe, 70 Ala. 339 (1881); 37 id. 399; 108 U. S. 199, 206.

[6] 2 Bl. Com. 505.

[1] See 1 Will. Exec. 585.

[2] Pratt v. Stewart, 49 Conn. 339 (1881). Powers as to realty, 24 Am. Law Reg. 689-706 (1885), cases.

[3] Beall v. New Mexico, 16 Wall. 540-42 (1872), cases; United States v. Walker, 109 U. S. 260-61 (1883), cases.

[4] Sims v. Waters, 65 Ala. 443 (1880). See also Conklin v. Egerton, 21 Wend. 432 (1839); Zebach v. Smith, 3 Binn. *69 (1810); 10 Ark. 465.

[5] See 5 Rawle, 264; 16 Wall. 540.

His guardian, or other suitable person, may then take out letters *cum testamento annexo.*

Administration pendente lite. While a suit continues — over an alleged will or the right of an appointment.

The incumbent's duty is limited to filing an inventory, caring for the assets, collecting and paying debts.[1]

Ancillary administration. Subordinate to another administration, and for collecting the effects of a non-resident.[2]

Any surplus beyond the claims of local creditors is paid over to the domiciliary representative.[3]

Foreign administration. Granted at decedent's domicil in another State or country.

Ground for a new probate, ancillary in nature. But a few courts hold that new letters need not be issued.[4]

Letters confer no authority beyond the limits of the State granting them. The title acquired by the administrator of the domicil is a fiduciary one, enforceable in another State only by permission of its laws. No State can be required to surrender the effects or debts due to an intestate domiciled elsewhere to the prejudice of its own citizens. Although the right of the domiciliary administrator may be recognized *ex comitate,* it is subject to the rights of creditors where the assets exist or the debtor resides.[5]

Limited administration. Restricted in time, power, or as to effects.[6]

Public administration. Conducted by a special public officer, or the guardians of the poor, where there is no relative entitled to apply for letters.

Special administration. Limited, either in time or in power.

The instrument given by the officer of probate to the person who proposes to administer upon the estate of an intestate is called the *letters of administration.* This instrument confers authority to take charge of and to settle the estate, collecting dues, paying debts, etc.; and comprises: a copy of the will, if there be a will and no executor; a copy of the decree of allowance of such will in probate; a certificate of the name of the appointee, his rights, duties, etc. The faithful discharge of his duties is secured by an *administrator's bond,* — an obligation entered into by the nominee, with sufficient sureties, and approved by the court.[1]

As against strangers letters of administration are not evidence of death, but merely of their own existence; *i. e.,* that the proceedings have been regularly had, and that the appointee is entitled to the office. Being like an exemplification, they need not be proved.[2] Compare LETTERS, 4; Testamentary.

An administrator represents the personal property of his decedent. He is a trustee thereof for creditors, distributees, and heirs; and is an officer of the court. He takes title from the time of his appointment. He stands in privity with the deceased, succeeding to all his rights, but not to his contract duties of a purely personal nature. He is liable to the amount of the assets. The nearest of kin is preferred for the office: descendants to ancestors; males to females; and, where there is no kin, a creditor of the estate. He is held to the care of a man of ordinary prudence,[3] and to the utmost good faith. Where there are two or more appointees, each is the other's agent; and all sue and are to be sued.

The chief duties of an administrator are to bury the deceased; give public notice of the grant of letters; make an inventory; collect the assets; pay the debts. He may not buy any part of the estate for himself; nor mix the estate's funds with his own; nor let the assets lie idle; nor use them to his own gain. On the more important matters he should seek and follow the direction of the court. For debts and improvements he is to first exhaust the personalty; after that he may convert realty. The law of the decedent's domicil governs the disposal of his personalty, the law of the place where situated his realty.[4]

See ADMINISTRARE; ASSETS; COMPROMISE; EXECUTOR; IMPROVIDENT; INCAPABLE; PERISHABLE; PRIVITY; SETTLE, 3; TRUST, 1; VOUCHEA; WITNESS.

ADMINISTRARE. L. To wait upon, serve; to dispose of, administer.

Plene administravit. He has fully administered. **Plene administravit præter.** He has fully administered except —.

The emphatic words of pleas by an executor or administrator: the former plea meaning that he has lawfully disposed of all assets that have come into his hands; the latter plea, that he has administered all assets except an amount which is not sufficient to satisfy the plaintiff's claim.

---

[1] See 4 Watts, 36; 16 S. & R. 420.

[2] 21 Cent. Law J. 186–90 (1885), cases.

[3] See 11 Mass. 263; 132 *id.* 452; 44 Ill. 202; 32 Barb. 190; 88 Pa. 131.

[4] See Wilkins *v.* Ellett, 108 U. S. 256 (1883); 2 Ala. 429; 18 B. Mon. 582; 18 Miss. 607; 12 Vt. 589.

[5] Moore, Adm'x, *v.* Jordan, 36 Kan. 275 (1887), cases, Johnston, J.; Story, Confl. Laws, § 512; Wyman *v.* Halstead, 109 U. S. 654 (1884), cases.

[6] See McArthur *v.* Scott, 113 U. S. 399 (1883), cases.

[1] See Beall *v.* New Mexico, 16 Wall. 543 (1872); Stovall *v.* Banks, 10 *id.* 583 (1870).

[2] Mutual Benefit Life Ins. Co. *v.* Tisdale, 91 U. S. 243 (1875); Devlin *v.* Commonwealth, 101 Pa. 276 (1882), cases.

[3] See Moore *v.* Randolph, 70 Ala. 584 (1881); Bowereox's Appeal, 100 Pa. 437 (1882).

[4] See generally Williams, and Schouler, on Executors, &c.; 2 Bl. Com. 489; 2 Kent, 409; 1 Pars. Contr 127; 13 How. 466–67.

Unless the defendant falsely pleads *plene adminis-travit* he is not liable to a judgment beyond the assets in his hands. The plea is not necessarily false because not sustained. The jury, if no *devastavit* is averred, must find the amount of the assets, if any, before a judgment can be rendered.[1]

See ACCIDERE, Quando, etc.; BONA, De bonis; DEV-ASTAVIT.

ADMIRALTY.

A court exercising jurisdiction over controversies arising out of the navigation of public waters; also, the system of jurisprudence which pertains to such controversies.

So named because, in England, originally held before the lord high admiral.[2]

"The judicial Power shall extend . . . to all cases of Admiralty and maritime Jurisdiction."[3]

The principal subjects of admiralty jurisdiction are maritime contracts and maritime torts, including captures *jure belli*, and seizures on water for municipal and revenue forfeitures. (1) Contracts, claims, or service, purely maritime, and touching rights and duties appertaining to commerce and navigation. (2) Torts and injuries of a civil nature committed on navigable rivers. Jurisdiction in the former case depends upon the nature of the contract, in the latter entirely upon the locality.[4]

The jurisdiction is not limited to tide-waters, but extends to all public navigable lakes and rivers, where commerce is carried on between different States, or with a foreign nation — wherever ships float or navigation successfully aids commerce.[5]

Courts of admiralty exist in all commercial countries, for the safety and convenience of commerce, the speedy decision of controversies where delay would often be ruin, and to administer the laws of nations in seasons of war, as to captures, prizes, etc. . . . A wide range of jurisdiction was necessary for the benefit of commerce and navigation: these needed courts acting more promptly than courts of common law and not entangled with the niceties and strictness of common-law pleadings and proceedings. . . . The acts of 1789 and 1845 save a concurrent remedy at common law in any Federal or State court, and secure a trial by jury as a matter of right in the admiralty courts. Congress may modify the practice in any respect it deems conducive to the administration of justice.[6]

By the act of September 24, 1789, § 9, the district courts have exclusive original cognizance "of all civil causes of admiralty or maritime jurisdiction; saving to suitors in all cases the right of a common-law remedy, where the common law is competent to give it."[1] The saving does not authorize a proceeding *in rem* to enforce a maritime lien, in any common-law court. Common-law remedies are not applicable to enforce such a lien, but are suits *in personam*, though such suits, under special statutes, may be commenced by attachment of property.[2]

The act of February 26, 1845, limits the powers granted by the act of 1789, as regards cases arising upon the "lakes, and navigable waters connecting said lakes;" limits jurisdiction to vessels of twenty tons burden or upward, enrolled or licensed for the coasting trade, or employed in commerce between places in different States; and grants a jury trial if either party demands it. The jurisdiction is expressly made concurrent with such remedies as may be given by State laws. Otherwise, the jurisdiction granted by the act of 1789 is exclusive in the district courts.[3]

Jurisdiction, in "civil cases," extends to all contracts, claims, and services essentially maritime: among which are bottomry bonds, contracts of affreightment and contracts for conveyance of passengers, pilotage on the high seas, wharfage, agreements of consort-ship, surveys of vessels, damages by the perils of the seas, the claims of material-men and others for the repair and outfit of ships belonging to foreign nations or to other States, and the wages of mariners; and also to civil marine torts and injuries, among which are assaults and other personal injuries, collisions, spoliation and damage, illegal seizures or other depredations of property, illegal disposition or withholding possession from the owners of ships, controversies between part owners as to the employment of ships, municipal seizures of ships, cases of salvage and marine insurance.[4]

Admiralty courts are international courts. As originally constituted they are the appropriate tribunals for controversies between foreigners.[5]

They have jurisdiction of collisions on the high seas between vessels owned by foreigners of different nationalities.[6]

They may estimate damages for death by negligence, when the court has jurisdiction of the vessel and of the subject-matter.[7]

In England there are two courts: the "instance" and the "prize" court, *qq. v.* The same judge presides in both. In the United States this double jurisdiction is vested in the district court.[8]

---

[1] Smith *v.* Chapman, 93 U. S. 42 (1876); 8 Wheat. 675; 5 Cranch, 19; 15 Johns. 323; 89 N. C. 416; 19 S. C. 252; 2 Kent, 417.

[2] 4 Bl. Com. 268.

[3] Constitution, Art. III, sec. 2.

[4] The Belfast, 7 Wall. 637 (1868), cases, Clifford, J.; New England Ins. Co. *v.* Dunham, 11 *id.* 29, 31 (1870).

[5] The Genesee Chief *v.* Fitzhugh, 12 How. 454-59 (1851), Taney, C. J.; The Hine *v.* Trevor, 4 Wall. 562-70 (1866), cases; The Belfast, 7 *id.* 639-41 (1868); The Eagle, 8 *id.* 20-26 (1868); New England Ins. Co. *v.* Dunham, 11 *id.* 23-29 (1870); *Exp.* Easton, 95 U. S. 70 (1877).

[6] The Genesee Chief, *supra;* N. E. Ins. Co. *v.* Dunham, *supra;* 2 Story, Const. § 1672; 1 Brown's Adm. 553; 20 F. R. 63.

[1] R. S., § 563, (8).

[2] The Belfast, 7 Wall. 644, 625 (1868); The Moses Taylor; 4 *id.* 428-31 (1866); The Hine, *ib.* 568 (1866).

[3] R. S. § 566; The Hine, 4 Wall. 569 (1866); The Eagle, 8 *id.* 20-26 (1868); 2 Kent, 365.

[4] *Exp.* Easton, 95 U. S. 68 (1877), Clifford, J. See also De Lovio *v.* Boit, 2 Gall. 398 (1815), Story, J.; 4 Woods, 287; 17 F. R. 887-88, cases.

[5] Thomassen *v.* Whitwell, 9 Bened. 115 (1877); The Belgenland, 114 U. S. 355, 361 (1885).

[6] The Luna, 13 Rep. 6 (E. D. Pa., 1881).

[7] *Exp.* Gordon, 104 U. S. 517-18 (1881), cases.

[8] 1 Kent, 353.

A "mixed case" in admiralty is a contract which does not depend altogether upon locality as the test of jurisdiction; as, a contract for supplies, a charter-party, and the like; but not a tort begun on land and completed on navigable water,[1] nor a policy of insurance upon a ship and its cargo against marine perils.[2]

The libelant propounds the substantive facts, prays for appropriate relief, and asks for process suited to the action, which is *in rem* or *in personam*. The respondent answers those facts by admitting, denying, or declaring his ignorance thereof, *and* alleges the facts of his defense to the case made by the libel. The proofs must substantially agree with the allegations. There are no common-law rules of variance or departure. The court grants relief on the case made out.[3]

The criminal jurisdiction of the Federal courts does not extend to the Great Lakes and their connecting waters; as, for example, the Detroit river. See SEA, High.[4]

See further ACCIDENT; CANAL; COLLISION, 2; CONSORT, 2; DAMAGES; FIDEJUSSOR; LAKES; LIBEL, 4; MARINE; MARITIME; MONITION; NAVIGABLE; PETITORY; RES, 2; SEA; STIPULATION, 1; TIDE; TORT, 2.

ADMISSION.[5] 1. Receiving: reception. Whence admit, admissible, inadmissible, non-admission.

Used of assenting to, allowing, or receiving — a claim, a will to probate, any other writing, or testimony.

Also applied to making a person a member of a privileged class or body, as of the legal profession, or of a partnership or association. See DELECTUS.

2. Recognition as fact or truth; acknowledgment, concession; also, the expression in which such assent is conveyed.

In evidence, applied to civil transactions, and to facts, in criminal cases, not involving criminal intent.[6]

In pleading, what is not denied is taken as admitted.

Direct or **express admission.** An admission made openly and in direct terms. **Implied admission.** Results from an act done or undone; as, from character assumed, from conduct or silence.

Incidental admission. Is made in another connection, or involved in some other fact admitted.

Judicial or **solemn admission.** So plainly made in pleadings filed, or in the progress of a trial, as to dispense with the stringency of some rule of practice.

Partial admission. In equity practice, delivered in terms of uncertainty, with explanation or qualification. **Plenary admission.** Without any qualification.[1]

Admissions are treated as "declarations against interest" and, therefore, probably true. In the absence of fraud they bind all joint parties and privies.[2]

The credibility of an admission is a question of fact. The admission of a right is not the same as of a fact. All the words must be considered. May be by a document, conduct, predecessor in title, agent, attorney, referee, joint party, trustee, officer, principal, husband, wife.[3]

Where the act of the agent will bind the principal, his admission respecting the subject-matter will also bind him if made at the same time, and constituting part of the *res gestæ*.[4]

But an act done by an agent cannot be varied, qualified, or explained, either by declarations, which amount to no more than a mere narrative of a past occurrence, or by an isolated conversation held, or an isolated act done, at a later period. The reason is, the agent to do the act is not authorized to narrate what he had done or how he had done it, and his declaration is no part of the *res gestæ*.[5]

For example, the declaration of the engineer of a train which met with an accident, as to the speed at which the train was running, made from ten to thirty minutes after the accident occurred, is not admissible against the company in an action by a passenger to recover damages for injuries sustained. "His declaration, after the accident had become a completed fact and when he was not performing the duties of engineer, that the train, at the moment the plaintiff was injured, was being run at the rate of eighteen miles an hour, was not explanatory of anything in which he was engaged. It did not accompany the act from which the injuries in question arose. It was, in its essence, the mere narrative of a past occurrence, not a part of the *res gestæ* — simply an assertion or representation, in the course of a conversation, as to a matter not then pending, and in respect to which his authority as engineer had been fully exerted. It is not to be deemed part of the *res gestæ* simply because of the brief period intervening between the accident and the making of the declaration. The fact remains that the occurrence had ended when the declaration in question was made, and the engineer was not in the act of doing anything that could possibly affect it. If his declaration had been made the next day after the accident, it would scarcely be claimed that it was admissible evidence against the company. And yet the circumstance that it was made between ten and twenty minutes — an appreciable period of time — after the

---

[1] The Plymouth, 3 Wall. 34-35 (1865), cases.

[2] New England Ins. Co. *v.* Dunham, 11 Wall. 1 (1870).

[3] Dupont de Nemours *v.* Vance, 19 How. 171 (1656); The Clement, 2 Curtis, 366 (1855).

[4] *Exp.* Byers, 32 F. R. 404 (1887), Brown, J.

[5] L. *ad-mittere*, to send to: receive.

[6] 1 Greenl. Ev. § 170.

---

[1] See 1 Greenl. Ev. §§ 194-211; 1 Chitty, Pl. 600.

[2] 1 Greenl. Ev. § 169.

[3] See Whart. Ev. Ch. XIII.

[4] Story, Agency, § 134. See also 1 Greenl. Ev. § 113.

[5] Packet Company *v.* Clough, 20 Wall. 540 (1874), Strong, J.; American Life Ins. Co. *v.* Mahone, 21 *id.* 157 (1874); Barreda *v.* Silsbee, 21 How. 164-65 (1858), cases; Whiteside *v.* United States, 93 U. S. 247 (1876); Xenia Nat. Bank *v.* Stewart, 114 *id.* 228 (1885), cases.

accident, cannot, upon principle, make this case an exception to the general rule. If the contrary view should be maintained, it would follow that the declaration of the engineer, if favorable to the company, would have been admissible in its behalf as part of the *res gestæ*, without calling him as a witness — a proposition that would find no support in the law of evidence. The cases have gone far enough in the admission of the subsequent declarations of agents as evidence against their principals. These views are fully sustained by adjudications in the highest courts of the States."

Contra. "As the declaration was made between ten and thirty minutes after the accident, we may well conclude that it was made in sight of the wrecked train, in the presence of the injured parties, and whilst surrounded by excited passengers. The engineer was the only person from whom the company could have learned of the exact speed of the train at the time. . It would seem, therefore, that his declaration, as that of its agent or servant, should have been received."

"The modern doctrine has relaxed the ancient rule that declarations, to be admissible as part of the *res gestæ*, must be strictly contemporaneous with the main transaction. It now allows evidence of them when they appear to have been made under the immediate influence of the principal transaction, and are so connected with it as to characterize or explain it. . . . What time may elapse between the happening of the event . . and the time of the declaration, and the declaration be yet admissible, must depend upon the character of the transaction itself. . . The admissibility of a declaration, in connection with evidence of the principal fact, as stated by Greenleaf, must be determined by the judge according to the degree of its relation to that fact, and in the exercise of a sound discretion; it being extremely difficult, if not impossible, to bring this class of cases within the limits of a more particular description. The principal points of attention are, he adds, whether the declaration was contemporaneous with the main fact, and so connected with it as to illustrate its character." [1]

See ACQUIESCENCE; COMPROMISE; CONFESSION, 2; DECLARATION, 1; DEMURRER: ESTOPPEL; EVIDENCE; PART, 1; SILENCE.

---

[1] Vicksburg & Meridian R. Co. *v.* O'Brien, 119 U. S. 99, 105–6 (Nov. 1, 1886), cases, Harlan, J.; Bradley, Woods, Matthews, and Gray, JJ., concurring; Waite, C. J., Field, Miller, and Blatchford, JJ., dissenting,— opinion, pp. 107–9, by Field, J., citing, as in point, the declaration of the engineer and the ruling in Hanover R. Co. *v.* Coyle, 55 Pa. 396, 402 (1867). And see Northern Pacific R. Co. *v.* Paine, 119 U. S. 560 (1877); N. J. Steamboat Co. *v.* Brockett, 121 *id.* 649 (1887). "The true rule is correctly stated by Greenleaf, with its limitations." Darling *v.* Oswego Falls Manuf. Co., 30 Hun, 279, 280–82 (1883), cases. See further, as to *res gestæ*, Little Rock, &c. R. Co. *v.* Leverett, 48 Ark. 338–43 (1886), cases — declaration by injured brakeman; Keyser *v.* Chicago, &c. R. Co., Sup. Ct. Mich. (1887), cases — declaration by an engineer: 36 Alb. Law J. 202, 203, cases; Williamson *v.* Cambridge R.

ADMIXTURE. See ACCESSION: CONFUSION, Of goods.

ADMONITION.[1] A judicial reprimand to an accused person about to be discharged. Whence admonitory.

ADOPT.[2] To choose: take, receive, accept. Whence adoption.

1. To make as one's own what formerly was not so; to appropriate: as, to adopt a symbol or design for a trade-mark, *q. v.*

2. To assent to what affects one's right; to approve, ratify: as, to adopt the unauthorized act of an agent; to adopt a by-law, a charter, a constitution, an amendment.

To "adopt" a route for the transportation of the mails is to take the steps necessary to cause the mail to be transported over that route. [3]

3. To take a stranger into one's family as son and heir; to accept the child of another as one's own child and heir. [4]

"Adopted child" and "adopted parent" are correlative expressions. "Adopting parent" and (but less frequently) "adopter" are also used.

Adoption, in this sense, is regulated by statute in each State. The child becomes in a legal sense the child of the adopted parent. At the same time it remains the child of its natural parents, and is not deprived of the right of inheriting from them, unless expressly so provided by statute. [5]

In the Roman law adoption was an act by which a person undertook to rear the child of another and appoint such child as his heir. Some special authority of law was necessary to constitute the relation. No right to adopt a child exists at common law. The methods known in modern law are by a decree of a competent court and by indenture. [6]

Adoption was unknown to the common law, but was recognized in the civil law from its earliest days. The effect was to make a stranger the son and heir of the adopting person. The stranger entered the family and came under the power of its head; he became as a child, and his children as grandchildren, of the adopter. Under the Spanish law as it existed while Texas was part of Mexico, no person having a legitimate child living could adopt a stranger as co-heir with his child. The statute law of that State has imported the civil law, modified in important respects. It gives the adopted party the position of a child so

Co., 144 Mass. 150 (1887) — declaration by conductor of a street car.

[1] L. *ad-monere*, to advise.
[2] L. *adoptare*, to choose.
[3] Rhodes *v.* United States, 1 Dev. 47 (1856).
[4] See Vidal *v.* Commagere, 13 La. An. 157 (1858): Webster.
[5] Wagner *v.* Varner, 50 Iowa, 534 (1879). See, as to inheriting lands in another State or country, Ross *v.* Ross, 129 Mass. 245–68 (1880), cases.
[6] Ballard *v.* Ward, 87 Pa. 361 (1879); Shafer *v.* Eneu, 54 *id.* 306 (1867), Strong, J.; 8 W. N. C. 14; 10 *id.* 80.

far as to make him an heir, but does not make him a member of the adopter's family. It allows him to inherit, to an extent, along with legitimate children.[1]

ADS. See VERSUS.

ADULT.[2] A person twenty-one or more years of age.

Where an assault becomes "aggravated, when committed by an adult male on a female or a child, or by an adult female on a child," "adult" means a person who has attained the age of twenty-one.[3]

Some processes may be served upon an adult member of a man's family. See AGE; INFANT; NEGLIGENCE.

ADULTERATE. To mix with food, drink, or drugs, intended for sale, other matter inferior in quality, and, perhaps, deleterious in character.

In some States no recovery can be had for a sale of adulterated liquors.

Watered milk may not be "adulterated" milk unless expressly declared so by statute.[4] See OLEOMARGARINE; POLICE, 2; SEAL, 5.

ADULTERY.[5] Criminal intercourse between a married person and one of the opposite sex whether married or single.[6]

Sexual connection between a married woman and an unmarried man or a married man other than her own husband.[7]

At common law adultery cannot be committed with a single woman. The child of such is *filius nullius*, possesses no inheritable blood, and cannot therefore be imposed as a legitimate heir upon a husband, for the mother has no husband, and cannot consequently occasion an adulteration of issue. The heinousness of the offense, by that law, consists in exposing an innocent husband to the maintenance of another man's child and to having it succeed to his estate. For the offense there lay, not an indictment, but a civil action for damages for the private wrong.[8]

By the civil law adultery could only be committed by the unlawful sexual intercourse of a man with a married woman. In the English ecclesiastical courts the offense is (or was) established by showing that the husband has had illicit intercourse with a married or an unmarried female.[9]

To sustain the charge there must be proof of actual marriage. Reputation and cohabitation (*q. v.*) are not enough; there must be strict proof of the fact.[1]

In allegations for divorce, although presumptive evidence alone is sufficient to establish the fact of adulterous intercourse, the circumstances must lead to it not only by fair inference but as a necessary conclusion; appearances equally capable of two interpretations, one of them innocent, will not justify the presumption of guilt. Evidence simply showing full and frequent opportunity for illicit intercourse is not alone sufficient.[2]

"Living in adultery" means living in the practice of adultery.[3] It is not necessary that the parties live together in the same house continually, as man and wife. An habitual illicit intercourse between them, though living apart, constitutes the offense.[4]

Adulterine. Children begotten in adultery.

See BIGAMY; CONDONE; CONVERSATION, 1; DIVORCE; POLYGAMY.

ADVANCE.[5] 1. To move forward on a list or calendar of causes, for early consideration: as, to advance a cause — whence advanced cause.

2. To supply beforehand; to loan before work is done or goods made: as, to advance materials or moneys.[6]

An advance of money on a contract is a payment made before an equivalent is received.[7]

In maritime insurance, has no fixed meaning; commonly refers to advances to a crew or on account of freight; may include money expended by a fishing vessel for bait.[8]

In a will, "advanced" and "loaned" may be interchanged.[9]

In a will, may not be restricted to "advancement" within the meaning of a statute, but may include any benefit conferred which the testator might have considered an appropriation of his estate.[10]

In its strict legal sense, "advances" does not mean gifts — advancements, but a sort of loan; and, in its ordinary sense, includes both loans and gifts — loans more readily, perhaps, than gifts.[11]

[1] Eckford v. Knox, 67 Tex. 204 (1886), cases, Willie, C. J. See also Barnhizel v. Ferrell, 47 Ind. 338 (1874); 14 Am. Law Reg. 682–84 (1875), cases; 1 South. Law Rev. 70–85 (1875), cases; 3 Cent. Law J. 397 (1876).

[2] L. *adultus*, grown up.

[3] George v. State, 11 Tex. Ap. 95 (1881). Compare Bell v. State, *id.* (1885): 21 Cent. Law J. 221, cases.

[4] People v. Tauerback, 5 Park. Cr. 311 (1864); 132 Mass. 11–14; 2 Q. B. D. 530. See generally "Adulteration of Food," 22 Am. Law Rev. 95–106 (1888), cases.

[5] L. *adulterare*, to make impure, corrupt.

[6] Miner v. People, 58 Ill. 60 (1871).

[7] Hood v. State, 56 Ind. 271–74 (1877); 27 Minn. 300.

[8] State v. Lash, 16 N. J. L. 384–90 (1833); State v. Wallace, 9 N. H. 517 (1838); Matchin v. Matchin, 6 Pa. 336–37 (1847). See Leviticus, xx, 10; Deut. xxii, 22–28.

[9] Commonwealth v. Call, 21 Pick. 511–13 (1839). See also State v. Fellows, 50 Wis. 65 (1880); 1 Crim. Law Mag. 579–82 (1880), cases; 1 Law Quar. Rev. 471–74 (1885).

[1] Miner v. People, 58 Ill. 60 (1871); 16 *id.* 85; Montana v. Whitcomb, 1 Monta. 362 (1871).

[2] Pollock v. Pollock, 71 N. Y. 141–42, 144–48 (1877), cases; Loveden v. Loveden, 2 Hagg. 1 (1810); 1 Whart. Ev. § 225.

[3] Goodwin v. Owen, 55 Ind. 249 (1876).

[4] Smith v. State, 39 Ala. 555 (1865); 14 *id.* 609.

[5] F. *avancer*, to go forward: *avant*, before.

[6] Powder Company v. Buckhardt, 97 U. S. 117 (1877), Hunt, J.

[7] Gibbons v. United States, 1 Dev. 51, § 145.

[8] Burnham v. Boston Mar. Ins. Co., 139 Mass. 39 (1885).

[9] Wright's Appeal, 89 Pa. 70 (1879).

[10] Barker v. Comins, 110 Mass. 488 (1872).

[11] Nolan's Executors v. Bolton, 25 Ga. 355 (1858).

A mortgage for "future advances" is valid at common law and throughout the United States, except where forbidden by local law.[1] See GUARANTY, 2.

Advancement. Giving, by anticipation, the whole or a part of what it is supposed a child will be entitled to on the death of the giver.[2]

A pure and irrevocable gift made by a parent to a child in anticipation of such child's future share of the parent's estate.[3]

A giving by a parent to a child or heir, by way of anticipation, of the whole or a part of what it is supposed the donee will be entitled to on the death of the party making it.[4]

"Advancements" means money or property given by a father to his children as a portion of his estate, and to be taken into account in the final partition or distribution thereof. "Advances" has a broader signification: it may characterize a loan or a gift, or money advanced, to be repaid conditionally.[5]

There is no intention to have a "gift" chargeable on the child's share of the estate. In "debt" the relation of debtor and creditor still exists.[6]

If, after an advancement, a will be made, the intention of the testator with respect thereto is a matter of fact determinable from the will and extrinsic testimony.[7]

Proof that gifts were made is not sufficient: it must appear that they were intended as advancements.[8]

Advancement is always a question of intention; and this must be proven to have existed at the time of the transaction. Thus, declarations of a parent that money, for which he held a note, was an advancement will establish it as such. The declarations must be of the res gestæ, accompanying the act.[9] See HOTCHPOT.

ADVANTAGE. See BENEFIT; COMMODUM; INTEREST, 1.

ADVENTURE.[10] 1. An enterprise of hazard.

2. A partnership for a single transaction.

3. Goods sent abroad to be disposed of for the benefit of the owner.

Also called a *marine* adventure; and evidenced by a *bill of adventure*.

In marine insurance, synonymous with "perils." Describes the enterprise or voyage insured against.[1]

ADVERSARY. See ADVERSE, 2.

ADVERSE.[2] 1. Acting against or in a contrary direction; opposed to; conflicting with, contrary to, the interest of another. In some senses, opposed to *amicable*.

As, an adverse — claim, conveyance, employment, enjoyment, interest, judgment, party, possession, proceeding, service, suit, title, verdict, use, qq. v.

2. Biased, hostile: as, an adverse witness.

Adversary.[3] Having an opposite party; adverse; not amicable.

As, an adversary — action, judgment, proceeding.

ADVERSUS. See A, 3; VERSUS.

ADVERTISEMENT.[4] Information given by hand-bill or newspaper. See LETTER, 3; REWARD, 1.

Official advertisement. Such as is made by some public authority and in pursuance of law.

Advertisement in a newspaper, under direction of law, is equivalent to notice; as, of a proceeding in court, of the dissolution of a partnership. See PUBLICATION, 1.

The exclusive right to employ a particular method of advertising, as by a card displaying paints of various colors, is not the subject of a copyright.[5]

ADVICE. Counsel, opinion; information given, or, perhaps, consultation had, as to action or conduct. Compare ADVISE; INOPS, Consilii. See INFLUENCE.

As per advice. On a bill of exchange, deprives the drawee of authority to pay the bill until in receipt of the letter of advice: the drawer's letter containing information as to paying the bill.[6] See under LETTER, 3.

ADVISE. Where a statute authorizes a trial judge to "advise" the jury to acquit an accused person, a request by counsel that the

---

[1] Lawrence v. Tucker, 23 How. 27 (1859), cases; Jones v. Guaranty, &c. Co., 101 U. S. 626 (1879); Nat. Bank of Genesee v. Whitney, 103 id. 99 (1880).

[2] (Osgood v. Breed's Heirs, 17 Mass. 358 (1821), Parker, C. J.

[3] Yundt's Appeal, 13 Pa. 580 (1850); 89 id. 341.

[4] Wallace v. Reddick, 119 Ill. 156 (1886), Scott, C. J.; Grattan v. Grattan, 18 id. 170 (1856), cases, Skinner, J.; Kintz v. Friday, 4 Dem., N. Y., 542–43 (1886), cases.

[5] Chase v. Ewing, 51 Barb. 612 (1868).

[5] Weatherhead v. Field, 26 Vt. 668 (1854).

[7] Wright's Appeal, 89 Pa. 70 (1879).

[6] Comer v. Comer, 119 Ill. 180 (1886).

[9] Merkel's Appeal, 89 Pa. 343 (1879); Holliday v. Wingfield, 59 Ga. 208 (1877); Dillman v. Cox, 23 Ind. 442 (1864); Fellows v. Little, 46 Vt. 35 (1865); Clark v. Wilson, 27 Md. 700 (1867); Eshleman's Estate, 74 Pa. 47 (1873); Dunham v. Averill, 45 Conn. 87 (1877); Rickenbacker v. Zimmerman, 10 S. C. 115–16 (1877), cases; 67 Law Times, 261.

[10] F. aventure, chance: L. adventurus, about to happen. Compare MISADVENTURE.

[1] Moores v. Louisville Underwriters, 14 F. R. 233 (1882), Hammond, J.

[2] L. adversus, opposed to.

[3] Ad'versary.

[4] Advertise'; adver'tisement or -tise'ment.

[5] Ehret v. Pierce, 18 Blatch. 302 (1880).

[6] See Byles, Bills, 91.

court "instruct" the jury to acquit should be denied.[1] Compare ADVICE; INSTRUCT, 2.

Advisable. See DISCRETION, 2.

Advisor. See COMMUNICATION, Privileged, 1; ATTORNEY.

Advisory. Containing counsel or a suggestion, yet not concluding or binding.

The verdict of a jury on an issue out of chancery is advisory;[2] a judge's opinion on the facts in a case may be regarded as advisory;[3] a nomination to an office may be an advisory designation.

ADVOCATE.[4] See JUDGE-ADVOCATE.

An assistant; an associate in conducting a lawsuit.

A person who makes a profession of presenting cases orally.

"Of advocates, or (as we more generally call them) counsel, there are two species or degrees: barristers and sergeants."[5]

In the United States no distinction is made between an advocate and an attorney, q. v.

ADVOWSON.[6] Taking into protection. The right of presentation to a church or ecclesiastical benefice.

Advowsons are (were) appendant, or in gross; and presentative, collative, or donative.[7]

ÆDIFICATA. See SOLUM, Ædificata.

ÆQUITAS. L. Equity.

Æquitas sequitur legum. Equity follows the law.

Where the law, or the common law, is ineffectual, equity affords relief, following at the same time the rules of law.[8] See EQUITY.

AEROLITE. See ACCRETION.

ÆS. L. Money.

Æs alienum. Another's money. **Æs suum.** One's own money.

The principle of bankrupt and insolvent laws is fairly expressed by the phrase "æs alienum," which, in Roman law, signified a debt. The property of a debtor, to the extent of his indebtedness, belongs to his creditors.[9]

ÆSTIMATIO. See CAPUT, Æstimatio.

AFFAIRS. Things done or to be done; business interests.

A word of large import. A receiver who has the management of the "affairs of a railroad com-

pany" must necessarily have control and management of the road.[1]

AFFECT. To act upon; to concern: as, cases affecting public ministers.

Often used in the sense of acting injuriously upon a person or thing; as in a proviso that an act shall not affect any confirmed claim to lands.[2]

AFFECTION. See CONSIDERATION, 2.

AFFIDAVIT.[3] A voluntary oath, before some judge or officer of a court, to evince the truth of certain facts; as, the facts upon which a motion is grounded.[4]

Affiant. One who makes an affidavit.

An affidavit is simply a declaration, on oath, in writing, sworn to by the declarant before a person who has authority to administer oaths.[5]

It does not depend upon the fact whether it is "entitled" in any cause or in a particular way. Without a caption it is an affidavit.[6]

It is not necessary that the party sign the statement, unless a statute expressly so require. It is the official certificate which gives authenticity to the written oath.[6]

In common parlance, any form of legal oath which may be taken.[7]

Hence, in a statute, may mean simply an oral oath.[7]

The officer must sign the jurat; otherwise the document is not an affidavit.[8]

The certificate is no part of the affidavit, but the *prima facie* evidence that it is the affidavit of the person by whom it purports to have been made.[9]

Counter affidavit. An affidavit made or filed in opposition to the averments contained in another affidavit.

Supplemental affidavit. An affidavit containing averments upon the same subject-matter as another affidavit previously presented, and designed to remedy some defect in that other.[10]

---

[1] People v. Horn. 70 Cal. 18 (1886); Cal. Penal Code, § 1118.

[2] Watt v. Starke, 101 U. S. 252 (1879).

[3] Nudd v. Burrows, 91 U. S. 439 (1875).

[4] L. *advocatus*, one called upon.

[5] 3 Bl. Com. 26.

[6] Advow'zŭn. L. *advocatio*, patronage.

[7] 2 Bl. Com. 21–22; 21 E. L. & Eq. 417.

[8] 2 Bl. Com. 350; 3 *id.* 441; 1 Story, Eq. § 64; 10 Pet. 210; 15 How. 299.

[9] 3 Pars. Contr. 428.

---

[1] Tompkins v. Little Rock, &c. R. Co., 15 F. R. 13 (1882).

[2] Ryan v. Carter, 93 U. S. 83 (1876).

[3] L. *affidavit*, he has made oath: *ad fidem dare*, to pledge faith for.

[4] 3 Bl. Com. 304; 2 Tex. Ap. 503.

[5] Harris v. Lester, 80 Ill. 311 (1875), Scott, C. J.

[6] Hagardine v. Van Horn, 72 Mo. 371 (1880). See 8 Iowa, 320; 16 N. J. L. 125.

[7] Baker v. Williams, 12 Barb. 557, 530 (1850). See 77 N. C 331; 28 Wis. 463.

[8] Morris v. State, 2 Tex. Ap. 503 (1877); State v. Richardson, 34 Minn. 118 (1885); 18 *id.* 90.

[9] Hitsman v. Garrard, 16 N. J. L. 125 (1837); Hagardine v. Van Horn, 72 Mo. 371 (1880).

[10] See Callan v. Lukeus, 89 Pa. 136 (1879); 1 T. & H. § 423.

Among the more common affidavits in use in civil practice are:

Affidavit of cause of action, which avers that a just cause of action exists.

Affidavit of claim, which verifies the statements of facts upon which a claim or demand is made.

Affidavit of defense, which verifies the statements of facts upon which a defendant resists a demand made upon him. See DEFENSE, 2, Affidavit, etc.

Affidavit of or *to the merits* (q. v.), which is to the sufficiency of the facts which constitute a defense in a civil action, instead of resistance upon technical grounds.

Affidavit to hold to bail, which is that the cause of action, brought for a civil injury, is valid.

Affidavits serve to verify allegations of fact not already matters of record, and thereby qualify them for judicial action; also, to initiate remedies, giving to statements the impress of good faith and probable cause. They are no part of the record in a case unless specially made so.[1]

Compare COMPLAINT, 2; DEPOSITION. See APPARERE, De non, etc.; CAPTION, 2; JURAT; KNOWLEDGE, 1; OATH; RECORD.

AFFILIATION. See FILIATION.

AFFINITAS. L. Nearness; affinity.

Affinitas affinitatis. The tie between the respective kindred of a married couple.

Affines. Relations by marriage.

AFFINITY. Relation by marriage. See AFFINITAS.

The tie which arises from marriage between the husband and the blood relations of the wife, and between the wife and the blood relations of the husband.[2] Opposed, *consanguinity*.

There is no affinity between the blood relations of the husband and of the wife.[3] See CONSANGUINITY; RELATION, 3.

AFFIRM.[4] 1. To aver a thing as established or certain, or as existing, or as provable as a fact. Whence affirmative, affirmation.

Affirmative (1), *adj.* Asserting as true; declaratory of what exists or is to be or to be done; positive. Opposed, *negative*.

As, affirmative or an affirmative — allega-

tion, averment, condition, covenant, defense, evidence, pleading, representation, statute, warranty, words, *qq. v.*

(2), *n.* The affirmative: the party who maintains or supports. Opposed, *the negative*.

The burden of proof rests upon him who holds the affirmative of an issue.[1] See PROOF, Burden of.

Affirmative pregnant. An affirmative allegation implying a negative in favor of the adverse party.

Opposed, *negative pregnant:* a negative allegation involving or admitting of an affirmative implication, or, at least, an implication favorable to the adverse party.[2] See NEGATIVE.

Affirmatively. (1) In positive terms; by positive testimony, and not by way of inference.

Error in judicial action, not being presumed, must be shown affirmatively.[3]

(2) In favor of what is proposed; approvingly.

A legislative committee is said to report a bill affirmatively, or negatively.

2. To make binding what before was not obligatory, but voidable; to confirm, to ratify, *qq. v.* Opposed, *disaffirm*. Whence affirmance, disaffirmance.

An infant, to avoid a deed, must disaffirm within a reasonable time after his majority is attained. While the decisions differ as to what constitutes a disaffirmance, the preponderance of authority is that mere inertness or silence, continued for a period less than prescribed by the statute of limitations, unless accompanied by voluntary affirmative acts manifesting an intention to assent to the conveyance, will not bar his right to avoid the deed. He cannot disaffirm while infancy continues.[4] See DISABILITY; RESCISSION; VOIDABLE.

3. To support or confirm: as, for a court of review to affirm the judgment or order of a lower court. Opposed, *reverse*. Whence affirmance, affirmed. See CURIA, Per curiam.

4. To attest by a solemn declaration, made in a judicial inquiry, to speak the truth. Whence affirmant, affirmation.

An affirmation, which is generally made by such persons as interpret the words of Scripture "Swear

---

[1] 65 Pa. 31; 100 U. S. 232.

[2] 1 Bl. Com. 434.

[3] Paddock *v.* Wells, 2 Barb. Ch. 333 (1847); 1 Denio, 26, 187; 29 Me. 545.

[4] F. *afermer*, to fix; L. *ad-firmus*, steadfast.

[1] 1 Greenl. Ev. § 74; 119 Ill. 357.

[2] Gould, Plead. 295; Steph. Pl. 331.

[3] 101 U. S. 601.

[4] Sims *v.* Everhardt, 102 U. S. 309, 312 (1880), cases; Brazee *v.* Schofield, *id.* (1889); Dawson *v.* Helmes, 30 Minn. 113 (1882), cases; Wilson *v.* Branch, 77 Va. 71–72 (1883), cases; Catlin *v.* Haddox, 49 Conn. 492 (1882), cases; Nathans *v.* Arkwright, 66 Ga. 186 (1880); Adams *v.* Beall, Sup. Ct. Md. (1887), cases: 8 Atl. Rep. 664; 26 Am. Law Reg. 713–15 (1887), cases; Bishop, Contr. §§ 936–44, cases.

not at all," etc., as prohibitory of an oath, does not, like an oath, involve an appeal to the Supreme Being.

A common form is, "You do solemnly, sincerely, and truly declare and affirm, that you will state the truth," etc. Upon assent to this interrogation the affirmant is bound as by oath, and liable to punishment as for perjury. See OATH; PERJURY.

AFFIRMANTI. See PROBARE, Probatio.

AFFIX. See FIXTURE; SEAL, 1.

AFFRAY.[1] The fighting of two or more persons in some public place to the terror of his majesty's subjects.[2]

When persons come together without a premeditated design to disturb the peace, and suddenly break out into a quarrel among themselves.[3]

More of a private nature than a "riot."[3]

If the fighting be in private it is an "assault." Actual or attempted violence is essential; the "terror" is presumed. An abettor is a principal.[2] See ABET; ACCIDENT.

AFFREIGHTMENT. See FREIGHT.

AFORE. Before; formerly; previously.

Aforesaid. Spoken of formerly. See SAID.

Aforethought. Conceived beforehand. See MALICE.

AFRICAN. See CITIZEN; COLOR, 1; SLAVERY.

AFTER. Further off, behind: subsequent to a date or event; exclusive of; subject to.

Where time is to be computed "after" a day that day is excluded.[4]

In the devise to A, "after" providing for B—subject to, after taking out, deducting or appropriating.[5]

Does not necessarily refer to time; may refer to order in point of right or enjoyment. "After settling my estate" is equivalent to "subject to the settlement."[6]

"After the charges herein," and "after the payment of my debts," means subject to the charges, subject to the payment of the debts.[7] See ON.

A contract to pass a title "after" payment of the

purchase price is to be understood as if it read "upon" payment.[1] See MATURITY, 2.

After-acquired. Obtained after some event: as, property acquired after a will was made, or after an adjudication in bankruptcy, or after a judgment is recovered. See ACQUIRE.

After-discovered. Came to light or was disclosed after an event or occurrence: as, after-discovered evidence, an after-discovered principal. See AGENT; AUDITA QUERELA; DISCOVERY, 3.

AFTERNOON. See DAY.

A complaint for not closing a saloon "at nine o'clock" and keeping it open till "past eleven in the afternoon" is not bad for failing to show that nine o'clock at night was meant.[2]

AG. Against; agreeing.

AGAINST. In opposition to; opposed; contrary to; adversely to. Compare CONTRA.

An enactment that neither party shall be allowed to testify "against" each other, as to any transaction with the deceased person whose estate is interested in the result, has been construed to allow the representative of the decedent to compel the opposite party to testify *for* the estate.[3]

A verdict in disobedience of instructions upon a point of law may be said to be "against law."[4]

Against the form of the statute. In an indictment alleges that a statute has been broken. See further FORM, 2, Of statute.

Against the peace. Words in use to charge a breach of the peace. See PEACE, 1.

Against the will. Words used to charge violence. See WILL, 1.

AGE. A period in life at which a person may do an act which, before that time, he could not do; "of age."

The period at which one attains full personal rights and capacity.

The time of life when a particular power or capacity becomes vested; as, in the phrases age of consent, age of discretion, qq. v.[5]

Full age. Twenty-one; majority.

Attained the day preceding the anniversary of birth. Considered as arbitrarily fixed, but very generally adopted.[6]

An infant is liable, as for deceit, for an injury re-

---

[1] F. *affraier*, to terrify,—4 Bl. Com. 145. "It affrighteth or maketh afraid,"—3 Coke, 158. L. L. *ex frediare*, to break the peace: disturb, frighten,—Skeat. L. *frigus*, shudder from fear,—Webster.

[3] 4 Bl. Com. 145; Order of Friends v. Garrigus, 104 Ind. 139 (1884); 70 Ala. 28; 33 Ark. 178; Rosc. Cr. Ev. 270; Arch. Cr. Pl. 1709.

[3] People v. Judson, 11 Daly, 83 (1849), Daly, J.—Astor Place Riot Case.

[4] Sheets v. Selden, 2 Wall. 190 (1864); 2 Hill, 355.

[6] Hooper v. Hooper, 9 Cush. (1851); 9 Pet. 470.

[6] Lamb v. Lamb, 11 Pick. *378 (1831), Shaw, C. J.; Minot v. Amory, 2 Cush. 387 (1848).

[7] King v. King, 14 R. I. 146 (1883); *ib.* 516. See also 63 Wis. 301, 573, 588; 9 H. L. Cas. 1.

[1] Hawley v. Kenoyer, 1 Wash. T. 611 (1879).

[2] People v. Husted, 52 Mich. 624 (1884).

[3] Dudley v. Steele, 71 Ala. 426 (1882).

[4] Declez v. Save, 71 Cal. 553 (1887); 40 *id.* 545; 4 Bosw. 262.

[5] [Abbott's Law Dict.

[6] 1 Bl. Com. 463; 2 Kent, 233.

ulting from his fraudulent representation that he is
f full age.[1] See ACKNOWLEDGMENT, 2; MUTUAL, 1.

Lawful age. The period in life when a
person may do a particular act, or serve in a
given relation.

Non-age. Under the age at which the
law has conferred ability to perform an act;
minority.

At common law a male at twelve may take the
oath of allegiance; at fourteen choose a guardian,
and, if his discretion be proved, make a will of personalty; at seventeen be an executor; at twenty-one is
at his own disposal, may alien his property and make
all contracts. A female, by the common law, may, at
seven, be betrothed or given in marriage; at nine is
entitled to dower; at twelve is of years of maturity,
may consent to marriage, and, if proved to have sufficient discretion, may bequeath her personalty; at
fourteen is of years of legal discretion, and may
choose a guardian; at seventeen be an executrix; at
twenty-one dispose of herself and her lands.[2]

A male from eighteen to forty-five is liable to mili-
ary service; at twenty-five is eligible as a Representative, at thirty as a Senator, and at thirty-five as
President.

See ADULT; INFANT; INFLUENCE; INSANITY; SEDUC-
TION; WHEN.

AGENDO. See ARREST, 2 (3).

AGENT.[3] A person employed by another
to act for him. Opposed, *principal*.

Agency. The relation between two persons as principal and agent.

The term agent includes many classes of persons to
which distinctive appellations are given; as, a factor,
broker, attorney, cashier, director, auctioneer, clerk,
partner, supercargo, consignee, ship's husband, master
of a vessel, *qq. v.*

The relation is founded upon contract, but not for
the doing of an unlawful act or an act of a strictly
personal nature.

General agent. An agent empowered to
transact all business of a particular kind.
Special agent. An agent employed to do
a single act or for a special transaction.

A "special agency" exists when there is a
delegation of authority to do a single act; a
"general agency" when there is a delegation
to do all acts connected with a particular
trade, business, or employment.[4]

To constitute one a general agent it is not necessary
that he should have done before an act the same *in
specie* with that in question. It is enough if the trans-

action involves the same general power that he has
usually exercised, though applied to a new subject-
matter.[1]

The principal is responsible for the acts of his general agent when acting within the general scope of
his authority, and the public cannot be supposed to be
cognizant of any private instructions; but where the
agency is special and temporary, and the agent exceeds his employment, the principal is not bound.[2]

The doctrine of general agency does not apply to
non-trading partnerships: as to them there is no presumption of authority to support the act of a partner.[3]

Public agent. A person by whom a
power of government is exercised.

Public agents represent the legislative, judicial, and
executive departments of government. They have
such power only as has been specifically conferred
upon them.[4]

Sub-agent. A person selected by an
agent to perform a part or all of the duties of
the employment.

An agent is answerable to his principal for the act
of his sub-agent although the principal knows that the
sub-agent has been employed.[5]

When an agent has power to employ a sub-agent
the acts of the latter, or notice given him in the
transaction of the business, have the same effect as if
done or received by the principal.[6]

Universal agent. One who is appointed
to do all the acts which the principal personally can do, and which he may lawfully delegate the power to another to do.[7]

Such agency may potentially exist; but it is difficult
to conceive of its practical existence, since it puts the
agent completely in the place of the principal.[7]

An infant, or *feme covert* (her husband consenting),
may serve another as agent; but not so a person who
has an adverse interest or employment.[8]

---

[1] Rice v. Boyer, 108 Ind. 472–80 (1886), cases.

[2] 1 Bl. Com. 463.

[3] L. *agens, agentis*, doing, acting.

[4] Story, Agency, § 17; *ib.* §§ 127, 133; Keith v. Hersch-
berg Optical Co., 48 Ark. 145 (1886), cases, Smith, J.;
1 Ind. 288; 35 Iowa, 281; 102 Mass. 225; 9 N. H. 263;
4 N. Y. 421; 16 *id.* 133, cases.

---

[1] Commercial Bank of Erie v. Norton, 1 Hill, 504
(1841); Merchants' Bank v. State Bank, 10 Wall. 650
(1870); Mining Co. v. Anglo-Californian Bank, 104 U. S.
192 (1881).

[2] Minn v. Commission Co., 15 Johns. 54 (1818); Scott
v. McGrath, 7 Barb. 55 (1849), cases; Adriatic Ins. Co.
v. Treadwell, 108 U. S. 365–66 (1883); Bohart v. Oberne,
36 Kan. 289 (1887); Bickford v. Menier, Ct. Ap. N. Y.
(Dec. 13, 1887); 26 Cent. Law J. 236; *ib.* 239–41 (1888),
cases; 2 Kent, 620; Smith, Contr. 363; cases *ante*.

[3] Pease v. Cole, 53 Conn. 60–65 (1885), cases. The
question was whether one member of a partnership
for conducting a theater could bind his partner by a
promissory note in the name of the firm, the copartner having no knowledge of the transaction.

[4] Whiteside v. United States, 93 U. S. 257 (1876), cases;
Anthony v. County of Jasper, 101 *id.* 699 (1879); *Exp.*
Virginia, 100 *id.* 347 (1879); Virginia v. Rives, *ib.* 313 (1879).

[5] Barnard v. Coffin, 141 Mass. 40 (1886), cases.

[6] Hoover v. Wise, 91 U. S. 310 (1875), cases; Story,
Agency, §§ 452, 454.

[7] Story, Agency, § 21.

[8] Wharton, Agency, § 14; Story, Agency, § 4.

The act of an agent, done in the usual way in the line of his employment, binds the principal.[1] His authority is limited to the usual and ordinary means of accomplishing the business intrusted to him.[2]

Knowledge in the agent is knowledge in the principal.[3]

The rule that notice to the agent is notice to the principal applies not only to knowledge acquired by the agent in the particular transaction, but to knowledge acquired in a prior transaction and present to his mind at the time he is acting as agent, provided it be of a character he may communicate to his principal without breach of professional confidence. The general rule, that the principal is bound by the knowledge of his agent, is based on the principle of law that it is the agent's duty to communicate his knowledge and the presumption that he will perform that duty.[4]

Where the principal has employed the agent to do an act upon the existence of a fact peculiarly within the latter's knowledge, and of the existence of which the execution of the power is a representation, a third person, dealing with the agent in good faith, may rely upon such representation, and the principal be estopped from denying the truth of the representation.[5]

But where communication by the agent would prevent him from consummating his own fraudulent purpose, the knowledge he possesses will not be imputed to the principal. In this sense, for example, a director of a corporation, acting wholly for himself, cannot be treated as the agent of the corporation. Uncommunicated notice received by the agent in prosecuting his private business will not bind the employer.[6]

An agent's act affecting negotiable paper requires specific authority.[7]

He is to exercise the highest good faith toward his principal.

He may make no profit secretly out of funds belonging to the principal.[8] See TRUST, 1.

The principal is answerable for the agent's act of negligence (q. v.) done in the course of the employment.[9]

He should name the principal as the contracting party in the body of a contract, and sign as agent.[1]

A note made by an agent within the principal un named in the body, but signed "B, agent for A," or "B for A," is the note of A, the principal. But inserting "for," "in behalf of," or "as" the principal, and signing the name of the agent, does not make the contract the principal's.[2]

In a bill payable to and indorsed by "B, agent," the word "agent" is a *designatio personæ*, and he may show by parol that he was merely an agent, as the plaintiff knew.[3]

Only where the power as given is under seal need the agent use the principal's name with a seal.[4] See further SEAL, 1.

Under a deed of trust a person may be the agent of another to buy and sell, without exposing the donor's bounty to liability for the agent's former debts.[5] See further TRUST, 1.

An agent who discloses the name of his principal is not liable on a contract, unless he agrees to be held.[6] The principal may sue on a contract made in the name of his agent.[7] But where a third party discovers the undisclosed principal he may sue either the principal or the agent.[8]

Where the principal and the agent are liable on a contract, each continues liable until satisfaction is made.[9]

An agency is dissolved (1) by revocation — (a) by the principal, except when the power is "coupled with an interest" or given for value, is part of a security, or a severable portion is executed and there exists no indemnity for the rest. Revocation takes effect from the time of notice. (b) The agent may renounce at any time, paying damages, if any, as to the part unexecuted. (2) By termination — by insanity or death, except when coupled with an interest; not, necessarily, by marriage or bankruptcy. (3) By extinction of the subject-matter or of the principal's power over the same. (4) By operation of law, in various ways. (5) By complete execution of the trust.[10]

See further ADMISSION, 2; ATTORNEY; COLLECTION;

---

[1] Barreda v. Silsbee, 21 How. 164–65 (1858), cases; Hoffman v. Hancock Mut. Life Ins. Co., 92 U. S. 164 (1875), cases; Whiteside v. United States, 93 *id.* 257 (1876), cases.

[2] Williams v. Getty, 31 Pa. 461 (1858).

[3] Hoover v. Wise, 91 U. S. 310 (1875), cases; Smith v. Ayer, 101 *id.* 320 (1879); Vicksburg, &c. R. Co. v. O'Brien, 119 *id.* 105 (1886).

[4] The Distilled Spirits, 11 Wall. 366–68 (1870), cases, Bradley, J.

[5] Bank of Batavia v. New York, &c. R. Co., Ct. Ap. N. Y. (1887): 7 Cent. Rep. 822. Cases *pro* and *con*, 26 Am. Law Reg. 576–81 (1887), cases.

[6] Innerarity v. Merchants' Nat. Bank, 139 Mass. 333–35 (1885), cases; Wilson v. Second Nat. Bank of Pittsburgh, Sup. Ct. Pa. (1886): 6 Cent. Rep. 756; Frenkel v. Hudson, 82 Ala. 162–63 (1886), cases.

[7] 1 Pars. Contr. 62; The Floyd Acceptances, 7 Wall. 676 (1878); Anthony v. County of Jasper, 101 U. S. 699 (1879).

[8] Northern Pacific R. Co. v. Kindred, 3 McCrary, 631 (1881), cases.

[9] Philadelphia, &c. R. Co. v. Quigley, 21 How. 209–10

(1858), cases; The Clarita, 23 Wall. 12 (1874); The Cahill, 9 Bened. 353–54 (1878), cases.

[1] Gottfried v. Miller, 104 U. S. 527 (1881), cases.

[2] Barlow v. Congregational Society, 8 Allen, 460, 463–64 (1864), cases, Gray, J.

[3] Bartlett v. Hawley, 128 Mass. 92 (1876), Gray, C. J.; 29 Minn. 121; 38 Ohio St. 444–45.

[4] Stanton v. Camp, 4 Barb. 276 (1848); Whitney v. Wyman, 101 U. S. 392 (1879).

[5] Nichols v. Eaton, 91 U. S. 725–30 (1875), cases.

[6] Whitney v. Wyman, 101 U. S. 392, 396 (1879); Cragin v. Lovell, 109 *id.* 194, 198 (1883), cases.

[7] New Jersey Steam Nav. Co. v. Merchants' Bank, 6 How. 381 (1848); Ford v. Williams, 21 *id.* 289 (1858).

[8] Wharton, Agency, § 464, cases; Merrill v. Kenyon, 48 Conn. 317 (1880), cases; Beymer v. Bonsall, 79 Pa. 300 (1875); N. Y., &c. Steamship Co. v. Harbinson, 15 F. R. 688 (1883), cases; ib. 694–96, cases.

[9] Story, Agency, § 295; Wharton, Agency, § 473; Beymer v. Bonsall, 79 Pa. 300 (1875).

[10] Story, Agency, §§ 462–500; Frink v. Roe, 70 Cal. 309 (1886); 2 Kent, 643; 4 Pet. 344.

LEGATUS; DESCRIPTIO; DIRECTOR; DISABILITY; FARE, Qui facit; INTEREST, 2 (2), Coupled, etc.; LIVERY-N; MANAGING; PARTNERSHIP; PRINCIPAL, 4; PROXY; TIFICATION; RES, 2, Gestæ; SERVANT, 3; TORT. 2.

AGGRAVATION.[1] Whatever adds to e weight of an act — in its consequences or ilt. Opposed, *mitigation.*

Something done by the defendant, on e occasion of committing the trespass, hich to some extent is of a different gal character from the principal act comained of.

As, where a plaintiff declares in trespass for enter-g his dwelling-house, and alleges in addition that e defendant also destroyed goods in the house and saulted the domestics.[2] See DAMAGES, Special.

Aggravated. Increased, in severity or normity: as, aggravated assault and batry, which is a more serious offense than mple assault and battery, *q. v.*

AGGREGATE. See CORPORATION, Ag-egate.

AGGREGATIO MENTIUM. L. Colction of purposes; collected intentions; greement.

Essential to a contract; where there is a misunder-nding, wanting.[3]

Not the origin of "agreement." That derivation is suggested by the harmony of intention which is sential.[4] See AGREEMENT; ASSENT.

AGGRIEVED.[5] Damaged, injured, ex-sed to loss: as, that the party aggrieved ay appeal or have a writ of error.

The "party aggrieved" is he against whom l appealable order or judgment has been tered;[6] a party prejudiced by the judg-ent;[7] one against whom error has been mmitted by a decree or judgment entered;[8] e whose pecuniary interest is directly af-cted by the order or decree — whose right property may be established or divested r the order or decree.[9]

Before a person can be said to be "aggrieved," so to be entitled to an appeal within the meaning of 296 of the code of New York, the adjudication must ve binding force against his rights, his person, or property. The fact that an order may remotely

---

1 L. *aggravare*, to add to a load: *gravis*, heavy.

Hathaway *v.* Rice, 19 Vt. 107 (1846), Royce, C. J. e also Steph. Plead. 257; 3 Am. Jur. 287–313.

Utley *v.* Donaldson, 94 U. S. 49 (1876).

1 Pars. Contr. 6.

F. *agrever*, to overwhelm: L. *ad-gravis.*

Ely *v.* Frisbee, 17 Cal. 261 (1861).

People *v.* Pfeiffer, 59 Cal. 91 (1881); 8 *id.* 315

State *ex rel. v.* Boyle, 6 Mo. 59 (1878).

Dietz *v.* Dietz, 38 N. J. E. 485 (1884).

or contingently affect interests which a receiver rep-resents does not give him a right of appeal.[1]

In the New York act of 1858, the party aggrieved by proceedings relative to any assessment for local im-provements in the city of New York may apply to vacate the same. This refers to the person injured by the proceedings. The injury must be a direct, not a remote or consequential, result.[2]

AGIST.[3] Originally, to feed cattle in the king's forest: a service performed for a con-sideration by officers called "agisters" or "gist-takers." Now, to pasture animals for pay.

Agistment. Where a man takes in a horse or other cattle to graze and depasture in his grounds.[4]

Agister. One who takes the cattle of an-other into his own ground to be fed for a consideration to be paid by the owner.

He has a lien for the keep; and may maintain tres-pass or trover against a stranger for taking the ani-mals away.[5]

While he does not insure the safety of an animal he is responsible for ordinary negligence in the care he takes of it.[6]

He, and not the owner, is liable for injuries done by beasts prone to commit trespasses.[7]

AGNATI. See NATUS, Agnati.

AGNOSTIC. See OATH.

AGREE.[8] To concur in thought; to unite in mental action, be of one mind, assent. Opposed, *disagree.*

May be read "grant;" as where a grantor agrees that no building shall be erected on an adjoining lot.[9]

Arbitrators, judges, and jurors, are said to agree, and to disagree.

Agreed balance. See BALANCE.

Agreed statement of facts. Facts sub-mitted as true to a court, for an opinion upon the law in the case. See CASE, 2, Stated.

Agreement. Union of minds to a thing; concurrence of intention; mutual assent. More specifically, a mutual agreement, a contract.

Consists of two or more persons being of

---

1 Ross *v.* Wigg, 100 N. Y. 246 (1885), Earl, J.

2 Matter of Walter, 75 N. Y. 357 (1878); 91 *id.* 2; 100 *id.* 246; 141 Mass. 208; 143 *id.* 235.

3 F. *giste*, abode: L. *jacere*, to lie.

4 2 Bl. Com. 452.

5 Bass *v.* Pierce, 16 Johns. 596 (1853).

6 Story, Bailm. § 443, cases.

7 Rossell *v.* Cottom, 31 Pa. 526–29 (1858), cases; Red-dick *v.* Newburn, 76 Mo. 424 (1882); Kemp *v.* Phillips, 55 Vt. 69 (1883). Case of agistment of 1,200 head of cattle. Teal *v.* Bilby, 123 U. S. 572 (1887).

8 F. *agreer*, to receive with favor.

9 Hogan *v.* Barry, 143 Mass. 538 (1887).

the same mind, intention, or meaning, concerning the matter agreed upon.[1]

The expression by two or more persons of a common intention to affect their legal relations.[2] See UNDERSTANDING.

In the Statute of Frauds is not understood in the loose sense of a promise or undertaking, but in its more proper and legal sense of a mutual contract on consideration between two or more parties.[3]

In a popular sense frequently declares the engagement of one person only. When a man "agrees" to pay money or to do some other act, the word is synonymous with "promise," "engage."[4]

In popular signification means no more than concord, the union of two or more minds, concurrence of views and intention. Every thing done or omitted by the compact of two or more minds is universally and familiarly called an agreement. Whether a consideration exists is a distinct idea which does not enter into the popular notion. In most instances any consideration, except the voluntary impulse of minds, cannot be ascribed to the numberless agreements that are made daily. . In its broad sense, synonymous with the concord of two or more minds, or mutual assent. If there is nothing to limit the meaning, regards promises only, not their consideration.[5]

In which ever sense understood in the Statute of Frauds the requirement is that it be in writing — if not to be performed within a year.[6]

The meaning of the contracting parties is their agreement.[7]

Also, the writing which preserves the evidence of the reciprocal promises.

Articles of agreement. The memorandum of the terms of an agreement; an agreement in writing.

Should state the names and residence of the parties, the subject-matter, the promises to be performed, the date, and any other elements of the contract.

See AGGREGATIO; ASSENT; CONTRACT; CONVENTIO; PARTY, 2; MERGER, 2; PERFORMANCE; RESCISSION.

AGRICULTURE. A person engaged in agriculture is engaged in raising cereals and stock. "Agriculture," in its general sense, is the cultivation of the ground for the purpose of procuring vegetables and fruits for the use of man and beast; or, the act of preparing the soil, sowing and planting seeds, dressing the plants, and removing the crops. In this sense the word includes gardening or horticulture, and the raising or feeding of cattle and other stock. In a more common and appropriate sense — that species of cultivation which is intended to raise grain and other field crops for man and beast; "husbandry," as defined by Webster.[1]

A person who cultivates a one-acre lot and is also a butcher and a day laborer is not "engaged in agriculture," within the meaning of an exemption law.[1]

A person is "actually engaged in the science of agriculture" when he derives the support of himself and family, in whole or in part, from the tillage and cultivation of fields. He must cultivate something more than a garden, though it may be less than a field. If the area cultivated can be called a *field*, the employment is "agriculture," as well in contemplation of law as by the etymology of the word. This condition being fulfilled, the uniting of other business not inconsistent with the pursuit of agriculture will not take away the protection of a law exempting one horse, harness, and a plow from levy and sale.[2]

See CROP; CULTIVATION; HORSE; IMPLEMENTS; TOOLS.

AID.[3] 1. Help; assistance; support.

Aid and abet. In common parlance, assistance, co-operation, encouragement.[4]

Assistance rendered by acts, words of encouragement, or support; or presence, actual or constructive, to render assistance should it become necessary.[5] See DECOY.

Aider and abettor. One who assists another in the accomplishment of a common design or purpose.

He must be aware of and consent to the design.[6]

Mere presence is not enough: something must be said or done showing consent to the felonious purpose and contributing to its execution.[7]

Aiders and abettors cannot be punished under a statute which creates a felony, unless the statute applies to all who are guilty, and not alone to the person actually committing the offense. Thus under a statute for confining in the penitentiary "any woman who shall endeavor to conceal the birth of her bastard child," aiders and abettors cannot be punished.[8] See CONSPIRACY; FELONY; PRINCIPAL, 5; LIQUOR, *ad fin.*

---

[1] Leake, Contr. 12.

[2] [Anson, Contr. 3.

[3] [Wain v. Warlters, 5 East, *17 (1804), Ellenborough, C. J.

[4] Packard v. Richardson, 17 Mass. 131 (1821), Parker, C. J.

[5] Sage v. Wilcox, 6 Conn. 85-94 (1826), Hosmer, C. J. See also Packard v. Richardson, 17 Mass. 131-34 (1821); Marcy v. Marcy, 9 Allen, 10-11 (1864), Bigelow, C. J.; Woodworth v. State, 20 Tex. Ap. 382 (1886); 31 F. R. 249.

[6] Marcy v. Marcy, 9 Allen, 10-11 (1864).

[7] Whitney v. Wyman, 101 U. S. 396 (1879), Swayne, J.

[1] Simons v. Lovell, 7 Heisk. 515 (1872), Sneed, J.

[2] Springer v. Lewis, 22 Pa. 193 (1853), Woodward, J.; 62 Me. 526; 64 Ga. 128.

[3] F. *aider*: L. *adjutare* (*ad-jurare*), to help.

[4] United States v. Gooding, 12 Wheat. 476 (1827), Story, J.

[5] Rainford v. State, 59 Ala. 108 (1877), Stone, J.

[6] Adams v. State, 65 Ind. 574-75 (1879), cases, Hawk, J.; United States v. Snyder, 14 F. R. 555 (1882): 1 Sup. R. S. 358; 127 Mass. 17.

[7] Kemp v. Commonwealth, 80 Va. 450 (1885), cases.

[8] Frey v. Commonwealth, 83 Ky. 190 (1885). See generally 18 Cent. Law J. 446 (1884) — *Canad. Law Times.*

Aid and comfort. In treason, any overt act which, if successful, would advance the interests of a treasonable design.[1]

Actual assistance is not essential.[1]

The subject of a foreign nation who furnished munitions of war to the Confederates, or did an act which would have rendered him liable to punishment for treason had he owed allegiance to the United States, gave "aid and comfort" to the rebellion, within the meaning of the act of March 12, 1863 (12 St. L. 820), and cannot recover the proceeds of property captured and paid into the treasury.[2]

Municipal aid. Assistance rendered by a municipal or a *quasi* municipal corporation, as, a township or a county, toward some work of internal improvement. Whence *aid bonds.*[3]

A steam grist-mill may or may not be a work of that nature.[4]

The legislature of a State, unless restrained by the organic law, has the right to authorize a municipal corporation to take stock in any work of internal improvement, to borrow money to pay for it, and to levy a tax to repay the loan. And this authority can be conferred in such a manner that the object may be attained with or without the sanction of a popular vote.[5] See BOND, Municipal; CORPORATE, Purpose.

2. Cure, remedy, supply. Whence aid and aider by verdict. See VERDICT.

Aid societies. See BENEFIT, Society.

AIR. A qualified property may be had in the air or atmosphere.[6]

The private owner of property has a natural right to purity of air; and, formerly, a like right to its free passage. Easements relative thereto are: a right to pollute it to an extent justified by the customary business of the locality; and, to send noise through it.[7]

No man may so use the air as to injure his neighbor. To poison or materially change it is a nuisance.[8]

An easement in the air coming over another's land cannot be acquired in the United States.[1]

Upon a conveyance, the right to air coming over other land of the grantor is implied as an easement of necessity.[2]

The right to pure air is an incident to land. While in cities the causes of pollution cannot be as easily traced as in sparsely inhabited places, yet, when the source of a well-defined nuisance is definitely known, the courts will protect the rights of any person injured by it. Each case must rest upon its own merits. The rule by which a court will be guided is the maxim that every one must so use his own property as not to injure another.[3]

See HEALTH; NUISANCE; OCCUPANCY; PROPERTY, Qualified; UTERE, Sic, etc.

A. J. See A, 3.

ALASKA. See TERRITORY, 2.

Congress has power, in its discretion, to prohibit the importation, manufacture, and sale of intoxicating liquors in the district of Alaska, and to make the violation of the prohibition a crime.[4]

ALCOHOL. See DISTILLER; LIQUOR.

An act of Congress approved May 20, 1887 (24 St. L. 69), the substance of which has been enacted in many of the States, provides —

"Section 1. That the nature of alcoholic drinks and narcotics, and special instruction as to their effects upon the human system, in connection with the several divisions of the subject of physiology and hygiene, shall be included in the branches of study taught in the common or public schools, and in the military and naval schools, and shall be studied and taught as thoroughly and in the same manner as other like required branches are in said schools, by the use of text-books in the hands of pupils where other branches are thus studied in said schools, and by all pupils in all said schools throughout the Territories, in the military and naval academies of the United States, and in the District of Columbia, and in all Indian and colored schools in the Territories of the United States.

"Sec. 2. That it shall be the duty of the proper officers in control of any school described in the foregoing section to enforce the provisions of this act; and any such officer, school director, committee, superintendent, or teacher who shall refuse or neglect to comply with the requirements of this act, or shall neglect or fail to make proper provisions for the instruction required and in the manner specified by the first section of this act, for all pupils in each and every school under his jurisdiction, shall be removed from office, and the vacancy filled as in other cases.

"Sec. 3. That no certificate shall be granted to any person to teach in the public schools of the District of Columbia or Territories, after January 1, 1888, who has not passed a satisfactory examination in physiology and hygiene, with special reference to the nature and

---

[1] [United States v. Greathouse, 4 Saw. 458 (1863), Field, J.

[2] Young v. United States, 97 U. S. 62 (1877).

[3] See 4 Neb. 455; 104 Ill. 285.

[4] Township of Burlington v. Beasley, 94 U. S. 310 1876); Osborne v. County of Adams, 106 id. 181 (1882).

[5] Thomson v. Lee County, 3 Wall. 330 (1865); James v. Milwaukee, 16 id. 159 (1872); Kenicott v. The Supervisors, ib. 452 (1872); Railroad Co. v. County of Otoe, ib. 667 (1872); Town of Concord v. Savings Bank, 92 U. S. 625 (1875); Fairfield v. County of Gallatin, 100 id. 47 (1879); Quincy v. Cooke, 107 id. 549 (1882); Ottawa v. Carey, 108 id. 123 (1883); Lewis v. City of Shreveport, ib. 286 (1883); City of Savannah v. Kelly, ib. 184 (1883); Grenda County Supervisors v. Bragden, 112 id. 261 1884), cases.

[6] 2 Bl. Com. 14.

[7] 10 A. & E. 590; 4 DeG. & S. 315; 11 H. L. C. 650; 10 C. B. 268; 19 W. R. 804; 4 Bing. N. C. 183.

[8] Appeal of Penn. Lead Co., 96 Pa. 116, 123 (1880); 2 Ld. Ray. 1163.

---

[1] Randall v. Sanderson, 111 Mass. 119 (1872), cases; 54 N. Y. 439; 25 Tex. 238; 17 Am. L. Reg. 440, note.

[2] Wash'b. Easem. 618; 115 Mass. 204; 34 Md. 1.

[3] Sellers v. Parvis, &c. Co., 30 F. R. 166 (1886).

[4] Nelson v. United States, 30 F. R. 112 (1887).

the effects of alcoholic drinks and other narcotics upon the human system."

ALDERMAN.[1] Originally, a senior: a superior in wisdom or authority.

A word of frequent occurrence among the Anglo-Saxons. All princes and rulers of provinces, all earls and barons, were aldermen in a general sense: but the word applied more particularly to certain chief officers.

In modern times, an officer in municipal corporations who is a kind of "assessor" to the chief magistrate.[2]

In England he sat with the bishop at the trial of causes, applying the common, while the latter expounded the ecclesiastical, law. Aldermen also sat as justices of assize, and exercised such powers of government as were conferred by the charters of their cities or towns, in that character taking cognizance of both civil and criminal matters. The term has designated an officer having judicial as well as civil power, in England from a period beyond the Conquest.[3]

In American cities "the aldermen" are a legislative body with limited judicial power, as, in matters of internal police; in some cities they hold separate courts and exercise magisterial authority.[4]

In some cities their sole functions are those of a magistrate of a court not of record and of limited statutory jurisdiction in civil and criminal matters: corresponding, in these respects, to justices of the peace in boroughs and townships. See COUNCIL, 2; JUSTICE, 2; MAGISTRATE.

ALE. See LIQUOR.

ALEATORY.[5] Depending upon an event the outcome of which is unknown; resting upon a contingency.

Applied, mainly, to annuities and insurance contracts. It is of the essence of all aleatory contracts that there should be risk on one side or on both sides.[6]

ALIA. See ALIUS.

ALIAS. L. 1. Otherwise; also used for—

Alias dictus. Otherwise called.

Alias, in the expression "A, *alias* B," denotes that those names are different descriptions of the same person. The word was formerly employed in connection with *dictus*—otherwise called. The use of *alias* alone to express the whole meaning has long obtained. The term has become familiar as equivalent to "otherwise called" or "otherwise known as." Generally the true name precedes the *alias dictus*. The term so used will avoid a variance or misnomer.[7]

2. At another time; formerly; before.

An *alias* execution is a process issued, upon a *scire facias* or otherwise, where the original execution has been returned, lost, or legally extinguished as a writ. It is another and different execution actually issued at a different time.[1]

ALIBI. L. In another place; elsewhere. The defense that at the time laid in the charge of an offense the accused was in another place.

Being proven, the conclusion is "not guilty."

The evidence on the part of the defendant must outweigh the testimony that he was at the place charged.[2]

The defense must cover the time when the offense is shown to have been committed, so as to preclude the possibility of presence at the *locus in quo*. This impossibility is to be proven like any other fact.[3]

The court, without discrediting the defense in the particular case, may observe generally that the defense is open to suspicion, because it offers opportunity and temptation to employ false witnesses, and because it may mislead through a mistake of honest witnesses as to the precise day and hour.[4]

ALIEN.[5] 1, *n.* One born in a strange country under obedience to a strange prince, or out of the liegeance of the king.[6]

One born out of the king's dominion or allegiance.[7]

A citizen or subject of a foreign state.[8]

In California a "non-resident alien" who may take by succession is one who is neither a citizen of the United States nor a resident of that State.[9]

Alienage; alienism. The legal status or condition of an alien.

Alien born. A naturalized citizen or subject.

Alien enemy. One who owes allegiance to an adverse belligerent.[10]

Alien friend. A citizen or subject of a friendly power; one whose country is at peace with ours.[11]

By the common law a person born within the dominion of the United States is a natural-born citizen

---

1 Roberts v. Church, 17 Conn. 145 (1845).

2 Commonwealth v. Webster, 5 Cush. 319, 323 (1850).

3 Briceland v. Commonwealth, 74 Pa. 469 (1873); State v. Northrup, 48 Iowa, 583 (1878); People v. O'Neil, 59 Cal. 259 (1881); Ware v. State, 67 Ga. 349 (1881); Savage v. State, 18 Fla. 975 (1882); State v. Beaird, 34 La. An. 106 (1882).

4 See State v. Blunt, 59 Iowa, 469 (1882); Dawson v. State, 62 Miss. 243 (1884); 6 Crim. Law Mag. 655-63 (1885), cases; 22 Am. Law Rev. 297-98 (1888), cases.

5 L. *alienus*, strange, a stranger.

6 [Coke, Litt. 128 b.

7 1 Bl. Com. 373.

8 Milne v. Huber, 3 McLean, 219 (1843); 2 Kent, 50.

9 State v. Smith, 70 Cal. 156 (1886); Civil Code, § 672

10 1 Kent, 72.

11 [1 Bl. Com. 372.

---

1 A. S. *ealderman*, elder-man, elder: *eald*, old.

2 Brown's Law Dict.; Spelman, Gloss.

3 Purdy v. People, 4 Hill, 409, 387 (1842), Walworth, Ch. See 1 Hume, Eng. 69.

4 [Bouvier's Law Dict.]

5 Pronounced ā'-le-ă-tō-ry. L. *alea*, a die: chance.

6 Moore v. Johnston, 8 La. An. 489 (1852); Henderson v. Stone, 6 Mart. 690 (1823); May, Ins. § 5.

7 Kennedy v. People, 39 N. Y. 250-52 (1868); 3 Salk. 238; 4 Johns. 118.

whatever the status of his parents. An exception is made of the children of ambassadors.[1]

An "alien born" may not purchase lands for his own use, for the king is thereupon entitled to them. One reason is that if he could purchase, the nation might in time become subject to foreign influence. But he may acquire personalty, which is of a movable nature; besides that, trade demands this indulgence. As a consequence he may maintain actions concerning personalty, and dispose of it by will. An "alien enemy," however, has no rights unless by the sovereign's special favor.[2]

By the common law an alien may *take* lands by purchase, though not by descent; in other words, while he cannot take by the act of the law he may take by the act of the party. But he has no capacity to *hold* lands, and they may be seized into the hands of the sovereign. Until so seized, the alien has complete dominion over them. In this regard alien friends and alien enemies are alike. The title is devested by office-found,[3] *q. v.*

Disabilities as to holding realty have been removed in the States. See LAND, Public.

At common law an alien is protected in his person, as to such property as he may own, in his relative rights, and in his reputation. In return for protection he is required to pay taxes. He cannot become President, nor, in some States, governor. Seven years after he has been naturalized he may be elected to Congress. Unnaturalized, he could not be adjudged a bankrupt, he cannot take out a copyright, nor can he exercise any political right. See PATENT, 2; TRADE-MARK.

See further ALLEGIANCE; CITIZEN; DENIZEN; IMMIGRATION; NATURALIZE.

Alien and sedition laws. See SEDITION.

2, *v.* To transfer; to alienate, *q. v.*

Alienable. Admitting of transfer from one person to another. **Inalienable,** less frequently **unalienable,** not subject to transfer or devestment.

" Inalienable rights " are such rights as cannot be bartered, given or taken away except in punishment of crime.[4]

An "unalienable right" is one which cannot be surrendered to government or society, because no equivalent can be received for it, and one which neither the government nor society can take away, because they can give no equivalent. Of such is the right of conscience.[5]

ALIENATE. See ALIENATIO.

To transfer property to another; to make a thing another man's.

In common law to alienate realty is voluntarily to part with ownership in it, by bargain and sale, conveyance, gift, or will.[1]

The right, originally, was a right in the owner of realty to divert it from his heir.[1]

To transfer or convey a title.[2]

An entry to foreclose does not do this.[2]

Alienee. He to whom property — realty, is transferred. **Alienor.** He by whom realty is transferred.

Alienation. Any method whereby an estate is voluntarily resigned by one man and accepted by another, whether that be effected by sale, gift, marriage, settlement, devise, or other transmission of property by the mutual consent of the parties.[3]

An act whereby one man transfers the property and possession of lands, tenements, or other things, to another.[4]

A transfer short of a conveyance of the title is not an alienation of an estate.[5]

Absolute alienation. A transfer of realty without condition or qualification.

Conditional alienation. A transfer of realty made to rest upon some event yet to happen, or upon some act yet to be done; as, a covenant to convey an estate. See CONDITION.

Blackstone describes four modes of alienation or transfer of title to real estate which he calls "common assurances:" by matter *in pais* or deed; by matter of record in the courts; by special custom; by devise.[6]

See CONVEYANCE, 2; MORTGAGE; TRANSFER.

ALIENATIO. L. Transfer, alienation.

From *alienare*, to make to be the property of another: *alienus*, another.

Alienatio rei præfertur juri accrescendi. The alienation of a thing is preferred in law to its accumulation. Alienation, rather than the accumulation, of property is favored.[7]

Limitations upon alienation, imposed by public policy or by general statutes, are designed to prevent perpetuities and accumulations of realty in corpora-

---

[1] Town of New Hartford *v.* Town of Canaan, 54 Conn. 40–45 (1886), cases.

[2] 1 Bl. Com. 372.

[3] Fairfax *v.* Hunter, 7 Cranch, 619–21 (1813), Story, J.; Conrad *v.* Waples, 96 U. S. 289–90 (1877); Phillips *v.* Moore, 100 *id.* 212 (1879); Hauenstein *v.* Lynham, *ib.* 484 (1879).

[4] Butchers' Union Co. *v.* Crescent City Co., 111 U. S. 756 (1884), Field, J.

[5] Hale *v.* Everett, 53 N. H. 60 (1868).

[1] [Burbank *v.* Rockingham Mut. Fire Ins. Co., 24 N. H. 558 (1852). See also Lane *v.* Maine Mut. Fire Ins. Co., 12 Me. 48 (1835); 13 R. I. 622.

[2] Huntress *v.* Place, 137 Mass. 409 (1884).

[3] 2 Bl. Com. 287.

[4] Boyd *v.* Cudderback, 31 Ill. 119 (1863); 1 N. Y. 48.

[5] Masters *v.* Madison County Ins. Co., 11 Barb. 630, 629 (1852).

[6] United States *v.* Schurz, 102 U. S. 397 (1880); 2 Bl. Com. 294.

[7] See 2 Bl. Com. 175, 288; 3 Kent, 507; 4 *id.* 131, 441; 59 Pa. 342; 76 Va. 144.

tions and ecclesiastical bodies, and to protect creditors against fraud by debtors. But there is no reason why a person who is solvent should not make another, who parts with nothing, an object of bounty, thereby protecting him from the ills of life, the vicissitudes of fortune, improvidence, etc.[1] See ACCUMULATION; TRUST, 1.

ALIENI. See under ALIUS.

ALIKE. See EQUAL; EQUIVALENT.

ALIMONY.[2] Support; provision; allowance for necessaries or maintenance.

1. An allowance made to a woman for her support out of her husband's estate, after a divorce *a mensa et thoro*.[3]

Applicable to all allowances, whether annual or in gross, made to a wife upon a decree of divorce — either from bed and board or from the bond of matrimony.[4]

Alimony pendente lite or **temporary.** An allowance at the institution of the suit to pay the expenses thereof and to supply the wife with necessaries. **Permanent alimony.** An allowance for future maintenance at the time a divorce is decreed.

Originally allowed because the wife was without other means of support or of obtaining the money necessary to defray her expenses in the suit, the husband owning everything. Where she has sufficient separate property that reason does not exist.[5]

Not the separate property of the wife, but a portion of the husband's estate for her subsistence. At her death arrears belong to the husband, subject to the payment of her debts.[6]

The amount, which is largely discretionary with the court, is usually proportioned to the rank of the parties, and is, ordinarily, about one-third of their joint income.[7]

The allowance is based upon the existence of the marriage relation, the ability of the husband, and the circumstances of the wife.[8]

To entitle the wife to permanent alimony there must have been a valid marriage; by the common law the marital relation must continue to exist — a rule generally changed by statute; the separation must be by decree; and she must not be the guilty party — except in a few of the States. An independent suit for an allowance is not maintainable. In a few States a gross sum is given. The right ceases upon re-cohabitation.

A wife under sentence of separation from bed and board is entitled to make a domicil for herself; and, by her next friend, she may sue her husband for the alimony decreed.[1]

Consult the statutes and decisions of each State. See DIVORCE.

2. In Louisiana the necessary expenses of a municipality; also, funds therefor.

The duty of levying a tax to pay registered judgments is subordinate to the duty of first providing for "the necessary alimony or support of the city."[2]

"The duty of providing for the alimony of the city is lodged in the discretion of the common council, in the legal exercise of which the courts may not interfere."[3]

ALIO; ALITER. See under ALIUS.

ALIUD. See CONCEAL. 5.

ALIUNDE. See under ALIUS.

ALIUS. L. Another, other; different. Plural, *alii*.

Alia enormia. Other wrongs. See ENORMIA; INTER, Alia.

Alieni generis. Of another kind.

Alieni juris. Under another's right or authority. See JUS, Sui, etc.

Alio intuitu. Under another aspect.

Alios. Other persons. Whence *et al.*, and *et als.*, q. v. See also A, 3.

Aliter. In another manner; otherwise — held or decided.

Introduces an exception to a rule or general principle.

Aliunde. From another — person, place, or source.

Designates evidence derived from an extrinsic source; as, testimony offered to contradict, vary, or explain the terms of a written instrument, or to explain an ambiguity therein.[4] Compare DEHORS. See PAROL, 2, Agreement.

ALIVE. See DEATH.

When an animal is stolen "alive" it is not necessary, in the indictment, to state the fact: the law presumes it; but when dead, that fact must be stated.[5]

ALL. Compare A, 4; EVERY; OMNIS.

May mean "each" or "every one."[6]

In the acts of legislatures, as in common parlance, "all," being a general rather than a universal term, is to be understood in one sense or the other according to the demands of sound reason.[7]

---

[1] Nichols v. Eaton, 91 U. S. 725 (1875). As to restraints in wills, see 18 Cent. Law J. 307–8 (1884), cases.

[2] L. *alimonia: alere*, to nourish, support, supply.

[3] 1 Bl. Com. 441; 1 Kent, 128; 36 Ga. 319; 18 Ill. 40; 93 N. C. 420.

[4] Burroughs v. Purple, 107 Mass. 432 (1871), cases, Gray, J.

[5] Westerfield v. Westerfield, 36 N. J. E. 197 (1882); Collins v. Collins, 80 N. Y. 1, 11–12 (1880).

[6] Holbrook v. Comstock, 16 Gray, 110 (1860), cases.

[7] 1 Bl. Com. 441–42; Bacon v. Bacon, 43 Wis. 203 (1877).

[8] Daniels v. Daniels, 9 Col. 150–51 (1886), cases.

(4)

---

[1] Barber v. Barber, 21 How. 590–98 (1858), cases. As to right to, after divorce, see 24 Am. Law Reg. 1–21 (1885), cases; and generally 26 *id.* 33–37 (1887), cases.

[2] Marchand v. New Orleans, 37 La. An. 18 (1886).

[3] United States v. New Orleans, 31 F. R. 537 (1887).

[4] 1 Greenl. Ev. § 291.

[5] Kollenberger v. People, 9 Col. 266 (1886); 1 Whart. Cr. L. § 359.

[6] Sherburne v. Sischo, 143 Mass. 442 (1887); Towle v. Delano, 144 *id.* 100 (1887).

[7] Kieffer v. Ehler, 18 Pa. 391 (1852); Stone v. Elliott, 11 Ohio St. 258 (1860).

All cases. See CASE, 1.

All faults. See FAULT, 2.

All-fours. Entirely alike.

Cases or decisions are said to be or to run "upon all-fours" when alike in such circumstances as affect their determination. The expression is metaphorical — from the running of mated quadrupeds.

All rights reserved. See RESERVE, 2.

ALLEGARE. L. To lay before one: to relate, allege.

Allegans contraria non est audiendus. He who alleges contradictory things is not to be listened to.

"A man shall not blow hot and cold." In Scotch phrase, no man may "approbate and reprobate." [1] See ESTOPPEL.

Allegans turpitudinem. See TURPITUDE, Allegans, etc.

Allegata et probata. Allegations and proofs.

A rule of evidence is, that the *allegata* and the *probata* must agree: the proofs must correspond with the averments. [2] See ALLEGATION.

ALLEGATION. Statement of what one can prove; positive assertion; an averment in pleading. See ALLEGARE.

Alleged. Asserted; claimed, claimed to be; charged: as, an alleged — fact, forgery, offense, deed, will, signature, execution.

Material allegation. Such an averment in the pleadings of an opponent as requires answer — by explanation or denial. Opposed, **immaterial allegation.**

A material allegation is one which is essential to the claim or defense, which could not be stricken from the pleading without leaving it insufficient. [3]

Defensive or responsive allegation. An averment by way of defense. **Rejoining allegation.** Complainant's reply to a defensive allegation. [4]

The rule is that the proof must correspond with the allegations in a declaration (or bill), but the requirement is fulfilled if the substance of the declaration is proved. The purpose of the rule is that the opposite party may be fairly apprised of the specific nature of the questions involved in the issue. Formerly the rule was applied with great strictness, but the modern decisions are more liberal and reasonable.

The rule established by recent statutes and decisions is that no variance between the allegation of a pleading and the proofs offered to sustain it shall be deemed "material" unless of a character to mislead the opposite party in maintaining his action or defense on the merits. Irrespective of statutes, however, no variance ought ever to be regarded as material where the allegation and proof substantially correspond. [1]

See ANSWER, 3; DESCRIPTION, 4; REDUNDANCY; SAID; VARIANCE.

ALLEGHENY CITY. See COMMON, 2.

ALLEGIANCE. [2] The tie, or *ligamen* which binds the subject to the king in return for that protection which the king affords the subject. [3]

When acknowledgment was made to the absolute superior, who was vassal to no man, it was in early times no longer called the oath of fealty (*q. v.*), but the oath of allegiance: therein the tenant swore to bear faith to his sovereign lord, in opposition to all men, without any saving or exception. . . There is an implied, original, and virtual allegiance owing from every subject to his sovereign, antecedently to any express promise. [3]

Acquired allegiance. Such allegiance as is due from a naturalized citizen. [4]

Local allegiance. Such allegiance as is due from an alien, or stranger born, as long as he continues within the king's dominions and protection. [4]

Natural allegiance. Such allegiance as is due from all men born within the king's dominions, immediately upon their birth. Also called *absolute* or *permanent* allegiance. [4]

Allegiance is nothing more than the tie or duty of obedience of a subject to the sovereign whose protection he is under. Allegiance *by birth* arises from being born within the dominions and under the protection of a particular sovereign. . . A person born on the ocean is a subject of the prince to whom his parents owe allegiance. The child of an ambassador is a subject of the prince whom he represents, although born under the actual protection and in the dominions of a foreign prince. [5]

Allegiance is the obligation of fidelity and obedience which the individual owes to the government under which he lives, or to his sovereign in return for the protection he receives. . It may be an absolute and permanent obligation, or a qualified and temporary one. The citizen or subject owes an absolute and permanent allegiance to his government or sovereign or, at least, until, by some open and distinct act, he renounces it and becomes a citizen or subject of another

---

[1] See Broom, Max. 169, 294; 60 Cal. 600; 10 Mass. 163; 50 Mich. 126; 70 Pa. 274; 61 Wis. 261; 62 *id.* 67, 326.

[2] 10 Pet. 209; 2 Sumn. 209; Story, Eq. Pl. § 257; 71 Ala. 80.

[3] [Rhemke *v.* Clinton, 2 Utah, 236 (1879): Civil Pract. Act, § 66; Lusk *v.* Perkins, 48 Ark. 247 (1886).

[4] See 3 Bl. Com. 100.

---

[1] Nash *v.* Towne, 5 Wall. 698–99 (1866), Clifford, J. Brown *v.* Pierce, 7 *id.* 211 (1868).

[2] F. *a-ligance*, homage: L. *ad-ligare*, to tie, bind.

[3] 1 Bl. Com. 366–69; 20 Johns. 191–92.

[4] 1 Bl. Com. 369–70; 44 Pa. 501.

[5] Inglis *v.* Trustees of Sailors Snug Harbor, 3 Pet. 155 (1830), Story, J.; Shanks *v.* Dupont, *ib.* 242 (1830).

government or sovereign. An alien whilst domiciled in the country owes a local and temporary allegiance, which continues during the period of his residence.[1]

At common law natural allegiance could not be renounced except by permission of the sovereign to whom it was due.[2] This was changed by the act of Congress of July 27, 1868,[3] and by statute of 33 Vict. c. 14, May 10, 1870.

Whether natural allegiance revives upon return of the naturalized citizen to his native country is not settled.[4]

See EXPATRIATION; INDIAN; NATURALIZATION; TREASON; WAR.

ALLEY. See ROAD; WAY.

When not qualified by "private," is conventionally understood, in its relation to towns and cities, to mean a narrow street in common use.[5]

ALLISION. See COLLISION.

ALLOCATUR. L. It is allowed.

The name of a writ permitting a thing requested.

As, an order or proceeding — to remove an indictment, to stay execution of a sentence, that special bail be furnished, that a *quo warranto* issue, that a bill of costs be referred to an auditor.

Non allocatur. It is not allowed.

Special allocatur. The allowance of a writ of error required in particular cases.

ALLODIAL.[6] From the low Latin *allodium:* every man's own land, which he possesses in his own right, without owing any rent or service to a superior — property, in the highest degree. Opposed, *feodum,* a fee.[7]

Wholly independent, and held of no superior.[8]

Held in free and absolute ownership.[9]

"All lands . . are declared to be allodial, and feudal tenures are prohibited" — constitution of Wisconsin. This means little more than if the framers had said "free" or "held in free and absolute ownership," as contradistinguished from feudal tenures, the prohibition of which, with their servitudes and attendant hindrances to free and ready transfer of realty, constituted the chief object of the provision.[10] See FEE, 1 (1); TENURE, 1.

ALLONGE.[1] A paper attached to a bill or note for such indorsements as the original paper itself will not hold.

When an indorsement is made on a paper attached to and made part of a note, such paper is called an "allouge." The reason for using it is, there is no room on the note for the indorsement. This does not mean that there must be an actual physical impossibility of writing the indorser's name on the original paper. All that the mercantile law requires is that when it is inconvenient to write on the back of the note the real contract between the vendor and vendee, which, if so written, would pass the title, it may be written on another paper and attached to it with like effect. There are cases showing that an assignment of a number of notes at once, by a separate paper, never attached to either of the notes or intended to be, is not an indorsement.[2]

ALLOPATHY. See MEDICINE.

ALLOT. 1. To set apart a thing to a person as his share: as, to allot a fund, land. Whence allottee, allotment.

As usually understood, to set apart a portion of a particular thing or things to some person: as, to allot to a widow a portion of her husband's estate.[3]

2. To assign, appoint: as, to allot the justices of the Supreme Court to circuits.

ALLOW. To approve of, sanction; to permit, consent to. Opposed, *disallow.* See PERMIT; SUFFER.

In its ordinary sense, to grant, admit, afford, or to yield, to grant license to, permit. Implies a power to grant some privilege or permission.[4]

Allowance. The act of permitting or giving; also, whatever is given as a share or portion.

As, to allow, and the allowance of — an account, alimony, an amendment, an appeal, a bill of exceptions, a claim, a pardon, a pension, a sum to an insolvent.

"Allowing" claims against estates: the sanction or approbation which the court gives to the acts of an executor or administrator as manifested by his account.[5]

Allowance to a widow of money in lieu of dower: something substituted by way of compensation for another thing.[6]

---

[1] Carlisle *v.* United States, 16 Wall. 154 (1872), Field, J.

[2] 1 Bl. Com. 369; 2 Kent, 449; 8 Op. Att.-Gen. 139; 9 *id.* 356.

[3] R. S. § 1999.

[4] Whart. Confl. L. § 6; 18 Am. Law Reg. 595, 665 (1879).

[5] Bailey *v.* Culver, 12 Mo. Ap. 183 (1882).

[6] Ger. *al-ód,* all one's own: the whole estate, — Skeat.

[7] 2 Bl. Com. 105.

[8] 2 Bl. Com. 47, 60.

[9] 3 Kent, 495, 488, 498.

[10] Barker *v.* Dayton, 28 Wis. 384 (1871), Dixon, C. J. See 1 Washb. R. P. 16, 41; 9 Cow. 513.

[1] Al-lŭnj'. F. *allonger,* to lengthen.

[2] Crosby *v.* Roub, 16 Wis. 626–27 (1863); Folger *v.* Chase, 18 Pick. 67 (1836); French *v.* Turner, 15 Ind. 62 (1860); Osgood *v.* Artt, 17 F. R. 577 (1883); Story, Bills, § 204, Prom. Notes, §§ 121, 151.

[3] Glenn *v.* Glenn, 41 Ala. 586 (1868.)

[4] Doty *v.* Lawson, 14 F. R. 901 (1883).

[5] Gildhardt's Heirs *v.* Starke, 1 How., Miss., 457 (1837).

[6] Glenn *v.* Glenn, 41 Ala. 584, 586 (1868).

Allowance to a child or other dependent: ordinarily, only another name for a gift or gratuity.[1]

The honorable discharge of a soldier from service does not restore him allowances forfeited by desertion included in which is a bounty), that is, everything which could be recovered from the government in consideration of enlistment and services. The forfeiture must first be removed.[2]

ALLOY. See COIN.

ALLUVIO. L. That which is washed to a place.

Alluvio maris. The washing of the sea.

Jure alluvionis. By right of alluvion. See ALLUVION.

ALLUVION. By the common law the addition made to land by the washing of the sea, a navigable river or other stream, whenever the increase is so gradual that it cannot be perceived in any one moment of time.[3] See ALLUVIO.

An addition to riparian land, gradually and imperceptibly made by the water to which the land is contiguous. It is different from "reliction" and the opposite of "avulsion."[4] See AVULSION; DERELICTION, 1.

The test as to what is gradual and imperceptible is, that, though the witnesses may see from time to time that progress has been made, they could not perceive it while going on. Whether it is the effect of natural or artificial causes makes no difference. The right to future alluvion is a vested right. It is an inherent and essential attribute of the original property. The title to the increment rests in the law of nature. It is the same with that of the owner of a tree to its fruits, and the owner of flocks and herds to their natural increase. The maxim *qui sentit onus debet sentire commodum* lies at its foundation. The owner takes the chances of injury and of benefit arising from the situation of the property. If there be a gradual loss he must bear it; if a gradual gain, it is his. The principle applies alike to streams that do, and to those that do not, overflow their banks, and where dykes and other defenses are, and where they are not, necessary to keep the water within its proper limits.[4]

It is generally conceded that the riparian title attaches to subsequent accretions to the land affected by the gradual and imperceptible operation of natural causes. But whether it attaches to land reclaimed by artificial means from the bed of the river, or to sudden accretions produced by unusual floods, is a question which each State decides for itself. By the

common law such additions to land on navigable (tide) waters belong to the crown.[1]

The right to alluvion depends upon the fact of the contiguity of the estate to the river. The accretion belongs to the strip of land to which it attaches, rather than to a larger portion from which the strip, when sold, was separated.[2]

See ACCESSION; ACCRETION; BATTURE; RIPARIAN.

ALMS-HOUSE. A house appropriated to the use of the poor.[3]

Within the meaning of an act exempting property from taxation, will include a house used solely for the "purpose of affording pecuniary and other relief to persons of Swiss origin in need of assistance."[3]

ALONE. See SEPARATE, 2.

A granted to B, for the use of C "alone," the right to take water anywhere on his donation. *Held*, that "alone" signified that the grant was for the "sole" benefit of C.[4]

ALONG. Over against in length; lengthwise of. Compare BY, 1; PARALLEL.

"By the length of, as distinguished from across; lengthwise of;" as, a railway along a highway.[5]

A sidewalk "along the line" of land does not import that the sidewalk must at all points touch or be parallel to such line.[6]

"Along a line" means up to, extending to, reaching to, that line.[7]

In the expression "on, over, and along" an alley, is synonymous with on or over, not by the side of.[8]

An insurable interest on property of a railroad "along its route" means property in proximity to the rails upon which the engines run: which may be outside the lines of the roadway or lawfully within those lines.[9]

"Along the bank" of the Chattahoochee is definite enough to exclude the idea that any part of the river or its bed was not to be within the State of Georgia — by the cession of her unsettled territory to the United States in 1802. The call excludes the idea that a line was to be traced at the edge of the water as that may be at one time or another; — it is for "the bank," the fast land which confines the water of the river in its channel or bed in its whole width. Wherever the bed may be it belongs to Georgia, and not to Alabama. The line is to be determined, in each trial, by the jury.[10]

[1] Taylor v. Staples, 8 R. I. 179 (1865). See also Bacon v. Bacon, 43 Wis. 203 (1877).

[2] United States v. Landers, 92 U. S. 79, 80 (1875), Field, J.; 13 Op. Att.-Gen. 198.

[3] Lovingston v. St. Clair County, 64 Ill. 58, 60 (1872), cases, Thornton, J.

[4] County of St. Clair v. Lovingston, 23 Wall. 68 (1874), Swayne, J. See 18 La. An. 122; 2 Bl. Com. 262; 3 Kent, 428; 2 Washb. R. P. 58, 452.

[1] Barney v. City of Keokuk, 94 U. S. 337 (1876), Bradley, J. See also New Orleans v. United States, 10 Pet. 717 (1836); 16 F. R. 816.

[2] Saulet v. Shepherd, 4 Wall. 508 (1866).

[3] People ex rel. Swiss Society v. Commissioners of Taxes, 36 Hun, 311 (1885): Webster.

[4] Salem Capital Flour Mills Co. v. Stayton Water-Ditch & Canal Co., 33 F. R. 154 (1887).

[5] County of Cook v. Great Western R. Co., 119 Ill. 225 (1886): Webster.

[6] Commonwealth v. Franklin, 133 Mass. 570 (1882).

[7] Benton v. Horsley, 71 Ga. 626 (1883).

[8] Heath v. Des Moines, &c. R. Co., 61 Iowa, 14 (1883).

[9] Grand Trunk R. Co. v. Richardson, 91 U. S. 472 (1875). See also 13 Metc. 99; 42 Me. 585-86; 27 Alb. L. J. 385.

[10] Howard v. Ingersoll, 13 How. 416-17 (1851).

ALS. See ALIUS, Alios.

ALSO. In wills, most frequently points out the beginning of a new devise or bequest. Imports no more than "item," and may mean the same as "moreover," but not the same as "in like manner."[1] Compare LIKEWISE.

ALTER.[2] To make a thing different from what it was; as, by cutting out a brand-mark.[3]

The word implies "another." A thing which ceased to exist can in no proper sense be said to be "altered." If altered it has merely changed its form or nature, but still has an existence. Thus, in forgery making may be by an original fabrication or by merely changing a thing already made into another thing. An altered note is still a note.[4]

To "alter judicial districts" means to change them. It is not a violation of usage to speak of the increasing or diminishing of a given number as an alteration or change in the number.[5]

Alteration. 1. A change or substitution of one thing for another: as, the alteration of a way.[6] See ADDITION, 1.

2. An act done upon an instrument by which its meaning or language is changed.

If what is written or erased has no tendency to produce this result or to mislead it is not an "alteration." The term applies to the act of the party entitled under the instrument and imports some fraud or improper design to change its effect. The act of a stranger is a mere "spoliation" or mutilation of the instrument, and does not change its legal operation as long as the original writing remains legible, and, if it be a deed, any trace of the seal remains.[7]

Material alteration. Such alteration as changes the language or meaning of the contract in a material particular. *Immaterial alteration.* Such merely verbal change as does not vary the contract in an essential particular.[8]

Suspicious alteration. Such change, apparent upon inspection, as would lead a man of ordinary caution to infer that the instru-ment had been illegally tampered with; or such apparent change in the language as would deter such person from accepting the instrument as reliable evidence of indebtedness or of an obligation.

That is a "material alteration" which causes the instrument to speak a language different in legal effect from what it originally spoke;[1] or which gives the instrument a different legal effect.[2]

A material alteration made without consent after execution avoids the instrument; but not so as to words which the law would supply. The question of materiality is for the court. If attested as made before execution does not detract from credit; nor, if it is against the interest of the holder. If suspicious upon its face, the law presumes nothing, but leaves questions of time, person, and intent, to the decision of a jury. If immaterial, presumed to have been made before execution. But some authorities require explanation before any altered instrument can be admitted in evidence.[3]

It will not be presumed that a party would sign a document with material clauses interlined or in the margin. The rule is strict as to negotiables. The burden of explaining alterations in ancient writings is not imposed when they are taken from their proper repository. Formal blanks may always be filled.[4]

The material alteration of a written contract by a party to it discharges a party who does not authorize or consent to the alteration, because it destroys the identity of the contract and substitutes a different agreement. Any change which alters the contract, whether increasing or diminishing liability, is "material."[5]

Some authorities hold that where there are no particular circumstances of suspicion the presumption of law is that the alteration was made contemporaneously with the execution, giving as a reason that a deed cannot be altered after its execution without fraud, which is never assumed without proof; other authorities hold the presumption to be the other way, and require an explanation of the alteration before the deed can be admitted in evidence.[6]

In the absence of proof the presumption is that a correction by erasure in a deed (a patent to land) was made before execution. This doctrine rests upon principle. "A deed cannot be altered after it is executed without fraud or wrong; and the presumption is against fraud or wrong." The cases are not uniform in this country, but the most stringent ones leave the question to the jury.[7]

---

[1] Evans v. Knorr, 4 Rawle, 68–70 (1833), cases; 22 Ill. 366.

[2] L. L. *alterare;* L. *alter,* other, another.

[3] Smith v. Brown, 1 Wend. 236 (1828).

[4] Haynes v. State, 15 Ohio St. 457 (1864).

[5] People v. Sassovich, 29 Cal. 484 (1866).

[6] Johnson v. Wyman, 9 Gray, 189 (1857), Shaw, C. J.

[7] [1 Greenl. Ev. § 566.

[8] See Woodworth v. Bank of America, 19 Johns. 391 (1821): 10 Am. Dec. 267–73 (1879), cases.

---

[1] 1 Greenl. Ev. § 565; 9 Baxt. 462.

[2] Eckert v. Pickel, 59 Iowa, 547–48 (1882); 51 *id.* 675; 30 Minn. 154; 76 Va. 545, 544; 18 Ct. Cl. 565.

[3] 1 Greenl. Ev. §§ 564–68; 61 Ala. 269; 2 Bl. Com. 308.

[4] 1 Whart. Ev. §§ 621–32, 732, cases.

[5] Mersman v. Werges, 112 U. S. 141 (1884), cases, Gray, J.; Angle v. Northwestern Mut. Life Ins. Co., 92 *id.* 342 (1875).

[6] Malarin v. United States, 1 Wall. 288 (1863), Field, J.

[7] Little v. Herndon, 10 Wall. 31 (1869), cases, Nel

A voluntary alteration of any instrument under seal, in a material part, to the prejudice of the obligor or maker, avoids it — unless done with the assent of the parties affected. Such act differs from spoliation by a stranger, or accidental alteration by mistake, in which case the instrument retains its effect. In respect to commercial paper the rule is more stringent, the law casting on the holder the burden of disproving any apparent material alteration on the face of the paper. The ground of the rule is public policy to insure the protection of the instrument from fraud and substitution. The purpose is to take away the motive for alteration by forfeiting the instrument on discovery of the fraud.[1]

See FORGE, 2; NOTE, 2, Raised; RATIFICATION.

ALTERNATIVE.[2] Offering a choice between two acts, courses, or things: as, an alternative — covenant, obligation, judgment.

An alternative writ commands the respondent to do a certain thing or show cause why he should not do it: as, an alternative *mandamus,*[2] q. v.

Alternative pleadings are ill; and alternative judgments, decrees, and sentences are, as a rule, invalid. See OR, 2; RELIEF, 2.

ALWAYS. See PROVIDED.

AM, Amended, amendment; American.

AMALGAMATE. See CONSOLIDATE, Associations.

AMBASSADOR. See MINISTER, 3.

AMBIGUITAS. See AMBIGUITY.

AMBIGUITY.[4] The effect of words that have either no definite sense or a double sense.[5]

Ambiguity or duplicity are predicable only of language as to which it is needful to make a choice of readings; while "indistinctness," "obscurity," and "uncertainty" include these, and also cases of language devoid of sense or which does not present any meaning with clearness or precision. The case of a blank left for a name should be deemed an uncertainty.[6]

Patent ambiguity. Such ambiguity as appears upon the face of the writing itself. **Latent ambiguity.** Where a writing is perfect and intelligible upon its face, but, from some circumstance admitted in proof,

a doubt arises as to the applicability of the language to a particular person or thing.[1]

Ambiguitas patens is that which appears to be ambiguous upon the instrument. *Ambiguitas latens* is that which seems certain and without ambiguity for anything that appears upon the instrument, but there is some collateral matter out of the deed that breeds the ambiguity.[2]

A "latent ambiguity" is where you show that words apply equally to two different things or subject-matters.[3]

Evidence is then admissible to show which thing or subject was intended.[3]

Difficulty in applying the descriptive portion of a deed to the external object usually arises from a latent ambiguity, which, having its origin in, is to be solved by, parol evidence.[4]

A "patent ambiguity" means an inherent ambiguity which cannot be removed either by the ordinary rules of legal construction or by the application of extrinsic and explanatory evidence, showing that impressions *prima facie* unintelligible are yet capable of conveying a certain, definite meaning.[5]

The court has to do with cases of patent ambiguity; the jury with a case of latent ambiguity. When the intention cannot be ascertained the defect is incurable.

Ambiguitas verborum latens verificatione suppletur; nam quod ex facto oritur ambiguum verificatione facti tollitur. A latent ambiguity of words is supplied by evidence; for whatever arises ambiguous from a fact [extrinsic] may be removed by evidence of the fact.[6]

Quoties in verbis nulla est ambiguitas, ibi nulla expositio contra verba fienda est. As long as in the words there is no ambiguity, then no interpretation contrary to the words is to be made.[7]

A cardinal canon of interpretation, both of deeds and of statutes. The words, the context, and the subject-matter, are to be considered equally with the effect and consequences or the spirit and reason, if not before them.[8]

---

[1] Stokeley v. Gordon, 8 Md. 505–9 (1855).

[2] [Lord Bacon, Max. Reg. 23 (25), Law Tracts, 99–100. Approved, Lathrop v. Blake, 23 N. H. 60 (1851); Lycoming Mut. Ins. Co. v. Sailer, 67 Pa. 112 (1870); Deery v. Cray, 10 Wall. 270 (1869); Hawkins v. Garland, 76 Va. 152 (1882). See 1 Greenl. Ev. §§ 297–300; 1 Whart. Ev. §§ 956–57, 961, 1006.

[3] Smith v. Jeffryes, 15 M. & W. *562 (1846), Alderson, B.; Webster v. Paul, 10 Ohio St. 534 (1860); 40 Ark. 241.

[4] Reed v. Proprietors of Locks, 8 How. 290 (1850); Moran v. Prather, 23 Wall. 501 (1874).

[5] Brown v. Guice, 46 Miss. 302 (1872), Peyton, C. J.

[6] Bacon, Max. 23; Broom, Max. 608; 2 Kent, 557; 13 Pet. 97; 100 Mass. 60; 8 Johns. 90; 67 Pa. 112.

[7] Broom, Max. 617; 2 Bl. Com. 379; 8 Mass. 201.

[8] Dame's Appeal, 62 Pa. 420 (1869), Sharswood, J.; 66 *id.* 136, 251; 34 La. An. 227, 957.

---

son, J., quoting Campbell, C. J., in Doe v. Catomore, 71 E. C. L. 746 (1851).

[1] Neff v. Horner, 63 Pa. 330–31 (1869), cases. See also Batchelder v. White, 80 Va. 108 (1885), cases; Fuller v. Green, 64 Wis. 165 (1885), cases; State v. Churchill, 48 Ark. 437–40 (1886), cases; 2 Daniel, Neg. Inst. §§ 1373–75, cases; 30 Alb. Law J. 245–49 (1884), cases; Bishop, Contr. §§ 745–76, cases.

[2] L. *alter,* other.

[3] [3 Bl. Com. 273, 111.

[4] L. *ambiguus,* doubtful.

[5] [Ellmaker v. Ellmaker, 4 Watts, 90 (1835), Gibson, C. J.

[6] Abbott's Law Dict.

A latent ambiguity in a will, which may be removed by extrinsic evidence, may arise: (1) When the will names a person as the object of a gift, or a thing as the subject of it, and there are two persons or things that answer such name or description; or (2) when the will contains a misdescription of the object or subject, as where there is no such person or thing in existence; or, if in existence, the person is not the one intended, or the thing does not belong to the testator. When a careful study of the testator's language, applied to the circumstances by which he was surrounded, discloses an inadvertency or mistake in a description of a person or thing which can be corrected without adding to his language — thus making a different will, — the correction should be made.[1]

One Gilmer, after making bequests to two Presbyterian churches in Illinois, and other bequests, left the rest of his estate "to be divided equally between the board of foreign missions and the board of home missions." *Held*, that there was a latent ambiguity respecting the object of the residuary gift, but that the ambiguity could be removed by extrinsic evidence; that the evidence introduced, taken in connection with the bequests to the Presbyterian churches, showed that the testator meant the Board of Foreign Missions and the Board of Home Missions of the Presbyterian Church of the United States of America, of which he was a member and an officer, and not any board of missions controlled by the Baptist, Methodist, Episcopalian, or other denomination.[2]

AMBULATORY.[3] 1. Moving about from one place to another; not held in any one place; not stationary.

The court of common pleas while it followed the king's household was said to be ambulatory.

2. Not fixed in legal character; not yet settled past alteration; revocable.

In this category is a sheriff's return until filed; and a will, to the last moment of testamentary rationality.

Voluntas testatoris est ambulatoria usque ad mortem. The will of a testator is ambulatory (alterable, revocable) up to his death.[4]

AMBUSH. The act of attacking an enemy unexpectedly from a concealed station. A concealed station where troops or enemies lie in wait to attack by surprise; an ambuscade. Troops posted in a concealed

place, for attacking by surprise.[1] See DISGUISE.

AMENDMENT.[2] 1. Correction of a fault; the curing of a defect; alteration for the better; improvement. Whence amendatory.

"Amend," in its most comprehensive sense, means to better. . . When a defendant is allowed to withdraw one plea or answer and to substitute another which rightly sets out his defense, it is a change for the better — an "amendment."[3]

Also, the writing or instrument made or proposed, which embodies the improvement.

Used of the correction, proposed or actually made: of an error in the pleadings or proceedings in a pending cause; of changes in bills, statutes, and ordinances, by lawmakers; of alterations in charters and by-laws: of changes in constitutions.

Material amendment. In pleading, such change in the substance of a party's case as destroys its former identity and occasions surprise (*q. v.*) in his adversary.

At common law, proceedings being *in fieri* till judgment, the courts allow amendments up to that point. After judgment enrolled, no amendment is permitted at a subsequent term; for only during the first term is the record in the breast of the court.[4] See further RECORD, 2.

An indictment, being a finding upon the oaths of the grand jury, can be amended only by their consent. See INDICTMENT.

Allowing amendments is incidental to the exercise of all judicial power, and indispensable to the ends of justice. Usually to permit or refuse any particular amendment rests in the discretion of the court; the result is not assignable for error.[5]

An appellate court will regard as made such amendment to a verdict as should have been made in the court below.[6]

A bill in equity may be amended, when found defective in parties, in prayers for relief, or in the omission or mistake of some fact or circumstance connected with the substance of the case, but yet not forming the substance itself, or for putting in new matter to meet the allegations in the answer. That is to say, by amendment the plaintiff may not make a new bill.[7]

---

[1] Patch *v.* White, 117 U. S. 217-19 (1886), cases, Bradley, J. See also Senger *v.* Senger's Executor, 81 Va. 694-97 (1886), cases; Webster *v.* Morris, 66 Wis. 397 (1886), cases; 64 *id.* 355.

[2] Gilmer *v.* Stone, 120 U. S. 586, 588-90 (1887), cases, Harlan, J. In Hannen *v.* Moulton, 23 F. R. 5-11 (1885), a devise of 1,500 acres of land was held defective on account of a latent ambiguity. See generally 5 Am. Law Reg. 140-43 (1866), cases.

[3] Am'bulatory. L. *ambulare*, to walk or move about.

[4] Coke, Litt. 112 *b*; 2 Bl. Com. 502; 4 Ves. 210; 10 *id.* 379; 143 Mass. 231; 1 Story, Eq. § 606 *a*.

[1] Dale County *v.* Gunter, 46 Ala. 142 (1871), Peck, C. J.

[2] F. *amender*: L. *emendare*, to free from fault.

[3] [Diamond *v.* Williamsburg Ins. Co., 4 Daly, 500 (1873), Daly, C. J.

[4] 3 Bl. Com. 407-8.

[5] Tilton *v.* Cofield, 93 U. S. 166 (1876); International Bank *v.* Sherman, 101 *id.* 406 (1879); Tiernan *v.* Woodruff, 5 McLean, 138 (1850), cases; 11 F. R. 781; 13 *id.* 653-55, cases; 132 Mass. 194.

[6] Shaw *v.* North Penn. R. Co., 101 U. S. 567 (1879).

[7] Shields *v.* Barrow, 17 How. 144 (1854); Story, Eq. Pl. § 884.

In reference to amendments of equity pleadings generally, the courts have found it impracticable to lay down a rule for all cases. Their allowance, at every stage, must rest in discretion — a discretion depending largely upon the special circumstances of each case. But the ends of justice should never be sacrificed to mere form, nor by a too rigid adherence to technical rules of practice. Where the application comes after the litigation has continued some time, or when granting it would cause serious inconvenience or expense to the opposite side, great caution should be exercised. Where it would materially change the very substance of the case made by the bill, and to which the parties have directed their proofs, an amendment should rarely, if ever, be permitted.[1] See JEOFAIL.

2. Amendments to constitutions are made in pursuance of directions contained in the instruments themselves.[2]

What here follows relates, as will be seen, to the Constitution of the United States.

"The Congress, whenever two thirds of both Houses shall deem it necessary, shall propose Amendments to this Constitution, or, on the Application of the Legislatures of two thirds of the several States, shall call a Convention for proposing Amendments, which, in either Case, shall be valid to all Intents and Purposes, as Part of this Constitution, when ratified by the Legislatures of three fourths of the several States, or by Conventions in three fourths thereof, as the one or the other Mode of Ratification may be proposed by the Congress; Provided . that no State, without its Consent, shall be deprived of its equal Suffrage in the Senate."[3]

The President's approval of a proposed amendment is not necessary.[4]

The amendments themselves thus far made (May, 1888) are designated as "Articles in Addition to, and Amendment of the Constitution," etc., and are numbered "Articles I, II," etc., up to XV.

Upward of one hundred amendments were proposed by the minorities in the several conventions that adopted the Constitution. The First Congress referred them to a committee of one member from each State. Twelve articles were agreed to for submission to the States. The first two, relating to the number and the pay of the members of the lower House, were rejected, and the remaining ten ratified, December 15, 1791.[5]

Most of these ten amendments are denials of power which had not been expressly granted, and which cannot be said to have been "necessary and proper for carrying into Execution" other powers. . . They

tend to show that in the judgment of those wl adopted the Constitution there were powers creat(by it which grew out of the aggregate of powers co ferred upon the government, or out of the sovereign instituted.[1]

They left the authority of the States where the found it, and added nothing to the already existir powers of the United States.[2]

The feeling that the Constitution as proposed f(ratification contained no formal Bill of Rights led 1 the adoption of the ten amendments. All are designe to operate as restraints upon the general Governmen most of them are for the protection of the privat rights of persons and property. Notwithstanding th reproach, however, there are many provisions in th original instrument of this latter character.[3]

The provisions of the fifteen amendments will b found quoted and commented upon under the follov ing titles:

I — ASSEMBLY; LIBERTY, 1, Of speech, Of the pres RELIGION.

II, III — MILITIA.

IV — SEARCH, Warrant.

V — CRIMINATE; INDICTMENT; JEOPARDY; PROCESS, Due, etc.; TAKE, 8.

VI — CRIME.

VII — JURY, Trial by.

VIII — BAIL, 2; FINE, 2; PUNISHMENT, Cruel, etc.

IX, X — CONSTITUTION, p. 238; POWER, 3.

XI -- SUIT, p. 990.

XII -- ELECTORS, Presidential.

XIII, XIV, XV — CITIZEN.

And see generally CONSTITUTION; EXPRESSIO; GO\ ERNMENT; STATE, 3 (2).

AMENDS. Reparation; compensation fo wrong done; satisfaction.

By 24 Geo. II (1751), c. 24, re-enacted in sever: States, a tender of amends to the party injured by mistake made by a magistrate, acting as such, is a ba to a contemplated action.[4]

Any sum may be tendered, because, in torts, th standard of damages is uncertain and the party is a likely to recover at trial less than more than the sur tendered.[5]

In some States a like tender may be made by a mir ister or a magistrate who marries a minor without th consent of the parent or guardian; also, for involur tary trespasses committed by constables, revenu officers, and perhaps some other ministerial officers.

See COMPENSATION, 2–4; DISTRESS; TENDER, 2.

---

[1] Hardin v. Boyd, 113 U. S. 761 (1885), Harlan, J. Approved, Richmond v. Irons, 121 id. 47, 46 (1887); Couhrough v. Adams, 70 Cal. 378 (1886): 17 id. 235.

[2] See Prohibitory Amendment Cases, 24 Kan. 709–12 (1881); Re Constitutional Convention, 14 R. I. 651 (1883).

[3] Constitution, Art. V

[4] Hollingsworth v. Virginia, 3 Dall. 378 (1798).

[5] See 1 Story, Const. §§ 301–5; 1 McMaster, Hist. Peop. U. S. 501, 555. While the proposed Constitution was before the people for adoption, the explanation that it

did not need a Bill of Rights — the Government bein " limited," having only such powers as were speciall granted to it — "satisfied not one State." 2 Bancrof Const. 241–42, et seq.

[1] Legal Tender Cases, 12 Wall. 535 (1870), Strong, .

[2] United States v. Cruikshank, 92 U. S. 522 (1875 Twitchell v. Pennsylvania, 7 Wall. 325–27 (1868), case:

[3] Kring v. Missouri, 107 U. S. 226 (1882), Miller, J. Se also Spies v. Illinois (Anarchists' Case), 123 id. 1! (1887), cases; 8 Saw. 262.

[4] 3 Bl. Com. 16.

[5] 3 Shars. Bl. Com. 16; 3 Watts, 317; 5 S. & R. 209, 51

[6] See Arch. Pract. 1372, 1174, 1273.

AMERCE.[1] To be amerced, or *à mercie*, is to be at the king's mercy with respect to a fine to be imposed. Later, simply to be fined. Whence amercement.

Before the jury deliver their verdict the plaintiff is to appear in court, by himself or attorney, to answer the amercement to which he is liable in case he fails in his suit, as a punishment for his false claim. The amercement is disused, but the form remains. It was an arbitrary amount, unliquidated; a "fine" was a fixed sum imposed upon one not a party for some fault or misconduct.[2]

Now used of a mulct or penalty imposed by a court upon its own officers for neglect of duty. In several States, also, amercement is the remedy against a sheriff for failing to levy an execution or make return of proceeds of a sale according to statute.[3]

AMERICA. See DISCOVERY, 1; STATE, 3 (2), p. 966.

American. In the general mind now describes a descendant of Europeans, born in America, and is especially applied to an inhabitant of the United States.[4]

AMI. F. A friend. Also spelled *amy*. Compare AMICUS.

Alien ami. An alien friend. See ALIEN, 1.

Prochein ami. Next friend.

One admitted by a court to prosecute for an infant, because otherwise the infant might be prejudiced by the refusal or neglect of his guardian. He is a species of attorney; and the court controls his actions.[5] See FRIEND, Next; GUARDIAN, Ad litem.

AMICABLE. Friendly; agreed to; prosecuted by consent of all parties; opposed to adverse, adversary: as, an amicable action, an amicable *scire facias* to revive a judgment, mortgage, or other lien.

An amicable lawsuit is a suit instituted seriously but in a friendly spirit, that some matter in controversy, by judicial decree, may be settled definitely, as cheaply and with as little delay as possible.[6]

AMICUS. L. A friend. Compare AMI.

Amicus curiæ. A friend of the court.

Imports friendly intervention of counsel to remind the court of some matter of law which has escaped its notice and in regard to which it appears to be in danger of going wrong. It is not his function to take upon himself the management of a cause.[1]

AMNESTY. Has no technical meaning in the common law: is merely the synonym of "oblivion," which, in English law, is the synonym of "pardon." The literal meaning is "removal from memory."[2]

Properly belongs to international law, applying to rebellions which by their magnitude are brought within that law.[2]

"Pardon" is remission of guilt; "amnesty" an act of oblivion or forgetfulness.[3]

By act of May 22, 1872, the political disabilities imposed by the third section of the XIVth Amendment were removed from all persons except members of the thirty-sixth and thirty-seventh Congresses, officers in the judicial, military, and naval service, heads of departments, and foreign ministers, of the United States.[4] See OATH, Of office; PARDON.

AMONG. Intermingled with.

Commerce among the States cannot stop at the external line of each State, but may be introduced into the interior. . . Comprehensive as "among" is it may properly be restricted to that commerce which concerns more States than one. . . Commerce among the States must of necessity be commerce with the States.[5] See COMMERCE.

Each child has a share where a power is distributed "amongst" children.[6] See BETWEEN.

AMORTISE. See MORTMAIN.

AMOTION.[7] Turning out; removal.

1. Turning out the legal proprietor of an estate in realty before the termination of the estate;[8] an eviction. See EVICTION; OUSTER.

2. Removal of a corporate officer from office, as distinguished from depriving a member of his privilege of membership[9]— expulsion, disfranchisement.

This right, for just cause, is a common-law incident to all corporations. Where the appointment is during good behavior, or the removal is for a specified cause, an opportunity to be heard should be afforded.[9]

Among the various causes are — *first*, such as have no immediate relation to the office yet are in them-

---

[1] F. *amercier*, to fine: L. *merces*, wages, detriment, pains.

[2] 3 Bl. Com. 376, 275; 4 *id*. 379–80.

[3] Abbott, Bouvier, Law Dicts.

[4] [Beardsley *v*. Bridgeport, 53 Conn. 493 (1885), Pardee, J., where the word is used in a charitable bequest.

[5] Tidd, Pract. 100, n; Tucker *v*. Dabbs, 12 Heisk. 19–20 (1883); 10 Abb. Pr. 40.

[6] Thompson *v*. Moulton, 2 La. An. 537 (1868); Lord *v*. Veazie, 8 How. 255 (1850), Taney, C. J.

[1] Taft *v*. Northern Transp. Co., 56 N. H. 416 (1876), Cushing, C. J. See also 11 Pitts. Leg. J. 321–22 (1864); 109 U. S. 68; 2 Mass. 215; 11 Tex. 698; 11 Gratt. 656.

[2] Knote *v*. United States, 10 Ct. Cl. 407 (1874).

[3] *Exp*. Law, 35 Ga. 296 (1865): Pardoning Power, 11 Op. Att.-Gen. 228 (1865).

[4] 17 St. L. 142. See, as to President granting a general amnesty, 8 Am. Law Reg. 513–32, 577–89 (1869), cases.

[5] Gibbons *v*. Ogden, 9 Wheat. 194, 196, 227 (1824), Marshall, C. J.; 14 How. 573; 3 Wall. 782; 9 *id*. 43.

[6] 4 Kent, 343.

[7] L. *a-movere*, to move from, remove.

[8] [3 Bl. Com. 198–99.

[9] See 2 Kent, 297; Bouvier, cases.

selves of so infamous a nature as to render the offender unfit to execute any public franchise — but
indictment and conviction must then precede; *second*,
such as are only against his oath and the duty of his
office as a corporator and amount to a breach of the
tacit condition annexed to his office: *third*, such as
are offenses not only against the duty of his office, but
are indictable at common law.[1] See TENURE, Of office.

AMOUNT. See DESCRIPTION, 1, 4; DIS-
PUTE; EXCEEDING; MORE OR LESS; SUM.

AMPLIARE. See JUDEX, 2, Boni, etc.

AMUSEMENT. See ENTERTAINMENT;
GAME, 2; RIGHT, 2 (2), Civil rights; THEATER;
TICKET.

AN. See A, 4; AD; ANTE; ANY.

ANALOGY. See ARGUMENTUM, A simile.

ANARCHY.[2] The absence of government; a state of society in which there is no
law or supreme power.[3]

"If the conspiracy had for its object the destruction
of the law and government, it had for its object the
bringing about of practical anarchy. And when murder has resulted from the conspiracy and the perpe-
trators are on trial for the crime, whether or not they
were anarchists may be a proper circumstance to be
considered in connection with other circumstances,
with a view of showing what connection, if any, they
had with the conspiracy and what were their purposes
in joining it."[3]

See further as to case cited, ACCESSARY; CHAL-
LENGE, 4; CHARACTER; CHARGE, 2 (2, c); CONSPIRACY;
COURTS, United States; CRIMINATE; DOUBT, Reason-
able; JURY; MALICE; OPINION, 2.

ANCESTOR.[4] The last person actually
seized of an inheritance.[5]

In the law of descents the prepossessor of
an estate.[6]

The ascendant of an intestate in the right
line, as father, mother, grandfather, grand-
mother.[7]

The person from whom an estate descends;
not a progenitor, in the popular acceptation.[8]

It is the *immediate*, and not the *remote*, ancestor
from whom the estate descends.[9]

---

[1] Rex *v.* Richardson, 1 Burr. 538 (1758), Mansfield,
C. J.; 1 B. & Ad. 936; L. R., 5 H. L. 636. See generally 24 Cent. Law J. 99 (1887), cases.

[2] Gk. *anarchi'a*, lack of government: *an'archos*,
without a chief.

[3] [Spies *et al. v.* People, 122 Ill. 253 (Sept. 14, 1887),
Magruder, J.,—"Anarchists' Case." [Webster's Dict.
Same case, 9 Cr. Law Mag. 829, 926-35, cases; 12 N. E.
Rep. No. 16; 18 Chic. Leg. News, 309, 411.

[4] F. *ancessour*, a fore-goer: L. *antecessor: ante ce-
dere*, to go before.

[5] 2 Bl. Com. 209, 443; 2 Kent, 404, 419.

[6] [McCarthy *v.* Marsh, 5 N. Y. 275 (1851).

[7] [Valentine *v.* Wetherill, 31 Barb. 659 (1859).

[8] Bailey *v.* Bailey, 25 Mich. 188 (1872).

[9] Murphy *v.* Henry, 35 Ind. 450 (1871).

After the rule was adopted that inheritances might
ascend, the ancestor was the person from whom the
inheritance devolved upon the heir, and a child might,
therefore, be the ancestor of his parent.[1]

Common ancestor. The parent from
whom designated persons have sprung.

In the Ohio statute of descents the ancestor is any
one from whom the estate is inherited. The ancestor
from whom it must "have come to the intestate" is
he from whom it was immediately inherited. Such
ancestor takes the place of the first purchaser under
the English canons of descent.   . No remote ancestor has any favorable estimation here. Neither
the primary definition nor the legal sense of the word
agrees with the most popular and obvious signification. He from whom the estate was immediately inherited is the ancestor, the *propositus*, from whom
the estate came.[2]

Embraces collaterals as well as lineals through
whom an inheritance is derived, and refers to the immediate ancestor.[3]

Uncles, aunts, and other collateral "antecessors"
who are not in fact "ancestors" are sometimes designated as "collateral ancestors." In its ordinary import
"ancestors" includes only those from whom the person spoken of is lineally descended on the father's or
the mother's side. When used in a sense different
from its ordinary import of lineal antecessors, so as
to embrace all the blood relatives preceding the person referred to, it is qualified or enlarged by some
other term.[4]

"Maternal ancestor" in the Massachusetts statute
of 1851, c. 211 (relating to illegitimate children), is
limited to progenitors in the direct ascending line, according to the common meaning and the only sense in
which "ancestor" is used throughout the statute of
descents and distributions.[5]

See further CONSANGUINITY; DESCENT; HEIR; IN-
HERIT.

ANCHOR. See A, 3, A 1; APPURTE-
NANCE; FURNITURE, Of ship.

A vessel fastened to a pier is not "lying at anchor;"[6] nor is a vessel purposely beached, though
having an anchor out for caution.[7]

ANCIENT.[8] 1. Created, made, conceded, or established at a day now long past;
beginning with a period indefinitely early;
dating from a time so remote as to acquire
or have attached some right or privilege ac-
accorded in view of long continuance: as,

---

[1] Lavery *v.* Egan, 143 Mass. 391 (1887), Field, J.

[2] Lessees of Prickett *v.* Parker, 3 Ohio St. 396-97
(1854). See also Gardner *v.* Collins, 2 Pet. 91 (1829).

[3] Wheeler *v.* Clutterbuck, 52 N. Y. 71 (1873).

[4] Banks *v.* Walker, 3 Barb. Ch. 446-47 (1848), Walworth, Ch.

[5] Pratt *v.* Atwood, 108 Mass. 42 (1871), Gray, J.

[6] Walsh *v.* N. Y. Floating Dry-Dock Co., 77 N. Y. 453
(1879).

[7] Reid *v.* Lancaster Fire Ins. Co., 19 Hun, 286 (1879).

[8] F. *ancien*. L. *antianus*, of a former time, old.
Formerly, antient,—2 Bl. Com. 99; 3 *id.* 274; 4 *id.* 380.

ancient — demesne, house, lights, wall, writings, qq. v.

2. A corruption or misprint of *enceinte*, pregnant — infirm: as, an ancient witness. See DEPOSITION.

ANCILLARY.[1] Auxiliary; subordinate; incidental; additional.

The king's court is not ancillary to any other.[2] Thus also are or may be related — one constitutional power to another;[3] implied powers in a corporation;[4] a writ of *certiorari* to a writ of *habeas corpus; a capias*, originally, to a summons, judgment or decree, to secure obedience or enforcement; a sequestration to preserve from waste movables on mortgaged property;[5] a commission to aid the court by hearing and report;[6] one bill in equity to another bill;[7] an attachment to another proceeding;[8] an action in aid of an execution at law to the original suit;[9] an act toward the performance of an agreement;[10] an administration (*q. v.*) subordinate to another;[11] parol testimony in some relations;[12] an outbuilding, to a dwelling-house; a statute, to a constitutional amendment.[13]

ANCIPITIS. See USUS, ANCIPITIS.

AND. Compare ET.

Construed to mean "or" (and "or" to mean "and") when necessary to give effect to the intention — of parties to contracts, of testators, of law-makers; but not so when the evident intent would thereby be defeated.[14] See further OR, 2.

ANGER. See ASSAULT; MALICE.

ANIMAL. Any irrational being, as distinguished from man.

In a common sense, a quadruped; not, a bird or a fowl.[15]

In discussions in the cases as to what is included by "animals" in the law of property and of larceny, in duty laws, in statutes punishing malicious mischief, and the like, the term is limited by notions of property. . . Steady progress has been made toward the recognition of all sentient life as deserving legal protection, irrespective of the property aspect.[16]

While the use in a particular context or statute may be limited by the general meaning and purpose, the term, in jurisprudence, may include any living creature not human or rational.[1]

In a statute against cruelty to animals includes wild and noxious animals, unless the purpose of the statute or the context indicates a limited meaning.[2]

Animals are distinguished as *domitæ naturæ*, of a tame disposition; and *feræ naturæ*, of a wild disposition — wild by nature.

Animals of a "base" nature are such as are not fit for food, but are kept for pleasure, curiosity or whim.

In such animals as are of a tame nature, a man may have as absolute a property as in any inanimate being; because they continue perpetually in his occupation, and will not stray from his house or person unless by accident or fraudulent enticement, in which cases the owner does not lose his property. The stealing or forcible abduction of such property is also felony: for these are things of intrinsic value, serving for the food of man or for the uses of husbandry. But in animals *feræ naturæ* a man can have no absolute, merely a qualified, property — *per industriam*, by reclaiming and making them tame by art, industry, training, or by so confining them within his own immediate power that they cannot escape and use their natural liberty; — *propter impotentiam* or *ratione impotentiæ*, on account of their own inability, as, in young animals, until they can fly or run away; — *propter privilegium*, by virtue of privilege, as of game within a liberty. While these creatures, reclaimed from the wildness of their nature, thus continue qualified or defeasible property they are as much under the protection of the law as if the owner's absolutely and indefeasibly. It is also as much a felony to steal such of them as are fit for food as to steal tame animals; but not so if they are kept only for pleasure, curiosity or whim, as dogs, bears, cats, parrots, singing-birds; because their value is then not intrinsic, but depends purely upon the caprice of the owner, though the taking is such an invasion of property as may amount to a civil injury and be redressed by a civil action.[3]

At common law larceny may be committed of a collar or chain attached to an animal not itself the subject of property.[4]

A property in dogs (*q. v.*) is now recognized under laws providing for their registration and taxation.[5]

---

[1] An'-cil-la-ry. L. *ancillaris, ancilla*, a handmaid.

[2] 3 Bl. Com. 98.

[3] Legal Tender Cases, 12 Wall. 535 (1870).

[4] 1 Pars. Contr. 141.

[5] Dupasseur *v.* Rochereau, 21 Wall. 136 (1874).

[6] Forbes Street, 70 Pa. 138 (1871).

[7] Christmas *v.* Russell, 14 Wall. 82 (1871).

[8] Cooper *v.* Reynolds, 10 Wall. 314 (1870).

[9] Claflin *v.* McDermott, 12 F. R. 375 (1882).

[10] 1 Story, Eq. § 762.

[11] 1 Story, Eq. § 583.

[12] Wall *v.* Dovey, 60 Pa. 213 (1869).

[13] 109 U. S. 20; 111 *id.* 522. So also an attachment may be, 48 Ark. 200; and one section in a charter to another section, 31 F. R. 218.

[14] Litchfield *v.* Cudworth, 15 Pick. 27 (1833); 14 *id.* 453; United States *v.* Fisk, 3 Wall. 447 (1865); Dumont *v.* United States, 98 U. S. 143 (1878); 55 Vt. 470.

[15] Reiche *v.* Smythe, 13 Wall. 165 (1871).

[16] [Abbott's Law Dict.

[1] [Abbott's Law Dict.]

[2] Commonwealth *v.* Turner, 145 Mass. 300 (Nov. 23, 1887); Pub. Sts. ch. 207, § 53.

[3] 2 Bl. Com. 390-94. See also 2 Kent, 349-50; Buster *v.* Newkirk, 20 Johns. *75 (1822) — as to a deer wounded by one and captured by another person; State *v.* Krider, 78 N. C. 482 (1878) — as to fish (in a pond ?); Swift *v.* Gifford, 2 Low. 112-15 (1872), cases, — as to a harpooned whale; Ghen *v.* Rich, 8 F. R. 159 (1881), cases, — as to a dead whale found floating.

[4] 4 Bl. Com. 235.

[5] See Morewood *v.* Wakefield, 133 Mass. 241 (1882);

The owner of an animal or the person who has the exclusive control of it is liable for injuries which he negligently suffers it to commit. This liability stands upon the ground of actual or presumed negligence. If the injury is committed while trespassing upon and the owner is responsible for damage directly resulting as a natural consequence. In other cases he may be liable although there is no trespass and the animal is rightfully in its place; as where the injury comes from the vicious disposition or mischievous habits of the animal of which the owner had previous actual notice; or where, without actual notice, the disposition and habits are so universal among the species that notice is presumed, as in the case of wild and savage beasts. The owner or keeper of such animals, without actual or implied notice of their character, is bound at his peril to keep them at all times and in all places properly secured, and is responsible to any one who without fault in himself is injured by them.[1]

Animals *feræ naturæ*, as a class, are known to be mischievous; and the rule is well settled that whoever undertakes to keep any such animal in a place of public resort is or may be liable for injuries inflicted by it on a party who is without fault. It is not necessary to aver negligence in the keeper, as the burden is upon the defendant to disprove that implied imputation; it is enough to aver ferocity in the animal and knowledge of that fact in the defendant. Certain animals *feræ naturæ* may doubtless be domesticated to such an extent they may be classed with tame animals; but as they are prone to relapse into their wild habits and to become mischievous, the rule is that if they do so, and the owner becomes notified, they will thereafter be viewed as not having been thoroughly and safely domesticated.[2]

See ACCESSION; AGIST; ALIVE; AT LARGE; BAIT, 2; CATTLE; CRUELTY, 3; DAMAGE, Feasant; DISTRESS; ESTRAY; FENCE; GAME, 1; IMPLEMENTS; LEVANT; MAIM, 2; NUISANCE; OYSTER; PARTUS; POUND, 2; BOUND, 2 (2); STOCK; 1; TEAM; TRESPASS; VICIOUS; WANTON; WARRANTY, 2; WARREN; WORRY; WOUND.

Harrington v. Miles, 11 Kan. 483–84 (1873), cases: 15 Am. Rep. 356, cases; State v. Doe, 79 Ind. 9 (1881), cases; Jemison v. Southwestern R. Co., 75 Ga. 445 (1885).

[1] Lyons v. Merrick, 105 Mass. 76 (1870), Colt, J.; Hewes v. McNamara, 106 *id.* 281 (1871); Maun v. Weiand, 81* Pa. 253–55 (1875), cases; Marble v. Ross, 124 Mass. 47–49 (1878), cases; Linnehan v. Sampson, 126 *id.* 510–11 (1879), cases; Muller v. McKeeson, 73 N. Y. 198–204 (1878), cases; Lynch v. McNally, *ib.* 349 (1878); State v. Harriman, 75 Me. 562 (1884); 56 Ala. 402; 49 Conn. 113; 69 Ga. 447; 75 Ill. 141; 88 *id.* 132; 35 Ind. 178; 34 Mich. 283; 7 Pa. 331; 15 *id.* 188; 51 Vt. 18; 38 Wis. 307; 2 Alb. L. J. 101; 20 *id.* 6, 104; 46 Am. R. 425.

As to animals trespassing on a railroad track, see Kansas City, &c. R. Co. v. Kirksey, 48 Ark. 376 (1886), cases.

[2] Congress & Empire Spring Co. v. Edgar, 99 U. S. 651–56 (1878), Clifford, J., citing many cases. The plaintiff below, one Mrs. Edgar, while visiting Congress Spring park, Saratoga, N. Y., was injured by a deer. The jury awarded her $6,500 damages, and the judgment therefor was affirmed by the circuit court for

ANIMUS. L. Mind; disposition; intention, will.

Animo. With, from, or in, mind or intention: as, in *eo animo, ex animo, malo animo, quo animo,* qq. v.

Animus, animum (objective form), mind or intention, **animo,** with intention or design — *cancellandi,* of canceling; *capiendi,* of seizing or taking; *dedicandi,* of dedicating or donating; *defamandi,* of defaming; *donandi,* of giving; *ferandi,* of stealing; *lucrandi,* of gaining; *manendi,* of remaining; *morandi,* of staying, remaining; *possidendi,* of possessing, appropriating; *recipiendi,* of receiving; *republicandi,* of republishing; *revertendi,* of returning; *revocandi,* of revoking; *testandi,* of making a will.

ANNEX.[1] To put in permanent connection with; to attach.

As, to annex — a fixture to a freehold; a condition to an estate; a covenant to land; one writing to another, as, an exhibit to a petition or affidavit of claim; one town to another town.[2]

Figuratively, a penalty or punishment is said to be annexed to an act.[3]

Annex incidents. To show what things are customarily treated as incidental and accessorial to the principal thing.[4]

Actual annexation. Such annexation as exists in point of fact: as, that of a fixture to a freehold. **Constructive annexation.** Exists in inference of law; as, that of a deed to land, that of a key to a house.

A fixture is "annexed to the freehold" when fastened to or connected with it. Mere juxtaposition, or the laying of an object, however heavy, on the freehold, does not amount to an annexation.[5]

A deposition taken under a commission is sufficient in the northern district of New York and by the United States Supreme Court. See also Twigg v. Ryland, 62 Md. 385–88 (1884), cases: 24 Am. Law Reg. 191, 196–97, cases; Meracle v. Down, 64 Wis. 323 (1885); Laherty v. Hogan, 13 Daly, 533 (1886); State v. Donahue. N. J. L. (1887), cases: 10 Atl. Rep. 150; 26 Am. Law Reg. 773–78 (1887), cases.

"If an ox gore a man or a woman that they die . . . and if the ox were wont to push with his horn in time past, and it hath been testified to his owner, and he hath not kept him in, but that he hath killed a man or a woman, the ox shall be stoned, and his owner also shall be put to death." Exodus, xxi, 28, 29.

[1] F. *annexer:* L. *annectere,* to knit, tie, bind to.
[2] 100 U. S. 530; 74 Me. 180.
[3] 1 Bl. Com. 415.
[4] 1 Greenl. Ev. § 294.
[5] Merritt v. Judd, 14 Cal. 64 (1859): 2 Sm. L. C. 296.

ciently annexed or connected to the commission by the envelope and official seal.[1]

Will annexed to letters. See ADMINISTER, 4.

ANNI; ANNO. See ANNUS.

ANNOYANCE. See NUISANCE; USUS, Sic utere, etc.; WANTON.

ANNUALLY. Applied to the payment of interest imports, not an undertaking to pay at the end of a year, but at the end of every year during the period of time, fixed or contingent.[2]

A note payable in five years from date "with interest annually" implies that the interest begins to run from the making of the note.[3] See ANNUS; YEAR.

ANNUITY.[4] A yearly sum stipulated to be paid to another in fee or for life or years, and chargeable only on the person of the grantor.[5]

A yearly sum chargeable upon the person of the grantor.[6]

A "rent-charge" is a burden imposed upon lands.[6]

An annuity is a stated sum payable annually, unless otherwise directed. It is neither "income" nor "profits," nor does it vary with them, though a certain fund may be provided out of which the sum is payable.[7] See INDIAN.

Annuitant. One who is entitled to an annuity.

Annuity table. A table exhibiting the probable longevity of a person at any particular age.

Based upon statistics, and of use in matters of life insurance and dower. See further TABLE, 4.

Life annuity. An annuity limited upon another's life — the engagement or the sum of money promised.[8]

An annuity payable to the annuitant and his heirs is a personal fee; neither curtesy nor dower are incidents thereto. It is assignable, and bequeathable; and may be an asset in case of insolvency. Remedies for its non-payment are: debt, covenant, action of annuity at common law.[9] It is also apportionable; and may be paid to a widow in lieu of dower.[10]

Since an annuity may be regarded as a legacy payable by a yearly instalment, the word "legacy," as used in a will, may comprise the word annuity.[1]

ANNUL. See NULL; REPEAL; RESCISSION; VACATE.

ANNUS. L. A year.

Anni nubiles. Marriageable years.

Infra annos nubiles. Within marriageable years — at common law the age of twelve in girls.[2]

Anno Domini. In the year of our Lord.

Abbreviated A. D. See ABBREVIATIONS; YEAR.

Annus luctus. The year of mourning.

Infra annum luctus. Within the year of mourning — sometimes called the "widow's year."

Roman and early Saxon law ordained that a widow should not remarry within a year after her husband's death: an inhibition which seems to have had reference to ascertaining the paternity of children.[3]

Supposed to be the origin also of a custom of wearing mourning dress.

Annus utilis. A serviceable year.

Anni utiles. The years during which a right may be asserted; as, the period during which one is not prevented by disability from availing himself of a statute of limitations.

ANONYMOUS. Designates a case reported with the names of the parties omitted. Abbreviated *Anon.*

ANOTHER. One other; any other

Larceny of the "personal goods of the United States" is within the words "personal goods of another" in the act of April 30, 1790.[4]

In the sense of another person, a co-party, is used in the titles of cases: as "A. B. v. C. D. and another." Compare ALIUS, Alios.

ANSWER. Response, reply; defense. Compare RESPONDERE.

1. In the sense of a response to a written or oral communication, see LETTER, 3; SILENCE.

2. A statement made in response to a question or interrogation propounded to a suitor, witness, or garnishee, in the course of a judicial inquiry. See further QUESTION, 1.

3. The formal written statement made by a defendant — to charges in a bill in equity, to a libel in admiralty or in divorce.

An answer is the most usual defense made to a bill in equity. It is given in upon oath; but where there are amicable defendants their answer may be taken without oath by consent of the plaintiff. This method

---

[1] Savage v. Birckhead, 20 Pick. 167 (1838); Shaw v. McGregory, 105 Mass. 100 (1870).

[2] Sparhawk v. Wills, 6 Gray, 164 (1856); Westfield v. Westfield. 19 S. C. 89–90 (1882).

[3] Winchell v. Coney, 54 Conn. 26, 30 (1886).

[4] L. L. *annuitas;* L. *annus,* a year.

[5] Coke, Litt. 144 b; 3 Kent, 460; 24 N. J. E. 356; 23 Barb. 216.

[6] 2 Bl. Com. 40; 10 Watts, 127; 23 Barb. 216.

[7] Booth v. Ammerman, 4 Bradf. 133–35 (1856), cases; Pearson v. Chace, 10 R. I. 456–57 (1873), cases; Bartlett v. Slater, 53 Conn. 107 (1885), cases.

[8] See 2 Bl. Com. 461.

[9] 3 Kent, 460, 471; Coke, Litt. 285; 4 Ves. 763; 5 *id.* 708.

[10] Blight v. Blight, 51 Pa. 420 (1866); Rudolph's Appeal,

10 *id.* 34 (1848); Lackawanna Iron, &c. Co.'s Case, 37 N. J. E. 27 (1883).

[1] Rudolph's Appeal, *ante; Exp.* M'Comb, 4 Bradf. 152 (1856); 12 N. Y. Leg. Obs. 182.

[2] 1 Bl. Com. 436; 2 Kent, 78.

[3] 1 Bl. Com. 457.

[4] United States v. Maxon, 5 Blatch. 362 (1866); 1 St. L. 116.

of proceeding was borrowed from the ecclesiastical courts.[1]

The parts of an answer are: the *title*, which tells whose answer it is and to whose bill; a *reservation* of advantages from any defects in the bill; the *substance*, whether the facts be of personal knowledge or rest upon information and belief; and a general *traverse* to the whole bill.

An answer must be responsive to all the material allegations in the bill.[2]

Unless the complainant have two witnesses, or one witness and corroborative circumstances, he will not be entitled to relief. The reason is, by calling upon the respondent to answer his allegations, the complainant admits that the answer will be evidence — equal to the testimony of any other witness; so that he cannot prevail unless the balance of proof is in his favor; to turn the scales, he must at least have circumstances which corroborate such single adverse witness.[3]

The answer must be responsive to the bill, and be sustained by the testimony of two witnesses, or of one witness corroborated by circumstances equivalent in weight to the testimony of another witness.[4]

If the alleged facts are not known to the defendant he should give his belief, if he has any; if none, he should say so and call for proof; otherwise he waives that branch of the controversy. A mere statement that he is without knowledge is not such admission as waives full proof.[5]

The answer of one defendant cannot be received against another, except where one so succeeds the other that his right devolves on the latter, making them privies in estate.[6]

An answer in equity must be signed by counsel. It must also deny or confess the material parts of the bill; it may confess and avoid (*q. v.*) the facts. If one of these things is not done the answer may be excepted to for insufficiency, and the defendant be compelled to put in a sufficient answer. A defendant cannot pray anything but to be dismissed the court; if he has any relief to ask he must do it by a cross-bill. After an answer is put in the plaintiff may amend his bill; and the defendant must then answer afresh. If the plaintiff finds sufficient confessed in the answer upon which to ground a decree he may proceed to a hearing upon the bill and answer; and in that case he takes the answer as true. Otherwise he replies generally, averring his bill to be true, certain, and sufficient, and the answer the reverse, as he is ready to prove: to which the defendant rejoins, averring the like on his side.[7]

See ADMIRALTY; ADMISSION, 2; ALLEGATION; AMENDMENT, 1; EQUITY, Bill; MASTER, 4; PLEA, 2; SHAM.

---

[1] 3 Bl. Com. 446–47.

[2] Roach *v.* Summers, 20 Wall. 170 (1873).

[3] Tobey *v.* Leonards, 2 Wall. 430 (1864); Moore *v.* Ullman, 80 Va. 310–11 (1885), cases; 9 Cranch, 160; 6 Wheat. 468; 4 Cliff. 266–67, 458–59, cases; 107 U. S. 232; 13 Pa. 70.

[4] Vigel *v.* Hopp, 104 U. S. 441 (1881); Morrison *v.* Durr, 122 *id.* 518 (1887); 109 *id.* 103; 2 Story, Eq. § 1528.

[5] Brown *v.* Pierce, 7 Wall. 211–12 (1868); 1 Johns. Ch. *107; 5 *id.* *248.

[6] Osborn *v.* United States Bank, 9 Wheat. 832 (1824).

[7] 3 Bl. Com. 447–49.

ANTAGONISM. See REPEAL; REPUGNANT.

ANTE. L. Before; hereinbefore.

Older form, *anti*, against. In compound words, *ante, anti, ant, an*. Anglo-Saxon, *and-*. Opposed, *post*. Compare ANTI; SUPRA.

Ante litem. See LIS, ANTE, etc.

Ante natus. See NATUS, ANTE, etc.

Antéa. Formerly.

ANTECEDENT. See SAID; SECURITY.

ANTE-DATE. See DATE.

ANTENUPTIAL. See NUPTIAL.

ANTI. L. Against; in opposition. Compare ANTE.

As used in compounds illustrated by such words as anti-license, anti-liquor, anti-monopoly, anti-oleomargarine, anti-prohibition (-ists), anti-saloon, anti-slavery.

ANTICIPATION.[1] Taking beforehand, or before a time.

1. Use in the present of what is to accrue or to becomes one's own as income or profit; dealing with income before it is due.

More specifically, alienation by a married woman, who has a separate estate by gift, of income not yet accrued.[2] Compare ADVANCEMENT; TRUST, 1.

2. Objection to issuing a patent, or to a patent granted, upon the ground that its subject-matter is identical with what is or was already known, whether patented or not.

Cases of anticipation are distinguished from cases of patentability or ingenuity, and from cases of new use, of substitution, and of combination.[3] See PATENT, 2.

ANTIENT. See ANCIENT, 1.

ANTIQUATED. See STALE.

ANY. Compare A, 4; EITHER.

In the expression, whether the county will construct "any road or bridge," extends to an indefinite number.[4]

May mean every; thus, in a statute of descents, "any father or mother" may embrace as well the case where all of a class have died in the life-time of the intestate as where only some one or more may have died.[5]

"For the foregoing purposes or any of them" means, in effect, "for the foregoing purposes and *every* of them."[5]

"Any railroad" may be taken distributively, in-

---

[1] L. *ante-capere*, to take beforehand.

[2] See 133 Mass. 174, 175; 3 Gray, 405; 12 Gratt. 425; 9 Ga. 201; 1 Ld. Cas. Eq. 520; 11 Ves. 221; Lewin, Trusts, 123.

[3] Merwin, Pat. Invent. 82.

[4] Dubuque County *v.* Dubuque, &c. R. Co., 4 Iowa, 4 (1853).

[5] McComas *v.* Amos, 27 Md. 141 (1868).

[6] Davidson *v.* Dallas, 8 Cal. 239, (1857).

cluding all railroads taken severally; as, in the expression, "any county may subscribe to the stock of any railroad in this State."[1]

"Any former deceased husband" in § 4162, Rev. St. Ohio, refers to any husband who has died; the expression is not confined to the case where a widow has had two or more husbands.[2]

APART. See ACKNOWLEDGMENT, 2; SEPARATE, 2.

APARTMENT. See BURGLARY; HOUSE.

APEX. See JUS, Apex, etc.; VEIN.

APOSTLE.[3] In English admiralty practice the copy of the record in an appealed case which is sent to the appellate tribunal.

APOTHECARY. See DRUGGIST; MERCHANT.

Any person who keeps a shop or building where medicines are compounded or prepared according to the prescriptions of physicians, or where medicines are sold.[4]

APPARATUS. See APPENDAGE; PROCESS, 2.

APPAREL. In exemption and duties laws "apparel," "wearing apparel," and "necessary wearing apparel" have their popular import.[5]

Cloth actually appropriated thereto may be regarded as apparel.[6]

In September, 1878, William Astor and family arrived home from Europe, bringing with them wearing apparel bought there for their use, to be worn during the season then approaching, and in quantity not excessive for persons of their means, habits, and station in life. A portion of the articles not having been worn duties were exacted on them, and the circuit court confirmed the action of the collector. The Supreme Court, reversing the lower court, held that under § 2505, Rev. St., exempting from duty "wearing apparel in actual use and other personal effects not merchandise," such articles as fulfill the following conditions are not subject to duty, viz.: 1, wearing apparel owned by the passenger and in condition to be worn at once without further manufacture; 2, apparel brought with him as passenger and intended for use by himself or his family who accompany him, not intended for sale, and not imported for other persons or to be given away; 3, apparel suitable for the season of the year immediately approaching at the time of arrival; 4, apparel not exceeding in quantity, quality, or value what the passenger is in the habit ordinarily

of providing for himself and family at that time, and keeping on hand for his and their reasonable wants, in view of their means, habits, and station in life, even though such articles have not been actually worn.[1]

See BAGGAGE; EXEMPTION; PARAPHERNALIA; PIN-MONEY.

APPARENT. 1. Readily seen; evident, self-evident; manifest: as, error apparent upon the face of a record. See APPARERE, De non, etc.; CONSTAT, 1; ERROR, 2 (3).

2. Existing in looks or appearance, and, perhaps, oftener not real than true and real; opposed to *actual:* as, apparent — authority, right or title; also opposed to **non-apparent:** as, an apparent or non-apparent easement, *q. v.*

An apparent right of possession is defeated by proof of a better, *i. e.*, an actual, right.[2]

When the owner of property clothes another with the apparent power of disposition a third party who is thereby induced to deal with that other will be protected as against the owner.[3]

A principal is held for the act of his agent clothed with apparent authority.[4]

The holder of mercantile paper is the apparent owner thereof.

Apparent danger. In the law of justifiable homicide such overt, actual demonstration, by conduct and acts, of a design to take life or to do great personal injury as makes killing apparently necessary.[5]

Apparent good order. Shipped "in apparent good order," in a bill of lading, does not change the legal effect of the bill. If a loss occurs the carrier is not precluded from showing that it proceeded from a latent defect in the package.[6]

APPARERE. L. To come into sight: to appear. Compare CONSTAT, 1.

De non apparentibus et non existentibus, eadem est ratio. Concerning things not appearing and things not existing, the rule (reason, conclusion) is the same. **Quod non apparet, non est.** What does not appear does not exist.

A thing which is not made to appear is regarded as if it could not be made to appear and did not therefore exist.

The record of a court of limited or inferior jurisdiction must show jurisdiction rightfully exercised;[7] but

---

[1] County of Chicot v. Lewis, 103 U. S. 167 (1880).

[2] Anderson v. Gilchrist, 44 Ohio St. 440 (1886). See also 41 N. J. E. 659; 9 S. C. 117.

[3] Gk. *apostolein'*, to send away.

[4] Revenue Act, 13 July, 1866, § 9: 14 St. L. 119.

[5] Maillard v. Lawrence, 16 How. 261 (1853); Greenleaf v. Goodrich, 101 U. S. 285 (1879); Re Steele, 2 Flip. 325-26 (1879), cases.

[6] Richardson v. Buswell, 10 Metc. 507 (1845); 33 Me. 535; 55 Barb. 389.

[1] Astor v. Merritt, 111 U. S. 202 (1884), Blatchford, J.

[2] 2 Bl. Com. 196.

[3] 46 N. Y. 325; 101 U. S. 575.

[4] 96 U. S. 86.

[5] [Evans v. State, 44 Miss. 773 (1870), Simrall, J.; Wesley v. State, 37 id. 349 (1859).

[6] The Oriflamme, 1 Saw. 178 (1870).

[7] 2 How. 341; 12 id. 253.

in courts of record of general jurisdiction all things are presumed to have been rightly done.[1]

A fact essential to the exercise, by a court of general jurisdiction, of a special power conferred upon it, must appear upon the face of the record.[2] See further PRÆSUMERE, Omnia, etc.

An affidavit is good for what it shows upon its face.[3]

A deed irregularly transcribed is not a record.[4]

An objection not of record will be disregarded.

The contents of a document in dispute must be proved.[5]

APPEAL.[6] 1. To apply to, as for relief; also, the application or action itself. Whence *appealable;* as, an appealable order.

May denote an application for relief to be obtained by a consideration or review of previous action: as, an appeal from listers to the selectmen of a town upon an alleged grievous assessment.[7]

2. To remove a cause to a higher court for review and retrial; also, the proceeding in itself considered.

Appeals are allowed in suits in equity, proceedings in courts of probate, orphans' or surrogate's courts, and in admiralty; from awards of arbitrators and referees; from municipal and tax assessments; on summary proceedings in criminal matters determined by committing magistrates; and in numerous other matters of code or statutory regulation.

Appeal lies to a final decree or judgment; in a few cases, also, upon an interlocutory order: as, in review of a commitment when authority in the lower court to act is disputed.[8]

Appellant. He who takes an appeal.

Appellee. The defendant in an appealed case.

Appellate. Having cognizance of appealed cases; accessible by appeal; concerning the judicial review of decisions: as, appellate — court, jurisdiction, power.

Appellate jurisdiction, q. v. Power to revise the decisions of the courts only, not the determinations of all inferior officers and boards.[9]

The secretary of the interior and the commissioner of the general land office in revising the acts of

subordinate officials exercise " supervisory " ra than appellate power in the sense in which " a late " is employed in defining the powers of cour justice.[1]

Appeal (*appellatio* in civil law) is defi *ab inferioris judicis sententia ad superio provocare:* the removal of a cause from sentence of an inferior to a superior ju or, as Blackstone expresses it, a compl to a superior court of an injustice done an inferior court.[2]

The remedy as known in England is in a g measure confined to causes in equity, ecclesiast and admiralty jurisdiction: as to each of whic jury intervenes. In courts proceeding accordin the civil law an appeal removes the whole of proceedings and usually, though not invariably, o the facts as well as the law to re-examination.[3]

A process of civil law origin. Removes a c entirely, subjecting the fact and the law to review retrial. A "writ of error," which is of common-law gin, removes nothing for re-examination but the l

While perhaps in most States an appeal fro court of general jurisdiction is in the nature of a of error,— whereby the appellate court passes the record as to facts and law, does not hear a tional evidence, but confines its adjudication to er appearing upon the record,— in Ohio the appeal i vacates without revisal all proceedings, and the is heard upon the same or other pleadings and n such testimony as may be offered in that court. subject is taken up *de novo,* as if the cause had n been tried.[4]

A final decree in chancery is taken to a higher c for review by appeal.[5]

The object of removing a cause from a justic the peace by an appeal is to obtain a new trial, n the same issue, in the higher court.[6]

In States which have adopted the name " appe for the review allowed of judgments governed by c of procedure, the proceeding is subject to so m statutory regulation, and in effect is so assimilate "writ of error," that it seems no longer possibl give a descriptive definition which shall be correct the various States and distinguish the two mode review.[7]

If a party to a suit is in no manner affected by v is decided he cannot be said to be a party to the cree, and, therefore, cannot appeal the case.[8]

[1] 11 Wall. 299–301.

[2] Chesterfield County v. Hall, 50 Va. 324 (1885).

[3] Lord v. Ocean Bank, 20 Pa. 384 (1853).

[4] McNitt v. Turner, 16 Wall. 361 (1872).

[5] See generally Broom, Max. 163, 166; 102 U. S. 202, 421; 104 *id.* 439; 4 Mass. 685; 8 *id.* 401; 55 Pa. 57; 76 Va. 301.

[6] L. *appellare,* to call upon, address.

[7] Leach v. Blakely, 34 Vt. 136 (1861).

[8] *Exp.* Virginia, 100 U. S. 342 (1879).

[9] See Hubbell v. McCourt, 44 Wis. 587 (1878), cases; Auditor v. Atkinson, &c. R. Co., 6 Kan. 505 (1870); Piqua Bank v. Knoup, 6 Ohio St. 391 (1856).

[1] Hestres v. Brennan, 50 Cal. 217 (1875); R. S. §§ 453, 2478.

[2] United States v. Wonson, 1 Gall. 13 (1812), Stor

[3] Wiscart v. Dauchy, 3 Dall. 327 (1796), Elswo C. J. See also United States v. Goodwin, 7 Cranch (1812); 22 How. 128; 103 U. S. 611. As to review facts in actions at law, see 22 Am. Law Rev. 26 (1888), cases.

[4] Mason v. Alexander, 44 Ohio St. 328 (1886), Spea

[5] McCollum v. Eager, 2 How. 61 (1844); 21 *id.* 445

[6] Rawson v. Adams, 17 Johns. *131 (1819).

[7] [Abbott's Law Dict. See 12 Mo. Ap. 186; 30 Minn.

[8] Farmers' Loan, &c. Co. v. Waterman, 106 U. S (1882); 108 *id.* 168.

Appeal bond. An obligation, with sureties, given by an appellant in order to remove a cause by appeal, and conditioned for the payment of damages and costs if he fails to " prosecute the appeal with effect," *q. v.*

If the judgment is affirmed the sureties, *proprio vigore,* become liable to the same extent as the principal for the damages and costs. In an appeal to a still higher court new sureties are required.[1]

An appeal bond, or a bond in error, is a formal instrument required and governed by the law, and, by nearly a century's use, has become a formula in legal proceedings, with a fixed and definite meaning. As the important right of appeal is greatly affected by it, it is not allowable, in practice, by a change in phraseology, to give it an effect contrary to what the statutes intend — as, in Federal practice, the acts of 1789 and 1803: R. S. §§ 1000, 1007, 1010, 1012. It would be against the policy of the law to suffer such deviations and irregularities. The rule followed in some States is a sound one, that if the condition of the bond substantially conforms to the requirements of the statutes it is sufficient, though it contain variations of language; and that if further conditions be superadded the bond is not therefore invalid, so far as it is supported by the statute, but only as to the superadded conditions.[2]

Court of appeals. Any court ordained to review the final decrees of another court; in several States the tribunal of last resort.

The highest court in Kentucky, Maryland, and New York. In Virginia and West Virginia it is known as the "supreme court of appeals;" in Delaware and New Jersey, as the "court of errors and appeals." In Texas the court is inferior to the supreme court. In England designates one of the two subdivisions of the supreme court of judicature as constituted by the acts of 1873 and 1875.

See ERROR, 2 (2, 3), Court of, Writ of; FINAL, 3; PAPER, 5; SUPERSEDEAS.

3. In old English law an accusation by a private subject against another of a heinous crime, demanding punishment on account of the particular injury suffered, rather than for the offense against the public.

Appellor: the accuser; **appellee:** the accused.

Originated, probably, when a private pecuniary satisfaction, called *weregild,* was paid to the party injured or to his relatives to expiate enormous crimes.[3]

Abolished in 1819, after the case of *Ashford* v. *Thornton.* See BATTEL.

APPEAR. The right to "appear" before a tribunal engaged in the transaction of particular business implies the right to be heard thereabout, — so far, at least, as the party is interested.[1]

Appearance. 1. Being apparent, *q. v.*

2. Having the form or semblance of. See COLOR, 2; FACIES.

3. Coming into court as a party to a suit; presence in court as a suitor. Used, particularly, of a defendant's presence, in person or by attorney.[2] Opposed, **non-appearance.**

An entry of appearance upon the record of a cause is to be interpreted by the practice of the particular court. Whatever is held to be a submission to its authority in the cause, whether coerced or voluntary, will be deemed an appearance.[3]

Made by entering of record the name of the party or his counsel, and at the request of either; also, by entering bail, answer, demurrer, or by any other act admitting that the defendant is in court, submitting to the jurisdiction. Originally, when pleadings were oral, made by actual presence in court.

An appearance may be *general* or *common,* or *special* or *conditional,* according as it is unqualified or unrestricted, or made for a specific purpose — as, to make a motion, or is coupled with a condition; *de bene esse,* when provisional on an event; *voluntary, compulsory,* or *optional,* according as it is entered freely, is compelled by plaintiff's action, or is made by one not obliged to appear, but who applies to do so, to save a right; *in person, by attorney, by next friend, by guardian,* or *by committee,* according as the party himself defends, or employs or is represented by another; *pro hac vice,* when in some special relation; *corporal,* when by defendant in person.

Corporal appearance is generally required in a criminal trial. In modern practice in civil actions appearing may be constructive or figurative.

An appearance is to be *entered* by a certain day, called the *appearance day;* to which day writs are made returnable. It is "general" when it is the stated day ordinarily observed; and "special" when some other day, as, the day appointed in a particular case.

On every return day in the term the person, at common law, had three days of grace beyond the day named in the writ in which to appear, and if he appeared on the fourth day inclusive, *quarta die post,* it

---

[1] Babbitt *v.* Finn, 101 U. S. 15, 13 (1879); Beall *v.* New Mexico, 16 Wall. 539 (1872).

[2] Kountze *v.* Omaha Hotel Co., 107 U. S. 395–96 (1882), cases; 11 Lea, 72.

[3] 4 Bl. Com. 312–17; 110 U. S. 526.

[1] Dundee Mortgage Trust Invest. Co. *v.* Charlton, 32 F. R. 194 (1887).

[2] See Schroeder *v.* Lahrman, 26 Minn. 88 (1879); Larrabee *v.* Larrabee, 33 Me. 102 (1851).

[3] Cooley *v.* Lawrence, 5 Duer, 610 (1855); Grigg *v.* Gilman, 54 Ala. 430 (1875).

was sufficient. Therefore, usually the court did not sit till the fourth or appearance day.[1]

An appearance is also entered in a book called the *appearance docket*, which exhibits, in a brief abstract, all the proceedings had in a cause.

For failure to appear after legal notice given, in cases, judgment may be taken "in default" of an appearance.

On cause shown, by petition to the court, an attorney may be permitted to "withdraw" his appearance, timely notice having first been given to the client.[2]

An appearance by a person admitted to practice is received as evidence of his authority; otherwise as to an attorney in fact.[3]

A general appearance waives all questions as to the service of process, and is, moreover, equivalent to a personal service. Its effect is not disturbed by the withdrawal of the attorney. The question of jurisdiction alone is saved.[4]

But, under the privilege of a special appearance, a person cannot avail himself of the advantage of a general appearance.[5]

See ABIDE· VENIRE.

APPENDAGE. See APPENDANT; INCIDENT; RAILROAD.

Where the question was whether a stereoscope, with views, was a "necessary appendage" to a schoolhouse, the court said that the words quoted, as used in a statute. referred to things connected with the building or designed to render it suitable for use as a schoolhouse.[6]

Under the same statute charts and maps to be hung upon the walls may be called "appendages" or "apparatus."[7]

Certainly a well would be a necessary appendage;[8] and, also, a fence around the school building.[9]

APPENDANT.[10] Annexed to another and superior thing; belonging to something as the principal thing; also, the thing itself thus attached: as, an incorporeal inheritance to another inheritance, one power to another power.[11]

Said of a thing which belongs to another

[1] 3 Bl. Com. 278, 290.

[2] United States v. Yates, 6 How. 608 (1848).

[3] See Osborn v. United States Bank, 9 Wheat. 830 (1824); Hill v. Mendenhall, 21 Wall. 454 (1874).

[4] Eldred v. Michigan Ins. Bank, 17 Wall. 551 (1873); Creighton v. Kerr, 20 *id.* 12 (1873); 6 How. 608; 29 Kan. 683; 29 Minn. 46.

[5] National Furnace Co. v. Moline Iron Works, 18 F. R. 863 (1884).

[6] School District v. Perkins, 21 Kan. 537 (1879).

[7] School District v. Swayze, 29 Kan. 216 (1883).

[8] Hemme v. School District, 30 Kan. 381 (1883).

[9] Creager v. Wright School District, Sup. Ct. Mich. (1886).

[10] L. *ad-pendere*, to hang to.

[11] [4 Kent, 316, 404; 2 Bl. Com. 33.]

thing as its principal and passes as an incident to the latter.[1]

Or, of a thing used with, related to, or dependent upon, another thing more worthy and agreeing in nature and quality with that other.[2] See APPENDAGE; APPURTENANCE.

APPERTAIN. One thing may appertain to another without adjoining or touching it.

Proof that pieces of land adjoin would not be proof that one appertained to the other. As a descriptive word in a deed "appertaining" imports use, occupancy; "adjoining" imports contiguity.[3] See ADJOINING; APPURTENANCE.

APPLICATION. 1. A written request, more or less formal, presented to a private person or to an official for the favorable exercise of his authority or discretion: as, an application for insurance[4] (*q. v.*), for an order of court, for a pardon, for remission of a fine.

2. Devoting, appropriating to an end or demand; also, the use or purpose itself to which a thing or fund has been set apart, distributed, or paid.

Misapplication. Improper or unlawful disposition or application.

It is not sufficient to aver simply that a defendant "willfully misapplied" trust funds: there must be averments to show how the application was made and that it was an unlawful one.[5]

Application of payments. The application of a general payment of money to the discharge of one or more of several demands.

The right must be exercised within a reasonable time after the payment and by an act which indicates an intention to appropriate. Where neither party has exercised the right the law presumes that the debtor intended to pay in the way which, at the time, was most to his advantage. Where, however, the interest of the debtor could not be promoted by any particular appropriation there is no ground for a presumption of any intention on his part, and the law then presumes that the payment was received in the way most advantageous to the creditor.[6]

The rule settled by the Supreme Court of the United States is that the debtor, or the party paying the money, may, if he chooses, direct its appropriation; if he fails so to do the right then devolves upon the cred-

[1] [Meek v. Breckenridge, 29 Ohio St. 448 (1876).

[2] Leonard v. White, 7 Mass. 8 (1810); Coke, Litt. 121 *b*, 122 *a*; 3 N. H. 192.

[3] Miller v. Mann, 55 Vt. 479 (1882), Veazey, J.

[4] See 25 Minn. 539; 133 Mass. 85.

[5] United States v. Britton, 107 U. S. 669 (1882); R. S. § 5209.

[6] Harker v. Conrad, 12 S. & R. 304 (1824), Gibson, J.; Pierce v. Sweet, 33 Pa. 157 (1859).

itor; and if he fails in this respect the law will make the application according to its own notions of justice. Neither party can make it after a controversy upon the subject has arisen between them.[1]

APPOINTMENT. Fixing, establishing: limitation, selection, designation.

1. Selection for the duties of an office or place of trust.

Appointee. The person so designated, until qualified.

A commission, regularly issued, is conclusive evidence of an appointment.[2]

Where a common council voted to ballot for a municipal officer, in pursuance of a power conferred by charter to "appoint" such officer, it was held that the ballot taken was intended to be an election, that is, an appointment.[3]

Appointments to office are intrinsically executive acts, whether made by a court, a municipal council, an executive officer, or other person or body. A particular appointment is complete when the last act required of the appointing power is performed.[3] See OFFICE, 1; RESIGNATION.

2. Exercise of the right to designate the person who is to take the use of realty.[4]

An authority given to another to be exercised over property in a manner and to an extent which he would not otherwise possess.[5]

Also called *power* of appointment.

Appointor. He who executes the power; the *donee*. He who confers the power is the *donor*. **Appointee.** He in whose favor the power is executed.[6]

General appointment. Such appointment as enables the donee to name, as appointee, whom he pleases — even himself. **Special appointment.** Such as restricts the donee to naming one or more appointees from among particular persons.

The latter dates from the creation of the power; the former from its exercise.

Where a person, having a general power of appointment, by deed or by will, executes it, the property is deemed in equity a part of his assets, subject to the demands of his creditors in preference to the claims of voluntary appointees or of legatees.[1]

Illusory appointment. Allotment of a nominal, not of a substantial, interest.[2]

The rule at common law was to require some allotment to each person where several appointees were intended. But the rule in equity requires a real, substantial portion in each appointee — a merely nominal allotment being viewed not only as illusory but as fraudulent.[3]

A devise to a corporation for a charitable use is an appointment rather than a bequest.[4]

The donee must be competent to dispose of an estate of his own in like manner. All donees, or their survivors, must join in executing the power. The donor's intention is to be strictly observed. A partial execution may be upheld. The estate vests in the appointee as if conveyed immediately by the donor.[5] See further POWER, 2; USE, 3.

APPORTIONMENT. A division into shares, portions or proportions; distribution into proportionate parts.

Division of a fund, or property, or other subject-matter, in shares proportioned to different demands, or appropriate to satisfy rival claims.[6] Whence non-apportionable, unapportionable.

Thus, we have the apportionment — of an *annuity* to a part of the year; of a *contract*, not entire, to the part performed; of *dividends*, or money, in stocks;[7] of sums payable toward the support or removal of an *incumbrance;* of *freight* earned previously to a disaster to an abandoned ship;[8] of *loss* and *damage* caused by a collision of vessels, both parties being in fault;[9] of *rent*, where the leasehold or reversion is transferred, partitioned, levied on for debt, or set-off in dower, or where there are several assignees, or the premises become untenantable;[10] of *Representatives*, decennially, according to the increase of population;[11] of corporate *shares*, when more have been subscribed for than the charter allows to be issued.[12]

---

[1] Nat. Bank of the Commonwealth *v.* Mechanics' Nat. Bank, 94 U. S. 439 (1876), cases; Nichols *v.* Knowles, 17 F. R. 495-96 (1881), cases; Bank of California *v.* Webb, 94 N. Y. 472 (1884), cases; McCurdy *v.* Middleton, 82 Ala. 137 (1885), cases; Sanborn *v.* Stark, 31 F. R. 18 (1887); 21 Cent. Law J. 473-79 (1885), cases. See also 9 Wheat. 720; 6 Cranch, 8; 1 Mass. 323; 88 Ind. 68-69, cases; 62 Miss. 8, 121, 500; 7 Oreg. 228; 59 Tex. 649; 55 Vt. 464, 543; 22 F. R. 570; 13 Am. Dec. 505. cases; 14 *id.* 694, cases; 1 Story, Eq. § 459 *b;* 2 Pars. Contr. 629.

[2] United States *v.* Le Baron, 19 How. 79, 73 (1856); 1 Cranch, 137; 10 Pet. 343; 10 Oreg. 520.

[3] State *ex rel.* Coogan *v.* Barbour, 53 Conn. 83, 85-90 (1885), cases.

[4] [2 Washb. Real Prop. 302.

[5] [Blagge *v.* Miles, 1 Story, 442 (1841), Story, J.

[6] [4 Kent, 316.]

---

[1] Brandies *v.* Cochrane, 112 U. S. 352 (1884), cases; Sewale *v.* Wilmer, 132 Mass. 134-35 (1882), cases.

[2] See 3 Kent, 343; Ingraham *v.* Meade, 3 Wall. Jr. 40 (1855).

[3] Sugden, Powers, 489; 4 Kent, 342.

[4] 2 Bl. Com. 376.

[5] 4 Kent, 324; 2 Story, Eq. §§ 1061-63; 2 Washb. R. P. 317-22, 298, 337.

[6] Abbott's Law Dict.

[7] 3 Kent, 470.

[8] 3 Kent, 333.

[9] 93 U. S. 302; 10 Bened. 658.

[10] 3 Kent, 469-71.

[11] 1 Kent, 230; Act 25 Feb. 1882: 22 St. L. 5.

[12] 1 Johns. Ch. 18; 1 Edw. 368.

At common law periodical payments, due at set times, were not apportionable.[1]

Guilt and negligence are unapportionable. See CONTRIBUTION.

APPRAISE.[2] To value; to estimate at a price, by authority of law.

Appraisement; appraisal; apprizal. The worth of property as estimated by an authorized person; also the act or proceeding by which the estimate is made.

An "apprizal" of property signifies a valuation of it, an estimation of its value, unless some other sense is plainly indicated.[3]

Appraisements are made—of the goods of a deceased; of articles set apart for the share or exemption of a widow; of the assets of an insolvent who has assigned his property for the benefit of creditors or who claims exemption of his statutory amount under proceedings in execution of a judgment; of property taken for public uses; of goods distrained for rent; of the goods of an importer.

Appraiser. One authorized to determine the value of an article or articles of property. See INDIFFERENT, 1.

Mercantile appraiser. An officer whose duty it is to ascertain the amount of business done by persons in the different mercantile pursuits and to regulate the tax or license fees to be paid by them on their business.

Government appraiser. The incumbent of a permanent office, selected by a collector of customs, and charged with the duty of valuing dutiable merchandise.

Merchant appraiser. An appraiser selected by an importer to act with a government appraiser.[4]

Re-appraiser. One chosen to make a second appraisement of dutiable goods.

The importer has a right to be present when re-appraisers view his goods. The re-appraisement is an apprizal on view, and the re-appraisers may ascertain the value of the merchandise by reasonable means, and determine what witnesses, if any, they will examine. The merchant appraiser who may be called in is not an "officer" within the meaning of Art. II of the Constitution; and the exaction of a fee for his compensation is not authorized.[5]

APPREHENSION.[6] Strictly, seizing and taking hold of a man, but may apply to detaining a person already in custody.[1] S ARREST, 2, 3; ATTACH, 2.

APPRENTICE.[2] A learner: a spec of servant usually "bound" for a term years, by indenture, to serve his master a be maintained and instructed by him.[3]

One bound to service for a term of ye: in order to learn a trade or art.[4] Wher apprenticeship. "Apprentice" is also us in a verbal sense.

"A young person bound by indenture t tradesman or artificer who, upon cert: covenants, is to teach him his mystery trade." To constitute an apprenticeship son thing is to be *learned:* this is the charact istic mark of the service to be performed.:

Ex vi termini implies service in some specific p fession, trade, or employment.[6]

This form of binding is usually done to person: trade in order to learn their art and mystery: bu may be done to husbandmen and others. The child: of poor persons, till twenty-one years of age, may apprenticed by the overseers of the poor to such are thought fitting; and these in turn may be cc pelled to take them.[7]

The "teacher" is called the *master.* The contr is signed by the immediate parties. The period c tinues till twenty-one in a male and eighteen in female, or longer by consent. The master takes place of the parent. He may discharge the apprent for reasonable cause. Each party is supposed to wi for the other's interest. At common law the contr is not assignable.[8]

Apprenticeship had its origin in days when the vi ous trades were encompassed with restrictions a: the persons who might enter them. Modern custo: which have so greatly relaxed the rules governing exercise of the arts and trades, have correspondin modified the strict characteristics of apprenticeshi Local statutes and decisions should be consulted

APPRIZAL. See APPRAISE.

APPROACH. See BRIDGE.

APPROBARE. L. To approve; lit ally, to test, try, prove good.

Qui approbat, non reprobat. He w approves cannot reject.

One cannot both accept and reject the same thi One may not both affirm and deny.

[1] 3 Kent, 469.

[2] F. *apreiser*, to value: L. *pretium*, price.

[3] Cocheco Manuf. Company v. Strafford, 51 N. H. 482 (1871), Doe, J.

[4] Belcher v. Linn, 24 How. 522 (1860): R. S. §§ 2609-10, 2946. See also Oelbermann v. Merritt, 19 F. R. 409 (1884); Oelbermann v. Merritt, 123 U. S. 356 (1887).

[5] Auff Mordt v. Hedden, 30 F. R. 360 (1886), Wheeler, J.

[6] L. *ad-prehendere*, to lay hold of.

[1] Regina v. Weil, 47 L. T. R. 632 (1883); s. c. 15 Rep.

[2] F. *apprendre*, to learn: L. *apprehendere*, to hold of, grasp.

[3] [1 Bl. Com. 426; 3 *id.* 26.

[4] [2 Kent, 261.

[5] Hopewell v. Amwell, 3 N. J. L. *425 (1808). See a State ex rel. v. Jones, 16 Fla. 316-18 (1878).

[6] *Re* Goodenough, 19 Wis. 277 (1865), Dixon, C. J.

[7] 1 Bl. Com. 426.

[8] 2 Kent, 261; 1 Bl. Com. 460.

[9] Abbott's Law Dict.

APPROBATE. See ALLEGARE, Allegans contraria, etc.

APPROPRIATE.[1] 1, *v.* (1) To take to one's self; to take as one's own — for one's self:[2] as, to appropriate running water; to appropriate the personalty of another is a conversion, an embezzlement, or larceny, *qq. v.* Whence appropriation, appropriator, appropriable. Compare ACQUIRE; OCCUPY.

To appropriate another's goods against his will is to take them from him to one's self with or without violence.[3] See CONVERSION, 3.

(2) To adopt as distinctively one's own: as, to appropriate a design or symbol for a trade-mark,[4] *q. v.*

(3) To reserve for a distinct purpose; to destine to a particular end: as, to appropriate property to an exclusive use, or a fund to the discharge of special demand.

A space is not appropriated to the use of passengers on board a vessel as long as one person is allowed an individual use of it.[5]

"Appropriated lands," in a pre-emption law: land applied to some specific use or purpose by virtue of law.[6]

In the expression "appropriate property of any individual to public uses," the term embraces every mode by which property may be applied to the use of the public. Whatever exists which public necessity demands may be thus appropriated.[7] See further DOMAIN, 1, Eminent.

A direction to an executor to "appropriate" funds is an implication that he is assumed to hold that which he is directed to appropriate.[8]

"Appropriations" in a will means a designation to a particular exclusive use.[9]

The "appropriation of public money" is the disposition of public moneys from the treasury by law;[6] — an authority from the legislature, given at the proper time and in legal form, to the proper officers, to apply sums of money out of that which may be in the treasury in a given year to specified objects or demands against the State.[10]

While, as referring to funds, "appropriate" and "apply" are often interchanged, "appropriate" may mean rather to decide that a certain fund shall be devoted to a specific purpose, and "apply" to make the expenditure in fact. See further APPLICATION, 2.

[1] L. *appropriare*, to make one's own — *proprius*.
[2] See 8 Oreg. 102; 9 *id.* 231.
[3] [Waters *v.* United States, 4 Ct. Cl. 393 (1868).
[4] 100 U. S. 95; 101 *id.* 53.
[5] United States *v.* Nicholson, 8 Saw. 164 (1882); R. S. § 4252.
[6] McConnell *v.* Wilcox, 2 Ill. 360, 359 (1837).
[7] Boston, &c. R. Corporation *v.* Salem, &c. R. Company, 2 Gray, 35 (1854), Shaw, C. J.
[8] Blake *v.* Dexter, 12 Cush. 568 (1853), Shaw, C. J.
[9] Whitehead *v.* Gibbons, 10 N. J. E. 233 (1854).
[10] Ristine *v.* State, 20 Ind. 338 (1863), Perkins, J.

APPROPRIATE. 2, *adj.* Adapted to the purpose: proper, fit, suitable, *q. v.*: as, the appropriate departments of the government;[1] appropriate legislation;[2] an appropriate remedy[3] or decree.[4]

APPROVE. 1. To accept as good or sufficient for the purpose intended. Opposed, *disapprove.* See APPROBARE.

Public sales are made on "approved, indorsed notes" when the purchaser gives his promissory note for the amount of a purchase, indorsed by another and approved by the seller. The approval of the note ratifies the sale.[5]

See SALE, On approval; RATIFICATION.

2. To deem of sufficient security: as, to approve a bond.

"Approved" indorsed on a bond by the judge of a court does not necessarily import more than that the bond is deemed a sufficient security to be accepted. It does not include a direction that the bond is to stand in lieu of another bond and that the other is discharged.[6]

3. To affirm as lawful and proper; to give judicial sanction to: as, to approve the report of an auditor, a master, or trustee. See CONFIRMATION, 3.

4. To concur in the propriety or expediency, the legality or constitutionality of; to give executive sanction to: as, to approve an ordinance proposed by the councils of a city, to approve an act of an Assembly or of Congress. See ACT, 2; PASS, 2; VETO.

5. To confess a felony or treason and accuse another as accomplice in order to obtain a pardon.

Approvement. The confession made in such case, and the act of making it.

Approver. He who makes such a confession.

The accused is the "appellee."

When a person indicted for treason or felony was arraigned he might confess the charge before plea pleaded and appeal or accuse some other as his accomplice, in order to obtain a pardon. This, allowed in capital cases only, was equivalent to an indictment, as the appellee was required to answer the charge. If proven guilty the judgment was against the appellee; and the approver was entitled to a pardon *ex debito justitiæ;* but if the appellee was acquitted the judgment was that the approver be condemned.[7] See ACCOMPLICE.

[1] 101 U. S. 770.
[2] 100 U. S. 345.
[3] 100 U. S. 311.
[4] 101 U. S. 398.
[5] Mills *v.* Hunt, 20 Wend. 435 (1838); Guier *v.* Page, 4 S. & R. 1 (1818).
[6] United States *v.* Haynes, 9 Bened. 25 (1877).
[7] 4 Bl. Com. 330; Rex *v.* Rudd, 1 Cowp. 335 (1775);

APPURTENANCE.[1] A right connected with the enjoyment or use of another thing as principal; also, the thing itself out of which the right grows as an incident.

Appurtenant. Connected with or pertaining to a thing of superior nature.

In strict legal sense land can never be appurtenant to land. A thing to be appurtenant to another thing must be of a different and congruous nature; such as an easement or servitude, or some collateral incident belonging to and for the benefit of the land. In Coke, Litt. 121 b, it is said that nothing can be appurtenant unless the thing agrees in quality and nature to the thing whereunto it appurtaineth; as a thing corporeal properly cannot be appurtenant to a thing corporeal, nor a thing incorporeal to a thing incorporeal. There are many other authorities to the same effect. In a case, therefore, where the words of a grant pass land " with its appurtenances " the law, in the absence of controlling words, will deem "appurtenances" to be used in its technical sense; and that construction will not be displaced until it is made manifest from other parts of the grant that some other thing was actually intended.[2]

Something appertaining to another thing as principal, and passing as an incident to such principal.[3]

A right not connected with the enjoyment or use of a parcel of land cannot be annexed as an incident to that land so as to become appurtenant to it.[4]

The expression "appurtenances of a ship" is not to be construed with reference to the abstract naked idea of a ship. The relation which the equipment bears to the actual service is to be looked at. "Appurtenances" is a word of wider extent than "furniture" (q. v.) and may be applied to many things which could not be so described with propriety in a contract of insurance. The tackle, apparel, and furniture form a part of every ship, but that is not a part which is only appurtenant as necessary for a special voyage.[5]

Compare APPENDANT; INCIDENT.

AQUA. L. Water.

Aqua cedit solo. Water passes with land: a grant of land conveys water rights.

One cannot bring an action to recover possession of a piece of water by the name of water only, by calculating its capacity, by superficial measurement, or l a general description, as for a pond, a water-cours etc. His action must be for so much land cover with water.[1]

Aqua currit, et debet currere, ut cu rere solebat. Water runs and should ru as it has been used to run: a running strea is to be let flow in its channel as nature h provided.

Running water must be used according 1 the order of nature. Thus, rain-water an drainage are to follow nature's channel — th course in which the water, peaceably an openly, has long been permitted to rnn.[2]

By the common law all riparian owners on th same stream have an equality of right to the use the water as it naturally flows, in quality and witho diminution in quantity except as created by a reaso able use for proper purposes. Hence, one may n throw back, nor divert, nor unreasonably detain, n deteriorate or poison the water. But exclusive use f twenty years may constitute a conclusive presumptic of right.[3]

A riparian owner on a stream must so use his rigl as not to injure the concomitant right of anothe owner, and subject to statutory regulations. Whe he owns land on one side his use extends to the midd thread of the stream. The right includes a right t erect mill dams and rights of fishery—both whic have their source in the ownership of the soil.[4]

A land owner has no better right to stop the flow a water-course which has its origin on his land than it arose elsewhere.[5]

No action can be maintained for changing th course or obstructing the flow of mere surface-wate by erections on adjoining land. A party cannot b his own act alone convert a flow of surface-water int a stream with the legal incidents of a natural wate course, but the right may be acquired by adverse use for the proper period.[6]

The courts will enjoin as a public and a private nu sance hydraulic mining which becomes injurious t navigation and destructive to the farms of riparia owners.[7]

A person operating a coal mine in the ordinary an usual manner may, upon his own land, drain or pum the water which percolates into the mine into a strear

---

Whiskey Cases (United States v. Ford), 99 U. S, 599 (1878); Oliver v. Commonwealth, 77 Va. 592 (1883).

[1] F. *apartenir*, to belong to: L. *ad-per-tinere*, to extend through to.

[2] United States v. Harris, 1 Sumn. 37-38 (1830), Story, J. See also Whitney v. Olney, 3 Mas. 281-83 (1823), Story, J.; 39 Ark. 135; 15 Cal. 186; 57 *id.* 14; 8 Allen, 291, 295; 28 Minn. 262; 53 N. H. 508; 15 Johns. 447; 93 N. Y. 549; 29 Ohio St. 648; 9 Oreg. 398; 10 S. & R. 53; 13 Pa. 495; 58 *id.* 253; 13 Am. Dec. 657-60, cases; 4 Kent. 467.

[3] [Harris v. Elliott, 10 Pet. *54 (1836), Thompson, J.

[4] Linthicum v. Ray, 9 Wall. 241 (1869), Field, J.

[5] Swift v. Brownell, 1 Holmes, 473-74 (1875), cases, Shepley, J.; The Witch Queen, 3 Saw. 202-3 (1874), cases; 2 Low. 40.

[1] 2 Bl. Com. 18.

[2] Kauffman v. Griesemer, 26 Pa. 412-16 (1856); Blanch ard v. Baker, 8 Me. *265 (1832); 2 Bl. Com. 395.

[3] Atchison v. Peterson, 20 Wall. 511 (1874), cases Tyler v. Wilkinson, 4 Mas. 400-2 (1827), cases, Story, J. Silver Spring Bleaching, &c. Co. v. Wanskuck Co., 1 R. I. 615 (1882); 3 Kent, 439.

[4] Holyoke Company v. Lyman, 15 Wall. 506 (1872 Clifford, J.

[5] Howe v. Norman, 13 R. I. 488 (1882).

[6] Dickinson v. Worcester, 7 Allen, 22 (1863), cases Stanchfield v. Newton, 142 Mass. 110 (1886).

[7] Woodruff v. North Bloomfield Gravel Mining Co 18 F. R. 753 (1884); 16 *id.* 25. See also 6 Col. 447, 530 92 N. Y. 480.

which forms the natural drainage of the basin, although the quantity of water may thereby be increased and its quality rendered unfit for domestic purposes by lower riparian owners. The use of the stream by such owners must *ex necessitate* give way to the interests of the community, in order to permit the development of the natural resources of the country and make possible the prosecution of the business of mining coal.[1]

On the mineral lands of the public domain in the Pacific States and Territories the doctrines of the common law are inapplicable, or applicable only in a very limited extent, to the necessities of miners, and inadequate to their protection; there, prior appropriation gives the better right to running waters to the extent in quantity and quality necessary for the uses to which the water is applied. What diminution of quantity or deterioration in quality will constitute an invasion of the rights of the first appropriator will depend upon the special circumstances of each case; and in controversies between him and parties subsequently claiming the water the question for determination is whether his use of the water to the extent of the original appropriation has been impaired by the acts of the other parties. Whether a court of equity will interfere to restrain acts of invasion upon the rights of the first appropriator will depend upon the character and extent of the injury alleged, whether it be irremedial in its nature, whether an action at law would afford adequate remedy, whether the parties are able to respond for the damages resulting from the injury, and other considerations ordinarily governing a court of equity in the exercise of its preventive process of injunction.[2]

The civil law acts upon the maxim that water is descendible by nature, that its usual flow should not be interfered with, and that its burden should be borne by the land through or over which it naturally flows, rather than by land through which it can be made to flow only by artificial means. The common law does not recognize this principle as to surface-water, but permits one to protect his premises against it, not regarding as injury any resulting inconvenience. The maxim of the civil law, *aqua currit*, etc., applies generally, in both systems, to running water, subject to such reasonable qualifications as the interests of agriculture require and the enjoyment of private property will permit. As an owner has the right to protect his lands from the violence of the current, or to improve the same by erecting embankments, and as this cannot be done without increasing the flow upon the opposite side, it follows that this must be permitted to some degree by all persons owning lands upon the stream, else the right cannot be exercised by any one of them.[3]

See ALLUVION; ICE; MILL, 1; RIPARIAN; SPRING; THREAD; WATER; WATER-COURSE.

Aquarium. See ENTERTAINMENT.

AQUATIC. See AQUA; RIPARIAN.

ARBITRARY.[1] Not governed by fixed rules; not defined by statute; discretionary: as, arbitrary punishment. See DISCRETION; JUDGE.

Without cause or reason shown; as, an arbitrary challenge.[2]

Arbitrarily. In a covenant not "arbitrarily" to withhold assent to an assignment of a lease means, without fair, solid, and substantial cause, and without reason given. A refusal grounded upon advice was held not arbitrary.[3] Compare SATISFACTORY.

ARBITRATION.[4] When the parties injuring and injured submit all matters in dispute, concerning any personal chattel or personal wrong, to the judgment of two or more arbitrators who are to decide the controversy.[5]

A like submission of *any* matter in dispute.

Although some jealousy is felt in allowing references of questions regarding realty, yet references have been had in cases of partition, disputed boundaries, waste by tenant, title of devisees, and generally upon titles. But crimes and misdemeanors are not subjects.[6]

Arbitrator. A private extraordinary judge chosen by the parties who have a matter in dispute, and invested with power to decide the same.[7]

Compulsory arbitration. When assent in one party is enforced by law, under a rule to refer. **Voluntary arbitration.** A reference freely consented to by both parties.

At common law, was *in pais* — by agreement out of court, with no compulsory power over witnesses. In pursuance of 9 and 10 Will. III (1698), c. 15, is *by rule of court* — by order of a court directing that a submission upon a matter not yet in court shall be made a rule of the court.

The statute enacts that all merchants and others who desire to end any controversy, suit, or quarrel (for which there is no remedy but by personal action or suit in equity) may agree that their submission of the suit to arbitration or umpirage shall be made a

---

[1] Pennsylvania Coal Co. *v.* Sanderson, 113 Pa. 126, 142–62 (1886), cases.

[2] Atchison *v.* Peterson, 20 Wall. 507, 511–16 (1874), cases, Field, J.; Bosey *v.* Gallagher, *ib.* 681–85 (1874), cases; Tartar *v.* Spring Creek Water & Mining Co., 5 Cal. 397 (1885); Sanford *v.* Felt, 71 *id.* 250 (1886), cases.

[3] Crawford *v.* Rambo, 44 Ohio St. 284, 282–87 (1886),

cases, Minshall. J. See also Barkley *v.* Wilcox, 86 N. Y. 143–48 (1881), cases.

[1] L. *arbitrarius*, capricious.

[2] 4 Bl. Com. 353.

[3] Treloar *v.* Bigge, L. R., 9 Ex. 154 (1874).

[4] L. *arbitrare*, to act as umpire: *arbiter*, a witness, a judge.

[5] 3 Bl. Com. 16.

[6] Brown's Law Dict.

[7] [Gordon *v.* United States, 7 Wall. 194 (1868), Grier, J.: Bouvier; 17 How. 394; 53 Barb. 595.

rule of the king's courts of record, and may insert such agreement in their submission or promise, or as the condition of the arbitration-bond; which agreement being proved upon oath by a witness thereto, the court shall make a rule that such submission and award shall be conclusive.[1]

A bond to abide the decision may be required. The arbitrators are the judges of both the law and the facts. They are not bound to disclose the grounds of their finding. They cannot modify or go beyond the precise question submitted; nor can they do general equity.[2]

Irregularities in appointing arbitrators, or in their proceedings, when apparent on the record, may be corrected by a writ of error; but those which are made so by extrinsic proof can be corrected only by the court below. Every presumption is made in favor of the award, unless flagrant error appears on the record. While the proceedings remain in court (that is, until the arbitrators are appointed), it must appear by the record that everything is regular, but after they are appointed the proceedings are out of court and need not be reduced to writing.[3]

The powers and duties of arbitrators are regulated by statute, and explanatory decisions, in each State.

Arbitrations are regarded favorably. If they settle the rights of the parties, and their award can be rendered certain by reference to documentary evidence, they will be sustained. An award which leaves nothing to be done to dispose of the matter except a ministerial act is sufficient.[4]

See further ABIDE; AWARD, 2; REFER, 1; UMPIRE.

Arbitration of exchange. See EXCHANGE, 3.

ARCHITECT. See LABORER.

Every person whose business it is to plan, design, or superintend the construction of buildings, ships, roads, bridges, canals, or railroads, shall be regarded as an architect and civil engineer: *Provided*, That this shall not include a practical carpenter who labors on a building.[5] See SPECIFICATION.

ARGUENDO. See ARGUMENTUM.

ARGUMENT. Proof or the means of proving, or inducing belief; a course or process of reasoning; an address to a jury, or a court. See ARGUMENTUM.

When a controverted question of fact is to be submitted to a jury for its determination either party has an absolute right to be heard in argument thereon. The power of the court is limited to imposing reasonable restrictions as to the time to be occupied.[6] See ATTORNEY.

---

[1] 3 Bl. Com. 17.

[2] 7 Morse, Arb. & Award, 181–83, cases.

[3] Wilcox v. Payne, 88 Pa. 157 (1878); Tobey v. County of Bristol, 3 Story, 800, 822 (1845); Corbin v. Adams, 76 Va. 61 (1881); Gaylord v. Norton. 130 Mass. 74 (1881).

[4] Cochran v. Bartle, 91 Mo. 646 (1887), cases.

[5] [Revenue Act, 13 July, 1866: 14 St. L. 121.

[6] Douglass v. Hill, 29 Kan. 529 (1883), cases; Foster v. Magill, 119 Ill. 82 (1886); 18 Cent. Law J. 363–68 (1884), cases.

Argument list. A calendar of cau for discussion and determination before court in banc, upon questions of law. £ BRIEF, 2.

Argumentative. By way of reasonir as, that a plea must not be argumentativ

Re-argument. A second or additior argument.

Sometimes ordered by a court of review when court wishes to hear counsel upon a material qu tion of law either not fully discussed in the first ar ment or passed by unnoticed and developed later the deliberations of the court.

ARGUMENTUM. L. Argument: l erally, that which makes clear or prov *Arguere*, to argue.

Arguendo. In reasoning, arguing. A breviated *arg*.

Applied to an observation made by a jud in rendering an opinion, incidental to t point under discussion and, therefore, r authoritative.

Argumentum a simile. Argume from a like case — from analogy.

Argumentum a simile valet in lege. j argument from an analogous case has weig in law. See SIMILIS.

Argumentum ab inconvenienti. A gument from a hardship, *q. v.*

ARISE. See JUDICIAL. Power.

ARIZONA. See TERRITORY, 2.

ARM OF THE LAW. See INJUNCTIC

ARM OF THE SEA. See SEA.

ARMA. L. Weapons; war, warfaı See ARMS, 2; LEX, Silent leges, etc.; V Vi, etc.

ARMED REBELLION. See WAR.

ARMS. Weapons, offensive or defensiv See ARMA.

1. Aggressive weapons; instruments of ; tack.

At common law one may carry arms for defen But going armed with dangerous or unusual weapo by terrifying the people, is a crime against the peac See DEFENSE, 1.

Playfully or wantonly pointing fire-arms at anoth which was an assault at common law, has been mε a statutory offense with increased punishment.

Discharging fire-arms within the limits of incor rated towns and cites is generally prohibited.

"A well regulated Militia, being necessary to ; security of a free State, the right of the people to kε and bear Arms, shall not be infringed."[3]

---

[1] 3 Bl. Com. 308.

[2] 1 Bl. Com. 143; 4 *id.* 149.

[3] Constitution, Amd. Art. II. Ratified Dec. 15, 17¦

This right is preserved, also, by the Bill of Rights of each State, and the exercise regulated by statute.

The right to bear arms is not a right granted by the Constitution; nor is it dependent upon that instrument for its existence. The Second Amendment declares that it shall not be infringed — by Congress.[1] See AMENDMENT, 2; POLICE, 2.

While it is true that that Amendment is a limitation upon the powers of Congress only, nevertheless, since all citizens capable of bearing arms constitute the reserved military force of the National government, a State cannot prohibit the people from keeping and carrying arms so as to deprive the United States of their rightful resource for maintaining the public safety.[2]

The right to bear arms for the common defense does not mean the right to bear them ordinarily or commonly, for individual defense, but refers to the right to bear them for the defense of the community against invasion or oppression. In order that he may be trained and efficient in their use, the citizen has the right to keep the arms of modern warfare and to use them in such manner as they may be capable of being used, without annoyance and hurt to others.[3]

By arms, in such connection, is meant such as are usually employed in civilized warfare and constitute the ordinary military equipment.[4] See TREASON; WAR; WEAPON.

2. Anything that may be used for defense or attack: as, staves, sticks, or other missiles, as well as fire-arms. Whence "force and arms." See FORCE, 2; VIOLENCE.

ARMY. See ENLISTMENT; MARTIAL LAW; NATURALIZAITON (R. S. § 2166); REINSTATE; STATION, 1; WAR.

ARPEN; ARPENT. A measure of land in use in this country, in the early French and Spanish times, nearly corresponding to the English acre.[5]

ARRAIGN.[6] To call upon to account or answer.[7]

To call a prisoner to the bar of the court to answer the matter charged upon him in the indictment.[8]

Arraignment. The act or proceeding of arraigning.

At common law the arraignment of a prisoner consists in calling him to the bar; in his holding up his hand — for identification; in reading the indictment to him — that he may understand the charge; in demanding, whether he is guilty or not guilty; and in inquiring how he will be tried — the common answer being "By God and my country."[1]

Constitutes no part of the trial, but is a preliminary proceeding. Until the party has pleaded, it cannot be known whether there will be any trial or not.[2]

In a State in which the constitution provides that the trial of crimes shall be by jury and the prisoner pleads "not guilty," it is mere mockery to ask him how he will be tried, for the constitution has already declared how that shall be. As soon as it judicially appears of record that the party has pleaded not guilty there is an issue which the court is bound to direct to be tried by a jury.[3]

Though a formal arraignment may be proper it is not essential to the power of the court to convict, when expressly waived by the accused; especially so since there are no longer the same reasons for the formalities of an arraignment that there were in ancient practice when proceedings were in Latin, and the accused could not appear with counsel, and, after a plea of not guilty, he was required to elect between trial by jury and ordeal or wager of battel.[4] See BATTEL.

The ancient formality is disused. The statutory requirement of furnishing the prisoner with a copy of the indictment takes the place of reading the indictment to him. The record should show that what took place amounted to an arraignment — as, the mention of the prisoner's presence in court, and that he was called upon to plead to the indictment.[5]

ARRAY.[6] Order; arrangement.

The whole body of jurors as arranged upon the panel. Whence challenge to the array.[7] See CHALLENGE, 4.

ARREAR.[8] Back, remaining back: unpaid, though due.

Arrears. Money unpaid after it is due: as, of interest, dividends, rent, taxes, wages, pensions, alimony, dower.

"In arrear" — overdue and unpaid.[9]

---

[1] United States v. Cruikshank, 92 U. S. 553 (1875), Waite, C. J.

[2] Presser v. Illinois, 116 U. S. 265 (1886), Woods, J.

[3] Andrews v. State, 3 Heisk. 177–89 (Ky., 1871), Freeman, J.

[4] Andrews v. State, 3 Heisk. 184, supra; 2 Humph. 158–59. See also State v. Reid, 1 Ala. 614–22 (1840), Collier, C. J.; Wright v. Commonwealth, 77 Pa. 470 (1875); 8 Phila. 610; 2 Litt., Ky., 90; 1 Kelly, Ga., 247–51; 2 Story, Const. §§ 1889–90; 8 Am. Rep. 22; 14 id. 380.

[5] See 12 How. 435; 6 Pet. 769: 4 Hall, L. J. 518.

[6] L. ad rationem ponere, to call to account, — 2 Hale, P. C. 216. F. aranier, to speak to, cite: raison, reason.

[7] State v. Weber, 22 Mo. 325 (1855).

[8] 4 Bl. Com. 322.

[1] 4 Bl. Com. 322–24. See 1 Steph. Hist. C. L. Eng. 297.

[2] United States v. Curtis, 4 Mas. 236 (1820), Story, J.

[3] United States v. Gilbert, 2 Sumn. 69 (1834), Story, J.; State v. Weber, 22 Mo. 325–27 (1855).

[4] Goodwin v. State, 16 Ohio St. 346 (1865), Day, J.

[5] Fitzpatrick v. People, 98 Ill. 260 (1881), Shelden, J. See also Lynch v. Commonwealth, 88 Pa. 193 (1878); Ray v. People, 6 Col. 231 (1882).

[6] F. arrai, preparation, order.

[7] 3 Bl. Com. 359; 4 id. 352.

[8] Old Eng. arere, rere, in the rear: F. riere; L. retro, backward.

[9] Hollingsworth v. Willis, 64 Miss. 157 (1886).

Said of money unpaid at the time it is due, that is, past due.[1]

"Arrear" implies that no part has been paid; "arrears" and "arrearage," that some part has been paid.[2] See RIEN.

ARREST.[3] 1, *v.* To delay, detain, stay, stop, withhold.

Arrest of judgment. If, while an issue of fact is regularly decided, it appears that the complaint was either not actionable or was not made with sufficient precision, the defeated party may supersede it by arresting or staying the judgment.[4]

Arrests of judgment arise from intrinsic causes appearing upon the face of the record. As, where the declaration varies totally from the original writ; where the verdict materially varies from the pleadings and issue thereon; or, when the case laid in the declaration is not sufficient in law upon which to found an action.[5]

An invariable rule is that whatever matter of law is alleged in arrest of judgment must be such matter as, upon demurrer, would have been sufficient to overthrow the action or plea.[5]

A defendant in a criminal prosecution, at any time before sentence, may offer exceptions to the indictment in arrest or stay of judgment; as, for want of sufficient certainty in setting forth either the person, the time, the place, or the offense.[6]

The motion should be predicated upon some defect which appears upon the face of the record.[7]

2, *n.* Taking a thing or a person into the custody of the law.

(1) In admiralty practice the technical term for an actual seizure of property.[8]

After an order of discharge from arrest the marshal is to restore the party to formal possession.[9] See AT-TACH, 2; RES, 2; SEIZURE.

(2) In civil practice apprehension of a person by virtue of lawful authority to answer the demand against him in a civil action.[10]

Restraint of the person — restriction of the right of locomotion.[1]

The causes are mainly torts — as, frauds upon creditors, breaches of promise to marry, non payment of taxes, non-compliance with the order of a court, professional or official misconduct.

May be made upon original, mesne, or final process.

(3) In criminal practice apprehending or detaining one's person in order to be forthcoming to answer an alleged or suspected crime.[2]

"Apprehension" (*q. v.*) is sometimes used distinctively for this species of arrest.

Taking, seizing, or detaining the person of another, touching or putting hands upon him in the execution of process, or any act indicating an intention to arrest, constitutes an arrest.[3] Usually effected by means of a —

Warrant of arrest. A written judicial order for the arrest of a person accused or suspected of having committed a crime.

This must be in writing, under the hand and seal of the magistrate, and state the cause of commitment, that it may be examined into, if necessary, upon a writ of *habeas corpus*.[4]

All processes for the arrest of a party are not included in the word "warrant" as used in the constitutional provision that no warrant shall issue for the arrest of a person but upon probable cause supported by oath or affirmation. A *capias*, or writ of arrest in a civil action, is not a warrant in the sense intended, and it is issued, at common law, as a matter of course, without oath. The warrant meant is an authority for the arrest of a person upon a criminal charge with a view to his commitment and trial. The arrest of a person upon a charge of insanity, for the purpose of his confinement, partakes more of the nature of a criminal than of a civil proceeding.[5]

Double arrest. Twice holding a defendant to bail for the same cause of action.

Not allowed except under very special circumstances. There cannot be an arrest in two places for the same cause of action.[6]

False arrest. Any restraint upon the liberty of a person without lawful cause; false imprisonment.

Malicious arrest. An arrest made without probable cause.

The malice necessary to sustain an action is not express malice or the specific desire to vex or injure

---

[1] Wiggin *v.* Knights of Pythias, 31 F. R. 125 (1887), Hammond, J.

[2] Webster's Dict.

[3] F. *arester*, to stay: L. *re-stare*, to stand back, to remain.

[4] [3 Bl. Com. 387.

[5] 3 Bl. Com. 393-94.

[6] 4 Bl. Com. 375. See also Delaware Canal Co. *v.* Commonwealth, 60 Pa. 371 (1869).

[7] Rountree *v.* Lathrop, 69 Ga. 539 (1882); People *v.* Kelly, 94 N. Y. 526 (1884).

[8] Pelham *v.* Rose, 9 Wall. 107 (1869), Field, J.; The Ottawanna, 20 *id.* 221-22 (1873).

[9] The Marys, 10 Bened. 561-62 (1879).

[10] [Gentry *v.* Griffith, 27 Tex. 462 (1864), Moore, J.

[1] [Hart *v.* Flynn, 8 Dana, 192 (Ky., 1839), Ewing, J.

[2] [4 Bl. Com. 289; Montgomery County *v.* Robinson, 85 Ill. 176 (1877).

[3] United States *v.* Benner, Bald. 239 (1830), Baldwin, J.; 1 Bl. Com. 137; 4 *id.* 290-91; 71 N. Y. 376; 92 *id.* 420; 4 Cr. L. M. 193-99.

[5] Sprigg *v.* Stump, 7 Saw. 289 (1881), Deady, J.

[6] See Hernandez *v.* Canobeli, 4 Duer, 642 (1855); 14 Johns. *347; 4 Yeates, 206.

another, but the willful doing of an unlawful act to the prejudice or injury of another.[1]

All persons within the jurisdiction of the court are liable to arrest on *civil process*, except — an ambassador and his servant; an attorney, suitor, or subpœnaed witness as such attending a lawful tribunal; a clergyman at divine service; an elector at a public election; a married woman on her contract; a lawmaker in attendance upon the legislative body; a soldier on military duty; sovereigns, governors of the States; and other persons, as provided in local statutes.

In the case of persons attending a tribunal or a legislature the privilege protects them not only during attendance, but also during the reasonable period required for going and returning,— *eundo, morando, et redeundo*, going, remaining, and returning.[2]

All persons in the public service are exempt, as a matter of public policy, from arrest upon *civil* process while thus engaged. The rule is different when the process is issued upon a charge of felony.[3]

May not be made in the presence of a court; nor on Sunday; nor, generally, at night.

When made upon final process merely giving bail does not authorize a discharge.

An unauthorized arrest renders the officer liable to trespass. This occurs when the process is materially irregular or informal, or issued from a court which has no jurisdiction, or when the wrong person is taken under legal process.[4]

All persons are liable to arrest on *criminal process* — except ambassadors and their servants. It may be made: 1. Under a warrant issued by a justice of the peace when he has jurisdiction; in a case of suspicion he is the sole judge of the probability. 2. By an officer without a warrant — when the peace is broken in his presence; and whenever he has probable cause to suspect that a felony has been committed and that the person he arrests is guilty; also, by watchmen, who keep watch and ward in towns, of all offenders, particularly night-walkers. 3. By a private person without a warrant — when the peace is broken in his presence; and whenever a felony has actually been committed and he has probable cause to know that the person he arrests was the perpetrator. 4. By hue and cry,[5] *q. v.*

---

[1] Johnson *v.* Ebberts, 11 F. R. 129 (1880), cases.

[2] See Bridges *v.* Sheldon, 18 Blatch. 516 (1880), cases; Atchison *v.* Morris, 11 F. R. 582 (1882), cases; Larned *v.* Griffin, 12 *id.* 590 (1882), cases: s. c. 14 Rep. 258; Nichols *v.* Horton, 14 F. R. 327, 329 (1882), cases; Jones *v.* Knauss, 31 N. J. E. 211-16 (1879), cases; Greer *v.* Young, Sup. Ct. Ill. (1887), cases: 26 Am. Law Reg. 372 (1887); *ib.* 377-82, cases; 11 N. E. Rep. 167; Palmer *v.* Rowan, Sup. Ct. Neb. (1888): 22 Am. Law Rev. 278-80 (1888), cases; 1 Greenl. Ev. §§ 316-17; 1 Whart. Ev. §§ 389-90.

[3] United States *v.* Kirby, 7 Wall. 486 (1868).

[4] 3 Bl. Com. 288-89; 1 Bouv. 183, cases.

[5] 4 Bl. Com. 289-94; Mitchell *v.* Lemon, 34 Md. 181 (1870), cases: Fleetwood *v.* Commonwealth, 80 Ky. 5 (1882); Neal *v.* Joyner, 89 N. C. 283-90 (1883), cases; Staples *v.* State, 14 Tex. Ap. 139-41 (1883), cases; Morley *v.* Chase, 143 Mass. 398 (1887), cases; Cooley, Torts, 174-75, cases.

May be made at night, and, for an indictable offense, on Sunday. Must be made within the jurisdiction of the court or at least of the State. The officer may use necessary force; but he may not kill one charged with a misdemeanor, in the act of escaping, and, rarely, one charged with a felony.[1]

One who is not a peace officer, *de jure* or *de facto*, by assuming to exercise the duties of such officer does not acquire more authority to make an arrest than any other private individual. In resisting arrest by such a person one may use only force enough to protect himself from the assault,— unless it is necessary to save his own life, or his person from great harm, in which case he may take life.[2]

See further BAIL, 1 (2); CAPERE; DURESS; ESCAPE, 2; HOUSE, 1; IMPRISON; OBSTRUCT, 3; PROSECUTION, Malicious; RESIST; REWARD, 1; SANCTUARY; SUSPICION; WARRANT, 2.

ARRIVAL.[3] Under a law imposing a forfeiture there may be an arrival of a vessel at a port without an actual entry or an attempt to enter the port.[4]

Perhaps an arrival "within" a port cannot be without an entry into the port.[4]

In navigation and revenue laws is sometimes used in the common sense of coming into port, and sometimes in the sense of coming into a port of entry or destination for a particular object connected with the voyage.[5]

Sometimes refers to a coming into a port for any cause or purpose. This may be the literal and general meaning with the lexicographers, but, in several cases, the term denotes a coming in for certain special objects of business and remaining there long enough to render an entry of the vessel proper, and a deposit of her papers with a consul prudent and useful. Thus it is when the vessel enters a port or harbor to close an outward or inward voyage. It is usually a coming to the place of the vessel's destination for her business and waiting to transact it.[6]

A vessel arrives at a port of discharge when she comes or is brought to the place where it is intended to discharge her and where the customary place of discharge is.[7]

As to arrival at destination of goods bailed to a common carrier, see CARRIER.

---

[1] 4 Bl. Com. 293; United States *v.* Rice, 1 Hughes, 562-66 (1875), cases; Reneau *v.* State, 2 Lea, 720 (1879). On federal arrests of State prisoners, see 18 Cent. Law J. 163-65 (1884), cases.

[2] Creighton *v.* Commonwealth, 83 Ky. 142 (1885).

[3] F. *arriver:* L. L. *ad-ripare*, to land, come to shore.

[4] [United States *v.* Open Boat, 5 Mas. 132 (1828), Story, J.; United States *v.* Shackford, *ib.* 447 (1828).

[5] Parsons *v.* Hunter, 2 Sumn. 422-23 (1836), Story, J.

[6] Harrison *v.* Vose, 9 How. 379-81 (1850), statutes, Woodbury, J.

[7] Simpson *v.* Pacific Mut. Ins. Co., 1 Holmes, 137-42 (1872), cases, Shepley, J. See also Gronstadt *v.* Witthoff, 15 F. R. 269, 271 (1883).

ARS. L. Skill in fitting or joining: skill, trade, calling, art.

Cuique, or **cuilibet, in sua arte perito, credendum est.** To one practiced in his art, confidence should be given.

The opinion of a person versed in a calling is to be received as evidence. Every one, also, is presumed to possess the skill ordinarily requisite to the due discharge of the demands or duties of his vocation.[1] See further EXPERT.

ARSENAL. See LAND, Public.

ARSON.[2] The malicious and willful burning of the house or out-house of another.[3]

The malicious burning of another's house.[4]

Burning any building so situated as to endanger a dwelling-house was felonious arson at common law.[5]

In some States statutes divide the offense into degrees, punishing most severely burnings which involve the greater danger to life. Statutes also impose punishments for the malicious burning of structures not the subject of arson at common law, without extending that name to include them.

At common law an offense against the right of habitation. Actual destruction of some integral part of the wood-work, not personalty, is necessary. The burning is "willful and malicious" when not accidental nor for the public welfare. By "house" is meant a dwelling-house or any out-building within the curtilage, q. v. Brief absence from the house is not regarded. If homicide results the act is also murder.

The offense may be committed by willfully setting fire to one's own house and thereby burning a neighbor's house.[6]

Burning one's own house to defraud insurers has been made indictable.[7] See BELONG; BURN.

ART. 1. A principle put into practice by means of some art, machine, manufacture, or composition of matter. See ARS.

"The Congress shall have Power . . To promote the Progress of Science and Useful Arts, by securing . . Inventors the exclusive Right to their . . Discoveries."[8]

In speaking of patenting an "art" the reference is not to an art in the abstract, without a specification of the manner in which it is to operate as a manufacture or otherwise, but to the art thus explained in the specification, and illustrated, when of a character so to be, by a machine or model or by drawings. It is the art so represented or exemplified, like the principle

so embodied, which the patent laws protect. In the English patent acts the word "art" is not used at all. And in ours, as well as in the Constitution, the word refers to a "useful art," or to a manufacture which is beneficial, and which, by the same law, is required to be described with exactness as to its mode of operation.[1]

"Useful art" is the general term used in the patent laws. An art may require one or more processes or machines to produce a certain result or manufacture. The arts of tanning, dyeing, making water-proof cloth, vulcanizing India-rubber, smelting ores, and numerous others, are usually carried on by processes, as distinguished from machines.[2]

Without attempting to define the term "art" with logical accuracy we take as examples of it something which, in their concrete form, exhibit what all concede to come within a correct definition, such as the art of printing, that of telegraphy, or that of photography. The art of tanning leather might also come within the category because it requires various processes and manipulations.[3]

Centuries ago discoveries were made in certain arts the fruits of which have come down to us, but the means by which the work was accomplished are at this day unknown. It would hardly be doubted, if one discovered an art thus lost, and it was a useful improvement, that he would be entitled to a patent. He would not literally be the original inventor; but he would be the first to confer on the public the benefit of the invention.[4] See DESIGN, 2; PATENT, 2; PROCESS, 2.

2. A description of the art of book-keeping, though entitled to the benefit of copyright, lays no foundation for an exclusive claim to the art itself.

The object of the one is explanation; of the other use. The former may be secured by copyright; the latter, if at all, by letters-patent.[5]

A copyright may be secured for models or designs intended to be perfected as works of the *fine arts* — painting and sculpture.[6] See COPYRIGHT.

American works of fine arts are importable free of duty.[7] See FURNITURE.

3. Trade; business; calling.

Words of art are understood as in the art or science; other words, in their popular or received import.[8]

When parties who are engaged in a particular business use terms which have acquired a well-defined meaning in that business, the supposition is that they intended the terms to have their ordinary technical meaning.[9]

A vessel was chartered to carry a cargo of oranges,

---

[1] 1 Bl. Com. 75; 2 Kent, 583; 21 How. 101; 9 Mass. 227.

[2] F. *arson*, incendiarism: L. *ardere*, to burn.

[3] 4 Bl. Com. 220; 40 Ala. 664; 20 Conn. *246.

[4] 2 Bishop, Cr. L. § 8.

[5] Hill v. Commonwealth, 98 Pa. 195 (1881); State v. McGowan, 20 Conn. *246–47 (1850).

[6] 4 Bl. Com. 220–23.

[7] 1 Whart. Cr. L. § 843; 32 Cal. 160; 51 N. H. 176; 19 N. Y. 537.

[8] Constitution, Art. 1, sec. 8, cl. 8.

---

[1] [Smith v. Downing, 1 Fish. P. C. 70–71 (1850), Woodbury, J.; French v. Rogers, ib. 142 (1850).

[2] Corning v. Burden, 15 How. 267 (1853), Grier, J.

[3] Jacobs v. Baker, 7 Wall. 397 (1868), Grier, J.

[4] Gayler v. Wilder, 10 How. 497 (1850), Taney, C. J.

[5] Baker v. Selden, 101 U. S. 105 (1879), Bradley, J.

[6] R. S. § 4952.

[7] Act 22 March, 1883: 22 St. L. 521.

[8] Maillard v. Lawrence, 16 How. 261 (1853); Moran v. Prather, 23 Wall. 499 (1874); Greenleaf v. Goodrich, 101 U. S. 284 (1879).

[9] South Bend Iron Works v. Cottrell, 31 F. R. 256 (1887).

the captain engaging to "take the northern passage." The cargo becoming damaged, the charterer libeled the vessel for the loss. The court below found that "northern passage" appeared to be a term of art, unintelligible without the aid of testimony, that the evidence concerning it was conflicting, but that it was immaterial to decide what it meant as the claimant was entitled to the least strict definition and the actual course of the vessel came within that definition. *Held*, that if the term was a term of art it should have been found by the court; and that if there was no passage known as the "northern," the vessel was bound to take the one which would carry it in a northerly direction through the coolest waters, and the court should have ascertained from the proof what passages vessels were accustomed to take and which passage the contract permitted.[1]

See ABBREVIATIONS; EXPERT; SCIENCE; TECHNICAL; TERM, 1.

ARTICLE.[2] 1. "A distinct portion or part, a joint or a part of a member, one of various things."

A word of separation to individualize and distinguish some particular thing from the general thing or whole of which it forms a part: as, an article in a newspaper, an article of merchandise.[3]

The radical word in the Greek means to join or to fit to as a part. It is only recently that it has been applied to goods or physical property, and then only in the sense of something that is separate and individual in itself, as salt is a necessary article, or a hammer is a useful article.[3]

When a carrier stipulates that he will not be liable in the carriage of baggage for an amount exceeding fifty dollars "upon any article," the reference is to any article coming under the denomination of baggage. The limitation would apply to the articles in a trunk, but not to the trunk as one article. "The article forwarded," in a similar special contract, may cover each of several articles so strapped together as to form one package.[3]

2. In the sense of a distinct portion, one of separate yet co-related parts, a clause in a contract, compact, or other formal document, is used in the expressions:

An article or articles — of agreement, of amendment, of association, of confederation, of impeachment, of partnership, of peace, of war, of separation, of shipping, *qq. v.*

In popular parlance "to article"[4] means to make and become bound by an article of agreement, *q. v.*

[1] The John H. Pearson, 121 U. S. 469, 472 (1887), Waite, C. J. Appeal from the Cir. Ct. for Mass.

[2] F. *article:* L. *articulus*, a small joint, a joint: Gk. *arein'*, to fit to as part.

[3] Wetzell *v.* Dinsmore, 4 Daly, 195 (1871), Daly, C. J. See also 6 Blatch. 68; 8 *id.* 257.

[4] See 1 Story, Eq. § 790.

Articled clerk. In England a person bound by indenture to a solicitor, that he may acquire the knowledge pertaining to the business of a solicitor.

Articulately. By separate or distinct propositions: as, to articulately propound in a libel in admiralty. See LIBEL, 2.

3. Precise point of time; the exact moment: as, to be in the article of death — *in articulo mortis.*

ARTIFICE. See COMMUNICATION, Privileged, 1; DECEIT; FRAUD.

ARTIFICIAL. 1. Pertaining to an art, trade, or profession; technical. See ART, 2, 3.

Artificially. A will is said to be "artificially" or "inartificially" drawn, according as it employs or does not employ technical or legal words and phrases and a lawyer-like arrangement of the matter. See CONSTRUCTION.

2. Made or devised by human law; opposed to *natural* — formed by the laws of God: as, an artificial body or person, *q. v.;* an artificial day, *q. v.*

3. Established by agreement between men; conventional; opposed to *natural* — made by nature: as, an artificial boundary, *q. v.*

ARTS. See ART.

AS. Compare SUCH.

While the omission of this word is not conclusive when the body of a complaint discloses a representative capacity in the defendant as the ground of action, where the scope and averments of the complaint harmonize with the omission the action may be considered against the defendant as an individual.[1]

As near as may be. See PROCEDURE.

As soon as. See IMMEDIATELY; POSSIBLE; SOON; WHENEVER.

As to. Compare QUOAD.

Recurring at the commencement of several devises does not necessarily indicate the commencement of a complete devise, independent of other limitations.[2]

ASCERTAIN. 1. To render definite or fixed: as, to ascertain the relief due.[3]

"The use in pleading of an averment is to ascertain that to the court which is generally or doubtfully expressed."[4]

[1] Bennett *v.* Whitney, 94 N. Y. 305 (1884). See also Cook *v.* Gray, 133 Mass. 110 (1882); 3 Cranch, C. C. 459.

[2] Gordon *v.* Gordon, 5 L. R., H. L. 254 (1871).

[3] See 2 Bl. Com. 65, 465. Swift wrote "A Proposal for correcting and ascertaining the English Tongue," and South (Sermons, V, 286) says that "success is intended for the wicked man, to ascertain his destruction."

[4] Van Vechten *v.* Hopkins, 5 Johns. 219 (1809).

To make sure or certain; to establish, determine, settle.[1]

This would seem to demand the observance of the usual mode of investigation, to determine the matter in question. Hence, where rent is to be "ascertained" by persons selected by the parties, notice of the time and place of hearing, with an opportunity for offering proofs, should first be given to the parties interested.[2]

2. To acquire information as to a fact; to become possessed of knowledge respecting an event or transaction; to learn the truth as to a matter capable of proof. See INQUIRY, 1; KNOWLEDGE, 1.

ASIDE. See SET ASIDE; STAND ASIDE.

ASPECT. A bill in equity may be framed with a "double aspect," embracing alternative averments, provided that each aspect entitles the complainant to substantially the same relief, and that the same defenses are applicable to each.[3] See RELIEF, 2.

ASPORTARE. L. To carry away.

Cepit et asportavit. He took and carried away. Words formerly used to charge an unlawful removal of personalty.

De bonis asportatis. For goods carried off. The name of an action of trespass for personalty unlawfully removed, withheld or converted. See ASPORTATION.

ASPORTATION. Carrying away or removing a thing — a chattel.

In larceny there must not only be a taking, but a carrying away. *Cepit et asportavit* was the old law-Latin expression. A bare removal from the place in which the goods are found is a sufficient asportation.[4] See ASPORTARE.

ASS. See CATTLE; HORSE.

ASSAULT.[5] An attempt or offer to beat another, without touching him.[6]

If one lifts up his cane or his fist, in a threatening manner at another, or strikes at but misses him — this is an assault, *insultus*, which Finch describes to be "an unlawful setting upon one's person."[6]

It is also inchoate violence, which is considerably higher than bare threats; and, therefore, though no actual suffering is proved, the party injured may have redress by action of trespass *vi et armis*, wherein he recovers damages as compensation for the injury.[6]

An offer or attempt by force to do corporal injury to another.[1]

As if one person strike at another with his hand or a stick, and miss him. If the other be stricken, it is a battery. Or if he shake his fist at another, or present a gun, or other weapon, within such a distance that a hurt might be given; or draw a sword and brandish it in a menacing manner. An intent to do some corporal injury must be coupled with the act.[1]

Any attempt or offer with force or violence to do a corporal hurt to another, whether from malice or wantonness, with such circumstances as denote at the time an intention to do it, coupled with a present ability to carry the intention into effect.[2]

An unlawful attempt, coupled with a present ability, to commit a violent injury upon the person of another.[3]

Assailant and *the assailed* designate, respectively, the person injuring and the person injured.

Abusive words cannot constitute the offense; nor can an act in defense of one's self, wife, child, servant, or property; nor an act in obedience to legal process. Unlawful imprisonment, undue liberty taken by an employer, teacher, physician, dentist, car conductor, or other person in a like position, is, or includes, an assault.

An assault with intent to commit a felony is a higher offense than simple assault.[4]

Remedies: indictment for breach of the peace; action for damages.

Son assault demesne. F. His own assault; his assault in the first instance.

"If one strikes me first, I may strike in my own defense; and, if sued for it, may plead *son assault demesne:* that it was the plaintiff's own original assault that occasioned it."[5] Compare MANUS, Molliter.

See further BATTERY; DEFENSE, 1; INDECENT; PROVOCATION.

ASSAYER. See COIN.

Any person or persons or corporation whose business or occupation it is to separate gold and silver from other metals or mineral substances with which such gold or silver, or both, are alloyed, combined, or united, or to ascertain or determine the quantity of gold or silver in an alloy or combination with other metals, shall be deemed an assayer.[6]

ASSEMBLY. An intentional meeting, gathering, or concourse of people: of three or

---

[1] Worcester's Dict.

[2] Brown *v.* Luddy, 11 Hun, 456 (1877).

[3] Adams *v.* Sayre, 70 Ala. 325 (1881); Fields *v.* Helmes, *ib.* 460 (1881); 17 How. 130.

[4] 4 Bl. Com. 232; Croom *v.* State, 71 Ala. 14 (1881).

[5] L. *ad-saltus*, a leap at: *salire*, to leap, spring.

[6] 3 Bl. Com. 120; 9 Ala. 82; 39 Miss. 524; 30 Hun, 427.

[1] United States *v.* Hand, 2 Wash. 437 (1810), Washington, J.; United States *v.* Ortega, 4 *id.* 534 (1825); Drew *v.* Comstock, 57 Mich. 181 (1885).

[2] Traver *v.* State, 43 Ala. 356 (1869), Peck, C. J.; Hays *v.* People, 1 Hill, 352–53 (N. Y.), 1841).

[3] Cal. Penal Code, § 240; People *v.* Gordon, 70 Cal. 468 (1886).

[4] People *v.* Devine, 59 Cal. 630 (1881).

[5] 3 Bl. Com. 120–21; 4 Blackf. 546; 4 Denio, 448.

[6] Revenue Act, 13 July, 1866, § 9: 14 St. L. 121.

more persons in one body; — of any number of persons in one place.

Assemblage. May be composed of things as well as persons.[1] — respects things only.[2]

Lawful assembly. Any congregating of people or citizens directed or permitted by the law of the place.

Civil assembly. A meeting of persons for purposes of trade, amusement, worship, or the like.

Political assembly. Any meeting of persons required by the constitution and laws of the place: as, that of law-makers — whence "Assembly" and "General Assembly" — also, that of the Federal electors, and that of voters at "primary assemblies."

Assemblyman. A member of the legislature of a State — possibly, by restriction, of the lower house. See LEGISLATURE.

Popular assembly. Any meeting of the people to deliberate over their rights and duties with respect to government; also, the House of Representatives in Congress, and the more numerous body in the legislature of a State.

"Congress shall make no law" prohibiting or abridging "the right of the people peaceably to assemble, and to petition the Government for a redress of grievances."[3]

The right of the people peaceably to assemble for lawful purposes existed long before the adoption of the Constitution. It is and always has been one of the attributes of citizenship under a free government. It was not therefore a right granted to the people by the Constitution. The government of the United States, when established, found it in existence with an obligation on the part of the States to afford it protection. The First Amendment operates upon the National government alone.[4] See PETITION, Right of.

In every meeting assembled for a lawful purpose there must necessarily exist an inherent power to preserve order and to remove by force any person who creates a disturbance. If it were not so, the guaranty of the constitution would be idle mockery. Religious meetings, for example, would lose their solemnity and usefulness if they could be turned into halls of disputation at the will of any individual.[5] See WORSHIP.

Unlawful assembly. When three or more do assemble themselves together to do an unlawful act, . . and part without

doing it or making any motion toward it.[1] See MOB; RIOT; ROUT.

ASSENT.[2] Agreement; approval; compliance; consent; willingness declared. Opposed, *dissent.*

Implies more than mere acceptance, — is an act of the understanding; while "consent" is an act of the feelings and will.[3] "Assent" respects matters of judgment; "consent" matters of conduct.[4]

Acceptance, approval, consent, ratification, and assent, are often interchanged.[5]

Express assent. Assent openly declared, in words spoken or written. **Implied assent.** Assent inferred from conduct.

Mutual assent. Assent given by all the parties to an act or contract; the meeting of the minds of the parties to any transaction.

Unless dissent is shown acceptance of a thing done for a person's benefit will be presumed; as in the case of a conveyance or a devise of land.

Assent must be *ad idem* — to the same thing, and in the same sense.[6]

"Mutual assent," which is the meeting of the minds of both of the parties to a contract, is vital to the existence of the contract. The obligation must be correlative: if there is none on one side there can be none on the other. Moreover, this requisite assent must be the work of the parties themselves: the law cannot supply it.[7]

Mutual assent of the parties to a modification is as indispensable as to the original making of a contract. Where there is a misunderstanding as to anything material the requisite mutuality of assent is wanting, the supposed contract does not exist, and neither party is bound. In the view of the law in such case there has been merely a negotiation resulting in a failure to agree. What has occurred is as if it were not.[8]

See KNOWLEDGE, 1; INQUIRY, 1; PEAMIT; PROTEST, 2; RATIFICATION; SATISFY, 1; SILENCE; UNDERSTANDING.

ASSERTORY OATH. See OATH, Official.

ASSESS.[9] 1. To rate or fix the proportion which each person is to pay of a tax; to

[1] Webster's Dict.

[2] Crabbe's Syn.

[3] Constitution, Amd. I. Ratified Dec. 15, 1791.

[4] United States v. Cruikshank, 92 U. S. 551-52 (1875), Waite, C. J.

[5] Wall v. Lee, 36 N. Y. 142-46 (1865), cases. See also 21 Wend. 149; 1 Gray, 182; 68 Pa. 474; 20 Alb. L. J. 124 (1879), cases.

[1] 4 Bl. Com. 146: 3 Coke, Inst. 176.

[2] L. *assentire*, to agree to.

[3] Webster's Dict.

[4] Crabbe's Syn.

[5] See Welch v. Sackett, 12 Wis. *257 (1860), Dixon, C. J.

[6] See 4 Wheat. 225; 1 Sumn. 218; 12 Mass. 461; 11 N. Y. 441; 1 Pars. Contr. 400; 2 Washb. R. P. 579.

[7] Mutual Life Ins. Co. v. Young, 23 Wall. 107 (1874), Swayne, J.

[8] Utley v. Donaldson, 94 U. S. 47-49 (1876), cases, Swayne, J.; First Nat. Bank of Quincy v. Hall, 101 *id.* 49-50 (1879); 109 *id.* 97.

[9] From L. *assessor*, an adjuster of taxes; originally a judge's assistant, one who sat by him: *assidere*, to sit near to. Compare ASSIZE.

tax. To adjust the shares of a contribution by several persons toward a common object according to the benefit received. To fix the value or the amount of a thing.[1]

To determine by rules of law a sum to be paid; to rate the proportional contribution due to a fund; to fix the amount payable by a person or persons in satisfaction of an established demand.[2]

Assessor. (1) An adviser to a court; an expert.

Nautical assessor. A person, possessing special knowledge in matters of navigation and of maritime affairs, who assists a court of admiralty.[3] Compare ALDERMAN.

(2) One who makes assessments for purposes of taxation or contribution.

A person charged by law with the duty of ascertaining and determining the value of property as the foundation of a public tax.[4]

Assessment. The act or proceeding by which a sum due or payable is determined; also, the sum itself as a payment or obligation.

As, an assessment — of the damages suffered by a plaintiff; of the value of property taken for public use; of money as the equivalent of a benefit or burden caused by a municipal improvement; of losses in insurance; of installments payable upon stock subscriptions; of a sum to be raised by taxation, and of the portions due from individuals.

Strictly speaking, an assessment of taxes is an official estimate of the sums which are to constitute the basis of an apportionment of a tax between the individual subjects of taxation within a district. As more commonly employed, consists in listing the persons, property, etc., to be taxed, and in estimating the sums which are to be the guide in an apportionment of the tax between them; — valuation is a part of it.[5]

In a broad sense taxes undoubtedly include assessments, and the right to impose assessments has its foundation in the taxing power of the government; but there is also a broad distinction between them. "Taxes" are public burdens imposed generally upon the inhabitants of the whole State, or upon some civil

division thereof, for governmental purposes without reference to peculiar benefits to particular individuals or property. "Assessments" have reference to impositions for improvements which are specially beneficial to individuals or property and which are imposed in proportion to the particular benefits supposed to be conferred. They are justified when the improvements confer special benefits and are equitable only when divided in proportion to such benefits.[1] See INSTALLMENT; JUST, 2; TAX, 2; VALUE.

Used of a business corporation, a rating or fixing, by the board of directors, of the proportion of his subscription which every subscriber is to pay, when notified of it and called upon.[2] See CALL, 2 (1).

Political assessment. See OFFICER.

2. To decide the degree of; to determine the extent of: as, to assess a punishment.

A statute providing that issues of fact in criminal cases shall be tried by a jury, "who shall assess the punishment in their verdict," refers to offenses as to which the limits of punishment are fixed by law and within which a discretion may be exercised.[3]

ASSETS.[4] Property sufficient to answer a demand — made by a creditor or a legatee upon an executor or administrator, or by a creditor upon an insolvent or a bankrupt.

Also, all the property of the estate of a decedent or of an insolvent.

"All the assets" of an insolvent company, of which a receiver takes possession in New York, means all the property, real and personal, of the company.[5]

The property of a deceased person appropriable to the payment of his debts; also, the entire property of a mercantile firm or trading corporation.[6]

Whatever is recovered that is of a salable nature and may be converted into ready money is called "assets" in the hands of the executor or administrator; that is "sufficient" or "enough" (French *assez*) to make him chargeable to a creditor or legatee, as far as such goods and chattels extend.[7]

Originally, that which is sufficient or

---

[1] [Bouvier's Law Dict.

[2] [Abbott's Law Dict.

[3] See The Clement, 2 Curt. 369 (1855); The Empire, 19 F. R. 559 (1884), cases.

[4] Savings, &c. Society v. Austin, 46 Cal. 509 (1873), Wallace, C. J.

[5] [People v. Weaver, 100 U. S. 545–46 (1879), Miller, J.: Cooley, Tax. 258; Bur. Tax. 198, § 94.

[1] Roosevelt Hospital v. Mayor of New York, 84 N. Y. 112–13 (1881), cases, Earle, J.; Palmer v. Stumph, 29 Ind. 333–36 (1868), cases; Chamberlain v. Cleveland, 34 Ohio St. 561–65 (1878), cases; Stephani v. Bishop of Chicago, 2 Bradw. 252–53 (1878); 1 Handy, 473; 3 Col. 462; 6 id. 113; 1 Wash. T. 576; Cooley, Tax. 147.

[2] [Spangler v. Indiana, &c. R. Co., 21 Ill. 278 (1859), Breese, J.

[3] Territory v. Romine, 2 N. M. 128 (1881); ib. 457.

[4] F. assez, sufficient: L. ad, to, for; satis, enough.

[5] Attorney-General v. Atlantic Mut. Life Ins. Co., 100 N. Y. 282 (1885).

[6] Vaiden v. Hawkins, 59 Miss. 419 (1882), Chalmers, C. J.

[7] 2 Bl. Com. 510, 244.

enough in the hands of the executor or administrator to make him chargeable to the creditors, legatees, and distributees of the deceased, so far as the personal property of the deceased, which comes to the hands of the executor or administrator, extends for purposes of administration. In an accurate legal sense, all the personal property of the deceased which is of a salable nature and may be converted into money is deemed assets. But the word is not confined to such property; for all other property of the deceased which is chargeable with, and applicable to, his debts or legacies is, in a large sense, assets.[1]

Though generally used to denote things which come to the representatives of a deceased person, the word includes anything, whether belonging to the estate of a deceased person or not, which can be made available for the payment of debts. Hence we speak of the assets of a money corporation, of an insolvent debtor, of an individual, of a private partnership. The word is likewise used for the "means" which a party has as compared with his liabilities.[2]

In the bankrupt law "assets" included all property chargeable with the debts of the bankrupt that came into the hands or under the control of the assignee.[3]

Legal assets. That portion of the assets of a deceased party which by law is directly liable in the hands of his executor or administrator to the payment of debts and legacies. Generally speaking they are such as can be reached by a suit at law against the executor or administrator, either by a common judgment or by a judgment upon a *devastavit*. More accurately speaking they are such as come into the hands and power of an executor or administrator, or such as, *virtute officii*, he is intrusted with by law to dispose of in the course of administration,— whatever he takes as executor or administrator, or in respect to his office. **Equitable assets.** All assets, chargeable with the payment of debts or legacies in equity, and which do not fall under the description of legal assets.[4]

Termed "equitable" because (1) to obtain payment out of them they can be reached only through the instrumentality of a court of equity, and (2) the rules of distribution by which they are governed differ from the rules for the distribution of legal assets. In general they are either created such by the intent of the party or result from the nature of the estate made chargeable.[4]

The property of a decedent available at common law for satisfying creditors is called "legal assets," and will be applied, at common law and in equity, in the ordinary course of administration, which gives debts of a certain nature priority over others. Where, however, the assets are available only in a court of equity they are termed "equitable assets," and, according to the maxim, that equality is equity, will, after satisfying those who have liens upon any specific property, be distributed among the creditors of all grades *pari passu*, without regard to legal priority.[1]

"Equitable assets" are such as the debtor has made subject to his debts generally, which would not be thus subjected without his act, and which can be reached only by a court of equity. They are divisible among the creditors in ratable proportions.[2]

Personal assets. Assets to which the executor or administrator is entitled; personalty. **Real assets.** Such assets as go to the heir by descent; assets by descent;[3] also, landed property.

"Personal assets" are chattels, money, and evidences of debt available for paying the debts of a bankrupt, insolvent, or decedent.

"Real assets" are such portion of the property of any such individual as consists of realty.

Assets are also *immediate* and *future*.[4]

At common law (originally for feudal reasons) lands in the hands of the debtor himself were not assets for the payment of debts; creditors could reach only the personalty and the profits of realty. Upon the death of the debtor, in case of intestacy, the land descended to the heir and the personalty to the executor. A creditor by a simple contract debt for satisfaction could look only to the personalty in the hands of the executor; while a creditor by a specialty in which the heir was named could reach the land itself in such heir's possession — his *assets by descent*. By will, however, the debtor might charge land with the prior payment of a debt.[5]

For the purpose of founding administration all simple contract debts are assets at the domicil of the debtor. A note given is merely evidence of the debt.[6]

See ACCIDERE, Quando; ACCOUNT, 1; ADMINISTER, 4; BANKRUPTCY; BONA; CONFORMITY; CREDITOR'S BILL; INSOLVENCY; LEGACY; MARSHAL, 2.

ASSIGN.[7] To point out, specify, signify which of several things; to select, appoint, fix. Whence assignable, assignment.

As, to assign — the particular in which a

---

[1] [1 Story, Eq. § 531.

[2] [Stanton v. Lewis, 26 Conn. 449 (1857); Hall v. Martin, 46 N. H. 342 (1865).

[3] Re Taggert, 16 Bankr. Reg. 353 (1877).

[4] [1 Story, Eq. §§ 551–52.

(6)

---

[1] [Silk v. Prime, 2 L. Cas. Eq., 4 Am. ed., 358, 353, cases.

[2] Catlin v. Eagle Bank, 6 Conn. 243 (1826), Hosmer, C. J. See also Freedman's Sav. & Trust Co. v. Earle, 110 U. S. 712–20 (1884); 2 Johns. Ch. 577.

[3] [2 Bl. Com. 244, 340, 510.]

[4] 4 Kent, 354.

[5] Hall v. Martin, 46 N. H. 341 (1865).

[6] Wayman v. Halstead, 109 U. S. 656 (1884), cases.

[7] F. *assigner*; L. *assignare*, to mark out to,

contract has been broken, that is, "the breach;" the matter in which alleged error was committed by an auditor, master, referee, court; dower, or the third of the deceased husband's realty; counsel for a prisoner on trial; a day for a hearing, trial, argument.

Assignment of errors. A pleading filed in an appellate court by a party who complains of errors committed by the court below.[1] See ERROR, 2 (3).

New or novel assignment. When a plaintiff in his replication, after an evasive plea, reduces a general wrong, as laid in his declaration, to a more particular certainty by assigning the injury afresh, with all its specific circumstances, in such manner as clearly to ascertain and identify it consistently with his general complaint.[2]

Not an admission of the facts alleged in the plea; merely an assertion that the plaintiff will not investigate the subject-matter.[3]

2. To set over something to another person; to transfer, convey.

Generally implies a writing. It is of all the right one has in any particular piece or pieces of property.[4] Compare LEASE.

The meanings vary with the subject-matter, but the general one is to set over or to transfer. As applied to movables, satisfied by a delivery.[5]

Assignable. Subject to lawful transfer; also, so transferable as to vest a right of action.[6] Opposed, *non-assignable.*

Assignor. He who transfers property to another person.

Assignee. He to whom property is transferred; more particularly he to whom an insolvent or a bankrupt makes over his whole estate for the benefit of his creditors.

In patent law one who has transferred to him in writing the whole interest of the original patent or any undivided part of such whole interest, in every portion of the United States. Compare GRANTEE (2); LICENSEE, 2.

In strict legal parlance does not designate an "indorsee" of paper.[7]

Assignee in fact. A person made an assignee by the act of another.

Assignee in law. A person made an assignee by the act of the law; as, an executor, an administrator, a trustee for creditors.

An executor, as taking by operation of law, may be deemed the assignee in law of the testator. But a legatee or devisee occupies no such position.[2]

Provisional assignee. One to whom the estate of a bankrupt is conveyed until the permanent assignee can be appointed.

Assigns. Assignees — persons to whom a grantee may potentially convey; as, in the phrase in deeds "heirs, executors, administrators, and assigns."[3]

Comprehends a line or succession of persons.[4]

Those to whom rights have been transmitted by a particular title, as by sale, gift, legacy, or other transfer or cession. Technically, designated the grantees of real estate in fee-simple; for convenience, came to embrace in its spirit all who succeeded to the title by any other means than by descent.[5]

Comprehends all those who take, immediately or remotely, from or under an assignor, whether by conveyance, devise, descent, or act of the law.[6]

In the phrase "lawful assigns or legal representatives," is used in a cognate sense with "legal representatives." Thus construed it means not assignees in fact, but assignees in law — those upon whom the right is devolved and vested by law, as, assignees in bankruptcy.[7]

Neither the word "assigns" nor the words "assigns forever" have any popular or technical meaning that could qualify a devise to a man and his "heirs."[8]

Includes a mortgagee.[9] See REPRESENTATIVE (1).

Not necessary in a deed as a word of limitation indicating the quantity of the estate granted or to empower the grantee to dispose of the estate.[10]

Assignment. A transfer of property to another for himself or creditors; also, the writing containing the evidence thereof.

The idea is essentially that of a transfer

---

[1] [Associates of the Jersey Company v. Davison, 29 N. J. L. 418 (1860).

[2] 3 Bl. Com. 311. See also 20 Johns. 43; Steph. Pl. 241.

[3] Norman v. Wescombe, 2 M. & W. 360 (1837).

[4] 2 Bl. Com. 327; 21 N. J. L. 389.

[5] Watkinson v. Ingleshy, 5 Johns. *591 (1810).

[6] [Thacker v. Henderson, 63 Barb. 279 (1862).

[7] Palmer v. Call, 2 McCrary, 530 (1881).

[1] See 3 Pars. Contr. 480.

[2] Hight v. Sackett, 34 N. Y. 451 (1866); 3 Hun, 419; 46 Ill. 31; 23 Wis. 295.

[3] See Baily v. De Crespigny, L. R., 4 Q. B. *186 (1869); Grant v. Carpenter, 8 R. I. 38 (1864); 34 Ala. 349; 28 Miss. 246; 19 N. Y. 344; 1 Curtis, 193.

[4] Ogden v. Price, 9 N. J. L. 169 (1827).

[5] [Watson v. Donnelly, 28 Barb. 658 (1859).

[6] Baily v. De Crespigny, L. R., 4 Q. B. *186 (1869), Hannen, J.; Brown v. Crookston Agricul. Association, 34 Minn. 547 (1886).

[7] South Pass of Mississippi, 16 Op. Att.-Gen. 157 (1878). Compare United States v. Gillis, 95 U. S. 407 (1877).

[8] Lawrence v. Lawrence, 105 Pa. 340 (1884).

[9] Brown v. Crookston Agr. Assoc., 34 Minn. 546 (1886).

[10] Salem Capital Flour Mills Co. v. Stayton Water-Ditch & Canal Co., 33 F. R. 154 (1887), Deady, J.

by one party to another of some species of property or valuable interest.[1]

When commercial paper, payable to bearer, is transferred by delivery, both the right of property and the right to sue pass thereby to the transferee; and this is frequently called an "assignment" of such chose in action. But such use of the term, which has grown up under the usages of commerce, is scarcely correct. Assignment proper is a transfer by writing.[2] See BEARER.

Domestic assignment. An assignment for the benefit of creditors, made by a debtor at the place of his domicil. *Foreign assignment.* Such assignment made in another State or county.[3]

Legal assignment. An assignment of an interest or of property, particularly of personal property, cognizable or enforceable in a court of law. *Equitable assignment.* A like transfer, and in a special sense referring to a chose in action or a thing not *in esse,* cognizable by a court of equity.

An "equitable assignment" is an agreement in the nature of a declaration of trust which a chancellor, though deaf to the prayer of a volunteer, never hesitates to execute when it has been made on a valuable or even good consideration.[4]

To make an assignment valid at law the subject must have actual or potential existence at the time of the grant or assignment. But courts of equity will support assignments not only of choses in action and of contingent interests and expectancies, but of things which, having no present actual or potential existence, rest in mere possibility; not indeed as a present positive transfer operative *in præsenti,* for that can only be of a thing *in esse,* but as a present contract to take effect and attach as soon as the thing comes *in esse:* as, an assignment of the oil to be obtained in a whaling voyage now in progress.[5]

To constitute an assignment in equity of a debt or other chose in action no particular form is necessary. Any order, writing, or act which makes an appropriation of a fund amounts to an equitable assignment of the fund. The reason is, the fund being a matter not assignable at law, nor capable of manual possession, an appropriation of it is all that the nature of the case

admits of, and therefore it is held good in a court of equity. As the assignee is generally entitled to all the remedies of the assignor, so he is subject to all equities between the assignor and his debtor. But, in order to perfect his title against the debtor, it is indispensable that the assignee should immediately give notice of the assignment to the debtor, for otherwise a priority of right may be obtained by a subsequent assignee or the debt be discharged by a payment to the assignee before such notice.[1]

An agreement to pay out of a particular fund, however clear in terms, is not an equitable assignment: a covenant in the most solemn form has no greater effect. Such intent and its execution are indispensable. The assignor must not retain control over the fund — an authority to collect, or power of revocation. The transfer must be of such a character that the fund-holder can safely pay, and is compellable to pay, though forbidden by the assignor. Then the fund-holder is bound from the time of notice. A bill of exchange or a check is not an equitable assignment *pro tanto.* But an order to pay out of a specified fund has always been held to be a valid assignment in equity and to fulfill all the requirements of the law.[2]

May be of part of a debt, without the consent of the debtor.[3] See DEPOSIT, 2; GIFT, 1.

Preferential assignment. An assignment with preferences: made to a trustee in favor of the claim of a particular creditor or creditors; as, that one or more creditors shall be paid in full before others receive anything.[4]

In the nature of a *special,* rather than of a *general,* assignment. But the latter is also opposed to a *particular* assignment or a transfer of part of the debtor's property.

In the absence of prohibitory legislation preferential assignments are valid.[5]

Voluntary assignment. Made of a debtor's own free will, for the benefit of creditors. *Compulsory assignment.* Made in pursuance of the mandate of law.[6]

A "voluntary assignment" means, presumably, an assignment of all of the debtor's property in trust to pay debts; as contradistinguished from a sale to a creditor in payment of his claim, and from a pledge

---

[1] [Hight *v.* Sackett, 34 N. Y. 451 (1866).

[2] Enloe *v.* Reike, 56 Ala. 504 (1876), Stone, J. See also Andrews *v.* Carr, 26 Miss. 578 (1853).

[3] As to effect of, see generally 26 Am. Law Reg. 509–12 (1887), cases; May *v.* First Nat. Bank of Attleboro, Sup. Ct. Ill. (1887), cases: 13 N. E. Rep. 806.

[4] Nesmith *v.* Drum, 8 W. & S. 10 (1844); Guthrie's Appeal, 92 Pa. 272 (1879); 2 Story, Eq. § 1040.

[5] 2 Story, Eq. §§ 1039–40; Mitchell *v.* Winslow, 2 Story, R. 638–44 (1843); Butt *v.* Ellett, 19 Wall. 544 (1873); Traer *v.* Clews, 115 U. S. 540 (1885), cases; Holroyd *v.* Marshall, 10 H. L. 209–20 (1862); 2 Bl. Com. 442.

[1] Spain *v.* Hamilton, 1 Wall. 624 (1863), Wayne, J.; Laclede Bank *v.* Schuler, 120 U. S. 516, 514 (1887), cases; 2 Story, Eq. § 1047, cases.

[2] Christmas *v.* Russell, 14 Wall. 84 (1871), Swayne, J. See also Wright *v.* Ellison, 1 *id.* 16 (1863); Trist *v.* Child, 21 *id.* 447 (1874), cases; Ketchum *v.* St. Louis, 101 U. S. 316–17 (1879), cases; Basket *v.* Hassell, 107 *id.* 614 (1882); Florence Mining Co. *v.* Brown, 124 *id.* 391 (1888); Lewis *v.* Traders' Bank, 30 Minn. 134 (1883), cases; Goodsell *v.* Benson, 13 R. I. 230 (1881), cases.

[3] James *v.* Newton, 142 Mass. 370–78 (1886), cases.

[4] See 2 Kent, 532.

[5] 1 Story, Eq. § 370; 2 *id.* § 1036.

[6] See 2 Kent, 397, 532.

or hypothecation as a security in the nature of a mortgage.[1]

A voluntary assignment for the benefit of creditors is a contract — a transfer in trust for a nominal consideration and the further consideration of a distribution of the proceeds of the assigned property among all the creditors.[2]

An assignment by a defendant, *pendente lite*, does not necessarily defeat the suit, but his assignee is bound by what is done against him. The assignee may come in by appropriate application and make himself a party, or he may act in the name of his assignor. Such assignment carries with it an implied license to use the assignor's name to protect the right assigned.[3]

Every demand connected with a right of property, real or personal, is assignable. But not — an officer's pay; a judge's salary; a soldier's pension; an action for fraud, negligence, or tort; a personal service or trust; a naked power; a right of entry for a condition broken; nor, without notice to the insurer, a policy of insurance; nor, at common law, a chose in action, or any right *pendente lite*.[4]

Where there is no restriction in any statute, in the articles of association or the by-laws, as to the disposition of property, the directors of a corporation may make an assignment for the benefit of its creditors.[5]

The assignee is bound by a covenant that runs with the land. See COVENANT.

An assignee for the benefit of creditors is a trustee for the creditors mainly, but, in some respects, for all parties.[6]

He is but the hand of the assignor in the distribution of his estate among his creditors. He enjoys the rights of the assignor only; he is bound where the assignor would be bound. He is not the representative of the creditors, and is not therefore clothed with their powers; nor is he a *bona fide* purchaser for value, but a mere volunteer only.[7]

After the trust has been executed the assignor's former interest revests in him, as if it had never been out of him.[8]

The title which vests in an assignee in bankruptcy by the assignment relates back to the date of filing the petition.[9] Such assignee represents the general or unsecured creditors, and his duties relate chiefly to their interests. As to every thing, except fraudulent conveyances and preferences, he takes as a purchaser

---

[1] [Dias *v.* Bouchand, 10 Paige, Ch. 461 (1843), Walworth, Ch.

[2] Blackburne's Appeal, 39 Pa. 165 (1861), Thompson, J.

[3] *Exp.* South & North Alabama R. Co., 95 U. S. 226 (1877), Waite, C. J.

[4] 1 Pars. Contr. 223; 3 *id.* 480.

[5] Hutchinson *v.* Green, 91 Mo. 375-76 (1886), cases.

[6] 2 Bl. Com. 480; 3 Pars. Contr. 465, 489.

[7] *Re* Fulton's Estate, 51 Pa. 211-12 (1865), Agnew, J.; Mellon's Appeal, 3 *id.* 129 (1859), Strong, J.

[8] Jacoby *v.* Guier, 6 S. & R. 451 (1821). As to the effect of assignor's fraud upon the assignment, see 21 Am. Law Rev. 901-35 (1887), cases; as to conflict of laws respecting assignments for creditors, 1 Harv. Law Rev. 259-64 (1888).

[9] Conner *v.* Long, 104 U. S. 230-44 (1881), cases; International Bank *v.* Sherman, 101 *id.* 406 (1879).

---

from the bankrupt with notice of all outstandin rights and equities. Whatever the bankrupt could to make the assigned property available for the ge eral creditors he may do, and he may recover pro erty conveyed in fraud of the rights of creditors an set aside fraudulent conveyances.[1]

To place parties on equal terms, an assignor of chose in action cannot be a witness against his a signee unless both are living and the latter's testimon can be obtained. Where there is entirety of interes declarations of the assignor, made previous to th transfer, bind the assignee; but, otherwise, he cann disparage the title of an innocent assignee or vende

Compare CONVEYANCE, 2; TRANSFER. See CHOS BANKRUPTCY; DAMNOSA, Hæreditas; LIS, Penden NOVATION; PERISHABLE; PREFER, 2; TRUST, 1; WITNES

ASSISE. See ASSIZE.

ASSISTANCE. Help, aid; furtherance.

Writ of assistance. A process issue from a court of equity to enforce a decree as, to place in possession a purchaser of mort gaged premises sold for a mortgage debt after he has received a deed.

Power to issue the writ results from the princip that jurisdiction to enforce a decree is co-extensiv with jurisdiction to hear and determine the rights the parties — that the court does complete justice h declaring the right and affording a remedy for its er joyment. But, as the execution cannot exceed th decree, the writ can issue only against a party boun by the decree.[4]

A purchaser under a decree for the foreclosure a mortgage has a right to the writ to obtain possessio as against parties and persons made tenants or tran ferees after the suit was begun.[5]

ASSIZE.[6] Originally, an assembly me for the purpose of ascertaining somethin judicially: a jury, or court; a session or sit ting; then the place where, as also the tim when, the session was held, the writ unde which it convened, the finding or resolution and the proceedings as a whole. Hence — regulation, an ordinance, a statute, — some thing determined and established; a tax o tribute of a definite amount; also, the reduc ing a thing to certainty — in number, quan tity, quality, weight, measure, time, place.

At first, the jury who tried a cause, "sitting t gether" for that purpose. Then, by a figure, th

---

[1] Dudley *v.* Easton, 104 U. S. 103 (1881), Waite, C. J

[2] 1 Greenl. Ev. §§ 190, 172.

[3] L. *assistere*, to approach: *ad-stare*, to stand by.

[4] Terrell *v.* Allison, 21 Wall. 291 (1874), cases, Field, J. Howard *v.* Milwaukee, &c. R. Co., 101 U. S. 849 (1879) Boyd *v.* United States, 116 *id.* 625 (1886).

[5] 2 Jones, Mort. § 1663; Watkins *v.* Jerman, 36 Kar 467 (1887), cases.

[6] F. *assise*, assembly — of judges; decree; impost O. F. *asseoir*, to sit near, assist a judge: L. *assidere* to sit near or together.

court or jurisdiction which summoned the jury by a commission of assize. Hence, the judicial assemblage held by the king's commission in the various counties were (and still are) termed, in common speech, "the assizes." By still another figure, an action for recovering possession of lands — because the sheriff summons a jury or assize.[1]

Designates the court, the place, or the time where the judges of the superior courts of Westminster try questions of fact, issuing out of those courts, ready for trial by jury. "The assizes" are the sittings of the judges at the various places they visit on their circuits, four times a year in vacation. "Assize" also sometimes denotes a jury, and sometimes a writ.[2]

"Assizes" is the word most in use in modern books. It often signifies a single court.

ASSOCIATE.[3] A person united with another in business, office, enterprise, or other interest.

Associates are persons united, or acting together by mutual consent or compact, in the promotion of some common object.[4]

Associate attorney or **counsel.** A lawyer who assists another in a cause; co-counsel; a colleague.

Associate in crime. A confederate in the commission of a criminal offense; an accomplice, q. v.

Associate judge or **justice.** A judge who serves with another on the same bench, in distinction from the "chief" justice, the "president" or "presiding" judge, q. v.

Association. 1. The act or state of being joined in common interest.

2. An organization of persons without a charter, for business, humanity, charity, culture, or other purpose; any unincorporated society or body.

3. A body of persons invested with some, yet not full, corporate rights and powers: as, a joint-stock association; a building and loan association.

When improvement of the members is the predominant idea, "society" seems to be the preferred word; and "company" or "partnership," when the idea is the making of profits.

"Association" *ex vi termini* implies agreement, compact, union of minds, purpose, and action. May apply to those who are already associated with persons named or those who may come in afterward: as, in acts of incorporation.[1]

Articles of association. The instrument which creates the union between the members of an incorporation, specifies the object and form of organization, the amount and shares of capital, the place of business, the corporators, etc.; and is distinguishable from the charter and the by-laws.

Where individuals voluntarily associate together and adopt a name or description intended to embrace all of its members, and under which its contracts are made and its business carried on, such company can neither sue nor be sued by the name adopted, but in the individual names as partners.[2]

To constitute a "partnership" there must be a community of interests for business purposes. Hence, *voluntary associations* or "clubs," for social and benevolent purposes and the like, are not proper partnerships, nor have their members the powers and responsibilities of partners. Thus, for example, while the members of a Masonic lodge may not be held as partners for a debt incurred by the lodge, each member who assented to or advised the outlay may be held liable as an individual.[3]

Associations for mutual benevolence among their own members are not associations for purely "charitable uses."[4]

The members of a committee, authorized to effect the incorporation of a voluntary association, who neglect to perfect the re-organization, may be held as partners as between themselves, and non-participating members of the association be relieved from liability.[5]

See BANK, 2 (2); BUILDING; BY-LAWS; CHARTER, 2; CHURCH; CLUBS; COMPANY, 2; CORPORATION; PARTNERSHIP; STOCK, 3 (2).

4. Association of words, see NOSCITUR.

---

[1] [Lechmere Bank v. Boynton, 11 Cush. 380, *ante.*

[2] Covington Drawbridge Co. v. Shepherd, 20 How. 232 (1857), Taney, C. J.; Beatty v. Kurtz, 2 Pet. *585 (1829), Story, J.; 27 Alb. Law J. 326-29 (1883), cases.

[3] See Thomas v. Ellmaker, 1 Pars. Sel. Eq. Cas. 98, 104, 111-12 (1844), cases; Laford v. Deems, 81 N. Y. 514 (1880); Ash v. Guie, 97 Pa. 499 (1881), cases; *Re* St. James's Club, 13 Eng. L. & Eq. 589 (1852); 3 Kent, 23; cases *infra.*

[4] Babb v. Reed, 5 Rawle, 150 (1835); Gorman v. Russell, 14 Cal. *535-38 (1860), cases. But some cases hold that Masonic lodges are "charities," — Duke v. Fuller, 9 N. H. 536 (1838); Burdine v. Grand Lodge, 37 Ala. 478 (1861); Indianapolis v. Grand Master, 25 Ind. 518 (1865); Savannah v. Solomon's Lodge, 53 Ga. 93 (1874). *Contra,* Bangor v. Rising Virtue Lodge, 73 Me. 428, 434 (1882) — the funds of a "public charity" are derived from gifts and devises, and it is open to the whole public, — Appleton, C. J.

[5] See Ward v. Brigham, 127 Mass. 24 (1879); Volger v. Ray, 131 *id.* 439 (1881); Ferris v. Thaw, 72 Mo. 446 (1880). As to unincorporated associations, see generally 17 Cent. Law J. 342-45 (1883), cases.

---

[1] 3 Bl. Com. 185, 57, 60; 4 *id.* 269, 424; 3 *id.* 221; 1 *id.* 148, 411.

[2] 3 Bl. Com. 58-59.

[3] L. *associatus*, joined to: *ad*, to; *socius*, a follower, companion.

[4] [Lechmere Bank v. Boynton, 11 Cush. 382, 379 (1853), Shaw, C. J.

ASSUME. To take to or upon one's self. See ASSUMPSIT.

A person who "assumes a lease" takes to himself or accepts the obligations and the benefits of the lessor under the contract.[1]

"Assumed" may be used in the sense of claimed; as, in saying that assumed facts must be proved before the main fact can be inferred.[2] Compare PRESUME.

ASSUMPSIT.[3] He engaged or agreed to do a thing.

Describes a contract, not under seal, made with another for his benefit; also, the common-law form of an action of trespass upon the case for damages or failure to perform such contract.[4]

"Debt" lies for an ascertained sum. "*Assumpsit*" originally lay for an unascertained sum, but may now be brought for a fixed sum.

Express assumpsit. An engagement in positive terms to do some particular thing; as, an obligation to pay a promissory note.

Implied assumpsit. An engagement which the law will infer from circumstances; such obligation as reason and justice dictate, and as the law presumes a man has contracted to perform; as, to pay a judgment, a forfeiture, or a penalty.[5]

The presumption in such case is that every man engages to do what duty or justice requires him to do.[6]

Indebitatus assumpsit. He, being indebted, undertook. The species of the action which charges a promise to pay from the mere fact that an indebtedness exists.

Rests upon an implied promise to pay what in good conscience ought to be paid.[6]

Called also *common* or *general assumpsit*.

The promise, the consideration (the facts out of which the obligation grows), and the breach, should be averred.[6]

Special assumpsit. The agreement, and the form of action therefor, which rests upon an express undertaking.

In declaring upon a special *assumpsit*, the undertaking should be set out in the precise terms used.

The action of *assumpsit* lies for — the worth of work done; the value of goods bought and delivered; money received which should not be retained; money spent for another at his request; a balance due on account; damages for injury from want of integrit or of care or skill assumed to be possessed or exerted See COUNT, 4 (1), Common.

Indebitatus assumpsit is founded on what the l terms an implied promise on the part of the defenda to pay what in good conscience he is bound to pay the plaintiff. . . The law never implies a promise pay unless some duty creates the obligation; and nev a promise to do an act contrary to duty or to law

Nunquam indebitatus, he never undertook, is t name of the general issue in the *indebitatus* speci but has been used, like *nil debet*, in debt on simp contract.

Non assumpsit. He has not unde taken, or did not undertake. The name the general denial in the foregoing actions.

Non assumpsit infra sex annos. He d not undertake within six years. The plea the statute of limitations in these action Compare ACTIO, Non accrevit, etc.

See further ACTION, 2; CASE, 3; CONTRACT; C ENANT; DEBET; DEBT; PROMISE.

ASSURANCE.[4] Certainty; warrant indemnity.

1. Legal evidence of the transfer of titl whereby every man's estate is assured him, and all controversies, doubts, and dif culties are prevented or removed.[5]

The *common assurances* of the realm are by matt *in pais*, by matter of record, by special custom, a by devise.[5]

Collateral assurance. An assurance addition to, or over and above, some oth assurance; as, a bond, to the covenants in mortgage.

Future assurance. Such transfer in t future as will cure a defect in a title, — a by removing an incumbrance, by procurir a quitclaim deed. Whence " covenant f future assurance." [6]

2. Insurance; in England, life-insuranc Whence assurer, the assured, re-assuranc See further INSURANCE.

ASTERISK. Indicates the words which the pages of the first edition of a te book or volume of reports began; enlarg

---

[1] Cincinnati, &c. R. Co. *v.* Indiana, &c. R. Co., 44 Ohio St. 314 (1886).

[2] Jenkins *v.* State, 62 Wis. 63 (1885).

[3] L. *assumpsit*, he has undertaken, he undertook: *assumere*, to take upon one's self.

[4] See 3 Bl. Com. 158-67; Carrol *v.* Green, 92 U. S. 513 (1875); Hendrick *v.* Lindsay, 93 *id.* 143 (1876); Boston, &c. Smelting Co. *v.* Smith, 13 R. I. 35 (1880), cases.

[5] 3 Bl. Com. 158, 159, 162; Lloyd *v.* Hough, 1 How. 159 (1843); Wallis *v.* Shelly, 30 F. R. 748 (1887).

[6] 3 Bl. Com. 155, 158.

[1] 3 Bl. Com. 162; Dermott *v.* Jones, 2 Wall. 9 (186 Nash *v.* Towne, 5 *id.* 702 (1866); Gaines *v.* Miller, U. S. 397 (1884); National Trust Co. *v.* Gleason, 77 N. 400 (1877).

[2] Bailey *v.* N. Y. Central R. Co., 22 Wall. 638 (1874), cases, Clifford, J.

[3] See 3 Bl. Com. 305, 308.

[4] F. *asseürer*, to make secure: L. *ad-sine-cura*.

[5] 2 Bl. Com. 294.

[6] [4 Kent, 468.

or annotated editions being printed as explained under A, 1, par. 3.

ASTUTE. When it is said that the courts are "not astute" to do a thing, (as, to infer fraud from negligence), the meaning is that they are disinclined, not disposed, to do the particular thing.

Thus, they are not only not predisposed but are reluctant or averse to accepting a conclusion involving intended wrong.

ASYLUM.[1] Retreat, refuge; protection, immunity.

1. A place of refuge and protection for criminals, and debtors.

"Asylum" includes not only place, but shelter, security, protection. Thus, within the meaning of the extradition treaty of 1868 (15 St. L. 629), a fugitive from justice in Italy "seeks asylum" in this country when he claims the use of a Territory as an asylum.[2] See EXTRADITION.

2. Immunity from law; as, the status of a public minister.

3. An institution for the unfortunate. See SECTARIAN.

AT. 1. The prefix *at-*, the Latin *ad*, q. v.

2. The English preposition, expressing the relation of presence, nearness in place or time, direction toward.[3]

The word is somewhat indefinite; it may mean "in," "within," or "near." Its primary idea is nearness, and it is less definite than *in* or *on*.[4]

"At the terminus" of a road may mean *near* the terminus.[4]

In ordinary speech, "at" more generally means "within" than "without." Thus, *at* a town or *at* a county means at some place within the town or county, rather than at a place without or even at the outermost verge of, but not in, such town or county. In indictments, where the utmost precision is necessary, the fact is generally stated to have been done at the place; and, if it were not done in the place, the venue would be wrong. "At," like "from," has not then, generally speaking, an exclusive signification: as, in the expression that a canal shall begin "at the District of Columbia."[5]

That "at a place" may not be equivalent to *in* the place, see IN, 1 (1).

Authority to construct a railroad from A to B, or beginning at A and running to B, confers authority to commence the road at some point within A, and to end it at some point within B. "At," like "from" and "to," is to be taken exclusively, according to the subject-matter.[1]

The description of a survey as beginning "at" a tree does not necessarily fix the point at the center of the tree. The deed may be interpreted in conformity with the practical effect given it by the parties, as by actual occupancy to a line beginning at the surface of the tree.[2]

Compare BY; IN, 1; INTO; NEAR; ON; TO; UPON, 1; WITHIN.

At interest. See INTEREST, 3.

At large. 1. In the full extent; in full; at length; *in extenso:* as, for a court to state at large that a thing should not be done; or for proceedings to be recorded at large, instead of by memoranda.[3]

2. Representing a State or district in its whole extent: as, a delegate, elector, or Congressman at large.

3. Applicable to all of a State, all the States, or the whole territory of the United States; general: as, statutes at large, the United States Statutes at Large.

4. In general; general, as opposed to special, particular, preferred, secured: as, the bearer at large, creditors at large.[4]

5. Unconfined; unrestrained; in the free exercise of natural freedom or propensities: as, an animal suffered to run at large.

"Running at large" means strolling about without restraint or confinement, as, wandering, roving, or rambling at will, unrestrained. The restraint need not be entirely physical; it may depend much upon the training, habits, and instincts of the animal. The sufficiency of the restraint is to be determined more from its effect, its controlling and restraining influence, than from the nature or kind of animal.[5]

Whether, in a given case, physical or moral power over the animal is necessary, depends upon its nature, age, character, habits, discipline, use, and other circumstances.[6]

---

[1] L. *asylum*, a place of refuge: Gk. *a'sylos*, undespoiled, unharmed.

[2] *Re* De Giacomo, 12 Blatch. 395 (1874), Blatchford, J.

[3] Webster's Dict.

[4] State (West Jersey R. Co.) *v.* Receiver of Taxes, 38 N. J. L. 302 (1876), Dixon, J.; State *v.* Ray, 50 Ala. 173 (1873), Peters, C. J.

[5] Chesapeake & Ohio Canal Co. *v.* Key, 3 Cranch, C. C. 606, 604 (1829), Cranch, C. J.; The Mohawk Bridge Co. *v.* Utica, &c. R. Co., 6 Paige, 562 (1837); Mason *v.* Brooklyn, &c. R. Co., 35 Barh. 377 (1861); Homer *v.* Homer, L. R., 8 C. D. 764 (1878); 28 Alb. L. J. 44.

[1] Union Pacific R. Co. *v.* Hall, 91 U. S. 348 (1875), cases, Strong, J.; Mason *v.* Brooklyn City, &c. R. Co., 35 N. Y. 377-78 (1861).

[2] Stewart *v.* Patrick, 68 N. Y. 454 (1877).

[3] See 3 Bl. Com. 392; 95 U. S. 420.

[4] See 2 Bl. Com. 467.

[5] Russell *v.* Cone, 46 Vt. 604 (1874), Peck, J.; Bertwhistle *v.* Goodrich, 53 Mich. 459 (1884).

[6] Jennings *v.* Wayne, 63 Me. 470 (1874), Dickerson, J. See also 52 Cal. 653; 49 Conn. 113; 53 Iowa, 632; 70 *id.* 462; 26 Kan. 268; 10 Metc. 382; 10 Allen, 151; 26 Minn. 157; 21 Hun, 249; 50 Vt. 130.

At law. 1. According to the course of the common law; in law, as opposed to "in equity" or according to the principles and procedure in courts of equity or chancery.

2. For the practice of law: as, an attorney or counselor-at-law. See ATTORNEY.

At least. Compare MORE OR LESS.

A publication sixteen months before a certain day was held valid under a statute directing that the publication should be made "at least six months" prior to that day.[1]

When a city charter requires that a resolution ordering work on a street shall lie over "at least four weeks after its introduction," a resolution introduced on a Monday may be acted upon on the fourth Monday thereafter.[2]

At length. See *At Large*, 1; ENTRY, II, 6.

At maturity. See MATURITY, 2.

At once. At one and the same time.[3]

At par. Of nominal value; worth the face value. See PAR, 2.

At sea. On the voyage. See SEA.

At sight. On view; on presentation. See SIGHT.

ATHEIST. One who disbelieves in the existence of a God who is the rewarder of truth and the avenger of falsehood.[4] See INFIDEL; OATH; RELIGION.

ATLANTIC. See CABLE, Submarine.

The Gulf of Mexico is not the "Atlantic coast."[5]

ATMOSPHERE. See AIR.

ATS. At suit of; equivalent to *ads — ad sectam.*

ATTACH.[6] 1. To tie to, fasten to, affix, annex, *q. v.*

2. To lay hold upon by legal authority; to seize, take, arrest. To take or touch,— a precise expression of the thing actually done.[7]

When used without qualification in a statute refers to the taking and holding of the person or property on mesne process, subject to the further order of the court or to the final judgment in the case.[8]

Attachment of the person. A writ in the nature of a *capias*, directed to the sheriff, and commanding him to attach or take up the defendant, and bring him into court;[1] also, the summary proceeding itself.

Employed to compel the appearance of a defendant; to enforce the attendance of a juror or a witness;[2] to bring before the court one charged with contempt.[3]

The officer makes caption of the person named in the same manner as upon an ordinary process for arrest. Instead, however, of holding him to bail he brings him corporally before the court, that he may do the thing required or show cause why he has not or should not do it. Fines for disobedience are often imposed. See CONTEMPT.

Attachment of property. An actual seizure of goods, that they may be held to satisfy the judgment which the plaintiff may recover.[4]

The object is to take out of the defendant's possession and transfer into the custody of the law, acting through its legal officer, the goods attached, that, if necessary, they may be seized in execution and be disposed of and delivered to the purchaser. Hence, in this sense, to attach is to take actual possession of the property.[5]

Originally, a writ issued out of the court of common pleas, grounded upon the non-appearance of the defendant at the return of the original writ. The sheriff was then commanded to attach him by taking gage, that is, certain of his property, which the defendant forfeited if he did not appear; or by making him find safe pledges or sureties for his appearance.[6]

Also the first and immediate process, without previous summons, upon actions of trespass *vi et armis* or for other injuries — trespasses against the peace, as, deceit and conspiracy, where the violence of the wrong requires a speedy remedy.[6]

Upon execution of a bond to discharge the attachment the latter becomes discharged, the grounds thereof are no longer in controversy, and the obligors become bound absolutely to pay such judgment as may be recovered.[7]

Attachment of vessel. Allowed after libel filed for work done, materials or supplies

---

[1] Hoffman *v.* Clark County, 61 Wis. 7 (1884); Ward *v.* Walters, 63 *id.* 43 (1885); *ib.* 314.

[2] Wright *v.* Forrestal, 65 Wis. 348 (1886).

[3] Platter *v.* Green, 26 Kan. 268 (1881).

[4] Commonwealth *v.* Hills, 10 Cush. 532 (1852), Dewey, J.

[5] New Haven Saw Mill Co. *v.* Security Ins. Co., 7 F. R. 847 (1881).

[6] F. *attacher*, to fasten, tack to: L. *attingere*, to touch,— 8 Conn. 334.

[7] Hollister *v.* Goodale, 8 Conn. 334 (1831), Hosmer, C. J.; Pennsylvania R. Co. *v.* Pennock, 51 Pa. 253 (1865).

[8] [Beardsley *v.* Beecher, 47 Conn. 414 (1879), Loomis, J.

[1] 3 Bl. Com. 443.

[2] 3 Bl. Com. 369.

[3] 4 Bl. Com. 283.

[4] Dunklee *v.* Fales, 5 N. H. 528 (1831), Richardson, C. J.; Bryant *v.* Warren, 51 *id.* 215 (1871).

[5] Hollister *v.* Goodale, 8 Conn. 334 (1831), Hosmer, C. J. See also Adler *v.* Roth, 2 McCrary, 447 (1881), cases; 5 Mass. 163; 12 *id.* 497; 3 Minn. 406; 51 Pa. 253; 55 Vt. 422; 76 Va. 318; 21 W. Va. 211.

[6] 3 Bl. Com. 280; Bond *v.* Ward, 7 Mass. *128 (1810).

[7] Ferguson *v.* Glidewell, 48 Ark. 201-4 (1886), cases *pro* and *con.*

furnished, wharfage due, etc., and is upon the interest of the owner or part-owner.

Domestic attachment. Issues against a resident of the State who is charged with fraud in contracting a debt or with remaining absent or absconding to defraud his creditors. **Foreign attachment.** Issues against a non-resident who evades service of process — in the view that a levy and sale of his property will serve the purpose of an appearance by him and meet the ends of justice.

A "foreign attachment" is a suit against a personal defendant by name; and, because of inability to serve process on him on account of non-residence, or for other reason mentioned in a statute, the suit is commenced by a writ directing the proper officer to attach sufficient property of the defendant to answer any judgment that may be rendered against him. It is like an admiralty proceeding *in rem.*[1]

The foundation of the proceeding is that the defendant is beyond, while his property is within, the reach of process.[2]

Attachment of property was introduced at an early date in London, chiefly to operate upon debtors who could not be arrested because not subject to jurisdiction. As these persons were "foreigners" the process was called *foreign* attachment or attachment of foreigners' goods.[3]

Execution-attachment. An attachment in execution of a judgment. A proceeding in satisfaction of a judgment — by seizing property, rights, or credits in the hands of a debtor or bailee of the defendant.

The proceeding of attachment of property was derived from the customary law of foreign attachment in London, legislatures having modified the use of it, from time to time, as seemed proper. At first it was merely ancillary to other proceedings — in the nature of a proceeding in equity intended to enjoin a person from parting with the property of an absent debtor in order to compel the debtor's appearance, and being, in default of an appearance, an adjudication of the property toward the liquidation of the demand.[4]

Proceedings by attachment are not purely *in rem;* they are rather proceedings against the interest of the defendant and those claiming under him.[5]

In New England attachment of a defendant's property, rights, and credits is an incident to a summons in all actions based upon contract. Elsewhere, the writ seems to issue only upon cause shown by affidavit, accompanied by a bond designed to secure the defendant in such damage as he may sustain on account of the proceeding. The ground upon which the writ may be obtained and the details of practice vary in the different States. Speaking generally, the remedy is allowed for an ascertainable amount due; the plaintiff acquires such rights as the defendant had at the time of the levy; the levy itself constitutes a lien; and attachments levied simultaneously share *pro rata.* In many States the defendant may substitute a bond with sureties, and thereupon resume possession of the property. An attachment is "dissolved" by final judgment entered for the defendant, or, on motion, for a substantial defect apparent upon the face of the proceedings.[1]

See GARNISH; ORDER, 2, Charging; RECEIPTOR; RES, 2; SEIZURE.

ATTACK. See ASSAULT; COLLATERALLY.

ATTAINDER.[2] Staining; corrupting: pollution of blood; extinguishment of inheritable quality of blood.

When sentence of death is pronounced the immediate, inseparable consequence at common law is attainder: the condemned is without the protection of the law, his estates are forfeited, his blood corrupted.[3]

The word is derived from *attincta:* the stain or corruption of a criminal capitally condemned. The party attainted lost all inheritable quality — he could neither receive nor transmit property or other rights of inheritance.[4]

Bill of attainder. A legislative act which inflicts punishment without a judicial trial.[5]

If the punishment be less than death, the act is termed a *bill of pains and penalties.*[5]

Bills of attainder (or acts of attainder as they were called when passed into statutes) were laws which declared certain persons attainted — their blood corrupted so that it lost heritable equality.[4]

"No Bill of Attainder . . shall be passed."[6] "No Attainder of Treason shall work Corruption of Blood, or Forfeiture except during the Life of the Person attainted."[7] "No State shall . pass any Bill of Attainder."[8]

Within the meaning of the Constitution bills of attainder include bills of pains and penalties. In these cases the legislative body, in addition to its legitimate functions, exercises the powers and offices of a judge: it assumes judicial magistracy; it pronounces upon

---

[1] The Hine v. Trevor, 4 Wall. 571 (1866), Miller, J.

[2] Pennsylvania R. Co. v. Pennock, 51 Pa. 250 (1865); Fitch v. Ross, 4 S. & R. *564 (1818).

[3] See Brandon, For. Att. 4.

[4] See Brandon, For. Att. 4; Drake, Att. §§ 4–5; Waples, Att. §§ 2–4.

[5] Megee v. Beirne, 39 Pa. 62 (1861); Doe v. Oliver, 2 Sm. L. C., 7 Am. ed., 809, cases.

[1] See Brandon; Drake; 1 Bouvier, 202–3. On attaching debts, see 18 Cent. Law J. 468 (1884), cases.

[2] F. *ateindre*, to convict, — Skeat. F. *attaindre*, to stain, accuse: L. *ad-tingere*, to reach to, touch, — Webster. L. *attinctus*, stained, blackened, — 4 Bl. Com. 380; 39 N. Y. 430; 4 Wall. 387.

[3] 4 Bl. Com. 380–89; 2 id. 251–56.

[4] [*Exp.* Garland, 4 Wall. 387 (1866), Miller, J.

[5] Cummings v. Missouri, 4 Wall. 323 (1866), Field, J.

[6] Constitution, Art. I, sec. 9, cl. 3.

[7] *Ibid.*, Art. III, sec. 3, cl. 2.

[8] *Ibid.*, Art. I, sec. 10.

the guilt of the party, without any of the forms or safeguards of trial; it determines the sufficiency of the proofs produced, whether conformable to the rules of evidence or otherwise; and it fixes the degree of punishment in accordance with its own notions of the enormity of the offense. Such bills are generally directed against individuals by name, but they may be against a whole class; and they may inflict punishment absolutely or conditionally.[1]

In England attainders of treason worked corruption of blood and perpetual forfeiture of the estate of the person attainted to the disinherison of those who would otherwise be his heirs. Thereby innocent children were made to suffer because of the offense of their ancestor. When the Constitution was framed this was felt to be a hardship — rank injustice. The provision was intended for the benefit of the children and heirs alone,— a declaration that the children should not bear the iniquity of the fathers. In this light is to be construed the Confiscation Act of 1862.[2]

Courts of justice were employed only to register the edict of Parliament and to carry the sentence into execution.[3]

In England bills of this sort have been usually passed in times of rebellion, of gross subserviency to the crown, or of violent political excitements.[4]

Shortly after the Revolution, acts of attainder were passed in several of the States. In England, by 33 and 34 Vict. (1870), attainder upon conviction is abolished. See TEST, Oath.

ATTEMPT. 1, *v.* To perform an act toward accomplishing a purpose; to do anything by physical exertion tending to produce an unlawful result.

To make an effort to effect an object; to make a trial or experiment; to endeavor; to use exertion to a purpose.[5]

2, *n.* In its largest signification, a trial or physical effort to do a particular thing.[6]

Can only be made by an actual ineffectual deed done in pursuance and in furtherance of the design.[7]

Consists of an act of endeavor to commit a particular offense, and an intent by that act alone, or in conjunction with other necessary acts, to commit it.[8]

Both these elements must be specifically charged.[5]

It is impossible to comprehend all cases in a definition that does not necessarily run into a mere enumeration of instances. There must be a combination of

intent and act — an intent to commit a crime and an act, done in pursuance thereof, which falls short of the thing intended. While preliminary preparations,— conditions not causes,— may co-exist with a guilty intent, they may not advance the conduct of the party beyond the sphere of mere intent.[1]

While "attempt" conveys the idea of physical effort to do an act, or to accomplish an end, "intent" expresses the quality of mind with which the act is done.[2]

An "intent" implies purpose only; an "attempt" both purpose and actual effort to carry the intent into execution.[3]

"Intent" indicates the purpose existing in the mind; "attempt" the act to be committed.[4]

A statutory punishment for an attempt to poison is not incurred by an unexecuted determination to poison, though preparation is made for the purpose; nor by the actual administration of a substance not poisonous, though believed to be so.[5]

Merely delivering poison to a person and soliciting him to place it in a spring is not "an attempt to administer poison" — the act not approximating sufficiently near to the commission of murder to establish an attempt to commit it, within the Pennsylvania act of March 31, 1860, § 82, which is a copy of 1 Vict. (1837), c. 85, sec. 3.[6]

When the attempt to commit the principal or ultimate offense is made, the distinct offense of attempting is complete.[7]

Every attempt to commit a felony not murder is a misdemeanor; and, generally, an attempt to commit a misdemeanor is a misdemeanor of the same nature. But merely "soliciting" another to do an act is not an attempt to do that act.[8]

It cannot be maintained as a universal principle that an attempt to commit a misdemeanor is, by the common law, a misdemeanor. The law has declared many acts to be misdemeanors where the purpose of the offender was not consummated, although, if consummated, it would have been an offense only of this grade. In such cases there must be an unlawful purpose and an act committed which would carry it into immediate execution, unless prevented by some counteracting force or circumstance.[9] See ADMINISTER, 1.

---

[1] Cummings *v.* Missouri, 4 Wall. 323 (1866), Field, J.

[2] Wallach *v.* Van Riswick, 92 U. S. 210 (1875), Strong, J. See also 2 Bl. Com. 256.

[3] Drehman *v.* Stifle, 8 Wall. 601 (1869).

[4] 2 Story, Const. § 1344.

[5] Commonwealth *v.* McDonald, 5 Cush. 367 (1850), Fletcher, J.

[6] Lewis *v.* State, 35 Ala. 387–88 (1860), cases, Stone, J.

[7] Uhl *v.* Commonwealth, 6 Gratt. 709 (1849).

[8] State *v.* Wells, 31 Conn. 212 (1862), Butler, J.; Gray *v.* State, 63 Ala. 73 (1879).

[1] United States *v.* Stephens, 12 F. R. 55 (1882), Deady, D. J.; 14 Cal. 160; 60 *id.* 71; 62 *id.* 297; 1 Whart. Cr. L. §§ 178, 181; 1 Bish. Cr. L. § 668.

[2] [State *v.* Marshall, 14 Ala. 414–15 (1848).

[3] Prince *v.* State, 35 Ala. 309 (1860); 14 Ga. 59.

[4] Stabler *v.* Commonwealth, 95 Pa. 321 (1880).

[5] State *v.* Clarissa, 11 Ala. 60 (1847).

[6] Stabler's Case, *supra.* See also Regina *v.* Williams, 47 E. C. L. 589 (1844); Regina *v.* Lewis, 38 *id.* 207 (1840); Regina *v.* St. George, *ib.* 193 (1840). Compare People *v.* Bush, 4 Hill, 133 (1843). See 2 Steph. Hist. Cr. L. Eng. 221–25.

[7] State *v.* Decker, 36 Kan. 720 (1887); Kan. Crim. Code, §§ 283, 121.

[8] 4 Bl. Com. 221, 241; Stabler's Case, *supra;* Smith *v.* Commonwealth, 54 Pa. 211–13 (1867), cases; Kelly *v.* Commonwealth, 1 Grant, 484 (1858); Rex *v.* Butler, 25 E. C. L. 441 (1834).

[9] Lamb *v.* State, Sup. Ct. Md. (1887), Bryan, J., deciding that the solicitation of a woman to take drugs to pro-

ATTEST.[1] To bear witness to: to signify, by subscription of his name, that the person has witnessed the execution of the particular instrument. Compare SIGN; SUBSCRIBE, 1.

In its strict sense to witness or bear witness to. The principal object in requiring that an instrument shall be executed in the presence of witnesses is that they may see that the same is properly and fairly executed. But the ordinary use of the word, as applied to the execution of deeds, requires that the witnesses should attest in writing: the principal end of which seems to be to preserve evidence that the instrument was executed in the presence of the required witnesses.[2]

To "attest" the publication of a paper as a last will, and to "subscribe" to that paper the names of the witnesses, are different things. Attestation is the act of the senses; subscription, the act of the hand: the one is mental, the other mechanical. To "attest" a will is to know that it was published as such, and to certify the facts required to constitute an actual and legal publication; but to "subscribe" a paper published as a will is only to write on the same paper the names of the witnesses for the purpose of identification. There may be a perfect attestation in fact without subscription.[3]

An "attesting" witness, under the Statute of Wills, is one who at the time of attestation would be competent to testify in court to the matter.[4]

The last requisite to the validity of a deed is the attestation or execution of it in the presence of witnesses; necessary rather for preserving the evidence than for constituting the essence of the deed.[5]

The number of witnesses necessary to a valid will, and whether there shall be any at all to a deed, and the particular facts to which they must certify, vary in the different States.[6]

See further DEED, 2; PRESENCE; WILL, 2; WITNESS.

2. To certify to the verity of a copy of a public document.

Referring to judicial writings or copies thereof, as the copy of the record of a judicial process, seems to intend an authentication by the clerk of the court so as to make them receivable as evidence.[1]

ATTORN.[2] To turn over: to transfer service to a new lord; to recognize as landlord the transferee of a leasehold.

Attornment. The consent of a tenant to the grant of his landlord.[3]

The acknowledgment by a tenant of a new landlord, and an agreement to become tenant to the purchaser.[4]

As the feudal obligation between lord and vassal was reciprocal, the lord could not alien his seigniory without the consent of the vassal. This consent was expressed by what was called "attorning"—professing to become the tenant of the new lord: a doctrine afterward extended to all leases for life or years. By 4 and 5 Anne (1706), c. 16, no longer necessary to complete a grant or conveyance.[5]

ATTORNEY.[6] One who is put in the place, stead, or "turn" of another to manage his affairs of law.[7] An attorney-at-law; a lawyer.

A person employed by another to act in his behalf; an agent.

Formerly, one who in any manner acted in behalf of another.[8]

Attorney-at-law. A person whose profession is to represent litigants in the management of their causes before the courts.

Attorney-in-fact. One who serves another as agent in the doing of a particular thing; an agent for the transaction of an act specified in a sealed instrument called a "letter" or "power" of attorney.

An attorney-at-law may act as an attorney-in-fact. Any one who may serve another as agent may be made an attorney-in-fact. Persons are often appointed attorneys-in-fact to transfer certificates of stock, to acknowledge satisfaction of mortgages, to transfer realty, to collect rents,—to attend to all one's business generally in a particular place or country. See DELEGATUS.

Persons acting professionally in legal formalities, negotiations, or proceedings by

---

cure an abortion is not within the act of 1868 of that State,—that the common-law rule was not altered by the act. Same case, 26 Am. Law Reg. 641 (1887); ib. 645-54, cases. See generally 17 Cent. Law J. 26-28, 45-50 (1883)—Irish Law Times (1882).

[1] L. *attestari*, to be a witness to. See TESTIS.

[2] Wright v. Wakefield, 4 Taunt. *223 (1812), Mansfield, C. J.

[3] [Swift v. Wiley, 1 B. Mon. 117 (Ky., 1840), Robertson, C. J. See also Re Downie's Will, 42 Wis. 76 (1877); 49 Conn. 249: Webster.

[4] [Jenkins v. Dawes, 115 Mass. 601 (1874), Gray, C. J.; 9 Pick. 350.

[5] 2 Bl. Com. 307. See also Ladd v. Ladd, 8 How. 31-39 (1850), cases.

[6] See Lord v. Lord, 58 N. H. 7 (1876); Dyer v. Dyer, 87 Ind. 17 (1882).

[1] Gass, &c. Manuf. Co. v. People, 4 Bradw. 515 (1879), cases, McAllister, J.

[2] At-türn'. F. *atorner*, to prepare, direct, dispose.

[3] Souders v. Vansickle, 8 N. J. L. 317 (1826).

[4] Lindley v. Dakin, 13 Ind. 389 (1859). See also Willis v. Moore, 59 Tex. 636 (1883); Lyon v. Washburn, 3 Col. 204-5 (1877); 1 Washb. R. P. 28.

[5] 2 Bl. Com. 288-89, 72.

[6] F. *attorner*, to attorn, q. v.

[7] 3 Bl. Com. 25.

[8] "Our only High Bishop, only attorney, mediator,"—A Short Catechism (1553). "Attornies are denied me, and therefore personally I lay my claim,"—Shakespeare, Rich. II (1595), Act ii, s. 3. "Baptism by an attorney, by a proxy,"—Donne, Sermons (1640), p. 794.

warrant or authority of their clients, may be regarded as "attorneys-at-law" within the meaning of that designation in this country.[1]

An attorney may be an "attorney-in-fact" or "private attorney," or an "attorney-at-law" or "public attorney." The former is one who is given authority by his principal to do a particular act not of a legal character. The latter is employed to appear for the parties to actions, or other judicial proceedings, and is an officer of the courts.[2]

The word "attorney" alone does not necessarily import that the person is an officer of a court;[2] but, standing unqualified, ordinarily it refers to an attorney-at-law.[3]

In this country the distinction between "attorney" or "solicitor" and "counsel" is practically abolished. The lawyer in charge of a case acts both as solicitor and counsel. His services in the one capacity and in the other cannot be distinguished.[4]

In practice when a member of the bar signs a common-law pleading it is as "attorney;" when he signs an equity pleading it is as "solicitor." The distinction arises merely from the two modes of proceeding. He is counsel and attorney of the court in either case.[5] In courts of admiralty his title is "proctor."

February 5, 1790, the Supreme Court "ordered that counsellors shall not practice as attornies nor attornies as counsellors in this court." August 12, 1801, it was "ordered that counsellors may be admitted as attornies" on taking the usual oath.[6]

Compare ADVOCATE; BARRISTER; COUNSEL; LAWYER; PROCTOR; SERGEANT.

In Federal courts a party may manage his cause personally, as prescribed by the rules of court.[7] So, also, in the courts of the States.

The form of oath taken and subscribed by a person applying for admission to practice before the Supreme Court is as follows: "I, ——, do solemnly swear (or affirm) that I will demean myself, as an attorney and counsellor of this court, uprightly and according to law, and that I will support the Constitution of the United States."

The order admitting an attorney to practice is a judgment of the court that a party possesses the requisite qualifications and is entitled to appear and to conduct causes. By virtue of this order he becomes an officer of the court, holding office during good behavior.[1]

He is an agent to conduct a suit to judgment and execution. The utmost good faith is exacted of him toward the court and his client. The authority in the court to remove him is intended to secure the exercise of this degree of fidelity.[2]

He is liable in damages for the want of such skill and care as members of the profession commonly possess and exercise in like matters.[3]

He is not answerable for anything said relative to the cause in hand, although it should reflect upon the reputation of another and even prove groundless; but otherwise if he goes out of the way of legitimate comment and willfully asperses character.[4] See SLANDER.

Without consent he cannot buy, except as trustee, an adverse interest touching the thing to which his employment relates.[5]

He has a lien on papers or on a fund in his hands, as well as a right of action, for the worth of his services.[6]

His fee cannot be included in damages sustained. The reasons are: there is no standard by which fees are measured, some attorneys charging more, and some clients being willing to pay more, than others; more counsel are sometimes employed than are necessary; and, if the rule were otherwise, the amount charged by attorneys and allowed by successful clients would be abused.[7]

He is answerable to the court for any misconduct calculated to bring discredit on the court and reproach upon the administration of justice.[8]

The power in a court to remove an attorney is included in the power to admit him to practice. This power will be exercised where his continuance in

---

[1] Savings Bank v. Ward, 100 U. S. 199 (1879), Clifford, J.

[2] [Hall v. Sawyer, 47 Barb. 119 (1866), Potter, J.

[3] Ingram v. Richardson, 2 La. An. 840 (1847); Clark v. Morse, 16 La. *576 (1841); 6 La. An. 706; People v. May, 3 Mich. 605 (1855).

[4] Re Paschal, 10 Wall. 493 (1870), Bradley, J. See 19 Am. Law Rev. 677 (1885) — as to relation in England; also The Nation, No. 964, p. 508.

[5] Stinson v. Hildrup, 8 Biss. 378 (1878), Drummond, J. See 3 Bl. Com. 25–29.

[6] Rules and Orders of the Supreme Court, 1 Cranch, xv, xvii.

[7] R. S. § 747.

[1] Exp. Garland, 4 Wall. 378 (1866), Field, J.

[2] Rogers v. The Marshal, 1 Wall. 651 (1863), cases; Randall v. Brigham, 7 id. 540 (1868), cases; Re Paschal, 10 id. 491, 496 (1870), cases.

[3] Savings Bank v. Ward, 100 U. S. 198, 195 (1879); Dundee Mortgage Co. v. Hughes, 20 F. R. 39 (1884); 24 Am. Law Reg. 197, 202–7 (1885), cases; Shattuck v. Bill, 142 Mass. 63–64 (1886), cases; 21 Am. Law Rev. 238–57 (1887), cases; 22 Cent. Law J. 60 (1886),— from Law Times (Eng.).

[4] 3 Bl. Com. 29; Munster v. Lamb, 49 L. T. R. 253 (1883); 28 Alb. Law J. 445; Stewart v. Hall, 83 Ky. 380–81, 383 (1885), cases; Weeks, Att'ys, § 110, cases; Cooley, Const. Lim. 443.

[5] Baker v. Humphrey, 101 U. S. 501 (1879), cases, Swayne, J.; Rodgers v. Marshall, 3 McCrary, 76, 82–85 (1881), cases.

[6] Re Paschal, 10 Wall. 483 (1870), cases; McPherson v. Cox, 96 U. S. 417 (1877); 2 Kent, 640. As to his lien for services, see generally 18 Abb. New Cases, 23–40 (1886), cases; as to his general or retaining lien, 20 Am. Law Rev. 727–40 (1886), cases; as to his special lien on judgments, ib. 821–47 (1886), cases; 21 id. 70–88 (1887), cases; acting for married women, 20 Cent. Law J. 365–368 (1885), cases.

[7] Oelrichs v. Spain, 15 Wall. 231 (1873), Swayne, J.

[8] Re Paschal, 10 Wall. 491 (1870), cases.

practice is incompatible with a proper respect of the court for itself, and of regard for the dignity of the profession, and where reprimand, suspension, or fine will not accomplish the end. Generally, opportunity to explain his conduct will be afforded him: the proceedings being *quasi* criminal; but for an act done in the presence of the court no formal allegation is necessary.[1]

It is laid down in all the books that a court has power to exercise summary jurisdiction over its attorneys to compel them to act honestly toward their clients, to punish them by fine and imprisonment for misconduct and contempts, and, in cases of gross misconduct, to strike their names from the roll. If regularly convicted of a felony, an attorney's name will be struck off the roll as of course; because he is rendered infamous. If convicted of a misdemeanor which imports fraud or dishonesty, the same course will be taken; as also for gross malpractice or dishonesty in his profession, or for conduct gravely affecting his character. Although it is not strictly regular not to grant a rule to show cause why he should not be struck off, without an affidavit making charges against him, yet, under the circumstances of a particular case, the want of an affidavit may not render disbarment proceedings void as *coram non judice*. Where an attorney commits an indictable offense, not in his character of attorney, and does not admit the charge, the rule is not inflexible that the court will not strike his name from the roll until he has been regularly indicted and convicted: there may be cases in which it is proper for the court to proceed without such previous conviction,—as where an attorney who had participated in "lynching" a prisoner made an evasive denial of the charge and failed to offer counter testimony to the evidence of his guilt, in itself clear. The proceeding is intended to protect the court from the official ministration of persons unfit to practice as attorneys therein. It is not a criminal proceeding and does not therefore violate the right of trial by jury. The proceeding, furthermore, when instituted in proper cases, is "due process of law." Special proceedings are provided for by statute in some of the States, requiring a formal information under oath to be filed, with regular proceedings and a trial by a jury. In the Federal courts the circumstances of each case must determine whether and when it is proper to dispense with a preliminary conviction.[2]

See further ADMISSION, 2; AGENT; CARE; CHAMPERTY; COMMUNICATION, Privileged, 1; COMPENSATION, 1; COMPROMISE; FEE, 2; CONTEMPT, 1; KNOWLEDGE, 1; MAINTENANCE; PETTIFOGGER; STIPULATION, 2; TRUSTEE; WOMAN.

---

[1] Bradley *v.* Fisher, 13 Wall. 354 (1871); *Re* Paschal, 10 *id.* 491 (1870); Randall *v.* Brigham, 7 *id.* 540 (1868); *Exp.* Garland, 4 *id.* 378 (1866); *Exp.* Steinman, 95 Pa. 220-39 (1880), cases, Sharswood, C. J.

[2] *Exp.* Wall, 107 U. S. 265, 273, 280, 287 (1882), cases, Bradley, J.; s. c. 13 F. R. 814, 820-23, cases. See also People *v.* Appleton, 105 Ill. 474 (1883); Farlin *v.* Sook, 30 Kan. 409 (1883). See generally, Weeks, Attorneys; Forsyth, Hist. Lawyers.

Attorney-general. 1. King's counsel.[1] 2. The head of the department of justice in the government of the United States.

The chief law-officer in the government of each State.

The former has a deputy in each judicial district, known as the "United States district attorney;" and the latter has a deputy in each county, known as the "district" or "county attorney," the attorney for the people, Commonwealth, State, or government. The attorney representing the United States is also often referred to as the attorney or counsel for the government. In the capacity of accusing and trying alleged violators of the criminal law, they are severally spoken of as the "prosecuting attorney"[2] or attorney for the prosecution.

The attorney-general of either government may appear by a special deputy attorney-general; and their subordinates, in districts and counties, by assistant district attorneys.

The attorney-general of the United States is not authorized, by the law creating and defining his office, to give legal opinions at the call of Congress. His duty to render such opinions is limited to calls from the President and the heads of departments,[3] *q. v.*

He manages government suits before the Supreme Court. His opinions are preserved in a series of reports known as the Opinions of the Attorneys-General, which include decisions rendered from 1791 to date.

The attorney-general of a State advises the governor, and exhibits informations in the name of the State.

Attorney, letter of, or power of. The instrument by which the authority of an attorney-in-fact is set forth.

This is *general*, when the authority is to act generally in the premises; and *special*, when limited to a particular act or acts. The former may be, in addition, *limited* or *unlimited*.

A power of attorney which authorizes the agent to vote is called a "proxy," *q. v.*

The authorization may be by parol or under seal: the latter is the method when an act under seal is to be done. The expression "letter" or "power" imports a sealed instrument.

All powers are strictly construed; general terms, in subordination to the particular subject-matter.[4]

The intention of the parties, not the letter, should control. The instrument should be construed to effectuate the object, if it can be ascertained.[5] See SEAL, 1.

---

[1] 3 Bl. Com. 27, 261; 4 *id.* 308; 1 Steph. Hist. Cr. L. Eng. 499.

[2] People *v.* Hallett, 1 Col. 359 (1871).

[3] Duty of Attorney-General, 15 Op. Att.-Gen. 475 (1878), cases; 1 Kent, 306; R. S. § 58.

[4] See Story, Agency, §§ 462, 500; 2 Kent, 643-46; 1 Pars. Contr. 94; 8 Pick. 493.

[5] Commonwealth *v.* Hawkins, 83 Ky. 251 (1885).

Attorney, warrant of. An instrument authorizing an attorney-at-law to appear in an action on behalf of the maker, or to confess a judgment against him.

The universal rule is to permit gentlemen of the bar to appear in causes without first procuring a warrant of attorney to appear.[1]

Frequently authorizes any attorney of a court of record to confess a judgment against the maker, in favor of a person named. It is generally under seal; and it must be for a sum certain. A common use is as a security in the hands of a creditor; it is then in some places popularly called a "judgment-note." May recite an accompanying bond, stating the terms upon which that was given; and be available only upon a breach of the condition in the bond — as, upon a default in paying money, in which event the creditor may procure a judgment at once without the delay of a suit, and, after that, have execution, etc. The form in general use also provides for the payment of costs and an attorney's commission out of the maker's property; releases the right to claim advantage from errors made in the proceedings; and waives stay of execution and exemption of property from levy and sale. The entry of one judgment exhausts the authority; after that the warrant is merged into the judgment — a higher species of security.[2] See COGNOVIT; CONFESSION, 1, Judgment.

AUCTION.[3] A public sale of property to the most favorable bidder.

A sale by consecutive bidding, intended to realize the highest price by competition for the article.[4]

When the law requires a sale of property to be made at public auction after due notice, it is for the purpose of inviting competition among bidders, that the highest price may be obtained.[5]

Auctioneer. A person who conducts an auction.

May refer to one who sells his own goods, as well as one who sells the goods of another, at public auction.[6]

Every person shall be deemed to be an auctioneer whose business it is to offer property at public sale to the highest and best bidder — excepting judicial or executive officers, and executors, administrators, and guardians, acting in their official capacity.[7]

An "auction" sale is a public competitive sale. The person who conducts it is an "auctioneer." It is part of his engagement to invite and excite competition, and to dispose of the property to the highest bidder. The practice originated with the Romans, who gave it the descriptive name of *auctio*, an increase, because the property was sold to him who offered the most for it. Military spoils were thus disposed of, the sales being conducted *sub hasta*, under a spear — stuck in the ground. (A modern popular phrase is "under the hammer.") Later came into use sale "by the candle" — while a candle burned one inch; and still later "Dutch auction" — an offer at a price above its value with a gradual lowering until some person purchased the article. In each method competition has been a necessary element.[1]

There may be a sale to the *lowest* bidder, as when land is sold for non-payment of taxes to any one who will take it for the shortest term.

A price may be set under which no sale will be permitted, provided public notice thereof be given beforehand.

Parties may unite to purchase in good faith.[2]

The conditions of sale should state whether or not the sale is "without reserve" and whether a right to bid is also reserved. A material error in the description of realty makes the sale voidable, *q. v.* A defaulting purchaser may be made to pay a deficiency on a resale, subject to the former conditions.[3] The auctioneer may not bid for himself nor by an agent, even though he offer a fair price: the reason being, the law will not permit a test to be made between interest and duty. Till a sale has been made he acts for the vendor; after the sale, for some purposes, as, to take the case out of the Statute of Frauds, he is agent for the buyer.[4] To exempt a sale of realty from the operation of that statute he must write the buyer's name in the memorandum of sale.[5] He has a special property in goods, and a lien for costs and commissions. If the vendor is undisclosed, he is liable as vendor. He is also liable for the want of due care and skill.[6]

He has all the liabilities of an ordinary agent. If he sells goods "as auctioneer," without naming the principal, he is liable as if selling for himself; and if the title proves defective, independently of the doctrine of implied warranty, he may be sued by the purchaser, as for money had and received, on the ground that the consideration has failed.[7]

See further BID; COMMERCE; CONCERN, For whom; JOBBER; SALE, Public; VENDUE.

---

[1] Osborn *v.* United States Bank, 9 Wheat. 830 (1824).

[2] See 3 Bl. Com. 397.

[3] L. *auctio*, increase: *augere*, to increase.

[4] [Hibler *v.* Hoag, 1 W. & S. 553 (1841); Campbell *v.* Swan, 48 Barb. 118 (1865).

[5] Porter *v.* Graves, 104 U. S. 174 (1881), Miller, J.

[6] City of Goshen *v.* Kern, 63 Ind. 473 (1878), Howk, C. J.

[7] Revenue Act, 13 July, 1866: 14 St. L. 119.

---

[1] Crandall *v.* State, 28 Ohio St. 481–82 (1876), Ashburn, J.

[2] See Smull *v.* Jones, 1 W. & S. 136 (1841); Piatt *v.* Oliver, 1 McLean, 301 (1837); Kearney *v.* Taylor, 15 How. 519 (1853); Smith *v.* Ullman, 58 Md. 189 (1882), cases.

[3] Weast *v.* Derrick, 100 Pa. 509 (1882).

[4] Veazie *v.* Williams, 8 How. 151–56 (1850), cases. As to that statute, see 19 Cent. Law J. 247–49 (1884), cases.

[5] Doty *v.* Wilder, 15 Ill. 410 (1854), cases; 2 Kent, 540; 13 Am. Dec. 398–400, cases.

[6] 3 Pars. Contr. 12.

[7] Seemuller *v.* Fuchs, 64 Md. 217 (1885), cases; Edgerton *v.* Michels, 66 Wis. 129 (1886), cases. Same cases, 24 Am. Law Reg. 250, 260; *ib.* 263–66, cases.

AUDIRE. L. To hear. Compare OYER.

Audi alteram partem. Hear the other side — the accused, the defendant.

No man is to be condemned unheard.[1] See NOTICE, 1, Judicial.

Audita querela. The complaint having been heard.

An *audita querela* lies where a defendant, against whom a judgment is recovered and who is therefore in danger of execution, may be relieved upon good matter of discharge which has happened since the judgment: as if the plaintiff has given him a general release, or if the defendant has paid the debt without procuring satisfaction to be entered on the record. In these and like cases, wherein the defendant has good matter to plead, but has had no opportunity of pleading it, an *audita querela* lies, in the nature of a bill in equity, for relief against the oppression. The writ is directed to the court below; states that the complaint of the defendant has been heard (*audita querela defendentis*); and, after setting out the matter of the complaint, directs the court to call the parties before it, and, having heard their allegations and proofs, to cause justice to be done between them.[2]

The writ was invented lest in any case there should be an oppressive defect of justice, where a party who has a good defense can not make it in the ordinary forms of law. But the indulgence shown in granting summary relief upon motion has rendered the writ almost useless.[2]

It is a judicial writ, founded upon a record, and directed to the court in which that record remains. It has the usual incidents of a regular suit. It is not a means for obtaining relief from negligence. The same end is now very generally secured by a motion.[3] See MOTION, 2.

AUDIT. Literally, he hears; a hearing. See AUDIRE.

1, *v.* To hear: to examine and adjust or certify.

2, *n.* The act or proceeding of officially examining and allowing or certifying, or of rejecting, a charge or account.

Auditor. One who hears: one who officially examines and allows as proper and lawful, or rejects as unlawful, the items of an account or accounts.

An officer of government whose duties are, chiefly, to examine, verify, and approve or reject, the accounts of those who have disbursed public moneys or furnished supplies.[1]

Termed *auditor-general, State auditor, county auditor, first auditor,* etc. Corresponding in duties is the comptroller (*q. v.*) of cities, States, and of the United States treasury.[2]

The office of public auditor belongs to the administrative department of government. Even where he is empowered to act upon his official judgment his functions are only *quasi* judicial.[3]

"To audit" an account is to hear, examine, adjust, pass upon and settle an account, and then to allow it.[4]

"To audit" is to examine and adjust an account or accounts. An "auditor" is a person authorized to examine an account or accounts, compare the charges with the vouchers, examine parties and witnesses, allow or reject charges, and state a balance.[5]

Such is the meaning when it is directed that a board of supervisors shall "audit and allow" the costs and expenses of a hearing to remove a county officer.[5]

In a statute providing that charges for making an examination of an insurance company shall be presented in an itemized bill, which shall be audited by the comptroller, "audit" means hear and examine, pass upon and adjust. In such case also the word plainly refers to a judicial investigation and decision as to the merits of a claim.[6]

An "auditor" is an agent or officer of the court who examines and digests an account for the decision of the court. He prepares the materials on which a decree may be made.[7]

He is an officer, either at law or in equity, assigned to state the items of debt and credit between parties and exhibit the balance.[8]

The term often designates an officer whose duties are properly those of a master.[9]

Originally, an auditor was an officer of the king, whose duty it was, at stated periods, to

---

[1] 1 Cush. 243; 46 N. Y. 119; 41 N. J. E. 659; 16 C. B. 416.

[2] 3 Bl. Com. 405–6.

[3] See Avery *v.* United States, 12 Wall. 307 (1870); 18 Ala. 778; 59 Cal. 139; 24 Me. 304; 20 Md. 320; 10 Mass. 101; 12 *id.* 270; 144 *id.* 13; 9 Johns. 221; 17 *id.* 484; 21 Barb. 435; 34 *id.* 515; 2 Hill, S. C., 298; 12 Vt. 56; 23 *id.* 324; 25 *id.* 168; 42 *id.* 165; 18 Wis. 571; 15 Am. Dec. 695.

---

[1] See R. S § 276.

[2] See R. S. §§ 268–73.

[3] State *v.* Brown, 10 Oreg. 222 (1882).

[4] Morris *v.* People, 3 Denio, 391 (1846); 68 Ga. 53.

[5] People *ex rel.* Benedict *v.* Supervisors, 31 N. Y. Supr. 419 (1881), Talcott, P. J.; Laws of 1874, ch. 323.

[6] Matter of Murphy, 31 N. Y. Supr. 594 (1881), Learned, P. J.

[7] Field *v.* Holland, 6 Cranch, 21 (1810), Marshall, C. J.

[8] Whitwell *v.* Willard, 1 Metc. 218 (1840), Shaw, C. J.

[9] Blain *v.* Patterson, 48 N. H. 152 (1868), Bellows, J.

examine the accounts of inferior officers and certify to their correctness. Later, the term designated an officer of the court of exchequer whose duty it was to take the accounts of the receivers of the king's revenue and "audit and perfect" them, without, however, putting in any charges; his office being merely to audit the accounts, that is, to ascertain their correctness. . . "To audit" is to examine, settle and adjust accounts — to verify the accuracy of the statements or items submitted.[1]

Where the items are numerous, the testimony questionable, and the accounts complicated, a court may make a general reference, with direction to state specifically such matters as either party may require or as the auditor may deem necessary.[2] See at end of Account, 1.

Auditors are called in by the courts to hear matters of detail which a court has not time to hear, and to inform the conscience of the court as to facts which are essential to be known before a particular decree or judgment can be pronounced.[3]

They are appointed to audit the accounts of assignees in insolvency, of trustees to sell realty, of executors, of administrators, of guardians, — when excepted to, or where distribution is to be made of a balance among rival claimants; also, to report upon the expediency of selling or mortgaging the realty of decedents; as to incumbrances affecting the interests of partitioners; sometimes, to report the facts, where a petition has been taken *pro confesso* but an account showing a balance against the respondent is essential; to examine the accounts of public officers; also, as to the satisfaction of judgments, as to the distribution of the proceeds of forfeited recognizances, of the proceeds of sales, etc. Or, a court may itself sit as a "court of audit," as, an orphans' or surrogate's court, in which at regular intervals large numbers of accounts are presented for approval.

Where the claimants to a fund are numerous the auditor is required to give public notice of the time and place of holding hearings. His specific duties may be defined in the order of his appointment; but statutes provide for his issuing subpœnas, for administering oaths and affirmations, and for procuring the attachment of contumacious witnesses. He reports the facts, not the testimony, and a schedule by which the fund may be distributed according to law. His rulings and recommendations are reviewable by the court upon exception filed by any aggrieved party. He is called upon to admit or reject items of costs, wages, rents, commissions, secured and unsecured claims, etc. In every case the statutes, decisions, rules and practice of the particular jurisdiction should be consulted. Compare Master, 4.

AUDITA. See Audire, Audita, etc.

AULA. L. A hall, or palace.

Aula regia or **regis.** The royal hall, or the king's hall.

A court established by the Conqueror, to advise the king in matters of great moment. It was composed of the king's great officers resident in his palace: the lords high constable, steward, treasurer, the lord chancellor, and others. These were assisted by persons learned in the laws — the king's justiciars or justices, and by the greater barons of parliament. Over all whom presided the chief justiciar.

Here will be noted the change in the meaning of the word "court" from royal household to tribunal of justice.

The court followed the king's household in all his expeditions. That being burdensome to litigants it was ordained by Magna Charta that the court should be held in some certain place — Westminster Hall.

In the reign of Edward I the court was subdivided into four distinct tribunals: chancery, king's bench, exchequer, and common pleas — the last being in a special sense the successor of the original *aula regis.*[1] See Chancellor, 1.

AUNT. See Ancestor; Consanguinity.

AUTER. See Autre.

AUTHENTIC.[2] In legal parlance, duly vested with all formalities and legally attested.[3]

Authentication. Official, legal attestation to a thing done: as, of a copy made of an act of legislation, or of the record in a court or other public office.

There does not appear to be any necessary or inherent meaning in the word "authenticated" as used in the act of June 19, 1876, amending Rev. St., § 5271, which relates to extraditions and requires the authentication to be in writing. Authentication in regard to original papers may be made by oral proof. A witness may swear to the verity and identity of the original, and that it would be received in the tribunals of the foreign country as evidence of the criminality of the accused. But when *copies* are offered they must be authenticated according to the law of the foreign country — for which the certificate of the principal officer of the United States is absolute proof.[4] See Faith, Full, etc.; Law, Foreign.

AUTHOR.[5] Within the meaning of the copyright law one who, by his own intellectual labor applied to the materials of his com-

[1] People v. Green, 5 Daly, 200 (1874), Daly, C. J. See 4 Coke, Inst. 107.

[2] Field v. Holland, *supra.*

[3] Miller's Appeal, 30 Pa. 490 (1858), Woodward, J.

[1] 3 Bl. Com. 37–40; 3 Steph. Com. 397–400.

[2] L. *authenticus*, written with one's own hand; original.

[3] [Downing v. Brown, 3 Col. 590 (1877): Webster.

[4] *Re* Fowler, 18 Blatch. 436 (1880), Blatchford, J.; s. c. 4 F. R. 311. See 1 Greenl. Ev. § 484; 1 Whart. Ev. § 700.

[5] L. *auctor*, an originator: *augere*, to increase.

position, produces an arrangement or compilation new in itself.[1]

See generally COPYRIGHT; HISTORY; LETTER, 3; LITERARY; MANUSCRIPT; PHOTOGRAPH; REVIEW, 3; SCIENCE.

AUTHORITY. 1. Power — delegated to an agent or exercised by virtue of an office, trust, or privilege.

Executive authority. Power vested in the President of the United States, or in the governor of a State; also, either of those officials himself considered in his political capacity, as opposed to the judicial and legislative branches of government.[2] **Judicial authority.** Official power in a court or judge. **Legislative authority.** Power conferred upon a legislative body.

Express authority. Power stated in terms more or less explicit. **Implied authority.** Such authority as is or is to be inferred from circumstances.

General authority. Power extending to all acts of a certain nature. **Special authority.** Authority confined to a single act or transaction.

Limited authority. Power restricted by instructions more or less precise. **Unlimited authority.** Authority not defined by words or instructions.

Naked authority. Power exercised by an agent solely for the benefit of the principal. **Authority coupled with an interest.** Power given for value to the agent, or as part of a security.

See further AGENT; DELEGATUS; INTEREST, 2; Coupled, etc.; PARTNER; also, APPARENT; CORPORATE; LAWFUL; POWER, 1; RATIFICATION.

2. The binding force of a constitution, treaty, statute, or ordinance.

Constituted authorities. Officers of government appointed under a constitution. **Constituting authorities.** The persons who appoint the former as their servants or agents.

3. Whatever is relied upon as declaring the law: (1) a constitution, treaty, statute, adjudication; (2) a text-book or treatise explanatory of organic, statute, or case law. Compare OPINION, 3; PRECEDENT.

AUTHORIZE. To confer power upon; to invest with lawful authority, *q. v.*

---

[1] [Atwill *v.* Ferrett, 2 Blatch. 46 (1846), Betts, J. See also 2 Kent, 373-74, 383; R. S. § 4952, cases.

[2] See Commonwealth *v.* Hall, 9 Gray, 267-68 (1857), Bigelow, C. J.

(7)

A government contract to be "authorized by law" must be made in pursuance of express authority given by statute or of authority necessarily inferable from some duty imposed upon, or from some power given to, the person assuming the contract.[1]

AUTRE. F. Another. Also spelled *auter.*

Autre action pendant. Another action pending. See PEND.

Autre droit. Another's right. See further DROIT.

Autre vie. Another's life. See VIE.

AUTREFOIS. F. Another time; formerly.

Autrefois acquit. Formerly acquitted.

Autrefois convict. Formerly convicted.

Pleas in bar of a second indictment for an offense of which the accused has already been acquitted or convicted. See further ACQUITTAL; CONVICTION, Former.

AUXILIARY. See ANCILLARY; EQUITY.

AVAIL.[2] To be of use or advantage; to answer the purpose; to have strength, force, or efficacy sufficient to the end:[3] as, in saying that a defense, a plea, or evidence will or will not avail the party.

Available. Suitable to the purpose: as, an available defense or plea; also, admitting of early conversion into ready money.

"Available means" are anything which can readily be converted into money; all that class of securities known in the mercantile world as representatives of value easily convertible into money; not necessarily, nor primarily, money itself.[4]

Avails. Profits, proceeds, funds.[5]

AVER. See AVERMENT.

AVERAGE.[6] Proportional payment: contribution to a loss or expense incurred at sea for the general benefit of several persons or several interests.

In its simple generic sense a loss, injury, or deduction not amounting to a total loss.[7]

General or gross average. That contribution to a loss or expense voluntarily incurred for the preservation of the whole, in

---

[1] Fifteen Per Cent. Contracts, 15 Op. A.-G. 236 (1877).

[2] F. *avaloir*, to be of use: L. *valere*, to be strong.

[3] [Webster's Dict.

[4] Brigham *v.* Tillinghast, 13 N. Y. 218-19 (1855).

[5] See 100 Mass. 233; 12 F. R. 371; 2 Bl. Com. 60.

[6] L. *averagium: averia*, cattle. Service a tenant owes his lord by horse, ox, or carriage therewith,— Blount's Law Dict. (1691). It meant use of horses, carriage, payment for carriage; hence, payment proportional — to horses employed, goods lost at sea, etc.,— Skeat.

[7] [Bargett *v.* Orient Ins. Co., 3 Bosw. 395 (1858).

which all who are concerned in the ship, freight, and cargo are to bear an equal part proportionable to their respective interests.[1]

Particular average. The damage or loss, short of total, falling directly upon particular articles of property.[1]

The liability or claim upon such articles from loss or damage to something else is "general" average.[2]

The rule as to general average is derived from the Rhodian law as adopted in the Roman jurisprudence. The Digest states the rule thus: If goods are thrown overboard to lighten a ship, the loss incurred for the sake of all shall be made good by the contribution of all. The case of jettison was used to illustrate the general principle. Now, as then, ship and cargo must have been placed in a common imminent peril; there must have been a voluntary sacrifice of property to avert that peril; and, by the sacrifice, the safety of the other property must have been successfully attained.[3]

The principle is that "what is given for the general benefit of all shall be made good by the contribution of all." General average is that contribution which is made by all who are parties to the same adventure toward a loss arising out of extraordinary sacrifices made, or extraordinary expenses incurred, by some of them for the common benefit of ship and cargo. The loss must be of an extraordinary nature, advisedly incurred, under circumstances of imminent danger, for the common benefit of ship and cargo; and it must have aided in the accomplishment of that purpose.[4]

Where the interests are temporarily separated, as by unloading the cargo to repair the vessel, and the expectation of resuming the voyage, from unforeseen circumstances, is not realized, as, for example, inability to make the vessel seaworthy, all the expense of protecting the different interests meanwhile is chargeable to general average.[5]

Passengers' baggage in daily use does not contribute to general average.[6]

AVERMENT.[7] A positive statement of the truth of a fact; a formal allegation in pleading.

Aver. To assert for the truth; to state in positive terms; to allege formally.

Averments are spoken of as "affirmative" and "negative," as "general" and "particular" or "specific," as "material" and "immaterial," as "unnecessary," "impertinent," etc., with substantially the same meaning as are "allegations." See ALLEGATION.

An averment in a declaration is a direct and positive allegation of fact, made in a manner capable of being traversed. It includes the idea of an affirmation to be made out by inference and induction.[1]

"The use in pleading of an averment is to ascertain that to the court which is generally or doubtfully expressed; so that the court may not be perplexed of whom, or of what, it ought to be understood; and to add matter to the plea to make doubtful things clear"—as, an averment in an action of slander.[2]

There is no particular form of words in use. The important matter is that each substantial fact be so averred as to be susceptible of a simple admission or denial. See VERIFY.

AVOCATION. See BUSINESS; EMPLOYMENT; TRADE.

AVOID.[3] 1. To cause to be or become empty: to render useless or void; to make inoperative or of no effect; to nullify. Opposed, *affirm, confirm.*

Avoidance. Setting aside; nullifying; rendering of no effect.[4] Compare VOID.

Some authorities assert that an infant's deed cannot be avoided except by an act equally solemn with the deed itself; some that it cannot be done by anything short of an entry; others that it may be done simply by another deed delivered to a different grantee. All agree, however, that acts which would be insufficient to avoid such a deed may amount to an affirmance,[5] *q. v.*

2. In pleading, to repel the consequence or inference which would logically follow a failure to deny the truth of an averment. More fully, to "confess and avoid."

Matter of avoidance. New matter which admits the declaration to be true, but shows, either that the defendant was never liable to the recovery claimed against him or that he has never been discharged from his original liability by something supervenient.[6] See further CONFESSION, 1.

AVOIRDUPOIS. See TON.

AVOW.[7] 1. To declare openly: to acknowledge and justify an act; opposed to *disavow.*

2. To make an avowry.

Avowant. He who makes an avowry.

Avowry. Upon an action of replevin being brought and a declaration delivered, the

[1] Padelford v. Boardman, 4 Mass. 549 (1808).

[2] Bargett v. Orient Ins. Co., *ante.*

[3] Columbian Ins. Co. v. Ashby, 13 Pet. 337-38 (1839), Story, J.

[4] McAndrews v. Thatcher, 3 Wall. 370, 376 (1865), Clifford, J. See also 3 Kent, 235.

[5] The Joseph Farwell, 31 F. R. 844 (1887), Toulmin, J.

[6] Heye v. North German Lloyd, 33 F. R. 65 (1887), cases, Brown, J.

[7] F. *averer,* to affirm as true: L. *ad,* to; *verum,* truth.

[1] Laughlin v. Flood, 3 Munf. 262 (1811).

[2] Van Vechten v. Hopkins, 5 Johns. 219 (1809).

[3] M. Eng. *avoiden,* to make empty, put out of the way.

[4] See 2 Bl. Com. 308.

[5] Irvine v. Irvine, 9 Wall. 627-28 (1869), Strong, J.

[6] Gould, Plead. 34, 13; 31 Conn. 177.

[7] L. *ad-vovere,* to vow to: *ad-vocare.*

distrainor, as defendant, makes "avowry," that *is*, he avows taking the distress in his own right or in the right of his wife, and sets forth the reason for it, as for rent-arrear, damage done, or other cause.[1]

If he justifies in another's right as his bailiff or servant, he is said to make "cognizance."[1] See Cognizance, 1.

AVULSION.[2] Alluvion or dereliction of land which is sudden and considerable.

As, where the course of a river is changed by a violent flood and thereby a man loses his ground; in which case he has, as his recompense, what the river has left in another place.[3] See further Alluvion.

AWARD.[4] 1, *v.* (1) To allow by judicial determination: as, for a court to award a writ of *habeas corpus* or other process.

(2) To adjudge as due; to allow; to find: as, for a jury or viewers to award damages, for arbitrators to award a claim.

2, *n.* The decision of a board of arbitrators; the finding of a referee; also, the writing which embodies such determination.

An award is the judgment of the arbitrator upon the matters submitted.[5]

No award. A plea to an action on an arbitration bond, that no legal award was made.

A valid award is equivalent to a judgment on a verdict. Feudal law did not permit a right in realty to pass by a mere award — lest an alienation should be made collusively without the consent of the superior. . . A party who disobeys an award is punishable as for contempt of court, unless the award be set aside for corruption or other misbehavior in the arbitrators.[6]

An award is an act of the parties performed through their agents, and assented to in advance.[7]

It can be impeached only for corruption, partiality, or gross misbehavior in the arbitrators, or for some palpable mistake as to the law or the facts. If so uncertain that it cannot be enforced, it is void.[8]

At common law it must be not only certain but final, disposing wholly of the controversy which properly forms the subject of the reference; otherwise it cannot be enforced.[9]

---

[1] 3 Bl. Com. 150; 21 N. J. L. 49.

[2] L. *avulsio: avellere*, to tear away.

[3] 2 Bl. Com. 262; 3 Washb. R. P. 452.

[4] Mid. Eng. *awarden:* F. *eswardier*, to examine, judge: *warder*, to take heed, keep. A thing for the parties to observe, — Skeat; Spel. Gloss.

[5] Halnon *v.* Halnon, 55 Vt. 322 (1883), Royce, C. J.

[6] 3 Bl. Com. 16–18.

[7] Babb *v.* Stromberg, 14 Pa. 399 (1850), Gibson, C. J.

[8] Herrick *v.* Blair, 1 Johns. Ch. 101 (1814), Kent, J.; 2 *id.* 551; Fairchild *v.* Adams, 11 Cush. 550 (1853); Perkins *v.* Giles, 53 Barb. 346 (1869); Russell *v.* Smith, 87 Ind. 466, 468 (1882).

[9] Connor *v.* Simpson, 104 Pa. 443 (1883); Morse, Arb., &c. 486.

Before a court of review every presumption will be made in favor of the validity of an award, unless flagrant error appears upon the face of the record itself.[1]

See further Abide; Arbitration.

AWAY. See Absent; Carry, 1.

Away-going. See Crop.

B.

B. Referring to a page or note, see A, 1.

In colonial times was imprinted with indelible ink upon the cheek of a person convicted of burglary.[2]

As an abbreviation, usually denotes bachelor, bail, bankruptcy, baron, bench, bill, bond, book:

B. B. Bail bond. See C. C. *et* B. B.

B. C. Bail court; bankruptcy cases.

B. E. Baron of the court of exchequer. See Baron, 3.

B. F. *Bonum factum*, a proper thing.

Formerly was indorsed upon the paper containing a decree, signifying that it was "approved."

B. R. *Bancus regis*, king's bench; bankruptcy reports; Bill of Rights.

B. S. *Bancus superior*, upper bench.

BABY ACT. A term of reproach originally applied to the disability of infancy when pleaded by an adult in bar of recovery upon a contract made while he was under age, but extended to any plea of the statute of limitations.

BACHELOR OF LAWS. See Degree.

BACK. To indorse, sign: as, to back a process or writ.

The warrant of a justice of the peace in one county must be backed, that is, signed, by a justice in another county, before it can be executed there. This practice prevailed for a long period prior to authorization by statute.[3]

Under extradition treaties, an officer of government, usually the secretary of state, may indorse or back a warrant of arrest.

BACK-GAMMON. See Game, 2,

BACK-WATER. See Mill, 1; Take, 8.

BAD. 1. When applied to "character," the jury must say whether want of chastity or of honesty was imputed.[4]

The charge of incontinency involved in the words "she is a bad, a loose, character," may be sufficiently averred by an *innuendo* without a *colloquium*. Such words of themselves impute incontinency. Whether

---

[1] Wilcox *v.* Payne, 88 Pa. 157 (1878).

[2] Jones *v.* Robbins, 8 Gray, 348 (1857), Shaw, C. J.

[3] 4 Bl. Com. 291.

[4] Riddell *v.* Thayer, 127 Mass. 490 (1879); Kedrolivansky *v.* Niebaum, 70 Cal. 218–19 (1886), cases.

or not the charge is true the jury must decide.[1] See CHARACTER; SLANDER.

2. In pleading — materially defective; ill; not good: as, a bad plea, bad pleading, a bad count. Compare ILL, 2; WELL, 2.

When evidence has not been given on a bad count, a general verdict will be entered on such of the good counts as are supported by proof.[2] See USUS, Utile per inutile, etc.

3. False, faulty: as, bad grammar, q. v.

Bad faith. See FAITH. Compare MALUS.

BADGE. 1. A mark or device worn by an officer of the peace for purposes of identification and perhaps of notification.

On demand, is ordinarily to be shown as evidence of authority to make an arrest.

2. Evidence of character.

A badge of fraud is a fact tending to throw suspicion upon a transaction, and calling for explanation;[3] as, possession of personalty by the alleged vendor.[4] See POSSESSION, Fraudulent.

"The provisions in the deed of assignment are at most but badges of fraud, susceptible of explanation, like all *indicia*, and may or may not be evidence of fraudulent intent."[5]

BADGER. To pester or worry; as, to badger a witness.[6] Compare BROWBEAT.

Originally, to follow up or pursue with eagerness, as the badger is hunted. See EXAMINATION, 9.

BAG. The sack, satchel, reticule or other like receptacle in which lawyers carry briefs and papers for use during the preparation, trial, hearing, or argument of cases, was formerly called, from the prevailing color of the material, the "green bag."

In the theatrical performances of Queen Caroline's time the lawyer is represented with a *green bag* in his hand; and such is the reference in the literature of Queen Anne's time; and, until a recent date, green bags were commonly carried by the majority of legal practitioners. The king's counselors, queen's counselors, the chancery lawyers, and the leaders of the common bar, were honored with the privilege of carrying red, purple, or blue bags. Indeed, the green bag was so uniformly associated with the profession in the reign of Anne that " to say that a man intended to carry a green bag was the same as saying that he meant to adopt the law as a profession."[7]

In the time of Charles II angry clients were accustomed to revile lawyers as "green-bag carriers."[8]

As to petty bag office, see HANAPER; PETIT.

---

[1] Vanderlip v. Roe, 23 Pa. 84 (1854).

[2] Haldeman v. Martin, 10 Pa. 372 (1849); Chaffey v. United States, 116 U. S. 442 (1886); *ib*. 427.

[3] Bump, Fraud. Convey. 31.

[4] 101 U. S. 229; 1 Pars. Contr. 529.

[5] Burr v. Clement, 9 Col. 11 (1885).

[6] [Webster's Dict.

[7] 5 Alb. Law J. 225 (1872).

[8] Wycherly, Plain Dealer.

BAGATELLE. See GAME, 2.

BAGGAGE. 1. Whatever a passenger takes with him for his personal use or convenience, according to the habits or wants of the particular class to which he belongs, either with reference to the immediate necessities or to the ultimate purpose of the journey.[1]

A contract to carry a person implies an undertaking to transport such a limited quantity of articles as are ordinarily taken by travelers for their personal use and convenience, the quantity depending upon the station of the party, the object and length of the journey, and other circumstances.[2]

To the extent that the articles carried by a passenger for his personal use exceed in quantity and value such as are usually carried by passengers of like station, pursuing like journeys, they are not baggage for which the carrier, by general law, is responsible as insurer. In cases of abuse by the passenger of the privilege which the law gives him, the carrier secures such exemption from responsibility, not, however, because the passenger, uninquired of, failed to disclose the character and value of the articles carried, but because the articles themselves, in excess of the amount usually or ordinarily carried, under like circumstances, would not constitute baggage within the meaning of the law.

In the case (Fraloff's, *infra*) in which the doctrine foregoing was enunciated, 275 yards of laces, alleged to be of the value of $75,000, and found by a jury to be worth $10,000, were held to constitute part of the wearing apparel of the defendant in error — a wealthy Russian. They were adapted to and exclusively designed for personal use, according to her convenience, comfort, or tastes, during an extended journey, upon which she had entered. They were not merchandise, and there was no evidence that they were intended for sale or for purposes of business. It was further decided that whether the laces were such articles in quantity or value as passengers of like station and under like circumstances ordinarily carry for their personal use, and to subserve their convenience, gratification, or comfort while traveling, was not a question for the jury, under instruction from the court, but for the court itself as a matter of law.[3]

The liability of the carrier attaches when the property, as baggage, passes into his hands with his con-

---

[1] Macrow v. Great Western Ry. Co., L. R., 6 Q. B. *622 (1871), Cockburn, C. J. See also Jordan v. Railway Co., 5 Cush. 72 (1849); Connolly v. Warren, 106 Mass. 148 (1870); 6 Hill, 586.

[2] Hannibal, &c. R. Co. v. Swift, 12 Wall. 274, 273 (1870), Field, J.

[3] N. Y. Central, &c. R. Co. v. Fraloff, 100 U. S. 29-30 (1879), Harlan, J.; Waite, C. J., Clifford, Hunt, Swayne, and Bradley, JJ., concurring; Field, Miller, and Strong, JJ., dissenting. See also Haines v. Chicago, &c. R. Co., 29 Minn. 161 (1882); Isaacson v. N. Y. Central, &c. R. Co., 94 N. Y. 283 (1884).

sent. He may refuse to receive property not properly baggage, but if he receives it knowingly, and no deception has been practiced upon him, he must carry it safely.[1]

The fare paid by a passenger includes the transportation of his baggage. The carrier has a lien therefor, and may detain the baggage until payment is made.[2]

The term has been held to include — a watch,[3] jewelry,[4] an opera glass,[5] surgical instruments,[6] a gun, a pistol,[7] a mechanic's tools,[8] manuscript,[9] books;[10] but not, samples of merchandise,[11] except when the carrier, being made aware of the contents of packages, takes them as baggage;[12] nor gold ornaments for presents;[13] nor money, except as to such limited amount as may be necessary for personal use.[14]

The possession of a baggage check by a passenger is evidence of the receipt of his baggage.[15]

Baggage is to be removed within a reasonable time after arrival, else the carrier may store the articles, charge reasonable rates for such service, and, in case of theft, loss, or destruction, be liable only as a warehouseman,[16] q. v. See also CARRIER.

2. As to the baggage of guests in hotels, see INNKEEPER.

BAIL.[17] 1, v. To deliver personalty to another as a bailment, q. v.

2, v. To deliver a defendant to sureties who give security for his appearance in court at the return of the writ.[18]

n. One or more of such sureties themselves.

A delivery or bailment of a person to his sureties, upon their giving (together with himself as principal) sufficient security for his appearance; he being supposed to continue in their friendly custody, instead of going to jail.[1]

The sureties undertake to surrender the defendant when he is called upon to answer the charge.[2]

Bailable. Admitting of bail; allowing or providing for release upon bail: as, a bailable — offense, action, process.

Bail-bond. The obligation entered into by the surety.

Takes the place of the body of the defendant, and is forfeited by his non-appearance according to the stipulation. It is not receivable under final process. The sheriff, constable, or marshal, as the case may be, is the obligee; in which respect the obligation differs from a recognizance, q. v. The plaintiff sues on the instrument as assignee of the officer to whom it was originally given, and, perhaps, by a writ of *scire facias*.[3] See C. C. ET B. B.

Bail-piece. A certificate from the record in a case that one or more persons named became bail in a certain sum of money.

Not in the nature of process; merely a record or memorial of the delivery of the principal to his bail, on security given.[4]

Originally written on a small *piece* of parchment.[5]

A surety may use this certificate as a warrant of arrest, and, by virtue thereof, deliver the principal over to an officer for confinement. See ONUS, Exoneretur.

Following are the common species of bail:

Bail above, or bail to the action. Sureties who jointly and severally undertake that if their principal, the defendant in an action, is "condemned," he will either pay the judgment or give himself up for imprisonment, or else that they will satisfy the judgment. **Bail below, or appearance bail.** Sureties who stipulate that a defendant will appear in court on the day named in the writ.[6]

Bail absolute. A person or persons who obligate themselves, usually to the State or Commonwealth, to pay a specified sum of money, in the event of another person (the principal) failing to account, in due form of law, for money entrusted to him as administrator, guardian, assignee, or other trustee.

Common or **straw bail.** One or more fictitious sureties whose names are entered as bail for matter of form, and who stipulate

[1] Hannibal, &c. R. Co. v. Swift, *ante;* Strouse v. Wabash, &c. R. Co., 17 F. R. 209 (1883). Left with railway porter, Bunch v. Great Western Ry. Co., L. R. 17 Q. B. D. 215 (1886): 2 Law Quart. Rev. 469-79 (1886), cases. See generally 18 Cent. Law J. 421-24 (1884), cases.

[2] Roberts v. Koehler, 30 F. R. 96 (1887), cases. Cases contra, 26 Am. Law Reg. 296-98 (1887).

[3] Jones v. Voorhees, 10 Ohio, 145 (1840); Clark v. Burns, 118 Mass. 277 (1875), cases.

[4] McGill v. Rowan, 3 Pa. 453 (1846).

[5] Toledo, &c. R. Co. v. Hammond, 33 Ind. 379 (1870).

[6] Hannibal, &c. R. Co. v. Swift, 12 Wall. 270 (1870).

[7] Chicago, &c. R. Co. v. Collins, 56 Ill. 217 (1870).

[8] Porter v. Hildebrand, 13 Pa. 133 (1850).

[9] Hopkins v. Westcott, 6 Blatch. 69 (1868).

[10] Doyle v. Kiser, 6 Ind. 242 (1855).

[11] Stimson v. Conn. Riv. R. Co., 98 Mass. 84 (1867), cases.

[12] Hoeger v. Chicago, &c. R. Co., 63 Wis. 100 (1885).

[13] The Ionic, 5 Blatch. 538 (1867); 4 Bosw. 225.

[14] Pfister v. Central Pacific R. Co., 70 Cal. 173 (1886); 31 Conn. 281; 25 Ga. 61; 22 Ill. 278; 33 id. 219; 56 id. 293; 5 Cush. 69; 98 Mass. 375; 41 Miss. 671; 44 N. H. 325; 9 Wend. 85; 25 id. 459; 6 Hill, 586; 30 N. Y. 594; 16 Pa. 67.

[15] 6 Col. 337; Redf. Car. 71, 73.

[16] See generally McCaffrey v. Canadian Pacific R. Co., 24 Am. Law Reg. 175-90 (1885), cases.

[17] F. *bailler*, to deliver, free from.

[18] [3 Bl. Com. 290.

[1] 4 Bl. Com. 297; 20 N. H. 161.

[2] Ramey v. Commonwealth, 83 Ky. 535 (1886).

[3] See 3 Bl. Com. 290.

[4] Nicolls v. Ingersoll, 7 Johns. *154 (1810).

[5] 3 Bl. Com. 291.

[6] [3 Bl. Com. 291.

that a defendant will appear. **Special bail.** Real, substantial bondsmen.

"Common" or "straw" bail are universal sureties — John Doe and Richard Roe, or other imaginary persons returned by the sheriff — standing pledges, for the purpose intended. They originally answered for the plaintiff in case he was amerced (*q. v.*) for making a false accusation.[1] See further DOE; STRAW.

"Special" bail may be required, by order of court in such cases as are particularly grievous, or when it is necessary that a defendant should be kept within the jurisdiction. Originally introduced to mitigate the hardships incident to imprisonment.[2]

"All persons shall be Bailable by sufficient Sureties, unless for Capital Offenses, where the proof is evident or the presumption great." This provision, quoted from the Great Law[3] of the Province of Pennsylvania, enacted in 1682, is also found in the constitutions of all the States. See EVIDENT.

Bail is taken by committing magistrates, by judges and commissioners of the courts, by clerks of some courts, and by other persons, as provided by statutes; but not, generally speaking, by justices of the peace on charges of homicide and certain other of the more heinous felonies, nor in charges of contempt of a court or of contempt of a legislature by a member thereof.[4]

"Excessive bail shall not be required."[5] What is "excessive" is for the court alone to determine. See EXCESSIVE.

Bail is not required of a municipal corporation; nor, as a rule, of persons in a fiduciary relation, sued as such.

A surety must generally be a freeholder to some amount, subject to process, and able to make a contract and to pay the amount of the bond. Ordinarily, common bail suffices from a defendant who is a freeholder. A non-resident plaintiff may have to furnish bail for the probable costs in his action.

The principal is regarded as delivered to his sureties as jailers of his own choosing. Their dominion is a continuance of the original imprisonment. Whenever they choose they may seize and deliver him up, in their own discharge; and, until this can be effected, they may imprison him. In this action they may be represented by an agent. They may pursue him into another State; they may arrest him on the Sabbath; and, if necessary, they may break and enter his house to arrest him. Being like a re-arrest by a sheriff of an escaping prisoner, they need no process. Their rights are alike in civil and criminal cases.

With the sureties there is an implied engagement by the principal that he will not leave the jurisdiction; and by the plaintiff, that he will do nothing to increase their risk or to affect their remedy.[6] See JUMP.

See also BIND; COMMISSIONER; DEPOSIT, In lieu, etc.; FIDEJUSSOR; JUSTIFICATION, 2; MAINPERNOR; PENALTY; PERFECT; SURETY.

---

[1] [3 Bl. Com. 274, 287, 290, 291, 295.]

[2] See 3 Bl. Com. 292, 287.

[3] Chapter LII: Linn, 120. See Wash. Law Rev., Oct. 25, Nov. 1, 15, 1882.

[4] See generally 20 Cent. Law J. 464–66 (1885), cases.

[5] Constitution, Amd. Art. VIII. 4 Bl. Com. 296–99.

[6] See Taylor *v.* Taintor, 16 Wall. 371 (1872), Swayne, J.;

BAILEE. See BAILMENT.

BAILIFF.[1] Originally, one put in charge of something.

An officer concerned in the administration of justice in a certain province.[2]

1. A servant, in a superior, ministerial capacity.[3]

A private person who has the custody and care of another's property.

He is liable to an action of account-render.[4]

2. An attendant who preserves order in and about the room where court is being held; a tipstaff, *q. v.*

3. A sheriff's officer or deputy.

Also called a bound or special bailiff.

The due execution of his duties is secured by an obligation with sureties.[5]

BAILIWICK.[6] A word, introduced by the Normans, and equivalent to "county." The liberty, province, or jurisdiction of a sheriff.[7] Compare PRECINCT.

BAILMENT.[8] A delivery of goods in trust, upon a contract, expressed or implied, that the trust shall be faithfully executed on the part of the bailee.[9]

A delivery of goods in trust upon a contract, expressed or implied, that the trust shall be duly executed, and the goods restored by the bailee as soon as the purpose of the bailment shall be answered.[10]

A delivery of a thing in trust for some special object or purpose, and upon a contract, expressed or implied, to conform to the object or purpose of the trust.[11]

When the identical thing delivered, though in an altered form, is to be restored, the contract is a "bailment," and the title to the property is not changed. But when there is no obligation to restore the specific article, and the receiver is at liberty to return another

---

Reese *v.* United States, 9 *id.* 21 (1869), Field, J.; 3 Bl. Com. 290–92. As to rights of sureties generally, see 1 Kans. Law J. 211–14 (1885), cases.

[1] The *-iff* is from the A. S. *reeve*, officer, steward,— 1 Bl. Com. 116. O. F. *bailler*, to keep in custody,— Skeat. See BAIL, 2; REEVE.

[2] Coke, Litt. 168 *b.*

[3] 1 Bl. Com. 427.

[4] See Coke, Litt. 172 *a;* 4 Watts, 422; 22 Ga. 161; 44 Barb. 453; 1 Story, Eq. § 446.

[5] 1 Bl. Com. 345.

[6] F. *baillie*, government; *bailler*, to have custody of; A. S. *wic*, dwelling, station, jurisdiction.

[7] 1 Bl. Com. 344; 2 *id.* 37.

[8] F. *bailler*, to deliver.

[9] 2 Bl. Com. 451, 395.

[10] 2 Kent, 559.

[11] Story, Bailm. § 2; Watson *v.* State, 70 Ala. 14 (1881).

thing of equal value, the title to the property being changed, the contract is a "sale,"[1] q. v.

Bail, v. To deliver a thing to a person upon his engaging to do something to or with it, and then either to return or to account for it.

Bailee. He who thus receives a thing bailed. **Bailor.** He who thus delivers a thing as bailed.

The purpose of the law of bailments is to ascertain, whenever the loss of or injury to a thing occurs, to what degree of care the bailee was bound and of what degree of negligence he has been guilty.[2]

Three kinds of bailments are recognized: That in which the trust is for the benefit — of the bailor, of the bailee, or of both bailor and bailee. In cases of the first kind, at least slight care is required; in cases of the second kind, great care; in cases of the third kind, ordinary care. The absence of the required degree of care constitutes negligence, for which the bailee is responsible.[3]

Sir William Jones, following the civil law, proposed, in 1790, this division: *Depositum*, gratuitous custody; deposit, q. v. *Mandatum*, gratuitous feasance; mandate, q. v. *Accommodatum* (q. v.), or *commodatum*, loan for use without pay; accommodation. *Pignus*, pledge, q. v. *Locatio*, or *locatum*, hiring,[4] q. v. See also LOAN, 1.

Each party has a qualified property (q. v.) in the subject of the bailment and may maintain an action with respect to it.[6]

Presumably, the bailor is entitled to the thing. The bailee is to do what the principal directed — restore the article or account to him for it. He "accounts" when he yields to the paramount right of immediate possession in a third person who is found to be the true owner.[6]

See also CARE; CARRIER; INNKEEPER; LARCENY; RES, Perit, etc.

BAIT. 1. To feed: to allure a dumb animal, by scented food, from the premises of its owner or from the highway.

The owner of an animal injured in this way may maintain an action upon the case for damages.

2. To attack with violence; to harass: as, to bait a bull with dogs.[7]

Pursuing rabbits with dogs is not baiting them. The term applies where the baited animal is tied to a stake or confined so that it cannot escape.[1]

BALANCE.[2] 1. Excess on one side of an account.

The conclusion or result of the debit and credit sides of an account.[3]

Implies mutual dealings, and the extension of debit and credit.[3]

2. Residue or remainder; as, the balance of an estate.[4]

General balance. Such sum of money as is due for services rendered by a person to whom two or more articles have been bailed for purposes of transportation, for the bestowal of work and labor, or on account of which money has been expended. See LIEN, Particular.

Net balance. Applied to the proceeds of a sale of stock, means, in commercial usage, the balance of the proceeds after deducting the expenses incident to the sale.[5]

In some States a balance found to be due from an executor, administrator, or guardian, may be entered of record as a judgment.

In suits arising out of mutual accounts the jury may find a balance due to the defendant which, by certificate of the court, becomes a judgment against the plaintiff.

Partial balance. A balance found upon a partial settlement of accounts, as between partners. **Final balance.** The balance at final settlement of a portion of the items of an account, or of all the items, and for a limited period of time or for the whole period covered by dealings or transactions.

An express promise by a partner to pay a partial balance is the most satisfactory evidence of an intention to separate the items included in the settlement from the rest of the joint affairs.

To constitute such an *agreed* final balance as will support an action by one partner against his copartner, the balance must have received the assent of both partners, binding them to an admission of its correctness.[6] See ACCOUNT, 1.

BALLET. See THEATER.

BALLOT.[7] n. A ball or a ticket used in voting; a paper embodying a vote; also, the whole number of votes cast. v. To decide by voting.

[1] Mallory v. Willis, 4 N. Y. 85 (1850), cases, Bronson, C. J.; Foster v. Pettibone, 7 id. 435 (1852), Ruggles, C. J.; Hyde v. Cookson, 21 Barb. 103 (1855); Marsh v. Titus, 3 Hun, 550 (1875); Story, Bailm. § 283; 2 Kent, 589. Grain in an elevator is "sold," 19 Cent. Law J. 268–69 (1884), cases.

[2] 2 Pars. Contr. 87.

[3] Story, Bailm. § 4.

[4] Jones, Bailm. 36.

[5] Bl. Com. 395, 452.

[6] The Idaho, 93 U. S. 579–80 (1876), cases, Strong, J.; Robinson v. Memphis, &c. R. Co., 16 F. R. 57 (1883), cases. See generally Coggs v. Bernard, 2 Ld. Ray. 909 (1704); 1 Sm. L. Cas. 369–454, cases. German Law, 2 Law Quar. Rev. 188–212 (1886).

[7] Pitts v. Millar, L. R., 9 Q. B. 382 (1874).

[1] Pitts v. Millar, *ante.*

[2] L. *bilanx*, having two scales.

[3] McWilliams v. Allen, 45 Mo. 574 (1870).

[4] Lopez v. Lopez, 23 S. C. 269 (1885); Skinner v. Lamp, 3 Ired. L. 155 (1842).

[5] Evans v. Waln, 71 Pa. 74 (1872).

[6] 2 Bates, Partn. § 861, cases.

[7] F. *ballotte*, a little ball for voting.

May refer to the decision of a juror or jurors, or to the preferences of persons qualified to elect the officers of a corporation or of a government.

In French dictionaries, defined as "the act of voting by balls or tickets by putting the same into a box or urn;" also as, "secret voting by means of a ball or ticket." The word did not change its meaning when adopted into the English language.[1]

As applied to elections of public officers, voting by ballot signifies a mode of designating an elector's choice of a person for an office by the deposit of a ticket, bearing the name of such person, in a receptacle provided for the purpose, in such a way as to secure to the elector the privilege of complete and inviolable secrecy in regard to the person voted for.[2]

This privilege of secrecy is the distinguishing feature of ballot voting. The object in view is the independence of the voter.[3]

Voting by ballot is a constitutional method of voting which cannot be changed by a statute. Its perpetuation is meant to secure the right to vote without having the voter's opinion of men or measures inquired into.[3] See TEST, Acts.

The natural import of "balloting at a national, State, or municipal election" is, balloting in and for the election of national, State, or municipal officers. The expression will not apply to ballots casts for or against a regulation like that of granting licenses for the sale of intoxicating liquors.[4]

Ballot-box. A receptacle for ballots; more precisely, such receptacle as is authorized by law.

"To stuff a ballot-box" means unlawfully, fraudulently, and clandestinely to place in a ballot-box, at a lawful election, ballots which have not been voted, with intent to affect the result of the election.[5] See ELECTION, 1; VOTE.

BAN; BANN.[6] Public proclamation or notice.

Banns of matrimony. Publication, by oral announcement, of an intended marriage, in a church or public chapel.

Affords opportunity to interpose legal objection to the marriage.[1]

BANC.[2] The seat occupied by the judges of a court; more particularly, a full bench, when all, or at least a majority, of the judges are present for the decision of questions of law, as distinguished from the practice of one or more members of the court sitting, with a jury, for the determination of questions of fact. Whence "banc days," and "sitting in banc." Compare BANK, 2 (1); BENCH.

BANK. 1. The earth bordering a watercourse, *q. v.*

The banks of a river are the earth which contains it in its ordinary state of high water.[3] See ALONG; BED, 2; RIPARIAN.

2. A bench.

(1) A judge's seat; also, a court sitting for the decision of matters of law — but for this "banc" is the word more generally used. See BANC; BENCH.

(2) An institution for the deposit, discount, or circulation of money.

May refer to the association, the office or place of business, or the managing officers as a body.[4]

The sense in which "bank" or "banks" is intended to be used is determined by their connection with what is said. An act to be done by a bank means an act to be done by those who have the authority to do it. If it be an act within the franchise for banking, or within the ordinary power of the bank, and it is done by the president and directors, or by their agents, we say the bank did it. If, however, an act is to be done relative to the institution, by which its charter is to be changed, the stockholders must do it, unless another mode has been provided by the charter. In one sense, after it has been done, we may say that the bank did it, but only so because what the stockholders have done becomes a part of the institution.[5]

Banks, in the commercial sense, are banks of deposit, of discount, or of circulation. Speaking strictly, the term "bank" implies a place for the deposit of money, as that is the most obvious purpose of such an institution. Originally, the business of banking consisted only in receiving deposits of bullion, plate, and the like, for safe-keeping. In time, bankers assumed to discount bills and notes, and to loan money

[1] State *v.* Shaw, 9 S. C. 138 (1877); Williams *v.* Stein, 38 Ind. 92 (1871).

[2] Brisbin *v.* Cleary, 26 Minn. 108 (1879), cases, Berry, J. See also Temple *v.* Mead, 4 Vt. 541 (1832); People *v.* Pease, 27 N. Y. 45, 57 (1863); Williams *v.* Stein, 38 Ind. 92, 95 (1871).

[3] Attorney-General *v.* Detroit Common Council, 58 Mich. 217 (1885).

[4] Commonwealth *v.* Howe, 144 Mass. 145 (1887),— upon an indictment for casting more than one ballot, contrary to Pub. Sts. *c.* 7, § 57.

[5] See R. S. § 5515; *Exp.* Siebold, 100 U. S. 373 (1879).

[6] A. S. *gebann:* L. L. *bandum, bannum,* a proclamation. Compare ABANDON; CONTRABAND.

[1] 1 Bl. Com. 439.

[2] F. *banc:* L. *bancus,* a bench.

[3] Pulley *v.* Municipality No. 2, 18 La. 537 (1841); Stone *v.* City of Augusta, 46 Me. 137 (1858); Howard *v.* Ingersoll, 13 How. 415–16 (1851); Houghton *v.* Chicago, &c. R. Co., 47 Iowa, 372 (1877); Halsey *v.* McCormick, 13 N. Y. 296 (1855).

[4] See Rominger *v.* Keyes, 73 Ind. 377 (1881).

[5] Gordon *v.* Appeal Tax Court, 3 How. 147–48 (1845), Wayne, J.

upon mortgage, pawn, or other security, and, at a still later period, to issue notes of their own intended as a circulating currency and a medium of exchange instead of gold and silver. Modern bankers frequently exercise any two or even all three of these functions; but it is still true that an institution prohibited from exercising more than one of them is a bank, in the strictest commercial sense.[1]

Bank; banker; banking. A banker is one who makes merchandise of money.[2]

"Banking," in its largest sense, includes the business of receiving deposits, loaning money, dealing in coin, bills of exchange, etc., and issuing paper money.[3]

In statutes "bank" usually designates an incorporated institution, and "banker" an unincorporated association exercising "banking privileges."[3]

The business of banking, as defined by law and custom, consists in the issue of notes payable on demand, intended to circulate as money where the banks are banks of issue; in receiving deposits payable on demand; in discounting commercial paper; making loans of money on collateral security; buying and selling bills of exchange; negotiating loans, and dealing in negotiable securities issued by the government, State and national, and municipal and other corporations.[4]

In Massachusetts "bank" applies to institutions incorporated for banking purposes, not to offices kept by individuals or copartnerships doing such banking business as they have been authorized to do.[5]

The term "banker" includes all the business of a money-changer.[6]

Having a place of business where deposits are received and paid out on checks and where money is loaned upon security is the substance of the business of a banker.[7] See MERCHANT.

The terms bank and banker include any person, firm, or company having a place of business where credits are opened by the deposit or collection of money or currency subject to be paid or remitted

upon draft, check, or order; or where money is advanced or loaned on stocks, bonds, bullion, bills of exchange, or promissory notes; or where stocks, bonds, bullion, bills of exchange, or promissory notes are received for discount or for sale.[1]

At common law the right of banking belongs to individuals, and is exercisable at pleasure.[2]

Bankable. Receivable as the equivalent of cash at a bank; receivable for discount by a bank: as, a bankable or non-bankable bill, or other paper.

Bank for savings; savings bank. A bank of deposit for the accumulation of small savings belonging to the industrious and thrifty.[3]

A bank for the receipt of small sums deposited by the poorer class of persons for accumulation at interest.[4]

An institution formed for the purpose of receiving deposits of money for the benefit of the depositors investing the same, accumulating the profit or interest thereof, paying such profit or interest to the depositor, or retaining the same for his greater security, and, further, of retaining the deposit itself.[5]

The primary relation of a depositor is that of a creditor and beneficiary of a trust. In case of insolvency, depositors stand as other creditors, with equal rights to be paid ratably out of the estate.[6]

National bank; national banking association. An institution, created under United States law, for banking purposes, as distinguished from a bank organized under the law of a State[7] — a *State bank.*

An association may be formed by any number of persons not less than five. They sign "articles of association," and acknowledge an "organization certificate" which states the name assumed, the place where operations are to be carried on, the amount of capital stock and the number of shares thereof, the names and residences of the shareholders, and the shares held by each. Upon filing in the office of the comptroller of the currency these documents, the

---

[1] Oulton v. German Savings, &c. Institution, 17 Wall. 118-19 (1872), cases, Clifford, J.; Bank for Savings v. The Collector, 3 id. 513-14 (1865). See Reninger v. Keyes, 73 Ind. 377 (1881).

[2] 2 Bl. Com. 475.

[3] Exchange Bank v. Hines, 3 Ohio St. 31-32 (1853), Bartley, C. J.; 16 How. 416; 14 Bankr. Reg. 96; 32 La. An. 531.

[4] Mercantile Bank v. New York, 121 U. S. 156 (1887), Matthews, J.

[5] May v. Butterworth, 106 Mass. 76 (1870); 108 id. 513.

[6] Hinckley v. Belleville, 43 Ill. 183 (1867).

[7] Warren v. Shook, 91 U. S. 710 (1875), Hunt, J. Act 3 March, 1865: 13 St. L. 252, 472.

---

[1] Revenue Act, 13 July, 1866, § 9: 14 St. L. 115; R. S. § 3407; Selden v. Equitable Trust Co., 94 U. S. 420-22 (1876).

[2] Bank of Augusta v. Earle, 13 Pet. 595 (1839). As to responsibility for correspondents and notaries, see 20 Am. Law Rev. 889-901 (1886), cases.

[3] Mercantile Bank v. New York, 121 U. S. 161 (1887), Matthews, J.

[4] Bank for Savings v. The Collector, 3 Wall. 513 (1865); McCollough's Com. Dict. 146. See also Johnson v. Ward, 2 Bradw. 274 (1878).

[5] Commonwealth v. Reading Savings Bank, 133 Mass. 19, 21-23 (1882), Devens, J.

[6] See People v. Mechanics' Sav. Inst., 92 N. Y. 9 (1883).

[7] See National Bank Act, 3 June, 1864; R. S. Tit. LXII, §§ 5133-5243.

association becomes, as from the date of the execution of its certificate of organization, a body corporate, empowered to used a corporate seal, have succession for twenty years, make contracts, sue and be sued, elect directors and appoint other officers; to prescribe, by the board of directors, by-laws, not inconsistent with law, for the conduct of general business, and the exercise of its privileges; " to exercise . . all such incidental powers as shall be necessary to carry on the business of banking; by discounting and negotiating promissory notes, drafts, bills of exchange, and other evidences of debt; by receiving deposits; by buying and selling exchange, coin, and bullion; by loaning money on personal security; and by obtaining, issuing, and circulating notes." [1]

The name to be adopted is subject to approval by the comptroller. [2] No other bank or banker, except a savings bank authorized by Congress, may use the word " national " as a portion of its title. [3]

Any old association may become a national association by the name prescribed in its organization certificate — the articles of association and the organization certificate being executed by a majority of the directors, the certificate declaring that the owners of two-thirds of the capital stock have authorized the directors to make such certificate and to convert the institution into a national association. The shares may continue for the same amount; and the former directors may be continued in office, with full power to perfect the re-organization, until others are elected. [4] The certificate of the comptroller is conclusive as to the completeness of the organization. [5]

The re-organization of a State bank does not relieve it from its former liabilities: it remains substantially the same institution under another name. [6]

National banking associations constitute no part of the Government. Designating a bank as a depositary of public moneys does not change the character of its organization, or convert its managers into public officers, or render the Government liable for its acts. [7]

An association may exist with or without power to issue circulation. [8] To obtain circulating notes an association must deposit with the comptroller United States bonds, as security for the redemption of such notes as it may issue; whereupon, within limits, notes of various denominations may be furnished by the comptroller. Associations may be authorized to issue notes payable in gold. [9]

One hundred thousand dollars is the minimum capital allowed, except in places not exceeding 6,000 inhabitants, when, by consent of the comptroller, the capital may be $50,000. Where the population exceeds 50,000, the capital must be at least $200,000. This capital is divided into shares of $100 each, which are personalty. Fifty per centum must be paid before organization, and the rest in monthly installments of ten per centum each. [1]

The act of May 1, 1886 (24 St. L. 18), empowers an association to increase its capital stock, in accordance with existing laws, to any sum approved by the comptroller, by a vote of the holders of two-thirds of the stock, notwithstanding the limit fixed in the original articles of association. By a like vote an association may change its name and location, the latter not to be more than thirty miles distant from the former location, after the comptroller has certified his approval.

Title to a share of stock passes when the owner delivers his certificate to the purchaser with authority to transfer the share on the books of the bank. [2] See further STOCK, 3 (2).

A national bank may hold such realty as is necessary for its immediate accommodation in the transaction of business; such as shall be mortgaged to it in good faith by way of security for debts previously contracted; such as shall be conveyed to it in satisfaction of debts previously contracted in the course of its dealings; such as it shall purchase at sales under judgments, decrees, or mortgages held by it, or shall purchase to secure debts due to it — title in the last case not to be held longer than five years. [3]

The circuit courts of the United States have jurisdiction of all suits by or against national banks established in the district for which the court is held, [4] irrespective of the amount in controversy or the citizenship of the parties. [5] State courts of its locality have jurisdiction of suits brought by it. [6] It may be sued in a place in a State other than where it is established. [7]

A national bank may not loan or discount on the security of its own stock, except to prevent loss. [8]

A national bank may go into liquidation and be closed by a vote of the holders of two-thirds of its stock. [9] In case of failure to pay its notes, the comptroller may appoint a receiver to wind it up. [10]

The Government has no priority of demand against an insolvent bank. [11]

National banks being designed to aid the Government in the administration of an important branch of the public service, the States can exercise only such control over them as Congress may permit. [12]

---

[1] R. S. §§ 5133–36.
[2] R. S. § 5134.
[3] R. S. § 5243.
[4] R. S. §§ 5154–55.
[5] Casey v. Galli, 94 U. S. 679 (1876).
[6] Coffey v. Nat. Bank of Missouri, 46 Mo. 143 (1870).
[7] R. S. § 5153; Branch v. United States, 12 Ct. Cl. 281 (1876).
[8] National Currency Acts, 11 Op. Att.-Gen. 334 (1865).
[9] R. S. § 5185.

[1] See Bailey v. Clark, 21 Wall. 284 (1874).
[2] Johnston v. Laflin, 103 U. S. 800, 804 (1880).
[3] R. S. § 5137; 2 Dill. 371.
[4] R. S. § 629, par. 10; 3 Dill. 298; 8 Wall. 506.
[5] 19 Alb. Law J. 182.
[6] Bank of Bethel v. Pahquioque Bank, 14 Wall. 383 (1871); Claflin v. Houseman, 93 U. S. 130 (1876); 101 Mass. 240.
[7] Casey v. Adams, 102 U. S. 66 (1880).
[8] R. S. § 5136.
[9] R. S. § 5220; 5 Biss. 499.
[10] R. S. § 5234, cases; Richmond v. Irons, 121 U. S. 47–50 (1887).
[11] Cook County Nat. Bank v. United States, 107 U. S. 445 (1882).
[12] Farmers', &c. Nat. Bank v. Dearing, 91 U. S. 33–34 (1875). See Veazie Bank v. Fenno, 8 Wall. 533 (1869).

Bank-bill; bank-note. A promissory note, issued by a bank under authority of law, payable on demand to the bearer.

Bank-notes differ from ordinary promissory notes only in the recognition of them by general consent, and by the law to an extent, as a substitute and equivalent for legal money. In other respects they are governed by the rules applicable to promissory notes payable to bearer.[1] See CURRENT, 2.

Bank cashier. See CASHIER.

Bank check. See CHECK; EXCHANGE, 2.

Bank director. See DIRECTORS.

Bank president. See ABSTRACT, 1; APPLICATION, 2; DIRECTORS.

Has no power by virtue of his office to bind the bank in an unusual manner, or in any undertaking outside of its customary routine of business. While the directors, or usage, may confer upon him special power, the authority inherent in his position is very slight.[2]

See generally ACCOUNT, 1; ADVANCES; CHARTER, 2; CIRCULATION; COLLECTION; DEPOSIT, 2 (2); DISCOUNT, 2; FUNDS; MONEYED; RESERVE, 7; TAX, 2; USURY.

BANKRUPT.[3] A trader who secretes himself, or does certain other acts tending to defraud his creditors.[4] See TRADER.

A person found, by the proper court, to be entitled or subject to have his property taken for distribution among his creditors, and he to be discharged from the legal obligation of past claims. In a loose sense, a person as to whose status such an adjudication may or would be made.

Bankrupt law. A law intended to secure the application of a debtor's effects to the payment of his debts, and to relieve him from the burden of them.[5]

Bankrupt system. The law, and the practice thereunder, respecting the division of a bankrupt's property among his creditors.

Bankruptcy. The status or condition of being a bankrupt; also, that branch of the law under which the assets of the estate of a bankrupt may be distributed among his creditors and he be discharged from the indebtedness.

Bankruptcy is a proceeding of an equitable nature — a sequestration of a debtor's property that the creditors may resort to, instead of to an ordinary suit at law or in equity.[1]

The object is equality of distribution of the assets among creditors not legally secured.[2] Another purpose, only second in importance to that, is speedy distribution of assets. Our statutes have been filled with provisions designed to secure the early discharge of the debtor and the speedy settlement of his estate.[3]

Bankrupt laws are for the benefit of the honest trader, his honest creditors, and public commerce.[4]

"The Congress shall have Power . . To establish . . uniform Laws on the subject of Bankruptcies throughout the United States."[5] See UNIFORM.

The English word "bankrupt" had its origin in incidents of trade. Whatever secondary or figurative meaning the word may have acquired, its primary and only legal meaning is that which confines it to *traders*. . As a state of "insolvency" usually precedes "bankruptcy," it is not surprising that the two words should sometimes be confounded. Insolvency is the generic term, comprehending bankruptcy as a species. A man may be insolvent without becoming a bankrupt, or having capacity to become such; and a bankrupt may prove to be entirely solvent. Mere insolvency never makes one a bankrupt without the concurrence of some act tending to the injury of his creditors.[6]

The line of partition between bankrupt and insolvent laws is not so distinctly marked as to enable a person to say with precision what belongs exclusively to the one and not to the other class of laws. It is said that laws which merely liberate the person are insolvent laws, and those which discharge the contract are bankrupt laws. Another distinction, more uniformly observed, is, insolvent laws operate at the instance of an imprisoned debtor, bankrupt laws at the instance of a creditor.[7]

Still another feature of insolvent laws is, the debtor is not discharged from the legal obligation to pay demands in full: he remains subject to suits and executions on account of unoutlawed claims.[8]

Fraudulent bankruptcy. Bankruptcy in which the debtor has practiced, or attempted to practice, some fraud upon creditors; as by not disclosing all of his assets, or by creating an unlawful preference.[9]

---

[1] See James v. Rogers, 23 Ind. 451, 453 (1864).

[2] Wheat v. Bank of Louisville, Sup. Ct. Ky. (1887), cases. Same case, 27 Am. Law Reg. 52 (1888); *ib.* 56–60, cases. See also 21 Cent. Law J. 144–46 (1885), cases.

[3] F. *banque*, a table or counter; *route*, trace, track: his "banque" was removed and no trace of it left,— 2 Bl. Com. 272. Ital. *banca rotta*, a broken bench: a money-changer's bench was broken up, on his failing in business,— Skeat. See 3 Story, 453.

[4] 2 Bl. Com. 285, 471.

[5] [2 Kent, 389; 2 Bl. Com. 474, 476; 109 U. S. 536.

---

[1] *Re* Weitzel, 7 Biss. 290 (1876).

[2] International Bank v. Sherman, 101 U. S. 406 (1879); Trimble v. Woodhead, 102 *id.* 650 (1880).

[3] Bailey v. Glover, 21 Wall. 346–47 (1874), Miller, J.; Jenkins v. International Bank, 106 U. S. 575–76 (1882); R. S. § 5057.

[4] 2 Bl. Com. 472, 475.

[5] Constitution, Art. I, sec. 8, cl. 4.

[6] Sackett v. Andross, 5 Hill, 343–44, 342 (N. Y., 1843), Bronson, J. See also 41 Conn. 505; 2 Bened. 203.

[7] Sturges v. Crowninshield, 4 Wheat. 194 (1819), Marshall, C. J.

[8] Martin v. Berry, 37 Cal. 222 (1869).

[9] See 4 Bl. Com. 156.

Private bankruptcy. Has been applied to cases of composition with creditors — resort to court for a discharge being thereby obviated.[1]

Voluntary bankruptcy. That in which the debtor avails himself of the law. **Involuntary** or **compulsory bankruptcy.** In which the debtor, by proceedings instituted by one or more creditors, is judicially decided to be bankrupt.

A case of voluntary bankruptcy is in the nature of a suit by the debtor against his creditors.[2]

Act of bankruptcy. An act by a debtor which exposes him to adverse proceedings in bankruptcy.

Under the Act of March 2, 1867, amended by Acts of June 22, 1874, and of July 26, 1876, acts of bankruptcy were certain acts done by a debtor six months before an adjudication was sought: as, — (1) departing from the State to defraud creditors; (2) remaining absent with that intent; (3) concealing himself to avoid service of process; (4) concealing or removing property to prevent its being attached, taken, or sequestered; (5) assigning or giving away property or rights, to delay, defraud, or hinder creditors; (6) being held in custody or imprisoned seven days on account of a claim over one hundred dollars; (7) making, in contemplation of insolvency, a transfer of property, confessing a judgment, procuring or suffering property to be taken on process, with intent to prefer a creditor or to defeat or delay the operation of the bankrupt law; (8) for a bank, banker, broker, merchant, trader, manufacturer, or miner, fraudulently to stop payment of commercial paper, or not to resume payment thereof, for fourteen days; (9) for a bank or banker to fail to pay a depositor within forty days.[3]

A debtor could have a jury trial upon any alleged act of bankruptcy.

Foreigners were exempt from the law; also, a citizen whose provable debts were less than three hundred dollars.

Proceedings were begun in the district court, by petition with annexed schedules of debts and assets. This petition was referred to the " register " — an auxiliary in matters of administration, — who ascertained whether the debts were above two hundred and fifty dollars; if so, the debtor was adjudged a bankrupt and his estate *ipso facto* became vested in the register. There then issued a warrant to the marshal to notify the creditors. In from ten to ninety days the creditors met and nominated an assignee, who, with his sureties, was to be approved by the court; whereupon, the register deeded the estate to the assignee, who proceeded to settle the business.[1]

Upon the commission of an act of bankruptcy the debtor's property becomes a common fund for the payment of his debts, he losing all right of proprietorship over it.[2]

When there exists no purpose to defraud, delay, or prefer, and the value of the estate remains unimpaired, before proceedings are begun the debtor can deal with the property.

Filing a petition is an attachment and an injunction — a *caveat* to all the world. After that, a person deals with the insolvent at his peril.[3]

A transfer designed to prevent equality of distribution, made within four months before petition filed, was held to be a fraud.[4] So was giving a note confessing judgment. But in all such cases the intention of the debtor was made the test.[5]

Property illegally transferred was recoverable by the assignee.[6]

Excepting attachments made within a prescribed period, and fraudulent dispositions, the assignee took title subject to all equities, liens, or incumbrances — in the same plight and condition as when the debtor held it.[6]

Under the acts of Congress a voluntary bankrupt was to pay thirty per centum of the provable claims, unless less was accepted by one-fourth in number and one-third in value of the creditors. A majority in number and three-fourths in value could accept a composition.

A discharge, which was a matter of favor, could be had one year after adjudication, an order having first been issued to such creditors as proved debts, to appear and show cause, if they knew of any, why the discharge should not be granted. And a discharge which had been granted could be annulled, within two years, for fraud undiscovered at the time of the discharge.

A discharge is no bar to an action on a judgment recovered after the discharge, in a suit commenced before the bankruptcy, pending when the discharge was granted, and upon a debt provable in bankruptcy.[7]

A United States law supersedes a State law.[8] But

---

[1] *Exp.* Vere, 19 Ves. *98 (1812).

[2] Wilson *v.* City Bank of St. Paul, 17 Wall. 481–82 (1873); United States *v.* Fox, 95 U. S. 672 (1877).

[3] R. S. § 5021, cases.

[1] See R. S. Tit. LXI: §§ 4972–5132.

[2] 2 Kent, 389; 2 Bl. Com. 474, 476.

[3] International Bank *v.* Sherman, 101 U. S. 406 (1879).

[4] Dutcher *v.* Wright, 94 U. S. 553 (1876), cases.

[5] Clarion Bank *v.* Jones, 21 Wall. 325 (1874); Clark *v.* Iselin, *ib.* 373 (1874); Watson *v.* Taylor, *ib.* 381 (1874); Little *v.* Alexander, *ib.* 500 (1874).

[6] Yeatman *v.* Savings Institution, 95 U. S. 764 (1877); Stewart *v.* Platt, 101 *id.* 738 (1879); 2 Bl. Com. 485.

[7] Dimock *v.* Revere Copper Co., 117 U. S. 559 (1886). See also Boynton *v.* Ball, 121 *id.* 457 (1887). See generally as to discharge, Laidley *v.* Cummings, 83 Ky. 606 (1886); Fuller *v.* Pease, 144 Mass. 390 (1887).

[8] Sturges *v.* Crowninshield, 4 Wheat. 196 (1819); Ogden *v.* Saunders, 12 *id.* 213 (1827); Baldwin *v.* Hale, 1 Wall. 228–31 (1863).

upon the repeal of a Federal law, a previously enacted State law becomes operative again.[1]

The convention which framed the Constitution had in view the English system.[2]

Bankrupt laws were passed by Congress in 1800, 1841, and 1867, but repealed, in each instance, after a comparatively brief operation. That of 1867, with its amendments, was repealed by act of June 7, 1878, the repeal taking effect September 1, 1878, without effect upon pending cases.[3]

Such laws have been in force in England for more than three centuries. They had their origin in the Roman law.[4]

See further AES, Alienum; CESSIO; COMPOSITION, 3; CONTEMPLATION; DEATH, Civil; HÆREDITAS, Damnosa; INSOLVENCY; PROCESS, 1, Legal.

BANNS. See BAN.

BAPTISTS, SEVENTH-DAY. See SUNDAY.

BAR. 1. A particular portion of a court room.

Named from the space inclosed by two bars or rails: one of which separated the judge's bench from the rest of the room; the other shut off both the bench and the area for lawyers engaged in trials from the space allotted to suitors, witnesses, and others.

Such persons as appeared as speakers (advocates, or counsel) before the court, were said to be "called to the bar," that is, privileged so to appear, speak and otherwise serve in the presence of the judges as "barristers." The corresponding phrase in the United States is "admitted to the bar."

Proceedings in open court are said to take place "at the bar of the court," or simply "at bar." The particular case being argued is the "case at bar;" and a person on trial for a crime is "the prisoner at the bar."

The figurative expression "before the bar of conscience" is not uncommon.

In still another sense "the bar" denotes the members of the legal profession; as in speaking of the bar of a county, of a State, of the United States. Whence, also, are "bar associations," which consist of lawyers united for the purpose of furthering the interests of their profession.

Barrister. A counselor, learned in the law, who pleads before courts, and undertakes the advocacy or defense of causes generally.

Inner barristers. Queen's counsel, admitted within the bar, in seats specially reserved for them.[1]

Outer or *utter barristers.* Junior counsel, who sit outside the bar. Compare SERGEANT.

Disbar. To expel an attorney from membership in the legal profession. See further ATTORNEY.

2. In a somewhat general way a **public bar** may be defined as a counter, table, shelf, or other similar device, designed and used for the purpose of facilitating the sale and delivery of liquors there kept to any one who may apply for them, to be then and there drunk, not in connection with meals, lunches or food.[2]

A lunch counter would not be such a bar merely because sales of liquor only are sometimes made there.[3]

3. An impediment; an obstacle. Whence the verbs "bar" and "debar," to prevent, cut off, defeat.

Plea in bar. A plea intended to overthrow an action; a plea which sets up an absolute or peremptory defense, as, payment.

Special plea in bar. New matter avoiding the inference of law on facts previously stated.

Temporary bar. A plea in bar which is effectual for a limited period only: as, "administered fully," until more assets come to hand.[3]

BARBED WIRE. See FENCE.

BARE. Compare NAKED.

BARGAIN.[4] 1, *n.* A mutual contract or agreement between two parties, the one to sell goods or lands, and the other to buy them.[5]

Any mutual undertaking.

"Bargain" more prominently, perhaps, than "agreement," brings into view the mutuality of a contract.[6]

2, *v.* To transfer in pursuance of a bargain; as, "to grant, bargain, and sell."

Bargainer. He who makes a bargain.

Bargainee. He who is to receive property under the contract of a bargain; the grantee in a deed of bargain and sale. See EARNEST; GRANT, 2; OFFER, 1.

[1] Tua v. Carriere, 117 U. S. 209 (1886).

[2] Nelson v. Carland, 1 How. 272, 277 (1843).

[3] See the Lowell Bill, as to partners, 19 Am. Law Rev. 32 (1885).

[4] Canada South. R. Co. v. Gebhard, 109 U. S. 536 (1883).

[1] See 3 Bl. Com. 26; The Nation, Dec. 20, 1883, No. 964.

[2] Commonwealth v. Rogers, 135 Mass. 539 (1883), Colburn, J.

[3] See 3 Bl. Com. 305; 1 Flip. 4; 60 Md. 125; 1 Oreg. 48.

[4] F. bargaigner, to chaffer: L. L. barca, a bark for merchandise.

[5] Hunt v. Adams, 5 Mass. *360 (1809), Parsons, C. J.; Packard v. Richardson, 17 id. *131-39 (1821).

[6] Sage v. Wilcox, 6 Conn. 85, 90 (1826).

Bargain and sale. A contract whereby the bargainer, for some pecuniary consideration, bargains and sells, that is, contracts to convey, land to the bargainee.[1]

Also used of transfers of personalty.

A contract to convey, for valuable consideration, by any words sufficient to raise a use in the bargainee.[2]

At common law, land can not pass without livery, *q. v.* In this contract the bargain vests the use, and the Statute of Uses then vests, that is, completes, the possession.[1]

The force of that statute is exhausted in transferring the legal title in fee-simple to the bargainee.[3] See Use, 3.

In a "bargain and sale" of personalty the thing becomes the buyer's the moment the contract is made, whether delivered or not. In an "executory agreement," the thing remains the property of the vendor till the contract is executed.[4]

Catching a bargain. An agreement to purchase an expectant estate at an inadequate price.

Applied to heirs dealing with their expectancies, and to reversioners and remainder-men dealing with property already vested in them, but of which the enjoyment is future, and is, therefore, apt to be underestimated by the giddy, the necessitous, the improvident, and the young.[5]

In most cases have concurred deceit and illusion as to other persons. The father, ancestor, or other relative, from whom was the expectation of the estate, has been kept in the dark. The expectant has been kept from disclosing his circumstances, and resorting to them for advice and relief. This misleads the ancestor. who has been induced to leave his estate, not to his heir or family, but to artful persons who have divided the spoil beforehand.[6]

To maintain parental and *quasi* parental authority, to prevent the waste of family estates, and to protect the heedless and necessitous from the designs of rapacity, relief is afforded in equity. The purchaser must establish not merely that there is no fraud, but "make good the bargain," that is, show that a fair and adequate (*q. v.*) consideration has been paid.[7] Compare *Unconscionable Bargain.*

Strike a bargain. To shake hands in attestation of an agreement; also, to come to an agreement.

From the old custom of shaking hands as necessary to bind a bargain.[8]

---

[1] 2 Bl. Com. 338; Slifer *v.* Beates, 9 S. & R. *177 (1822).

[2] [4 Kent, 495.

[3] Croxall *v.* Sshererd, 5 Wall. 282 (1866), cases.

[4] Benj. Sales, §§ 308, 310; Smith, Contr. 331; Smith *v.* Surman, 9 B. & C. 568 (1829).

[5] 1 Story, Eq. § 337.

[6] Chesterfield *v.* Janssen, 2 Ves. 157, 155 (1750), Hardwicke, Ld. C.

[7] 1 Story, Eq. §§ 335–36.

[8] 2 Bl. Com. 448.

Time bargain. A contract for the sale of stocks, provisions, or other commodity or article of merchandise, at a certain price on a future day, the vendor himself intending to purchase the thing, which is the subject of the proposed sale, before the day for the delivery has arrived. See further Wager, 2.

Unconscionable bargain. Such bargain as no man in his senses and not under delusion would make, on the one hand, and as no honest and fair man would accept, on the other, — being an inequitable and unconscientious bargain.[1]

A bargain of so unconscionable a nature and of such gross inequality as naturally leads to the presumption of fraud, imposition, or undue influence.[2]

A court of equity is not bound to shut its eyes to the evident character of a transaction where its aid has been sought to carry into effect an unconscionable bargain, but it will leave the party to his remedy at law; as, in salvage cases.[3]

BARGE. See Ship, 2; Vessel.

BARK. See Litera, Qui hæret, etc.

BARN. See Arson; Belong; Curtilage.

Within the meaning of a statute against arson, the building need not be used for storing provender.[4]

The word may include a building mainly used for storing tobacco.[5]

BARON.[6] 1. The man — one able to bear arms; one bound to render service to the king.[7] See Curtilage, 1.

2. A member of the nobility in the fifth and lowest degree.[7]

3. A judge of the court of exchequer.

"Barons of the realm" only were formerly appointed to the office;[8] as, "Park, B."

4. A lord; a husband.

Baron and femme. Man and woman; husband and wife.[9]

Covert-baron. One under coverture; a wife.[10] See Coverture.

---

[1] Chesterfield *v.* Janssen, *ante.*

[2] [1 Story, Eq. § 244.

[3] Mississippi, &c. R. Co. *v.* Cromwell, 91 U. S. 643 (1875). See Post *v.* Jones, 19 How. 160 (1856); The Emulous, 1 Summ. 210 (1832); The Brooks, 17 F. R. 548 (1883); 16 *id.* 144; 4 Del. Ch. 198; 27 Alb. L. J. 4 (1883).

[4] State *v.* Smith, 28 Iowa, 568 (1870).

[5] Ratekin *v.* State, 26 Ohio St. 420 (1875).

[6] L. L. *baro, varo*: L. *vir,* a man, — Webster. Ger. *bar,* a man: *beran,* to carry, — Skeat.

[7] 1 Bl. Com. 398–99.

[8] 3 Bl. Com. 44, 55–56.

[9] 1 Bl. Com. 432.

[10] 1 Bl. Com. 442.

BARRATRY.[1] 1. In maritime law, an act committed by the master or mariners of a ship, for some unlawful or fraudulent purpose, contrary to their duty to the owners, whereby the latter sustain injury.[2]

Consists in willful acts of the master or mariners, done for some unlawful or fraudulent purpose, contrary to their duty to the owners of the vessel.[3]

The act must not be accidental, nor caused by negligence — unless that is so gross as to amount to evidence of fraud. The intention need not be to promote one's own benefit. Any willful act of known criminality, or of malversation, operating to the prejudice of the owner, is barratry.[3]

All definitions agree that fraud is a constituent part of the act.[4]

2. Iu criminal law, **common barratry** is the offense of frequently exciting and stirring up suits and quarrels, either at law or otherwise.[5]

The proof must show at least three instances of offending.[6]

"A common barrator is a common mover or stirrer up or maintainer of suits, quarrels, or parties, either iu courts or in the country; in the country in three manners: in disturbance of the peace; in taking or detaining of the possession of houses, lands, or goods, etc., which are iu question or controversy, not only by force, but also by subtlety and deceit, and for the most part in suppression of truth and right; by false invention, and sowing of calumny, rumors, and reports, whereby discord and disquiet arise between neighbors."[7]

We have here strife and contention, and deceit or fraud, growing out of the compound origin and synonymous uses of the word. In the sense of "strife and contention," the word was used in connection with policies of insurance as late as the middle of the last century.[6]

BARREN. See LEVY; RENT; TRUST, 1.

BARRISTER. See BAR, 1.

BARTER.[1] A contract by which goods are exchanged for goods.[2]

The exchange of one commodity or article of property for another.[3]

The consideration, instead of being paid in money, as in the case of a sale, is paid in goods or merchandise susceptible of valuation.[4]

An agent empowered to sell cannot barter; and the principal may recover from an innocent transferee.[6] See EXCHANGE, 1; SALE.

BAS-RELIEF. See DESIGN, 2.

BASE. Inferior; of low degree.

Base animal. An animal which is unfit for food. See ANIMAL.

Base coin. Debased coin.[6]

Base fee. An estate in fee that ends whenever an annexed qualification requires it.[7] See FEE, 1.

Base services. Fit only for a person of servile rank.[8]

Base tenant. One bound to servile service.[9] See FEUD.

BASE BALL. See GAME, 2.

BASTARD.[10] One that is not only begotten, but born, out of lawful matrimony.[11]

Such child as is not born either in lawful wedlock, or within a competent time after its determination.[12]

One begotten and born out of lawful wedlock.[13]

The test is whether the husband of the woman who gives birth to the child is its father.[14]

In Virginia, one born out of wedlock, lawful or unlawful, or not within a competent time after the coverture is determined; or, if born out of wedlock, whose parents do not afterward intermarry, and the father acknowledges the child; or who is born in wedlock when procreation by the husband is for any cause impossible.[16]

Bastardize. To make out to be a bastard, an illegitimate or natural child.

---

[1] Sp. *barateria*, deceit, fraud,— 3 Pet. *230.

[2] Marcardier *v.* Chesapeake Ins. Co., 8 Cranch, 49 (1814), Story, J.

[3] Lawton *v.* Sun Mut. Ins. Co., 2 Cush. 511–12 (1848), Shaw, C. J.; Atkinson *v.* Great West. Ins. Co., 65 N. Y. 538–40 (1875), cases; 2 Wash. 66.

[4] Patapsco Ins. Co. *v.* Coulter, 3 Pet. *230 (1830).

[5] 4 Bl. Com. 134.

[6] Commonwealth *v.* M'Culloch, 15 Mass. *229 (1818); Commonwealth *v.* Tubbs, 1 Cush. 3 (1848).

[7] The Case of Barratry, 8 Coke, *72 (1612).

[8] Atkinson *v.* Great Western Ins. Co., 4 Daly, 16–20 (1871), Daly, C. J.

[1] F. *barat*, traffic.

[2] 2 Bl. Com. 446.

[3] Cooper *v.* State, 37 Ark. 418 (1881), English, C. J.

[4] Washington County *v.* Thompson, 12 Bush, 241 (1877), Cofer, J.

[5] Guerreiro *v.* Peile, 3 B. & Ald. 616 (1820).

[6] 6 Wheat. 333.

[7] [2 Bl. Com. 109.

[8] [2 Bl. Com. 62, 61.

[9] 2 Bl. Com. 148.

[10] F. *bastard: fils de bast*, son of a packsaddle — muleteers made beds of their saddles,— Skeat.

[11] 1 Bl. Com. 454.

[12] 2 Bl. Com. 247.

[13] 2 Kent, 208.

[14] Wilson *v.* Babb, 18 S. C. 69–70 (1882), Simpson, C. J.

[16] Smith *v.* Perry, 80 Va. 570 (1885), Lacy, J.

Bastardy. The offense of begetting an illegitimate child; also, the condition of being an illegitimate child — illegitimacy.

Bastardy process. The statutory mode of proceeding against the putative father of an illegitimate child, to secure maintenance for the child.

Bastardy bond. The obligation entered into by such father with the guardians of the poor, conditioned for the payment of the lying-in expenses, maintenance of the child, and, perhaps, such costs as may have been incurred and such fine as has been imposed.[1]

At common law there was no legal liability upon the father to support his bastard child. Now, at the instance of the mother, he can be made support it, by a "bastardy proceeding."[2]

A bastard is a *filius nullius*, son of nobody, or *filius populi*, son of the people. He has no inheritable blood,— has no heir except of his own body. He may, however, take by bequest or devise.[3]

He has a right to maintenance; his settlement is the same as his mother's at his birth; he takes her name, but he may acquire a name by reputation.[4]

Once a marriage is proven, nothing can impugn the legitimacy of issue short of proof of facts showing it to be impossible that the husband could be the father.[5]

By the civil law, and statutes in many States, the subsequent marriage of the parents legitimates children born prior thereto. This seems to be the law in Alabama, Georgia. Illinois, Indiana, Kentucky, Louisiana, Maine, Maryland, Massachusetts, Mississippi, Missouri, Ohio, Pennsylvania, Vermont, and Virginia.[6]

See ABANDON, 2 (2); ACCESS; ADULTERINE; CONCEAL, 4; FILIATION; MARRIAGE; PREGNANCY.

BATTEL.[7] Trial by combat or duel.

Also called **wager of battel, battle, battaile.**

In the nature of an appeal to Providence, under an apprehension and hope that Heaven would give the victory to him who had the right.

Introduced by the Conquerer; and used in the court-martial, or court of chivalry and honor, in appeals of felony, and in writs of right — the last and most solemn decision of real property.[8]

Recognized as the law of the land as late as 1818, in the case of *Ashford v. Thornton.*[9] Abolished by

statute 59 Geo. III (1819), c. 46.[1] Compare ORDEAL; WAGER, 1.

BATTERY.[2] The unlawful beating of another.[3]

Any unlawful touching of the person of another, either by the aggressor or by any person or thing set in motion by him.[4]

The least touching of another's person willfully, or in anger, is a battery. The law cannot draw the line between different degrees of violence, and therefore prohibits the first and lowest stage of it — every man's person being sacred and no other having a right to meddle with it in the slightest manner.[5]

In assessing damages the degree of violence is taken into account. See BEAT.

Every "battery" includes an "assault." The two offenses are joined in indictments, and the assault alone may be proved. Whence "assault and battery," which is — simple, when a mere touching or beating is intended; aggravated, when grievous bodily harm is inflicted, as by breaking a limb or disfiguring the face; felonious, when death is designed, or serious wounding with intent to commit a felony, when the end sought is a felony, at common law or by statute.[6] See ASSAULT.

While "battery" includes "assault," it does not include "an assault with a deadly weapon with intent to commit bodily harm."[7]

A battery may be lawful or justifiable, or unlawful. It is lawful: (1) when committed under authority, as by an officer in order to preserve the peace, or by a parent, master, teacher, or military officer, each of whom may correct moderately; (2) when in self-defense; that is, of self, wife, husband, child, parent, servant; (3) when in defense of one's own goods or possession. It is unlawful: (1) when it originates in malice — is committed in an angry, spiteful, insolent, or rude manner; (2) when it is the result of censurable carelessness.[8]

A trespasser who uses force may be summarily ejected. A person assailed need not wait till a blow has been dealt him. At the same time resistance must not exceed the degree of necessary defense — for it is the law that punishes. Any resistance in the offender to justifiable apprehension becomes a new battery.[9]

Whatever is attached to the person partakes of its inviolability: as, the skirt of the coat or dress, an object in the hand.

---

[1] See Gleason v. Commissioners, 30 Kan. 493 (1883).

[2] Stowers v. Hollis, 83 Ky. 549 (1886).

[3] 1 Bl. Com. 459; 2 *id.* 247–49; Gaines v. Hennen, 24 How. 553, 592 (1860); Gaines v. New Orleans, 6 Wall. 648 (1867); Smith v. Du Bose, Sup. Ct. Ga. (1887): 36 Alb. Law J. 344–48.

[4] 1 Bl. Com. 459.

[5] Patterson v. Gaines, 6 How. 589, 598 (1848). See also 18 Cent. Law J. 262–68, 305–7 (1884), cases.

[6] See 2 Kent, 210–14.

[7] L. *batuere*, to strike, beat.

[8] 3 Bl. Com. 337; 4 *id.* 346; Coke, Litt. § 294 *b*.

[9] 1 Barn. & Ald. 405.

---

[1] See generally United States v. Gibert, 2 Sumn. 68 (1834), Story, J.

[2] L. *batuere*, to beat.

[3] 3 Bl. Com. 120.

[4] 1 Saund. Pl. & Ev. *141; Kirland v. State, 43 Ind. 153 (1873); 3 Cooley, Bl. Com. 120, note.

[5] 3 Bl. Com. 120; Johnson v. State, 17 Tex. 517 (1856).

[6] See 4 Bl. Com. 216; 13 Allen, 317; 17 F. R. 266.

[7] People v. Helbing, 61 Cal. 621 (1882).

[8] See 3 Bl. Com. 120–21.

[9] See 2 Bishop, Cr. L. § 561.

To strike the horse which another person rides or drives is an assault. The owner is liable for a battery when his horse, left near a sidewalk, bites or kicks a passer-by.

The remedy in a civil court is an action of trespass *vi et armis* for damages; in a criminal court, indictment for assault and battery for the public wrong.[1]

While it is no defense to a civil action for an assault and battery that the acts complained of were committed in a fight engaged in by mutual consent, such consent may go in mitigation of the damages.[2]

See ABET; ARREST, 2; DEFENSE, 1; DURESS; FORCE; MANUS, Molliter; INJURY; PROVOCATION; WOUND.

BATTURE. "Accretion," which is the imperceptible augmentation of the soil on the shore of a stream, is called "alluvion" and sometimes "batture."[3]

A marine term, denoting a bottom of sand, stone or rock mixed together, and rising toward the surface of the water. From the French *battre*, to beat: beaten by the water. . An elevation of the bed of a river, under the surface of the water; also, sometimes, the same elevation of the bank, when it has risen above the surface of the water or is as high as the land on the outside of the bank.[4] See ACCRETION.

BAWD.[5] One who procures opportunities for persons of opposite sexes to cohabit in an illicit manner.[6]

Bawdy-house. A house of ill-fame; a house kept for the resort and unlawful convenience of lewd people of both sexes; a house resorted to for purposes of lewdness and prostitution.[7]

The prosecution having shown that the defendant is the keeper of a house alleged to be a common bawdy-house, testimony as to the general reputation of the house, of the persons who frequent it, and of the defendant, is admissible, as tending to show the real character of the house.[7]

Keeping a bawdy-house is indictable as a common nuisance at common law.[8] See HOUSE, 1, Of ill-fame; PROSTITUTE.

BAY-WINDOW. See LIGHTS, Ancient.

A jut or bay-window which is maintained without authority of law, which encroaches on the public highway, and is prejudicial to the interests of the community and of the rights of individual property owners, may be declared a public nuisance and its continuance restrained. As, a window built in the second story of a house, sixteen feet above the sidewalk and projecting three and a half feet beyond the property or building line.[1]

BE IT ENACTED. See ACT, 3.

BEACH. The land, between the lines of high and low water, over which the tide ebbs and flows; synonymous with shore, strand, flat.[2]

A deed of land described as bounded "on the beach" does not convey the shore below high-water mark, unless this boundary is controlled by other parts of the description.

Taking sea-weed from an uninclosed beach, and selling stones therefrom from time to time, may operate to disseize the true owner.[3]

BEACON. See COMMERCE; WRECK.

BEANS. See GRAIN.

BEAR. See DATE; INTEREST, 2 (3).

BEARER. He who bears or carries a thing; he who presents for payment a bill, check, or note, transferable by delivery.

A note payable to "A or bearer" is negotiable without indorsement, and payment may be demanded by any bearer as the person whom the maker promised to pay. The transferrer is not liable except on failure of the consideration. The holder is presumed to be owner for value; but any circumstance of suspicion, as theft of the instrument by a former holder, may require the present holder to prove that he gave value for the paper.[4]

The *bona fide* purchaser of a note payable to bearer, but stolen from the rightful holder, may recover the amount of it from the maker; otherwise, where the note is stolen directly from the maker.[5]

A note payable to bearer is said to be assignable by delivery; but really there is no "assignment" at all. The paper passes by mere delivery, the holder never makes title through any assignment, but claims as bearer. The note is an original promise by the maker to pay any person who shall become bearer; it is, therefore, payable to any and every person who successively holds the note *bona fide*, not by virtue of an assignment of the promise, but by the original, direct promise moving from the maker.[6]

See BLANK, 2; BOND; COUPON; NEGOTIATE, 2.

---

[1] 3 Bl. Com. 121; 4 *id.* 216; Kirland *v.* State, 43 Ind. 148–56 (1873), cases; State *v.* Davis, 1 Hill, S. C., 46 (1833).
[2] Barholt *v.* Wright, Sup. Ct. Ohio (1887), cases: 12 N. E. Rep. 185; 36 Alb. Law J. 3 (1887), cases.
[3] [Zeller *v.* Yacht Club, 34 La. An. 838 (1882), Todd, J.; 4 Hall's Law J. 518; 12 F. R. 295; 15 Wall. 650.
[4] Morgan *v.* Livingston, 3 Mart. 111 (1819), Martin, J.; *ib.* 11. See Municipality No. 2 *v.* Orleans Cotton Press, 18 La. 436 (1841).
[5] F. *baud*, gay, wanton: Ger. *bald*, bold, free.
[6] Dyer *v.* Morris, 4 Mo. 216 (1835).
[7] State *v.* Boardman, 64 Me. 529 (1874); McAlister *v.* Clark, 33 Conn. 92 (1865); State *v.* Hand, 7 Iowa, 411 (1858); Harwood *v.* People, 26 N. Y. 191 (1863); State *v.* Brunell, 29 Wis. 436 (1872), cases.
[8] Martin *v.* Stillwell, 13 Johns. *275 (1816).

[1] Reimer's Appeal, 100 Pa. 182, 190 (1882); Commonwealth *v.* Harris, 10 W. N. C. 10–15 (1881),— Philadelphia cases.
[2] [Doane *v.* Willcutt, 5 Gray, 335 (1855); 41 Conn. 14; 15 Me. 237; 48 *id.* 68.
[3] Litchfield *v.* Ferguson, 141 Mass. 97 (1886).
[4] 2 Bl. Com. 468; 2 Pars. Contr. 242; 14 Wall. 296; 17 Blatch. 2.
[5] Branch *v.* Commissioners, 80 Va. 432–34 (1885), cases.
[6] Bullard *v.* Bell, 1 Mas. 252 (1817), Story, J.; Thompson *v.* Perrine, 106 U. S. 592–93 (1882), cases; Chickaming *v.* Carpenter, *ib.* 666 (1882).

BEARING. See DATE; INTEREST, 2 (3).

BEAST. See ANIMAL.

Beasts of the plow. An ancient expression referring to animals employed in the ordinary uses of husbandry, or other actual labor in a lawful and useful industry.[1] See DISTRESS (3); HORSE.

BEAT. In law, not merely to whip, wound, or hurt; includes any unlawful imposition of the hand or arm.[2]

To commit a battery,[3] q. v.

BED. 1. The right of connubial intercourse; cohabitation, q. v. Whence **bed and board.** See DIVORCE.

2. The **bed of a river** is that soil so usually covered by water as to be distinguishable from the banks, by the character of the soil, or vegetation, or both, produced by the common presence and action of flowing water.[4] Compare BANK, 1.

BEE. See ANIMAL.

BEER. See LIQUOR; PROHIBITION, 2.

BEEVES. See NEAT.

BEFORE. See AFTER; ANTE; CORAM; ON.

Before the twenty-eighth of a month means by the twenty-seventh, at least.[5]

Before a given day excludes that day.[6]

Before the court. When a matter, by regular proceeding, is made to engage or receive the direct attention of a court, for the purpose of decision, it is said to be or to be pending "before the court." See DECISION; DICTUM.

A certificate by a clerk that a complaint was sworn to "before said court" raises a presumption that this was done in court.[7]

Before trial. May mean before pleading to the merits,[8] — implies that a suit has been commenced.[9]

BEGGING. See VAGRANT.

The act of a cripple who stands upon a sidewalk and in silence holds out his hand for money from passers-by is "begging for alms."[10]

BEGIN. See AFFIRM, 1; AT, 2; RUN, 5.

BEHALF. See INTEREST, 2 (1).

A witness called by a party testifies "in his behalf" though he testifies against his interest.[1]

BEHAVIOR. Manner of having, holding, or keeping one's self; personal carriage and demeanor; bearing, with respect to propriety, morals, and the requirements of law.

Disorderly behavior. See CONTEMPT; DISORDER, 2; ORDER, 4.

Good behavior. Bearing which conforms to the law.

All persons who are not of good fame may be bound over to good behavior — an expression of so great latitude as to leave much to be determined by the discretion of the magistrate.[2] See SUSPICION, 3.

Security to be of good behavior includes more than security to keep the peace; it is demanded with greater caution, and the recognizance is more easily forfeited.[3] See PEACE, 1.

Misbehavior. Improper, unlawful conduct.

A verdict will be set aside for gross misbehavior in the jury, the prevailing party, or his counsel; and an award will be set aside for misbehavior in the arbitrators or referee.[3]

A judge holds office for a specified term, if he shall "so long behave himself well." See TENURE, Of office.

Each house of Congress may punish its members for disorderly behavior.[4]

BEING. Compare IN, 3 (2), Esse.

An allegation that liquor was sold to S. and W. M., "being" minors, shows with sufficient certainty that those persons were minors.[5]

BELIEF. Conviction of mind, founded on evidence, that a fact exists — that an act was done, that a statement is true.[6]

The difference between "belief" and "knowledge" consists in the degree of certainty. Things which do not make a deep impression on the memory may be said to leave a "belief." Knowledge is firm belief.[7]

"Between mere belief and knowledge there is a wide difference;" for example, as to whether a lode or vein of gold or silver exists in a claim proposed for a patent.[8]

The distinction between the two words has become important where the contents of a paper are to be verified as true to the knowledge of the affiant, ex-

---

[1] Somers v. Emerson, 58 N. H. 49 (1876).

[2] Goodrum v. State, 60 Ga. 511 (1878).

[3] State v. Beverlin, 30 Kan. 613 (1883).

[4] Howard v. Ingersoll, 13 How. 427, 381, 416 (1851), Curtis, J.

[5] Metropolitan Nat. Bank of New York v. Morehead, 38 N. J. E. 500 (1884).

[5] Ward v. Walters, 63 Wis. 44 (1885).

[7] Tacey v. Noyes, 143 Mass. 451 (1887).

[8] Winship v. People, 51 Ill. 298 (1869).

[9] Horner v. Pilkington, 11 Ind. 442 (1858).

[10] Re Haller, 3 Abb. N. Cas. 65 (1877).

[1] Richerson v. Sternburg, 65 Ill. 272 (1872).

[2] 4 Bl. Com. 256; 1 Binn. 98, n; 2 Yeates, 437.

[3] 3 Bl. Com. 387; 4 id. 361.

[4] Constitution, Art. I, sec. 5, cl. 2.

[5] State v. Boucher, 59 Wis. 481 (1884).

[8] Giddens v. Mirk, 4 Ga. 369 (1848). See also State v. Grant, 76 Mo. 246 (1882).

[7] [Hatch v. Carpenter, 9 Gray, 274 (1857), Shaw, C. J.; 9 Cal. 62.

[8] Iron Silver Mining Co. v. Reynolds, 124 U. S. 383 (1888), Field, J.

cept as to a matter stated on "information and belief," which he must state he believes to be true.[1]

That may be ground for "suspicion" which will not evidence "belief."[2]

While a person may have reason to believe and yet disbelieve, he cannot "verily believe" without having good reason in fact.[3]

The grounds of belief are: credulity, experience, probability, induction. Experience constitutes the basis of belief in human testimony. Aid is derived from the experience of others. Belief in such testimony is a fundamental principle of our moral nature. This is strengthened by corroborating circumstances. Probability is determined by experience and reasoning combined. Induction tests probability.[4]

See ANSWER, 3; CERTAINTY; CREDIT, 2; DECEIT; FRAUD; KNOWLEDGE, 1; SUPPOSE; SUSPICION.

BELLIGERENT. See WAR.

BELL-ROPE. See OBSTRUCT, 1.

BELLS. See NUISANCE.

BELONG. In statutes referring to inhabitancy, the poor, etc., designates the place of a person's legal settlement, not merely his place of residence.[5]

Belonging to. In the Pennsylvania statute defining arson, includes all structures (as, for example, a barn) so near a dwelling-house on the same premises as to endanger the safety of the house in case of fire.[6] See ACCESSORY; INCIDENT.

BELOW. Compare ABOVE; INFRA.

BENCH. The judge's seat in a court.

Also, the judges themselves as a tribunal or a professional class: as, the common or common pleas bench, the supreme bench, a full or partial bench. Compare BAR, 1.

King's or **Queen's bench.** The supreme court of common law in England, now merged into the High Court of Justice.

Abbreviated K. B., and Q. B.

The king in person used to sit in this court: in theory it was always held before the sovereign. During the reign of a queen it is called the "Queen's bench." In the time of Cromwell it was styled the "upper bench." It succeeded the *aula regis*, q. v. Although supposed to follow the person of the sovereign, it was in fact held at Westminster. It consisted formerly of a chief justice and four associate justices — the sovereign conservators of the peace. The jurisdiction of the court, which was originally criminal and included trespasses, in time included all personal common-law actions between subjects, and actions of ejectment. It had also supervisory power

over inferior tribunals, magistrates, and corporations.[1]

Bencher. In England, a dignitary of the inns of court.

Each inn is presided over by a certain number of benchers who exercise the right of admitting candidates as members of their society and of ultimately calling them to the bar. They are selected from members who have distinguished themselves in their profession. They also exercise general supervision over the professional conduct of counselors who are members of the inn.[2]

Bench-warrant. Process of arrest issued against a person charged with a crime or a contempt of court.

1. A process issued against a person under indictment to bring him into court to answer the charge.

2. A process issued by a civil court for the apprehension of a person appearing to be guilty, under verified allegations, of an indictable civil injury; as, where a debtor, insolvent and believed to have defrauded or to be intending to defraud his creditors, is disposing of his effects or is about to remove with them from the jurisdiction.

The process may be issued by a judge on the *bench* (whence the name "bench" warrant), or by a judge at chambers.

The proceeding is interlocutory,— like a rule on a defendant to show cause why he should not be held to bail in an action *ex contractu;* and is limited to cases where there appears to be a strong presumption of fraud of some kind on one or more creditors. Hence, fraud is the matter to be alleged, controverted, and substantiated. The remedy is allowed without regard to the place where the fraud was perpetrated, as in actions of tort. The proceeding is not in the nature of a summary conviction, but simply an arrest for debt under the regulated supervision of a judge, instead of the arbitrary and badly controlled discretion of a party. Nor is the proceeding criminal: the fraud is treated as a private injury. The plaintiff files a preliminary affidavit showing, in at least general terms, probable cause to the satisfaction of the court. This affidavit also specifies the nature of the claim, whether a contract or not, and, that the amount of bail may be known, the amount of the claim. A hearing of the proofs is fixed, at which the defendant, who has been previously arrested and imprisoned or bailed, may deny all allegations and demand proof of the alleged facts.[3] See ATTACH, 2.

BENEFICE. A gratuitous donation, as, an estate by feudal tenure; also, an ecclesi-

[1] See Black v. Halstead, 39 Pa. 71 (1861); 56 *id.* 33; 67 *id.* 477; 79 *id.* 384; 81 *id.* 180; 82 *id.* 354.

[2] Commonwealth v. Lottery Tickets, 5 Cush. 374 (1850).

[3] Russell v. Ralph, 53 Wis. 332 (1881), cases.

[4] 1 Greenl. Ev. Ch. III.

[5] Reading v. Westport, 19 Conn. 564 (1849), Church, C. J.; 3 *id.* 467; 18 *id.* 425; 8 Vt. 45.

[6] Hill v. Commonwealth, 98 Pa. 195 (1881).

[1] See 3 Bl. Com. 41; 4 *id.* 265.

[2] Holthouse's Law Dict.

[3] Gosline v. Place, 32 Pa. 520 (1859), Lowrie, C. J.; Act 12 July, 1842.

astical living or church preferment given or held for life.[1]

BENEFICIARY. One who is entitled to the benefit of a contract or of an estate held by another.

The word, though a little remote from the original meaning of the expression "*cestui que trust*," is more appropriate for one who is a trustee or fide-commissary.[2] . See TRUST, Cestui, etc.

As a member of a beneficial society, see BENEFIT.

BENEFIT. Good, advantage; fruit, profit, use; aid.

As, in the expressions, assignment for the benefit of creditors, common or mutual benefit, benefit of a doubt, of clergy, of copyright, of a law. See BETTERMENT; USE, 2.

Only he for whose benefit a thing exists can complain of a non-recognition or abuse of his right; and he who retains the benefit of an act must bear the burden.[3] He who has enjoyed the fruit of an act cannot afterward deny the existence or validity of the act — as, that a bond is not valid,[4] that a law is unconstitutional,[5] or an act *ultra vires*. See COMMONUM.

Benefit society. An association incorporated for the purpose of receiving periodical payments from members, to be loaned or given to such members as may need pecuniary relief. Sometimes called *aid*, and *beneficial*, society.

Sick benefits. Aid, usually money, given to a person during the period of his illness or disability, on account of membership or insurance in a benefit or relief society.[6]

The recognition of a person as a member up to a short time before his death, in connection with the presumption that persons follow such regulations as they are under, is sufficient evidence of good standing to maintain an action upon a certificate.[7]

When a benefit certificate takes effect, so far as to vest an absolute right to the benefit money, at the death of the party to whom it issued, the same rule should hold which prevails as to wills and life policies of insurance, viz., that an express designation of the person is conclusive.[8]

---

[1] [4 Bl. Com. 107; 3 Kent, 494.

[2] 1 Story, Eq. 12 ed. § 321, note.

[3] Cowell v. Colorado Springs Co., 100 U. S. 55 (1879); Jones v. Guaranty, &c. Co., 101 *id*. 628 (1879); Peoples' Bank v. National Bank, *ib*. 181 (1879).

[4] United States v. Hodson, 10 Wall. 395 (1870).

[5] Daniels v. Tearney, 102 U. S. 421 (1880); 106 *id*. 481.

[6] See Poultney v. Bachman, 31 Hun, 49, 52–55 (1883), cases.

[7] Lazensky v. Knights of Honor, 31 F. R. 592 (1887); Knights of Honor v. Johnson, 78 Ind. 113 (1881).

[8] Thomas v. Leake, 67 Tex. 470 (1887), Willie, C. J. As to beneficiaries generally, see Lamont v. Grand Lodge, 31 F. R. 177, 181 (1887), cases. As to designation of beneficiary, see Hotel-Men's Association v. Brown, 32 *id*. 11 (1887).

A contract of membership must be read in the light afforded by the constitution and by-laws.[1] See ACCIDENT; ASSOCIATION.

Benefits accepted. See AGENT; ASSUMPSIT; CONTRACT, Implied; ESTOPPEL.

Benefits and burdens. Advantages and disadvantages; profits and losses; rights and duties. See BURDEN.

Beneficial. 1. For the assistance of members, as see, *Society*, above.

2. Entitled to receive the income or profit, as the beneficial owner of an estate. See BENEFICIARY.

3. Contributing to the end in view; supporting or maintaining rather than restricting or defeating; liberal. See CONSTRUCTION; STATUTE, Remedial; RES, 2, Ut, etc.

BENEVOLENCE; BENEVOLENT. "Benevolent," of itself, without anything in the context of a will to restrict its ordinary meaning, clearly includes not only purposes which are deemed charitable by a court of equity, but also any acts of kindness, good will or disposition to do good, the objects of which have no relation to technical charities.[1]

Hence, a devise to be applied "solely for benevolent purposes," in the discretion of a trustee, is not a charity. . . But "benevolent," when coupled with "charitable" or an equivalent word, or used in such connection or applied to such public institutions or corporations as to manifest an intent to make it synonymous with "charitable," has been given effect according to that intent.[2]

"Benevolence" is wider than "charity," in legal signification, but its meaning may be narrowed by the context.[3]

"Benevolent," applied to objects or purposes, may refer to such as are charitable or not charitable, in the legal sense. Acts of kindness, friendship, forethought, or good will, might properly be described as benevolent. It has therefore been held that gifts to trustees to be applied for "benevolent purposes" at their discretion, or to such "benevolent purposes" as they could agree upon, do not create a public charity. . . Where the word is used in connection with other words explanatory of its meaning, and indicating the intent of the donor to limit it to purposes strictly charitable, it has been held to be equivalent to "charitable."[4]

See ASSOCIATION; CHARITY.

---

[1] Splawn v. Chew, 60 Tex. 534 (1883); 67 *id*. 472. See also, generally, 22 Cent. Law J. 562–64 (1886), cases; *ib*. 277, cases.

[2] Chamberlain v. Stearns, 111 Mass. 268–69 (1873), cases, Gray, J.

[3] De Camp v. Dobbins, 31 N. J. E. 695 (1879), Beasley, C. J.; Thomson v. Norris, 20 *id*. 523 (1869), cases; 60 N. H. 533.

[4] Suter v. Hilliard, 132 Mass. 413–14 (1882), cases, En-

BENZINE. See OIL.

BEQUEATH. A gift of personal property by will.

Bequest. A gift of personalty by will; the clause in the instrument making the gift; the thing itself so given.

When the context requires it "bequeath" will be construed "devise"—which is of realty.[1] See DEVISE; LEGACY; WILL, 2.

BEST. See BID; EVIDENCE; KNOWLEDGE.

A testator made a bequest to his son-in-law in trust "to pay the income or such portion as he may consider best and at such time as he sees fit" to testator's granddaughter, an infant, during her life. *Held*, that the intent of the testator was to consider the welfare of the granddaughter; that the word "best" had more reference to withholding income than paying it: that the trustee was to pay only as he thought best to pay.[2] See DISCRETION, 2; IF.

BESTIALITY. See SODOMY.

BET.[3] A wager,—the act or the amount.

"Bet" and "wager" are synonymous terms, applied to the contract of betting and wagering and to the thing or sum bet or wagered. They may be laid upon games and upon things that are not games.[4]

A "bet" or wager is ordinarily an agreement between two or more that a sum of money or some valuable thing, in contributing which all agreeing take part, shall become the property of one or some of them on the happening in the future of an event at present uncertain; while the "stake" is the money or other thing thus put upon the chance. Each party gets a chance of gain from others, and takes a risk of loss of his own to them.[5]

"Illegal gaming implies gain and loss between the parties by betting, such as would excite a spirit of cupidity." A "purse," "prize," or "premium" is ordinarily some valuable thing offered by a person for the doing of something by others, into the strife for which he does not enter. He has not a chance of gaining the thing offered; if he abide by his offer, that he must give it over to some of those contending for it is reasonably certain. "Bet or stakes" and "bet or wager" have substantially the same meaning.[6]

dicott, J.; Saltonstall v. Sanders, 11 Allen, 470 (1865), Gray, J.; Jones v. Habersham, 107 U. S. 185 (1882); Adye v. Smith, 44 Conn. 60 (1876).

[1] Evans v. Price, 118 Ill. 599 (1886); Ladd v. Harvey, 21 N. H. 528 (1850); Lasher v. Lasher, 13 Barb. 109-10 (1852); Laing v. Barbour, 119 Mass. 525 (1876), cases.

[2] Bartlett v. Slater, 53 Conn. 110 (1885).

[3] For *abet*, to maintain.

[4] Woodcock v. McQueen, 11 Ind. 16 (1858), Perkins, J.

[5] Harris v. White, 81 N. Y. 539 (1880), Folger, C. J.; Commonwealth v. Wright, 137 Mass. 251 (1884).

A bet *on* an election means on the result of the election.[1] See GAME, 2; WAGER.

BETTER. See EQUITY.

BETTERMENT. 1. An improvement to realty which is more extensive than ordinary repair, and increases, in a substantial degree, the value of the property; melioration.

Betterment Acts. Statutes which secure to a purchaser of land for valuable consideration, without notice of an infirmity in the title, an interest in the land equal to the value of the improvements or melioration he may have made.

The rule of the common law is that the owner of land shall not pay an intruder or occupant for unauthorized improvements. This induces diligence in the examination of titles, and prevents wrongful appropriations. Chancery, borrowing from the civil law, made the first innovation upon the doctrine; and in time held that when a *bona fide* possessor made meliorations in good faith, under an honest belief of ownership, and the real owner for any reason went into equity, the court, applying the maxim that he who seeks equity must do equity, and adopting the civil law rule of natural equity, compelled the owner to pay for such industrial accessions as were permanently beneficial to the estate.[2]

The occupant must have peaceable possession, under color of title, and honestly believe that he is the owner of the land. Any instrument having a grantor and grantee, containing a description of the land, and apt words for their conveyance, gives color of title. Actual notice of an adverse title is proof of the absence of good faith.[3]

2. The additional value which a piece of property acquires from its proximity to a public improvement.[4] See COMPENSATION, 3.

BETWEEN. Often synonymous with "among," especially when employed to convey the idea of division or separate ownership of property held in common.[5]

It is as appropriate to say that property is to be divided "between" as "among" A, B, and C.[5]

[1] Commonwealth v. Avery, 14 Bush, 633 (1879).

[2] Parsons v. Moses, 16 Iowa, 444-46 (1864), cases, Dillon, J.

[3] Beard v. Dansby, 48 Ark. 186-87 (1886), cases. See generally Bright v. Boyd, 1 Story, 492-98 (1841); 2 *id.* 607 (1843); Griswold v. Bragg, 18 Blatch. 206 (1880); Wheeler v. Merriman, 30 Minn. 376 (1883); Effinger v. Hall, 81 Va. 102-6 (1885), cases; Green v. Biddle, 8 Wheat. 79 (1823); Jackson v. Loomis, (N. Y.), 15 Am. Dec. 347, cases; 19 Blatch. 94; 48 Conn. 581; 11 Me. 482; 74 *id.* 515; 13 Ohio, 308; 14 S. C. 338; 17 Vt. 109; 3 Pomeroy, Eq. § 1241, cases; 2 Story, Eq. §§ 799, 1237-38, cases; 1 Wash. R. P. 139, cases.

[4] See Foster v. Commissioners, 113 Mass. 335 (1882).

[5] Myres v. Myres, 23 How. Pr. 415-16 (1862). See also Ward v. Tomkins, 30 N. J. E. 4 (1878); 20 Conn. 122.

When "between" and "among" follow the verb "divide" their general signification is very similar, and in popular use they are synonymous — though "among" denotes a collection and is never followed by two of any sort, while "between" may be followed by any plural number, and seems to refer to the individuals of a class rather than to the class itself.[1]

"Between" persons implies, strictly speaking, between two parties to a division; but the reference may be to more than two persons.[2]

By the language "equally divided between my grandchildren," a testator may intend division between two families.[3]

Between two places excludes the *terminii*.[4]

Between two days excludes both days.[5] See DAY.

"Between eleven o'clock P. M. and five o'clock A. M." covers the period intervening between eleven o'clock at night and five o'clock in the morning of the succeeding day.[6]

BEYOND. See SEA.

BI. The Latin prefix, put for *dui*, twice, or from *bis*, twice, two.

BIAS.[7] Inclination of mind toward a particular object; an influential power which sways the judgment.[8]

In a juror, being under an influence which so sways his mind to one side as to prevent his deciding the cause according to the evidence.[8]

Not synonymous with prejudice.[8]

May show bias in a witness by relationship, sympathy, hostility, or prejudice.[9] See IMPARTIAL, 1; PREJUDICE.

BIBLE. See BLASPHEMY; CHRISTIANITY; HEARSAY, 4.

BICYCLE. Held to be a "carriage," within a statute forbidding fast driving.[10]

Not a "carriage" liable to toll, under the English Turnpike Act of 1883.[11]

A tricycle capable of being propelled by the feet, or by steam as an auxiliary, or alone, was held to be a "locomotive," within the English Highways and Locomotive Act of 1878.[12]

The park commissioners of New York, in their discretion, may prohibit bicycles in the parks of that city. An ordinance to that effect may be a "regulation" intended by the statute creating their office.[13]

An act which forbids the use of bicycles on a certain road, unless permitted by the superintendent of the road, is not unconstitutional.[1]

In the absence of legislative prohibition, riders of bicycles would seem to have the same rights on highways as those using any other vehicle.[2]

BID. In its most comprehensive sense, to make an offer; in its more ordinary acceptation, to make an offer at an auction;[3] the offer itself.

Also, the price at which a contractor will furnish material or do some other particular thing.

Bid off. One is said to bid off a thing when he bids at an auction and the thing is knocked down to him in immediate succession to his bid and as a consequence of it.[3]

Bidder. One who offers to give a designated price for property on sale at an auction.

By-bidding. Fictitious bidding; running up the price of an article, not to save it from sacrifice, but to mislead *bona fide* bidders; puffing.

Upset bid. A more liberal bid on property sold at public sale, offered to the court having jurisdiction in the proceeding, in order that the sale already made may be set aside, or confirmation thereof withheld, and that the new bid may be entertained, perhaps along with other bids. Whence *upset-bidder*, for the person who makes such offer.[4] (Local.)

The article offered for sale is to be delivered to the highest real bidder. If a minimum price is fixed notice thereof must be given. By-bidding, since it deceives and involves falsehood, is a fraud.[5] An agreement not to bid, that is, to prevent competition and possibly to cause a sacrifice of the property, is void, as against public policy. On a breach of a contract to pay a bid the measure of damages is the amount which would have been received if the contract had been kept.[6]

It was formerly the rule in England, in chancery sales, that, until confirmation of the master's report, the bidding would be "opened" upon a mere offer to advance the price ten per centum. But Lord Eldon expressed dissatisfaction with this practice, as tend-

[1] Senger *v.* Senger's Executor, 81 Va. 698 (1886), Richardson, J.

[2] Haskell *v.* Sargent, 113 Mass. 343 (1873).

[3] Stoutenburgh *v.* Moore, 37 N. J. E. 69 (1883).

[4] Revere *v.* Leonard, 1 Mass. *93 (1804).

[5] Bunce *v.* Reed, 16 Barb. 352 (1853); 5 Metc. 540.

[6] Hedderich *v.* State, 101 Ind. 570 (1884).

[7] F. *biais* a slant, slope: inclination to a side. L. L. *bifacem*, one who looks sideways.—Skeat.

[8] [Willis *v.* State, 12 Ga. 449–50 (1853).

[9] 1 Whart. Ev. §§ 408, 566.

[10] Taylor *v.* Goodwin, L. R., 4 Q. B. D. 228 (1879).

[11] Williams *v.* Ellis, L. R., 5 Q. B. D. 176 (1880).

[12] Parkyns *v.* Priest, L. R., 7 Q. B. D. 315 (1881).

[13] Matter of Wright, 29 Hun, 358 (1883).

[1] State *v.* Yopp, 97 N. C. 477 (1887).

[2] Cook, Highways. See 69 Law Times, 28 (1880); 25 Solic. J. & R. 4 (1880) — commenting on Taylor's and Williams' cases, *ante* — notes 10, 11.

[3] Eppes *v.* Mississippi, &c. R. Co., 35 Ala. 56 (1859), Walker, C. J.

[4] See Yost *v.* Porter, 80 Va. 855 (1885).

[5] Veazie *v.* Williams, 8 How. 151–52 (1850), cases; 2 Kent, 538.

[6] Wicker *v.* Hoppock, 6 Wall. 97–98 (1867), cases; James *v.* La Crosse, &c. R. Co., *ib.* 752 (1867); 4 Del. Ch. 491; 1 Cowp. 395.

ing to impair confidence in sales, to keep bidders from attending, and to diminish the amount realized, and his views were finally adopted in the statute of 30 and 31 Vict. (1867), c. 48, § 7. . . In this country his views were followed at au early day by the courts, and the rule has become almost universal that a sale will not be set aside for inadequacy of price unless the inadequacy be so great as to shock the conscience, or unless there be additional circumstances against its fairness; being very much the rule that always prevailed in Englaud as to setting aside a sale after a master's report had been confirmed. . If the inadequacy of price is so gross as to shock the conscience, or if, iu addition to gross inadequacy, the purchaser has been guilty of unfairness, or has taken any undue advantage, or if the owner of the property, or the party interested in it, has been for any other reason misled or surprised, the sale will be regarded as fraudulent and void, or the party injured will be permitted to redeem the property sold. Great inadequacy requires only slight circumstances of unfairness in the conduct of the party benefited by the sale to raise the presumption of fraud.[1]

See ADEQUATE, 1; AUCTION; RESPONSIBLE; SALE, Judicial.

BIGAMY.[2] The offense of having two husbands or wives at the same time, the one *de jure* and the other *de facto.*[3]

Strictly speaking, *bigamy* means "twice married," as its derivation shows. This was never an offense at common law; it was made an offense by the canonists. *Polygamy* is the proper term; but, by long usage, *bigamy* has come to mean the state of a man who has two wives, or a woman who has two husbands, at the same time.[4]

Whence bigamist (not a legal term), and bigamous.

The penalties of the offense are not incurred where one of a married couple has been absent and unheard of for a long period, as five to seven years, and the other party marries; nor, in some States, where one is sentenced to imprisonment for a long term, as for life; nor where there has been a legal dissolution of the relation for a cause not involving guilt, as for a contract made within the age of consent.[5]

The first wife is not admitted as a witness against her husband, because she is the true wife: but the sec-

ond wife, so called, may be, for she is not a wife at all; and so, *vice versa,* as to the second husband, so called.[1]

The first marriage may be proved by the admissions of the prisoner.[2]

Iu a criminal prosecution strict proof of an actual marriage is necessary; but in a civil suit an admission, or reputation and cohabitation, suffices.[3]

The act of Congress of July 1, 1862, provided that every person having a husband or wife living, who married another, whether married or single, in a Territory, or other place over which the United States had exclusive jurisdiction, was guilty of bigamy —

And should be punished by a fine of not more than five hundred dollars, and by imprisonment for a term of not more than five years.[4] That act was amended by act of March 22, 1882, to read as follows:

Section 1. "Every person who has a husband or wife living who, in a Territory or other place over which the United States have exclusive jurisdiction, hereafter marries another, whether married or single, and any man who hereafter simultaneously, or on the same day, marries more than one woman, in a Territory or other place over which the United States have exclusive jurisdiction, is guilty of polygamy, and shall be punished by a fine of not more than five hundred dollars and by imprisonment for a term of not more than five years; but this section [R. S. § 5352, as amended] shall not extend to any person by reason of any former marriage whose husband or wife by such marriage shall have been absent for five years, and is not known to such person to be living, and is believed by such person to be dead. not to any person by reason of any former marriage which shall have been dissolved by a valid decree of a competent court, nor to any person by reason of any former marriage which shall have been prouounced void by a valid decree of a competent court, on the ground of nullity of the marriage contract."

Sec. 2. If any male person cohabits with more than one woman, he shall be guilty of a misdemeanor, punishable by a fine of not more than three hundred dollars, and by imprisonment for not more than six months, or by both.

Sec. 5. Cause for challenge of a juror is: living or having lived in the practice of bigamy, polygamy, or unlawful cohabitation with more than one woman; or believing in the practice of bigamy, polygamy, etc. . . . An answer shall not be given in evidence in any criminal prosecution under the act. Declining to answer as a witness renders the person incompetent.

Sec. 6. The President may grant amnesty for offenses committed before the passage of the act.

Sec. 7. The issue of Mormon marriages, born before January 1, 1883, are legitimated.

---

[1] Graffam *v.* Burgess, 117 U. S. 191–92 (1886), cases, Bradley, J. See also Vass *v.* Arrington, 89 N. C. 13 (1883) — ten per cent. rule; Hansucker *v.* Walker, 76 Va. 753 (1882); Langyher *v.* Patterson, 77 *id.* 470 (1883); Central Pacific R. Co. *v.* Creed, 70 Cal. 501 (1886); Babcock *v.* Canfield, 36 Kan. 439 (1887).

[2] L. L. *bigamia; bi* for Gk. *di,* double; *gamia,* for Gk. *gámos,* marriage. Gk. *digamía,* — Skeat.

[3] 1 Bishop, Mar. & Div. § 296.

[4] Gise *v.* Commonwealth, 81 Pa. 432, 430 (1876), Paxson, J. See also 4 Bl. Com. 163; 2 Steph. Hist. Cr. L. Eng. 430; 1 Law Quar. Rev. 474–76 (1885).

[5] 2 Kent, 79–80; 4 Bl. Com. 164.

---

[1] 4 Bl. Com. 164.

[2] Miles *v.* United States, 103 U. S. 304, 311 (1880), cases.

[3] The Gaines Cases, 24 How. 605 (1860); 12 *id.* 472; 6 *id.* 597; State *v.* Johnson, 12 Minn. 476 (1867), cases: 93 Am. Dec. 241, 251–57, cases; 53 Pa. 132; 14 Tex. 468, 471; 2 Utah, 25.

[4] 12 St. L. 50: R. S. § 5352.

Sec. 8. "No polygamist, bigamist, or any person cohabiting with more than one woman, and no woman cohabiting with any of the persons described as aforesaid . . shall be entitled to vote at any election . . or be eligible for election or appointment to or be entitled to hold any office or place of public trust, honor, or emolument in, under, or for any such Territory or place, or under the United States."

Sec. 9. Declares all registration and election offices vacant, and provides for their being filled by a board of five persons, appointed by the President, until provision be made by the legislative assembly of the Territory as further directed by this section.[1]

Any man is a polygamist or bigamist, within the meaning of the last recited act, who having previously married one wife, still living, and having another at the time when he presents himself to claim registration as a voter, still maintains that relation to a plurality of wives, although from March 22, 1882, until the day he offers to register, he may not in fact have cohabited with more than one woman. . . The crime, under the acts of Congress, consists in entering into a bigamous or polygamous marriage, and is complete when the relation begins.[2] See RELIGION.

The offense of cohabiting with more than one woman, created by § 3 of the act of March 22, 1882, is committed by a man who lives in the same house with two women, and eats at their tables one-third of his time, or thereabouts, and holds them out to the world, by his language or conduct, as his wives. It is not necessary that he and the women, or either of them, shall sleep together.[3] See COHABIT, 2.

The uniform current of authority is, that for the purposes of prosecution the offense of bigamy or polygamy can be committed but once prior to the time the prosecution is instituted.[4]

See further Act of March 3, 1888, under POLYGAMY.

---

[1] 22 St. L. 30–32. See 116 U. S. 56–57; 118 id. 350.

[2] Murphy v. Ramsey, 114 U. S. 15, 35, 41 (1885), Matthews, J. Approved, 116 id. 72, infra.

[3] Cannon v. United States, 116 U. S. 55 (1885), Blatchford, J. Afterward, May 10, 1886, the court decided that it had no jurisdiction under the writ of error in the case, as see 118 U. S. 354–55.

[4] Exp. Snow, 120 U. S. 274, 281–86 (1887), cases, Blatchford, J. Snow was convicted of polygamy upon three indictments, exactly alike except that they covered different periods of time, and three sentences were imposed. He complied with the first sentence — paid a fine of $300, and remained in prison six months; and then demanded his release, claiming that his offense had been a continuing one, and that he could not be punished more than once for it. The Supreme Court held that under the theory of the lower court Snow might have been punished under an indictment entered every week during the continuance of the polygamous relation.

BILATERAL. Designates a contract executory on both sides, as, a sale. **Unilateral.** When one party makes no express agreement, but his obligation is left to implication of law, as, a guaranty. See CONTRACT, Bilateral, etc.

A bilateral record is a record introduced between parties and privies. A unilateral record is a record offered to show a particular fact as a prima facie case for or against a stranger.

BILGED. That state of a ship in which water is freely admitted through holes and breaches made in the planks of the bottom, occasioned by injuries, whether the ship's timbers are broken or not.[1]

BILL.[2] A statement of particulars, in writing, and more or less formal in arrangement.

Distinctive qualifying terms are frequently omitted, the relation or context indicating the sense. Thus "bill," standing alone, is often used for bill of exchange, bill in equity, bill of indictment, etc.

I. IN CONSTITUTIONAL LAW. A formal, public, written declaration of popular rights and liberties — restrictive of governmental power. See further RIGHT, 2, Bill of Rights.

II. IN LEGISLATION. The draft or form of an act presented to a legislature but not enacted. As, a bill of attainder, and money bills, qq. v.

"Act" is the appropriate term for the document after it has been passed by the legislature: it is then something more than a draft or form.[3]

See ACT, 3; PASS, 2; RIDER; SNAKE; TITLE, 2; VETO; YEAS AND NAYS.

III. IN MERCANTILE LAW. A written statement of the amount or items of a demand, or of the terms of an agreement or undertaking, particularly for the payment of money.[4]

As, a bank-bill; a due-bill; a bill rendered, payable, or receivable; a bill of adventure, of credit, of exchange, of lading, of parcels, of sale, of sight; a bill of health, of mortality; a bill obligatory or penal, or single. As to which see the descriptive or qualifying word.

Bill; bill obligatory; bill penal; bill single. A bond without a condition. An instrument acknowledging indebtedness, in

---

[1] Peele v. Merchants' Ins. Co., 3 Mas. 39 (1822), Story, J.

[2] L. L. billa, a writing: bulla, a papal bill; originally, a leaden seal, — Skeat.

[3] [Southwark Bank v. Commonwealth, 26 Pa. 450 (1856), Lewis, J.; 4 Wall. 387.

[4] Abbott's Law Dict.

a certain sum, to be paid on a day certain.[1]

Differs from a promissory note in having a seal affixed; yet, by the custom of merchants, binds without seal, witness, or delivery. It is subject to defalcation and set-off.[1]

A "bill" is a common engagement for money, given by one man to another. When with a penalty, called a "penal bill;" when without a penalty, a "single bill;" though the latter is most frequently used. By a "bill" is ordinarily understood a single bond without a condition.[2]

"Bill single," or simply "bill," without condition or penalty, was originally the plainest form. A "bill penal" or "penal bill" had a condition and penalty annexed. A "bill obligatory" in form was like either of these and had a seal. Bonds with conditions have superseded bills penal.

Bill payable. Any demand, usually evidenced by a writing, for money, subsisting against a person. **Bill receivable.** Any such demand, with respect to the person who is entitled to the money.

"Bills receivable" are promissory notes, bills of exchange, bonds and other evidences or securities, which a merchant or trader holds, and which are payable to him.[3]

Bill rendered. A creditor's written statement of his claim, itemized.

Not assented to by the debtor, as in an account stated. The creditor may sue for a larger sum.[4] See ACCOUNT, I.

IV. IN LEGAL PROCEDURE. A formal written statement of complaint to a court of justice.[5] As, the original bill in common-law practice; a bill in chancery or equity; a bill of indictment, of information, *qq. v.*

Also, a written statement or record of proceedings in an action.[1] As, a bill of exceptions, of costs, of particulars, a fee-bill,[5] *qq. v.*

Bill in chancery; bill in equity. A statement, addressed to a chancellor or a court of equity, of the facts which give rise to a complaint, with a petition for relief.

This may be an original bill or a bill not original, a cross-bill, a supplemental bill, a bill for discovery, of conformity, interpleader, peace or *quia timet*, review, revivor, foreclosure, a creditor's bill, *qq. v.*

A bill in equity corresponds to a declaration at law. Its parts are: 1, the address to the court; 2, the names of the parties; 3, the facts of complainant's case — the stating part; 4, a general charge of improper combination — the clause of confederation; 5, the pretenses or excuses respondent may have to offer in defense — the charging part; 6, allegations that the respondent's acts are contrary to equity, and that no adequate remedy is afforded at law — the clause of jurisdiction; 7, a prayer for answers to interrogations — the interrogating part; 8, a prayer for relief; 9, a prayer for process. Parts 4, 5, and 6 are omitted, except where fraud is to be specifically charged as an actual fact. The whole is sworn to by the complainant.

When a person has a cause which is redressible only in equity he commences his suit by preferring to the court a written statement of his case called a "bill in chancery" or a "bill in equity," which is in the nature of a petition to the court, sets forth the material facts, and concludes with a prayer for the appropriate relief or other thing required of the court, and for the usual process against the parties, against whom the relief or other thing is sought, to bring them before the court to make answer in the premises.[1]

The most general division of bills is those which are original and those which are not original. **Original bills** relate to some matter not before litigated in the court, by the same persons standing in the same interests. These bills may again be divided into those which pray, and those which do not pray, relief.[2]

Bills not original are, first, such as are an addition to, or a continuance or a dependency of, an original bill; or, second, such as are brought for the purpose of cross-litigation, or of controverting, suspending, or reversing some decree or order of the court, or of carrying it into execution. The first class of bills not original furnishes the means of supplying the defects of a suit, of continuing it, if abated, and of obtaining the benefit of it. These means are: by a supplemental bill; by an original bill in the nature of a supplemental bill; by a bill of revivor; by an original bill in the nature of a bill of revivor; by a bill of revivor and supplement. The second class includes: a cross-bill; a bill of review; a bill to impeach a decree upon the ground of fraud; a bill to suspend the opera-

[1] Farmers', &c. Bank v. Greiner, 2 S. & R. 115, 117 (1815), Tilghman, C. J.

[2] Tracy v. Talmage, 18 Barb. 462 (1854): Jacob's Law Dict.

[3] State v. Robinson, 57 Md. 501 (1881): Bouvier's Law Dict.

[4] Williams v. Glenny, 16 N. Y. 389 (1857).

[5] Abbott's Law Dict.

[1] Story, Eq. Pl. § 7.

[2] Story, Eq. Pl. §§ 16, 17; 16 F. R. 731.

tion of a decree; a bill to carry a former decree into execution; a bill partaking in some measure of one or more of both of these classes of bills.[1]

A **cross-bill** is brought by a defendant in a suit against the plaintiff in the same suit, or against other defendants in the same suit, or against both, touching the matters in question in the original bill. It is an auxiliary to the proceedings in the original suit, a dependency upon it — brings the whole dispute before the court for one decree. The two bills constitute one suit.[2]

New and distinct matters, not embraced in the original bill, cannot be introduced by the cross-bill; and new parties must be introduced by amendment of the bill.[2]

A **supplemental bill** is brought as an addition to an original bill to supply some defect in its original frame or structure, not the subject of amendment.[3]

May be filed by either party to his own bill, within a reasonable time — even after decree made, when a necessary party has been omitted, when further discovery is requisite, when some matter overlooked needs development, or when it is essential to bring out other matter in order to give full effect to the decree entered or to be entered on the original bill. The bill is not amendable after the parties are at issue, and witnesses have been examined. An answer to the new matter is prayed for.[3]

After hearing the proofs a bill may be so amended as to put in issue matters in dispute and in proof, but not sufficiently in issue by the original bill.[4] See AMENDMENT, 1.

See also ADEQUATE; ANSWER, 3; DEMURRER; DISMISS; EQUITY; FISHING, 2; IMPERTINENCE; MULTIFARIOUSNESS; PARTY, 2; PREJUDICE, 2; RELIEF, 2; REMEDY.

Original bill. 1. An ancient mode of commencing an action at law, particularly in the court of king's bench; sometimes termed a "plaint," and resembled the modern "declaration." Compare WRIT, Original.

2. In equity, a complaint relating to a dispute not before litigated by the same persons in the same interests. See page 121.

True bill. See IGNORE.

[1] Story, Eq. Pl. § 326.

[2] Story, Eq. Pl. § 389; Shields v. Barrow, 17 How. 145 (1854); Ayres v. Carver, ib. 595 (1854); Cross v. De Valle, 1 Wall. 14 (1863); Exp. Montgomery, &c. R. Co., 95 U. S. 225 (1877); Ayers v. Chicago, 101 id. 187 (1879); Nashville, &c. R. Co. v. United States, ib. 641 (1879); First Nat. Bank v. Flour Mills Co., 31 F. R. 584 (1887); 2 McCrary, 177; 50 Conn. 62; 105 Ill. 585; 21 W. Va. 247; 2 Daniel, Ch. 1548.

[3] Story, Eq. Pl. § 332.

[4] Graffam v. Burgess, 117 U. S. 195 (1886), cases.

BILLA. L. L. A bill: an original bill at law, or a bill of indictment.

Billa cassetur. That the bill be quashed. A judgment, at common law, for defendant, on a plea in abatement.[1] See QUASH.

Billa vera. A true bill.

BILLIARDS. See GAME, 2.

BIND. To place under a legal obligation, particularly that of a bond or covenant; to affect with a contract or a judgment; to affect with a thing done, or with a common relation; to obligate.

As, to bind, and to be bound or to become bound, by a contract made, by a judgment or decree entered or rendered, by legislation, by the act of a privy, a wife, a partner, or other agent, or by the declaration of an accomplice.

Binding. Establishing an obligation; creating a legal duty or necessity. See INSTRUCT, 2.

Binding out. To obligate as an apprentice, q. v.

Binding over. To obligate to appear as a witness, or as a defendant, at the time of trial, or to keep the peace, q. v.

Bound. Brought under an obligation, as by a covenant; charged with responsibility, as with a duty; obligated. See APPRENTICE; BOND; HOLD, 4; INDENTURE; OBLIGATE.

BIPARTITE. See PART, 1.

BIRD. See ANIMAL.

BIRTH. See ABANDON, 2 (2); NATUS; VENTER.

BIS. See BI.

BISSEXTILE. See YEAR.

BITTERS. See LIQUOR.

BLACK. See ACRE; CAP; GOWN; RENT.

BLACKLEG. A person who gets his living by frequenting race-courses and places where games of chance are played, getting the best odds and giving the least he can, but not necessarily by cheating.[2]

BLACK-LISTING. See BOYCOTTING.

An act of Wisconsin, approved April 8, 1887 (Laws, ch. 349), provides that: Any two or more employees who shall agree, combine, and confederate together for the purpose of interfering with or preventing any person or persons seeking employment from obtaining such employment, either by threats, promises or by circulating or causing the circulation of a so-called black-list, or by any means whatsoever, or for the purpose of procuring and causing the discharge of any employee or employees by any means whatsoever,

[1] [3 Bl. Com. 303.

[2] Barnett v. Allen, 3 H. & N. 379 (1858), Pollock, C. B.

shall be deemed guilty of a misdemeanor, and upon conviction shall be punished by imprisonment in the county jail for a period of not more than one month or by a fine not less than fifty dollars, or by both.

BLACK-MAIL.[1] 1. Rent reserved in work, grain, or the baser money. Opposed, *white rent:* rent paid in silver.[2]

A rent in grain, cattle, money, or other thing, anciently paid to men of influence, in the north of England, for protection against robbers.[3]

By statute 43 Eliz. (1601), c. 13, for preventing rapine on the northern borders, to imprison or carry away any subject in order to ransom him . . or to give or take any money or contribution, there called *black-mail,* in order to secure goods from rapine, is felony without benefit of clergy.[4]

2. In common parlance, extortion — the exaction of money for the performance of a duty, the prevention of an injury, or the exercise of an influence.[5]

Imports an unlawful service and an involuntary payment. Not unfrequently, the money is extorted by threats, or by operating upon the fears or the credulity, or by promises to conceal or offers to expose the weakness, the folly, or the crime of the victim. There is moral compulsion which neither necessity nor fear nor credulity can resist. The term, as universally regarded, implies an unlawful act; and though, from its indefiniteness and comprehensiveness, the offense is not classified as a distinct crime, it is nevertheless believed to be criminal. Therefore, to charge a man with "black-mailing" is equivalent to charging him with a crime.[6]

Worcester says that "black-mail" originally meant the performance of labor, the payment of copper coin, or the delivery of certain things in kind, as rent; and that the word was contrasted with "white rent," which was paid in silver. Spelman attributes the term "black" to the color of the coin; Jamieson to its illegality. Dean Swift used the term to signify "hush money," "money extorted under the threat of exposure in print for an alleged offense." Bartlett is the first lexicographer who confines its meaning to that sense, and the use of it to this country. . . The meaning is not legally confined to extortion by threats or other morally compulsory measure. The sense intended in any given case should be determined by a jury.[6] See EXTORTION; THREATENING LETTER.

---

[1] According to most of the authorities, *mail* is from the French *maille,* a small coin. It may come from the German *mahl,* tribute, or from the Gaelic, *mal,* a rent.

[2] See 2 Bl. Com. 42–43.

[3] See Termes de la Ley (1721).

[4] 4 Bl. Com. 244. See All the Year, vol. 30, p. 247.

[5] Edsall *v.* Brooks, 2 Robt. 33–34 (N. Y. Super. Ct. (1864), Monell, J. Same case, 17 Abb. Pr., o. s., 226; 26 How. Pr. 431.

[6] Edsall *v.* Brooks, 3 Robt. 293–95 (1865), Robertson, C. J. See 132 Mass. 264; 97 N. Y. 313; 13 Tex. Ap. 287.

BLACKS. See CITIZEN; SCHOOL, Separate; WHITE.

BLACKSMITH SHOP. See POLICE, 2.

Is not a nuisance *per se.* The business may be so carried on as not to annoy persons living in the vicinity.[1] See NUISANCE.

BLACKSTONE, SIR WILLIAM.

Born July 10, 1723. In 1736 he entered Pembroke College, Oxford, where he continued till 1741, when he began to study law. In 1746, at the end of the probationary period, he was called to the bar. Down to 1760 he seems to have been engaged in but two cases of importance. He passed much time in Oxford, taking an active interest in the affairs of the university.

About 1750 he began to plan his Lectures on the Laws of England. In 1753 he delivered his first course at Oxford. The next year he published his Analysis of the Laws of England, for the use of his numerous hearers. This analysis is founded on a similar work by Sir Matthew Hale.

A "broadsheet," dated Oxford, June 23, 1753, announcing that the "course of lectures" would begin "in Michaelmas Term next" (November), and were "calculated" for laymen as well as for lawyers, stated that "To this End it is proposed to lay down a general and comprehensive Plan of the Laws of *England;* to deduce their History; to enforce and illustrate their leading Rules and fundamental Principles; and to compare them with the Laws of Nature and of other Nations; without entering into practical Niceties, or the minute Distinctions of particular Cases." [2]

Mr. Viner having bequeathed to the University of Oxford a sum of money and the copyright of his Abridgment of Law, for the purpose of instituting a professorship of common law, Blackstone, on October 20, 1758, was elected first Vinerian professor, and, five days later, delivered his "Introductory Lecture on the Study of Law," afterward prefixed to his Commentaries. His lectures became celebrated throughout the kingdom.

He never acquired celebrity as an advocate. In *Tonson* v. *Collins* (1 W. Bl. 301, 321), he made an exhaustive argument in favor of the common-law right of literary property.

In 1765 appeared the first volume of his commentaries. The other three volumes were published during the next four years.

In 1766 he resigned the Vinerian professorship. In 1770 he was appointed a judge of the King's Bench, receiving then the honor of knighthood; and, a few months later, became a judge of the court of Common Pleas. In *Scott* v. *Shephard* (2 W. Bl. 892), the "squib case," wherein the difference between the actions of trespass and case was discussed, he dissented from the opinion of the majority of the court. See CASE, 3.

He died February 14, 1780. The notes of decisions which he had collected, and prepared for the press, were published in two volumes, in 1781, as directed in his will, by his brother-in-law, James Clitherow, Esq.[3]

---

[1] Foucher *v.* Grass, 60 Iowa, 507 (1883).

[2] 2 Law Quar. Rev. 83 (1896) — from a copy of the "broadsheet" found in 1885, in an old book.

[3] See generally Preface to 1 W. Bl. Reports.

American lawyers, with few exceptions, since the Revolution, have drawn their first lessons in jurisprudence from Blackstone's Commentaries. "That work was contemporaneous with our Constitution, and brought the law of England down to that day, and then, as now, was the authoritative text-book on its subject, familiar not only to the profession, but to all men of the general education of the founders of our Constitution." [1]

Blackstone first rescued the law of England from chaos. He did well what Coke tried to do one hundred and fifty years before: he gave an account of the law as a whole, capable of being studied, not only without disgust, but with interest and profit. His arrangement of the subject may be defective; but a better work of the kind has not yet been written, and, with all its defects, the literary skill with which a problem of extraordinary difficulty was dealt with is astonishing. He knew nearly everything, relating to the subject, worth knowing. [2]

"Its institutional value, and especially its historic value as an authentic and faithful mirror of the condition of the English Law as the result of legislation and adjudication, as it then existed, it is difficult to overestimate." [3]

BLAME. See DELICTUM; WRONG.

BLAND'S TABLES. See TABLE, 4.

BLANK. [4] 1, *adj.* (1) Of a white color: lacking something essential to completeness; not filled in or filled up with a word or words — names, amount, time, place, description, conditions, etc.: as, a blank certificate of stock, power of attorney, assignment, warrant.

(2) Unrestricted; indorsee not named: as, an indorsement in blank or a blank indorsement.

2, *n.* A space left in a written or printed paper, to be filled with words or figures in order to complete the sense.

Blanks. Forms of writs, deeds, leases, powers of attorney, and other instruments, printed with spaces left for writing in names, dates, sums, places, descriptions, conditions, and other matters peculiar to special cases. Often spoken of as *legal* blanks. See WRITING.

Powers of attorney to transfer stock are often executed in blank, the right to fill in the name of an attorney being implied. [1]

The blanks in a warranty of attorney to confess judgment need not be filled up. The idiom of the language admits of many things being understood which are not directly expressed. This is eminently so with the personal pronouns. [2]

The grantor in a deed conveying realty, signed and acknowledged, with a blank for the name of the grantee, may by parol authorize another party to fill up the blank. In such case before the deed is delivered to the grantee his name must be inserted by the party so authorized. [3]

Where a party to a negotiable instrument intrusts it to the custody of another for use, with blanks not filled, as against the rights of innocent third persons such instrument carries on its face implied authority in the receiver as agent to fill any blanks necessary to perfect it as an instrument; [4] but not to vary or alter material terms by erasing what is written or printed as part, nor to pervert the scope or meaning by filling blanks with stipulations repugnant to what was clearly expressed in the instrument before it was so delivered. [5]

A note payable to bearer and indorsed in blank is transferable by mere delivery, and any *bona fide* holder is effectually shielded from the defense of prior equities between the original parties. [6]

As between original parties the act of delivering the paper is authority for filling blanks conformably to their mutual understanding. If there is no express agreement the authority is general; and the burden of proof is on the defendant to show such agreement. [7]

In cases of blank indorsements possession is evidence of title. [8]

When blanks material in nature are filled up after execution, the instrument, as a deed, should be re-executed and re-acknowledged; but failure to do so would hardly defeat a vested interest. [9]

See ALTERATION, 2; BEARER; INDORSEMENT.

BLANKET. See INSURANCE, Policy of.

BLASPHEMY. [10] Denying the being or providence of the Almighty, or contumelious reproaching of Christ; also, profane scoffing at the holy scripture, or exposing it to contempt and ridicule. [11]

---

[1] Knote *v.* United States, 10 Ct. Cl. 399 (1874), Loring, J.

[2] 2 Steph. Hist. Cr. Law Eng. 214–15.

[3] 26 Am. Law Rev. 35 (1888), J. F. Dillon. See also Cooley's Bl. Com. vol. 1, p. v.

See generally preface to Chitty's edition of the Commentaries; 8 Alb. Law J. 290; 13 *id.* 104; 1 Allibone, Dict. Authors; 1 Am. Jur. 116; 1 Austin, Lect. 71; 104 Eclectic Mag. 703; 15 Law Mag. 292; 14 Leg. Obs. 143; 51 Macm. Mag. 350; 7 Pitts. Leg. J. 106; 5 West. Jur. 529.

[4] F. *blanc,* white.

[1] Denny *v.* Lyon, 38 Pa. 101 (1860); German Building Association *v.* Sendmeyer, 50 *id.* 67 (1865).

[2] Swecsey *v.* Kitchen, 80 Pa. 160 (1876), Agnew, C. J.

[3] Allen *v.* Withrow, 110 U. S. 128–29 (1884), cases.

[4] Bank of Pittsburgh *v.* Neal, 22 How. 108 (1859); Angle *v.* N. W. Mut. Life Ins. Co., 92 U. S. 338–39, 331, 337 (1875), cases.

[5] Goodman *v.* Simonds, 20 How. 360–61 (1857), cases; Michigan Bank *v.* Eldred, 9 Wall. 551–52 (1869), cases; 101 U. S. 572; 46 N. Y. 325.

[6] City of Lexington *v.* Butler, 14 Wall. 295 (1871).

[7] 3 Kent, 89; Davidson *v.* Lanier, 4 Wall. 456 (1866), Chase, C. J.

[8] 3 Kent, 90.

[9] 2 Pars. Contr. 563, 723.

[10] Gk. *blas-phēmein',* to speak ill or evil of.

[11] [4 Bl. Com. 59.

Maliciously reviling God or religion.[1]

An offense at common law. The reviling is an offense because it tends to corrupt the morals of the people and to destroy good order. Such offenses have always been considered independent of any religious establishment or the rights of the church. They are treated as affecting the essential interests of civil society. . . The people of the State of New York, in common with the people of this country, profess the general doctrines of Christianity, as the rule of their faith and practice; and to scandalize the author of these doctrines is not only, in a religious point of view, extremely impious, but even in respect to the obligations due to society is a gross violation of decency and good order. The free, equal, and undisturbed enjoyment of religious opinion, whatever it may be, and free and decent discussions on any religious subject, is granted and secured; but to revile, with malicious and blasphemous contempt, the religion professed by almost the whole community is an abuse of that right. Wicked and malicious words, writings and actions which go to vilify those gospels, continue, as at common law, to be an offense against the public peace and safety. They are inconsistent with the reverence due to the administration of an oath, and, among other evil consequences, they tend to lessen, in the public mind, its religious sanction.[1]

A malicious and mischievous intention is the broad boundary between right and wrong. This is to be collected from the offensive levity, scurrilous and opprobrious language, and other circumstances. The species of the offense may be classed as: 1, denying the being and providence of God; 2, contumelious reproaches of Jesus Christ; profane and malevolent scoffing at the scriptures, or exposing any part of them to contempt and ridicule; 3, certain immoralities tending to subvert all religion and morality. It is not necessary to the exercise of liberty of conscience and to freedom of religious worship that a man should have the right publicly to vilify the religion of his neighbors and of his country. It is open, public vilification of the religion of the country that is punished, not to force conscience by punishment, but to preserve the peace by an outward respect to the religion of the country, and not as a restraint upon the liberty of conscience.[2]

Consists in blaspheming the holy name of God, by denying, cursing, or contumeliously reproaching God, his creation, government, or final judging of the world.[3]

This may be done by language orally uttered, which would not be a libel, but it is not the less blasphemy if the same thing be done by language written, printed, and published, although when in this form it also constitutes the offense of libel.[2]

Speaking evil of the Deity with an impious purpose to derogate from the divine majesty, and to alienate the minds of others from the love and reverence of God. Purposely using words concerning God calculated and designed to impair and destroy the reverence, respect, and confidence due to Him, as the intelligent creator, governor and judge of the world. A willful and malicious attempt to lessen men's reverence of God, by denying his existence or his attributes as an intelligent creator, governor and judge of men, and to prevent their having confidence in Him as such.[1]

Blasphemous libel. The publication of writings blaspheming the Supreme Being, or turning the doctrines of the Christian religion into contempt and ridicule.[2]

Does not consist in an honest denial of the truths of the Christian religion, but in "a willful intention to pervert, insult, and mislead others by means of licentious and contumelious abuse applied to sacred subjects."[3]

The fullest inquiry, and the freest discussion, for all honest and fair purposes, one of which is the discovery of truth, is not prohibited. The simple and sincere avowal of a disbelief in the existence and attributes of a supreme, intelligent being, upon proper occasions, is not prevented. It is the design to calumniate and disparage the Supreme Being, and to destroy the veneration due Him, that is intended.[1]

See CHRISTIANITY; PROFANITY; RELIGION.

BLASTING. See NUISANCE.

If a voluntary act, lawful in itself, naturally results in injury to another, the doer must pay all damages which are the proximate consequence of the act, regardless of the degree of care exercised.[4] See NEGLIGENCE.

BLIND. See READING.

A blind man may make a contract or a will.

The handwriting of an attesting witness who has become blind may be proved as if he were dead — he being first produced and examined, if within the jurisdiction.[5]

Whether it is negligence for a blind man to travel upon a highway on foot, unattended, is a question for a jury.[6]

---

[1] People v. Ruggles, 8 Johns. *293–98 (1811), Kent, C. J.

[2] Updegraph v. Commonwealth, 11 S. & R. 406, 408 (Pa., 1824), Duncan, J.

[3] Commonwealth v. Kneeland, 20 Pick. 211–12 (Mass., 1838), Shaw, C. J.

[1] Commonwealth v. Kneeland, 20 Pick. 213, 220 (1838), Shaw, C. J.

[2] 3 Greenl. Ev. § 164.

[3] Regina v. Ramsay and Foote, 48 L. T. 734–40 (1883), cases, Coleridge, C. J., quoting Starkie. See Bradlaugh's Case, 4 Cr. Law Mag. 592 (1883); 17 Cent. Law J. 38 (1883) — Law Times (Eng.).

[4] Georgetown, &c. R. Co. v. Eagles, 9 Col. 544 (1886), cases. Eagles recovered damages for direct injury done to the roofs of houses from falling debris, and for loss of rents.

[5] 1 Starkie, Ev. § 341; 1 Greenl. Ev. §§ 365–67; 1 Whart. Ev. § 401.

[6] Sleeper v. Sandown, 52 N. H. 244, 250 (1872); 20 Am. Law Reg. 507–16 (1881), cases.

BLOCKADE. The investment of a seaport by a competent naval force, with a view of cutting off all communication of commerce.[1]

Every nation, of common right, as a municipal regulation, may declare what places shall be ports of entry and delivery, and enforce the regulation by such means and with such penalties as it pleases. The term does not apply to an embargo, like that of 1808. That exists only where the forces of one nation encompass the ports of another. A blockade interrupts trade and communication to neutrals.[2]

The President has a right to institute a blockade of ports in possession of persons in armed rebellion against the government, on principles of international law. Neutrals have a right to challenge the existence of a blockade *de facto*, and also the authority of the party exercising the right to institute it. They have a right to enter the ports of a friendly nation for purposes of trade and commerce, but are bound to recognize the rights of a belligerent engaged in actual war to use this mode of coercion for the purpose of subduing the enemy.[3]

Simple blockade. Such blockade as may be established by a naval officer acting upon his own discretion or under direction of superiors, without governmental notification. **Public blockade.** Is not only established in fact, but is notified, by the government directing it, to other governments.[4]

In the case of a simple blockade, the captors of prize property are bound to prove its existence at the time of the capture; while in the case of a public blockade, the claimants are held to proof of discontinuance in order to protect themselves from the penalties of attempted violation. The blockade of the rebel ports was of the latter sort. It is the duty of the belligerent government to give prompt notice of the discontinuance of a public blockade. If it fails to do so, proof of discontinuance may be otherwise made; but, subject to just responsibility to other nations, it must judge for itself when it can dispense with a blockade.[4]

Evidence of intent to violate a blockade may be collected from bills of lading, from letters and other papers found on board the captured vessel, from acts and words of the owners or hirers of the vessel and the shipper of the cargo and their agents, and from the spoliation of papers in apprehension of capture.[4]

No **paper** or constructive blockade is allowed by international law.[5] Compare EMBARGO.

BLOOD. 1. Relationship; stock; family; consanguinity.

To be "of the blood" of a person means to be descended from him or from the same common stock. All those are of the blood of an ancestor who may, in the absence of other and nearer heirs, take by descent from him.[1]

A person is "of the blood" of another who has any, however small a portion, of the same blood derived from a common ancestor. When it is intended to express any qualification, the word *whole* or *half* blood is used to designate it, or the qualification is implied from the context or from known principles of law. In the common law, "blood" was used in the same sense.[2] See SISTER.

Originally, feuds and estates descended to none not of the "blood of the first purchaser:" because what was given for personal service and merit ought not, it was held, to descend to any but heirs of the person.[3]

See ANCESTOR; ATTAINDER; CONSANGUINITY; DESCENT; PRIVY, 2; PURCHASER; RELATION, 3.

2. Temper of mind; state of the passions; disposition.

Cold blood. Undisturbed use of reason; calm deliberation. See COOLING TIME.

BLOW HOT AND COLD. See ALLEGARE, Allegans contraria, etc.

BOARD. A table.

1. What is served on a table as food; supplies for sustenance.

To board is to receive food as a lodger, or without lodgings, for compensation.[4]

Boarder. If a person comes upon a special contract to board, and to sojourn at an inn, in the sense of the law, he is not a guest, but a boarder.[5]

Where the host is only an innkeeper the presumption is that a temporary sojourner is a guest; but where he also carries on the business of keeping boarders, the question who is a guest and who a boarder is not so easily answered. The duration of the person's stay, the price paid, the extent of the accommodation afforded, the transient or permanent character of his residence or occupation, his knowledge or want of knowledge of any difference of accommodation afforded to or price paid by boarders and guests, are all to be considered.[6]

The keeper of a boarding-house receives only such persons as he chooses; an innkeeper must receive all who come, unless there exists a special reason for refusing entertainment.[7]

---

[1] 1 Kent, 146–47.

[2] United States *v.* The William Arthur, 3 Ware, 280–81 (1861).

[3] Prize Cases, 2 Black, 665, 635 (1862), Grier, J.

[4] The Circassian, 2 Wall. 150–51, 135 (1864), Chase, C. J.; 21 W. Va. 356.

[5] The Peterhoff, 5 Wall. 50 (1866).

[1] Den *v.* Jones, 8 N. J. L. 346 (1826); 2 Bl. Com. 202, 229, 227.

[2] Gardner *v.* Collins, 2 Pet. *87, *94 (1829), Story, J.

[3] 2 Bl. Com. 220, 56; 2 Pet. *87, *94.

[4] Pollock *v.* Landis, 36 Iowa, 652 (1873).

[5] Story, Bailm. § 477; Berkshire Woolen Co. *v.* Proctor, 7 Cush. 424 (1851); Johnson *v.* Reynolds, 3 Kan. 261 (1865).

[6] Hall *v.* Pike, 100 Mass. 497 (1868), Colt, J. See also 26 Ala. 371; 33 Cal. 597; 25 Iowa, 555; 36 *id.* 651; 53 Me. 163; 35 Wis. 118; 24 How. Pr. 62; 1 Pars. Contr. 628.

[7] Willard *v.* Reinhardt, 2 E. D. Sm. 148 (1853); Cady *v.* McDowell, 1 Lans. 486 (1869), cases.

A keeper of boarders must take at least ordinary care of his patron's property; an innkeeper must exercise the highest degree of care reasonably possible.

A boarder's goods are not now distrainable for rent due by his host.[1]

See further DISTRESS; INN; NECESSARIES; RESIDE. Compare GUEST; LONGER.

2. A table at which a council is held; hence, an authorized assembly. More particularly, a number of persons organized to execute a trust or to perform some other representative or official business.

As, a board — of aldermen,[2] of arbitrators,[2] of directors,[2] of examiners[2] of candidates for admission to the bar, of examiners of patents,[2] of health,[2] of inspectors,[2] of liquidation,[2] of pardons,[2] of property, of public works, of revisers,[2] of supervisors, of trade, of trustees, of viewers,[2] of visitors,[2] poor-board, stock[3] and exchange[2] boards.

BOAT. See VESSEL.

BODY. Compare CORPUS.

1. The physical person. The *natural* body or such as is formed by the laws of God, as distinguished from an *artificial* body or such as is devised by human laws.[3]

In an indictment for murder, the trunk, in distinction from the head and limbs.[4]

See ARREST, 2; MAYHEM; SECURITY, Personal.

Heir or issue of the body. See HEIR; ISSUE, 5; TAIL.

Body-lifting or snatching. See BURIAL.

2. A number of individuals considered collectively, usually organized for a common purpose: as, a legislative body.

An artificial body or that devised by human laws.[5]

An *artificial* body can do only what is authorized by its charter or by law; a *natural* person or body, whatever is not forbidden by law.[6]

Body corporate or **corporate body.** An artificial body; a corporation, *q. v.*

Body politic. The governmental, sovereign power: a city or a State.

A body to take in succession, framed as to its capacity by policy, and, therefore, called by Littleton a body politic; and it is termed a corporation or body politic, because the persons are made into a body, and are of capacity to take, grant, etc., by a particular name.[1]

"Body corporate and politic" is said, in the older books, to be the most exact expression for a public corporation or corporation having powers of government.

The body politic is the "social compact by which the whole people covenant with each citizen, and each citizen with the whole people, that all shall be governed by certain laws for the common good."[2]

While that compact does not confer power upon the whole to control purely private rights, it authorizes laws requiring each to so act as not to injure another — which is the very essence of government.[3] See CORPORATION, Public.

3. The physical part or portion of a thing.

Body of a county or **of a State.** A county or a State considered in its territorial entirety, as distinguished from a portion of the territory, and from the legal corporation.

Jurisdiction in admiralty extends over a locality within the body of a State connecting with navigable waters although not affected by the ebb and flow of the tide.[4] See COUNTY.

Body of an instrument. The substantial operative part; the essential provisions: as, the body of a contract, note, statute, will. See TITLE, 2.

4. A number of particulars taken together; a systematic collection: as, a body of laws.

BONA. L. 1, *adj.* Good: a feminine form of *bonus*, *q. v.*

2, *n.* Goods, property: personalty, movables, chattels; assets.

Literally, valuables: the plural of *bonum*, a thing of value. Fr. *biens*.

Bona immobilia. Immovables.

Bona mobilia. Movables.

Bona notabilia. Property of sufficient value to be noted in an account.[5]

Debts evidenced by promissory notes are *bona notabilia* at the domicil of the debtor.[6]

Bona parapherna, or **paraphernalia.** Goods over and above dower. See PARAPHERNALIA.

---

[1] Riddle v. Welden, 5 Whart. 9, 14 (1839); Stone v. Matthews, 7 Hill, 428 (1844).

[2] Which last word see.

[3] [1 Bl. Com. 467.

[4] Sanchez v. People, 22 N. Y. 149 (1860).

[5] 1 Bl. Com. 467.

[6] Paul v. Virginia, 8 Wall. 177 (1868); Baltimore, &c. R. Co. v. Harris, 12 *id.* 81 (1870).

---

[1] Lord Coke, quoted in People v. Morris, 13 Wend. 334 (1835): Vin. Abr. Corp. (A, 2).

[2] Constitution of Massachusetts.

[3] Munn v. Illinois, 94 U. S. 124 (1876), Waite, C. J.; 1 Bl. Com. 467.

[4] Genesee Chief, 12 How. 443 (1851); 1 Black, 580; 7 Wall. 637.

[5] See 2 Bl. Com. 509; 74 Me. 89.

[6] Moore v. Jordan, 36 Kan. 275 (1887), cases; Wyman v. Halstead, 109 U. S. 654 (1884), cases.

Bona peritura. Perishable property. See PERISHABLE.

Bona vacantia. Unclaimed property.[1]

Bona waviata. Property thrown away. See WAIF.

De bonis. As to goods; concerning property or assets.

De bonis asportatis. See ASPORTARE.

De bonis non. See ADMINISTER, 4.

De bonis propriis. Out of his own property.

Said of a judgment rendered against an executor or administrator, which is to be satisfied out of his property; as, when he has wasted the assets or falsely pleaded "no assets."

De bonis testatoris. Out of the property of the testator.

Describes a judgment rendered against an executor, which is to be satisfied out of the estate of the decedent.

Another form of judgment is *de bonis testatoris cum* (or *quando*) *acciderint:* out of the assets of the testator when they shall have come to hand.

Still another form is *de bonis testatoris si, et non si, de bonis propriis:* out of the assets of the testator if (there are any), and if not, out of his own property.

Even if it happens that the executor has received assets, still the judgment should be against him, in his representative character, to be levied out of the assets in his hands, when no *devastavit* is averred and proved, unless it appears that no such assets can be found; in which event the judgment may, if so ordered, be levied out of his own proper goods.[2]

Nulla bona. No goods; no property.

The return to an execution when no property is found on which to make a levy; also, the plea by a garnishee that he has in his possession nothing belonging to or no money due to the debtor.

BOND. That which binds; any instrument in writing that legally binds a party to do a certain thing. "Bond," "obligation," and "instrument in writing" are sometimes used as convertible terms.[3]

A deed whereby the obligor obliges himself, his heirs, executors, and administrators, to pay a certain sum of money to another at a day appointed.[1] See OBLIGE.

If that be all, the bond is "single" [or "common"]; but there is generally a condition added that if the obligor does a particular act the obligation shall be void, or else shall remain in full force: as, pay rent, perform a covenant, or repay the principal of a sum borrowed, with interest, which principal is usually one-half of a specified penal sum. In case this condition is not performed the bond becomes forfeited, or "absolute," at law, and charges the obligor, while living, and, after his death, descends upon his heir.[1]

A deed or obligatory instrument, in writing, whereby one binds himself to another to pay a sum of money or to do some other act.[2]

Contains an obligation with a penalty, and a condition which expressly mentions what is to be done and the time within which it must be done.[2]

At common law, and at the present time, imports a sealed instrument.[3]

Bonds are either negotiable or non-negotiable. The former pass ownership by mere delivery; the latter, by written transfer, duly signed, sealed, and, perhaps, attested.

Bond-book. A book in which original, perhaps official, bonds are executed or preserved.

Bondsman. One who by a sealed instrument engages that if another person (the principal) fails to do a specified thing he will pay a certain sum of money; a surety, *q. v.*

Counter-bond. A bond given in a judicial proceeding in opposition to another bond previously furnished by an adversary.

Thus, in replevin, the plaintiff may give a bond for the protection of the officer in taking the property and the defendant execute a counter-bond for holding it.

Forthcoming bond. Security that property levied upon will be produced when wanted. See further FORTHCOMING.

Income bonds. Corporate "income bonds" are bonds payable out of the net income of the corporation by which they are issued.

Such bonds may be negotiable or unnegotiable. They may be payable only out of the net income, or unconditionally. They may bear a fixed rate of interest, or be graduated by the amount of net earnings, or at a certain per centum thereof; and they may or may not have interest-coupons attached.[4]

---

[1] See 1 Bl. Com. 298.

[2] Smith *v.* Chapman, 93 U. S. 43 (1876), cases; McLaughlin *v.* Winner, 63 Wis. 128-29 (1885), cases; 29 Minn. 296.

[3] [Courand *v.* Vollmer, 31 Tex. 401 (1868), Morrill, C. J. Compare 108 U. S. 189; 110 *id.* 739.

[1] 2 Bl. Com. 340, 456.

[2] Boyd *v.* Boyd, 2 Nott & McC. *126 (S. C., 1819), Gantt, J.

[3] Koshkonong *v.* Burton, 104 U. S. 673 (1881), Harlan, J.

[4] See 25 Am. Law Reg. 553-61 (1886), cases.

Official bond. An obligation with sureties given by a public officer as security for the faithful discharge of the duties of his office. See OFFICER.

Public bond. The obligation of a nation, State, or public corporation, to pay money at or within a specified time; municipal, State, or government bonds.

Holders of government bonds must be presumed to have knowledge of the laws by authority of which they were created and put into circulation, and of all lawful acts done by government officers under these laws. The obligations of the United States under the five-twenty bonds, consols of 1865, are governed by the law-merchant regulating negotiable securities, modified only, if at all, by the laws authorizing their issue.[1]

Refunding bond. An obligation to pay back money in the event of it appearing that the money should not have been paid.

As, a bond to return the whole or a part of a legacy should the assets of the estate be found insufficient to pay all demands upon it.

Other terms descriptive of bonds are: administration, appeal, arbitration, bail, bottomry, distiller's, duty, estrepement, injunction, joint or joint and several, judgment, *post-obit*, replevin, *respondentia*, railway aid, qq. v.

In an action of debt upon a non-negotiable bond, the demand is for the penalty. The condition is no part of the obligation. A judgment for the penalty will be released on performance of the condition.[2]

See OBLIGATION, 3, 4; RECOGNIZANCE; CONDITION; DATE; FACE, 1; FAITHFULLY; HOLDER; MORTGAGE; PARTY, 2; PENALTY; SEAL, 1; SURETY.

School-district, city, county, State, railway aid, and other corporation bonds, payable to bearer, have the qualities of negotiable instruments. Therein depends their value, mainly.[3] They are the representatives of money because issued in negotiable form.[4]

The expectation being that they will be put upon distant markets, the purchaser is assured that conditions precedent to their lawful issue have been complied with. He is bound to know the law which confers the power to issue the bonds on the specified contingency; but that that contingency has happened is a question of fact not for him to decide.[5]

If any essential proceeding, prescribed by law, be dispensed with, the bonds will be invalid in the hands of a person not a *bona fide* purchaser. If a statute is referred to on the face of the bond, a dealer is supposed to know all of its requirements.[1]

When the purchaser has a certificate of a fact he need not inquire whether the fact is as certified.[2]

A recital of circumstances which bring it within the power of the proper authorities to issue the bonds estops denial of the truth of the circumstances.[3] The statute must confer power to issue the bonds, in express terms or by reasonable implication.[4] The holder is chargeable with notice of the statutory provisions and of recitals in the bond.[5]

The corporation acts through its agents, and whenever they have power to decide that a condition precedent has been met (as that the required portion of the voters of a town have petitioned for a subscription in aid of a railroad), their determination of that fact, or their recital of that determination in a series of bonds subsequently issued and held by *bona fide* purchasers, is binding upon the corporation. The recital is a decision of the fact by the appropriate tribunal; and proof that such recital is incorrect is no defense. But where there is no recital the question is open.[6]

The Supreme Court of the United States has uniformly held that where a statute confers power upon a municipal corporation, after the performance of certain precedent conditions, to execute bonds in aid of the construction of a railroad, or for other like purpose, and imposes upon certain officers — invested with authority to determine whether such conditions have been performed — the responsibility of issuing them when such conditions have been complied with, recitals by such officers that the bonds have been issued "in pursuance of," or "in conformity with," or "by virtue of," or "by authority of," the statute, import, in favor of *bona fide* purchasers for value, full compliance with the statute, and preclude inquiry as to whether the precedent conditions had been performed before the bonds had issued. But in all such cases the recitals have imported a compliance, in all substantial respects, with the statute giving authority to issue the bonds. Sound public policy forbids enlarging or extending the rule. Where the holder relies for protection upon mere recitals, in order to estop the corporation from showing that the bonds were issued in violation or without authority of law, the recitals should be clear and unambiguous.[7]

[1] Morgan v. United States, 113 U. S. 476, 490 (1885), limiting Texas v. White, 7 Wall. 700 (1868).

[2] Farni v. Tesson, 1 Black, 314 (1861); 2 Bl. Com. 341.

[3] Mercer County v. Hacket, 1 Wall. 95 (1863), Grier, J.; Commissioners of Knox County v. Aspinwall, 21 How. 539 (1858), Nelson, J.; Pompton v. Cooper Union, 101 U. S. 204 (1879); Wadsworth v. Supervisors, 102 *id.* 534 (1880); 19 Blatch. 371.

[4] Bailey v. N. Y. Central R. Co., 22 Wall. 636 (1874).

[5] Town of Coloma v. Eaves, 92 U. S. 487, 490, 486 (1875), cases, Strong, J.; Pana v. Bowler, 107 *id.* 539 (1882); North. Bank of Toledo v. Porter Township, 110

id. 616 (1884); Dixon County v. Field, 111 *id.* 93–94 (1883), cases.

[1] McClure v. Township of Oxford, 94 U. S. 432 (1876).

[2] Menasha v. Hazard, 102 U. S. 95 (1880); Sherman County v. Simons, 109 *id.* 735 (1884), cases.

[3] Buchanan v. Litchfield, 102 U. S. 290 (1880), cases; Louisiana v. Wood, *ib.* 294 (1880); 3 McCrary, 35.

[4] Wells v. Supervisors, 102 U. S. 625 (1880).

[5] Walnut v. Wade, 103 U. S. 695 (1880), cases.

[6] Commissioners v. Aspinwall, Pompton v. Cooper Union, *ante;* Bissell v. Jeffersonville, 24 How. 287 (1860); St. Joseph Township v. Rogers, 16 Wall. 659–66 (1872), cases; Marsh v. Fulton County, 10 *id.* 681 (1870).

[7] School District (Iowa) v. Stone, 106 U. S. 187 (1882), Harlan, J.; Pana v. Bowler, 107 *id.* 539–40 (1882), cases.

A municipal corporation without legislative authority cannot issue bonds in aid of any extraneous object. Every person at his peril must take notice of the terms of the law by which it is claimed the power to issue bonds is conferred. The particular law forms a part of the bonds, as if incorporated in them. The holder is chargeable with notice of all statutory provisions.[1]

Unlike business, the powers of municipal corporations, unless otherwise directed by express or implied grant, are limited to such as are governmental or administrative, to such as are necessary to conserve the purposes of their organism.[2]

A purchaser takes the risk of the genuineness of an official signature. This includes the official character of him who makes the signature.[3]

A statute which authorizes a town to contract a debt payable in money implies the duty to levy taxes to pay the debt, unless some other source of payment is provided. If there is no power in the legislature to authorize such levy, the statute and forms of contract based thereon are void.[4]

See AID, 1, Municipal; COUPON; STOCK, 3 (2); TAX, 2.

BONE-BLACK. See MANUFACTURE.

BONUS. 1. Lat. Good.

Bona fides. Good faith. See FIDES.

Boni judicis. See JUDEX, 2, Boni, etc.

2. Eng. (1) Not a gift or gratuity, but a sum paid for services, or upon a consideration in addition to or in excess of that which would ordinarily be given.[5]

A State may exact a bonus for the grant of a franchise, payable in advance or *in futuro* (as, one-fifth of the fare paid by passengers to a railroad company), although it affects the charge which the donee of the franchise will have to exact. Such bonus differs in principle from a tax on transportation between States, which is an interference and regulation of commerce.[6]

(2) A premium paid for the use of money beyond the legal rate of interest.

Although one portion of the sum be called interest and another portion a bonus, the contract is still usurious.[7]

Usury laws cannot be evaded by an understanding

which assumes the distinctness of a contract for the payment of additional interest as a bonus.[1]

BOOK. Any literary composition which is printed, or printed and bound into a volume.

1. In copyright law, the form of the publication is not material — the term may include a single sheet.

So held in 1809, under the statute of 8 Anne (1710), § 1;[2] and so held ever since.[3]

Under the copyright act of March 3, 1865, § 4, book includes every volume and part of a volume, together with all maps, prints, or other engravings belonging thereto, with a copy of any subsequent edition published with additions.[4]

A single sheet of music has been held to be a book;[2] so, a diagram of patterns;[3] but not a mere label,[6] nor a prices-current.[6] The test is the subject-matter, not the size, form, or shape.[3, 6]

Although the legal definition of the word may be more extensive than that given by lexicographers, including a sheet as well as a volume, yet it necessarily conveys the idea of thought or conceptions clothed in language or in musical characters, written, printed, or published. Its identity does not consist merely in ideas, knowledge or information communicated, but in the same conceptions clothed in the same words, making it the same composition. A "copy" of a book must, therefore, be a transcript of the language in which the conceptions of the author are clothed; of something printed and embodied in a tangible shape.[7] See CHART; COPYRIGHT; PRINT.

2. In post-office law, a pamphlet of twenty-four pages, consisting of a sheet and a half secured together by stitching, with a cover of four pages and a title-page, may be described as a book.[8] See MAIL, 2.

Book-account. An account evidenced by one or more books regularly kept in the particular business or calling.

Book of accounts; or account-book. A book in which are entered the transactions of the owner's business; a creditor's book of entries, exhibiting, in detail, the transactions had with a person alleged to be his debtor.

[1] National Bank of the Republic *v.* City of St. Joseph, 31 F. R. 219 (1887), cases, Wallace, J.

[2] Holmes *v.* City of Shreveport, 31 F. R. 121 (1887), Boarman, J.

[3] Anthony *v.* County of Jasper, 101 U. S. 699 (1879), Waite, C. J.

[4] Loan Association *v.* Topeka, 20 Wall. 658-67 (1874), cases, Miller, J.; Parkersburg *v.* Brown, 106 U. S. 500 (1882). See generally Phelps *v.* Lewiston, 15 Blatch. 151-53 (1878); Smith *v.* Ontario, *ib.* 269 (1878); Stewart *v.* Lansing, *ib.* 287 (1878); Commonwealth *ex rel.* Whelen *v.* Pittsburgh, 88 Pa. 66, 81 (1878); Pierce, Railroads, 87-109, cases; 26 Am. Law Reg. 209-22, 608-20 (1878), cases.

[5] Kenicott *v.* The Supervisors, 16 Wall. 471 (1872), Hunt, J.

[6] Baltimore & Ohio R. Co. *v.* Maryland, 21 Wall. 473, 457 (1874), Bradley, J. See 3 How. 145-46.

[7] Mutual Sav. Bank *v.* Wilcox, 24 Conn. *153 (1855).

[1] 3 Pars. Contr. 113-14; 17 Cent. L. J. 102-5 (1883), cases.

[2] Clementi *v.* Golding, 2 Campb. 32 (1809), Ellenborough, C. J. See 11 East, 244.

[3] Drury *v.* Ewing, 1 Bond, 540, 546 (1862), Leavitt, J.

[4] 13 St. L. 540; Lawrence *v.* Dana, 4 Cliff. 62 (1869), Clifford, J.

[6] Coffeen *v.* Brunton, 4 McLean, 516 (1849).

[6] Clayton *v.* Stone, 2 Paine, 382 (1835?).

[7] Stowe *v.* Thomas, 2 Wall. Jr. 565 (1853), Grier, J.; 2 Bl. Com. 406.

[3] United States *v.* Bennett, 16 Blatch. 351 (1879). See R. S. § 3893.

Action of book-account. A remedy for collecting a balance due upon such dealings as are proper matters of book-account; an action of book-debt.

An account-book, regularly kept, may be received as evidence. And book-accounts are assets.[1] But a tally, a board, a slate, or loose sheets of paper, can hardly be said to constitute a book of accounts.[2] Yet there are not a few decisions to the effect that an account need not be kept in a bound volume.[3]

Book-entries. Particulars of a transaction recorded in a book of accounts.

Book of original entries. A book exhibiting the first or original charges made under a contract concerning merchandise, work and labor done, or services rendered.

To be admissible in evidence, the entries must be contemporaneous with the facts to which they relate; they must be made by a person having personal knowledge of the facts; and they must be corroborated by his testimony, if he is living and accessible, or by proof of his handwriting, if he is dead, insane, or beyond the reach of process. The witness need not remember the facts, if he will testify that he believed the entry to be true as set down.

It is not necessary that the transaction should have been directly between the original creditor and debtor; nor that the entries should have been against the interest of the person making them.[4]

As book-entries are received to prevent a failure of justice, their admissibility is limited by this necessity.[5]

Questions in relation to books of entry as evidence stand upon a new footing since the passage of statutes making parties witnesses. Formerly, the book itself was evidence, and the oath of the party supplementary. Now, the party himself is a competent witness, and may prove his own claim as a stranger would have done before the statutes were passed.[6]

The rule is that books of original entries, properly proved, are evidence of work and labor performed and of goods sold and delivered. To this rule are several exceptions; as, that the invoice book of an agent is not evidence of the sale and delivery of goods nor of goods to be delivered, nor is an entry evidence that is not in the course of the party's business. Books of original entry were formerly received in evidence from necessity. Where the transaction admits of more satisfactory evidence, they should not be received. Now that the parties are witnesses, care is to be taken not to enlarge the rule. In several States the account is not to exceed a sum specified. While there should be some limit to the amount, much more depends upon the nature of the item, and upon the evidence, outside of the book, which naturally exists to prove the item. The charges should be reasonably specific. Lumping charges are not admissible; as, entries like these: "B. Corr, Dr. July 13, 1880. To repairing brick machine, $1,932;" "190 days' work;" "seven gold watches, $398;" "13 dollars for medicine and attendance on one of the general's daughters, in curing the whooping cough."[1]

The books of a corporation are public as to its members, who for a proper purpose may examine them. Inspection of the books of a public office is permitted to any one interested in them, but not, if liable to affect public interests injuriously; of this the head of the department is to judge. *Mandamus* is the remedy by which to obtain an inspection and copies of such books, in which the petitioner has an interest.[2] See PRODUCE, 1.

Books on medicine, agriculture, science, and the like, not being subjects of cross-examination, are not admissible as evidence. But an approved history, being a quasi-public document, is receivable to prove a general fact of ancient date, a general custom, or any like matter.[3] See EXPERT; HISTORY; SCIENTIFIC.

A record in a Bible or other book, by a deceased relative, as to pedigree (*q. v.*) is receivable as a declaration.[4]

The results of an examination of many books may sometimes be proved.[5] See ACCOUNT, 1.

Under statutes in some States, school-books and Bibles are exempted from levy and sale.

The pledgee of a book must use it carefully.[6]

See HORN, LETTER, LOO, MINUTE, PAPER, YEAR, BOOK; BAGGAGE; DOCUMENT; LOST, 2; MAIL, 2; OBSCENE; REFRESH; SUBPŒNA, Duces, etc.

BORN. See CHILD; NATUS.

BOROUGH. 1. A town, whether corporate or not, that sends burgesses to parliament.[7]

2. A town or city organized for purposes of government.[8]

In the United States, not extensively used with any precise meaning. In Connecticut and Pennsylvania,

[1] 1 Greenl. Ev. §§ 115–18; 55 Vt. 347; 3 Bl. Com. 368.

[2] Richardson v. Wingate, 10 West. Law J. 146 (1853), Matthews, J.

[3] Price v. The Earl, 1 Sm. L. C. 535–77, cases; 2 Harr., Del., 288; 4 *id.* 532; 12 Bankr. Reg. 390.

[4] Town of Bridgewater v. Town of Roxbury, 54 Conn. 217 (1886), cases.

[5] Chaffee v. United States, 18 Wall. 541 (1873), cases, Field, J.; Ætna Fire Ins. Co. v. Weide, 9 *id.* 680 (1869), cases; Burley v. German American Bank, 111 U. S. 216 (1884); 20 Wend. 74–76; 79 Iowa, 376; 132 Mass. 478; 59 Miss. 378; 21 W. Va. 301, 308–11; 1 Greenl. Ev. §§ 115–17, 120, 151–54, cases; 1 Whart. Ev. §§ 678–88, cases.

[6] Nichols v. Haynes, 78 Pa. 176 (1875).

[1] Corr v. Sellers, 100 Pa. 170–71 (1882), cases, Mercur, J.; Laird v. Campbell, *ib.* 159, 165 (1882); Vinal v. Gilman, 21 W. Va. 301 (1883).

[2] 1 Greenl. Ev. §§ 474–78, cases; 1 Whart. Ev. §§ 662, 663, cases.

[3] 1 Greenl. Ev. §§ 440, 497, cases; 1 Whart. Ev. §§ 664–70, cases. As to medical books see, especially, Marshall v. Brown, 50 Mich. 148 (1883); Boyle v. State, 57 Wis. 472, 478 (1883), cases; 60 Cal. 581.

[4] 1 Greenl. Ev. § 104.

[5] Burton v. Driggs, 20 Wall. 136 (1873).

[6] 2 Pars. Contr. 111.

[7] [1 Bl. Com. 114; 2 *id.* 82; 41 Mo. 175.

[8] See 1 Steph. Com. 116; 3 *id.* 191.

a part of a township having a charter for municipal purposes.

Borough and village may be duplicate names for the same thing.[1] See TOWN.

Borough English. A custom prevalent in some parts of England (chiefly in old boroughs) by which the youngest son inherited the father's estate.

So called to distinguish it from the Norman rule of primogeniture, *q. v.*

The oldest sons were provided for as they grew up; the younger remained at home and might have been left destitute but for this law.[2]

Burgess. 1. An inhabitant of a borough; also, the representative of a borough in the house of commons.

2. A magistrate of an incorporated town.

3. The chief administrative officer of an incorporated town.[3]

BORROW. While often used in the sense of obtaining a thing to be returned *in specie*, is not limited to that sense. There may be a borrowing where an equivalent is paid annually in the form of interest, though the contract be perpetual and the loan irredeemable.[4]

"Borrowing" imports a promise or understanding that what is borrowed will be repaid or returned, the thing itself or something like it of equal value, with or without compensation for the use of it. To borrow is reciprocal with "to lend."[5] See LOAN.

Under the usury laws of New York the word "borrower" includes any person who is a party to the original contract or in any way liable for the loan.[6]

Power to "borrow money," vested in public authorities, may not include power to issue bonds for the purpose — as, to erect a court-house.[7] See PURPOSE, Public; TENDER, Legal (2).

BOTE.[8] Compensation, recompense; satisfaction, amends.

Synonymous with French *estovers*, q. v. House-bote: sufficient wood from another's land to repair, or to be burnt in, one's house; whence *fire-bote*. Plough-bote, cart-bote: wood for making and repairing instruments of husbandry. **Hay-bote, hedge-bote:** wood for repairing hay, hedges, or fences.[9]

Theft-bote. Where a person who has been robbed takes his goods back, or receives other amends, upon an agreement not to prosecute the felon.[1]

Bote is supposed to be preserved in the expressions "What boots it," and "to boot."

BOTTLE. See LEAKAGE; SEAL, 5.

A demijohn holding four gallons is not a "bottle" within the meaning of a statute requiring imported liquors to be put up in packages of not less than one dozen bottles each.[2]

An indictment for the larceny of "bottles" of liquor was held not sustained by proof of the larceny of liquor in bottles belonging to the accused, into which he had drawn the liquor.[3]

BOTTOMRY. A contract in the nature of a mortgage on a ship: when the owner borrows money to enable him to carry on his voyage, and pledges the keel or *bottom* of the ship as security for the repayment.[4]

"Bottom" was formerly used for ship or vessel.

Bottomry bond. The instrument which evidences a contract of bottomry.

In the sense of the general maritime law, and independent of the peculiar regulations of the positive codes of different commercial nations, a contract for a loan of money on the bottom of a ship, at an extraordinary rate of interest, upon maritime risks, to be borne by the lender for a voyage, or for a definite period.[5]

Blackstone and others speak of bottomry contracts of the owner only, omitting those of the *master*, which are now the more common, and are strictly for the necessities of the ship.[6]

A contract by which the owner of a ship hypothecates or binds the ship as security for the repayment of money advanced for the use of the ship.[6]

The contract creates a lien on the ship enforceable in admiralty on arrival at the port of destination, but void in the event of loss before arrival. The hazard being extraordinary, the rate of interest is high.[7]

To justify giving the bond, it is essential that there be a necessity, as, for repairs, and a necessity for resorting to the bond to procure the proper funds. There is no such necessity when the master has funds or can get funds on the credit of the owner.[8]

The vital principle is that the case is one of unprovided and real necessity, and that neither master nor owner has funds or credit available.[7]

[1] Brown *v.* State, 18 Ohio St. 507 (1869).

[2] 1 Bl. Com. 75; 2 *id.* 83.

[3] Wharton's Law Dict.; 1 Bl. Com. 174.

[4] Appeal of Phila. & Reading R. Co., 39 Leg. Int. 98 (Pa., 1882); State *v.* School District, 13 Neb. 88 (1882).

[5] Kent *v.* Quicksilver Mining Co., 78 N. Y. 177 (1879), Folger, J.

[6] National Bank *v.* Lewis, 75 N. Y. 523 (1878), cases.

[7] Lewis *v.* Sherman County, 1 McCrary, 377 (1881).

[8] A. S. *bot*, profit; M. E. *bote, boote*.

[9] [2 Bl. Com. 35; 1 Wash. R. P. 99.

[1] [4 Bl. Com. 133; 16 Mass. 93; 44 N. H. 16.

[2] U. S. *v.* Demijohns of Rum, 8 F. R. 485 (1880).

[3] Commonwealth *v.* Gavin, 121 Mass. 54 (1876).

[4] [2 Bl. Com. 457.

[5] The Draco, 2 Sumn. 186, 175–89 (1835), cases, Story, J.

[6] Braynard *v.* Hoppock, 32 N. Y. 573 (1865), Wright, J.

[7] The Grapeshot, 9 Wall. 135 (1869), Chase, C. J.; 26 Wend. 575; 32 N. Y. 573.

[8] The Fortitude, 3 Sumn. 233–37 (1838), cases, Story, J.

Such contracts seem to have been first recognized among the ancient Rhodians. They are allowed for the benefit of commerce. When *bona fide*, they will be upheld by the courts with a strong hand. They cover accruing freight, as well as the ship itself. They are to be liberally construed.[1]

There is no prescribed form for a bond. Any words indicating the amount of the loan, the interest to be paid, the names of the contracting parties, the name of the vessel, the limits of the voyage as to ports and time, the nature of the risks, and the period for repayment, will ordinarily be sufficient.

The lien created takes precedence over other liens, except liens for seaman's wages.

The bonds are usually negotiable instruments.

See Hypothecation; Respondentia.

BOUGHT. See Buy; Note, 1.

BOULEVARD. Originally, a bulwark or rampart; afterward, a public walk or road on the side of a demolished fortification; now, a public drive.

Not, technically, a street, avenue, or highway, though a carriage-way over it is a feature. Refers to an area set apart for purposes of ornament, exercise, and amusement.[2]

BOUND, *v.* See Bailiff; Bind; Bond.

BOUND, *n.;* **BOUNDARY.** Bound: a limit: boundary: a visible line designating a limit. The terms are often interchanged.[3]

Bounds. The legal, imaginary line by which different parcels of land are divided.

The "bounds of a river" may refer to the center line of the river.[4]

Artificial boundary. An object erected by man for designating the limit of an ownership in land; as, a post, a fence, or other monument.

Natural boundary. Any natural object remaining where placed by nature; as, a spring, a stream, a tree.

Private boundary and *public* boundary are used.

The most material and most certain calls control those which are less material and less certain. A call for a natural object, as, a river, a stream, a spring, or a marked tree, controls both course and distance.[5]

Courses and distances yield to natural and ascertained objects. Artificial and natural objects called for have the same effect. In a case of doubtful construction the claim of the party in actual possession will be maintained.[6]

Monuments control courses, and specific courses a general course.[1]

On a question of private boundary, declarations of a particular fact, as distinguished from reputation, made by a deceased person, are not admissible unless it is shown that such person had knowledge of that whereof he spoke and was on the land or in possession of it when the declaration was made — as part of the *res gestæ*.[2]

Where a disputed boundary between States is settled, grants previously made by one of lands claimed by it, and over which it exercised political jurisdiction, but which, on the adjustment of the boundary, are found to be within the territory of the other State, are void, unless confirmed by the latter State; but such confirmation cannot affect the titles of the same lands previously granted by the latter State.[3]

See Abut; At, 2; Call, 2 (2); Confusion; Description; Line, 1; Monument, 1; Thread.

BOUNTY.[4] Money paid or a premium offered [usually by government] to encourage or promote an object, or procure a particular thing to be done. The context may restrict the meaning.[5]

"A premium offered or given to induce men to enlist into the public service." That is a proper and intelligent definition, indicating clearly that the word is only applicable to the payment made to the enlisted man, as the inducement for his service, and not as a premium paid to the man by whose procurement the recruit is mustered.[6]

Bounties have also been established for those who kill dangerous animals or noxious creatures, or who engage in a particular business or industry which it is desired to encourage, as in a fishery, or in the manufacture of salt.

While bounties are usually paid in money, they may be paid in land. Whence **bounty lands,** and **bounty-land** warrants.

Land or money, other than current salary or pay, granted by the government to a person entering the military or naval service, has always been called a bounty; and while it is by no means a "gratuity," because the promise to grant it is one of the considerations for which the soldier or sailor enters the service, yet it is clearly distinguishable from "salary" or pay measured by the time of service.[7]

---

[1] The Albro, 10 Bened. 671–72 (1879), cases; 1 Pet. *436–37: 3 Kent, 353; 2 Bl. Com. 457.

[2] People *ex rel.* Seaver *v.* Green, 52 How. Pr. 445 (1873), Faucher, J.

[3] See Webster's Dict.

[4] Walton *v.* Tift, 14 Barb. 221 (1852).

[5] Newsom *v.* Pryor, 7 Wheat. 10 (1810), Marshall, C. J.; Brown *v.* Huger, 21 How. 321 (1858).

[6] County of St. Clair *v.* Lovingston, 23 Wall. 62 (1874), cases, Swayne, J.

[1] Grand County *v.* Larimer County, 9 Col. 280 (1886).

[2] Hunnicutt *v.* Peyton, 102 U. S. 364, 363 (1880), cases. See generally 2 Washb. R. P. 630–38, cases; 1 Greenl. Ev. §§ 145, 301, cases; 1 Whart. Ev. §§ 185–91, cases; 28 Am. Law Reg. 546–48 (1880), cases. The highway as a boundary, 36 Alb. Law J. 305–8 (1887), cases.

[3] Coffee *v.* Groover, 123 U. S. 10 (1887), cases, Bradley, J. Boundary between Georgia and Florida.

[4] L. *bonitas*, goodness, gratuity: *bonus*, good.

[5] Fowler *v.* Selectmen of Danvers, 8 Allen, 84 (1864), Bigelow, C. J.

[6] Abbe *v.* Allen, 39 How. Pr. 488 (1870), Bacon, J.

[7] Five Per Cent. Cases, 110 U. S. 479 (1884), Gray, J.

General encouragements, held out to all persons indiscriminately, to engage in a particular trade or manufacture, whether in the shape of bounties or drawbacks, or other advantage, are always under legal control and may be discontinued at any time. Thus a law offering a sum for every bushel of salt manufactured in a State is a general law, regulative of internal economy, dependent for its continuance upon the dictates of public policy, and the voluntary good faith of the legislature. Such law does not belong to the class denominated "contracts," except so far as actually executed and complied with.[1]

BOX. See BALLOT-BOX; JURY-BOX.

BOYCOTTING. A combination between persons to suspend or discontinue dealings or patronage with another person or persons because of refusal to comply with a request made of him or them. The purpose is to constrain acquiescence or to force submission on the part of the individual who, by non-compliance with the demand, has rendered himself obnoxious to the immediate parties, and, perhaps, to their personal and fraternal associates.

The persons directly so confederating have hitherto as a class been employees as against either their own employer or the employer of others in a like business, or else of retail dealers as against a particular manufacturer or wholesale dealer.

The means employed have been the withdrawal of the custom and good-will in business of the immediate parties and of such others as they could influence.

The word may refer to the fact of combining or to the resolution as executed.

The practice takes its name from one Boycott, an agent for Lord Earne on certain estates in the western part of Ireland. Having lost favor with the tenants, from evictions and other harsh treatment, they agreed not to work for him, and the tradesmen of the community not to deal with him.[2]

"The word in itself implies a threat. In popular acceptation it is an organized effort to exclude a person from business relations with others by persuasion, intimidation and other acts which tend to violence, and thereby coerce him, through fear of resulting injury, to submit to dictation in the management of his affairs."[2]

Any such combination is, and ever has been, at common law, a conspiracy, the unlawfulness consisting in the agreement for the concerted action; and aptly illustrates the well-settled principle that two or more persons may not combine to do toward another what one individual of his own accord might not unlawfully do.

"The doctrine to be gathered from the cases seems to be that a conspiracy of this kind ceases to be legal when the means designed . . . are characterized by force, threats, intimidation, molestation, improper interference, or compulsion."[1]

It is against the criminal law for a number of men to band together for the purpose, through the power of combination, of injuring the business of another, by parading before his door, by placarding themselves with the word "boycott," by advising passers-by not to patronize the establishment, by distributing circulars filled with accusations and justifying the boycott, and by other devices calculated to induce the public to keep away from the alleged wrong-doer,—provided that the persons so engaged use force, threats, or intimidation. To constitute intimidation it is not necessary that there should be an overt act of violence or any direct threat by word of mouth: it is enough if the attitude of the accused was intimidating; and this may be shown by their numbers, methods, placards, circulars, and other devices. If the attitude and method is such as to deter any of the complainant's customers, even the most timid, from entering his place of business, or to inspire any portion of the general public with a sense of danger in ignoring their appeals, there is intimidation. In New York procuring money from another with his consent obtained by fear, induced by threat to do or to continue an injury to his property, constitutes "extortion;" and every person present when the money, or the agreement under which it was paid, is obtained, and who aids and abets the person to whom it is paid, by personal participation or by silently acquiescing in the threats made by his associates speaking in their joint behalf, is liable as a principal, and he need not be present when the money is actually received.[2]

Associations have no more right to inflict injury upon others than have individuals. All combinations and associations designed to coerce workmen to become members or to interfere with, obstruct, vex or annoy them in working or in obtaining work because they are not members, or to induce them to become members; or designed to prevent employers from making a just discrimination in the wages paid to the skillful and the unskillful, the diligent and the lazy, the efficient and the inefficient; and all associations designed to interfere with the perfect freedom of employers in the proper management of their lawful business, or to dictate the terms upon which their

---

gheny Co., Pa. (April 21, 1888), Slagle, J.: 35 Pitts. Leg. J. 399, 405. See "England under Gladstone," McCarthy.

[1] 10 Va. Law J. 799 (Sept., 1886), Atkins, J., in Crump v. Commonwealth. Affirmed, May 24, 1888.

[2] People v. Wilzig, 4 N. Y. Cr. R. 403 (O. & T. N. Y. Co., June, July, 1886), Barrett, J. Sometimes called Theiss's Case. N. Y. Penal Code, §§ 552–53. See also People v. Lenhardt, ib. 317 (June, 1886).

---

[1] Salt Company v. East Saginaw, 13 Wall. 379 (1871), Bradley, J. See also Commissioners v. Woodstock Iron Co., 83 Ky. 153 (1886), cases.

[2] Brace Brothers v. Evans et al., C. P. No. 1, Alle-

business shall be conducted by means of threats of injury or loss, by interference with their property or traffic, or with their lawful employment of other persons, or designed to abridge any of those rights,—are *pro tanto* illegal combinations; and all acts done in furtherance of such intentions by such means and accompanied by damage are actionable.[1]

An act of Wisconsin, approved April 2, 1887 (Laws, ch. 287), provides that: Any two or more persons who shall combine, associate, agree, mutually undertake, or concert together for the purpose of willfully or maliciously injuring another in his reputation, trade, business or profession, by any means whatever, or for the purpose of maliciously compelling another to do or perform any act against his will, or preventing or hindering another from doing or performing any lawful act, shall be punished by imprisonment in the county jail not more than one year, or by fine not exceeding five hundred dollars.[2]

See further COMBINATION, 2; CONSPIRACY; INJURY, Irreparable; STRIKE, 2. Compare BLACK-LISTING. See also ASSEMBLY, Unlawful; RIOT.

BRAKEMAN. See ADMISSION, 2; NEGLIGENCE.

BRANCH. See RAILROAD.

BRAND. To burn; to mark, stamp.

In common parlance, to mark. What was formerly done by a hot iron in the way of marking packages is now done by the stencil plate. In referring to marks upon packages of merchandise, the use of stencil plates is denominated " branding " quite as often as otherwise. " To brand " has become an equivalent expression with to stamp and to mark.[3] See BURN.

BRAWL. A noisy quarrel; uproar.

" Brawl " and " tumult " are correlative terms. They refer to the same kind of disturbance of the peace, produced by the same class of agents, and well define one and the same offense.[4] See PEACE, 1.

BREACH. Breaking, violation, infraction.

1. A violation of duty or obligation. 2. The part of a declaration which charges the violation of a contract. See DAMAGES.

Breach of close. An unlawful entry upon land. See CLOSE, 3.

Breach of contract or **covenant.** A failure to observe the conditions of a contract. See CONTRACT; COVENANT.

Breach of pound. The forcible removal of a thing lawfully impounded. Also called *pound-breach.* See POUND, 2.

Breach of prison. Escape from lawful confinement in a prison. Also called *prison-breach.* See ESCAPE, 1 (2).

Breach of privilege. Violation of the privilege of a legislature. See PRIVILEGE, 4.

Breach of promise. Failure to solemnize a contract of marriage, *q. v.*

Breach of the peace. Disturbance of the public order. See PEACE, 1.

Breach of trust. Violation of the duty imposed by an instrument creating a trust; also, willful misappropriation of a thing bailed. See TRUST, 1.

Breach of warranty. Where a contract of warranty is broken in any of its conditions. See WARRANTY.

Continuing breach. Describes acts in violation of one's duty, continuous or repeated at short intervals.

BREAD ACTS. Statutes providing for the sustenance of persons confined in jail for civil causes have been so called.[1]

BREAD AND WATER. To be fed on bread and water was part of the punishment imposed under the Great Law of the province of Pennsylvania (1682) for swearing, profanity, cursing, drunkenness, and offenses of like grade.[2]

This is also sometimes made the diet of persons held in confinement who refuse to obey reasonable prison-rules.

BREAK. 1. To sever by fracture; to part or divide with force or violence; also, to lay open or uncover.

Break bulk. For a bailee to open a box or package intrusted to his custody and fraudulently appropriate the contents.[3] See LARCENY, By bailee.

Break doors. To remove the fastenings of a house with force, so that a person, as, an officer executing process, may enter. See HOUSE.

Break ground. See FREIGHT, Affreightment; SAILING.

---

[1] Old Dominion Steamship Co. *v.* McKenna, U. S. Cir. Ct., S. D. N. Y. (Feb. 25, 1887), cases, Brown, J.: 30 F. R. 48, 35 Alb. Law J. 208, 26 Am. Law Reg. 423–32, cases, 18 Abb. N. Cas. 262, 281, cases. See also State *v.* Glidden, 55 Conn. 76 (April, 1887): 35 Alb. Law J. 348, 3 N. E. Rep. 849; 9 Cr. Law Mag. 1–17 (Jan., 1887), cases; 21 Am. Law Rev. 41–69 (Feb., 1887), cases; *ib.* 509–32 (1887), cases; State *v.* Stewart, Sup. Ct. Vt. (May, 1887), cases: 36 Alb. Law J. 9–11 (1887); 35 *id.* 203, 224–26 (1887), cases; 22 Am. Law Rev. 233 (April, 1888), cases; 3 Kans. Law J. 273 (1886).

[2] Compare Penn. Acts 8 May, 1869, 14 June, 1872, 20 April, 1876: Purd. Dig. 1172. Applied, Brace Brothers *v.* Evans *et al., ante.*

[3] Dibble *v.* Hathaway, 11 Hun, 575–76 (1877), Bockes, J.

[4] State *v.* Perkins, 42 N. H. 465 (1861).

[1] See 49 Conn. 87, 89; 91 U. S. 300; 3 Bl. Com. 416; 1 Brightly, T. & H. § 1426.

[2] Laws of Prov. of Penn., Linn, 110–111.

[3] 1 Pick. 375; 4 Mass. 580.

Break jail or **prison.** To escape from a place of lawful confinement. See ESCAPE, 1.

Break seals. See SEAL, 1, 4.

2. In burglary and house-breaking, to remove any part of the house, or of the fastenings provided to secure it against intrusion, with intent to commit a felony.

Such breaking is *actual* when force is used; and *constructive* when an entry is effected by fraud, conspiracy, or threat.[1] See further BURGLARY.

3. To violate a duty or engagement: as, to break a contract. See BREACH.

4. To establish, in a judicial proceeding, the invalidity of an alleged will. See CONTEST.

BREAST OF THE COURT. This expression, much used by the older writers, seems to mean the sound discretion, the conscience and judgment, of the judge or judges of a court.

During the term the record is in the breast of the court.[2]

In a trial *per testes* the judge is left to form in his own breast his sentence upon the credit of the witnesses examined.[3]

The liberty of considering all questions in an equitable light might leave the decision of every question entirely in the breast of the judge.[4]

BREVE. L. A writ; literally, short, brief, *q. v.* Also, an original writ. Plural, **brevia.**

Brevia were originally in the form of letters. They tersely stated the matter in question — *rem quæ est breviter narrat.* The species came to be known by some important word or phrase in the writ itself, or from the subject-matter; and this word or phrase, in turn, was transferred to the form of action in the prosecution of which the writ (*breve*) was procured.[5]

BREWER. See LIQUOR.

Every person, firm, or corporation who manufactures fermented liquors of any name or description, for sale, from malt, wholly or in part, or from any substitute thereof.[6] Compare DISTILLER.

BRIBERY. 1. In old English, theft, rapine, open violence, official extortion.

The rapacious dignitary was styled the *briber*, and he was said *to bribe* when he boldly grasped his prey; now, the tempter is the briber and the recipient the bribed.[7]

2. When a judge, or other person concerned in the administration of justice, takes any undue reward to influence his behavior in office.[1]

Giving (and perhaps offering) to another anything of value or any valuable service, intended to influence him in the discharge of a legal duty. It does not apply to a mere moral duty.[2]

The later and broader doctrine is that any attempt to influence an officer in his official conduct, whether in the executive, legislative, or judicial department of the government, by the offer of a reward or pecuniary consideration, is an indictable common-law misdemeanor.[3]

A candidate for a judgeship who pledges himself, if elected, to serve at a less salary than that provided by law, virtually bribes the masses to vote for him.[4]

Bribery in a judge of the United States courts, of a member of Congress, or of any officer of the United States, is punishable.[5]

The general election laws of Pennsylvania prohibiting bribery include caucuses as well as elections for State officers; and the constitutional prohibition against violation of any "election law" includes any law intended to purify elections, then or thereafter in force.[6] See CANDIDATE.

One who bribes another cannot maintain an action to recover the money.[7] Compare CORRUPT, 2.

BRIDGE. A structure of wood, iron, brick, or stone, ordinarily erected over a river, brook, or lake, for the more convenient passage of persons and beasts and the transportation of baggage.[8]

A structure, usually of wood, stone, brick, or iron, erected over a river or other watercourse, or over a ravine, railroad, etc., to make a continuous roadway from one bank to another.[9]

Formerly and strictly, the word, unqualified, imported a structure that had a pathway. In this sense

---

[1] See Timmons v. State, 34 Ohio St. 427-31 (1878), cases; 68 N. C. 207; 85 Pa. 54; 2 Chitty, Cr. L. 1092.

[2] 3 Bl. Com. 407; 105 Ill. 608, 669.

[3] 3 Bl. Com. 336.

[4] 1 Bl. Com. 62; 112 U. S. 190.

[5] Coke, Litt. 73 b, 54 b; Steph. Pl. *27.

[6] Revenue Act, 13 July, 1866: 14 St. L. 117.

[7] Marsh, Lect. Eng. Lang. 249.

[1] 4 Bl. Com. 139; 65 Ill. 65.

[2] Dishon v. Smith, 10 Iowa, 221 (1859).

[3] State v. Ellis, 33 N. J. L. 103 (1868). See also 62 Cal. 493; 135 Mass. 530.

[4] People ex rel. Bush v. Thornton, 25 Hun, 465-66 (1881), cases. See also State v. Elting, 29 Kan. 399, 402-4 (1883), cases; Hall v. Marshall, 80 Ky. 553, 563-66 (1882), cases.

[5] R. S. §§ 5449-51, 5499-5502.

[6] Leonard v. Commonwealth, 112 Pa. 607, 626 (1886).

[7] Clark v. United States, 102 U. S. 322 (1880). See generally People v. Sharp, 10 N. Y. St. R. 522-77 (1887), cases, etc.

[8] Enfield Bridge Co. v. Hartford, &c. R. Co., 17 Conn. 56 (1845), Williams, C. J.

[9] Webster's Dict.; Madison County v. Brown, 89 Ind.

a *railroad* bridge, being in the nature of a viaduct, is not a violation of a franchise for an ordinary toll-bridge.[1] See RAILROAD.

The word includes the structure itself and such abutments as are necessary to make the structure accessible and useful; but exactly what constitutes a bridge in a particular case is a question of fact.[2]

The approaches to a bridge, within reasonable limits, are a part of the bridge.[3] See ABUTMENT.

Free bridge. A bridge owned and maintained, usually by the public, free of charge to travelers. **Toll bridge.** A chartered bridge, with the right in its owners to collect toll in reimbursement of the cost of construction, repairs, etc.

Private bridge. A bridge for the use of individuals, generally its owners. **Public bridge.** A bridge which constitutes a part of the public highway, whether free or toll. See TOLL, 2.

A bridge is to be maintained (the repair being equal to the service expected) by its owner, whether a county, a township, a municipality, or a company. But the person or persons, as, a railway company, who makes the structure a necessity, is to make repairs; if he fails in this duty, the public authorities must make them at his expense.[4]

If a bridge is not kept in repair, redress may be had in court by indictment for maintaining a nuisance, by injunction, by *quo warranto*, by *mandamus*, and by suit for special damage suffered by any individual person.

A State may erect a bridge over a river, provided inter-State navigation is not thereby unreasonably obstructed.[6]

What the form and character of bridges over a navigable stream should be, that is, of what height and materials, and whether with or without draws, are matters for regulation by the particular State or States authorizing the construction, subject only to the paramount authority of Congress to prevent unnecessary obstruction to free navigation. Until Congress intervenes in such cases, and exercises its authority, the power of the State is plenary.   . Bridges are

merely connecting lines of turnpikes, streets, and railroads; and the commerce over them may be much greater than that on the streams which they cross. A break in the line of railroad communication from the want of a bridge may produce greater inconvenience to the public than the obstruction of navigation caused by a bridge with proper draws. In such cases the local authority can best determine which of the two modes of transportation should be favored.[1]

Congress can empower a private corporation to occupy navigable waters within a State, and appropriate the soil under them, in order to construct a bridge for the purposes of inter-State commerce, against the protest of the State.[2]

The act of Congress of June 16, 1886, authorizing the construction of a railroad bridge across Staten Island Sound, known as "Arthur Kill," and establishing the same as a post-road, is within the power to regulate commerce, to open up commercial communication between the States. Such privilege may be exercised without the consent of the State in which the structure is to be placed. The grant is, in effect, of the use of the soil, not an assumption of exclusive jurisdiction. The right of the State is not property susceptible of pecuniary compensation as "private property" taken for public use.[3]

Speaking generally, a chartered bridge will not be allowed near another bridge, nor near a ferry, having an older franchise.[4]

See COMMERCE; DRAWBRIDGE; FERRY; NAVIGATION.

BRIEF.[5] A concise statement; an epitome; an abridgment.

Sometimes used in a verbal sense, to reduce to the form of a brief, etc. See STATE, 1.

Brief of title. An abstract of the deeds, judicial proceedings, etc., which affect a title to realty. See further ABSTRACT, 2. Compare also SEA-BRIEF.

1. In very old law, a writ. See BREVE.

2. An abridged statement of a party's case, prepared by his counsel, usually for the information of the court on the matters of law involved.[6] See PAPER, 5.

In England the essentials of a case as prepared in writing by the solicitor or attorney for the use of the barrister who is to conduct the case in court is called "the brief" in the case. In America the term designates the memorandum counsel take into court or to a

52 (1883). See 5 South. Law Rev. 733–35 (1880), cases; 37 Me. 461; 132 Mass. 312; 41 Ohio St. 52; 110 U. S. 566; 6 Iowa, 455; Ang. Highw. § 35.

[1] Proprietors of Bridges v. Hoboken Land Co., 1 Wall. 149–51 (1863), cases; s. c., 2 Beasley, 503. See also Smith Bridge Co. v. Bowman, 41 Ohio St. 56–58 (1884).

[2] Tollard v. Willington, 26 Conn. 582–83 (1857), cases; Bardwell v. Jamaica, 15 Vt. 442 (1843).

[3] Rush County v. Rushville, &c. R. Co., 87 Ind. 505 (1882); Driftwood Valley Turnpike Co. v. Bartholomew County, 72 id. 236–38 (1880), cases; Whitcher v. Somerville, 133 Mass. 455 (1885).

[4] Penn. R. Co. v. Borough of Irwin, 85 Pa. 336 (1877); Shelby County v. Deprez, 87 Ind. 510–13 (1882), cases.

[5] Pennsylvania v. Wheeling Bridge Co., 13 How. 562 (1851); People v. Kelly (East River Bridge), 5 Abb. N. Cas. 383, 439 (1879); 5 McLean, 425.

[1] Hamilton v. Vicksburg, &c. R. Co., 119 U. S. 281–82 (1886), Field, J.

[2] Decker v. Baltimore & N. Y. R. Co., 30 F. R. 724–28 (1887), cases, Wallace, J.

[3] Stockton, Attorney-General v. Baltimore, &c. R. Co., 32 F. R. 9, 16 (1887), cases, Bradley, J. Same case, 36 Alb. Law J. 371.

[4] See 3 Bl. Com. 219; 4 id. 167; Enfield Toll Bridge v. Hartford, &c. R. Co., 17 Conn. 40, 56 (1845), cases.

[5] F. bref: L. brevis, short.

[6] Gardner v. Stover, 43 Ind. 357, 356 (1873).

hearing before an auditor, master, or other commissioner, to assist in elucidating the law, and, perhaps, the facts in a particular case; also, the statement of the law (statutes, decisions, etc.) supposed to apply to a case pending before a court of review, and filed for the information of the court and of opposing counsel.[1]

Briefless. Without briefs; without business requiring the preparation of briefs; without clients.

Within the meaning of the rules of an appellate court, a "brief" is a statement of a case for the information of the court. It should furnish aid in deciding the case—show why the judgment below should be either reversed or affirmed.[1]

After the trial or argument of a cause, though the counsel of one of the parties gives notice that he will furnish the court a brief of authorities, a decision may be rendered without giving time for the preparation of the brief. The reception of briefs being for the assistance of the court, the judges, who are presumed to know the law, are not bound to receive them.[2]

BRING INTO COURT. See PAYMENT.

BRING SUIT. See BROUGHT; SUIT.

BRISTLES. See HAIR.

BRITISH. See STATUTE.

BROKER.[3] An agent employed to make bargains and contracts between other persons in matters of trade, commerce or navigation, for a compensation commonly called *brokerage*.[4]

Brokerage. The business of a broker; also, his remuneration or commission. Formerly spelled *brokage* and *brocage*.

The term "broker" is no longer limited to a person employed to negotiate contracts for the sale or exchange of goods, but is extended to almost every branch of business—to realty as well as to personalty.[5]

The term is applied, ordinarily, to one acting for others.[6]

A broker is a middleman, an intervenor between the buyer and the seller: a factor or agent who acts for one or the other.[7]

Brokers take their names from the kinds of contracts they negotiate. The more common classes are the following:

Bill and note brokers. These negotiate the purchase and sale of bills of exchange and promissory notes.

They impliedly warrant that the paper is as represented, with respect to the genuineness of signatures, but not as to the solvency of parties.[1]

Their usefulness would be destroyed if a purchaser was to be affected with their knowledge as to the character of the paper they offer in market for discount.[2] See *Exchange Broker*.

Commercial broker. A person who negotiates sales of merchandise, or contracts for freights, for other persons.

Within the meaning of the internal revenue laws a person who negotiates sales or purchases in the names of the parties primarily liable; not, one authorized to sell in his own name or on his own account.[3]

Any person or firm whose business it is, as a broker, to negotiate sales or purchases of goods, wares, or merchandise, or to negotiate freights and other business for the owners of vessels, or for the shippers, or consignors, or consignees of freight carried by vessels, shall be regarded as a commercial broker.[4]

Exchange broker. A broker who negotiates bills of exchange, foreign or domestic.

Every person, firm, or company, whose business it is to negotiate purchases or sales of stocks, bonds, exchange, bullion, coined money, bank-notes, promissory notes, or other securities, for themselves or others, shall be regarded as a broker.[4] Compare *Bill* and *Stock Broker*.

Insurance broker. A person who negotiates contracts of insurance.

He is agent for both parties. An insurance agent is, ordinarily, the employee of the insurer only. See INSURANCE, Broker.

Merchandise broker. A broker who negotiates sales of merchandise without having possession or control of it. See FACTOR.

Pawnbroker. A person, usually licensed, who loans money, in small sums, at usurious interest, on the security of pledges of personalty. See further PAWN.

Produce-broker. A person whose occupation it is to buy and sell agricultural or farm-products.[5]

Not, then, one who sells from his own farm, or goes from house to house to sell his own produce.[6]

---

[1] Gardner v. Stover, *ante*.

[2] Van Dolsen v. Abendroth, N. Y. City, Mar. Ct., 15 Rep. 472 (1883).

[3] In Mid. Eng. an agent, a witness of a transaction. Probably allied to A. S. *bru'can*, to use, employ,—Skeat.

[4] Story, Agency, § 28; 83 N. Y. 381, *infra*.

[5] Little Rock v. Barton, 33 Ark. 448, 444–49 (1878), cases, Turner, S. J.

[6] Warren v. Shook, 91 U. S. 710 (1875), Hunt, J.

[7] [United States v. Simons, 1 Abb. U. S. 472–73 (1870), McCandless, J.

---

[1] Baxter v. Duren, 29 Me. 439–41 (1849), cases; Morrison v. Currie, 4 Duer, 82–85 (1854), cases; Aldrich v. Jackson, 5 R. I. 219 (1858).

[2] Moorehead v. Gilmore, 77 Pa. 122. Agency: Worthington v. Cowles, 112 Mass. 30; 1 Dan. N. Inst. § 740 a.

[3] [Slack v. Tucker, 23 Wall. 329 (1874).

[4] [Revenue Act, 13 July, 1866: 14 St. L. 117, 116.

[5] United States v. Simons, *ante*.

Real estate broker. A broker who negotiates sales of realty.

He may also negotiate loans on mortgages, let houses, lease lands, collect rents, etc.

Inasmuch as acting for both parties in an exchange of lands, involves inconsistent duties he can recover remuneration from neither party, notwithstanding an express promise by one of the parties to pay a percentage, unless it clearly appears that each principal had full knowledge of all the circumstances connected with his employment by the other which would naturally affect his action, and had assented to the double employment. When such knowledge and assent are shown, he may recover from either party.[1]

Ship broker. A broker who negotiates sales of ships, freighting of vessels, etc. See *Commercial Broker.*

Stock broker. A broker who buys and sells shares in corporations. See ORDER, Stop, 2; RINGING UP; STOCK, 3, Exchange.

Ordinarily, a broker never buys or sells in his own name, nor has he possession of the goods; wherein he differs from a "factor" or commission merchant. His business is to bring buyer and seller together; but he need not actually negotiate the bargain. Unless there is a special agreement to the contrary, he earns his commission when he procures a party with whom the principal is satisfied, and who actually contracts for the purchase of the property at a price acceptable to the owner. But he must establish his employment and that his agency was the procuring cause of the sale. Pending an authorized negotiation at private sale, the owner cannot take the business out of the broker's hands, complete the sale, and then refuse to pay the commission.[2] The owner must have a good reason for refusing to fulfill his agreement to pay the broker for his services. Usage, in the absence of an express contract, determines the value of the services.[3] When the broker does not disclose his principal he may be held as principal. See REALIZE.

BRONZES. See FURNITURE.

BROOD. See PARTUS.

BROTHEL. See BAWDY-HOUSE.

BROTHER. See BLOOD, 1; CONSANGUINITY; DESCENT, Canons of.

[1] Bell *v.* McConnell, 37 Ohio St. 399–402 (1881), cases.

[2] See McGavock *v.* Woodlief, 20 How. 227 (1857); Walker *v.* Osgood, 98 Mass. 348 (1867): 93 Am. Dec. 171–78, cases; Keys *v.* Johnson, 68 Pa. 43–44 (1871), cases; Sibbald *v.* Bethlehem Iron Co., 83 N. Y. 381–82 (1881), cases; Vinton *v.* Baldwin, 88 Ind. 105–6 (1882), cases; Viaux *v.* Old South Society, 133 Mass. 10 (1882), cases; Armstrong *v.* Wann, 29 Minn. 127–28 (1882), cases; Barry *v.* Schmidt, 57 Wis. 172 (1883); Hamlin *v.* Schulte, Sup. Ct. Minn. (1887): 26 Am. Law Reg. 106 (1887); *ib.* 109–15, 543–68 (1887), cases; 20 Cent. Law J. 466–68 (1885), cases; Chic. Leg. Adv. (1885): 9 Va. Law J. 515, 2 Kans. Law J. 242; 22 Cent. Law J. 126–29 (1886), cases; 21 Am. Law Rev. 705–14 (1887), cases; 26 Cent. Law J. 75–77 (1888), cases.

[3] Koch *v.* Emmerling, 22 How. 74 (1859).

BROTHERHOODS. See COMMUNITY, 3.

BROUGHT. Commenced.

In the legislation of Congress on the subject of limitation of actions, "commenced" and "brought" mean the same thing.[1]

A suit is brought when it is instituted or commenced.[2] See COMMENCE, Action.

BROWBEAT. To depress or bear down with haughty, stern looks, or with arrogant speech and dogmatic assertions; to bear down by impudence: as, to browbeat a witness.[3] Compare BADGER. See EXAMINATION, 9.

BRUTALITY. See CRUELTY; WHIPPING-POST.

BUBBLE ACT. The statute of 6 Geo. I (1720), c. 18 (enacted after the South Sea project had beggared half the nation), made all unwarrantable undertakings by unlawful subscriptions, then known as "bubbles," subjects of *præmunire.*[4]

By 6 Geo. IV (1825), the greater portion of that statute was repealed, and illegal companies left to be dealt with by the common law.[5]

"Bubble Acts" and "bubble companies" are still in use in speaking of persons who have been defrauded by subscribing to the stock of companies organized either without real capital or business, or with capital but for dishonest speculation.

BUCKET-SHOP. See WAGER, 2.

BUGGERY. See SODOMY.

BUGGY. See WAGON.

BUILDING. In its broadest sense, an erection intended for use and occupation as a habitation or for some purpose of trade, manufacture, ornament, or use, constituting a fabric or edifice, such as a house, a store, a church, a shed.[6]

A structure of considerable size, intended to be permanent or at least to endure for a considerable time.[7]

The "commencement" of a building imports some work and labor on the ground, the effect of which is apparent, as, beginning to dig the foundation, or other work of like description, which every one can readily recognize as the commencement of a building,[8] —

[1] Goldenberg *v.* Murphy, 108 U. S. 163 (1883), Waite, C. J.; 119 *id.* 475.

[2] Berger *v.* Commissioners, 2 McCrary, 485 (1880): Act of Congress, 1875, § 1.

[3] Webster's Dict.

[4] 4 Bl. Com. 117.

[5] 4 Chitty, Bl. Com. 117.

[6] Truesdell *v.* Gay, 13 Gray, 312 (1859), Bigelow, C. J.

[7] Stevens *v.* Gourley, 97 E. C. L. 112 (1859), Byles, J.

[8] Brooks *v.* Lester, 36 Md. 70 (1872).

work being done with the purpose then formed to continue it to the completion of the building.[1]

The idea in all the cases which concern a "new" building is newness of structure in the main mass — the entire change of external appearance, which denotes a different building from that which gave place to it, though into the composition of the new structure some of the old parts may have entered. This newness of construction must be in the exterior, the main plan of the building, not in the interior arrangements.[2]

See ADDITION, 1; ALTER; BURGLARY; ERECT, 1; HOUSE, 1; LOSS, Total; SPECIFICATION, 1; STRUCTURE; SUPPORT, 2.

Building or building and loan associations. Co-operative associations, usually incorporated, for the purpose of accumulating money and loaning it to their members upon the security of their real estate.

Each member makes a monthly payment upon each share of his stock, and such members as borrow from the association pay, in addition, interest upon the sums loaned to them. When the stock, from the payments of the monthly installments upon shares and from the accumulation of interest, reaches its par value, the mortgages given by the borrowers are canceled, and the non-borrowers receive in cash the par of their shares of stock.

Buildings, public. See LAND, Public.

Builder. A person whose business it is to construct buildings, vessels, bridges, canals, or railroads, by contract.[3] See CONTRACTOR.

He who undertakes to build a house impliedly agrees with every person who may have occasion to use it that he will exert, in the construction, such skill, care, and foresight as may be expected of a man of at least ordinary caution.[4]

The occupant of a house likewise agrees not to overload a floor; and, that every part of the premises, in and out of doors, to which the public are admitted, shall be reasonably guarded against accident. See CARE; DUTY, 1; MANSLAUGHTER; NEGLIGENCE; RES, Perit, etc.

As to the expense of changes made in plans and specifications, see *Watson* v. *Jones,* under CONTRACT, Executed, and *Phillips Construction Co.* v. *Seymour,* under COVENANT.

BULK. See BREAK.

BULLDOZE. See BALLOT; CONSPIRACY.

BULLION. Uncoined gold and silver, either smelted, refined, or in the condition in which it is used for coining.

Fr m an early period, has been associated with or employed as a term denoting money.[5] See BANK, 2 (2).

---

[1] Kelly *v.* Rosenstock, 45 Md. 392 (1876), cases.

[2] Miller *v.* Hershey, 59 Pa. 69 (1868), cases.

[3] See Revenue Act, 13 July, 1866; 14 St. L. 121.

[4] 1 Addison, Torts, § 569; People *v.* Buddensieck, 4 N. Y. Cr. R. 230, 250–72 (1886), cases.

[6] Counsel *v.* Vulture Mining Co., 5 Daly, 77 (1874).

BUNDLING. See SEDUCTION.

BURDEN. That which is borne: charge, obligation, duty; also, disadvantage. Compare BENEFIT; INCUMBRANCE; ONUS.

Burdensome. Grievous, oppressive: as, a burdensome contract.

Burden of proof. The obligation imposed upon a party who alleges the existence of a fact or thing necessary in the prosecution or defense of an action, to establish it by proof.[1]

Sometimes spoken of simply as "the burden." See further PROOF, Burden of.

BUREAU. See BOARD, 2; DEPARTMENT; HEALTH; LABOR, 1.

BURGESS. See BOROUGH.

BURGLAR.[2] He that by night breaketh and entereth into a mansion-house with intent to commit a felony.[3]

Burglarious. Intending to commit burglary.[4]

Burglary. Originally, the robbery of a dwelling; now, breaking and entering the house of another in the night-time with intent to commit a felony, whether the felony be actually committed or not.[5]

"House-breaking" describes the same offense, the time not being regarded.

Burglary, or nocturnal house-breaking, has always been looked upon as a very heinous offense; not only because of the terror that it naturally carries with it, but also as it is a forcible invasion and disturbance of that right of habitation which every individual might acquire even in a state of nature.[6]

By "night" is meant the period between total disappearance of daylight in the evening and its reappearance the next morning. The disappearance is total when a face can no longer be discerned. See NIGHT.

By "mansion-house" is meant a dwelling-house: any building actually used for human habitation and not permanently abandoned. It includes incidental out-buildings which are parcel of the dwelling-house. By statutes, extended to stores or shops. A single room may be such habitation: the injured owner being he who has the right of possession. See CURTILAGE.

There must be both a "breaking" and an "entering." "Breaking" means the removal of some portion

---

[1] People *v.* McCann, 16 N. Y. 66 (1857); Willett *v.* Rich, 142 Mass. 357 (1886).

[2] F. *burglar,* a burg-thief: a house-breaker: L. *latro,* a robber.

[3] Coke, 3 Inst. 63; 4 Bl. Com. 224; 29 Ind. 80; 34 La. An. 49; 53 Md. 153.

[4] See 14 Tex. Ap. 664.

[5] Anderson *v.* State, 48 Ala. 666 (1872): 3 Chitty, Crim. Law, 1101.

[6] 4 Bl. Com. 223.

of the house intended for security against intrusion. This may be by lifting a latch or a window, or by getting in through artifice or conspiracy; but not by raising a window already open, pushing back a door standing ajar, or by other entrance already made, except as to a chimney, which is as much closed as the nature of things will permit. The breaking may be of an inner or chamber door, or for purposes of egress. The least degree of "entering" with any part of the body, or with an instrument held in the hand, is sufficient; and it may be before, as well as after, the breaking.

The "intent" must be to commit a robbery, a murder. a rape, or other felony, whether the crime be actually perpetrated or not. If such specific intent is absent the act is a mere "trespass."[1]

Where the accused had himself, concealed in a chest, transferred to an express car, intending to rob the messenger, his acts were held to constitute a breaking and entering.[2]

The common-law definition has been modified and different degrees of the offense have been established, in some of the States.

See ACCESSARY; ACCOMPLICE; CRIME; DEFENSE, 1; EXTRADITION, 1; FELONY; INDICTMENT; MANSLAUGHTER.

BURIAL. "Burial ground" and "cemetery" may be used synonymously.[3]

To take up a dead body without lawful authority is a misdemeanor at common law. But there can be no larceny of the body, although there may be of the shroud.[4]

Preventing the burial of a dead body is indictable.

After interment, control over a body is in the next of kin. If they differ as to the disposition to be made of it, a court of equity may not afford assistance to either party.[5]

A stone vault in a cemetery used for the interment of dead bodies, though wholly above ground, is not a "building" or "other erection or inclosure," within the meaning of the penal code of New York.[6]

For sanitary reasons, a State may forbid the exhumation and removal of a corpse, without a permit being first procured.[7] See HEALTH; SEPULCHER.

---

[1] 4 Bl. Com. 224; Commonwealth v. Glover, 111 Mass. 402 (1873), cases; Walker v. State, 63 Ala. 50 (1879), cases.

[2] Nichols v. State, 68 Wis. 416 (1887), cases.

[3] Jenkins v. Andover, 103 Mass. 104 (1869).

[4] See 28 Alb. Law J. 106–8 (1883), cases; Re Wong Yung Quy, 6 Saw. 442, infra.

[5] See Re Beckman Street, 4 Bradf. Sur. 502 (1856); Bogert v. Indianapolis, 13 Ind. 138 (1859); Wynkoop v. Wynkoop, 42 Pa. 293, 301 (1862); Pierce v. Swan Point Cemetery, 10 R. I. 227, 235 (1872); Craig v. First Presby. Church, 88 Pa. 42, 52 (1878); Weld v. Walker, 130 Mass. 423 (1881), cases; Griffith v. Charlotte, &c. R. Co., 23 S. C. 39–42 (1885), cases; Johnston v. Marinus, 18 Abb. N. Cas. 72–77 (1886), cases; 10 Alb. Law J. 70 (1874), cases; 16 Am. Law Reg. 155 (1877), cases; 24 id. 591–600 (1885), cases; 19 Am. Law Rev. 251–70 (1885); Bishop, Contr. § 237.

[6] People v. Richards, N. Y. Ct. Ap. (Jan. 17, 1888): Pen. Code, §§ 498, 404.

[7] Re Wong Yung Quy, 6 Saw. 442 (1880).

BURNED. See LOST, 2.

BURNING. In the law of arson (q. v.), to·materially destroy the integrity of some portion of the house of another.[1]

Burning in the hand and left cheek was anciently a mode of punishment.[2] See C, 2; F, 1; T, 2.

Prior to 30 Geo. III (1790), c. 48, the penalty for treason was being burned alive;[3] and so, anciently, as to arson.[4] But victims seem to have been first deprived of sensation, as by strangling.[5]

As a punishment for military offenses, branding has been used to a very limited extent.

See BRAND; PUNISHMENT; WITCHCRAFT.

Burning fluid. See OIL.

BURSTING. In an insurance policy, which excepts a loss from the bursting of a boiler, synonymous with explosion, q. v.

BUSINESS. A word of large signification, denoting the employment or occupation in which a person is engaged to procure a living.[6]

"Business" and "employment" are synonymous terms, signifying that which occupies the time, attention, and labor of men for purposes of a livelihood or for profit. A calling for the purpose of a livelihood.[7] See EMPLOYMENT; HAPPINESS.

"Labor" may be business, but it is not necessarily so; and "business" is not always labor. The making of a contract is business, but not labor.[8] See LABOR, 1; TRADE.

"Other business," in the expression "works, mines, manufactory, or other business," is ejusdem generis with the species of business described by the preceding words, and imports, in a Wages Act, business of the same general character.[9]

"Ten per cent. on the business" of a partnership may mean ten per centum of the result of the business, that is, of the profits.[10]

Business corporation. In the Bankruptcy Act of 1867, had a broader meaning than "trading" corporation; was held to include a railroad corporation,[11] and an insurance company.[12]

---

[1] See 40 Ala. 669; 46 Cal. 356; 110 Mass. 403.

[2] 4 Bl. Com. 370.

[3] 4 Bl. Com. 204, 376, 407.

[4] 4 Bl. Com. 222.

[5] 4 Bl. Com. 377. See 1 Steph. Hist. Cr. Law Eng. 476–77.

[6] Goddard v. Chaffee, 2 Allen, 395 (1861), Merrick, J.

[7] [Moore v. State, 16 Ala. 413 (1849); 52 id. 21; 71 id. 62; 28 N. J. L. 545; 23 N. Y. 244.

[8] [Bloom v. Richards, 2 Ohio St. 396–403 (1853), cases.

[9] Pardee's Appeal, 100 Pa. 412 (1882).

[10] Funck v. Haskell, 132 Mass. 582 (1882).

[11] Adams v. Boston, &c. R. Co., 1 Holmes, 30 (1870); Winter v. Iowa, &c. R. Co., 2 Dill. 488 (1873).

[12] Re Independent Ins. Co., 1 Holmes, 104 (1872).

While "business" in § 37 of that act had a broader meaning than the word "commercial," used in the same section, such scope was not given it as to supersede "commercial" and "moneyed," or to leave these words without practical signification.[1]

Business hours. The business hours of the community generally.[2]

The hours when business is ordinarily transacted, down to the beginning of the hours of rest in the evening, except as to paper payable at a bank or by a banker.[3]

Business paper. Commercial paper; negotiable instruments. See NEGOTIABLE.

Business usages. See CUSTOM; USAGE.

Course of business. An act done according to the rules or methods which prevail in business generally or in a particular line or branch of business is said to be done in the "due," "ordinary," "regular," or "usual" course of business.

One who takes commercial paper before its maturity, and without notice, actual or otherwise, of any defense thereto, receives the paper in the due course of business and becomes a holder for value.[4]

Under the Bankruptcy Acts sales not made in the usual and ordinary course of the business of the debtor were *prima facie* evidence of fraud on creditors; as, where a retail dealer disposed of his stock at wholesale.[5]

Place of business. The place where one habitually or chiefly transacts his business duties is his usual or principal place of business.

"Usual place of business" means the place where one's business is carried on openly; the place which has public notoriety as one's usual place of business.[6]

The "principal place of business" is no test of residence, either of a natural person or of a corporation.[7]

See BANK, 2 (2); CARRY ON; COMMERCE; CUSTOM; INCOME; LABOR, 1; LICENSE, 3; MERCHANT; PROFIT, 1; RESIDE; SUNDAY; TAX, 2; TRADE.

BUST. See DESIGN, 2.

BUTCHER. See PEDDLER; POLICE, 2; RETAILER.

BUTTAL. See ABUT.

BUTTERINE. See OLEOMARGARINE.

---

[1] Sweatt v. Boston, &c. R. Co., 3 Cliff. 351 (1871).

[2] Derosia v. Winona, &c. R. Co., 18 Minn. 154 (1872).

[3] Cayuga County Bank v. Hunt, 2 Hill, 635, 638 (N. Y., 1842); Lunt v. Adams, 17 Me. 231 (1840); Flint v. Rogers, 15 *id.* 69 (1833).

[4] Brooklyn City R. Co. v. Nat. Bank of the Republic, 102 U. S. 25-28 (1880), cases.

[5] Act of 1867, § 35; Walbrun v. Babbitt, 16 Wall. 581 (1872), cases.

[6] [Bank of Columbia v. Lawrence, 1 Pet. *583 (1828); Stevenson v. Primrose, 8 Porter, 155 (Ala., 1838): 33 Am. Dec. 287.

[7] Guinn v. Iowa Cent. R. Co., 14 F. R. 324 (1882); McCabe v. Illinois Cent. R. Co., 13 *id.* 827 (1882).

BUY. To acquire by giving a consideration, usually money; to purchase, *q. v.*

To buy a note, as opposed to discount a note, see DISCOUNT, 2.

Buy in. To cause property to be offered at public sale, and then to become the purchaser thereof. See AUCTION.

Buying titles. See SEISIN, Disseisin.

Buyer. He who becomes the owner of a thing by paying the price asked; he who acquires or purchases; a purchaser.

See CAVEAT, Emptor; REDEEM; SALE; WAGER, 2.

BY. 1. Near, near to; by the side of; beside — all denoting exclusion.

Used descriptively in a grant, not "in immediate contact with." but "near to" the object.[1]

"By land of A " means along the line of A's land.[2]

A grant of land bounded "by" a fresh-water stream, whether navigable or unnavigable, conveys the soil to the middle line of the stream.[3] See ALONG.

A contract for the doing of a thing "by" a certain day means on *or* before that day.[4] See DAY.

Authorized "by" may mean "in" this State.[5]

By-bidding. See BID.

By-road. See WAY, Private.

By-standers. See TALES.

2. With, through, as the means or mode; as, by the book, by the uplifted hand. See OATH. Compare PER.

3. According to; by authority, direction, or allowance of: as, by agent, by writing filed, by the court, by act and operation of law, by statute, *qq. v.* See also ACCORDING; FORCE, 2.

Staying proceedings until an issue is determined by final judgment in another case may mean to stay the proceedings "according to" the judgment.[6]

4. May be used instead of "to;" as in the sentence "a person whose name is not known by the complainant."[7]

BY-LAW.[8] 1. A law affecting a single village or township; a rule governing the inhabitants of a locality.

"The by-law [of a borough] has the same effect within its limits, and with respect to the persons upon

---

[1] Wilson v. Inloes, 6 Gill, 153 (Md., 1847).

[2] Peaslee v. Gee, 19 N. H. 277 (1848).

[3] The Magnolia v. Marshall, 39 Miss. 110, 117, 134 (1860).

[4] Coonley v. Anderson, 1 Hill, 519, 522 (N. Y., 1841); Rankin v. Woodworth, 3 P. & W. 48 (Pa., 1831). See Higley v. Gilmer, 3 Monta. 437 (1880).

[5] State v. Overton, 16 Nev. 149 (1881).

[6] Haubert v. Haworth, 78 Pa. 83 (1875).

[7] Commonwealth v. Griffin, 105 Mass. 175 (1870).

[8] Scan. *byr*, a town, a village,— Skeat. A. S. *bilage*, a private law,— Webster. "A law made *obiter*, or by the by," Termes de la Lay (1721).

whom it lawfully operates, as an act of Parliament has upon the subjects at large."[1]

2. A rule or law of a corporation for its own government.

An act of legislation; therefore the formalities required by the charter for its passage must be observed. It may be in the form of a "resolution," although that is not necessarily a by-law.[2]

By-laws are the orders and regulations which a corporation, as one of its legal incidents, has power to make, and which is usually exercised to regulate its own action and concerns and the rights and duties of its members among themselves.[3] See CHARTER, 2; ORDINANCE, 1.

C.

C. 1. In connection with references to statutes means chapter. See STATUTE, 2.

2. In Rhode Island, as late as 1785, was branded upon the forehead as part of the punishment for counterfeiting.

3. As an abbreviation, may also denote case, chancellor, chancery, chief, circuit, civil, code, commissioner, common, counsel, court, criminal, crown:

C. A. Chancery appeals; court of appeals.

C. A. V. *Curia advisari vult.* The court wishes to consider the matter. See further CURIA, Advisari, etc.

C. B. Chief baron; common bench.

C. C. *Cepi corpus;* chief commissioner; circuit, city, or county court; chancery, civil, criminal, or crown cases; civil code.

C. C. J. Circuit, city, or county court judge.

C. C. P. Code of civil procedure: court of common pleas.

C. D. Commissioners' (patent) decisions.

C. J. Chief justice; circuit judge.

C. J. B. Chief judge in bankruptcy.

C. L. Civil law: common law.

C. L. P. Common law procedure.

C. O. D. Collect (*q. v.*) on delivery.

C. P. Common pleas (court).

C. q. t. (or *c. q. t.*). *Cestui que trust.* q. v.

C. R. Chancery reports; *curia regis*, the king's court.

---

[1] Hopkins v. Mayor of Swansea, 4 M. & W. *640 (1839), Ld. Abinger, C. B.

[2] Drake *v.* Hudson River R. Co., 7 Barb. 539 (1849). Compare Compton *v.* Van Volkenburgh, &c. R. Co., 34 N. J. L. 185 (1870).

[3] Commonwealth *v.* Turner, 1 Cush. 496 (1848), Shaw, C. J.

C. t. a. (usually, *c. t. a.*). *Cum testamento annexo*, with the will attached. See ADMINISTER, 4.

CABINET. See DEPARTMENT; PRESIDENT.

CABLE. See COMMERCE; TELEGRAPH.

The act of Congress approved February 29, 1888 (25 St. L. 41), entitled an act to carry into effect the International Convention of March 14, 1884, for the protection of submarine cables, provides:

"Section 1. That any person who shall willfully and wrongfully break or injure, or attempt to break or injure, or who shall in any manner procure, counsel, aid, abet, or be accessory to such breaking or injury, or attempt to break or injure, a submarine cable, in such manner as to interrupt or embarrass, in whole or in part, telegraphic communication, shall be guilty of a misdemeanor, and, on conviction thereof, shall be liable to imprisonment for a term not exceeding two years, or to a fine not exceeding five thousand dollars, or to both fine and imprisonment, at the discretion of the court."

"Sec. 2. That any person who by culpable negligence shall break or injure a submarine cable in such manner as to interrupt or embarrass, in whole or in part, telegraphic communication, shall be guilty of a misdemeanor, and, on conviction thereof, shall be liable to imprisonment for a term not exceeding three months, or to a fine not exceeding five hundred dollars, or to both fine and imprisonment, at the discretion of the court."

Sec. 3. The foregoing sections shall not apply to a person who breaks or injures a cable in an effort to save life or limb, or to save his own or any other vessel: *Provided*, that he takes reasonable precautions to avoid such breaking or injury.

"Sec. 4. That the master of any vessel which, while engaged in laying or repairing submarine cables, shall fail to observe the rules concerning signals that have been or shall hereafter be adopted by the parties to the convention with a view to preventing collisions at sea: or the master of any vessel that, perceiving, or being able to perceive the said signals displayed upon a telegraph ship engaged in repairing a cable, shall not withdraw to or keep at a distance of at least one nautical mile; or the master of any vessel that seeing or being able to see buoys intended to mark the position of a cable when being laid or when out of order or broken, shall not keep at a distance of at least a quarter of a nautical mile, shall be guilty of a misdemeanor, and on conviction thereof, shall be liable to imprisonment for a term not exceeding one month, or to a fine of not exceeding five hundred dollars."

Sec. 5. The master of any fishing vessel who shall not keep his implements or nets at a distance of at least one nautical mile from a vessel engaged in laying or repairing a cable, or at a distance of at least a quarter of a nautical mile from a buoy intended to mark the position of a cable when being laid or when out of order or broken, shall be guilty of a misdemeanor, and on conviction be liable to imprisonment for a term not exceeding ten days, or to a fine not exceeding two hundred and fifty dollars, or to both fine and imprisonment, at the discretion of the court: *Provided, however,* that fishing vessels, on perceiving or being able to perceive the said signals displayed on a telegraph ship, shall be allowed such time as may be necessary to obey the notice thus given, not exceeding twenty-four hours, during which period no obstacle shall be placed in the way of their operations.

Sec. 6. A person commanding a ship of war of the United States or of any foreign state for the time being bound by the convention, or a ship specially commissioned by such government or state, may exercise and perform the duties vested in and imposed on such officer by the convention.

Sec. 7. Any person having the custody of the papers necessary for the preparation of the statements provided for in article ten of the convention who shall refuse to exhibit them or shall violently resist persons having authority according to said article to draw up statements of facts in the exercise of their functions, shall be guilty of a misdemeanor, and on conviction thereof shall be liable to imprisonment not exceeding two years, or to a fine not exceeding five thousand dollars, or to both fine and imprisonment, at the discretion of the court.

Sec. 8. The penalties provided for the breaking or injury of a cable shall not be a bar to a suit for damages.

Sec. 9. When an offense against this act shall have been committed by means of a vessel, or of any boat belonging to it, the master of such vessel shall, unless some other person is shown to have been in charge, be deemed to have been navigating the same, and he liable to be punished accordingly.

Sec. 10. Unless the context of this act otherwise requires, the term "vessel" shall be taken to mean every description of vessel used in navigation, in whatever way it is propelled; "master" every person having command or charge of a vessel; and "person" to include a body of persons, corporate or incorporate. "Convention" shall mean the International Convention for the Protection of Submarine Cables, made at Paris, May 14, 1884, and proclaimed by the President of the United States May 22, 1885.

Sec. 11. The provisions of the Revised Statutes, from § 4300 to 4305 inclusive, for the summary trial of offenses against the navigation laws, shall extend to offenses against sections four and five of this act.

Sec. 12. This act shall apply only to cables to which the convention for the time being applies.

Sec. 13. The district courts of the United States shall have jurisdiction over all offenses against this act and of all suits of a civil nature arising thereunder, whether the infraction complained of shall have been committed within or outside of the territorial waters of the United States: *Provided,* that in case such infraction is committed outside of said waters the vessel is a vessel of the United States. From decrees and judgments, appeals and writs of error shall be allowed as now provided by law in other cases. Criminal actions and proceedings shall be prosecuted in the district court for the district within which the offense was committed, and when not committed within any judicial district, then in the district court for the district within which the offender may be found; and suits of a civil nature may be commenced in the district court for any district within which the defendant may be found and shall be served with process.

CADET. See GRADUATE.

Naval cadets, by settled usage which has the force of law, are appointed by certificates under the hand and seal of the secretary of war. They are inferior officers who, for purposes of instruction, may be required to serve as officers, non-commissioned officers, or privates.[1]

CADIT. See QUÆSTIO, Cadit.

CÆTERA. See ADMINISTER, 4; ET, Etc.

CALENDAR. 1. The division of time into years, months, weeks, and days, and a register of them.

The *pontifex maximus* on the first of every month proclaimed — Lat. *calare* — the month, with its festivals and the time of the new moon. From *calare* was derived "calendar." The first day of the month in the Roman calendar was called the *calendæ,* the calends.[2]

Calendar month. A solar month, known as January, February, etc.; distinguished from a lunar **month** of twenty-eight days. See further MONTH.

2. A list of causes arranged for trial or argument; a list; a docket.[3]

The calendar of a criminal court gives the names of offenders and prosecutors, the nature of the charges, from what magistrates certified, numbers and terms of the cases, and like particulars.

The calendar of a civil court contains the names of the parties plaintiff and defendant, the names of counsel, the nature of the demand in each case, the defense or plea, the number and term of the case, and, in courts of review, the name of the lower court from which removed.

CALIFORNIA. See CHINESE; PUEBLO.

CALL. 1, *v.* (1) To require a prisoner to present himself and answer the indictment, in the immediate presence of the court, is to call him to or before the bar.[4] See ARRAIGN.

(2) To admit to the rights and privileges of a practitioner of law is to call a student-at-law to the bar.

In England, "call-day" is the day in each term when those who have been students are admitted to practice law.

Call a case. For a judge to announce that a cause is about to be placed on a particular list, or to proclaim that a cause on

---

[1] Babbitt *v.* United States, 16 Ct. Cl. 203, 215–17 (1880). See United States *v.* Morton, 112 U. S. 1, 3 (1884). As to cadet-engineers, see also United States *v.* Redgrave, 116 *id.* 474 (1886); United States *v.* Perkins, *ib.* 483 (1886).
[2] Rives *v.* Guthrie, 1 Jones L. 86–87 (N. C., 1853), Nash, C. J.
[3] See Titley *v.* Kaehler, 9 Bradw. 539 (1881).
[4] [4 Bl. Com. 322.]

such list may now be determined by a trial by a jury or by argument before the court.

Call a list or **docket.** To inquire publicly in open court as to what causes on a list are ready for trial; also, to call for trial or argument certain causes already set or fixed for such determination.[1]

Whence, in the practice of some courts, the "first," the "second," and perhaps the "third" call of a case or list; also "the call."

Call a jury. To draw the names of persons to serve as a jury, out of the names of all of those who have been summoned as jurors.

Call a party. To call aloud his name in open court, and to command him to appear in order to perform some duty.

Call the plaintiff. At common law, when counsel for the plaintiff perceives that his client has not made out a case, the client may withdraw from the court room: whereupon the crier is required to call the plaintiff. If he does not answer the call (made thrice in succession), judgment of nonsuit is entered.[2]

The nonsuit is more eligible for the plaintiff than a verdict against him.[2]

Call a witness. To call his name aloud in, and perhaps about, the room of the court at which he has been subpœnaed to appear, before an attachment issues for disobedience.

Also, to present a witness for examination in a trial or hearing then in progress.

Recalling a witness, who has been once examined and dismissed, is a matter almost wholly within the discretion of the trial court.[3] See PRODUCE, 1.

2, *n.* (1) A notice or demand by the directors of a stock corporation upon a subscriber to pay money on account of his shares.

The word may refer to the resolution, its notification, or the time when it becomes payable.[4]

A court of equity may enforce payment of stock subscriptions though there have been no calls for them by the company. . . Subscriptions are in the nature of a fund for the payment of debts, and calls may be made whenever funds are needed for such payment. . . A formal call need not be made before a bill in equity is filed: filing the bill is equivalent to a call.[5] See PUT, 3; STOCK, 3 (2).

(2) A designation of the limit of a boundary.

A "locative call" refers to a physical object rather than to a course or distance. See further BOUNDARY.

CALLING. See BUSINESS.

CAMP-MEETING. See WORSHIP.

The Massachusetts statute of 1867, c. 57, which prohibits a person, during the time a camp or field meeting is being held for religious purposes, and within one mile of the place, from maintaining a building for vending provisions or refreshments without permission of the officers of the meeting, and which provides that a person having a regular and established place of business shall not be required to suspend his business, is constitutional.[1]

The Pennsylvania act of May 8, 1878,[2] prohibits disposing of any kind of merchandise, within one mile of any camp-meeting held for religious worship, under a fine of not more than one hundred dollars or imprisonment of not more than six months, or both; the act not applying to persons having written permit from the managers of the meeting, nor to persons regularly engaged in business, nor to farmers who sell the products of their farms upon the same. And the act of March 23, 1876,[3] provides that a judge of the court of common pleas of the particular county may appoint as policemen such persons as the association may designate; each to possess the powers of a constable; to enforce obedience to all reasonable regulations of the association not inconsistent with the constitution and laws of the State; to detain offenders twelve hours, if need be, exclusive of Sunday, until they can be carried before the nearest justice of the peace; and to wear a metallic shield with "camp police" and the name of the association inscribed thereon, in plain view — except when employed as detectives.

CAMPBELL'S ACT. See ACTIO, Personalis, etc.

CAN. Compare CASE, 4.

CANAL. Applied to an artificial passage for water, includes the banks, and refers to the excavation or channel as a receptacle for the water.[4]

As used in an Internal Improvement Act, a navigable public highway, for the transportation of persons and property. . . There must be a canal fitted in all respects for navigation and open to public use before benefits can accrue to the owner to overcome his claim for damages.[5]

The title of owners of land abutting on a canal extends to the line of the canal, subject to the use of the bank by the owners of the canal for purposes of commerce.[6]

---

[1] See Blanchard *v.* Ferdinand, 132 Mass. 391 (1882).
[2] [3 Bl. Com. 376.
[3] Keating *v.* Brown, 30 Minn. 10 (1832).
[4] Ambergate, &c. R. Co. *v.* Mitchell, 4 Ex. R. *543 (1849), Parke, B.
[5] Hatch *v.* Dana, 101 U. S. 214–15 (1879), Strong, J.

[1] Commonwealth *v.* Bearse, 132 Mass. 542, 551 (1882).
[2] P. L. 63.
[3] P. L. 9.
[4] Bishop *v.* Seeley, 18 Conn. *394 (1847).
[5] Kennedy *v.* City of Indianapolis, 103 U. S. 604 (1880), Waite, C. J.
[6] Morgan *v.* Bass, 14 F. R. 454 (1882).

A general grant of premises upon the bank of a river, in which is constructed a canal, conveys the grantor's right to the river's center. Where the canal company, as such, has the right only to use the bed and water, at dissolution such right reverts to the proper owners.[1]

Navigable water situated as is the Illinois and Lake Michigan canal,—a highway for commerce between ports and places in different States,—is public water of the United States, within admiralty jurisdiction, although the canal is wholly within the body of the State of Illinois.[2]

See COMMERCE; TOLL, 2.

CANCEL.[3] 1. To draw lines over the face of an instrument, in the forms of lattice-work. 2. To obliterate, deface, efface, expunge; to do away with, set aside, strike out of existence. 3. To satisfy, pay.

A deed may be rendered of no effect by delivering it up to be canceled; that is, to have lines drawn over it in the form of lattice-work: though the phrase is now used figuratively for any manner of obliteration or defacing it.[4]

To draw cross-lines over the face of an instrument is a common mode of showing an intention thereby to make an end of it as an instrument in force. In earlier times, when few persons could write, the mass of men could manifest their intention, with pen and ink, only by unlettered marks. . . When the instrument is so marked by the maker as to show clearly that the act was designed to be a canceling, that act becomes effectual as a revocation of a will by canceling.[5]

Cancel is not a technical word. In a statute of wills it is presumed to retain its popular meaning. . . A canceled bond or note has meant exclusively a bond or note over which lattice-work lines have been drawn. . . Revocation of a will by cancellation means by any act done to the paper which, in common understanding, is regarded as cancellation when done to any other instrument.[6]

In a contract, may not be equivalent to rescind; may mean no more than "doing away with" an existing agreement upon the terms, with the consequences, mentioned.[7]

Cancellation will be ordered, by a court of equity, of a writing which was obtained without consideration, or which became a nullity, or which may cause injury to the plaintiff, or be used to vex him after the evidence to impeach it has been lost, or which may throw a cloud over his title.[8]

Cancellation destroys a deed, annulling all covenants, as far as the deed is executory. It will not revest in the grantor an estate once completely transferred to another.[1]

"Canceling an executed contract is an exertion of the most extraordinary power of a court of equity. The power ought not to be exercised except in a clear case, and never for an alleged fraud unless the fraud be made clearly to appear; never for alleged false representations unless their falsity is certainly proved, and unless the complainant has been deceived and injured by them."[2] See PATENT, 2.

Compare NULL; RESCISSION; VACATE; VOID.

CANDIDATE. One who seeks or aspires to some office or privilege, or who offers himself for the same.

In a constitutional provision that any person who, while a candidate for office, shall be guilty of bribery, etc., is used in that popular sense: any one who seeks an office, whether nominated or not.[3]

See BRIBERY; LEGAL, Illegal; LIBEL, 8; LIBERTY, 1, Of the press.

CANISTER. See CASE, 4.

CANON.[4] A rule; a law.

Canon law. Ecclesiastical law.

In particular, a body of ecclesiastical laws relative to matters over which the church of Rome had or claims to have had jurisdiction.[5]

Compiled from opinions of the fathers, decrees of councils, and decretal epistles and bulls of the holy see. Received, in England, by immemorial custom, or else by consent of parliament; otherwise, ranked as unwritten law.[5]

Canons of construction. Rules of construction, q. v.

Canons of descent or of inheritance. The rules which regulate the descent of inheritances; the rules according to which estates are transmitted from ancestor to heir.[6] See further DESCENT.

CAP. When a person, who has been sentenced to capital punishment by hanging, is about to be executed, it is customary to place over his head and neck a sack or bag, which, from the color of the material, is called the **white cap** or **black cap**, and, generally, the **"death cap."**

In England and Canada, when a judge formally passes sentence of death upon a prisoner, he usually

---

[1] Day v. Pittsburgh, &c. R. Co., 44 Ohio St. 415 (1886); Pittsburgh, &c. R. Co. v. Bruce, 102 Pa. 33 (1882).

[2] Exp. Boyer, 109 U. S. 632 (1884).

[3] L. L. cancellare, to draw lines across: L. cancelli, lattice-work. Compare CHANCERY.

[4] 2 Bl. Com. 309.

[5] Warner v. Warner's Estate, 37 Vt. 362–63 (1864).

[6] Evans's Appeal, 58 Pa. 243–44 (1868), Strong, J. See also Ladd's Will, 60 Wis. 189–99 (1884), cases, Cassoday, J.

[7] Winton v. Spring, 18 Cal. 455 (1861); Weil v. Jones, 53 id. 47 (1878).

[8] 1 Story, Eq. §§ 692–711; 17 Blatch. 145.

[1] See 4 Kent, 452; 1 Greenl. Ev. § 265.

[2] Atlantic Delaine Company v. James, 94 U. S. 214 (1876), Strong, J. Approved, Union R. Co. v. Dull, 124 id. 188 (1888), Harlan, J.

[3] Leonard v. Commonwealth, 112 Pa. 624 (1886): Webster; Const. Penn. Art. VIII, sec. 9.

[4] Gk. kanōn', a reed, rod, rule.

[5] 1 Bl. Com. 82, 79, 19. See 2 Steph. Hist. Cr. L. Eng. 440; 25 Hen. VIII, c. 19; 1 Eliz. c. 1.

[6] 2 Bl. Com. 208.

wears a "black cap." Some writers trace the practice to the ancient custom by which rulers covered the head on occasions of great solemnity; while other writers find its origin in a prohibition against persons in holy orders (from which class the judges were largely selected) imposing the death penalty — as officials of the church. Since it was obligatory that such sentences should be pronounced, the judges, on such occasions, were supposed to lay aside their ecclesiastical character by "covering the clerical tonsure " with the black cap which all judges in early days wore as a part of their official dress.[1]

CAPACITY. Ability to take, do, act: competency, qualification, fitness, power. See CAPAX.

1. Power or fitness to perform a particular legal act; mental qualification: as, capacity to enter into a contract, disposing or testamentary capacity.

Capacity for guilt: will joined with an act.[2]

The test of capacity to make an agreement or a conveyance is, that a man shall have the ability to understand the nature and effect of the act in which he is engaged.[3] See INFLUENCE.

2. Character or function, relation or office, invested or conferred by law: as, capacity to act as an executor, administrator, guardian, trustee, referee, judge, sheriff, or other officer.

Whence also fiduciary, judicial, ministerial capacity; professional capacity; men in public capacity — see LIBEL, 5; DESCRIPTIO, Personæ.

CAPAX. L. Receiving or containing: able, fit for; having capacity, q. v.

Capax doli. Competent to intend wrong, to commit a crime. **Doli incapax:** incapable of committing crime. See further DOLUS.

Capax negotii. Competent to transact business.

CAPERE. L. To take, seize; to arrest.

Capias. That you take. A common-law writ commanding the sheriff to take a defendant into custody.

Named from the emphatic word in the writ when expressed in Latin.

Has come to designate the whole class of writs by which arrests are made by a constable, sheriff, or marshal. The species are:

Capias ad respondendum. That you take for answering: arrest (and imprison) the defendant so that you have him in person before the court on a certain day to answer the plaintiff's complaint.

Serves the purpose of compelling an appearance in court, on the part of a defendant, in actions of tort, in which damages are claimed, as, in actions for slander, libel, false arrest, malicious prosecution, and other trespasses. Being the species of the writ most frequently issued, is often designated as a or the " capias."[1] See PROCESS, 1.

Capias ad satisfaciendum. That you take for satisfying: arrest (and imprison) the defendant so that you may have him in court on a given day, in order that he may then and there pay the plaintiff such debt, damages, and costs as he may recover. Abbreviated *ca. sa.*

At common law, after this writ no other process could be issued against a debtor's property. The early use of the writ has been restricted by statutes abolishing imprisonment for debt or facilitating the discharge of debtors, in cases in which no fraud is shown to have been practiced.[2]

Capias in withernam.[3] That you take in reprisal; that you distrain for a distress.

A writ for seizing property of a distrainor on account of property concealed, eloigned, or otherwise withheld by him so that it could not be replevied.[4] See ELOIGN.

Capias utlagatum. That you arrest the outlaw, q. v.

Cepi. I have taken, or arrested. The distinctive word in old Latin forms of returns of service to orders for making arrests.

Cepi corpus. I have taken the body, — arrested the defendant. Abbreviated C. C.

Cepi corpus et bail bond. I have arrested the defendant and discharged him on a bail bond. Abbreviated C. C. et B. B.

Cepi corpus et committitur. I have arrested and imprisoned the defendant. Abbreviated C. C. et C.

Cepi corpus et est custodia. I have arrested the defendant and he is in custody.

Cepi corpus et est languidus. I have arrested the defendant and he is sick. See LANGUIDUS.

Cepi corpus et paratum habeo. I have arrested the defendant and have him in readiness. See ARREST, 2; BAIL, 1 (2).

Cepit. He took. The emphatic word in the Latin writs of trespass for taking personalty, and in declarations in trespass and replevin. Still used as descriptive of the action,

---

[1] See 22 Am. Law Rev. 121 (1888).
[2] 4 Bl. Com. 20.
[3] Eaton v. Eaton, 37 N. J. L. 113 (1874); 2 Bl. Com. 290.

---

[1] See 3 Bl. Com. 414.
[2] See 4 Bl. Com. 319.
[3] With'-er-nam is A. S. *widher*, against, and *niman*, to seize.
[4] See 3 Bl. Com. 149.

as in replevin for a mere taking — when the action is said to be " in the *cepit*." See Non Cepit.

Cepit et abduxit. He seized or took and led away — a person, or a living chattel.

Cepit et asportavit. He took and carried away — an inanimate thing, goods. See AS-PORTARE; CARRY, 1.

Cepit in alio loco. He took in another place — than that declared upon. A plea in replevin justifying the taking and claiming a return.

Non cepit. He did not take. The general issue in replevin : denies taking and detaining.

CAPIAS. See CAPERE, Capias.

CAPITA. See CAPUT, Capita.

CAPITAL.[1] 1, *adj.* For which death is the penalty : as, a capital offense.

Probably from "decapitation," once a common mode of executing the sentence of death.

Those judgments are capital which extend to the life of the offender, and consist, generally, in his being hanged by the neck till dead.[2] See DEATH, Penalty.

2, *n.* Money or property invested in a business enterprise.

The actual estate, whether in money or property, which is owned by an individual or a corporation.[3]

The chief thing, the head, the beginning and basis of an undertaking or enterprise. . . "Capital" and "capital stock," in ordinary parlance, when applied to combinations or associations for transacting business, have the same meaning, the former being an abbreviation of the latter.[4]

Used with respect to the property of a corporation or association, the term "capital" has a settled meaning. It applies only to the property or means contributed by the stockholders as the fund or basis for the business or enterprise for which the corporation or association was formed. . . Referring to the property of individuals in any particular business, the term has substantially the same import. It then means the property taken from other investments or uses and set apart for and invested in the special business, and in the increase, proceeds or earnings of which property, beyond expenditures incurred in

its use, consists the profits made in the business.[1]

It does not, any more than when used with respect to corporations, embrace temporary loans in the regular course of business.[1] See MONEYED.

"Capital stock," or "shares of capital stock," signifies the sum upon which calls may be made upon the holders of the stock of a corporation, and upon which dividends are declared.[2] See further STOCK, 3 (2).

CAPITATION. See TAX, 2.

CAPTION. 1. A taking, a seizure, *q. v.;* an arrest; a capture, *q. v.* See also CAPERE.

Recaption. When any one deprives another of his personal property, or wrongfully detains his wife, child, or servant.[3]

The owner of the goods, and the husband, parent, or master, may claim and retake them wherever he finds them, so that it be not attended with a breach of the peace. The owner may have this only opportunity to do himself justice.[3] See DEFENSE, 1.

2. The heading of a legal document, in which is shown the time when, the place where, and the person by whose authority, it was prepared or executed.

This use of the word is not warranted by its derivation — *captio,* a taking, and not *caput,* a head; but it is quite common in law books.

Though usual, is not necessary to an affidavit.[4]

When an inferior court, in obedience to the mandate of the king's bench, transmitted an indictment to the crown office, it was accompanied with its history — naming the court in which, the jurors by whom, and the time and place when and where, it was found. All this was entered of record by the clerk of the superior court immediately before the indictment, and was called the " caption," but was not then and is not now a part of the indictment itself.[5]

See AFFIDAVIT; COMMENCE, Indictment; TITLE, 2.

CAPTURE. A taking, seizure. See CAPERE.

In the law of marine insurance, any unlawful taking by force, including a piratical taking as well as such as is made *jure belli.*[6]

Synonymous with prize (*q. v.*), as used in Europe. The popular use of a taking by force or violence from without, to which a vessel in the course of a maritime adventure might be exposed, corresponds with the use in marine insurance.[6]

A taking by the enemy of a vessel or its cargo as prize, in time of open war, or by

---

[1] L. *capitalis,* chief: *caput,* the head.

[2] 4 Bl. Com. 376.

[3] People *v.* Commissioners, 23 N. Y. 219 (1861), Comstock, C. J.

[4] San Francisco *v.* Spring Valley Water Works, 63 Cal. 529 (1883), Thornton, J.; Gas Light Co. *v.* Assessors, 31 La. An. 477 (1879), Manning, C. J.

[1] Bailey *v.* Clark, 21 Wall. 286–87 (1874), Field, J.

[2] Sanger *v.* Upton, 91 U. S. 60, 47 (1875), Swayne, J.

[3] [3 Bl. Com. 4.

[4] Harris *v.* Lester, 80 Ill. 311 (1875).

[5] People *v.* Bennett, 37 N. Y. 122 (1867); *Exp.* Bain, 121 U. S. 7 (1887): Starkie, Cr. Pl. p. 287.

[6] Dole *v.* New England Mut. Mar. Ins. Co., 6 Allen, 386–90 (1863), Bigelow, C. J. See Fifield *v.* Ins. Co. of Penn., 47 Pa. 176–77, 189 (1864), cases.

way of reprisal, with intent to deprive the owner of it.[1]

This was probably the primary idea in instruments of marine insurance. Losses of ships and cargo engaged in commerce, by the public enemy, were the most to be apprehended and provided against. But usage, and the course of decisions by the courts, have very much widened this meaning, and it now may embrace —

The taking of a neutral ship and cargo by a belligerent *jure belli;* also, the taking forcibly by a friendly power, in time of peace, and even by the government itself to which the assured belongs.[1]

Technically, a taking by military power; a seizure, a taking by civil authority.[2]

"Captured property" may mean property seized or taken from hostile possession by the military or naval forces of the United States.[3]

As to **recapture,** see POSTLIMINY. See also RANSOM.

CAPUT. L. A head, the head; an individual.

Æstimatio capitis. The value of a head: the worth of a life.

In Saxon law, a prescribed sum to be paid for an unlawful taking of another man's life. In modern law, the amount of damages recoverable for causing a death.

Capita. Heads: bodies; individual persons.

Per capita. By heads: according to the individuals. Opposed, *per stirpes,* by the ancestor.

In distributing the personalty of an intestate, the persons entitled thereto are said to take *per capita* when they claim in their own rights as in equal degree of kindred, and not in right of another — *per stirpes.* This rule of succession was borrowed from the civil law. The common-law rule was the *per stirpes* rule.[4]

Caput lupinum. A wolf's head: an outlawed felon — who might be knocked on the head like a wolf.[5]

Caput mortuum. A dead head: a matter of no legal validity; a thing void as to all persons and for all purposes.[6]

CAR. See CARRIER, Common; RAILROAD.

Car load. A contract for a certain number of car loads of ice was held not void for uncertainty, that the quantity contemplated could be made certain by averment and proof.[1] See also CARRIAGE, 1.

CARDS. See GAME, 2.

CARE. Attention, caution, circumspection, vigilance, diligence.

Due care. In cases where the gist of the action is negligence, implies not only that a party has not been negligent or careless, but that he has been guilty of no violation of law in relation to the subject-matter or transaction which constitutes the cause of action.[2]

Great care. The degree of attention which a very thoughtful man exercises toward securing his own interests.

Ordinary care. That degree of care which every person of ordinary prudence takes of his own concerns.[3]

In the law of bailment, that degree of care which, under the same circumstances, a person of ordinary prudence would take of the particular thing were it his own.[4]

Ordinary care, skill, and diligence is such a degree of care, skill, and diligence as men of ordinary prudence, under similar circumstances, usually employ.[5]

Ordinary care implies the exercise of reasonable diligence, and reasonable diligence, as between a corporation and its employees, implies such watchfulness, caution, and foresight as, under all the circumstances of the particular service, a corporation controlled by careful, prudent officers ought to exercise.[6]

The same degree of care which a railroad company should take in providing and maintaining its machinery must be observed in selecting and retaining its employees, including telegraphic operators. Ordinary care on its part implies, as between it and its employees, not simply the degree of diligence which is customary among those intrusted with the management of railroad property, but such as, having respect to the exigencies of the particular service, ought reasonably to be observed. It is such care as, in view of the consequences that may result from negligence on the part of employees, is fairly commensurate with the perils or dangers likely to be encountered. . A degree of care ordinarily exercised in such matters may not be due, or reasonable, or proper care, and therefore not ordinary care, within the meaning of the law.[6]

---

[1] Schreiber *v.* Butler, 84 Ind. 576 (1882).

[2] Jones *v.* Inhabitants of Andover, 10 Allen, 20 (1865), Bigelow, C. J.

[3] 2 Pars. Contr. 87, tit. Bailment.

[4] [Heathcock *v.* Pennington, 11 Ired. L. 643 (1850), Ruffin, C. J.

[5] Brown *v.* Lynn, 31 Pa. 512 (1858), Williams, J.

[6] Wabash Ry. Co. *v.* McDaniels, 107 U. S. 460–61 (1882), Harlan, J. See also 25 Ind. 197; 74 Me. 497; 104 Mass. 104; 132 *id.* 426; 58 N. H. 528; 10 Oreg. 254; 41 Eng. C. Law, 425.

---

[1] Mauran *v.* Alliance Ins. Co., 6 Wall. 10 (1867), Nelson, J.

[2] United States *v.* Athens Armory, 2 Abb. C. C. 137 (1868).

[3] United States *v.* Padelford, 9 Wall. 540 (1869).

[4] See 2 Bl. Com. 517, 218; 49 Conn. 222; 143 Mass. 239; 91 N. Y. 445–47.

[5] 4 Bl. Com. 320.

[6] See 96 U. S. 195–96.

Reasonable care. The care and foresight which men of ordinary prudence are accustomed to employ.[1]

Care exercised in proportion to the danger of doing harm to others.[2]

A relative term, with no fixed meaning. The caution which persons of ordinary prudence would exercise in any given case is "reasonable care" in law. That care which under some circumstances would be reasonable care might under other circumstances be gross negligence.[3]

Slight care. The degree of care which every man of common sense, though inattentive to his own affairs, applies to them.[4]

See further CARRIER; CAUTION; DILIGENCE; DUTY, 1; KNOWLEDGE, 1; NEGLIGENCE; PRUDENCE.

CARGO. Goods on board of a vessel.[5]

All the merchandise and effects laden on board a ship, exclusive of persons, rigging, ammunition, provisions, guns, etc. What is laden on board as merchandise.[6]

Generally speaking, the entire load of the ship.[7]

See BOTTOMRY; CHARTER-PARTY; COLLISION, 2; DISPATCH; HYPOTHECATE; SAIL; SALVAGE; SHIP, 2.

CARICATURE. See LIBEL, 5.

CARLISLE TABLES. See TABLE, 4.

CARNAL. See KNOWLEDGE, 2.

CARPENTER. See CONTRACTOR; MANUFACTURER.

CARRIAGE. 1. The act of carrying: transportation, conveyance; also, that which carries or conveys.

To the ordinary mind, does not convey the idea of a railroad or street railway car, nor of a wheeled vehicle for the transportation of merchandise or products used in ordinary business. The idea is a vehicle for the transportation of persons for pleasure or business, drawn by horses or other draught animals over the ordinary streets and highways of the country, and not that of a "car" used upon a railroad or street railway expressly constructed therefor. As yet, in this country, the vehicles used for transporting passengers on railroads and street railways are generally called cars, occasionally coaches; seldom, if ever, carriages. The definition given by the older lexicographers of "carriage" was very general and indefinite, while that given in our own times is more in consonance with the restricted meaning of the word

as understood by people in general. In a bill of lading therefore, a "carriage" will not include a street car.[1]

See BICYCLE; CARRIER; FREIGHT; VEHICLE.

2. Manner of carrying one's self, behavior. See BEHAVIOR; LASCIVIOUS.

CARRIER. One who engages to transport persons or property.

Common carrier. One who undertakes, for hire or reward, to transport the goods of such as choose to employ him, from place to place.[2] **Private** or **special carrier.** One who agrees in a special case, with some private individual, to carry for hire.[3]

A common carrier holds himself out "in common," that is, to all persons who choose to employ him, as ready to carry for them.[3]

If it is his legal duty to carry for all alike, who comply with the terms as to freight, etc., he is a common carrier; if he may carry or not, as he deems best, he is but a private individual, and may make such contracts as suit himself.[4]

A private carrier, like an ordinary bailee for hire, is only liable for the injury or loss of the goods intrusted to him when it results from the failure of himself or his servant to exercise ordinary care. He is not bound to carry for any person unless he enters into a special agreement to do so.[5] He is not an insurer, but must use care and skill.[6] The bailor must prove negligence.

A common carrier is bound to carry for all who offer such goods as he is accustomed to carry, and who tender reasonable compensation for carrying them. If he refuses to perform his obligation in this respect he may be held liable in damages.[6]

Common carriers are classified as carriers of goods or merchandise, and as carriers of passengers. Their office is *quasi* public: the public have an interest in the faithful discharge of the duties. Their property, being devoted to a public use, may be regulated by the legislature.[7]

I. Common Carrier of Goods or Merchandise. To him "common carrier" and "carrier" are applied by way of pre-eminence. His relation, at common law, is that of insurer against all losses except such as result from an act of God or of the public enemy. As against any other cause of loss, the law conclu-

---

[1] [Johnson v. Hudson River R. Co., 6 Duer, 646 (1857).

[2] Dexter v. McCready, 54 Conn. 172 (1886), Park, C. J.

[3] Read v. Morse, 34 Wis. 318 (1874), Lyon, J. See also 100 U. S. 195; 1 Flip. 13.

[4] [2 Pars. Contr. 87; 20 N. Y. 69.

[5] Seamans v. Loring, 1 Mas. 142 (1816), Story, J.

[6] [Thwing v. Great West. Ins. Co., 103 Mass. 406–7 (1869), cases, Gray, J.

[7] Macy v. Whaling Ins. Co., 9 Metc. 366 (1845); 113 U. S. 49.

---

[1] [Cream City R. Co. v. Chicago, &c. R. Co., 63 Wis. 97 (1885), Taylor, J.

[2] Dwight v. Brewster, 1 Pick. 53 (1882), Parker, C. J.

[3] Allen v. Sackrider, 37 N. Y. 342 (1867), Parker, J. See also 3 Wend. 161; Story, Contr. § 752, a.

[4] Piedmont Manuf. Co. v. Columbia, &c. R. Co., 19 S. C. 364 (1883), Simpson, C. J.

[5] Varble v. Bigley, 14 Bush, 702–6 (1879), cases.

[6] The Margaret, 94 U. S. 497 (1876), cases. See also 25 Am. Law Reg. 451–61 (1886), cases.

[7] See Munn v. Illinois, 94 U. S. 113, 130 (1876). See generally 1 Sm. L. Cas. 406–41, cases.

sively presumes negligence on his part — a rule which proceeds upon the ground of public policy. He and his employer are not on equal terms: the property is within his power, and it would be difficult for the owner to prove misconduct. He may limit the operation of this rule by a special agreement — just and reasonable in itself, not against legal policy, and not exempting him from liability for negligence or misconduct.[1]

Toward avoiding the effects of an overpowering cause, ordinary diligence only is exacted.[2]

He may regulate his business by such rules as are in themselves reasonable, consistent with law and public policy, and distinctly made known to shippers.[3]

For a reasonable cause he may refuse to receive goods.

The common law does not require him to charge equal rates for carriage.[4]

He has a right to know both the general nature and the value of packages offered for carriage.[5] But the law does not exact of him knowledge of the contents of a package, nor permit him, in cases free from suspicion, to require information as to the contents, as a condition to transportation.[6]

He has a lien for freight, q. v.

On the service of legal process, he may surrender goods into the custody of the law.[7]

The fair result of the cases limits his liability, where no special contract exists, to his own line. But if he undertakes the entire service, he cannot make another carrier the agent of the consignor or consignee.[8]

II. Common Carrier of Passengers. His duty is to carry all persons who apply for transportation, if his accommodations are sufficient and there exists no reasonable objection to the persons.[9]

He may make reasonable regulations for the comfort and safety of the passengers. For non-compliance with a proper regulation, he may expel a passenger. Each passenger is to take at least ordinary care of himself. The carrier is expected to exercise the highest degree of vigilance — he represents that all the means of conveyance are sound, and that his employees will use the utmost of human foresight toward preventing accidents and securing a safe journey.[1]

The engagement of a railroad company is to carry its passengers safely; for an injury arising from a defect in its road, which could have been guarded against by the exercise of proper care, it will be liable in damages. Though a carrier of passengers is not, like a carrier of property, an insurer against all accidents except those caused by an act of God or the public enemy, it is charged with the utmost care and skill in the performance of its duty; which implies not merely the most attention in respect to the movement of cars, but to the condition of the road, and of its ties, rails,— all appliances essential to the safety of the train and passengers. For injuries through negligence, to which the passenger does not contribute by his own act, it is liable.[2]

In guarding passengers from dangers not incident to ordinary railway travel, the rule of liability is less stringent than in the case of the ordinary perils from appliances, servants, and operation of trains; but in no case must the carrier expose the passenger to extra-hazardous dangers that might readily be discovered or anticipated by reasonable and practicable care and foresight.[3]

The standard of duty should be according to the consequences that may ensue from carelessness. The rule has its foundation in public policy. It is approved by experience, and sanctioned by the plainest principles of reason and justice. The courts should not relax it. The terms in question do not mean all the care and diligence the human mind can conceive of, nor such as will render the transportation free from any possible peril, nor such as would drive the carrier from his business. . . The rule is beneficial to both parties. It tends to give protection to the traveler, and warns the carrier against the consequences of delinquency.[4]

---

[1] See Southern Express Co. v. Caldwell, 21 Wall. 267–72 (1874), cases; York Co. v. Illinois Central R. Co., 3 id. 111–13 (1865), cases; N. Y. Central, &c. R. Co. v. Lockwood, 17 id. 359–84 (1873), cases; Bank of Kentucky v. Adams Express Co., 93 U. S. 181 (1876); Brown v. Adams Express Co., 15 W. Va. 816–26 (1879), cases.

[2] Memphis, &c. R. Co. v. Reeves, 10 Wall. 189–91 (1869), cases.

[3] New York Central & Hudson River R. Co. v. Fraloff, 100 U. S. 27 (1879).

[4] 2 Pars. Contr. 173.

[5] Muser v. Holland, 17 Blatch. 414–15 (1880), cases.

[6] Nitro-Glycerine Case, 15 Wall. 535–36 (1872), cases; State v. Goss, 59 Vt. 271 (1886), cases.

[7] 2 Pars. Contr. 207.

[8] Michigan Central R. Co. v. Manufacturing Co., 16 Wall. 324 (1872); Ogdensburg, &c. R. Co. v. Pratt, 22 id. 129 (1874); Bank of Kentucky v. Adams Express Co., 93 U. S. 181 (1876); St. Louis Ins. Co. v. Railroad Co., 104 id. 157–59 (1881); Myrick v. Michigan Central R. Co., 107 id. 106–10 (1882), cases; Atchison, &c. R. Co. v. Denver, &c. R. Co., 110 id. 680 (1884); Keep v. Indianapolis, &c. R. Co., 3 McCrary, 208, 214–19 (1881), cases; Aigen v. Boston, &c. R. Co., 132 Mass. 425 (1882), cases; Central Trust Co. v. Wabash, &c. R. Co., 31 F. R. 248 (1887), cases. On the carriage of freight generally, see 23 Cent. Law J. 79 (1886), cases.

[9] Pearson v. Duane, 4 Wall. 615 (1866).

---

[1] Philadelphia, &c. R. Co. v. Derby, 14 How. 486 (1852); Hall v. Memphis, &c. R. Co., 15 F. R. 57, 69–97 (1882), cases.

[2] Vicksburg & Meridian R. Co. v. O'Brien, 119 U. S. 109 (1886), Field, J.

[3] Chicago, &c. R. Co. v. Pillsbury, Ill. Sup. Ct. (Nov. 11, 1887): 26 Cent. Law J. 288; ib. 290–92 (1888), cases. The plaintiff took aboard non-union laborers (under police protection) who went into the smoking-car with other passengers, among whom was Pillsbury. The train, while stopping at a crossing (not a station), was boarded by a mob who attacked the laborers, and shot Pillsbury. The company was held liable in damages for his death, on the ground that the attack might have been foreseen and the death of the passenger averted.

[4] Indianapolis, &c. R. Co. v. Horst, 93 U. S. 296–97 (1876), cases, Swayne, J. See also 26 Cent. Law J. 50–55 (1888), cases; Hyman v. Pennsylvania R. Co., Sup. Ct. Pa. (1888).

He is liable for the slightest fault. He cannot by special contract exempt himself from liability for negligence or misconduct. The burden of disproving negligence rests upon him. He must show by affirmative evidence that he exercised the requisite degree of care.[1]

What will be misconduct on the part of servants toward a passenger cannot be defined by a rule applicable to every case, but must depend upon the particular circumstances in which they are required to act. In the enforcement of reasonable regulations established by the carrier for the conduct of its business, the servant may be obliged to use force. But the law will not protect the carrier if the servant uses excessive or unnecessary force.[2]

A passenger upon a railroad, taking a drawing-room car, has a right to assume that the car is there under a contract with the railroad corporation, and that the servants in charge of the car are its servants, for whose acts, in the discharge of their duty, it is liable.[3]

The negligence of a servant of a palace-car company whose car forms part of the carrier's train is negligence in the railroad company, though an additional sum has been paid to the former company.[1] See SLEEPING-CAR.

See further ACCIDENT; ACT, 1, Of God; BAGGAGE; BAILMENT; COMMERCE; DELIVERY, 1; EXPRESS COMPANY; LIEN; NEGLIGENCE; PASSENGER; POLICY, 1; RAILROAD; RIGHT, 2, Civil Rights Acts; STOPPAGE; TORT, 2; TUG-BOAT; WAREHOUSEMAN; WHARFINGER.

CARRY. 1. In the law of larceny, "carry" is not the same as "carry away." "Did take and carry away" is the translation of "*cepit et asportavit*," used in indictments when processes and records were in Latin. "Away" or some other word must be subjoined to "carry" to modify its general signification.[4] See LARCENY.

"Take and haul away" has the same meaning as take and carry away.[5]

2. To bear: as, to "carry a concealed weapon."

Locomotion is not essential.[6] See further WEAPON.

3. When a party becomes entitled to the payment of costs as an incident to a verdict in his favor, the verdict is said to "carry costs." See DAMAGES.

4. That to carry safely is the obligation of a common carrier, see CARRIER.

Carry on. A single act pertaining to a particular business will not constitute one as "carrying on" or engaged in that business.[1]

Making a contract in Colorado to build and to deliver in Ohio certain machinery was held not "carrying on" business in Colorado.[2] See further FIND, 2.

Carry stock. When a broker buys stock and holds it on account of a customer, he is said to "carry stock."[3]

CART. See WAGON.

CARTA. See CHARTA.

CASE. 1. That which happens or comes about; an occurrence; a circumstance to which something applies. Compare CASUS.

In the Revised Statutes, § 5392, limiting perjury to oaths in a case in which the law authorizes an oath to be administered, "case" is not confined to a suit or proceeding in court. The meaning is, the law must authorize the oath under the circumstances existing; as, in justifying bail.[4]

The expression "all cases" often signifies all cases of a particular class only. The generality of the words will be restrained by the context and the general scheme of the instrument.[5]

The words "in case he lives" imply a condition as explicitly as "if," "upon," and the like, and express a contingency.[3] See THEN; UPON, 2.

2. A state of facts which furnishes occasion for the exercise of the jurisdiction of a court of justice.[7]

A question contested before a court of justice; an action or suit in law or equity.[8]

An action, suit, or cause, qq. v.

In the sense of "a state of facts involving a question for discussion or decision, a cause or suit in court," will include a question pending before a commission authorized to hear and determine matters pertaining to railroads.[9]

The word is applied in New York to at least three abstract ideas: a suit or action at law; the combination of facts upon which each party relies to sustain

[1] Pennsylvania Co. v. Roy, 102 U. S. 456 (1880), cases; Hart v. Penn. R. Co., 112 id. 338–43 (1884), cases; Waterbury v. N. Y. Central, &c. R. Co., 17 F. R. 671, 674–93 (1883), note; 22 Am. Law Rev. 198–202 (1888), cases.

As to contract for non-liability for negligence, see also Griswold v. New York, &c. R. Co., 53 Conn. 385–86 (1885), cases, pro and con.; Lake Shore, &c. R. Co. v. Spangler, 44 Ohio St. 476 (1886); Little Rock, &c. R. Co. v. Eubanks, 48 Ark. 465 (1886), cases.

[2] New Jersey Steamboat Co. v. Brockett, 121 U. S. 646–47 (1887), cases. As to servants, see 23 Cent. Law J. 127 (1886) — Justice of the Peace (Eng.).

[3] Thorpe v. N. Y. Central & Hudson River R. Co., 76 N. Y. 402 (1879).

[4] Commonwealth v. Adams, 7 Gray, 45 (1856); Commonwealth v. Pratt, 132 Mass. 247 (1882).

[5] Spittorff v. State, 108 Ind. 172 (1886).

[6] Owen v. State, 31 Ala. 389 (1858), Rice, C. J.

[1] Weil v. State, 52 Ala. 20–21 (1875); United States v. Jackson, 1 Hughes, 532 (1875).

[2] Cooper Manuf. Co. v. Ferguson, 113 U. S. 735 (1885).

[3] Peckering v. Demerritt, 100 Mass. 421 (1868).

[4] United States v. Volz, 14 Blatch. 17 (1876).

[5] Phillips v. State, 15 Ga. 521 (1854); 27 Ark. 564; 11 Ohio St. 252; 18 Pa. 388; 118 U. S. 491.

[6] Robert's Appeal, 59 Pa. 72 (1868).

[7] Kundolf v. Thalheimer, 12 N. Y. 596 (1855), Gardiner, C. J.

[8] Exp. Towles, 48 Tex. 433 (1877), Roberts, C. J.

[9] Smith v. City of Waterbury, 54 Conn. 177 (1886).

his side of a controversy; and the aggregation of papers and evidence presented to an appellate court on the argument of an appeal.[1]

Case in judgment. The facts which constitute the case under consideration or already decided.

Case law. That part of the jurisprudence of a country which is deducible from the decisions rendered by the courts; law made by decided cases.

Case reserved. When the jury find a verdict generally for the plaintiff, but subject to the opinion of the court on the special case stated by counsel on both sides with regard to a matter of law.[2]

Case stated. When the parties submit to the court a written statement of the facts in the case as they agree upon them, to obtain a decision upon the question of law arising out of the facts. Also called a "case agreed upon," or "case made."

A case stated is a substitute for a special verdict,[3] q. v.

If a question of mere law arises in the course of a cause in chancery, it is referred, for an opinion, to the king's bench or the common pleas, upon a case stated for that purpose, wherein all the material facts are admitted, and the point of law is submitted to their decision.[4]

Cases and controversies. By "cases and controversies," in the judicial article of the Constitution, are intended the claims of litigants brought before the courts for determination by such regular proceedings as are established by law or custom for the protection or enforcement of rights, or the prevention, redress, or punishment of wrongs. Whenever the claim of a party under the Constitution, laws, or treaties takes such a form that the judicial power is capable of acting upon it, it becomes a case. The term implies the existence of present or possible adverse parties whose contentions are submitted to the court for adjudication.[5]

The term "controversies," if distinguishable from "cases," is so in that it is less comprehensive than the latter, and includes only suits of a civil nature.[6] See CONTROVERSY; JUDICIAL, Power.

See also ADMIRALTY; FICTITIOUS; LEADING; MERITS; OVERRULED; REPORT, 1 (2); TABLE, Of cases.

---

[1] [15 Alb. Law J. 242 (1877).
[2] [3 Bl. Com. 378.
[3] Whitesides v. Russell, 8 W. & S. 47 (1844).
[4] 3 Bl. Com. 453.
[5] Re Pacific Railway Commission, 32 F. R. 255 (1887), Field, J.

---

3. In pleading, a term for "action on the case," "trespass on the case," "special action of trespass on the case"—a common-law form of action.

A generic term, embracing many different species of actions, those of most frequent use being *assumpsit* and trover.[1]

A remedy for all personal wrongs committed without force — where the injury is consequential. Called "case" because the plaintiff's whole cause of complaint is set forth at length.[2]

Where the act done is in itself an immediate injury the remedy is by an action of trespass *vi et armis.* Where there is only a culpable omission, or where the act is not immediately injurious, but only consequentially and collaterally so, the remedy is by an action on the special case for the damages consequent on such act or omission.[3]

Where any special consequential damage arises, which could not be foreseen and provided for in the ordinary course of justice, the party is allowed, by common law and by statute of Westminster 2, c. 24, to bring a special action on his own case, by a writ formed according to the peculiar circumstances of his particular grievance.[4] See CASUS, Consimili casu.

The action of case lies for a tort not committed with force, actual or implied; for a tort committed forcibly where the matter affected was not tangible, as for an injury to a right of way or to a franchise; for an injury to a relative right; for an injury resulting from negligence; for a wrongful act done under legal process regularly issued from a court of competent jurisdiction; for a wrongful act committed by defendant's servant without his order, but for which he is still responsible; for the infringement of a right given by statute; for an injury done to property of which the plaintiff has the reversion only.

Damages not necessarily resulting from the act complained of must be alleged specially. The plea "not guilty" raises the general issue; and under this plea almost any matter of defense, except the statute of limitations, may be given in evidence. In some States the distinction between "trespass" and "case" has been abolished.

See AMENDMENT, 1; DAMAGES, Special; TRESPASS.

4. A chest, box, or package.

By statute 35 and 36 Vict. (1872), c. 77, s. 23, no explosive or inflammable substance shall be taken into a mine "except in a case or canister," etc. *Held*, that "case" means something solid and substantial in the nature of a canister, and that a package like a bag of linen or calico was not contemplated.[5]

---

[1] [Carrol v. Green, 92 U. S. 513 (1875), Swayne, J.
[2] [3 Bl. Com. 122, 154.
[3] 3 Bl. Com. 123; Scott v. Shepherd, 2 W. Bl. 892 (1773): 1 Sm. L. C., Part I, *754-69; Cooley, Torts, 70; 36 Conn. 182, 186.
[4] 3 Bl. Com. 122-23, 50-51.
[5] Foster v. Diphwys Casson Slate Co., L. R., 18 Q. B. D. 428 (1887).

CASH. In all sales for cash the money must be paid when the property is delivered.[1]

A sale for cash is a sale for the money in hand.[2]

But when a factor is directed to sell grain for cash, evidence may be given of a well-established custom to allow the purchaser to receive the grain, and call for the money in a few days after delivery.[2, 3]

Where goods are sold for cash, but the delivery is unconditional and without fraud or mistake, the title vests in the vendee notwithstanding the cash was not in fact paid.[3]

The idea of a sale on credit is that the vendee is to have the thing sold on his assumption to pay, and before actual payment.[4]

See CREDIT; CURRENT, 2; MONEY; PLACE, 1, Of delivery, payment; SALE; VALUE.

CASHIER. An officer or agent whose business is mainly to take care of the money of an institution, of a private person, or of a firm.

The cashier of a bank is the executive officer through whom the financial operations are conducted. He receives and pays out its moneys, collects and pays its debts, receives and transfers its commercial securities. Tellers and other subordinate officers are under his direction, and are, as it were, the arms by which designated portions of his functions are discharged.[5]

Evidence of powers habitually exercised with the acquiescence of the directors of the bank defines and establishes, as to the public, those powers — provided the charter is not violated.[6]

He is the general financial agent. He acts, or is presumed to act, according to general practice, and the course of business; and this binds the bank in favor of one who possesses no other knowledge.[7]

See AGENT; BANK, 2 (2); CHECK; DEPOSIT, 2.

[1] Bliss v. Arnold, 8 Vt. 255 (1836).

[2] Steward v. Scudder, 24 N. J. L. 101 (1853).

[3] Foley v. Mason, 6 Md. 49 (1854), cases.

[4] Merchants' Nat. Bank of Memphis v. Nat. Bank of Commerce, 91 U. S. 95 (1875), Strong, J.

See also 24 Am. Law Reg. 514–19 (1885), cases; 20 Cent. Law J. 304–7 (1885), cases; 1 Cal. 45; 54 id. 218; 4 Mass. 245; 103 id. 17; 5 Allen, 91; 27 N. Y. 378; 62 id. 513; 69 id. 148; 9 Johns. 120; 19 id. 144; 39 Barb. 283; 1 Ohio, 189; 34 Pa. 344; 28 Gratt. 165.

[5] Merchants' Nat. Bank v. State Nat. Bank, 10 Wall. 650 (1870), cases, Swayne, J.

[6] Ibid. 604, 644; Moores v. Citizens' Nat. Bank of Piqua, 111 U. S. 156, 169 (1884), cases.

[7] Case v. Citizens' Bank of Louisiana, 100 U. S. 454 (1879); Martin v. Webb, 110 id. 14 (1884); Xenia Bank v. Stewart, 114 id. 224 (1885); Knickerbocker Life Ins. Co. v. Pendleton, 115 id. 344 (1885); Bostwick v. Van Voorhis, 91 N. Y. 353 (1883); Merchants' Bank v. Jeffries, 21 W. Va. 504 (1883); 20 Cent. Law J. 126–30 (1885), cases; 133 Mass. 22; Story, Agency, §§ 114–15; Whart. Ag. §§ 684–87; 3 Am. Law Rev. 612–40 (1869), cases; Bank. Mag., July, 1860. As to his signature, see Robinson v. Kanawha Valley Bank, 44 Ohio St. 448 (1886).

CASK. See EMPTY.

CASSETUR. See QUASH.

CAST. To transfer, invest with, place upon; as, in saying that the law casts the legal ownership of the property of an intestate upon the administrator,[1] or casts the estate upon the heir.[2]

Cast away. For a vessel to be lost, to be irrecoverable by ordinary means, to perish.[3]

Casting vote. See VOTE.

CASTIGATORY. See SCOLD.

CASTLE. See HOUSE, 1; MANOR.

CASUAL.[4] That which happens by accident or is brought about by an unknown cause. Compare REGULAR.

Casual ejector. A nominal defendant in the action of ejectment at common law.

By a fiction he was supposed to have entered and ejected the lawful possessor.[5]

Casual pauper or **poor.** A person who is assisted under the poor laws in a district other than that of his lawful settlement. Whence "casuals." See further POOR.

Casualty. An inevitable accident, q. v.

"Unavoidable casualty," in common use in leases, comprehends only damage or destruction arising from supervening and uncontrollable force or accident. By strict definition, an event or accident which human prudence, foresight, and sagacity cannot prevent.[6] See ACT, 1, Of God; INSURANCE.

CASUS. L. A thing that happens: an occurrence; a combination of circumstances; an event; a case, q. v.

Casus fœderis. The case of the treaty: the case contemplated in a compact or contract.[7]

Casus fortuitous. An inevitable occurrence or accident.[8]

Casus major. An unusual accident.[9] See ACCIDENT; ACT, 1, Of God.

Casus omissus. A case not provided for. A combination of circumstances overlooked,

[1] 143 Mass. 392; 52 Pa. 232; 7 Wheat. 107

[2] 36 Cal. 332.

[3] 1 Wash. 372; 3 id. 382; 4 Dall. 412.

[4] L. casualis, happening by chance.

[5] 3 Bl. Com. 202.

[6] [Welles v. Castles, 3 Gray, 325 (1855), Bigelow, J. See also Thompson v. Tillotson, 56 Miss. 36 (1878).

[7] See 1 Kent, 49.

[8] See 3 Kent, 217, 300; Whart. Neg. §§ 113, 553.

[9] Story, Bailm. § 240.

or deemed unimportant, in a statute or a contract.

Where the letter of a statute would have been enlarged to include an occurrence, had the legislature foreseen it, the courts will bring the case within the spirit of the statute.[1]

But, under this rule, a court may not go so far as virtually to make a law.[2]

Consimili casu. In like case.

To quicken the diligence of the clerks in chancery, who were much attached to ancient precedents, it was provided by statute of Westm. 2, 13 Edw. I (1285), c. 24, that when "in one case a writ shall be found in the chancery, and *in a like case* falling under the same right and requiring like remedy, no precedent of a writ can be produced, the clerks shall agree in forming a new one; and if they cannot agree, it shall be adjourned to the next parliament." . . This provision might have answered all the purposes of a court of equity.[3]

CATALOGUE. See COPYRIGHT.

CATCHING. See BARGAIN.

CATCHPOLE. Formerly, an officer, as a deputy-sheriff or a constable, who made arrests.

He was supposed to catch the prisoner by the *poll* — the head, or neck. The term now expresses contempt or derision.

CATTLE.[4] Domestic animals generally; animals useful for food or labor.

"Sheep, oxen, swine, and horses, which we in general call cattle, may be estrays."[5]

Not only domesticated horned animals, but also swine, horses, asses, and mules.[6]

In an indictment "steer" may be used for "cattle" or "neat cattle."[7]

Within the meaning of a penal statute, "buffaloes" may not be cattle.[1]

See ANIMAL; DAMAGE-FEASANT; FEED; FENCE; HEIFER; HOG; HORSE; PERISHABLE; PROVISIONS.

CAUCUS. See BRIBERY.

CAUSA. L. That which operates to produce an effect; that on account of which a thing is done; that which supplies a motive, or constitutes a reason.

Causa causans. The originating, efficient cause; the immediate cause. **Causa causæ causantis.** The cause of the cause operating; i. e., the near, not the direct, cause.[2] See CAUSE, 1.

Causa mortis. See DONATIO, Mortis, etc.

Causa proxima, non remota, spectatur. The near cause, not the removed, is considered. See at length CAUSE, 1, Proximate, etc.

Causa sine qua non. A cause without which a thing cannot be or exist: as, a cause without which an injury could not have occurred.[3]

Causa turpis. An unlawful motive or purpose: an immoral or illegal consideration.

Ex turpi causa non oritur actio. Out of an illegal consideration an action cannot arise: no court will aid a party who founds his claim for redress upon an illegal act.[4] See further DELICTUM, In pari, etc.

CAUSE. 1. Eng. (1) That which produces or effects a result; that from which anything proceeds, and without which it would not exist.[5]

Proximate cause. The nearest, the immediate, the direct cause; the efficient cause; the cause that sets another or other causes in operation; the dominant cause. **Remote cause.** The removed, the distant, the indirect, the intermediate cause.

The law concerns itself only with the direct cause of an event — that force or influence which, in the order of causation, is nearest to the effect or result under consideration, and is sufficient of itself to produce the result.

The principle is of frequent application in the law of insurance: and in cases of involuntary negligence, as distinguished from wanton or intentional injuries.

[1] See 1 Shars. Bl. Com. 61; 2 *id.* 260; 4 *id.* 302.

[2] See United States *v.* Union Pacific R. Co., 91 U. S. 85 (1875); Hobbs *v.* McLean, 117 *id.* 579 (1886).

[3] 3 Bl. Com. 50–51.

[4] L. L. *catalla*, movables. In old English, "cattle" had not that meaning,— Marsh, Eng. Lang. 246. From L. *capitalis*, the head or chief. Compare "pecunia-ry," and "feud." When wealth consisted in heads of cattle (*capita, capitalia*), the word which designated them came to include all kinds of property. In the Elizabethan age "quick cattle" meant live stock. In time "chattel" denoted dead, inanimate property; and "cattle" sensate possessions. Wiclif, in 1380, translated Luke viii, 44, "a woman that spendid all hir catel in leechis;" and Chaucer, in 1388, wrote that an avaricious man "hath hope in his catel." See Trench, Glossary, 29.

[5] 1 Bl. Com. 298.

[6] See United States *v.* Mattock, 2 Saw. 149–51 (1872); Decatur Bank *v.* St. Louis Bank, 21 Wall. 299 (1874); Ohio, &c. R. Co. *v.* Brubaker, 47 Ill. 462 (1868); Toledo, &c. R. Co. *v.* Cole, 50 *id.* 186 (1869); Hubotter *v.* State, 32 Tex. 484 (1870); 27 *id.* 726; 45 *id.* 84.

[7] State *v.* Lange, 22 Tex. 591 (1858); State *v.* Abbott, 20 Vt. 537 (1848).

[1] State *v.* Crenshaw, 22 Mo. 458 (1856).

[2] See 12 Wall. 399; 95 U. S. 132; 4 Gray, 398.

[3] 111 U. S. 241.

[4] The Florida, 101 U. S. 43 (1879); 2 Pet. *539; 87 Ind. 273; 45 Iowa, 241.

[5] Webster's Dict.

If we could deduce from the cases the best possible expression of the rule, it would remain after all to decide each case largely upon the special facts belonging to it, and often upon the very nicest discriminations. One of the most valuable criteria furnished by the authorities is to ascertain whether any new cause has intervened between the fact accomplished and the alleged cause. If a new force or power has intervened, of itself sufficient to stand as the cause of the misfortune, the other must be considered as too remote.[1]

No difficulty attends the application of the maxim when the causes succeed each other in the order of time. When one of several successive causes is sufficient to produce the effect (for example, to cause a loss), the law will never regard an antecedent cause of that cause, or the *causa causans*, q. v. But when there are two concurrent causes, the predominating efficient one must be regarded as the proximate, when the damage done by each cannot be distinguished. And certainly that cause which set the other in motion, and gave to it its efficiency for harm at the time of the disaster, must rank as predominant.[2]

What is the proximate cause of an injury is ordinarily a question for the jury. It is not a question of science or of legal knowledge. It is to be determined as a fact, in view of the circumstances of fact attending it. The primary cause may be the proximate cause of a disaster, though it may operate through successive instruments, as an article at the end of a chain may be moved by a force applied to the other end, that force being the proximate cause of the movement, as in the oft cited case of the squib thrown in the market-place. The question always is, Was there an unbroken connection between the wrongful act and the injury, a continuous operation? Did the facts constitute a continuous succession of events, so linked together as to make a natural whole, or was there some new and independent cause intervening between the wrong and the injury? It is admitted that the rule is difficult of application. But it is generally held that, to warrant a finding that negligence, or an act not amounting to wanton wrong, is the proximate cause of an injury, it must appear that the injury was the natural and probable consequence of the negligent or wrongful act, and that it ought to have been foreseen in the light of attending circumstances. . . We do not say that even the natural and probable consequences of a wrongful act or omission are in all cases to be chargeable to the misfeasance or non-feasance. They are not when there is a sufficient and independent cause operating between the wrong and the injury. In such a case the resort of the sufferer must be to the originator of the intermediate cause. But when there is no intermediate efficient cause, the original wrong must be considered as reaching to the effect, and proximate to it. The inquiry must, therefore, always be whether there was any intermediate cause, *disconnected from the primary fault*, and self-operating, which produced the injury. Here lies the difficulty. But the inquiry must be answered in accordance with

common understanding. In a succession of events an interval may always be seen by an acute mind between a cause and its effect, though it may be so imperceptible as to be overlooked by a common mind. Thus, if a building be set on fire by negligence, and an adjoining building be destroyed without any negligence in the occupants of the first building, no one would doubt that the destruction of the second building was due to the negligence that caused the destruction of the first. Yet in truth, in a very legitimate sense, the immediate cause of the burning of the second building was the burning of the first. The same might be said of the burning of the furniture in the first. Such refinements are too minute for rules of social conduct. In the nature of things, there is in every transaction a succession of events, more or less depending upon those preceding, and it is the province of a jury to look at this succession of events or facts, and ascertain whether they are naturally and probably connected with each other by a continuous sequence, or are dissevered by new and independent agencies; and this must be determined in view of the circumstances existing at the time.[1]

The question is not what cause was nearest in time or place to the catastrophe. The proximate cause is the efficient cause, the one that necessarily sets the other causes in operation. The causes that are merely incidental or instruments of a superior or controlling agency are not the proximate causes and the responsible ones, though they may be nearer in time to the result. It is only when the causes are independent of each other that the nearest is, of course, to be charged with the disaster. The proximate cause is the dominant cause, not the one which is incidental to that cause, its mere instrument, though the latter may be nearest in place and time to the loss.[2]

The jury must determine whether the facts constitute a continuous succession of events, so linked together that they become a natural whole, or whether the chain of events is so broken that they become independent, and the final result cannot be said to be the natural and probable consequence of the primary cause — the negligence of the defendant.[3]

When several proximate causes contribute to an accident and each is an efficient cause, without the operation of which the accident would not have happened, it may be attributed to all or to any of the causes.[4]

That some agency intervenes between the original wrong and the injury does not necessarily bring the cause within the rule. It is firmly settled that the intervention of a third person, or of other and new

---

[1] Mutual Ins. Co. v. Tweed, 7 Wall. 52 (1868), Miller, J.; Travelers' Ins. Co. v. Seaver, 19 *id*. 542 (1873).

[2] Howard Fire Ins. Co. v. Transportation Co., 12 Wall. 199 (1870), Strong, J.

[1] Milwaukee, &c. R. Co. v. Kellogg, 94 U. S. 474-76 (1876), Strong, J. In this case a mill was destroyed by fire communicated from an elevator, and to the elevator from a boat.

[2] Ætna Fire Ins. Co. v. Boon, 95 U. S. 130, 133 (1873), cases, Strong, J. See also Crandall v. Goodrich Transp. Co., 16 F. R. 75 (1883).

[3] Pennsylvania R. Co. v. Hope, 80 Pa. 377-78 (1876), cases, Agnew, C. J.; Hoag v. Lake Shore, &c. R. Co., 85 *id*. 297-98 (1877), cases.

[4] Ring v. City of Cohoes, 77 N. Y. 90 (1879), Earl, J.; Reiper v. Nichols, 31 Hun, 495 (1884), cases

causes, does not preclude a recovery, if the injury was the natural and probable result of the original wrong.[1]

Everything which induces or influences an accident does not necessarily and legally cause it.   . There can be no fixed rule defining a proximate cause. Much must depend upon the circumstances of each case.[2]

Strictly, the law knows no cause but a responsible human will. When such a will negligently sets in motion a natural force that acts upon and with surrounding conditions, the law regards such human action as the cause of resulting injury.[3]

Whether a particular act of negligence is the proximate cause is a question of fact to be determined by the jury under instructions.[3]

The unlawful act of a third person, though directly induced by the original wrong of the defendant, is not to be attributed to the original wrong as a proximate cause of the damage.[4] See ACT, 1, Of God; BLASTING; CONSEQUENCES; DAMAGES.

(2) The occasion for action; that by reason of which a thing is done; reason or ground for action.

The origin or foundation of a thing, as of a suit or action; a ground of action.[5]

Cause of action. The right which a party has to institute and carry through a proceeding.[6]

The act on the part of the defendant which gives the plaintiff his cause of complaint.[7]

Jurists have found it difficult to define a cause of action. It may be said to be composed of the right of the plaintiff and the obligation, duty, or wrong of the defendant.[8]

A wrong committed or threatened.[1]

A plaintiff must show himself entitled to the relief called for by the facts stated in his complaint. The allegations, the evidence, and the findings should correspond in legal intent.[1]

The expression implies not only a right of action, but that there is some person in existence who is qualified to institute process. The right must be capable of being legally enforced; and so there must be a person to be sued.[2]

The elements are: a right possessed by the plaintiff, and an infringement of such right by the defendant.[3]

Where the distinction between "trespass" and "case" is abolished, the plaintiff in his petition may present such facts as show a blending of those common-law forms of action.[3] See LIMITATION, 3, Statute of.

To "show cause of action" is to exhibit the facts upon which a right of action rests. The practice is resorted to in actions of tort to reduce the amount of bail required, as where it will appear that the cause of action is purely technical or is of a very ordinary nature.

See MERITORIOUS; SPLIT.

For cause. See CHALLENGE, 4; REMOVE, 2.

Good cause. Has no certain meaning in a stipulation for canceling a contract.[4]

Probable cause. Within the meaning of the law relating to actions for malicious prosecutions,— a reasonable cause of suspicion, supported by circumstances sufficiently strong in themselves to warrant a cautious man in the belief that the person accused is guilty of the offense with which he is charged.[5]

Such a state of facts in the mind of the prosecutor as would lead a man of ordinary caution and prudence to believe, or entertain an honest and strong suspicion, that the person arrested is guilty.[6]

The existence of such facts and circumstances as would excite the belief in a reasonable mind, acting on the facts within the knowledge of the prosecutor, that the person

---

[1] Billman v. Indianapolis, &c. R. Co., 76 Ind. 168–71 (1881). See also Louisville, &c. R. Co. v. Krinning, 87 id. 354–55 (1882), cases; 12 Bradw. 153.

[2] Spaulding v. Winslow, 74 Me. 534–35 (1883), cases. See also Jucker v. Chicago, &c. R. Co., 52 Wis. 152–53 (1881), cases; N .Y. Express Co. v. Traders' Ins. Co., 132 Mass. 382–85 (1882); Nelson v. Chicago, &c. R. Co., 30 Minn. 77 (1882); Ransier v. Minneapolis, &c. R. Co., 32 id. 334 (1884), cases; Georgetown, &c. R. Co. v. Eagles, 9 Col. 547 (1886), cases; 14 Pet. 99; 10 Wall. 191; 66 Ga. 750; 4 Gray, 412; 76 Mo. 293; 8 Kent, 374; 4 Am. Law Rev. 201–16 (1870), cases; 4 South. Law Rev. 759–68 (1878), cases; Whart. Neg. § 73.

[3] Adams v. Young, 44 Ohio St. 86–91 (1886), cases, Follett, J. Sparks, negligently thrown from a mill smoke-stack, set fire to a stable one hundred feet away, from which a second building, two hundred feet distant, took fire, and from that the building in suit, sixty feet distant. See same and other cases, 25 Am. Law Reg. 568–70 (1886).

[4] The Young America, 31 F. R. 753 (1887), cases, Wallace, J.

[5] United States v. Rhodes, 1 Abb. C. C. 33 (1866): Burrill.

[6] [Meyer v. Van Collem, 28 Barb. 231 (1858).

[7] Jackson v. Spittall, L. R., 5 C. P. *552, 544 (1870), Brett, J.

[8] Veeder v. Baker, 83 N. Y. 160 (1880), Earl, J. See

also Rodgers v. Mutual Endowment Association, 17 S. C. 410 (1881).

[1] Miller v. Hallock, 9 Col. 453 (1886), cases, Beck, C. J.

[2] Fruitt v. Anderson, 12 Bradw. 430 (1883).

[3] Atchison, &c. R. Co. v. Rice, 36 Kan. 600 (1887), Valentine, J.

[4] Cummer v. Butts, 40 Mich. 322 (1879).

[5] Munns v. Dupont, 3 Wash. 37 (1811), Washington, J.; 2 Denio, 617; 97 U. S. 645; 37 Md. 318, 381.

[6] Bacon v. Towne, 4 Cush. 238 (1849), Shaw, C. J. See also Mitchell v. Wall, 111 Mass. 497 (1873); Heyne v. Blair, 62 N. Y. 22 (1875); Stacey v. Emery, 97 U. S. 645 (1878), cases.

charged was guilty of the crime for which he was prosecuted.[1]

When information as to the commission of a crime is believed, and is such, and from such sources, that the generality of business men of ordinary care, prudence, and discretion would prosecute upon it under the same conditions.[2]

The constitutional provision that a warrant of arrest can issue only "upon probable cause, supported by oath or affirmation," contemplates an oath or affirmation by the person who, of his own knowledge, deposes to the facts which constitute the offense; the mere belief of the affiant is insufficient.[3]

"Probable cause for making an information" does not mean actual and positive cause. The complaint may be made upon information and belief.[4]

Prize courts deny damages or costs where there has been probable cause for a seizure. Probable cause exists where there are circumstances sufficient to warrant a reasonable ground of suspicion, even though not sufficient to justify condemnation.[5]

There is no substantial difference between "probable cause" and "reasonable cause" of seizure.[6] See PROSECUTION, Malicious.

Reasonable cause. A fact which would suggest to persons of average intelligence the same inference or action; such facts as would constrain a person of ordinary caution and sagacity to pursue a particular course of conduct; legal cause or excuse; probable cause.

In the law of homicide, reasonable cause or ground to apprehend harm or death. A bare fear, unaccompanied by any overt act indicative of the supposed intention, will not warrant a killing, if there is no actual danger.[7] See further DEFENSE, 1.

The reasonable cause which will justify a husband or wife in abandoning the other is, in Pennsylvania at least, that which would entitle the party so separating himself or herself to a divorce.[8] See ABANDON, 2 (1).

Reasonable cause to believe a debtor insolvent exists when the condition of his affairs is known to be such that prudent business men would conclude that he could not meet his obligations as they mature in the ordinary course of business.[1]

A recital in the certificate of a magistrate that "satisfactory cause" has been shown for issuing a warrant of arrest is not equivalent to a statement that he is satisfied that there is "reasonable cause" to believe that the charge contained in the preliminary affidavit is true.[2]

To avoid, as a fraudulent preference in the Bankrupt Act, a security taken for a debt, the creditor must have had such knowledge of facts as to induce a reasonable belief of his debtor's insolvency. . . Reasonable cause "to believe" and "to suspect" are distinct, in meaning and effect.[3] See PREFER, 2.

(3) An action at law, a suit at law or in equity; a judicial proceeding.

In any legal sense, action, suit, and cause are convertible terms.[4]

"Case" is more limited, importing a collection of facts with the conclusions thereon. A "cause" pends, is postponed, appealed, removed; whereas a "case" is made, vested, argued, decided, etc.[5]

See ACTION, 2; ADMIRALTY; CASE, 2; CHANCERY; JOINDER; SUIT; TITLE, 2.

2. Fr. A case; a trial.

Cause celebre. A celebrated trial; plural, *causes celebres.*

In French law, resembles a "State trial" in English law. Among English and American writers, a trial, or a reported case, famous for the parties and the facts involved.

CAUSEWAY. See BRIDGE.

CAUTELA. L. Caution; providence; care; heed.

Ad majorem cautelam. For the sake of the greater caution. **Ex abundanti cautela.** Out of extreme caution. **Ex majore cautela.** By way of greater vigilance.

Applied to the use of apparently superfluous words and the doing of things seemingly supererogatory, from an apprehension that otherwise some right may be yielded or prejudiced, some power or privilege waived, or an estoppel created: as where formal, technical, and synonymous terms are employed in instruments; where slightly varying averments are made in pleading: where special statutory power to do a thing is conferred, on the supposition that power may not already exist.[6]

CAUTION. Attention to the effect of a thing about to be done; regard to contingencies; forethought; care. See CAUTELA.

---

[1] Wheeler v. Nesbitt, 24 How. 551-52 (1860), Clifford, J.

[2] [Hamilton v. Smith, 39 Mich. 226-29 (1878), cases, Graves, J. See also Burton v. St. Paul, &c. R. Co., 33 Minn. 191 (1885), cases; 1 Am. Ld. Cas. 213; 23 Ind. 67; 12 Bradw. 635; 52 Me. 505; 76 Mo. 670; 20 Ohio, 129; 28 Iowa, 49; 45 Tex. 544.

[3] United States v. Tureaud, 20 F. R. 623-24 (1884), cases, Billings, J. See also Swart v. Kimball, 43 Mich. 451 (1880).

[4] State v. Davie, 62 Wis. 308 (1885).

[5] [The Thompson, 3 Wall. 162 (1865), cases, Davis, J.

[6] Stacey v. Emery, 97 U. S. 646 (1878).

[7] Wiggins v. People, 93 U. S. 478-80 (1876), cases, Clifford, J.

[8] Gordon v. Gordon, 48 Pa. 234 (1864); Butler v. Butler, 1 Pars. Sel. Cas. Eq. 337 (1849).

[1] Merchants' Nat. Bank v. Cook, 95 U. S. 346 (1877), cases, Hunt, J.; Dutcher v. Wright, 94 id. 557 (1876), cases; Stucky v. Masonic Bank, 108 id. 74 (1883).

[2] May v. Hammond, 144 Mass. 152 (1887), cases.

[3] Grant v. First Nat. Bank of Monmouth, 97 U. S. 81 (1877), Bradley, J.

[4] Exp. Milligan, 4 Wall. 112 (1866), Davis, J.

[5] 18 Conn. App. 10.

[6] 6 Wheat. 108; 2 Saw. 150; 59 Pa. 333.

Cautionary. By way of warning; made or done in anticipation of a change in circumstances; providing for an adverse contingency.

Cautionary judgments may sometimes be entered or confessed to bind lands or to charge special bail.

Cautionary orders are intended to provide for indemnity against loss by reason of an injunction issued.[1]

CAVEAT. L. Let him take heed; let him beware.

A formal notice or warning to an officer or a court not to do a specified act; as, not to probate a will, grant letters of administration, issue letters-patent for an invention or for land,—until the person procuring the order can be heard in opposition to the contemplated act or proceeding.[2]

Caveator. He who interposes a caveat. *Caveatee.* He against whom a caveat is interposed.

Protects the rights of one person against rights which, without it, might arise in favor of another person out of the proposed proceeding. Thus, for example, it secures time to perfect an invention without the risk of a patent being granted to another — allows an opportunity to show priority of invention and title.[3]

Caveat actor. Let the doer beware.

Caveat emptor. Let the buyer beware.

A purchaser of property must examine and judge for himself as to its title and quality, unless dissuaded by representations.

In the absence of fraud or an express warranty, the purchaser of realty has no relief against a defect in the title, or for the unsuitableness of the land for a particular purpose, either of which an examination, which he was free to make, would have revealed. And so as to personalty, in the absence of imposition or of an express assurance, no warranty of title or of quality is implied. The maxim does not apply where a specific article is ordered for a known purpose, nor where merchandise is sold not by sample nor under the inducement of an express warranty, but with opportunity for thorough inspection. In other cases a warranty is implied that the article will reasonably answer the purpose for which it is ordinarily used.

Where there is neither fraud nor warranty, and the buyer receives and retains the goods without objection, he waives his right to object afterward. Where the buyer has no opportunity to inspect, and no warranty is given, the law implies the condition that the thing shall fairly answer the description in the contract.[4]

The fundamental inquiry is whether, under the circumstances of the case, the buyer had the right to rely and necessarily relied upon the judgment of the seller.[1]

The rule applies to a purchaser at a judicial sale: he takes the defendant's interest only.[2]

See COMMENDATIO; DECEIT; DICTUM, Gratis; FRAUD, Actual; SALE, Judicial; SAMPLE; SOUND, 2 (2).

Caveat venditor. Let the seller take heed.

This maxim of the civil law expresses a doctrine contrary to the rule of *caveat emptor* of the common law. An implied warranty of title on the sale of a chattel is common to both systems; but while in the civil law a fair price implies a warranty also of the soundness of the article, by the common law, as seen above, to make the vendor answerable for the quality there must be either an express warranty or fraud on his part. The civil law maxim applies to executory sales, to contracts for goods to be manufactured or produced, and to sales where the buyer has no opportunity to inspect the article purchased.[3]

Caveat viator. Let the traveler take care.

A traveler upon a highway must use reasonable care in detecting and avoiding defects in the road.[4] See SIDEWALK; STREET.

CEASE. See RATIO, Cessante, etc.

Where a lot was to revert if a school-house "ceased" to stand on it for two years, and none was built, *held*, that the lot did not revert. A thing cannot "cease" until after it has begun.[5]

Insurance conditioned to be void if the premises "cease to be operated" as a factory was held not void because of a temporary suspension on account of yellow fever.[6]

CEDE. See CESSION.

CEMETERIES. See BURIAL.

CENSUS. A rating, numbering, valuing, assessing.

"Representatives and direct Taxes shall be apportioned among the several States . according to their respective numbers. . The actual Enumeration shall be made within three Years after the first Meeting of the Congress of the United States, and within every subsequent Term of ten Years, in such Manner as they shall by Law direct."[7]

In connection with the ascertainment of the number of inhabitants, the act of Congress provides for inquiries as to age, birth, marriage, occupation, and

---

[1] R. S. § 718.
[2] See Slocum *v.* Grandin, 38 N. J. E. 488 (1884).
[3] R. S. § 4902.
[4] Miller *v.* Tiffany, 1 Wall. 309 (1863); Barnard *v.* Kellogg, 10 *id.* 388 (1870); 2 Kent, 478; 1 Story, Eq. § 212; 3 Bl. Com. 165.

[1] Kellogg Bridge Co. *v.* Hamilton, 110 U. S. 116, 112-15 (1884), cases; Wissler *v.* Craig, 80 Va 32 (1885): Burwell *v.* Fauber, 21 Gratt. 463 (1871), cases.
[2] Oslerberg *v.* Union Trust Co., 93 U. S. 428 (1876); 105 Ill. 339.
[3] See Wright *v.* Hart, 18 Wend. 453 (1837), Walworth, Ch.; *ib.* 432; Hargous *v.* Stone, 5 N. Y. 81-84 (1851), cases.
[4] Cornwell *v.* Commissioners, 10 Excheq. *774 (1855).
[5] Jordan *v.* Haskell, 63 Me. 192 (1874).
[6] Pass *v.* Western Assurance Co., 7 Lea, 707 (1881).
[7] Constitution, Art. I, sec. 2, cl. 3. See R. S. tit. XXXI.

other matters of general interest. For a refusal to answer an inquiry a small penalty is imposed. There is no attempt to inquire into private affairs, nor are the courts called upon to enforce answers to inquiries. Similar inquiries usually accompany the taking of a census of every country, and they are not deemed to encroach upon the rights of the citizen.[1]

CENT. See COIN.

CENTER. See FILUM; ROAD, 1; STREET.

CEPI; CEPIT. See CAPERE, Cepi, Cepit.

CERA. See SEAL, 1.

CERTAIN. Known, established, definite: as, a certain date, a certain instrument. See CERTUM; CUSTOM; DEBT.

Since "uncertain" may include any doubt, whether reasonable or unreasonable, a jury should not be told that if they feel uncertain that a witness is to be believed, they should acquit.[2]

Certainty. 1. Assurance; confident belief: freedom from doubt or failure; also, that which is established beyond question. Compare CONTINGENCY; THEN: WHEN.

The certainty of the law is of the highest consequence. See HARDSHIP.

Moral certainty. A state of impression produced by facts in which a reasonable mind feels a sort of coercion or necessity to act in accordance with it.[3]

The phrase, borrowed from the publicists and metaphysicians, signifies only a very high degree of probability. . Proof beyond a reasonable doubt is proof to a moral certainty, as distinguished from an absolute certainty. As applied to a judicial trial for crime, the two phrases are synonymous and equivalent; each has been used by eminent judges to explain the other.[4] See further DOUBT, Reasonable.

2. Distinctness, accuracy, clearness of statement; opposed to uncertainty and ambiguity, *q. v.*

Generally refers to written language.

In pleading, statement of alleged facts so clear and explicit as to be readily understood by the opposite party who is to make answer, by the jury which is to find the truth, and by the court which is to pronounce judgment.[5]

Consists in alleging the facts necessary to be stated, so distinctly as to exclude ambigu-

ity and make the meaning of the averments clearly intelligible.[1]

Three degrees of certainty were formerly recognized: *Certainty to a common intent* — words used in their ordinary sense, but susceptible of a different meaning. This degree was required in defenses and in instruments of an ordinary nature. *Certainty to a certain intent in general* — the meaning ascertainable upon a fair and reasonable construction, without recurrence to possible facts which do not appear. This degree was required in indictments and declarations. *Certainty to a certain intent in particular* — such technical accuracy of statement as precluded all question, inference, or presumption. This was required in estoppels and as to disfavored pleas.[2]

A negotiable instrument must have certainty as to payor, payee, amount, time, fact of payment, and, perhaps, place of payment.[3]

A postal card containing the words "Send us pice of counter screen" was held to present a case of incurable uncertainty; and the judge properly refused to submit to the jury to determine whether "pice" meant "piece" or "price."[4]

CERTIFICATE.[5] A writing giving assurance that a thing has or has not been done, that an act has or has not been performed, that a fact exists or does not exist.

To "certify" is to testify to in writing: to make known or establish as a fact. The word is not essential to a "certificate:" it is enough that the law calls a statement a certificate.[6] See CHECK, Certified.

Certificates are such as are authorized or required by law, and such as are purely voluntary. "Authorized or required by law" are: a certificate of a balance due, of costs, of a divorce, that a married woman has been decreed a *feme sole* trader, that a bankrupt has been discharged, that an alien has been naturalized, that a physician is qualified to practice medicine; a certificate of copyright, or of a trademark registered; a certificate that a document is authentic, or genuine; an officer's return of service of process. "Voluntary" certificates include: certificates of benefits receivable, of check, of deposit, of interest, of loan, of no defense, of search, of stock, of scrip, of transfer, a receiver's certificate, *qq. v.*

Voluntary certificates are not conclusive evidence of the facts they state, except where, otherwise, an innocent party would be the loser. Certificates required by law of officers are conclusive of the facts

---

[1] *Re* Pacific Railway Commission, 32 F. R. 250 (1887), Field, J.; R. S. § 2171.

[2] State *v.* Ah Lee, 7 Oreg. 258 (1879).

[3] Montana *v.* McAndrews, 3 Monta. 165 (1878), Wade, C. J.: Bur. Circ. Ev. 199.

[4] Commonwealth *v.* Costley, 118 Mass. 23 (1875), Gray, C. J. See also United States *v.* Guiteau, 10 F. R. 164 (1882).

[5] See Andrews *v.* Whitehead, 18 East, 102, 107 (1810).

[1] [Gould, Pleading, IV, sec. 24.

[2] See Coke, Litt. 303 *a;* Gould, Plead. III, sec. 52; Steph. Plead. 380; 3 Cranch, C. C. 56; 5 Conn. 423; 9 Johns. 314.

[3] See 1 Parsons, Notes & Bills, 30, 37; 24 Am. Law Reg. 719–24 (1885), cases; 59 Iowa, 649.

[4] Cheney Bigelow Wire Works *v.* Sorrell, 142 Mass. 442 (1886).

[5] L. *certificatus,* assured, made certain.

[6] State *v.* Schwin, 65 Wis. 213 (1886): Webster.

mentioned, but fraudulent procurement may be shown. Certificates authorized by statute are evidence of such facts only as the officer may certify under the statute.[1]

2. A writing made by a court, a judge or an officer thereof, and properly authenticated, to give notice to another court of a thing done in the court *a quo*. See OPINION, 3, Division of.

CERTIORARI. L. To be certified. A writ by which the record of a proceeding in a lower court is removed into a higher court for review.

The emphatic word in the Latin writ, which read: *quia certis de causis certiorari volumus*, for as much as concerning certain causes we wish to be certified. From *certior*, the comparative of *certus*, known, established. See CERTUM.

After indictment found, a writ of *certiorari facias* [that you cause to be certified] may be had to certify and remove the indictment, with all the proceedings thereon, from any inferior court of criminal jurisdiction into the court of king's bench.[2]

The writ, at common law, issued out of chancery or the king's bench, directed, in the king's name, to the judges or officers of the inferior courts, commanding them to return, before him, the record of a cause depending before them, that the party may have more sure and speedy justice or such other justice as he shall assign to determine the cause.[3]

The writ has been extended, and the practice under it regulated, by statutes in each State. Speaking generally, it is employed for removing statutory proceedings for completion, when the lower court fails to do so; it serves as an auxiliary process to obtain a full return to other process; it effects a review of the determinations of special tribunals, commissioners, and magistrates; it secures an inspection of the record where a writ of *habeas corpus* has been sued out. Unless a statute directs otherwise, or palpable injustice will be done, it does not lie to review a decision based on a matter of fact, nor as to a matter resting in discretion; nor does it lie for an error in formality, substantial justice being dispensed.

The application for the writ must disclose a proper case upon its face. The plaintiff may have to furnish security for the demand, with interest and costs, before the writ will operate as a *supersedeas*, q. v.

The judgment is that the proceedings be quashed or affirmed, in whole or in part. At common law neither party recovered costs.

At common law, also, the writ was granted to a prosecutor as a matter of right, and to a defendant as a matter in discretion.[1]

Will not, in general, be issued where the party has another remedy, as by appeal.[2]

Bill of certiorari. An original bill, in equity, to remove a cause into a higher court.

States the proceedings in the lower court, the incompetency in the powers of such court to do complete justice, etc. Rarely used in the United States.[3]

CERTUM. L. Perceived, determined: definite, known, certain.

Certum est quod certum reddi potest. That is certain which can be made certain — or reduced to a certainty.

When the law requires certainty, that is accepted for certainty which, by computation or testimony, can be shown to be already certain; as, in questions respecting the sum to be paid on a negotiable instrument, the liquidation of damages for non-performance of a contract, reasonable time, and the like.[4]

CESSANTE. See RATIO, Cessante, etc.

CESSER. A ceasing; formerly, neglect of duty. Also, a yielding up, a cession, *q. v.*: as, the cesser of an interest conferred by a will.[5]

CESSIO. L. A giving up; surrender. See CESSION.

Cessio bonorum. A surrender of goods. In civil law, an assignment for the benefit of creditors.

Discharged the debtor to the extent of the property made over; and exempted him from imprisonment. French, *cession des biens*.[6]

CESSION. A yielding up; transfer. See CESSIO.

Cede: to give up, yield up.[7] Compare ABANDON, 1.

Concession. A grant, as of lands, between sovereignties. **Recession.** A reconveyance by a sovereign.

Thereby public property passes from one government to the other, but private property remains as before, and with it those municipal laws which are designed to secure its peaceful use and enjoyment. As a matter of course, all laws, ordinances, and regulations in conflict with the political character, institu-

---

[1] See 1 Whart. Ev. §§ 120–26, cases; 10 Oreg. 247.

[2] 4 Bl. Com. 320.

[3] [Dean *v.* State, 63 Ala. 154 (1879); 18 Fla. 523; 15 Blatch. 386; 108 U. S. 31.

---

[1] See 4 Bl. Com. 321; *Exp.* Hitz, 111 U. S. 766 (1884).

[2] Alabama Great Southern R. Co. *v.* Christian, 82 Ala. 309 (1886), cases.

[3] Story, Eq. Pl. § 298; 2 Hale, Pl. Cr. 215.

[4] See 1 Bl. Com. 78; 2 *id.* 143; 2 Kent, 480; 2 Black, 504; 99 U. S. 439; 101 *id.* 633; 9 Col. 279; 73 Ga. 92; 80 Va. 761; 59 Wis. 500; 61 *id.* 183; 66 *id.* 427; 67 *id.* 434.

[5] 91 U. S. 724.

[6] See 2 Bl. Com. 473; 1 Kent, 422; 15 Wall. 605; 32 F. R. 1.

[7] Somers *v.* Pierson, 16 N. J. L. 184 (1837).

tions, and constitution of the new government are at once displaced.[1] See LAND, Public; PUEBLO.

CESTUI. He; that one; the one. Also spelled *cestuy*. See ADDENDA.

Pronounced cĕst-wē̤. A law-French term, corresponding to the classic French *c' est lui (celui)*: it is for him that, etc. Plural, *cestuis*.

Cestui que trust. He for whom a trust exists, or was created: the beneficiary under a trust.[2]

The *que* is pronounced kŏ. See further TRUST, Cestui, etc.

Cestui que use. He for whom a use — exists: he for whose benefit land is held by another.[3] See further USE, 3, Cestui, etc.

Cestui que vie. He for whose life — land is held by another:[4] he whose life measures the duration of an estate.[5]

CF. An abbreviation of the Latin *conferre*, compare.

Used in references to analogous cases or subjects.

CH. An abbreviation of chancellor, chapter, chief.

CHAIN. See ABSTRACT; EVIDENCE, Circumstantial; OBLIGATION, 1.

It is incorrect to speak of a body of circumstantial evidence as a "chain," and allude to the different circumstances as the "links." A chain cannot be stronger than its weakest link. The metaphor may perhaps be correctly applied to the ultimate and essential facts necessary to conviction in a criminal case; but it is not true that every minor circumstance introduced to sustain the ultimate facts must be proven with the same degree of certainty.[6]

CHAIRMAN. See DESCRIPTIO, Personæ.

CHALLENGE.[7] 1. A request to fight — to fight a duel.

Whether made by word or letter, is indictable at common law. Tends to a breach of the peace. He who knowingly carries a challenge for another is guilty of the offense.[8] See PRIZE-FIGHT.

2. Objection to the legality of a vote about to be cast. See BALLOT.

3. Objection to a cause being tried before a particular judge on account of alleged bias, prejudice, interest, or other disqualification.

4. Objection to a juror or jurors drawn to try a cause.

Challenge to the array. An exception to the whole panel in which the jury are arrayed or set in order by the sheriff in his return.[1]

The reason which, before awarding the *venire*, would be sufficient to cause it to be directed to the coroner or to elisors, will be sufficient to quash the array when made by an officer of whose partiality there is any fair ground of suspicion; also, if the sheriff arrays the panel under the direction of either party.[1]

Challenge to the polls. An exception to particular jurors.

Lies for any matter showing disqualification. Also known as "principal challenge" and as the "challenge for cause."

Challenge for cause. For which a reason is assigned,— to the array or to the polls.

An objection to a particular juror; and may be "general"—that he is disqualified from serving in any case, or "particular"—that he is disqualified from serving in the action on trial.[2]

Challenge for favor. Of the same nature and effect as a principal challenge "propter affectum."

Peremptory challenge. For which no reason is assigned.

Principal challenge. 1. "Propter defectum" — for disability: as, alienage, infancy, unsound mind, insufficient property. 2. "Propter affectum" — for bias or partiality: as, opinion formed; of kin to a party, or of the same fraternity or corporation; his attorney, servant, or tenant, or entertained by him; promised money for verdict; sued by exceptant in an action involving legal malice; being formerly a juror or an arbitrator in the matter; influenced by scruples against the punishment. 3. "Propter delictum" — for an offense committed: as, convicted of treason, forgery, perjury, or other *crimen falsi*.[3]

A juror unsuccessfully challenged for cause may be challenged peremptorily. In felonies, at common law, thirty-five peremptory challenges were allowed the accused; at present the number is about twenty in capital cases; in civil cases, if allowed at all, only to a very limited extent. The State is allowed peremptory challenges in capital cases, the number varying in the different States.

When a challenge for bias, actual or implied, is disallowed, and the juror is peremptorily challenged and

[1] Chicago & Pacific R. Co. *v.* McGlinn, 114 U. S. 547 (1885), Field. J.

[2] 2 Bl. Com. 328.

[3] 2 Bl. Com. 328; 4 Kent, 301; 1 Washb. R. P. 163.

[4] 2 Bl. Com. 123; *ib.* 461.

[5] [1 Washb. R. P. 88.

[6] Clare *v.* People, 9 Col. 123 (1886), Helm, J.

[7] Mid. E. *chalenge*, a claim: F. *chalonge*, a dispute, accusation.

[8] See 4 Bl. Com. 150; 3 East, 581; 6 Blackf. 20; 1 Dana, 524.

[1] 3 Bl. Com. 359.

[2] Cal. Penal Code, § 1071; 70 Cal. 11.

[3] See 3 Bl. Com. 361-65; 4 *id.* 352; 29 Kan. 690; 17 S. & R. 162.

excused, and a competent juror is obtained in his place, no injury is done the accused, if, until the jury is completed, he has other peremptory challenges which he can use.[1]

Experience has shown that one of the most effective means to free the jury-box from men unfit to be there is the exercise of the peremptory challenge. . . The number of challenges must necessarily depend upon the discretion of the legislature, and may vary according to the condition of different communities, and the difficulties in them of securing intelligent and impartial juries.

Originally, by the common law, the crown could challenge peremptorily without limitation as to number. By an act passed in the time of Edward I, the right was restricted to challenges for cause. But, by rule of court, the crown was not obliged to show cause till the whole panel was called. Those not accepted on the call were directed to stand aside; and if a full jury was not otherwise obtained, the crown was required to show cause against those jurors; if no sufficient cause appeared, the jury was completed from them.

The right to challenge is the right to reject, not to select, a juror. If from those who remain an impartial jury is obtained, the constitutional right of the accused is maintained.[2]

Challenges are to be made before the jury is sworn. In the Federal courts the justness of a challenge is determined by the judge, without the aid of triors.[3]

See JURY; OPINION, 2; TRIORS; VOIR DIRE.

CHAMBER. A room in a house, used for purposes of a dwelling, of an office, or of a court. See HOUSE, 1; STAR-CHAMBER; SURVEY, Of land.

Chambers. In London, the offices of barristers.

Chambers, or **at chambers.** A private room or other place where parties may be heard and orders made by a judge, in such matters as the law does not require shall be considered in open court or by a full court. Of such are acts done in a court room while the court is not in session.

Jurisdiction at chambers is incidental to and grows out of the jurisdiction of the court itself. It is the power to hear and determine, out of court, such questions arising between the parties to a controversy as might well be determined by the court itself, but which the legislature has seen fit to intrust to the judgment of a single judge, out of court, without requiring them to be brought before the court in actual session. It follows that the jurisdiction of a judge at chambers cannot go beyond the jurisdiction of the court to

which he belongs, or extend to the matters with which his court has nothing to do.[1]

" A judge at chambers " is simply a judge acting out of court.[2] See VACATION.

CHAMPERTY.[3] A bargain with a plaintiff or defendant, *campum partire*, to divide the land or other matter sued for between them, if they prevail: whereupon the champertor is to carry on the party's suit at his own expense. . . The purchasing of a suit or right of suing.[4]

Champart, in the French law, signifies a similar division of profits, being a part of the crop annually due to the landlord by bargain or custom.[4]

Champertor. One who purchases or promotes another's suit; a person chargeable with champerty. **Champertous.** Infected with champerty.

Champerty is the unlawful maintenance of a suit in consideration of some bargain to have a part of the thing in dispute, or some profit out of it.[5]

A common example is (or was) the case of a contract by an attorney to collect a claim for a percentage.[6] Also of a champertous character are: purchases of demands involving litigation, of pretended titles, and like claims which cannot be realized upon except by lawsuit.[7]

As between an attorney and his client, it is essential that the attorney prosecute the suit at his own expense.[8]

Where the right to compensation is not confined to an interest in the thing recovered, but gives a right of action against the party, though pledging the avails of the suit as security for payment, the agreement is not champertous.[9]

Some courts have ruled that if the fact that a suit is being prosecuted upon a champertous contract comes to the knowledge of the court in any proper manner, it should refuse longer to entertain the proceeding. Other courts have held, what seems supported by the better reason, that the fact that there is a champertous contract for the prosecution of a cause of action is no ground of defense thereto, and can only be set up by the client against the attorney when the champertous agreement is sought to be enforced. . . The tendency is to relax the common-law doctrine so as to

---

[1] Spies v. Illinois (The Anarchists' Case), 123 U. S. 168 (Nov. 2, 1887), Waite, C. J.; Hopt v. Utah, 120 *id.* 436 (1887).

[2] Hayes v. Missouri, 120 U. S. 70-71 (1887), cases, Field, J.

[3] R. S. § 819; Reynolds v. United States, 98 U. S. 157 (1878).

---

[1] Pittsburg, Ft. W., &c. R. Co. v. Hurd, 17 Ohio St. 146-47 (1866).

[2] Whereatt v. Ellis, 65 Wis. 644 (1886).

[3] Sham'-perty.

[4] 4 Bl. Com. 153. See 2 Story, Eq. § 1048; 4 Hughes, 563; 10 F. R. 533; 53 Ind. 317; 22 Wend. 405.

[5] Stanley v. Jones, 7 Bing. *377 (1831), Tindal, C. J.

[6] See Ackert v. Baker, 131 Mass. 437-38 (1881), cases; McPherson v. Cox, 96 U. S. 404, 416 (1877); Atchison, &c. R. Co. v. Johnson, 29 Kan. 227 (1883), cases.

[7] 2 Story, Eq. §§ 1048-57.

[8] Phillips v. South Park Com'rs, 119 Ill. 637 (1887).

[9] Blaisdell v. Allen, 144 Mass. 395 (1887), cases.

permit greater liberality of contracting between attorney and client than was formerly allowed, for the reason that the condition of society which gave rise to the doctrine has, in a great measure, passed away. In some States the common-law rule is altogether repudiated.[1]

The English common law and statutes against maintenance and champerty had their origin, if not their necessity, in a different state of society from that which prevails at the present time. When the doctrine was established, lords and other large landholders were accustomed to buy up contested claims against each other, or against commoners with whom they were at variance, in order to harass and oppose those in possession. On the other hand, commoners, by way of self-defense, thinking that they had title to land, would convey part of their interest to some powerful lord, in order, through his influence, to secure their pretended right. The want of sufficient written conveyances, and records of titles, and the feudal relation of villein and liege lord, afforded facilities for the combinations and oppressions which followed this state of things. The power of the nobles became mighty in corrupting the fountains of justice. To remedy these evils, the law against both maintenance and champerty was introduced.[2]

CHANCE. A thing happens by chance to a person which is neither brought about nor pre-estimated by his understanding.[3] See GAME, 2; MEDLEY.

CHANCELLOR.[4] 1. In England, several officers bear this name.

Chancellor of the exchequer. A high officer of the crown, who sometimes sat in court, sometimes in the exchequer chamber, and, with the regular judges of the court, saw that matters were conducted to the king's advantage. His chief duties now concern the management of the royal revenue. Under the Judicature Act of 1873, he is deprived of his judicial functions.[5] See EXCHEQUER.

---

[1] Courtright v. Burnes, 13 F. R. 317 (1882), cases, McCrary, J.; ib. 323-29, cases; s. c. 3 McCrary, 63, 68-75, cases. See generally Fowler v. Callam, 102 N. Y. 397 (1886).

[2] Hovey v. Hobson, 51 Me. 64 (1863), Dickerson, J. See also 29 Ala. 680; 70 id. 118, 179; 17 Ark. 624; 40 Conn. 570; 57 Ga. 264; 73 Ill. 13; 89 id. 183; 5 T. B. Mon. 416; 1 Pick. 416; 132 Mass. 388; 4 Mich. 538; 13 Ired. L. 198; 4 Duer, 275; 13 Ohio St. 175; 2 Baxt. 457; 29 Wis. 506; 19 Alb. Law J. 468-69 (1879), cases; 19 Cent. Law J. 402-8 (1884), cases; 24 id. 198 (1887), cases.

[3] [Goodman v. Cody, 1 Wash. T. 335 (1871).

[4] F. chancelier; L. L. cancellarius: a cancellando, from canceling — illegal letters-patent,— 4 Coke, Inst. 88; 3 Bl. Com. 46. He stood near the screen, cancellus, before the judgment seat,— Skeat. See also 1 Campbell's Lives Ld. Ch. 1-2.

[5] 3 Bl. Com. 44, 55.

Lord chancellor. The presiding judge in the court of chancery.

In the courts of the Roman emperors he was a chief scribe or secretary, afterward invested with judicial powers and supervision over other officers. From the empire the name passed to the church: every bishop had a chancellor, the principal judge of his consistory. And when the modern kingdoms were established, almost every state preserved its chancellor, with different jurisdictions and dignities. In all of them he had supervision of such instruments of the crown as were authenticated in the most solemn manner. When seals came into use he had the custody of the king's great seal.[1]

The office is created by delivery of the king's great seal into the custody of the nominee. He becomes a privy counsellor by his office and prolocutor of the house of lords by prescription. He appoints all justices of the peace. Being formerly an ecclesiastic, presiding over the king's chapel, he became keeper of the king's conscience, visitor to all hospitals and colleges of the king's founding, and patron of certain of the king's livings. He is the general guardian of all infants, idiots, and lunatics; he superintends all charitable uses. These powers belong to him apart from the extensive jurisdiction he exercises in his judicial capacity in the court of chancery.[1] See CHANCERY, 1; WOOLSACK.

Vice chancellor. One of a class of equity judges who held court independently of the lord chancellor, but whose decisions were reviewable in his court. They perhaps originally acted in his place.

2. In the United States, the judge of a court of equity.

As a judicial title, in use in Alabama, Delaware, Kentucky, Mississippi, and New Jersey. See CHANCERY, 2.

3. A person sitting as a judge in equity; as in saying that a circumstance in a case would cause a " chancellor " to hesitate to enter a decree in favor of a particular person. See TITLE, Marketable.

CHANCERY.[2] 1. In England, the highest court next to parliament.

Originally consisted of two distinct tribunals: an ordinary court, or court of common law; and an extraordinary court, or court of equity.

The " ordinary court " was the more ancient. It had jurisdiction in proceedings to cancel letterspatent, in cases of traverse of office, and the like; and of personal actions against officers of the court. Whenever any such cause came to an issue of fact, the chancellor, having no power to summon a jury,

---

[1] 3 Bl. Com. 46, 47, 49.

[2] Chancery: L. L. cancellaria, the record-room of a chancellor,— Skeat. L. cancelli, bars, lattice.— to keep off the people,— 3 Chitty, Bl. Com. 46.

sent the record to the court of king's bench for trial. Out of this ordinary tribunal also issued original writs under the great seal, commissions of charitable uses, of bankruptcy, of lunacy, etc.; for which the court was said to be always open: whence called the *officina justitiæ*.[1]

The "extraordinary court" became the court of greatest consequence. When the courts of law, which followed strictly the directions of the original writs, pronounced a harsh or imperfect judgment, application for redress was at first made to the king in person and his counsel; they, in time, referred the matter to the chancellor and a select committee, or, by degrees, to the chancellor alone,—the referee being empowered to mitigate the severity or to supply the defects of the judgment pronounced in the courts of strict law, upon consideration of all the circumstances in each case.[2] See CHANCELLOR.

The equitable jurisdiction of the court grew out of the exigencies of the times and of judicial administration: as from petitions to the king in council; cases as to which the precedents furnished no form of action for a remedy; cases calling for relief from fraud, accident, mistake, forfeiture; cases involving uses and trusts. The well-defined development of its distinct exercise dates from the time of Edward I (about 1300); but its character was crude until the time of Cardinal Woolsey and Sir Thomas Moore, under Henry VIII (1509–47). Lord Bacon reduced the practice to somewhat of a system. But Sir Heneage Finch (about 1680) so laid the foundation of modern equity jurisprudence as to have been called "the father of equity." Later lord chancellors, notably Hardwicke and Mansfield, extended and improved the system.[3]

Under the Judicature Act of 1873 the court of chancery became the Chancery Division of the High Court of Justice, retaining its former extraordinary jurisdiction; with part of its former ordinary jurisdiction transferred to the Court of Appeal, and the rest to the Courts of Common Law.

A too severe application of common-law rules brought the court of chancery into existence. . . The body of chancery law is nothing else than a system of exceptions — of principles applicable to cases falling within the letter, but not within the intention, of particular rules.[4]

2. In the United States, "chancery" corresponds to "equity," and a "court of chancery" to a "court of equity," that is, a court exercising equitable powers.

Here equity jurisprudence has grown up chiefly since the close of the last century, the English court of chancery being followed as a model. In some of the States, and in the national tribunals, chancery powers are exercised by the common-law courts.[5] See further EQUITY.

[1] 3 Bl. Com. 47–48.
[2] 3 Bl. Com. 49–50, 50–55.
[3] See 1 Story. Eq. §§ 41–52; 3 Bl. Com. 53–55; 1 Kent. 494.
[4] Pennock v. Hart, 8 S. & R. 377 (1822), Gibson, J.
[5] 1 Story, Eq. §§ 54–58; 1 Pomeroy, Eq. §§ 1–42; 3 Story, Const. §§ 506–7, 644–45.

CHANGE. See ALTER; FUNDAMENTAL; PARTY, 2; VENUE.

'CHANGE. See EXCHANGE, 3.

CHANNEL. The main channel is that bed of a river over which the principal body of water flows.[1] See AQUA, Currit, etc.; NAVIGABLE.

CHAPTER. See STATUTE, 2.

CHARACTER. The qualities impressed by nature or habit on a person, which distinguish him from other persons. These constitute his real character; while the qualities he is supposed to possess constitute his estimated character or reputation. . . "Reputation" may be evidence of character, but it is not character itself.[2]

That which a person really is, in distinction from that which he may be reputed to be.[3]

Character [reputation] is the slow-spreading influence of opinion, arising from the deportment of a man in society.[4]

In many cases it has been said that the regular mode of examining a witness is to inquire whether he knows the general character of the person whom it is intended to impeach, but in all such cases the word "character" is used as synonymous with "reputation." What is wanted is the common opinion, that in which there is general concurrence; in other words, general reputation or character attributed. That is presumed to be indicative of actual character.[5]

General character. The estimation in which a person is held in the community where he has resided.

Ordinarily, the members of that community are the only proper witnesses to testify to such character.

Evidence of character is founded on opinion, and a witness testifying as to the general character of another must have the means of knowing such character.[6]

Good character. Good general reputation for one, several, or many qualities — as, for honesty, chastity, veracity, peaceableness, integrity.

Moral character and conduct may be proven: to afford a presumption that the person is not guilty of a criminal act; to affect the damages where the amount depends upon character and conduct; to impeach or confirm the veracity of a witness.

[1] St. Louis, &c. Packet Co. v. Keokuk Bridge Co., 31 F. R. 757 (1887), Love, J.
[2] [Carpenter v. People, 8 Barb. 608 (1850), Welles, J.
[3] Andre v. State, 5 Iowa, 394 (1857), Woodward, J.
[4] Trial of Hardy, 24 St. Tr. 1079 (1795), Erskine (Ld.), *arguendo*.
[5] Knode v. Williamson, 17 Wall. 588 (1873), Strong, J. See State v. Egan, 59 Iowa, 637 (1882).
[6] Douglass v. Tousey, 2 Wend. 354 (1829).

In civil suits the character of a party is not admissible in evidence unless the nature of the action involves his general character or directly affects it. In the case of a tort, when the defendant is charged with fraud from mere circumstances, evidence of his general character is receivable to repel it. Such evidence will be rejected, whenever the general character is involved by the plea only and not by the nature of the action. Character in regard to a particular trait is not in issue, unless the trait is involved in the matter charged.[1]

The bad character of the plaintiff may be shown in suits for damages for seduction, breach of promise to marry, slander, libel, and malicious prosecution, qq. v. The burden of proof is on the assailant.[2]

In homicide, evidence of previous good character may be made the basis on which to form a doubt.[3] But when the evidence is positive and satisfactory, good character cannot overcome the presumption of guilt;[4] against facts strongly proven, good character cannot avail.[5]

The old rule, that evidence of the good character of the defendant is not to be considered unless other evidence leaves the mind in doubt, has been much criticised; the weight of authority is now against it. If evidence of reputation is admissible at all its weight should be left to be determined by the jury in connection with all the other evidence in the case. The circumstances may be such that an established reputation for good character, if it is relevant to the issue, would alone create a reasonable doubt, although without it the other evidence would be convincing.[6]

A witness called to impeach the veracity of another witness may be asked: "Is the character of the witness for truth on a par with that of mankind in general?" In English courts the inquiries are: "Are you acquainted with the character of the witness? What is his general character? Would you believe him under oath?"[7]

Courts differ as to whether the general reputation of a witness for truth and veracity is the true and sole criterion of his credit, or whether the inquiry may not properly be extended to his entire moral character and estimation in society. They also differ as to the right to inquire of the impeaching witness whether he would believe the other on his oath. All agree, however, that the first inquiry must be restricted either to his general reputation for truth and veracity, or to his general character; and that it cannot be extended to particular facts or transactions, for the rea-

son that while every man is supposed to be fully prepared to meet those general inquiries, it is not likely he would be prepared, without notice, to answer as to particular acts.[1]

Unwillingness to believe a man under oath must be based upon two facts: that the witness knows the reputation for veracity among the man's neighbors, and that such reputation is bad.[2]

Proof of a general disposition to do a thing is not proof of that thing. Thus, proof of a habit of gambling when drunk is not proof that the person gambled when drunk on a particular day; nor will proof of a habit of loaning money at a usurious interest prove that a loan was made in a particular instance.[3]

See further BAD, 1; CHASTE; COMMUNICATION, Privileged, 1; REPUTATION; SUSPICION, 3.

CHARGE. 1, v. To lay on, to place under or upon, as, a burden, a duty, a trust. Opposed, **discharge**, q. v.

(1) To place under a duty or obligation with respect to knowing or doing: as, to charge one with notice of such facts or information as inquiry (q. v.) would disclose, or with notice of what the law requires; to charge an acceptor or indorser by presentment.[4]

(2) To impose, upon a person or thing, the duty or obligation of paying money: as, to charge the estate of a decedent with a debt; to charge a legacy upon land devised; to charge a purpart in partition with owelty. See LEGACY; OWELTY.

(3) To enter, in an account, an item of money due. See ACCOUNT, 1.

(4) To place upon one the burden of crime or guilt; to accuse of a wrong or offense; to indict.

The implication is, usually, that the offense has been alleged according to the forms of law — that legal process has issued.[5] See *Charge*, n. (2, b).

(5) For a jury to be charged with the fate of a prisoner,[6] see JEOPARDY.

(6) To instruct in the nature of a duty imposed: as, for a judge or a coroner to charge a jury.

Chargeable. Subject to charge; capable of being or of becoming charged;[7] as, to be

---

[1] 1 Greenl. Ev. §§ 54–55, cases; 4 Wall. 471; 26 Alb. L. J. 364. As to evidence of, in civil cases, see particularly Simpson v. Westenberger, 28 Kan. 757–62 (1882), cases.

[2] 1 Whart. Ev. §§ 47–56, cases.

[3] Kilpatrick v. Commonwealth, 31 Pa. 216 (1858).

[4] United States v. Freeman, 4 Mas. 510 (1827).

[5] Commonwealth v. Webster, 5 Cush. 325 (1850); 59 Cal. 601; 62 id. 29; 50 Md. 233.

[6] Commonwealth v. Leonard, 140 Mass. 470, 479 (1886), cases, Field, J.; 26 Cent. L. J. 515–19 (1888), cases.

[7] State v. Randolph, 24 Conn. *367 (1856); Langhorne v. Commonwealth, 76 Va. 102 (1882); State v. Rush, 77 Mo. 519 (1883).

---

[1] Teese v. Huntingdon, 23 How. 11–13 (1859), cases, Clifford, J. See, generally, as to evidence, 25 Cent. Law J. 146 (1887), cases.

[2] Spies et al. v. People, 122 Ill. 208 (1887).

[3] Thompson v. Bowie, 4 Wall. 471 (1866), cases.

[4] 94 U. S. 432; 101 id. 697.

[5] Day v. Inhabitants of Otis, 8 Allen, 478 (1864), Bigelow, C. J.

[6] State v. Connor, 5 Coldw. 3:3 (1868).

[7] 46 Vt. 625; 107 Mass. 426.

chargeable with a loss;[1] a tax chargeable on land; a pauper chargeable upon a district.

"Chargeable," in its ordinary acceptation as applicable to the imposition of a duty or burden, signifies capable of being charged; subject, liable, proper to be charged.[2]

2, *n.* A burden, duty, obligation, responsibility, or disability — imposed upon a person or attached to a thing. Opposed, **discharge** (which see).

(1) Charge upon a Thing. Whatever is in the nature of a lien or incumbrance (*qq. v.*) resting upon an object of property and to be satisfied out of it or out of the proceeds of it: as, a legacy to be paid out of land. Of this nature also are assessments and taxes upon realty,[3] *qq. v.*

Charges. (a) Pecuniary impositions upon property — real estate.

(b) Book-entries of moneys due.

(c) Expenses incurred in settling an estate.[4] See ACCOUNT, 1.

(d) Referring to litigation, something more than costs, *q. v.*

(e) In equity pleading, allegations in denial or avoidance of a defense.

Charge and discharge. Describes the mode formerly pursued in accounting before a master: the complainant exhibited the items of his claim in a form called a charge, while the respondent exhibited contrary items or claims by way of discharge — as, a release.[5]

Charging order. An order of court that stock shall stand pledged to the payment of a judgment. See further ORDER, 2.

Charging part. Allegations, in a bill in equity, intended to anticipate and controvert the answer.[6]

Collateral charge. An obligation in a bond binding the heir, executor, and administrator, — descends upon the heirs and holds assets by descent.[7]

Overcharge. In a statute providing for recovery from a railroad company "for any overcharge," signifies, as ordinarily, a charge of more than is permitted by law.[1]

See also RENT-CHARGE; SURCHARGE.

(2) Charge upon a Person. Anything in the nature of a burden, or of a duty or obligation, resting upon one or more individuals.

While in this substantive sense the word "charge" may have a meaning corresponding to any one of the foregoing verbal senses, it distinctly signifies:

(a) The duty of paying money.

(b) Responsibility for a wrong or an offense, as for negligence or crime, particularly the latter — formal accusation of criminal conduct.

An accusation, made in a legal manner, of illegal conduct.[2]

May imply an original complaint made in the first instance preliminary to a formal trial.[3] See INDICTMENT.

(c) Instruction judicially given by the judge of a court to a jury in regard to their duty as jurors, in particular to a traverse jury as to their duty in finding a verdict.

An authoritative exposition of the law which it is incumbent upon the jury to obey.[4]

Delivered to grand jurors before they proceed to consider indictments and presentments; and to petit or common jurors before they retire to deliberate over the evidence in a particular case.

General charge. Instruction upon a case in its entirety. **Special charge.** Made, at the request of counsel for a party, upon one or more points in the case.

It is clearly error to charge upon a conjectural state of facts, of which no evidence has been offered. The instruction presupposes that there is some evidence before the jury which they may think sufficient to establish the facts hypothetically assumed in the opinion of the court; and if there is no evidence which they have a right to consider, then the charge does not aid them in coming to a correct conclusion, but the tendency is to mislead and embarrass them. It may induce them to indulge in conjectures, instead of weighing the testimony.[5]

Where there is an entire absence of testimony, or it is all one way, and its conclusiveness is free from doubt, it is competent for the court to direct the jury to find accordingly.[6]

---

[1] 101 U. S. 19.

[2] Walbridge *v.* Walbridge, 46 Vt. 625 (1874).

[3] See Harris *v.* Miller, 71 Ala. 34 (1881); 59 *id.* 317; 69 *id.* 127; 25 *id.* 333.

[4] [Goodwin *v.* Chaffee, 4 Conn. 166 (1822).

[5] See Daniel, Chanc. Pract. 1173.

[6] See Story, Eq. Pl. § 31.

[7] [2 Bl. Com. 340.

[1] Woodhouse *v.* Rio Grande R. Co., 67 Tex. 418 (1887), Stayton, A. J.

[2] Tompert *v.* Lithgow, 1 Bush, 180 (1866).

[3] Ryan *v.* People, 79 N. Y. 598 (1880); 16 Nev. 91.

[4] See Commonwealth *v.* Porter, 10 Metc. 285–86 (1845).

[5] United States *v.* Breitling, 20 How. 254 (1857), Taney, C. J.; Goodman *v.* Simonds, *ib.* 359 (1857); Michigan Bank *v.* Eldred, 9 Wall. 553 (1869).

[6] Meguire *v.* Corwine, 101 U. S. 111 (1879); *ib.* 697.

When, after giving a party the benefit of every inference that can fairly be drawn from all the evidence, it is insufficient to authorize a verdict in his favor, it is proper for the court to give the jury a peremptory instruction for the other party.[1]

The court may sum up the facts, and submit them, with the inferences of law, to the judgment of the jury. But care is to be taken to separate the law from the facts, and to leave the latter, in unequivocal terms, to the jury, as their true and peculiar province.[2]

With the charge of the court upon matters of fact, and with its commentaries upon the weight of evidence, the Supreme Court has nothing to do; such observations are understood to be addressed to the jury merely for their consideration as the ultimate judges of matters of fact, and entitled to no more importance than the jury choose to give them.[3]

But, as the jurors are the triors of the facts, an expression of opinion by the court should be so guarded as to leave the jury free in the exercise of their own judgments.[4]

A general statement will be taken in connection with the facts in the particular case.[5]

In some States the court neither sums up the evidence, nor expresses an opinion upon a question of fact, the charge being strictly confined to questions of law, leaving the evidence to be discussed by counsel, and the facts to be decided by the jury without comment or opinion by the court. But most of the States have adopted the English practice, where the judge always sums up the evidence, and points out the conclusions which in his opinion ought to be drawn from it; submitting them, however, to the judgment of the jury. The judge of a Federal court may express his opinion on the facts.[5]

At a trial by jury in a Federal court the judge may express his opinion upon the facts; the expression, when no rule of law is incorrectly stated and all facts are ultimately submitted to the determination of the jury, cannot be reviewed by writ of error; and the power of the court in this respect is not controlled by a State statute forbidding judges to express an opinion upon the facts.[7] Nor can a State constitution prohibit the judges of the Federal courts from charging juries with regard to matters of fact.[8]

No error is committed in refusing a prayer for instructions consisting of a series of propositions, presented as an entirety, if some of them should not be given to the jury.[9]

It is not error to refuse to give an instruction asked for, even if correct in point of law, provided those given cover the entire case and submit it properly to the jury.[1]

Failure to embrace all the issues in one instruction is not error, if they are included in those given, which, on the whole, are correct, not contradictory, nor calculated to mislead.[2]

Although an instruction, considered by itself, is too general, yet if it is properly limited by others, so that it is not probable that it could have misled the jury, the judgment will not be reversed.[3]

If the court has laid down the law fully and correctly, it is not bound to repeat an instruction in terms varied to suit the wishes of a party.[4]

Where a charge embraces several distinct propositions, a general exception to it will not avail the party if any one of the propositions is correct.[5]

Where any portion of the charge is correct, an exception to the entire charge will not be sustained.[6]

A nice criticism of words will not be indulged when the meaning of the instruction is plain and obvious, and cannot mislead the jury.[7]

Exceptions to a charge are made after the jury retire; and each must cover a distinct point or part only. See further DIRECT, 2; INSTRUCT, 2; JURY, Trial by; NONSUIT; POINT.

CHARGE D'AFFAIRES. See MINISTER, 3.

CHARITY. 1. In its widest sense, all the good affections men ought to bear toward each other; in a restricted and common sense, relief of the poor.[8]

The benevolence which limits itself to giving alms to the poor comes within the restricted definition but falls far short of that true charity which has its origin in the two great sources of all good deeds — the love of God and the love of man.[9]

In considering what is lawful to be done on the Lord's day, "charity" includes everything which proceeds from a sense of moral

---

[1] Marshall v. Hubbard, 117 U. S. 419 (1886), cases.

[2] M'Lanahan v. Universal Ins. Co., 1 Pet. 182 (1828), Story, J.

[3] Carver v. Jackson, 4 Pet. 80 (1830), Story, J.; Hayes v. United States, 32 F. R. 663 (1887), cases.

[4] Tracy v. Swartwout, 10 Pet. 96 (1836), McLean, J.; Games v. Stiles, 14 id. 327 (1840).

[5] Northern Bank v. Porter Township, 110 U. S. 615 (1884), cases; 6 Wheat. 264.

[6] Mitchell v. Harmony, 13 How. 130 (1851), Taney, C. J.

[7] Vicksburg & Meridian R. Co. v. Putnam, 118 U. S. 553 (1886), cases, Gray, J.

[8] St. Louis, &c. R. Co. v. Vickers, 122 U. S. 360 (1887).

[9] Worthington v. Mason, 101 U. S. 149 (1879); Beaver v. Taylor, 93 id. 54 (1876), cases.

[1] Laber v. Cooper, 7 Wall. 566 (1868); Indianapolis, &c. R. Co. v. Horst, 93 U. S. 295 (1876); The Schools v. Risley, 10 Wall. 115 (1869); Wheeler v. Winn, 53 Pa. 127–29 (1866).

[2] Muehlhausen v. St. Louis R. Co., 91 Mo. 346 (1886), Norton, C. J.

[3] Spies et al. v. People, 122 Ill. 245–46 (1887), cases.

[4] Northwestern Mut. Life Ins. Co. v. Muskegon Bank, 122 U. S. 510 (1887), cases.

[5] Lincoln v. Claflin, 7 Wall. 132, 139 (1868); Johnston v. Jones, 1 Black, 221 (1861).

[6] Boogher v. N. Y. Life Ins. Co., 103 U. S. 98 (1880), cases.

[7] Rogers v. The Marshal, 1 Wall. 654 (1863).

[8] Morice v. Bishop of Durham, 9 Ves. *405 (1804), Sir William Grant. Approved, Same v. Same, 10 id. *540 (1805), Lord Eldon.

[9] Price v. Maxwell, 28 Pa. 36, 35 (1857), Lewis, C. J.

duty, or a feeling of kindness and humanity, and is intended wholly for the relief or comfort of another, and not for one's own benefit or pleasure.[1]

Charity is active goodness. It is doing good to our fellow-men. It is fostering those institutions that are established to relieve pain, to prevent suffering, and to do good to mankind in general or to any class or portion of mankind. The term no doubt takes on shades of meaning from the Christian religion.[2] See further SUNDAY.

2. A gift, devise, or trust, intended to promote a charitable use.

In law, charity and charitable use are convertible terms. The latter was originally employed in contradistinction to "superstitious use," and designated such "good and worthy use" as was deemed not within the purview of statute 23 Hen. VIII (1532), c. 10, which abolished certain uses invented by the clergy. But, inasmuch as that statute swept away many meritorious uses, statute 1 Edw. VI (1547), c. 14, was passed to legalize, as recited in the preamble, several "good and godly uses" — such as schools for educating the youth, provision for the poor, etc. This preamble became the germ of the law of "charitable uses." Before 1547, such uses had never been grouped together as a distinct class, and peculiar principles applied to them.   Since the enactment of statute 43 Eliz. (1601), c. 4, no uses have been regarded as "charitable" except uses within the letter or spirit of that statute; and these are wholly "public" in nature.[3]

What is a charity is rather a matter of description than of definition.[4]

A charity is a gift for a public use; as, a gift in aid of the poor, to learning, to religion, to a humane object.[5]

A precise definition of a legal charity is hardly to be found in the books. The one most commonly used in modern cases, originating in the judgment of Sir William Grant, confirmed by that of Lord Eldon, in Morice's Case, 9th and 10th Vesey, ante — that those purposes are considered charitable which are enumerated in the statute of 43 Elizabeth, or which by analogy are deemed within its spirit and intendment — leaves something to be desired in point of certainty, and suggests no principle. Mr. Binney, in his argument in the Girard Will Case, p. 41 (1844), defined a charitable or pious gift to be "whatever is given for the love of

God, or for the love of your neighbor, in the catholic and universal sense — given for these motives, and to these ends — free from the stain or taint of every consideration that is personal, private and selfish;" and this definition was approved in Price's Case, 28th Pa. ante. A more concise and practical rule is that of Lord Camden, adopted by Chancellor Kent, by Lord Lyndhurst, and by the Supreme Court of the United States — "A gift to a general public use, which extends to the poor as well as the rich." Jones v. Williams, Ambl. 652 (1767); Coggeshall v. Pelton, 7 Johns. Ch. 294 (1823); Mitford v. Reynolds, 1 Phil. Ch. 191 (1842); Perin v. Carey, 24 How. 506 (1860).[1]

A charity, in the legal sense, may be more fully defined as a gift, to be applied consistently with existing laws, for the benefit of an indefinite number of persons, either by bringing their minds or hearts under the influence of education or religion, by relieving their bodies from disease, suffering, or constraint, by assisting them to establish themselves in life, or by creating or maintaining public buildings or works, or otherwise lessening the burdens of government.[1]

It is immaterial whether the purpose is called "charitable" in the gift itself, if it is so described as to show that it is charitable in its nature.[1]

A testator must be taken to have used the word "charitable" in its legal sense.[2]

The statute of Elizabeth is the principal source of legal charities, — has become the general rule of charities. The signification of the word is chiefly derived from it, and not from the popular understanding of "good affection" between men, nor of relief of the poor.[3]

That statute names as distinct charities: 1, relief of the aged, impotent, and poor; 2, maintenance of sick and maimed soldiers and mariners; 3, schools of learning; 4, free schools; 5, scholars in the universities; 6, houses of correction; 7, repair of bridges, ports, havens, causeways, churches, sea-banks, highways; 8, the education and preferment of orphans; 9, marriage of poor maids; 10, support and help of young tradesmen, handicraftsmen, persons decayed; 11, relief and redemption of prisoners or captives; 12, aid of the poor in paying taxes; 13, setting out of soldiers.[4]

These charities are but instances under three general classes: 1, relief and assistance of the poor and needy; 2, promotion of education; 3, maintenance of public buildings and works. The inquiry in each case

---

[1] Doyle v. Lynn & Boston R. Co., 118 Mass. 197 (1875), cases, Gray, C. J.

[2] Allen v. Duffie, 43 Mich. 7 (1880), Cooley, J.

[3] Owens v. Missionary Society, 14 N. Y. 385, 389, 397. 403 (1856), Selden, J. See also Baptist Association v. Hart, 4 Wheat. 2, 27 (1819); ib., App. 1; 17 How. 151-52, 155; 9 Ves. *405; 30 Kan. 638; 2 Bl. Com. 273; 2 Story, Eq. §§ 1135-49.

[4] Perin v. Carey, 24 How. 494 (1860), Wayne, J.

[5] Kain v. Gibboney, 101 U. S. 365 (1879), Strong, J.

[1] Jackson v. Phillips, 14 Allen, 555-56 (1867), Gray, J. See also Detwiller v. Hartman, 37 N. J. E. 353 (1883); White v. Ditson, 140 Mass. 352 (1885); Humane Society v. Boston, 142 id. 27 (1886). Definitions collected, Protestant Episcopal Education Society v. Churchman, 80 Va. 762-63 (1885).

[2] Howe v. Wilson, 91 Mo. 49 (1886).

[3] Town of Hamden v. Rice, 24 Conn. *355 (1856), Ellesworth, J.

[4] Ould v. Washington Hospital, 95 U. S. 309-11 (1877), Swayne, J.

is: Is the purpose of the gift within the principle and reason of the statute, although not expressly named in it.[1]

Gifts for repairing a church, for building an organ gallery, for erecting and maintaining a parsonage, for the worship of God, for the advancement of Christianity, for the benefit of ministers of the gospel, have been held to be valid charities.[2]

The statute of Elizabeth was simply remedial and ancillary to the common law.[3] Courts of equity had, and still have, an original and inherent common-law jurisdiction over charities, except in a few States, as in Maryland, North Carolina, and Virginia.[4]

While the provisions of the statute of Elizabeth have been re-enacted in some States, in others new purposes have been enumerated. In Connecticut, the District of Columbia, Maryland, New York, North Carolina, and Virginia, the statute seems to have been repudiated; in Georgia, Indiana, Iowa, Kentucky, Massachusetts, Rhode Island, Vermont, and in some other States, it is still in force.[5]

A good charitable use is "public," not in the sense that it must be executed openly and in public, but in the sense of being so general and indefinite in its objects as to be deemed of common and public benefit. Each individual benefited may be private, and the charity may be distributed in private and by a private hand. Opposed is a "private charity:" not a public or general charity, in view of the statute of Elizabeth or of a court of chancery, but an association for the mutual benefit of the contributors and of no others. Such a case wants the essential element of indefiniteness in the immediate objects, if not that of gratuity in the contribution.[6]

A charitable use is essentially shifting. When a trust defines the beneficiaries with certainty, it is rather private than public. "Charity begins where uncertainty of the beneficiaries begins."[7]

When private property is appropriated to the sup-

port of education for the benefit of the public without any view to profit, it constitutes a charity which is purely public.[1]

Trusts for public charitable purposes must be for the benefit of an indefinite number of persons; for, if all the beneficiaries are personally designated, the trust lacks the element of indefiniteness, which is one characteristic of a legal charity. If the founder describes the general nature of the trust, he may leave the details of its administration to be settled by trustees under the superintendence of a court of chancery.[2]

If the general object of a bequest is pointed out, or if the testator has provided a means of doing so by the appointment of trustees with that power, the gift will be treated as sufficiently definite for judicial cognizance.[3]

When a charitable trust has been fully constituted, and the funds have passed into the hands of the institution or organization intended for its administration, the court of chancery becomes its legal guardian and protector, and will take care that the objects of the trust are duly pursued, and the funds rightfully appropriated. But where contributions to a charity are proposed to be made upon certain express conditions, the rights of the donors stand upon contract; and if the conditions are not performed, their obligation to contribute is discharged.[4]

A devise to a corporation in favor of a charity is valid.[5]

There is no implication, in such case, that the corporation is of a "religious" nature.[6]

Where there is a valid devise to a corporation in trust for charitable purposes, the sovereign may enforce the execution of the trust, by changing the administrator, if the corporation be dissolved, or, if not, by modifying and enlarging its franchises, provided the trust be not perverted, and no wrong be done to the beneficiaries.[7]

Equity will not enforce a trust whose object is the propagation of atheism, infidelity, immorality, or hostility to the existing forms of government.[8]

The essentials to a valid charity are: ability in the donor; capacity in the donee; an instrument or means whereby it is given; a thing to be given;[5] a legal purpose; a gift not absolute, but available through the medium of a trust.[9]

Equity will not administer a foreign charity, unless it be valid under the laws of both States, and the

---

[1] Jackson v. Phillips, 14 Allen, 551 (1867), cases, Gray, J.

[2] Bishop's Residence Co. v. Hudson, 91 Mo. 676 (1887), cases.

[3] Ould v. Washington Hospital, ante.

[4] Kain v. Gibboney, Ould v. Hospital, ante; Vidal v. Girard's Executors, 2 How. 155 (1844); Howe v. Wilson, 91 Mo. 49 (1886), cases; 80 Va. 773; 107 U. S. 167.

[5] See 1 Bouvier, 304, cases.

[6] Saltonstall v. Sanders, 11 Allen, 456, 464 (1865), cases, Gray, J. See also Jones v. Habersham, 107 U. S. 174 (1882), cases; s. c. 3 Woods, 443; Beckwith v. The Rector, 69 Ga. 569 (1882); De Wolf v. Lawson, 61 Wis. 480 (1884); Protestant Epis. Education Society v. Churchman, 80 Va. 718 (1885); Kent v. Dunham, 142 Mass. 216, 218 (1886).

[7] Dodge v. Williams, 46 Wis. 98, 91–103 (1882), cases, Ryan, C. J.; Fontain v. Ravenel, 17 How. 384 (1854).

[1] Gerke v. Archbishop Purcell, 25 Ohio St. 247, 243 (1874), White, J.

[2] Russell v. Allen, 107 U. S. 167 (1883), cases, Gray, J.; American Academy of Arts v. Harvard College, 12 Gray, 596 (1832), Shaw, C. J.

[3] Howe v. Wilson, 91 Mo. 52 (1886), Black, J. See also Webster v. Morris, 66 Wis. 366 (1886).

[4] Printing House v. Trustees, 104 U. S. 727 (1881), Bradley, J.

[5] Perin v. Carey, Vidal v. Girard's Executors, ante.

[6] De Wolf v. Lawson, 61 Wis. 480 (1884).

[7] Girard's Executors v. Philadelphia, 7 Wall. 14–15 (1868); Philadelphia v. Fox, 64 Pa. 182 (1870).

[8] Manners v. Library Company, 93 Pa. 172 (1880), cases; Jones v. Habersham, 107 U. S. 189 (1882), cases.

[9] Owens v. Missionary Society, 14 N. Y. 335 (1856).

CHART   171   CHARTER

trustee has capacity to receive and carry out the trust.[1]

By the law of England, before the statute of Elizabeth, and by the law of this country at the present day (except where restricted by statute or decision, as in Virginia, Maryland, and New York), trusts for public charitable purposes are upheld under circumstances as to which private trusts would fail. Being for objects of permanent interest and benefit to the public, they may be perpetual in their duration; and the instruments creating them should be so construed as to give them effect if possible, and to carry out the general intention of the donor, when clearly manifested, even if the particular form and manner pointed out by him cannot be followed.[2]

Board of charities. A board of public charities, in several of the States, is a body of commissioners, appointed by the governor of each State (possibly by and with the consent of one of the houses of the legislature), and charged with the duty of examining into the condition of all charitable, reformatory or correctional institutions in the State; having regard, in particular, to the methods of government and instruction, the official conduct of trustees or officers, the finances, buildings, etc.

See AMERICAN; ASSOCIATION, 3; BENEVOLENCE; CY PRES; INDIGENT; LEGACY; MARSHAL, 2; MASSES; MORTMAIN; PROTESTANT; SUBSCRIBE, 2; VISIT, 2.

CHART. As used in the copyright law, does not include sheets of paper exhibiting tabulated or methodically arranged information.

In the Copyright Act of 1790, where the word was first used, a chart was a marine map, as is shown by all the dictionaries of the time. A definition covering such a sheet of paper was introduced into Worcester's dictionary in 1864, and into Webster's in 1865. The word, in the present act, is separated from the word "book," and kept with the word "map" and other words of artistic import, thus showing an intention to continue its use in the sense of a chart of the class of maps, and other works of art.[3] See COPYRIGHT. Compare MAP.

CHARTA. L. Paper; a writing; a charter. See MAGNA CHARTA; OFFICINA; CHARTARUM.

CHARTER. 1. A deed is sometimes called a charter from its materials.[4] See CHARTA.

Charter-land. Land held by deed under certain rents and free services; book-land. Opposed, *folk-land;* which was held by an assurance in writing.[5] See MANOR.

Charter-party. A contract by which the owner lets his vessel to another for freight.[1]

A contract by which an entire ship, or some principal part thereof, is let to a merchant for the conveyance of goods on a determined voyage to one or more places.[2]

All contracts under seal were anciently called "charters," and divided into two parts, one for each party. Whence *charta-partita:* a writing divided; like an indenture (*q. v.*) at common law.[3]

Charterer. He who hires a vessel under a "charter-party." *Charter-money.* The sum agreed to be paid for the use of the vessel.

Charge of navigating the vessel may be retained by the owner or assumed by the hirer.

The contract is generally effected through a broker acting for the ship-owner.

A ship thus chartered is opposed to a "general ship."

The instrument is not usually under seal. It names the vessel, master, and contract parties; and specifies the tonnage, the times and places for loading and discharge, the charter-money, and the allowance for delay. It is a commercial instrument, subject to the rules applicable to other commercial contracts. It is to be construed liberally, in agreement with the intention of the parties, the usages of trade in general and of the particular trade.[4]

An action *in rem* cannot be maintained for the breach of a charter-party when the voyage was not undertaken, and no part of the cargo delivered on board.[5]

See DEFECT; DISPATCH; FREIGHT; LADING, Bill of; SAIL.

2. The primary meaning — a deed or sealed instrument — is obsolete. Used alone, the word now refers to certain instruments which emanate from government, in the nature of letters-patent.[6]

The king's grants, whether of lands, honors, liberties, franchises, or aught besides, are contained in charters or letters-patent,[7] *q. v.*

Charter of incorporation. The instrument evidencing the act of a legislature, governor, court, or other authorized department or person, by which a corporation is or was created.

The charter of a *private* corporation, duly accepted, is an executed contract. It is construed

---

[1] Taylor *v.* Trustees of Bryn Mawr College, 34 N. J. E. 101 (1881), cases: 13 Rep. 20.

[2] Russell *v.* Allen, *ante;* 13 Wall. 723. See generally 23 Cent. Law J. 364–68 (1886), cases.

[3] Taylor *v.* Gilman, 24 F. R. 633–34 (1885), cases, Wheeler, J.

[4] 2 Bl. Com. 295.

[5] 2 Bl. Com. 90.

---

[1] Spring *v.* Gray, 6 Pet. 164 (1832), Marshall, C. J.

[2] Vandewater *v.* Mills, 19 How. 91 (1856), Grier, J.; Ward *v.* Thompson, 22 *id.* 333 (1859).

[3] 2 Kent, 201.

[4] Lowber *v.* Bangs, 2 Wall. 744 (1864); 113 U. S. 40; 115 *id.* 353.

[5] The Missouri, 30 F. R. 384 (1887), cases.

[6] See 1 Story, Const. § 161.

[7] 2 Bl. Com. 346; 1 *id.* 108, 473.

strictly, against the corporation, and in favor of the public. Nothing passes but what is granted in explicit terms. The charter of a *municipal* corporation is not a contract.[1]

The charter of a bank is a franchise, and not taxable if a fair price has been paid for it and accepted in lieu of taxation. No power of sovereignty will be held to be surrendered, unless expressed in terms too plain to be mistaken.[2]

A power reserved by the legislature to alter, amend, or repeal a charter authorizes it to make any alteration or amendment of a charter, granted subject to such power, which will not defeat or substantially impair the object of the grant or of any right vested under it, and which the legislature may deem necessary for securing either that object or a public right.[3]

To "create" a charter is to make one which never existed before. To "renew" a charter is to give a new existence to one which has been forfeited, or which has lost its vitality by lapse of time. To "extend" a charter is to give one which now exists greater or longer time in which to operate than that to which it was originally limited.[4]

It is a well settled rule of construction of grants to corporations, whether public or private, that only such powers and rights can be exercised under them as are clearly comprehended within the words of the act or derived therefrom by necessary implication, regard being had to the objects of the grant. Any ambiguity

or doubt arising out of the terms used by the legislature must be resolved in favor of the public.[1]

See CORPORATION; FUNDAMENTAL; IMPAIR; RAILROAD; ULTRA VIRES.

CHASE. See GAME, 1.

CHASTE. Actually pure as to conduct and principle; virtuous.

Chaste character. Personal virtue; moral purity.

Refers not to reputation but to moral qualities — to what a person really is.[2]

Actual personal virtue — actually chaste and pure in conduct and principle.

Applies to one who, having fallen, has subsequently reformed and become chaste.[3]

Although a female, from ignorance or other cause, may have so low a standard of propriety as to commit or permit indelicate acts or familiarities, yet, if she have enough of the sense of virtue that she would not surrender her person, unless seduced to do so under a promise of marriage, she cannot be said to be a woman of "unchaste character" within the meaning of a statute punishing seduction under a promise of marriage.[4]

Chastity. The virtue which prevents unlawful sexual commerce.

Offenses against chastity are: fornication, adultery, incest, seduction, lascivious carriage, keeping or frequenting houses of prostitution, bigamy, marrying the husband or wife of another, obscene libels, sodomy, bestiality.

Solicitation of chastity. Inviting another to commit adultery or fornication.

A solicitation is not an attempt. Until some forbidden overt act is committed, the law will not detect and punish the intent. The contrary rule would be impracticable.[5]

Charges of unchaste conduct are seldom made in direct words; usually by insinuation. However made, they are slanderous when they convey to the mind of the hearers the meaning that the person in question is unchaste.[6]

See ATTEMPT; BAD, 1; PRETIUM, Pudicitiæ.

CHATTEL. Things personal include not only things movable, but something more: the whole of which is comprehended under the general name of "chattels," which Coke says is a French word signifying goods — from the technical Latin *catalla*, which meant, primarily, beasts of husbandry, and,

---

[1] Dartmouth College *v.* Woodward, 4 Wheat. 518, 624 (1819), Marshall, C. J.; *ib.* 708, 712, Story, J.

[2] Jefferson Branch Bank *v.* Skelly, 1 Black, 446 (1861); Thomas *v.* West Jersey R. Co., 101 U. S. 82 (1879),

[3] Close *v.* Glenwood Cemetery, 107 U. S. 476 (1882), cases, Gray, J. See also Union Passenger Ry. Co. *v.* Philadelphia, 101 *id.* 539–40 (1879); Spring Valley Water Works *v.* Schottler, 110 *id.* 352–53 (1884); County of Santa Clara *v.* South. Pacific R. Co., 18 F. R. 406–8 (1883). Although an attempt to shake or limit the conclusion reached in the Dartmouth College Case was made in Bank of Toledo *v.* Toledo, 1 Ohio St. 622 (1853), and in other cases at about the same time, the doctrine was re-asserted and even generalized and extended by the Supreme Court in Piqua Branch *v.* Knoop, 16 How. 369 (1853); Dodge *v.* Woolsey, 18 How. 331 (1855), and cases, *ib.* 380, 384. Much space would be needed for expounding the decisions which have applied the doctrine, and for tracing its application to different kinds of charters. To do so is the less necessary because the legislatures have become accustomed to grant charters subject to a general reserved power to alter or repeal them. There are, no doubt, a few corporations chartered before 1819, and some created since, without reservation of such power, which are independent of legislative changes made without their assent; but the great mass of private corporations now active are subject to a right reserved to the legislature to make changes. Addison, Contr. *2, Am. ed., A. & W. (1888), note. See also New Orleans *v.* Great Southern Tel., &c. Co., Sup. Ct. La. (Feb. 23, 1888); 26 Cent. Law J. 233; *ib.* 234–36 (1888), cases.

[4] Moers *v.* Mayor, &c. of Reading, 21 Pa. 201 (1853), Black, C. J.

---

[1] Minturn *v.* Larue, 23 How. 436 (1859), Nelson, J.; 76 Va. 961; 77 *id.* 219.

[2] [State *v.* Carron. 18 Iowa, 375–76 (1865), cases; State *v.* Prizer, 49 *id.* 532 (1878); 5 *id.* 391; 59 *id.* 636; 70 *id.* 454; 28 Minn. 52.

[3] Carpenter *v.* People, 8 Barb. 608–9 (1850).

[4] State *v.* Brinkhaus, 34 Minn. 285 (1885), Mitchell, J.

[5] Smith *v.* Commonwealth, 54 Pa. 211–14 (1867), cases; 14 *id.* 226; 7 Conn. 270; 1 Bish. Cr. L. § 767.

[6] Kedrolivansky *v.* Niebaum, 70 Cal. 218 (1886).

secondarily, all movables in general. In Normandy, a chattel stood opposed to a fief or feud.[1] See further CATTLE.

Any species of property not real estate or freehold.[2]

Chattel personal. Chattels personal are, strictly, things movable: which may be annexed to or attendant on the person of the owner, and carried about with him from one part of the world to another.[3]

Such are animals, household stuff, money, jewels, grain, garments, and everything else that can be put in motion and transferred from place to place;[3] also, choses in action; and slaves were.

Chattel real. Chattels real, says Coke, are such as concern, or savor of, the realty; as, terms for years of land, estates by a statute-merchant, statute-staple, or the like.

These are called real chattels, as being interests issuing out of, or annexed to, real estate: of which they have one quality, viz., immobility, which denominates them "real;" but want the other, viz., a sufficient, legal, indeterminate duration; and this want it is that constitutes them "chattels." The utmost period for which they can last is fixed and determinate, either for a space of time certain, or till a particular sum of money be raised out of a particular income; so that they are not equal, in law, to the lowest estate of freehold,— a lease for another's life.[4]

See FIXTURE; GOODS; MORTGAGE; PROPERTY; SALE.

CHAUD-MEDLEY. See MEDLEY.

CHEAT.[5] Cheats which are punishable at common law may be described to be deceitful practices in defrauding or endeavoring to defraud another of his known rights by means of some artful device, contrary to the plain rules of common honesty.[6]

Many acts which would be denounced as cheats by the principles of morality are not legally cheats.[7]

To "cheat and defraud" does not necessarily import the commission of an indictable offense. Therefore, in charging a conspiracy to cheat and defraud, the means proposed must be set out, for the information of the court and of the defendant.[8]

A cheat or fraud, indictable at common law, must be such as would affect the public, such as common prudence cannot guard against: as, using false weights and measures (q. v.), or false tokens (q. v.), or where there is a conspiracy to cheat.[1]

Technically, the offense is "false pretenses." Spoken of one in relation to his vocation, the word is defamatory and actionable.[2]

See COVIN; DECEIT; PRETENSES; SWINDLE.

CHECK.[3] An order on a bank to pay the holder a sum of money at the bank, on presentment of the order and demand of the money.[4]

A draft or order upon a bank or banking house, purporting to be drawn upon a deposit of funds for the payment at all events of a certain sum of money to a certain person therein named, or to him or his order, or to the bearer, and payable instantly on demand.[5]

When accepted, it is an appropriation of so much money of the drawer in the hands of the drawee to the payment of an admitted liability on the part of the drawer. The drawer must have an account with the bank, and, perhaps, money on deposit.[6]

The payee of a check, before it is accepted by the drawee, cannot maintain an action upon it against the latter, as there is no privity of contract between them.[7]

A check is not an inland bill of exchange, though like it. Unlike a bill, it is drawn upon a bank or banker and against funds on deposit; acceptance of it stops denial of funds; no grace is allowed on it; it is not due until payment is demanded; the drawer is not discharged by laches in the holder in presenting it for payment, except to the extent of injury done him; and the death of the drawer rescinds authority in the bank to pay the check. In other respects checks are governed by the rules applicable to inland bills of exchange and promissory notes. When drawn outside of the State in which the bank is located, they are like foreign bills of exchange.[8]

A check is to be presented or indorsed over to another holder within such time as is reasonable, taking into view all the circumstances of the case. The holder

---

[1] [2 Bl. Com. 385–86; 19 Ill. 584; 13 Johns. *94.

[2] 2 Kent, 342.

[3] 2 Bl. Com. 387.

[4] 2 Bl. Com. 386. See Insurance Co. v. Haven, 95 U. S. 251 (1877); Hyatt v. Vincennes Nat. Bank, 113 id. 415 (1885); Putnam v. Westcott, 19 Johns. *76 (1821); 2 Kent, 342.

[5] F. escheat: from fraud used by lords of manors to procure escheats.

[6] Hawkins, Pl. Cr., b. 1, c. 23, § 1.

[7] See People v. Miller, 14 Johns. *372 (1817).

[8] Commonwealth v. Wallace, 16 Gray, 223 (1860), Dewey, J.

---

[1] Rex v. Wheatly, 2 Burr. 1127 (1760), Mansfield, C. J.; 3 Bl. Com. 165. See 7 Johns. *201; 12 id. *293; 14 id. *372.

[2] Heard, Lib. & Sl. §§ 16, 28, 46; 6 Cush. 185; 5 Wend. 263; 2 Pa. 187.

[3] Mid. E. chek, a stop: F. eschec, a "check at chessplay." Cheque is from exchequer, and erroneous,—Skeat; Webster.

[4] [Bullard v. Randall, 1 Gray, 606 (1854), Shaw, C. J.; 10 Oreg. 35.

[5] 2 Daniel, Neg. Inst. § 1566 (1879): 28 Gratt. 170.

[6] See Merchants' Nat. Bank v. State Nat. Bank, 10 Wall. 647–48 (1870), cases; Espy v. Bank of Cincinnati, 18 id. 604, 619–20 (1873); Gordon v. Müchler, 34 La. An. 604 (1882); 12 Rep. 514.

[7] First Nat. Bank of Washington v. Whitman, 94 U. S. 343–47 (1876), cases; 100 id. 689.

[8] Re Brown, 2 Story, 513 (1843); Merchants' Bank v. State Bank, Espy v. Bank, supra; Levy v. Laclede Bank, 18 F. R. 193 (1883).

can sue the drawer, if payment is refused; and the drawer, in such case, has *assumpsit* against the bank for breach of contract. The holder cannot sue the bank.[1]

Checks, regular upon their face, pass as money.[2]

A bank is not bound to take notice of memoranda and figures on the margin of a check, which a depositor places there merely for his own convenience, to preserve information for his own benefit; and in such case, the memoranda and figures are not a notice to the bank that the particular check is to be paid only from a particular fund. So, too, a mark on a deposit ticket, if intended to require a particular deposit to be kept separate from other deposits, must be in the shape of a plain direction, else such a duty will not be imposed on the bank.[3]

Certified check. A check marked "good" by the banker.

Implies that there are funds in the bank with which to pay it, that the same are set apart for its satisfaction, and that they will be so applied when the check is presented for payment.[4]

The act of certifying is equivalent to an acceptance of the check. The object is to enable the holder to use the check as money. The bank charges the check to the account of the drawer; credits it in a certified check account; and, when paid, debits that account with the amount. The bank thus becomes the debtor of the holder.[4]

Memorandum check. A check having "Memorandum" or "Mem." written across its face.

A memorandum of indebtedness given by a borrower. In the hands of a third person, for value, has the force of a check without restriction.[5]

The check takes the place of a note, as for a temporary loan. It is not designed to be presented at bank, but is for redemption at the time agreed upon.[6]

Raised check. A check increased in the amount for which it was drawn, by fraudulent alteration, *q. v.*

When money has been been paid upon a raised check by mistake, neither party being in fault, it may be recovered as paid without consideration. If neither party's negligence caused the injury the holder must bear the loss. When a person sends such paper to the bank upon which it is drawn, for information, the bank

is presumed to know the drawer's signature and the state of his account. Unless the attention of the bank officer is directed beyond these two matters, his response that the check is good will be limited to them, and will not be extended to the genuineness of the filling-in or of the check as to the payee or the amount.[1]

See BANK, 2; CASHIER; DEPOSIT, 2; DONATIO, Mortis, etc.; NEGOTIABLE; ORDER, I.

CHEESE. See OLEOMARGARINE; POLICE. 2.

CHEMISTRY. See CORONER; EXPERT; PROCESS, 2.

CHICKEN. See ANIMAL; DAMAGE-FEASANT; CRUELTY, 3; NUISANCE; TRESPASS; WORRY.

CHIEF.[2] The head: principal; leading; above, higher, or preceding another or others. Compare PRIMARY.

Chief Executive. The President of the United States. See PRESIDENT.

Chief justice. The presiding judge of a court of errors and appeals. See further JUDGE.

In chief. A shortened form of the phrase "examination in chief:" the first examination of a witness by the party who calls him; the direct examination of a witness.[3] See EXAMINATION, 9.

Tenant in chief. See FEUD.

CHILD. 1. An infant — in the popular senses. See ABANDON, 2 (2); ABORTION; CURTESY; VENTER.

2. One of tender years; a young person; a youth. See CRUELTY, 2; INFANT; SERVITUDE, 1, Involuntary.

3. A legitimate descendant in the first degree.

4. A legitimate descendant in any degree; but, in this case, "children" is the word used; offspring, issue or descendants generally.

In common parlance, "children" does not include any other than the immediate descendants in the first degree of the ancestor. But it may include others, as where it appears from a will that there are no other persons in existence who will answer the description of children except descendants of a degree remoter than the first; or, where there could not be any of the first degree at the time or in the event contemplated by the testator; or where he has shown by other words that he used the word "children" as synonymous with descendants, or issue, or to designate or

---

[1] Bank of the Republic *v.* Millard, 10 Wall. 156 (1869). See generally 26 Cent. Law J. 339–42 (1888), cases.

[2] Poorman *v.* Woodward, 21 How. 275 (1858); Downey *v.* Hicks, 14 *id.* 240 (1852).

[3] State Nat. Bank of Springfield *v.* Dodge, 124 U. S. 346 (1888). Blatchford, J.

[4] Merchants' Bank *v.* State Bank, Espy *v.* Bank, Bank *v.* Whitman, *ante;* Bank of British North America, 91 N. Y. 110 (1883).

[5] Story, Prom. Notes, § 499; 16 Pick. 535; 32 N. J. L. 96; 11 Paige, 612.

[6] See Turnbull *v.* Osborne, 12 Abb. Pr. 201–7 (1872),

---

[1] Espy *v.* Bank of Cincinnati, 18 Wall. 604, 619 (1873).

[2] F. *chef,* head, top.

[3] 1 Greenl. Ev. § 445.

include illegitimate offspring, grandchildren, or step-children. But, ordinarily, the reference is to descendants in the first degree only.[1]

The word is generally a word of purchase; but not so in the case of a grant in the present tense to a man and his children, he having no child, as in *Wild's Case.*[2]

While the word "children" will include a grandchild,[3] the presumption of law is against such construction.[4]

The word itself intends only legitimate children.[5]

Children become emancipated at twenty-one. Their duties to their parents arise out of natural justice, and compensation. At common law they are not bound to support an infirm or indigent parent; but otherwise, now, by statute. They may defend the parent's person, but may not commit crime at his command.[6]

In a contest for the possession of a child, the welfare of the child is the controlling consideration. The father will be given the custody of it, unless he is shown to be unfit or incompetent for that office, or unless the welfare of the child demands a different disposition.[7]

See further ADOPT, 3; AGE; AGENT; BASTARD; DESCENDANT; DIE, Without, etc.; FAMILY; HEIR; INFANT; ISSUE, 5; NAME, 1; NEGLIGENCE; ORPHAN; PARENT; PATER, Partus, etc.; PERPETUITY; RAISE; SHELLEY's CASE; WITNESS.

CHINA, DECORATED. See PAINTING.

CHINESE. See BURIAL; CITIZEN; COMMERCE: LAUNDRIES; POLICY, 2; QUARANTINE, 2; RIGHT, Civil Rights Act; TREATY; WHITE.

The **Burlingame treaty of July 28, 1868,** declares, Art. 6, that "Chinese subjects visiting or residing in the United States, shall enjoy the same privileges, immunities, and exemptions in respect to travel and residence, as may be enjoyed by the citizens or subjects of the most favored nation," and, reciprocally, as to citizens of the United States in China.

Appeals from the Pacific coast induced the Government to request a modification of the treaty. This resulted in the **supplemental treaty of November 17, 1880,** the first article of which provides that "whenever in the opinion of the government of the

United States, the coming of Chinese laborers to the United States, or their residence therein, affects or threatens to affect the interests of that country, or to endanger the good order of the said country or of any locality within the territory thereof, the government of China agrees that the government of the United States may regulate, limit or suspend such coming or residence, but may not absolutely prohibit it. The limitation or suspension may be reasonable and shall apply only to Chinese who may go to the United States as laborers . . and immigrants shall not be subject to personal maltreatment or abuse; " and the second article of which provides that " Chinese subjects, whether proceeding to the United States as teachers, students, merchants, or from curiosity, together with their body and household servants, and Chinese laborers who are now in the United States, shall be allowed to go and come of their own free will and accord, and shall be accorded all the rights, privileges, immunities, and exemptions which are accorded to the citizens and subjects of the most favored nation." [1]

The **act of May 6, 1882,** c. 126 (22 St. L. 58), entitled " An act to execute certain stipulations relating to Chinese," as amended by the act of **July 5, 1884,** c. 220 (23 St. L. 115) — the words in italics being introduced by the act of 1884, while those in brackets were in the act of 1882, but were stricken out by the amendatory act — provides as follows:

Whereas, in the opinion of the government of the United States, the coming of Chinese laborers to this country endangers the good order of certain localities within the territory thereof, therefore be enacted,—

Section 1. That from and after the [expiration of ninety days next after the] passage of this act, and until the expiration of ten years, the coming of Chinese laborers to the United States be, and the same is hereby, suspended; and during such suspension it shall not be lawful for any Chinese laborer to come *from any foreign port or place,* or, having so come, [after the expiration of said ninety days,] to remain within the United States.

Sec. 2. The master of any vessel who shall knowingly bring within the United States on such vessel and land, *or attempt to land,* or permit to be landed, any Chinese laborer, from any foreign place, shall be deemed guilty of a misdemeanor, and, on conviction thereof, shall be punished by a fine of not more than five hundred dollars for each and every laborer so brought, and may *also* be imprisoned for a term not exceeding one year.

Sec. 3. The foregoing sections shall not apply to Chinese laborers who were in the United States on the 17th of November, 1880, or who shall have come into the same before the expiration of ninety days next after the passage of *the act to which* this act *is amendatory, nor shall said sections apply to laborers,* [and] who shall produce to such master before going on board such vessel, and to the collector of the port at which such vessel shall arrive, the evidence hereinafter required of his being one of the laborers in this section mentioned; nor shall the foregoing sections

[1] See Mowatt *v.* Carow, 7 Paige, 339 (1838), Walworth, Ch.; Palmer *v.* Horn, 84 N. Y. 520–21 (1881): Ingraham *v.* Meade, 3 Wall. Jr. 42 (1855); Rogers *v.* Weller, 5 Biss. 168 (1870); Feit *v.* Vanatta, 21 N. J. E. 84 (1870); Winsor *v.* Odd Fellows' Association, 13 R. I. 150 (1880); Butler *v.* Ralston, 69 Ga. 489 (1882); Bates *v.* Dewson, 128 Mass. 334 (1880).

[2] 3 Coke, *17 (1599); Cannon *v.* Barry, 59 Miss. 289, 300 (1881), cases; Bannister *v.* Bull, 16 S. C. 227 (1881).

[3] *Re* Paton, 41 Hun, 500 (1886); *Re* Brown, 29 *id.* 417 (1883), cases.

[4] Pugh *v.* Pugh, 105 Ind. 555 (1885); 94 *id.* 407, cases; Smith *v.* Smith, 24 S. C. 214 (1885).

[5] Minot *v.* Harris, 132 Mass. 531 (1882).

[6] See 1 Bl. Com. 453; 4 *id.* 28; 4 Kent, 345: People *v.* Turner, 55 Ill. 283–86 (1870).

[7] *Re* Scarritt, 76 Mo. 565, 584 (1882), cases.

[1] See Treaty of 1868, 16 St. L. 739; Treaty of 1880, 22 St. L. 826; Heong *v.* United States, 112 U. S. 536, 542 (1884); Act 1884, *ib.* 543; 124 *id.* 627.

apply to the case of any master whose vessel, being bound to a port not within the United States, shall come within the jurisdiction of the United States by reason of being in distress or in stress of weather, or touching at a port on its voyage to any foreign port or place: provided that all laborers brought on such vessel shall *not be permitted to land except in case of absolute necessity, and must* depart with the vessel on leaving port.

Sec. 4. For the purpose of properly identifying Chinese laborers who were in the United States on the 17th of November, 1880, or who shall have come into the same before the expiration of ninety days next after the passage of *the act to which* this act *is amendatory,* and in order to furnish them with the proper evidence of their right to go from and come to the United States, [of their free will and accord,] as provided by the *said act and the* treaty between the United States and China dated November 17, 1880, the collector of customs of the district from which any such laborer shall depart from the United States shall, in person or by deputy, go on board each vessel having on board any such laborer, and cleared or about to sail from his district for a foreign port, and on such vessel make a list of all such laborers, which shall be entered in registry books kept for that purpose, in which shall be stated the *individual, family, and tribal* name *in full, the* age, occupation, *when and where followed,* last place of residence, physical marks or peculiarities, and all facts necessary for the identification of each of such laborers, which books shall be safely kept in the custom-house; and every such laborer so departing from the United States shall be entitled to, and shall receive, free of any charge or cost, upon application therefor, from the collector, or his deputy *in the name of said collector, and attested by said collector's seal of office,* at the time such list is taken, a certificate, signed by the collector or his deputy, and attested by his seal of office, in such form as the secretary of the treasury shall prescribe, which certificate shall contain a statement of the *individual, family, and tribal* name *in full,* age, occupation, *when and where followed,* [last place of residence, personal description, and facts of identification,] of the laborer to whom the certificate is issued, corresponding with the said list and registry in all particulars. In case any laborer, after having received such certificate, shall leave such vessel before her departure, he shall deliver his certificate to the master of the vessel, and, if such laborer shall fail to return to such vessel before her departure from port, the certificate shall be delivered by the master to the collector of customs for cancellation. The certificate herein provided for shall entitle the laborer to whom the same is issued to return to and re-enter the United States upon producing and delivering the same to the collector of customs of the district at which such laborer shall seek to re-enter; *and said certificate shall be the only evidence permissible to establish his right of re-entry;* and upon [delivery] *delivering* of such certificate by such laborer to the collector of customs at the time of re-entry, said collector shall cause the same to be filed in the custom-house and duly canceled.

Sec. 5. Any Chinese laborer mentioned in section four being in and desiring to depart from the United States by land, shall have the right to demand and receive, free of charge or cost, a certificate of identification similar to that provided for in section four to be issued to such laborers as may desire to leave the United States by water; and it is hereby made the duty of the collector of customs of the district next adjoining the foreign country to which said laborer desires to go to issue such certificate, free of charge or cost, upon application by such laborer, and to enter the same upon registry books kept as provided for in section four.

Sec. 6. In order to the faithful execution of [articles one and two of the treaty in] *the provisions of* this act, [before mentioned,] every Chinese person other than a laborer, who may be entitled by said treaty [and] *or* this act to come within the United States, and who shall be about to come to the United States, shall *obtain the permission of and* be identified as so entitled by the Chinese government, or *of such other foreign government of which at the time such person shall be a subject,* in each case, [such identity] to be evidenced by a certificate issued [under the authority of said] *by such* government, which certificate shall be in the English language, [or, if not, accompanied by a translation into English, stating such right to come,] *and shall show such permission, with the name of the permitted person in his or her proper signature,* and which certificate shall state the *individual, family, and tribal* name *in full,* title or official rank, if any, the age, height, and all physical peculiarities, former and present occupation or profession, *when and where and how long pursued,* and place of residence [in China] of the person to whom the certificate is issued, and that such person is entitled [conformably to the treaty in] *by* this act [mentioned] to come within the United States. *If the person so applying for a certificate shall be a merchant, said certificate shall, in addition to above requirements, state the nature, character, and estimated value of the business carried on by him prior to and at the time of his application as aforesaid; Provided, That nothing in this act, nor in said treaty, shall be construed as embracing within the meaning of the word " merchant " hucksters, peddlers, or those engaged in taking, drying, or otherwise preserving shell or other fish for home consumption or exportation. If the certificate be sought for the purpose of travel for curiosity, it shall also state whether the applicant intends to pass through or travel within the United States, together with his financial standing in the country from which such certificate is desired. The certificate provided for in this act, and the identity of the person named therein, shall, before such person goes on board any vessel to proceed to the United States, be viséd by the indorsement of the diplomatic representative of the United States in the foreign country from which said certificate issues, or of the consular representative of the United States at the place from which the person is about to depart; and such representative whose indorsement is so required is hereby empowered, and it shall be his duty, before indorsing such certificate, to examine into the truth of the statements set forth in said certificate, and, if he shall find that any of the statements therein contained are untrue, it shall be his duty to refuse to indorse the same. Such certificate, viséd as aforesaid,* shall be prima facie evidence of the fact set forth therein, and shall be produced to the collector of customs [or his deputy] of the port at which the person shall arrive, *and afterward produced to the proper authorities of the United States whenever lawfully demanded, and shall be the sole evidence permissible on the part of the person producing the same to establish a right of entry; but said certificate may be controverted, and the facts therein stated disproved, by the United States authorities.*

Sec. 7. Any person who shall knowingly and falsely alter or substitute any name for the name written in such certificate, or forge any such certificate, or knowingly utter any forged or fraudulent certificate, or falsely personate any person named in any such certificate, shall be deemed guilty of a misdemeanor; and, upon conviction thereof, shall be fined in a sum not exceeding one thousand dollars, and imprisoned in a penitentiary for a term of not more than five years.

Sec. 8. The master of any vessel arriving from any foreign place shall, at the same time he delivers a manifest of the cargo, and, if there be no cargo, then at the time of making a report of the entry of the vessel pursuant to law, in addition to the other matter required to be reported, and before landing, or permitting to land, any Chinese passengers, deliver and report to the collector of customs of the district in which such vessels shall have arrived a separate list of all Chinese passengers taken on board his vessel at any foreign place, and all such passengers on board the vessel at that time. Such list shall show the names of such passengers, (and if accredited officers of the Chinese *or of any other foreign* government traveling on the business of that government, or their servants, with a note of such facts,) and the names and other particulars, as shown by their respective certificates; and such list shall be sworn to by the master in the manner required by law in relation to the manifest of the cargo. Any [willful] refusal or *willful* neglect of any such master to comply with the provisions of this section shall incur the same penalties and forfeiture as are provided for a refusal or neglect to report and deliver a manifest of cargo.

Sec. 9. Before any Chinese passengers are landed from any such vessel, the collector or his deputy shall proceed to examine such passengers, comparing the certificates with the list, and with the passengers; and no passengers shall be allowed to land from such vessel in violation of law.

Sec. 10. Every vessel whose master shall knowingly violate any provision of this act shall be deemed forfeited to the United States, and shall be liable to seizure and condemnation in any district into which such vessel may enter, or in which she may be found.

Sec. 11. Any person who shall knowingly bring into, or cause to be brought into, the United States by land, or who shall [knowingly] aid or abet the same, or aid or abet the landing from any vessel of any Chinese person not lawfully entitled to enter, shall be deemed guilty of a misdemeanor, and shall, on conviction, be fined in a sum not exceeding one thousand dollars, and imprisoned for a term not exceeding one year.

Sec. 12. No Chinese person shall be permitted to

(12)

enter by land without producing to the proper officer of customs the certificate required of persons seeking to land from a vessel. And any person found unlawfully here shall be caused to be removed to the country whence he came, [by direction of the President,] and at the cost of the United States, after being brought before some justice, judge, or commissioner of a United States court, and found to be one not lawfully entitled to remain; *and in all such cases the person who brought, or aided in bringing, such person to the United States, shall be liable to the United States for all necessary expenses incurred in such investigation and removal; and all peace officers of the several States and Territories are hereby invested with the same authority as a marshal or United States marshal in reference to carrying out the provisions of this act, or the act of which this is amendatory, as a marshal or deputy marshal of the United States, and shall be entitled to like compensation, to be paid by the same officers. And the United States shall pay all charges for the maintenance and return of any person having the certificate prescribed by law as entitling such person to come into the United States, who may not have been permitted to land by reason of any provision of this act.*

Sec. 13. This act shall not apply to diplomatic and other officers of the Chinese *or other* governments traveling upon the business of that government, whose credentials shall be taken as equivalent to the certificate in this act mentioned, and shall exempt them and their body and household servants from the provisions of this act as to other Chinese persons.

Sec. 14. Hereafter no court shall admit Chinese to citizenship; and all laws in conflict with this act are hereby repealed.

Sec. 15. *The provisions of this act shall apply to all subjects of China and Chinese, whether subjects of China or any other foreign power; and* the words "Chinese laborers" shall be construed to mean both skilled and unskilled laborers and Chinese employed in mining.

Sec. 16. *Any violation of any provision of this act, or of the act of which this is amendatory, the punishment of which is not otherwise herein provided for, shall be deemed a misdemeanor, punishable by fine not exceeding one thousand dollars, or by imprisonment for not more than one year, or both fine and imprisonment.*

Sec. 17. *Nothing contained in this act shall be construed to affect any proceeding, criminal or civil, begun under the act of which this is amendatory; but such proceeding shall proceed as if this act had not been passed.*

The convention between the United States and China for excluding Chinese laborers from coming to the United States, signed at Washington March 12, 1888, was as follows: (See ADDENDA.)

"Whereas, on the 17th day of November, A. D. 1880, a treaty was concluded between the United States and China for the purpose of regulating, limiting, or suspending the coming of Chinese laborers to, and their residence in, the United States;

"And whereas the government of China, in view of the antagonism and much deprecated and serious disorders to which the presence of Chinese laborers has given rise in certain parts of the United States, desires to prohibit the emigration of such laborers from China to the United States;

" And whereas the government of the United States and the government of China desire to coöperate in prohibiting such emigration, and to strengthen in other ways the bonds of friendship between the two countries; "

Now, therefore, the President of the United States has appointed Thomas F. Bayard, secretary of state, as his plenipotentiary; and the Emperor of China has appointed Chang Yen Hoon, minister of the third rank of the Imperial Court, etc., as his plenipotentiary; and the said plenipotentiaries have agreed upon the following articles:

ARTICLE I.

"The high contracting parties agree that for a period of twenty years, beginning with the date of the exchange of the ratifications of this convention, the coming, except under the conditions hereinafter specified, of Chinese laborers to the United States shall be absolutely prohibited; and this prohibition shall extend to the return of Chinese laborers who are not now in the United States, whether holding return certificates under existing laws or not.

ARTICLE II.

"The preceding article shall not apply to the return to the United States of any Chinese laborer who has a lawful wife, child, or parent in the United States, or property therein of the value of one thousand dollars, or debts of like amount due him and pending settlement. Nevertheless, every such Chinese laborer shall, before leaving the United States, deposit, as a condition of his return, with the collector of customs of the district from which he departs, a full description in writing of his family, or property, or debts, as aforesaid, and shall be furnished by said collector with such certificate of his right to return under this treaty as the laws of the United States may now or hereafter prescribe and not inconsistent with the provisions of this treaty; and should the written description aforesaid be proved to be false, the right of return thereunder, or of continued residence after return, shall in each case be forfeited. And such right of return to the United States shall be exercised within one year from the date of leaving the United States; but such right of return to the United States may be extended for an additional period, not to exceed one year, in cases where by reason of sickness or other cause of disability beyond his control, such Chinese laborer shall be rendered unable sooner to return — which facts shall be fully reported to the Chinese consul at the port of departure, and by him certified, to the satisfaction of the collector of the port at which such Chinese subject shall land in the United States. And no such Chinese laborer shall be permitted to enter the United States by land or sea without producing to the proper officer of the customs the return certificate herein required.

ARTICLE III.

" The provisions of this convention shall not affect the right at present enjoyed by Chinese subjects, being officials, teachers, students, merchants, or travelers for curiosity or pleasure, but not laborers, coming to the United States and residing therein. To entitle such Chinese subjects as are above described, to admission into the United States they may produce a certificate from their government or the government where they last resided, viséd by the diplomatic or consular representative of the United States in the country or port whence they depart.

" It is also agreed that Chinese laborers shall continue to enjoy the privilege of transit across the territory of the United States in the course of their journey to or from other countries, subject to such regulations by the government of the United States as may be necessary to prevent said privilege of transit from being abused.

ARTICLE IV.

"In pursuance of Article III of the Immigration Treaty between the United States and China, signed at Pekin on the 17th day of November, 1880, it is hereby understood and agreed that Chinese, laborers, or Chinese of any other class, either permanently or temporarily residing in the United States, shall have for the protection of their persons and property all rights that are given by the laws of the United States to citizens of the most favored nation, excepting the right to become naturalized citizens. And the government of the United States re-affirms its obligation, as stated in said Article III, to exert all its power to secure protection to the persons and property of all Chinese subjects in the United States.

ARTICLE V.

" Whereas, Chinese subjects, being in remote and unsettled regions of the United States, have been the victims of injuries in their persons and property at the hands of wicked and lawless men, which unexpected events the Chinese government regrets, and for which it has claimed an indemnity the legal obligation of which the government of the United States denies; and whereas the government of the United States, humanely, considering these injuries and bearing in mind the firm and ancient friendship between the United States and China, which the high contracting parties wish to cement, is desirous of alleviating the exceptional and deplorable sufferings and losses to which the aforesaid Chinese have been subjected; therefore, the United States, without reference to the question of liability therefor (which as a legal obligation it denies), agrees to pay on or before the first day of March, 1889, the sum of two hundred and seventy-six thousand six hundred and nineteen dollars and seventy-five cents ($276,619.75) to the Chinese minister at this capital, who shall accept the same, on behalf of his government, as full indemnity for all losses and injuries sustained by Chinese subjects as aforesaid, and shall distribute the said money among the said sufferers and their relatives.

ARTICLE VI.

" This convention shall remain in force for a period of twenty years, beginning with the date of the exchange of ratifications; and if, six months before the expiration of the said period of twenty years, neither government shall formally have given notice of its termination to the other, it shall remain in full force for another like period of twenty years."

The act of 1882 was framed in supposed conformity with the provisions of the supplemental treaty of 1880.[1] See REPEAL.

General or ambiguous expressions in the act are to be construed so as to make them conform to the treaty. . "Chinese laborers" means those who come here with the intention to labor and enter into competition with the labor of the country.[2]

"Laborer" is used in its popular sense, and does not include any persons but those whose occupation involves physical toil, and who work for wages, or with a view of disposing of the product or result of their labor to others.[3]

A Mongolian was not entitled to become a citizen under the Revised Statutes as amended in 1875. He is not a "white person" within the meaning of those words as used in the naturalization laws.[4] See express prohibition, sec. 14, act of July, 1884, ante.

A Chinaman who left this country between May 6, 1882, and July 5, 1884, and returned after the latter date, is entitled to land upon complying with the requirements of the act of 1882; such provisions of the act of 1884 as relate to evidence of identity not being retroactive.

A person who, while abroad, has lost by theft a certificate issued under § 4 of the act of 1882, may land on his return to the port whence he sailed (no one having meanwhile presented the certificate) on proving these facts, and identifying himself as the person to whom the certificate was issued.

A district court may, under R. S. § 753, issue a *habeas corpus* where a Chinaman is prevented from landing by the master of a vessel, by direction of the customs authorities, under the provisions of the foregoing acts; there being nothing in those acts, or in the treaty, making the decision of the customs officers final, or ousting the courts of jurisdiction.[5]

CHOLERA. See QUARANTINE, 2.

CHOOSE. See ELECT.

CHOSE.[6] A thing recoverable by an action at law: a thing, personalty.

Chose in action. A thing of which one has the right, but not the possession.[7] **Chose in possession.** Personalty in possession, in actual enjoyment.

Property in chattels personal may be either "in possession," — where a man has not only the right to enjoy, but has the actual enjoyment of, the thing; or else it is "in action," — where he has only a bare right, without any occupation or enjoyment. In the latter case the possession may be recovered by a suit or action at law: whence the thing so recoverable is called a thing or "chose in action " — as, money due on a bond, or recompense for breach of a contract.[1]

The general definition of "chose in action" is, a right not reduced into possession. A note, bond, or other promise not negotiable, is denominated a chose in action, before the promisor or obligor is liable to an action on it, as well as after. A note for money, payable on time, is a chose in action as soon as made.[2]

The term "chose in action" is one of comprehensive import. It includes the infinite variety of contracts, covenants, and promises which confer on one party the right to recover a personal chattel or a sum of money from another by action. A debt secured by a bond and mortgage is an example.[3]

In its enlarged sense, a chose in action may be considered as any right to damages, whether arising from the commission of a tort, the omission of a duty, or the breach of a contract.[4]

At common law a chose in action was not assignable. To make over a right of going to law was encouraging, it was thought, litigiousness. But in equity, at an early day, an assignment was viewed as a declaration of trust, and an agreement to permit the assignee to use the name of the assignor, for purposes of recovery — the transferee being rather an attorney in fact than an assignee.[5]

Bills of exchange, by the law-merchant, and promissory notes, by statute of 3 and 4 Anne (1705), c. 9, were made exceptions to the common-law rule; and so were bills of lading, by statute of 18 and 19 Vict. (1855), c. 111. By the Judicature Act of 1873 choses are assignable in all cases.

The assignee, except in the case of negotiable instruments, although without notice, takes the chose subject to all equities existing between the debtor and the assignor.[6]

The assignee cannot proceed in equity to enforce, for his own use, the legal right of his assignor, merely upon the ground that he cannot maintain an action at law in his own name. So held where the owner of letters-patent assigned them, with claims for damages

---

[1] *Re Low Yam Chow*, 7 Saw. 548-50 (Sept., 1882).

[2] *Re Moncan*, 8 Saw. 350-56 (Oct., 1882): s. c. 14 F. R. 44.

[3] *Re Ho King*, 8 Saw. 438 (1883). See also 13 F. R. 286, 291; 17 *id.* 634; 18 *id.* 28; 19 *id.* 184, 490; 22 *id.* 519; 23 *id.* 329, 441.

[4] R. S. § 2169; *Re Ah Yup*, 5 Saw. 155 (1878); 2 Kent, 72.

[5] United States v. Jung Ah Lung, 124 U. S. 621 (Feb. 13, 1888), affirming 25 F. R. 141. Opinion by Blatchford, J.; Harlan, Field, and Lamar, JJ., dissenting as to identification without the certificate:

[6] Shöse. F. from L. *causa*, action, suit at law.

[7] 4 Bl. Com. 135.

---

[1] 2 Bl. Com. 388, 396, 442.

[2] Haskell v. Blair, 3 Cush. 535 (1849), Metcalf, J.

[3] Sheldon v. Sill, 8 How. 449 (1850), Grier, J.; 37 Alb. Law J. 44-46 (1888), cases.

[4] Magee v. Toland, 8 Port. 40 (Ala., 1839). See also 4 Ala. 351; 72 Ga. 51; 34 La. An. 608; 5 Mas. 82; 4 Denio, 82; 14 S. C. 538; 43 Wis. 32.

[5] 2 Bl. Com. 442; 4 *id.* 135; 1 Pars. Contr. 227.

[6] Hill v. Wanzer, 17 How. 367-68 (1854), cases; 20 Blatch. 277.

for infringement, and the assignee filed a bill to recover the damages. In such case the assignee must bring an action at law, in the name of the assignor, to his own use.[1]

See ASSIGN, 2; ATTACH, 2; CHAMPERTY; DONATIO; HUSBAND.

CHRISTIAN. One who believes or assents to the doctrines of Christianity, as taught by Jesus Christ in the New Testament, or who, being born of Christian parents or in a Christian country, does not profess any other religion, or does not belong to any one of the other religious divisions of man.[2] See NAME, 1.

Christianity. The system of doctrines and precepts taught by Christ; the religion founded by Christ.

Christianity is said to be part of the common law. "Christianity is parcel of the laws of England; and, therefore, to reproach the Christian religion is to speak in subversion of the law."[3]

" The essential principles of natural religion " and " of revealed religion are a part of the common law, so that any person reviling or subverting or ridiculing them may be prosecuted at common law."[4]

"The true sense of the maxim is that the law will not permit the essential principles of revealed religion to be ridiculed and reviled."[5]

Christianity is a part of the common law of Pennsylvania in the qualified sense that its divine origin and truth are admitted, and therefore it is not to be maliciously and openly reviled and blasphemed against, to the annoyance of believers or the injury of the public.[6] Not Christianity founded upon any particular religious tenets; but Christianity with liberty of conscience to all men.[7]

The maxim does not mean that Christianity is an established religion; nor that its precepts, by force of their own authority, form part of our system of municipal law; nor that the courts may base their judgments upon the Bible; nor that religious duties may be penally enforced; nor that legal discrimination in favor of Christianity is allowed.[8]

The best features of the common law, especially those which regard the family and social relations, if not derived from, have at least been improved and strengthened by, the prevailing religion and the teachings of its sacred Book. But the law does not attempt to enforce the precepts of Christianity on the ground of their sacred character or divine origin. Some of those precepts, though we may admit their continual and universal obligation, we must nevertheless recognize as being incapable of enforcement by human laws. Those precepts, moreover, affect the heart, and address themselves to the conscience; while the laws of the state can regard the outward conduct only: for which reasons Christianity is not a part of the law of the land in any sense which entitles the courts to take notice of and base their judgments upon it, except so far they can find that its precepts and principles have been incorporated in and made a component part of the law of the State.[1]

The maxim can have no reference to the law of the National government, since the sources of that law are the Constitution, treaties, and acts of Congress.[2]

See further LAW, Common; BLASPHEMY; HOLIDAY; POLICY, 2; RELIGION; SUNDAY.

CHROMO. See COPYRIGHT; PRINT.

CHURCH. A temple or building consecrated to the honor of God and religion; or, an assembly of persons, united by the profession of the same Christian faith, met together for all religious worship.[3]

Among those whose polity is congregational or independent, a body of persons associated together for the purpose of maintaining Christian worship and ordinances.[4]

A " religious society " may be a body of persons associated for worship, omitting the sacraments.[4]

" Church " and " society " popularly denote the same thing: a religious body organized to sustain public worship.[5]

A school-house in which religious services are held on Sunday is not a " church."[6]

The right to organize voluntary religious associations to assist in the expression and dissemination of any religious doctrine, and to create tribunals for the

[1] N. Y. Guaranty Co. v. Memphis Water Co., 107 U. S. 214 (1882), cases. See R. S. § 723.

[2] [Hale v. Everett, 53 N. H. 50 (1868), Sargent, J. On the "Arrest and Trial of Jesus," see 36 Alb. Law J. 334–88 (1887); Greenleaf, Test. Evangelists, &c.

[3] Taylor's Case, Ventris, 293 (1676), Hale, C. J. See Rex v. Woolston, 2 Strange, 834 (1729); 4 Bl. Com. 59; 2 Steph. Hist. Cr. L. Eng. 438.

[4] Case of Evans, 2 Burn. Ec. L. 185 (1780), Mansfield, C. J.

[5] Lives of Chief Justices, vol. 3, p. 417, Ld. Campbell.

[6] Vidal v. Girard's Executors, 2 How. 198 (1844), Story, J.

[7] Updegraph v. Commonwealth, 11 S. & R. 399 (1824).

[8] See 13 Alb. Law J. 366 (1876); 21 Am. Law Reg. 201, 329, 537 (1873); People v. Ruggles, 8 Johns. *294 (1811), Kent, C. J.; Chapman v. Gillett, 2 Conn. 43 (1816); Updegraph v. Commonwealth, 11 S. & R. 399–401 (1824);

State v. Chandler, 2 Harr., Del., 562 (1837); Shover v. State, 10 Ark. 263 (1850); Bloom v. Richards, 2 Ohio, 390 (1853); Lindenmuller v. People, 33 Barb. 560–68 (1861); Sparhawk v. Union Passenger Ry. Co., 54 Pa. 432 (1867); Hale v. Everett, 53 N. H. 204 (1868); Board of Education v. Minor, 23 Ohio St. 246–54 (1872); 20 Alb. Law J. 265, 285 (1879).

[1] Cooley, Const. Lim. 472, cases.

[2] See Wheaton v. Peters, 8 Pet. 591 (1834); Pennsylvania v. Wheeling, &c. Bridge Co., 13 How. 519 (1851).

[3] Robertson v. Bullions, 9 Barb. 95 (1850).

[4] [Silsby v. Barlow, 16 Gray, 330 (1860); Anderson v. Brock, 3 Me. *247 (1825).

[5] Society v. Hatch, 48 N. H. 396 (1869).

[6] State v. Midgett, 85 N. C. 538 (1881). See also 9 Cranch, 326; 16 Conn. 291; 3 Harr., Del., 257; 88 Ind. 131; 16 Mass. 498; 3 Paige, Ch. 301; 3 Tex. 288.

decision of controverted questions of faith within the association, and for the ecclesiastical government of all individual members, congregations, and officers within the general association, is unquestioned. All who unite themselves to such a body do so with an implied assent to this government, and are bound to submit to it. . . Each member is bound by the law of the society,—the written organic law, books of discipline, collections of precedents, usages and customs. The civil courts have only to do with the rights of property: they cannot revise an act of discipline, excommunication, etc., though they may inquire whether such act was the act of the church or of persons who did not constitute the church.

Where property is in dispute, the civil court inquires:

(1) Was the property or fund devoted, by the express terms of the gift, grant, or sale by which it was acquired, to the support of a specific doctrine or belief, or was it acquired for the general use of the society for religious purposes, with no other limitation? If so, when necessary to protect a trust, the court will inquire into the faith or practice of the parties claiming the use or control of the property, and see that it is not diverted from the trust.

(2) Is the society of the strictly independent form of government, owing no submission to any organization outside of the congregation? If so, the rights of conflicting claimants are determined by the ordinary rules which govern voluntary associations—the will of the majority, the decision of chosen officers, or otherwise. Those who adhere to the acknowledged organism by which the body is governed are entitled to the use of the property. No inquiry is made into the opinions of those who comprise the legal or regular organization.

(3) Is the society one of a number united to form a more general body of churches, with ecclesiastical control in the general association over the individual members and societies? The tribunals of such association decide all questions of faith, discipline, rule, custom, or government. When a right of property depends on one of those questions, and that has been decided by the highest tribunal within the organization to which it has been carried, the civil courts accept that decision as final. The local society is but a member of a larger organization, under its control and bound by its judgments.[1]

Church and state. See RELIGION.

See also ASSEMBLY, Civil; BANNS; CANON, Law; CHRISTIANITY; CONGREGATION; PARISH, 1; PEW; SANCTUARY, 1; SCHISM; SUBSCRIBE, 2; WORSHIP.

---

[1] Watson v. Jones, 13 Wall. 713, 722-31 (1871), cases, Miller, J. The litigation grew out of dissension, due primarily to differences of opinion upon the subject of slavery, among the members of the Third or Walnut Street Presbyterian Church, of Louisville, Ky. See also Bouldin v. Alexander, 15 id. 131, 140 (1872); Same v. Same, 103 U. S. 330 (1880); Hennessey v. Walsh, 55 N. H. 515, 526 (1875); Stack v. O'Hara, 98 Pa. 232 (1881); Graff v. Greer, 88 Ind. 13:-32 (1882), cases; Hadley v. Mendenhall, 89 id. 186, 152-56 (1883), cases; Whitecar v. Michenor, 37 N. J. E. 6 (1883), cases; State v. Rector, 45 N. J. L. 230 (1883); 12 Am. Law Reg. 201, 329, 537 (1873), cases; 15 id. 276-82 (1876), cases; Relations of Civil Law to Church Polity, etc. (1875), Hon. William Strong.

CIDER. See LIQUOR.

CIRCUIT. A division of country visited by a judge for the dispensing of justice, as for the trial of causes; also, the periodical journey itself.

The judges of assize and of *nisi prius* are twice a year sent around the kingdom to try, by a jury of the respective counties, the truth of such matters of fact as are then under dispute in the courts at Westminster Hall. Formerly, the itinerant justices made their circuits once in seven years; but Magna Charta directed that they be sent into every county once a year. They usually went in the vacations, after Hilary and Trinity terms.[1]

The custom is retained in a few of the States.

Circuit court. See COURT, Circuit.

CIRCUITY. A round-about course: indirect action, or procedure.

Circuity of action. An indirect or round-about mode of suing: where a party by an indirect proceeding makes two or more actions necessary, when justice could be obtained by a single action involving a more direct course.

To prevent circuity of action, a court of equity often entertains jurisdiction upon this ground alone; and to avoid it, cross-demands and judgments are set off against each other.

Circuitus est evitandus. Circuity is to be avoided.[2]

CIRCULAR. 1, *adj.* Going around or about, from beginning to end: as, circular mileage, *q. v.*

2. *n.* In the post-office laws, a printed letter, which, according to internal evidence, is being sent in identical terms to several persons.

The date, names of sender and addressee, and typographical corrections, may be written on such circular.[3]

A circular is a paper intended to be issued to a great number of persons, or for general circulation. In the form of a letter, may be described in an indictment, as, a "letter and circular."[4] See MAIL, 2; POST-OFFICE.

CIRCULATION. Whatever passes from person to person, as, money, currency; also, the fact and the extent of a thing's being circulated.

Certificates of indebtedness issued by a person or a corporation are not taxable as "circulation," under Rev. St., § 3408, unless calculated or intended to circulate or to be used as money.[5]

---

[1] 3 Bl. Com. 57-58; 4 id. 422, 424; 1 Steph. Hist. Cr. L. Eng. 100.

[2] 18 Ct. Cl. 457; 15 M. & W. 208.

[3] Act 3 March, 1879; 20 St. L. 300, 1 Sup. R. S. 456.

[4] United States v. Noelke, 17 Blatch. 557 (1880); Commerford v. Thompson, 2 Flip. 615 (1880).

[5] United States v. Wilson, 106 U. S. 620 (1882). See

The act of February 8, 1875, c. 35, sec. 19 (18 St. L. 311), provides "that every person, firm, association other than national banking associations, and every corporation, State bank, or State banking association, shall pay a tax of ten per centum on the amount of their own notes used for circulation and paid out by them." This act is to be construed in connection with the internal revenue law; is designed to provide a currency for the country, and to restrain the circulation of notes not issued by authority of Congress. An order by A in favor of B, or bearer, upon C for "five dollars in merchandise at retail," paid out by A and used as circulation, is not a note within the meaning of the act. Only such notes as are in law negotiable, so as to carry title in their general circulation from hand to hand, are the subjects of taxation under the act.[1]

A certificate by a national bank that a person named has deposited in it a certain sum, payable to the order of himself on return of the certificate properly indorsed, and understood not to be payable until a day agreed upon, is not forbidden.[2] See Bank, 2 (2); Tax, 2.

CIRCUMSTANCES. 1. Surroundings: the particulars which accompany an act or fact; *res gestæ, q. v.*

Reference to "surrounding circumstances" is made to ascertain the precise nature of a subject-matter or to explain terms used.

Circumstantial. Consisting in or pertaining to attendant circumstances or facts; afforded by what naturally accompanies: as, circumstantial evidence, *q. v.* See Case, 1.

"Circumstance" and "fact" are often interchanged. When a conviction depends upon circumstantial evidence, it often happens that one or more of the ultimate or essential matters may appropriately be called a "circumstance," to be established beyond a reasonable doubt.[3]

2. A person's qualifications, status or condition, material, moral, and perhaps mental.

In a law providing that letters testamentary shall not be granted, unless a bond be filed, to a person whose "circumstances do not afford adequate security" for the due administration of the estate, the reference is not exclusively to pecuniary responsibility. Thrift, integrity, good repute, and stability of character are "circumstances."[4] See Pecuniary.

"In failing circumstances," applied to a bank, means, in Missouri, a state of uncertainty whether the bank will be able to sustain itself, depending on favorable or unfavorable contingencies, which in the course of business may occur, and over which its officers have no control.[5]

Poverty is not such "extraordinary circumstance" as will defeat the rule of diligence in civil procedure in the Federal courts.[1]

CIRCUS. See Theater.

CITE. To call, command, summon.

1. To notify a party of a proceeding against him.

2. To refer to or quote in support of a proposition; as, to cite a case or authority.

Citation. 1. Originally, a process to call a party before an ecclesiastical court.[2]

2. Official notice to appear and answer in a proceeding.

In this sense, used in the practice of courts of probate, surrogates' and orphans' courts; and in practice upon writs of error, as, writs from the Supreme Court.

A notice to the opposite party that a thing is about to be done, as, that a record is about to be transferred to another court, where he may appear, or decline to appear, as his judgment or inclination may direct.[3]

"Citation" and "notice" are not synonymous. A citation must be directed to some officer and be served by him; and, if issued by a court having a seal, must be under the seal of such court. It must contain the names of the persons upon whom service is to be had, unless in the case of unknown heirs who are served by publication. A notice is much less formal: it is not necessarily under seal, although issued by a court of record, and it may be served by a person not an officer.[4]

3. The act of quoting an authority; also, the authority itself. Compare Precedent, 2.

CITIZEN. In the Roman government, seems to have designated a person who had the freedom of the city, and the right to exercise all political and civil privileges of the government. There was also, at Rome, a partial citizenship, including civil but not political rights. Complete citizenship embraced both.[5]

One who owes to government allegiance, service, and money by way of taxation, and to whom the government, in turn, grants and guarantees liberty of person and of conscience, the right of acquiring and possessing property, of marriage and the social relations,

---

also Philadelphia, &c. R. Co. *v.* Pollock, 19 F. R. 403 (1884); United States *v.* White, *ib.* 723 (1884).

[5] Hollister *v.* Zion's Co-operative Institution, 111 U. S. 62 (1884); 8 Wall. 533; 96 U. S. 366; *Re* Aldrich, 16 F. R. 369 (1883).

[1] Hunt, Appellant, 141 Mass. 519 (1886): R. S. § 5183.

[2] Clare *v.* People, 9 Col. 124 (1886), Helm, J.

[3] Martin *v.* Duke, 5 Redf. 599 (1882), Rollins, Sur.

[4] Dodge *v.* Mastin, 17 F. R. 665 (1883).

[1] Whalen *v.* Sheridan, 10 F. R. 661 (1880); 91 U. S. 249; 96 *id.* 618.

[2] [3 Bl. Com. 100.

[3] [Cohens *v.* Virginia, 6 Wheat. 411 (1821), Marshall, C. J.

[4] Perez *v.* Perez, 59 Tex. 324 (1883).

[5] Thomassen *v.* State, 15 Ind. 151 (1860), Perkins, J.; White *v.* Clements, 39 Ga. 259-62 (1869).

of suit and of defense, and security in person, estate, and reputation.[1]

A State may deny all her "political rights" to an individual, and he yet be a citizen. The rights of office and suffrage are political purely. A citizen enjoys "civil rights."[1]

For convenience it has been found necessary to give a name to membership in a political community or nation. The object is to designate by title the person and the relation he bears to the nation. For this purpose the words "subject," "inhabitant," and "citizen" have been used, and the choice between them is sometimes made to depend upon the form of the government. "Citizen" is now more commonly employed, however, and as it has been considered better suited to the description of one living under a republican government, it was adopted by nearly all of the States upon their separation from Great Britain, and was afterward adopted in the Articles of Confederation and in the Constitution. Used in this sense it is understood as conveying the idea of membership in a nation, and nothing more.

Whoever was one of the people of either of the States when the Constitution was adopted became *ipso facto* a citizen — a member of the nation created by its adoption. . . Disputes have arisen as to whether or not certain persons or classes of persons were part of the people at the time, but never as to their citizenship, if they were.

Additions might be made by birth, and by naturalization.

The Constitution does not, in words, say who shall be natural-born citizens. To ascertain that, resort must be had to the common law, with the nomenclature of which the framers were familiar. At common law, all children born in a country of parents who were its citizens became themselves, upon their birth, citizens. These were natives, or natural-born citizens, as distinguished from aliens or foreigners. Some authorities include as citizens children born within the jurisdiction without reference to the citizenship of their parents. As to this class there have been doubts, but not as to the other class.

Sex has never been made one of the elements of citizenship in the United States. The Fourteenth Amendment did not affect the citizenship of women any more than that of men: it prohibited the State from abridging any of her privileges and immunities (q. v.), as a citizen of the United States, but it did not confer citizenship on her. That she had before its adoption. The right of suffrage was not co-extensive with citizenship before the adoption of the Amendment, nor was it added thereby.[2]

Citizen and "legal voter" are not synonymous terms. Minors and females may be citizens, yet they are not legal voters.[3]

[1] Amy v. Smith, 1 Litt. *342 (Ky., 1822), Mills, J. Approved, Van Valkenburg v. Brown, 43 Cal. 51 (1872).

[2] Minor v. Happersett, 21 Wall. 166-67, 170, 175 (1874), Chase, C. J. See also Dred Scott v. Sandford, 19 How. 404, 422 (1856), Taney, C. J.; 2 Kent, 258; 3 Story, Const. § 1687; 25 Cent. Mag. 178.

[3] People v. Town of Oldtown. 88 Ill. 205 (1878); United States v. Anthony, 11 Blatch. 202 (1873).

A person may be a citizen of the United States and of a State, and as such have different rights. Citizens are the members of the political community to which they belong. They are the people who compose the community, and who, in their associated capacity, have established or submitted themselves to the dominion of a government for the promotion of their general welfare and the protection of their individual as well as of their collective rights.[1]

By the definition usually given, a citizen is an "inhabitant of a city, town, or place," and so would include every person dwelling in the place named; but the term is subject to various limitations, depending upon the context. It may indicate a permanent resident, or one who remains for a time or from time to time.[2]

Citizenship implies residence with intention of remaining permanently at the particular place.[3] See INHABITANT; RESIDENT.

The word does not necessarily include the element of descent or inheritance, nor of sex, nor of race, nor of right to co-operate in government, nor of property.[4]

Citizenship as affected by the Thirteenth, Fourteenth, and Fifteenth Amendments to the Constitution:

The object sought by these Amendments was "the freedom of the slave (African) race, the security and firm establishment of that freedom, and the protection of the freedman from the oppressions of those who had exercised dominion over him." But the letter and spirit of the Amendments "apply to all cases coming within their purview, whether the party concerned be African or not."[5]

Amendment XIII. "Neither slavery nor involuntary servitude, except as a punishment for crime whereof the party shall have been duly convicted, shall exist within the United States, or any place subject to their jurisdiction." Ratified December 18, 1865.

Amendment XIV. "All persons born or naturalized in the United States, and subject to the jurisdiction thereof, are citizens of the United States and of the State wherein they reside. No State shall make or enforce any law which shall abridge the privileges or immunities of citizens of the United States; nor shall any State deprive any person of life, liberty, or property, without due process of law; nor deny to any person within its jurisdiction the equal protection of the laws." Ratified July 28, 1868.

Amendment XV. "The right of citizens of the United States to vote shall not be denied or abridged

[1] United States v. Cruikshank, 93 U. S. 549, 542 (1875), Waite, C. J.; Dred Scott Case, *ante*.

[2] Union Hotel Co. v. Hersee, 79 N. Y. 461 (1880).

[3] Winn v. Gilmer, 27 F. R. 817 (1886); 25 Am. Law Reg. 706 (1886); ib. 710-14, cases. As affecting citizenship, 31 Alb. Law J. 465 (1885) — consular instructions.

[4] See 16 Alb. Law J. 24, 176 (1877); 25 Am. Law Reg. 1-14 (1886), cases; 24 Cent. Law J. 540 (1887), cases; 11 Ohio, 27; Abbott, cases.

[5] Slaughter-House Cases, *post*.

by the United States or by any State on account of race, color, or previous condition of servitude." Ratified March 30, 1870.

In the case of each Amendment, Congress is given express power to enforce the provisions thereof by appropriate legislation.

The series have a common purpose: to secure to the negro race all the civil rights the white race enjoy;—to raise the colored race into perfect equality of civil rights with all others in the State;—to take away all possibility of oppression by law because of race or color;—to secure equal protection of the laws.

They are limitations on the power of the States, and enlargement of the powers of Congress. To carry out their purpose they are to be construed liberally.

The XIIIth Amendment forbids all forms of involuntary slavery — African slavery, Mexican peonage, Chinese coolie trade. It declares the personal freedom of all the human race within the jurisdiction of the United States. After the slave had been emancipated, certain States so curtailed his rights that his freedom was of little value: in this originated the XIVth Amendment. The laws being still administered by the white man alone, the XVth Amendment was adopted to make the negro a voter.

The XIVth Amendment conferred citizenship on the negro, defines citizenship in the United States *and* in the States, and protects the privileges and immunities of *citizens of the United States* from hostile legislation by the States. That is, it not only gave citizenship, but it denies a State power to withhold equal protection of the laws, and gives Congress power to enforce its provisions by appropriate legislation, as, by removal of a cause from a State to a Federal court. Its enforcement is left to the discretion of Congress. In an especial sense it makes one law for black and for white. It does not enumerate rights, but speaks in general terms. It confers a new constitutional right: exemption from discrimination between persons and classes of persons by action of any State; it does not refer to action by a private individual.[1]

The XIVth Amendment intended not only that there should be no arbitrary deprivation of life or liberty, or arbitrary spoliation of property, but that equal protection and security should be given to all under like circumstances in the enjoyment of their personal and civil rights; that all persons should be equally en-

titled to pursue their happiness and acquire and enjoy property; that they should have like access to the courts of the country for the protection of their persons and property, the prevention and redress of wrongs, and the enforcement of contracts; that no impediment should be interposed to the pursuits of any one except as applied to the same pursuits by others under like circumstances; that no greater burdens should be laid upon one than are laid upon the others in the same calling and condition, and that in the administration of criminal justice no different or higher punishment should be imposed upon one than is prescribed to all for like offenses. . The Amendment does not interfere with the "police power" of the States — a regulation designed not to impose unequal or unnecessary restrictions upon any one, but to promote, with as little individual inconvenience as possible, the general good. . . Class legislation, discriminating against some and favoring others, is prohibited, but legislation which, in carrying out a public purpose, is limited in its application, if within the sphere of its operation it affects alike all persons similarly situated, is not within the Amendment.[1]

The XIVth Amendment forbids an ordinance which, though expressed in general terms, is directed against a particular class, as Chinese convicts, by imposing a degrading punishment, like that of cutting off the queue.[2]

An administration of an ordinance for carrying on a lawful business (that of a laundry), which makes discriminations founded upon differences of race between persons otherwise in similar circumstances, violates the XIVth Amendment.[3]

The XVth Amendment merely invests citizens of the United States with the constitutional right of exemption from discrimination in the enjoyment of the elective franchise on account of race, color, or previous condition of servitude.[4]

No one of the Amendments confers power on Congress to punish private persons who, acting without authority of the State, invade rights protected by the Amendments.[5]

See further CONSPIRACY; RIGHT, 2, Civil Rights; SCHOOL, Separate; SERVITUDE, 1; SUFFRAGE; VAGRANT; WAR. See also ALIEN, 1; ALLEGIANCE; CHINESE; CORPORATION, Private; DENIZEN; DOMICIL; EXPATRIATION; NATURALIZE; PERSON; PRIVILEGE, 1; STATE, 3 (2); SUFFRAGE; TERRITORY, 2; WHITE.

CITY.[6] 1. An incorporated town or borough, which, in England, is or has

---

[1] Slaughter-House Cases, 16 Wall. 36, 70–71 (1873), Miller, J. Regarded a "servitude" in property.

Strauder *v.* West Virginia, 100 U. S. 306, 310 (1879), Strong, J. S., a negro, tried for murder, had been denied a removal of the cause into a circuit court. Virginia *v.* Rives, ib. 318 (1879),—in which a mixed jury was denied.

Exp. Virginia, 100 U. S. 344–48 (1879), Strong, J. That State petitioned for the discharge of one Coles, a county judge, indicted for excluding a colored man from a jury. Bush *v.* Kentucky, 107 *id.* 118–19 (1882), cases.

Missouri *v.* Lewis, 101 U. S. 30–31 (1879), Bradley, J. Regarded a regulation of jurisdiction.

Neal *v.* Delaware, 103 U. S. 385–86 (1880), Harlan, J.; United States *v.* Woods, 106 *id.* 637–44 (1882), Woods, J.; United States *v.* Reese, 92 *id.* 214, 218 (1875), Waite, C. J.

---

[1] Barbier *v.* Connolly, 113 U. S. 31–32 (1885), Field, J. See also Pace *v.* Alabama, 106 *id.* 584 (1882); Railroad Tax Case (County of San Mateo *v.* South. Pacific R. Co.), 8 Saw. 251, 302 (1882); Civil Rights Cases, 109 U. S. 3, 11, 23, 24 (1883); 93 N. Y. 446.

[2] Ah Kow *v.* Nunan, 5 Saw. 552, 562 (1879).

[3] Yick Wo *v.* Hopkins, 118 U. S. 356, 365 (1886).

[4] United States *v.* Cruikshank, 92 U. S. 542 (1875); United States *v.* Harris, 106 *id.* 637 (1882).

[5] Le Grand *v.* United States, 12 F. R. 577, 583–85 (1882).

[6] L. *civitas*, citizens in a community: *civis*, a citizen.

been the see of a bishop.[1] An incorporated town.[2]

The word "city" may include a town,[3] *q. v.*

2. A municipal corporation of the larger class, with powers of government confided in officers who are usually elected by popular vote.

A political division of a State, for the convenient administration of the government.[4]

An instrumentality, with powers more or less enlarged, according to the requirements of the public, and which may be increased or repealed at the will of the legislature.[4]

In a few States cities are of the first class, of the second class, etc., according to population.[6]

Under a constitutional power to organize cities and villages, the legislature is authorized to classify municipal corporations, and an act relating to any such class may be one of a general nature.[6]

City purpose. Any public improvement for the common benefit and enjoyment of all the citizens.[7]

Each case must depend largely upon its own facts.[7]

City vouchers are non-negotiable. See under NEGOTIATE, 2.

See generally CHARTER, 2; CORPORATION, Municipal; COUNCIL, 2; FIRE, Department; HEALTH, Board of; OFFICER; ORDINANCE, 1; PARK, 2; POLICE, 3; RECORDER, 2; SEWER; SIDEWALK; STREET; TELEGRAPH.

CIVIL. Pertaining to the citizen (Lat. *civis*) — the free inhabitant of an independent city, in distinction from the government, the soldier, the peasant, the ecclesiastic, and persons of other classes.[8]

1. Contrasted with *barbarous* or *savage*, *natural* or *uncivilized*, denotes a state of society reduced to order and regular government: as in speaking of civil — liberty, government, rights, society, *qq. v.*

2. Originating or existing among, pertaining to, or affecting, fellow-citizens of the same state or nation, and opposed to *foreign:* as, a civil — commotion, rebellion, war, *q. v.*

3. Accorded by just and equal laws; as opposed to *political* or that which is actually or practically enjoyed under law: as, again, civil — rights or liberty, *qq. v.*

4. Existing in contemplation of law; attributable under municipal law; and contrasted with *natural:* as, civil — life, death, disability, *qq. v.*

5. Concerning the rights of and wrongs to individuals considered as private persons, in contradistinction to *criminal* or that which concerns the whole political society, the community, state, government: as, civil — action, case, cause, code, court, damage, injury, jurisdiction, law, obligation or responsibility, proceeding, procedure, process, remedy, report, side, *qq. v.*

6. Pertaining to the administration of government, and contrasted with *military* and *ecclesiastical:* as, civil — office, officer, tenure, *qq. v.*

"Civil" is used, in contradistinction to "barbarous" or "savage," to indicate a state of society reduced to order and regular government; to "criminal," to indicate the private rights and remedies of men as members of the community, in contrast to those which are public, and relate to the government; to "military" and "ecclesiastical;" to "natural" or "foreign." In the Constitution, seems to be contradistinguished from "military," to indicate the rights and duties relating to citizens generally, as distinct from those of persons engaged in the land and naval service of the government.[1]

Civiliter mortuus. Civilly dead. See *Civil*, 4.

CLAIM.[2] A challenge by a man of the propriety [property] or ownership of a thing which he has not in possession, but which is wrongfully detained from him.[3]

In a juridical sense, a demand of some matter as of right made by one person upon another, to do or to forbear to do some act or thing as a matter of duty.[4]

A more limited but equally explicit definition is that given by Lord Dyer in *Stowel's Case.*[4, 3]

The assertion, demand, or challenge of something as a right, or the thing thus demanded or challenged.[5]

---

[1] 1 Bl. Com. 114.

[2] Van Riper *v.* Parsons, 40 N. J. L. 4 (1878).

[3] People *v.* Stephens, 62 Cal. 236 (1882): Cal. Const., Art. X, sec. 19.

[4] New Orleans *v.* Clark, 95 U. S. 654 (1877), Field, J.

[6] See Kilgore *v.* Magee, 85 Pa. 411 (1877); 77 *id.* 346; 88 *id.* 258; 96 *id.* 422; 106 *id.* 377; 15 W. N. C. 209; 32 Kan. 431; 82 Mo. 388.

[6] State *ex rel.* Attorney-General *v.* Hudson, 44 Ohio St. 139 (1886), cases; Heck *v.* State, *ib.* 539 (1886).

[7] People *v.* Kelly, 76 N. Y. 487 (1879).

[8] A "civil" man once was one who fulfilled all the duties flowing from his position as a *civis*, and his relations to the other members of the *civitas* to which he belonged, and "civility" was the condition in which those duties were recognized and observed. Trench, Glossary, &c., 36.

[1] [1 Story, Const. § 791.

[2] L. *clamare*, to call out, demand.

[3] Stowel *v.* Zouch, 1 Plow. 359 (1568), Lord Dyer.

[4] Prigg *v.* Pennsylvania, 16 Pet. 615 (1842), Story, J.

[5] Fordyce *v.* Godman, 20 Ohio St. 14 (1871), Scott, J.

The subject-matter of a claim is the facts or circumstances out of which the claim arises or by reason of which the supposed right accrues.[1]

Something asked for or demanded on the one hand and not admitted or allowed on the other.[2]

When the demand is admitted it is not a mere claim, but a debt. It no longer rests in mere clamor or petition, but is something done upon which an action may be maintained. Thus, "a claim upon the United States" (R. S. § 3477) is something in the nature of a demand for damages arising out of some alleged act or omission of the government, but not yet provided for or acknowledged by law.[2]

Every account upon which any sum of money or other thing is or is claimed to be due to the person presenting it is a claim or demand; but every claim or demand is not an "account." The terms, however, may be used synonymously.[3]

May refer to such debt or demand against a decedent as might have been enforced against him in his life-time by personal action for the recovery of money, and upon which only a money judgment could have been rendered.[4]

Claims against an estate are those in existence at the death of the deceased. Other claims are properly denominated "expenses of administration."[5] See DEMAND, 1.

Referring to public lands, relates to a settler's right or improvement on land the fee of which is in the government.[6]

Within the meaning of Rev. St., § 3438, providing for the punishment of any person who prefers a claim (pension) against the Government, knowing the same to be false, "claim" is not used in the sense of a demand theretofore presented, but of a demand then existing, and known to be wrongful. The act of presenting it in the first instance is denounced as a crime.[7]

Under that section one is guilty who presents a claim which he believes to be just, but seeks to substantiate by the affidavit of a person who, to his knowledge, certifies to a fact of which the affiant knows nothing.[8]

Adverse claim. See POSSESSION, Adverse.

Claim and delivery; claim-bond. See REPLEVIN, 1.

Claim of title. See COLOR, 2. Of title.

Claimant. 1. One who demands a thing as a matter of right.

2. One who has filed a claim as the law requires.[1]

3. In admiralty, a person admitted to defend a libel *in rem*, q. v.

A *bona fide* claimant to land is one who supposes that he has a good title and knows of no adverse claim.[2] See FAITH, Good.

Under pre-emption laws "claim" and "claimant" are frequently used in connection with the right to acquire title to a part of the public lands upon compliance with the laws.[3]

Counter-claim. A cross-demand, existing in favor of a defendant. Includes recoupment and set-off.

"Counter" means contrary to, contrary way, opposition; and "claim," the demand of anything that is in the possession of another, the right to demand of another.[4]

The term of itself imports a claim opposed to, or which qualifies, or at least in some degree affects, the plaintiff's cause of action or the right to the relief to which he would otherwise be entitled by his action. "Consists of a set-off or claim by way of recoupment, or is in some way connected with the action stated in the complaint."[5]

Is broader than "set-off;" includes not only demands the subject of set-off and recoupment, but equitable demands.[6]

Under the laws of many States, if the claim and counter-claim are both established, the latter reduces the former; but if the counter-claim alone is established, judgment is recovered for the amount of it. See further SET-OFF.

Non-claim. Omission or neglect to make a demand; failure to assert a claim within the time limited by law.

"An infant shall lose nothing by non-claim, or neglect to demand his right."[7]

A statute of non-claim has all the characteristics of a statute of limitations.[8]

See AFFIDAVIT, Of claim; COURTS, United States; DISCLAIMER; INTERPLEAD; QUITCLAIM; RECLAIM; STALE.

[1] Fordyce v. Godman, *ante*.

[2] Dowell v. Cardwell, 4 Saw. 228 (1877), Deady, J.

[3] Stringham v. Supervisors, 24 Wis. 600 (1869), Dixon, C. J.; 43 *id.* 644; 56 *id.* 170, 245; 40 Ala. 147.

[4] Fallon v. Butler, 21 Cal. 32 (1862), Field, C. J.; McCausland's Estate, 52 *id.* 577 (1878); 9 *id.* 616; 36 *id.* 23, 88; 46 *id.* 100; 9 Oreg. 391; 2 N. Y. 254; 43 *id.* 413.

[5] Dodson v. Nevitt, 5 Monta. 520 (1885); McLaughlin v. Winner, 63 Wis. 128 (1885).

[6] Bowman v. Torr, 3 Iowa, 574 (1856); United States v. Wilcox, 4 Blatch. 388-89 (1859).

[7] United States v. Rhodes, 30 F. R. 433 (1887), Brewer, J.

[8] United States v. Jones, 32 F. R. 482 (1887), Simonton, J.

[1] [Adams v. Worrill, 46 Ga. 295 (1872).

[2] Morrison v. Robinson, 31 Pa. 459 (18_8): 1 Wash. 79. See also 12 F. R. 152.

[3] United States v. Spaulding, 3 Dak. 92-93 (1882).

[4] [Great Western Ins. Co. v. Pierce, 1 Wyom. 49-50 (1872). Fisher, C. J.

[5] Dietrich v. Koch, 35 Wis. 626 (1874), Lyon, J.: 24 How. Pr. 329, 332; 22 Barb. 143; 21 N. Y. 191, 196; 63 *id.* 549; 40 Ark. 78; 7 Ind. 523; 2 Pars. Contr. 741; Roberts v. Donovan, 70 Cal. 112 (1886), cases. In actions *ex delicto*, see 20 Cent. Law J. 363-65 (1885), cases.

[6] Roberts v. Donovan, 70 Cal. 112 (1886), cases; Cal. Code Civ. Proc., § 438.

[7] 1 Bl. Com. 465.

[8] Williamson v. McCrary, 33 Ark. 470 (1878).

CLANDESTINE. See CONVEYANCE, 2, Fraudulent; DISTRESS; FRAUD.

CLASS. Persons or things ranked together for like action, for similar or uniform treatment, as possessing a common attribute, or as being in the same category.

Used of legatees, obligees, and other persons;[1] of cities;[2] of legislation.[3] See CITY, 2; ENUMERATION; LEGACY.

CLAUSE. A separate portion: a part of a written instrument.

One of the subdivisions of a written or printed document.[4]

Clauses take their names from the nature of the provision intended to be made by them. Of the more common are: clause of jurisdiction — in a bill in equity; clause of accruer; commerce, dictionary, enacting, guaranty, penal, residuary, and sweeping clause, *qq. v.*

CLAUSUM. L. A close; an inclosure.

Quare clausum fregit (pl. *fregerunt*). Wherefore he broke the close. The emphatic words in the old Latin writ commanding a defendant to show cause why he made an alleged unlawful entry upon plaintiff's land.

Abridged to trespass *quare clausum, qu. cl. fr.*, and *q. c. f.* See CLOSE, 3; TRESPASS.

CLEAN. See HAND, 4; LADING, Bill of.

CLEAR. 1, *v.* To clear out a highway is to clear it out for all the purposes to which it is dedicated.[5]

"Clearing land," in the absence of words of limitation, means removing therefrom all the timber of every size, except taking out the stumps.[6]

2, *adj.* Free from, as, from taxes: said of an annuity.[7]

Clear yearly value: free from all out-go.[8]

Clearly. "Clearly established by satisfactory proof" is equivalent to established by proof beyond reasonable doubt.[9]

To require insanity, as a defense in homicide, to be proved by evidence which "clearly preponderates" is practically saying that it must be proved beyond all doubt or uncertainty.[10]

CLEARANCE. A certificate from the collector of customs at a port that a vessel has complied with the customs and health laws, and has permission to sail.[1]

CLEARING-HOUSE. The object of a clearing-house association is to effect at one time and place the daily exchanges between the banks which are members of the association, and the payment of the balances resulting from such exchanges.[2]

Sending a note through the clearing-house is not a formal demand for immediate payment made during business hours, but it is equivalent to leaving the note at the bank for collection from the maker on or before the close of banking hours.[2] See LOAN, Certificate.

CLEARLY. See CLEAR, 2, Clearly.

CLERGY. Persons in holy orders; ecclesiastics, as a class; also, benefit of clergy.

Clergyable. Admitting or entitled to the benefit of clergy.

Benefit of clergy. Exemption from capital punishment, anciently allowed to churchmen, and, later, to laymen.

Originated in the regard princes had for the church, and the ill use made of that regard. In time, extended to the laity, and made to include all felonies. The claimant "prayed his clergy." If he could read a psalm correctly (usually, the fifty-first), he obtained a trial before twelve "clerks," *q. v.* They heard him on oath, with his witnesses and compurgators, who attested their belief in his innocence.[3]

Abolished in England by 7 and 8 Geo. IV (1827), c. 28; and in Federal practice by act of April 30, 1790. Was part of the common law of the older States.[4]

Clergyman. See COMMUNICATION, Privileged, 1.

CLERK. 1. A member of the clergy.

The clergy, as they engrossed almost every other branch of learning, were remarkable for their study of the law. The judges were usually created out of the sacred order, and all the inferior officers were supplied by the lower clergy, which occasioned their successors to be denominated "clerks."[5]

2. A person employed to keep records: as, a clerk of a court.

Clerk of courts. The chief clerk of the courts of quarter sessions and oyer and terminer. (Penn.) See PROTHONOTARY; MINUTES, 1.

---

[1] 16 Pick. 132; 17 Wend. 52.

[2] 85 Pa. 401; 106 *id.* 377; 32 Kan. 431; 82 Mo. 388; 44 Ohio St. 139, 589.

[3] 109 U. S. 24.

[4] Eschbach *v.* Collins, 61 Md. 499 (1883).

[5] Winter *v.* Peterson, 24 N. J. L. 528 (1854).

[6] Seavey *v.* Shurick, 110 Ind. 496 (1886); Harper *v.* Pound, 10 *id.* 35 (1857).

[7] Hodgeworth *v.* Crawley, 2 Atkyns, 393 (1793).

[8] Tyrconnel *v.* Ancaster, 2 Ves. Sr. 504 (1754).

[9] People *v.* Hamilton, 62 Cal. 385 (1882).

[10] Coyle *v.* Commonwealth, 100 Pa. 580, 577 (1882).

---

[1] See R. S. §§ 4197, 4200, 4207.

[2] Nat. Exchange Bank *v.* Nat. Bank of North America, 132 Mass. 148 (1882).

[3] 4 Bl. Com. 356.

[4] See R. S. § 5329; 1 Bish. Cr. L. § 936; 1 Chitty, Cr. L. 667; 1 Steph. Hist. Cr. L. Eng. 459–72.

[5] 1 Bl. Com. 17.

Clerical error. See ERROR, 2 (1); REC-ORD, 2, Judicial.

3. A person employed to keep minutes, accounts, and the like.

A person, employed in an office, public or private, for keeping records, whose business is to write or register in proper form the transactions of the tribunal or body to which he belongs.[1]

An employee who attends to sales no further than delivering goods manufactured, and keeping a memorandum of the delivery for a temporary purpose, is not a "clerk" within the meaning of the rule which requires proof of the original entries.[2] See AGENT; SERVANT, 3; ENTRY; II, 1.

CLIENT.[3] One who employs a lawyer professionally.

Clientage. The patronage of clients; professional patronage.

A client is one who applies to an advocate for counsel and defense; one who retains an attorney, is responsible to him for his fees, and to whom the attorney is responsible for the management of the suit.[4]

Sergeants and barristers may take upon them the protection of suitors, plaintiffs and defendants, who are therefore called their "clients," like the dependents upon the Roman orators.[5]

Among the Romans, the "patron" was the legal adviser of the client, maintained and defended him in his lawsuits — cared for his interests, both public and private. The "client" contributed toward the marriage portion of the patron's daughter, to his ransom, to the costs and penalties of lost lawsuits, to the expense of any public office held by the patron. Neither could accuse, testify or vote against the other. The relation resembled kinship. It was the glory of illustrious families to have many clients.[6] See ATTORNEY; COMMUNICATION, Privileged, 1.

CLOSE. As a verb and an adjective, preserves its vernacular senses, except in the compound "foreclose," q. v.; as a noun, has the technical meaning noted below.

1, v. (1) To end, terminate, complete: as, to close a bargain or negotiation.[7]

(2) In a statute providing that places where intoxicating liquors are sold shall be "closed on Sundays," the meaning is that sales shall be entirely stopped, the traffic shut off effect-ually, so that drinking and the conveniences of drinking shall be no longer accessible.[1]

A saloon is not "closed," within the meaning of a law requiring such places to be closed at certain times, as long as it is possible for persons desiring liquor to get in peaceably, whether by an outside entrance or any other, or as long as a customer, who is inside at the time for closing, remains inside. And it is not important that there is no one attending bar, if the liquor is accessible, nor is it important that no liquor is sold.[2]

2, adj. Not proper for public inspection; hence, sealed on the outside: as, a close writ or roll; opposed to patent in letters-patent. See PATENT, 1 (1).

Not admitting corporators generally to vote for officers: as, a close corporation, q. v.

3, n. An interest in the soil.[3]

Taking sheaves from another's close is equivalent to a taking from his land.[3]

A portion of land, as, a field inclosed by a hedge, fence, or other sensible inclosure.[4]

Every unwarrantable entry on another's soil the law entitles a trespass by "breaking his close:" the words of the writ of trespass commanding the defendant to show cause quare clausum querentis fregit. For every man's land is, in law, inclosed and set apart from his neighbor's land.[5] See CLAUSUM; ENCLOSURE; INCLOSE.

CLOTHE. See VEST.

CLOTHING. See APPAREL; EXEMPTION.

CLOUD. "Cloud," and the fuller and more frequent expression "cloud upon the title," import that there is in existence something which shows a prima facie right in a person to an interest in realty in the possession of another.

A cloud exists upon a title where an instrument is outstanding which is void, or an unfounded claim is set up which complainant has reason to fear may at some time be used injuriously to his rights.[6]

Questions as to what constitutes a cloud upon a title and what character of title the complainant must

[1] People v. Fire Commissioners, 73 N. Y. 442 (1878), Allen, J. See also Ross v. Heathcock, 57 Wis. 96 (1883).

[2] Sickles v. Mather, 20 Wend. 72, 74 (1838).

[3] F. client, a suitor: L. cliens, one who hears, listens to advice.

[4] McFarland v. Crary, 6 Wend. 312 (1830).

[5] 3 Bl. Com. 28; 2 id. 64.

[5] See 2 Bl. Com. 21; Wharton's Law Dict.

[7] See 18 Barb. 60; 43 Sup. Ct., N. Y., 454.

[1] Kurtz v. People, 33 Mich. 282 (1876); People v. Cummerford, 58 id. 331 (1885); 49 id. 337; 52 id. 566. See also 59 Ala. 64; 47 Conn. 276; 65 Ga. 568; 57 Ill. 370; 68 id. 420.

[2] People v. Cummerford, 58 Mich. 328 (1885), cases, Morse, C. J.

[3] Richardson v. Brewer, 81 Ind. 108 (1881).

[4] Lochlin v. Casler, 52 How. Pr. 45 (1875).

[5] 3 Bl. Com. 209.

[5] Chipman v. City of Hartford, 21 Conn. 495 (1852); Ward v. Chamberlain, 2 Black, 444-45 (1862), cases; Waterbury Savings Bank v. Lawler, 46 Conn. 245 (1878); Teal v. Collins, 9 Oreg. 92 (1881).

have, to secure relief in equity, are decided upon principles long established. Prominent among them are: that the title of the complainant must be clear; that the pretended title, which is alleged to be a cloud upon it, must not only be clearly invalid or inequitable, but must be such as may, in the present or at a future time, embarrass the real owner in controverting it.[1]

Independently of statutes, the object of a bill to remove a cloud upon a title, and to quiet the possession, is to protect the owner of the legal title from being disturbed in his possession or harassed by suits in regard to that title; and the bill cannot be maintained without clear proof of both possession and legal title in the plaintiff.[2]

The remedy is to cancel the instrument;[3] or to annul or modify the proceeding or record which creates the cloud. Where the illegality of an agreement, deed, or other instrument, appears upon the face of it, so that its nullity can admit of no doubt, a court of equity will not direct it to be canceled or delivered up. There can be no danger that lapse of time may deprive the party of his full means of defense. Such a paper cannot, in strictness, be said to create a cloud, nor be a means of vexatious litigation, or of serious injury.[4]

A bill in equity lies to remove a cloud upon the title to realty where there is not a plain, adequate, and complete remedy at law.[5]

The jurisdiction of a court of equity is an independent source or head of jurisdiction, not requiring any accompaniment of fraud, accident, mistake, trust, account, or any other basis of equitable intervention.[6]

The decree, unless otherwise expressly provided by statute, is not a judgment *in rem*, establishing a title in land, but operates *in personam* only, by restraining the defendant from asserting his claim, and directing him to deliver up his deed to be canceled, or to execute a release to the plaintiff.[7]

See QUIET. Compare COLOR, 2, Of title.

CLUB LAW. The use of force or violence for the redress of wrong, actual or alleged.

CLUBS. Associations of persons for the promotion of a common purpose.

In this sense "club" has no very definite meaning. Clubs are formed for all sorts of purposes, and there is no uniformity in their constitutions and rules.[6]

A club of persons may own intoxicating liquors, and employ one member as steward to deliver drinks to other members upon the presentation of checks which are sold by the steward, the money received being used to buy other liquors as the property of the club, without violating a law forbidding the keeping of intoxicating liquors with intent to sell them.[1]

By-laws, which vest in a majority the power of expulsion for a minor offense, are, so far, void. The power of disfranchisement which destroys the member's franchise must be conferred by statute; it is never sustained as an incidental power except on conviction for an infamous offense, or for the commission of an act against the society which tends to its injury.[2] See ASSOCIATION.

CO. 1. An abbreviation of company and of county. See COMPANY, 1.

2. The Latin *con* (q. v.) used as a prefix, and meaning: with, together with, joined with — and, hence, companion, fellow, associate: as in co-administrator, co-conspirator, co-defendant, co-executor, co-heir, co-obligor, co-partner, co-plaintiff, co-salvor, co-surety, co-tenant, co-trespasser — in which the person spoken of possesses the characteristics of another person whose office or relation is more particularly mentioned. See each of those simple words; also JOINT.

COACH. A kind of carriage, distinguished from other vehicles chiefly as being a covered box, hung on leathers, with four wheels.[3] See RAILROAD; WAGON.

COAL. See ACQUA, Currit, etc.; MINERAL; WASTE, 2.

COASTING TRADE. By act of Congress of February 18, 1793, commercial intercourse carried on between different districts in different States, between different districts in the same State, and between different places in the same district, on the seacoast or on a navigable river.[4]

The reference is to vessels engaged in the domestic trade, plying between ports in the United States, as distinguished from vessels engaged in the foreign trade or plying between a port of the United States and a port in a foreign country.[5]

COAT OF ARMS. See HEIRLOOM.

COCK-FIGHTING. See CRUELTY, 3; GAME, 2.

[1] Phelps v. Harris, 101 U. S. 374–75 (1879), cases; Gilman v. Van Brunt, 29 Minn. 272 (1882), cases.

[2] Frost v. Spitley, 121 U. S. 556 (1887), cases, Gray, J.; Harland v. Bankers' & Merchants' Tel. Co., 32 F. R. 308 (1887).

[3] Fox v. Blossom, 17 Blatch. 356 (1879), cases.

[4] 1 Story, Eq. § 700a.

[5] Russell v. Barstow, 144 Mass. 130 (1887). Where the alleged owner is in possession he cannot maintain a writ of entry without abandoning the possession.

[6] Dull's Appeal, 113 Pa. 510, 515–18 (1886), cases. See also Holland v. Challen, 110 U. S. 24 (1884); Pomeroy, Eq. J. § 1398.

[7] Harte v. Sansom, 110 U. S. 155 (1884), cases.

[8] Commonwealth v. Pomphret, 137 Mass. 567, 564 (1884). See 59 Ala. 34; 79 Ill. 85; 48 Ind. 21; 32 Iowa, 405; 55 Md. 566; 8 Q. B. D. 373.

[1] Commonwealth v. Pomphert, *ante*.

[2] Evans v. Philadelphia Club, 50 Pa. 107 (1865). See generally 5 Alb. Law J. 226 (1872), cases; Dawkins v. Antrobus, 37 Eng. R. 237 (1881); Louhat v. Le Roy, 40 Hun, 546 (1886), cases.

[3] Turnpike Co. v. Neil, 9 Ohio, 12 (1839).

[4] Steamboat Co. v. Livingston, 3 Cow. 747 (1825).

[5] [San Francisco v. Navigation Co., 10 Cal. 507 (1858), cases.

CODE.[1] A reduction and revision of the law and procedure of a political community, upon one or more general subjects, and the enactment of this new, systematized statement as one statute.

An enactment of a more or less complete system of law, or of procedure, or of both law and procedure, upon one or more general subjects.

Codification. The act or process of reducing all the law upon one or more general subjects to a code.

The reduction of the existing law to an orderly written system, freed from the needless technicalities, obscurities, and other defects which the experience of its administration has disclosed.[2]

Codify. To reduce to the form of a code. *Uncodified:* not reduced to a code.

Codifier. One who makes or assists in making a code.

" A code ought to be based upon the principle that it aims at nothing more than the reduction to a definite and systematic shape of the results obtained and sanctioned by the experience of many centuries.[3]

The codes of New York have been the most celebrated and influential in this country. In that State the work of codification began under the constitution of 1846. Commissioners reported as complete the codes of Civil and Criminal Procedure in 1850, the Political Code in 1859, the Penal Code in 1864, and the Civil Code in 1865. Each of these has since been revised. The code of Civil Procedure, with some changes, has been adopted in Arizona, Arkansas, California, Colorado, Connecticut, Dakota, Idaho, Indiana, Iowa, Kansas, Kentucky, Minnesota, Mississippi, Missouri, Montana, Nebraska, Nevada, North Carolina, Ohio, Oregon, South Carolina, Utah, Washington, Wisconsin, and Wyoming; and the code of Criminal Procedure, in Arizona, Arkansas, California, Dakota, Idaho, Indiana, Iowa, Kansas, Kentucky, Minnesota, Montana, Nebraska, Nevada, Oregon, Utah, Washington, Wisconsin, and Wyoming. California and Dakota have also adopted the substance of the other three codes. Other States have partial revisions or consolidations sometimes called " codes." The New York codes are said to have also had an influence in framing the system adopted in England by the Judicature Act of 1873.[4]

In 1886 a codification of civil and criminal statutes was adopted in Alabama; a code of civil procedure in

Connecticut; and a civil code in Virginia, taking effect January 1, 1888.

A large portion of the modern codes is but declaratory of the common law as expounded by the courts.[1]

A code is a general collection or compilation of laws by public authority; a collection and compilation of general statutes. . The rule is, that when a statute is revised, or when one statute is framed from another, some parts being omitted, the parts so omitted are annulled. It must be presumed that the legislature has declared its entire will.[2] See REVISE.

CODICIL.[3] A supplement to a will, or an addition made by the testator, annexed to, and to be taken as part of, a testament: being for its explanation, or alteration, or to make some addition to, or else some subtraction from, the former disposition of the testator.[4]

A clause added to a will after its execution; the purpose of which usually is to alter, enlarge, or restrain the provisions of the will, or to explain, confirm, and republish it.[5]

Part of the will, to be construed with it, as one entire instrument. . . But the will is not altered by the codicil, except by express words or necessary implication. It is to be deemed altered by necessary implication where a subsequent provision is inconsistent with and repugnant to a prior provision. But where they can stand together, both shall have effect.[5]

The effect of republication of the will by the addition of a codicil is to bring both instruments to the same date.[6] See WILL, 2.

COERCION. Compulsion: constraint; duress.

Direct or positive coercion. When a person by physical force is compelled to do an act against his will.

Implied or legal coercion. When a person, under legal subjection to another, is induced to do an act involuntarily.

As free will is necessary to accountability, a person acting under coercion has no will. But the command of a superior to an inferior, of a parent to a child, of

---

[1] F. *code;* L. *codex,* a tablet, a book. Codify, codifier, and codification are pronounced cŏd'—.

[2] 3 Stephen, Hist. Cr. L. Eng. 351.

[3] Mr. Justice Stephen.

[4] See 19 Alb. Law J. 192 (1879) — David Dudley Field; 1 Kent, 475, note; Edinb. Rev., Oct., 1869; Abbott, Bouvier, Law Dicts.

[1] Cincinnati v. Morgan, 3 Wall. 293 (1865).

[2] Mobile, &c. R. Co. v. Weimer, 49 Miss. 739 (1874). See also Sedgw. Stat. 429. See generally 3 South. Law Rev., o. s., 222 (1874); 2 *id.,* N. s., 215 (1876); 3 *id.* 573 (1877); 6 *id.* 1 (1880); 19 Am. Law Rev. 14–17 (1884); 20 *id.* 1–47, 315–38 (1886); 21 *id.* 194–203 (1887); 2 Law Q. Rev. 125 (1886); 35 Alb. Law J. 244–47, 264, 321 (1887); 36 *id.* 224 (1887); 37 *id.* 221–23 (1888); 26 Cent. Law J. 257 (1888); 22 Am. Law Rev. 1–29, 57–65 (1888); 4 Kans. Law J. 258 (1886) — Law Counselor.

[3] L. *codicillus,* a little book or writing.

[4] 2 Bl. Com. 500. See 4 Kent, 531.

[5] Lamb v. Lamb, 11 Pick. 375 (1831), Shaw, C. J. See Dunham v. Averill, 45 Conn. 79 (1877); Grimball v. Patton, 70 Ala. 631 (1881); Fairfax v. Brown, 60 Md. 58 (1882).

[6] Hatcher v. Hatcher, 80 Va. 173 (1885).

a master to a servant, or of a principal to his agent, does not. ordinarily, amount to coercion.

If a wife acts in company with her husband in the commission of a tort or a crime other than treason, homicide, or other heinous felony, it is presumed, at common law, that she acted under coercion and without guilty intent. But non-coercion may be proved.[1] See DURESS; WILL, 2.

COGNATI. See NATUS, Cognati.

COGNIZANCE.[2] 1. Recognition; acknowledgment.

When a defendant in replevin justifies a distress of goods in another's right as his bailiff or servant, he is said to make cognizance; that is, he acknowledges the taking, but insists that it was legal.[3] Compare AVOWRY; RECOGNIZANCE.

2. Judicial recognition; judicial power; jurisdiction.

A word of the largest import, embracing all power, authority, and jurisdiction: as in the provision that a particular court shall have full cognizance of capital crimes.[4]

COGNOVIT. L. He has confessed or acknowledged it.

Cognovit actionem. He has confessed the action. Sometimes called a *cognovit*.

An acknowledgment by a defendant that an action brought against him is rightly brought, and that the sum named is due to the plaintiff.[5]

An unsealed confession of judgment given to the plaintiff after suit is brought. A warrant of attorney is under seal and given before suit is entered.[6] See ATTORNEY, Warrant of.

COHABIT.[7] 1. The primary meaning is to dwell with some one, not merely to visit or to see that one.[8]

In criminal statutes, to live together as husband and wife.

As, in the act of Congress of March 22, 1882, c. 47, forbidding polygamy.[9]

To live together in the same house as married persons live together, or in the manner of husband and wife.[1]

2. In a popular sense, sometimes found in statutes and decisions, includes the idea of occupying the same bed, and sexual intercourse.[2]

Cohabitation. As a fact presumptive of marriage, not a sojourn, nor a habit of visiting, nor even a remaining with for a time. . . Neither cohabitation nor reputation of marriage, nor both, is marriage. Conjoined, they are evidence from which a presumption of marriage arises. The legal idea of cohabitation is that which carries with it a natural belief that it results from marriage only. To cohabit is to live or dwell together, to have the same habitation; so that where one lives and dwells there the other always lives and dwells. The Scotch expression, "the habit and repute" of marriage, conveys the true idea better, perhaps, than our own. When we see a man and a woman constantly dwelling together, we obtain the first idea in the presumption of marriage; and when we add to this that the parties thus constantly living together are reputed to be man and wife, and so taken and received by all who know them both, we take the second step in the presumption of the fact of a marriage. Marriage is the cause, these follow as the effect. . An inconstant habitation and a divided reputation of marriage carry with them no full belief of an antecedent marriage as the cause. Irregularity in these elements of evidence is at once a reason to think that there is irregularity in the life itself which the parties lead: unless attended by independent facts, which aid in the proof of marriage. Without concomitant facts to prove marriage, such an irregular cohabitation and partial reputation of marriage avail nothing in the proof of marriage.[3]

See CONNONATION; DESERTION, 1; LASCIVIOUS; MARRIAGE; REPUTED.

COIN. A piece of metal stamped and made legally current as money.[4]

"Coin" and "coinage" apply to the stamping of metal in some way so as to give them currency.[5]

"The Congress shall have Power . . To coin Money, regulate the Value thereof, and of foreign

---

[1] 4 Bl. Com. 28–29; State v. Shee, 13 R. I. 536 (1882), cases; State v. Boyle, ib. 538 (1882); 51 Me. 308; 97 Mass. 547; 103 id. 71; 65 N. C. 398; 1 Greenl. Ev. § 28; 2 Whart. Ev. § 1256; 1 B. & H. Ld. Cr. Cas. 76–87, cases; 2 Steph. Hist. Cr. L. Eng. 99–110.

[2] Kŏg'-nĭ-, or kŏn'-i-zans. F. *cognoissance*, knowledge: L. *cognoscere*, to know,—Skeat. Also cognisance, and, formerly, conusance.

[3] 3 Bl. Com. 150.

[4] Webster v. Commonwealth, 5 Cush. 400 (1850), Shaw, C. J. See also 68 N. Y. 101; 2 Bl. Com. 38; 3 id. 86, 298; 4 id. 278.

[5] Smith, Contracts, 280.

[6] 3 Bl. Com. 397.

[7] L. *con*, with; *habitare*, to have often, *i. e.*, abide with,—54 Me. 366.

[8] [Calef v. Calef, 54 Me. 366 (1867), Appleton, C. J.

[9] Cannon v. United States, 116 U. S. 55, 74–75 (1885).

[1] Jones v. Commonwealth, 80 Va. 20 (1885), Fauntleroy, J.

[2] See 1 Bishop, Mar. & D. § 777, note, cases; 116 U. S. 75; 4 Paige, 425. As a married right, 19 Cent. Law J. 142 (1884), cases.

[3] Yardley's Estate, 75 Pa. 211 (1874), Agnew, C. J. See also Brinckle v. Brinckle. 34 Leg. Int. 428 (1877); Hynes v. McDermott, 91 N. Y. 459–62 (1883), cases; Teter v. Teter, 88 Ind. 498 (1883), cases; Appeal of Reading Fire Ins. & Trust Co., 113 Pa. 208 (1886), cases; 1 Whart. Ev. §§ 84–85, cases.

[4] United States v. Bogart, 9 Bened. 315 (1878), Wallace, J.; 5 Phila. 403; 16 Gray, 240.

[5] Meyer v. Roosevelt, 25 How. Pr. 105 (1863).

Coin." [1] "No State shall . coin Money" or "make any Thing but gold and silver Coin a Tender in Payment of Debts." [2] See TENDER, 2 (2), Legal Tender Acts.

The gold coins of the United States shall be a one-dollar piece, which, at the standard weight of twenty-five and eight-tenth grains, shall be the unit of value; a quarter-eagle, or two and a half dollar piece; a three-dollar piece; a half-eagle, or five-dollar piece; an eagle, or ten-dollar piece; and a double eagle, or twenty-dollar piece.

The silver coins shall be [a trade-dollar,] [3] a half-dollar or fifty-cent piece, a quarter-dollar or twenty-five-cent piece, a dime or ten-cent piece. The weight of [the trade-dollar shall be four hundred and twenty grains troy; the weight of] the half-dollar, twelve grams and one-half of a gram; the quarter-dollar and the dime, respectively, one-half and one-fifth of the weight of said half-dollar.

The standard of both gold and silver coins shall be such that of one thousand parts by weight nine hundred shall be pure metal and one hundred of alloy. The alloy of the silver coins shall be of copper. The alloy of the gold coins shall be of copper, or of copper and silver; but the silver shall in no case exceed one-tenth of the whole alloy.

The minor coins shall be a five-cent piece, a three-cent piece, and a one-cent piece; and their weight, respectively, seventy-seven and sixteen-hundredths grains troy, thirty grains, and forty-eight grains. The alloy of the five and three cent pieces shall be of copper and nickel, three-fourths to one-fourth; the alloy of the one-cent piece, ninety-five per centum of copper and five per centum of tin and zinc.

Any gold coins in the treasury, when reduced in weight by natural abrasion more than one-half of one per centum below the standard weight, shall be re-coined. [4]

There shall be coined silver dollars of the weight of four hundred and twelve and a half grains troy of standard silver, as provided in the act of January 18, 1837 (5 St. L. 137). [5]

Foreign coins. The value of foreign coins as expressed in the money of account of the United States shall be that of the pure metal of such coin of standard value; and the values of the standard coins in circulation of the various nations of the world shall be estimated annually by the director of the mint, and be proclaimed on the first day of January by the secretary of the treasury. [6]

The valuation thus made is conclusive upon custom-house officers and importers. [7]

All foreign gold and silver coins received in pay-ment for moneys due to the United States shall, before being issued in circulation, be coined anew. [1]

See ATTACHMENT, Execution; CURRENT, 2; MONEY.

COLD. See COOLING.

COLLATERAL. [2] Does not depart from its non-legal, popular signification.

1. Applied to a person or personal relation — that which is by the side, and not in the direct line: as collateral or a collateral — ancestor, charge, consanguinity, descent, heir, inheritance, kindred, kinsmen, relatives, qq. v.

2. Said of a right or a thing — depending upon another as the more important; additional to some other as principal: as collateral or a collateral — assurance, covenant, deed, estoppel, fact, issue, limitation, obligation, promise, security, undertaking, warranty, qq. v.

Collaterally attack or **impeach.** To question the validity of a thing done in court, in an independent proceeding: [3] as to collaterally attack a judgment or a judicial sale, qq. v.

Not permitted, except for fraud, of a matter regularly adjudicated by proper authority. See ADJUDICATION, Former.

Collaterals. 1. Collateral kinsmen. 2. Collateral securities, q. v.

COLLEAGUE. See ASSOCIATE, Counsel, Judge.

COLLECT. To gather together: to bring into the custody of one person.

1. To gather the assets of a decedent's estate: as for one to collect the goods of the estate for safe-keeping, until a will is proven and an executor qualified, or an administrator appointed. [4]

2. To receive or obtain money.

Collector. (1) A public officer charged with the duty of exacting and receiving payment of moneys due the government, as of taxes, or of customs or revenue duties. See DUTY, 2.

(2) A private person employed to demand and receive payment of money; a collecting agent, q. v.

Collection. The act or fact of claiming and receiving payment of money.

In New York, a guaranty of the collection of a demand, or that it may be collected, or is collectible,

---

[1] Constitution, Art. I, § 8, cl. 5.

[2] Ibid. § 10, cl. 1. See generally Bronson v. Rods, 7 Wall. 247-54 (1868), Chase, C. J.

[3] Act 3 March, 1887 (24 St. L. 634), provides for the exchange and retirement of the trade-dollar.

[4] R. S. §§ 3511-15.

[5] 1 Sup. R. S. p. 306: Act 28 Feb., 1878.

[6] Act 3 March, 1873: R. S. § 3564.

[7] Arthur, Collector v. Richards, 23 Wall. 246 (1874); Cramer v. Arthur, 102 U. S. 612 (1880); Hadden v. Merritt, 115 id. 25 (1885).

---

[1] Act 9 Feb., 1793: R. S. § 3566.

[2] L. collateralis, side by side: con, by; latus, side.

[3] See generally 25 Cent. Law J. 387 (1887), cases.

[4] 2 Bl. Com. 510.

means that payment can be obtained either by demand or by resort to the proper legal remedy.[1] See RE-COVER.

Collect on delivery.

The initials C. O. D. mean collect on delivery, that is, deliver upon payment of the charges due to the seller for the price and to the carrier for the carriage of the goods. The initials have acquired a fixed meaning which the courts and juries may recognize from their general information.[2]

The contract of the carrier is not only for the safe carriage and delivery of the goods to the consignee, but also that he will collect the price and the charges due thereon, and return the price to the consignor. Should the goods be destroyed by any other agency than an act of God or of a public enemy, the carrier is liable, as in other cases.[3] See CARRIER, Common.

Collecting agent or agency.

A collection to be made by a collecting agent imports an undertaking by such agent himself; not that he receives a claim for transmission to another for collection, for whose negligence he is not to be responsible.[4]

For collection. Indorsed on negotiable paper, restrains negotiability. The indorser may prove that he was not the owner and did not mean to give title to it or to its proceeds when collected. Such indorsement is not intended to give currency or circulation to the paper; its effect is limited to an authority to collect.[5]

There is a marked difference of opinion, expressed in the adjudged cases, respecting the liability of a collecting banker for the manner in which the notary, to whom notes are delivered for presentment and protest, discharges his duty. . . The supreme court of New York, in *Allen* v. *Merchants' Bank of New York*,[6] said that "a note or bill of exchange left at a bank and received for the purpose of being sent to a distant

place for collection, would seem to imply, upon a reasonable construction, no other agreement than that it should be forwarded with due diligence to a competent agent to do what should be necessary in the premises. The person leaving the note is aware that the bank cannot personally attend to the collection, and that it must therefore be sent to some distant or foreign agent," and that there was nothing which could imply an assumption for the fidelity of the agent. The case being carried to the court of errors, the foregoing decision was reversed, and the doctrine declared that the bank was responsible for all subsequent agents employed in the collection of the paper.[1] The reversal was by a vote of fourteen senators against ten. The decision has since been followed in New York, and its doctrine adopted in Ohio. But in the courts of other States it has been generally rejected and the views expressed by the supreme court approved. In *Dorchester and Milton Bank* v. *New England Bank* it was held by the supreme court of Massachusetts that when notes or bills, payable at a distant place, are received by a bank for collection, without specific instructions, it is bound to transmit them to a suitable agent at the place of payment, for that purpose; and that when a suitable sub-agent is thus employed, in good faith, the collecting bank is not liable for his neglect or default.[2]

In the supreme courts of Connecticut, Maryland, Illinois, Wisconsin, and Mississippi, the doctrine of the supreme courts of New York and Massachusetts, in the cases cited, has been approved and followed.[3]

The indorsement upon a check " For collection; pay to the order of A," is notice to purchasers that the indorser is entitled to the proceeds.[3]

Whether a stipulation in a note for the payment of the expenses of collection is enforceable under statutes allowing costs or statutes against usury, or whether such stipulation renders the instrument so uncertain as to destroy its negotiable quality, are questions not uniformly settled.[4]

COLLEGE.[5]

1. In the civil law, corporations were called *collegia*, from the idea of individuals being gathered together.[6]

Tres faciunt collegium: three form a corporation.[6]

2. An organized assembly.

---

[1] See Moakley v. Riggs, 19 Johns. 70 (1821); Taylor v. Bullen, 6 Cow. 626 (1827); Cumpston v. McNair, 1 Wend. 460 (1828); Backus v. Shipherd, 11 Wend. 634 (1834); Loveland v. Shepard, 2 Hill, 139 (1841).

[2] State v. Intoxicating Liquors, 73 Me. 279 (1882), Peters, J. See also United States Express Co. v. Keifer, 59 Ind. 267 (1877); American Express Co. v. Lesem, 39 Ill. 333 (1866).

[3] See Pilgreen v. State, 71 Ala. 368 (1882); The Illinois, 2 Flip. 420 (1879); Higgins v. Murray, 73 N. Y. 252, 254 (1878); Wagner v. Hallack, 3 Col. 184 (1877); Gibson v. American Express Co., 1 Hun, 389 (1874); Baker v. Boucicault, 1 Daly, 26–27 (1860); cases *supra.*

[4] Hoover v. Wise, 91 U. S. 310–15 (1875), cases: Hunt, Field, Swayne, Davis, Strong, JJ., and Waite, C. J., concurring; Miller, Clifford, and Bradley, JJ., dissenting.

[5] Sweeney v. Easter, 1 Wall. 173–74 (1863), cases.

[6] 15 Wend. 487 (1836), cases.

[1] 22 Wend. 227–44 (1839), cases.

[2] Britton v. Niccolls, 104 U. S. 761–63 (1881), Field, J. See also First Nat. Bank of Lynn v. Smith, 132 Mass. 227 (1882); Exchange Nat. Bank v. Third Nat. Bank, 112 U. S. 381–93 (1884), cases; Central R. Co. v. First Nat. Bank of Lynchburg, 73 Ga. 383 (1884); Bank of Sherman v. Weiss, 67 Tex. 333–35 (1887), cases. The bank is liable for misappropriation by the agent; Power v. First Nat. Bank of Ft. Benton, 6 Monta. 251 (1887), cases; 35 Alb. Law J. 185–90, cases *contra.* See 18 Cent. Law J. 165–70 (1884), cases; 20 Am. Law Rev. 889–901 (1886), cases.

[3] Bank of the Metropolis v. First Nat. Bank of Jersey City, 19 F. R. 302 (1884), cases.

[4] Merchants' Nat. Bank v. Sevier, 14 F. R. 662, 667–75 (1882), cases.

[5] L. *con-ligere*, to bring together, assemble.

[6] 1 Bl. Com. 460.

Electoral college. The body of electors chosen by the people, in pursuance of the XIIth Amendment, to elect a President and a Vice-President of the United States.[1] See ELECTORAL.

3. Referring to an institution of learning, may more naturally apply to the place where a collection of students is contemplated than to the hall or building intended for their accommodation.[2]

In a statute exempting colleges and academies from taxation, means a seminary of learning: not the assemblage of the professors and students, nor the trustees in their corporate capacity, but certain property belonging to them, with the edifices and the lands whereon the same are erected.[3] See ABODE; CHARITY, 2; ENDOWMENT, 2; MEDICAL; PERMANENT; SCHOOL, Public.

COLLISION.[4] A striking together or impact of two bodies — vehicles or vessels, more commonly the latter.

Includes "allision" — when a stationary body is struck by a moving body; also, injuries from one thing being rubbed or pressed against another — as one vessel lying alongside of another.[5]

1. As to collisions between vehicles, see ACCIDENT; CARRIER, Common; NEGLIGENCE; ROAD, 1, Law of.

2. A vessel engaged in commerce is liable for damage occasioned by a collision, on account of the complicity, direct or indirect, of the owner, or the negligence or want of care or skill of the navigator. The reason is, the owner employs the master and the crew. Any fault is imputed to him, and his vessel is liable. Otherwise when the person in fault does not stand in the relation of agent to the owner.[6]

Where neither vessel is in fault, a loss rests where it falls; where both vessels are in fault, the damages are proportioned equally; where one vessel alone is in fault, it pays all damages. When both vessels are in fault, an innocent person, as, a shipper or consignee, who is injured, may recover of either vessel or of its owner all the loss, and may pursue his remedy at common law, or in admiralty by proceedings *in rem* or *in personam*.[7] For suits *in personam*, the United States courts, as courts of admiralty, have not exclusive jurisdiction, the right to any common-law remedy being expressly saved by statute (R. S. § 563).[1]

Under the act of March 3, 1851 (R. S. §§ 4282–87), the owner is entitled to a limitation of liability to the value of his interest in the ship and in her earned freight, at the termination of the voyage,—which may he by loss of the ship at sea. The subsequent repair of a wrecked vessel, giving her increased value, is not an element; nor is any insurance had on the vessel: that being a collateral and personal interest. And the right to proceed for a limitation of liability is not lost by a surrender of the vessel to the underwriters.[2]

The limitation may be claimed by way of defense, or by surrendering the ship or by paying her value into court. The latter method is necessary when the owner desires to bring all claimants into concourse for distribution.[3]

Where both vessels are in fault, the one that suffers least is decreed to pay the other the amount necessary to make them equal; that is, one-half the difference between the respective losses.[4] The decree should be, not *in solido* for all damages and costs, but severally against each vessel for one-half thereof, any balance unrecovered from one to be paid by the other vessel, and to the extent of her stipulated value beyond the moiety due from her.[5]

Where the collision is between foreign vessels on the high seas, the Federal courts have jurisdiction, the first court that obtains it exercising it under the general maritime law as understood in the courts of the country.[6]

See further ACCIDENT, Inevitable; ACTOR, 1, Sequitur; ADMIRALTY; LIBEL, 4; RES; RESTITUTIO; TUG.

COLLOQUIUM. L. A speaking together: a conversation.

An averment, in an action for slander, that the defendant spoke the words in a certain conversation (*in quodam colloquio*) he had with another person, concerning the plaintiff.

When the words are actionable in themselves, a *colloquium*, averring a speaking of and concerning the plaintiff, is sufficient. When the words have a slanderous meaning, not of their own intrinsic force, but by reason of the existence of some extraneous

---

[1] See 2 Story, Const. §§ 1438–74; 15 Alb. Law J. 220 (1877).

[2] [Stanwood v. Peirce, 7 Mass. 460 (1811), Parsons, C. J.

[3] [State v. Ross, 24 N. J. L. 498 (1854), Haines, J.,— Case of the College of New Jersey.

[4] L. *collidere*, to strike together.

[5] See The Moxey, 1 Abb. Adm. 73 (1847); Wright v. Brown, 4 Ind. 96 (1853); The City of Baltimore, 5 Bened. 474 (1872).

[6] Sturgis v. Boyer, 24 How. 123 (1860), Clifford, J.; The Clarita, 23 Wall. 11 (1874).

[7] Union Steamship Co. v. N. Y. & Va. Steamship Co., 24 How. 313 (1860), Clifford, J.; The Continental, 14 Wall. 355 (1871); The Atlas, 93 U. S. 302 (1876); The Juniata, *ib.* 337 (1876); Vanderbilt v. Reynolds, 16 Blatch. 84–91 (1879), cases; The Clara, 102 U. S. 203 (1880), cases; The Benefactor, *ib.* 214 (1880).

[1] Schoonmaker v. Gilmore, 102 U. S. 118 (1880), cases.

[2] The City of Norwich, 118 U. S. 469, 489–506 (1886), Bradley, J.: Waite, C. J., Field, Woods, and Blatchford, JJ., concurring; Matthews, Miller, Harlan, and Gray, JJ., dissenting — *ib.* pp. 526–41. The other cases, The Scotland, *ib.* 507, and The Great Western, *ib.* 520, being considered in the same connection.

[3] The Great Western, 118 U. S. 520 (1886). See also Norwich Co. v. Wright, 13 Wall. 104, 116–28 (1871), cases; The Benefactor, 103 U. S. 246 (1880).

[4] The North Star, 106 U. S. 20, 17–22 (1882), cases, Bradley, J. See, as to dividing the loss, 2 Law Q. Rev. 357–63 (1886).

[5] The Stirling, 106 U. S. 647 (1882), cases, Waite, C. J.

[6] The Belgenland, 104 U. S. 355, 361 (1885), cases.

fact, this fact must first be averred as inducement, and then there must be a *colloquium*, averring a speaking of or concerning the plaintiff. Lastly, the word "meaning," or *innuendo*, is used to connect the matters thus introduced with the particular words laid, showing their identity, and drawing what is the legal inference from the whole declaration that such was, under the circumstances thus set out, the meaning of the words.[1] See INNUENDO; SLANDER.

COLLUSION.[2] An agreement between persons to defraud another of his rights by the forms of law or to obtain an object forbidden by law.[3] Whence collusive. See FRAUD.

COLONIES. See INDEPENDENCE; LAW, Common; RELIGION; STATE, 2 (2, b); TAX, 2; WRECK.

COLOR. 1. Darkness of skin from presence of African blood.

The phrase " persons of color " embraces, universally, not only all persons descended wholly from African ancestors, but also those who have descended in part only from such ancestors, and have a distinct admixture of African blood.[4]

"Colored" race means "African" race.[5]

In 1866, in Virginia, "colored person" was substituted for "negro," which word before that time included "negro" and "mulatto." The act of February 27, 1866, like the Code of 1849, provided that "every person having one-fourth or more negro blood shall be deemed" a colored person.[6] See CITIZEN; SCHOOL, Separate; WHITE.

2. Appearance; apparent reality, validity, or legality; also, pretense.

Colorable. Existing in aspect merely: not real: as, a colorable abridgment or alteration of a copyrighted production, imitation of a trade-mark, assignment, claim or defense, change of possession, title, *qq. v.*

Colorless. Without intimation as to motive or preference.

Colorless will. A will characterized by a general intent to effect a stated disposition of property, without intimation as to the motives for making the several gifts, or with-

out indication of preference for any beneficiary, class, or object.

Where a general and a particular intent are expressed, the latter, in a case of doubt as to the testator's meaning, is made to yield to the former.[1] See CY PRES; WILL, 2.

Color of law. Pretense or semblance of legal right or authority.[2] See EXTORTION.

Color of office. Pretense or semblance of official right to do an act by one who has no right; pretended authority of office. See further OFFICER, De facto; OFFICIUM, Colore.

Color of title. That which in appearance is title, but which in reality is no title.[3]

The resemblance or appearance of title. Whenever an instrument, by apt words of transfer from grantor to grantee, in form passes what purports to be the title, it gives color of title.[4]

May be made through a conveyance, a bond, a contract, or bare possession under a parol agreement. Whether the title be weak or strong is of no importance. What is color of title is a matter of law for the court. If good faith be a necessary element in the claim, that is for a jury. . . A claim under a conveyance, however inadequate to carry the true title, and however incompetent the grantor, is such a claim under color of title, and one which will draw to the possession of the grantee the protection of the statute of limitations, other requisites of the statutes being complied with.[5] See POSSESSION, Adverse. Compare CLOUD, On title.

Give color. To admit the appearance of right in favor of an adverse party.

"In trespass, if the defendant desires to refer the validity of his title to the court, he may state his title specially, and at the same time 'give color' to the plaintiff, or suppose him to have an appearance of title, had indeed in point of law, but of which a jury are not competent to judge."[6]

"Giving color" is a phrase borrowed from the ancient rhetoricians. In pleading it signifies an apparent or *prima facie* right; and the meaning of the rule that every pleading in confession and avoidance must give color is, that it must admit an apparent right in the opposite party, and rely, therefore, on some new matter by which that apparent right is defeated. . . The kind of color which is naturally

---

[1] Carter *v.* Andrews, 16 Pick. 6 (1834), Shaw, C. J. See also 23 Pa. 82; 53 *id.* 421; 1 Greenl. Ev. § 417.

[2] L. *colludere*, to co-act in a fraud: *con-ludere*, to play together.

[3] See Baldwin *v.* Mayor of New York, 45 Barb. 369 (1856): s. c. 30 How. Pr. 30, quoting Bouvier and others.

[4] Johnson *v.* Town of Norwich, 29 Conn. 408 (1861), Storrs, C. J. See also Van Camp *v.* Board of Education, 9 Ohio St. 411 (1859); 9 Ired. L. 384; 31 Tex. 67.

[5] Clark *v.* Directors of Muscatine, 24 Iowa, 275 (1868); People *v.* Hall, 4 Cal. 399–404 (1854); 37 Miss. 209.

[6] Jones *v.* Commonwealth, 80 Va. 543–44 (1885).

---

[1] See Schouler, Wills, § 476, cases; 1 Redf. Wills, *433, cases.

[2] See United States *v.* Deaver, 14 F. R. 599 (1882).

[3] Wright *v.* Mattison, 18 How. 56–59 (1855), cases.

[4] Hall *v.* Law, 102 U. S. 466 (1880), Field, J.

[5] Wright *v.* Mattison, *supra.* See also 26 Am. Law Reg. 409–19 (1887), cases; 4 Saw. 529; 4 Dill. 555–56; 10 F. R. 536; 33 Cal. 676; 33 Ga. 242; 66 *id.* 170; 23 Ill. 510; 69 *id.* 140; 30 Iowa, 486; 32 Md. 358; 27 Minn. 62–63; 79 N. C. 491; 38 Vt. 345; 6 Wis. 536.

[6] 3 Bl. Com. 309.

latent in the structure of all regular pleadings in confession and avoidance is "implied color," to distinguish it from the kind which, in instances, is formally inserted in the pleading, and known as "express color." To the latter, the term usually applies.[1]

Colore officii. By color of office. See COLOR, 2, Of office.

COLT. See HORSE.

COLUMBIA. See COURTS, United States; DISTRICT, Of Columbia.

COM. See CUM.

COMBAT. A combat in which both parties enter willingly is "mutual."

A person who enters into a combat armed with a concealed deadly weapon may use it to protect his life, if his adversary, who struck the first blow, resorts to such a weapon; and he will not be guilty of assault with intent to murder unless he intended from the first to use the weapon if necessary to overcome his antagonist.[2] See FIGHT.

COMBINATION. 1. In the law of patents, the union of different elements.

A combination is patentable only when the several elements of which it is composed produce by their joint action a new and useful result, or an old result in a cheaper or otherwise more advantageous way.[3]

Limitations and provisos imposed by the inventor will be construed strictly against him, as in the nature of disclaimers.[4]

A combination may be infringed when some of its elements are employed and for others are used mechanical equivalents known to be such when the patent was granted.[5]

See further NOVELTY; EQUIVALENT, 2; PATENT, 2.

2. In penal and criminal laws (as in a statute providing that one common carrier may not combine with another for any purpose), a coalition, union, mutual agreement, or other blending, for any purpose whatever; as, for creating a monopoly.[6]

A combination between the manufacturers of a patented article (a balance shade-roller), intended not to restrict production but simply to maintain a fair and uniform price, and to prevent the injurious effects to producers and consumers of fluctuating prices caused by undue competition, is not in restraint of trade or against public policy.[1]

A combination is criminal whenever the act to be done has a necessary tendency to prejudice the public or to oppress individuals by unjustly subjecting them to the power of the confederates, and giving effect to the purposes of the latter, whether of extortion or mischief.[2]

The gist of the offense is the conspiracy. If the motives of the confederates be to oppress, or the means unlawful, or the consequences to others injurious, it is a conspiracy. Thus, a confederation to raise or depress the price of stocks, labor, merchandise, or the natural products, is a conspiracy.[2]

A confederation or conspiracy by an associated body of ship-owners, which is calculated to have and has the effect of driving the ships of other persons, and those of the plaintiff in particular, out of a certain line of trade,— even though the immediate object be not to injure the plaintiff but to secure to the conspirators a monopoly of the carrying trade between certain ports,— is, or may be, indictable, and therefore actionable, if private and particular damage can be shown. To warrant the court in granting an interim injunction he who complains must show that he has or will sustain "irreparable damage," that is, damage for which he cannot obtain adequate compensation without the special interference of the court.[4]

"If a large number of men, engaged for a certain time, should combine together to violate their contract, and quit their employment together, . . it would surely be a conspiracy to do an unlawful act, though of such a character that, if done by an individual, it would lay the foundation of a civil action only, and not of a criminal prosecution."[5]

See BOYCOTTING; CONSPIRACY; STRIKE, 2; TRADE, Restraints; TRADES-UNIONS.

COME. See APPEARANCE, 3; RESIDE; VENIRE.

COMES. L. See CONSTABLE; COUNTY.

COMFORT. Whatever is necessary to give security from want, and furnish reasonable physical, mental, and spiritual enjoyment.

So held where an executor was directed to pay the testator's widow as much of a certain fund as is "necessary for her comfort."[6] See AM, 1.

---

[1] Stephen Plead., Tyl. ed., 206, 210. See Gould, Pl. 322; 2 Chitty, Pl. 555.

[2] Aldrige v. State, 59 Miss. 255 (1881), Chalmers, C. J.

[3] Stephenson v. Brooklyn R. Co., 114 U. S. 157 (1885); Thatcher Heating Co. v. Burtis, 121 id. 286, 295 (1887), cases.

[4] Sargent v. Hall Safe and Lock Co., 114 U. S. 86 (1885), cases.

[5] Rowell v. Lindsay, 113 U. S. 102 (1885), cases. See also Booth v. Parks, 1 Flip. 381 (1884), cases; Hill v. Sawyer, 31 F. R. 282 (1887), cases; 20 Wall. 368; 92 U. S. 357; 109 id. 420; 111 id. 103; 17 F. R. 80, cases; 19 id. 509, cases.

[6] Watson v. Harlem, &c. Navigation Co., 52 How. Pr. 353 (1877).

[1] Central Shade-Roller Co. v. Cushman, 143 Mass. 364 (1877); Craft v. McConoughy, 79 Ill. 346 (1875). See generally as to combinations for stifling competition, 20 Am. Law Rev. 195-216 (1886), cases.

[2] Commonwealth v. Carlisle, Brightly's Rep. 40 (Pa., 1821), Gibson, J. See Commonwealth v. Gallagher, 2 Pa. L. J. Rep. 64 (1844).

[3] Morris Run Coal Co. v. Barclay Coal Co., 68 Pa. 173, 186-88 (1871), cases. See also Vanarsdale v. Laverty, 69 id. 103, 108 (1871) — an agreement not to employ one as a teacher.

[4] Mogul Steamship Co. v. M'Gregor, Gow & Co., L. R., 15 Q. B. D. 476, 482 (1885), Coleridge, C. J.

[5] Commonwealth v. Hunt et al., 4 Metc. 131 (1842), Shaw, C. J.

[6] Forman v. Whitney, 2 Keyes, 168 (1865).

COMITATUS. See COUNTY, Power of.

COMITY.[1] Courtesy: deference, from good feeling or feeling of equality.

Comity of nations, or between States. Expresses the basis upon which one independent sovereignty applies within its own territory the laws of another sovereignty, in a matter as to which the latter or its citizen is concerned.[2]

Upon this basis rest observances under extradition treaties, q. v. And some adjudications upon the estates of decedents and insolvents are respected, between the States, to the extent that reciprocity obtains.

Comity obtains to permit the corporations of one State to pursue a lawful business in another State.[3]

Judicial comity. The respect which tribunals of independent jurisdictions entertain for the decisions of each other, in the determination of questions involving reference to extra-territorial law.

The Federal courts adopt the construction given to a State's constitution or statutes by the courts of that State, whatever the opinion as to their soundness, except where the highest State court has given different constructions, and rights have been acquired under the earlier construction; in which case they follow the latter;[4] except, also, in interpreting a contract between States, whether the contract is in the shape of a law or of a covenant by State agents;[5] and except in cases where the Constitution, a treaty, or a statute of the United States, provides otherwise.[6] They give a change in construction the same effect in its operation upon existing contract rights that they give to a legislative amendment — they make it prospective.[7] But they are not bound by decisions upon commercial law.[8]

Where the law of a State is not settled, it is the right and the duty of the Federal courts to exercise their own judgment; as they always do in reference to the doctrines of commercial law and general jurisprudence. So, when contracts have been entered into, and rights have accrued thereon under a particular state of the decisions, or where there has been no decision, of the State tribunals, the Federal courts claim the right to adopt their own interpretation of the law applicable to the case, although a different interpretation may be adopted by the State courts after such rights have accrued. But even in such cases, for the

sake of harmony and to avoid confusion, the Federal courts will lean to an agreement of views with the State courts if the question seems to them balanced with doubt. As, however, the object of giving to the National courts jurisdiction to administer the laws of the States in controversies between citizens of different States was to institute independent tribunals which it might be supposed would be unaffected by local prejudices, it is their duty to exercise an independent judgment in cases not foreclosed by previous adjudication.[1]

COMMAND. See MANDATE; PROHIBERE; RATIHABITIO.

COMMENCE. In several uses has a somewhat technical import:

Commencement of a building. Work done on the ground the effect of which is apparent. See further BUILDING.

Commencement of an action, prosecution, or suit. Such inception of judicial proceedings as affects the several defendants; as saves the cause from the bar of the statute of limitations, q. v.; or as assures the jurisdiction, when collaterally questioned.

In civil actions, at common law, suing out or issuing the writ "commences" an action; in equity practice, filing the bill, or, perhaps, issuing and endeavoring to serve the subpœna; under codes of procedure, service or publication of the summons.[2] See BROUGHT.

Before an action can be commenced, the cause of action must be complete, — the day for payment must have passed, a precedent condition must have been performed; the plaintiff must have the necessary privity, and as against the particular defendant; in the case of a tort there must be a legal injury (q. v.), and, possibly, the act must not amount to an untried felony; where there is a breach of a public duty, particular damage must have resulted to the plaintiff.[3]

Commencement of an indictment. The most common form (derived from England) is "The jurors of the people of the State of ——, in and for the body of the county of ——, upon their oath present," etc.[4] Compare CAPTION, 2.

---

[1] L. *comitas*, urbanity: *comis*, friendly.

[2] See Story, Confl. Laws, §§ 28, 33-38.

[3] Cowell v. Saratoga Springs Co., 100 U. S. 59 (1879); Memphis, &c. R. Co. v. Alabama, 107 *id*. 581, 585 (1882), cases.

[4] Fairfield v. County of Gallatin, 100 U. S. 52 (1879), cases; Caroll County v. Smith, 111 *id*. 563 (1884), cases.

[5] Jefferson Branch Bank v. Skelly, 1 Black, 436 (1861); Wright v. Nagle, 101 U. S. 793 (1879).

[6] Oates v. Nat. Bank of Montgomery, 100 U. S. 246 (1879), cases.

[7] Machine Co. v. Gage, 100 U. S. 676 (1879); Douglass v. County of Pike, 101 *id*. 687 (1879).

[1] Burgess v. Seligman, 107 U. S. 33-34 (1882), cases, Bradley, J. See also Pana v. Bowler, *ib*. 541 (1882), cases; Norton v. Shelby County, 118 *id*. 439 (1886).

[2] See generally 26 Cent. Law J. 31-33 (1888), cases; 2 McCrary, 189; 4 Woods, 108; 11 F. R. 217; 17 *ia*. 475; 10 Ark. 120, 479; 19 Cal. 557; 21 *id*. 351; 45 *id*. 125; 30 Ga. 873; 1 Ind. 276; 11 *id*. 48, 354; 8 Iowa, 309; 9 *id*. 178; 10 *id*. 308, 418; 16 *id*. 59; 3 A. K. Marsh. 18; 5 Bush, 435; 15 Mass. 455; 7 Me. 370; 33 Mich. 112; 42 Miss. 241; 36 *id*. 40; 5 N. H. 225; 47 *id*. 24; 37 N. Y. 122; 10 Barb. 318; 6 Cow. 471, 519; 17 Johns. 65; 36 Pa. 474; 24 *id*. 124; 15 *id*. 293; 1 R. I. 17; 11 Humph. 303; 10 Tex. 155; 28 *id*. 713; 30 *id*. 494; 42 Vt. 552; 55 *id*. 355; 6 W. Va. 336.

[3] See 21 Cent. Law J. 401-12 (1885), cases.

[4] People v. Bennett, 37 N. Y. 122 (1867).

COMMENDATIO. L. Commending; recommending.

Simplex commendatio non obligat. A mere recommendation does not bind: the expression of an opinion does not constitute a warranty. Abridged, *Simplex commendatio.*

A false assertion of value, when no warranty is intended, is not a ground of relief to a purchaser: the assertion is a matter of opinion, which does not imply knowledge, and in which men may differ. Every person reposes at his peril in the opinion of others, when he has equal opportunity to form and exercise his own judgment.[1]

"The law recognizes the fact that men will naturally overstate the value and qualities of the articles which they have to sell." A buyer has no right to rely upon mere "dealer's talk."[2] See CAVEAT, Emptor; WARRANTY, 2.

COMMERCE.[3] In its simplest signification, an exchange of goods; but in the advancement of society, labor, transportation, intelligence, care, and various mediums of exchange, become commodities and enter into commerce.[4]

The interchange or mutual change of goods, productions, or property of any kind, between nations or individuals.[5]

"Transportation" is the means by which "commerce" is carried on.[6]

Commercial. Concerning commerce, trade, or traffic; pertaining to the customs of merchants, or to the law-merchant; mercantile: as, commercial or a commercial — broker, corporation, domicil, law, paper, regulation, term, qq. v.

Commercial law is not peculiar to one State nor dependent upon local authority, but arises out of the usages of the commercial world. The Federal courts are not controlled by the decisions of the courts of a State upon matters of commercial law.[6]

Mercantile law is a system of jurisprudence acknowledged by all commercial nations. Upon no subject is it of more importance that there should be,

as far as practicable, uniformity of decision throughout the world.[1] See NEGOTIABLE.

Commercial agency. See COMMUNICATION, Privileged, 2.

Commercial traveler. See below, and DRUMMER; MERCHANT.

In some connections "commerce" relates to dealings with foreign nations; "trade," to mutual traffic among ourselves, or to the buying, selling, or exchange of articles among members of the same community.[2]

The application of the term commerce is generally discussed with reference to the provision (called the commerce or commercial clause of the Constitution) that "The Congress shall have Power . . . To regulate Commerce with foreign Nations and among the several States, and with the Indian Tribes."[3]

By force of this provision, the subject, the vehicle, the agent, and their various operations, become the objects of commercial regulation by Congress.[4,5]

Commerce is more than traffic. It embraces, also, transportation by land and water, and all the means and appliances necessarily employed in carrying them on.[6]

A term of the widest import, comprehending intercourse for the purpose of trade in any and all its forms, including the transportation, purchase, sale, and exchange of commodities.[7]

Commercial intercourse between nations and parts of nations, in all its branches.[8]

"To regulate" this trade and intercourse is to prescribe the rules by which it shall be conducted.[8]

Commerce comprehends navigation,[4] including navigation on rivers and in ports;[9] transportation of

---

[1] 2 Kent, 485, cases; Gordon v. Parmelee, 2 Allen, 214 (1861), Bigelow, C. J.; Hull v. Field, 76 Va. 605 (1882); Tenney v. Cowles, 67 Wis. 594 (1886); Dillman v. Nadlehoffer, 119 Ill. 575 (1887), cases.

[2] Kimball v. Bangs, 144 Mass. 323 (1887), Morton, C. J.; Mooney v. Miller, 102 *id.* 220 (1869); Gordon v. Butler, 105 U. S. 557 (1881); Southern Development Co. v. Silva, 125 *id.* 256 (1888).

[3] L. *commercium,* trade: *con,* with; *merx,* goods.

[4] Gibbons v. Ogden, 9 Wheat. 1, 229 (1824), Marshall, Chief Justice.

[5] Council Bluffs v. Kansas City, &c. R. Co., 45 Iowa, 349 (1876), Miller, C. J. See also People v. Raymond, 34 Cal. 497 (1868).

[6] Brooklyn, &c. R. Co. v. Nat. Bank of Republic, 102 U. S. 31–32 (1880); *ib.* 55.

[1] Goodman v. Simonds, 20 How. 364 (1857); 12 Am. L. Reg. 473 (1873).

[2] People *v.* Fisher, 14 Wend. 15 (1835), Savage, C. J. See also People v. Brooks, 4 Denio, 436 (1847); Sears v. Commissioners, 36 Ind. 270–80 (1871).

[3] Constitution, Art. I, sec. 8, cl. 3.

[4] Gibbons v. Ogden, *ante.*

[5] Council Bluffs v. Kansas City, &c. R. Co., *ante.*

[6] Chicago, &c. R. Co. *v.* Fuller, 17 Wall. 568 (1873): 2 Story, Const. §§ 1061–62.

[7] Welton v. Missouri, 91 U. S. 280, 275 (1875), Field, J.; Webber v. Virginia, 103 *id.* 350 (1880); Walling v. Michigan, 116 *id.* 454 (1886); Robbins v. Taxing District, 120 *id.* 497 (1887); 122 *id.* 358; 128 *id.* 129.

[8] Henderson v. Mayor of N. Y. City, 92 U. S. 270 (1875), Miller, J.; Gloucester Ferry Co. v. Pennsylvania, 114 *id.* 203 (1885).

[9] Gilman v. Philadelphia, 3 Wall. 724 (1865); South

passengers;[1] intercourse by telegraph.[2], [5] But it does not concern matters of trade and traffic between citizens of the same State; as, a trade-mark or a policy of insurance.[3]

"Commerce with foreign Nations" refers to commerce between citizens of the United States and subjects of foreign countries; foreign commerce. Commerce "among (*q. v.*) the several States" refers to commerce between citizens of different States; domestic commerce.[3] Commerce "with the Indian Tribes" applies only to cases where the tribe is wholly within the limits of a State.[4]

Commerce being national in its operation is placed under the protecting care of the National government.[5] Commercially this is but one country, and intercourse is to be as free as due compensation to the carrier interest will allow. Local interference is forbidden.[6] The power is vested in Congress to insure uniformity of commercial regulations, where such uniformity is practicable, and as against conflicting State regulations. The non-exercise of the power is equivalent to a declaration that it shall be free from restrictions.[7]

It is not everything that affects commerce that amounts to a "regulation" of it; as, local regulations of ferries, of hackmen, millers, inn-keepers, warehousemen.[8], [9]

Each State retains absolute control over its own territory, highways, bridges, corporations, etc.[6]

The powers vested in Congress keep pace with the progress of the country, and adapt themselves to the new developments of time and circumstances. . . They were intended for the government of the business to which they relate at all times, and under all circumstances.[6]

Commerce by *water* was principally in the minds of the framers of the Constitution; transportation on land being then in vehicles drawn by animals.[6]

The Constitutional provision covers property transported as an article of commerce from foreign countries, or from another State, from hostile or interfering State legislation, until mingled with part of the general property of the country, and protects it, after it

has entered the State, from burdens imposed by reason of its foreign origin.[1]

In every case where a State law has been held null, it created, in the way of a tax, a license, or a condition, a direct burden upon commerce or interfered with its freedom;[2] it regulated or impeded commerce or discriminated between its own citizens and outsiders, prejudicially to the latter.

For example, a State cannot require a license to sell foreign goods remaining in the packages in which they were imported: that would operate as a tax on the goods.[2], [3] Nor may it discriminate against peddlers;[4] nor against commercial travelers or drummers;[1] nor against sewing machine companies.[5] It may not tax sales of foreign liquors, unless domestic liquors are taxed in equal degree;[6] nor tax passengers, freight, or cars brought into, taken from, or carried through its borders to or from other States or countries.[7] It may not exact wharfage solely of a vessel laden with articles not products of the State; nor impose tonnage duties upon foreign vessels, to pay quarantine expenses;[8] nor collect tonnage duties of its own citizens, engaged in commerce within its own limits,[9] except as to a vessel owned by a resident of a city, for city purposes and not for the privilege of trading;[10] nor may it exact a premium for a vessel brought to its ports;[11] nor require a sum for each passenger brought from a foreign country;[12] nor extort money to prevent immigration;[13] but it may require a list of passengers, with their ages, occupations, etc.[14] What it may do to keep out paupers and convicts, in the absence of legislation by Congress, has not as yet been decided.[15]

---

[1] Welton *v.* Missouri, and other cases, *ante.*

[2] Sherlock *v.* Alling, 93 U. S. 103 (1876).

[3] Brown *v.* Maryland, 12 Wheat. 436 (1827); Cook *v.* Pennsylvania, 97 U. S. 566 (1878).

[4] Ward *v.* Maryland, 12 Wall. 418 (1870); Walling *v.* Michigan, 116 U. S. 454 (1886).

[5] Howe Machine Co. *v.* Gage, 100 U. S. 678 (1879).

[6] Tiernan *v.* Rinker, 102 U. S. 123 (1880).

[7] State Freight Tax, 15 Wall. 232 (1872); State Tax on Railway Receipts, *ib.* 284 (1872); Gloucester Ferry Co. *v.* Pennsylvania, 114 U. S. 203 (1885); Pickard *v.* Pullman Southern Car Co., 117 *id.* 34 (1886); Philadelphia, &c. Steamship Co. *v.* Pennsylvania, 122 *id.* 326, 338–46 (1887), cases, Bradley J., explaining State Tax on Railway Receipts, *supra.*

[8] Peete *v.* Morgan, 19 Wall. 581 (1873); Cannon *v.* New Orleans, 20 *id.* 577 (1874).

[9] State Tonnage Tax, 12 Wall. 204 (1870).

[10] The North Cape, 6 Biss. 505 (1876); Wheeling, &c. Transportation Co. *v.* Wheeling, 99 U. S. 273 (1878).

[11] Steamship Co. *v.* Port-Wardens, 6 Wall. 31 (1867).

[12] Passenger Cases, 7 How. 283 (1849); People *v.* Compagnie Transatlantique, 107 U. S. 59–60 (1882), cases; Wiggins Ferry Co. *v.* East St. Louis, *ib.* 374–75 (1882), cases; 92 *id.* 266–69.

[13] Chy Lung *v.* Freeman, 92 U. S. 275 (1875). But Congress may regulate it by imposing a duty to mitigate incidental evils; Head Money Cases, 112 *id.* 580 (1884).

[14] City of New York *v.* Miln, 11 Pet. 102 (1837); 92 U. S. 265–69.

[15] Henderson *v.* Mayor of N. Y. City, 92 U. S. 260 (1875).

Carolina *v.* Georgia, 93 U. S. 13 (1876); Western Union Tel. Co. *v.* Pendleton, 122 *id.* 358 (1887); 115 *id.* 203.

[1] Steamboat Co. *v.* Livingston, 3 Cow. 713 (1825); People *v.* Raymond, 34 Cal. 497 (1868).

[2] Western Union Telegraph Co. *v.* Atlantic, &c. Tel. Co., 5 Nev. 109 (1869).

[3] Trade-Mark Cases, 100 U. S. 96, 95 (1879); County of Mobile *v.* Kimball, 102 *id.* 697 (1880); Gloucester Ferry Co. *v.* Pennsylvania, 114 *id.* 197 (1885).

[4] United States *v.* Holliday, 3 Wall. 417–18 (1865); United States *v.* Forty-Three Gallons of Whiskey, 108 U. S. 494 (1883).

[5] Pensacola Telegraph Co. *v.* Western Union Tel. Co., 96 U. S. 9 (1877).

[6] Baltimore, &c. R. Co. *v.* Maryland, 21 Wall. 474, 472, 470 (1874).

[7] Gilman *v.* Philadelphia, and other cases, *ante.*

[8] State Tax on Railroad Receipts, 15 Wall. 293 (1872).

[9] Munn *v.* Illinois, 94 U. S. 135 (1876).

A State may not grant an exclusive right to maintain telegraph lines within its borders.[1] Nor may it prohibit the driving of cattle into it, during certain months.[2]

Inter-State commerce cannot be taxed at all, even though the same amount of tax should be laid on domestic commerce, or that which is carried on wholly within the State. The negotiation of sales of goods which are in another State, for the purpose of introducing them into the State in which the negotiation is made, is inter-State commerce. Therefore, a State statute imposing a license tax upon "drummers" and others selling by sample is unconstitutional as applied to citizens of other States.[3]

If the power to tax inter-State or foreign commerce exists, it has no limit but the discretion of the State, and might be exercised in such a manner as to drive away the commerce, or to load it with an intolerable burden, seriously affecting the business and prosperity of other States; and if those States, by way of retaliation, or otherwise, should impose like restrictions, the utmost confusion would prevail in our commercial affairs. This state of things actually existed under the Confederation.[4]

A statute requiring locomotive engineers to be licensed by a board of examiners, and prescribing penalties for its violation, is not unconstitutional, as a regulation of inter-State commerce, even when applied to the case of an engineer operating a locomotive attached to a train running between points in different States.[5]

Some statutes also conflict with the prohibition on the States against levying imposts or duties on imports or exports. But since this provision refers exclusively to articles brought from foreign countries, a State may tax auction sales or other property when there is no discrimination against citizens or products of another State. A purchaser of goods from abroad, which are at his risk until delivered, is not an importer, and the goods may be taxed.[6]

A State may authorize the building of bridges or dams over navigable rivers, provided they do not materially obstruct navigation.[7] See SPAN.

State legislation is not forbidden on matters either local in nature or operation, or intended to be mere aids to commerce, for which special regulations can more effectually provide; such as harbor pilotage, beacons, buoys, and navigable rivers within a State, if free navigation is not thereby impaired. With respect to all such subjects Congress, by non-action, declares that, until it deems fit to act, they may be controlled by State authority. . . The States have as full control over their purely internal commerce as Congress has over inter-State and foreign commerce. . . But as far as an exercise of the power relates to matters which are purely national in character, and require uniformity of regulation affecting all the States, the power is exclusive in Congress.[1]

It is Congress, not the judicial department, that is to regulate commerce. The courts can never take the initiative on this subject. They interpose to prevent or redress acts done or attempted under the authority of unconstitutional State laws: the non-action of Congress, in the cases, being deemed an indication of its will that no exaction or restraint shall be imposed.[2]

The power in Congress is paramount over all legislative powers which, in consequence of not having been granted to Congress, are reserved to the States. It follows that any legislation of a State, although in pursuance of an acknowledged power reserved to it, which conflicts with the actual exercise of the power of Congress over commerce, must give way before the supremacy of the national authority. As the regulation of commerce may consist in abstaining from prescribing positive rules for its conduct, it cannot always be said that the power to regulate is dormant because not affirmatively exercised. And when it is manifest that Congress intends to leave commerce free and unfettered by positive regulations, such intention would be contravened by State laws operating as regulations of commerce as much as if these had been expressly forbidden. In such cases, the existence of the power in Congress has been construed to be exclusive, withdrawing the subject as the basis of legislation altogether from the States. There are many cases, however, where the acknowledged powers of a State may be so exerted as to affect foreign or inter-State commerce without being intended to operate as commercial regulations. If such regulation conflicts with the regulation of the same subject by Congress, either as expressed in positive laws or as implied from the absence of legislation, such State legislation, to the extent of that conflict, must be regarded as annulled. To draw the line of interference between the two fields of jurisdiction, and to define and declare the instances of unconstitutional encroachment, is a judicial question often of much difficulty, the solution of which, perhaps, is not to be found in any single and exact rule of decision. Some

[1] Pensacola Telegraph Co. v. Western Union Tel. Co., 96 U. S. 9 (1877).

[2] Hannibal, &c. R. Co. v. Husen, 95 U. S. 465 (1877).

[3] Robbins v. Taxing District of Shelby County, Tennessee, 120 U. S. 497 (March 7, 1887), Bradley, J.; Waite, C. J., Field, and Gray, JJ., dissenting; 121 id. 246; Exp. Asher, 23 Tex. Ap. 662 (1887): 27 Am. Law Reg. 77 (1888); ib. 89–94, cases; 25 Cent. Law J. 26 (1887).

[4] Philadelphia & Southern Steamship Co. v. Pennsylvania, 122 U. S. 326, 346 (1887), Bradley, J.; Brown v. Maryland, 12 Wheat. 446 (1827), Marshall, C. J.

[5] Smith v. Alabama, 124 U. S. 465 (1888), Matthews, J.; Bradley, J., dissenting. Act of Ala. 28 Feb., 1887.

[6] Waring v. Mayor of Mobile, 8 Wall. 110 (1868); Woodruff v. Parham, ib. 123 (1868); Hinson v. Lott, ib. 148 (1868).

[7] Willison v. Blackbird Creek Marsh Co., 2 Pet. 245 (1829); Wheeling Bridge Case, 18 How. 421 (1855); Gilman v. Philadelphia, 3 Wall. 724 (1865); Escanaba, &c. Transp. Co. v. Chicago, 107 U. S. 683, 687 (1882), cases.

[1] County of Mobile v. Kimball, 102 U. S. 696–99 (1880), Field, J.

[2] Transportation Co. v. Parkersburg, 107 U. S. 701, 704 (1882), Bradley, J. See generally Re Watson, 15 F. R. 511, 514–31 (1882), cases; Kaeiser v. Illinois Central R. Co., 18 id. 153 (1883).

lines of discrimination, however, have been drawn in the various decisions of the Supreme Court.[1]

See further BONUS, 2 (1); IMMIGRATION; INDIAN; INSPECTION, 1; LIEN, Maritime; NAVIGABLE; POLICE, 2; PRIVILEGE, 2; PROHIBITION, 2; QUARANTINE, 2; REGULATE; TAX, 2; TONNAGE; WAREHOUSE; WHARFAGE.

A statute of a State, intended to regulate, to tax, or to impose any other restriction upon the transmission of persons or property or telegraphic messages from one State to another, is not within that class of legislation which the States may enact in the absence of legislation by Congress; and such statutes are void even as to that part of such continuous conveyance as is within the limits of the State.[2]

The case of *The Wabash, &c. R. Co.* v. *Illinois*, declared unconstitutional a statute of Illinois which enacted that if any railroad company within that State should charge or receive for transporting passengers or freight of the same class, the same or a greater sum for any distance, than it charged for a larger distance, it should be liable to a penalty for unjust discrimination. The defendant company discriminated against a shipper at Gilman and in favor of a shipper at Peoria, by charging more for the haul from Gilman although eighty-six miles nearer New York City, the place of unloading. This decision was followed by the act of Congress of February 4, 1887, " An act to regulate commerce," known as the **Inter-State Commerce Act** (24 St. L. 379), which is here reprinted entire —

Section 1. The provisions of this act shall apply to any common carrier or carriers engaged in the transportation of passengers or property wholly by railroad, or partly by railroad and partly by water when both are used, under a common control, management, or arrangement, for a continuous carriage or shipment, from one State or Territory of the United States, or the District of Columbia, to any other State or Territory of the United States, or the District of Columbia, or from any place in the United States to any adjacent foreign country, or from any place in the United States through a foreign country to any other place in the United States, and also to the transportation in like manner of property shipped from any place in the United States to a foreign country and carried from such place to a port of trans-shipment, or shipped from a foreign country to any place in the United States and carried to such place from a port of entry either in the United States or an adjacent foreign country: *Provided, however*, That the provisions of this act shall not apply to the transportation of passengers or property, or to the receiving, delivering, storage, or handling of property, wholly within one State, and not shipped to or from a foreign country from or to any State or Territory as aforesaid.

The term "railroad" as used in this act shall include all bridges and ferries used or operated in connection with any railroad, and also all the road in use by any corporation operating a railroad, whether owned or operated under a contract, agreement, or lease; and the term "transportation" shall include all instrumentalities of shipment or carriage.

All charges made for any service rendered or to be rendered in the transportation of passengers or property as aforesaid, or in connection therewith, or for the receiving, delivering, storage, or handling of such property, shall be reasonable and just; and every unjust and unreasonable charge for such service is prohibited and declared to be unlawful.

Sec. 2. That if any common carrier subject to the provisions of this act shall, directly or indirectly, by any special rate, rebate, drawback, or other device, charge, demand, collect, or receive from any person or persons a greater or less compensation for any service rendered or to be rendered than it charges, demands, collects, or receives from any other person or persons for doing for him or them a like and contemporaneous service in the transportation of a like kind of traffic under substantially similar circumstances and conditions, such common carrier shall be deemed guilty of unjust discrimination, which is hereby prohibited and declared to be unlawful.

Sec. 3. That it shall be unlawful for any common carrier subject to the provisions of this act to make or give any undue or unreasonable preference or advantage to any particular person, company, firm, corporation, or locality, or any particular description of traffic, in any respect whatsoever, or to subject any particular person, company, firm, corporation, or locality, or any particular description of traffic, to any undue or unreasonable prejudice or disadvantage in any respect whatsoever.

Every common carrier subject to the provisions of this act shall, according to their respective powers, afford all reasonable, proper, and equal facilities for the interchange of traffic between their respective lines, and for the receiving, forwarding, and delivering of passengers and property to and from their several lines and those connecting therewith, and shall not discriminate in their rates and charges between such connecting lines; but this shall not be construed as requiring any such common carrier to give the use

---

[1] Smith v. Alabama, 124 U. S. 473 (1888), Matthews, J. See Tests of Regulation, 1 Harv. Law Rev. 159–84 (1887), cases.

[2] Wabash, St. Louis & Pacific R. Co. v. Illinois, 118 U. S. 557, 560–77 (Oct. 25, 1886), cases, Miller, J.; Field, Harlan, Woods, Matthews, and Blatchford, JJ., concurring; Waite, C. J., Bradley, and Gray, JJ., dissenting, pp. 577–96, opinion by Bradley, J.

In the case of The Reading Railroad Co. v. Pennsylvania, commonly called the Case of the State Freight Tax, 15 Wall. 232 (1872), it was held that a tax upon freight taken up within a State and carried out of it, or taken up outside of the State and brought within it, is an unlawful burden on inter-State commerce. In Fargo v. Michigan, 121 U. S. 230 (April 4, 1887), it was held that a State statute which levies a tax upon the gross receipts of railroads for the carriage of freight and passengers into, out of, or through the State, is also unconstitutional. See Reading Railroad Case explained, ib. 240, Wabash Railway Case, ib. 247, and other cases, ib. 242–46. The State may of course tax money after it has passed the stage of compensation for carrying persons or property, ib. 230. The Wabash Railway case ruled the case of The Commonwealth v. Housatonic R. Co., 143 Mass. 266 (Jan. 7, 1887).

of its tracks or terminal facilities to another carrier engaged in like business.

Sec. 4. That it shall be unlawful for any common carrier subject to the provisions of this act to charge or receive any greater compensation in the aggregate for the transportation of passengers or of like kind of property, under substantially similar circumstances and conditions, for a shorter than for a longer distance over the same line, in the same direction, the shorter being included within the longer distance; but this shall not be construed as authorizing any common carrier within the terms of this act to charge and receive as great compensation for a shorter as for a longer distance: *Provided, however,* That upon application to the commission appointed under the provisions of this act, such common carrier may, in special cases, after investigation by the commission, be authorized to charge less for longer than for shorter distances for the transportation of passengers or property; and the commission may from time to time prescribe the extent to which such designated common carrier may be relieved from the operation of this section of this act.

Sec. 5. That it shall be unlawful for any common carrier subject to the provisions of this act to enter into any contract, agreement, or combination with any other common carrier or carriers for the pooling of freights of different and competing railroads, or to divide between them the aggregate or net proceeds of the earnings of such railroads, or any portion thereof; and in any case of an agreement for the pooling of freights as aforesaid, each day of its continuance shall be deemed a separate offense.

Sec. 6. That every common carrier subject to the provisions of this act shall print and keep for public inspection schedules showing the rates and fares and charges for the transportation of passengers and property which any such common carrier has established and which are in force at the time upon its railroad, as defined by the first section of this act. The schedules printed as aforesaid by any such common carrier shall plainly state the places upon its railroad between which property and passengers will be carried, and shall contain the classification of freight in force upon such railroad, and shall also state separately the terminal charges and any rules or regulations which in any wise change, affect, or determine any part or the aggregate of such aforesaid rates and fares and charges. Such schedules shall be plainly printed in large type, of at least the size of ordinary pica, and copies for the use of the public shall be kept in every depot or station upon any such railroad, in such places and in such form that they can be conveniently inspected.

Any common carrier subject to the provisions of this act receiving freight in the United States to be carried through a foreign country to any place in the United States shall also in like manner print and keep for public inspection, at every depot where such freight is received for shipment, schedules showing the through rates established and charged by such common carrier to all points in the United States beyond the foreign country to which it accepts freight for shipment; and any freight shipped from the United States through a foreign country into the United States, the through rate on which shall not have been made public as required by this act, shall, before it is admitted into the United States from said foreign country, be subject to customs duties as if said freight were of foreign production; and any law in conflict with this section is hereby repealed.

No advance shall be made in the rates, fares, and charges which have been established and published as aforesaid by any common carrier in compliance with the requirements of this section, except after ten days' public notice, which shall plainly state the changes proposed to be made in the schedule then in force, and the time when the increased rates, fares, or charges will go into effect; and the proposed changes shall be shown by printing new schedules, or shall be plainly indicated upon the schedules in force at the time and kept for public inspection. Reductions in such published rates, fares, or charges may be made without previous public notice; but whenever any such reduction is made, notice of the same shall immediately be publicly posted and the changes made shall immediately be made public by printing new schedules, or shall immediately be plainly indicated upon the schedules at the time in force and kept for public inspection.

And when any such common carrier shall have established and published its rates, fares, and charges in compliance with the provisions of this section, it shall be unlawful for such common carrier to charge, demand, collect, or receive from any person or persons a greater or less compensation for the transportation of passengers or property, or for any services in connection therewith, than is specified in such published schedule of rates, fares, and charges as may at the time be in force.

Every common carrier subject to the provisions of this act shall file with the commission hereinafter provided for copies of its schedules of rates, fares, and charges which have been established and published in compliance with the requirements of this section, and shall promptly notify said commission of all changes made in the same. Every such common carrier shall also file with said commission copies of all contracts, agreements, or arrangements with other common carriers in relation to any traffic affected by the provisions of this act to which it may be a party. And in cases where passengers and freight pass over continuous lines or routes operated by more than one common carrier, and the several common carriers operating such lines or routes establish joint tariffs of rates or fares or charges for such continuous lines or routes, copies of such joint tariffs shall also, in like manner, be filed with said commission. Such joint rates, fares, and charges on such continuous lines so filed as aforesaid shall be made public by such common carriers when directed by said commission, in so far as may, in the judgment of the commission, be deemed practicable; and said commission shall from time to time prescribe the measure of publicity which shall be given to such rates, fares, and charges, or to such part of them as it may deem it practicable for such common carriers to publish, and the places in which they shall be published; but no common carrier party to any such joint tariff shall be liable for the failure of any other common carrier party thereto to observe and adhere to the rates, fares, or charges thus made and published.

If any such common carrier shall neglect or refuse to file or publish its schedules or tariffs of rates, fares, and charges as provided in this section, or any part of the same, such common carrier shall, in addition to other penalties herein prescribed, be subject to a writ of *mandamus*, to be issued by any circuit court of the United States in the judicial district wherein the principal office of said common carrier is situated or wherein such offense may be committed, and if such common carrier be a foreign corporation, in the judicial circuit wherein such common carrier accepts traffic and has an agent to perform such service, to compel compliance with the aforesaid provisions of this section; and such writ shall issue in the name of the people of the United States, at the relation of the commissioners appointed under the provisions of this act; and failure to comply with its requirements shall be punishable as and for a contempt; and the said commissioners, as complainants, may also apply, in any such circuit court of the United States, for a writ of injunction against such common carrier, to restrain such common carrier from receiving or transporting property among the several States and Territories of the United States, or between the United States and adjacent foreign countries, or between ports of transshipment and of entry and the several States and Territories of the United States, as mentioned in the first section of this act, until such common carrier shall have complied with the aforesaid provisions of this section of this act.

Sec. 7. That it shall be unlawful for any common carrier subject to the provisions of this act to enter into any combination, contract, or agreement, expressed or implied, to prevent, by change of time schedule, carriage in different cars, or by other means or devices, the carriage of freights from being continuous from the place of shipment to the place of destination; and no break of bulk, stoppage, or interruption made by such common carrier shall prevent the carriage of freights from being and being treated as one continuous carriage from the place of shipment to the place of destination, unless such break, stoppage, or interruption was made in good faith for some necessary purpose, and without any intent to avoid or unnecessarily interrupt such continuous carriage or to evade any of the provisions of this act.

Sec. 8. That in case any common carrier subject to the provisions of this act shall do, cause to be done, or permit to be done any act, matter, or thing in this act prohibited or declared to be unlawful, or shall omit to do any act, matter, or thing in this act required to be done, such common carrier shall be liable to the person or persons injured thereby for the full amount of damages sustained in consequence of any such violation of the provisions of this act, together with a reasonable counsel or attorney's fee, to be fixed by the court in every case of recovery, which attorney's fee shall be taxed and collected as part of the costs in the case.

Sec. 9. That any person or persons claiming to be damaged by any common carrier subject to the provisions of this act may either make complaint to the commission as hereinafter provided for, or may bring suit in his or their own behalf for the recovery of the damages for which such common carrier may be liable under the provisions of this act, in any district or circuit court of the United States of competent jurisdiction; but such person or persons shall not have the right to pursue both of said remedies, and must in each case elect which one of the two methods of proceduro herein provided for he or they will adopt. In any such action brought for the recovery of damages the court before which the same shall be pending may compel any director, officer, receiver, trustee, or agent of the corporation or company defendant in such suit to attend, appear, and testify in such case, and may compel the production of the books and papers of such corporation or company party to any such suit; the claim that any such testimony or evidence may tend to criminate the person giving such evidence shall not excuse such witness from testifying, but such evidence or testimony shall not be used against such person on the trial of any criminal proceeding.

Sec. 10. That any common carrier subject to the provisions of this act, or, whenever such common carrier is a corporation, any director or officer thereof, or any receiver, trustee, lessee, agent, or person acting for or employed by such corporation, who, alone or with any other corporation, company, person, or party, shall willfully do or cause to be done, or shall willingly suffer or permit to be done, any act, matter, or thing in this act prohibited or declared to be unlawful, or who shall aid or abet therein, or shall willfully omit or fail to do any act, matter, or thing in this act required to be done, or shall cause or willingly suffer or permit any act, matter, or thing so directed or required by this act to be done not to be so done, or shall aid or abet any such omission or failure, or shall be guilty of any infraction of this act, or shall aid or abet therein, shall be deemed guilty of a misdemeanor, and shall, upon conviction thereof in any district court of the United States within the jurisdiction of which such offense was committed, be subject to a fine of not to exceed five thousand dollars for each offense.

Sec. 11. That a commission is hereby created and established to be known as the Inter-State Commerce Commission, which shall be composed of five commissioners, who shall be appointed by the President, by and with the advice and consent of the Senate. The commissioners first appointed under this act shall continue in office for the term of two, three, four, five, and six years, respectively, from the first day of January, A. D. 1887, the term of each to be designated by the President; but their successors shall be appointed for terms of six years, except that any person chosen to fill a vacancy shall be appointed only for the unexpired term of the commissioner whom he shall succeed. Any commissioner may be removed by the President for inefficiency, neglect of duty, or malfeasance in office. Not more than three of the commissioners shall be appointed from the same political party. No person in the employ of or holding any official relation to any common carrier subject to the provisions of this act, or owning stock or bonds thereof, or who is in any manner pecuniarily interested therein, shall enter upon the duties of or hold such office. Said commissioners shall not engage in any other business, vocation, or employment. No vacancy in the commission shall impair the right of the remaining commissioners to exercise all the powers of the commission.

Sec. 12. That the commission hereby created shall have authority to inquire into the management of the business of all common carriers subject to the provisions of this act, and shall keep itself informed as to the manner and method in which the same is conducted, and shall have the right to obtain from such common carriers full and complete information necessary to enable the commission to perform the duties and carry out the objects for which it was created; and for the purposes of this act the commission shall have power to require the attendance and testimony of witnesses and the production of all books, papers, tariffs, contracts, agreements, and documents relating to any matter under investigation, and to that end may invoke the aid of any court of the United States in requiring the attendance and testimony of witnesses and the production of books, papers, and documents under the provisions of this section.

And any of the circuit courts of the United States within the jurisdiction of which such inquiry is carried on may, in case of contumacy or refusal to obey a subpœna issued to any common carrier subject to the provisions of this act, or other person, issue an order requiring such common carrier or other person to appear before said commission (and produce books and papers if so ordered) and give evidence touching the matter in question; and any failure to obey such order of the court may be punished by such court as a contempt thereof. The claim that any such testimony may tend to criminate the person giving such evidence shall not excuse such witness from testifying; but such evidence or testimony shall not be used against such person on the trial of any criminal proceeding.

Sec. 13. That any person, firm, corporation, or association, or any mercantile, agricultural, or manufacturing society, or any body politic, or municipal organization complaining of anything done or omitted to be done by any common carrier subject to the provisions of this act in contravention of the provisions thereof, may apply to said commission by petition, which shall briefly state the facts; whereupon a statement of the charges thus made shall be forwarded by the commission to such common carrier, who shall be called upon to satisfy the complaint or to answer the same in writing within a reasonable time, to be specified by the commission. If such common carrier, within the time specified, shall make reparation for the injury alleged to have been done, said carrier shall be relieved of liability to the complainant only for the particular violation of law thus complained of. If such carrier shall not satisfy the complaint within the time specified, or there shall appear to be any reasonable ground for investigating said complaint, it shall be the duty of the commission to investigate the matters complained of in such manner and by such means as it shall deem proper.

Said commission shall in like manner investigate any complaint forwarded by the railroad commissioner or railroad commission of any State or Territory, at the request of such commissioner or commission, and may institute any inquiry on its own motion in the same manner and to the same effect as though complaint had been made.

No complaint shall at any time be dismissed because of the absence of direct damage to the complainant.

Sec. 14. That whenever an investigation shall be made by said commission, it shall be its duty to make a report in writing in respect thereto, which shall include the findings of fact upon which the conclusions of the commission are based, together with its recommendation as to what reparation, if any, should be made by the common carrier to any party or parties who may be found to have been injured; and such findings so made shall thereafter, in all judicial proceedings, be deemed *prima facie* evidence as to each and every fact found.

All reports of investigations made by the commission shall be entered of record, and a copy thereof shall be furnished to the party who may have complained, and to any common carrier that may have been complained of.

Sec. 15. That if in any case in which an investigation shall be made by said commission it shall be made to appear to the satisfaction of the commission, either by the testimony of witnesses or other evidence, that anything has been done or omitted to be done in violation of the provisions of this act, or of any law cognizable by said commission, by any common carrier, or that any injury or damage has been sustained by the party or parties complaining, or by other parties aggrieved in consequence of any such violation, it shall be the duty of the commission to forthwith cause a copy of its report in respect thereto to be delivered to such common carrier, together with a notice to said common carrier to cease and desist from such violation, or to make reparation for the injury so found to have been done, or both, within a reasonable time, to be specified by the commission; and if, within the time specified, it shall be made to appear to the commission that such common carrier has ceased from such violation of law, and has made reparation for the injury found to have been done, in compliance with the report and notice of the commission, or to the satisfaction of the party complaining, a statement to that effect shall be entered of record by the commission, and the said common carrier shall thereupon be relieved from further liability or penalty for such particular violation of law.

Sec. 16. That whenever any common carrier, as defined in and subject to the provisions of this act, shall violate or refuse or neglect to obey any lawful order or requirement of the commission in this act named, it shall be the duty of the commission, and lawful for any company or person interested in such order or requirement, to apply, in a summary way, by petition, to the circuit court of the United States sitting in equity in the judicial district in which the common carrier complained of has its principal office, or in which the violation or disobedience of such order or requirement shall happen, alleging such violation or disobedience, as the case may be; and the said court shall have power to hear and determine the matter, on such short notice to the common carrier complained of as the court shall deem reasonable; and such notice may be served on such common carrier, his or its officers, agents, or servants, in such manner as the court shall direct; and said court shall proceed to hear and determine the matter speedily as a court of equity, and without the formal pleadings and proceedings applicable to ordinary suits in equity, but in such manner as to do justice in the premises; and to this end such court shall have power, if it think fit, to direct and prosecute, in such mode and by such persons as it may appoint, all such inquiries as the court may think needful to enable it to form a just judgment in the matter of such petition; and on such hearing the report of said commission shall be *prima facie* evidence of the matters therein stated; and if it be made to appear to such court, on such hearing or on report of any such person or persons, that the lawful order or requirement of said commission drawn in question has been violated or disobeyed, it shall be lawful for such court to issue a writ of injunction or other proper process, mandatory or otherwise, to restrain such common carrier from further continuing such violation or disobedience of such order or requirement of said commission, and enjoining obedience to the same; and in case of any disobedience of any such writ of injunction or other proper process, mandatory or otherwise, it shall be lawful for such court to issue writs of attachment, or any other process of said court incident or applicable to writs of injunction or other proper process, mandatory or otherwise, against such common carrier, and if a corporation, against one or more of the directors, officers, or agents of the same, or against any owner, lessee, trustee, receiver, or other person failing to obey such writ of injunction or other proper process, mandatory or otherwise; and said court may, if it shall think fit, make an order directing such common carrier or other person so disobeying such writ of injunction or other proper process, mandatory or otherwise, to pay such sum of money not exceeding for each carrier or person in default the sum of five hundred dollars for every day after a day to be named in the order that such carrier or other person shall fail to obey such injunction or other proper process, mandatory or otherwise; and such moneys shall be payable as the court shall direct, either to the party complaining, or into court to abide the ultimate decision of the court, or into the treasury; and payment thereof may, without prejudice to any other mode of recovering the same, be enforced by attachment or order in the nature of a writ of execution, in like manner as if the same had been recovered by a final decree *in personam* in such court. When the subject in dispute shall be of the value of two thousand dollars or more, either party to such proceeding before said court may appeal to the Supreme Court of the United States, under the same regulations now provided by law in respect of security for such appeal; but such appeal shall not operate to stay or supersede the order of the court or the execution of any writ or process thereon; and such court may, in every such matter, order the payment of such costs and counsel fees as shall be deemed reasonable. Whenever any such petition shall be filed or presented by the commission it shall be the duty of the district attorney, under the direction of the attorney-general of the United States, to prosecute the same; and the costs and expenses of such prosecution shall be paid out of the appropriation for the expenses of the courts of the United States. For the purposes of this act, ex-

cepting its penal provisions, the circuit courts of the United States shall be deemed to be always in session.

Sec. 17. That the commission may conduct its proceedings in such manner as will best conduce to the proper dispatch of business and to the ends of justice. A majority of the commission shall constitute a quorum for the transaction of business, but no commissioner shall participate in any hearing or proceeding in which he has any pecuniary interest. Said commission may, from time to time, make or amend such general rules or orders as may be requisite for the order and regulation of proceedings before it, including forms of notices and the service thereof, which shall conform, as nearly as may be, to those in use in the courts of the United States. Any party may appear before said commission and be heard, in person or by attorney. Every vote and official act of the commission shall be entered of record, and its proceedings shall be public upon the request of either party interested. Said commission shall have an official seal, which shall be judicially noticed. Either of the members of the commission may administer oaths and affirmations.

Sec. 18. That each commissioner shall receive an annual salary of seven thousand five hundred dollars, payable in the same manner as the salaries of judges of the courts of the United States. The commission shall appoint a secretary, who shall receive an annual salary of three thousand five hundred dollars, payable in like manner. The commission shall have authority to employ and fix the compensation of such other employees as it may find necessary to the proper performance of its duties, subject to the approval of the secretary of the interior.

The commission shall be furnished by the secretary of the interior with suitable offices and all necessary office supplies. Witnesses summoned before the commission shall be paid the same fees and mileage that are paid witnesses in the courts of the United States.

All of the expenses of the commission, including all necessary expenses for transportation incurred by the commissioners, or by their employees under their orders, in making any investigation in any other places than in the city of Washington, shall be allowed and paid, on the presentation of itemized vouchers therefor approved by the chairman of the commission and the secretary of the interior.

Sec. 19. That the principal office of the commission shall be in the city of Washington, where its general sessions shall be held; but whenever the convenience of the public or of the parties may be promoted or delay or expense prevented thereby, the commission may hold special sessions in any part of the United States. It may, by one or more of the commissioners, prosecute any inquiry necessary to its duties, in any part of the United States, into any matter or question of fact pertaining to the business of any common carrier subject to the provisions of this act.

Sec. 20. That the commission is hereby authorized to require annual reports from all common carriers subject to the provisions of this act, to fix the time and prescribe the manner in which such reports shall be made, and to require from such carriers specific answers to all questions upon which the commission may need information. Such annual reports shall show in etail the amount of capital stock issued, the amounts aid therefor, and the manner of payment for the ame; the dividends paid, the surplus fund, if any, and ie number of stockholders; the funded and floating ehts and the interest paid thereon; the cost and value f the carrier's property, franchises, and equipment; ie number of employees and the salaries paid each lass; the amounts expended for improvements each ear, how expended, and the character of such imrovements; the earnings and receipts from each ranch of business and from all sources; the operatig and other expenses; the balances of profit and oss; and a complete exhibit of the financial operaions of the carrier each year, including an annual alance-sheet. Such reports shall also contain such iformation in relation to rates or regulations conerning fares or freights, or agreements, arrangeients, or contracts with other common carriers, as ie commission may require; and the said commission ay, within its discretion, for the purpose of enabling ; the better to carry out the purposes of this act, precribe (if in the opinion of the commission it is practiable to prescribe such uniformity and methods of eeping accounts) a period of time within which all ommon carriers subject to the provisions of this act hall have, as near as may he, a uniform system of acounts, and the manner in which such accounts shall e kept.

Sec. 21. That the commission shall, on or before the rst day of December in each year, make a report to ie secretary of the interior, which shall he by him ansmitted to Congress, and copies of which shall be istributed as are the other reports issued from the iterior department. This report shall contain such iformation and data collected by the commission as ay he considered of value in the determination of uestions connected with the regulation of commerce, ogether with such recommendations as to additional gislation relating thereto as the commission may eem necessary.

Sec. 22. That nothing in this act shall apply to the arriage, storage, or handling of property free or at reuced rates for the United States, State, or municipal overnments, or for charitable purposes, or to or from airs and expositions for exhibition thereat, or the issunce of mileage, excursion, or commutation passenger ckets; nothing in this act shall he construed to proihit any common carrier from giving reduced rates to iinisters of religion; nothing in this act shall be conrued to prevent railroads from giving free carriage) their own officers and employees, or to prevent the rincipal officers of any railroad company or comanies from exchanging passes or tickets with other ilroad companies for their officers and employees; id nothing in this act contained shall in any way oridge or alter the remedies now existing at comon law or by statute, hut the provisions of this act e in addition to such remedies: *Provided*, That) pending litigation shall in any way he affected by is act.

Sec. 23. That the sum of one hundred thousand ollars is herehy appropriated for the use and puroses of this act for the fiscal year ending June 30, . D. 1888, and the intervening time anterior thereto.

Sec. 24. That the provisions of sections eleven and

eighteen of this act, relating to the appointment and organization of the commission herein provided for, shall take effect immediately, and the remaining provisions of this act shall take effect sixty days after its passage. See ADDENDA.

March 22, 1887, President Cleveland appointed the following commissioners: Thomas M. Cooley, of Michigan, for the term of six years; William R. Morrison, of Illinois, for the term of five years; Augustus Schoonmaker, of New York, for the term of four years; Aldace F. Walker, of Vermont, for the term of three years; Walter L. Bragg, of Alabama, for the term of two years. At the first meeting of the commission, March 31, Mr. Cooley was chosen chairman.[1]

April 4, 1887, in the circuit court of Oregon, in a case concerning the transportation of goods by the Oregon and California Railroad (which lies wholly within Oregon), destined for San Francisco, Judge Deady, after explaining that the act "does not include or apply to all carriers engaged in inter-State commerce, but only to such as use a railway or railway and water-craft under common control or management for a continuous carriage or shipment of property from one State to another," held that it does not "apply to the carriage of property by rail wholly within the State, although shipped from one destined to a place without the State, so that such place is not in a foreign country."[2]

June 15, 1887, the commission summarized its conclusions upon the construction to be placed upon the fourth section of the act, in the following language:

First. That the prohibition against a greater charge for a shorter than for a longer distance over the same line, in the same direction, the shorter being included within the longer distance, as qualified therein is limited to cases in which the circumstances and conditions are substantially similar.

Second. That the phrase "under substantially similar circumstances and conditions" in the fourth section, is used in the same sense as in the second section; and under the qualified form of the prohibition in the fourth section carriers are required to judge in the first instance with regard to the similarity or dissimilarity of the circumstances and conditions that forhid or permit a greater charge for a shorter distance.

Third. That the judgment of carriers in respect to the circumstances and conditions is not final, but is subject to the authority of the commission and of the courts, to decide whether error has been committed, or whether the statute has been violated. And in case of complaint for violating the fourth section of the act the burden of proof is on the carrier to justify any departure from the general rule prescribed by the statute by showing that the circumstances and conditions are substantially dissimilar.

Fourth. That the provisions of section one, requiring charges to be reasonable and just, and of section two, forbidding unjust discrimination, apply when

---

[1] The first and the present secretary of the commission is Edward A. Moseley; and the present auditor is C. C. McCain.

[2] *Exp.* Koehler, 1 I. C. R. 28; 30 F. R. 867.

exceptional charges are made under section four as they do in other cases.

Fifth. That the existence of actual competition which is of controlling force, in respect to traffic important in amount, may make out the dissimilar circumstances and conditions entitling the carrier to charge less for the longer than for the shorter haul over the same line in the same direction, the shorter being included in the longer in the following cases:

1. When the competition is with carriers by water which are not subject to the provisions of the statute.

2. When the competition is with foreign or other railroads which are not subject to the provisions of the statute.

3. In rare and peculiar cases of competition between railroads which are subject to the statute, when a strict application of the general rule of the statute would be destructive of legitimate competition.

Sixth. The commission further decides that when a greater charge in the aggregate is made for the transportation of passengers or the like kind of property for a shorter than for a longer distance over the same line in the same direction, the shorter being included in the longer distance, it is not sufficient justification therefor that the traffic which is subjected to such greater charge is way or local traffic, and that which is given the more favorable rates is not.

Nor is it sufficient justification for such greater charge that the short-haul traffic is more expensive to the carrier, unless when the circumstances are such as to make it exceptionally expensive, or the long-haul traffic exceptionally inexpensive, the difference being extraordinary and susceptible of definite proof.

Nor that the lesser charge on the longer haul has for its motive the encouragement of manufactures or some other branch of industry.

Nor that it is designed to build up business or trade centres.

Nor that the lesser charge on the longer haul is merely a continuation of the favorable rates under which trade centres or industrial establishments have been built up.

The fact that long-haul traffic will only bear certain rates is no reason for carrying it for less than cost at the expense of other traffic.[1]

Where the conditions are dissimilar there is no prohibition; a doubt should be solved in favor of the object of the law.[2]

Railroads doing an express business are within the act; independent express companies are not.[3]

A road wholly within a State, but used as a means of conducting inter-State traffic by companies owning connecting inter-State roads, is subject to the provisions of the act.[4]

The act does not embrace *carriers wholly by water,* though they may also be engaged in the like commerce and as such be rivals of the carriers which the act undertakes to control. Perhaps the most influential reasons for omitting them were that the evils of corporate management have not been so obvious in their case as in that of carriers by land, and their rates of transportation were so low that they were seldom complained of even when unjustly discriminating. The fact that in their competition with carriers by land they were at a disadvantage had some influence in propitiating public favor, inasmuch as they appeared to operate as obstacles to monopoly and as checks upon extortion.[1]

May 25, 1887, the following rules of practice were adopted by the commission (Report for 1887, p. 127):—

I. When at Washington the commission will hold its general sessions at 11 o'clock A. M. daily, except Saturdays and Sundays, for the reception and hearing of petitions and complaints, and the transaction of such other business as may be brought before it. The sessions will be held at the office of the commission in the Sun Building, No. 1315 F street northwest. When special sessions are held at other places such regulations as may be necessary will be made by the commission.

II. Applications under the fourth section of the act for authority to charge less for longer than for shorter distances for the transportation of passengers or property must be made by petition addressed to the commission by the carrier or carriers desiring the relief. The petition must state with particularity the extent of the relief desired and the points at and between which authority is asked to charge less for longer distances; the reasons for the relief sought must also be set forth, and the facts upon which the application is founded. The petition must be verified by some officer or agent of the carrier in whose behalf it is presented, to the effect that the allegations of the petition are true to the knowledge or belief of the affiant. Notice must be published by a petitioner in not less than two newspapers along the line of the road having general circulation, for at least ten days prior to the presentation of a petition, stating briefly the nature of the relief intended to be applied for and the time when the application will be presented, and proof of each publication must be filed with the petition.

III. Upon the presentation of a petition for relief an investigation will be made by the commission at a time and place to be designated, when testimony will be received for and against the prayer of the petition. After investigation the commission will make such order as may appear to be just and appropriate upon the facts and circumstances of the case.

IV. Complaints under section 13 of the act of anything done or omitted to be done by any common carrier subject to the provisions of the act, in contravention of the provisions thereof, must be made by petition, which must briefly state the facts which are claimed to constitute a violation of the act, and must be verified by the petitioner, or by some officer or agent of the corporation, society, or other body or organization making the complaint, to the effect that

---

[1] Report, 1887, pp. 64, 84–85. See *ib.* 18–20. *Re* Petition of Louisville & Nashville R. Co., and others.

[2] Missouri Pacific R. Co. *v.* Texas & Pacific R. Co., 31 F. R. 862 (June 21, 1887), Pardee, J.

[3] *Re* Express Companies, 1 I. C. R. 677–83 (Dec. 28, 1887), Walker, C. See also Report, 1887, pp. 12–14. As to sleeping and parlor car companies, and transporters of mineral oil, see *ib.* 15.

[4] Heck *v.* East Tennessee, &c. R. Cos. (Feb. 17, 1888).

[1] Report of 1877, pp. 11–12.

the allegations of the petition are true to the knowl-edge or belief of the affiant.

The complainant must furnish as many written or printed copies of the complaint or petition as there may be parties complained against to be served. When a complaint is made the name of the carrier complained against must be set forth in full, and the address of the petitioner and the name and address of his attorney or counsel, if any, must be indorsed upon the complaint.

The commission will cause a copy of the complaint to be served upon each common carrier complained against, by mail or personally, in its discretion, with notice to the carrier or carriers to satisfy the complaint or to answer the same in writing within the time specified.

V. A carrier complained against must answer the complaint made within twenty days from the date of the notice, unless the commission shall in particular cases prescribe a shorter time for the answer to be served, and in such cases the answer must be made within the time prescribed. The original answer must be filed with the commission, at its office in Washington, and a copy thereof must at the same time be served upon the complainant by the party answering, personally or by mail. The answer must admit or deny the material allegations of fact contained in the complaint, and may set forth any additional facts claimed to be material to the issue. The answer must be verified in the same manner as the complaint. If a carrier complained against shall make satisfaction before answering, a written acknowledgment of satisfaction must be filed with the commission, and in that case the fact of satisfaction without other matter may be set forth in the answer filed and served on the complainant. If satisfaction be made after the filing and service of an answer, a supplemental answer setting forth the fact of satisfaction may be filed and served.

VI. If a carrier complained against shall deem the complaint insufficient to show a breach of legal duty, it may, instead of filing an answer, serve on the complainant notice for a hearing of the case on the complaint, and in case of the service of such notice, the facts stated in the complaint will be taken as admitted. The filing of an answer will not be deemed an admission of the sufficiency of the complaint, but a motion to dismiss for insufficiency may be made at the hearing.

VII. Adjournments and extensions of time may be granted upon the application of parties in the discretion of the commission.

VIII. Upon issue being joined by the service of answer, the commission, upon request of either party, will assign a time and place for hearing the same, which will be at its office in Washington, unless otherwise ordered. Witnesses will be examined orally before the commission, except in cases when special orders are made for the taking of testimony otherwise. The petitioner or complainant must in all cases prove the existence of the facts alleged to constitute a violation of the act, unless the carrier complained of shall admit the same, or shall fail to answer the complaint. Facts alleged in the answer must also be proved by the carrier, unless admitted by the petitioner on the hearing.

In cases of failure to answer, the commission will take such proof of the charge as may be deemed reasonable and proper, and make such order thereon as the circumstances of the case appear to require.

IX. Subpœnas requiring the attendance of witnesses will be issued by any member of the commission in all cases and proceedings before it, and witnesses will be required to obey the subpœnas served upon them requiring their attendance or the production of any books, papers, tariffs, contracts, agreements, or documents relating to any matter under investigation or pending before the commission.

Upon application to the commission authority may be given, in the discretion of the commission, to any party to take the deposition of any witnesses who may be shown, for some sufficient reason, to be unable to attend in person.

June 15, 1887, this rule was modified to the extent that where a cause is at issue on petition and answer, each party may proceed at once to take depositions of witnesses in the manner provided by sections 863 and 864 of the Revised Statutes of the United States, and transmit them to the secretary of the commission, without making any application to, or obtaining any authority from, the commission for that purpose.

X. Upon application by any petitioner or party amendments may be allowed by the commission, in its discretion, to any petition, answer, or other pleading in any proceeding before the commission.

XI. Copies of any petition, complaint, or answer, in any matter or proceeding before the commission, or of any order, decision, or opinion by the commission, will be furnished upon application by any person or carrier desiring the same, upon payment of the expense thereof.

XII. Affidavits to a petition, complaint, or answer may be taken before any officer of the United States, or of any State or Territory, authorized to administer oaths.

The history of the development of the railroad system of the United States, with relation to inter-State commerce and to the corporate abuses which led to the passage of the foregoing act of 1887, may be summarized as follows:—

When the grant of the power to regulate commerce was made, the commerce between the States was insignificant—carried on by coastwise vessels and other water-craft, sailed or rowed, within the interior. The inter-State commerce on land was little, and its regulation was by the common law. To a few associations of regular carriers of passengers on definite routes exclusive rights were granted, in the belief that otherwise the regular transportation would not be adequately provided for.

For regulation of commerce on the ocean and other navigable waters Congress passed the necessary laws; but not until 1824 (in the case of *Gibbons* v. *Ogden*) was it settled that such waters of a State as constitute a highway for inter-State commerce are subject to Federal legislation equally with the high seas. But Congress still abstained from regulating commerce by land—leaving even the Cumberland road, a national highway, to the supervision of the States through which it should be built.

When the application of steam to vessels as a motive power so stimulated internal commerce as to necessitate improved highways, these, both turnpikes and canals, were State creations, the General government merely making some appropriations for canals. It was natural that the States should control these highways, so long as there was no discrimination against the citizens of other States. When, in 1830, steam power was applied to land vehicles, the same reasons for State control prevailed.

For a long time Federal regulation of inter-State commerce was purely negative, merely restraining excessive State power, through the judicial department, in isolated cases. Thus, the corporations monopolizing commerce made the law for themselves — State power and common law being inadequate to complete regulation and National power not yet being put forth. The circumstances of railroad development tended to make this indirect and abnormal law-making unequal and oftentimes oppressive. Later, when the promoters of railroads were viewed as public benefactors, laws were passed, under popular clamor, allowing municipalities to use public money and public credit in aid of roads. So much money thus lent (to irresponsible parties) was lost, that constitutional amendments were adopted prohibiting such use of the public money or credit.

The inadequate business of many roads led to destructive competition, to the undue favoring of large dealers, and secret arrangements in the form of special rates, rebates, and drawbacks, underbilling. reduced classification, or whatever else might be best adapted to keep the transaction from a public not deceived but practically helpless through dependence. Intelligent shippers, even the favored ones, realized that any reasonable, non-discriminating, permanent schedule of rates was preferable to one so fluctuating and untrustworthy as to make business contracts virtually lottery ventures.

Special terms were often made with large shippers to increase the volume of business, in order either to attract purchasers of stock, justify some demand for an extension of line or other large expenditure, or to assist in making terms in a consolidation or strengthen the demand for a larger share in a pool.

Whatever the motive. the allowance of a special rate or rebate was not only unjust, wronging and often ruining the small dealer, but it was also demoralizing,— sufferers, doubtful of obtaining redress in the courts, becoming parties to the evil by seeking similar favors.

The discriminations applied to places not less than to persons, often resulting, through necessities artificially created, in charging more for a short than for a long haul on the same line in the same direction, so that towns with superior natural advantages withered away under the mischievous influence.

Not less conspicuous were the evils of the free transportation of persons, causing the corruption of some public officials and subjecting others to unjust and cruel suspicion, all leading to a deterioration of the moral sense of the community. Railroads themselves were in cases the sufferers, the demand for passage often partaking of the nature of blackmail.

In addition to these evils, rates, through the absence of competition or the consolidation of competing

roads, were kept oppressively high; they were also changed at pleasure, and without notice. Secret dealings made the public unable to judge of the reasonableness of charges. Such publications of tariffs as were made were so complicated as not to be intelligible to the uninitiated, and rather tended to increase the difficulties.

Still another evil was the strengthening of a class feeling between those whose interests demanded harmony.

The manipulation of capital stocks for the benefit of managers and to the destruction of the interest of the owners resulted in great wrong, directly to individuals and indirectly to the public. The large fortunes amassed in a short time by some officials created in the public mind suspicion and an unfair prejudice against railroad management in general, which developed into an unfortunate breach between the public and all railroad corporations.

In short, the manifest misuse of corporate powers created an irresistible demand for "National legislation, and this very naturally, because the private gains resulting from corporate abuse were supposed to spring, to some extent at least, from excessive burdens imposed upon that commerce which the nation ought to regulate and protect." In response to this demand the act of 1887 lays down rules to be observed by the carriers to which its provisions apply, which are intended to be rules of equity and equality, and "to restore the management of the transportation business of the country to public confidence." [1]

COMMISSION.[2]   Doing, performing; execution.

1. An undertaking, without recompense, to do a thing for another person; a gratuitous bailment, *q. v.*

2. (1) Formal written authority from a court to do something pertaining to the administration of justice: as, a commission to ascertain whether one is a bankrupt, or a lunatic; a commission to take depositions or testimony, *qq. v.*

A writ or process issued, under seal, by the special order of a court.[3]

(2) Formal authority from a government

---

[1] See Report of Commission, 1887, pp. 2–10.

That report presents the views of the board upon the following general subjects: The carriers subject to its jurisdiction, pp. 11–15; the long and short haul clause of the act, 15–23; the filing and publication of tariffs, 23–24; general supervision of the carriers subject to the act, 24–27; proceedings before the commission, 27–28; expense of hearings, 28–29; annual reports from carriers, 29–30; classification of passengers and freight, 30–32; voluntary association of railroad managers, 33–36; reasonable charges, 36–41; general observations, 41–42; amendments of the law, 42–43, 14–15.

[2] L. *committere*, to place with, intrust to: *con*, with; *mittere*, to send.

[3] [Tracy *v.* Suydam, 30 Barb. 115 (1859); Boal *v.* King, 6 Ham., Ohio, 13 (1833), cases.

for the doing of something belonging to the exercise of its powers.

Imports, *ex vi termini*, written authority from a competent source.[1] Compare WARRANT, 2.

(3) The body or board of persons intrusted with the performance of some public service or duty: as, to revise statutes, codify laws, fix the boundary lines between States, enforce the inter-State commerce act.

The instrument evidences the fact of the appointment, *q. v.*, and the nature and extent of the powers conferred.[2]

Commissioner. Such person as has a commission, letters-patent, or other lawful authority, to examine any matter or to execute any public office.[3]

An officer of a court, appointed to assist it in administering justice in a particular case or cases. Compare MASTER, 4.

The supreme court of California appoints, and may at any time remove, three persons of legal learning and personal worth to assist the court in the performance of its duties, and in the disposition of the undetermined causes now pending. Each commissioner holds office for the term of four years, and during that period may not engage in the practice of the law. The court appoints one as chief commissioner.[4] Whence C., and C. C.

An officer who assists in the administration of government, being usually charged with administering the laws relating to some one department thereof: as, the commissioner of agriculture, of a circuit court, of a county, of deeds, of education, of fisheries, of the general land-office, of highways, of Indian affairs, of internal revenue, of patents, of pensions.[5] See MINISTERIAL.

Commissioner of bail. An officer authorized to take bail for hearings or trials before a court and jury, in cases admitting of release from confinement when the accused can furnish bail.

Commissioner of the circuit courts. See under COURTS, United States.

Commissioner of deeds. An officer authorized to take acknowledgments and depositions, and to probate accounts.

County commissioners. See COUNTY.

3. Compensation for services rendered. The plural, commissions, is often used.

A percentage on price or value.[1]

A sum allowed as compensation to a servant, factor, or agent, who manages the affairs of another, in recompense for his services.[2]

"Commission" generally signifies a percentage upon the amount of money involved in the transaction, as distinguished from "discount," which is a percentage taken from the face value of the security or property negotiated.[3]

A reasonable commission is allowed to administrators, assignees, auctioneers, brokers, executors, receivers, and other agents or trustees, *qq. v.* But the service must be completed, and due care and skill and perfect fidelity have been employed. The amount is a reasonable percentage upon the sum received or paid out, and is regulated by custom, or by the discretion of the appointing authority.

Commission merchant. A factor, *q. v.*

COMMIT. To intrust to; to confide in.

1. To delegate a duty to a person or persons. See COMMISSION; COMMITTEE.

2. To send to a place of confinement a person found to be a lunatic.

May contemplate a sending without an adjudication by a court or a magistrate.[4] See LUNACY.

3. To send to prison a person, charged with or convicted of a crime.

Commitment. The act of sending an accused or convicted person to prison; also, the warrant by virtue of which the incarceration is made.

"To commit" was regarded as the separate and distinct act of carrying a party to prison, after having taken him into custody by force of a warrant of commitment.[5]

Commitment, Warrant of. Written authority to commit a person to prison or custody, until a further hearing in the matter as to which he is charged can be had, or until he is discharged by due course of law; a *mittimus*; a *committitur.*

Committing. Authorized to hear charges of crime, and to discharge or take bail for trial before a jury.

Committing magistrate. Any (inferior) officer empowered to hear charges of crime and to commit the accused to prison or accept bail for their appearance before a higher

[1] United States v. Reyburn, 6 Pet. *364 (1832).

[2] Marbury v. Madison, 1 Cranch, 155 (1803); Lessee of Talbot v. Simpson, 1 Pet. C. C. 94 (1815); United States v. Vinton, 2 Sumn. 307 (1836).

[3] [Jacob's Law Dict.; 14 N. J. L. 428.

[4] Cal. Statutes, 1885, p. 161. Similar provision was made in Kansas in 1887,— Laws, c. 148; and on March 5, three commissioners were appointed by the governor, with the consent of the senate,— 36 Kan. R. lii.

[5] See Index, Revised Statutes.

[1] Brennan v. Perry, 7 Phila. 243 (1869).

[2] [Ralston v. Kohl, 30 Ohio St. 98 (1876), Scott, J.

[3] Swift v. United States, 18 Ct. Cl. 57 (1883).

[4] Cummington v. Wareham, 9 Cush. 585 (1852).

[5] [French v. Bancroft, 1 Met. 504 (1840), Shaw, C. J. See also 112 Mass. 62; 133 id. 400.

court; as, a justice of the peace, some aldermen, mayors, and commissioners of bail.

If the offense is not bailable, or the party cannot find bail, he is to be committed to the county gaol by the *mittimus* of the justice, or warrant under his hand and seal, containing the cause of his commitment; there to abide till delivered by due course of law.[1]

Commitment for crime being only for safe-keeping, when bail will answer the purpose it is generally taken. The warrant is in the name of the State; is under the hand and seal of the magistrate; shows his authority, and the time and place of issue; describes the prisoner by name; specifies the place of confinement, and is directed to the keeper thereof; states that the party has been charged on oath with a particular offense. When the offense is bailable the direction is "to keep in safe custody for want of sureties, or until discharged by due course of law;" when not bailable, "until discharged by due course of law;" and when for further examination of the charge, "for further hearing."[2] See BAIL, 1 (2); CAPERE, Capias, Cepi.

COMMITTEE. One or more persons to whom a matter is referred for examination, deliberation, superintendence, action, or recommendation.

An individual or a body to which others have committed or delegated a particular duty, or who have taken upon themselves to perform it in the expectation of their act being confirmed by the body they profess to represent or to act for.[3]

More particularly, a person appointed by a court to take charge of the person or the estate, or of both, of a lunatic, habitual drunkard, or spendthrift.

The committee of a lunatic is a bailiff whose power is limited to the mere care of the estate under the direction of the court.[4]

The civil law assigned a *tutor* to protect the person, and a *curator* to manage the estate. . To prevent sinister practices the next of kin was seldom appointed committee of the person, but generally manager of the estate, accountable to the court, to the representative of the lunatic, and to the lunatic himself upon recovery.[5]

But now, for committee of the person, the next of kin is favored; and for committee of the estate, the heir at law.[6]

COMMITTITUR. See COMMIT, 3; INTERIM.

COMMODATUM. See ACCOMMODATUM.

COMMODITY.[1] Convenience, privilege, profit, gain; popularly, goods, wares, merchandise.

Within the meaning of the constitution of Massachusetts "commodities" embraces everything which may be the subject of taxation,— including the privilege of using a particular branch of business or employment: as, the business of an auctioneer. of an attorney, of a tavern-keeper, of a retailer of liquors.[2]

"Commodity" is a general term, and includes the privilege and convenience of transacting a particular business.[3] See MONOPOLY; STAPLE.

COMMODUM. L. Convenience, benefit, advantage.

Nullus commodum capere potest de injuria sua propria. No one advantage shall take of his own wrong-doing — as a cause of action or of defense.

Applies where a partner retires from a firm, and fails to give notice of the change: where a person inadvertently or fraudulently mingles grain of his own with higher-priced grain belonging to another; where a tenant for years or for life cuts down trees and then claims them; where a grantor attempts to dispute the validity of the title he has conveyed; where one party binds another to a condition impossible to be performed, or does something to prevent or hinder performance.

The maxim applies only to the extent of undoing an advantage gained against the right of another, not to taking away a right previously possessed.[4]

Thus, also, an admission, whether of law or of fact, which has been acted upon by another, is conclusive against the person who made it.[5]

Qui sentit commodum, sentire debet et onus. He who enjoys the benefit, ought also to bear the burden. He who enjoys the advantage of a right takes the accompanying disadvantage — a privilege is subject to its condition.

Illustrated in the rights and liabilities arising out of the relation of principal and agent, grantor and grantee, lessor and lessee, attorney and client, husband and wife, innkeeper and guest, a carrier and the public — the principle pervades the law in all its branches.[6]

On this principle rests the law of alluvion: the

---

[1] 4 Bl. Com. 300; 3 *id.* 134; 112 Mass. 62.

[2] See 4 Bl. Com. 296–300; 4 Cranch, 129; 17 F. R. 156; 9 N. H. 185; 6 Humph. 391.

[3] Reynell *v.* Lewis, 15 M. & W. *529 (1846), Pollock, C. B.

[4] Lloyd *v.* Hart, 2 Pa. 478 (1846), Gibson, C. J.

[5] 1 Bl. Com. 306; 3 *id.* 427.

[6] Shelford, Lunacy, 137, 140, 441.

[1] L. *commodus*, convenience.

[2] [Portland Bank *v.* Apthorp, 12 Mass. 256 (1815), Parker, C. J.

[3] Commonwealth *v.* Lancaster Savings Bank, 123 Mass. 495 (1878); Connecticut Ins. Co. *v.* Commonwealth, 133 *id.* 163 (1882); Gleason *v.* McKay, 134 *id.* 424-25 (18·3). cases; Hamilton Company *v.* Massachusetts, 6 Wall. 649 (1867); 24 How. Pr. 492.

[4] See Broom, Max. *279; State *v.* Costin, 89 N. C. 516 (1883).

[5] See 1 Greenl. Ev. §§ 207-9.

[6] See Cooper *v.* Louanstein, 37 N. J. E. 305 (1883); Mundorff *v.* Wickersham, 63 Pa. 89 (1869), cases.

owner takes the chances of injury and of benefit arising from situation.[1] Compare ONUS, Cum onere.

COMMON. 1, *adj.* (1) Belonging to, or participated in, by several or more persons; mutual: as, a common — ancestor, benefit, labor or service, master, property, recovery, tenants in common,[2] *qq. v.*

(2) Originating with, or subsisting for, the people at large; belonging to, or affecting, the public; not private, but public or general, *q. v.*: as, a common or the common — bench, carrier, council, fishery, highway, inn, law, nuisance, pleas, right, schools, way, *qq. v.*

(3) Ordinary, usual, customary, familiar; opposed to special: as, common or a common — appearance, *assumpsit*, assurance, bail, bar, bond, care or diligence, costs, count, informer, intendment, intent, jury, mortgage, seal, stock, traverse, warranty, *qq. v.*

(4) Frequent, habitual: as, common offenders — barrator, drunkard, gambler, prostitute, scold, thief, *qq. v.*

Three distinct acts of sale of liquors are necessary to constitute a "common" seller. Such has been the rule as to common barrator, and other cases of this nature.[3]

(5) Ordinary; manual; opposed to mental or intellectual: as, common labor, *q. v.*

2, *n.* The common field; ground set apart for public uses.[4]

The waste grounds of manors (*q. v.*) were called "commons."[5]

Land appropriated to a public common may not be diverted to other uses, to the prejudice of individuals who have purchased lots adjoining it.[6]

Where privileges of a public nature are beneficial to private property, as in the case of land upon a public square, the enjoyment of the privileges will be protected, by injunction, against encroachment.[7] See DEDICATION, 1.

Common, or **right of common.** A profit which a man hath in the lands of another:

as, to feed his beasts thereon, to catch fish, to cut wood.[1]

Commoner. A person invested with a right of common.

Existed between the owner of a manor and his feudal tenants,— for the encouragement of agriculture. The tenant's right was to pasture his cattle, provide necessary food and fuel for his family, and repair his implements of husbandry, from the lord's land.[2]

An incorporeal hereditament. The right usually meant is **common of pasture**: the right of feeding beasts on another's land. There was also *common of estovers:* the liberty of taking necessary wood, for use of house or farm — house-bote, fire-bote, hay-bote, hedge-bote, etc.; *common of piscary:* the liberty of fishing (*q. v*) in another's water; *common of turbary:* a right to dig turf; *common in the soil:* a right to dig for minerals, etc. All the species result from the same necessity — the maintenance and carrying on of husbandry.

Commonable beasts. Beasts of the plow; beasts which manure the ground.

Inter-commoning. Where the beasts of adjacent manors have immemorially fed upon adjoining commons.

Commons of pasture were *appendant,* when regularly annexed to arable land,— for the support of commonable beasts; *appurtenant,* when annexed to lands in other lordships,— for the support of all kinds of animals, and arose neither from necessity nor from any connection of tenures; *in gross* or *at large,* when annexed to a man's person, by grant to him and his heirs; *because of vicinage,* when the inhabitants of adjoining townships intercommoned.[3] See FEUD.

The right of common, with many of its old common-law incidents, was formerly recognized in this country, particularly in the middle and eastern States.[4]

[1] County of St. Clair *v.* Lovingston, 23 Wall. 69 (1874).

[2] Chambers *v.* Harrington, 111 U. S. 352 (1884).

[3] Commonwealth *v.* Tubbs, 1 Cush. 3 (1848), Dewey, J.

[4] Patterson *v.* McReynolds, 61 Mo. 203 (1875); Crawford *v.* Mobile, &c. R. Co., 67 Ga. 416 (1881).

[5] 2 Bl. Com. 32.

[6] See Emerson *v.* Wiley, 10 Pick. 315 (1831); Carr *v.* Wallace, 7 Watts, 394 (1838); Abbott *v.* Mills, 3 Vt. 525 (1831); State *v.* Trask, 6 *id.* 364 (1834).

[7] Wheeler *v.* Bedford, 54 Conn. 248–49 (1886), cases: 2 Story, Eq. § 927; High, Inj. § 551. An injunction to prevent inclosing part of a town common or public park, by the owner of a lot adjoining the lot of complainant.

[1] 2 Bl. Com. 32.

[2] 3 Kent, 408.

[3] 2 Bl. Com. 33–35; 3 *id.* 237.

[4] See Watts *v.* Coffin, 11 Johns. *495 (1814),— as to lands in the city of Hudson, Columbia county, N. Y.; Livingston *v.* Ten Broeck, 16 *id.* *15 (1819),— town of Livingston, same county; Leyman *v.* Abeel, *ib.* *30 (1819),— Catskill patent; Van Rennselaer *v.* Radcliff, 10 Wend. *639 (1833),— town of Guilderland, Albany county.

See also Western University of Pennsylvania *v.* Robinson *et al.*, 12 S. & R. *29 (1824), and Carr *v.* Wallace, 7 Watts, 394 (1838),— both as to one hundred acres of land in the town of Allegheny, Pa. (now constituting the parks in the central portion of the city), in which the State, in 1787, created the right of "common of pasture" in the purchasers of "in-lots" in the plan of lots laid out and sold by the State for the purpose of raising money with which to pay public debts. In 1819 the legislature, without the consent of the owners of those lots, granted fifty acres of these "commons" to the university named, but the supreme court, in Robinson's Case, held that the State

COMMONS, HOUSE OF. See PAR-
LIAMENT.

COMMONWEALTH. The common or
public weal: the republic; the state, or a
State; the people, qq. v.

"The commonwealth or public polity of the kingdom." [1] Blackstone also wrote it "common wealth." [2]

The legal title of a few of the States, as of
Kentucky, Massachusetts, Pennsylvania, Virginia.

COMMORANT.[3] Inhabiting, dwelling,
residing; as, in saying that a person is or is
not commorant in a particular place. Whence
commorancy.[4]

COMMORIENTES. L. Those who die
at the same time, from the same accident or
calamity. See SURVIVE, 2.

COMMOTION. A "civil commotion"
is an insurrection of the people for general
purposes, though it may not amount to a rebellion, in which there is usurped power.[5]

COMMUNE. See COMMUNISM.

COMMUNICATION. Information imparted by one person to another.

Confidential communication. Information imparted between persons who occupy
a relation of trust and duty; a privileged communication.

Privileged communication. 1. Information imparted which the law does not require to be disclosed in a judicial or legislative
examination.

Public policy forbids the disclosure of matters
which the law regards as confidential, and as to which
it will not allow confidence to be violated.[1]

The rule, at common law, does not extend to confessions made to clergymen. This has been changed
by statute in some States, as in Iowa, Michigan, Missouri, New York, and Wisconsin.[2]

Confidence between husband and wife, as to the interests of either, is forever inviolable.[3]

A lawyer who has counseled with a client cannot
disclose information received from him. The inhibition includes a clerk or a student in the lawyer's office;
and applies also to a scrivener or a conveyancer. But
a legal adviser may testify as to "negotiations" between clients who later become adversaries. The rule
does not cover a disclosure of an intention to break the
law, nor testamentary communications, nor information obtained outside of the professional relation.[4]

A communication to a medical attendant is not
privileged. A few of the States (among others, those
mentioned above) have conferred the immunity, excepting consultations for criminal purposes.[5] See
INFORMATION, 1.

State secrets are privileged. This embraces communications to any high officer of state, and consultations with the executive, or a committee of the legislature.[6]

Prosecuting attorneys are privileged as to confidential matters.[7] See ACCOMPLICE.

Communications between a party and a witness, by
way of preparation for trial, are privileged.[8]

Neither arbitrators, judges, nor jurors can be compelled to disclose the grounds of their findings.[9] See
JURY, Grand.

Ties of blood create no privilege.[10]

Telegrams (q. v.) are not protected.[11]

2. In the law of slander and libel, false
matter not actionable, because the circum-

---

had only the right of soil, subject to the right of common, which latter right the lot-holders could release
or modify at pleasure, with the concurrence of the
legislature. Some three years later, at the request
of a large majority of the lot-owners, the legislature
granted ten acres of the same common to trustees
representing the Presbyterian Church in the United
States, for the uses of a theological seminary. After
the lapse of several years, during which more than
$25,000 had been expended in improvements, one Carr,
who had acquiesced in this disposition of the common
ground, by suit in court questioned the validity of the
grant to the trustees. The supreme court held that
by failing to complain at the proper time he had approved what had been done.

See also Thomas v. Marshfield, Mass., 10 Pick. 364
(1830), and Phillips v. Rhodes, 7 Metc. 322 (1843),—as
to rights of common in a beach; and Hall v. Lawrence, 2 R. I. 218 (1852),— which concerned a similar
right at Newport, in 1776. On the origin of rights of
common, see 3 Law Q. Rev. 373-98 (1887).

[1] 4 Bl. Com. 127.

[2] 3 Bl. Com. 9.

[3] Cŏm'-mo-rant. L. commorari, to abide.

[4] See 3 Bl. Com. 364; 4 id. 273; Wright v. Smith, 74
Me. 497 (1883): Me. Laws, 1876, c. 93.

[5] [Langdale v. Mason, 2 Marsh. Ins. 792 (1780), Ld.
Mansfield; May, Ins. § 403.

[1] Totten v. United States, 92 U. S. 107 (1875).

[2] 1 Greenl. Ev. §§ 247-48, cases; 1 Whart. Ev. §§ 596-
98, cases.

[3] 1 Greenl. Ev. §§ 254, 334; 1 Whart. Ev. §§ 427-32; 113
Mass. 160; 46 Barb. 158; 35 Vt. 379.

[4] 1 Greenl. Ev. §§ 237-46; 1 Whart. Ev. §§ 576-93; 74
Me. 543; 101 Mass. 193.

[5] 1 Greenl. Ev. § 248; 1 Whart. Ev. § 606: Connecticut
Mut. Life Ins. Co. v. Union Trust Co., 112 U. S. 254
(1884); Gartside v. Connecticut Mut. Life Ins. Co., 76
Mo. 449-53 (1882), cases, statutes.

[6] 1 Greenl. Ev. §§ 250-51; 1 Whart. Ev. §§ 604-5, cases;
Worthington v. Scribner, 109 Mass. 488-93 (1872), cases;
Totten v. United States, 92 U. S. 105 (1875); Hartranft's
Appeal, 85 Pa. 433 (1878); Rex v. Hardy, 24 How. St.
Tr. 815 (1794); 15 Op. Att.-Gen. 9, 378, 416; 50 Md. 626.

[7] Vogel v. Gruaz, 110 U. S. 311, 316 (1884), cases;
1 Whart. Ev. § 603.

[8] 1 Whart. Ev. § 594.

[9] 1 Whart. Ev. §§ 599-601; 1 Greenl. Ev. §§ 249, 252.

[10] 1 Whart. Ev. § 607; 14 Ill. 89; 3 Wis. 456; L. R., 18
Eq. 649.

[11] 1 Whart. Ev. §§ 595, 617.

stances gave the defendant a right to make the statement.

The occasion on which the communication was made rebuts the inference arising, *prima facie*, from a statement prejudicial to the character of the plaintiff, and puts it upon him to prove that there was malice in fact — that the defendant was actuated by motives of personal spite or ill-will, independent of the occasion on which the communication was made.[1]

" Privileged " in this connection means simply that the circumstances under which the communication was made were such as to repel the legal inference of malice, and to throw upon the plaintiff the burden of offering evidence of its existence beyond the mere falsity of the charge.[2]

A communication made *bona fide* upon any subject-matter in which the party communicating has an interest, or in reference to which he has a duty, is privileged, if made to a person having a corresponding interest or duty, although it contains criminatory matter which, without this privilege, would be slanderous and actionable.[3]

Where a person is so situated that it becomes right, in the interests of society, that he should tell a third person certain facts, then if he *bona fide* and without malice does tell them it is a privileged communication. The jury must say whether the statement was made in good faith.[4]

In some instances a voluntary imparting of information will be justified; in others the privilege applies only to information in response to inquiries. The subject may be one that is privileged, and a communication on that subject be unprivileged. If the restraints imposed by law upon the publicity to be given the communication be disregarded, the communication is unprivileged and actionable, although made from the best of motives. The act of communicating defamatory matter to a person with respect to whom there is no privilege is without legal justification or excuse. Good faith and honest belief will not justify defamation.[5]

In the law of libel, privileged communications are: 1. When an author or publisher acted in *bona fide* discharge of a public or private duty, legal or moral; or in the prosecution of his own rights or interests. 2. Anything said or done by a master in giving the character of a servant who has been in his employment.

3. Words used in the course of a legal or judicial proceeding, however harsh. 4. Publications duly made in the ordinary mode of parliamentary proceedings. . In these cases the complainant must show express malice, by construction of the matter, or by facts accompanying the matter or the parties.[1]

In some jurisdictions the privilege is spoken of as " absolute," that is, it rests upon grounds of policy, requiring freedom in debate or argument, and in giving testimony — in which cases proof of even actual malice is not received, unless it be as to the last: as, for utterances by a legislator, judge, advocate, or witness; and as " presumptive," that is, in which the plaintiff may prove absence of good faith or actual malice: as, communications in discharge of social duties; when the author or recipient has a legal interest to be promoted; answers to legitimate inquiries; characters given to servants; statements to sellers as to credit of buyers; notices protective of one's interests or in discharge of a corporate duty.[2]

Utterances in the course of church discipline, to or of a member of the church, are not actionable unless express malice be proved.[3] See LIBEL, 5; SLANDER.

COMMUNIS. See ERROR, 1, Communis.

COMMUNISM. A name given to schemes of social innovation which have for their common starting-point the overthrow of absolute rights of ownership in private property as an institution. Most theories further comprehend the regulation of industry and the sources of livelihood, as well as of the domestic relations, and some involve the abrogation of all central authority in a State, and the substitution of that of the commune.[4]

It is the latter feature that constitutes a distinction between communism and socialism.[4] See ANARCHY; GOVERNMENT; NIHILIST.

COMMUNITY.[5] 1. Unity; mutuality: as, community of interest or of intention. See PARTNERSHIP.

2. In Louisiana, Texas, California, and perhaps in New Mexico and Arizona, a species of partnership created between husband and wife by the contract of marriage, in acquisitions of property made or received during the continuance of that relation.

This community is *conventional* when formed by express agreement in the contract

---

[1] Wright *v.* Woodgate, 2 Cromp., M. & R. 577 (1835), Parke, B.

[2] Lewis *v.* Chapman, 16 N. Y. 373 (1857), Selden, J.

[3] Harrison *v.* Bush, 5 Ellis & B. *347-48 (1855), Campbell, C. J.

[4] Davies *v.* Snead, L. R., 5 Q. B. *611 (1870), Blackburn, J. See Waller *v.* Loch, 7 Q. B. D. 621-22 (1881); Marks " Baker, 23 Minn. 164-65 (1881), cases; Erber *v.* Dun, 12 F. R. 530 (1882); Trussell *v.* Scarlett, 18 *id.* 214, 216-20 (1882), cases; Locke *v.* Bradstreet, 22 *id.* 771 (1885); 26 Am. Law Reg. 681-93 (1887), cases.

[5] King *v.* Patterson, 49 N. J. L. 421, 419-33 (1887), cases, Depue, J. The plaintiff (above) published in his " mercantile agency notification sheet " the false information that the defendant had executed a chattel mortgage upon her stock of goods.

[1] White *v.* Nicholls, 3 How. 286-92 (1845), cases, Daniel, J. As to newspaper publications, see 21 Cent. Law J: 86-9), 430-55 (1885), cases.

[2] See O'Donaghue *v.* M'Govern, 23 Wend. *29 (1840); Howard *v.* Thompson, 21 *id.* 325 (1839).

[3] Coombs *v.* Rose, 9 Blackf. *157 (1846), cases. *Contra,* Fitzgerald *v.* Robinson, 112 Mass. 371-78 (1873), cases; Magrath *v.* Finn, 16 Alb. Law J. 186 (1877) — Irish Common Pleas.

[4] [Worcester's Dict.

[5] L. *communis,* common

of marriage; *legal,* when it arises by operation of law — as where there is no express stipulation.

At the dissolution of the relation the effects are divided equally, as between heirs.[1]

Statutes upon the subject proceed upon the theory that the marriage, in respect to property acquired during its existence, is a community, of which each spouse is a member, equally contributing by his or her industry to its prosperity and possessing an equal right to succeed to the property after dissolution, in the event of surviving the other. To the community all acquisitions by either, whether made jointly or separately, belong. No form of transfer or mere intent of parties can overcome this positive rule of law. All property is common property, except that owned previous to marriage or acquired after the relation has ceased. The presumption is against separate ownership. A purchase made with separate funds must be affirmatively established by clear and decisive proof. The husband has the entire control of the common property; and it is liable for his debts.[2]

3. A society of people having common rights, interests, or privileges in matters of property, representation, etc.

An association by which each member surrenders his property into one common stock for the mutual benefit of all during their joint lives, with the right of survivorship, reserving to each member the right to secede at any time during his life, is not prohibited by law.[3]

4. A society of people possessing common political interests; a political society. See STATE, 2 (2).

COMMUTATION.[4] Putting one thing for another; substitution.

As, of a tax, for a personal service; an annuity to a tribe of Indians, for goods; rations to a soldier, for money;[5] an artificial limb, for its value in money.[6]

Commutation of punishment. The substitution of a less for a greater penalty or punishment;[7] the change of one punishment for another and different punishment, both being known to the law.[8] See PARDON.

Commutable; commutative. Capable or admitting of substitution; not interchangeable for another — of less or equal

value or degree. Opposed, incommutable, incommutative, non-commutable.

COMPACT. An agreement or contract — between independent sovereignties.[1]

Original or **social compact.** The implied contract of association of individuals in a community, by which, in return for the benefits of the association, the individual surrenders such of his natural freedom as is necessary for the good of society.

Thereby, whatever power the individual had to punish offenses against the law of nature is vested in the magistrate — the sovereign power.[2] See BODY, 2, Corporate.

COMPANY. **1.** The member of a partnership (*q. v.*) whose name does not appear in the name of the firm.

The use of the collective designation " & Co.," as part of the name of a firm, creates a presumption that there is a partner in addition to the person or persons whose names are given; but this presumption is rebuttable. Statutes in Louisiana and New York forbid the use of the addition unless an actual partner is represented by it; but a fanciful title, such as " Eureka Co.," may still be used; and the reference may be to a person under disability. Such statutes are intended to protect persons who give credit to, not those who obtain credit from, a firm.[3]

2. Applied to persons engaged in trade, those united for the same purpose or in a joint concern.[4]

" Company " or " association," when used in the Revised Statutes, acts or resolutions of Congress, in reference to corporations, shall be deemd to embrace the words " successors and assigns of such company or association " in like manner as if these last-named words, or words of similar import, were expressed.[5]

The simple word " company " will include individuals as well as corporations.[6]

Often designates a numerous association, chartered or unchartered. Every unincorporated company is a partnership.

See ASSOCIATION; PARTNERSHIP, Limited; STOCK, 3 (2); BUBBLE; EXPRESS; PROSPECTUS; RAILROAD; TELEGRAPH; TRANSPORTATION.

---

[1] La. Civ. Code, 2375, 2393; 10 La. 146, 172, 181; 12 *id.* 598. See as to Texas, Hanrick v. Patrick, 119 U. S. 172 (1886), cases.

[2] Tibbetts *v.* Fore, 70 Cal. 244–45 (1886), cases; Schuyler *v.* Broughton, *ib.* 283 (1886), cases.

[3] Schriber *v.* Rapp (Harmony Society), 5 Watts, 351, 360 (1836); Baker *v.* Nachtrieb, 19 How. 126 (1856); Speidel *v.* Henrici, 120 U. S. 377 (1887).

[4] L. *commutare,* to exchange with.

[5] United States *v.* Lippitt, 100 U. S. 663, 670 (1879).

[6] R. S. § 4788.

[7] Lee *v.* Murphy, 22 Gratt. 799, 798–800 (1872), cases.

[8] *Exp.* Janes, 1 Nev. 321 (1865).

[1] See 8 Wheat. 92; 11 Pet. 185; 1 Bl. Com. 45.

[2] 1 Bl. Com. 233, 299; 3 *id.* 160; 4 *id.* 8, 71, 382. See 1 Shars. Bl. Com. 232; Atlantic Monthly, June, 1887, p. 750, article by A. L. Lowell, who undertakes to show that the theory, first propounded in 1594 by Richard Hooker, adopted by Hobbs, Locke, Rousseau, the framers of the constitution of Massachusetts, and Kant, has been made the servant of absolutism, democracy, revolution, and transcendental ethics.

[3] 1 Bates, Partn. §§ 191, 198, cases; Gay *v.* Seibold, 97 N. Y. 476 (1884); Lauferty *v.* Wheeler, 11 Daly, 197 (1882); Zimmerman *v.* Erhard, 83 N. Y. 76 (1880); Kent *v.* Mojoiner, 36 La. An. 259 (1884).

[4] Palmer *v.* Finkham, 33 Me. 36 (1851), Shepley, C. J.

[5] R. S. § 5: Act 25 July, 1866.

[6] Chicago Dock Co. *v.* Garrity, 115 Ill. 164 (1885).

COMPARATIVE. See JURISPRUDENCE; NEGLIGENCE.

COMPARISON. See HANDWRITING.

COMPENSATION. That return which is given for something else — a consideration: as, the compensation of an office.[1]

Compensatory. Serving as an equivalent; making amends: as, compensatory damages, *q. v.*

1. Recompense; remuneration: as, for services rendered by an officer, agent, attorney, trustee.

When not fixed by agreement, evidence of the amount ordinarily charged in like cases is admissible. The service, however, must be lawful. An agreement to pay a contingent compensation for professional services in prosecuting a claim against the government, pending in a department, is not unlawful.[2]

In a constitutional provision that the "compensation" of any public officer shall not be increased or diminished during his term of office, applies to officers who receive a fixed salary from the public treasury, not to such minor officers as are paid by fees taxed or allowed for each item of service as it is rendered.[3]

When Congress has said that a sum appropriated shall be "in full compensation" of the services of a public officer, the courts cannot allow him a greater sum. The appropriation of a fixed sum as compensation, followed by the appropriation of a round sum as "additional" pay, evinces an intention not to allow further compensation during the period specified. So, a statute which fixes the annual salary of an officer at a designated sum without limitation as to time, is not abrogated by subsequent enactments appropriating a less amount for his services for a particular fiscal year, but containing no words which expressly or impliedly modify or repeal it.[4] See COMMISSION, 3; CONTINUANCE, 3; COUNT, 4 (1), Common; EXPERT; IMPAIR; LEGAL; SALARY.

2. Remuneration for loss of time, necessary expenditures, and for permanent disability, if such be the result.[5]

As, compensation for personal injuries caused by another's negligence. See DAMAGES.

3. Amends for privation of a thing; an equivalent for property taken for a public use.

Just compensation. Private property cannot be taken for a public use without just compensation being made or secured. This means pecuniary recompense equivalent in value to that of the property.[1]

"Just" intensifies the meaning of "compensation"—imports that the equivalent shall be real, substantial, full, ample.[2]

Nearly all of the authorities agree that "just compensation" consists in making the owner good, by an equivalent in money, for the loss he sustains in the value of his property by being deprived of a portion of it.[3]

In determining the value of land appropriated for public purposes, the same considerations are to be regarded as in the sale of property between private persons. The inquiry is, What is the property worth in the market, viewed not merely with reference to the uses to which it is at the time applied, but with reference to the uses to which it is plainly adapted; that is to say, what is it worth from its availability for valuable purposes. . . So many and varied are the circumstances to be taken into the account that it is perhaps impossible to formulate a rule to govern its appraisement in all cases. Exceptional circumstances will modify the most carefully guarded rule. As a general thing, the compensation is to be estimated by reference to the uses for which the property is suitable, having regard to the existing business or wants of the community, or such as may be reasonably expected in the immediate future.[4]

When an incorporated company appropriates land, the measure of compensation is the difference between the value of the property before and after the taking, and as affected by the taking.[5] See DOMAIN, Eminent; POLICE, 2; STREET; TAKE, 8.

4. In equity, something to be done for, or money to be paid to, a person, equal in value or amount to the right or thing of which he has been deprived.

Ordinarily decreed as incidental to other relief sought by the bill, or where there is no adequate remedy at law, or where a peculiar equity intervenes.[6]

Compensation may be decreed where the court cannot grant the specific relief prayed for. Thus, if a plaintiff was originally entitled to specific performance of a contract of sale, but it so happens that before the final decree it becomes impracticable for the defendant to make a conveyance, so that the specific relief sought for cannot be decreed, the court will not

---

[1] Searcy *v.* Grow, 15 Cal. 123 (1860).

[2] Stanton *v.* Embrey, 93 U. S. 548 (1876).

[3] Supervisors of Milwaukee *v.* Hackett, 21 Wis. *617–18 (1867), Dixon, C. J.

[4] United States *v.* Fisher, 109 U. S. 143 (1883); United States *v.* Mitchell, *ib.* 146 (1883); United States *v.* Langston, 118 *id.* 389 (1886).

[5] Parker *v.* Jenkins, 3 Bush, 591 (1868).

---

[1] Council Bluffs R. Co. *v.* County of Otoe, 16 Wall. 674 (1874). Strong, J.

[2] Virginia, &c. R. Co. *v.* Henry, 8 Nev. 171 (1873), Whitman, C. J.

[3] Bigelow *v.* West Wisconsin R. Co., 27 Wis. 487 (1871), cases, Lyon, J.

[4] Mississippi, &c. Boom Co. *v.* Patterson, 98 U. S. 407–8 (1878), Field, J.

[5] See Lake Erie, &c. R. Co. *v.* Kinsey, 87 Ind. 516–21 (1882), cases; Shenango, &c. R. Co. *v.* Braham, 79 Pa. 452 (1875), cases; 39 Ala. 171–72; 42 *id.* 8; 46 *id.* 579; 69 Ga. 322; 133 Mass. 255, 433; 34 Miss. 227; 36 *id.* 300; 17 N. J. L. 47; 20 *id.* 252; 38 *id.* 155; 14 Ohio, 175; 9 Oreg. 379–80; 2 Kent, 338; Pierce, Railr. 210, 212, 224.

[6] 2 Story, Eq. Ch. XIX.

turn the plaintiff over to seek his damages in an action at law, but will proceed directly to decree him compensation.[1] See CONDITION, Precedent, Subsequent.

5. A mode of extinguishing a debt, and takes place, by mere operation of law, where debts equally liquidated and demandable are reciprocally due.[2]

COMPERUIT. See DIES, Comperuit.

COMPETENT. Answering the requirement of the law; legally able, fit, or qualified: also, proper or admissible as evidence. Whence competency; incompetent, incompetency.

A judge is said to be incompetent to hear a cause in which he is interested; and an infant, or a married woman, incompetent to contract for an article not a necessary.

All witnesses that have their reason, except such as are infamous, or, at common law, are interested in the event of the cause, are competent, but the jury must judge of their credibility,[3] *q. v.*

Competency is a question for the court. Every witness is presumed to be competent. Ordinarily, incompetency is to be objected to when first known or discovered — before the witness is sworn and his testimony found to be unfavorable.[4] See further EVIDENCE, Competent; WITNESS.

COMPETITION. See MONOPOLY; POLICY, 2; TRADE, Restraints.

Competitive examinations. See SERVICE, 3, Civil.

COMPILE. To copy from various authors into one work. Implies the exercise of judgment in selecting and combining the extracts.[5]

A compiler may take existing materials from sources common to all writers, and, by arranging them in combination in a new form, give them an application unknown before. Others may use the materials, but not his improvement. The "fair use" which is allowable applies to the materials, not to another's plan and arrangement.[6]

A compilation made from original sources is a new work. The fact of originality may be proved by another than the author. A compiler is an "author," within the meaning of the Constitution and the copyright laws. . A compilation, which is the result of labor devoted to gathering from original sources and to arranging in convenient form facts open to be published by any one, is a new work. . . "Colorable differences" applies to devices intended to cover a literary piracy, not to real and substantial differences.[1]

A compilation made from voluminous public documents, and arranged to show readily the date and order of historic events, may be copyrighted. Such publications are valuable sources of information and require labor, care, and some skill in their preparation.[2] See further ABRIDGE; PIRACY, 2; REPORT, 1 (2); REVIEW, 3.

COMPLAINT. 1. A formal charge that a person named has committed an offense, preferred before a magistrate or a tribunal authorized to inquire into the probable truth of the accusation.

Refers to a proceeding before a magistrate.[3] But may include an indictment.[4] Implies that an oath has been administered.[5]

A complaint is the initial proceeding in criminal prosecutions and examinations before magistrates, and is made upon oath. If a jurat be attached, and it be properly certified by the magistrate, as is frequently the case, it will be essentially an "affidavit." But a complaint is not necessarily an affidavit, nor are they understood as convertible terms. For, though a complaint may be reduced to writing and subscribed, it need not be certified by the magistrate, since the fact may otherwise appear from his record. And it may be merely formal, made by one who has little, if any, knowledge about the facts, and the examination consist of the depositions of other witnesses. An "affidavit," on the other hand, as the term is ordinarily used, is a sworn statement of facts or a deposition in writing, and includes a jurat — a certificate of the magistrate showing that it was sworn to before him, including the date, and sometimes also the place.[6]

2. The first pleading filed by a plaintiff in a civil action.

The first pleading in an action; containing a statement of the cause of action, with a demand for the appropriate relief to which the party may be entitled.[7]

Complainant. One who prefers a charge of crime; also, he who institutes a civil suit, particularly a suit in equity.

See DECLARATION, 2; PLAINT. Compare AUDIRE, Audita, etc.

COMPLETE. See CAUSE, 2, Of action; INCHOATE; PERFECT.

---

[1] Mason's Appeal, 70 Pa. 29–30 (1871), cases; 77 *id.* 227; 75 *id.* 483; 13 Ves. 73, 287.

[2] See Dorvin *v.* Wiltz, 11 La. 520 (1856); Stewart *v.* Harper, 16 *id.* 181 (1861).

[3] 3 Bl. Com. 369. As to moral status, see 19 Am. Law Rev. 343–58 (1885), cases; as to mental status, *ib.* 583–92 (1885), cases.

[4] 1 Greenl. Ev. § 50; 1 Whart. Ev. §§ 391–411, 418–2).

[5] Story's Ex'rs *v.* Holcombe, 4 McLean, 313 (1847).

[6] Lawrence *v.* Dana, 4 Cliff. 75–86 (1869), cases.

[1] Bullinger *v.* Mackey, 15 Blatch. 555, 558 (1879), cases.

[2] Hanson *v.* Jaccard Jewelry Co., 32 F. R. 203 (1887), Thayer, J.; Drone, Copyr. 152–54, cases.

[3] Commonwealth *v.* Davis, 11 Pick. *436 (1831).

[4] Commonwealth *v.* Haynes, 107 Mass. 197 (1871).

[5] Campbell *v.* Thompson, 16 Me. 120 (1839).

[6] State *v.* Richardson, 34 Minn. 117–18 (1885), cases, Vanderburgh, J. Extradition Act, R. S. § 5278.

[7] M'Math *v.* Parsons, 26 Minn. 247 (1879).

COMPOS. L. Having control of; possessing power over.

Compos mentis. Having capacity of mind; sound in mental faculties; of sound mind. **Non compos mentis.** Not of sound mind; lunatic; insane. See INSANITY.

COMPOSITION. 1. In the law of copyright, the invention or combination of the parts of a work — literary, musical, or dramatic: as, in the case of a letter, discourse, or book; or of an opera; but not of a mere exhibition, spectacle, or scene.[1] See BOOK, 1; COPYRIGHT; DRAMA; OPERA.

2. In the law of patents, a mixture or chemical combination. See PATENT, 2; PROCESS, 2.

3. Payment of part in satisfaction of the whole of a debt. See COMPOUND, 3.

Composition in bankruptcy or **insolvency.** A contract by which creditors agree to accept a part of their demands, and to discharge the debtor from liability for the rest.

An arrangement between a creditor and his debtor for the discharge of the debt, on terms or by means different from those required by the original contract or by law.[2]

This may be by a composition agreement so called, by a letter of license, or by a deed of inspectorship. See LICENSE; INSPECTION, 3.

A strict composition agreement is an agreement whereby the creditors accept a sum of money, or other thing, at a certain time or times, in full satisfaction and discharge of their respective debts.[2]

Obviates the necessity of a discharge by the court; if made in good faith and fairly and strictly conducted, will be upheld. The agreement is evidenced by an instrument signed by the debtor and the creditors, and called a composition *deed*, although, at common law, such instrument is not necessary.[3] See ACCORD; BANKRUPTCY; PREFER, 2.

COMPOUND. 1, *v.* (1) To put parts together to form a whole. See COMPOSITION.

(2) To add interest to principal for a new principal. See INTEREST, 2 (3).

(3) To "compound" a debt is to abate a part on receiving the residue. Demands are compounded when adjusted by payment of part in satisfaction of the whole.[1] See COMPOSITION, 3.

(4) To take goods, or other amends, upon an agreement not to prosecute a person for a crime.

Compounding a misdemeanor is sometimes allowed by leave of court, as affecting the individual, he having a right of action for damages. Compounding a felony is, at common law, an offense of an equivalent nature [to the felony], and is, besides, an additional misdemeanor against public justice by contributing to make the laws odious.[2] See BOTE, Theft; LEGAL, Illegal.

By stat. 25 Geo. II (1752), c. 36, advertising a reward for the return of things stolen, "no questions to be asked," subjects the advertiser and the printer to a forfeiture of £50 each.[3]

2. *adj.* See INTEREST, 2 (3); LARCENY.

COMPRISE. See INCLUDE.

COMPROMISE.[4] An agreement in settlement of a controverted matter.

The yielding of something by each of two parties.[5]

A mutual yielding of opposing claims; the surrender of some right or claimed right in consideration of a like surrender of some counter-claim.[6]

Compromises are highly favored in law.

An "offer" to do something by way of compromise of a controversy, as, to pay a sum of money, to allow a certain price, to deliver certain property, and like offers, made to avoid litigation, is not receivable in evidence against the maker as an admission. If the offer is plainly for a compromise, the rule is to presume it to have been made without prejudice — it is open to explanation. But an admission made during or in consequence of the offer is receivable.[7]

To admit evidence of an offer to compromise litigation would discourage the amicable settlement of disputes. When the object is to buy peace, an offer will be excluded.[8] See PREJUDICE, Without.

If the right surrendered is of doubtful validity, its surrender may be a valuable consideration for the promise.[6]

---

[1] Martinetti *v.* Maguire, 1 Abb. U. S. 362 (1867); The "Iolante" Case, 15 F. R. 439 (1883); 17 F. R. 595, cases; 9 Am. Law Reg. 33; 23 Bost. L. R. 397.

[2] [4 South. Law Rev. 639–75, 805–42 (1878), cases.

[3] Clarke *v.* White, 12 Pet. 178 (1838); 20 Cent. Law J. 385–88 (1885), cases; 3 McCrary, 608; 21 Cal. 122; 49 Conn. 105; 75 Ind. 127; 30 Kan. 361; 80 Ky. 614; 71 N. C. 70; 92 Pa. 474; 100 *id.* 164; R. S. § 5103; 2 Kent, 309, *b.*

[1] [Haskins *v.* Newcomb, 2 Johns. *408 (1807), Kent, Chief Justice.

[2] [4 Bl. Com. 136. See Smith, Contr. 226.

[3] 4 Bl. Com. 133.

[4] L. *com-promittere*, to mutually promise; to arbitrate.

[5] Bellows *v.* Sowles, 55 Vt. 399 (1883).

[6] Gregg *v.* Wethersfield, 55 Vt. 387 (1883); *ib.* 397; 10 Neb. 360; 2 Wis. *6.

[7] West *v.* Smith, 101 U. S. 273 (1879), cases; Home Ins. Co. *v.* Baltimore Warehouse Co., 93 *id.* 548 (1876); 1 Pet. 222; 16 Op. Att-Gen. 250; 87 Ind. 465; 4 La. 456; 50 Md. 45; 44 N. J. L. 174; 1 Greenl. Ev. § 192; 2 Whart. Ev. § 1090.

[8] International, &c. R. Co. *v.* Ragsdale, 67 Tex. 27

An administrator may compound a debt, if for the benefit of the estate;[1] and so may a partner for the benefit either of himself or of the firm — statutes in many of the States making a release of one joint debtor not a release of others.[2]

The courts, are inclined to favor a compromise fairly made by an attorney at law, and will uphold it for good reason shown.[3] See ACCORD.

COMPTROLLER, or CONTROLLER. One who keeps a counter-roll, a duplicate register, of accounts: an officer charged with the duty of verifying accounts in the fiscal department of government.

In the treasury there are two comptrollers, designated as the first and the second. Their duties are prescribed by statute.[4] See BANK, 2 (2).

In 1880 there was published, by direction of the treasurer, a volume of the decisions of the first comptroller, of a general character; and, in 1881, a second volume. Since 1882, one volume a year has been issued under authority of a resolution of Congress of August 3, 1882. In the introduction to volumes one, two, and three, more especially to volume three, will be found an outline of the nature and extent of the important jurisdiction exercised by the first comptroller, and of the nature of the powers exercised by accounting officers generally, as compared with strictly judicial power.

COMPULSORY. Involuntary; constrained: as, a compulsory — arbitration, assignment, condition, nonsuit, payment, process, *qq. v.* See VOLUNTARY.

Compulsion. Coercion; duress, *qq. v.* Compare BOYCOTTING.

COMPURGATORS. Neighbors of a person, made a defendant in a criminal or a civil action, who testified under oath that they believed he swore to the truth.[5] See further WAGER, 1, Of law.

COMPUTARE. L. To sum up; to account, *q. v.*

Insimul computassent. They settled an account together.

An averment that a balance was struck by the parties to an account, and that the defendant, against whom the balance appeared, promised, by implication of law, to pay it to the plaintiff.[6]

Plene computavit. He has accounted in full.

A plea in the action of account-render that the defendant has fully accounted.

Quod computet. That he account,— *computent*, that they account.

An interlocutory judgment in account-render or action of account, at law or in equity, that the defendant render an account before an auditor or a master.[1]

COMPUTE. See under CERTUM; COMPUTARE; DAY; TIME.

CON. 1. A form of *cum* (q. v.), in compound words.

2. An abbreviation of *contra*, and of conversation, *qq. v.*

CONCEAL. To hide, keep from view, cover up, secrete; to prevent discovery of; to withdraw from reach; to withhold information.

1. To hide or secrete a physical object from sight or observation.[2]

The act of March 2, 1799, authorizing the seizure of "concealed" goods, subject to duty, requires that the goods be secreted — withdrawn from view. It does not apply to a mere removal, though fraudulent.[3]

To "conceal property" in order to prevent its being taken on process includes not only physical concealment — literal secreting or hiding, but also the doing of any act by which the title of a party is concealed,— his property so covered up that it cannot be reached by process. The provision may apply to realty as well as to personalty.[4]

A horse may be "concealed" by destroying the means of identifying him. The word includes all acts which render the discovery or identification of property more difficult.[5]

A "concealed weapon" is a weapon willfully covered or kept from sight.[6] See further WEAPON.

2. To shelter from observation; to harbor; to protect. See HARBOR, 1.

3. To withdraw to a place where one cannot be found; to abscond, *q. v.*

"Concealment by a debtor to avoid the service of summons" involves an intention to delay or prevent creditors from enforcing their demands in the ordinary legal modes. It may be by the debtor's secreting himself upon his own premises, or by departing secretly to a more secure place, in or out of the county of his residence.[7]

(1887), cases; Chicago, &c. R. Co. v. Catholic Bishop, 119 Ill. 531 (1887).

[1] Jeffries v. Mutual Life Ins. Co. of New York, 110 U. S. 309-10 (1884), cases.

[2] 1 Bates, Partn. §§ 382, 387, cases.

[3] Whipple v. Whitman, 13 R. I. 512-15 (1882), cases; Township of North Whitehall v. Keller, 100 Pa. 108 (1882); Holker v. Parker, 7 Cranch, 452 (1813).

[4] See R. S. §§ 269, 273.

[5] See 3 Bl. Com. 341-48.

[6] 3 Bl. Com. 164; 81 N. Y. 271.

---

[1] 3 Bl. Com. 164; 1 Story, Eq. § 548.

[2] [Gerry v. Dunham. 57 Me. 339 (1869).

[3] United States v. Chests of Tea, 12 Wheat. 486 (1827).

[4] [O'Neil v. Glover, 5 Gray, 159 (1855); 4 Cush. 453.

[5] State v. Ward, 49 Conn. 442 (1881).

[6] Owen v. State, 31 Ala. 389 (1858).

[7] Dunn v. Salter, 1 Duv. 345 (1864). **See also Frey v.** Aultman, 30 Kan. 182, 184 (1883).

Leaving a place, requesting that false information of the person's movements be given, is concealment.[1]

4. To contrive to prevent the discovery or disclosure of a fact.

When the operation of a statute of limitations is to be suspended if the debtor "conceals the cause of action," there must be an arrangement or contrivance of an affirmative character to prevent subsequent discovery.[2]

To "conceal the death of a bastard child" is a misdemeanor. The time was when the mother had to prove, by at least one witness, that the infant was dead-born; if she could not she was presumed to be guilty of murder.[3] See AIDER AND ABETTER.

The fact that the owner of stolen goods does not know of the theft does not amount to a "concealment of the larceny" on the part of the thief, within a provision that where a thief conceals his crime the period of concealment is not to be included within the period of limitation.[4]

5. To neglect or forbear to disclose information; to withhold intelligence of a fact which in good faith ought to be communicated.[5]

In insurance law, concealment is the intentional withholding of any fact material to the risk, which the assured, in honesty and good faith, ought to communicate to the underwriter. . . That is a "material fact" the knowledge or ignorance of which naturally influences the judgment of the underwriter in making the contract, or in estimating the degree and character of the risk, or in fixing the rate of the premium.[6] See further REPRESENTATION, 1 (2).

"Fraudulent concealment" is the suppression of something which a party is bound to disclose. The intention to deceive must clearly appear. The test is, whether one party knowingly suffered the other to deal under a delusion.[6]

"Undue concealment," which amounts to fraud in the sense of a court of equity, and for which it will grant relief, is the non-disclosure of those facts and circumstances which one party is under some legal or equitable obligation to communicate to the other, and which the latter has a right not merely in *foro conscientiæ*, but *juris et de jure*, to know.[7]

Deliberate concealment is equivalent to deliberate falsehood.[8]

In making a contract, each party is bound to communicate his knowledge of the material facts, provided he knows that the other party is ignorant of them, and they are not open and naked, or equally within the reach of the party's observation, and that there is an obligation to communicate truly and fairly, by confidence reposed, or otherwise.[1] See FRAUD.

Aliud est celare, aliud tacere. It is one thing to conceal, another to be silent.

Silence is not concealment — where matters are equally open for the exercise of judgment. See CAVEAT, Emptor; SILENCE.

CONCEPTION. See QUICKENING; PREGNANCY; VENTER.

CONCERN. To affect the interest of, be of importance to, a person. See INTEREST, 1.

Sales of property for charges by a bailee, or for taxes, "for whom it may concern," mean for the unknown or non-claiming owner.

A policy of insurance "on account of whom it may concern," or with equivalent terms, will be applied to the interests of the persons who ordered it, provided they had authority to insure. Thus, an agent, factor, carrier, bailee, trustee, consignee, mortgagee, or any other lien-holder may insure the property to the extent of his own interest, and, by the use of the words in question, for all other persons, to the extent of their respective interests, when he has previous authority or subsequent ratification.[2]

Concerning. In R. S., § 3894, which provides that no letter "concerning lotteries" shall be carried in the mails, refers to letters sent out to advertise lotteries.[3]

Concerns. Under a statute exempting persons from turnpike tolls when traveling on "ordinary domestic business of family concerns," a physician going to visit his patients is not exempt.[4]

CONCESSION. See CESSION.

CONCLUDE.[5] 1. To close, end, terminate; to finish, complete.

Conclusion. (1) An ending or closing, as of an instrument or a pleading. See DECLARATION, 2; INDICTMENT; PLEA, 2.

(2) The last argument to a court, or the last address to a jury. See BURDEN, Of proof.

(3) An inference or deduction: as, a conclusion of fact, or of law. See PRESUMPTION.

2. To put an end to, close up; to be final; to estop, bar, preclude.[6]

[1] North v. McDonald, 1 Biss. 59 (1854).

[2] Boyd v. Boyd, 27 Ind. 429 (1867).

[3] 4 Bl. Com. 198, 358.

[4] Free v. State, 13 Ind. 324 (1859).

[5] See Gerry v. Dunham, 57 Me. 339 (1869).

[6] Magee v. Manhattan Life Ins. Co., 92 U. S. 93 (1875), Swayne, J.; Bartholmew v. Warner, 32 Conn. 103 (1864).

[7] 1 Story, Eq. § 207; Paul v. Hadley, 23 Barb. 524 (1857).

[8] Crosby v. Buchanan, 23 Wall. 454 (1874).

[1] 4 Kent, 482, note (a).

[2] Hooper v. Robinson, 98 U. S. 536, 538 (1878), Swayne, J.; Robbins v. Firemen's Fund Ins. Co., 16 Blatch. 127 (1879).

[3] Cummerford v. Thompson, 2 Flip. 614 (1880).

[4] Centre Turnpike Co. v. Smith, 12 Vt. 216 (1840).

[5] L. *claudere*, to shut up, close.

[6] See Hilliard v. Beattie, 58 N. H. 112 (1877).

Conclusive. Determinative, decisive; not to be questioned, controverted, or contradicted, nor requiring support. **Inconclusive:** presumptive, rebuttable.

As, in speaking of a judgment, or of a return of service that is conclusive, and of conclusive and inconclusive evidence or presumptions, *qq. v.*

A party who fails to assert his right, after receiving notice of a proceeding affecting it, is said to be " concluded " by the judgment.

CONCUBINAGE. "Concubinage" and "prostitution" have no common-law meaning. In their popular sense they include all cases of lewd intercourse,[1] *q. v.* See also PROSTITUTION.

CONCUR. 1. To go along together; to co-exist: as, in saying that in malicious prosecution malice and want of probable cause must concur.

Concurrent. Co-existing; having effect, operation, or validity at one and the same time: as, a concurrent or concurrent — agreements, covenants, or promises, consideration, jurisdiction, negligence, possession or seisin, remedies, *qq. v.*

2. To entertain like views; to agree: as, to concur in an opinion, and concurring opinion. Opposed to dissent. See OPINION, 3.

CONDEMN. To pronounce wrong.

1. To sentence; to adjudge.

Condemnation. A sentence or judgment which condemns a person to do, give, or pay something; or which declares that his claim or pretensions are unfounded.

Condemnation money. Money which the law sentences a party to pay;[2] also, in appeal bonds, the damages that may be awarded against the appellant, by judgment of the court.[3]

Bail above or bail to the action undertake that if the defendant is condemned in the action he will pay the costs and the condemnation, or else that they will.[4] See APPEAL, 2, Bond.

2. To declare forfeited: as, to condemn merchandise offered for sale in violation of a revenue law.

In Federal practice, proceedings in such cases are *in rem*, against the thing as offending. Whence the title of cases: United States *v.* Chests of Tea, Boxes of Cigars, Gallons of Whiskey. See RES.

3. To confiscate as contraband of war. See CONFISCATE.

4. To declare a vessel to be a prize, or unfit for service.[1] See PRIZE, 3.

5. To adjudge necessary for the uses of the public: as, to condemn private property under the power of eminent domain. See DOMAIN, 2.

A condemnation of lands is a purchase of them *in invitum;* the title acquired is a quitclaim.[2]

6. To judicially determine that realty, out of its rents and profits, clear of reprises, will not satisfy a judgment within a prescribed period, as, seven years. See INQUEST, Of lands.

CONDITIO. L. A stipulation, proviso, condition, *q. v.*

Conditio sine qua non. A condition without which (a thing can) not (exist); an indispensable prerequisite.

Melior est conditio. See DELICTUM, In pari, etc.

CONDITION. 1. State, status, predicament.[3]

2. A restriction placed upon the use of a thing.[4]

Some quality annexed to real estate by virtue of which it may be defeated, enlarged, or created upon an uncertain event; also, a quality annexed to a personal contract or agreement.[5]

The uncertain event itself; and the clause, in the instrument, which expresses the contingency.

An estate upon condition is such that its existence depends upon the happening or not happening of some uncertain event, whereby the estate may be either originally created, or enlarged, or finally defeated.[6]

An estate upon condition *implied* in law is where a grant of an estate has a condition annexed to it inseparably, from its essence and constitution, although no condition is

---

[1] People *v.* Cummons, 56 Mich. 545 (1885), Campbell, J.

[2] Lockwood *v.* Saffold, 1 Ga. 74 (1846).

[3] Doe *v.* Daniels, 6 Blackf. 9 (1841); 107 U. S. 381-92.

[4] 3 Bl. Com. 291.

---

[1] See 1 Kent, 101; 3 *id.* 103; 3 Wall. 28, 170, 514, 603; 5 *id.* 1, 28; 11 *id.* 268, 308; 106 U. S. 316.

[2] Lake Merced Water Co. *v.* Cowles, 31 Cal. 217 (1866).

[3] See Dunlap *v.* Mobley, 71 Ala. 105 (1881).

[4] See Ayling *v.* Kramer, 133 Mass. 13 (1882), cases.

[5] [Selden *v.* Pringle, 17 Barb. 465 (1854); Laberee *v.* Carleton, 53 Me. 213 (1865).

[6] 2 Bl. Com. 152, 154, 340. See also 4 Kent, 152; Adams *v.* Copper Co., 4 Hughes, 593-94 (1880); 31 Conn. 475; 39 Ga. 207; 31 Mich. 49; 1 Nev. 53; 70 N. Y. 309.

expressed in words: as, that proper use shall be made of a franchise. . . An estate on condition *expressed* in the grant itself is where an estate is granted with an express qualification annexed, whereby the estate shall either commence, be enlarged, or defeated, upon performance or breach of such qualification or condition.[1]

As respects realty, a "charge" is a devise with a bequest out of the subject-matter; and a charge upon the devisee personally is an estate on condition.[2] A "condition" is made by a grantor, and only he or his heir can take advantage of a breach.[3] A "covenant" is made by both grantor and grantee.[4] A "limitation" ends the estate without entry or claim; and a stranger may take advantage of the determination.[5]

Conditional. Subject to, or dependent upon, a condition; opposed to *unconditional:* as, a conditional — contract, conveyance, fee, guaranty, indemnity, liability, obligation, pardon, sale, *qq. v.*

Words which create a condition are "provided," "on account of," "if," and other words expressive of the intention. "Upon condition" is appropriate, but does not of necessity create an estate upon condition.[6]

Condition precedent. Such condition as must happen or be performed before the estate can vest or be enlarged. **Condition subsequent.** A condition upon the failure or non-performance of which an estate already vested may be defeated.[7]

Thus, if an estate for life be limited to A upon his marriage with B, the marriage is a condition precedent. Examples of conditions subsequent are: a grant of a fee-simple with a right to re-enter upon non-payment of the rent reserved; an estate held upon the condition that the grantee does not remarry, or continues to live at a certain place.

A "condition precedent" is one which must happen before either party becomes bound by the contract. A "condition subsequent" is one which follows the performance of the contract, and operates to defeat and annul it upon subsequent failure of either party to comply with the condition.[8]

Whether a qualification, restriction, or stipulation is a condition precedent or subsequent depends upon the intention of the parties, as gathered from the whole instrument.[1]

A condition precedent must be literally observed; a condition subsequent, tending, as it does, to destroy the estate, is not favored, and is construed strictly.[2]

No one can take advantage of a "condition subsequent" annexed to an estate in fee but the grantor or his heir, or the successor of an artificial person; and if they do not see fit to assert their right to enforce a forfeiture on that ground, the title remains unimpaired in the grantee. . . In what manner the reserved right of the grantor must be asserted depends upon the character of the grant. If it be a private grant, that right must be asserted by entry or its equivalent. If the grant be a public one, it must be asserted by judicial proceedings authorized by law, the equivalent of an inquest of office at common law, or there must be some legislative assertion of ownership of the property on account of a breach of the condition.[3]

Failure to perform a "condition precedent" bars relief; but equity will relieve against a forfeiture under a "condition subsequent" upon the principle of compensation, when that principle can be applied, giving damages, if damages should be given, and the amount is ascertainable. . If a "condition subsequent" be possible at the time of making it, and becomes afterward impossible to be complied with, by the act of God, the law, or the grantor, the estate of the grantee, being once vested, is not thereby divested, but becomes absolute.[4]

Where an act is to be performed by the plaintiff before the accruing of the defendant's liability under his contract, the plaintiff must prove either his performance of such condition precedent, or an offer to perform it which the defendant rejected, or his readiness to fulfill the condition until the defendant discharged him from so doing, or prevented the execution of the matter which the contract required him to perform. . . Conditions precedent may be waived by the party in whose favor they are made. Where the conditions are dependent and of the essence of the contract, the performance of one depends upon the performance of another, and the prior condition must be first performed. In cases where either party may be compensated for a breach, the conditions are mutual and independent.[5]

When a condition subsequent is broken, relief may be had upon equitable terms; but when the condition is a precedent one, and neither fulfilled nor waived, no right or title vests, and equity can do nothing for the party in default: as, where an assured is to pay the premium before the assurer shall be bound.[6]

---

[1] 2 Bl. Com. 152, 154, 340.

[2] See 4 Kent, 604; 12 Wheat. 498.

[3] See 2 Bl. Com. 155; 4 Kent, 122, 127; 21 Wall. 63; 3 Gray, 142; 41 N. J. L. 76; 19 N. Y. 100.

[4] 2 Coke, Litt. 70; 2 Pars. Contr. 31; 6 Barb. 386.

[5] 16 Me. 158; 3 Gray, 142; 5 Neb. 407.

[6] Stanley v. Colt, 5 Wall. 165 (1866); Sohier v. Trinity Church, 109 Mass. 19 (1871); Casey v. Casey, 55 Vt. 520 (1883).

[7] 2 Bl. Com. 154; Towle v. Remsen, 70 N. Y. 309 (1877).

[8] Story, Contr. §§ 40, 42-43; Jones v. United States, 96 U. S. 27-29 (1877), cases; Redman v. Ætna Fire Ins. Co., 49 Wis. 438 (1880); 17 Nev. 415; 35 N. H. 450; 47 Barb. 262.

[1] Lower v. Bangs, 2 Wall. 736, 746 (1864), cases; 70 N. Y. 311; 2 Bl. Com. 156-57; 4 Kent, 130.

[2] 2 Bl. Com. 154; 4 Kent, 125; 3 Pet. 374; 9 Wheat. 841.

[3] Schulenberg v. Harriman, 21 Wall. 63 (1874), cases, Field, J.

[4] Davis v. Gray, 16 Wall. 229 (1872), cases, Swayne, J.

[5] Jones v. United States, 96 U. S. 27-29 (1877), cases, Clifford, J.; Lower v. Bangs, 2 Wall. 736, 746 (1864), cases; Ruch v. Rock Island, 97 U. S. 693, 696 (1878), cases; The Tornado, 108 *id.* 352 (1883).

[6] Giddings v. Northwestern Mut. Life Ins. Co., 102 U. S. 111 (1880). See 2 Story, Eq. §§ 1302-11.

Repugnant conditions. Such conditions as tend to the subversion of the estate; such as totally prohibit the alienation or use of property conveyed.

Conditions which prohibit alienations to particular persons, or for a limited period, or subject to particular uses, are not subversive of the estate: they do not destroy or limit its alienable or inheritable character. Hence, property may be conveyed in fee and yet be exempted from use as a slaughter-house, soap-factory, distillery, livery-stable, tannery, machine-shop, or place where intoxicating liquors are manufactured, sold, or stored.[1]

Conditions are also distinguished as: *affirmative* or *positive*, prescribing the doing of a positive act, and opposed to such as are *negative; as collateral*, regarding some act incidental to another act; as *compulsory*, expressly requiring the doing of an act; as *consistent*, agreeing with each other or others, and opposed to such as are *inconsistent; as copulative*, for the doing of related things, and opposed to such as are *single*, for the performance of one thing only; as *disjunctive*, for the doing of one of several things; as *express*, stated in express words, and opposed to such as are *implied*, imposed by inference of law; as *possible*, performable, however difficult, and opposed to such as are *impossible*, or not performable.

Although words in a deed or devise are sufficient to create a condition, the breach of which would forfeit the estate, the courts lean against such a construction, and hold that words which may be treated as a covenant or restriction do not amount to a condition.[2]

See AFTER; CONDONATION; CONTRACT; DEFEASANCE; IF; PERFORMANCE; PROMISE; PROVIDED; REPRESENTATION, 1; SALE: TERM, 2; TRADE; WHEN.

CONDONATION.[3] Forgiveness by a husband or a wife of a breach, in the other, of marital duty.

The free, voluntary, and full forgiveness and remission of a matrimonial offense.[4]

Unless accompanied by that operation of the mind, even cohabitation, without fraud or force, is insufficient to establish condonation.[4]

A mere inference of law from proven facts. It is

the remission, by one of the parties, of an offense which the other has committed against the marriage, on condition of being afterward treated with conjugal kindness. While the condition remains unbroken, remedy for the condoned offense is barred. In cases of "connivance" (*q. v.*) no injury is done.[1]

Condonation of cruel treatment is conditioned upon the treatment ceasing.[2] See DIVORCE.

CONDUCT. See BEHAVIOR; DISORDER, 2; ESTOPPEL, Equitable.

A declaration of the result of a popular election may be included in power conferred upon the managers to "conduct" the election.[3]

CONFECTIONER. See MANUFACTURER; SUNDAY.

Selling liquors by the drink is not part of the business of a confectionery, and is not covered by a "confectioner's" license[4]

CONFEDERACY.[5] A league, or compact; a combination.

1. An improper agreement or combination alleged against defendants in equity: whence "clause of confederacy" in a bill in equity.

2. A (criminal) conspiracy,[6] *q. v.*

3. A political confederation, *q. v.*

CONFEDERATION.[5] A compact. An agreement between states or nations by which they unite for mutual welfare.

Confederation, Articles of. The instrument under which the compact between the Thirteen States was formed.

The full title was "Articles of Confederation and perpetual union between the States of New Hampshire," etc. The Articles were reported July 12, 1776; recommended for adoption November 17, 1777; ratified by eight States July 9, 1778, and by the last State (Maryland) March 1, 1781. The First Congress thereunder met March 2, 1781. The Articles continued in force to March 4, 1789, when the first Congress under the Constitution met.[7] See STATE, 3 (2).

Confederation of Southern States; Confederate States of America. See GOVERNMENT, De facto; MONEY, Lawful; OATH, Of office; STATE, 3 (2); WAR.

---

[1] Cowell *v.* Colorado Springs Co., 100 U. S. 57-58 (1879), cases, Field, J. See Camp *v.* Cleary, 76 Va. 143 (1882), cases; Case *v.* Dwire, 60 Iowa, 444 (1883), cases; Smith *v.* Barrie, 56 Mich. 317-20 (1685), cases; Munroe *v.* Hall, 97 N. C. 210 (1887). In wills, see Webster *v.* Morris, 66 Wis. 386-88 (1886), cases; 19 Cent. Law J. 122-26, 462-67 (1884), cases; 30 Alb. Law J. 4-8 (1884), cases.

[2] Adams *v.* Valentine, 33 F. R. 4 (1887), cases, Wallace, J.

[3] L. *condonare*, to remit, pardon.

[4] Betz *v.* Betz, 2 Robt. 696 (N. Y., 1864), Barbour, J.

[1] [2 Bish. Mar. & Div. §§ 33-34; 1 *id.* § 95 *a.* See also Morrison *v.* Morrison, 142 Mass. 362-65 (1886), cases; 23 Ark. 615; 28 Ga. 286; 73 Ill. 500; 34 Ind. 369; 60 *id.* 258; 140 Mass. 528; 32 Miss. 289; 8 Oreg. 224.

[2] Rose *v.* Rose, 87 Ind. 481 (1882). See generally Ohio Law J., Aug. 23, 1884.

[3] Blake *v.* Walker, 23 S. C. 526 (1885).

[4] New Orleans *v.* Jans, 34 La. An. 667 (1882).

[5] L. *con-fœderare*, to unite by covenant: *fœdus*, a league.

[6] See State *v.* Crowley, 41 Wis. 284 (1876).

[7] See R. S. p. 7; 1 Story, Const. § 225; Owings *v.* Speed, 4 Wheat. 420 (1820); 1 Bancroft, Const. 3-118 (1884).

CONFESSIO. L. Acknowledgment; admission; confession.

Confessio facti. Admission of a fact.

Confessio juris. Admission of the law — of the effect of a thing in law.

The latter is not received in evidence, for the party may not know the legal effect of a thing, as of an instrument.[1] See DECREE, Pro confesso; IGNORANCE.

CONFESSION. Acknowledgment; admission.

1. In civil law, the admission of a fact as true, existing, binding, or valid.

Confession and avoidance. The act or proceeding by which a party admits the truth of an allegation he proposes to answer, and then states matter intended to avoid the legal inference which may be drawn from the admission.

Some pleas of this sort are in justification or excuse — show that the plaintiff never had any right of action, because the act charged was lawful; while other pleas are in discharge — show that a right of action once existed, but that it is released by some subsequent matter.[2] See AVOID, 2; COLOR, 2; MATTER, 3, New.

Confession of action. A plea confessing the complaint, in whole or in part.[3]

An admission of a cause of action, as alleged in the declaration, to the extent of its terms.[4]

Confession of judgment. A voluntary submission to the jurisdiction of the court, giving, by consent and without the service of process, what could [might] otherwise be obtained by complaint, summons, and other formal proceedings.[5] See ATTORNEY, Warrant of; COGNOVIT.

2. In criminal law, acknowledgment of guilt.[6]

Direct, indirect, or incidental confession. An acknowledgment of criminal intent, made like an "implied admission" (q. v.) in civil cases.[7]

Judicial confession. A confession made before a magistrate or in a court, in the course of legal proceedings. **Extra-judicial confession.** Such as is made elsewhere than before a magistrate or in court; and embraces not only explicit and *express* confessions of crime, but all admissions from which guilt may be implied.[1]

Naked confession. A confession uncorroborated by other proof of the *corpus delicti.*[2]

Voluntary confession. The presumption is that all confessions are voluntary: free from promise or threat. The state of mind must be brought about by the accused's own independent reasoning.[3]

A confession, when the free prompting of a guilty conscience, unincited by hope or fear, is evidence. It is receivable although obtained by artifice, by liquor given, or under promise of some collateral good, or made to a physician, parent, or spiritual adviser. At common law, an attorney is the only protected confidant.[4]

The practice is to inquire of the witness whether the prisoner had been told, in effect, that it would be better for him to confess, or worse for him if he did not confess. The judge, exercising a legal discretion, and governed by extreme caution, receives or rejects the proposed proof.[5] See further ACCOMPLICE; ADMISSION, 2; COMMUNICATION, Privileged, 1.

CONFESSIONAL. See COMMUNICATION, Privileged, 1.

CONFIDENCE. See COMMUNICATION; CREDIT; FAITH; FIDUCIARY; TRUST, 1; USE, 2.

CONFINEMENT. See PRISON.

CONFIRMATION. Making firm what was before infirm.[6]

1. Affirmation; ratification, q. v.

2. A secondary or derivative conveyance, defined by Coke to be "a conveyance of an estate or right *in esse*, whereby a voidable estate is made sure and unavoidable, or whereby a particular estate is increased."[7]

3. The judicial sanction of a court: as, the confirmation of a sale.[8]

A decree of confirmation upon a judicial sale is a judgment of the court, which determines the rights of the parties. Before confirmation, the whole proceed-

---

[1] 1 Greenl. Ev. §§ 96, 203.

[2] Steph. Pl. 72, 79, 220; 1 Chitty, Pl. 540; 2 id. 644; 3 Bl. Com. 310; 31 Conn. 177.

[3] [3 Bl. Com. 303, 3J7.

[4] Hackett v. Railroad Co., 35 N. H. 397 (1857).

[5] First Nat. Bank of Canandaigua v. Garlinghouse, 53 Barb. 619 (1868).

[6] 1 Greenl. Ev. § 170.

[7] 1 Greenl. Ev. § 214.

[1] [1 Greenl. Ev. § 216; 1 Cliff. 23; 28 Mo. 230.

[2] 1 Greenl. Ev. § 217.

[3] Commonwealth v. Sego, 125 Mass. 213 (1878); Speer v. State, 4 Tex. Ap. 479-86 (1878), cases; People v. McGloin, 91 N. Y. 247 (1883).

[4] 1 Greenl. Ev. ch. XII.

[5] 1 Greenl. Ev. § 219. And see Hopt v. Utah, 110 U. S. 584-87 (1884), cases; 4 Bl. Com. 357; 1 B. & H. Lead. Cr. Cas, 112, note; 59 Cal. 457; 68 Ga. 663; 34 La. An. 17-18; 89 N. C. 629.

[6] [Coke, Litt. 295.

[7] 2 Bl. Com. 325; 1 Inst. 295; Litt. §§ 515, 516, 531; Langdeau v. Hanes, 21 Wall. 530 (1874).

[8] Langyher v. Patterson, 77 Va. 473 (1883).

ing is *in fieri*, and under the control of the court. Until confirmation, the accepted bidder is not regarded as the purchaser. Whether the sale will be confirmed depends upon the circumstances of each case, and the sound discretion of the court in view of fairness, prudence, and the rights of all concerned.[1]

CONFISCATE.[2] To transfer property from private to public use; to forfeit property to the prince or state.[3]

Usage tends to confine the word to seizures of property by way of punishment of a breach of allegiance, or in the exercise of rights given by the laws of war.[4]

" Confiscation " is the act of the sovereign against a rebellious subject. " Condemnation " as prize is the act of a belligerent against another belligerent. Confiscation may be effected by such means, summary or arbitrary, as the sovereign, expressing its will through lawful channels, may please to adopt. Condemnation as prize can only be made in accordance with principles of law recognized in the common jurisprudence of the world. Both are proceedings *in rem*, but confiscation recognizes the title of the original owner to the property, while in prize the tenure of the property is qualified, provisional, and destitute of absolute ownership.[5]

Confiscation Acts of 1861 and **1862.** The act of August 6, 1861, and the act of July 17, 1862.[6]

Made in exercise of the war powers of the Government. The right to make such laws exists alike in civil and foreign war. Congress determines what property shall be taken.[7]

The proceedings are justified as an exercise of belligerent rights against a public enemy, and are not a punishment for treason. Hence, the pardon of an act of treason will not restore rights of property previously condemned.[8]

The act of 1862, as explained by a resolution of the same date, provided that forfeiture of realty should not extend beyond the life of the offender. Passing this act was an exercise of war powers, not a criminal proceeding.[9] Its design was to strengthen the Government and to enfeeble the enemy by taking from the adherents of that enemy the power to use their property in aid of the hostile cause. It provided for the

seizure and condemnation of the life-estate, with the fee left in the heirs.[1]

The act of 1861 made property a lawful subject of capture and prize. The object of the act of 1862 was to confiscate the property of traitors by way of punishment for countenancing the rebellion.[2]

The act of 1862, generally known as *the* Confiscation Act, and the joint resolution of the same day explanatory thereof, must be construed together. In a sale of property thereunder, all that could be sold was a right to the property seized, terminating with the life of the offender. Such sale does not affect the rights of a mortgagee in favor of a third person. The property goes to the Government or to the purchaser *cum onere*.[3]

Debts and credits, which are intangible, are nowhere confiscated.[4] See ATTAINDER; PARDON; PROHIBITION, 2; WAR.

CONFLAGRATION. See FIRE, Department; NECESSITY; TAKE, 8.

CONFLICT. Striking together; meeting in collision; opposition, as of authority, interest, jurisdiction, titles.

Conflict of laws. Opposition of laws upon the same object; whether of the same or of different jurisdictions.

As between different States, there is more or less disagreement in the laws relating to marriage and divorce, legitimacy, pending suits, judgments, intestate estates, assignments by insolvents, bills and notes, remedies, and some other subjects.

The laws of each State affect all persons, property, contracts, acts and transactions within its boundaries. Foreign laws are allowed to bind foreign-made transactions unless they injuriously affect citizens, violate statutes, or are opposed to good morals or public policy. Realty is governed by the law of the place where it is situated; personalty, by the law of the owner's domicil.[5]

See COMITY; COMMERCE; LAW, Foreign; MARSHAL, 1, (2); PLACE, Of contract, delivery, payment; PROPERTY; REPEAL.

CONFORMITY. Agreement; adjustment.

A bill in equity filed by an executor or administrator, when he finds the affairs of the estate so much involved that he cannot safely administer the estate except under the

---

[1] Brock *v.* Rice, 27 Gratt. 815–16 (1876), cases; Terry *v.* Coles's Executor, 80 Va. 703–7 (1885), cases.

[2] L. *confiscare*, to transfer to the public purse: *fiscus*, a purse.

[3] Ware *v.* Hylton, 3 Dall. 234 (1796); 12 Mo. Ap. 234.

[4] See 1 Bl. Com. 299; 1 Kent, 52.

[5] Winchester *v.* United States, 14 Ct. Cl. 48 (1879), Davis, J.

[6] 12 St. L. 319, 590.

[7] Miller *v.* United States, 11 Wall. 308, 312–13 (1870); Alexander's Cotton, 2 *id.* 419 (1864).

[8] Semmes *v.* United States, 91 U. S. 27 (1875).

[9] Bigelow *v.* Forrest, 9 Wall. 350, 338 (1869); Miller *v.* United States, 11 *id.* 304, 268 (1870); Day *v.* Micou, 18 *id.* 160 (1873).

(15)

---

[1] Wallach *v.* Van Riswich, 92 U. S. 207 (1875); Waples *v.* Hays, 108 *id.* 8 (1882).

[2] Kirk *v.* Lynd, 106 U. S. 319 (1882); Phœnix Bank *v.* Risley, 111 *id.* 125 (1884).

[3] Shields *v.* Schiff, 124 U. S. 356 (1888), Bradley, J.; Avegno *v.* Schmidt, 35 La. An. 585 (1883): 113 U. S. 300 (1885).

[4] 1 Kent, 64–65. See further 4 Cranch, 415; 6 *id.* 286; 8 *id.* 122, 128; 13 Wall. 351; 15 *id.* 591; 20 *id.* 92; 2 Dill. 555; Chase, Dec. 259; 111 U. S. 125, 52; 96 *id.* 176.

[5] See Story, Wharton, Conf. of Laws.

direction of court, is called a "bill of conformity."[1]

The suit is against the creditors generally, for the purpose of having all their claims adjusted, and a final decree made settling the order and payment of the assets.

So called because the plaintiff undertakes to "conform" to the decree, or because the creditors are compelled to conform thereto.[1]

CONFRONT. To bring face to face.

The constitutional provision that the accused shall be "confronted with the witnesses against him" means that the witnesses on the part of the State shall be personally present when the accused is on trial;[2] or that they shall be examined in his presence, and be subject to cross-examination by him.[3]

If witnesses are absent by the procurement of the accused, competent evidence of the testimony they gave on a previous trial will be received.[4]

A person accused of a crime is deprived of his right of appearing in person and of being confronted with the witnesses against him if the jury view the *locus in quo* without his presence.[5] See DECLARATION, 1, Dying.

CONFUSION. Mixing, intermixture; intermingling, blending; confounding.

Confusion of boundaries. Where the boundary lines of different titles are conflicting, disputed, or uncertain; also, that branch of equity jurisprudence which ascertains such boundaries, *q. v.*

Confusion of debts. The concurrence of two adverse rights to the same thing in one and the same person.[6]

Confusion of goods. Intermixture of the goods of different owners so that the separate properties are indistinguishable.

Applies to the mixing of chattels of one and the same general description. "Accession" (*q. v.*) is where various materials are united in one product.[7]

He who causes a confusion of goods must bear whatever loss or disadvantage results.

The general rule that governs cases of intermixture of property has many exceptions. It applies in no case where the goods intermingled remain capable of identification, nor where they are of the same quality or value; as where guineas are mingled, or grain of the same quality. Nor does the rule apply where the intermixture is accidental, or even intentional, if not wrongful. All authorities agree, however, that if a man willfully and wrongfully mixes his own goods with those of another owner, so as to render them indistinguishable, he will not be entitled to his proportion, or any part, of the property; certainly not, unless the goods of both owners are of the same quality and value. Such intermixture is a fraud. And so, if a wrong-doer confounds his own goods with goods which he suspects may belong to another, and does this with intent to mislead or deceive that other, and embarrass him in obtaining his right, the effect must be the same.

. . Even where the articles are of the same kind and value, the wronged party has a right to the possession of the entire aggregate, leaving the wrong-doer to reclaim his own, if he can identify it, or to demand his proportional part. So held where bales of cotton, of different weight and grade, were purposely intermixed to render identification of particular bales impracticable.[1]

Confusion of rights or **titles.** In civil law, when titles to the same property unite in the same person.

"Confusion" in the civil law is synonymous with "merger" in the common law.[2]

CONGEABLE.[3] Permissible; done lawfully.

"If his entry were congeable, it will be considered as limited by his right."[4]

CONGREGATION. An assemblage or union of persons for a religious purpose.[5]

A voluntary association of individuals or families, united for the purpose of having a common place of worship, and to provide a proper teacher to instruct them in religious doctrines and duties, and to administer the ordinances.[6] See CHURCH.

CONGRESS. See CONSTITUTION.

"All legislative Powers herein granted shall be vested in a Congress of the United States, which shall consist of a Senate and House of Representatives."[7]

"The House of Representatives shall be composed of Members chosen every second Year by the

---

[1] 1 Story, Eq. §§ 544-45.

[2] Westfall v. Madison Co., 62 Iowa, 427 (1883).

[3] Howser v. Commonwealth, 51 Pa. 338 (1865).

[4] Reynolds v. United States, 98 U. S. 158-60 (1878), cases; United States v. Angell, 11 F. R. 43 (1881); 34 La. An. 121.

[5] People v. Lowrey, 70 Cal. 193 (1886).

[6] Woods v. Ridley, 11 Humph. 198 (1840); Story, Prom. Notes, § 439.

[7] 1 Schouler, Pers. Prop. 41, 40-54.

[1] The Idaho, 93 U. S. 585-86 (1876), cases, Strong, J. See also Jewett v. Dringer, 30 N. J. E. 291-311 (1878), cases; Queen v. Wernwag, 97 N. C. 383 (1887); 11 Wall. 369; 21 *id.* 64; 1 Saw. 306; 14 Ala. 695; 44 *id.* 609; 31 Ill. 282; 36 *id.* 150; 12 Me. 243; 56 *id.* 566; 8 Md. 301; 21 Pick. 298; 6 Gray, 134; 14 Allen, 376; 107 Mass. 123; 10 Mich. 433; 22 *id.* 311; 31 *id.* 215; 25 Minn. 88; 12 Mo. Ap. 284-85; 33 N. H. 433; 39 *id.* 557; 57 *id.* 514; 10 N. Y. 213; 24 *id.* 595; 6 Hill, 461; 24 Pa. 246; 20 Wis. 615; 20 Vt. 333; 2 Bl. Com. 405; 2 Kent, 365.

[2] Palmer v. Burnside, 1 Woods, 182 (1871).

[3] Cŏn'-ge-able. F. *congé*, leave; L. *commeare*, to go and come.

[4] Ricard v. Williams, 7 Wheat. 107 (1822), Story, J.; Litt. § 279.

[5] [Runkel v. Winemiller, 4 H. & M'H. 452 (1799).

[6] Baptist Church of Hartford v. Witherall, 3 Paige, Ch. 301 (1832), Walworth, Ch.

[7] Constitution, Art. I, § 1. On the powers of Congress, see 2 Bancroft, Const. VII, VIII; *ib.* abr. ed. 292-325 (1884),— summarizes the discussions in the original constitutional convention.

People of the several States, and the Electors in each State shall have the Qualifications requisite for Electors of the most numerous Branch of the State Legislature."[1]

"No Person shall be a Representative who shall not have attained to the Age of twenty-five Years, and been seven Years a Citizen of the United States, and who shall not, when elected, be an Inhabitant of that State in which he shall be chosen."[2]

"Representatives . . shall be apportioned among the several States . . . according to their respective Numbers . . . excluding Indians not taxed. . ."[3]

"When vacancies happen in the Representation from any State, the Executive Authority thereof shall issue Writs of Election to fill such Vacancies."[4]

"The House of Representatives shall chuse their Speaker and other Officers. . ."[5]

"The Senate shall be composed of two Senators from each State chosen by the Legislature thereof, for six years; and each Senator shall have one vote."[6]

One-third of the Senators are chosen every second year. "If Vacancies happen by Resignation or otherwise, during the Recess of the Legislature of any State, the Executive thereof may make temporary Appointments until the next Meeting of the Legislature, which shall then fill such Vacancies."[7]

"No Person shall be a Senator who shall not have attained to the Age of thirty Years, and been nine Years a Citizen of the United States, and who shall not, when elected, be an Inhabitant of that State for which he shall be chosen."[8]

"The Vice President . . . shall be President of the Senate, but shall have no Vote, unless they be equally divided."[9]

"The Senate shall chuse their other Officers, and also a President pro tempore, in the Absence of the Vice President, or when he shall exercise the Office of President of the United States."[10]

"The Times, Places and Manner of holding Elections for Senators and Representatives, shall be prescribed in each State by the Legislature thereof; but the Congress may at any time by Law make or alter such Regulations, except as to the Places of chusing Senators."[11]

"The Congress shall assemble at least once in every Year, and such Meeting shall be on the first Monday in December, unless they shall by Law appoint a different Day."[12]

"Each House shall be the Judge of the Elections, Returns and Qualifications of its own Members, and a Majority of each shall constitute a Quorum to do Business; but a smaller Number may adjourn from day to day, and may be authorized to compel the Attendance of absent Members, in such Manner, and under such Penalties as each House may provide."[1]

"Each House may determine the Rules of its Proceedings, punish its Members for disorderly Behavior, and, with the Concurrence of two-thirds, expel a Member."[2]

"Each House shall keep a Journal of its Proceedings, and from time to time publish the same, excepting such Parts as may in their Judgment require Secrecy; and the Yeas and Nays of the Members of each House on any question shall, at the Desire of one-fifth of those Present, be entered on the Journal."[3]

"Neither House, during the Session of Congress, shall, without the Consent of the other, adjourn for more than three days, nor to any other Place than that in which the two Houses shall be sitting."[4]

"The Senators and Representatives shall receive a Compensation for their Services, to be ascertained by Law, and paid out of the Treasury of the United States. They shall in all Cases, except Treason, Felony and Breach of the Peace, be privileged from Arrest during their Attendance at the Session of their respective Houses, and in going to and returning from the same; and for any Speech or Debate in either House, they shall not be questioned in any other Place."[5]

"No Senator or Representative shall, during the Time for which he was elected, be appointed to any civil Office under the Authority of the United States, which shall have been created, or the Emoluments whereof shall have been encreased during such time; and no Person holding any office under the United States, shall be a member of either House during his Continuance in Office."[6]

"All Bills for raising Revenue shall originate in the House of Representatives; but the Senate may propose or concur in Amendments as on other Bills."[7]

It is provided by statute that Representatives shall be chosen in single districts;[8] and that the elections shall take place on the Tuesday next after the first Monday of November.[9] Vacancies are filled as may be provided by State laws.[10] Votes must be by written or printed ballot: other votes are of no effect.[11]

For the election of Senators it is provided that the legislature of each State, chosen next preceding the expiration of the time for which any Senator was elected to represent such State in Congress, shall, on the second Tuesday after the meeting and organization thereof, proceed to elect a Senator.[12] At least one

---

[1] Constitution, Art. I, § 2, cl. 1.
[2] Constitution, Art. I, § 2, cl. 2.
[3] Constitution, Art. I, § 2, cl. 3.
[4] Constitution, Art. I, § 2, cl. 4.
[5] Constitution, Art. I, § 2, cl. 5.
[6] Constitution, Art. I, § 3, cl. 1.
[7] Constitution, Art. I, § 3, cl. 2.
[8] Constitution, Art. I, § 3, cl. 3.
[9] Constitution, Art. I, § 3, cl. 4.
[10] Constitution, Art. I, § 3, cl. 5.
[11] Constitution, Art. I, § 4, cl. 1.
[12] Constitution, Art. I, § 4, cl. 2.

[1] Constitution, Art. I, § 5, cl. 1.
[2] Constitution, Art. I, § 5, cl. 2.
[3] Constitution, Art. I, § 5, cl. 3.
[4] Constitution, Art. I, § 5, cl. 4.
[5] Constitution, Art. I, § 6, cl. 1.
[6] Constitution, Art. I, § 6, cl. 2.
[7] Constitution, Art. I, § 7, cl. 1.
[8] R. S. § 23: Acts 2 Feb., 30 May, 1872.
[9] R. S. § 25: Acts 2 Feb., 1872, 3 March, 1875.
[10] R. S. § 26: Act 2 Feb., 1872.
[11] R. S. § 27: Acts 28 Feb., 1871, 30 May, 1872; 76 Mo. 148.
[12] R. S. § 14: Act 25 July, 1866.

vote must be taken every day, during the session, until a person is chosen.[1] An existing vacancy is filled at the same time and in the same way;[2] and a vacancy occurring during the session is filled by election, the proceedings for which are had on the second Tuesday after the legislature has organized and has had notice of the vacancy.[3]

When Congress convenes, the president of the Senate administers the oath of office to its members;[4] and takes charge of the organization. The clerk of the preceding House of Representatives makes a roll of the Representatives-elect, and places thereon the names of those persons whose credentials show that they were regularly elected in accordance with the law.[5] If the clerk cannot serve, from sickness, absence, etc., the sergeant-at-arms of the preceding House performs this duty.[6]

In 1866 the salary of members of Congress was fixed at $5,000, and mileage, by the most usual route, at twenty cents a mile. In 1873 the salary was raised to $7,500; and in 1874 reduced to $5,000.[7]

See further, as to powers, such subjects as ACT, 3; BANKRUPTCY; CENSUS; COMMERCE; COIN; CONFEDERATION; CONTEMPT, 2; COPYRIGHT; COURTS, United States; DUTIES; ELECTORAL; FRANK; IMPEACH, 4; JOURNAL; LAND, Public; LOBBY; MARQUE; NATURALIZE; OATH, Of office; PATENT, 2; PIRACY, 1; POST-OFFICE; PRESIDENT; REVENUE; SWEEPING CLAUSE; TENDER, 2, Legal; TENURE, Of office; TERRITORY, 2; TREATY; VETO; WAR; WEIGHTS; WELFARE; YEAS AND NAYS.

CONJUNCTIVE. See DISJUNCTIVE.

CONJURATION. See WITCHCRAFT.

CONNECTING. See CONNECTION, 1.

CONNECTION. 1. "Railroad connection" means either such a union of tracks as to admit the passage of cars from one road to another, or such intersection of roads as to admit the convenient interchange of freight and passengers.[8]

The word conveys no implication of a right to connect business with business.[9]

The "connections" of a steamer, referred to in a policy of insurance, may refer to regular connections only.[10]

Connecting line. In the sense of the Georgia act of 1874, is where any railroad at its terminus, or any intermediate point along its line, joins another, or where two railroads have the same terminus; or where a railroad is adjacent to another and capable of being joined to it by a switch, either at its terminus or wherever along its line they meet or converge, and the right is given to make such connection, whether it be voluntarily granted or not.[1] See COMMERCE.

2. Any relation by which one society is linked or united to another.[2]

3. "Connections" is more vague than "relations." In popular phrase, a wife's relations are her husband's connections; but connections, unless they are also relations, never take by the statute of distributions.[3] See RELATION, 3.

4. "Guilty connection," applied to a man and a woman, imports carnal connection.[4]

CONNIVANCE.[5] Intentional failure or forbearance to see or actually know that a tort or offense is being committed; willful neglect to oppose or prevent; specifically, assent or indifference, by a husband, to immoral behavior by his wife.

It has been repeatedly held, under 20 and 21 Vict. (1857), c. 85, and similar statutes in this country, that a husband's connivance at his wife's prostitution bars subsequent complaint or cause of action on his part. The connivance need not be active: it is sufficient if it be made to appear that there has been a course of criminal conduct of which he actually was or must have been cognizant. Total indifference may justify inference of original consent.

It has also been held that if he once consents to her fall from virtue he cannot complain of any other act naturally resulting from such fall; but that doctrine carried too far would deprive a man of all hope, however repentant he may be, and however he may strive to win his wife to repentance. No authority decides that, under all circumstances, connivance at one act is an absolute bar to a divorce for a prior act as to which consent was not given, expressly or by implication.[6]

To be a bar to a decree for divorce the fact must appear that the libelant either desired and intended, or at least was willing, that the libelee should err. "A corrupt intention," it has been said, "is necessary to constitute connivance."[7]

See COLLUSION; CONDONATION; CRIME, Recriminate; DIVORCE; VOLO, Volenti, etc.

CONSANGUINITY.[8] The connection or relation of persons descended from the same stock or common ancestor;[9] blood-relationship. Opposed, *affinity*, q. v.

[1] R. S. § 15: Act 25 July, 1866.

[2] R. S. § 16: Act 25 July, 1866.

[3] R. S. § 17: Act 25 July, 1866.

[4] R. S. § 28: Act 1 June, 1798.

[5] R. S. § 31: Acts 21 Feb., 1867, 3 March, 1863.

[6] R. S. §§ 32-33: Act 21 Feb., 1867.

[7] R. S. § 35: Act 26 July, 1866, 3 Mar., 1873, 20 Jan., 1874.

[8] Philadelphia, &c. R. Co. v. Catawissa R. Co., 53 Pa. 20, 59 (1866); 60 Md. 269.

[9] Atchison, &c. R. Co. v. Denver, &c. R. Co., 110 U. S. 676-79 (1884).

[10] Schroeder v. Schweizer Lloyd Mar. Ins. Co., 60 Cal. 478 (1882).

[1] Logan v. The Central R. Co., 74 Ga. 684, 693 (1885).

[2] [Allison v. Smith, 16 Mich. 433 (1868).

[3] Storer v. Wheatley, 1 Pa. 507 (1845), Gibson, C. J.

[4] State v. Georgia, 7 Ired. L. 324 (1847).

[5] L. con-*nivere*, to close the eyes, wink at.

[6] Morrison v. Morrison, 142 Mass. 363-65 (1886), cases.

[7] Robbins v. Robbins, 140 Mass. 530-31 (1886), cases. See also 2 Bishop, Mar. & D. § 17; 34 Am. Law Reg. 98-100 (1886), cases.

[8] L. *consanguineus:* con, together; *sanguis*, blood.

[9] 2 Bl. Com. 202.

Consanguinei. Blood relations.

Consanguineal; consanguineous. Of the same blood or ancestor.

The subject is of importance in the law of inheritance and marriage.

Lineal consanguinity. Subsists between persons of whom one is descended in a direct line from the other. **Collateral consanguinity.** Subsists between persons who descend from the same stock or ancestor, but not one from the other.[1]

The common ancestor is the *stirps* or root, the *stirpes*, trunk or common stock, whence the relations branch out.[1]

The method of computing degrees in the canon law, adopted into the common law, is, to begin at the common ancestor (*propositus*) and reckon downward: and in whatever degree the two persons or the most remote of them is distant from the common ancestor, that is the degree in which they are related. . . The method in the civil law is to count upward, from either of the persons related, to the common stock, and then downward to the other, reckoning a degree for each person both ascending and descending.[2]

The canonists take the number of degrees in the longest line; the civilians, the sum of the degrees in both lines.[3]

The canon law rule prevails in the United States.

See ANCESTOR; DESCENT; INCEST.

CONSCIENCE. The moral sense; the sense of right and justice.

There are many cases against natural justice which are left wholly to the conscience of the party, and are without redress, equitable or legal.[4]

Human laws are not so perfect as the dictates of conscience, and the sphere of morality is more enlarged than the limits of civil jurisdiction. There are many duties, belonging to the class called "imperfect obligations," which are binding on conscience, but which human laws do not and cannot undertake directly to enforce. But when the aid of a court of equity is sought to carry into execution such a contract, then the principles of ethics have a more extensive sway.[5] See RIGHT, 1; FAITH.

Conscionable. In accord with strict honesty and justice: as, a conscionable appraisement or inventory of the articles of a decedent's estate. **Unconscionable.** Contrary to probity, fair-dealing, or what a fair-minded man would do or refrain from doing: as, an unconscionable contract or bargain, *q. v.*

Conscionable is an ill-contrived word: from conscience-able, or conscible (not now in use).[6]

Conscious. The expression, in a charge, "conscious of what he (a prisoner alleged to be insane) was doing," refers to the real nature, the true character, of the act as a crime, not to the mere act itself.[1]

Conscience of the court. To "inform the conscience of the court" is to furnish a court such data as will enable it to decide a matter discreetly and equitably.

Thus, the verdict of a jury out of chancery is intended to inform the conscience of the chancellor.[2]

Conscience, court of. The title of a court for the recovery of debts not exceeding forty shillings, formerly existing in some districts of England, as, in London, for the benefit of trade.

Examinations were summary, on the oath of the parties and witnesses. Such order was made as seemed consonant with equity and conscience. In 1846 jurisdiction was transferred to the county courts.[3]

Conscience, rights of. The constitutional declaration that "no human authority can control or interfere with the rights of conscience," refers to the right to worship the Supreme Being according to the dictates of the heart: to adopt any creed or hold any opinion whatever on the subject of religion; and to do, or to forbear to do, any act, for conscience sake, the doing or forbearing from which is not prejudicial to the public weal.[4]

Where liberty of conscience would impinge on the paramount right of the public it ought to be restrained. . . There are few things, however simple, that stand indifferent in the view of all the sects.[4]

"The constitution of this State secures freedom of conscience and equality of religious right. No man can be coerced to profess any form of religious belief or to practice any peculiar mode of worship, in preference to another. . . Beyond this, conscientious doctrines and practices can claim no immunity from the operation of general laws made to promote the welfare of the whole people." . "So long as no attempt is made to force upon others the adoption of a belief, so long is conscience left in the enjoyment of its natural right of individual decision."[5]

See further BLASPHEMY; EQUITY; HOLIDAY; RELIGION; SUNDAY.

CONSENSUAL. See CONSENT.

CONSENSUS. L. Perceiving or feeling alike: agreement; consent.

Consensus facit legem. Consent makes the law: the terms of a contract, lawful in

---

[1] [2 Bl. Com. 203–4; 45 Pa. 432.

[2] 2 Bl. Com. 205–7.

[3] 4 Kent, 412; 2 Coke, Litt. *158; 1 Williams, Ex. 364; 45 Pa. 432–33.

[4] 1 Story, Eq. §§ 14, 2.

[5] 2 Kent, 490; 1 Story, Eq. § 206; 1 Johns. Ch. 630.

[6] Skeat, Etym. Dict.

[1] Brown v. Commonwealth, 78 Pa. 128 (1875).

[2] Watt v. Starke, 101 U. S. 252 (1879).

[3] See 3 Bl. Com. 81.

[4] Commonwealth v. Lesher, 17 S. & R. 160 (1827), Gibson, C. J.

[5] Specht v. Commonwealth, 8 Pa. 322 (1848), Bell, J.

its purposes, constitute the law as between the parties.

Consensus, non concubitus, facit matrimonium. Consent, not intercourse, creates marriage.

Consensus tollit errorem. Consent removes error: the effect of a mistake is obviated or waived by concurrence.

Applies to an irregularity or a matter of mere form in procedure. A defect in substance, pleaded over, is still demurrable.[1]

Also applies to voluntary payments of illegal exactions, where recovery could have been prevented.[2]

Qui tacet consentire videtur. He who is silent is regarded as consenting: silence gives consent.

A man who is fully aware of what is being done against his interest cannot remain passive and afterward resist the disadvantage his silence has caused.[3] Nor can a person complain of the effect of words uttered in his presence, when he should have denied their truth.[4]

The maxim is to be construed as applying only to those cases where the circumstances are such that a party is fairly called upon to deny or to admit his liability. But if silence may be interpreted as assent where a proposition is made to one which he is bound to deny or admit, so also it may be if he is silent in the face of facts which fairly call upon him to speak.[5] See ESTOPPEL; SILENCE.

CONSENT. Agreement of mind; concurrence of wills; approval. Compare ASSENT; CONSENSUS.

An agreement of the mind to what is proposed or stated by another.[6]

The synonym of assent, acquiescence, concurrence; agreement or harmony of opinion or sentiment.[7]

Implies assent to some proposition submitted. In cases of contract, means the concurrence of wills. Supposes a physical power to act, a moral power of acting, and a serious, determined, and free use of these powers.[8]

The theory of the law in regard to acts done and contracts made by parties, affecting their rights, is, that in all cases there must be a free and full consent to bind the parties. Consent is an act of the reason, accompanied with deliberation. . . Hence, if consent is obtained by meditated imposition, circumvention, surprise, or undue influence, it is to be treated as a delusion, and not as a deliberate and free act of the mind. . . Upon this ground the acts of a person *non compos mentis* are invalid.[1]

Consent rule. See EJECTMENT.

Consensual. 1. Formed by mere consent.

In civil law, a contract of sale is consensual; not so a contract of loan. In the case of a sale, upon consent given, the parties have reciprocal actions; in the case of a loan, there is no action till the thing is delivered.[2]

2. In the sense of resting upon mere consent, all contracts, except marriage, may be said to be consensual.

See ACQUIESCENCE; AGE; DECREE; DURESS; RATIFICATION.

CONSEQUENCES. Persons of sound mind are held to intend whatever are the natural and necessary consequences of their acts: they are supposed to know what these consequences will be.

Experience has shown the rule to be a sound one, and one safe to be applied in criminal as well as in civil cases. Exceptions to it undoubtedly arise, as where the consequences likely to flow from the act are not matters of common knowledge, or where the act or the consequence is attended by circumstances tending to rebut the ordinary probative force of the act or to exculpate the intent of the agent.[3]

The law does not undertake to charge a person with all the possible consequences of a wrongful act, but only with its probable and natural result; otherwise the punishment would often be disproportioned to the wrong. thereby impeding commerce and the ordinary business of life, and rendering the rule impracticable. Although the damages may arise remotely out of the cause of action, or be, to some extent, connected with it, yet if they do not flow naturally from it, or could not, in the ordinary course of events, have been expected to arise from it, they are not sufficiently proximate to authorize a recovery.[4] See CAUSE, 1; DELIBERATION; INTENT; NEGLIGENCE.

Consequential. See CASE, 3; DAMAGES.

CONSERVATOR. One who preserves, or has the charge of a matter or thing, as, of the peace, *q. v.*

In Connecticut and Illinois, the committee of a lunatic or distracted person.[5]

[1] See Rogers v. Cruger, 7 Johns. *611 (1808); Morrison v. Underwood, 5 Cush. 55 (1849); Cushing v. Worrick, 9 Gray, 386 (1857); Wilkinson's Appeal, 65 Pa. 190 (1870).

[2] Chicago & Northwestern R. Co. v. United States, 104 U. S. 687 (1881).

[3] See 99 U. S. 581; 20 Conn. 98; 41 N. H. 465; 9 Barb. 17; 2 Pars. Contr. 759.

[4] 1 Greenl. Ev. § 197.

[5] Day v. Caton, 119 Mass. 515-16 (1876), cases.

[6] Plummer v. Commonwealth, 1 Bush, 78 (1866).

[7] Clem v. State, 33 Ind. 431 (1870).

[8] Howell v. McCrie, 36 Kan. 644 (1887), Simpson, C.

[1] 1 Story, Eq. §§ 222-23.

[2] See Hare, Contracts, 85-86.

[3] Clarion Bank v. Jones, 21 Wall. 337 (1874), Clifford, J. See also Reynolds v. United States, 98 U. S. 167 (1878); 5 Cush. 305; 4 Bl. Com. 197.

[4] Smith v. Western Union Tel. Co., 83 Ky. 115 (1885).

[5] Treat v. Peck, 5 Conn. *280 (1824); Hutchins v. Johnson, 12 id. 376 (1837); Nuetzel v. Nuetzel, 13 Bradw. 542 (1883).

The duties of a conservator of the estate of a ward are defined, in a general way, by statute. He acts independently of the ward, and is alone responsible for his acts. Debts incurred by the ward prior to the appointment of the conservator remain claims against the ward alone.[1]

CONSIDERATION.[2] 1. Deliberation, mature reflection.

"It is considered" is equivalent to "it is adjudged" by the court.[3]

The corresponding Latin formula is *consideratum est per curiam*. It imports that a judgment is the act of the law, pronounced by the court, after due deliberation and inquiry.[4]

The phrase is not an essential part of a judgment in a criminal case.[5]

2. That which the party to whom a promise is made does or agrees to do in exchange for the promise.[6]

The reason which moves a party to enter into a contract. . . The civilians hold that in all contracts there must be something given in exchange, something that is mutual or reciprocal. This thing, which is the price or motive of the contract, is called the consideration.[7]

Something esteemed in law as of value in exchange for which a promise is made.[8]

The "motive" for entering into a contract and the "consideration" of the contract are not the same. Nothing is consideration that is not regarded as such by both parties. It is the price voluntarily paid for a promisor's undertaking. Expectation of results will not constitute a consideration.[9]

That which one party to a contract gives or does or promises in exchange for what is given or done or promised by the other party.[10]

The proper test is detriment to the promisee. All our "considerations" would be "reasons" (*causæ*) in the Roman law; but it does not follow that all "reasons" — *e. g.*, desire to aid a meritorious object, or to benefit a member of one's own family — are considerations in our sense. And though all "considerations" are reasons, many of them are so slight that as mere reasons they would be entitled to little weight. With us, there must be a material *quid pro quo*, something given or surrendered in return, no matter how slight, to make the promise binding.[10]

---

[1] Brown *v.* Eggleston, 53 Conn. 119 (1885).

[2] L. *considerare*, to view attentively.

[3] Terrill *v.* Auchauer, 14 Ohio St. 85 (1862).

[4] 3 Bl. Com. 396, 130.

[5] State *v.* Lake, 34 La. An. 1070 (1882); State *v.* Bassett, *ib.* 1110 (1882); 39 Wis. 393.

[6] Phœnix Life Ins. Co. *v.* Raddin, 120 U. S. 197 (1887), Gray, J.

[7] [2 Bl. Com. 443.

[8] [Bishop, Contr. § 38, citing definitions.

[9] Philpot *v.* Gruninger, 14 Wall. 577 (1871), Strong, J.

[10] 1 Whart. Contr. § 493.

Void for want of consideration are: a promise to make a gift, the promisee surrendering nothing; a warranty given after a sale; a promise to pay for unsolicited past services; a promise to pay toward a religious or charitable object, when purely gratuitous; promises to pay debts that have been released.[1]

Any damage to another, or suspension or forbearance, is a foundation for an undertaking, and will make it binding; though no actual benefit accrues to the party undertaking.[2]

It is not absolutely necessary that a benefit should accrue to the person making the promise. It suffices that something valuable flows from the person to whom it is made; and that the promise is the inducement to the transaction. In the case of a letter of credit given by A to B, the person who, on the faith of that letter, trusts B, has a remedy against A although no benefit accrued to him.[3]

Damage to the promisee constitutes as good a consideration as benefit to the promisor.[4]

Any benefit, delay, or loss to either party. More fully, either a benefit to the party promising, or some trouble or prejudice to the party to whom the promise is made.[5]

If there is a benefit to the defendant or a loss to the plaintiff consequent upon and directly resulting from the defendant's promise in behalf of the plaintiff, there is a sufficient consideration moving from the plaintiff to enable him to maintain an action upon the promise to recover compensation.[6]

A valuable consideration may consist either in some right, interest, profit, or benefit accruing to the one party, or some forbearance, detriment, loss, or responsibility given, suffered, or undertaken by the other.[7]

"Any damage or suspension of a right, or possibility of a loss occasioned to the plaintiff by the promise of another, is a sufficient consideration for such promise, and will make it binding, although no actual benefit accrues to the party promising." This rule is sustained by a long series of adjudged cases.[8]

The performance of gratuitous promises depends wholly upon the good-will which prompted them, and will not be enforced by the law. The rule is that, to support an action, the promise must have been made upon a legal consideration moving from the promisee to the promisor. To constitute such consideration there must be either a benefit to the maker of the promise, or loss, trouble, or inconvenience to, or a charge or obligation resting upon, the party to whom the promise is made.[9]

---

[1] 1 Whart. Contr. §§ 494-95.

[2] Pillans *v.* Van Mierop, 3 Burr. 1673 (1765), Yates, J.

[3] Violett *v.* Patton, 5 Cranch, 150 (1809), Marshall, C. J.

[4] Townsley *v.* Sumrall, 2 Pet. 182 (1829), Story, J.; United States *v.* Linn, 15 *id.* 314 (1841).

[5] 2 Shars. Bl. Com. 443 (1859).

[6] Piatt *v.* United States, 22 Wall. 507 (1874), Clifford, J.

[7] Currie *v.* Misa, L. R., 10 Ex. 162 (1875), Lush, J.

[8] Hendrick *v.* Lindsay, 93 U. S. 148 (1876), Davis, J. Purports to quote Pillans *v.* Van Mierop, *supra*.

[9] Cottage Street M. E. Church *v.* Kendall, 121 Mass.

A valuable consideration may consist either in some right, interest, profit, or benefit accruing to the one party, or some extension of time of payment, detriment, loss, or responsibility given, suffered, or undertaken by the other.[1]

Executed consideration. An act already done, or value already given; a consideration already received or wholly past.

Executory consideration. A promise to do or to give something in the future; a consideration to be rendered.[2]

Good consideration. That of blood, or natural affection between near relatives.

Valuable consideration. Money, marriage, work done, services rendered, or the like.

Each is viewed as an equivalent. The former is founded in motives of generosity, prudence, and natural duty; the latter in motives of justice.[3]

"Good consideration" sometimes means a consideration which is valid in point of law; and it then includes a meritorious, as well as a valuable, consideration. But it is more often used in contradistinction to valuable consideration.[4]

By "consideration" as defined to be any benefit, delay, or loss to either party to a contract, is all that is meant by "valuable consideration." The distinction between "good" and "valuable" consideration is largely speculative.[5]

Moral consideration. The duty to perform, voluntarily, an obligation which is no longer enforceable in law.

This is sufficient to support an executed contract; and it will serve as a consideration for a new promise: as, a promise to pay a debt contracted in infancy, or outlawed, or discharged by a decree in bankruptcy. In such cases the moral duty was once a legal duty.[6]

The duty to perform a positive promise, not contrary to law or public policy, or obtained by fraud or mistake, is an obligation in morals, and a sufficient consideration for an express promise.[7] See OBLIGATION, 1.

Considerations are also distinguished as: *concurrent*, such as arise at the same time, or under· promises made simultaneously; as *continuing*, executed in part only; as *entire*, incapable of division or severance, unapportionable — if part is illegal, all is illegal; as *equitable*, based upon moral duty, moral; as *express*, stated in words, oral or written; as *gratuitous*, founded on no detriment to the promisee;[1] as *implied*, not stated in words, yet regarded in law as the consideration; as *legal*, valid in law, and as opposed to such as is *illegal, invalid, immoral*;[2] as *impossible*, such as, in the nature of things, cannot be performed, and not such as is merely very difficult;[3] as *nominal*, consisting of a sum or value purely nominal, as that of "one dollar;" and as *sufficient*, such as satisfies the requirement of law.

A valid consideration is absolutely necessary to a contract. An engagement without it is a *nudum pactum*, and totally void; as, a promise to make a gift.[4] The purpose is to prevent the too free-handed, the improvident, the reckless, from binding themselves to the performance of undertakings either wasteful of their means or else affording no reciprocal advantage.[5] But any degree of reciprocity will take an agreement out of this category.[4] See PACT, Nude.

Common examples of valid considerations are: prevention of litigation; forbearance to enforce a well-founded claim; assignment of a debt or right; work and service; trust and confidence; advances made, or liability incurred, in consequence of a subscription of money.

A seal imports a consideration.

Every bond, from the solemnity of the instrument, and every promissory note, from the subscription, carries with it internal evidence that a sufficient consideration has passed.[6]

A good consideration will not avail when the contract tends to defraud creditors or others of their rights. A valuable consideration will always support a contract in a court of common law, and, if adequate, in a court of equity.[7]

However small the consideration, if given in good faith, it will support the contract.[8]

A past consideration will not support a promise unless requested beforehand. A previous request is implied from service accepted or benefits received.[9]

529-30 (1877), cases, Gray, C. J.; University of Des Moines v. Livingston, 57 Iowa, 307 (1881).

[1] Nat. Bank of the Republic v. Brooklyn City, &c. R. Co., 102 U. S. 46 (1880), Clifford, J. See also 6 Col. 192; 17 Conn, 517; 58 N. H. 443.

[2] See Bishop, Contr. §§ 76-82, cases; Leake, Contr. 18; 1 Story, Contr. § 22; 1 Whart. Contr. § 493.

[3] 2 Bl. Com. 297, 444. See 4 Kent, 464; 1 Story, Eq. § 354; Bishop, Contr. § 42, cases; 58 Ala. 307; 20 Cal. 224-25; 9 Barb. 225.

[4] [1.Story, Eq. § 354. See 3 Cranch, 157.

[5] See 1 Whart. Contr. § 497.

[6] See Bishop, Contr. § 44, cases; 1 Pars. Contr. 431-36; 1 Story, Contr. § 590; 1 Whart. Contr. § 512; Leake, Contr. 86, 615; 2 Bl. Com. 445; 25 How. Pr. 484.

[7] Bentley v. Lamb, 112 Pa. 484 (1886): 23 Am. Law Reg. 635-36 (1886), cases.

[1] 1 Whart. Contr. § 494; M. E. Church v. Kendall, *ante*.

[2] See 1 Pars. Contr. 479.

[3] [1 Pars. Contr. 460.

[4] See 2 Bl. Com. 445.

[5] See Broom, Philosophy of Law, 38.

[6] See 2 Bl. Com. 446; Whart. Contr. § 495; Smith, Contr. 13.

[7] See 2 Bl. Com. 444, 297.

[8] Lawrence v. McCalmont, 2 How. 452 (1844); Bish. Contr. § 45, cases.

[9] 1 Pars. Contr. 427, 474.

A consideration subsequently arising may cure a deed defective for want of a consideration.[1]

The consideration of a written contract may be shown by parol.[2]

As to the parties to a deed, the consideration clause is *prima facie* evidence, with the effect only of a receipt, open to explanation and contradiction, not to defeat the deed as a conveyance, but to show the true consideration.[3]

See further ADEQUATE, 1; CONTRACT; CONVEYANCE, 2, Voluntary; DELIBERATION; FAITH, Good; FORBEARANCE; LEGAL, Illegal; NEGOTIABLE; SECURITY, 1; VALUE, Received; VOID.

CONSIGN.[4] 1. In civil law, for a debtor, under the direction of a court, to deposit with a third person an article of property for the benefit of a creditor.

Consignation. A deposit which a debtor makes, by authority of court, of the thing which he owes, in the hands of a third person.[5]

2. In mercantile law, to send or transmit goods to a merchant or factor for sale. . . The radical meaning of the word, which is of French origin, is to deliver or transfer as a charge or trust.[6]

Modern usage extends the meaning to transmission, by the agency of a common carrier, of merchandise or other movables for custody, sale, etc.

Consignee.[7] The factor or agent to whom merchandise or other personal property is consigned. **Consignor.** He who makes a consignment of personal property.

Consignment. Property intrusted to a common carrier for delivery to a person named in the bill of lading; also, the act or transaction by which the property is transported. See BAILMENT; CARRIER; FACTOR; LADING, Bill of.

CONSIMILI. See CASUS, Consimili.

CONSISTENT. See CONDITION; CUSTOM; REPEAL.

CONSISTING. Is not synonymous with "including," which implies that there may be other objects in the same category, though not specified. The words "consisting of" will be limited to the things specifically mentioned.[1]

The devise "I give all my worldly goods, consisting of household furniture, money, cattle, likewise my house and the lot I now occupy," was held not to pass other realty than that particularly designated.[1]

CONSOLIDATE. To unite or merge into one; to combine; to amalgamate.

To unite into one mass or body, as, to consolidate various funds; to unite in one, as, to consolidate legislative bills.[2]

Consolidation of actions. A direction that one of several pending actions, involving the same facts and issues, shall be tried, the result of the trial to be an adjudication of all the causes; or else that all the actions proceed to trial and judgment as one suit.

Sometimes termed the "consolidation rule."[3]

Allowed in suits against several insurers; in suits on separate promissory notes of the same date; but not in actions upon independent contracts, nor where claims have different guarantees; nor in actions upon distinct penalties.

The United States courts may consolidate actions of a like nature, or relative to the same question, as they deem reasonable.[4]

Consolidation of associations. Union or merger into one, of two or more companies or corporations organized for the same, or for some related, purpose. In England, "amalgamation."

Whether the consolidation of two companies works a dissolution of both, and the creation of a new corporation, depends upon the intention of the legislature.[5]

A sale by one corporation of all of its property to another corporation, is, as against creditors not assenting thereto, fraudulent and void.[6]

When two companies unite or become consolidated under the authority of law, until the contrary appears the presumption is that the united or consolidated company has all the powers and privileges, and is subject to all the restrictions and liabilities, of the companies out of which it was created.[7]

---

[1] Jones v. N. Y. Guaranty, &c. Co., 101 U. S. 627 (1879).

[2] See 1 Greenl. Ev. §§ 32, 26; 71 Ala. 95; 55 Pa. 504; 57 *id.* 410; 13 R. I. 95.

[3] Allen v. Kennedy, 91 Mo. 328 (1886), cases.

[4] L. *con-signare*, to mark, seal: to register, attest. In civil law a consignment of money was sealed up,— Bouvier.

[5] Weld v. Hadley, 1 N. H. 304 (1818).

[6] Gillespie v Winberg, 4 Daly, 320 (1872), Daly, C. J.

[7] Con-si-nee'; con-sin'-or.

---

[1] Farrish v. Cook, 6 Mo. Ap. 328, 331 (1878).

[2] Indep. District of Fairview v. Durland, 45 Iowa, 56 (1876), Seevers, C. J.

[3] See Gould, Plead., IV, s. 103; Cox, Com. L. Pr. 239; 59 Miss. 126.

[4] R. S. § 921; Keep v. Indianapolis, &c. R. Co., 3 McCrary, 302 (1882): 10 F. R. 455.

[5] Central R. Co. v. Georgia, 92 U. S. 670–76 (1875), cases; Branch v. Charleston, *ib.* 677, 682 (1875), cases; Green County v. Couness, 109 *id.* 106 (1883); Tyson v. Wabash R. Co., 11 Biss. 510 (1883); Woodruff v. Erie R. Co., 93 N. Y. 615–16 (1883).

[6] Hibernia Ins. Co. v. St. Louis, &c. Transp. Co., 4 McCrary, 432 (1882).

[7] Tennessee v. Whitworth, 117 U. S. 147 (1886), cases.

CONSORT. 1. A companion.

Consortship. Fellowship, companionship, *consortium*, q. v.

2. A vessel that keeps company with another vessel.

Consort-ship. A contract between owners of wrecking vessels to share mutually with each other moneys awarded as salvage, whether earned by one vessel or by both.[1]

Prevents mischievous competitions, and collisions. When made for an indefinite time, continues until dissolved by notice; not dissolved by mere removal of a master. Enforceable in admiralty, against property or its proceeds in the custody of the court.[1]

CONSORTIUM. L. Union of lots or chances: companionship; society; conjugal fellowship and assistance.

The right which a husband has to the conjugal fellowship of the wife, to her company, coöperation, and aid in every conjugal relation. . . He is not the master of the wife, and can maintain no action for the loss of her services as his servant. His interest is expressed by the word *consortium*. Some acts of a stranger to the wife are of themselves invasions of the husband's right and necessarily injurious to him; others may or may not injure him, according to their consequences: in which cases the injurious consequences must be proved, and that the husband actually lost her company and assistance.[2]

Per quod consortium amisit. By which he lost her assistance.

For a common battery upon the person of the wife trespass for damages is to be brought by husband and wife jointly; but, if, by reason of the maltreatment, he is deprived of her company and assistance, he has a separate remedy therefor.[3]

CONSPIRACY.[4] A combination of two or more persons, by some concerted action, to accomplish a criminal or unlawful purpose, or to accomplish a purpose, not in itself criminal or unlawful, by criminal or unlawful means.[5]

The unlawful combination or agreement of two or more persons to do an act unlawful in itself, or to do a lawful act by unlawful means.[6]

When two or more persons, in any manner or through any contrivance, positively or tacitly come to a mutual understanding to accomplish a common, unlawful design. . . A combination formed by two or more persons to effect an unlawful end, they acting under a common purpose to accomplish that end.[1]

The combination of two or more persons to do something unlawful, as a means or as an ultimate end. Many acts not indictable come within this definition. It is sufficient if the end proposed, or the means employed, are, by reason of the power of combination, particularly dangerous to the public interests or injurious to some individual, although not criminal.[2]

At common law the gist of the offense is the unlawful agreement. The offense is complete without an overt act—the law punishes the unexecuted intent.[3]

While, by statute, in many of the States, some overt act is necessary, the final result of such act does not vary the legal character of the offense.[4]

As known at common law conspiracy is not defined in any act of Congress as an offense against the United States, nor is it, therefore, cognizable as such in her courts.[5]

The act of Congress of May 17, 1879,[6] which is a substitute for the act of March 2, 1867,[7] provides that: "If two or more persons conspire either to commit any offense against the United States or to defraud the United States in any manner for any purpose, and one or more of such parties do any act to effect the object of the conspiracy, all the parties to such conspiracy shall be liable to a penalty of not more than ten thousand dollars, or to imprisonment for not more than two years, or to both fine and imprisonment in the discretion of the court."

Although by that enactment something more than the common-law definition is necessary to complete the offense, to wit, some act done to effect the object of the conspiracy, it remains true that the combination of minds in any unlawful purpose is the foundation of the offense. The conspiracy is for *any* fraud or offense against the United States.[8]

---

[1] Andrews *v.* Wall, 3 How. 571 (1845), cases, Story, J.

[2] Bigaouette *v.* Paulet, 134 Mass. 124 (1883), W. Allen, J. See also Winsmore *v.* Greenbank, Willes, 577 (1745): Bigelow, Ld. Cas. Torts, 328, 333–40, cases; Jones *v.* Utica, &c. R. Co., 40 Hun, 351 (1886).

[3] 3 Bl. Com. 140.

[4] L. *con*, together; *spirare*, to breathe, whisper.

[5] [Commonwealth *v.* Hunt, 4 Metc. 123, 121 (1842), Shaw, C. J. Approved in Spies *et al. v.* People (Anarchists' Case), 122 Ill. 213 (1887); Heaps *v.* Dunham, 95 *id.* 586 (1880); 3 Greenl. Ev. § 89.

[6] Buffalo Lubricating Oil Co. *v.* Everest, 30 Hun, 588 (1883); 17 F. R. 147.

[1] United States *v.* Babcock, 3 Cent. Law J. 144 (1876), Dillon, J.; United States *v.* Nunnemacher, 7 Biss. 120 (1876).

[2] [Commonwealth *v.* Waterman, 122 Mass. 57 (1877), cases, Colt, J.

[3] United States *v.* Walsh, 5 Dill. 60 (1878); United States *v.* Martin, 4 Cliff. 162–63 (1870), cases; 16 Blatch. 24–25; 97 Pa. 405.

[4] State *v.* Norton, 23 N. J. L. 40–46 (1850); Hazen *v.* Commonwealth, 23 Pa. 363–64 (1854), cases.

[5] United States *v.* Martin, 4 Cliff. 160 (1870).

[6] 1 Sup. R. S. p. 484: 21 St. L. 4.

[7] R. S. § 5440.

[8] United States *v.* Hirsch, 100 U. S. 34–35 (1879). See also 1 Low. 266; 11 Blatch. 168; 16 *id.* 15, 21; 2 Woods,

As soon as the conspiracy is formed and an act is done in pursuance thereof, the crime is consummated. In three years thereafter the bar of the statute of limitations is complete.[1]

An overt act, being necessary, must be alleged.[2]

Also punishable by acts of Congress are (or have been) conspiracies: to prevent a person from accepting or exercising an office; to deter a person from attending court as a party, witness, or juror; to impede the due course of justice, with intent to deny equal protection of the laws; to prevent a person from supporting a Federal elector or a member of Congress;[3] to destroy a vessel or the goods aboard with intent to injure any underwriter or lender of money;[4] to levy war against the United States;[5] to obtain approval of false claims for lands, pensions, etc.[6]

But no provision of the Constitution authorizes Congress to enact a law under which two or more free white citizens can be punished for conspiracy or going in disguise to deprive another free white citizen of a right accorded by the law of the State to all classes of persons.[7]

At common law a general allegation of a conspiracy to effect an object criminal in itself is sufficient, although the indictment omits all charges of the particular means employed.[8]

When the criminality consists in an unlawful agreement to promote a criminal or illegal purpose, that purpose must be clearly and fully stated in the indictment. When the criminality consists in the agreement to promote a purpose not of itself criminal or unlawful, by the use of fraud, force, falsehood, or other criminal or unlawful means, such intended use of fraud, etc., must be set out in the indictment.[9]

The connection of the members being once shown every act and declaration of each member, in pursuance of the common purpose, is the act and declaration of all.[10]

175, 197; 3 *id.* 47; 4 Dill. 128, 145, 407; 5 *id.* 58; 3 Hughes, 553; 12 F. R. 250; 32 *id.* 534, *infra*.

[1] United States *v.* Owen, 32 F. R. 534 (1887).

[2] United States *v.* Reichert, 32 F. R. 142 (1887). Field, J.

[3] R. S. §§ 1980, 5518-19.

[4] R. S. § 5364.

[5] R. S. § 5336.

[6] See R. S., Index, "Conspiracy."

[7] United States *v.* Harris, 106 U. S. 637-44 (1882), cases. Declared unconstitutional the act of Congress of April 20, 1871: R. S. § 5519. See also Baldwin *v.* Franks, 120 U. S. 678 (1887).

[8] See Commonwealth *v.* Fuller, 132 Mass. 566 (1882); United States *v.* De Griff, 16 Blatch. 24-25 (1879), cases; Barras *v.* Bidwell, 3 Woods, 47 (1876); Hazen *v.* Commonwealth, 23 Pa. 363-64 (1854), cases; Rex *v.* Gill & Henry, 2 B. & Ald. *205 (1818); 109 U. S. 199; 113 *id.* 104.

[9] Commonwealth *v.* Hunt, 4 Metc. 126 (1842), Shaw, C. J. See also 4 Bl. Com. 136; 3 *id.* 126; 3 Ala. 360; 6 *id.* 765; 12 Conn. 101; 30 *id.* 507; 25 Ill. 17; 30 Me. 132; 48 *id.* 218; 1 Mich. 220; 4 *id.* 444; 15 N. H. 394; 16 Johns. 592; 76 N. Y. 247; 41 Wis. 278; 2 Q. B. D. 59; 11 Q. B. 245; 10 Cox, Cr. Cas. 325.

[10] 1 Greenl. Ev. § 111; 64 Ind. 473; 87 *id.* 28; 88 *id.* 15; 66 Ga. 693.

If one concur, proof of agreement to concur is not necessary. As soon as the union of wills for the unlawful purpose is perfected the offense is complete. The joint assent may be established as an inference from other facts.[1]

It is not necessary to prove that the accused came together and agreed, in terms, to have a common design, and to pursue it by common means. It is enough to prove that they pursued the same objects, often by the same means, one performing one part, another another part of the same, so as to complete it with a view to the attainment of that same end.[2]

Every person entering into a conspiracy already formed is in law a party to all the acts done by any of the other parties, before or afterward, in furtherance of the common design.[3]

It makes no difference in the degree of responsibility that some of the conspirators were not present at the consummation of the design.[4]

If the act of one, proceeding according to the common intent, terminates in a criminal result, though not the particular result meant, all are liable. That is, a person may be guilty of a wrong he did not specifically intend, if it came naturally, or even accidentally, through some other specific or general evil purpose.[5]

He who conspires with others to do such an unlawful act as will probably result in the taking of human life is presumed to have understood the consequences which might reasonably be expected from carrying it into effect, and to have assented thereto.[6]

"He who inflames people's minds, and induces them, by violent means, to accomplish an illegal object, is himself a rioter, though he takes no part in the riot." . If he awakes into action an indiscriminate power, he is responsible. If he gives directions vaguely and incautiously, and the persons receiving them act according to what he might have foreseen would be the understanding, he is responsible.[7]

Such declarations of a conspirator as are in furtherance of the common design can be introduced against the other conspirators. Declarations which are merely narrative as to what has been or will be done may be admitted against him who made them or in whose presence they were made. . . The rule that the conspiracy must first be established *prima facie* before the acts of one confederate can be received in evidence against another cannot well be enforced where the proof depends upon a vast number of iso-

---

[1] Spies *et al. v.* People, 122 Ill. 213 (1887), citing 2 Bish. Cr. Law, § 190.

[2] Spies *v.* People, *ib.* 170, citing 3 Greenl. Ev. § 93.

[3] Spies *v.* People, *ib.* 179, citing 3 Greenl. Ev. § 93.

[4] Spies *v.* People, *ib.* 177, 253, citing Williams *v.* People, 54 Ill. 422 (1870); Brennan *v.* People, 15 *id.* 517 (1854); Whart. Hom. § 338.

[5] Spies *v.* People, *ib.* 225, quoting 1 Bish. Cr. Law, § 636, cases.

[6] Spies *v.* People, *ib.* 226, 229, cases; 1 Whart. Cr. Law, § 225 *a.*

[7] Spies *v.* People, *ib.* 198, 224, 230, quoting Regina *v.* Sharpe, 3 Cox, C. C. 288 (1848), Wilde, C. J.; 1 Bish. Cr. Law, §§ 640-41; Queen *v.* Most, L. R., 7 Q. B. D. 244 (1881).

lated circumstances. In any case, where the whole evidence shows that a conspiracy actually existed, it will be considered immaterial whether the conspiracy was established before or after the introduction of the acts and declarations of the members.[1]

A simple conspiracy is not the subject of a *civil action* unless it results in actual damage to the person aimed at. If such damage, but not the combination, is proven, the plaintiff is entitled to a verdict against any defendant shown to have committed an unlawful act.[2]

A bill in equity will not lie against persons (pilots) who have confederated to destroy the business of the owner of a vessel by publications in newspapers, by instituting suits, and in other ways. The injured person has adequate remedies at law for each of those acts.[3]

See ACCOMPLICE; BOYCOTTING; COMBINATION, 2; INDICTMENT; PROSECUTION, Malicious; SEDITION; STRIKE, 2; TRADES-UNIONS.

CONSTABLE.[4] 1. Originally, an officer who regulated matters of chivalry, tournaments, and feats of arms, performed on horseback.

2. An officer appointed to preserve the peace, and to execute the processes of a justice of the peace.[5]

Constabulary. Pertaining to or consisting of peace-officers. **Constablery.** The jurisdiction of a constable.

High constable. 1. A constable, or "lord high constable," in the primitive sense above noted. 2. The chief police officer in a town or city: the *chief* constable.

Petty constable. 1. An inferior officer in every town and parish, subordinate to a high constable.[6] 2. An officer charged with keeping the peace within a county or other district, and with executing such processes as are issued by justices of the peace.

Special constable. A person appointed to execute a warrant on a particular occasion or to co-operate in preserving the peace on a special emergency. See ARREST, 2; COUNTY, Power of; MARSHAL, 1 (3); PEACE, 1.

CONSTAT. L. 1, *v.* It appears: literally, it is established, certain, made manifest. Compare CONSTATE.

Non constat. It does not appear; it does not follow: it is not certain. *Non constitit:* it did not appear.

" Before judgment, *non constat,* the accused may be innocent."[1] "*Non constat* by the record, who gave notice."[2] " Whether the title was to come from him, and when, and on what conditions, *non constat.*"[3] "*Non constituit* whether a felony was committed till the principal was attainted."[4]

2, *n.* A certificate of what appears upon record as to a matter in question.

Thus, an exemplification of the enrollment of letters-patent under the great seal was called a "constat."[5]

There may be a possession of a vessel under a claim of title " with a constat of property."[6]

CONSTATE.[7] To establish, ascertain; to evidence, testify, prove.

" Unless there has been some violation of the charter or the constating instruments " of the corporation, the directors will not be personally liable."[8]

CONSTITUENT. See AGENT.

CONSTITUTED. See AUTHORITY, 2.

CONSTITUTION.[9] Originally, an important decree or edict. Later, the laws and usages which gave a government its characteristic features — the organic law.[10]

The constitution of England consists of customs, statutes, common laws, and decisions of fundamental importance. American constitutions are enacted; but the meaning of much of them is found in decided cases.[10]

The English constitution is a growth. Rights in favor of the Commons were established as follows: (1) In the reign of Henry III (1216–72), participation in levying taxes and in legislation, and control of applications for supplies. (2) In the reign of Edw. III (1326–77), enlarged participation in levying taxes and in legislation; inquiry into public abuses; impeachment of public ministers. (3) In the reigns of Hen. IV, V, and VI (1399–1461), the exclusive right to impose taxes; the right to grant supplies to the sovereign upon redress of grievances; larger participation in legislation; control of the administration; impeachment of ministers; and certain rights of privilege — freedom of speech in Parliament, freedom from arrest

---

[1] Spies *v.* People, *ib.* 237–39; State *v.* Winner, 17 Kan. 298 (1876); 1 Greenl. Ev. § 111; Roscoe, Cr. Ev. 414–15.

[2] Buffalo Lubricating Oil Co. *v.* Everest, 30 Hun, 588 (1883), cases.

[3] Francis *v.* Flinn, 118 U. S. 385 (1886).

[4] F. *conestable:* L. *comes stabuli,* count of the stable.

[5] [1 Bl. Com. 355.

[6] [1 Bl. Com. 355.

[1] 16 Wall. 370.

[2] 59 Wis. 652.

[3] 53 Pa. 396.

[4] 4 Bl. Com. 323. See also 6 Wheat. 229; 34 La. An. 1134.

[5] Coke, Litt. 225.

[6] The Tilton, 5 Mas. 468 (1830), Story, J.

[7] Con-state'. L. *con-stare,* to stand firm, be certain, known. See CONSTAT.

[8] Ackerman *v.* Halsey, 37 N. J. E. 363 (1883), Runyon, Ch.

[9] L. *constituere,* to make to stand together, to establish.

[10] Lieber, Encyc. Am., tit. Constitution.

during attendance upon Parliament, and the right of deciding upon election returns.[1]

An act of extraordinary legislation by which the people establish the structure and mechanism of their government, and in which they prescribe fundamental rules to regulate the motion of the several parts.[2]

The body of rules and maxims in accordance with which the powers of sovereignty are habitually exercised.[3]

Although, in some sense, every State may be said to have a constitution, the expression "constitutional government" applies to those States only whose fundamental rules or maxims prescribe how those shall be chosen who are to exercise the sovereign powers, and impose restraints upon that exercise, for the purpose of protecting individual rights, and of shielding them against any assumption of arbitrary power.[3]

If the constitution is unwritten there may be laws or documents which declare some of its important principles; as, in England, in the cases of the Magna Charta, Petition of Rights. Habeas Corpus Act, Bills of Rights. and the Common Law as the expositor of those charters.[3]

In America, the principle of constitutional liberty is that sovereignty resides in the people; and, as they could not collectively exercise the powers of government, written constitutions were agreed upon. These instruments create departments for the exercise of sovereign powers; prescribe the extent and methods of the exercise, and, in some particulars, forbid that certain powers, which would be within the compass of sovereignty, shall be exercised at all. Each constitution is, moreover, a covenant on the part of the people with each individual thereof, that they have divested themselves of the power of making changes in the fundamental law except as agreed upon in the constitution itself.[3]

A **written** constitution establishes iron rules, which, when found inconvenient, are difficult of change; it is sometimes construed by technical rules of verbal criticism rather than in the light of great principles; and it is likely to invade the domain of legislation, instead of being restricted to fundamental rules, and thereby to invite demoralizing evasions. An *unwritten* constitution is subject to perpetual change at the will of the law-making authority; against which there can be no security except in the conservatism of that authority, and in its responsibility to the people, or, if no such responsibility exists, then in the fear of resistance by force.[1]

Our **State constitutions** are forms of government ordained and established by the people in their original sovereign capacity to promote their own happiness and permanently secure their rights, property, independence, and common welfare. They are deemed compacts in the sense of their being founded on the voluntary consent or agreement of a majority of the qualified voters of the State. A constitution is in fact a fundamental law or basis of government, and falls strictly within the definition of "law" as given by Blackstone,— a rule of action prescribed by the supreme power in a state, regulating the rights and duties of the whole community. It is in this light that the language of the Constitution of the United States contemplates it; for it declares that this constitution, etc., "shall be the supreme Law of the land."[2]

A constitution is the letter of attorney from the people.[3]

Constitutions guard the rights of personal security, personal liberty, private property, and of religious professions and worship.[4]

Constitutions are mainly for the protection of minorities. In times of excitement and distress, their rights are most likely to be sacrificed.[5]

By the Revolution the transcendant powers of Parliament devolved upon the people. A portion of this power they delegated to the government of the United States. Such as remained they bestowed upon the governments of the States, with certain express limitations and exceptions. The **Federal Constitution** confers powers particularly enumerated; that of each State is a grant of all powers not excepted. The former is construed strictly against those who claim under it; the latter, strictly against those who stand upon the exceptions, and liberally in favor of the government itself. The Federal government can do whatever is author-

[1] See 4 Bl. Com. Ch. XXXIII; 3 Law Quar. Rev. 204-10 (1887).

[2] Eakin v. Raub, 12 S. & R. 347 (1825), Gibson, J. See also Wabash, &c. R. Co. v. People, 105 Ill. 240 (1883), Walker, J.

[3] [Cooley, Princ. Const. Law, 22-23; Const. Lim. 2-3. See also Hurtado v. California, 110 U. S. 531-32 (1884), Matthews, J.

[1] [Cooley, Princ. Const. Law, 22-23.

[2] 1 Story, Const. §§ 333-39.

[3] 1 Sharswood, Bl. Com. *147, note.

[4] 1 Kent, 407.

[5] Bunn v. Gorgas, 41 Pa. 446 (1862).

ized, expressly or by clear implication; the government of a State, whatever is not prohibited.[1]

The Federal Constitution went into effect the first Wednesday of March, 1789. September 14, 1786. commissioners from five States met at Annapolis, and recommended that a general convention be held at Philadelphia, to revise the Articles of Confederation. February 21, 1787, the congress of the confederation made a similar recommendation. May 25, 1787, the delegates assembled, organized, and, about four months later, to wit, September 17th, adjourned, having drafted a "Constitution of the United States of America." June 21, 1788, the document, as a constitution, was ratified by the ninth State. September 13, 1788, Congress set the time for choosing Presidential electors, appointing March 4, 1789, as the day, and New York City as the place, when and where the new Government of the United States should begin operations.[2] See CONFEDERATION, Articles of; NATIONAL.

The Constitution was ordained and established by "the people of the United States." It was not necessarily carved out of existing State sovereignties, nor was it a surrender of powers already existing in State institutions, for the powers of the States depend upon their own constitutions; and the people of every State had the right to modify and restrain them, according to their own views of policy or principle. On the other hand, it is clear that the sovereign powers vested in the State governments, by their respective constitutions, remained unaltered and unimpaired, except so far as they were granted to the government of the United States. "The powers not delegated to the United States by the Constitution, nor prohibited by it to the States, are reserved to the *States* respectively, or to the *people*." (Amd. Art. X.) The government, then, can claim no powers which are not granted to it, and the powers actually granted must be such as are expressly given, or given by necessary implication. . . The instrument is to have a reasonable construction, according to the import of its terms; and where a power is expressly given in general terms, it is not to be restricted to particular cases, unless that construction grows out of the context expressly, or by necessary implication. The words are to be taken in their natural and obvious sense, not in a sense unreasonably restricted or enlarged. It unavoidably deals in general language. It did not suit the purpose of the people in framing this great charter of our liberties to provide for minute specifications of its powers, or to declare the means by which these powers should be carried into execution. It was foreseen that this would be a perilous and difficult, if not an impracticable, task. The instrument was intended to endure through a long lapse of ages. It could not be foreseen what new changes and modifications of power might be indispensable to effectuate the general objects; and restrictions and specifications, which, at the pres-

ent, might seem salutary, might, in the end, prove the overthrow of the system itself. Hence its powers are expressed in general terms, leaving the legislature, from time to time, to adopt its own means to effectuate legitimate objects, and to mould and model the exercise of its powers, as its own wisdom, and the public interests, require.[1]

The Federal government is one of enumerated powers. The question respecting the extent of the powers actually granted will continue to arise, as long as our system shall exist. There is no phrase in the instrument which excludes incidental or implied powers, and which requires that everything granted shall be expressly and minutely described. Even the Tenth Amendment, framed for the purpose of quieting the excessive jealousies which had been excited, omits the word "expressly," and declares only that the powers "not delegated to the United States, . . nor prohibited by it to the States, are reserved to the States respectively, or to the people;" thus leaving the question, whether the particular power, which may become the subject of contest, has been delegated to the one government or prohibited to the other, to depend upon a fair construction of the whole instrument. A constitution, to contain an accurate detail of all the subdivisions of which its great powers will admit, and of all the means by which they may be carried into execution, would partake of the prolixity of a legal code, and could scarcely be embraced by the human mind. Its nature, therefore, requires that only its great outlines should be marked, its important objects designated, and the minor ingredients which compose those objects be deduced from the nature of the objects themselves. The powers given imply at least the ordinary means of execution. The government which has a right to do an act, and has imposed on it the duty of performing that act, must be allowed to select the means.

But this use of means is not left to general reasoning. To the enumerated powers is added that of making "all Laws which shall be necessary and proper for carrying into Execution the foregoing Powers, and all other Powers vested by this Constitution in the Government of the United States, or in any Department or Officer thereof." (Art. I, sec. 8, cl. 18.) "Necessary" (q. v.) does not here import an absolute physical necessity, so strong that one thing to which another may be termed necessary cannot exist without that other. If this clause does not enlarge it cannot be construed to restrain the powers of Congress, or to impair the right of the legislature to exercise its best judgment in the selection of measures to carry into execution the constitutional powers of the government.[2]

The revolution which established the Constitution was not effected without immense opposition. Fears were entertained that the very powers which were

[1] Sharpless v. Mayor of Philadelphia, 21 Pa. 160-64, 172-73 (1853), cases, Black, C. J.; 17 *id.* 119; 52 *id.* 477; 13 Conn. 125; 46 N. Y. 401; 16 How. 428.

[2] See R. S. p. 17; Century Mag., Sept., 1887; Bancroft, Const.

[1] Martin v. Hunter's Lessee, 1 Wheat. 324-27 (1816), Story, J.; Gibbons v. Ogden, 9 *id.* 187 (1824), Marshall, C. J.

[2] M'Culloch v. State of Maryland, 4 Wheat. 405-23 (1819), Marshall, C. J.,—upon the constitutionality of the act of April 10, 1816, incorporating the Bank of the United States. See also Legal Tender Case, 110 U. S. 441 (1884); *Exp.* Yarbrough, *ib.* 651, 658 (1884).

essential to union might be exercised in a manner dangerous to liberty.[1]

The rule laid down in *M'Culloch* v. *Maryland* has ever since been accepted as a correct exposition of the Constitution. It is settled that the words "all Laws which shall be necessary and proper for carrying into Execution" powers expressly granted or vested have a sense equivalent to the words: laws, not absolutely necessary indeed, but appropriate, plainly adapted to constitutional and legitimate ends; laws not prohibited, but consistent with the letter and spirit of the Constitution; laws really calculated to effect objects intrusted to the government. It was needful only to make express grants of general powers, coupled with a further grant of such incidental and auxiliary powers as might be required for the exercise of the powers expressly granted. Perhaps the largest part of the functions of the government have been performed in the exercise of implied powers.[2]

It is indispensable to keep in view the objects for which the powers were granted. If the general purpose of an instrument of any nature is ascertained the language of its provisions must be construed with reference to that purpose and so as to subserve it. And there are more urgent reasons for looking to the ultimate purpose in examining the powers conferred by the Constitution than there are for construing any other instrument. We do not expect to find in a constitution minute details. It is necessarily brief and comprehensive. It prescribes outlines, leaving the filling up to be deduced from these outlines. . . The powers conferred upon Congress must be regarded as related to each other, and all means for a common end. Each is but part of a system, a constituent of one whole. No single power is the ultimate end for which the Constitution was adopted. A subordinate object is itself a means designed for an ulterior purpose. It is impossible to know what those non-enumerated powers are, and what their nature and extent, without considering the purposes they were intended to subserve. Those purposes reach beyond the mere execution of all powers definitely intrusted to Congress and mentioned in detail. . In the nature of things, enumeration and specification of all the means or instrumentalities, necessary for the preservation and fulfillment of acknowledged duties, were impossible. They are left to the discretion of Congress, subject only to the restrictions that they be not prohibited and be necessary and proper for carrying into execution the enumerated powers. . . The existence of a power may be deduced fairly from more than one of the substantive powers expressly defined. . . Congress has often exercised powers not expressly given nor ancillary to any single enumerated power. These are *resulting* powers, arising from the aggregate powers. Illustrative instances of the recognition and exercise of such powers are found in the right to sue, and to make contracts; the oath required of officers;

building a capitol or Presidential mansion; the penal code; the census "of free white persons in the States," as to persons not free and in the Territories; the collection of statistics; carrying the mails, and punishing offenses against the postal laws; improving harbors; establishing observatories, light-houses, break-waters; the registry and construction of ships, and the government of seamen; the United States bank — for the convenience of the treasury and internal commerce, and to which the government subscribed one-fifth of the stock, although the bank was a private corporation doing business for its own profit; priority of debts due to the United States over other creditors; the Legal Tender Acts of 1862 and 1863.[1]

Constitutions are instruments of a practical nature, founded on the common business of human life, adapted to common wants, designed for common use, and fitted for common understandings.[2]

A constitutional provision is "self-executing" or "self-enacting" when it supplies the rule by which the right given may be enjoyed and protected, or the duty imposed may be enforced. It is not self-executing when it merely indicates the principles, without laying down rules by means of which those principles may be given the force of law. . . Some provisions are mandatory; others, without legislation, are dormant.[3]

Constitutional. 1. Relating to the framing or formation of a written constitution: as, a constitutional convention.

2. Based upon, secured, or regulated by a constitution: as, constitutional — governments, liberty, rights.

3. Authorized by a particular constitution, whether written or unwritten.

Unconstitutional. Contrary to the principles or rules of a constitution. Whence constitutionality, unconstitutionality.

An "unconstitutional" law either assumes power not legislative in its nature, or is inconsistent with some provision of the Federal or State constitution.[4]

A State legislature cannot pass a law conflicting with the rightful authority of Congress, nor perform a judicial or executive function, nor violate the popular privileges reserved by the Declaration of Rights, nor change the organic structure of the government, nor exercise any other power prohibited in the consti-

---

[1] Barron v. Mayor of Baltimore, 7 Pet. *250, 247 (1833).

[2] Hepburn v. Griswold, 8 Wall. 614-15 (1869), Chase, C. J. This power (Art. I, sec. 8, cl. 8) "was so clearly necessary that without cavil or remark it was unanimously agreed to" by the members of the Constitutional convention; 2 Bancroft, Const. 149.

[1] Legal Tender Cases, 12 Wall. 533-47 (1870), cases, Strong, J.; (Second) Legal Tender Case, 110 U. S. 439 (1884); *Exp.* Yarbrough, *ib.* 658 (1884); Holmes v. Jennison, 14 Pet. 571 (1840).

[2] 1 Story, Const. § 451; *ib.* § 419; 7 Tex. Ap. 210; 24 N. Y. 486. See also Burks v. Hinton, 77 Va. 29 (1883).

[3] Cooley, Const. Lim. 99-101; Groves v. Slaughter, 15 Pet. 500 (1841); 92 U. S. 214; 10 F. R. 503; 9 Cal. 341; 33 id. 487; 48 id. 279; 13 Ill. 1; 60 id. 390; 62 id. 38; 64 id. 41; 68 id. 286; 89 Ind. 115; 24 La. An. 214; 2 Mich. 500; 7 id. 488; 29 id. 108; 8 Miss. 14; 62 Mo. 444; 81 Pa. 482; 20 Gratt. 733; 9 W. Va. 703.

[4] Commonwealth v. Maxwell, 27 Pa. 456 (1856).

tution. The judiciary, in clear cases, has always exercised the right to declare such acts void. But beyond this there lies a vast field of power, granted to the legislature by the general words of the constitution, and not reserved, prohibited, or given away to others: their use of which is limited only by their own discretion. The constitution gives a list of the things the legislature may do. For the judiciary to extend that list would be to violate the letter and the spirit of the organic law itself. The people rely for faithful execution of the powers given to the legislature on the wisdom and honesty of that department, and on the direct accountability of the members to their constituents. The mere abuse of power was not meant to be corrected by the judiciary — for judges can be imagined to be as corrupt and wicked as legislators. And the general principles of justice, liberty, and right, not contained or expressed in the body of the constitution itself, are not elements for a judicial decision upon the constitutionality of an enactment.[1]

To justify a court in pronouncing an act unconstitutional, in whole or in part, it must be able to vouch some exception or prohibition clearly expressed or necessarily implied. To doubt is to favor constitutionality. That meaning of words is to be taken which will support the statute.[2]

A separable portion of an act may be unconstitutional, and the rest be valid, provided the law as a whole can be executed.[3]

The rule is to enforce statutes as far as they are constitutionally made, rejecting those provisions only which show an excess of authority, conformably to the settled maxim *ut res magis*, etc.[4]

The opposition between the Constitution and the law should be such that the judge feels a clear and strong conviction of their incompatibility.[5]

"Let the end be legitimate, let it be within the scope of the Constitution, and all means which are appropriate, which are plainly adapted to that end, which are not prohibited, but consist with the letter and spirit of the Constitution, are constitutional. Where the law is not prohibited, and is really calculated to effect any of the objects intrusted to the government, for the court to undertake to inquire into the degree of its necessity would be to pass the line which circumscribes the judicial departments, and to tread on legislative ground."[6]

---

[1] Sharpless *v.* Mayor of Philadelphia, 21 Pa. 160–64 (1853), cases, Black, C. J.

[2] Commonwealth *v.* Butler, 99 Pa. 540 (1882), Sharswood, C. J.; State *v.* Hipp, 38 Ohio St. 219 (1882).

[3] United States *v.* Reese, 92 U. S. 221 (1875); Virginia Coupon Cases, 114 *id.* 305 (1885); Presser *v.* Illinois, 116 *id.* 263 (1886), cases; Spraigue *v.* Thompson, 118 *id.* 90, 95 (1886); Baldwin *v.* Franks, 120 *id.* 689 (1887); State *v.* Kelsey, 44 N. J. L. 29 (1882).

[4] Adler *v.* Whitbeck, 44 Ohio St. 575 (1886); 15 Ohio, 645. See also Black *v.* Trower, 79 Va. 127–28 (1884), cases; Reid *v.* Morton, 119 Ill. 118, 129 (1886); 83 Ky. 68.

[5] Fletcher *v.* Peck, 6 Cranch, 128 (1810); County of Livingston *v.* Darlington, 101 U. S. 410 (1879), cases.

[6] M'Culloch *v.* Maryland, 4 Wheat. 421, 423 (1819), Marshall, C. J.; Hepburn *v.* Griswold, 8 Wall. 614–15 (1869); Legal Tender Cases, 12 *id.* 538 (1870).

The duty to declare an act of Congress repugnant to the Constitution is one of great delicacy, only to be performed where the conflict is irreconcilable. Every doubt is to be resolved in favor of constitutionality.[1]

The reasons against the unconstitutionality should at least preponderate; if they are equally balanced, the court should declare the statute valid.[2]

Proper respect for a co-ordinate branch of the government requires the Federal courts to give effect to the presumption that Congress will pass no act not within constitutional power. This presumption should prevail unless the lack of authority is clearly demonstrated. At the same time, the government being one of delegated, limited, and enumerated powers, every valid act must find in the Constitution some warrant for its authority.[3]

See AMENDMENT, 2; CITIZEN; COURTS, United States; FEDERALIST; IMPAIR; LAW, Supreme; LEGISLATURE; POLITICS; PREAMBLE, 1; RELIGION; RIGHTS, Bill of; STATE, 3 (2); TAX, 2; TENDER, 2, Legal.

CONSTRUCTION.[4] 1. Putting together, ready for use; building; erecting: applied to houses, vessels,[5] railroads,[6] machines.[7] See BUILD; ERECT; CONTRACTOR.

2. Drawing conclusions respecting subjects that lie beyond the direct expression of the text, from elements known from and given in the text — conclusions within the spirit, though not within the letter, of the text.[8]

"Interpretation" is the art of finding out the true sense of any form of words; that is, the sense which their author intended to convey.[8]

In common use, "construction" embraces all that is covered by both synonyms.[9]

Rules of construction have for their object the discovery of the true intent and meaning of instruments — the thought expressed.[10]

Where the language is transparent there is no room for the office of construction. There should be no construction where there is nothing to construe.[11]

Liberal construction. Such construction as enlarges or restrains the letter of an agreement or instrument so as more effectually to accomplish the end in view. Also called *equitable* construction. **Strict construction.** Such as limits the application

---

[1] Mayor of Nashville *v.* Cooper, 6 Wall. 251 (1867); 20 *id.* 668.

[2] Cherokee County *v.* State, 36 Kan. 339 (1887), cases.

[3] United States *v.* Harris, 106 U. S. 635 (1882), Woods, J. See 2 Story, Const. § 1243.

[4] L. *construere*, to put together.

[5] Sprague, 180; 103 Mass. 227.

[6] 11 Iowa, 17; 115 Mass. 400.

[7] 17 How. 72.

[8] Lieber, Hermen., Ham. ed., 44, 11; 36 N. J. L. 209; 2 Pars. Contr. 491.

[9] [Cooley, Const. Lim. *38.

[10] People *v.* May, 9 Col. 85 (1885).

[11] Lewis *v.* United States, 92 U. S. 621 (1875), Swayne, J.; Benn *v.* Hatcher, 81 Va. 34 (1885).

to cases clearly described by the words used; a close adherence to words. Also called *literal* construction.[1]

By a liberal interpretation of a letter of guaranty we do not mean that the words should be forced out of their natural meaning; simply that they should receive a fair and reasonable interpretation, so as to attain the object for which the instrument is designed and the purpose to which it is applied.[2]

Other expressions are: *artificial, forced* or *strained, refined, reasonable* construction.

A reasonable construction of an instrument, as of the Constitution, means that in case the words are susceptible of two senses, the one strict, the other more enlarged, that should be adopted which is most consonant with the apparent intent.[3]

The object is not to make or modify the instrument, but to find the sense. Hence, the whole document is to be construed together. This is to be done by the court, except when the writing contains technical words, or terms of art, or when it is introduced collaterally, or when its effect depends upon extrinsic circumstances — in which cases the duty devolves upon the jury.[4]

It is a cardinal rule in the construction of all instruments that, if possible, effect should be given to all parts and to every clause, *ut res magis*, etc.[5]

See further CONDITION; CONSTITUTION; CONSTRUCTIVE; CONTRACT; COVENANT; DEED, 2; EXPOSITIO; EXPRESSIO; FORFEITURE; FRANCHISE, 1; GRANT; IMPAIR; INSTRUMENT, 3; INSURANCE, Policy; NOSCITUR; PUNCTUATION; REPEAL; REPUGNANT; STATUTE; TRUST, 1; USUS, Utile, etc.; VERBUM; WILL, 2; WORD.

CONSTRUCTIVE. Determined by construction: inferred or implied, presumed or imputed; opposed to actual: as,

Constructive — annexation, appropriation, assent or consent, attachment, breaking, close, contempt, conversion, damages, delivery, fraud, larceny, levy, loss, malice, notice, possession, presence, service, taking, treason, trust, *qq. v.*

CONSUETUDO. L. Custom; usage; practice.

Consuetudo est altera lex. Custom is another law.

Consuetudo interpres legum. Custom is the expounder of laws.[6]

Consuetudo loci observanda. The custom of the place is to be conformed to. See CUSTOM.

CONSUL.[1] "Consul," "consul-general," and "commercial agent," in the Revised Statutes, denote full, principal and permanent consular officers, as distinguished from subordinates and substitutes.[2]

"Deputy consul" and "consular agent" denote officers subordinate to such principals, exercising the powers and performing the duties within the limits of their consulates or commercial agencies respectively, the former at the same ports or places, and the latter at ports or places different from those at which such principals are located respectively.[3]

"Vice-consuls," and "vice-commercial agents" denote consular officers, who shall be substituted, temporarily, to fill the places of consuls-general, consuls, or commercial agents, when they shall be temporarily absent or retired from duty.[4]

"Consular officer" includes consuls-general, consuls, commercial agents, deputy consuls, vice-consuls, vice-commercial agents, consular agents, and none others.[5]

The word "consul" shall be understood to mean any person invested by the United States with and exercising the functions of consul-general, vice-consul-general, consul or vice-consul.[6]

A "consul" is an officer of a particular grade in the consular service; in a broad generic sense, the word embraces all consular officers of whatever grade.[7]

Under treaties, consuls have had conferred upon them judicial authority over their own countrymen: as in the decision of controversies in civil cases; the administration of estates; the registering and certifying of wills, contracts, etc. When residing in a country of different political and religious institutions, they have also a limited criminal jurisdiction over their countrymen.[8]

Consuls are approved and admitted by the local sovereign. If guilty of illegal or improper conduct, the *exequatur* (q. v.) which has been given may be revoked, and they may be punished, or sent out of the country, at the option of the offended government. In

---

[1] [Bouvier's Law Dict.; 1 Wash. T. 351; 1 Shars. Bl. Com. 87; 23 Cent. Law J. 483 (1886), cases.

[2] Lawrence *v.* McCalmont, 2 How. 449 (1844), Story, J.; Crist *v.* Burlingame, 62 Barb. 355 (1862).

[3] [1 Story, Const. § 419.

[4] Goddard *v.* Foster, 17 Wall. 142 (1872), cases; Beardsley *v.* Hotchkiss, 30 Hun, 613 (1883); 1 Law Quar. Rev. 466 (1885).

[5] May *v.* Saginaw County, 32 F. R. 632 (1887).

[6] 116 U. S. 622.

(16)

[1] L. *consulere*, to consult.

[2] R. S. § 1674, par. 1.

[3] *Ibid.*, par. 2.

[4] *Ibid.*, par. 3.

[5] *Ibid.*, par. 4.

[6] Act 1 Feb. 1876; R. S. § 4130.

[7] Dainese *v.* United States, 13 Ct. Cl. 74 (1879).

[8] See R. S. § 4083; 11 F. R. 607.

civil and criminal cases they are subject to the local law in the same manner as other foreign residents owing a temporary allegiance to the state. A trading consul, in all that concerns his trade, is liable as a native merchant.[1]

See further DIPLOMATIC; MINISTER, 3.

CONSUMMATE.[2] Complete, finished, perfected, entire; opposed to inchoate, *q. v.*

An estate by curtesy is consummate on the death of the wife.[3]

Consummation. In the law of marriage, copulation.[4] See CUM, Copula; MARRIAGE.

CONSUMPTION. See LEGACY; LOAN, 1; TAX, 2, Indirect.

CONTAGIOUS. See DISEASE; DISORDER, 1; HEALTH.

CONTAINED. See PREMISES, 3.

Buggies insured as "contained in" a livery-stable were destroyed while in a factory for repairs. *Held*, that the words quoted were a warranty as to property whose use did not require removal.[5]

The description of a horse as "contained in" a barn, in a policy against lightning, was held not to be a contract that the horse was to be kept all the time in the barn. "Danger from lightning exists almost wholly in the summer season, when stock of all kinds upon farms is kept in the fields. A policy which covered stock only when in the barn would not furnish indemnity."[6]

Household furniture, described in a policy as "contained in" a certain house, was removed, without the insurer's knowledge, to a house on another street, where it was destroyed by fire. *Held*, that as the statement of locality was to be construed as a continuing warranty, the insured could not recover.[7]

A seal-skin dolman, insured as wearing apparel by a policy describing it as "contained in" a particular dwelling-house, was burned while in the store of a furrier, to which it had been sent for repair. *Held*, that the insurer was liable, although the risk was increased: temporary removal or absence being necessarily incident to the use of such property, and presumptively contemplated by the parties.[8]

CONTEMPLATION. Bankrupt and insolvent laws provide that acts done "in contemplation" of bankruptcy or insolvency shall be void.

The bankrupt act of 1841, by the phrase "contemplation of bankruptcy," did not intend contemplation solely of being a bankrupt, but contemplation of actually stopping business because of insolvency and incapacity to carry it on.[1]

The debtor must have contemplated more than a state of insolvency,— an act of bankruptcy, or an application to be declared a bankrupt.[1]

In the act of 1867, the phraseology is "in contemplation of insolvency or bankruptcy." This was held not to require an absolute inability to pay all debts in full on a close of business; only that the debtor could not pay his debts in the ordinary course of business.[2]

See BANKRUPTCY; INSOLVENCY.

CONTEMPORANEA. See EXPOSITIO.

CONTEMPT.[3] Disrespect; willful disregard of the authority of a court or legislature.

1. To the head of summary proceedings is referred the method, immemorially used by the superior courts, of punishing contempts by attachment. . . Contempts are either **direct** [sometimes called *criminal*], which openly insult or resist the powers of the courts or the persons of the judges who preside there; or else are **consequential** [sometimes called *constructive*], which, without such gross insolence or direct opposition, plainly tend to create a universal disregard of their authority.

The principal instances are: 1. Those committed by inferior judges and magistrates — by acting unjustly, oppressively, or irregularly in administering justice; disobeying writs issuing out of the superior courts by proceeding in a cause after it is put a stop to or removed by writ of prohibition, *certiorari*, error, *supersedeas*, etc. 2. Those committed by sheriffs, bailiffs, jailors, and other officers of the court — by abusing the process of the law or deceiving the parties; by acts of oppression, extortion, collusive behavior, or culpable neglect of duty. 3. Those committed by attorneys (*q. v.*), who are also officers of court — by gross fraud and corruption, injustice to their clients, or other dishonest practice. 4. Those committed by jurymen — by making default when summoned, refusing to be sworn or to give a verdict, accepting entertainment at the cost of a party, etc. 5. Those committed by witnesses — by making default when summoned, by refusing to be sworn or examined, by prevaricating in their evidence. 6. Those committed by parties — by disobedience to a rule or order, by non-payment of costs, non-performance of awards, etc. 7. Those committed by any other persons — as

---

[1] Coppell *v.* Hall, 7 Wall. 553 (1868), cases; The Anne, 3 Wheat. 445–46 (1818); 1 Kent, 53.

[2] Con-sum'-mate.

[3] 2 Bl. Com. 128; 17 Ct. Cl. 173.

[4] See 1 Bl. Com. 435.

[5] London, &c. Fire Ins. Co. *v.* Graves, 12 Ins. Law J. 308 (1883), cases,— Superior Ct. Ky.: 43 Am. Rep. 34; Longueville *v.* Western Assur. Co., 51 Iowa, 553 (1879).

[6] Haws *v.* Fire Association of Philadelphia, 114 Pa. 434 (1886).

[7] Lyons *v.* Providence Washington Fire Ins. Co., 14 R. I. 109 (1883), reversing Same *v.* Same, 13 *id.* 347.

[8] Noyes *v.* Northwestern Nat. Ins. Co., 64 Wis. 419–21 (1885), cases.

---

[1] Arnold *v.* Maynard, 2 Story, 353 (1854); Morse *v.* Godfrey, 3 *id.* 386 (1844); Everett *v.* Stone, *ib.* 453 (1844).

[2] Rison *v.* Knapp, 1 Dill. 194–95 (1870), cases; Martin *v.* Toof, *ib.* 206, 211 (1870); Re Smith, 13 Rep. 296 (1881): R. S. § 5110; 4 Bankr. Reg. 203; 21 How. Pr. 420; 61 Wis. 635.

[3] L. *contemptus*, scorn: *temnere*, to despise.

in cases of forcible rescue, disobedience to the prerogative writs.

Some of these contempts may arise in the face of the court — as by rude and contumelious behavior, obstinacy, perverseness, prevarication, breach of the peace, or other willful disturbance; others, in the absence of the party — as by disobeying the writ, rule, or other process of the court; perverting a writ or process to purposes of private malice, extortion, or injustice; speaking or writing contemptuously of the court or judges acting in their judicial capacity; printing false accounts (or even true accounts, without permission) of causes pending in judgment; anything, in short, that demonstrates a gross want of that respect without which the authority of the courts, among the people, would be lost.

The process of attachment for contempts must necessarily be as ancient as law itself. Laws without authority to secure their administration from disobedience would be nugatory. The power, therefore, to suppress a contempt by an immediate offender results from the first principles of judicial establishments, and must be an inseparable attendant upon every superior tribunal.

If the contempt be committed in the face of the court the offender may be instantly apprehended and imprisoned, in the discretion of the judges. But in matters that arise at a distance, if the judges upon affidavit see sufficient ground they may rule the suspected party to show cause why he should not be attached; in a flagrant case the attachment may be issued in the first instance. Once in court, the party must either stand committed or put in bail, in order to answer upon oath such interrogatories as shall be administered to him for the better information of the court with respect to the circumstances of the contempt. These interrogatories are in the nature of a charge or accusation, to be exhibited within a reasonable period, as, four days. If the party can clear ["purge," q. v.] himself upon oath, he is discharged. If he confesses the contempt, the court may fine or imprison him. This mode of trial, which is derived from the courts of equity, is sanctioned by immemorial usage.[1]

While a justice of the peace has no power to punish a contempt committed before him, he may bind the party to answer an indictment for obstructing the administration of justice, and to be of good behavior meanwhile.[2]

The act of Congress of March 2, 1831, "declaratory of the law concerning contempts of court," limits the power of the circuit and district courts to three classes of cases: 1, where there has been misbehavior of a person in the presence of a court, or so near thereto as to obstruct the administration of justice; 2, where there has been misbehavior of any officer of a court in his official transactions; 3, where there has been diso-

bedience or resistance by any officer, party, juror, witness, or other person, to any lawful writ, process, order, rule, decree, or command of a court.[1]

Such has always been the power of the courts, both of common law and of equity. The exercise of the power has a twofold object: to punish disrespect to the court or its order, and to compel performance of some act or duty. In the former case, the court must judge for itself of the nature and extent of the punishment. In the latter case, the party refusing to obey should be fined and imprisoned until he performs the act or shows that it is not in his power to do it.[2]

When a contempt is committed *in facie curiæ*, the punishment is generally summary; when committed elsewhere, initial proceedings are necessary, with notice, and opportunity to defend. A common initial process is a rule to show cause why an attachment or warrant for contempt should not issue, of which service should be made. In a proceeding to punish for criminal contempt, personal notice of the accusation is indispensable.[3]

2. The power in a legislature to determine the rules of its proceedings, and to punish for disorderly behavior, includes power to enforce its rules in the customary way — by attachment as for contempt.

The necessity for the existence and exercise of this incidental power rests upon the principle of self-preservation.[4]

There is in the Constitution no express authority for the power. Neither House of Congress is a court of judicature, as was Parliament originally. The Houses may punish for disorderly conduct or for failure to attend sessions; may decide contested elections, determine the qualifications of members, impeach officers of government. Where, in an examination necessary to the performance of these duties, a witness proves contumacious, he may be fined and imprisoned; but this can never be extended to an inquiry into his private affairs, on the plea that he is a debtor to the United States — that is a matter exclusively for the judiciary.[5]

[1] *Exp.* Robinson, 19 Wall. 510–11 (1873), Field, J.; Fischer v. Hayes, 19 Blatch. 13, 18 (1881); Worden v. Searls, 121 U. S. 121–26 (1887); R. S. § 725; 10 F. R. 629-33, cases.

[2] *Re* Chiles, 22 Wall. 168 (1874), Miller, J.; *Exp.* Hollis, 59 Cal. 408 (1881). See generally 22 Cent. Law J. 464–66 (1886), cases. History of constructive contempt, 33 Alb. Law J. 145–47 (1886), cases.

[3] Wheeler & Wilson Manuf. Co. v. Boyce, 36 Kan. 356 (1887); Rapalje, Cont. § 96.

[4] 1 Kent, 236–37; 2 Story, Const. §§ 305–17.

[5] Kilbourn v. Thompson, 103 U. S. 168, 181–205 (1880), cases, Miller, J. It had been alleged that Jay Cooke & Co., bankrupts, who were indebted to the United States, were interested in a "real-estate pool" in Washington, D. C., and that their trustee had settled with the associates of the firm to the disadvantage of the creditors. The House of Representatives authorized a committee to be appointed to investigate the matter. Kilbourn, being subpœnaed, appeared before the committee, but refused to give the names of the

[1] 4 Bl. Com. 283–88. See 21 Conn. 199; 65 Ind. 508; 49 Me. 392; L. R., 9 Q. B. 224; 25 Ala. 81; 16 Ark. 384; 25 Miss. 883; 37 N. H. 450; 29 Ohio, 330; 8 Oreg. 487; 13 R. L 427; 29 Am. Law Reg. 81, 145, 217, 289, 361, 425 (1881).

[2] Albright v. Lapp, 26 Pa. 101 (1856); The Queen v. Lefroy, L. R., 8 Q. B. 137–40 (1873).

The case of *Anderson* v. *Dunn* [1] declared that representative bodies possess inherently the power to punish for contempt. For sixty years this decision stood unquestioned. The repeated and unqualified declarations of the principle by courts and text-writers are to be traced to that case. The case of *Kilbourn* v. *Thompson* seems to deny that general and unlimited power exists inherently. [2]

A city council is not a legislature; nor is it vested with judicial functions; and its members are not chosen with reference to their fitness to exercise such functions. To allow it the right to imprison for refusal to answer any inquiry the whole body or one of its committee may choose to make would be a dangerous invasion of the rights and liberties of the citizen. . . The legislature cannot confer upon municipal bodies or officers, not courts of justice nor exercising judicial power, authority to imprison and punish without the right of appeal or of trial by jury. [3]

CONTENTS. 1. The clause, in a bill of lading, "shipped in good order . . contents unknown," acknowledges only fair external appearance; it includes no implication as to quantity, quality, or condition of the article: so that a shipper must prove the actual good condition of the contents. [4] See CARRIER.

2. In the Judiciary Act of September 24, 1879, § 11, in the phrase "any suit to recover the contents of any promissory note or other chose in action," means the sum named therein, payable by the terms of the instrument itself. [5]

An action to recover damages for a refusal to accept and pay for merchandise purchased under an oral contract is a suit to recover the "contents . . of a chose in action," within the act of March 3, 1887. The quoted words were taken from the judiciary act of 1789. Primarily they were intended to apply to commercial instruments, such as promissory notes, acceptances, and bonds, in which the sum promised is familiarly spoken of as the "contents" of such instrument. [1]

A suit to enforce the specific performance of a contract is a suit to recover the contents of a chose in action, within the meaning of § 629, Rev. St. [2]

3. In the House of Lords the "contents" are those who assent to, and the "non-contents" those who oppose, a bill.

CONTEST. [3] To make the subject of litigation; to litigate; to dispute or resist.

Contestable. Disputable; subject to resistance in a court; opposed to *non-contestable.*

Contestant. A litigant; a suitor.

To contest an election means to deny the legality thereof; to contest a will, to resist the probate of a writing alleged to be a will,— see INFLUENCE; ISSUE, 3, Feigned.

Some policies of insurance, by covenant on the part of the insurer, are not contestable after a certain period, as, three years, for a matter which arose prior to the end of that period.

CONTESTATIO. See LIS, Contestatio.

CONTEXT. See CONSTRUCTION.

CONTIGUOUS. In actual close contact; touching; near.

A relative term; referring to a building, means in close proximity to the same. [4]

A building any particular number of feet, as twenty-five, from a detached dwelling, is not "contiguous" to it. [5]

The charter of a water-works company provided that it should not prevent the city council from granting to persons "contiguous" to the Mississippi river the privilege of laying pipes to the river for their own use. *Held,* that no lot can be contiguous unless it fronts on the river or is separated only by a public highway, with no private owner intervening, or, possibly, on a block or square so situated. [6] Compare ADJACENT; ALONG.

---

members of the pool, or to produce designated books and papers. The House ordered the speaker to issue his warrant, directed to Thompson, the sergeant-at-arms, to arrest Kilbourn, who, when brought before the House, still refused to impart the desired information. For this contempt he was committed to the custody of Thompson until he would obey the original subpoena, meanwhile to be confined in the common jail of the District. At the end of forty-five days he was released on a *habeas corpus,* and at once sued the speaker, the committeemen, and the sergeant-at-arms for forcible arrest, and imprisonment. The members of the House were held protected from prosecution; but a verdict for $60,000 damages was recovered against Thompson. This verdict being set aside as excessive, on the second trial $39,000 were awarded. This sum was reduced to $20,000, and paid by order of Congress, with interest, and costs. See MacArthur & Mackey, 401–32 (1883); 23 St. L. 467; *Re* Pacific Railway Commission, 32 F. R. 251–53 (1887).

[1] 6 Wheat. 204 (1821).

[2] *Exp.* Dalton, 44 Ohio St. 150–53 (1886), cases.

[3] Whitcomb's Case, 120 Mass. 123–24, 120–23 (1876), cases, Gray, C. J.

[4] Clark v. Barnwell, 12 How. 283 (1851).

[5] Barney v. Globe Bank, 5 Blatch. 115 (1862).

[1] Simons v. Ypsilanti Paper Co., 33 F. R. 193–94 (1888), Brown, J.

[2] Shoecraft v. Bloxham, 124 U. S. 730 (1888).

[3] L. *con-testari,* to call to witness.

[4] Arkell v. Commerce Ins. Co., 69 N. Y. 193 (1877); 10 Hun, 26.

[5] Olson v. St. Paul, &c. Fire Insurance Co., 35 Minn. 433 (1886).

[6] New Orleans Water-Works Co. v. Ernst, 32 F. R. 6 (1887), Billings, J., following Water-Works Co. v. Rivers, 115 U. S. 674 (1885), which concerned the St. Charles Hotel, five blocks from the river. Compare New Orleans Water-Works Co. v. Louisiana Sugar Co., 125 *id.* 18 (1888).

CONTINGENCY.[1] An event which may happen; a possibility. A fortuitous event which comes without design, foresight, or expectation.

A remainder which depends upon an uncertainty is a "contingent" remainder. An expense which depends upon some future uncertain event is a "contingent" expense.[2]

"Contingencies," in an estimate of expenses, means expenses not yet ascertained, as yet unknown, uncertain, such as may or may not be incurred.[2]

Contingency with a double aspect. Occurs where remainders are so limited that one is a substitute for the other, in the event of the latter failing, and not in derogation of the latter.[3]

As, a grant to A for life, and if he have a son, then to the son in fee, and if no son, then to B.

Contingent. Possible; liable to occur; dependent upon an uncertainty: as, contingent or a contingent — damage, demand or liability, devise or legacy, estate or interest, fee or compensation, remainder, use, *qq. v.*

Applied to a use, remainder, devise, bequest, or other legal right or interest, implies that no present right exists, that whether a right ever will exist depends upon a future uncertain event.[4]

An estate will not be held contingent unless decided terms are used, or it is necessary to infer that a contingency was meant to carry out other parts of the will.[5]

As a rule, contingent interests are assignable, devisable, and descendible.[6]

See also ABSOLUTE; AFTER; CERTAIN; THEN; UPON, 2; WHEN.

CONTINUANCE. 1. After an issue or demurrer has been joined, as well as in previous stages of a proceeding, a day is given, and entered upon the record, on which the parties are to appear from time to time as the exigence of the case may require. The giving of this day is called the "continuance," because thereby the proceedings are continued without interruption from one adjournment to another.[7]

2. Adjournment, postponement, to another term of court.

May be had on account of — the absence of a material witness, who has been subpœnaed, unless the opposite party admits what such witness would testify to; inability to obtain the evidence of a witness out of the State in time for trial; detention of a party in a public service; sickness or death of a party or of counsel; commission outstanding for taking testimony; amendment to pleadings which occasions surprise; filing a bill of discovery. An affidavit to the alleged fact constituting the ground for continuance is required. See AMENDMENT, 1; NISI.

Puis darrein continuance. Since the last adjournment or term of court. A plea by which the defendant takes advantage of a matter which has arisen since he entered his original defense.[1]

As, that the plaintiff, who was then a *feme sole*, has married; or that she has given a release.[1]

In effect, a pleading of facts occurring since the last stage of the suit, whatever that be, provided it precedes the trial.[2]

Confesses the matter which was before in dispute. Not allowed if a continuance has intervened between the time when the matter arose and when it was pleaded: for the defendant is guilty of neglect, and is, besides, supposed to rely upon his former plea. Nor is it allowed after a demurrer has been determined, or a verdict been given: because relief may be had by motion.[3]

The appointment of a successor in office, after proceedings by *mandamus* are begun, may be set up by a plea *puis darrein continuance.*[4] See CONTINUANDO; DISCONTINUANCE.

3. "Continuance in office," in a constitution prohibiting the legislature from increasing the compensation of any public officer during such period, means continuance under one appointment.[5] See COMPENSATION, 1.

CONTINUANDO. L. By continuing; by continuance.

In trespasses of a permanent nature, where the injury is continually renewed, the declaration may allege that the injury has been committed by continuation from one given time to another. This is called "laying the action with a *continuando.*" The plaintiff is not then compelled to bring a separate action for each day's separate offense. But where the trespass is by one or several acts, each terminating in itself, and being once done cannot be done again, it cannot be laid with a *continuando;* yet if there be repeated acts of trespass committed (as, cutting a certain number of trees), they may be laid to be done, not continually, but at divers days and times within a given period;[6] or on a given day and "on divers other days and times between" that and another particular day.[7]

---

[1] L. *con-tingere*, to touch; to relate to, happen.

[2] People *v.* Yonkers, 39 Barb. 272 (1863). See also 16 Op. Att.-Gen. 413; 30 Me. 384.

[3] See Fearne, Cont. Rem. 373.

[4] Jemison *v.* Blowers, 5 Barb. 692 (1849); Haywood *v.* Shreve, 44 N. J. L. 104 (1882).

[5] Weatherhead *v.* Stoddard, 58 Vt. 623 (1886), cases.

[6] Kenyon *v.* See, 94 N. Y. 563 (1884).

[7] [3 Bl. Com. 316.

[1] [3 Bl. Com. 295. See Steph. Pl. 64.

[2] [Waterbury *v.* McMillan, 46 Miss. 640 (1872).

[3] 3 Bl. Com. 296; 4 Del. Ch. 352.

[4] Thompson *v.* United States, 103 U. S. 480, 483 (1880).

[5] Smith *v.* City of Waterbury, 54 Conn. 176 (1886).

[6] 3 Bl. Com. 212.

[7] Gould. Plead. 86-96; State *v.* Bosworth, 54 Conn. 1 (1886); 58 N. H. 41.

CONTINUING. Extending from one time or condition to another: as, a continuing — consideration, breach, damage, guaranty, nuisance, *qq. v.* See also PRESUMPTION.

CONTINUOUS. 1. Uninterrupted; unintermitted; unbroken: as, a continuous adverse use;[1] that a custom (*q. v.*) must be continuous; a continuous carriage, passage, trip, or voyage.[2] See CARRIER, Common; LADING, Bill of.

2. As applied to an "injury," recurring at repeated intervals, of repeated occurrence; of the same sort of damnification an actual continuous mischief would be.[3] Compare CONTINUANDO.

Non-continuous. A grant of a right or easement (*q. v.*) in land is "non-continuous" when the use of the premises by the grantee will be only intermittent and occasional, and not embrace the entire beneficial occupation and improvement of the land.[4]

CONTRA. L. Against; in opposition to; to the contrary effect; contrary.

Standing alone (1) denotes opposition of counsel to matters urged in argument, as "A. B., *contra;*" (2) indicates cases or authorities which do not agree with others cited. See CON, 2; COUNTER.

Contra bonos mores. Against good morals, *q. v.*

Contra formam statuti. Against the form (*q. v.*) of the statute.

Contra pacem. Against the peace, *q. v.*

Contra proferentem. Against the proposer. See VERBUM, Verba fortius, etc.

CONTRABAND.[5] Contrary to a ban — a public proclamation.

Contraband of war. Prohibited by the laws of war. Describes goods which a neutral may not furnish to a belligerent.

Articles manufactured and primarily or ordinarily used for military purposes in time of war are always contraband. Articles which may be used for war or peace according to circumstances are contraband only when actually destined to the use of the belliger-

ent. Articles exclusively used for peaceful purposes are not contraband, though liable to seizure for violation of blockade or siege. Contraband articles contaminate non-contraband, if belonging to the same owner. In ordinary cases the conveyance of contraband articles attaches only to the freight.[1]

Provisions, and money, destined for hostile use, are contraband.[2]

Treaty provisions enumerate the articles which shall be deemed contraband.

CONTRACT.[3] 1, *n.* (1) An agreement, upon sufficient consideration, to do or not to do a particular thing.[4]

A compact between two or more parties.[5]

An agreement in which a party undertakes to do, or not to do, a particular thing.[6]

In the Constitution, as elsewhere, the agreement of two or more minds, for considerations proceeding from one to the other, to do, or not to do, certain acts. Mutual assent to the terms is of the very essence.[7]

An interchange, by agreement, of legal rights.[8]

A deliberate engagement between competent parties, upon a legal consideration, to do, or to abstain from doing, some act.[9]

A promise from one or more persons to another or others, either made in fact or created by the law, to do or refrain from some lawful thing; being also under the seal of the promisor, or being reduced to a judicial record, or being accompanied by a valid consideration, or being executed, and not being in a form forbidden or declared inadequate by law.[10]

In its widest sense includes *records* and *specialties*, but is usually employed to designate simple or parol contracts; *i. e.*, not only verbal and unwritten contracts, but all contracts not of record or under seal. This is strictly the legal signification, inasmuch as the existence of a consideration which is necessary to constitute a parol agreement is not requisite, or rather

---

[1] 59 Ind. 411; 4 De G. J. & S. 199; 18 F. R. 115.

[2] 4 Saw. 114; 12 Weekly Dig. (N. Y.) 375.

[3] Wood *v.* Sutcliffe, 8 Eng. L. & Eq. 220 (1851).

[4] Jamaica Pond Aqueduct Corporation *v.* Chandler, 9 Allen, 164 (1864), Bigelow, C. J.; Fetters *v.* Humphreys, 18 N. J. E. 262 (1867).

[5] *Contrabannum*, in mediæval Latin, is *merces banno interdictæ*. "The sovereign of the country made goods contraband by an edict prohibiting their importation or their exportation,"— Woolsey, Int. Law, § 192; *ib.* §§ 192-99. See BAN.

[1] The Peterhoff, 5 Wall. 58 (1866), Chase, C. J.

[2] The Commercen, 1 Wheat. 387 (1816); United States *v.* Dickelman, 92 U. S. 626 (1875); 1 Kent, 138-43.

[3] L. *con-trahere*, to draw together: for minds to meet.

[4] 2 Bl. Com. 442, quoting some previous author.

[5] Fletcher *v.* Peck, 6 Cranch, 136 (1810), Marshall, C. J.

[6] Sturges *v.* Crowninshield, 4 Wheat. 197 (1819), Marshall, C. J. See also *ib.* 656, 682; 11 Pet. *572; 109 U. S. 288; 113 *id.* 464; 71 Ala. 432; 34 La. An. 45; 30 Tex. 422; 4 Tex. Ap. 321.

[7] Louisiana *v.* Mayor of New Orleans, 109 U. S. 288 (1883), Field, J.; Chase *v.* Curtis, 113 *id.* 464 (1885).

[8] 1 Whart. Contr. § 1.

[9] Story, Contr. § 1; also 1 Pars. Contr. 6.

[10] Bishop, Contr. § 22, where definitions from other books are quoted.

is presumed, in obligations of record and in specialties.[1]

There must be a person able to contract; a person able to be contracted with; a thing to be contracted for; a sufficient consideration; words clearly expressing the agreement; and the assent of both parties to the same thing in the same sense.[2]

A contract is resolvable into proposal and acceptance; the proposal not to bind beyond a reasonable time, and, until accepted, may be conditional. The place and time of acceptance are the place and time of the contract. The assent must be definite; nonrefusal is not enough.[3] See UNDERSTANDING. Compare TRANSACTION.

(2) The language, written or unwritten, which evidences a mutual engagement or exchange of promises.

Does not, like "deed," "bond," or "promissory note," necessarily import a written instrument.[4] It applies to agreements obligating both parties, hence not to bills and notes.[5]

Generally, "agreement" is the weaker, more vernacular word, "contract" the more technical and forcible. "Agreement" is more apt to be used of an engagement formed by actual negotiation, but not embodied in the most solemn formality of writing, seal, etc.; "contract," where the intention is to embrace the whole range of enforcible obligations created by mutual consent. "Bargain" seems to be used like "contract" in importing a consideration and full legal obligation; like "agreement" in implying actual negotiation and assent rather than definite legal formalities.

In the best use "contract" does not embrace obligations which society imposes for reasons of general expediency, only obligations founded upon assent of parties; nor a mere moral obligation, unrecognized by law, deducible from a promise unsupported by a consideration; nor a judgment; nor, generally, a charter, nor a license from government; nor is a public office the subject of a contract. Marriage is rather a civil or social status than a contract. Obligations in which there is no apparent mutuality have been excluded: mutuality of assent and of act being of the essence of a contract.

Formerly, lawyers spoke of "obligations" (meaning bonds, in which "obliged" is a formal term), "covenants," and "agreements" — the last word being used as "contract" is now used.[6]

2, v, adj. Agreed to; stipulated; undertaken; incurred.

A "debt contracted" may include a debt founded upon a tort.[7]

---

[1] Story, Contr. § 1; also 1 Parsons, Contr. 6; Bishop, Contr. §§ 103, 140, 151, 162.

[2] Justice v. Lang, 42 N. Y. 497 (1870).

[3] 1 Whart. Contr. Chap. I.

[4] Pierson v. Townsend, 2 Hill, 551 (1842).

[5] Safford v. Wyckoff, 4 Hill, 456 (1842).

[6] [Addison, Contr. *1-2, Am. ed., A. & W. (1888), note] See also Bishop, Contr. §§ 191-92, 107.

[7] Re Radway, 3 Hughes, 631 (1877); State v. O'Neil, 7 Oreg. 142 (1879).

Contractual. Arising out of a contract: as, a contractual relation. Whence *non-contractual.*

Besides the general distinctions noted below, contracts are: *accessory,* when assuring the performance of another contract; *aleatory,* when performance depends upon an uncertainty: as, an annuity, a contract of insurance; *consensual,* when dissolvable by mere consent; *dependent,* when made to rest upon some connected act to be done by another — opposed to *independent,* in which the acts have no inter-relation; *parol,* when verbal or in writing but not under seal — opposed to *sealed* contract, which is a specialty; *personal,* when relating to personalty, or else requiring some action of a person — opposed to *real,* which regards realty, q. v.; *quasi,* when the relation existing is analogous to that of a contract, and the law attaches similar consequences; *separable* or *severable,* when divisible, not entire, q. v.; *simple,* when evidenced neither by a specialty nor by a record: *specialty* (q. v.), when under seal; *verbal,* when simple or parol. See also FIDUCIARY; HAZARDOUS; MARITIME; ONEROUS; QUASI; WAGERING.

More general and important distinctions are the following:

Absolute contract. An agreement to do or not to do something at all events. **Conditional contract.** An executory contract, the performance of which depends upon a condition — precedent or subsequent.[1]

Bilateral contract. Two promises given in exchange for and in consideration of each other. **Unilateral contract.** A binding promise not in consideration of another.

A bilateral contract becomes unilateral when one of the promises is fully performed.[2]

In a suit upon a unilateral contract, it is only where the defendant has had the benefit of the consideration, for which he bargained, that he can be held bound.[3]

Divisible contract. A contract the consideration of which is, *by its terms,* susceptible of apportionment on either side so as to correspond to the unascertained consideration on the other side. **Entire contract.**

---

[1] Story, Contr. §§ 39-40.

[2] Langdell, Sum. Contr. §§ 183, 12; Butler v. Thompson, 92 U. S. 415 (1875); 6 Col. 324.

[3] Richardson v. Hardwick, 106 U. S. 255 (1882), cases.

A contract the consideration of which is entire on both sides. The entire fulfillment of the promise by either is a condition precedent to the fulfillment of any part by the other.[1]

Examples of a divisible contract are an engagement to pay a person the worth of his services as long as he will do certain work; or, to give a certain price for every bushel of so much grain as corresponds to a sample. The criterion is, the extent of the consideration on either side is indeterminate until the contract is performed.[1]

A contract by which one subscribes for a copy of a book, to be published, delivered, and paid for in parts, is entire.[2]

Special contract. (1) A contract under seal; a specialty, *q. v.*

(2) A contract incidental to another as the original or principal; as, for extra work or material in the construction of a house. See *Dermott* v. *Jones*, page 249.

(3) A contract specially entered into, or with peculiar provisions in distinction from such ordinary terms as, in the absence of a particular agreement, the law supplies.

As, that made with an employee for compensation, and that with a common carrier (*q. v.*) in limitation of his liability at common law.

Express contract. When the agreement is formal, and stated either verbally or in writing. **Implied contract.** When the agreement is matter of inference and deduction.

The distinction between them is in the mode of proof. In an "implied contract" the law supplies that which, not being stated, must be presumed to have been the agreement intended.[3]

Express contracts are sometimes said to be of record, by specialty, or by simple contract. See DEBT, Of record, etc.; JUDGMENT.

An "express contract" exists where the terms of the agreement are openly uttered and avowed at the time of the making; as, to pay a stated price for certain goods. An "implied contract" is such as reason and prejudice dictate, and which therefore the law presumes that every man undertakes to perform; as, to pay the worth of services requested of another; as, to pay the real value of goods delivered without agreement as to price. A species of implied contract, annexed to all other contracts, conditions, and covenants, is, that if one party fails in his part of the agreement he will pay the other party any damages thereby sustained.[4]

An implied contract is co-ordinate and commensurate with *duty*, and whenever it is certain that a man ought to do a particular thing the law supposes him to have promised to do that thing.[1]

In that large class of transactions designated in the law as implied contracts, the assent or convention which is an essential ingredient of an actual contract is often wanting. Thus, if a party obtain the money of another by mistake, it is his duty to refund it, from the general obligation to do justice which rests upon all persons.[2]

A contract may be inferred when it is found that there is an agreement and an intention to create a contract, although that intention has not been expressed in words of contract. A contract is also sometimes said to be implied when there is no intention to create a contract, and no agreement of parties, but the law has imposed an obligation which is enforced as if it arose *ex contractu*, instead of *ex lege*.[3]

The distinction between express and implied contracts may well be indicated by saying that the former are actual, the latter constructive, imputed by law rather because justice requires treating parties as if under contract than because of any real supposition that they have contracted.[4]

Joint contract. A contract by which the parties together are bound to perform the obligation or are entitled to receive the benefit of it. **Several contract.** A contract by which the individuals are separately concerned.

Where there is more than one person on either side the contract will be construed as a joint right or obligation, unless it be made several by the terms of the contract.[3] See further JOINT.

Executed contract. A contract whose object has been performed. **Executory contract.** One in which a party binds himself to do, or not to do, a particular thing.[6]

A contract may either be "executed," as if A agrees to change horses with B, and they do it immediately, in which case the possession and the right are transferred together; or it may be "executory," as if they agree to change next week. In the latter case the right only vests, and their reciprocal property in each other's horse is "in action;" for a contract executed conveys a chose in possession, a contract executory, a chose in action.[7]

A "contract executed" is one in which nothing remains to be done by either party, and where the transaction is completed at the moment the agreement is made. An "executory contract" is a contract to do some future act. A contract to sell personalty is executory, while a completed sale by delivery is ex-

---

[1] Story, Contr. §§ 25–26; Pars. Contr. 517; 2 McCrary, 169; 3 *id.* 130, 144–46, cases.

[2] Barrie v. Earle, 144 Mass. 4 (1886).

[3] Story, Contr., § 11; Leake, Contr. 11.

[4] 2 Bl. Com. 443; 3 *id.* 158–66.

[1] Illinois Central R. Co. *v.* United States, 16 Ct. Cl. 333 (1880), Drake, C. J. See also 55 Vt. 417; 2 Kent, 450.

[2] Pacific Mail Steamship Co. *v.* Joliffe, 2 Wall. 457 (1864); Milford *v.* Commonwealth, 144 Mass. 65 (1887).

[3] Inhabitants of Milford *v.* Commonwealth, 144 Mass. 65 (1887), Field, J.

[4] Addison, Contr. *2, Am. ed., A. & W. (1888), note.

[5] Story, Contr. §§ 53–55.

[6] [Fletcher *v.* Peck, 6 Cranch, 136 (1810), Marshall, C. J.

[7] 2 Bl. Com. 443.

ecuted; but as to which is meant the language may not always be decisive. An undertaking may be of the nature of both.[1]

In an "executory contract" it is stipulated by the agreement of minds, upon sufficient consideration, that something is to be done or not to be done by one or both of the parties. Only a slight consideration is necessary. On the other hand, a contract is "executed" where every thing that was to be done is done, and nothing remains to be done; as, a grant actually made. This requires no consideration to support it: a gift consummated is as valid as anything can be.[2]

An executed contract stands for and against all parties. To the extent that an invalid contract is not performed, it is voidable.[3]

While a special contract remains executory the plaintiff may sue upon it. When it has been fully executed according to its terms, and nothing remains to be done but to pay the price, he may sue upon the contract, or in *indebitatus assumpsit*, and rely upon the common counts. In either case the contract will determine the rights of the parties. But when he has been guilty of fraud, or has willfully abandoned the work, leaving it unfinished, he cannot recover in any form of action. When he has in good faith fulfilled the contract, but not in the manner or not within the prescribed time, and the other party has sanctioned or accepted the work, he may recover upon the common counts in *indebitatus assumpsit*. In that case he must produce the contract upon the trial, and it will be applied as far as it can be traced; but if, by the fault of the defendant, the cost of the work or material has been increased, so far the jury may depart from the contract prices. In such case the defendant may recoup any damages sustained by plaintiff's deviations from the contract, and not induced by himself, both as to the manner and the time of performance.[4]

Pre-contract. An engagement which renders a person unable to enter into another legal contract; in particular, a contract of marriage which renders void a subsequent marriage.[5]

Sub-contract. A contract, by one who has engaged to do a thing, with another who agrees to do all or a part of that thing. See CONTRACTOR.

A contract, procured by fraud, or for an immoral purpose, or against an express enactment, or in general restraint of trade, or contrary to public policy, will be declared void.

[1] Story, Contr. §§ 22-23.
[2] Farrington *v.* Tennessee, 95 U. S. 683 (1877), cases, Swayne, J.
[3] Thomas *v.* West Jersey R. Co., 101 U. S. 85 (1879).
[4] Dermott *v.* Jones, 2 Wall. 9 (1864), Swayne, J.; Chicago *v.* Tilley, 103 U. S. 146, 154 (1880), cases; Cutter *v.* Powell, 2 Sm. L. Cas. 1-60, cases; Chitty, Contr., 612; 49 Conn. 203; 30 Kan. 328.
[5] 1 Bl. Com. 435; Bishop, Mar. & D. § 53.

For cases other than those within the Statute of Frauds, there is no prescribed form.

At common law, damages for breach of contract is the only remedy; in equity, specific performance (*q. v*) may be had. Where one party refuses to perform his part the other has an immediate right of action, and need not wait for the time of performance.[1] See VALUE, Market.

A mere assertion that the party will be unable or will refuse to perform his contract is not sufficient; it must be a distinct, unequivocal, absolute refusal to perform the promise, and be treated and acted upon as such by the promisee.[2]

The complaint must aver a promise and a breach thereof.[3]

It is well settled that the plaintiff may recover as a part of the **damages** for the breach of a special contract such profits as would have accrued from the contract as the direct and immediate result of its fulfillment.[4] "These are part of the contract itself, and must have been in the contemplation of the parties when the agreement was entered into. But if they are such as would have been realized from an independent and collateral undertaking, although entered into in consequence and on the faith of the principal contract, they are too uncertain and remote to be considered part of the damages."[5] That is, the damages "must be such as might naturally be expected to follow the violation of the contract; and they must be certain in their nature and as to the cause from which they proceed. The familiar rule that the damages must flow directly and naturally from the breach is a mode of expressing the first; and that they must be the proximate consequence, and not be speculative or contingent, are modifications of the last."[6] In cases of executory contracts for the purchase of personalty, ordinarily the measure of damages is the difference between the contract price and the market price when the contract is broken. This rule may be varied where

[1] Grau *v.* McVicker, 8 Biss. 18-20 (1874), cases, Drummond, J.; Burtis *v.* Thompson, 42 N. Y. (Hand), 246 (1870); Cort *v.* The Ambergate, &c. R. Co., 6 E. L. & E. 230, 234-37 (1851), cases.
[2] Benjamin, Sales, 2 ed. § 568. Approved, Smoot's Case, 15 Wall. 48 (1872), cases; Dingley *v.* Oler, 117 U. S. 503 (1886), cases; Johnstone *v.* Milling, 16 Q. B. D. 467, 470, 473 (1886), cases.
[3] Du Brutz *v.* Jessup, 70 Cal. 75 (1886).
[4] Masterton *v.* City of Brooklyn. 7 Hill, 67 (1845), Nelson, C. J.,—the leading case: United States *v.* Speed, 8 Wall. 84 (1868); United States *v.* Behan, 110 U. S. 342 (1884); Insley *v.* Shepard, 31 F. R. 873 (1887). In Masterton's case it was also said that "the plaintiff may recover the difference between the cost of doing the work, and what he was to receive for it, making a reasonable reduction for the less time engaged, and the release from the care, trouble, risk, and responsibility attending the full execution of the contract."
[5] Fox *v.* Harding, 7 Cush. 522 (1851), Bigelow, J.
[6] Griffin *v.* Colver, 16 N. Y. 489 (1858). See also Booth *v.* Rolling Mill Co., 60 *id.* 492 (1875), cases; White *v.* Miller, 71 *id.* 133 (1877), cases; Billmeyer *v.* Wagner, 91 Pa. 94 (1879); 48 *id.* 407; 11 Atl. Rep. 300; Kendall Bank Note Co. *v.* Commissioners, 79 Va. 573 (1884).

the contract is made in view of special circumstances in contemplation of both parties.[1]

When a party sues for a part of an entire indivisible demand, and recovers judgment, he cannot subsequently maintain an action for another part of the same demand.[2]

Where a writing is the sole repository of an agreement, its construction is a matter of law for the court. Words are to be taken in the meaning usually attached to them. But a true interpretation requires that they be applied to the subject-matter, the situation of the parties, and the usual and known course of business. The common meaning of expressions, otherwise clear, may thus be modified by parol, without invasion of the rule which makes the writing the only proper evidence of the agreement.[3]

In construing contracts, especially those of a distinct class (like policies of insurance), in regard to which, owing to long and constant use of forms substantially alike, there has grown up a common and general use of language which may be said to constitute *jus et norma loquendi*,— it is not safe to adopt the mere etymological meaning of words, nor the definition which lexicographers give them. It is often necessary to ascertain whether a word or phrase has acquired a special or peculiar meaning, or whether it is used with any restricted signification by authors or jurists or those conversant with the business to which it relates.[4]

Contracts are to be construed according to their plain meaning to men of understanding, and not according to forced or artificial constructions.[1]

The court seeks to place itself in the place of the parties, and to view the circumstances as they viewed them.[2]

Where the meaning is not clear the court takes the light of the circumstances in which the contract was made, and the practical interpretation the parties by their conduct may have given it.[1]

When the language is ambiguous, the practical interpretation given by the parties is entitled to great, if not controlling, influence.[3]

Such practical construction will always prevail over the literal meaning.[4]

It is a fundamental rule that the courts may look not only to the language employed, but to the subject-matter and the surrounding circumstances, and avail themselves of the light the parties possessed when the contract was made.[5]

Written instruments are always to be construed by the court, except when they contain technical words or terms of art, or when the instrument is introduced in evidence collaterally, or where its effect depends not merely on the construction and meaning of the instrument but upon extrinsic facts and circumstances, in which case the inference to be drawn from it must he left to the jury. . It is for the jury to say what is the meaning of peculiar expressions, but it is for the court to decide what is the meaning of the contract.[2]

It is the business of the courts to enforce contracts, not to make or modify them.[6]

The law of contracts, in its widest extent, may be regarded as including nearly all the law which regulates the relations of human life. All social life presumes it, rests upon it: out of contracts, express or implied, declared or understood, grow all rights, all duties, all obligations, all law. Almost the whole procedure of human life is the continual fulfillment of contracts. . Implied contracts are co-ordinate and commensurate with *duty*, with what a man ought to do. These, in particular, form the warp and woof of actual life. To compel the performance of contract duties, the law exists. The well-being of society may be measured by the degree in which the law construes contracts wisely; eliminating whatever is of fraud or error, or otherwise wrongful; and carrying them into their full and proper effect and execution. These results the law seeks by means of principles; that is, by

---

[1] Western Union Tel. Co. v. Hall, 124 U. S. 444, 453 (1888), cases, Matthews, J. The plaintiff brought suit for damages for the non-delivery of a message instructing the addressee to buy 10,000 barrels of petroleum, the price of which, when the message should have been delivered, was $1.17 per barrel, but when received had advanced to $1.35 per barrel. The addressee did not purchase. *Held*, that the plaintiff, having suffered no actual loss, could recover only nominal damages, not the contingent profit he might have made by buying and selling.

In Hadley v. Baxendale, 9 Exch. *354 (1854), it was said "the damages for which compensation is allowed are such as naturally and ordinarily flow from the breach; such as may be supposed to have entered into the contemplation of the parties when they made the contract, or such as, according to the ordinary course of things, might be expected to follow its violation." The rule as here expressed has been frequently followed in this country, as see Murdock v. Boston, &c. R. Co., 133 Mass. 15 (1882); Bodkin v. Western Union Tel. Co., 31 F. R. 136 (1887); Poposkey v. Munkwitz, 68 Wis 330 (1887), cases; and cases *ante*.

"In an action for a breach of contract to deliver iron the plaintiff recovers the difference between the contract price and the market price at the date of the refusal to fulfill the contract." Roberts v. Benjamin, 124 U. S. 64 (1888), cases, Blatchford, J.

[2] Baird v. United States, 92 U. S. 432 (1877); Warren v. Comings, 6 Cush. 103 (1850), cases.

[3] Palmer v. Clark, 106 Mass. 387 (1871), Colt, J. See Bishop, Contr. §§ 379–82, cases.

[4] Dole v. New Eng. Mut. Ins. Co., 6 Allen, 386 (1863), Bigelow, C. J.

[1] Lowher v. Bangs, 2 Wall. 737 (1864), cases; Nash v. Towne, 5 *id*. 699 (1866), cases.

[2] Goddard v. Foster, 17 Wall. 142 (1872), cases, Clifford, J.; Dewelley v. Dewelley, 143 Mass. 513 (1887); 20 Pick. 503.

[3] Chicago v. Sheldon, 9 Wall. 54 (1869); Topliff v. Topliff, 122 U. S. 131 (1887).

[4] District of Columbia v. Gallaher, 124 U. S. 510 (1888); Rowell v. Doggett, 143 Mass. 487 (1887).

[5] Merriam v. United States, 107 U. S. 441 (1882), cases, Woods, J. See also United States v. Gibbons, 109 *id*. 200, 203 (1883).

[6] The Harriman, 9 Wall. 173 (1869); 10 *id*. 171.

means of truths, ascertained, defined, and so expressed as to be practical and operative.[1]

See further AGREEMENT; ART, 3; ASSENT; ASSIGN, 2; ASSUMPSIT; CERTAINTY; COMPACT; CONDITION; CONSIDERATION, 2; CONTRACTOR; CONTRACTUS; COVENANT; CONVENTIO; CUSTOM; DAMAGES; DESCRIPTION, 4; DISABILITY; DURESS; DUTY, 1; EARNEST; EXCEPTION, 1; FRAUD; GRANT; IMPLIED; INFLUENCE; INSANITY, 2 (4); LEGAL; LET, 1 (2); LETTER, 3; LICENSE, 3; MERGER, 2; NOVATION; OBLIGATION; OFFER, 1; OPTION; PACT; PAROL, 2; PARTNERSHIP; PARTY, 2; PERFORMANCE; PLACE, Of contract; POSSIBLE; PRIVITY; PROMISE; RATIFICATION; READING; REFORM; RES, Perit, Ut res; RESCISSION; REVIVAL; SALE; SATISFACTORY; STULTIFY; SUBROGATION; SUNDAY; TIME; TRADE; USUS, Utile; VALUE; VOID; WAIVER; WAR.

CONTRACTOR.

The primary meaning is one who contracts; one of the parties to a bargain; he who agrees to do anything for another.

One who contracts with a government to furnish provisions or supplies or to do work; one who agrees to construct a portion of a work, as, a railroad.[2]

Standing alone, or unrestrained by the context or particular words, may mean a sub-contractor or a person remotely engaged under a contract and doing the work, as well as an original contractor.[3]

Although, in a general sense, every one who enters into a contract may be called a "contractor," yet that word, for want of a better, has come to be used with special reference to a person who, in the pursuit of an independent business, undertakes to do specific jobs of work for other persons without submitting himself to their control in respect to the petty details of the work. . . The true test is to ascertain whether one who renders the service does so in the course of an independent occupation, representing the will of his employer only as to the *result* of his work and not as to the means by which it is accomplished. . If he submits himself to the discretion of his employer as to the details of the work, fulfilling his will not merely as to the result but also as to the means by which that result is to be attained, the contractor becomes a servant in respect to the work.[4]

The ordinary relation of principal and agent, master and servant, does not subsist in the case of an independent employee or contractor who is not under the immediate direction of the employer.[5]

See Phillips Construction Co. v. Seymour, under COVENANT; RESPONDEAT.

CONTRACTUS.

L. A drawing together: a meeting of minds; a contract. See FORUM; LOCUS.

Ex contractu. By virtue of a contract. Applied to a right or a duty founded upon a contract relation. Opposed, *ex delicto:* by force of a wrongful act, or tort.

Whence actions *ex contractu* and *ex delicto*. See ACTION, 2; DELICTUM.

The civil law refers the greater part of rights and duties to the head of obligations *ex contractu* and *quasi ex contractu:* express and implied contracts.[1]

CONTRADICT.

See PAROL; REBUT.

CONTRARY.

A verdict "contrary to law" is contrary to the principles of law applicable to the facts which the jury were to try.[2] See AGAINST.

CONTRAVENE.

To conflict, oppose. Whence contravention.

A right which militates with another right is sometimes called a "contravening equity."[3]

CONTRIBUTION.

The share provided by or due from one of several persons to assist in discharging a common obligation or in advancing a common enterprise.[4]

Contributive; contributory. Helping to bring about a result; directly contributing to an injury: as, contributory negligence, q. v.

"Contributory" is also used in the sense of contributor: a person liable to contribution to the assets of a company which is being wound up, q. v.

A right to contribution exists where a debt owed by several persons jointly is collected from one; when one of two or more sureties pays the sum for which both or all are bound; when one co-devisee or co-distributee pays a charge upon land devised or descended; when a partner pays more than his share of the firm's debts; where recourse to private property is had to pay the debt of an insolvent corporation; where a co-insurer pays the whole loss; where a party-wall or a division-fence is constructed or repaired.[5]

Equal contribution to discharge a joint liability is not inequitable, even as between wrong-doers, although the *law* will not, in general, support an action to enforce it where the payments have been unequal.[6]

---

[1] 1 Pars. Contr. 1–5; 2 Bl. Com. 443; 3 Law Quar. Rev. 166–79 (1887).

[2] Kent v. N. Y. Central R. Co., 12 N. Y. 631 (1855).

[3] Mundt v. Sheboygan, &c. R. Co., 31 Wis. 457 (1872), Dixon, C. J.; 12 N. Y. 631; 5 How. Pr. 454; 25 Minn. 524.

[4] Shearman & Redf., Neg. §§ 76–77: quoted, 71 Me. 322; 7 Lea, 373; 57 Tex. 510. See also Carter v. Berlin Mills Co., 58 N. H. 52–58 (1876), cases; Edmundson v. Pittsburgh, &c. R. Co., 111 Pa. 319 (1885); 86 id. 159; 17 Mo. 121.

[5] Cunningham v. International R. Co., 51 Tex. 511

(1879), cases. See also Robinson v. Blake Manuf. Co., 143 Mass. 532 (1887); 27 Conn. 274; 45 Ill. 455; 3 Gray, 349; 4 Allen, 134; 11 id. 419; 125 Mass. 232; 66 N. Y. 184; 46 Pa. 213; 57 id. 374; 9 M. & W. *73.

[1] 2 Bl. Com. 443.

[2] [Bosseker v. Cramer, 18 Ind. 45 (1862); Candy v. Hanmore, 76 id. 128 (1881).

[3] 101 U. S. 739.

[4] [Abbott's Law Dict.

[5] See 1 Story, Eq. §§ 484–505.

[6] Selz v. Unna, 6 Wall. 336 (1867), Clifford, J.; 28 Conn. 455; 1 Bibb, 562.

The remedy in equity is more effective; as, between co-sureties.[1]

But there is "no contribution between wrong-doers." This rule applies appropriately only to cases where there has been *intentional* violation of law, and where the wrong-doer is to be presumed to have known that the act was unlawful.[2] It fails when the injury grows out of a duty. resting primarily upon one of the parties, and but for his negligence there would have been no cause of action against the other. . . A servant is liable to his master for the damages recovered against him in consequence of the negligence of the servant.[3]

A municipality, made to pay damages for an injury resulting from the negligence of a private citizen, may recover the amount from the citizen.[4] See AVERAGE, General; JOINT.

CONTROL. See PROHIBITION; REGULATE.

In a contract by a railroad company concerning the roads which it might "control," held to refer to the immediate or executive control which it exercised by officers and agents acting under instructions from the board of directors.[5]

The "control" is a necessary incident to the "regulation" of the streets of a city.[6]

CONTROLLER. See COMPTROLLER.

CONTROVERSY. Any issue, whether of a civil or criminal nature; a case, *q. v.*

A dispute arising between two or more persons.[7]

A civil proceeding; as, that the judicial power of the United States shall extend "to Controversies to which the United States shall be a Party; — to Controversies between two or more States," etc.[8]

A controversy between citizens is involved in a suit whenever any property or claim of the parties capable of pecuniary estimation is the subject of litigation, and is presented by pleadings for judicial determination.[9]

See further CASE, 2, Cases, etc.; DISPUTE; MATTER; PROBATE; REMOVE, 2.

CONTUMACY.[10] Refusal or neglect to appear or to answer in a court; contempt for

the order of a court or legislature. Whence contumacious. See CONTEMPT.

CONUSANCE. See COGNIZANCE.

CONUSOR. See RECOGNIZANCE.

CONVENIENTLY. See SOON.

Whatever it is the duty of an officer to do in the performance of service enjoined by law, and which may be accomplished by the exercise of reasonable diligence, that he can "conveniently" do.[1]

CONVENTIO. L. A coming together: agreement, engagement.

Conventio vincit legem. Agreement takes the place of the law: the express understanding of parties supersedes such understanding as the law would imply.

Parties are permitted to make law for themselves where their agreements do not violate the express provisions of any municipal law nor injuriously affect the interests of the public.[2]

Setting aside the application of a general rule of law is not intended.[3]

CONVENTION. A general term for any mutual engagement, formal or informal. See CONVENTIO.

Conventional. Agreed upon; created by act of parties — by agreement; opposed to *legal* — created by construction and operation of law: as, a conventional estate for life;[4] a conventional community, *q. v.*

There are postal conventions between nations; and constitutional conventions by delegates chosen to frame constitutions, *q. v.* Compare RECONVENTION.

CONVERSATION. 1. The etymological meaning (which see, below) seems to be preserved in the offense termed *criminal conversation:* adultery regarded as an injury to the husband, entitling him to damages in a civil action.[5]

The abbreviation "crim. con." has acquired a fixed and universal signification which the courts will take notice of without proof.[6]

The development of the word has been substantially as follows: L. *conversatio*, frequent use, habitual abode, intercourse: *conversari*, to turn to often, to dwell, live with.

(1) Manner of living; habits of life; behaving, behavior; conduct; life.

---

[1] White, Ld. Cas. 60; 1 Ld. Cas. Eq. 100; 13 Am. Law Reg. 529.

[2] Bailey v. Bussing, 28 Conn. 458-61 (1859), cases; The Atlas, 93 U. S. 315 (1876), cases; The Hudson, 15 F. R. 167 (1883), cases; 13 Bradw. 565.

[3] Merryweather v. Nixon, 2 Sm. L. C. 483, 480, cases; Chicago City v. Robbins, 2 Black, 418 (1862); Robbins v. Chicago City, 4 Wall. 657 (1866).

[4] Clinton, &c. R. Co. v. Dunn, 59 Iowa, 619 (1882), cases; Cooley, Torts, p. 145.

[5] Pullman Palace Car Co. v. Missouri Pacific R. Co., 3 McCrary, 647 (1882).

[6] Chicago Dock Co. v. Garrity, 115 Ill. 164 (1885).

[7] Barber v. Kennedy, 18 Minn. 226 (1872); 33 *id.* 350; 77 Va. 125.

[8] Constitution, Art. III, sec. 2; 2 Dall. 431-32; 109 U. S. 477; Story, Const. § 1668.

[9] Gaines v. Fuentes, 92 U. S. 20 (1875), Field, J.; Searl v. School District, 124 *id.* 199 (1888), cases, Matthews, J.

[10] L. *contumax*, stubborn, obstinate.

---

[1] Guerin v. Reese, 33 Cal. 297 (1867).

[2] Little Rock, &c. R. Co. v. Eubanks, 48 Ark. 467 (1886); 22 N. Y. 249.

[3] Story, Agency, § 368; 14 Gray, 446; 52 Pa. 96; 10 Wall. 644.

[4] 2 Bl. Com. 120.

[5] 3 Bl. Com. 139.

[6] Gibson v. The Cincinnati Enquirer, 5 Cent. Law J. 381 (1877); Same v. Same, 2 Flip. 125 (1877). See Wales v. Miner, 89 Ind. 118 (1883); 15 Am. Law Reg. 451-69 (1876), cases.

As, in the expressions: "of upright conversation;"[1] "the filthy conversation of the wicked,"[2] — *i. e.*, their lascivious life; "the conversation of the wives chaste conversation."[3]

(2) Intimate relation, association; companionship; familiar intercourse.

(3) Sexual acquaintance; illicit intimacy.

2. Familiar discourse; oral communication. See COMMUNICATION; COLLOQUIUM; DECLARATION, 1.

CONVERSION. Changing into another state or condition.

1. Of partnership debts: the changing of their original character and obligation with the consent of the creditors; so that, if they are originally joint debts of all the partners, they become, by consent, the separate debts of one partner; or if they are the separate debts of one partner, they become, by like consent, the joint debts of all the partners.[4]

2. In equity, money which, according to a will or agreement, is to be invested in land is regarded as realty; and land which is to be converted into money is regarded as money, and treated accordingly.[5]

Whence the doctrine of **equitable conversion**; whence, also, **reconversion**: the change of property, once converted, into other property of the former species.

The application to deeds and wills of the principle which treats that as done which ought to be done.[6]

A conversion will be regarded as such only for the purposes of the will, unless a different intention is distinctly indicated.[7]

An implied direction to sell land, for the payment of legacies, works an equitable conversion. The immediate effect of such direction is to break the descent, by vesting the estate in the trustee clothed with power to sell, and to confer on the legatees, not an interest in the land, but simply a right to the proceeds of the sale, in designated proportions,— which is a mere chose in action.[8]

When the purpose for which the conversion was to take place totally fails, the property is regarded as being what it is in fact, no conversion then taking place.

"To establish a conversion, the will must direct it absolutely or out and out, irrespective of all contingencies. The direction to convert must be positive and explicit, and the will, if it be by will, or the deed, if it be by contract, must decisively fix upon the land the quality of money. The direction to sell must be imperative."[1]

A naked or merely discretionary power to sell, unless, perhaps, coupled with an interest, does not effect a conversion.[2]

Where land is to be sold, and legatees interested in the proceeds elect to take it as such, it then becomes bound by liens.[3]

There is no conversion where a widow elects to take against a will directing a sale.[4]

To effect a *reconversion*, an election to take the land, instead of the proceeds, must be by an unequivocal act on the part of all persons interested.[5]

Intention is the governing rule as to conversions.[6]

3. Any unauthorized dealing with another's personalty as one's own.

The exercise of dominion and control over property inconsistent with and in defiance of the rights of the true owner or party having the right of possession.[7]

This may be *actual*, and either *direct* or *constructive*.

It is not necessary that there be a manual taking of the thing, nor that the defendant has applied it to his own use. The one inquiry is: Does he exercise a dominion over it in exclusion or in defiance of the plaintiff's right? If so, that is a conversion, be it for his own or another's use.[6]

Trover and conversion. The action for damages for a conversion, maintainable by him who has the right to immediate possession.[9]

The property may be a deed, a negotiable security, money, a copy of a record, an untamed animal reclaimed, trees or crops severed, liquors adulterated, or goods confused.

Includes using a thing without right, or in excess of license; misuse — detention, delivery in violation of

[1] The King's Bible (1611) — Psalms, xxxix, 14.
[2] 2 Pet. ii, 7.
[3] 1 Pet. iii, 1-2.
[4] Story, Partn. § 369.
[5] Seymour v. Freer, 8 Wall. 214 (1868).
[6] Chew v. Nicklin, 45 Pa. 87 (1863); De Wolf v. Lawson, 61 Wis. 477-78 (1884), cases; Effinger v. Hall, 81 Va. 107 (1885).
[7] Johnson v. Holifield, 82 Ala. 127-28 (1886), cases.
[8] Beatty v. Byers, 18 Pa. 107 (1851).

[1] Anewalt's Appeal, 42 Pa. 416 (1862), cases; Jones v. Caldwell, 97 id. 45 (1881), cases; Hammond v. Putnam, 110 Mass. 235 (1872); 8 Ves. 388; 19 id. 424.
[2] Bleight v. Bank, 10 Pa. 131 (1848); Chew v. Nicklin, 45 id. 84 (1863); Dundas's Appeal, 64 id. 325 (1870).
[3] Brownfield v. Mackay, 27 Pa. 320 (1856); Brolasky v. Gally, 51 id. 513 (1866); Evans's Appeal, 63 id. 183 (1869).
[4] Hoover v. Landis, 76 Pa. 354 (1874).
[5] Beatty v. Byers, 18 Pa. 107 (1851); Evans's Appeal, *supra*; 8 Va. Law J. 513 (1884).
[6] See generally Fletcher v. Ashburner, 1 Brown, C. C. *497 (1779); 1 W. & T. Lead. Cas. Eq. 1118-71, cases; 1 Story, Eq. §§ 562-71, 790-93; 2 id. §§ 1212-30; 2 Kent, 230, 476; Craig v. Leslie, 3 Wheat. 577-78, 582 (1818); 10 Pet. *563; 5 How. 233; 4 Del. Ch. 72; 15 B. Mon. 118; 27 Md. 563; 3 Gray, 180; 63 N. C. 332, 381; 5 Paige, Ch. 172; 6 id. 448; 13 R. I. 507.
[7] Badger v. Hatch, 71 Me. 565 (1880), Barrows, J.
[8] Bristol v. Burt, 7 Johns. *258 (1810), Per curiam.
[9] 3 Bl. Com. 152; 127 Mass. 64; 1 Sm. L. C. 230; 89 Ind. 245.

orders, or non-delivery and even a wrongful sale, by a bailee; improper seizure or sale by an officer; not an accidental loss, nor mere non-feasance.[1] An original unlawful taking is conclusive; but where the original taking is lawful, and the detention only is illegal, a demand and refusal to deliver is necessary and must be shown.[2]

The action of trover and conversion, though originally for damages against one who had *found* and appropriated the goods of another, now reaches all cases where one has obtained such goods by any means, and has sold or used them, without assent, or has refused to deliver them on demand.[3]

The measure of damages is the value of the property at the time of the conversion, with legal interest.[4]

As to what is conversion of public moneys by public officers, see Revised Statutes, §§ 5488, 5496.

See further DETINUE; REPLEVIN; TROVER.

CONVEYANCE.[5] A carrying from place to place; also, transmission, transfer, from one person to another.

1. Transportation,— the act, or the means employed.

Public conveyance. A vessel or vehicle employed for the general conveyance of passengers. **Private conveyance.** A vessel or vehicle belonging to and used by a private individual.[6]

An omnibus used to carry, free of charge, guests of a hotel to and from railroad stations is not a "public" conveyance.[7] See VEHICLE.

2. Transfer of title to realty; and, the instrument by which this is done.

Properly, the term does not relate to a disposition of personalty, although sometimes so used,[8] as see under *Fraudulent Conveyance.*

The conveyance or transfer of title to vessels is regulated by the act of July 29, 1850, re-enacted into Rev. St. as § 4192.

To "convey" real estate is, by an appropriate instrument, to transfer the legal title from the present owner to another.[9]

In a deed, is equivalent to "grant."[1] See COVENANT, 1.

Imports an instrument under seal.[2]

May include a lease,[3] or a mortgage.[4]

Is simply a deed which passes or conveys land from one man to another,[5] or conveys the property of lands and tenements from man to man.[6] Evidences an intention to abandon the land.[7]

Involves a transfer of a freehold estate.[8]

Absolute conveyance. A conveyance entirely executed; not conditional, as in the case of a mortgage, *q. v.*

Adverse conveyance. A conveyance opposed to another conveyance; one of two or more conveyances passing or pretending to pass rights which are inconsistent with each other.

As, two or more transfers of absolute ownership in the same piece of land to different persons. See POSSESSION, Adverse.

Conveyances at common law. Some of these may be called o*riginal* or *primary*, those by means whereof the benefit or estate is created or first arises; others, *derivative* or *secondary*, those whereby the benefit or estate originally created is enlarged, restrained, transferred, or extinguished.[9]

Original are: feoffment, gift, grant, lease, exchange, partition. Derivative are: release, confirmation, surrender, assignment, defeasance — each of which presupposes some other conveyance precedent.[9]

Conveyances under the Statute of Uses. Such as have force and operation by virtue of that statute.[10]

They are: covenant to stand seized to uses, bargain and sale, lease and release, deed to lead or declare the use of another more direct conveyance, deed or revocation of a use.[11]

At common law, words of conveyance were give, grant, bargain and sell, alien, enfeoff, release, confirm, quitclaim, *qq. v.* The meaning of these terms has been somewhat modified.[12]

---

[1] 3 Bl. Com. 152, etc., *ante.*

[2] 1 Chitty, Pl. 179; 126 Mass. 132; 2 Greenl. Ev. § 644.

[3] Boyce *v.* Brockway, 31 N. Y. 493 (1865), cases; 61 *id.* 477; 68 *id.* 524; 10 Johns. 172. See also 9 Ark. 55; 2 Cal. 571; 19 Conn. 319; 10 Cush. 416; 2 Allen, 184; 36 Me. 439; 85 N. C. 340; 39 N. H. 101; 48 *id.* 406; 10 Oreg. 84; 9 Heisk. 715; 39 Vt. 480; L. R., 7 Q. B. 629; 9 Ex. 89.

[4] Grimes *v.* Watkins, 59 Tex. 140 (1883); 46 *id.* 402; 6 *id.* 45. As to limitation of actions, see 21 Cent. Law J. 245-47 (1885), cases.

[5] F. *convier*, to transmit: L. *conviare*, to accompany.

[6] Ripley *v.* Insurance Co., 16 Wall. 338 (1872), Chase, C. J.; Oswego *v.* Collins, 38 Hun, 170 (1885).

[7] City of Oswego *v.* Collins, 38 Hun, 171 (1885).

[8] Dickerman *v.* Abrahams, 21 Barb. 561 (1854).

[9] Abendroth *v.* Town of Greenwich, 29 Conn. 365 (1860); Edelman *v.* Yeakel, 27 Pa. 29 (1856).

[1] Patterson *v.* Carneal, 3 A. K. Marsh.* 621 (1821); Lambert *v.* Smith, 9 Oreg. 193 (1881).

[2] Livermore *v.* Bagley, 3 Mass. 510-11 (1807).

[3] Jones *v.* Marks, 47 Cal. 246 (1874).

[4] Odd Fellows' Savings Bank *v.* Banton, 46 Cal. 607 (1873); Babcock *v.* Hoey, 11 Iowa, 377 (1860); Pickett *v.* Buckner, 45 Miss. 245 (1871); Rowell *v.* Williams, 54 Wis. 639 (1882). See N. Y. R. S. 762, § 38; 2 *id.* 137, § 7.

[5] Brown *v.* Fitz, 13 N. H. 285 (1842); Klein *v.* McNamara, 54 Miss. 105 (1876).

[6] 2 Bl. Com. 309.

[7] 2 Bl. Com. 10.

[8] Hutchinson *v.* Bramhall, 42 N. J. E. 385 (1886).

[9] 2 Bl. Com. 309, 324; 9 Oreg. 187.

[10] 2 Bl. Com. 309, 327.

[11] 2 Bl. Com. 338-39.

[12] Richardson *v.* Levi, 67 Tex. 367 (1887).

The forms of conveyance are prescribed by statutes in many States; but such statutes are generally deemed directory only, not mandatory; and the common-law modes are recognized as effectual. Conveyance by bargain (*q. v.*) and sale is the mode ordinarily practiced.

Whatever be the form or nature of the conveyance, if the grantor sets forth on the face of the instrument, by way of recital or averment, that he is possessed of a particular estate in the premises, which estate the deed purports to convey, or if the possession is affirmed in the deed in express terms or by necessary implication. the grantor and persons in privity with him, are estopped from denying that he was so possessed. The estoppel works upon the estate, and binds an after-acquired title.[1] See ABANDON, 1; CONDITION; DEED, 2; DELIVERY, 4; ESTOPPEL; INFLUENCE; RECORD; TRANSFER; UNDER AND SUBJECT.

Fraudulent conveyance. In a general sense, any transfer of property, real or personal,[2] which is infected with fraud, actual or constructive; more specifically, such transfer of realty by a debtor as is intended or at least operates to defeat the rights of his creditors. **Voluntary conveyance.** A transfer without valuable consideration.

Celebrated statutes upon this subject, adopted by the States, are: (1) 13 Elizabeth (1571), c. 5, which declares void conveyances of lands, and also of goods, made to delay, hinder, or defraud *creditors;* unless "upon good [valuable] consideration, and *bona fide*," to a person not having notice of such fraud. (2) 27 Elizabeth (1585), c. 4, made perpetual by 39 Eliz. (1597), c. 18, s. 31, which provides that voluntary conveyances of any estate in lands, tenements, or other hereditaments, and conveyances of such estates with clause of revocation at the will of the grantor, are also void as against *subsequent purchasers* for value. The effect of the last statute is, that a person who has made a voluntary settlement of landed property, even on his own children, may afterward sell the property to any purchaser, who, even though he has notice of the settlement, will hold the property; but, otherwise, if the settlement is founded on a valuable consideration.[3] These statutes are to be liberally construed in suppression of fraud.[4]

The object of 13 Elizabeth was to protect creditors from frauds practiced under the pretense of discharging a moral obligation toward a wife, child, or other relative. It excepts the *bona fide* discharge of such obligation. Hence, a voluntary conveyance, as to creditors, is not necessarily void.[4] The object of 27 Elizabeth was to give protection to subsequent purchasers against mere volunteers under prior conveyances. As between the parties such conveyances are binding.[5]

In England, all voluntary conveyances are void as to subsequent purchasers, with or without notice, although the original conveyance was *bona fide*, upon the ground that the statute infers fraud.[1]

In New York, only voluntary conveyances, originally fraudulent, are held to be within the statute.[2] In Massachusetts, a conveyance, to be avoided, must have been fraudulent, not merely voluntary, at its inception.[3] In Pennsylvania, the grantor must have intended, by his voluntary conveyance, to withdraw his property from the reach of his future creditors;[4] any such creditor must prove that fraud on him was intended: a man need not provide for indebtedness he does not anticipate and which may never occur.[5] And the Supreme Court of the United States holds, what is the settled doctrine generally, that if a person, natural or artificial, solvent at the time, without actual intent to defraud creditors, disposes of his property for an inadequate consideration, or makes a voluntary conveyance of it, subsequent creditors are not injured;[6] that a conveyance for value (as for marriage) will be upheld, however fraudulent the purpose of the grantor, if the grantee had no knowledge thereof.[7]

A deed made to prevent a recovery of damages for a tort is fraudulent and void.[8]

Conveyances to defraud creditors are also indictable; expressly made so by 13 Elizabeth, c. 5, § 3.[9]

The conveyance to a wife, in payment of a debt owing by her husband, is not voluntary, nor fraudulent as to other creditors; but there must have been a previous agreement for repayment.[10]

See further DECLARATION, 1; FRAUD; HINDER; POSSESSION, Fraudulent; PREFERENCE; SETTLE, 4.

Mesne conveyance. A conveyance between others; an intermediate transfer.

Reconveyance. A transfer of realty back to the original or former grantor.

Conveyancer. One who makes a business of drawing deeds of conveyance of land, and, perhaps, of examining titles.

One whose business it is to draw deeds, bonds, mortgages, wills, writs, or other legal papers, or to examine titles to real estate.[11]

---

[1] Van Rensselaer v. Kearney, 11 How. 322 (1850), cases; French v. Spencer, 21 *id.* 240 (1858); Apgar v. Christophers, 33 F. R. 203 (1887), Wales, J.

[2] See Livermore v. Bagley, 3 Mass. *510–11 (1807).

[3] Williams, Real Prop. 76.

[4] 1 Story, Eq. §§ 352–53, 362; 4 Kent, 462–64.

[5] 1 Story, Eq. § 425.

[1] 1 Story, Eq. § 426.

[2] Sterry v. Arden, 1 Johns. Ch. *269–70 (1814); s c. 12 Johns. *554 (1815); 6 Cowen, 603; 8 *id.* 406; 8 Paige, 165.

[3] Beal v. Warren, 2 Gray, 450, 451 (1854).

[4] McKibbin v. Martin, 64 Pa. 356 (1870).

[5] Harlan v. Maglaughlin, 90 Pa. 297–98 (1879), cases; Hoak's Appeal, 100 *id.* 62 (1882), cases.

[6] Graham v. La Crosse, &c. R. Co., 102 U. S. 153 (1880), cases, Bradley, J.

[7] Prewit v. Wilson, 103 U. S. 24 (1880), cases. See Barbour v. Priest, *ib.* 293 (1880); Clark v. Killian, *ib.* 766 (1880); 17 F. R. 425–28, cases; Sexton v. Wheaton, 8 Wheat. 242 (1823); 1 Am. L. C. *36, 55; Twyne's Case, 1 Sm. L. C. *33, 39; 18 Am. Law Reg. 137.

[8] Johnson v. Wagner, 76 Va. 590 (1882), cases.

[9] Regina v. Smith, 6 Cox, Cr. C. 31, 36 (1852).

[10] Bates v. McConnell, 31 F. R. 588 (1887); *ib.* 591, note. See generally 24 Am. Law Reg. 489–90 (1885), cases; 22 Cent. Law J. 124 (1886), cases, — remedy by execution.

[11] Revenue Act, 13 July, 1866, § 9; 14 St. L. 118.

Conveyancing. That branch of the law which treats of transfers of realty.

Includes the examinations of titles, and the preparation of instruments of transfer. In England, Scotland, and some of our larger cities, it is a highly artificial system of law, with a distinct class of practitioners.[1]

CONVICT.[2] 1, *v.* To find guilty of a criminal offense, by verdict of a jury.

2, *n.* One who has been found guilty of a crime; in particular, one who is serving a sentence for the commission of a crime.

Convicted. Found guilty of the crime whereof one stands indicted: which may accrue from his confessing the offense and pleading guilty, or by his being found so by verdict of his country.[3]

A man is "convicted" when he is found guilty or confesses the crime before judgment had.[4]

Incapable of holding office or testifying because "convicted of crime" intends a verdict of guilt *and* judgment thereon.[5]

Conviction. 1. Used to designate a particular stage of a criminal prosecution triable by a jury, the ordinary legal meaning is, the confession of the accused in court, or the verdict returned against him by the jury, which ascertains and publishes the fact of his guilt.[6]

"Judgment" or "sentence" is the appropriate word to denote the action of the court before which the trial is had, declaring the consequences to the convict of the fact thus ascertained.[6] See SENTENCE.

The finding by the jury that the accused is guilty; but, in legal parlance, often denotes the final judgment of the court.[7]

The act of convicting or overcoming one; in criminal procedure, the overthrow of the defendant by the establishment of his guilt according to some known legal mode — a plea of guilty or verdict of a jury.[8]

The term may be used in such connection as to have a secondary or unusual meaning, which would include the final judgment of the court.[5]

In many cases refers to a finding of guilt by a verdict or plea of guilty, and not to the sentence in addition.[1]

Opposed, *acquit, acquitted, acquittal,* q. v.

Former conviction. A plea that the accused has already been tried and convicted of the offense charged. Opposed, former acquittal.

Second convictions, or even second trials, after legal conviction or acquittal, are not allowed. The pleas of *autrefois convict* and *autrefois acquit* are grounded upon the universal maxim of the common law that no man is to be brought into jeopardy of his life more than once for the same offense. The defense must be pleaded, and it must be alleged and proved by the former record that the conviction or acquittal was legal, and based on the verdict of a jury duly impaneled and sworn, else the plea will be subject to demurrer.[2]

A plea which shows that the former sentence has been reversed for error is not a good bar.[3] See further JEOPARDY. Compare ADJUDICATION, Former.

Summary conviction. (1) Such sentence as may be pronounced by a court without the intervention of a jury.

At common law, peculiar to punishment for contempts, *q. v.*

(2) A trial of an offense against the excise or revenue laws, determined by the commissioner of the particular department or by a justice of the peace.[4]

(3) A sentence pronounced by a committing magistrate, without a hearing and verdict by a jury.

This is what is generally meant. It is provided for by statute, for the punishment of the lighter offenses; and intended to secure the accused a speedy trial, as well as to relieve society and the higher courts of the annoyance of jury trials in petty cases. But the proceeding is in derogation of the constitutional right of trial by jury, and statutory directions are to be strictly pursued. Appeal to a court having a jury is allowed, within a short period, as five days; so that, in reality, these convictions are only submitted to by offenders. See further SUMMARY.

See also INDICTMENT; JURY, Trial by; VAGRANT.

2. Firm belief. See ABIDING; DOUBT, Reasonable.

[1] Bouvier's Law Dict.

[2] L. *con-vincere,* to completely overcome.

[3] [4 Bl. Com. 362.

[4] Shepherd *v.* People, 25 N. Y. 406 (1862), cases; 1 Bish. Cr. L. § 223.

[5] Faunce *v.* People, 51 Ill. 313 (1869); Smith *v.* State, 6 Lea, 639 (1881).

[6] Commonwealth *v.* Lockwood, 109 Mass. 325-40 (1872), cases, Gray, J.; Dwar. Stat., 2 ed., 683.

[7] Blaufus *v.* People, 69 N. Y. 109 (1877), cases, Folger, J.; Schiffer *v.* Pruden, 64 *id.* 52 (1876); 5 Bush, 204; 48 Me. 127; 3 Mo. 602; 25 Gratt. 853; 12 Ct. Cl. 201.

[8] United States *v.* Watkinds, 7 Saw. 91-93 (1881), Deady, J.

[1] Quintard *v.* Knoedler, 53 Conn. 487-88 (1885); Bishop, Stat. Cr. § 348; Whart. Cr. Pr. & Pl. § 935. *Quære.* In a prosecution, alleging a "former conviction," do not these words denote "final judgment," and can they be predicated of a suspended judgment? — White *v.* Commonwealth, 79 Va. 611, 615 (1884).

[2] Coleman *v.* Tennessee, 97 U. S. 525-31 (1878), cases, Clifford, J.

[3] Cooley, Const. Lim. 326-28, cases; 1 Bish. Cr. L. §§ 651-80; Whart. Cr. Pl. § 435; Moore *v.* State, 71 Ala. 308 (1882), cases: 4 Cr. Law Mag. 429.

[4] See 4 Bl. Com. 280-83.

CONVINCE. To overcome or subdue: to satisfy the mind by proof.[1] See DOUBT, Reasonable.

COOLING TIME. Time for passion to subside and reason prevail; time for reflection.

A man, when assailed with violence or great rudeness, is inspired with a sudden impulse of anger, which puts him upon resistance before he has had time for cool reflection. If, during that period, he attacks his assailant with a weapon likely to endanger his life, and death ensues, it is regarded as done through heat of blood or violence of anger, and not through malice.[2] See MALICE; PROVOCATION.

COOPER. See MANUFACTURER.

CO-OPERATIVE. See ASSOCIATION; TRADES-UNION.

CO-ORDINATE. See JURISDICTION, 2.

COPARCENARY. The estate held where lands of inheritance descend from the ancestor to two or more persons.[3]

Coparceners. Co-heirs are called co-parceners, and parceners: they may be compelled to make "partition."

All parceners make but one heir. They have the unities of interest, title, and possession of joint-tenants. No unity of time is necessary; for the heir of a parcener and surviving parcener are coparceners. Parceners always claim by *descent;* joint-tenants by purchase. They sue and are to be sued jointly. They may not have an action for waste against each other: that can be prevented by partition. Each has a distinct moiety, with no survivorship. Possession being severed by partition, they become tenants in severalty; when one aliens his share they become tenants in common. Where they divide amicably each elects a share by seniority, which is a personal privilege. Under a writ in partition, the sheriff, by the verdict of a jury (or commissioners) divides and assigns the parts.[3]

In the old sense, includes males and females; in modern English usage, is limited to females.[4]

Of comparatively little practical importance at present. With us, heirs take as tenants in common.[5] See HOTCH-POT; PARTITION; TENANT.

COPARTNER. See PARTNER.

COPPERS. See COIN.

COPY. A true transcript of an original writing.[6]

A reproduction or transcript of language, written or printed, or of a design, device, picture, or work of art.[1] Compare TRANSCRIPT.

Certified or office copy. A copy made and attested by the officer who is intrusted with the custody of an original writing, and authorized to make copies.

Every document of a public nature, as to which inconvenience would be occasioned by a removal, and which the party has a right to inspect, may be proved by a duly authenticated copy.[2]

Examined copy. A copy compared with the original, or with an official record thereof.

Exemplified copy. A copy attested under the seal of the proper court; an exemplification (*q. v.*) of record.

An examined copy of a record is evidence where the removal of the original would inconvenience the public. Fraud or mistake therein can be readily detected.[3] See RECORD, Judicial.

A copy of a will may be received in probate.[4]

Where an original is lost, or withheld after notice to produce, a copy will be received.[5]

To be evidence, a copy must also be complete.[6]

In making examined copies, the comparing witnesses should change hands, so that the listening witness may in turn become the reading witness.[7]

Such copy should be proved by some one who has compared it with the original.[8]

The rule that a copy of a copy is not admissible evidence is correct in itself, when properly understood and limited to its true sense. The rule properly applies to cases where the copy is taken from a copy, the original being still in existence and capable of being compared with it, for then it is a second remove from the original; or where it is a copy of a copy of a record, the record being in existence, by law deemed as high evidence as the original, for then it is also a second remove from the record. But it is quite a difficult question whether it applies to cases of secondary evidence where the original is lost, or the record of it is not deemed as high evidence as the original, or where the copy of a copy is the highest proof in existence.[9]

A letter-press copy is receivable, the original being lost. While secondary at best, a copy from such a copy, the original being lost, has been allowed.[10]

---

[1] Evans v. Rugee, 57 Wis. 626 (1883).

[2] Commonwealth v. Webster, 5 Cush. 308 (1850), Shaw, C. J. See also Abernethy v. Commonwealth, 101 Pa. 322 (1882); 71 Ala. 485; 3 Gratt. 594; Whart. Hom. 448; 1 Russ. Cr. 667.

[3] 2 Bl. Com. 187–90; 3 *id.* 227.

[4] 4 Kent, 366.

[5] 1 Washb. R. P. 415.

[6] Dickinson v. Chesapeake, &c. R. Co., 7 W. Va. 412 (1874); Bouvier.

(17)

[1] Abbott's Law Dict.

[2] Stebbins v. Duncan, 108 U. S. 50 (1882), cases; Shutesbury v. Hadley, 133 Mass. 247 (1882), cases; Booth v. Tiernan, 109 U. S. 208 (1883).

[3] 1 Greenl. Ev. § 91.

[4] 1 Williams, Ex. 364.

[5] 1 Greenl. Ev. § 508.

[6] Commonwealth v. Trout, 76 Pa. 382 (1874).

[7] 1 Whart. Ev. § 94.

[8] McGinniss v. Sawyer, 63 Pa. 267 (1869).

[9] Winn v. Patterson, 9 Pet. *677 (1835), Story J.

[10] See Goodrich v. Weston, 102 Mass. 363 (1869), cases; 1 Cush. 189; 7 Allen, 561; 3 McCrary, 169; 37 Conn. 555; 57 Ga. 50; 73 Ill. 161; 18 Kan. 546; 19 La. An. 91; 35 Md. 123; 44 N. Y. 172; 1 Whart. Ev. §§ 90–109, cases.

COPYHOLD. Lords of manors, from time out of mind, having permitted villains to enjoy their possessions without interruption, in a regular course of descent, the common law, of which custom is the life, gave the villains title to prescribe against the lords, and, on performance of the same services, to hold the lands under the lord's will, that being in conformity with the customs of the manor as preserved and evidenced by the rolls of the courts-baron.[1]

In England, to-day, a copyhold, in a general way, distinguishes a customary tenure from a freehold.

COPYRIGHT. An exclusive right to the multiplication of the copies of a production.[2]

The sole right of printing, publishing and selling one's literary composition or book.[3]

A copyright gives the author or the publisher the exclusive right of multiplying copies of what he has written or printed.[4]

The word may be understood in two senses. The author of a literary composition has an undoubted right at common law to the piece of paper on which his composition is written, and to the copies he chooses to make of it for himself or others. . . The other sense is, the exclusive right of multiplying copies: the right of preventing others from copying, by printing or otherwise, a literary work which the author has published; the exclusive right of printing a published work, that being the ordinary mode of multiplying copies.[5]

The word is used indifferently for **common-law copyright:** copyright before publication; and **statutory copyright:** copyright after publication. It is also made a synonym for "literary property" — the exclusive right of an owner publicly to read or exhibit his work; but this is not strictly correct.[6]

A copyright secures the proprietor against the copying by others of the original work, but does not confer upon him a monopoly in the intellectual conception which it expresses. The law originated in the recognition of an author's right to be protected in the manu-

script which is the title of his literary property. It does not rest upon the theory that the author has an exclusive property in his ideas or in the words in which he has clothed them. . No person, for example, can acquire an exclusive right to appropriate the information contained in a translation, chart, map or survey. . Frequently, it is necessary to determine whether the defendant's work is the result of his own labor, skill, and use of materials common to all, or is an appropriation of the plaintiff's work, with colorable alterations and departures intended to disguise the piracy. He may work on the same original materials, but he cannot evasively use those already collected and embodied by the skill, industry, and expenditure of another.[1]

The earliest evidence of the recognition of copyright is found in the charter of the Stationers' Company, granted by Philip and Mary, and in the decrees of the court of star-chamber. The first statute was 8 Anne (1710), c. 19; passed for the protection and encouragement of learned men. This statute gave the author and his assigns the sole liberty to print his work for fourteen years; the *author* to be entitled to an extension for another like term. But, the better opinion is that the common law, before that statute, admitted the exclusive right in the author, and his assigns, to multiply copies of his own original literary composition, for injunctions to protect this right were granted in equity. At all events, it has long been settled that the common-law right was taken away by the statute, and, hence, that it has existed, if at all, by force of some subsequent statutory provision.[2]

With us, before the adoption of the Constitution, it may be doubted whether there was any copyright at common law. Some of the States had passed laws recognizing and securing the right. All power in the States to legislate upon the subject became vested in Congress. " The Congress shall have power .
To promote the Progress of Science and useful Arts, by securing for limited Times to Authors and Inventors the Exclusive Right to their respective Writings and Discoveries." [3] Under this authority various general acts have been passed, from that of May 31, 1790, to that of June 18, 1874; all which, as re-enacted, constitute §§ 4948 to 4971 of the Revised Statutes, known as the title or chapter on " Copyrights."

"Any citizen of the United States or resident therein, who shall be the author, inventor, designer, or proprietor of any *book, map, chart, dramatic or musical composition, engraving, cut, print, or photograph or negative thereof, or of a painting, drawing, chromo, statue, statuary, and of models or designs intended to be perfected as works of the fine arts,* and the executors, administrators, or the assigns of any such person shall, upon complying with the provision of this chapter, have the sole liberty of printing, re-

---

[1] 2 Bl. Com. 95, 90, 147; Williams, R. P. 333.

[2] [Stephens *v.* Cady, 14 How. 530 (1852), Nelson, J. See R. S. § 4952.

[3] [Stowe *v.* Thomas, 2 Wall. Jr. 567 (1853), Grier, J.

[4] Perris *v.* Hexamer, 99 U. S. 675 (1878), Waite, C. J.

[5] Jefferys *v.* Boosey, 4 H. L. C. 919–20 (1854), Parke, B.; Cappell *v.* Purday, 14 M. & W. 316 (1845), Pollock, C. B.

[6] See Drone, Copyr. 100.

[1] Johnson *v.* Donaldson, 18 Blatch. 289–90 (1880), cases, Wallace, J. See also *Re* Brosnahan, 18 F. R. 64-65 (1883).

[2] See 2 Bl. Com. 406–7; 2 Kent, 373; Millar *v.* Taylor, 4 Burr. 2408 (1769); Stevens *v.* Gladding, 17 How. 454 (1854); 18 *id.* 165; 2 Story, 100; 5 McLean, 32; 6 *id.* 128; 15 Alb. Law J. 445, 465 (1877); Drone, 1.

[3] Constitution, Art. I, sec. 8, cl. 8.

printing, publishing, completing, copying, executing, finishing, and vending the same; and, in case of a dramatic composition, of publicly performing or representing it, or causing it to be performed or represented by others." R. S. § 4952.

"The printing, publishing, importation, or sale of any book, map, chart, dramatic or musical composition, print, cut, engraving, or photograph, written, composed, or made by any person *not a citizen* of the United States nor resident therein," is not to be construed as prohibited. R. S. § 4971. No mention being here made of paintings. drawings, chromos, statues, statuary, models, or designs, there would seem to be nothing to prevent a resident owner from copyrighting any such, although the work of a foreigner.[1] See further PROPRIETOR, 1.

"Engraving, cut, and print" (R. S. § 4952) apply only to pictorial illustrations or works connected with the fine arts; and no *prints* or *labels* designed to be used for any other article of manufacture shall be entered under the copyright law, but may be registered in the patent office.[2] See PRINT.

Manufacturers of designs for molded decorative articles, titles, plaques, or articles of pottery or metal, subject to copyright, may put the copyright mark upon the back or bottom of such articles, or in such other place upon them as it has heretofore been usual for manufacturers to employ.[3]

The period is twenty-eight years from the time of recording the title; with a right of renewal for fourteen years, in the author, inventor, or designer, or his widow or children, being still a citizen or resident. R. S. §§ 4953–54.

A printed copy of the title (not title-page) of the book, map, chart, etc., or a description of the painting, drawing, etc., or a model or design of the work of art, as the case may be, is to be deposited with or mailed to the Librarian of Congress; and, within ten days after publication, two complete copies of the best edition of each book or other article is also to be sent to him.[4]

The print of a type-writer will be accepted. See TITLE, 2, Book.

Notice of copyright must be given by some imprint on the title,—leaf, face, or front-piece. The shortest form is "Copyright, 1888, by A. B." The penalty for an unauthorized notice is one hundred dollars.

"Registered" is not the equivalent of "copyright."[5]

"Right of translation reserved," or "All rights reserved," secures the right to translate or to dramatize the production. See DRAMA; RESERVE, 2.

Assignments must be in writing, and recorded within sixty days.

A separate copyright must be taken out for each volume or number of a periodical, or variety, or description.

In the case of a painting, statue, model, or design, a photograph of "cabinet" size must accompany the description and application.

No affidavit or formal application is required.

At present, 1888, the fees are: fifty cents each for recording a title, description, etc., for a certificate, or a duplicate certificate; and one dollar for each assignment.[1]

The right is infringed when another person produces a substantial copy of the whole or of a material part of the thing copyrighted.[2]

To constitute an invasion of copyright it is not necessary that a large portion of a work be copied in form or in substance. If so much is taken that the value of the original is sensibly diminished, or the labors of the original author substantially, to an injurious extent, appropriated, that is an infringement. Courts look to the nature and objects of the selections made, the quantity and value of the materials used, and the degree in which the use may prejudice the sale or diminish the profits, or supersede the object of the original work.[3]

Evidence of the coincidence of errors, the identity of inaccuracies, affords strong proof of copying; so does coincidence of citation, and identity in plan and arrangement. Equity may not relieve where the amount copied is small and of little value, where there is no bad motive, where there is a well-founded doubt as to the legal title, or long acquiescence or culpable neglect in seeking redress. A copyright thus differs from a patent-right, which admits of no use at all without license.[4]

Recent decisions afford more ample protection to copyright than the earlier ones; they restrict the privilege of subsequent writers within narrower limits.[4, 3]

A production, published under a *nom de plume*, and not copyrighted, becomes public property; and the use of the assumed name is not a trade-mark which will protect against republication.[5]

An action for the penalty for infringement, provided by R. S. § 4965, abates by the death of the defendant.[6]

See further ABRIDGE; ART, 2; BOOK, 1; CHART; COMPILE; COMPOSITION, 1; DEDICATION, 2; DIRECTORIES; IDENTITY, 2; LETTER, 3; MANUSCRIPT; PHOTOGRAPH; PIRACY, 2; REPORT, 1 (2); REVIEW, 3; SCIENCE; SECURE, 1; TRANSLATION; USUS, Ancipitis, Utile, etc. Compare PATENT, 2; TRADE-MARK.

---

[1] Drone, Copyr. 232. But see Yuengling v. Schile, 20 Blatch. 458–63 (1882).

[2] Act 18 June, 1874: 1 Sup. R. S. 41.

[3] Act 1 Aug. 1882: 22 St. L. 181; amending R. S. §§ 4962, 959.

[4] See Merrell v. Tice, 104 U. S. 561 (1881); Donelly v. Ives, 13 Rep. 390 (S. D. N. Y., 1882); 1 Blatch. 618.

[5] Higgins v. Keuffel, 30 F. R. 627 (1887).

[1] Upon application to the Librarian of Congress, printed directions for securing a copyright will be furnished free of charge.

[2] Perris v. Hexamer, 99 U. S. 674 (1878).

[3] Folsom v. Marsh, 2 Story, 116 (1844); Lawrence v. Dana, 4 Cliff. 81–83 (1869), cases.

[4] Lawrence v. Dana, 4 Cliff. 74–75, 80 (1869), cases; R. S. §§ 4964–65.

[5] Clemens ("Mark Twain") v. Belford, 11 Biss. 461 (1883): 15 Rep. 227; 14 F. R. 720.

[6] Schreiber v. Sharpless, 17 F. R. 589 (1883). See generally *ib.* 593–603, cases. R. S. §§ 4964–67, providing penalties for infringements, explained,— Thornton v. Schreiber, 124 U. S. 613–16 (1888), Miller, J.

CORAM. L. Before; in the presence of.
Coram nobis. Before us. **Coram vobis.**
Before you.

Designate, the first, a writ of error designed to review proceedings before the same court which is alleged to have committed the error; and the second, a writ for a review by a higher court. See further ERROR, 3.

Coram non judice. Before one not a judge; by a court without jurisdiction. See further JUDEX, Coram.

CORD. One hundred and twenty-eight cubic feet.

A contract for the sale of wood or bark by the cord calls for such number of cubic feet.[1]

CORDIALS. See LIQUOR.

CORN. See GRAIN.

CORNER. In the language of gambling speculation, when an article of commerce is so engrossed or manipulated as to make it scarce or plenty in the market at the will of the gamblers, and its price thus placed within their power.[2] See COMBINATION, 2.

CORNERS. See FOUR.

CORODY. See PENSION, 2.

CORONER.[3] 1. An officer who has principally to do with pleas of the crown, or such wherein the king is more immediately concerned.[4]

2. A county officer who inquires into the causes of sudden or violent deaths, while the facts are recent and the circumstances unchanged.[5]

The lord chief justice is the chief coroner of all England; and there are usually four coroners for each county. The office is of equal antiquity with that of sheriff; was ordained with his, to keep the peace, when the earls gave up the wardship of the county. Much honor formerly appertained to the office, which might be for life.

According to Blackstone, the duties of the office, which are principally judicial, are largely defined by 4 Edw. I (1276), and consist in inquiring (whence coroner's inquest) when any person is slain, or dies suddenly, or in prison, concerning the manner of his death. This must appear upon view of the body, at the place where death happened, by a jury of four to six persons. If any person be found guilty of homicide the coroner is to commit him to prison for further trial, and to inquire as to his property, which is for-

feited thereby; and he is also to certify the whole of the inquisition, with the evidence, to the court of king's bench or to the next assizes. Another branch of his office was to inquire generally concerning shipwrecks, and treasure-trove. His ministerial office is as the sheriff's substitute: when exception is taken to the sheriff, for suspicion of partiality, process is awarded to the coroner for execution.[1] See SHERIFF.

The object of an inquest is to seek information and secure evidence in case of death by violence or other undue means. It is the coroner's duty to act only when there is reasonable ground to suspect that a death was so caused; the power is not to be exercised capriciously, and arbitrarily against all reason.[2]

The welfare of society and the interests of public justice alike demand that an inquest should be thorough. Statutory provisions are, therefore, to be liberally construed, with a view to the accomplishment of the end desired. They are to be so construed that the coroner may be thereby authorized to employ such medical, surgical, or other scientific skill as may be necessary, in his judgment, in the particular case, and to charge his county with payment of the reasonable expense thereof.[3]

In Massachusetts, the office was abolished in 1877. The governor appoints as examiners "men learned in the science of medicine," who hold autopsies, and, in cases of death from violence, notify the district attorney and a justice of that fact.[4]

CORPORAL. 1. Relating to the body of a person; bodily: as, corporal punishment, q. v.; corporal seizure or touching. See ARREST, 2; CORPUS.

2. Affecting a thing externally; as, a corporal oath,—taken with the hand upon the Gospels. See OATH.

3. In person: as, a corporal appearance. Compare CORPOREAL.

CORPORATE. See CORPORATION, Corporate.

CORPORATION. A creature of the crown, created by letters-patent.[5]

An artificial being, indivisible, intangible, and existing only in contemplation of law.[6]

As all personal rights die with the person, and as the necessary forms of investing a

---

[1] Kennedy v. Oswego, &c. R. Co., 67 Barb. 167 (1867). See Buffalo v. O'Malley, 61 Wis. 258 (1884).

[2] Kirkpatrick v. Bonsall, 72 Pa. 158 (1872), Agnew, J.

[3] L. *coronator; corona*, a crown.

[4] 1 Bl. Com. 346.

[5] Commonwealth v. Gray, 5 Cush. 309 (1850), Shaw, Chief Justice.

---

[1] 1 Bl. Com. 346–48; 4 *id.* 274; 7 Q. B. D. 514; 20 Ga. 336; 10 Humph. 346; 73 N. Y. 45.

[2] Lancaster County v. Mishler, 100 Pa. 627 (1882).

[3] Jameson v. Bartholomew County, 54 Ind. 530 (1876), Howk, C. J. See also Dearborn County v. Bond, 88 *id.* 102 (1882); Sandford v. Lee County, 49 Iowa, 148 (1878); Cook v. Multnomah County, 7 Oreg. 170 (1879); 6 Am. Law Reg. 385–400 (1858).

[4] Laws of 1877, c. 200.

[5] Kirk v. Nowill, 1 T. R. 124 (1786), Mansfield, C. J.

[6] Dartmouth College v. Woodward, 4 Wheat. 636 (1819), Marshall, C. J.; United States Bank v. Deveaux, 5 Cranch, 88 (1809); Bank of Augusta v. Earle, 13 Pet. 587 (1839); 1 Black, 295.

series of individuals, one after the other, with the same identical right, would be inconvenient, if not impracticable, it has been found necessary, when for the advantage of the public that particular rights should be continued, to constitute artificial persons who may maintain a perpetual succession. These artificial persons are called "bodies politic," "bodies corporate," or "corporations."[1]

The great object of a corporation is to bestow the character and properties of individuality on a collective and changing body of men.[2]

A private corporation is merely an association of individuals united for a special purpose, and permitted to do business under a particular name, and have a succession of members without dissolution.[3]

The privilege of exercising the particular right, by grant of the sovereign, is a franchise.[4] Compare *Corporation Aggregate*.

The constitutions of several States provide that the term corporation " shall be construed to include all associations and joint-stock companies having any of the powers and privileges of corporations not possessed by individuals or partnerships."[5]

In England, the tendency seems to have been to confine the term to its original sense as implying non-liability of members for corporate debts; and, if this exemption is not to be accorded, to call the body a "public company." . The current of American decisions has been to the effect that the word embraces an association formed under general laws, with stockholders, directors, a president, etc.; and that such a body is not a *quasi* corporation (*q. v.*), nor a joint-stock company, nor a limited partnership.[6] See Association; Company.

If the essential franchises of a corporation are conferred upon a joint-stock company, it is none the less a corporation for being called something else.[7]

Being the mere creature of law, each possesses only those properties which the charter of its creation confers upon it, expressly or as incidental to its very existence. These are such as are supposed best calculated to effect the object for which it was created.

Among the most important are immortality and individuality: "properties by which a perpetual succession of many members are considered as the same, and may act as a single individual."[1]

The members and their successors are as one person in law, with one will — that of the majority; and with prescribed rules which take the place of natural laws.[2]

The sovereign's consent is necessary to the erection of a corporation. With respect to corporations which exist by force of the common law, as, the king himself and bishops, this consent is implied; so, also, as to corporations, like the city of London, whose charter rests on prescription. His consent is expressly given by act of parliament or by charter. He may grant the power to a subject as his agent.[3]

The powers of a corporation aggregate are: to have perpetual succession; to sue and be sued; to hold lands; to have a common seal; to make by-laws; — with all the rights necessarily incident to these general powers.[4]

The duty of a corporation is to act up to the end or design for which it was created. To enforce this duty all corporations may be " visited "— by the founder or his representative in the case of a lay corporation; by the endower, his heirs or assigns, in the case of an eleemosynary corporation.[5]

A corporation is dissolved by a statute assented to; by the natural death of all its members; by surrender of its franchises; by forfeiture of its charter, through negligence or abuse of its franchises.[6]

The objects for which corporations are created are such as the government wishes to promote. They are deemed beneficial to the country; and it is this benefit that constitutes the consideration of the grant.[7]

The United States may be deemed a corporation;[8] so may a State;[9] and so, a county. All corporations were originally modeled upon a state or nation; whence they are still called " bodies politic."[10] See *Municipal* and *Public Corporation*.

The species of corporations are the following:

Aggregate corporation. Consists of many persons united together into one society, and is kept up by a perpetual succession of members, so as to continue forever.

Corporation sole. Consists of one person only and his successors, incorporated in order to give them legal capacities and advantages,

---

[1] 1 Bl. Com. 467, 123.

[2] Providence Bank v. Billings, 4 Pet. *562 (1830), Marshall, C. J.

[3] [Pembina Mining Co. v. Pennsylvania, 125 U. S. 189 (1888), Field, J.

[4] [2 Bl. Com. 37. See also 4 Ark. 351; 40 Ga. 637; 76 Ill. 573; 6 Kan. 253; 40 N. H. 578; 1 Ohio St. 642; 45 Wis. 592; 1 Hill, N. Y., 620.

[5] Const. N. Y., 1849, Art. 8, § 3; Cal., 1849, Art. 4, § 33; Mich., 1850, Art. 15, § 11; Kan., 1859, Art. 12, § 6; Minn., 1857-58, Art. 10, § 1.

[6] 1 Abbott, 291; Falconer v. Campbell, 2 McLean, 195 (1840); Oliver v. Liverpool, &c. Ins. Co., 100 Mass. 538 (1868): 10 Wall. 566 (1870).

[7] Fargo v. Louisville, &c. R. Co., 10 Biss. 277 (1881).

[1] Dartmouth College v. Woodward, 4 Wheat. 636 (1819); 97 U. S. 666; 101 *id.* 83; 1 Bl. Com. 468.

[2] 1 Bl. Com. 468.

[3] 1 Bl. Com. 472-74. As to names of corporations, see 23 Cent. Law J. 531 (1886), cases.

[4] 1 Bl. Com. 475-78.

[5] 1 Bl. Com. 480.

[6] 1 Bl. Com. 485.

[7] Dartmouth College v. Woodward, 4 Wheat. 637 (1819); 101 U. S. 83.

[8] United States v. Hillegas, 3 Wash. 73 (1811).

[9] Indiana v. Woram, 6 Hill, 38 (1843); 2 Johns. Cas. 58, 417; 1 Abb. U. S. 22; 35 Ga. 315.

[10] McIntosh, Hist. Eng. 31-32.

particularly that of perpetuity, which in their natural persons they could not have had; as, the king, by force of the common law, and a bishop or parson.[1]

A "corporation aggregate" is a collection of individuals united into one collective body, under a special name, and possessing certain immunities, privileges, and capacities in its collective character which do not belong to the natural persons composing it.[2]

A "corporation aggregate" consists of many persons united together into one society, and kept up by a perpetual succession of members, so as to continue forever.[3]

A "corporation sole" consists of a single person who is made a body corporate and politic in order to give him some legal capacities and advantages, especially that of perpetuity; as, a minister seized of lands in right of the parish.[3]

A "corporation aggregate" is a true corporation, but a "corporation sole" is one individual, being a member of a series of individuals, who is invested by a fiction with the qualities of a corporation. The capacity or office is here considered apart from the particular person who from time to time may occupy it.[4]

Ecclesiastical corporation. When the members composing the corporation are entirely spiritual persons, as, a bishop, a parson, and the like; for the furtherance of religion and perpetuating the rights of the church. **Lay corporation.** A corporation composed of secular persons; and in nature either civil or eleemosynary.

Civil corporation. Such corporation as is erected for a temporal purpose. **Eleemosynary corporation.** Such corporation as is constituted for the perpetual distribution of the free alms or bounty of the founder to such persons as he has directed.[5]

Of the "civil" sort are: those erected for the good government of a town or district; those for the advancement and regulation of manufacturers and commerce; those for special purposes — as for medical science, natural history, etc.[5] See *Municipal* and *Private Corporation.*

Of the "eleemosynary" kind are hospitals for the relief of the poor, the sick, the impotent; and colleges for the promotion of piety and learning.[5]

"Eleemosynary corporations" are incorporated for perpetuating the application of the bounty of the donor to the specified objects of that bounty[6] — the

distribution of the free alms and bounty of the founder as he has directed.[1]

An "eleemosynary corporation" is a private charity, constituted for the perpetual distribution of the alms and bounty of the founder.[2]

A corporation for religious and charitable purposes, endowed solely by private benefactions, is a "private eleemosynary" corporation, although created by a charter from the government.[3]

Close corporation. In this the majority of the persons to whom the corporate powers have been granted, on the happening of vacancies among them, have the right of themselves to appoint others to fill such vacancies, without allowing the corporators in general any choice in the selection of such new officers. **Open corporation.** In which all the corporators have a vote in the election of officers.[4]

Commercial corporation. See BUSINESS, Corporation.

Foreign corporation. A corporation created by or under the laws of another State, government, or country.[5] **Domestic or home corporation.** A corporation created under the law of the place where it exists or exercises its powers.

A corporation exists only by force of law, and can have no legal existence beyond the bounds of the sovereignty by which it is created. It dwells in the place of its creation. It is not a "citizen," within the meaning of the Constitution, and cannot maintain a suit in a Federal court against a citizen of a different State from that by which it was created, unless the persons who compose the corporate body are all citizens of that State. The legal presumption is that its members are citizens of the State in which alone the body has a legal existence.[6]

By comity, if not forbidden by its charter, nor by the laws of that State, a corporation may exercise its powers in another State.[7]

---

[1] Dartmouth College *v.* Woodward, 4 Wheat. 668, 672-79 (1819), Story, J.

[2] Allen *v.* McKean, 1 Sumn. 299 (1833): 2 Kent, 274. See also 12 Mass. 557; 9 Barb. 90; 27 *id.* 306; 8 N. Y. 533; Ang. & A. Corp. § 39.

[3] Society for Propagating the Gospel *v.* New Haven, 8 Wheat. 480 (1823).

[4] McKim *v.* Odom, 2 Bland, Ch. 416, n. (1829).

[5] Daly *v.* National Life Ins. Co., 64 Ind. 6-8 (1878).

[6] Ohio & Mississippi R. Co. *v.* Wheeler, 1 Black, 295-96 (1861), cases, Taney, C. J.; Paul *v.* Virginia, 8 Wall. 177-82 (1868), cases; Chicago, &c. R. Co. *v.* Whitton, 13 *id.* 283 (1871); Sewing Machine Case, 18 *id.* 575 (1873); Doyle *v.* Continental Ins. Co., 94 U. S. 535 (1876); Cowell *v.* Colorado Springs Co., 100 *id.* 59 (1879); Memphis, &c. R. Co. *v.* Alabama, 107 *id.* 585 (1882); Philadelphia Fire Association *v.* New York, 119 *id.* 117-18 (1886), cases.

[7] Christian Union *v.* Yount, 101 U. S. 352 (1879); St. Louis *v.* Ferry Co., 11 Wall., 429 (1870).

---

[1] 1 Bl. Com. 469.

[2] Dartmouth College *v.* Woodward, 4 Wheat. 667 (1819), Story, J.

[3] Overseers of the Poor *v.* Sears, 22 Pick. 125-28 (1839), Shaw, C. J.; 7 Mass. 447; 22 Wend. 70; 1 Hill, 620; 19 N. Y. 39; 2 Kent, 273.

[4] Maine Anc. Law, 181.

[5] 2 Bl. Com. 470-71.

[6] Dartmouth College *v.* Woodward, 4 Wheat. 640, 647, 630 (1819), Marshall, C. J.

No State need allow the corporations of another State to do business within its jurisdiction unless it chooses, with perhaps the exception of commercial corporations; but if it does, without limitation, the corporation comes in as it has been created.[1]

The State which recognizes foreign corporations can impose such conditions on its recognition as it chooses, not inconsistent with the Constitution and laws of the United States. If it permits them to do business without limitation, express or implied, they carry with them all their chartered rights, and may claim all their chartered privileges which can be used away from their legal home. By doing business away from home they do not change their citizenship; they simply extend their field of operations.[2]

But a State may not impose a limitation upon the power of a foreign corporation to make contracts within the State for carrying on commerce between the States. Doing a single act of business in a State, with no purpose of doing other acts there, does not bring a corporation within a statute requiring a foreign corporation, before it can carry on business in the State, to file a certificate showing places of business, agents, etc.[3]

Undoubtedly a corporation of one State, employed in the business of the general government, may do such business in other States without obtaining a license from them. . It is not every corporation, lawful in the State of its creation, that other States may be willing to admit within their jurisdiction; such, for example, as a corporation for lotteries. And even when the business is not unlawful the State may wish to limit the number of corporations belonging to its class, or to subject their business to such contract as would be in accordance with the policy governing domestic corporations of a similar character. The States may, therefore, require for the admission within their limits of the corporations of other States such conditions as they may choose. . The only limitation, upon such power arises where the corporation is in the employ of the Federal government, or where its business is strictly commerce, inter-State or foreign.[4]

Moneyed corporation. Any corporation with banking powers, or power to make loans on pledges or deposits, or to make contracts of insurance.[5]

Quasi corporation. A phrase applied to a body which exercises certain functions of a corporate character, but which has not been created a corporation by any statute, general or special.[1]

Such auxiliaries of the State as a county, school-district, township, and other like involuntary corporations with liabilities not as great as those of municipal corporations.[2]

Of such are the inhabitants of a school district;[3] commissioners of schools,[4] and boards of education;[5] overseers of the poor;[6] the commissioners or supervisors of a county,[7] q. v.; commissioners of roads;[8] the governor of Tennessee;[9] a levee district organized by statute to reclaim land;[10] — any body invested with corporate powers *sub modo*, for a few specified purposes only, and which may sue and be sued.[11] See under *Public Corporation*, Quasi, etc.

Municipal corporation. A public corporation (q. v.) created by the government for political purposes and having subordinate and local powers of legislation; an incorporation of persons inhabitants of a particular place, or connected with a particular district, enabling them to conduct its local civil government. Merely an agency instituted by the sovereign for the purpose of carrying out in detail the objects of government.[12]

Essentially a revocable agency — having no vested right to any of its powers or franchises — the charter or act of erection being in no sense a contract with the State — and therefore fully subject to the control of the legislature, which may enlarge or diminish its territorial extent or its functions, change or modify its internal arrangement, or destroy its very existence, with the mere breath of arbitrary discretion. While it thus exists in subjection to the will of the sovereign, it enjoys the rights and is subject to the liabilities of any other corporation, public or private. This is the very object of making it a body politic, giving it a legal entity and name, a seal by which to act in solemn form, a capacity to contract and be contracted with, to sue and be sued, a *persona standi in judicio*, to

---

[1] Relfe v. Rundle, 103 U. S. 225 (1880).

[2] Baltimore, &c. R. Co. v. Koontz, 104 U. S. 11–13 (1881), cases, Waite, C. J.; National Steamship Co. v. Tugman, 106 id. 120–21 (1882), cases; St. Clair v. Cox, ib. 355–56 (1882); Canada Southern R. Co. v. Gebhard, 109 id. 537 (1883).

[3] Cooper Manufacturing Co. v. Ferguson, 113 U. S. 727, 732 (1885).

[4] Pembina Mining Co. v. Pennsylvania, 125 U. S. 186, 189–90 (1888), cases, Field, J.

[5] See 2 N. Y. Rev. St., 7 ed., 1371; Gillet v. Moody, 3 N. Y. 485 (1850); Hill v. Reed, 16 Barb. 287 (1853); 48 id. 464; 6 Paige, 497.

[1] School District v. Insurance Co., 103 U. S. 708 (1880), Miller, J.

[2] Levy Court v. Coroner, 2 Wall. 508 (1864); Barnes v. District of Columbia, 91 U. S. 552 (1875); 7 Mass. 169; 109 id. 213.

[3] 33 Conn. 298; 26 Ind. 310; 37 Iowa, 542; 22 Me. 564; 13 Mass. 193; 23 Mo. 418.

[4] 1 Miss. 328; 18 Johns. 407.

[5] 38 Ohio St. 54.

[6] 44 Ala. 566.

[7] 8 Johns. 422; 20 Barb. 294; 1 Cow. 670; 16 S. & R. 286.

[8] 1 Spears (S. C.), 218.

[9] 8 Humph. 176.

[10] 51 Cal. 406.

[11] 51 Cal. 406; 10 N. Y. 409; 18 Barb. 567; 4 Wheat. 531; Angell & A. Corp. § 24; Boone, Corp. § 10.

[12] Philadelphia v. Fox, 64 Pa. 180–81 (1870), Sharswood, J., quoting 2 Kent, 275; Glover, Munic. Corp. 1. See also 33 Cal. 142, 145; 60 Ga. 544; 37 Iowa, 544; 26 La. An. 481; 29 Minn. 450–51; 52 Mo. 311; 6 Baxt. 171; 2 Utah, 403; 2 Kent, 268; Ang. & A. Corp. § 15.

hold and dispose of property, and thereby to acquire rights and incur responsibilities. These franchises were conferred upon it for the purpose of enabling it the better to effect the design of its institution, the exercise of certain of the powers of government, subordinate to the legislature, over a part of the territory of the State. But all this affects its relations to other persons, natural or artificial: it does not touch its relation to the State, its creator.[1]

In the exercise of its duties, including those most strictly local or internal, a municipal corporation is but a department of the State. The legislature may give it all the powers such a being is capable of receiving, making it a miniature State within its locality; or it may strip it of every power, leaving it a corporation in name only. . . The municipality may act through its mayor, its common council or legislative department, its supervisor of streets, commissioner of highways, board of public works, etc., provided it acts within the province committed to its charge. Whether its agents be appointed or elected is immaterial.[2]

What portions of a State shall be within the limits of a city is a proper subject of legislation — however thick or sparse the settlement.[3]

Property held for public uses — such as public buildings, streets, squares, parks, wharves, fire-engines, engineering instruments: whatever is held for governmental purposes — cannot be subjected to the payment of the debts of the city. Its public character forbids such an appropriation. The obligation of its contracts survives dissolution. Equity will apply its property to the payment of its debts; after which, surplus realty may revert to the grantor, and personalty vest in the State. The private property of individuals cannot be taken for its debts, except through taxation. The doctrine of some States, that such can be reached directly on an execution against the municipality, has not been generally accepted.[4]

The general doctrine that, being the creature of the law, a municipal corporation can only act as provided by its organic law, and that if its agents fail to observe the forms and methods prescribed by that law, in any substantial particular, their acts are not the acts of the corporation,— has been greatly modified, by the decisions of the Supreme Court, in its application to bonds issued by agents when the rights of *bona fide* purchasers are involved.[5]

A municipal corporation can exercise such powers only as are granted in express words or are necessarily or fairly implied in or incident to those powers, and such as are essential to the declared objects of the corporation.[6]

The earliest form of corporation was, probably, the municipality or city, which necessily exacted for the control or local police of the marts or crowded places of the empire. These cities became a bulwark against despotism.[1] See CITY; ORDINANCE, 1; RIOT.

National corporation. A corporation created by Congress to assist in "carrying into execution" one or more of the powers vested by the Constitution in the government of the United States.

Of such are the national banking associations.[2] See GRANT, 3; LAND, Public.

Political corporation. See *Public Corporation.*

Private corporation. An association of individuals united for some common purpose, and permitted by the law to use a common name, and to change its members without a dissolution of the association.[3]

Its powers are such as are conferred by statute; and its charter is the measure thereof. The enumeration of these powers excludes all others.[4]

Its charter is a contract, not to be "impaired," *q. v.*

Public corporation. Such corporation as exists for political purposes only; as, a town, a city, a county. But, strictly speaking, public corporations are such only as are founded by the government for public purposes, where the whole interests belong also to the government.[5]

If, therefore, the foundation be "private," though under the charter of the government, the corporation is private, however extensive the uses to which it is devoted. . . A hospital or a college founded by a private benefactor is a private corporation, although dedicated by its charter to general charity.[6]

In popular meaning nearly every corporation is "public" inasmuch as they are created for the public benefit. Yet if the whole interest does not belong to the government, or if the corporation is not created for the administration of political or municipal power, it is a "private" corporation. Thus, all bank, bridge, turnpike, railroad, and canal companies are private corporations. In these and similar cases, in a certain sense, the uses may be called public, but the corporations are private, as much so as if the franchises were

[1] Philadelphia *v.* Fox, *ante.*

[2] Barnes *v.* District of Columbia, 91 U. S. 544, 541 (1875), cases, Hunt, J. See also 108 *id.* 121; 109 *id.* 287. On revoking powers of municipal corporations, see Supervisors *v.* Luck, 80 Va. 226–27 (1885), cases.

[3] Kelly *v.* Pittsburgh, 104 U. S. 80 (1881); 92 *id.* 310–12.

[4] Meriwether *v.* Garrett, 102 U. S. 501, 511–19 (1880), cases, Waite, C. J.; Broughton *v.* Pensacola, 93 *id.* 268 (1876); Claiborne Co. *v.* Brooks, 111 *id.* 410 (1884).

[5] Phelps *v.* Town of Yates, 16 Blatch. 193 (1879), Wallace, J.

[6] Dillon, Munic. Corp. 89, cases; Brenham *v.* Water

Co., 67 Tex. 553 (1887). See generally 26 Cent. Law J. 179 (1888), cases.

[1] McIntosh, Hist. Eng. 31–32; 1 Bl. Com. 468, 472; Liverpool Ins. Co. *v.* Massachusetts, 10 Wall. 574 (1870), Miller, J.

[2] See generally 21 Cent. Law J. 428–29 (1885), cases; 21 Am. Law Rev. 258–69 (1887), cases.

[3] Baltimore & Ohio R. Co. *v.* First Baptist Church, 108 U. S. 330 (1883), Field, J.; County of Santa Clara *v.* Southern Pac. R. Co., 18 F. R. 402 (1883); 8 Saw. 264; 15 Rep. 674.

[4] Thomas *v.* West Jersey R. Co., 101 U. S. 82 (1879).

[5] Dartmouth College *v.* Woodward, 4 Wheat. 668–69 (1819), Story, J.

vested in a single person. The delegation of the right of eminent domain, to be used for private emolument as well as for public benefit, does not clothe a corporation with the inviolability or immunity of public officers performing public functions.[1]

Public corporations are so called because they are but parts of the machinery employed in carrying on the affairs of the State; — auxiliaries of the State in the business of municipal rule; — political divisions of State, originating in the necessities and conveniences of the people. Their officers are local agents of the State.[2]

A public corporation is a mere instrumentality of the State for the better administration of the government in matters of local concern.[3] It is a local agency of the government creating it; its powers are such as belong to sovereignty. Property and revenue necessary for the exercise of these powers become part of the machinery of government. To permit a creditor to seize and sell these, in order to collect a debt, would be to permit him in a degree to destroy the government itself.[4]

A public corporation can exercise no power not given by its charter or some other statute of the State.[5]

It is now well settled that the charter of a public corporation may be changed, modified, or repealed, as the exigencies of the public service or the public welfare may demand; unless the organic law otherwise provides.[6]

Public and other municipal corporations represent the people, and are to be protected against the unauthorized acts of their officers and agents, when this can be done without injury to third parties. This is necessary in order to guard against fraud and peculation. Persons dealing with such officers or agents are chargeable with notice of the power the corporation possesses.[6]

Quasi public corporations: corporations technically private, but yet of a *quasi* public character having in view some general public enterprise, in which the public interests are directly involved to such an extent as to justify conferring upon them important governmental powers, such as an exercise of the right of eminent domain. Of this class are railroad, turnpike, and canal companies; and corporations strictly private, the direct object of which is to promote public interests, and in which the public have no concern, except the indirect benefits resulting from the promotion of trade, and the development of the resources of the country.[1]

It is a misnomer to attach the name "*quasi* public corporation" to a railroad company, for it has none of the features of such corporations, if we except its qualified right of eminent domain, which it has because of the right reserved to the public to use its way for travel and transportation. Its road may be a *quasi* public highway, but the company itself is a private corporation, and nothing more.[2]

Corporate. Relating to a corporation.

Corporate authorities. In the constitution of Illinois, Art. 9, § 5, municipal officers who are either directly elected by the people or are appointed in some mode to which they have given their assent.[3]

Corporate existence. Dates from the time when full authority to transact business is possessed by a corporation, as from the filing of articles with the secretary of State.[4]

Corporate purpose. In some States, as in Illinois, taxation by public corporations must be for corporate purposes. This means such purposes as are germane to the objects of the welfare of the municipality or at least have a legitimate connection with those objects and a manifest relation thereto.[5]

The reference is to a tax which is to be expended in a manner promoting the general prosperity and welfare of the municipality which levied it.[6]

The purpose must be germane to the general scope of the object for which the corporation was created.[7]

The expression will include money expended for a court-house, jail, poor-house; the opening and keeping of a common highway; the erection and maintenance of a bridge; a donation to secure the location of a school;[8] and, perhaps, also, money expended in developing the natural resources for manufacturing purposes.[9] Compare PURPOSE, Public.

Corporate rights. "Franchises or peculiar privileged grants" of the nature of corporeal property.[10]

---

[1] Randle v. Delaware & Raritan Canal Co., 1 Wall. C. C. 290 (1849), Grier, J.; Sweatt v. Boston, &c. R. Co., 3 Cliff. 346 (1871).

[2] Commissioners of Laramie County v. Commissioners of Albany County, 92 U. S. 310–312 (1875), cases, Clifford, J.; 2 Kent, 305.

[3] United States v. New Orleans, 98 U. S. 393 (1878), Field, J.

[4] Klein v. New Orleans, 99 U. S. 150 (1878), Waite, C. J.

[5] Mt. Pleasant v. Beckwith, 100 U. S. 524 (1879).

[6] Thomas v. City of Richmond, 12 Wall. 356 (1870), Bradley, J.

On changes in public corporations affecting property and rights of creditors, see 21 Am. Law Rev. 14–40 (1887), cases.

[1] Miners' Ditch Co. v. Zellenbach, 37 Cal. 577 (1869), Sawyer, C. J.

[2] Pierce v. Commonwealth, 104 Pa. 155 (1883); 6 Col. 8; 11 Kan. 608; 3 Hill, 567, 570; 1 N. H. 273; 1 Wall. Jr. 275. See generally 22 Cent. Law J. 148 (1886), cases.

[3] Gage v. Graham, 57 Ill. 146–47 (1870), cases.

[4] Hurt v. Salisbury, 55 Mo. 314 (1874).

[5] People v. Dupuyt, 71 Ill. 651 (1874); Livingston County v. Wieder, 64 id. 432 (1872).

[6] Burr v. City of Carbondale, 76 Ill. 455 (1875).

[7] Wrightman v. Clark, 103 U. S. 260 (1880), cases; Ottawa v. Carey, 108 id. 121–22 (1883), cases.

[8] County of Livingston v. Darlington, 101 U. S. 411–13 (1879), cases.

[9] Hackett v. Ottawa, 99 U. S. 94 (1878), cases.

[10] Warner v. Beers, 23 Wend. 154 (1840); 7 Hill, 283; 2 Bl. Com. 37.

Corporator. Usually, a member of a corporation, in which sense it includes a stockholder; also, one of the persons who are the original organizers or promoters of a new corporation.[1]

The corporators are not the corporation, for either may sue the other.[2]

Incorporate, *v.* To form into an artificial body; to create a corporation out of natural persons.

Incorporate, *adj.* The same as corporate, *q. v.*

Incorporated. United into one body; constituted a legal entity or person. *Unincorporated:* not existing as a corporation.

Incorporation. The act of uniting natural persons into a creature of the law; also, a body incorporated, that is, a corporation — a use not favored.

"Incorporation" is the act by which the political institution called a corporation is created.[3]

See further AGENT; AMOTION; BANK, 2 (2); BODY, 2; BOND; BY-LAW, 2; CAPITAL, 2; CHARITY, 2; CHARTER, 2; CONSOLIDATION; DIRECTOR; DISSOLVE, 2; DISTRINGAS; DIVIDEND, 3; DOMAIN, 1, Eminent; FIND, 2; FRANCHISE, 1; INSPECTION, 2; LEGISLATURE; MANAGER; MEETINGS; MINUTES, 2; MORTMAIN; ORGANIZE; PERPETUAL; PERSON; POLICE, 2; PROPERTY; PROSPECTUS; PROXY; RAILROAD; RECEIVER; RESIDENCE; SEAL, 1, Common; SOUL; STOCK, 3; SUCCESSION; TAKE, 8; TAX, 2; TORT, 2; ULTRA VIRES; VISIT, 2; VOTING, Cumulative; WARRANTUM.

CORPOREAL. Having a body: material in nature; substantial; palpable.

Incorporeal. Immaterial; intangible; insensible; existing in thought; ideal.

In the Roman law, *res corporales* were objects of property apprehensible by the senses; *res incorporales* objects apprehensible by the mind only. A right of way over another's land, an obligation to pay money, an undivided interest in land, were examples of the latter species of property; while the land itself and the money when paid were examples of the former species.[4]

Hereditaments are spoken of as corporeal and incorporeal. See HEREDITAMENT; CORPUS.

CORPSE. See BURIAL.

CORPUS. L. A body; also, the principal thing, the essential part, the substance.

In several phrases it means the body or person of an individual, as see under CAPERE; HABERE.

The *corpus* of an estate is the material object, or species of property, of which the estate is composed. It is this which, generally, is vested in a trustee, in distinction from the income of the estate, which is allotted to the beneficiary.[1]

The *corpus* of a railroad is the roadway, embankment, superstructure, and equipment.[2]

Corpus comitatus. The body of the county. See BODY, 3.

Corpus delicti. The essential element of an offense: the fact that the particular crime alleged has been actually committed.

To warrant a conviction for murder there must be direct proof either of the death, as by the finding and identification of the corpse, or of criminal violence adequate to produce death and exerted in such manner as to account for the disappearance of the body. The *corpus delicti* in murder has two components: death as the result, and the criminal agency of another as the means. Where there is direct proof of the one, the other can be established by circumstantial evidence.[3]

The *corpus delicti* must be proved like any other fact, that is, beyond a reasonable doubt, and that doubt is for the jury. A confession alone is not regarded as sufficient proof. The State must first produce sufficient evidence to send the case to the jury, and the jury are first to be satisfied, from that evidence, that the crime has been committed.[4]

The doctrine applies to other crimes, as, larceny. The possession of the fruits of a crime may do away with direct proof of the *corpus delicti*.[5]

Corpus Juris Civilis. See PANDECTS.

CORRELATIVE OBLIGATIONS. See ASSENT.

CORRESPONDENCE. See COMMUNICATION, Privileged, 2; LETTER, 3.

CORROBORATING. See CIRCUMSTANCES; EVIDENCE.

CORRUPT. 1. To taint, vitiate: as, to corrupt the blood, *q. v.*

2. To do an act for unlawful gain.

Corruption. An act done with intent to gain an advantage not consistent with official duty and the rights of others; something forbidden by law:[6] as, certain acts by arbitra-

[1] [Gulliver v. Roelle, 100 Ill. 147 (1881).
[2] Memphis City v. Dean, 8 Wall. 73 (1868), cases; Davenport v. Downs, 18 id. 627 (1873), cases.
[3] Ang. & A. Corp. § 5; Toledo Bank v. Bond, 1 Ohio St. 642 (1853).
[4] See Hadley, Rom. Law, 158-61.

[1] See Kountz v. Omaha Hotel Co., 107 U. S. 395 (1882); 67 Pa. 476; 70 id. 501; 75 id. 119.
[2] Jackson v. Ludeling, 99 U. S. 521 (1878); 106 id. 311.
[3] Ruloff v. People, 18 N. Y. 179, 182 (1858).
[4] Gray v. Commonwealth, 101 Pa. 386 (1882); Udderzook v. Commonwealth, 76 id. 340 (1874); Pitts v. State, 43 Miss. 480-82 (1870), cases; United States v. Williams, 1 Cliff. 25 (1858); 4 Crim. Law Mag. 902-12 (1883).
[5] See examples, 20 Blatch. 236; 10 F. R. 470; 26 Miss. 157; 59 id. 545; 15 Wend. 147; 14 Tex. Ap. 560; 1 Greenl. Ev. § 214; Whart. Cr. Ev. § 324.
[6] [Bouvier's Law Dict.

tors, election or other officers, trustees; a champertous contract; a contract for usury.

In an indictment for corrupt misbehavior in office the act must be distinctly charged as done knowingly and with a corrupt motive.[1]

See AWARD, 2; BRIBERY.

COST.[2] Of an article purchased for exportation: the price given for it, with every incidental charge, paid or supposed to be paid, at the place where the article is exported.[3]

Cost price. The price actually paid for a thing.[4]

COSTS. The expenses of an action recoverable from the losing party.[5]

An allowance to a party for expenses incurred in conducting his suit.[6]

The sums prescribed by law as charges for services enumerated in the fee-bill.[7]

"Fees" are a compensation to an officer for services rendered in the progress of a cause. Originally, fees were demandable the instant the services were rendered; but indulgence, ripened into a custom, and which has received the sanction of judicial decision, provides that the party should not be called upon to pay them till after the determination of the cause; when, to avoid suit for a trifling demand, it became the practice to include them in the execution as if they were a part of the successful party's costs.[7]

When a party in a litigated proceeding is duly adjudged to pay costs, his liability is not restricted to the disbursements and expenses which the opposite party may be entitled to receive, but extends to the fees of the officers of the court for services rendered therein. When these united sums are taxable in the case they constitute "the costs" for which he is liable. If the successful party collects them, he is trustee of the fees. As against the paying party, all the items are costs.[8]

Includes all charges fixed by statutes, as compensation for services rendered by officers of the court in the progress of a cause.[9]

Bill of costs. A statement of the items of costs incurred in a suit,—presented for taxation to an officer of the court.

In this connection "costs" means taxable costs.[1] The statement gives the names of the witnesses, days in attendance, and mileage.

Carry costs. A verdict is said to carry costs when he for whom it is found becomes entitled to the payment of all costs as an incident to the verdict.

Certificate of costs. A memorandum signed by the judge who tries a cause, that, under the law, a party is entitled to costs.[2]

Cost-bond. The bond or other security required of a party to a proceeding for the payment of such costs, if any, as may be awarded against him.

Costs de incremento. Costs by increase; increased costs — adjudged by the court in addition to such as the jury assess.

Before the statute of Gloucester, costs were enrolled as increase of damages. After the statute, juries taxed the damages, and costs, separately. When the amount so taxed was not sufficient to pay the costs of the suit, the plaintiff prayed that the officer might tax the costs inserted in the judgment: this was the origin of costs de incremento.[3]

Costs of prosecution. Costs incurred in conducting a prosecution; not, expenses in resisting the prosecution.[4]

Costs of suit. The expenses incurred pending a suit, as allowed by the court.[5]

May include commissions upon money collected by execution.[6]

Costs of the day. Costs incurred in preparing for trial on a particular day,—according to notice of trial given by a party.[7]

Costs of the term. May include only the expense of travel and attendance of the party, the clerk's and witnesses' fees.[8]

Costs that have accrued. In the compromise of a suit, costs that would follow the judgment.[9]

Costs to abide event. If the event is the same to the party who had the verdict at the former trial, he gets his costs; otherwise, the costs of the first trial are lost.[10]

---

[1] Boyd v. Commonwealth, 77 Va. 55-56 (1883), cases; 2 Whart. Cr. L. § 2518.

[2] L. con-stare, to "stand at."

[3] [Goodwin v. United States, 2 Wash. 499 (1811); 2 Mas. 398.

[4] [Buck v. Burk, 18 N. Y. 340 (1858).

[5] [Stanton County v. Madison County, 10 Neb. 308 (1880); State v. Dyches, 28 Tex. 542 (1866).

[6] Musser v. Good, 11 S. & R. *248 (1824), Gibson, J.

[7] Apperson v. Mut. Benefit Life Ins. Co., 38 N. J. L. 390 (1876), Depue, J.

[8] Janes's Appeal, 87 Pa. 431 (1878).

[9] Markham v. Ross, 73 Ga. 105 (1884); Davis v. State, 33 id. 533 (1863).

[1] Doe v. Thompson, 22 N. H. 219 (1850); Childs v. New Haven, &c. R. Co., 135 Mass. 572 (1883).

[2] See 3 Bl. Com. 214, 401.

[3] 3 Bl. Com. 399; Day v. Woodworth, 13 How. 372 (1851).

[4] State v. Wallin, 89 N. C. 578 (1883).

[5] [Norwich v. Hyde, 7 Conn. *534 (1829).

[6] Kitchen v. Woodfin, 1 Hughes, 340 (1877).

[7] See 3 Bl. Com. 357; Adams, Eq. 343.

[8] Thurston v. Mining Co., 1 R. I. 288 (1850).

[9] Tallassee Manuf. Co. v. Glenn, 50 Ala. 489 (1876).

[10] Jones v. Williams, L. R., 8 Q. B. 283 (1873); 2 Ex. Div. 287, 354; 3 id. 262.

Double costs; treble costs. 1. English practice. *Double costs:* common costs and half as much more. *Treble costs:* three times the amount of the costs incurred by a party in an action; common costs, half of these, and half of the latter.

"Double costs" were estimated by first allowing the prevailing party single costs, including witnesses' expenses, counsels' fees, etc., and then half the amount of the single costs, without deducting counsels' fees, etc. "Treble costs" consisted of single costs, half the single costs, and half of that half.[1]

Payment of treble costs was imposed for violation of certain statutes, as that of 29 Eliz. (1586), c. 4, against extortion by sheriffs on final process. Double and treble costs were repealed by 5 and 6 Vict. (1842), c. 97. Since then, only "party and party" costs, or reasonable costs, are taxable.

2. American practice. *Double costs:* in New York, and South Carolina, common costs and one-half more. *Treble costs:* common costs and three-fourths more.[2]

In Pennsylvania, double and treble costs mean double and treble the single costs.[3]

These additional costs seem to be given as compensation in cases of willful trespass or of vexatious litigation.

Interlocutory costs. Such costs as are given on various motions and proceedings in the course of a suit. **Final costs.** Such as depend upon the final event of the suit. To these the term "costs" generally applies.[4]

Security for costs. Security required of a plaintiff who is a non-resident of the State, that if he is defeated in his action he will pay all the costs thereof.

Until this is furnished he may not be allowed to proceed in his action. The defendant waives his right by taking any step in the cause after he has notice that the plaintiff is a non-resident. A general affidavit of defense may be first required. The law of the particular jurisdiction should be consulted for information as to details.[5]

Taxation of costs. Official adjustment of the amount of costs incurred in a case, or to which the prevailing party is entitled.

Costs are a necessary appendage to a judgment. The maxim is *victus victori in expensis condemnatus est,* the defeated, to the prevailing party, in the expenses is condemned. The common law allowed no costs to either party. If the plaintiff failed, he was "amerced;" if he recovered, the defendant was "at mercy" for detaining the amount of the debt. This in time was viewed as a hardship, and statute of 6 Edw. I (1277), c. 1, called the Statute of Gloucester, and which has been adopted in the States, was passed, giving costs in all cases where the plaintiff recovered damages. But no costs were allowed the defendant till the statute of 23 Hen. VIII (1531), c. 15, which, with later statutes, gave him, if he prevailed, such costs as the plaintiff would have received had he recovered.[1]

To prevent trifling and vexatious actions of trespass, it was enacted by 43 Eliz. (1600), c. 6, and 22 and 23 Car. (1670), c. 9, that where the jury awarded less damages than forty shillings the plaintiff should be allowed no more costs than damages, unless the judge certified that the freehold or title to the land chiefly came in question. But 8 and 9 Wm. III (1696), c. 11, provided that in actions wherein it appeared that the trespass was willful and malicious, and so certified by the judge, the plaintiff should recover full costs. These statutes are in force in a few of the States.[2]

The statute of Charles is restricted to actions of trespass *quare clausum fregit,* and of assault and battery; for in no other case is it possible to give the certificate. Moreover, to entitle the plaintiff to full costs, the judge's certificate must be made "at the trial of the cause;" that is, before final judgment.[3] In Pennsylvania currency, the forty shillings are equal to $5.33: the English shilling sterling not having been adopted.[4]

Costs are regulated entirely by statute, as to both item and amount. The Federal fee bill act of 1853, made section 983, Rev. St., provides that: "The bill of fees of the clerk, marshal, and attorney, and the amount paid printers and witnesses, and lawful fees for exemplifications and copies of papers necessarily obtained for use on trial in cases where by law costs are recoverable in favor of the prevailing party, shall be taxed by a judge or clerk of the court, and be included in and form a portion of a judgment or decree against the losing party. Such taxed bills shall be filed with the papers in the cause."

In the Federal courts, the prevailing party in common-law actions recovers costs in all cases, except when otherwise provided by an act of Congress.[5]

Section 968, Rev. St., providing that the prevailing party shall not be allowed costs when the recovery is less than $500, is imperative; the court has no discretion to allow costs where the judgment is under that sum.[6] See MARSHAL, 1 (2); PREVAIL.

The government, at common law, neither pays nor

---

[1] [Wharton's Law Dict.; 1 Chitty, Pr. 27; Brightly, Costs, 298.

[2] Patchin v. Parkhurst, 9 Wend. 443 (1832); 1 Harp. L. (S. C.) 440.

[3] Welsh v. Anthony, 16 Pa. 256 (1851); 2 Rawle, 201. See 34 N. J. L. 530.

[4] See Goodyear v. Sawyer, 17 F. R. 8–9 (1883).

[5] See 1 Daniel, Ch. Pr. 30; 10 Ves. 287; 18 F. R. 105; 18 Rep. 114; 18 How. Pr. 462; 60 Md. 375; 9 Wend. 262.

[1] 3 Bl. Com. 399–400; Day v. Woodworth, 13 How. 372 (1851); Antoni v. Greenhow, 107 U. S. 781 (1882); 26 Am. Law Reg. 693–98 (1878), cases; 17 F. R. 10–11; 29 Minn. 430.

[2] 3 Bl. Com. 214, 401; Winger v. Rife, 101 Pa. 152 (1882).

[3] Simonds v. Barton, 76 Pa. 485–37 (1874), cases; Towers v. Vielie, 1 Johns. Cas. 221 (1799).

[4] Chapman v. Calder, 14 Pa. 358 (1850).

[5] United States v. Treadwell, 15 F. R. 534 (1883); R. S. §§ 823, 983.

[6] Gibson v. Memphis, &c. R. Co., 31 F. R. 553 (1887).

receives costs; under statute, it may.[1] In admiralty, costs are left to the discretion of the court.[2] In equity, they are largely within the discretion of the chancellor.[3] In criminal law, in cases of conviction of felony, the prisoner pays the costs if he has property, and, in cases of acquittal, the government pays them; while in misdemeanors the accused, if convicted, is sentenced to pay them; and if acquitted he may be required to pay them where there was *prima facie* evidence of guilt; or the prosecutor may have to pay them; or, again, they may be divided between the prosecutor and the accused; or there may be authority for the government alone defraying them. If the accused cannot pay them he may have to remain in prison until discharged under the insolvent laws of the State. Costs do not bear interest.

See ATTORNEY; DAMAGES; DOCKET; FEE, 2.

COUNCIL. 1. An advisory body selected to assist the governor of a State in his official determinations.

King's councils. To assist him in the discharge of his duties, the maintenance of his dignity, and the exertion of his prerogative, the law has assigned the sovereign a diversity of councils with which to advise, to wit: the high court of parliament; the peers of the realm assembled at call; the judges of the courts of law; but, principally, his *privy council* (by way of eminence *the* council), an assembly of the king and such as he wills, in his palace.[4]

A governor's council is still retained in a few States.[5]

2. The ordinance-making body in a municipal corporation.

Usually in the plural form "councils;" whereof *common* and *select* council are the branches.

The organization and powers of such bodies are determined by statute.[6]

The city council of Boston, for example, is not a "legislature." It has no power to make "laws," but merely to pass ordinances upon such local matters as the legislature may commit to its charge. Neither branch is vested with any judicial functions whatever. Nor are its members chosen with a view to their fitness for the exercise of such functions.[7] See further CITY; CONTEMPT, 2; ORDINANCE, 1; TRIBUNAL.

COUNSEL; COUNSELLOR. See ATTORNEY, 2.

CONSILIUM. See INOPS.

COUNT. 1, *v.* In the sense of to compute, see ACCOUNT; DISCOUNT.

2. In the sense of to refer to a statute, compare RECITE.

3, *n.* In the sense of earl or *comes*, see SHERIFF.

4. In pleading, a distinct statement of the cause of action or of the ground of accusation.

Peculiar, therefore, to a declaration or an indictment. From the French *conte;* a narrative.

(1) In civil procedure at common law, is sometimes synonymous with declaration, its original signification; but now is generally considered as a part of a declaration, wherein the plaintiff sets forth a distinct cause of action.[1]

Where the plaintiff's complaint embraces a single cause of action and he makes one statement of it that statement is called, indifferently, a "declaration" or a "count." But where his suit embraces two or more causes of action (each of which of course requires a different statement), or when he makes two or more different statements of one and the same cause of action, each statement is called a "count," and all of them, collectively, constitute the "declaration,"[2] q. v.

Common counts. Distinct statements of a cause of action so varied as to correspond with the possible state of the proof.

In the common action of *assumpsit*, q. v., they are, ordinarily, for money—had and received, paid, lent, or due upon an account stated; perhaps, also, for the worth of work done and materials furnished: whence called "money" counts.[3] See CONTRACT, Implied.

Special count. States the facts peculiar to the case in hand.[4]

One object in inserting two or more counts in a declaration, when there is in fact but one cause of action, is to guard against the danger of an insufficient statement of the cause, where a doubt exists as to the legal sufficiency of one or another of two or more different modes of declaring. But the more usual end proposed is to accommodate the statement of the cause, as far as may be, to the possible state of the proof exhibited on the trial.

In *assumpsit*, under a declaration containing a special count on a promissory note, and also the common counts, a note varying from the one specially pleaded is admissible under the common counts, as evidence of money had and received, in connection with evi-

---

[1] 3 Bl. Com. 400; 3 Cranch, 73; 2 Wheat. 395; 12 *id.* 546; 5 How. 29; 3 Pa. 153.

[2] The Scotland, 118 U. S. 519 (1886).

[3] See 2 Daniel, Ch. Pr. 1515-21; Goodyear *v.* Sawyer, 17 F. R. 6 (1883), cases.

[4] 1 Bl. Com. 227-32.

[5] See 70 Me. 570.

[6] See Dillon, Munic. Corp. 326.

[7] Whitcomb's Case, 120 Mass. 123 (1876), Gray, C. J.

---

[1] [Cheetham *v.* Tillotson, 5 Johns. [4]435 (1809).

[2] Gould, Pl. 158.

[3] See, as to money had and received, Barnett *v.* Warren, 82 Ala. 557 (1886); 20 Cent. Law J. 326-30 (1885), cases, as to *quantum meruit.*

[4] See Nash *v.* Towne, 5 Wall. 702 (1866).

dence that the defendant admitted his indebtedness on the note.[1]

Counts for contract and trespass, being dissimilar in kind, cannot be joined.[2] See BAD, 2; DUPLICITY; JOINDER.

(2) In criminal procedure, each count in an indictment imports a different offense; is, in effect, a separate indictment.[3]

When a verdict is silent as to one or more counts and finds guilt as to others, presumably the jury found the defendant not guilty as to the former counts.[4]

See INDICTMENT; SENTENCE.

COUNTER. Contrary, in opposition to. See CONTRA.

As a prefix, denotes that one thing is, or is placed, in antagonism to some other: as, a counter-affidavit, counter-bond, counter-claim, counter-evidence, counter-plea, counter-proof, counter-statement, counter-surety,— for each of which see the simple substantive. Compare CROSS, 3.

COUNTERFEIT, v. To make something falsely and fraudulently in the semblance of that which is true; also, the thing so made.

n. A spurious imitation intended to resemble something which is not.[5]

Refers, ordinarily, to imitations of money or of securities. But a trade-mark (*q. v.*) may be counterfeited.

The resemblance of the spurious to the genuine must be such, possibly, as to deceive a person using ordinary caution.[6]

"False, forged, and counterfeit," said of counterfeiting Treasury notes, necessarily imply that the instrument so characterized is not genuine, but only purports to be, or is in the similitude of the genuine instrument.[7]

It is not necessary in an indictment, under § 5457, Rev. St., to allege that the act of counterfeiting was done with intent to defraud; such intent, if an element of the crime, is implied in the allegation of "falsely" making.[8]

On counterfeiting the securities of the United States, see Rev. St. § 5413.[9]

Counterfeiting, passing, or possessing with intent to utter or pass, within the United States, the notes, or other securities of any foreign government, is punishable by fine and imprisonment at hard labor; and so is having in one's possession, without lawful authority, any plate therefor or printing from the same.[1]

Under the power "to define and punish offenses against the law of nations," and to "regulate commerce with foreign nations," Congress may provide for punishing as a crime the counterfeiting, within the United States, of the notes of foreign banks or corporations, although they be not the obligations of the foreign government.[2]

See FALSE; FORGE, 2; GENUINE; GUILT; OBLIGATION, 2; SIMILITUDE; SPURIOUS; UTTER.

COUNTERPART. One of the parts of an indenture which lay opposite or counter to each other.[3] A duplicate copy.

Indentures were originally written twice on the same sheet of parchment with a space in the middle — where it was afterward divided.[3]

When the several parts of an indenture are interchangeably executed by the parties that part or copy which is executed by the grantor is called the *original*, and the rest *counterparts*.[4]

COUNTERSIGN. 1. To sign on the opposite side.

2. To sign in addition to another, as the superior officer, and in attestation of authenticity.[5] See SIGN, Countersign.

COUNTERVAIL. To operate with equal effect: to deserve equal consideration.

An equitable right which is as important or well founded as another which is being pressed for the more favorable recognition, is spoken of as a "countervailing equity."

COUNTRY.[6] 1. In its primary meaning, signifies place; in a larger sense, the territory or dominions occupied by a community, or even waste and unpeopled sections or regions of the earth; but its metaphorical meaning (which is no less definite and well understood) in common parlance, in historical and geographical writings, in diplomacy, legislation, treaties, and international codes, denotes the population, the nation, the state, the government, having possession and dominion over the country.[7] See PLACE, 1.

As used in the revenue laws, embraces all the possessions of a foreign state, however widely separated,

---

[1] Hopkins *v.* Orr, 124 U. S. 513 (1888), cases.

[2] Gould, Pl. 159; 3 Bl. Com. 295; 58 N. H. 41.

[3] United States *v.* Malone, 20 Blatch. 140 (1881): R. S. § 1024; s. c. 13 Rep. 67.

[4] State *v.* McNaught, 36 Kan. 627 (1887), cases.

[5] Queen *v.* Hermann, 4 Q. B, D. 287 (1879). See 1 Stew., Ala., 386; 1 Ohio St. 187.

[6] United States *v.* Bogart, 9 Bened. 315 (1878).

[7] [United States *v.* Howell, 11 Wall. 432, 436 (1870), Miller, J. See 2 Flip. 557; 13 F. R. 96; Const. Art. I, sec. 8, cl. 6.

[8] United States *v.* Otey, 31 F. R. 68 (1887).

[9] See also United States *v.* Bennett, 17 Blatch. 358 (1879); 22 F. R. 390.

[1] Act 16 May, 1884: 23 St. L. 22.

[2] United States *v.* Arjona, 120 U. S. 479 (1887), Waite, Chief Justice.

[3] [Burrill's Law Dict.

[4] 2 Bl. Com. 296.

[5] See Smith, Eq. 212, 181; 101 U. S. 22.

[6] F. *contree:* L. *contra*, opposite: that which lies opposite to a city.

[7] United States *v.* "The Recorder," 1 Blatch. 225 (1847), Betts, J.

which are subject to the same supreme executive and legislative control.[1] See INDIAN, Country.

2. The inhabitants of a district from which a jury is to be summoned; a jury.

Trial by jury is also called trial *per pais*, or *per patrian*, by the country.[2]

By the policy of the ancient law the jury was to come *de vicineto*, from the neighborhood of the place where the cause of action was laid. For, living in the neighborhood, they were properly the very country, or *pais*, to which both parties had appealed, and were supposed to know beforehand the characters of the parties and their witnesses. But this convenience being overbalanced by the fact that jurors coming from the immediate neighborhood naturally intermixed their prejudices and partialities in the trial, the early practice became so far relinquished that the jury now comes from the body of the county at large, and not *de vicineto*, from the particular neighborhood.[3] See VENUE.

Conclude to the country. To tender an issue of fact for trial by a jury.

God and my country. The answer, at common law, of a prisoner arraigned for trial. See ARRAIGN.

Put upon the country. To submit a matter in dispute to a jury.

The full expression, on the part of the plaintiff, is, "And this the said A prays may be inquired of by the country;" on the part of the defendant, "And of this the said B puts himself upon the country."[4] Compare PAIS; PATRIA.

COUNTY. Originally, a province governed by a count,— the earl or alderman to whom the government of the shire was intrusted.[5]

A civil division of the territory of England.[6]

The terms "the county" and the "people of the county" may be convertible; so, too, "the county" and the "commissioners of the county."[7]

The city of St. Louis, under the constitution of Missouri of 1875, though not a county as that word is ordinarily used in the constitution, is in a qualified sense a county, being a "legal subdivision of the State" which bears county relations to the State, and having many important attributes of a county.[8]

A county is not a corporation, but a mere political organization of a certain portion of the territory within the State, particularly defined by geographical limits, for the more convenient administration of the laws and police power of the State, and for the convenience of the inhabitants.[1]

Such organization is invested with certain powers, delegated by the State, for the purpose of civil administration; and for the same purpose is clothed with many characteristics of a body corporate. It is a *quasi* corporation, for in many respects it is like a corporation. But the power to sue and be sued is expressly conferred by statute.[1]

In the Revised Statutes, or in any act or resolution of Congress, the word county shall include a "parish" or any other equivalent subdivision of a State or Territory.[2]

"Establishing" a county is setting apart certain territory to be in the future organized as a political community, or *quasi* corporation for political purposes; "organizing" a county is vesting in the people of the territory such corporate rights and powers.[3]

County corporate. A city or town, with more or less territory annexed, to which, out of special favor, the king has granted the privilege to be a county of itself, and not to be comprised within another county.[4]

Similar to this are the counties of Philadelphia, New York, and Boston.[5]

Foreign county. Another county than the one in which a matter arises or is drawn in question.

Body of a county. 1. The territorial limits of a county. See BODY, 3.

2. The people of a county collectively considered. See VENUE.

County bridge. See BRIDGE.

County court. 1. A name for a class of courts having civil jurisdiction in controversies of medium grade, varied powers in the charge and care of persons and estates within legal guardianship, a limited criminal jurisdiction, appellate jurisdiction over justices of the peace, and numerous powers and duties in the administration of county affairs.[6]

2. In England, a court of great antiquity,

---

[1] Stairs *v.* Peaslee, 18 How. 526 (1855), Taney, C. J. See Campbell *v.* Barney, 5 Blatch. 221 (1864).

[2] 3 Bl. Com. 349; 4 *id.* 348.

[3] 3 Bl. Com. 359-60.

[4] 3 Bl. Com. 313.

[5] [1 Bl. Com. 116; Eastman *v.* Clackamas Co., 32 F. R. 29 (1887).

[6] 1 Bl. Com. 113.

[7] County Court *v.* Sievert, 58 Mo. 201 (1874); Carder *v.* Fayette County, 16 Ohio St. 369 (1865).

[8] State *v.* Finn, 4 Mo. Ap. 350 (1877).

[1] Hunter *v.* Commissioners, 10 Ohio St. 520 (1860); Harris *v.* Supervisors, 105 Ill. 451 (1883); Washer *v.* Bullitt County, 110 U. S. 564 (1884); Faulkner *v.* Hyman, 142 Mass. 54 (1886); Vincent *v.* Lincoln Co., 30 F. R. 749-53 (1887), cases; 33 Ark. 497; 14 Fla. 321; 2 Kan. 128; 50 Md. 245; 8 Minn. 504; 10 Nev. 552; 7 Ohio St. 109; 10 F. R. 545.

As to suits by and against counties, see 19 Cent. Law J. 185-88 (1884), cases.

[2] Act 13 July, 1866: R. S. §§ 1-2.

[3] State *v.* Parker, 25 Minn. 219 (1878); 23 *id.* 40.

[4] [1 Bl. Com. 120.

[5] See State *v.* Finn, 4 Mo. Ap. 347 (1877).

[6] [Abbott's Law Dict.

incident to the jurisdiction of the sheriff. It seems to have had cognizance of purely personal actions and of some real actions; but it was not a court of record.[1]

Since 1846, a tribunal, established under 9 and 10 Vict. c. 95, in upward of five hundred districts, none within the city of London; and at present invested with a common-law jurisdiction over demands not exceeding £50, an equity jurisdiction where the amount involved does not exceed £500, together with certain jurisdiction in probate, admiralty, and bankruptcy.[2]

County officer. One by whom a county performs its usual political functions,— its functions of government; who exercises "continuously, and as a part of the regular and permanent administration of government, its public powers, trusts, or duties."[3]

He may be the auditor, commissioner, supervisor, treasurer, or other functionary of the county. Local statutes usually designate who shall be considered county officers, and prescribe their duties.

County purpose. May include only the ordinary purposes, as the ordinary expenses, of a county.[4]

County seat. See PERMANENT.

Power of the county. The male inhabitants of a county, over fifteen years of age, whom the sheriff may command to aid him in preserving the peace, executing process, arresting felons, etc.; the *posse comitatus*.[5]

See SHERIFF; CORONER; WARRANT, 2.

COUPLED. See INTEREST, 2 (2), Coupled.

COUPON.[6] Something "cut off" from another thing: a distinct part of a document or instrument, intended to be separated from the body thereof and used as evidence of something connected with it or mentioned in it.

Coupon bond. Ordinarily, by "coupon" is meant a part of a transferable bond or certificate of loan, designed to be separated therefrom and used as evidence of interest due by the terms thereof. The original or primary obligations are called *coupon bonds*.

An instrument complete in itself, and yet composed of several distinct instruments, each of which is in itself as complete as the whole together.[1]

Such coupons are merely interest warrants or interest-certificates — written contracts for the payment of a definite sum of money on a given day.[2]

Most of the bonds of municipal bodies and private corporations are issued in order to raise funds for works of large extent and cost, and their payment is therefore made at distant periods. Coupons for the installments of interest are usually attached, in the expectation that they will be paid as they mature, however distant the period for the payment of the principal. These coupons, when severed from the bonds, are negotiable and pass by delivery. They then cease to be incidents, become in fact independent claims; and they do not lose their validity, if for any cause the bonds are canceled or paid before maturity, nor their negotiable character, nor their ability to support separate actions. Once severed from the bonds, and having matured, they are in effect equivalent to separate bonds for the different installments of interest.[3]

The holder is enabled to collect the interest at the time and place named, or to transfer the coupon to another who may collect it, without the trouble of presenting the bond itself. This is a convenience to the foreign holder. The device tends to enhance the marketableness of interest-bearing securities, and is favored by the courts.[4]

The form does not change their nature. That they are payable at a particular place does not make it necessary to aver or prove a presentation for payment there.[5]

Suit may be maintained upon a coupon without producing the bond; but the provisions in the bond must be recited in such a general way as to explain the relation the coupon originally held, and still holds, to it. Recovery may then be had for the face amount, with interest from the day when payment was unjustly refused, and exchange at the place of payment.[4]

When a coupon upon its face refers to the bond, the purchaser is chargeable with notice of all that the bond contains.[6]

These separable obligations bear interest after their maturity. An unpaid coupon left on a bond is not of itself evidence that the bond is dishonored.[7]

Interest coupons are instruments of a peculiar nature. Title to them passes by mere delivery. A

[1] See 3 Bl. Com. 35; 3 Law Quar. Rev. 1–13 (1887).

[2] See 1 Abbott, Law Dict. 299; 59 Law Times, 379 (1875).

[3] [Sheboygan County v. Barker, 3 Wall. 96 (1866), Grier, J. See Re Whiting, 2 Barb. 517 (1848); Re Carpenter, 7 id. 34 (1849); State, ex rel. v. Glenn, 7 Heisk. 472 (1872).

[4] McCormick v. Fitch, 14 Minn. 257 (1869). See also 23 Ohio St. 339; 1 Sneed, 637.

[5] 1 Bl. Com. 343; 4 id. 122; Regina v. Brown, 1 Carr. & M. *314 (1841).

[6] Koo'-pŏng. F. from couper, to cut, cut off.

[1] 2 Daniel, Neg. Inst. § 1488 (1879). See Myers v. York, &c. R. Co., 43 Me. 239–40 (1857); Ethoven v. Hoyle, 13 C. B. 372 (1853).

[2] Aurora City v. West, 7 Wall. 105 (1868), cases.

[3] Clark v. Iowa City, 20 Wall. 589 (1874), cases, Field, J.; Hartman v. Greenhow, 102 U. S. 684 (1880); Walnut v. Wade, 103 id. 696 (1880); Thompson v. Perrine, 106 id. 592 (1882); Kerr v. City of Corry, 105 Pa. 282 (1884).

[4] City of Kenosha v. Lamson, 9 Wall. 477, 482–85 (1869), Nelson, J.

[5] Walnut v. Wade, 103 U. S. 695 (1880).

[6] McLure v. Township of Oxford, 94 U. S. 432 (1876), Waite, C. J.

[7] Indiana & Illinois Central R. Co. v. Sprague, 103 U. S. 761–63 (1880), cases.

transfer of possession is presumptively a transfer of title.[1]

When issued by competent authority they pass into the hands of a *bona fide* purchaser for value before maturity, freed from any infirmity in their origin. As with other negotiable paper mere suspicion that there may be a defect of title in the holder, or knowledge of circumstances which would excite suspicion as to his title in the mind of any prudent man, is not sufficient to impair the title of the purchaser. That result will only follow where there has been bad faith on his part.[2]

Being complete instruments, capable of sustaining separate actions without reference to the maturity of the bond, the statute of limitations begins to run from the time when they respectively mature.[3] See BOND; EX, 3; IMPAIR.

Coupon note. A promissory note with coupons attached, which, in number, correspond to the payments of interest.

The original note may be secured by a mortgage. A form in Iowa reads thus:

$——.   —— —— 1888.

On the —— day of ——, 188—, I promise to pay to —— —— or order, —— dollars. Being semi-annual interest to that date on my note for —— dollars, due —— 188—. Payable at ——.

No. ——.   —— ——.

Coupon stamp. The Government furnishes collectors of its revenue books of stamps having coupons attached, to be used when taxes are paid on spirits.

There are nine coupons to each stamp representing a decimal, all printed between the stamp and the stub. Upon the receipt of a distiller's tax, for example, the officer detaches a stamp with such number of coupons attached as corresponds to the number of proof-gallons in the cask, as shown by the gauger's return. Unused coupons remain with the stub; if detached, they are of no value.[4]

Coupon ticket. Sets or books of tickets issued by carriers of passengers, providing that for each trip had, according to the terms of the contract, a ticket shall be detached or

canceled, are called "coupon tickets" or tickets in the "coupon form."

When the carriage is confined to the issuing line, the ticket is a contract to carry according to its own terms; but when there is one ticket for carriage over that line and other tickets as passports over other lines, the first carrier is ordinarily only agent for the others, except in cases of express contract to the contrary.[1] See CARRIER, Common.

COURSE. 1. The direction of a line with reference to a meridian. See BOUNDARY; HEARSAY, 3; MONUMENT, 1.

2. Routine; practice; procedure. Compare CURSUS.

Course of an action. Progressive action in a suit or proceeding not yet determined.[2]

Due course or **process of law.** Law in its regular administration. See further PROCESS, 1.

"Due course" and "due process" of law mean the same thing.[3]

Of course. Said of a thing done in the common manner of proceeding, and which does not require special allowance of a judge of the court.

Many rules and citations are taken or had, as "of course," by application to the clerk or prothonotary of the court.

3. The usual way or mode; usage; custom.

Course of business, or **of trade.** The way ordinarily pursued in a particular calling. See BUSINESS; TRADE.

"Due course of trade," with respect to the negotiation of a note, is where the holder has given for it money, goods, or credit at the time of receiving it, or has on account of it sustained some loss or incurred some liability.[4]

Course of a voyage. The customary track between ports. See DEVIATION.

COURT.[5] 1. According to Cowel, the house where the king remains with his reti-

---

[1] Ketchum v. Duncan, 96 U. S. 662 (1877).

[2] Cromwell v. County of Sac, 96 U. S. 57 (1877), Field, J.; Murray v. Lardner, 2 Wall. 110–121 (1864), cases.

[3] Koshkonong v. Burton, 104 U. S. 668, 675 (1881). See Virginia Coupon Cases, 114 *id.* 269–340 (1885); generally, 1 Wall. 83, 175, 384; 3 *id.* 327; 10 *id.* 68; 11 *id.* 139; 14 *id.* 232; 15 *id.* 355; 19 *id.* 83; 21 *id.* 354; 92 U. S. 502, 569; 93 *id.* 502; 94 *id.* 351, 463, 741, 801; 96 *id.* 659; 97 *id.* 96, 272; 99 *id.* 112, 362, 434, 499, 686; 101 *id.* 87, 677; 104 *id.* 505; 105 *id.* 370, 733; 106 *id.* 663; 107 *id.* 529, 539, 568, 711, 769; 15 Blatch. 343–46; 16 *id.* 54; 17 *id.* 4; 18 *id.* 383; 26 Conn. 121; 53 Ind. 191; 109 Mass. 88; 112 *id.* 53; 49 Me. 507; 2 Nev. 199; 57 N. H. 397; 82 N. C. 382; 66 N. Y. 14; 44 Pa. 63; 22 Gratt. 833; 1 Daniel, Neg. Inst. Ch. XLVII.

[4] R. S. § 3313.

(18)

[1] See Baltimore, &c. R. Co. v. Harris, 12 Wall. 65 (1870); Hudson v. Kansas Pacific R. Co., 3 McCrary, 249 (1882); Keep v. Indianapolis, &c. R. Co., *ib.* 208, 214–19 (1882), cases; Quimby v. Vanderbilt, 17 N. Y. 313 (1858); Milnor v. New York & New Haven R. Co., 53 *id.* 363, 369–71 (1873), cases; Kessler v. New York & Hudson R. Co., 61 *id.* 541 (1875); Hartan v. Eastern R. Co., 114 Mass. 44 (1873); Wolff v. Central R. Co., 68 Ga. 653 (1882); 23 Conn. 457; 29 Vt. 421; 26 Ala. 733.

[2] Williams v. Ely, 14 Wis. *238 (1861), Dixon, C. J.

[3] Adler v. Whitbeck, 44 Ohio St. 569 (1886).

[4] [Kimbro v. Lytle, 10 Yerg. 428 (1837), Reese, J.; Merchants' Bank v. McClelland, 9 Col. 608 (1886).

[5] F. *cort, curt, court,* a court or yard; also, a tribunal: L. *cortis,* a court-yard, court, palace: L. *cors,* an inclosure: co-, together; *hort-us,* a garden, yard,—Skeat. Orig. from L. *cers,* a pen, a fortified place, a palace,—Müller, Science Lang. 269. Compare CURTILAGE.

nue; also, the place where justice is administered.

These two meanings, in the beginning, were closely connected. For, in early history, when the king was actually the fountain and dispenser of justice, nothing could be more natural than that subjects who had complaints of ill-treatment to make should use the expression "the court," in speaking of the journey to the place where the king was domiciled, and the application to him preferred, usually in the court of the palace, for interference and redress. Anciently, then, the "court," for judicial purposes, was the king and his attendants; later, those who sojourned or traveled with him, to whom he delegated authority to determine controversies and to dispense justice.[1]

The earlier courts were merely assemblages, in the court-yard of the baron or of the king himself, of those whose duty it was to appear at stated times, or upon summons. Traces of this constitution of courts remain in tribunals for the trial of impeachments, and in the control exercised by legislatures over the organization of courts of justice, as constituted in modern times. Indeed, parliament is still the "High Court of Parliament," and in Massachusetts the united legislative bodies are entitled the "General Court."[2]

A place where justice is judicially administered.[3]

The more effectually to accomplish the redress of private injuries, courts of justice are instituted to protect the weak from the insults of the strong, by expounding and enforcing those laws by which rights are defined and wrongs prohibited.[4]

As the executive power of the law is vested in the king, courts of justice, which are the medium by which he administers that law, originate with this power of the crown. . . . He is represented by his judges.[5]

In every court there must be: an *actor*, plaintiff, who complains of an injury; a *reus*, defendant, who is called upon to make satisfaction; and a *judex*, judicial power to examine the truth of the fact, determine the law arising thereon, and, for injury done, by its officers to apply the remedy.[5]

A tribunal established for the public administration of justice, and composed of one or more judges, who sit for that purpose at fixed times and places, attended by proper officers.[7]

An organized body, with defined powers, meeting at certain times and places for the hearing and decision of causes and other matters brought before it, and aided in this by its officers, viz., attorneys and counsel to present and manage the business, clerks to

record and attest its acts and decisions, and ministerial officers to execute its commands and secure order in its proceedings.[1]

Proceedings at another time and place or in another manner than that specified by law, though in the personal presence and under the direction of a judge, are *coram non judice*, and void.[2]

The definition given by Coke (and Blackstone) lacks fullness: it is limited to the *place* of a court. There must also be the presence of the officers constituting the court, the judge or judges certainly, and probably the clerk authorized to record the action taken; time must be regarded, too, for the officers of a court must be present at the place and time appointed by law. To give existence to a court, then, its officers, and the time and place of holding it, must be such as are prescribed by law. . . . "Open court" conveys the idea that the court must be in session, organized for the transaction of judicial business. It may mean public, free to all.[3]

A permanent organization for the administration of justice; not a special tribunal provided for by law, occasionally called into existence and ceasing to exist with particular exigencies.[4] See further TRIBUNAL.

2. The judge charged with deciding the law in a given case; as opposed to the jury, who are triers of the fact.

The term "court" may mean the "judge" or "judges" of the court, or the judge and the jury, according to the connection, and the object of its use.[5] See JUDGE; JUDICIARY.

For the speedy, universal, and impartial administration of justice the law has appointed a variety of courts, some with a more limited, others with a more extensive jurisdiction; some to determine in the first instance, others upon appeal and by way of review. Of these the most important are:

Civil court. A court instituted for the enforcement of private rights and the redress of private wrongs; any court which administers civil law. Criminal court. Any tribunal for the redress of public wrongs — crimes and misdemeanors. Ecclesiastical court. Such judicatory as enforces law made by a religious body for its own government. See CHURCH.

Court of law, or court of common law. Any court which administers justice according to the principles and forms of the com-

---

[1] [Abbott's Law Dict.
[2] [Bouvier's Law Dict.
[3] 3 Bl. Com. 23: Coke, Litt. 58.
[4] 3 Bl. Com. 2.
[5] 3 Bl. Com. 23–24; 1 *id.* 270.
[6] 3 Bl. Com. 25; 34 Ill. 360; 14 F. R. 178.
[7] *Mason v. Woerner*, 18 Mo. 570 (1853), Gamble, J.

[1] [Burrill's Law Dict.
[2] See *Wightman v. Karsner*, 20 Ala. 451 (1852); *Brumley v. State*, 20 Ark. 78 (1859).
[3] *Hobart v. Hobart*, 45 Iowa, 503 (1877), Beck, J. See *Lewis v. Hoboken*, 42 N. J. L. 379 (1880).
[4] [*Shurburn v. Hooper*, 40 Mich. 505 (1879); *Streeter v. Paton*, 7 *id.* 348 (1859), Manning, J.
[5] See *Gold v. Vermont Central R. Co.*, 19 Vt. 482 (1847); *Michigan Central R. Co. v. Northern Indiana R. Co.*, 3 Ind. 245 (1851); 13 R. I. 401.

mon law. **Court of chancery, or of equity.** A court which proceeds wholly according to the principles of equity, *q. v.*

Court of original jurisdiction. Such court as is to exercise jurisdiction over a matter in the first instance. **Court of appellate jurisdiction.** Is organized to review causes removed from another court or courts. **Court of general jurisdiction.** Takes cognizance of all causes, civil or criminal, of a particular nature. **Court of limited or special jurisdiction.** May have cognizance over a few matters only.

Inferior court. A court subordinate to another; or, a court of limited jurisdiction. **Superior court.** A court with controlling authority over some other court or courts, and with certain original jurisdiction of its own. **Supreme court.** A court of the highest jurisdiction; also, a court higher than some other court or courts, but not necessarily of last resort.

Inferior courts. All courts from which an appeal lies are "inferior" to the court to which their judgments may be carried — as are the circuit and district courts of the United States, but they are not, therefore, "inferior courts" in the technical sense as applying to courts of a special and limited jurisdiction, which are created on such principles that their judgments, taken alone, are entirely disregarded, and the proceedings must *show* their jurisdiction.[1] See further APPARERE, De non, etc.

Superior courts. Courts in Connecticut, Delaware, Georgia, Massachusetts, and North Carolina, whose jurisdiction extends throughout the whole of a defined district or of the whole State. In a few other States, the title of a court or courts organized in a particular city or county, additional to the general system; as in one or more counties of Illinois, Indiana, Maine, Maryland, and Michigan.

Supreme courts. The supreme courts of New Hampshire, Pennsylvania, and Vermont, the "supreme courts of appeal" of Virginia and West Virginia, and the "supreme judicial courts" of Maine and Massachusetts, in addition to their appellate powers, exercise an additional jurisdiction, more or less general, in the issuing of the prerogative writs of *mandamus*, prohibition, *quo warranto*, etc. In New Jersey the supreme court is the highest court of law of original jurisdiction; and in New York a court, next to the court of appeals, with certain general original jurisdiction coupled with some appellate powers. In Connecticut the court of last resort is called the "supreme court of errors." In most, if not quite all, of the other States, the name supreme court, for a court possessing the general characteristics above described, is applied to the court of last resort.[1] As to the Supreme Court of the United States, see page 278.

Court of record. A court in which the acts and judicial proceedings are enrolled on parchment for a perpetual memorial and testimony. . . All such are the king's courts; no other has authority to fine and imprison: so that the erection of a new jurisdiction with this power makes it instantly a court of record. **Court not of record.** Originally, the court of a private man, whom the law would not intrust with discretionary power over the fortune or liberty of his fellow-subjects: as, the courts-baron and other inferior jurisdictions where the proceedings were not enrolled or recorded, and which could hold no plea of a matter cognizable by the common law, unless under the value of forty shillings, nor of any forcible injury, not having process of arrest.[2]

The existence or truth of what is done in a court not of record can, if disputed, be tried and determined by a jury; but nothing can be averred against a "record,"[2] *q. v.*

A court of record is a judicial, organized tribunal having attributes and exercising functions independently of the person of the magistrate designated generally to hold it, and proceeding according to the course of the common law.[3]

The power to fine and imprison was not an indispensable attribute of a court of record. In modern law, the fact that a permanent record is kept may not stamp this character upon a court; since numerous courts of limited or special jurisdiction are obliged to keep records and yet are held to be courts not of record.[4]

Courts of record are sometimes distinguished by the possession and use of a *seal.*

There is high authority for making the fact that a court is a court of record the test which confers upon its proceedings, in a particular case (falling within the general scope of its jurisdiction), the presumption of jurisdiction, rather than the fact that it is a superior court of general common-law powers.[5]

---

[1] [Kempe *v.* Kennedy, 5 Cranch, 185 (1809), Marshall, C. J. See M'Cormick *v.* Sullivant, 10 Wheat. 199 (1825); *Exp.* Watkins, 3 Pet. *205 (1830); Grignon *v.* Astor, 2 How. 341 (1844); Kennedy *v.* Georgia State Bank, 8 *id.* 611 (1850); *Exp.* Lathrop, 118 U. S. 113 (1886); Cooley, Const. Lim. 508–9, cases.

[1] See 2 Abbott's Law Dict.

[2] [3 Bl. Com. 24–25, 331. See 10 Watts, 24; 34 Cal. 422; 23 Wend. 377; 37 Mo. 29.

[3] See *Exp.* Gladhill, 8 Metc. 170 (1844), Shaw, C. J.

[4] See 1 Bouvier's Law Dict. 426.

[5] Davis *v.* Hudson, 29 Minn. 35 (1881); Freeman, Judgm. § 122, cases.

Minor terms descriptive of courts are: **Court above** or **ad quem.** To which a cause is taken from another and inferior court. Opposed, **court below** or **a quo:** such lower court, from which the cause is removed. **Local court.** For the trial of causes within comparatively narrow territorial limits: also, the court of a State, as opposed to the court of the United States to which a cause may be removed. **Full court.** A session of a court at which all the members are present.

Other terms descriptive of special courts will be found explained in their alphabetical places, as see, in addition to the entries following, APPEAL; ARBITRATION; ERROR, 2 (3); IMPEACH, 4; MOOT; MARTIAL; NISI PRIUS; OYER AND TERMINER; PROBATE.

See also phrases beginning BREAST; BY; DAY; FRIEND; LEAVE; OUT; OPEN.

And see related terms, such as ATTORNEY; BENCH; CHAMBER; CLERK; COMITY; CONSTITUTION; CONTEMPT, 1; COSTS; CRIER; DEPOSITION; DISCRETION, 3-5; JUDGE; JUDGMENT; JUDICIAL; JUDICIARY; JURISDICTION, 2; JURY; LAW; NEWSPAPER; NOTICE, 1, Judicial; PAYMENT; PLEADING; PRÆSUMPTIO; PROCEDURE; RECORD, 2; RULE, 2; SESSION; TERM, 4; VACATION.

Compare CURIA; FORUM.

COURTS OF ENGLAND. Statutes of 36 and 37 Vict. c. 66, and 38 and 39 Vict. c. 77, both of which went into effect November 1, 1875, consolidated into one supreme court of judicature the high court of chancery, and the courts of queen's bench, common pleas, exchequer, admiralty, probate, and divorce and matrimonial causes. The supreme court has two divisions: the high court of justice and the court of appeal; the former of which has original and some appellate jurisdiction, and the latter appellate and some original jurisdiction. The lord chief justice is president of the former court, the lord chancellor of the latter.

To the high court of justice there are five *divisions:* chancery; queen's bench; common pleas; exchequer; probate, divorce, and admiralty. To each of these divisions are assigned the judges of the old courts similarly named, and the jurisdictions of those courts. Each division has its series of reports; another series comprises the decisions of the court of appeal — "appeal cases."

Besides these courts of superior jurisdiction are numerous others of inferior or local jurisdiction, and also ecclesiastical courts.[1] See JUDICATURE, Acts.

As to the older English courts, see[2] ADMIRALTY; AULA; CHANCERY; CORONER; COUNTRY, 2; COUNTY, Court, 2; EXCHEQUER; FEUDS; KING; ORDINARY, 2; OYER; PLEA, 1; STAR-CHAMBER.

COURTS OF SCOTLAND. The court of session, the supreme civil court, consists of two divisions of four judges each, who together form the *inner house,* and of five judges (lords ordinary) who form the *outer house.* The judges of the outer house are judges of the first instance, with co-ordinate authority, except as to certain classes of cases appropriated to the junior, the second junior, and the third junior lord ordinary, respectively. The inner house, which is mainly a court of review, consists of the first division, presided over by the lord president, and the second division, presided over by the lord justice clerk. No action can be brought in the court of session for an amount under twenty-five pounds.[1]

COURTS OF THE STATES. There is no uniformity among our States as to the number, name, or organization of their courts. Each State has some tribunal of last resort, with numerous subordinate tribunals; but the mode in which they are created, the extent of their jurisdiction, the selection of the judges and their terms of office and duties, are matters upon which each State legislates for itself. By name these courts are: a supreme court, court of appeals, or court of errors and appeals; courts of common pleas, county courts, or circuit courts for one or more counties; orphans', probate, or surrogates' courts; courts of sessions; recorders' courts; city courts; superior courts; district courts; aldermen's or justices' courts.

For an account of which, see those titles, and the names or titles and references on page 275.

COURTS OF THE UNITED STATES. "The judicial Power of the United States shall be vested in one supreme Court, and in such inferior Courts as the Congress may from time to time ordain and establish."[2]

"The judicial Power shall extend to all Cases, in Law and Equity, arising under this Constitution, the Laws of the United States, and Treaties made, or which shall be made, under their Authority; — to all Cases affecting Ambassadors, other public Ministers and Consuls; — to all Cases of admiralty and

---

[1] See Preface to 15 Moak's Reports, i-xv; 2 Law Q. Rev. 1-11 (1886).

[2] 3 Bl. Com. Ch. III-VI.

---

[1] See 37 Alb. Law J. 4-7 (1888)

[2] Constitution, Art. III, sec. 1.

maritime Jurisdiction; — to Controversies to which the United States shall be a Party; — to Controversies between two or more States; — between a State and Citizens of another State; — between Citizens of different States; — between Citizens of the same State claiming Lands under Grants of different States, and between a State, or the Citizens thereof, and foreign States, Citizens or Subjects." [1] See POWER, 3.

The judges are appointed by the President, by and with the advice and consent of the Senate; and they hold office during good behavior. [2]

The oath taken by justices of the Supreme Court, the circuit and the district judges, is as follows:

"I, —— ——, do solemnly swear (or affirm) that I will administer justice without respect to persons, and do equal right to the poor and to the rich, and that I will faithfully and impartially discharge and perform all the duties incumbent on me as justice of the Supreme Court of the United States, according to the best of my abilities and understanding, agreeably to the Constitution and laws of the United States: So help me God." [3]

The organization of the system of courts (except as to the Supreme Court) was commenced by the act of September 24, 1789, known as the Judiciary Act, q. v.

The laws of the several States, except where the Constitution, treaties, or statutes of the United States otherwise provide, are to be regarded as "rules of decision in trials at common law" in the courts of the United States, in cases where they apply. [4]

This includes the rules of evidence prescribed by the laws of the States in which the United States courts sit. [5] See further DECISION, Rules of.

August 8, 1791, Chief Justice Jay, in answer to an interrogation by the attorney-general, announced that "this court consider the practice of the king's bench, and of chancery, in England, as affording outlines for the practice of this court; and that they will, from time to time, make such alterations therein as circumstances may render necessary." [6]

Remedies at common law and in equity are not according to the practice of the State courts, but according to the principles of common law and equity as distinguished in England, whence we derive our knowledge of those principles. [7]

The blending of equitable and legal causes of action in one suit is not permissible. But in suits in equity in the circuit and district courts the forms and modes of proceeding shall be according to the principles, rules and usages belonging to courts of equity. This requirement is obligatory. [1]

In the following cases and proceedings jurisdiction is exclusive in the courts of the United States: [2] 1. Of all crimes and offenses cognizable under the authority of the United States. [3] 2. Of all suits for penalties and forfeitures incurred under the laws thereof. [4] 3. Of all civil causes of admiralty or maritime jurisdiction, saving to suitors the right of such remedy as the common law is competent to give. 4. Of all seizures under Federal law not within admiralty and maritime jurisdiction. 5. Of all cases arising under patent-right [5] or copyright laws. [6] 6. Of all matters in bankruptcy. [7] 7. Of all controversies of a civil nature where a State is a party, except between a State and its own citizens, citizens of other States or aliens. [8]

The courts mentioned have power to issue all writs, not specifically provided for by statute, which may be necessary for the exercise of their respective jurisdictions and agreeable to the usages and principles of law. [9]

A re-examination, by writ of error, may be had in the Supreme Court, of a final judgment or decree in any suit in the highest court of a State, where there is drawn in question the validity of a treaty or statute of, or an authority exercised under, the United States, and the decision is against their validity; or the validity of a statute of, or an authority exercised under, a State, on the ground of repugnance to the Constitution, treaties, or laws of the United States, and the decision is in favor of their validity; or where any title, right, privilege, or immunity is claimed under the Constitution, a treaty or a statute of, or commission held or authority exercised under, the United States, and the decision is against the title, right, etc., specially set up or claimed. [10]

The record from the State court of last resort must present a "Federal question," that is, the Constitution, a law, or a treaty, of the United States must have been drawn in question and its authority denied or evaded. [11]

It is not enough that a Federal question was presented for decision. It must affirmatively appear that the decision was necessary to the determination of the cause, and that the judgment rendered could not have been given without deciding it. [12]

---

[1] Constitution, Art. III, sec. 2. See 2 Bancroft, Const. 195-206.

[2] Constitution, Art. II, sec. 2, cl. 2.

[3] R. S. § 712: Act 24 Sept. 1789.

[4] R. S. § 721, cases.

[5] Potter v. Third Nat. Bank of Chicago, 102 U. S. 165 (1880), cases.

[6] Rules and Orders, Supreme Court, 1 Cranch, xvi.

[7] Thompson v. Central Ohio, &c. R. Cos., 6 Wall. 137 (1867), cases.

[1] R. S. § 913, cases; Hurt v. Hollingsworth, 100 U. S. 103 (1879), cases; Herklotz v. Chase, 32 F. R. 433 (1887).

[2] R. S. § 711: various Acts, and cases.

[3] See 2 Dall. 393; 4 Saw. 634; 53 Pa. 112; 2 Woods, 468.

[4] See 47 Md. 242; 74 Ill. 217; 95 Mass. 301.

[5] See 7 Johns. *145; 60 N. Y. 459; 24 Iowa, 231; 103 Mass. 501; 40 Me. 430; 15 Mich. 265.

[6] See 47 N. Y. 535.

[7] See 119 Mass. 434; 3 Neb. 437; 72 N. Y. 159; 69 N. C. 464.

[8] See 29 Ark. 649; 27 La. An. 329; 2 Hill, N. Y., 159.

[9] R. S. § 716; Rosenbaum v. Bauer, 120 U. S. 450 (1887), cases; 10 Wheat. 51; 15 Wall. 427; 21 id. 289; 94 U. S. 672; 5 Blatch. 309.

[10] R. S. § 709, cases; 1 Sup. R. S. p. 138.

[11] Williams v. Bruffy, 102 U. S. 255 (1880).

[12] Brown v. Atwell, 92 U. S. 329 (1875); Home Ins. Co. v. City Council, 93 id. 121 (1876); Gold-Washing, &c.

Writs of error to the State courts have never been allowed as of right, that is, as of course. It is the duty of the justice to whom application is made, under Rev. St. § 709, to ascertain, from the record of the State court, whether any question, cognizable on appeal, was decided in the State court, and whether the case, on the face of the record, will justify re-examination. When the case is urgent the motion for the writ may be permitted to be made in open court. But if it appears that the decision of the Federal question was so plainly right as not to require argument, and especially if it accords with well-considered judgments in similar cases, the writ will not be awarded.[1]

At the trial some title, right, privilege, or immunity must have been "specially set up or claimed" under the Constitution, laws, or treaties of the United States.[2]

The "inferior courts" (which phrase see, page 275) established are: Circuit courts, District courts, Territorial courts, the Supreme Court of the District of Columbia, and the Court of Claims.

Congress can vest no part of its power in a State court;[3] nor in a military commission.[4] During the rebellion the President had power to establish provisional courts at the seat of war, as an incident to military occupation.[5] See WAR.

By consent of a State, Congress may impose duties upon the tribunals of a State, not incompatible with State duties.[6]

Supreme Court of the United States.

This court, as seen, was established by the Constitution itself.[7]

"In all cases affecting Ambassadors, other public Ministers and Consuls, and those in which a State shall be a party, the supreme Court shall have original Jurisdiction. In all the other Cases before mentioned [page 276], the supreme Court shall have appellate Jurisdiction, both as to Law and Fact, with such Exceptions and under such Regulations as the Congress shall make."[1]

Congress cannot extend this original jurisdiction, since in all other cases the Court's jurisdiction must be appellate.[2]

But the extent of the appellate jurisdiction is not limited by the Constitution to any particular form or mode; and the appellate is broader than the original jurisdiction.[3]

In view of the practical construction put upon the Constitution by Congress and the courts, the Supreme Court has expressed an unwillingness to say that it is not within the power of Congress to grant to the inferior courts jurisdiction in cases where that Court has been vested by the Constitution with original jurisdiction.[4]

The Court has power to issue a writ of prohibition to a district court proceeding as a court of admiralty and maritime jurisdiction; also, a writ of *mandamus*, in a case warranted by the principles and usages of law, to an inferior Federal court or to a person holding a Federal office; where a State, a public minister, a consul or vice-consul is a party;[5] also, to issue writs of *habeas corpus;*[6] writs of *scire facias*, and all other writs not especially provided for by statute, which may be necessary for the exercise of its jurisdiction and agreeable to the principles and usages of law.[7] The justices, individually, may grant writs of *habeas corpus*, of *ne exeat*, and of injunction,[8] *qq. v.*

The Court exercises *appellate jurisdiction* as follows: (1) By writ of error from the final judgment of a circuit court, or of any district court exercising the powers of a circuit court, in civil actions brought there by original process, or removed there from the court of a State, and in final judgments of any circuit court in civil actions brought from the district court, where the matter in dispute, exclusive of costs, exceeds $5,000.[9] (2) Upon appeal from the decree of a circuit court in cases of equity and of admiralty, where the sum in controversy, exclusive of costs, exceeds $5,000.[10] (3) And in certain other cases in admiralty, for which see act of February, 1875, 18 St. L. 315. (4) Upon appeal, or error upon a certificate of differ-

Co. v. Keyes, 96 *id.* 203 (1877); Daniels v. Tearbey, 102 *id.* 417 (1880); Brown v. Colorado, 106 *id.* 96 (1882); New Orleans Waterworks Co. *v.* Louisiana Sugar Refining Co., 125 *id.* 29 (1888), cases; 99 *id.* 71, 99; 107 *id.* 319; 111 *id.* 361; 112 *id.* 127; 114 *id.* 133; 116 *id.* 548; 21 Wall. 639.

[1] Spies v. Illinois (The Anarchists' Case), 123 U. S. 163 (Nov. 2, 1887), Waite, C. J.; Twitchell v. Pennsylvania, 7 Wall. 324 (1868), Chase, C. J. Anarchists' Case commented on, 27 Am. Law Reg. 33–47 (1888), cases; 1 Harv. Law Rev. 306–26 (1888).

[2] Brooks v. Missouri, 124 U. S. 394 (Jan. 23, 1888), Waite, C. J.; French v. Hopkins, *ib.* 524 (1888).

[3] Martin v. Hunter's Lessee, 1 Wheat. 330 (1816); 7 Conn. 243; 17 Johns. 9.

[4] *Exp.* Milligan, 4 Wall. 121 (1866).

[5] The Grapeshot, 9 Wall. 132 (1869). As to criminal jurisdiction generally, see United States v. Clark, 26 Am. Law Reg. 703–9 (1887), cases; also, Circuit, etc., Courts, *post.*

[6] United States v. Jones, 109 U. S. 520 (1883); 1 Kent, 400.

[7] To be the "bulwark of a limited Constitution against legislative encroachment," — Federalist, lxxviii.

[1] Constitution, Art. III, sec. 2, cl. 2. See Act of 1789, s. 13: R. S. § 687.

[2] *Exp.* Vallandigham, 1 Wall. 252 (1863), cases.

[3] *Exp.* Virginia, 100 U. S. 341–42 (1879), cases.

[4] Ames v. Kansas, 111 U. S. 469 (1884).

[5] R. S. § 688, cases.

[6] R. S. § 751, cases.

[7] R. S. § 716, cases.

[8] R. S. §§ 717, 719, 752, cases.

[9] R. S. § 691, cases: Act 16 Feb. 1875: 1 Sup. R. S. p. 136.

[10] R. S. § 692, cases; Act 16 Feb. 1875. See CIRCUIT COURT, p. 280.

ences of opinion between the judges of a circuit court.[1] (5) Upon appeals in prize cases.[2] (6) In patent and copyright cases; in revenue cases; in alleged abridgment of the rights of citizenship.[3] (7) In cases from the judgment or decree of the supreme court of the District of Columbia or of any Territory, when the matter in dispute, exclusive of costs, exceeds $1,000 and as to the supreme court of the said District $2,500,[4] and of Washington Territory, $2,000;[5] except in cases involving the validity of a patent or copyright, or in which is drawn in question the validity of a treaty or statute of or an authority exercised under the United States, in which cases appeal or error lies regardless of the sum or value in dispute.[6] In cases in the court of claims, decided for the plaintiff, the sum being over $3,000 or his claim forfeited.[7] (8) In capital cases and cases of bigamy or polygamy from Utah Territory.[8] (9) In cases involving a Federal question, as see page 277. (10) Where a court dismisses or remands a cause to a State court.

Its criminal jurisdiction includes such proceedings against public ministers or their domestic servants as a court of law can have consistently with the law of nations.[9]

The judges of the Supreme Court consist of a chief justice and eight associate justices, any six of whom constitute a quorum;[10] the latter have precedence according to the dates of their commissions, or, where the dates are the same, according to age.[11]

The number of members was originally five; in 1807, it was made six; in 1837, eight; and in 1863, nine.

The Court holds one term, annually, at Washington City, commencing on the second Monday of October, and such special terms as it may find necessary.[12] Provision is made for adjournments when a quorum does not attend.[13]

The Court appoints a clerk, a marshal, and a reporter of its decisions.[14]

The ceremony observed in opening and closing the Court is as follows: When the marshal appears, at twelve o'clock noon (in advance of the justices), at the north door of the court room, the crier raps on the desk three times, for the audience to come to order and to rise from their seats. When the chief justice enters the door the crier announces "The honorable, the chief justice and associate justices of the Supreme Court of the United States!" As the justices seat themselves, after ascending the platform, the crier proclaims: "O yez! O yez! O yez! All persons having business before the honorable, the Supreme Court of the United States, are admonished to draw near and give their attention, for the Court is now sitting. God save the United States and this honorable Court!" At four o'clock P. M., on intimation (usually a gesture) from the chief justice, or at such other time as he may indicate, the crier announces: "This honorable Court is now adjourned until to-morrow at twelve o'clock," or until "Monday, at twelve o'clock."

Circuit courts of the United States. These are courts of the "circuits" into which the country is divided; each circuit being composed of at least three "judicial districts." In number and territorial jurisdiction the courts correspond with the following circuits:

First.— Maine, New Hampshire, Massachusetts, and Rhode Island.

Second.— Vermont, Connecticut, and New York.

Third.— New Jersey, Pennsylvania, and Delaware.

Fourth.— Maryland, Virginia, West Virginia, North Carolina, and South Carolina.

Fifth.— Georgia, Florida, Alabama, Mississippi, Louisiana, and Texas.

Sixth.— Ohio, Michigan, Kentucky, and Tennessee.

Seventh.— Indiana, Illinois, and Wisconsin.

Eighth. — Minnesota, Iowa, Nebraska, Missouri, Kansas, Arkansas, and Colorado.

Ninth.— California, Oregon, and Nevada.[1]

For the second circuit an additional judgeship was created by the act of March 3, 1887 (24 St. L. 492). The "senior judge" sits in election proceedings (R. S. §§ 2011-14), unless absent or unable to serve, in which event the "junior judge" may act.

There are also courts called "circuit courts" for particular districts within Alabama, Arkansas, and Mississippi.[2]

A circuit court consists of a justice of the Supreme Court, called the "circuit justice," a "circuit judge" for the circuit having the same powers as the circuit justice, and the "district judge" of the district where the circuit court is held. Any two of these officials may hold court. The "circuit justice," sitting apart, may try cases; during every two years he must attend .

[1] R. S. §§ 693, 697, cases.
[2] R. S. §§ 695-96, cases.
[3] R. S. § 699, cases.
[4] Act 25 Feb. 1879: 1 Sup. R. S. p. 149.
[5] R. S. §§ 702, 706, cases.
[6] R. S. §§ 702, 706, cases.
[7] R. S. § 707, cases.
[8] Act 23 June, 1874: 1 Sup. R. S. p. 108.
[9] R. S. § 4063, cases.
[10] R. S. § 673: Act 10 April, 1869.
[11] R. S. §§ 674-75: Acts 24 Sept. 1789, 25 June, 1868.
[12] R. S. § 684: Acts 23 July, 1866, 24 Jan. 1873.
[13] R. S. § 685: Acts 29 April, 1802, 21 Jan. 1829.
[14] R. S. § 677: various Acts, 1789 to 1867.

[1] R. S. § 604: various Acts, 1789 to 1876.
[2] See R. S. § 603; 1 Sup. R. S. p. 87.

at least one term of court in the district.[1] By consent of the parties the district judge may vote on an appeal from his own decision; but judgment is to be rendered in conformity with the opinion of the presiding judge.[2] When a circuit justice, or all the judges, are disqualified from any cause, a case may be certified to the most convenient circuit, or the judge thereof may be requested to hold the court.[3]

Each court appoints its own clerks and their deputies.[4]

Each court also appoints as " commissioners " as many discreet persons, none of them being a marshal or his deputy, as may be deemed necessary;[5] but they are not considered officers of the court.[6] They are authorized to hold persons to security of the peace, and for good behavior in cases arising under Federal law,[7] to take bail and affidavits required in another circuit or a district court.[8] They may imprison or bail offenders;[9] discharge poor convicts;[10] administer oaths and take acknowledgments;[11] apprehend fugitives from justice.[12] They are required to conform their proceedings in criminal cases to the practice in the State courts as far as practicable.[13] They are impliedly authorized to keep a docket, and entitled to docket fees.[14]

The jurisdiction of the circuit courts is such as Congress confers.[15] A general description of the *original jurisdiction* is, that it extends (subject to some limitations founded upon residence) to civil suits involving more than $2,000,— (by act of March 3, 1887,— prior thereto $500) exclusive of costs, and arising under the Constitution, laws, or treaties of the United States, or in which the United States are plaintiffs, or in which the controversy is between different States, or citizens of a State and foreign States, citizens, and subjects; also of crimes under the laws of the United States. They have no *appellate jurisdiction* over the district courts.[16] By act of March 3, 1875,[17] a

new definition was given of the jurisdiction, which is very comprehensive, and has been held to be a substitute for and implied repeal of the provisions of the Revision of 1873.[1] See further act of March 3, 1887, page 281.

The $2,000 provision relates to the amount "in dispute," not to the amount claimed.[2] The Supreme Court has power of review where the matter in dispute exceeds the sum or value of $5,000, exclusive of costs.[3]

The matter in dispute may be made up of distinct demands each less than $2,000, and although title be acquired by assignment.[4]

The jurisdiction is co-extensive with the limits of the State.[5] Where there are two districts in a State, a citizen of such State is liable to suit in either district, if served with process.[6]

The fact that a nominal or immaterial party resides in the same State with one of the actual parties will not defeat the jurisdiction.[7]

The court, not being a foreign court, adopts and applies the law of the State.[8]

The facts on which jurisdiction rests must, in some form, appear on the face of the record of each suit; as, for example, the fact of citizenship.[9]

More specifically, the *original jurisdiction* includes: cases arising under — laws providing internal revenue, postal laws, patent laws, copyright laws; proceedings for penalties incurred by a merchant vessel in carrying passengers; suits by or against a national banking association; matters involving the elective franchise and other civil rights belonging to citizens of the United States; also, *exclusive jurisdiction* of all crimes and offenses cognizable under the authority of the United States, except when otherwise provided, and *concurrent jurisdiction* with the district courts of offenses cognizable therein.[10]

In an admiralty cause by consent, and in a patent cause in equity under rules made by the Supreme Court, the court may impanel a jury of five to twelve persons to determine the issue of fact.[11] But except-

---

[1] R. S. § 610: Act 10 April, 1869.

[2] R. S. § 614: Acts 24 Sept. 1789, 29 April, 1802, 2 March, 1867.

[3] R. S. §§ 615, 617: various Acts, and cases; Supervisors v. Rogers, 7 Wall. 175 (1868).

[4] R. S. §§ 619, 624: various Acts.

[5] R. S. §§ 627–28: various Acts.

[6] *Exp.* Van Orden, 3 Blatch. 167 (1854).

[7] R. S. § 727: various Acts.

[8] R. S. § 945: various Acts.

[9] R. S. §§ 1014–15: various Acts.

[10] R. S. § 1042: Act 1 June, 1872.

[11] R. S. § 1778: various Acts.

[12] R. S. § 5270: Acts and cases.

[13] R. S. § 1014; United States v. Harden, 4 Hughes, 456 (1881).

[14] Phillips v. United States, 33 F. R. 164 (1887).

[15] Sewing Machine Cases, 18 Wall. 577 (1877).

[16] See R. S. § 629: various Acts and cases.

[17] 18 St. L. 470: 1 Sup. R. S. p. 173.

[1] Osgood v. Chicago, &c. R. Co., 6 Biss. 332 (1875).

[2] Brooks v. Phœnix Mut. Life Ins. Co., 16 Blatch. 188 (1879).

[3] 1 Sup. R. S. p. 136; R. S. §§ 691–92; 100 U. S. 6, 147, 158, 444, 457; 101 *id.* 231; 102 *id.* 177; 103 *id.* 673, 755; 106 *id.* 579.

[4] Bernheim v. Birnbaum, 30 F. R. 885 (1887).

[5] Shrew v. Jones, 2 McLean, 78 (1840).

[6] M'Micken v. Webb, 11 Pet. *38 (1837); Vore v. Fowler, 2 Bond, 294 (1869); 10 Blatch. 307.

[7] Walden v. Skinner, 101 U. S. 589 (1879).

[8] Tennessee v. Davis, 100 U. S. 271 (1879).

[9] Continental Life Ins. Co. v. Rhoads, 119 U. S. 239 (1886), cases; Menard v. Goggan, 121 *id.* 253 (1887).

[10] R. S. § 629: Act 3 March, 1875: 18 St. L. 470.

[11] Act 16 Feb. 1875, c. 77: 18 St. L. 315. See 98 U. S. 440; 101 *id.* 6, 247; 102 *id.* 218.

ing these cases, reference to referees, and some exceptions in bankruptcy, the trial of all issues of fact is by jury.[1] By stipulation filed, the court may find the facts in the nature of a general or special verdict,[2] *q. v.*

This court has power to issue writs of error to the district courts on final judgments in civil cases at common law. An appeal may be had to it from a final decree of a district court of equity, admiralty, or maritime jurisdiction, except prize causes where the matter in dispute exceeds the sum or value of fifty dollars, exclusive of costs;[3] the writ of error or appeal being taken out within one year from the removal of any disability.[4] Provision is made for the removal of causes into this court when the district judge is disqualified by interest, etc.[5] The court is always open for interlocutory proceedings in equity causes.[6] The opinion of the presiding judge or justice prevails, in cases of difference;[7] and in criminal proceedings, upon request, the point of difference is to be certified to the Supreme Court, but the cause may proceed, if that can be done without prejudice to the merits.[8] In cases of non-attendance of the judges, the marshal, or the clerk. may adjourn the court.[9] See OPINION, 3, Difference of.

Jurisdiction of writs of error in criminal cases comprises sentences of imprisonment and fines in excess of $300. Within a year thereafter, a petition to the circuit court for a writ of error may be presented; the writ, if allowed, to be accompanied with a bond to prosecute the suit and abide the judgment.[10]

The circuit courts are co-ordinate tribunals, constituting a single system, and the decision of any one of them ought to be regarded as decisive of the question involved, until otherwise determined by the Supreme Court.[11]

The act approved March 3, 1887 (24 St. L. 552), provides that the first section of the act of March 3, 1875 (18 St. L. 470), be amended to read as follows:

That the circuit courts of the United States shall have *original cognizance*, concurrent with the courts of the several States, of all suits of a civil nature, at common law or in equity, where the matter in dispute exceeds, exclusive of interest and costs, the sum or value of two thousand dollars, and arising under the Constitution or laws of the United States, or treaties made, or which shall be made, under their authority, or in which controversy the United States are plaintiffs or petitioners, or in which there shall be a controversy between citizens of different States, in which the matter in dispute exceeds, exclusive of interest and costs, the sum or value aforesaid, or a

[1] R. S. § 648; 1 Sup. R. S. p. 175; 100 U. S. 208.

[2] R. S. § 649; 12 Wall. 275; 19 *id.* 81; 101 U. S. 569; 20 Blatch. 266.

[3] R. S. §§ 631, 633, 636: Acts and cases.

[4] R. S. § 635: Act 1 June, 1872.

[5] R. S. § 637: several Acts.

[6] R. S. § 638: several Acts.

[7] R. S. § 650: Act 1 June, 1872.

[8] R. S. § 651: Act 1 June, 1872.

[9] R. S. §§ 671-72: several Acts.

[10] Act 3 March, 1879: 20 St. L. 374.

[11] Welles *v.* Oregon R. & N. Co., 8 Saw. 612 (1883); 1 Flip. 388.

controversy between citizens of the same State claiming lands under grants of different States, or a controversy between citizens of a State and foreign states, citizens, or subjects, in which the matter in dispute exceeds, exclusive of interest and costs, the sum or value aforesaid, and shall have *exclusive cognizance* of all crimes and offenses cognizable under the authority of the United States, except as otherwise provided by law, and *concurrent jurisdiction* with the district courts of the crimes and offenses cognizable by them. But no person shall be arrested in one district for trial in another in any civil action before a circuit or district court; and no civil suit shall be brought before either of said courts against any person by any original process of [or] proceeding in any other district than that whereof he is an inhabitant; but where the jurisdiction is founded only on the fact that the action is between citizens of different States, suit shall be brought only in the district of the residence of either the plaintiff or the defendant; nor shall any circuit or district court have cognizance of any suit except upon foreign bills of exchange, to recover the contents of any promissory note or other chose in action in favor of any assignee, or of any subsequent holder of [if [1]] such instrument be payable to bearer and be not made by any corporation, unless such suit might have been prosecuted in such court to recover the said contents if no assignment or transfer had been made; and the circuit courts shall also have appellate jurisdiction from the district courts, under the regulations and restrictions prescribed by law.

Sec. 2. That any suit of a civil nature, at law or in equity, arising under the Constitution or laws of the United States, or treaties made, or which shall be made, under their authority, of which the circuit courts of the United States are given original jurisdiction by the preceding section, which may now be pending, or which may hereafter be brought, in any State court. may be *removed* by the defendant or defendants therein to the circuit court of the United States for the proper district[;] any other suit of a civil nature, at law or in equity, of which the circuit courts of the United States are given jurisdiction by the preceding section, and which are now pending, or which may hereafter be brought, in any State court, may be removed into the circuit court of the United States for the proper district by the defendant or defendants therein being non-residents of that State; and when in any suit mentioned in this section there shall be a controversy which is wholly between citizens of different States, and which can be fully determined as between them, then either one or more of the defendants actually interested in such controversy may remove said suit into the circuit court of the United States for the proper district. And where a suit is now pending, or may be hereafter brought, in any State court, in which there is a controversy between a citizen of the State in which the suit is brought and a citizen of another State, any defendant, being such citizen of another State, may remove such suit into the circuit court of the United States for the proper district, at any time before the trial thereof, when it shall be

[1] Newgass *v.* New Orleans, 33 F. R. 196 (1888).

made to appear to said circuit court that from prejudice or local influence he will not be able to obtain justice in such State court, or in any other State court to which the said defendant may, under the laws of the State, have the right, on account of such prejudice or local influence, to remove said cause: *Provided*, That if it further appear that said suit can he fully and justly determined as to the other defendants in the State court, without being affected by such prejudice or local influence, and that no party to the suit will be prejudiced by a separation of the parties, said circuit court may direct the suit to he remanded, so far as relates to such other defendants, to the State court, to be proceeded with therein. At any time before the trial of any suit which is now pending in any circuit court or may hereafter he entered therein, and which has heen removed to said court from a State court on the affidavit of any party plaintiff that he had reason to believe and did believe that, from prejudice or local influence, he was unable to obtain justice in said State court, the circuit court shall, on application of the other party, examine into the truth of said affidavit and the grounds thereof, and, unless it shall appear to the satisfaction of said court that said party will not be able to obtain justice in such State court, it shall cause the same to he remanded thereto. Whenever any cause shall be removed from any State court into any circuit court of the United States, and the circuit court shall decide that the cause was improperly removed, and order the same to be remanded to the State court from whence it came, such remand shall he immediately carried into execution, and no appeal or writ of error from the decision of the circuit court so remanding such cause shall be allowed.

That section 3 of said act shall read as follows:

Sec. 3. That whenever any party entitled to remove any suit mentioned in the next preceding section, except in such cases as are provided for in the last clause of said section, may desire to remove such suit from a State court to the circuit court of the United States, he may make and file a petition in such suit in such State court at the time, or any time hefore the defendant is required by the laws of the State or the rule of the State court in which such suit is brought to answer or plead to the declaration or complaint of the plaintiff, for the removal of such suit into the circuit court to be held in the district where such suit is pending, and shall make and file therewith a bond, with good and sufficient surety, for his or their entering in such circuit court, on the first day of its then next session, a copy of the record in such suit, and for paying all costs that may be awarded by the said circuit court if said court shall hold that such suit was wrongfully or improperly removed thereto, and also for their appearing and entering special bail in such suit if special hail was originally requisite therein. It shall then be the duty of the State court to accept said petition and bond, and proceed no further in such suit; and the said copy heing entered as aforesaid in said circuit court of the United States, the cause shall then proceed in the same manner, as if it had been originally commenced in the said circuit court; and if in any action commenced in a State court the title of land be concerned, and the parties are citizens of the same State, and the matter in dispute exceed the sum

or value of two thousand dollars, exclusive of interest and costs, the sum or value being made to appear, one or more of the plaintiffs or defendants, before the trial, may state to the court, and make affidavit if the court require it, that he or they claim and shall rely upon a right or title to the land under a grant from a State, and produce the original grant, or an exemplification of it, except where the loss of public records shall put it out of his or their power, and shall move that any one or more of the adverse party inform the court whether he or they claim a right or title to the land under a grant from some other State, the party or parties so required shall give such information, or otherwise not be allowed to plead such grant or give it in evidence upon the trial; and if he or they inform that he or they do claim under such grant, any one or more of the party moving for such information may then, on petition and bond, as hereinbefore mentioned in this act, remove the cause for trial to the circuit court of the United States next to be holden in such district; and any one of either party removing the cause shall not he allowed to plead or give evidence of any other title than that by him or them stated as aforesaid as the ground of his or their claim.

Sec. 2. That whenever in any cause pending in any court of the United States there shall be a *receiver* or *manager* in possession of any property such receiver or manager shall manage and operate such property according to the requirements of the valid laws of the State in which such property shall he situated in the same manner the owner or possessor thereof would he bound to do if in possession thereof. Any receiver or manager who shall willfully violate the provisions of this section shall he deemed guilty of a misdemeanor, and shall on conviction thereof he punished by a fine not exceeding three thousand dollars, or by imprisonment not exceeding one year, or by both said punishments, in the discretion of the court.

Sec. 3. That every receiver or manager of any property appointed hy any court of the United States may he sued in respect of any act or transaction of his in carrying on the business connected with such property, without the previous leave of the court in which such receiver or manager was appointed; but such suit shall be subject to the general equity jurisdiction of the court in which such receiver or manager was appointed, so far as the same shall he necessary to the ends of justice.

Sec. 4. That all *national banking associations* established under the laws of the United States shall, for the purposes of all actions by or against them, real, personal or mixed, and all suits in equity, he deemed citizens of the States in which they are respectively located; and in such cases the circuit and district courts shall not have jurisdiction other than such as they would have in cases between individual citizens of the same State.

The provisions of this section shall not he held to affect the jurisdiction of the courts of the United States in cases commenced by the United States or by direction of any officer thereof, or cases for winding up the affairs of any such hank.

Sec. 5. That nothing in this act shall be held, deemed, or construed to repeal or affect any jurisdiction or right mentioned either in sections 641, or in 642, or in 643, or in 722, or in title 24 of the Revised Statutes of the United States, or mentioned in section 8 of the act of Congress of which this act is an amendment, or in the act of Congress approved March 1st, 1875, entitled "An act to protect all citizens in their civil or legal rights."

Sec. 6. That the last paragraph of section 5 of the act of Congress, approved March 3d, 1875, entitled "An act to determine the jurisdiction of circuit courts of the United States, and to regulate the removal of causes from State courts, and for other purposes," and section 640 of the Revised Statutes, and all laws and parts of laws in conflict with the provisions of this act, be, and the same are hereby repealed: *Provided*, That this act shall not affect the jurisdiction over or disposition of any suit removed from the court of any State, or suit commenced in any court of the United States, before the passage hereof except as otherwise expressly provided in this act.

Sec. 7. That no person related to any justice or judge of any court of the United States by affinity or consanguinity, within the degree of first cousin, shall hereafter be appointed by such court or judge to or employed by such court or judge in any office or duty in any court of which such justice or judge may be a member.[1] See ADDENDA.

Section 1 of the act of March 3, 1887, does not apply in determining a question of jurisdiction on an application for the removal of a cause.[2]

The circuit court cannot take cognizance of a suit against a party in a district of which he is not a resident.[3]

Before the act of 1887, a controversy between citizens of different States could be brought in any Federal court where the defendant could be served with process. That act confines the plaintiff to the district of which the defendant is an inhabitant, and that wherein the plaintiff himself resides.[4]

In a case involving a single controversy, where the jurisdiction depends upon citizenship, the right of removal is governed by clause 2 of section 2 of the act of 1887, and can be exercised only by non-resident defendants. Clause 3 of that section, like clause 2 of section 2 of the act of 1875, governs that class of cases only where there are two or more controversies involved in the same suit and one of them is wholly between citizens of different States. Under the act of 1887, the right of removal in the latter cases is limited to one or more of the defendants actually interested in such separable controversy, and does not extend to the plaintiff.[5]

Section 2 of the act of 1887, does not change the practice as to defendants seeking a removal on the ground of prejudice or local influence.[6]

A formal affidavit by the defendant that he believes that he cannot obtain justice because of prejudice or local influence is not sufficient: the fact must be shown by oral testimony or by affidavit. The affidavit may be filed in the State court and a certified copy be sent to the circuit court.[1]

Only when the court can plainly see that its jurisdiction is being fraudulently invoked will it deny the privilege of increasing the *ad damnum* by amendment.[2]

The Supreme Court cannot review an order remanding a suit removed under the act of 1887, begun, removed, and remanded after that act went into effect.[3] Nor has the court jurisdiction where the suit was removed before the approval of that act, but not remanded until thereafter;[4] nor where the order to remand was made while the act of 1875 was in force, and the writ of error not brought until after the passage of the act of 1887. Until the act of 1875 there was no such jurisdiction; and the provision in that act was repealed by the act of 1887, without reservation as to pending cases, the proviso in the repealing section having reference "only to the jurisdiction of the circuit court and the disposition of the suit on its merits."[5] See further REMOVE, 4.

District courts of the United States.
Each State consists of one or more "districts" for the convenient administration of United States law. Each district has its "district court" held by a resident judge.[6]

The judge appoints a clerk of the court, with one or more deputies.[7] A deputy may do any act permissible in the clerk.[8]

The court has jurisdiction over all admiralty and maritime causes, all proceedings in bankruptcy, and all penal and criminal matters cognizable under the laws of the United States, exclusive jurisdiction over which is not vested in the circuit or Supreme Court.

More specifically, this jurisdiction comprises: non-capital crimes committed within the district or upon the high seas, except the cases mentioned in Revised Statutes, Title "Crimes," section 5412; cases of piracy, when no·circuit court is held in the district; suits for penalties and forfeitures, in general; suits at common law brought by the United States or any officer thereof; suits in equity to subject realty to the payment of internal revenue

---

[1] See acts of 1877 and 1875 compared, 21 Am. Law Rev. 310-16 (1887).

[2] Fales *v.* Chicago, &c. R. Co., 32 F. R. 679 (1887).

[3] County of Yuba *v.* Pioneer Gold Mining Co., 32 F. R. 183 (1887), Sawyer, J. *Contra*, ib. 675, 84.

[4] Gavin *v.* Vance, 13 F. R. 85 (1887), Hammond, J.

[5] Western Union Tel. Co. *v.* Brown, 32 F. R. 342 (1887), Brewer, J.

[6] Hills *v.* Richmond, &c. R. Co., 33 F. R. 81 (1887), Newman, J.

[1] Short *v.* Chicago, &c. R. Co., 33 F. R. 114 (1887). Brewer, J.

[2] Davis *v.* Kansas City, &c. R. Co., 32 F. R. 863 (1887).

[3] Morey *v.* Lockhart, 123 U. S. 56 (1887).

[4] Wilkinson *v.* Nebraska, 123 U. S. 286 (1888).

[5] Sherman *v.* Grinnell, 123 U. S. 679 (1887), Waite, C. J.

[6] R. S. § 551: various Acts.

[7] R. S. §§ 555, 558: various Acts.

[8] Confiscation Cases, 20 Wall. 111 (1873). See 1 Woods, 213.

tax; suits for forfeitures or damages as debts due to the United States by Rev. St., section 3490; causes arising under the postal laws; civil causes in admiralty and maritime law; some offenses against civil rights — Rev. St., Title XXIV; suits by or against any national bank within the district; suits by aliens for torts in violation of the law of nations or of a treaty; certain suits against consuls or vice-consuls; and original bankruptcy proceedings.[1]

Trial of issues of fact, except in equity, admiralty and maritime proceedings, is by jury.[2] (See page 277, column 1, page 280, column 2.)

The time for holding the sessions of the various courts is provided for;[3] also, the circumstances under which special terms may be held;[4] also, adjournments by the marshal;[5] and certifying cases into the circuit court, in case of disability or disqualification in the district judge.[6] The judge of one district may be designated to hold court in another district within the same circuit.[7] In cases of vacancy all processes are to be continued to the next stated term after the qualification of a successor; except that in States having two or more districts the judge of any such district may hold court.[8]

Territorial courts of the United States. The Territories are legislative governments, and their courts legislative courts. Congress, in the exercise of its powers in the organization and government of the Territories, combines the powers of both the Federal and State authorities.[9] The phrase "courts of the United States" is sometimes used to include these courts in the Territories, but not so in the Constitution itself.[10]

In Arizona the judicial power is vested in a supreme court and such inferior courts as the legislative council may provide. In the other organized Territories the power is vested in a supreme court, district courts, probate courts, and in justices of the peace.[11]

The supreme court, which consists of a chief justice and two associate justices, appointed for four years, holds an annual term at the seat of government of the Territory.

---

[1] R. S. § 563: various Acts.
[2] R. S. § 566: various Acts.
[3] R. S. § 572: various Acts.
[4] R. S. § 581: various Acts.
[5] R. S. § 583: various Acts.
[6] R. S. §§ 587–89, 601: several Acts; 1 Gall. 338; 97 U. S. 146.
[7] R. S. §§ 592–97: various Acts.
[8] R. S. §§ 602–3: various Acts.
[9] Scott v. Jones, 5 How. 374 (1847); Benner v. Potter, 9 id. 241 (1850).
[10] United States v. Haskins, 3 Saw. 271 (1875); 1 Fla. 198.
[11] R. S. § 1907: various Acts.

Each Territory is divided into three districts, and a district court is to be held by a justice of the supreme court as prescribed by law. Terms for causes in which the United States are not a party are held in the counties designated by the laws of the Territory. The supreme and district courts possess chancery and common-law powers. Review of a final decision in a district court by the supreme court is regulated by the territorial legislature. The district courts have the same jurisdiction, in cases arising under the Constitution and laws, as is vested in the Federal circuit and district courts. A marshal and attorney are appointed by the President and Senate; and a clerk, by each supreme court judge in his district.

An appeal or writ of error to the Supreme Court at Washington is allowed where the Constitution, an act of Congress, or a treaty is brought in question. There is also an appeal where the value in dispute exceeds $1,000; except in Washington Territory, as to which this limit is $2,000.[1]

Justices of the peace are not given jurisdiction where the title to land may be in dispute, or where the claims exceed one hundred dollars. See further TERRITORY, 2.

Supreme Court of the District of Columbia. This court, which may be embraced in the expression "courts of the United States,"[2] was established by the act of March 3, 1863, consists of six justices appointed by the President and the Senate, and has the same jurisdiction as circuit and district courts, with cognizance in divorce cases.

Actions are maintainable against inhabitants of the District, or persons found therein. It has common-law and chancery jurisdiction according to the laws of Maryland of May 3, 1802. It has appellate jurisdiction from the police court of the District, from justices of the peace in cases involving less than fifty dollars, and from the decisions of the commissioner of patents.[3] Any final judgment or decree, involving over $2,500 in value, may be re-examined in the Supreme Court of the United States; and so too, by special allowance, as to cases involving a less amount, where the questions of law are of great importance.[4]

Court of Claims of the United States. The court in which the United States consents to be sued.

Consists of a chief justice and four judges, appointed by the President and the Senate; holds an annual session at Washington, beginning on the first Monday in December. Members of Congress are forbidden to practice in the court. A quorum consists of three judges; and the concurrence of three is necessary to a judgment.[5]

---

[1] R. S. §§ 702, 706: various Acts, and cases.
[2] Embry v. Palmer, 107 U. S. 9–10 (1882); Noerr v. Brewer, 1 MacArthur, 507 (1874).
[3] See generally R. S., Index.
[4] Act 25 Feb. 1879: 1 Supl. R. S. p. 149; R. S. § 706.
[5] R. S. §§ 1049–58: Act 23 June, 1874; 1 Ct. Cl. 3 3.

Its jurisdiction extends to all claims founded upon any law of Congress, any regulation of an executive department, any contract, express or implied, with the Government; to claims referred to it by either House of Congress; to set-offs, counter-claims, claims for damages, and other claims on the part of the United States against plaintiffs in said court.[1]

Its jurisdiction is limited to *contracts*. To constitute an implied contract there must have been a consideration moving to the United States, or they must have received the money charged with a duty to pay it over, or the claimant must have had a lawful right to it when received.[2]

The court has no equitable jurisdiction.[3]

For torts committed by an officer or agent of the United States, whether a remedy should be furnished, Congress has reserved for its own determination.[4]

The court may enter a judgment on a set-off against the claimant.[5]

An alien may sue, provided the like right is accorded an American citizen to prosecute claims against his government.[6]

The common-law rule which excludes interested parties as witnesses is observed; but, at the instance of the solicitor of the United States, a claimant may be required to testify.[7]

The court may appoint commissioners to take testimony.[8]

Suits in this court are not suits at common law; hence, trial by jury is not a right in a claimant.[9]

The court has never felt bound by the strict rules of pleading incident to actions in courts of common law or in equity. It seeks to administer justice by simple and convenient forms, and makes such interlocutory orders as will lead to the doing of complete justice without prolonged litigation.[10]

The limitation of writs is six years after the claim has accrued, with the usual allowance in cases of disability.[11]

Prior to 1855 claimants were heard by Congress. This court was established, in that year, to relieve Congress, to protect the government by regular investigation, and to benefit claimants by affording them a certain mode of examining and adjudicating claims.

---

[1] R. S. § 1059: several Acts, and cases.

[2] Knote v. United States, 95 U. S. 156 (1877).

[3] Bonner v. United States, 9 Wall. 160 (1869).

[4] Langford v. United States, 101 U. S. 344 (1879); Nichols v. United States, 7 Wall. 126 (1868); Gordon v. United States, 2 id. 561 (1864); 8 id. 269.

[5] R. S. § 1061. See 17 Wall. 209; 12 Ct. Cl. 317.

[6] R. S. § 1068. See 6 Ct. Cl. 171, 192; 9 id. 254; 11 Wall. 178.

[7] R. S. §§ 1079-80. See United States v. Clark, 96 U. S. 37 (1877).

[8] R. S. §§ 1071, 1080.

[9] M'Elrath v. United States, 12 Ct. Cl. 317 (1876).

[10] Brown v. District of Columbia, 17 Ct. Cl. 310 (1881), cases.

[11] R. S. § 1069. See 107 U. S. 124.

Originally it was a court in name, for its power extended only to the preparation of bills to be submitted to Congress. In 1863 the number of judges was increased from three to five, its jurisdiction was enlarged, and it was authorized to render final judgment, subject to appeal to the Supreme Court and to an estimate by the secretary of the treasury of the amount required to pay each claimant. Congress repealed this provision for an estimate — as inconsistent with the finality essential to judicial decisions; since which time the court has exercised all the functions of a court. It is one of those "inferior courts" which Congress may establish.[1]

As at first organized, the court was an auditing board authorized to pass upon claims submitted to it, and to report to the secretary of the treasury. He submitted to Congress, for an appropriation, such confirmed claims as he approved, with no right of appeal in the claimant. The jurisdiction of the court has received frequent additions by the reference of cases to it under special statutes, and by other changes in the general law; but the principle originally adopted of limiting its general jurisdiction to cases of contract, remains.[2]

Appeal lies from it to the Supreme Court in the exercise of the general jurisdiction of the latter. And an appeal taken before the right therefor has expired is not vacated by an appropriation by Congress of the amount necessary to pay the judgment.[3]

The act approved March 3, 1887 (24 St. L 505), provides, That the court of claims shall have jurisdiction to hear and determine the following matters:

First. All claims founded upon the Constitution of the United States or any law of Congress, except for pensions, or upon any regulation of an executive department, or upon any contract, express or implied, with the government of the United States, or for damages, liquidated or unliquidated, in cases not sounding in tort, in respect to which claims the party would be entitled to redress against the United States either in a court of law, equity, or admiralty if the United States were suable: *Provided, however,* That nothing in this section shall be construed as giving to either of the courts herein mentioned, jurisdiction to hear and determine claims growing out of the late civil war, and commonly known as "war claims," or to hear and determine other claims, which have heretofore been rejected, or reported on adversely by any court, department, or commission authorized to hear and determine the same.

Second. All set-offs, counter-claims, claims for damages, whether liquidated or unliquidated, or other demands whatsoever on the part of the government of the United States against any claimant against the government in said court: *Provided,* That no suit

---

[1] United States v. Klein, 13 Wall. 144 (1871), Chase, Chief Justice.

[2] Langford v. United States, 101 U. S. 344-45 (1879), Miller, J.; Gordon v. United States, 117 id. 697 (1864), Taney, C. J.; 1 Dev. Ct. Cl. 41-53; 17 Ct. Cl. 1-29: 7 South. Law Rev. 781-811 (1882).

[3] United States v. Jones, 119 U. S. 477 (1886), Waite, C. J. Explains Gordon v. United States, and other cases.

against the government of the United States, shall be allowed under this act unless the same shall have been brought within six years after the right accrued for which the claim is made.

Sec. 2. That the district courts of the United States shall have concurrent jurisdiction with the court of claims as to all matters named in the preceding section where the amount of the claim does not exceed one thousand dollars, and the circuit courts of the United States shall have such concurrent jurisdiction in all cases where the amount of such claim exceeds one thousand dollars and does not exceed ten thousand dollars. All causes brought and tried under the provisions of this act shall be tried by the court without a jury.

Sec. 3. That whenever any person shall present his petition to the court of claims alleging that he is or has been indebted to the United States as an officer or agent thereof, or by virtue of any contract therewith, or that he is the guarantor, or surety, or personal representative of any officer, or agent, or contractor so indebted, or that he, or the person for whom he is such surety, guarantor, or personal representative has held any office or agency under the United States, or entered into any contract therewith, under which it may be or has been claimed that an indebtedness to the United States has arisen and exists, and that he or the person he represents has applied to the proper department of the government requesting that the account of such office, agency, or indebtedness may be adjusted and settled, and that three years have elapsed from the date of such application and said account still remains unsettled and unadjusted, and that no suit upon the same has been brought by the United States, said court shall, due notice first being given to the head of said department and to the attorney-general of the United States, proceed to hear the parties and ascertain the amount, if any, due the United States on said account. The attorney-general shall represent the United States at the hearing of said cause. The court may postpone the same from time to time whenever justice shall require. The judgment of said court or of the Supreme Court of the United States, to which an appeal shall lie, as in other cases, as to the amount due, shall be binding and conclusive upon the parties. The payment of such amount so found due by the court shall discharge such obligation. An action shall accrue to the United States against such principal, or surety, or representative to recover the amount so found due, which may be brought at any time within three years after the final judgment of said court. Unless suit shall be brought within said time, such claim and the claim on the original indebtedness shall be forever barred.

Sec. 4. That the jurisdiction of the respective courts of the United States proceeding under this act, including the right of exception and appeal, shall be governed by the law now in force, in so far as the same is applicable and not inconsistent with the provisions of this act; and the course of procedure shall be in accordance with the established rules of said respective courts, and of such additions and modifications thereof as said courts may adopt.

Sec. 5. That the plaintiff in any suit brought under the provisions of the second section of this act shall file a petition, duly verified with the clerk of the respective court having jurisdiction of the case, and in the district where the plaintiff resides. Such petition shall set forth the full name and residence of the plaintiff, the nature of his claim, and a succinct statement of the facts upon which the claim is based, the money or any other thing claimed, or the damages sought to be recovered and praying the court for a judgment or decree upon the facts and law.

Sec. 6. That the plaintiff shall cause a copy of his petition filed under the preceding section to be served upon the district attorney of the United States in the district wherein suit is brought, and shall mail a copy of the same, by registered letter, to the attorney-general of the United States, and shall thereupon cause to be filed with the clerk of the court wherein suit is instituted an affidavit of such service and the mailing of such letter. It shall be the duty of the district attorney upon whom service of petition is made as aforesaid to appear and defend the interests of the government in the suit, and within sixty days after the service of petition upon him, unless the time should be extended by order of the court made in the case, to file a plea, answer, or demurrer on the part of the government, and to file a notice of any counter-claim, set-off, claim for damages, or other demand or defense whatsoever of the government in the premises: *Provided*, That should the district attorney neglect or refuse to file the plea, answer, demurrer, or defense, as required, the plaintiff may proceed with the case under such rules as the court may adopt in the premises; but the plaintiff shall not have judgment or decree for his claim, or any part thereof, unless he shall establish the same by proof satisfactory to the court.

Sec. 7. That it shall be the duty of the court to cause a written opinion to be filed in the cause, setting forth the specific findings by the court of the facts therein, and the conclusions of the court upon all questions of law involved in the case, and to render judgment thereon. If the suit be in equity or admiralty, the court shall proceed with the same according to the rules of such courts.

Sec. 8. That in the trial of any suit brought under any of the provisions of this act, no person shall be excluded as a witness because he is a party to or interested in said suit; and any plaintiff or party in interest may be examined as a witness on the part of the government.

Section 1079 of the Revised Statutes is hereby repealed. The provisions of section 1080 of the Revised Statutes shall apply to cases under this act.

Sec. 9. That the plaintiff or the United States, in any suit brought under the provisions of this act shall have the same rights of appeal or writ of error as are now reserved in the statutes of the United States in that behalf made, and upon the conditions and limitations therein contained. The modes of procedure in claiming and perfecting an appeal or writ of error shall conform in all respects, and as near as may be, to the statutes and rules of court governing appeals and writs of error in like causes.

Sec. 10. That when the findings of fact and the law applicable thereto have been filed in any case as provided in section six of this act, and the judgment or decree is adverse to the government, it shall be the duty of the district attorney to transmit to the attorney-general of the United States certified copies of all the papers filed in the cause, with a transcript of the testimony taken, the written findings of the court, and his written opinion as to the same; whereupon the attorney-general shall determine and direct whether an appeal or writ of error shall be taken or not; and when so directed the district attorney shall cause an appeal or writ of error to be perfected in accordance with the terms of the statutes and rules of practice governing the same: *Provided*, That no appeal or writ of error shall be allowed after six months from the judgment or decree in such suit. From the date of such final judgment or decree interest shall be computed thereon, at the rate of four per centum per annum, until the time when an appropriation is made for the payment of the judgment or decree.

Sec. 11. That the attorney-general shall report to Congress, and at the beginning of each session of Congress, the suits under this act in which a final judgment or decree has been rendered giving the date of each, and a statement of the costs taxed in each case.

Sec. 12. That when any claim or matter may be pending in any of the executive departments which involves controverted questions of fact or law, the head of such department, with the consent of the claimant, may transmit the same, with the vouchers, papers, proofs, and documents pertaining thereto, to said court of claims, and the same shall be there proceeded in under such rules as the court may adopt. When the facts and conclusions of law shall have been found, the court shall report its findings to the department by which it was transmitted.

Sec. 13. That in every case which shall come before the court of claims, or is now pending therein, under the provisions of an act entitled "An act to afford assistance and relief to Congress and the executive departments in the investigation of claims and demands against the government," approved March 3, 1883, if it shall appear to the satisfaction of the court, upon the facts established, that it has jurisdiction to render judgment or decree thereon under existing laws or under the provisions of this act, it shall proceed to do so, giving to either party such further opportunity for hearing as in its judgment justice shall require, and report its proceedings therein to either House of Congress or to the department by which the same was referred to said court.

Sec. 14. That whenever any bill, except for a pension, shall be pending in either House of Congress providing for the payment of a claim against the United States, legal or equitable, or for a grant, gift, or bounty to any person, the House in which such bill is pending may refer the same to the court of claims, who shall proceed with the same in accordance with the provisions of the act approved March 3, 1883, entitled an "Act to afford assistance and relief to Congress and the executive departments in the investigation of claims and demands against the government," and report to such House the facts in the case and the amount, where the same can be liquidated, including any facts bearing upon the question whether there has been delay or laches in presenting such claim or applying for such grant, gift, or bounty, and any facts

bearing upon the question whether the bar of any statute of limitation should be removed or which shall be claimed to excuse the claimant for not having resorted to any established legal remedy.

Sec. 15. If the government of the United States shall put in issue the right of the plaintiff to recover the court may, in its discretion, allow costs to the prevailing party from the time of joining such issue. Such costs, however, shall include only what is actually incurred for witnesses, and for summoning the same, and fees paid to the clerk of the court.

Sec. 16. That all laws and parts of laws inconsistent with this act are hereby repealed.

For additional information as to the powers and practice of the United States courts see particular terms, such as ADMIRALTY; BANKRUPTCY; CITIZEN; COMITY; CONSTITUTION; CONTEMPT, 1; COSTS; DEPOSITION; DISCRETION, 3-5; GOWN, 1; JURISDICTION, 2; LAW, Common, Supreme; MARSHAL, 1 (2); PROCEDURE; REMOVAL, 2; RES, 2; STATE, 3 (2); SUIT, 3; VENUE; WITNESS.

COURT-MARTIAL. See MARTIAL.

COURT-YARD. See COURT, 1; CURTILAGE.

COUSIN. Sometimes means a cousin by marriage.

A similar usage obtains as to the words "nephew" and "niece." A person speaking of another by his name and relationship is likely to be most accurate as to the name.[1] See CONSANGUINITY.

COVENANT.[2] 1. A promise under seal: as, a covenant to pay rent.[3]

May be used not in its limited, technical sense of a promise evidenced by a sealed instrument, but in the wider sense of any contract in general.[4]

Although words of proviso and condition may be construed as words of covenant, if such be the apparent intent and meaning of the parties, covenant will not arise unless it can be collected from the whole instrument that, on the part of the person sought to be charged, there was an agreement, or an engagement, to do or not to do some particular act.[5]

A covenant or convention is a clause of agreement in a deed, whereby either party may stipulate for the truth of certain facts, or bind himself to perform, or give, something to or for the other.[6]

Thus, the grantor of land may covenant that he has a right to convey, or for the grantee's quiet enjoyment, or the like; the grantee may covenant to pay rent, or to keep the premises in repair,[6] etc.

[1] Cloak v. Hammond, 52 Law Times, 134, 97 (1886): 35 Alb. Law J. 66.

[2] F. *covenant, convenant*, agreement: L. *convenire*, to come together, agree.

[3] [Greenleaf v. Allen, 127 Mass. 253 (1879).

[4] Riddle v. McKinney, 67 Tex. 32 (1886), Gaines, A. J.

[5] Hale v. Finch, 104 U. S. 268-69 (1881), cases, Harlan, J.; 52 Tex. 226.

[6] [2 Bl. Com. 304.

Covenantor. He who makes a covenant. **Covenantee.** He in whose favor a covenant is made.

Express covenant. A covenant explicitly stated in words. **Implied covenant.** Such covenant as is inferred or imputed in law from words used.[1]

Express covenants are also called covenants *in deed;* and implied covenants, covenants *in law.* Any words, such as "I covenant," "I agree," "I bind myself," plainly showing an intent to be bound, raise an express covenant; while a covenant may be implied from the use of such words as "grant," "bargain and sell," "give," "demise,"[2] *q. v.*

Joint covenant. A covenant that binds all the covenantors together as one person. **Several covenant.** Such as binds each covenantor separately. **Joint and several covenant.** Binds all covenantors together, or each singly.

When the legal interest in a covenant and in the cause of action thereon is joint, the covenant is joint, although in its terms it may be several, or joint and several.[3] See further JOINT.

Dependent covenant. A covenant in which the obligation for performance is conditioned upon performance of another covenant, made prior or at the same time. **Independent covenant.** In this the duty of performance rests solely upon the terms of the covenant in itself considered, irrespective of the performance or non-performance of any other covenant.

A "dependent covenant" rests upon the prior performance of some act or condition, and until the condition is performed the other party is not liable to an action on his covenant. Under an "independent covenant" either party may recover damages from the other for injuries received by a breach of the covenants in his favor; and it is no excuse for the defendant to allege a breach of covenants on the part of the plaintiff.[4]

If the whole is to be performed on one side, before anything else is to be done on the other side, the covenants are dependent, and performance is a condition precedent. But if something is to be done one side, before the whole can be performed on the other, the covenants are independent. . . . A dependent stipulation is a condition, performance of which must be averred and proved in order to a recovery. Mutual and independent stipulations are not conditions, but each party has a remedy by action for non-performance by the other, by showing performance on his own part.[1]

Whether a covenant is dependent or independent is determined, in each case, by the intention of the parties as it appears on the instrument, and by the application of common sense; to which intention, when once discovered, all technical forms of expression must give way.[2]

Mutual covenants. Covenants as to which the thing to be done by one party is the consideration of the thing to be done by the other.

When a specified thing is to be done by one party as the consideration of the thing to be done by the other party, the covenants are mutual, and also dependent, if they are to be performed at the same time; and if, by the terms or nature of the contract, one is first to be performed as the condition of the obligation of the other, that which is first must be done or tendered before the party who is entitled to its performance can sustain a suit against the other party. If a day is fixed for the performance of a mutual covenant, the party whose duty it is to perform or tender performance first must do it on that day, or show his readiness to do it, else he cannot recover for non-performance by the other party. But both at common law and in chancery there are exceptions, growing out of the nature of the thing to be done and the conduct of the parties. The case of part performance, possession, etc., in chancery, where time is not of the essence of the contract, or has been waived by acquiescence, is an example of the latter; and the case of contracts for building houses, railroads, etc., in which the means of the builder and his labor become combined and affixed to the soil, or mixed with materials and money of the owner, afford examples at law.[3]

When mutual covenants go to the whole consideration on both sides they are mutual conditions, the one precedent to the other; where they go to a part only, a remedy lies on one covenant to recover damages for a breach of it, but it is not a condition precedent.[2]

Real covenant. Such a covenant as affects realty, binding it in the hands of the covenantor, his grantee or devisee. **Personal covenant.** A covenant obligatory upon the maker only, or to the extent of his personalty.

If the covenantor covenants for himself and his "heirs," his covenant is real, and descends upon the heirs, who are bound to perform it, provided they have assets by descent; if he covenants also for his

[1] See Conrad v. Morehead, 89 N. C. 34 (1883).

[2] See 4 Kent, 468, 473.

[3] Capen v. Barrows, 1 Gray, 379 (1854), cases, Metcalf, J. See Calvert v. Bradley, 16 How. 596 (1853).

[4] Bailey v. White, 3 Ala. 331 (1842), Collier, C. J.

[1] White v. Atkins, 8 Cush. 370 (1851), cases, Shaw, C. J.; Matthews v. Jenkins, 80 Va. 467–68 (1885), cases.

[2] Lowber v. Bangs, 2 Wall. 736 (1864), cases; Lewis v. Chisolm, 68 Ga. 44–45 (1883), cases; Neis v. Yccum, 16 F. R. 170 (1883), cases; The Tornado, 108 U. S. 351 (1883); Cutter v. Powell, 2 Sm. L. C. 22–66, cases.

[3] Phillips, &c. Construction Co. v. Seymour, 91 U. S. 650 (1875), Miller, J.

"executors" and "administrators," both his personal and real assets stand pledged for the performance.[1]

A real covenant has for its object something annexed to, or inherent in, or connected with, land or other real property; and runs with the land, so that the grantee is invested with it, and may sue upon it for any breach happening in his time.[2]

Of covenants real the most important are *covenants for title*, which assure the full enjoyment of whatever the deed purports to convey: the covenants — of seisin, of a right to convey, for quiet enjoyment, against incumbrances, for further assurance, and of warranty, *qq. v.* In the United States they are sometimes called "full covenants."[3]

Other covenants relating to realty are: a covenant to convey; against nuisances or a particular use; to renew a lease.[4]

An article of agreement for the sale of land is a covenant to convey the land.[5] A covenant of a right to convey means that the covenantor has the capacity and a right to transfer the land in question: the same as a covenant of seisin,[6] *q. v.*

A covenant "runs with the land" when either the liability to perform it, that is, its burden, or the right to take advantage of it, that is, its benefit, passes to the assignee of the land.[7]

Covenants running with the land are: those annexed to the estate, such as the ancient warranty, now represented by the usual covenants of title; and those which are attached to the land itself, such as the rights of common or easements. Species of the latter class, to be enforceable against the assignees of the covenantor, must "touch and concern" or "extend to the support of" the land conveyed.[8]

On covenants to stand seized to uses, see USE, 3.

Other terms by which covenants are distinguished are: *affirmative*, that a thing has been or shall be done, and opposed to *negative*, not to do a thing; *alternative* or *disjunctive*, affording an election between things to be done; *auxiliary*, relating to another covenant as the principal, and discharged with it; *collateral*, connected with a grant, but not relating immediately to the thing, and opposed to *inherent*, affecting the particular property immediately; *concurrent*, to be performed at the same time with another; *declaratory*, limiting or directing a use; *executed*, performed, and opposed to *executory*, to be performed in the future; *general*, relating to lands generally and placing the covenantee in the position of a specialty creditor, and opposed to *special*, relating to particular land and giving the covenantee a lien thereon; *transitive*, passing over to the representatives of the maker, and opposed to *intransitive*, limited to the covenantor himself.

A grantor, conveying by deed of bargain and sale, by way of release or quitclaim of all his right and title to a tract of land, if made in good faith, without fraudulent representation, is not responsible for the goodness of the title beyond the covenants in his deed. He conveys nothing more than the estate of which he is possessed at the time; his deed does not pass an interest not then in existence. If the vendee has contracted for a particular estate, or for an estate in fee, he must take the precaution to secure himself by proper covenants of title. This principle is applicable to a deed of bargain and sale by release or quitclaim, in the strict sense of that species of conveyance. If the deed bears on its face evidence that the grantor intended to convey and that the grantee expected to become invested with an estate of a particular description or quality, and that the bargain had proceeded upon that footing, then, although it may not contain covenants of title in the technical sense, still the legal effect of the instrument will be as binding upon the grantor in respect to the estate thus described as if a formal covenant to that effect had been inserted; at least so far as to estop him from ever afterward denying that he was seized of the particular estate at the time of conveyance.[1]

In the absence of a recital estopping the grantor as to the character of his title or the quantum of interest to be conveyed, a covenant of general warranty, where the estate conveyed is the present interest of the grantor, does not operate as an estoppel to pass a title subsequently acquired.[2]

2. An action, or a form of action, at common law to recover damages for the breach of a contract under seal.

A covenant to do or to omit a direct act is a species of express contract, the breach of which is a civil injury. The remedy for any disadvantage or loss is by a *writ of covenant*, which directs the sheriff to command the defendant generally to keep his covenant with the plaintiff or to show good cause to the contrary. If the defendant continues refractory, or the covenant is already so broken that it cannot be specifically performed, the subsequent proceedings set forth with precision the covenant, the breach, and the loss

---

[1] 2 Bl. Com. 304.

[2] Davis *v.* Lyman, 6 Conn. 255 (1826), Hosmer, C. J.

[3] Rawle, Cov. Title, 24–27, 318.

[4] See 4 Kent, 473.

[5] See Espy *v.* Anderson, 14 Pa. 308 (1850); 11 Ill. 194; 19 Ohio, 347; 4 Md. 498; 19 Barb. 639.

[6] 2 Wash. R. P. 648; 10 Me. 91; 10 Cush. 134.

[7] Savage *v.* Mason, 3 Cush. 505 (1849); Shaber *v.* St. Paul Water Co., 15 Rep. 339 (1883); Spencer's Case, 1 Sm. L. C. *120–83, cases.

[8] Norcross *v.* James, 140 Mass. 189 (1885), cases, Holmes, J.: 25 Am. Law Reg. 64.

(19)

[1] Van Rennselaer *v.* Kearney, 11 How. 322–23 (1850), cases, Nelson, J.

[2] Hanrick *v.* Patrick, 119 U. S. 175–76 (1886), cases, Matthews, J.; Rawle, Cov. Tit. 333.

which has happened thereby; whereupon the jury will give damages in proportion to the injury sustained.[1]

Performance of a condition precedent (*q. v.*), if there is any such condition, must be averred.[2]

"Debt" will lie where the damages are liquidated.

Under the plea of *non est factum* (he did not make it), the defendant may show any fact contradicting the making of the instrument; as, personal incapacity, or that the deed was fraudulent, was not executed by all the parties, or was not delivered.

In Pennsylvania the defendant may plead "covenants performed with leave, etc.," that is, with leave, after notice to the plaintiff, to offer in evidence anything that amounts to a lawful defense. "Covenants performed, *absque hoc*" (without this) admits the execution, but puts the plaintiff to proof of performance.

. . "Covenants performed," although in substance a denial of the breach alleged, is an affirmative plea, and does not put the execution of the instrument in issue. "*Absque hoc*" puts in issue the performance on the part of the plaintiff as alleged by him. "With leave, etc.," implies an equitable defense, such as arises out of special circumstances, which the defendant intimates he means to offer in evidence.[3]

See CONDITION; CONTRACT; FACTUM, Non est; POSSIBILITY; PROVIDED; SEIZIN; WARRANTY, 1.

COVER. See COVERT; DISCOVERY.

COVERT.[4] 1. Covered, protected: as, a pound covert. See POUND, 2.

2. Implied, inferred: as, a covert condition.

3. Under the disability of marriage; married. **Discovert.** Unmarried, whether said of a widow or of a spinster.

Covert baron. A wife: under the protection of her husband or baron,[5] *q. v.*

Feme covert. A married woman: under the wing, protection or cover of her husband.[5]

Coverture. The condition of a woman during marriage. **Discoverture.** Not subject to the disability of being married.

Used as pleas in abatement, *q. v.*, and in speaking of the rights and liabilities of married women generally. See further DISABILITY; FEME, Covert; HUSBAND.

COVIN.[6] "A contrivance between two to defraud or cheat a third."[7]

"A secret assent determined in the hearts of two or more to the prejudice of another."[3]

Covinous. Collusive, fraudulent.

An example is where a tenant for life or tail secretly conspires with another that he shall recover the land held by such tenant to the prejudice of the reversioner.

COW. See ANIMAL; CRUELTY, 3.

A distinction between cow and heifer may or may not be intended in penal statutes,[1] and in a statute exempting a cow from sale on execution.[2] See HEIFER.

CR. Criminal; crown.

CRAFT. See VESSEL.

CRANK. Has no necessary defamatory meaning, any more than to say of one that he is capricious or subject to vagaries or whims.[3]

Does not necessarily imply that a man has been guilty of a crime, nor tend to subject him to ridicule or contempt. If the word has such import it should at least be averred and proven.[3]

CRAVE. See OYER.

CREATE. See CHARTER, 2.

CREDIBLE.[4] 1. Worthy of belief; deserving of confidence. See CREDIT, 1.

2. Entitled to be heard as a witness; competent. Competent to give evidence, and worthy of belief.

The English statute as to the execution of wills prior to 1838 required witnesses to be "credible." This was held to mean such persons as were not disqualified from giving testimony by imbecility, interest, or crime.[5]

This rule has been followed in Connecticut, Kentucky, Massachusetts, Mississippi, South Carolina, and several other States.[6]

As used in a statute requiring that a will disposing of realty shall be attested by credible witnesses, is equivalent to competent; not as meaning, in the loose popular sense, a person of good moral character and reputation in fact, and personally worthy of belief, but a person entitled to be examined in a court of justice, though subject to have his actual credit weighed and considered by the court or jury; and to be examined upon the question whether the will was duly executed, and by a person of disposing mind.[7]

Credibility. Being entitled to be believed; worthiness of belief.

In deciding upon the credibility of a witness it is usual to inquire whether he is capable of knowing a

---

[1] 3 Bl. Com. 156–57.

[2] 1 Chitty, Pl. 116.

[3] Farmers', &c. Turnpike Co. *v.* McCullough, 25 Pa. 304 (1855); 4 Dall. 439; 5 Pa. 199; 8 *id.* 272; 25 *id.* 303; 38 *id.* 75; 70 *id.* 194; 79 *id.* 336; 96 *id.* 239–40. See Act 25 May, 1887: P. L. 271.

[4] Küv'-ert. F. *couvrir*, to cover.

[5] [1 Bl. Com. 442.

[6] F. *couvenir*, to agree, covenant.

[7] Mix *v.* Muzzy, 28 Conn. 191 (1859): Ld. Ellenborough.

[8] Girdlestone *v.* Brighton Aquarium, 3 Ex. Div. 142 (1878): Termes de la Ley (1708, 1721).

---

[1] King *v.* Cook, 1 Leach, Cr. C. 123 (1774); 2 East, P. C. 616.

[2] Carruth *v.* Grassie, 11 Gray, 211 (1858); Pomeroy *v.* Trimper, 8 Allen, 400 (1864).

[3] Walker *v.* Chicago Tribune Co., 29 F. R. 827 (1887), Blodgett, J.

[4] L. *credere*, to believe, trust; also, to lend.

[5] 1 Jarman, Wills, 124.

[6] Fuller *v.* Fuller, 83 Ky. 350 (1885), cases.

[7] [Haven *v.* Hilliard, 23 Pick. 18 (1839), Shaw, C. J.; Amory *v.* Fellows, 5 Mass. *228 (1809), Parsons, C. J.; Jones *v.* Larrabee, 47 Me. 476 (1860), Appleton, J.; 38 Md. 424; 26 Conn. 416; 18 Ga. 40; 58 N. H. 8; 14 Tex. Ap. 72.

thing, and the particular thing, thoroughly; whether he was actually present; what attention he gave to the occurrence; and whether he honestly relates the affair as he remembers it.[1]

Credibility depends upon veracity and capacity to observe.[2] Literal coincidence of oral statements may afford ground for suspicion.[3] Affirmative testimony is the strongest.[4] When the credit due to witnesses is equal, preponderance is to be given to number.[5] Credibility is for the jury.[6] See further CHARACTER; COMPETENCY; IMPEACH, 3; WITNESS.

CREDIT. 1. In its primary sense, as a noun and a verb, imports reliance upon something said or done as the truth: belief or faith in testimony.

Discredit. To diminish the reliance to be placed upon testimony on any account whatever, and not necessarily for want of veracity in a person or for want of genuineness in a document. Compare IMPEACH, 2; INFAMY.

General credit. The general credit of a witness is his character as a credit-worthy man. **Particular credit.** Credit as a witness in a particular action.[7] See CREDIBLE.

2. The capacity of being trusted.[8]

The trust reposed in an individual, by those who deal with him, that he is able to meet his engagements.[9]

In an enlarged commercial sense, implies reputation and confidence; a basis on which the possessor may trade without immediate payment.[10]

The term also comprehends what is due to another person; and, again, time given in which to pay for a thing bought.

Credit is, strictly, a benefit as a means to procure property, and is not in itself recognized as property. Its whole office is to obtain trust. It is available to another by gift, sale, etc. Given gratuitously, it is a loan; given for a consideration, a *sale* of credit.[6]

Every contract for labor, not paid for in advance, is a contract upon credit; because the labor, when once performed, cannot be recalled. It is otherwise where property is to be paid for on delivery, for a delivery need not be made.[11]

---

[1] See 1 Greenl. Ev. §§ 2, 49, 431; 3 Bl. Com. 369.
[2] 1 Whart. Ev. § 404.
[3] 1 Whart. Ev. § 413.
[4] 1 Whart. Ev. § 415.
[5] 1 Whart. Ev. § 416.
[6] 1 Whart. Ev. §§ 391, 417.
[7] Bemis v. Kyle, 5 Abb. Pr. 233 (1867).
[8] Dry Dock Bank v. American Ins. Co., 3 N. Y. 356 (1850).
[9] [Owen v. Branch Bank at Mobile, 3 Ala. 267 (1842).
[10] [Rindge v. Judson, 24 N. Y. 71 (1861).
[11] Ketchum v. City of Buffalo, 14 N. Y. 365 (1856).

Credit, bill of. "No State . . shall emit Bills of Credit,"[1] that is, issue paper intended to circulate through the community, for its ordinary purposes as *money*, and redeemable at a future day.[2]

A paper issued by the sovereign power, containing a pledge of faith, and designed to circulate as money.[3]

The term may cover certificates of indebtedness, bearing interest;[2] but not bills of a bank chartered by a State, even though the State be the sole stockholder,[8] nor, even if it pledges its credit for their payment, in case the bank fails to redeem them.[4]

Credit, letter of. A letter written by one merchant or correspondent to another requesting him to credit the bearer with a sum of money.[5] See LETTER, 3, Of credit.

Mutual credits. In laws of set-off, "a knowledge on both sides of an existing debt due to one party, and a credit by the other party, founded on and trusting to such debt, as a means of discharging it."[6] See ACCOUNTS, Mutual; DEBTS, Mutual.

Creditor. In a strict literal sense, he who voluntarily trusts or gives credit to another, upon bond, bill, note, book, or simple contract, for money or other property. In a liberal sense, he who has a legal demand for money or other property which has come to the hands of another, without the consent of the former, but by mistake or accident, and to the payment or possession of which, or to compensation in damages therefor, he is entitled upon the ground of an implied promise. In a still more general sense, he who has a right by law to demand and recover of another a sum of money on any account whatever.[7]

Not simply a person to whom a debt is due, but a person to whom any obligation is due,— the last not being the usual meaning.[8]

---

[1] Constitution, Art. I, sec. 10, cl. 1.
[2] Craig v. Missouri, 4 Pet. 431 (1830), Marshall, C. J.
[3] Briscoe v. Bank of Kentucky, 11 Pet. 314 (1837), McLean, J.
[4] Darrington v. Bank of Alabama, 13 How. 16 (1851). See Legal Tender Case, 110 U. S. 443 (1883); Virginia Coupon Cases, 114 *id.* 283 (1885); 2 Story, Const. §§ 1362-64; 4 Kent, 408.
[6] Mechanics' Bank v. N. Y. & New Haven R. Co., 4 Duer, 586 (1855); McCulloch's Commercial Dict.
[6] 2 Story, Eq. § 1435; Munger v. Albany City Nat. Bank, 85 N. Y. 590 (1881), Folger, C. J.
[7] [Stanley v. Ogden, 2 Root, 261 (1795).]
[8] [New Jersey Ins. Co. v. Meeker, 37 N. J. L. 300 (1875), Beasley, C. J.

One who has the right to require the fulfillment of an obligation or contract.[1] Compare DEBTOR.

The term may merely designate a person. Thus, although the relation of debtor and creditor has been dissolved, the person who was the "debtor" in a contract for usurious interest may testify against him who was the "creditor."[2]

No one, unsolicited, may make himself the creditor of another.[3] See NEGOTIABLE.

Domestic creditor. A creditor resident within the county or the State of the debtor's domicil, or where his property is situated. *Foreign creditor.* One who resides within another jurisdiction.[4]

Execution creditor. A creditor who has obtained a levy upon property belonging to his debtor.

Existing creditor. A person who becomes the creditor of another after the latter has made an invalid transfer of his property, and before the invalidity has been removed.[5]

General creditors, or *creditors at large.* Creditors of an insolvent whose claims are to be satisfied *pro rata* out of any balance left after the claims of secured or favored creditors have been paid.

Judgment creditor. He whose claim has been merged into a judgment against his debtor, and under which, generally, execution may be had.

Junior creditor. A person who becomes a creditor after some other has become a creditor; also termed a "younger," "later," or "subsequent" creditor, and particularly used with reference to the validity of the liens of judgment creditors.

Lien creditor. A creditor who has for evidence of his claim a judgment, mortgage, or other lien regularly entered of record.

Preferred creditor. A creditor who the law, or the debtor, has directed shall be paid before others. See PREFER, 2.

Secured creditor. A creditor who has the possession of, or a lien upon, property of his debtor, as security for the payment of his claim. Opposed, *unsecured creditor.*

Subsequent or *future creditors; existing creditors; prior creditors.* See ASSIGN; CONVEYANCE, Fraudulent; RECEIVER; STOCK, 3 (2); SUFFER.

Creditor's bill. A bill in equity filed by one or more creditors of a deceased person for an account of the assets and a settlement of the estate of the decedent.

A single creditor may file his bill for payment of his own debt, and seek a recovery of assets for this purpose only. But the more usual course is for one or more creditors to file a bill by and on behalf of himself or themselves, and all other creditors who shall come under the decree, for an account of the assets, and a due settlement of the estate. The principle is that as equality is equity the assets should be distributed without that preference allowed at common law. The usual decree is, *quod computet:* that the master take the accounts between the deceased and all his creditors; and an account of all the personal estate of the deceased in the hands of the executor or administrator, the same to be applied in payment of the debts and other charges, in a due course of administration. Thereafter, a creditor may not carry on a suit at law except as the court of equity may allow.[1]

Such a bill lies for a discovery of assets. The court will proceed to a final decree on the merits. The usual decree is for an account; but where the representative of the deceased admits assets, the decree is for immediate payment.[2]

It is no doubt generally true that a creditor's bill, to subject his debtor's interests in property to the payment of the debt, must show that all remedy at law had been exhausted. And, generally, it must be averred that judgment has been recovered for the debt, that execution has been issued, and that it has been returned *nulla bona.* The reason is, until such a showing is made, it does not appear, in most cases, that resort to a court of equity is necessary, in other words that the creditor is remediless at law. But a fruitless execution is not necessary to show that the creditor has no adequate legal remedy. Thus, when the debtor's estate is a mere equitable one, which cannot be reached by any proceeding at law, there is no reason for requiring attempts to reach it by legal processes.[3]

In Illinois a creditor's bill is defined to be a bill by which a creditor seeks to satisfy his debt out of some equitable estate of the defendant which is not liable to a levy and sale under an execution at law.[4]

CREDIT-MOBILIER.[5] A company or bank formed for advancing money on personal estate, generally with the declared ob-

[1] Hardy *v.* Norfolk Manuf. Co., 80 Va. 423 (1885), Lacy, J.

[2] Gifford *v.* Whitcomb, 9 Cush. 483 (1852), cases, Bigelow, J.; 28 Minn. 153.

[3] Gurnee *v.* Bausemer, 80 Va. 872 (1885), cases.

[4] On enjoining creditors from proceeding in a foreign jurisdiction, see 23 Cent. Law J. 268 (1886), cases.

[5] McAfee *v.* Busby, 69 Iowa, 331 (1886); 38 *id.* 215.

[1] 1 Story, Eq. §§ 546–49; Richmond *v.* Irons, 121 U. S. 44 (1887), cases.

[2] Kennedy *v.* Creswell, 101 U. S. 645–46 (1879), cases.

[3] Case *v.* Beauregard, 101 U. S. 690–91 (1879), cases, Strong, J.

[4] Newman *v.* Willetts, 52 Ill. 98 (1869): Chancery Code, §§ 36–37.

[5] Krā'-dē-mō-bē-le-ā'. F. *crédit,* credit; *mobilier,* movable, personal: L. *mobilis,* movable.

ject of promoting industrial enterprises, such as the construction of railways, the sinking of mines, and the like.[1]

CREW. See REVOLT; SHIP.

Whenever, in a statute, the words "master" and "crew" occur in connection with each other, "crew" embraces all the officers as well as the common seamen — the ship's company; as, in the act of March 3, 1835, § 3, which punishes cruelty by a master or other officer, toward the crew.[2]

CRIER. One who proclaims: an officer of a court whose duty it is to announce the opening and adjournment of the court; to call the names of suitors, jurors, and witnesses; to proclaim that the acknowledgment of a sheriff's deed is about to be taken, or a special return received of the distribution made of the proceeds of a sale by the sheriff; and to make various other proclamations of a public nature, under the directions of the judges of the court.[3]

On the assembling of the Supreme Court the proclamation made by the marshal is in these words: "The honorable the chief justice and associate justices of the Supreme Court of the United States. Oyez! oyez! oyez! all persons having business before the honorable, the Supreme Court of the United States, are admonished to draw near and give their attention, for the court is now sitting. God save the United States and this honorable Court."

"Let the cryer make proclamation and say, O yes, O yes, O yes, Silence is commanded in the Court, While the Justices are sitting, upon pain of imprisonment. After silence is Commanded, The Cryer shall make a proclamation saying: All manner of persons that have anything to doe, at this Court, Draw Nigh and give your attendance, and if any person shall have any Complaint to enter, or suit to prosecute, Let them Draw near, and they shall be heard."[4]

CRIM. CON. See CONVERSATION, 1.

CRIME. An act committed or omitted in violation of a public law either forbidding or commanding it.[5] See CRIMEN.

A wrong of which the law takes cognizance as injurious to the public, and punishes in what is called a criminal proceeding prosecuted by the State in its own name or in the name of the people or the sovereign.[6]

A crime is a breach and violation of the public rights and duties due to the whole community in its social aggregate capacity;

a public wrong. Distinguished from a private wrong, which is a civil injury or tort.[1]

Crime and misdemeanor are synonymous terms; though, in common usage, "crimes" denotes such offenses as are of a deeper and more atrocious dye; while smaller faults, and omissions of less consequence, are comprised under the gentler name of "misdemeanors."[1] See MISDEMEANOR, 2.

In short, the term "crime" embraces any and every indictable offense.[2]

Yet it is not synonymous with "felony."[3]

Capital crime. A crime punishable with death. See PUNISHMENT, Capital.

High crime. Used, with no definite meaning, in prosecutions by impeachment; merely serves to give greater solemnity to the charge.

High crimes and misdemeanors are such immoral and unlawful acts as are nearly allied and equal in guilt to felony, yet, owing to some technical circumstance, do not fall within the definition of felony.[4]

Infamous crime. Offenses which rendered the perpetrator infamous at common law were treason, felony, and the *crimen falsi*.[5] See further INFAMY.

Statutory crime. An act which has been made a criminal offense by enactment of a legislature. **Common-law crime,** or **crime at common law.** Any indictable offense at common law.

All offenses against the government of the United States are of statutory origin: no common-law offense can be committed against it.[6] See LAW, Common.

Crimes may be classified as offenses against the sovereignty of the state; against the public — peace, health, justice, trade, policy, property; against the lives and persons of individuals; against private property; against the currency, and public and private securities; against religion, decency, and morality; against the law of nations, *qq. v.*

Established principles are: That the trial of all crimes, except in cases of impeachment, shall be by jury, and in the State where the same was committed; but when not committed within any State, the trial shall be at such place as Congress may have directed.[7] No person shall be held to answer for a capital, or otherwise infamous crime, unless on presentment or indictment of a grand jury, nor be subject for the

---

[1] [Worcester's Dict.

[2] United States *v.* Winn, 3 Sumn. 212 (1838), Story, J.

[3] See R. S. § 715.

[4] Laws of Province of Penn. (1682): Linn, 128.

[5] 4 Bl. Com. 5.

[6] *Re* Bergin, 31 Wis. 386 (1872). See 1 Bish. Cr. L. § 32.

[1] [4 Bl. Com. 5; 3 *id.* 2.

[2] See People *v.* Police Commissioners, 39 Hun, 510 (1886); 7 Conn. 185; 60 Ill. 168; 32 N. J. L. 144; 9 Wend. 212; 9 Tex. 340; 24 How. 102; 26 Vt. 208; 41 *id.* 511; 2 N. Y. Rev. St. 70, § 22.

[3] County of Lehigh *v.* Schock, 113 Pa. 379 (1886).

[4] State *v.* Knapp, 6 Conn. 417 (1827); 1 Russ. Cr. 61. See Const. Art. II, sec. 4; 24 How. 102.

[5] People *v.* Toynbee, 20 Barb. 189 (1855).

[6] United States *v.* Britton, 108 U. S. 206 (1885); United States *v.* Walsh, 5 Dill. 60 (1878).

[7] See Constitution, Art. III, sec. 2, cl. 3.

same offense to be twice put in jeopardy of life and limb; nor be compelled in any criminal case to be a witness against himself, nor be deprived of life, liberty, or property without due process of law.[1] In all criminal prosecutions the accused shall enjoy the right of a speedy and public trial by an impartial jury of the State and district wherein the crime shall have been committed, which district shall have been previously ascertained by law, and to be informed of the nature and cause of the accusation; to be confronted with the witnesses against him; to have compulsory process for obtaining witnesses in his favor, and to have the assistance of counsel for his defense.[2] No *ex post facto* law shall be passed — by Congress or by any State.[3]

The foregoing principles restrict the power of the United States government, and do not affect State legislation. But the same principles, expressed in identically or substantially the same language, are also found in the constitutions of the States, as part of the rights which are declared to be excepted out of the general powers of government, and not delegated to the law-enacting department.

See in detail the names of particular crimes; also ACCESSARY; ACCIDENT; AID, 2; ATTEMPT; BAIL, 2; CAUSE, 2; CHARACTER; COMMIT, 3; COMPACT, Social; COMPOUND, 4; CONFESSION, 2; CONFRONT; CONVICT; COSTS; DAMAGES; DECEIT, 2; DECOY; DEGREE, 2; DELIBERATION, 3; DRUNKENNESS; DUEL; DOUBT, Reasonable; EQUITY; EVIDENCE; EXTRADITION; FACTUM, Ex post; FELONY; FINE, 2; FORFEITURE; GUILTY; IGNORANCE; INDICTMENT; INFAMY; INNOCENT, 2; INSANITY, 2 (6); INTENT; JEOPARDY; JURY, Trial; MERGER, 3; OBSCENE; PARDON; POLICE, 2, 3; PREMEDITATE; PRESENT, 1; PROCESS, 1; PUNISH; RATIFICATION; REVOLT; REWARD, 1; SENTENCE; WAIVER; WILL, 1; WITNESS; WRONG. Compare CRIMEN; DELICTUM.

Criminal. 1, *adj.* Involving the commission of an offense against the public; also, pertaining to the law upon the subject of public wrongs or crimes. Opposed to *civil*, q. v.

As, criminal or a criminal — act, action, case, contempt, conversation, court, information, intent, jurisdiction, law, libel, offense, procedure, process, prosecution, *qq. v.*

2, *n.* A person who has committed an indictable offense against the public. Compare CONVICT, 2.

Criminate. To exhibit evidence of the commission of an indictable offense; to show or prove to be guilty of crime.

No person "shall be compelled in any Criminal Case to be a witness against himself." [4]

---

[1] See Constitution, Amd. V.

[2] See Constitution, Amd. VI.

[3] See Constitution, Art. I. sec. 9, cl. 3; sec. 10, par. 1. As to criminal jurisdiction in the Federal courts see under COURTS, United States, and 26 Am. Law Reg. 703-9 (1887), cases.

[4] Constitution, Amd. V.

A witness cannot be compelled *to* answer a question which may expose him to a penalty or punishment.[1] A statement made under compulsion cannot be used to show guilt: confessions (*q. v.*) are to be free and voluntary.[2] But a party cannot claim this privilege. The danger to prosecution must be real. Exposure to civil liability, or to police prosecution, will not excuse. The court determines as to the reasonableness of the objection. Waiver of part of the privilege waives all. Pardon and statutes of indemnity do away with protection.[3]

If an accused person offers himself as a witness in his own behalf to disprove the charge he thereby waives his privilege as to all matters connected with the offense.[4]

An accused may be cross-questioned as to whether he has not been convicted of other charges of crime.[5]

A party on trial for violating an election law who testifies that he did not write names unlawfully entered in a registration book may be compelled, on cross-examination, to write the names in the presence of the jury, as evidence in rebuttal.[6]

Excriminate. To free from a charge or suspicion of crime; to exculpate. Whence excriminatory.

Incriminate. To charge with crime; to criminate; to inculpate. Whence incriminatory.

Recriminate. To charge crime back upon an accuser; particularly, for the respondent in divorce proceedings to acknowledge the offense charged and to make a counter-accusation against the libelant. Whence recrimination, recriminative, recriminatory.

Recrimination as a bar to divorce is not limited to a charge of the same nature as that alleged in the libel. It is sufficient if the counter-charge is a cause for divorce of equal grade. Thus, in Massachusetts, a respondent charged with adultery may reply that the libelant was at the time serving a sentence in the State prison.[7]

CRIMEN. L. A crime, a fault; literally, a judicial decision, or that which is subjected to a judicial decision; an accusation of wrong.

---

[1] 1 Greenl. Ev. § 451.

[2] Emery's Case, 107 Mass. 180 (1871); United States *v.* Prescott, 2 Dill. 405 (1872); 1 Den. Cr. Cas. 236.

[3] See United States *v.* M'Carthy, 18 F. R. 87 (1883); Youngs *v.* Youngs, 5 Redf. 505, 509-11 (1882), cases; *Exp.* Reynolds, 20 Ch. D. 294 (1882); 1 Whart. Ev. §§ 533-40; 2 Crim. Law Mag. 313. That court to decide, see also *Exp.* Stice, 70 Cal. 53 (1886).

[4] Spies *et al. v.* People, 122 Ill. 235 (1887); Whart. Cr. Ev. § 432.

[5] State *v.* Pfefferle, 36 Kan. 92-96 (1886), cases: 35 Alb. Law J. 63.

[6] United States *v.* Mullaney, 32 F. R. 370 (1887), Brewer, J.

[7] Morrison *v.* Morrison, 142 Mass. 362 (1886), cases; Handy *v.* Handy, 124 *id.* 395 (1878), cases.

Crimen falsi. The crime of deceiving or falsifying. At common law, any offense involving falsehood, and which might injuriously affect the administration of justice by the introduction of falsehood and fraud.[1]

The exact extent and meaning of the expression is nowhere stated with precision. In the Roman law it included every species of fraud and deceit.[1]

Offenses included, at common law, are: forgery, perjury, subornation of perjury, suppression of testimony by bribery or by conspiracy to procure the non-attendance of witnesses, conspiracy to accuse an innocent person of crime, barratry, counterfeiting money or an official seal, making or dealing by false weights or measures, falsification of records. To this list others have been added by statute.

The effect of a conviction for a crime of this class is infamy,[2] *q. v.*

Crimen læsæ majestatis. The crime of wounding majesty: treason, *q. v.*

Flagrans crimen. A crime being committed. *Flagrante crimine.* While a criminal act is being committed; literally, a crime in its very heat.

Locus criminis. The place of a crime — where committed.

Particeps criminis. One who takes part in a crime; an accomplice. See PARTICEPS.

CRIMINAL; CRIMINATE. See under CRIME, p. 294.

CRITICISM. See REVIEW, 3.

CROP. That which is cropped, cut, or gathered;[3] the valuable part of what is planted in the earth; fruit; harvest. Compare CULTIVATION; FRUCTUS.

Crop-time. That portion of the year which is occupied in making and gathering the crops.[4]

Away-going crop. A crop sown by a tenant who will be no longer tenant at harvest-time; that is, a crop which is sown before but ripens after the end of the tenant's term.

Where the term of a tenant for years depends upon a certainty, as if he holds from midsummer for ten years, and in the last year he sows a crop, which is not cut before the end of his term, the landlord shall have the crop; for the tenant knew the expiration of his term, and it was his own folly to sow what he could never reap the profit of. Otherwise, however, where

the lease depends upon an uncertainty, as, the life of some one, or an act of God.[1]

But now, generally, where the lease ends in the spring, the tenant has the crop of *winter* grain sown the autumn before; and the straw is part of the crop. See EMBLEMENTS.

Growing crop. Any annual crop raised by cultivation.

In some States, regarded as personalty, and leviable with a right to harvest it; in a few States, realty.

Whether a contract for the sale of a growing crop is for "an interest in or concerning lands," to be in writing under the Statute of Frauds, seems to be answered in conformity with the intention of the parties. And so as to growing grass, growing trees, and fruits; although, according to some cases, emblements only are to be considered as chattels, while the spontaneous growth of the land remains a part of it, at least, until ripe and ready for removal. Whenever the parties connect the land and its growth together the growth comes within the statute.[2]

"The lien of a mortgage on a growing crop continues on the crop after severance, whether remaining in its original state or converted into another product, so long as the same remains on the land of the mortgagor." Such lien is not lost by a tortious removal by a person having constructive notice of the lien; and the mortgagee may maintain an action for the conversion.[3]

Outstanding crop. A crop in the field — not gathered and housed, without regard to its state. It is "outstanding" from the day it commences to grow until gathered and taken away.[4] See FAIR; HARVEST.

Cropper. One who, having no interest in the land, works it in consideration of receiving a portion of the crop for his labor.[5]

One hired to work land and to be compensated by a share of the produce.[6]

He has no estate in the land; his possession is that of the landlord, who must divide off to the cropper his share of the crops. A "tenant" has an estate in the land, and a right of property in the crops. Until division, the right of property and of possession in the whole crop is the tenant's.[7]

Where the contract is that the land-owner shall give the cropper a part of the produce after paying all advances, and the crop has been divided, the cropper is not a tenant, but a mere employee; the ownership of the entire crop is in the land-owner, and if the cropper

---

[1] [1 Greenl. Ev. § 373. See also Barbour v. Commonwealth, 80 Va. 288 (1885).

[2] See United States v. Block, 4 Saw. 212–13 (1877), cases; Barker v. People, 20 Johns. *460 (1823); Webb v. State, 29 Ohio St. 358 (1876).

[3] [Webster's Dict.

[4] Martin v. Chapman, 6 Port. 351 (Ala., 1838).

[1] 2 Bl. Com. 145.

[2] 3 Pars. Contr. 31; 3 Kent, 477; 4 *id.* 73; 1 Wash. R. P., 4 ed. p. 9; 3 Bl. Com. 10; Freeman, Exec. 113, cases; Benj. Sales, 120; 59 Tex. 637.

[3] Wilson v. Prouty, 70 Cal. 197 (1886); Cal. Civ. Code, § 2972.

[4] Sullins v. State, 53 Ala. 476 (1875), Brickell, C. J.

[5] [Frye v. Jones, 2 Rawle, *12 (1829).

[6] Steel v. Frick, 56 Pa. 175 (1867); Adams v. McKesson, 53 *id.* 83 (1866).

[7] Harrison v. Ricks, 71 N. C. 10 (1874), cases.

forcibly, or against consent, takes the crop from the possession of the owner, the taking constitutes larceny, robbery, or other offense, according to the circumstances.[1] See DISTRESS, 4, 5.

CROSS. 1, *v.* To intersect, *q. v.*

Crossing. Before a person enters upon a railroad crossing he must use all his senses, take all the precaution he reasonably can, to ascertain that he may cross in safety.[2]

Cross-walk. See SIDEWALK.

2, *n.* (1) A mark, instead of his name, made by a person who cannot write, or is disabled from writing. See SIGNATURE.

(2) The character × is sometimes used to indicate " cross-examination."[3]

3, *adj.* In the inverse order; counter; made by the opposite party.

Applied to things which are connected in subject-matter, but run counter to each other.[4]

As, a cross — action, appeal, bill, demand, error, examination or question, interrogatory, remainder, *qq. v.*

CROWN. The sovereign; the royal power; also, that which concerns or pertains to the ruling power — the king or queen.

In use, similar to our terms State, Commonwealth, Government, People.[5]

Crown case. A criminal prosecution.

Crown debt. A debt due to the government.

Crown law. Criminal law.

Crown office, or side. The criminal side of the court of King's or Queen's bench.

Crown paper. A list of criminal cases awaiting hearing or decision.

Crown pleas, or pleas of the crown. Criminal causes. Opposed, *common pleas:* civil actions between subject and subject.

The king, in whom centers the majesty of the whole people, is the person supposed to be injured by every infraction of public rights, and is the proper prosecutor.[6] See KING.

CRUEL. See CRUELTY; PUNISHMENT.

CRUELTY. Ill-treatment; maltreatment; abuse; unnecessary infliction of pain,

generally physical; immoderate, unrestrained chastisement; violence; inhuman conduct.

Not usually employed in speaking of a battery, malicious mischief, mayhem, or other like act with respect to which the parties are viewed as members of the community; but in cases where they sustain a special relation, as, that of husband and wife, parent and child, guardian and ward, teacher and pupil.

1. Cruelty as between Husband and Wife. Such cruelty as causes injury to life, limb, or health, or creates danger of such injury, or a reasonable apprehension of such danger.[1]

Actual personal violence or the reasonable apprehension of it; such course of treatment as endangers life or health, and renders cohabitation unsafe.[2]

The last definition, which accords with the present doctrine of the English courts,[3] has been frequently approved.[4]

Anything that tends to bodily harm and thus renders cohabitation unsafe; or, as expressed in the older decisions, that involves danger of life, limb, or health.[5]

Not, mere austerity of temper, petulance of manner, rudeness of language, want of civil attention and accommodation, or even occasional sallies of passion that do not threaten harm,— which merely wound the feelings without being accompanied by bodily injury or actual menace.[5]

Extreme cruelty. Any conduct, in one of the married parties, which furnishes reasonable apprehension that the continuance of cohabitation would be attended with bodily harm to the other.[6]

It is now generally held that any unjustifiable conduct, on the part of either the husband or the wife, which so grievously wounds the mental feelings or so destroys the peace of mind as to seriously impair the bodily health or endanger the life, or such as in any other manner endangers the life, or such as destroys the legitimate objects of matrimony, constitutes "extreme cruelty " under statutes, although no personal or physical violence be inflicted or even threatened.[7] Compare INDIGNITY. See DIVORCE.

---

[1] Parrish *v.* Commonwealth, 81 Va. 1, 7, 12 (1884), cases; Taylor, Landl. & T. 21. See also Hammock *v.* Creekmore, 48 Ark. 265 (1886).

[2] Ormsbee *v.* Boston, &c. R. Co., 14 R. I. 103–8 (1883), cases.

[3] 18 S. C. 60–64.

[4] [Abbott's Law Dict.

[5] See 106 U. S. 208.

[6] 4 Bl. Com. 2; 3 *id.* 40.

[1] [Bailey *v.* Bailey, 97 Mass. 378 (1867), cases, Chapman, J.; Peabody *v.* Peabody, 104 *id.* 197 (1870).

[2] [Butler *v.* Butler, 1 Pars. Eq. Cas. 344, 339–44 (Pa., 1849), cases, King, J.

[3] Gordon *v.* Gordon, 48 Pa. 238 (1865), Strong, J.

[4] Jones *v.* Jones, 66 Pa. 498 (1871), Agnew, J.; May *v.* May, 62 *id.* 210–11 (1869); 76 *id.* 357.

[5] Latham *v.* Latham, 30 Gratt. 321 (Va., 1878), Staples, J.

[6] Morris *v.* Morris, 14 Cal. *79 (1859), Cope, J.

[7] Carpenter *v.* Carpenter, 30 Kan. 744 (1883), cases, Valentine, J. See also Holyoke *v.* Holyoke, 78 Me. 410–11 (1886), cases; Powelson *v.* Powelson, 22 Cal. 361 (1863); generally, 19 Ala. 307; 36 Ga. 296; 88 Ill. 248; 57

2. Cruelty to Children. Inordinate chastisement of children of tender years — under fourteen.

Beginning with New York in 1875 (under the act of April 21, of that year), societies for the prevention of cruelty to children have been very generally formed. These societies, by statute, are authorized to prosecute persons who maltreat children, or employ them at hard labor in mines, mills, and factories, beyond a certain number of hours a day, or who sell or employ their services as acrobats or as beggars, or as servants about drinking saloons, places of low amusements, houses of prostitution, and like resorts. Abuses which had been characterized as misdemeanors are thus, in effect, brought within the category of acts of cruelty.[1]

3. Cruelty to Animals. The infliction of pain upon dumb animals, without just cause.

Until within recent years ill-usage of a dumb animal was viewed merely as a wrong to the owner's property; no degree of ill-treatment amounted to a misdemeanor unless so inhuman as to shock, and, indirectly, to demoralize beholders: in which case the act became indictable as a public nuisance.[2]

The present view is that, for its own sake, all sentient life is to be protected from the wanton and unnecessary infliction of pain.[3]

To protect animals from cruelty, societies, similar in scope and power to those for children, have been organized in the United States and Europe.

Under the Great Law of the Province of Pennsylvania, ordained in 1682, those who frequented "such rude and riotous sports and practices as . . bull-baitings, cock-fightings, with such like . . shall be reputed and fined as breakers of the peace, and suffer at least ten days' imprisonment at hard labor in the house of correction, or forfeit twenty shillings."[4]

Severe pain inflicted for the mere purpose of causing pain or of indulging vindictive passion is "cruel;" and so is pain inflicted without justifiable cause, but with reasonable cause to know that it is produced by wanton or reckless conduct.[5]

"Cruelty" includes both the willfulness and cruel temper of mind with which the act is done and the pain inflicted. An act merely accidental, or not giving pain, is not cruel in the ordinary sense.[6]

The distinction is between the infliction of such chastisement as is necessary for the training or discipline by which animals are made useful, and the beating or needless infliction of pain which is dictated by a cruel disposition, by violent passions, a spirit of revenge, or reckless indifference to the sufferings of others.[1]

In the statute of 12 and 13 Vict. (1849) c. 92, cruelty means the unnecessary abuse of any animal — domestic bird or quadruped;[2] and in 45 Vict. (1881) c. 712, the intentional infliction upon any animal of pain that in its kind, degree, object or circumstances, is unreasonable.

Under 12 and 13 Vict. c. 92, § 2, dishorning cattle is not an offense, the operation being skillfully performed.[3]

In the New York act of 1874, c. 12, § 8, cruelty includes every act, omission, or neglect whereby unjustifiable physical pain, suffering, or death is caused or permitted.

By the California act of 1874 cruelty includes every act, omission, or neglect whereby unnecessary or unjustifiable physical pain or suffering is caused or permitted.

The Pennsylvania act of 1869 forbids wantonly or cruelly ill-treating, overloading, beating, or otherwise abusing any animal, or being interested in any place kept for the purpose of fighting or baiting any bull, bear, dog, cock, or other creature.

In the Arkansas act of 1879 "needlessly killing" an animal refers to an act done without any useful motive, in a spirit of wanton cruelty, or for the mere pleasure of destruction.[4]

The Tennessee statute of 1881 is designed to protect animals from willful or wanton abuse, neglect, or cruel treatment; not from the incidental pain or suffering that may be casually or incidentally inflicted by the use of lawful means of protection against particular animals.[5]

Letting loose a captive fox to be hunted (and which is captured) by dogs is cruelty, within Mass. Pub. Sts. c. 207, § 53. There is nothing in the general purpose of the statute that prevents it from including all animals, whether wild and noxious or tame and useful, within the common meaning of the word "animal." The statute does not define an offense against the rights of property in animals, nor against the rights of the animals protected by it, but against public morals, which the commission of cruel and barbarous acts tends to corrupt.[6] See MALICE; MAIM, 2; NEEDLESS; TORTURE; WANTON; WOUND.

Ind. 568; 10 Iowa, 133; 13 id. 266; 52 id. 511; 18 Kan. 371, 419; 24 Mich. 482; 26 id. 417; 37 id. 604; 40 id. 493; 45 id. 151; 49 id. 417; 56 id. 543; 8 N. H. 315; 58 id. 144; 24 N. J. E. 338; 30 id. 119, 215; 73 N. Y. 369; 14 Tex. 356; 50 Wis. 254; 26 Alb. L. J. 83.

[1] See Delafield Children (1876); Washington Humane Society Act, 13 Feb. 1885: 23 St. L. 302.

[2] United States v. Jackson, 4 Cranch, C. C. 483 (1834); Grise v. State, 37 Ark. 458 (1881).

[3] State v. Avery, 44 N. H. 394 (1862).

[4] Laws of Prov. of Penn. Ch. XXVI; Linn, 114.

[5] Commonwealth v. Lufkin, 7 Allen, 581 (1863), Hoar, J.

[6] Commonwealth v. McClellan, 101 Mass. 35 (1869), Chapman, C. J.

[1] [State v. Avery, 44 N. H. 394 (1862), Bellows, J.

[2] Bridge v. Parsons, 3 Best & S. 382 (1863): 32 Law J. 95. See Bates v. M'Cormick, 9 Law T. R. 175 (1863); Morrow's Case, 9 Pitts. Law J. 86 (1879).

[3] Callaghan v Society for Prevention of Cruelty, 37 Eng. R. 813 (1885), cases: 16 Cox's Cr. Cas. 101.

[4] Grise v. State, 37 Ark. 456 (1881).

[5] Hodge v. State, 11 Lea, 532 (1883). See also R. S. Wis. § 445.

[6] Commonwealth v. Turner, 145 Mass. 300 (1887).

The Massachusetts Society for the Prevention of Cruelty to Animals is a "charity." There is no pecuniary benefit in it for any of its members; its work in the education of mankind in the proper treatment of domestic animals is instruction in a duty incumbent on us as human beings. Its hospital for animals, if established by a bequest or other gift, would be treated as a charity. It has a humane, legal, and public or general purpose; and, whether expressed or not in the Statute of 43 Elizabeth, comes within the equity of that statute. . . An institution is both benevolent and charitable which educates men in the diseases of the domestic animals, and the proper means of dealing with them, even if it also inculcates the duty of kindness and humanity to them, and provides appropriate means of discharging it.[1]

Common carriers, by land or water, from one State to another, may not confine cattle, sheep, swine, or other animals, for a longer period than twenty-eight consecutive hours, without unloading them for rest, water, and feeding, for at least five consecutive hours, unless prevented from unloading by storm or other accidental cause. The hours in transit on connecting roads are to be taken into the account. If such unloaded animals are not properly fed and watered by their owner, the transporter shall care for them, and have a lien for the service. Willful failure to comply with the foregoing provisions exposes the offender to a penalty of $100 to $500. An exception is made in favor of cars and boats in which the animals have proper food, water, space, and opportunity to rest. Penalties are recoverable by civil action in the name of the United States, in the circuit or district court held within the district where the violation was committed, or the person or corporation resides or carries on business.[2]

The lien is enforceable by petition filed in the district court within the district where it attached, or the owner or custodian of the property resides. The court is to issue process suited to the case for the collection of the debt, costs, penalties, and charges.[3]

CRUISE. Any voyage for a given purpose. Imports a definite place, as well as time of commencement and termination.[4]

CRY. See AUCTION; CRIER; PAIS.

CUCKING-STOOL. See SCOLD.

CUILIBET. See ARS, Cuilibet, etc.

CUJUS. See SOLUM, Cujus, etc.

CUL DE SAC. Fr. The bottom of a bag. A street open at one end; a blind alley.

CULPA. L. A fault; negligence; guilt.

Lata culpa. Gross negligence. **Levis culpa.** Ordinary negligence. **Levissima**

culpa. Slight negligence.[1] Compare DELICTUM; DOLUS.

Whence exculpatory, inculpatory, exculpation.

Culpabilis. Guilty. **Non culpabilis.** Not guilty.

Non culpabilis was abbreviated upon the minutes "non cul." To this plea the clerk, on behalf of the sovereign, replied that the prisoner was guilty, as he was ready to prove. The formula for this reply was **cul. prit.,** i. e., *culpabilis partus verificare.*[2]

Whence "culprit." But that word may come from *culped,* which is from *culpe,* to charge with a crime;[3] or it may be a corruption of *culpate,* an accused person.[4]

The expression **non cul et de hoc,** still used in the records of a few criminal courts of general jurisdiction, is an abridgment of the sentence *non culpabilis et de hoc se ponit supra Deum et patriam,* not guilty and of this he puts himself upon God and his country. See ARRAIGN; CULPABLE.

CULPABLE. Censurable; criminal. See CULPA.

Applied to an omission to preserve the means of enforcing a right, "censurable" is more nearly an equivalent than "criminal."[5] See NEGLIGENCE, Culpable.

CULTIVATION. See AGRICULTURE; BETTERMENT; CROP; IMPROVE.

Being in a state of cultivation is the converse of being in a state of nature. Whenever lands have been wrought with a view to the production of a crop they must be considered as becoming and continuing in "a state of cultivation" until abandoned for every purpose of agriculture and designedly permitted to revert to a condition similar to the original one.[6]

"Fit for cultivation" refers to that condition of soil which will enable a farmer, with a reasonable amount of skill, to raise regularly and annually by tillage grain or other staple crops.[7]

CULVERT. A water-way or passage, whether of wood or stone, square or arched.[8]

CUM. L. With, together with; along with; in connection with; wholly.

In compounding words, the *m* remains before *b, p, m;* assimilates before *l, n, r;* changes into *n* before other consonants; is rejected before a vowel or *h.*

---

[1] Massachusetts Society, &c. v. Boston, 142 Mass. 27–28 (1886), Devens, J.

[2] Act 3 March, 1873: R. S. §§ 4386–89.

[3] Act 27 Feb. 1877: R. S. § 4390.

[4] [The Brutus, 2 Gall. 526, 539, 268 (1815); Marsh. Ins. 196, 199, 520.

[1] Jones, Bailm. 8; Story, Bailm. § 18; 8 Barb. 378; 34 La. An. 1129.

[2] 4 Bl. Com. 339; 6 Cal. 232; 2 Sumn. 67.

[3] Webster's Dict.

[4] Skeat's Etym. Dict.

[5] Waltham Bank v. Wright, 8 Allen, 122 (1864).

[6] Johnson v. Perley, 2 N. H. 57 (1819).

[7] Keeran v. Griffith, 34 Cal. 581 (1868); 13 Ired. L. 37; 29 Kan. 596.

[8] Oursler v. Baltimore, &c. R. Co., 60 Md. 367 (1883).

Designates a being or bringing together of several objects; also, completeness, perfection of an act,— intensifies the signification of the simple word. See CON, 1.

Cum copula. With connection; with intercourse.

A promise to marry in the future, *cum copula*, did not, at common law, constitute a valid marriage; otherwise, for some purposes, by the canon law.[1]

Cum onere. With the charge or incumbrance. See further ONUS, Cum, etc.

Cum testamento annexo. With the will attached. See ADMINISTER, 4.

CUMULATIVE.[2] More of the same kind; superadded to other of the same nature; additional.

As, a cumulative or cumulative — evidence or testimony, legacy, offense, remedy, sentence or judgment, statute, voting, *qq. v.*

CUR. See CURIA.

CURABLE. See CURE, 2.

CURATOR. L. A guardian; a committee, *q. v.*

The guardian of the estate of a ward, as distinguished from the guardian of his person.[3]

Curator ad hoc. A guardian for this — special purpose.

Curator ad litem. A guardian for the suit; a guardian *ad litem*, q. v.

CURE.[4] 1. In the original sense of taking care or charge of, instead of the later sense of healing, is used in the sea-law which requires that a seaman is to be "cured" at the expense of the ship of sickness, or injury sustained in the ship's service, to the end of the voyage.[5]

The obligation to "cure," as the old cases say, or to give "medical treatment," as the later cases term it, continues only to the end of the particular voyage.[6]

2. To remedy, correct, remove.

Want of authority in an agent is cured by the principal when he adopts the agent's act.

A general appearance cures antecedent irregularity of process, a defective service, etc.[7]

Formal defects in pleading are cured by pleading over without demurrer.[1]

A verdict cures a defective statement of a title or cause of action.[2] See AID, 2; BAD, 2; CERTAINTY.

Curable. Admitting of remedy or rectification. **Incurable.** Said of ambiguities, defects in pleading, defects in powers, etc.

Curative. Designed to correct an error or defect.

As, an act passed to relieve from some hardship or inconvenience caused by the careless use of language in a former statute.

An invalid public contract may be confirmed and made binding by curative statutes.[3]

CURED-MEAT. Was given the meaning at the residence (Memphis, Tenn.) of a purchaser, when that differed from the meaning at the residence (Atchison, Kan.) of the seller.[4]

CURIA. L. A court of justice; a court, or the court. Compare FORUM.

Curia advisari vult. The court desires to deliberate — over the matter: the court reserves its decision, for the present. Abbreviated *cur. ad. vult.*, and *c. a. v.*

Originally, an entry upon the record of a cause, just argued, indicating that a decision would be rendered by and by. Later, it denoted a suspension of judgment until the court could examine the matter fully.

Curia regis. The king's court.

Per curiam. By the court.

A formula by which a judge may express the assent of the court to a thing asked, or by which a court may make any order whatever.

Prefixed to a decision, may imply that the law in the case is too well settled to require either argument or elucidation.[5]

Rectus in curia. Right (unimpeached) in court, or before a court.

The condition of a person who stands before a court with no charge of misconduct preferred against him, or cleared or purged of a charge.

See under ACTUS; AMICUS; CURSUS.

CURRENT.[6] 1. Now running or passing; now present; now being created or received; existing in present time.

As, a current — account, balance, earnings, motion, value, year, *qq. v.*

---

[1] Cheney v. Arnold, 15 N. Y. 345 (1857); 2 Pars. Contr. 79.

[2] L. *cumulus*, a heap.

[3] Duncan v. Crook, 49 Mo. 117 (1871); 21 Pa. 333; 1 Bl. Com. 460.

[4] L. *cura*, care, charge.

[5] See Reed v. Canfield, 1 Sumn. 202 (1832); The City of Alexandria, 17 F. R. 393–95 (1883), cases.

[6] The John B. Lyon, 33 F. R. 187 (1887), Blodgett, J.

[7] Creighton v. Kerr, 20 Wall. 12 (1873).

[1] United States v. Noelke, 17 Blatch. 559, 561 (1880).

[2] Lincoln Township v. Cambria Iron Co., 103 U. S. 415 (1880); 7 How. 721; 53 Ind. 283; 87 *id.* 37; 3 Monta. 452.

[3] Randall v. Kreiger, 23 Wall. 147 (1874), cases; Ritchie v. Franklin County, 22 *id.* 75 (1874).

[4] Treadwell v. Anglo-American Packing Co., 18 F. R. 22 (1882). And see Featherston v. Rounsaville, 73 Ga. 617 (1884).

[5] Letzkus v. Butler, 69 Pa. 281 (1871).

[6] L. *currere*, to run, flow, move.

2. Circulating as money; received as money; lawful as money.

Current funds. Current money; par funds, or money circulating without any discount.

A bill of exchange drawn for "current funds" entitles the holder to coin or its equivalent.[1]

Gold, silver, or anything equivalent thereto, and convertible at pleasure into the same.[2]

"In current funds," as used in a bank-check, means in money; and the insertion of the words does not impair negotiability.[3]

Commencing with the first issue in this country of notes declared to have the quality of legal tender, it has been a common practice for makers of commercial bills, checks, and notes, to indicate whether the same are to be paid in gold or silver, or in such notes; and the term "current funds" has been used to designate any of these, all being current and declared to be legal tender. It was intended to cover whatever was receivable and current by law as money, whether in the form of notes or coin.[3]

Current money. Money received as such in common business transactions; the common medium in barter and exchange.[4]

Current notes. Bank-notes convertible into specie, or redeemable in gold, silver, or an equivalent.[5]

Current price or *value.* See VALUE.

Currency. Primarily, a passing or flowing — something which passes from hand to hand. In monetary affairs, not necessarily cash; it is equally applicable to anything used as a circulating medium, and generally accepted as a representative of values of property.[6]

Bank-notes, or other paper money, issued by authority, and continually passing, as and for coin.[7]

The money which passes at a fixed value, from hand to hand; money which is authorized by law.[8]

Includes both coined and paper *money;* not all bank-notes in circulation, for all such are not necessarily money. Whatever is at a discount is not money

nor currency. National bank-notes, although not legal tender, are as much currency as treasury notes, which are legal tender. Therefore, a certificate of deposit promising repayment "in currency" may be deemed negotiable,— it is payable in money.[1]

In an indictment, the words "of the currency current" are equivalent to "current as money."[2] See PAR, 2; TENDER, 2, Legal.

CURSE. See BLASPHEMY.

CURSUS. L. A running: way, mode, practice. See DE, Cursu.

Cursus curiæ lex curiæ. The practice of a court is the law of the court.

Established, inveterate practice will be adhered to: it is supposed to be based upon principles of justice and public convenience. But a court of error does not generally notice the practice of another court. In short, every court, especially every court of equity, makes its own practice.[3] Compare ERROR, 1, Communis.

CURTESY.[4] 1. Where a man marries a woman seized of an estate of an inheritance (that is, of land and tenements in fee-simple or fee-tail), and has by her issue, born alive, capable of inheriting the estate, on her death he holds the land for life as tenant by the curtesy of England.[5]

An estate by the curtesy is the interest to which the husband is entitled upon the death of the wife, in the lands or tenements of which she was seized in possession, in fee-simple or in tail, during their coverture, provided they had lawful issue born alive which might by possibility inherit the estate as heir to the wife.[6]

When a man marries a woman, seized at any time during the coverture of an estate of inheritance, in severalty, in coparcenary, or in common, and has issue by her, born alive, and which might by possibility inherit the same estate as heir to the wife, and the wife dies in the life-time of the husband, he holds the land during her life "by the curtesy of England."[7]

---

[1] Galena Ins. Co. *v.* Kupfer, 28 Ill. 335 (1862).

[2] [Lacy *v.* Holbrook, 4 Ala. 90 (1842); 9 *id.* 289; 34 Ill. 292; 9 Ind. 135; 47 Iowa, 672; 44 Pa. 457.

[3] Bull *v.* First Nat. Bank of Kasson, 123 U. S. 112 (1887), Field, J.

[4] [Stalworth *v.* Blum, 41 Ala. 321 (1867); 3 T. B. Mon. 166; 21 La. An. 624; 5 Lea, 96; 1 Dall. 124; 9 Mo. 697.

[5] Pierson *v.* Wallace, 7 Ark. 293 (1847); Fleming *v.* Nall, 1 Tex. 247 (1846); Moore *v.* Gooch, 6 Heisk. 105 (1871); 64 N. C. 381; 5 Cow. 187; 5 Humph. 485.

[6] [Chicago Fire, &c. Ins. Co. *v.* Keiron, 27 Ill. 507 (1862), Caton, C. J.

[7] [Same *v.* Same, *ib.* 506, Walker, J.: Wharton.

[8] Butler *v.* Paine, 8 Minn. 329 (1863): Bouvier.

---

[1] Klauber *v.* Biggerstaff, 47 Wis. 560–61 (1879), cases, Ryan, C. J. See also 30 Ill. 399; 32 *id.* 77; 35 *id.* 163; 14 Mich. 379; 27 *id.* 197; 61 N. C. 23; 1 Ohio, 115, 119.

[2] Commonwealth *v.* Griffiths, 126 Mass. 252 (1879).

[3] Broom, Max. 133, 135; 7 Ct. Cl. 332.

[4] L. *curialitas,* attendance upon the lord's court or *curtis; i. e.,* being his vassal or tenant. Or, "by the courts of England,"—2 Bl. Com. 126. From F. *courtesie,* favor (to the husband),—28 Barb. 345.

[5] [2 Bl. Com. 126.

[6] Westcott *v.* Miller, 42 Wis. 465 (1877), Cole, J.

[7] Billings *v.* Baker, 28 Barb. 344 (1859); 4 Kent, 27. See also 7 How. 54; 1 Sumn. 271; 1 McLean, 478; 2

Under old common law, as soon as a child was born the father began to have a permanent interest in the lands, he became one of the *pares curtis*, did homage to the lord, and was called tenant by the curtesy "initiate." He could do many acts to charge the land, but his estate was not "consummate" till the death of the wife.[1]

The requisites are: a legal marriage; an actual seizin or possession in the wife — wherefore no curtesy can be had in a remainder or a reversion; issue born alive, during the life of the mother, capable of inheriting the estate; and, the death of the wife.[1]

Adopted as a common-law estate in all of the older States, though somewhat modified in some of them. The right is expressly created by statute in Delaware, Kentucky, Maine, Massachusetts, Minnesota, New Hampshire, Rhode Island, Vermont, and Wisconsin. In Alabama, Connecticut, Illinois, Maryland, Mississippi, Missouri, New Jersey, North Carolina, Tennessee, and Virginia it is recognized by the courts as an existing estate. In California it is not allowed; realty being there held in common, and the survivor taking one-half in severalty. In Georgia the husband takes an absolute estate in all the property. In Kansas he takes one-half absolutely, upon her decease without a will; and if without issue, he takes all absolutely. In Louisiana their relation to their property does not admit of curtesy. In Nebraska the estate is given, unless she had issue by a former husband who would take the estate. In New York it would seem that she may defeat a right by conveyance. In Ohio, Oregon, and Pennsylvania issue is not necessary. In South Carolina he takes his share in fee. In Texas any property is the common property of both. In Dakota, Indiana, Michigan, and Nevada the estate seems to be abolished.

In many of the States curtesy is given, by statute, in equitable estates of which the wife is seized. The right extends to equities of redemption, contingent uses, and moneys directed to be laid out in lands for the benefit of the wife.[2]

In the absence of fraud, a husband who is embarrassed may convey his curtesy to a trustee for the benefit of his wife and children, for a consideration valuable in equity.[3] Compare DOWER.

2. A voluntary act of kindness.

An act of kindness toward another person, of the free will of the doer, without previous request or promise of reward, has sometimes been called a "voluntary curtesy."

From such act the law implies no promise for remuneration. If it were otherwise, one man might impose a legal obligation upon another against his will. Hence the phrases "a voluntary curtesy will not support an *assumpsit*," but that "a curtesy moved by a previous request will."[4] See PROTEST, 2.

MacA. 63; 15 Ark. 483; 43 Miss. 633; 8 Neb. 525; 14 S. C. 907; 8 Baxt. 361; 6 Mo. Ap. 416, 549.
[1] 2 Bl. Com. 127.
[2] See 1 Washburn, Real Prop., 4 ed., 164, 166 (1876).
[3] Hitz v. Nat. Metropolitan Bank, 111 U. S. 722 (1884).
[4] See Lampleigh v. Brathwait, 1 Sm. L. C. *222; Holthouse.

CURTILAGE. 1. Originally, the land with the castle and out-houses, inclosed often with high walls, where the old barons sometimes held court in the open air. Whence *court-yard*.[1]

2. The court-yard in the front or rear of a house, or at its side; any piece of ground lying near, inclosed, used with, and necessary for the convenient occupation of the house.[2]

A fence or inclosure of a small piece of land around a dwelling-house, usually including the buildings occupied in connection with the dwelling-house, the inclosure consisting either of a separate fence or partly of a fence and partly of the exterior of buildings so within this inclosure.[3]

If a barn, stable, or warehouse be parcel of the mansion-house, and within the same common fence, though not under the same roof nor contiguous, a burglary may be committed therein; for the capital house protects and privileges all its branches and appurtenances, if within the same curtilage or homestall.[4]

It is perhaps unfortunate that this term, which is found in English statutes, and which is descriptive of the common arrangement of dwellings, and the yards surrounding them, in England, should have been perpetuated in our statutes. It is not strictly applicable to the common disposition of inclosures and buildings constituting the homestead of the inhabitants of this country. In England dwellings and out-houses of all kinds are usually surrounded by a fence or stone-wall, inclosing a small piece of land embracing the yards and out-buildings near the house constituting what is called the court. Such precautionary arrangements have not been necessary in this country.[5]

Nothing is implied as to the size of the parcel of land.[6]

In Michigan, includes more than an inclosure near the house.[5]

In § 4347, code of Alabama, defining arson in the second degree, includes the yard or space near a dwelling-house, within the same inclosure, and used in connection with it by the household; as, a barn which opens into such yard, in part separating it from another inclosure.[7]

Under a mechanics' lien law, a jury may determine the necessary curtilage to which a lien extends.[8]

[1] Coddington v. Dry Dock Co., 31 N. J. L. 485 (1863).
[2] [People v. Gedney, 10 Hun, 154 (1877): Bac. Abr.
[3] Commonwealth v. Barney, 10 Cush. 481, 483 (1852), Dewey, J. Approved, 140 Mass. 289.
[4] 4 Bl. Com. 225; 1 Hale, P. C. 558; 61 Ala. 58; 31 Me. 523.
[5] People v. Taylor, 2 Mich. 251 (1851).
[6] Edwards v. Derrickson, 28 N. J. L. 45 (1859); Same v. Same, 29 id. 474 (1861).
[7] Washington v. State, 82 Ala. 32 (1886).
[8] Keppel v. Jackson, 3 W. & S. 320 (1842); 5 Rawle, 291.

CURVES. See RAILROAD.

CUSTODIA. L. Keeping, custody; literally, watch, guard, care.

In custodia legis. In the custody of the law. See CUSTODY.

CUSTODY. See CUSTODIA. 1. Care, possession, charge: as, the custody of a child, of a lunatic, of a ward;[1] the custody of a deposit, or of funds.

Custody of property, as contradistinguished from legal possession, is that charge to keep and care for the owner, subject to his direction, and without any adverse right, which every servant possesses with regard to goods confided to his care.[2]

2. Detention by lawful authority.

Custody of the law. Property lawfully taken by virtue of legal process is in the custody of the law.[3]

In this category are goods lawfully levied upon by a marshal, sheriff, or constable; goods impounded;[4] property in the hands of a receiver, *q. v.;* money paid into court.

Such property, for the time being, is not liable to be again seized in execution by the officer of any other court.[5]

But the court of a State cannot by this device prevent the collection of Federal taxes.[5]

3. A person under lawful arrest is said to be in custody or in the custody of the law. See RESCUE.

A sentence that a prisoner "be in custody till his sentence is complied with," imports actual imprisonment.[7]

CUSTOM.[8] That length of usage which has become law; a usage which has acquired the force of law. Often used synonymously with "usage."[9]

A law established by long usage. A universal custom becomes common law.[10]

"The law or rule which is not written, and which men have used for a long time, supporting themselves by it in the things and

reasons with respect to which they have exercised it."[1]

"Usage," strictly speaking, is the evidence of a "custom."[2]

"Custom" is the making of a law; "prescription," the making of a right.[3]

Customary. Originating in long usage: as, customary incidents or rights; customary dispatch, *q. v.;* customary estate, freehold,[4] service,[5] tenant;[4] customary law: common law.

General customs. The universal rule of the whole kingdom, forming the common law, in its stricter and more usual signification. **Particular customs.** Such as, for the most part, affect only the inhabitants of particular districts;[6] a local or special custom.

A general custom is a general law.[7]

"General" customs are such as prevail throughout a country and become the law of the country. "Particular" customs are such as prevail in some county, city, town, or other place.[8]

The chief corner-stone of the laws of England is general immemorial custom, or common law, from time to time declared in the decisions of the courts of justice; which decisions are preserved among the public records, explained in the reports, and digested for general use by the sages of the law. . . Our practice is to make custom of equal authority with the written law,— when it is not contradicted by that law. "For, where is the difference, whether the people declare their assent to a law by suffrage, or by a uniform course of acting accordingly?" . . It is one of the marks of English liberty that our common law depends upon custom; which carries this internal evidence of freedom along with it, that it probably was introduced by the voluntary consent of the people.[9] See LAW, Common.

Particular customs are doubtless the remains of that multitude of local customs out of which the common law was collected, at first by Alfred. For reasons that have been long forgotten, particular counties, cities, towns, and manors were indulged with the privilege of abiding by their own customs. Such, for example, are the customs of London. These particular customs must be proved to exist, and appear to be: legal, that is, be immemorial; continued—the right uninterrupted; peaceable—acquiesced in; reason-

---

[1] 1 Bl. Com. 303; 3 *id.* 427.

[2] [People *v.* Burr, 41 How. Pr. 296 (1871).

[3] [Gilman *v.* Williams, 7 Wis. *334 (1859).

[4] 3 Bl. Com. 12, 146.

[5] Buck *v.* Colbath, 3 Wall. 341 (1865), cases.

[6] Keely *v.* Sanders, 99 U. S. 442 (1878).

[7] Smith *v.* Commonwealth, 59 Pa. 324 (1868).

[8] F. *custume:* L. L. *costuma: con,* together, very; *suere,* to make one's own —have it one's own way,— Skeat. Compare CUSTOMS; CONSUETUDO.

[9] Walls *v.* Bailey, 49 N. Y. 471 (1872), Folger, J.; Hursh *v.* North, 40 Pa. 243 (1861); Bishop, Contr. § 444.

[10] Wilcox *v.* Wood, 9 Wend. 349 (1832), Savage, C. J.

---

[1] Strother *v.* Lucas, 12 Pet. *446 (1838).

[2] See 3 Pars. Contr. 239.

[3] Lawson, Usages & Customs, 15, n. 2.

[4] 2 Bl. Com. 149.

[5] 3 Bl. Com. 234.

[6] 1 Bl. Com. 67.

[7] United States *v.* Arredondo, 6 Pet. 715 (1832).

[8] Bodfish *v.* Fox, 23 Me. 95 (1843); 12 Pet. *446.

[9] 1 Bl. Com. 73-74.

able — no sufficient legal reason be assignable against the custom; certain — ascertained or ascertainable; compulsory — not left to one's option, to use or not to use; and consistent — with each other, if not, then they could never have been assented to. Customs in derogation of the common law are strictly construed.[1]

In few States do any purely local customs, such as have just been explained, exist. And such customs are to be carefully distinguished from "usages of trade or business." These are everywhere allowed their just influence and operation. A usage of trade and business clearly proved to exist, to be ancient, notorious, reasonable, and consistent with law, is permitted to explain the meaning of ambiguous words in written contracts, and to control the mode and extent of their rights where the parties have been silent. But it is never admitted against the expressed agreement of the parties, nor in violation of any statute or well-established rule of law. The current of decisions of late years has been to restrain and limit the allowance and influence of special usages.[2]

The courts take judicial notice of general customs. Particular or special customs are to be alleged and proved.[3]

Evidence of a temporary custom of which the party to be affected has no knowledge is not admissible against him.[4]

Where the object is to interpret a contract it is not necessary to prove all the elements of a custom necessary to make a law.[5]

To establish the validity of a custom the usage must have existed so long as to become generally known, and it must be clearly and distinctly proved. The concurrent testimony of a large number of witnesses increases the probability of its being generally known. This is illustrated in the case of a custom which authorizes the captain of a steamboat to insure it for the benefit of the owner without his express direction.[6]

Evidence of a custom or usage of trade is resorted to in order to ascertain and explain the meaning and intention of the parties to a contract: on the theory that they knew of its existence and contracted with reference to it. It is never received if it is inconsistent with the contract, if it contradicts or varies directly or by necessary implication express stipulations, if it would subvert a settled rule of law, or if there is no contract in reality.[7] See RINGING UP.

The uncontradicted testimony of one witness may be sufficient to establish a custom.[1]

Customary rights and incidents are such as universally attach to the subject-matter of a contract in the place where the contract is made. These also are impliedly annexed to the terms of a contract unless expressly excluded.[2] See USE, 2, Usage; Usus, Malus usus, etc.

Custom of merchants. A system of customs, originating among merchants, and allowed for the benefit of trade as part of the common law.

Of such are certain rules relating to bills of exchange (as, that of allowing days of grace), to mercantile contracts, to the sale, purchase, and barter of goods, to freight, insurance, shipping, partnerships.[3] Constitutes the *lex mercatoria* or law merchant. See MERCHANT, Law.

Customs of London. Particular customs relating chiefly to trade, apprentices, widows, orphans, and local government.

Good only by special usage; and tried by the certificate of the mayor and alderman, by the mouth of their recorder.[4]

CUSTOMERS. See BOYCOTTING; GOOD WILL.

CUSTOMS. Taxes upon goods or merchandise imported or exported.[5]

The duties, toll, tribute, or tariff payable upon merchandise exported or imported.[6]

They are the inheritance of the king from almost immemorial time. Denominated, in ancient records, *costuma*, from the French *coustom* or *coutom*, toll or tribute; which in turn is from *coust*, price, charge, cost.[6]

Customs were exactions maintained by the crown or lords upon the grounds of immemorial usage. In time, only duties upon merchandise, and as regulated by law, remained.

Common phrases are: customs appraiser, customs collector, customs commissioner, customs laws. See DUTIES, 2; REFUNDS; SMUGGLE.

CUT. 1. A wound made with an instrument having an edge.[7] See BATTERY; MAYHEM; STAB; WOUND.

2. An impression made upon paper or cloth from an engraved block or plate. See COPYRIGHT.

Compare COUPON; TAIL. See TIMBER; WASTE.

---

[1] 1 Bl. Com. 76–79; Lindsay v. Cusimano, 12 F. R. 506 (1882); 110 U. S. 499.

[2] 1 Shars. Bl. Com. 78; Coxe v. Heisley, 19 Pa. 246–48 (1852), cases, Black, C. J.

[3] 1 Greenl. Ev. § 5; 1 Whart. Ev. §§ 298, 331.

[4] Wootters v. Kauffman, 67 Tex. 493 (1887), cases.

[5] Carter v. Philadelphia Coal Co., 77 Pa. 290 (1875); Morningstar v. Cunningham, 110 Ind. 333–35 (1886), cases; 1 Cooley, Bl. Com. 76, note.

[5] Adams v. Pittsburgh Ins. Co., 95 Pa. 355–56 (1880), cases.

[7] Bliven v. Screw Company, 23 How. 431 (1859); Insurance Companies v. Wright, 1 Wall. 470–72 (1863); Thompson v. Riggs, 5 id. 679 (1866); Barnard v. Kellogg, 10 id. 390 (1870); Robinson v. United States, 13 id. 365

(1871); Tilley v. County of Cook, 103 U. S. 162 (1880), cases; The Dora Mathews, 31 F. R. 620 (1887), cases.

[1] Wootters v. Kauffman, *ante.*

[2] 1 Greenl. Ev. § 405; 1 Whart. Ev. § 969. See generally Wigglesworth v. Dallison, Dougl. 190 (1779): Sm. L. C., 8 ed., vol. I, pt. II, 928–65, cases.

[3] 2 Pars. Contr. 539; 1 Bl. Com. 75.

[4] 1 Bl. Com. 75, 76; 3 id. 334.

[5] See 1 Story, Const. § 949.

[5] 1 Bl. Com. 313–14, note (v).

[7] State v. Patza, 3 La. An. 514 (1848), cases.

CUTLERY. A generic term, often used to describe razors, scissors, and shears, as well as knives for table, pocket, and other uses.[1]

"Sheep shears" are included within the word, as used in Schedule C of the Tariff Act of March 3, 1883.[1]

The name of an imported article is not the sole guide by which to classify it for duty; its uses, especially when new and a substitute for other articles, should be considered. Thus "hair clippers" should be rated as "cutlery."[2] See DUTIES.

CY PRES.[3] As near; as near as; as near as can be.

The rule of construction that the intention of a testator, who seeks to create a charity, is to be given effect as far as is consistent with the rules of law[4] is known as the *cy près* doctrine.

Refers to the judicial power of substituting a charity which approaches another, the original, charity, in nature and character.[5]

Where the particular intention cannot be given effect, the words will be construed so as to give effect to the general intention evinced, and that as near to the particular intention as the law permits.

The doctrine modifies the strictness of the common law, as to a condition precedent to the enjoyment of a personal legacy. When a literal compliance with the condition becomes impossible from unavoidable circumstances, and without default in the legatee, it is sufficient that the condition is complied with as near as it practically can be.[6]

Borrowed from the Roman law, by which donations for public purposes were applied, when illegal *cy prés*, to other and legal purposes.[7] Or, originated in the indulgence shown to the ignorance of testators who devised to the unborn son of an unborn son.[8]

A leading and illustrative case is that of *Jackson v. Phillips*,[9] decided in Massachusetts in 1867. The will created a trust " for the preparation and circulation of books and newspapers, the delivery of speeches, lectures, and such other means as in their [the trustees'] judgment will create a public sentiment that will put an end to negro slavery in this country," and " for the benefit of fugitive slaves escaping from the slave-holding States." While litigation upon the will

was in progress, the Thirteenth Amendment, abolishing slavery, was adopted (1865); and the fund in question was ultimately applied to the New England Branch of the American Freedman's Union Commission.

The general doctrine has been approved in all of the New England States except Connecticut, in Illinois, and in Mississippi. In some States the doctrine has not been decided; in Pennsylvania it obtains where a designated class of beneficiaries become extinct;[1] in Alabama, Indiana, Iowa, Maryland, New York, North Carolina, South Carolina, and Virginia, it seems to be repudiated.[2,3]

The Supreme Court of the United States, in its latest decisions, favors the doctrine.[3] See CHARITY, 2.

D.

D. 1. As an abbreviation may signify, in addition to the words noted below, dictionary, *dictum*, digest, division.

2. In the old action of ejectment stood for *demissione*, by demise, *q. v.*

3. In the apportionment of jurisdiction to the United States courts is used for "District:" as, E. D., M. D., N. D., S. D., and W. D.,— eastern, middle, northern, southern, and western district.

D. B. E. *De bene esse*, conditionally. See DE, Bene, etc.

D. B. N. *De bonis non*, of effects unadministered. See ADMINISTER, 4.

D. C. District court; District of Columbia.

D. C. L. Doctor of the civil law. See DOCTOR.

D. J. District judge.

D. P. *Domus procerum*, House of Lords.

D. R. Declaration of Rights.

D. S. Deputy sheriff.

D. S. B. *Debitum sine brevi*, debt without a writ. See DEBET, Debitum, etc.

DAILY. See DAY.

DAKOTA. See TERRITORY, 2.

DAM. The work or structure raised to obstruct the flow of water in a stream; also,

---

[1] Simmons Hardware Co. *v.* Lancaster, 31 F. R. 445 (1887).

[2] Koch *v.* Seeberger, 30 F. R. 424 (1887).

[3] *Cy prés;* pronounced, cī-prā'. Law Fr. *cy*, contracted from *icy*, now *ici*, here.

[4] See Coster *v.* Lorillard, 14 Wend. 308 (1835), Savage, C. J.

[5] [4 Kent, 508 (b) 1; 2 *id*. 288 (a).

[6] [1 Story, Eq. § 291. See *Re* Brown's Will, 18 Ch. Div. 65 (1881).

[7] See 1 Story, Eq. § 1169.

[8] Williams, Real Prop. 264.

[9] 14 Allen, 539, 549, 574–96, cases, Gray, J.

---

[1] Act 26 May, 1876: P. L. 211.

[2] See Bispham, Eq. § 130 (1882); 1 Col. Law T. 8–14 (1887), cases.

[3] See Loring *v.* Marsh, 6 Wall. 337 (1867); Perin *v.* Carey, 24 How. 465 (1860); Fontain *v.* Ravenel, 17 *id*. 369 (1854); Vidal *v.* Girard, 2 *id*. 127 (1844); Jackson *v.* Phillips, 14 Allen, 588 (1867).

See generally 38 Ala. 305; 22 Conn. 54; 30 *id*. 113; 4 Ga. 404; 25 *id*. 420; 16 Ill. 231; 35 Ind. 198; 46 *id*. 172; 18 B. Mon. 635; 40 Me. 302; 50 Mo. 167; 33 N. H. 296; 20 N. J. E. 522; 28 N. Y. 308; 34 *id*. 584; 17 S. & R. 88; 45 Pa. 27; 63 *id*. 465; 4 R. I. 439; 7 *id*. 252; 3 S. C. 509; 27 Tex. 173; 2 W. Va. 310.

the pond of water created by the obstruction.[1] See AQUA, Currit, etc.; MILL, 1; NAVIGABLE; RIPARIAN; TAKE, 8.

DAMAGE. Detriment; deprivation; injury; loss.

Etymologically, a thing taken away; the lost thing, which a party is entitled to have restored, that he may be made whole again.[2] See DAMNUM; LOSS.

Loss caused by malice or negligence in another person, or from inevitable accident. Interchanged with "injury." *q. v.*

Referring to a collision between vessels, the injury directly and necessarily resulting from the collision.[3]

When a bill of lading recites that the goods are received in good order and that the carrier will "not be accountable for weight, contents, packing, and damage," "damage" refers to injuries to the goods at the time of receipt.[4]

Damage-feasant.[5] Doing damage.

Said of animals trespassing upon land. To insure identification, the injured person may distrain them.[6]

A person is not justified in killing animals or fowls found trespassing upon his land. He should impound them, or sue for the damage they do. They are valuable property, the destruction of which is not necessary to the protection of his rights. A notice of an intention to kill the animals or fowls, if not shut up, is a threat to do an illegal act.[7]

DAMAGES. The compensation which the law will award for an injury done.[8]

A species of property given to a man by a jury as a compensation and satisfaction for some injury sustained.[9]

The plaintiff has no certain demand till after verdict; but when the jury has assessed his damages and judgment is given thereon, he instantly acquires, and the defendant loses, a right to that specific sum.

The verdict and judgment fix and ascertain the plaintiff's inchoate title; they do not give, they define, his right.[9]

The recompense that is given by a jury to the plaintiff for the wrong the defendant hath done unto him.[10]

A compensation, recompense, or satisfaction to the plaintiff for an injury actually received by him from the defendant.[1]

The legal injury is the standard by which the compensation is to be measured: the injured party is to be placed, as near as may be, in the situation he would have occupied if the wrong had not been committed.[2]

When it is said that a person is or will be responsible (or be required to respond) or liable or answerable "in damages," the meaning is, he may or will be required by law to furnish a money equivalent for the injury he has done.

Actual or **single damages.** Compensation for the real loss or injury. **Increased, double,** or **treble damages.** Single damages, as found by a jury, enhanced by the court.[3]

The statutes of nearly every State provide for the increase of damages where the injury complained of results from neglect of duties imposed for the better security of life and property, and make that increase, in some cases, even quadruple the actual damages. Experience favors this legislation as the most efficient mode of preventing, with the least inconvenience, the commission of injuries. The decisions of the highest courts have affirmed the validity of such legislation. The injury actually received is often so small that in many cases no effort would be made by the sufferer to obtain redress, if the private injury were not supported by the imposition of punitive damages.[4] See FENCE.

Civil damages. Injuries sustained either to one's rights as a citizen of a State and of the United States, or else to his relative rights as a member of a family, and aside from any view of the act complained of as an offense to the public and punishable in the criminal tribunals.

Civil Damage Laws. (1) Statutes which confer upon colored persons individual rights of action in the civil courts for any discrimination against them and in favor of white persons on account of race, color, or previous condition of servitude. See RIGHT, Civil Rights Act.

(2) Statutes which confer a right of action in a civil court upon the wife, family, or a near

---

[1] [Colwell *v.* Water Power Co., 19 N. J. E. 248 (1868).

[2] [Fay *v.* Parker, 53 N. H. 342 (1872).

[3] Memphis, &c. Packet Co. *v.* Gaeger Transportation Co., 10 F. R. 396 (1882).

[4] The Tommy, 16 F. R. 601, 603 (1883).

[5] Fäz'-ant.

[6] 3 Bl. Com. 6–7; 50 Mich. 32.

[7] Clark *v.* Keliher, 107 Mass. 409 (1871); Johnson *v.* Patterson, 14 Conn. 3–12 (1840), cases; Matthews *v.* Fiestel, 2 E. D. S. 90 (N. Y., 1853).

[8] Kansas City, &c. R. Co. *v.* Hicks, 30 Kan. 292 (1883), Brewer, J.

[9] 2 Bl. Com. 438; 3 *id.* 153.

[10] Coke, Litt. 257 *a:* Rosenfield *v.* Express Co., 1 Woods, 137 (1871); 17 N. J. L. 482.

(20)

[1] 2 Greenl. Ev. § 253; Dow *v.* Humbert, 91 U. S. 299 (1875), Miller, J. See also Shugart *v.* Egan, 83 Ill. 57 (1876); Tetzner *v.* Naughton, 13 Bradw. 153 (1882); Scripps *v.* Reilly, 38 Mich. 23 (1878); 9 Heisk. 850; 26 Ga. 271; 16 Johns. 143; 55 Vt. 164.

[2] Wicker *v.* Hoppock, 6 Wall. 99 (1867), Swayne, J.

[3] See Berry *v.* Fletcher, 1 Dill. 71 (1870), Dillon, Circ. J.; Lobdell *v.* New Bedford, 1 Mass. *153 (1804); Welsh *v.* Anthony, 16 Pa. 256 (1851); 10 Oreg. 342.

[4] Missouri Pacific R. Co. *v.* Humes, 115 U. S. 523 (1885), Field, J.

relative of a person who lost his life or who has sustained injuries in consequence of intoxicating liquor having been sold or given to him in violation of law.[1]

The Massachusetts statute contemplates that the habitual drunkenness of a husband or wife, parent or child, is a substantial injury to those bound together in domestic relations, and gives the right to recover damages in the nature of a penalty, not only for any injury to the person or property, but for the shame and disgrace brought upon them. Hence, the right of a son to recover damages does not depend upon the question whether he is dependent upon the father for support or not, but solely upon the relation.[2] See POLICY, 1, Public.

Compensatory damages.

Such damages as measure the actual loss, and are allowed as amends therefor. **Exemplary, punitive, or vindictive damages.** Such damages as are in excess of the actual loss, and allowed, in theory, where a tort is aggravated by evil motive — actual malice, deliberate violence or oppression, or fraud.

Exemplary damages are sometimes called "smart money."[3]

All rules of damages are referred to compensation or punishment. Compensation is to make the injured party whole; exemplary damages are something beyond this, and are inflicted with a view to punishing the defendant.[4]

It is undoubtedly true that the allowance of any thing more than an adequate pecuniary indemnity for a wrong suffered is a departure from the principle upon which damages in civil suits are awarded. But although, as a rule, the plaintiff recovers merely such indemnity, yet the doctrine is too well settled now to be shaken that exemplary damages may in certain cases be assessed. As the question of intention is always material in an action of tort, and as the circumstances which characterize the transaction are, therefore, proper to be weighed by the jury in fixing the compensation of the injured party, it may well be considered whether the doctrine of exemplary damages cannot be reconciled with the idea that compensation alone is the true measure of redress. But jurists have chosen to place the doctrine on the ground, not that the sufferer is to be recompensed, but that the offender is to be punished; and, although some text-writers and courts have questioned its soundness, it has been accepted as the rule in England and in most of the States of this country. It has also received the sanction of the Supreme Court. Discussed and recognized in *Day* v. *Woodworth*, 13 How. 371 (1851), it was more

accurately stated in *The Philadelphia, Wilmington & Baltimore Railroad Co.* v. *Quigley*, 21 How. 213 (1858): Mr. Justice Campbell, who delivered the opinion of the court, saying — "whenever the injury complained of has been inflicted maliciously or wantonly, and with circumstances of contumely or indignity, the jury are not limited to the ascertainment of a simple compensation for the wrong committed against the aggrieved person. The malice spoken of in this rule is not merely the doing of an unlawful or injurious act: the word implies that the wrong complained of was conceived in the spirit of mischief, or criminal indifference to civil obligations." Although this rule was announced in an action for libel it is equally applicable to suits for personal injuries received from the negligence of others. Redress commensurate with such injuries should be afforded. In ascertaining its extent the jury may consider all the facts which relate to the wrongful act of the defendant, and its consequences to the plaintiff; but they are not at liberty to go further, unless it was done willfully, or was the result of that reckless indifference to the rights of others which is equivalent to an intentional violation of them. In that case the jury are authorized, for the sake of public example, to give such additional damages as the circumstances require. The tort is aggravated by the evil motive, and on this rests the rule of exemplary damages.[1]

"Exemplary," "punitive," and "vindictive" damages are synonymous terms. In cases of personal torts, such as assault and battery, slander, libel, seduction, criminal conversation, malicious arrests and prosecutions, seizure of goods, where the element of fraud, malice, gross negligence, cruelty, oppression, brutality, or wantonness intervened, exemplary or punitive damages may be recovered. And, since what would be a severe verdict to one of limited means might be but a trifle to one of large means, and the reason of the rule fail, evidence of the defendant's ability to respond in damages may always be given in evidence.[2]

Constructive damages.

Such damages as are imputed in law from an act of wrong to another person.

Contingent damages.

Such damages as may or may not occur or be suffered; such

---

[1] See Berthold v. O'Reilly, 74 N. Y. 511–30 (1878), cases; 84 Ill. 195; 57 Ind. 171; 48 Iowa, 588; 50 *id.* 34; 29 Kan. 109; 130 Mass. 366; 133 *id.* 54–55; 67 Me. 517; 41 Mich. 475; 20 Alb. Law J. 204–5 (1879), cases; 19 Cent. Law J. 208–10 (1884), cases.

[2] Taylor v. Carroll, 145 Mass. 96 (1887).

[3] See 36 Conn. 185.

[4] Berry v. Fletcher, 1 Dill. 71 (1870).

---

[1] Milwaukee & St. Paul R. Co. v. Arms, 91 U. S. 492–93 (1875), Davis, J. See also Missouri Pacific R. Co. v. Humes, 115 *id.* 521 (1885); Barry v. Edmunds, 116 *id.* 562–64 (1886), cases; Denver, &c. R. Co. v. Harris, 122 *id.* 609–10 (1887), cases; 1 Kan. Law J. 74, 118–22 (1885), cases; 3 *id.* 369–75 (1886).

[2] Brown v. Evans, 8 Saw. 490 (1883), cases, Sabin, J.: s. c., 17 F. R. 912. See also Nagle v. Mullison, 34 Pa. 53 (1859), cases; Chicago, &c. R. Co. v. Scurr, 59 Miss. 461 (1882); Louisville, &c. R. Co. v. Guinan, 11 Lea, 103–5 (1883), cases; 71 Ala. 293; 50 Conn. 583; 76 Ill. 223; 92 *id.* 97; 63 Ind. 57; 39 Mich. 211; 36 Mo. 230; 53 N. H. 342; 56 *id.* 456; 35 N. Y. 25; 76 Va. 137; 41 Wis. 284; 1 Kent, 630; 2 Sedgw. Dam. 323; 2 Greenl. Ev. § 253; 23 Alb. Law J. 44 (1881), cases; 18 Cent. Law J. 143–46 (1884), cases.

as depend upon an event which may or may not happen.

Continuing damages. Damages incurred or suffered between two dates, as the beginning and the end of an act, and more or less separated in time. See CONTINUANDO.

Direct or **immediate damages.** Such damages as result from an act without the intervention of any intermediate controlling or self-efficient cause. **Consequential** or **resulting, indirect** or **remote damages.** Not produced without the concurrence of some other event attributable to the same origin or cause.

"Direct damages" include the damages for all such injurious consequences as proceed immediately from the cause which is the basis of the action, not merely for the consequences which invariably or necessarily result and which are always provable under the general allegation of damages in the declaration; but also other direct effects which have in the particular instance naturally ensued, and, to be recovered for, must be alleged specially. "Consequential damages" are those which the cause in question naturally but indirectly produced.[1]

All "remote damages" are consequential, but all "consequential damages" are by no means remote.[2]

Excessive damages. Damages awarded by a jury, so much larger in amount than what are justly due as to indicate that the jurors must have been influenced by partiality, prejudice, passion, or ignorance; also called *inordinate* and *unreasonable* damages.

Inadequate damages. Damages which, for some such reason, are grossly less than the sum actually due; also called *insufficient* damages.

Verdicts for excessive or inadequate damages are set aside by the courts — the evidence of misapprehension or disregard of duty, on the part of the jury being clear beyond question.[3]

General damages. Such damages as by implication of law result from an act, and are awarded in the sound discretion of the jury, without evidence of particular loss.[4]

Special damages. Losses which are the natual, but not the necessary, consequence of the act; a loss which is peculiar to the particular case.

Special damages must be particularly averred in the declaration,— for notice to the defendant, and thereby to prevent surprise at the trial. They result as the natural but not as the necessary consequence of the act complained of.[1] See PER, QUOD.

Liquidated damages. Damages definitely ascertained by agreement of the parties or by the judgment of a court. **Unliquidated damages.** Such damages as are not so determined.

Care must be taken to distinguish between cases of "penalties," strictly so called, and cases of "liquidated damages." The latter properly occur when the parties have agreed that, in case one party shall do a stipulated act or omit to do it, the other party shall receive a certain sum as the just, appropriate and conventional amount of the damages sustained by such act or omission. In cases of this sort courts of equity do not interfere to grant relief, but deem the parties entitled to fix their own measure of damages; provided always that the damages do not assume the character of extravagance, or of wanton and unreasonable disproportion to the nature or extent of the injury. On the other hand, those courts will not suffer their jurisdiction [to grant relief in the case of a penalty, if compensation can be made] to be evaded merely by the fact that the parties have called a sum damages which is, in fact and in intent, a penalty.[2] See further PENALTY.

Nominal damages. A trivial sum awarded where a mere breach of duty or infraction of right is shown, with no serious loss sustained. **Substantial damages.** A sum awarded as compensation for injury actually suffered; compensatory damages, *q. v.*

Whenever a right is invaded the law infers damage, and will award, *pro forma*, some small sum at least; as, one cent, six and one-quarter cents — half of an American shilling, etc.[3]

Failure to show actual damages, and the inference that none have been sustained, do not necessarily render a case trivial.[4]

A judgment for one cent, damages for trespass upon a mining claim, entered upon a special verdict for "nominal damages," if in other respects proper, will not be set aside for uncertainty in the verdict. "Nominal damages" refers to some trifling sum. In such a case the doctrine of *de minimis* should be invoked.[5]

Prospective damages. A loss which, in all probability, will be sustained by a plaint-

---

[1] 1 Sutherland, Damages, 19, 20; 50 N. H. 513.

[2] Sedgwick, Damages, 7 ed., 90, 101.

[3] Barry v. Edmunds, 116 U. S. 565 (1886); 2 Story, 670; Borland v. Barrett, 76 Va. 137 (1882); Phillips v. London, &c. R. Co., 5 Q. B. D. 78 (1879); 21 Alb. Law J. 62; 88 Ind. 389; 59 Tex. 259; 2 Sedgw. Dam. 334.

[4] See Smith v. St. Paul, &c. R. Co., 30 Minn. 172 (1883).

[1] See 1 Sutherl. Dam. 763; Roberts v. Graham, 6 Wall. 579 (1867); Mitchell v. Clark, 71 Cal. 167, 168 (1886); Atchison, &c. R. Co. v. Rice, 36 Kan. 602-3 (1887); 33 Cal. 689; 43 Conn. 567; 84 Ill. 195; 121 Mass. 393; 78 Pa. 73; 1 Chitty, Pl. 395; 2 Sedgw. Dam. 606.

[2] 2 Story, Eq. § 1318. See 1 Am. Dec. 331; 30 Am. R. 6; 12 Am. Law Rev. 286-300 (1878), cases; 19 Cent. Law J. 282-90, 302-5 (1884), cases.

[3] Mayne, Damages, 5; Sedgwick, Dam. 47.

[4] Paterson v. Dakin, 31 F. R. 685 (1887).

[5] Davidson v. Devine, 70 Cal. 519 (1886).

iff; indemnity for losses which will "almost to a certainty happen."[1] Termed **speculative damages** when the probability that a circumstance will exist as an element for compensation becomes conjectural.

The lack of certainty in the measurement of damages is no reason for refusing compensation. The law is full of instances where there is the same uncertainty, and where the jury determine what is reasonable compensation. All that is necessary is that there be certainty of damage as a direct result, and not a case of *damnum absque injuria*.[2]

On a *contract* to pay money at stipulated periods there may be as many suits as there are installments. On a *tort* there is but one action, and in that the party must have full justice: hence the courts anticipate a loss likely to occur in the future.[3]

When one party enters upon the performance of a contract, incurs expense therein, and, being willing to perform, is, without fault of his own, prevented by the other party, his loss will consist of two distinct items of damage: his outlay and expenses, less the value of materials on hand: and the profits he might have realized by performance. The first item he may recover in all cases; and the second (the profits), when they are the direct fruit of the contract, and not too remote or speculative. If the party injured by the stoppage of a contract elects to rescind the contract he cannot recover for outlay or for loss of profits; only for the value of services actually performed, as upon a *quantum meruit*.[4]

Damages for the breach of a contract are limited to such as are the natural and proximate consequences of the breach, such as may fairly be supposed to enter into the contemplation of the parties when they made the contract, and such as might naturally be expected to result from its violation.[5] See further under CONTRACT.

But if a party can save himself from loss arising from a breach of contract at trifling expense or with reasonable exertion, it is his duty to do so.[6] See INDEMNITY, 1.

The right to compensation for damages to the person or for *personal injuries* is well recognized at common law. Any limitation by the legislature to a sum less than the actual damages is in conflict with the right of remedy by due course of law reserved to the

individual for injury to his person, in the constitution of each State.[1]

In an action for a personal injury the plaintiff is entitled to recover compensation, so far as it is susceptible of an estimate in money, for the loss and damage caused to him by the defendant's negligence, including not only expenses incurred for medical attendance, and a reasonable sum for his suffering, but also a fair recompense for the loss of what he would otherwise have earned in his trade or profession, and has been deprived of the capacity of earning, by the wrongful act of the defendant. To assist the jury in making such an estimate, standard life and annuity tables, showing at any age the probable duration of life, and the present value of a life annuity, are competent evidence, but not absolute guides.[2]

In a statute providing that actions for tort for assault, battery, imprisonment, or other "damage to the person," shall survive to the representative, the tort must affect the person directly — not the feelings or the reputation, as in cases of breach of promise, slander, and malicious prosecution. The substantial cause of action must be a bodily injury, or damage of a physical character, whether trespass or case lie.[3]

At common law no damages were recoverable for the loss of a human *life*. The reason was: life transcended all moneyed value; or, because, under feudal law, the property of a felon was forfeited to the crown, so that nothing remained wherewith to satisfy private demands. The life of a subject, as far as capable of proprietorship, was the property of the government; the justice which was to be satisfied was public justice; the deceased and his family were only regarded as members of the state; the public, through the government, inflicted the punishment and received the amercement, and, as far as necessity existed, provided for the family, and, therefore, private redress or satisfaction was excluded. The effect of the action now allowed by statute (as to which see below) is, *pro tanto*, to relieve the state of a public charge; the suit for damages becomes a private action.[4]

The common-law rule has been changed in most of the States by statutes which follow closely 9 and 10 Vict. (1846), known as "Lord Campbell's Act." Proceeding upon the theory that the widow, the children, and perhaps the parents, have a pecuniary interest in the life of the deceased, these statutes provide that for the benefit of such relatives an action for damages may be maintained against the person by whose wrongful act the deceased lost his life, the act being of such a nature that the deceased, had he survived, could himself have had an action for the personal injury.

The right of recovery, then, being purely statutory, the amount recoverable for a death rests with the dis-

[1] See 2 Addison, Torts, 1391. To realty, see 26 Am. Law Reg. 281-92, 345-59 (1887), cases. As to future damages, see 36 Alb. Law J. 84-89, 104-9 (1887), cases.

[2] Omaha Horse R'y Co. *v.* Cable Tram-Way Co., 32 F. R. 733-34 (1887), Brewer, J.

[3] Miller *v.* Wilson, 24 Pa. 120 (1854), Black, C. J.; Stilson *v.* Gibbs, 53 Mich. 283-84 (1884), Cooley, C. J.; 2 Bing. 240.

[4] United States *v.* Behan, 110 U. S. 338, 344-46 (1884), cases, Bradley, J. Approved, Lovell *v.* St. Louis Mut. Life Ins. Co., 111 *id.* 274 (1884).

[5] Murdock *v.* Boston & Albany R. Co., 133 Mass. 15 (1882), Morton, C. J.

[6] Miller *v.* Mariners' Church, 7 Greenl. *55-56 (1830); Wicker *v.* Hoppock, 6 Wall. 99 (1867), cases.

[1] Cleveland, &c. R. Co. *v.* Rowan, 66 Pa. 400 (1870); Thirteenth Street R'y Co. *v.* Boudrou, 92 Pa. 481 (1880).

[2] Vicksburg & Meridian R. Co. *v.* Putnam, 118 U. S. 554-56 (1886), cases, Gray, J.

[3] Norton *v.* Sewall, 106 Mass. 145 (1870), cases, Gray, J.

[4] The E. B. Ward, 4 Woods, 149 (1883), Billings, J.; s. c. 17 F. R. 259. See generally Grosso *v.* Delaware, &c. R. Co., Sup. Ct. N. J. (1888), cases; 25 Am. Law Reg. 307-9 (1886), cases.

cretion of the legislature. In the District of Columbia this amount is $10,000;[1] in some States, as in Massachusetts, Connecticut, New York, and Pennsylvania, $5,000; but the amount recoverable for personal injuries generally remains unlimited,[2] — in Massachusetts it is $4,000.[3]

In the absence of an act of Congress or a statute of a State giving a right of action therefor, a suit in admiralty cannot be maintained in the courts of the United States to recover damages for the death of a human being on the high seas, or on waters navigable from the sea, which was caused by negligence.[4]

Where the death is caused by negligence the only damages recoverable are for the injury to the relative rights of the surviving members of the family, and are compensatory in nature. Where, therefore, a child is free, lives apart from his parents, and in no way contributes to their support, they cannot maintain an action to recover damages for his death. When the child is not free the parents can recover only the value of his services during minority, and the expenses caused by the injury and death.[5]

In all cases the amount of damages must depend very much on the good sense and sound judgment of the jury upon all the facts and circumstances of the particular case. If the suit is brought by the party there can be no fixed measure of compensation for the pain and anguish of body and mind, nor for the loss of time and care in business, or the permanent injury to health and body. So when the suit is brought by the representative the pecuniary injury resulting from the death to the next of kin is equally uncertain and indefinite.[6]

In some States statutes provide that no action will lie for a wrong committed elsewhere, without proof of the existence of a similar right in the place where the wrong was committed.[7]

See also ACTIO, Personalis; AGGRAVATION; COMMENCE, Action; CONDEMNATION; COSTS; INDEMNITY; INJURY, 2; INNOCENT, 1; INSPECTION, 2; INTEREST, 3; LAY, 2; MALICE; MEASURE; NEGLIGENCE; PROFIT, 2; RECOUP; REMIT, 3; ROAD; SOLATIUM; SOUND, 1; RESTITUTIO; TAKE, 8; TIMBER; TORT; TRESPASS; TROUBLE.

[1] Act of Congress, 17 Feb., 1885: 23 St. L. 307.

[2] See *Exp.* Gordon, 104 U. S. 517 (1881); Dennick *v.* Central Railroad of New Jersey, 103 *id.* 17 (1880); Mobile Life Ins. Co. *v.* Brame, 95 *id.* 759 (1877); The Charles Morgan, 2 Flip. 275 (1878); Davies *v.* Lathrop, 12 F. R. 356 (1882); Barrett *v.* Dolan, 130 Mass. 366 (1881); Laws Conn., 1877, c. 78, s. 1; 24 Conn. 575; 45 Me. 209; 9 Cush. 108; 18 Mo. 162; 16 Barb. 54; 15 N. Y. 432; 44 Pa. 175.

[3] Act of 1887.

[4] The Harrisburg, 119 U. S. 199, 204–12 (1886), cases, Waite, C. J.

[5] Lehigh Iron Co. *v.* Rupp, 100 Pa. 95, 98 (1882).

[6] Illinois Central R. Co. *v.* Barron, 5 Wall. 105–6 (1866), cases, Nelson, J.; The City of Panama, 101 U. S. 464 (1879); 18 N. Y. 543.

[7] McDonald *v.* Mallory, 77 N. Y. 550 (1879), cases; Leonard *v.* Columbia Steam Nav. Co., 84 *id.* 53 (1881), cases. See Richardson *v.* N. Y. Central R. Co., 98 Mass. 89 (1867), cases; Woodard *v.* Michigan, &c. R. Co., 10 Ohio St. 122 (1859); Bruce's Adm. *v.* Cincinnati

DAMNUM. L. That which is taken away: loss; damage; legal hurt or harm. Plural, *damna:* legal losses. *Damnificatus,* injured. *Damnosa,* hurtful.

Ad damnum. To the loss; "to the damage of plaintiff (so many) dollars."

The clause, at the end of a common-law declaration, in which the plaintiff sets out the money amount of the loss he has suffered in consequence of the act he complains of; also, the amount itself so set out.[1]

Ad quod damnum. To what damage.

A writ, at common law, by which the sheriff was to inquire by a jury what damage it would be to the sovereign, or to a subject, to grant a fair, market, highway, or other like franchise.[2]

An inquisition *ad quod damnum* designates the remedy given by statute for the assessment of damages suffered from an exercise of the right of eminent domain, or in consequence of some public improvement.

Damnificatus. Injured, damaged, damnified.

Quantum damnificatus. How much he is injured.

The name of an issue by which damages, to be awarded in equity, may be ascertained by a jury.

This was the course in former times, and may still be the practice in cases of a complicated nature; but the same inquiry may now generally be made by a master.[3] See PENALTY.

Non damnificatus. He is not injured.

The plea in the case of an action on a covenant to indemnify and save harmless, — in the nature of a plea of performance.

If there was any injury the plaintiff must reply to such plea. Not the plea when the condition is to "discharge and acquit."[4]

Damnosa hæreditas. A hurtful or burdensome inheritance; an expensive asset.

By the Roman law the heir was liable to the full extent of his ancestor's liabilities.

The term has been applied to property of a bankrupt which is a charge or an expense to the creditors.

The assignee need not regard such property as an asset; he may, instead, leave the creditor to prove his claim; or, possibly, he may assign the burden to

R. Co., 83 Ky. 174, 180 (1885); Burns *v.* Grand Rapids, &c. R. Co., Sup. Ct. Ind. (1888), cases: 37 Alb. Law J. 228.

[1] 2 Greenl. Ev. § 260; 108 U. S. 176; 9 Bened. 241

[2] See 2 Bl. Com. 271.

[3] 2 Story, Eq. § 795.

[4] Wicker *v.* Hoppock, 6 Wall. 99 (1867), cases; Steph. Pl. 388.

another, as, a pauper; but not so in insolvency, in which case the process is voluntary.[1]

Damnum absque injuria. A loss without injury: deprivation without legal injury; a loss for which the law provides no remedy. Opposed, *injuria absque damno:* injury without legal damage.

There are many cases of loss for which no relief or equivalent in money can be afforded. Examples: unintended hurt, while due care is being exercised; harm done from taking a medicine prescribed by a person known not to be a physician; patronage drawn off by competition in business;[2] an improvement in a machine, which does not infringe the rights of a prior patentee;[3] waste by a tenant in fee, as affecting the interest of the heir; defamatory words proven to be true.[4]

Every public improvement, while adding to the convenience of the people at large, affects more or less injuriously the interests of some individuals.[5]

When the exercise of a right, conferred by law for the benefit of the public, is attended with temporary inconvenience to private parties, in common with the public in general, they are not entitled to damages therefor.[6]

Damnum fatale. A fated loss; a loss ordained by fate — beyond the control of man.

In the civil law, a loss for which a bailee was not liable: as, a loss by shipwreck, lightning, or other like casualty; also, a loss from fire or from pirates.[7]

Included all accidents occasioned by an "act of God or public enemy," and, perhaps, also, others which would not now be considered as due to "irresistible force."[8] See ACCIDENT, Inevitable; ACT, 1, Of God.

See DE MELIORIBUS, Damnis; REMITTITUR, Damnum.

DANGER. In the law of self-defense "apparent danger" means such overt, actual demonstration, by conduct and acts, of a design to take life or to do some great personal injury, as makes killing apparently necessary for self-preservation.[9] See IMMEDIATE.

Dangerous. Said of a weapon, means such as is likely to cause death or to produce great bodily harm. See further WEAPON.

Dangers of navigation. The ordinary perils which attend navigation.[1]

Includes dangers arising from shallow waters at the entrance of harbors;[1] also, unavoidable dangers from a bridge across a river.[2]

Dangers of the river. The natural accidents incident to river navigation; not, such accidents as may be avoided by the exercise of that skill, judgment, or foresight which are demanded from persons in the particular occupation.[3]

Includes dangers from unknown reefs, suddenly formed in the channel, and not discoverable by the use of care.[4]

Dangers of the sea or *seas.* Stress of weather, winds and waves, lightning, tempests, and other extraordinary occurrences, as understood in a marine policy; not, the ordinary perils which every vessel must encounter.[5]

Accidents, peculiar to navigation, of an extraordinary nature, or arising from an irresistible force or overwhelming power which cannot be guarded against by the ordinary exertions of human skill and prudence.[6]

All unavoidable accidents from which common carriers, by the general law, are not excused unless they arise from the act of God.[7]

The phrases "dangers of the sea," "dangers of navigation," and "perils of the seas," employed in bills of lading, are convertible expressions.[6] See further ACT, 1, Of God; PERIL.

DARE. L. To give; to transfer. See DEDIMUS.

Nemo dat qui non habet. No one gives who does not have.

Nemo dat quod non habet. No one can give what he does not own.

[1,3] Pars. Contr. 466, 492; American File Co. *v.* Garrett, 110 U. S. 295 (1884), cases.

[2] 3 Bl. Com. 224.

[3] Burr *v.* Duryee, 1 Wall. 574 (1863).

[4] 3 Bl. Com. 219, 125.

[5] Miller *v.* Mayor of New York, 109 U. S. 395 (1883). See Broom, Max. 1; 1 Sm. L. C. 244; Sedg. Dam. 29, 111; 20 How. 148; 108 U. S. 331; 109 *id.* 329; 119 *id.* 284; 32 F. R. 568; 17 Conn. 302; 83 Ky. 218; 97 N. C. 482; 94 N. Y. 129; 86 Pa. 401; 98 *id.* 84; 113 *id.* 126; 16 Op. Att.-Gen. 480; 66 Ga. 69, 308; 71 *id.* 734; 34 La. An. 312, 496, 506, 857, 974, 996; 74 Me. 171; 133 Mass. 489; 11 Lea, 737; 59 Tex. 517; 25 Vt. 49.

[5] Hamilton *v.* Vicksburg, &c. R. Co., 119 U. S. 285 (1886).

[7] See Story, Bailm. 471; 2 Kent, 594.

[8] Thickstun *v.* Howard, 8 Blackf. 536 (1847).

[9] Evans *v.* State, 44 Miss. 773 (1870).

[1] [Western Transportation Co. *v.* Downer, 11 Wall. 133 (1870).

[2] The Morning Mail, 17 F. R. 545 (1883).

[3] Hill *v.* Sturgeon, 35 Mo. 213 (1864); 28 *id.* 323.

[4] Hibernia Ins. Co. *v.* St. Louis, &c. Transportation Co., 17 F. R. 478 (1883).

[5] Hazard *v.* New England Marine Ins. Co., 8 Pet. *585 (1834), M'Lean, J.

[6] [Tuckerman *v.* Stephens, &c. Transportation Co., 32 N. J. L. 323 (1867); 33 *id.* 565.

[7] Dibble *v.* Morgan, 1 Woods, 411 (1873).

[6] Baxter *v.* Leland, 1 Abb. Adm. 352 (1848), cases; 3 Ware, 215; 2 Curtis, 8; 56 Barb. 442; 3 Kent, 300.

Qui non habet, ille non dat. He who does not own, cannot transfer.[1] See TRANS-FERRE; REDDARE.

DARRAIGN. See DERAIGN.

DARREIN. See CONTINUANCE, Puis, etc.

DARTMOUTH COLLEGE CASE. See CHARTER, 2; CORPORATION.

DATE.[2] The primary signification is time "given" or specified,— in some way ascertained and fixed.[3]

The time when an instrument was made, acknowledged, delivered, or recorded; the clause or memorandum which specifies that fact; and the time from which its operation is to be reckoned.[4]

In the ancient form the clause ran: *datum apud,* etc., specifying the place and time; thence called the *datum* clause, afterward shortened to "date."

False date. Implies a date purposely incorrect.

Misdate. An erroneous date, made so intentionally or unintentionally.

A date is not a necessary part of a document. Another day than that named may be shown to be the true date, except where there is collusion.[5]

A deed is considered as executed on the nominal date, unless the contrary be made to appear; it speaks from the day of delivery; and it is valid whether it bears no date, or has a false or an impossible date, provided the real day when it was given can be established.[6]

The purpose of a date in a bill or note is to fix the day of payment; if such day is indicated, that is sufficient.[7] See DESCRIPTION; RELATION, 1.

DAY. 1. The time between one midnight and the next succeeding midnight.[8] See NIGHT.

The civil day begins and ends at 12 o'clock P. M. The word "day," used alone in a statute or contract, means, unless restricted to a shorter period, the twenty-four hours.[9]

2. The time between sunrise and sunset; day-time, *q. v.*

3. The business hours of a day.

Artificial day; solar day. From the rising to the setting of the sun. **Natural day.** The whole twenty-four hours; midnight to midnight.[1]

Daily. "Advertisement in a daily newspaper" (*q. v.*) may refer to a paper issued every day of the week but one.[2]

Day in court. A day set for appearing in a court; a day on which a person may be heard as to a matter affecting his rights.

It is an old maxim that every one is entitled to his day in court. This means that day on which the cause is reached for trial in pursuance of the forms and methods prescribed by law.[3] See CONTINUANCE; NOTICE, 1.

Days of grace. Three additional days in which to pay a negotiable bill or note after its maturity. See further GRACE, Days of.

Day's work. See SERVICE, 1.

Day-time. That portion of the twenty-four hours during which a man's person and countenance are discernible.[4] See BURGLARY.

Judicial day; juridical day. A day for judicial proceedings; a day for exercising judicial power; a court day. Opposed, *non-judicial, non-juridical day.*

Non-judicial days are legal holidays and Sundays. Judicial proceedings in civil matters on such days are generally void. See DIES, Dominicus, etc.; HOLIDAY; SUNDAY.

Peremptory day. A day assigned for a hearing without further postponement.

See APPEARANCE, 3; LAW-DAY; RETURN-DAY; RUNNING DAY. Compare DIES.

"In the space of a day all the twenty-four hours are usually reckoned, the law generally rejecting all fractions of a day, in order to avoid disputes."[5]

Common sense and common justice equally sustain the propriety of allowing "fractions of a day" whenever it will promote the purposes of substantial justice.[6]

[1] See 16 Wall. 550; 23 *id.* 128; 4 Cliff. 311, 360; 71 Ala. 288; 100 Mass. 24; 4 Wend. 619.
[2] L. *datum,* a thing given.
[3] Bement v. Trenton Locomotive Co., 32 N. J. L. 515 (1866); 2 Bl. Com. 304.
[4] See Orcutt v. Moore, 134 Mass. 48 (1883).
[5] 1 Whart. Ev. §§ 976–78, cases; 2 Greenl. Ev. §§ 12–13, cases.
[6] 2 Bl. Com. 304, 307; Raines v. Walker, 77 Va. 92 (1883), cases; 19 How. 73; 33 Me. 446.
[7] Daniel, Neg. Inst. §§ 83–85, cases; 1 Ames, Bills, etc., 145.
[8] Pulling v. People, 8 Barb. 385 (1850); Kane v. Commonwealth, 89 Pa. 522 (1879); Haines v. State, 7 Tex. Ap. 33 (1879).
[9] Benson v. Adams, 69 Ind. 354 (1879), cases; Helphenstein v. Vincennes Nat. Bank, 65 *id.* 589 (1879); 2 Bl. Com. 141.

[1] See People v. Hatch, 33 Ill. 137 (1863).
[2] Richardson v. Tobin, 45 Cal. 30, 33 (1872).
[3] Ketchum v. Breed, 66 Wis. 92 (1886), Cassoday, J.; 81 Va. 759.
[4] Trull v. Wilson, 9 Mass. 154 (1812); 4 Bl. Com. 224.
[5] 2 Bl. Com. 141.
[6] *Re* Richardson, 2 Story, 577 (1843); Lapeyre v. United States, 17 Wall. 198 (1872); United States v. Norton, 97 U. S. 170 (1877); Burgess v. Salmon, *ib.* 383 (1878); First Nat. Bank of Cincinnati v. Burkhardt, 100 *id.* 689 (1879); Louisville v. Portsmouth Savings Bank, 104 *id.* 474–79 (1881), cases; 11 F. R. 214; 37 Ill. 239; 69 Ind. 353; 28 Pa. 518.

The maxim is now chiefly known by its exceptions. When private rights depend upon it, the courts inquire into the hour at which an act was done, a decree entered, an attachment laid, or a title accrued.[1]

When an officer has neglected to note upon a writ of execution the hour and minute at which the writ was delivered to him, the precise time may be established by evidence.[2]

It has become the rule in the construction of a contract, when the time to be computed is one or more days, weeks or years, to exclude the day of the date or event, whether by the contract the time is to be reckoned from date, from the day of the date, or from some act or event. The day is not divided, because not only is a day a natural unit of time, but it is a fair presumption that the parties did not intend to divide a day, since the time to be computed is made up of days as units of time; and the day is excluded because to include it would require an act, which, by the contract, was to be done in one day from date, to be done on the day of the date, which is against the apparent intention of the parties. But whenever it is necessary to divide a day in order to carry into effect the intention of the parties, this may be done; and the rule of excluding the day is not applied when a different intention appears on the face of the contract; and no such general rule obtains when acts are to be done within one or more hours, for example, after the date of the contract.[3]

In computing time, days are counted according to the following rules:

1. When a contract, a statute, or a rule of court prescribes a definite number of days within which an act must be done (as, make a payment, take an appeal, file a plea or pleading, serve a notice), the first day is excluded and the last day included: the first and last days are never both included.[4]

2. An intervening Sunday is frequently omitted, especially when the days are less than a week.[5]

3. When the last day is Sunday, or a legal holiday, the act may be done on the day following — except as to days of grace.[4,5] See further under Time.

See After; Afternoon; At; Between; By; For; From; On or Before; When; Within; — Month; Time; Year.

DE. A Latin preposition denoting: away from, out of, arising from; of, about, concerning, with regard to; for, on account of, because of, by.

With adjectives, forms adverbial expressions; as, *de novo*, anew.

In compounds, denotes separation, departure, removal: cessation or negation of the fundamental idea; sometimes, a strengthening of that idea.

---

[1] Maine v. Gilman, 11 F. R. 216 (1882), cases.

[2] Hale's Appeal, 44 Pa. 439 (1863).

[3] Hitchings v. Edmands, 132 Mass. 339 (1882), Field, J.; Ward v. Walters, 63 Wis. 44 (1885), cases.

[4] See 2 Pars. Contr. 364; 19 Conn. 376; 12 Iowa, 186; 9 N. H. 304; 37 Mo. 574; 28 Barb. 284; 16 Pa. 14.

[5] See 31 Cal. 240, 271; 12 Ga. 93; 53 Ill. 87; 46 Mo. 17; 29 Pa. 522; 40 *id.* 372; 17 Gratt. 109.

[6] See 3 Cush. 137; 27 N. J. L. 68; 20 Wend. 205.

De bene esse. For the well being: provisionally, conditionally. Abbreviated *d. b. e.*

Characterizes an act or proceeding viewed as sufficient for the time being.

The entry of record of the name of an attorney as counsel for a defendant is termed an appearance *de bene esse*, when such appearance is not to be conclusive unless subsequently ratified.

The examination of a witness *de bene esse* may be had when he is an important witness, and there is danger of losing his testimony from death or absence. His deposition (*q. v.*) may be taken, but not used at trial unless he has since died, or is abroad or beyond reach of process.[1]

De bonis. Of, for, or concerning goods or property. See phrases under Bona.

De cursu. Of course; as a matter of course.

De donis. Concerning grants. See under Donum.

De facto. In fact; as a matter of fact. Opposed, *de jure:* by right, by legal right or title. See Factum; Government.

De gratia. From favor, indulgence. Opposed, *de jure:* of right.

De homine replegiando. For replevying a man. See Replevin, 2.

De incremento. Of the increase. See Costs.

De injuria. Of wrong. See Replication.

De jure. Of or by right. See *De facto; De gratia.*

De lunatico inquirendo. For inquiry as to lunacy, *q. v.*

De medietate linguæ. Of half tongue: half of each language or nationality. See Medietas.

De melioribus damnis. Of the better damages; of the abler ones the damages.

Where a loss is assessed against several defendants the plaintiff may elect to claim satisfaction of those most able to pay. See Contribution.

De mercatoribus. Concerning merchants, *q. v.*

De minimis. See Lex, De minimis, etc.

De non apparentibus. See Apparere, De non, etc.

De novo. From the first; anew. See Venire, De novo.

De partitione facienda. For division to be made. See Partitio.

De retorno habendo. For having return; to have a return, *q. v.*

---

[1] See 2 Daniel, Ch. Pr. 111; 25 Cent. Law J. 244, 579. (1887), cases.

De son tort. F. Of his own wrong. See TORT, 1.

De terris. Out of the lands.

As, a judgment *de terris*, for arrears of dower.[1]

De una parte. Of one part or party. See PARS.

De ventre. See VENTER.

De vicineto. From the vicinage or country. See COUNTY, 2; VICINITY.

DEAD. See ALIVE; ANIMAL; BURIAL; DEATH; FREIGHT; PLEDGE.

Dead-head. A person other than an officer, agent, or employee, of a railroad or other company, who is permitted to travel without paying fare.[2] See COMMERCE, Act of 1887, sec. 22, p. 206.

Dead-letter law. See OBSOLETE.

Deadly. See WEAPON.

DEAF. See INFLUENCE; WILL, 2; WITNESS.

A deaf mute who does not and cannot be made to understand any matter of business, except of the most simple character, cannot manage his own affairs or select an agent to transact them.[3]

A statute required that a stationary bell be rung or a whistle sounded at a railroad crossing, before a train passed. A deaf mute who saw a train approaching, as to which no warning was given, attempted to cross the track and was injured. *Held*, that he could not recover damages.[4]

DEAL. To traffic; to transact business; to trade.[5]

Said of a bank, may mean to buy and sell for gain, and include sales on commission.[6]

Dealer. One who trades, buys or sells;[7] one who buys to sell again;[8] one who makes successive sales a business.[9]

One who slaughters animals and sells the meat as food is not a " dealer " within the meaning of a statute requiring dealers who buy and sell merchandise to take out a license.[10] See PEDDLER; RETAIL.

Dealer's talk. See COMMENDATIO, Simplex, etc.

---

[1] Haven v. Bartholomew, 57 Pa. 126 (1868).

[2] [Gardner v. Hall, 61 N. C. 22 (1866).

[3] Perrine's Case. 41 N. J. E. 410–12 (1886), cases, Runyon, Ch.: 25 Am. Law Reg. 776 (1886); *ib.* 778–80.

[4] Ormshee v. Boston, &c. R. Co., 14 R. I. 102 (1883).

[5] Vernon v. Manhattan Co., 17 Wend. 526 (1837).

[6] Bates v. State Bank, 2 Ala. 465–68 (1841); Fleckner v. United States Bank, 8 Wheat. 349, 351 (1823); 11 Wis. 334.

[7] Berks County v. Bertolet, 13 Pa. 524 (1850).

[8] Norris v. Commonwealth, 27 Pa. 495 (1856); 33 *id.* 381.

[9] Overall v. Bezeau, 57 Mich. 507 (1877), Cooley, C. J.

[10] State v. Yearby, 82 N. C. 561 (1880); 80 *id.* 479. See also 44 Ala. 29; 79 Ill. 178; 65 Me. 284; 12 Lea, 282; 21 Vt. 484.

DEATH. Cessation of life; extinction of political existence. See LIFE.

Civil death. Extinction of civil rights.

A bankrupt is regarded as civilly dead;[1] so is an insolvent corporation, to the extent that its property may be administered as a trust fund for creditors and stockholders.[2]

Formerly, if a man was banished or abjured the realm, or entered a monastery, before the law he was civilly dead — *civiliter mortuus*. Then, a monk, like a dying man, could make a will, or leave his next of kin to administer as if he had died intestate. Since, also, the act determined a lease for life, conveyances for life were usually made for the term of one's " natural life."[3]

A convict, in the penitentiary, is civilly dead, and cannot be sued.[4]

Natural death. Death from the unassisted operation of natural causes; death by visitation of the Creator. **Violent death.** Death caused by human agency. See CORONER.

A person who for seven years has not been heard of by those who would naturally have heard of him, had he been alive, is presumed to be dead; but the law raises no presumption as to the precise time of death. That he died before the end of that period may be presumed, it appearing that he encountered a special peril or came within the range of some impending or immediate danger which might reasonably be expected to destroy life.[5] See DIE, Without children.

Death by the hands of justice. The execution of a person convicted of crime in any form allowed by law.[6] See under DIE.

Death penalty. Punishment by deprivation of life; capital punishment. **Death sentence.** A sentence involving death. **Death warrant.** An order for the execution of a person who has been sentenced to punishment by death.

The manner of inflicting the punishment of death shall be by hanging.[7]

The language of a death-sentence is believed to be substantially as follows: " A B, having been convicted of the felony with which you stand charged, and of the crime of murder in the first degree [or other capi-

---

[1] International Bank v. Sherman, 101 U. S. 406 (1879).

[2] Graham v. La Crosse, &c. R. Co., 102 U. S. 161 (1880).

[3] 1 Bl. Com. 132; 2 *id.* 257; 6 Johns. 118; Mo. R. S. 1855, p. 642.

[4] Rice County v. Lawrence, 29 Kan. 161 (1883).

[5] Davie v. Briggs, 97 U. S. 633–34 (1878), cases; Newell v. Nichols, 75 N. Y. 86–90 (1878), cases; Evans v. Stewart. 81 Va. 733–38 (1886), cases; Doe v. Nepean, 2 Sm. L. C. 510; 1 Greenl. Ev. § 41; 2 Whart. Ev. §§ 1274–78, cases; 92 Am. Dec. 704–3, cases.

[6] Breasted v. Farmers' Life & Trust Co., 8 N. Y. 303 (1853).

[7] R. S. § 5324.

ta] offense], the sentence of the law is, that for this offense you be taken hence to the jail of the county, whence you came, and thence, at such time as the governor of the State [or, the President of the United States] may, by his warrant, appoint, to the place of execution, and that you be then and there hanged by the neck until you be dead. And may God have mercy upon your soul."

The wording of a recent death-warrant was: Commonwealth of Pennsylvania, —— ——, governor of said commonwealth, to —— ——, high sheriff of the county of Allegheny, sends greeting:

Whereas, At a court of oyer and terminer and general jail delivery held at Pittsburgh in and for the county of Allegheny at September session, 1885, a certain —— —— was tried upon a certain indictment charging him with the crime of murder, and was, on the 13th day of November, 1885, found guilty of murder in the first degree, and was thereupon, to wit, November 19, 1885, sentenced by the said court, that he, the said —— ——, be taken thence to the jail of Allegheny county, whence he came, and thence to the place of execution at such time as the governor of this commonwealth by his warrant may appoint, and there and then he be hanged by the neck until he be dead. Now, therefore, this is to authorize and require you, the said —— ——, high sheriff of the county of Allegheny as aforesaid, or your successor in office, to cause the sentence of the said court to be executed upon the said —— —— between the hours of 10 A. M. and 3 P. M., on Thursday, the 23d day of February, Anno Domini, one thousand eight hundred and eighty-eight, in the manner directed in the seventy-sixth section of the act of general assembly of this commonwealth, approved the 31st day of March, A. D., 1860, entitled an act to consolidate, revise and amend the laws of this commonwealth relating to penal proceedings and pleadings, and for so doing this shall be your sufficient warrant.

Given under my hand and the great seal of the State at Harrisburg this 20th day of January, in the year of our Lord one thousand eight hundred and eighty-eight, and of the commonwealth the one hundred and twelfth. —— ——,

Secretary of the commonwealth.

Punishment by death is known as "the extreme penalty of the law." It is not viewed as an equivalent, even in murder, nor as retaliation, but as the highest penalty man can inflict, and tending most to personal security.[1] See further CAP; EXECUTION, 3; PUNISHMENT, Capital.

Death watch. Special guard appointed, a few days (perhaps eight to fourteen) before execution, to observe the actions of a prisoner under sentence of death, in order to discover and defeat any plan formed or attempt made to effect his escape, and to prevent him from committing suicide; also, the occasion for taking such extra precaution, and, the number of days during which the precaution is exercised.

[1] 4 Bl. Com. 13, 376.

The persons who actually perform the service may be designated as the "day" and the "night" watch.

See also ACCIDENT, Insurance; DIE; ABATEMENT, 4; ACTIO, Personalis; AGENT; BURIAL; CONCEAL, 1; DAMAGES; DECEDENT; DECLARATION, 1, Dying; DEODAND; DONATIO; HOMICIDE; INSURANCE; MORTALITY; POLICE, 2; REVIVE; SURVIVE. Compare MORS.

DEBAR. See BAR, 3.

DEBATE. See LIBERTY, 1, Of speech; PRIVILEGE, 4.

DEBAUCH. In French, *debauche*, from the shop: to entice away from work or duty; to entice and corrupt. Referring to a woman, at first meant to seduce, then to seduce and violate: in which twofold sense it is used in law.[1]

DEBENTURE. 1. A custom-house certificate that an importer is entitled to a drawback.[2]

2. A bond in the nature of a charge on government stock, or on the stock of a public company.[3] See DEBET.

A security issued by a public (usually, a railway) company, and may be a mortgage of its lands and stock. It is in the form of a promissory note, subject to strict regulations as to transfers, and has coupons attached for the payments of interest.[4]

The word does not admit of accurate definition. It expresses an acknowledgment of a debt by either a corporate body or a large partnership.[5]

"You may have mortgage debentures, which are charges of some kind upon property; or you may have debentures which are bonds. . You may also have a debenture which is nothing more than an acknowledgment of debt, or you may have an instrument like this in question, which is a statement by two directors that a company will pay."[5]

DEBET. L. He owes; from *debere: de habere*, to have a thing of some one. Compare ASSUMPSIT.

Debet et detinet. He owes and withholds.

The form of the writ of debt is sometimes in the *debet* and *detinet*, and sometimes in the *detinet* only: that is, the writ states, either that the defendant owes and unjustly detains the debt or thing in question, or only that he unjustly detains it. The writ is brought in the *debet* as well as in the *detinet*, when sued by one of the original contracting parties who personally

[1] [Koenig v. Nott, 2 Hilt. 329 (N. Y., 1859), Daly, F. J.: 8 Abb. Pr., o. s., 389.

[2] Act of Congress, 2 March, 1799, s. 80.

[3] [Mozley & Whiteley's Law Dict.

[4] [Brown's Law Dict.]

[5] British India Steam Navigation Co. *v.* Commissioners of Internal Revenue, 44 L. T. 378 (1881), Grove, J. See also *Re* Rogers' Trusts, 1 Drew. & S. 341 (1860).

[6] 44 L. T. 381, *supra*, Lindley, J. See Jones, Ry. Sec. § 72.

gave the credit, against the other who personally incurred the debt, or against his heirs, if they are bound
to the payment; as, by the obligee against the obligor.
But if brought by or against an executor for a debt
due to or from the testator, this, not being his own
debt, shall be sued for in the *detinet* only. So, also,
if the action be for goods, or corn, or a horse, the writ
shall be in the *detinet* only, for nothing but a sum of
money, for which I (or my ancestor in my name) have
personally contracted, is properly considered my debt.[1]

Debit. He owes. See under DEBT, 2.

Debitum. A thing due or owing; an obligation; a debt, *q. v.*

Debitum in præsenti, solvendum in futuro.
An obligation existing in the present, dis-
chargeable in the future.

Describes any class of obligations complete at the
present day, though payable in the future.[2]

Debitum sine brevi. Debt without a writ
or declaration. Written also *debitum*, and
debit, sans breve; and abbreviated *d. s. b.*

1. When an action at common law was
begun by original bill, the allegations in
which resembled the allegations in a modern
declaration, the action was said to be by bill,
or by bill without a writ,— other actions
being founded upon an original writ.

2. In the practice of several States, a debt
confessed by warrant of attorney and entered of record, either with or without a
declaration accompanying it. See further
ATTORNEY, Warrant of.

Nihil, or nil, debet. He owes nothing.
The plea which forms the general issue in an
action of debt upon a parol contract.[3]

DEBRIS. See AQUA, Currit, etc.

DEBT. Whatever one owes.[4] See DEBET.

1. A liquidated demand.

A sum of money due by certain and express agreement.[5]

As, by a bond for a determinate sum, by a bill or
note, by a special bargain, or as rent reserved on a
lease: in which cases the amount is fixed, specific,
does not depend upon subsequent valuation to settle it.[6]

Frequently, a sum of money reduced to a
certainty, and distinguished from a claim for
uncertain damages.

As, in statutes of set-off, where there are mutual
debts between plaintiff and defendant. . . If we

regard the original, *debitum*, a thing due or owing,
there is no reason why compensation for a breach of
contract may not be "due," although not reduced to
a certain sum. This enlarged sense, at least, may
best answer the intent of the legislature.[1]

A sum of money due by contract.

It is not essential that the contract be express, nor
that it fix the precise amount to be paid.[2]

That for which an action of debt will lie —
a sum of money due by certain and express
agreement. In a less technical sense, any
claim for money; in a more enlarged sense,
any kind of a just demand.[3]

In its most general sense, that which is due
from one person to another, whether money,
goods, or services; that which one is bound
to pay to or perform for another.[4]

Standing alone, is as applicable to a sum of money
promised at a future day as to a sum now due and
payable. The former is a debt *owing*, the latter a
debt *due.* . . A sum in all events payable is a debt,
without regard to the time of payment. A sum payable upon a contingency is not a debt.[5] See DUE, 1.

Liability in a borrower to be sued is not essential.[6]

The idea is that one has bound himself to pay
money which he may be compelled to pay.[7]

"Whatever is due to a man under any form of obligation or promise." Coke says that *debitum* signifies
not only a debt for which an action of debt lies, but,
generally, any duty to be yielded or paid.[8]

A fixed and certain obligation to pay
money or some other valuable thing, in the
present or in the future.[9]

Any contract whereby a determinate sum
of money becomes due and is not paid, but
remains in action, is a "contract of debt."

In this light the word comprehends a variety of acquisitions, usually divided into debts — of record, by
special contract, and by simple contract.

A *debt of record* is a sum of money which
appears to be due by evidence of a court of
record; a *debt by specialty*, a sum acknowledged to be due by an instrument under
seal; a *debt by simple contract* is evidenced

---

[1] 3 Bl. Com. 156.
[2] 13 Pet. 494; 11 Mass. 270; 30 Minn. 7; 29 Pa. 151.
[3] 3 Bl. Com. 305; Steph. Pl. 174.
[4] Rodman *v.* Munson, 13 Barb. 197 (1852).
[5] 3 Bl. Com. 154; McElfresh *v.* Kirkendall, 36 Iowa,
226 (1873).

[1] Frazer *v.* Tunis, 1 Binn. 262 (1808), Tilghman, C. J.
[2] United States *v.* Colt, 1 Pet. C. C. 146 (1815), Washington, J.
[3] New Haven Saw Mill Co. *v.* Fowler, 28 Conn. 108
(1859).
[4] Kimpton *v.* Bronson, 45 Barb. 625 (1866), cases; 7
N. Y. 197; 24 *id.* 290.
[5] People *v.* Arguello, 37 Cal. 525 (1869).
[6] Mayor of Baltimore *v.* Gill, 31 Md. 390 (1869).
[7] Scott *v.* City of Davenport, 34 Iowa, 218 (1872).
[8] New Jersey Ins. Co. *v.* Meeker, 37 N. J. L. 301 (1875);
Burrill; Bowen *v.* Hoxie, 137 Mass. 531 (1884); 3 Metc.
526; 113 U. S. 463.
[9] [Appeal of City of Erie, 91 Pa. 402 (1879).

by mere oral testimony or by an unsealed note.[1]

Antecedent debt. See SECURITY (3), Collateral.

Mutual debts. Moneys due or owing by two persons to each other; debts reciprocally due.

"Mutual debts," "dealing together," and "indebted to each other," in statutes of set-off, are of the same import.[2]

"Mutual debts" and "mutual credits," in § 5013, Rev. St., are correlative expressions. What is a debt on one side is a credit on the other. In case of bankruptcy only such credits as must in their nature terminate in debts are the subject-matter of set-off,[3] q. v. Compare CREDIT, Mutual.

Present or existing, prior, and future or subsequent debts. See CONVEYANCE, 2, Fraudulent; SECURITY, 1.

Privileged debt. A debt payable before other debts — in the event of insolvency.

Results from the character of the creditor, as, a State or the United States; or form the nature of the debt, as, funeral expenses.

Priority of payment of debts due to the government is founded upon motives of public policy, to secure revenue.[4]

Public debt. A national or State obligation; a public security; rarely, if ever, the obligation of a town.[5]

"The validity of the public debt of the United States, authorized by law, including debts incurred for payment of pensions and bounties for services in suppressing insurrection or rebellion, shall not be questioned. But neither the United States nor any State shall assume or pay any debt or obligation incurred in aid of insurrection or rebellion against the United States, or any claim for the loss or emancipation of any slave; but all such debts, obligations and claims shall be held illegal and void."[6]

2. The non-payment of any such definite sum of money being regarded as an injury, the remedy afforded is known as the **action of debt** or simply "debt:" the form of action to compel the performance of the contract.

This is the shortest and surest remedy, particularly where the debt arises upon a specialty. But if A verbally agrees to pay B a certain price for a certain parcel of goods, and fails in the performance, an action of debt will lie against A; for this is also a deter-

minate contract; but if he agrees for no settled price, he is liable upon a special "action on the case," according to the nature of the contract.[1]

The action lies whenever a sum certain is due to the plaintiff, or a sum which can readily be reduced to a certainty — a sum requiring no future valuation to settle its amount:[2] a sum which can be ascertained from fixed data by computation.[3]

It is not material in what manner the obligation was incurred or by what it is evidenced, if the sum is capable of being definitely ascertained. Nor is it necessarily founded upon a contract.[2]

The action lies for *money* only. On an obligation to pay or deliver any other article, covenant is the remedy, and the recovery is of a compensation in damages.[4] See ASSUMPSIT; COVENANT, 2.

Debit. To charge as due or owing; also the sum so charged.

Debtor. One who owes another anything, or is under obligation, arising from express agreement, implication of law, or the principles of natural justice, to render and pay a sum of money to another.[5]

The correlative *debtee* has been in use.[6]

One who is under obligation to discharge some duty, or to pay damages for its non-performance, is a debtor, as really as one who is under obligation by bond to pay a sum of money.[7]

Joint debtor. One of several persons who jointly owe a sum of money; a co-obligor. See JOINT.

As to "absconding" and "absent" debtors, see those terms; also, CONCEAL, 3.

A person, without request or assent, cannot make another his debtor by paying his debt, as, taxes;[8] otherwise, as to honoring commercial paper, as see ACCEPT, 2.

The rule is that "the debtor must seek the creditor," and pay or tender payment of the debt when due.[9]

Indebted. The state of being in debt, absolutely, and not conditionally — as is a surety or an indorser.[10]

Implies a debt presently payable; as, in an affidavit for an attachment.[11]

---

[1] [2 Bl. Com. 464-66; 3 *id.* 154, 166. See 2 Story, 450; 2 Wash. 385; 11 Ark. 355; 15 Ind. 282; 1 Nev. 589; 40 N. J. E. 178; 13 Barb. 77; 38 Ohio St. 570; 51 Vt. 86.

[2] Pate v. Gray, 1 Hempst. 157 (1831).

[3] Libby v. Hopkins, 104 U. S. 307-8 (1881), cases.

[4] United States v. State Bank, 6 Pet. *35 (1832).

[5] Morgan v. Cree, 46 Vt. 786 (1861).

[6] Constitution, Amd. XIV, sec. 4.

[1] 3 Bl. Com. 155.

[2] Stockwell v. United States, 13 Wall. 542 (1871).

[3] Mills v. Scott, 99 U. S. 29 (1878); 7 Wall. 79, 80.

[4] Minnick v. Williams, 77 Va. 760 (1883); Story, Contr. § 969.

[5] Stanly v. Ogden, 2 Root, 262 (1795).

[6] 3 Bl. Com. 18.

[7] New Haven Saw Mill Co. v. Fowler, 28 Conn. 108 (1859); 34 Iowa, 213.

[8] Homestead Co. v. Valley R. Co. 17 Wall. 167 (1872); Gurnee v. Bansemer, 80 Va. 872 (1885), cases.

[9] Johnston v. Hargrove, 81 Va. 121 (1885).

[10] See St. Louis Perpetual Ins. Co. v. Goodfellow, 9 Mo. 153 (1845).

[11] Trowbridge v. Sickler, 42 Wis. 420 (1877), cases.

Indebtedness. The condition of owing money; also, the amount owed; indebtment.

May include an obligation for future payment equally with that presently due;[1] and may be by contract or tort.[2]

The "indebtedness" that may be created by a city in excess of a certain percentage on its taxable property includes an agreement of any kind to pay money where no suitable provision has been made for the prompt discharge of the obligation.[3]

See ACCORD; ACCOUNT, 1; ACKNOWLEDGMENT, 1; ADMINISTER, 4; BANKRUPTCY; CERTUM; CHARGE, 2 (2); CLAIM; COMPOSITION, 3; CONTRACT; DEMAND; EXEMPTION; EXTINGUISH; FLOATING; FUND; GUARANTY, 2; INCUR; INSOLVENCY; LIABILITY; LIEN; MERGER, 2; NOVATION; PAY; PENALTY; PRE-EXISTING; PREFERENCE; PRIOR; PRISON; RECOGNIZANCE; RECOVERY; RELEASE; RESCISSION; SUBROGATION; TAKE, 8; TAX, 2; TENDER, 2.

DECAPITATION. See CAPITAL, 1.

DECAY. See PERISHABLE; SOUND, 2 (1).

DECEDENT.[4] A deceased person whose estate is being settled. See ADMINISTER, 4; CREDITOR, Bill; DISTRIBUTION, 2; PART, 1; PROBATE; RESIDUE; WILL, 2.

DECEIT. Any device or false representation by which one man misleads another to his injury.

A fraudulent misrepresentation, by which one man deceives another, to the injury of the latter.[5]

Deceit practiced to induce one to enter into a contract may be *active*, as where falsehood and misrepresentation are actually used by one party to deceive the other; or *passive*, as where a vendor knows that a purchaser is under a delusion influencing his judgment in favor of purchasing, and yet suffers him to complete his purchase.[6]

Other examples are: where one sells what is not his own, or sells unwholesome provisions;[7] or falsely represents his credit to a mercantile agency.[8]

While every deceit comprehends a lie, it is more than a lie — on account of the view with which it is practiced, of its being coupled with some dealing, and of the injury it is calculated to occasion, and does occasion. But a mere lie thrown out at random without intention to hurt anybody, and which a plaintiff was foolish enough to believe, will not support an action.[1]

Formerly the remedy was by a "writ of deceit;" now, unless otherwise provided by statute, it is by an action of trespass on the case.

Besides the special action on the case there is also an "action of deceit," which gives damages in particular cases of fraud, principally where one man does anything in the name of another, by which he is deceived or injured. But an action on the "case" for damages, in the nature of a writ of deceit, is the usual remedy.[2]

To a recovery it is essential that the *defendant:* (1) actually made a false representation of a material fact, by words or acts unambiguous in import;[3] (2) knew the falsity, or did not know the truth, of the representation[4] — the word "deceit" of itself imports this;[5] (3) intended that the plaintiff should act upon the representation — the essence of the injury;[1,6] and that the *plaintiff:* (1) acted upon the representation; (2) to his actual damage;[7] (3) because he was ignorant of the falsity of the representation, and believed it to be true.[7]

The defendant or his agent must have been guilty of some moral wrong; legal fraud alone will not support the action.[8]

The plaintiff must prove representations of material facts which are false, and which induced him to act; and either that the defendant knew the representations to be false, or that, the facts being susceptible of knowledge, he represented, as of his own knowledge, that they were true, when he had no such knowledge.[9]

It is not only necessary to establish the telling of an untruth, knowing it to be such, with intent to induce the person to whom told to act upon it, but also that he altered his condition in consequence, and suffered damage thereby. If it appears affirmatively that although he altered his condition, after hearing the untruth, he was not induced to do it as a consequence, but did it independently, the action fails.[10]

In a recent case the plaintiff averred that he had been induced to purchase the lease, good-will, and fixtures of a livery-stable, upon false, fraudulent, and deceitful representations by the defendant that he owned the lease, was in peaceable possession, etc.

---

[1] Pittsburgh, &c. R. Co. *v.* Clarke, 29 Pa. 151 (1857); Law *v.* People, 87 Ill. 393 (1877).

[2] Mattingly *v.* Wulke, 2 Bradw. 172 (1878), cases.

[3] Sackett *v.* New Albany, 88 Ind. 479 (1883); Valparaiso *v.* Gardner, 97 *id.* 6–7 (1884).

[4] De-ce′-dent.

[5] Farwell *v.* Metcalf, 61 Ill. 374 (1871), Thornton, J.

[6] [Smith, Contr. 206.

[7] 3 Bl. Com. 166.

[8] Eaton *v.* Avery, 18 Hun, 44 (1879).

[1] Pasley *v.* Freeman, 3 T. R. 56 (1789), Buller, J.; *ib.* 63, Ashhurst, J.

[2] 3 Bl. Com. 165.

[3] Halls *v.* Thompson, 1 Smedes & Mar. 481 (1843), cases.

[4] Gibbs *v.* Odell, 2 Coldw. 133 (1865), cases; Stone *v.* Covell, 29 Mich. 363 (1874).

[5] Farwell *v.* Metcalf, 61 Ill. 374–75 (1871), cases.

[6] Lord *v.* Goddard, 13 How. 210 (1851), cases; Farwell *v.* Metcalf, 61 Ill. 375 (1871), cases; Bigelow, Torts, 31.

[7] Cases *supra* and *infra.*

[8] Erie City Iron Works *v.* Barber, 106 Pa. 125, 138, 140 (1884), cases.

[9] Cole *v.* Cassidy, 138 Mass. 439 (1885), Morton, C. J.; 117 *id.* 195; 103 *id.* 382.

[10] Ming *v.* Woolfolk, 116 U. S. 599, 602–3 (1886), cases, Woods, J.; Southern Development Co. *v.* Silva, 125 *id.* 250 (1888); Patterson *v.* Wright, 64 Wis. 289 (1885).

To support an action of tort, it was held that the plaintiff must show: that the representations were untrue, were known by the defendant to be untrue, were calculated to induce him to act, and he, believing them, was induced to act accordingly; that the representations must have been both false and fraudulent; that a positive statement of a falsehood, or the suppression of a material fact which the defendant ought to have known, would constitute the falsity; that if any essential point, requisite to maintaining the action, was wanting, recovery could not be had; and that the defendant, after judgment against him, was not entitled to an exemption of his property from execution for debt.[1]

Where the fraudulent concealment or misrepresentation is made by the vendor of land, as to its nature, quality, quantity, situation, or title, the representation must be in reference to a material thing unknown to the vendee from want of examination, or from want of opportunity to be informed. And if the buyer trusts to representations not calculated to impose upon a man of ordinary prudence, or if he neglects means of information easily within his reach, he must suffer the consequences of his own folly and credulity. The vendee must show, further, that some deceit was practiced for the purpose of putting him off his guard, or that special confidence was reposed in the representations of the vendor, and that the contract was made upon the strength of that confidence. To support the action there must be fraud as distinguished from mere mistake.[2]

Where the question is as to misrepresentation of facts peculiarly within the defendant's knowledge, "the mere fact that the person deceived to his hurt had means of learning the truth, had he made diligent inquiry, is not necessarily fatal to the right to recover."[3]

Thus, a distinct statement by the seller of a patent-right that he owned the right, knowing it to be false, and with intent to deceive the buyer, and on which statement the buyer acted to his injury, will sustain an action, even if the buyer might have discovered the fraud by searching the records of the patent office.[4]

See AGE, Full; CAVEAT, Emptor; CONCEAL, 5; CONSPIRACY; ESTOPPEL; PROSPECTUS; WARRANTY, 2. Compare DOLUS; FRAUD; PRETENSE.

DECEM. See TALES.

DECENT. See INDECENT.

DECEPTION. 1. In the sense of a false representation to induce credit or confidence, see DECEIT; ESTOPPEL; FRAUD, Actual.

2. In the sense of stratagem to discover crime, see COMMUNICATION, Privileged, 1; DECOY.

DECISION. The result of the deliberations of one or more persons, official or unofficial; the judicial determination of a question.

Somewhat more abstract or more extensive than "judgment" or "decree," [1] qq. v.

The "decision" of a court is its judgment; its "opinion" is the reason given therefor. The former is recorded upon its rendition, and can be changed only through an application to the court. The latter is the property of the judges, subject to modification until transcribed in the records.[2]

Decide. Includes the power and right to deliberate, to weigh the reasons for and against, to see which preponderate, and to be governed by that preponderance.[3]

Judicial decision. The determination of a court, in a cause. **Extra-judicial decision.** A determination beyond the limits of authority; a ruling which transcends jurisdiction.

A decision determines no more than what is necessary to the case in hand,—does not go beyond the limits of what is required by the exigencies of the case.[4]

At most, decisions are only evidence of what the laws are, and are not of themselves laws. They are often re-examined, reversed, and qualified by the courts themselves, whenever found to be defective, ill-founded, or otherwise incorrect. The laws of a State are understood to mean the rules and enactments promulgated by the legislative authority thereof, or long established local customs having the force of law.[5]

Decision, rules of. The laws of the several States, except where the Constitution, treaties, or statutes of the United States otherwise require or provide, shall be regarded as rules of decision in trials at common law, in the courts of the United States, in cases where they apply.[6]

This embraces the statute and common law of a State, including statutes relating to the law of evidence in civil cases at common law.[7] In criminal cases the laws of the State in existence in September 24, 1789, are the rules of decision.[8]

[1] Cox v. Highley, 100 Pa. 249, 252 (1882). See also 1 Chitty, Pr. 832; Bigelow, Torts, 9; Cooley, Torts.
[2] Clark v. Edgar, 12 Mo. Ap. 352 (1882).
[3] Arthur v. Wheeler & Wilson Manuf. Co., 12 Mo. Ap. 340 (1882).
[4] David v. Park, 103 Mass. 503 (1870), cases; Watson v. Atwood, 25 Conn. 320 (1856).

[1] See Abbott, Law Dict.; 26 Moak, 449; 55 Vt. 582.
[2] [Houston v. Williams, 13 Cal. 27 (1859), Field, J.
[3] Commonwealth v. Anthes, 5 Gray, 253 (1855). See 43 Md. 629; 16 Moak, 86.
[4] Hauenstein v. Lynham, 100 U. S. 490 (1879); Trade-Mark Cases, ib. 96 (1879); Wright v. Nagle, 101 id. 796 (1879); State v. Baughman, 38 Ohio St. 459 (1882); 10 Oreg. 114.
[5] Swift v. Tyson, 16 Pet. 18 (1842), Story, J.; Nat. Bank of the Republic v. Brooklyn City, &c. R. Co., 102 U. S. 29 (1880); 1 Bl. Com. 69.
[6] R. S. § 721: Act 24 Sept. 1789, § 34.
[7] M'Niel v. Holbrook, 12 Pet. *89 (1838).
[8] United States v. Reid, 12 How. 361 (1851).

Rules of State practice acted upon by the Federal courts, as obligatory upon them, are also included — they have the efficacy of rules adopted by express order of those courts.[1]

Not included are decisions upon general principles of law, for the reasons already given.[2]

The provision does not apply to proceedings in equity, or in admiralty, or to criminal offenses against the United States. The Federal courts follow the decisions of the highest court of a State on questions which concern merely the constitution or laws of that State; also, a course of those decisions, whether founded on statutes or not, which has become a rule of property within the State; also in regard to rules of evidence in actions at law; also in reference to the common law of the State, and its laws and customs of a local character when established by repeated decisions.[3] See COMITY, Judicial; PROCEDURE.

English decisions. See at end of STATUTE, 2.

Compare DECISUM. See COMITY, Judicial; DICTUM, 2; IMPAIR; OPINION, 1 (2); REPORT, 1 (2).

DECISORY. See OATH, Decisory.

DECISUM. L. Cut off, settled, decided; a decision, a precedent.

Stare decisis, et non quieta movere. To stand by precedents and not to disturb what is settled: follow decided cases; adhere to precedents. Shortened to *stare decisis.*

Once a point of law is firmly settled by a decision, that decision rules like cases subsequently arising.

When a court has once laid down a principle of law as applicable to a certain state of facts, for the sake of the stability and certainty of the law it will apply that principle to all future cases where the facts are substantially the same.[4]

Stability and certainty in the law are of the first importance. The certainty of a rule is often of more importance than the reason of it.[5]

Where there has been a series of decisions by the highest tribunal, the rule *stare decisis* is regarded as impregnable — except by legislative enactment.[6] This is true in a special sense where the law has become settled as a rule of property, and titles have been acquired on the strength thereof.[7]

The maxim contemplates points actually involved and argued. The results established, not the reasons assigned, make the case an authority. In considering the soundness of the doctrine enunciated courts of concurrent or of foreign jurisdiction pay regard to the thoroughness of the arguments of counsel, the ability, learning, and jurisdictional authority of the court, and the care and research bestowed in preparing the opinion. The meaning, moreover, is to be drawn from the opinion as a whole.

The maxim is not applied to a case decided contrary to principle, nor to a decision considered merely as a judgment between the immediate parties, nor to decisions upon scientific theories, as, of insanity.[1]

See COMITY, Judicial; COURTS, United States, "Federal question," page 277.

DECLARANT. See DECLARE, 4.

DECLARATION. 1. An assertion or statement explicitly made.

Any statement of material matters of fact sworn to and subscribed is a written declaration.[2]

A declaration which accompanies and qualifies an act is part of it; but when made of a thing that is past it is mere hearsay.[3]

Made contemporaneously, and by a person interested in the matter, a declaration is admissible as original evidence: (1) when the fact of the making is in question; (2) when the inquiry is as to expressions of bodily feelings — their existence or nature;[4] (3) in cases of pedigree,[5] *q. v.*; (4) when part of the *res gestæ.*[6]

The declarations of an injured party, made *after* the injury has happened or the cause of suffering occurred, with regard to the facts of the injury or the cause of the suffering, may not be shown, in an action for damages by such person; nor may his declarations with regard to past suffering or pain, or past conditions of body or mind, be shown. Some authorities seem to oppose the last proposition, especially where the declarations are made to a physician or surgeon while examining the party as a patient. Declarations, however, with regard to present suffering or present condition of the body or mind may generally be shown by any person who heard them; but there are authorities also seemingly opposed to this proposition.[7]

---

[1] United States *v.* Douglass, 2 Blatch. 214 (1851); The Mayor *v.* Lord, 9 Wall. 413 (1869).

[2] Swift *v.* Tyson, *ante.* See generally Watson *v.* Tarpley, 18 How. 520 (1855); Thompson *v.* Phillips, Baldw. 246 (1830); Sonstiby *v.* Keeley, 11 F. R. 580-81 (1882), cases; Burt *v.* Keyes, 1 Flip. 61 (1861); 112 U. S. 255.

[3] Bucher *v.* Cheshire R. Co., 125 U. S. 555 (1888), cases, Miller, J.

[4] Moore *v.* Albany, 98 N. Y. 410 (1885), Earl, J.

[5] N. W. Forwarding Co. *v.* Mahaffey, 36 Kan. 157 (1887); White *v.* Denman, 1 Ohio St. 115 (1853).

[6] Harrow *v.* Meyers, 29 Ind. 470 (1868); 88 *id.* 568.

[7] Reed *v.* Ownby, 44 Mo. 206 (1869); Hihn *v.* Courtis, 31 Cal. 402 (1866); Pioche *v.* Paul, 22 *id.* 110 (1863).

[1] See generally 25 Am. Law Reg. 745-57 (1886), cases; 77 Va. 24-25; 68 Ga. 797; 100 Ind. 422; 41 N. J. E. 479; 5 Johns. 258; 22 Barb. 97, 106; 9 Oreg. 470; 10 *id.* 66; 78 Pa. 500; 87 *id.* 286; 62 Wis. 138, 151, 194; 63 *id.* 138, 151, 194; 1 Bl. Com. 69; 1 Kent, 477; Cooley, Const. 57; Wells, Res. Adj., &c. 527, 583.

[2] United States *v.* Ambrose, 108 U. S. 340 (1883), Miller, J.: R. S. § 5392.

[3] Long *v.* Colton, 116 Mass. 416 (1876); Bender *v.* Pitzer, 27 Pa. 335 (1856).

[4] Travelers' Ins. Co. *v.* Mosley, 8 Wall. 404 (1869); Roosa *v.* Boston Loan Co., 132 Mass. 439 (1882), cases; Commonwealth *v.* Felch, *ib.* 23 (1882); 1 Greenl. Ev. § 102; 1 Whart. Ev. § 268.

[5] 1 Greenl. Ev. §§ 103-4; 1 Whart. Ev. §§ 202-25.

[6] 1 Greenl. Ev. §§ 108-9, 111-14; 1 Whart. Ev. §§ 258-63.

[7] Atchison, &c. R. Co. *v.* Johns, 36 Kan. 781-83 (1887),

After one's death his former declarations are admissible as secondary evidence when on a matter: (1) of general interest;[1] (2) of ancient possession;[2] (3) against interest — before the controversy arose, and it was the deceased's duty to know the facts;[3] (4) when in the nature of a dying declaration.

A declaration by an agent binds his principal, and by a partner binds his copartner, when made during the continuance of the relation and while the particular transaction is pending.[4]

After a person has made a sale of personalty he stands as a stranger to the title, and his declaration respecting the title is not binding on the vendee. Such declaration is admissible only when it appears from independent evidence that both vendor and vendee were engaged in a common purpose to defraud the creditors of the vendor, and that the admission had such relation to the execution of the purpose as to constitute part of the *res gestæ*.[5]

The declaration of a conspirator, to bind his fellows, must be made while acting in furtherance of the common design.[6] See CONSPIRACY.

Declaration of intention. A formal, solemn asseveration by an alien that it is his *bona fide* intention to become a citizen. See NATURALIZATION.

Declaration of Rights. See RIGHT, 2, Declaration, etc.

Declaration of trust. An acknowledgment that property, the title to which the declarant holds, belongs, in whole or in part, to another; also, the writing in which such acknowledgment is made. See TRUST, 1.

Dying declaration. A statement of a material fact concerning the cause and circumstances of a homicide, made by the victim under the solemn belief of impending death.[7]

Such declaration as is made by the party, relating to the facts of the injury of which he afterward dies, under the fixed belief and moral conviction that his death is impending and certain to follow almost immediately, without opportunity of repentance, and in the absence of all hope of avoidance; when he has despaired of life and looks to death as inevitable and at hand.[1]

An exception to the rule rejecting hearsay evidence is made in the case of dying declarations. The general principle on which they are admitted is, they are declarations made in extremity, when the party is at the point of death, when every hope of this world is gone; when every motive to falsehood is silenced, and the mind is induced by the most powerful considerations to speak the truth. A situation so solemn is considered as creating an obligation equal to that imposed by a positive oath administered in a court of justice.[2]

The person must have been qualified to testify, and the declaration must be complete. The competency of the evidence is to be determined by the court; its weight by the jury. If resting in memory, the substance of all that was stated may be given. The declaration may be by signs.[3]

Declarations of the deceased are admissible upon a trial for murder only as to those things as to which he would have been competent to testify if sworn as a witness in the cause: they must relate to facts only, not to mere matters of opinion. It is essential to the admissibility of such declarations, and it is a primary fact to be proved by the party offering them, that they were made under a sense of impending death. But it is not necessary that they be stated at the time to be so made; it is enough if it satisfactorily appears in any mode that they were made under that sanction, whether it be directly proved by the express language of the declarant, or be inferred from his evident danger, from the opinions of the medical or other attendants expressed to him, or from his conduct or other circumstances of the case. Such declarations must relate to the circumstances of the death; they cannot be received as proof when not connected as *res gestæ* with the death.[4]

See further ADMISSION, 2; ESTOPPEL; HEARSAY; PAROL, 2, Evidence; RES, Gestæ.

2. A statement in legal form of the plaintiff's cause of action.[5]

The plea by which a plaintiff in a suit at law sets out his cause of action, as the word "complaint" is in the same sense the technical name of a bill in chancery.[6]

The first pleading filed in a suit is the declaration, *narratio*, count; anciently called the "tale." In this the plaintiff sets forth his cause of complaint at length;

cases, Valentine, J. See generally 22 Cent. Law J. 509 (1886), cases.

[1] 1 Greenl. Ev. §§ 128–40; 1 Whart. Ev. §§ 185–200, 252.

[2] 1 Greenl. Ev. §§ 131–46; 1 Whart. Ev. § 201.

[3] 1 Greenl. Ev. §§ 147–55; 1 Whart. Ev. §§ 226–37.

[4] 1 Greenl. Ev. §§ 112–14, 174–76; 2 Whart. Ev. § 1192.

[5] Winchester Manuf. Co. *v.* Creary, 116 U. S. 165 (1885); Jones *v.* Simpson, *ib.* 611 (1886); Robertson *v.* Pickrell, 109 *id.* 616 (1883); Moses *v.* Dunham, 71 Ala. 177 (1881); Roberts *v.* Medbery, 132 Mass. 101 (1882), cases; Scheble *v.* Jordon, 30 Kan. 354 (1883); Barbour *v.* Duncanson, 77 Va. 76 (1883); Frink *v.* Roe, 70 Cal. 316–19 (1886).

[6] 1 Greenl. Ev. § 111; 2 Whart. Ev. §§ 1205–6.

[7] People *v.* Olmstead, 30 Mich. 435 (1874).

[1] Starkey *v.* People, 17 Ill. 21 (1855), cases.

[2] Rex *v.* Woodcock, 2 Leach, Cr. Cas. 567 (1789), Eyre, Ch. B.; 1 Greenl. Ev. § 156.

[3] 1 Greenl. Ev. §§ 151–61 *b*; Whart. Cr. Ev. § 292; People *v.* Shaw, 63 N. Y. 40 (1875); Walker *v.* State, 39 Ark. 226 (1882).

[4] People *v.* Taylor, 59 Cal. 640, 645 (1881), cases. See generally 19 Cent. Law J. 128–29 (1884), cases; 1 Kan. Law J. 134 (1885), cases.

[5] Smith *v.* Fowle, 12 Wend. 10 (1834), Savage, C. J.

[6] United States *v.* Ambrose, 108 U. S. 340 (1883), Miller, J.

t being, indeed, only an amplification of the original writ (*q. v.*) upon which his action is founded, with the additional circumstances of time and place when and where the injury was committed.[1]

A declaration contains a succinct statement of the plaintiff's case, and generally comprises the following parts: (1) The title and the date — the court, day and year, term, and number of the case; (2) the venue — State and county; (3) the commencement — A B, by his attorney or in person, complains of C D, for that, heretofore, etc.; (4) the body — which consists of: (a) the inducement (*q. v.*) — introductory matter; (b) the averments — allegations of performance of precedents by the plaintiff; (c) the counts — statements of injuries by the defendant; (5) the conclusion — "to the damage of plaintiff —— dollars; and thereupon (or wherefore) he brings suit.[2]

See further AMENDMENT, 1; CONSOLIDATE, Actions; COUNT, 4; CURE, 2; DAMAGES, General; DESCRIPTION, 4; PLEADING; SUIT, 1.

Declaratory. Rendering clear what was before obscure: giving a clear statement; making certain what might remain in doubt; explanatory; elucidatory: as, a declaratory covenant, act, statute, law.

The "declaratory part of the law" is that portion whereby the rights to be observed and the wrongs to be eschewed are clearly defined and laid down.[3]

A "statute declaratory" of the common law states what that law is, as where a custom has almost fallen into disuse or become disputable.[4]

A declaratory statute removes uncertainty as to the rule of law when decisions or prior enactments conflict. It may elucidate existing common or statute law.

Magna Charta was for the most part declaratory of the principal grounds of the fundamental laws of England.[5]

A large portion of our modern codes is but declaratory of the common law as expounded by the courts.[6]

Statutes declaratory of the meaning of former acts are not uncommon. By the courts they are regarded with respect, as expressive of the legislative opinion, and, so far as they can act upon subsequent transactions, they are of binding force. But they cannot operate to disturb rights acquired before their enactment, or to impose penalties for lawful acts done before their passage. The construction of an existing statute is a judicial function.[7] See DECLARE.

---

[1] 3 Bl. Com. 293; 5 Johns. 435.

[2] See 1 Chitty, Pl. 356; 7 Ark. 282; 12 Wend. 10.

[3] 1 Bl. Com. 54.

[4] 1 Bl. Com. 86.

[5] 1 Bl. Com. 127.

[6] Cincinnati City *v.* Morgan, 3 Wall. 293 (1865).

[7] Stockdale *v.* Atlantic Ins. Co., 20 Wall. 340 (1873); Koshkonong *v.* Burton, 104 U. S. 678 (1881); Salters *v.* Tobias, 3 Paige, 344 (1832).

Declare.[1] To announce clearly as fact or truth.

1. To aver, affirm, allege in express terms: as, to declare a person innocent or guilty.

2. To announce, pronounce, decide: as, to declare a contract illegal or void, or a statute unconstitutional.

3. To state or set forth as a cause of action.

4. To proclaim as due: as to declare a dividend, *q. v.*

"In no part of the application did the assured promise that he would not practice any pernicious habit. He 'declared' that he would not. To 'declare' is to state, assert, publish, utter, announce, announce clearly some opinion or resolution; while to 'promise' is to agree, 'pledge one's self, engage, assure or make sure, pledge by contract.' The assured declared, as a matter of intention, that he would not practice any pernicious habit. Was this declaration of future intention false? There is no allegation, much less proof, that it was so. The assured might well have intended to adhere to his declaration in the most perfect good faith, and yet in a moment of temptation have been overcome by this insidious enemy"[2] — intoxicating liquor, from the use of which the assured was attacked with *delirium tremens* and died.

"Declare and affirm" may be equivalent to promise and affirm.[3]

For a judge to "declare the law," is for him to charge the law arising upon the evidence.[4]

5. To determine what shall constitute; to define.

Declaring that a certain act shall constitute an offense, is "defining" that offense.[5]

Declarant. 1. One who states a thing as a fact; he who asserts a thing for the truth.

2. One who avers the truth of a matter as the basis of a cause of action. See DECLARATION, 2.

DECORATION DAY. See HOLIDAY.

DECOY. "Decoy letters" are, ordinarily, letters prepared and mailed for the purpose of detecting criminals.

It is no objection to a conviction upon evidence produced by means of a decoy letter that the prohibited act was discovered by such a letter addressed to a person who had no actual existence. There is a class of cases in respect to larceny and robbery in which it is held that when one person procures, or originally induces, the commission of the act the doer cannot be convicted — because the taking was not against the will of the owner. Many frauds upon the postal,

---

[1] L. *declarare*, to make clear.

[2] Knecht *v.* Mutual Life Ins. Co., 90 Pa. 121 (1879), Paxson, J.

[3] Bassett *v.* Denn, 17 N. J. L. 433 (1840).

[4] Crabtree *v.* State, 1 Lea, 270 (1878).

[5] United States *v.* Arjona, 120 U. S. 488 (1887).

revenue, and other laws, can effectually be discovered only by means of decoys.[1]

Where the guilty intent to commit crime has been formed, any one may furnish opportunities or even lend assistance to the criminal, to expose him. . . But no court will countenance a violation of positive law or contrivances for inducing a person to commit a crime.[2]

Exceptions to the principle exist in two cases: (1) Where it is a condition to an offense that it should be "against the will" of the party injured, as in prosecutions for rape, highway robbery, and assaults not offenses against the public peace, there must be an acquittal when it appears that the party alleged to be injured invited the commission of the offense. (2) Where there are physical conditions of an offense inconsistent with a trap, so that these conditions cannot exist where there is a trap, the defendant must be acquitted; as when the door of a house is opened by its owner to give a burglar entrance.

Judge Benedict, in *United States* v. *Bott*, 11 Blatch. 346 (1873), and Judge Drummond, in *Bates* v. *United States*, 10 F. R. 92 (1881), decided that it is no defense to an indictment under Revised Statutes, sec. 3993 (act of July 12, 1876), for sending an obscene book by mail, that the book was sent to a detective who gave a fictitious name. Contra, *United States* v. *Whittier*, supra.[3]

A "decoy" or "test" letter should get into the mail in some of the ordinary ways provided by the postal authorities, and as part of the "mail matter."[4]

DECREE.[5] The decision, judgment, or sentence of a court of equity, admiralty, probate, or divorce jurisdiction.

A sentence or order of a court of equity, pronounced on hearing and understanding all the points in issue, and determining the right of all the parties to the suit, according to equity and good conscience.[6]

A judgment in a suit, equitable in nature, rendered by a court exercising equitable powers.[7]

---

[1] United States v. Whittier, 5 Dill. 39–41 (1878), cases, Dillon, Cir. J.

[2] *Ibid.*, 45, Treat, J.

[3] Note by Francis Wharton, Bates's Case, 10 F. R. 97–100, cases. See also note to Speiden v. State, 3 Tex. Ap. 156 (1871), in 30 Am. Rep. 129, cases; Saunders v. People, 38 Mich. 222 (1878); People v. Collins, 53 Cal. 185 (1878); State v. Jansen, 22 Kan. 498 (1879), cases; Commonwealth v. Cohen, 127 Mass. 282 (1879); Wright v. State, 7 Tex. Ap. 574 (1880); People v. Noelke, 94 N. Y. 137 (1883); 19 F. R. 39; 1 Bish. Cr. L. § 262; 25 Alb. Law J. 184 (1882); 15 Irish L. T. 583.

[4] United States v. Rapp, 30 F. R. 822 (1887), Neuman, J.

[5] L. *decretum: de cernere*, to decide literally, to separate.

[6] 2 Daniel, Ch. Pr. 986.

[7] See McGarrahan v. Maxwell, 28 Cal. 85 (1865); 3 Bl. Com. 451.

Like a judgment at law, it is the sentence pronounced by the court upon the matter of right between the parties, and is founded on the pleadings and proofs in the cause.[1] See JUDGMENT.

A draft of a decree made by the judge for convenience, that counsel might see in a general way what decree he was prepared to enter, cannot be considered a decree; and in such case the word "decree" on the clerk's docket cannot amount to an entry of the paper as a decree. The word may mean "decree to be entered," or "stands for decree," as well as decree "entered."[2]

Decrees in equity operate only upon the person.[3]

Decretal. In the nature of a final decree.

When an "order" (which is interlocutory, and made on motion or petition), in an event resulting from a direction contained in it, may lead to the termination of the suit in like manner as a decree at the hearing, it is called a "decretal" order.[4]

Interlocutory decree. A decree which directs an inquiry as to a matter of law or fact preparatory to a final decision. **Final decree.** A decree which finally decides and disposes of the merits of the whole cause, and reserves no further question or direction for the future judgment of the court, so that it will not be necessary to bring the cause again before the court for decision.[5]

A decree is "interlocutory" when it finds the general equities, and the cause is retained for reference, feigned issue, or consideration, to ascertain some matter of fact or law when it again comes under the consideration of the court for final disposition.[6]

A decree is "interlocutory" which leaves anything to be done to afford completely the relief contemplated. Such a decree may always, in a pending cause, on a rehearing, be altered at the sound discretion of the chancellor, however great the lapse of time.[7]

A decree is "final" which finally disposes of the subject of litigation so far as the court making it is concerned. . It is the last decree necessary to give the parties the full and entire benefit of the judgment. . . A decree is not the less final because some further order may become necessary to carry it into effect.[8]

When the decree decides the right to the property in contest, and directs it to be delivered up, or to be

---

[1] Rowley v. Van Benthuysen, 16 Wend. 383 (1836).

[2] Fairbanks v. Amoskeag Nat. Bank, 32 F. R. 573 (1887), Colt, J.

[3] Wilson v. Joseph, 107 Ind. 491 (1886), cases: 26 Am. Law Reg. 48 (1887); *ib.* 50–54, cases.

[4] [Brown, Law Dict.: 22 Mich. 201.

[5] [Beebe v. Russell, 19 How. 285 (1856), Wayne, J.; Whiting v. Bank of United States, 13 Pet. 15 (1839).

[6] Kelley v. Stanberry, 13 Ohio, 421 (1844).

[7] Wright v. Strother, 76 Va. 857, 859 (1882); *ib.* 69, 162; 77 *id.* 806.

[8] Mills v. Hoag, 7 Paige, 19 (1827), Walworth, Ch. Cited, 19 How. 285; 10 Wall. 587. See 10 Paige, 131.

sold, or that the defendant pay a sum of money to the complainant, and the complainant is entitled to have such decree carried immediately into execution, the decree must be regarded as a "final" one to that extent.[1]

"The current of decisions fully sustains the rule laid down by the late Chief Justice,"[2] in the foregoing case.

It is not unusual in courts of equity to enter decrees determining the rights of parties, and the extent of the liability of one party to another, giving at the same time a right to apply to the court for modification and directions. It has never been doubted that such decrees are "final." They are all that is necessary to give to the successful party the full benefit of the judgment.[3]

A "final decree" conclusively settles all the legal rights of the parties involved in the pleadings.[4] See further FINAL, 3.

A final decree in equity may be modified or set aside: by an appeal within the time prescribed by law; by a bill of review, filed within such time, charging error apparent upon the record; and by an original bill charging fraud or newly discovered evidence.[5]

Decrees are also classified as: *decrees by default*, against parties who do not appear, in which case the plaintiff takes such decree as he can stand by; *decrees by consent*, in which the form depends upon agreement; *decrees pro confesso*, by admission, in which the form depends upon the case made by the bill — as see below; and *decrees on the hearing*, which vary with the nature of the suit and the relief prayed for.[6]

A bill to "suspend a decree" seeks to avoid or suspend the operation of the decree. A bill to "carry a decree into execution" lies when, from any cause, without further aid, a decree cannot be executed.

A decree taking a bill *pro confesso*, or in default of an answer, is intended to prepare the case for final decree. Its effect is like that of a default at common law, by which the defendant is deemed to have admitted all that is well pleaded in the declaration. The matters in the bill do not pass *in rem judicatam* until the final decree is made — which may be against the plaintiff.[1]

The court will decree what is proper upon the statements in the bill assumed to be true.[2]

When a bill contains a joint charge against several defendants one of whom makes default, the correct mode of proceeding is to enter a default and a formal decree *pro confesso* against such one, and proceed with the cause upon the answers of the other defendants. The defaulting defendant has lost his standing in court: he is not entitled to service of notices; nor to adduce evidence, nor to be heard at the final hearing — he cannot appear in any way. If the suit should be decided against the complainant on the merits, the bill will be dismissed as to all the defendants alike — the defaulter included; but if in the complainant's favor he will be entitled to a final decree against all. A final decree on the merits against the defaulting defendant alone, pending the continuance of the cause, would be incongruous and illegal.[3]

A final decree affirmed by the highest court is conclusive as between the parties,[4] and as binding as a judgment at law.[5] When there are no words of qualification indicating a privilege to take further proceedings, it will be presumed to have been rendered upon the merits.[6]

The language of a decree is construed with reference to the issue put forward by the prayer for relief and the other pleadings, and which these show it was meant to decide.[7] See EQUITY; RELIEF, 2; REVIEW, 2; TERM, 4.

DECREPIT. A "decrepit person" may mean one who is disabled, incapable or incompetent, from physical or mental weakness or defects produced by age or other cause, to such an extent as to render him comparatively helpless in a personal conflict with one possessed of ordinary health and strength.[8]

DEDICATION.[9] Appropriation to public uses of some right or property: as, the dedication of a highway, landing, square, park, land for school purposes; the dedication of an invention, or of a literary or musical composition.

---

[1] Forgay v. Conrad, 6 How. 204 (1848), Taney, C. J.; Winthrop Iron Co. v. Meeker, 109 U. S. 183 (1883); District of Columbia v. Washington Market Co., 108 *id.* 242 (1883); Parsons v. Robinson, 122 *id.* 114-15 (1887).

[2] Thomson v. Dean, 7 Wall. 346 (1868), cases, Chase, Chief Justice.

[3] Stovall v. Banks, 10 Wall. 587 (1870), Strong, J.; 2 Daniel, Ch. Pr. 641.

[4] French v. Shoemaker, 12 Wall. 98 (1870). See also 70 Ala. 571; 34 Ark. 130; 9 Fla. 47; 105 Ill. 26; 3 Md. 505; 22 Mich. 201; 2 Miss. 326; 10 Nev. 405; 12 Johns. 508; 14 Wend. 542; 1 Ohio St. 520; 1 Heisk. 526; 1 Wash. T. 174.

[5] Huntington v. Little Rock, &c. R. Co., 3 McCrary, 585 (1882).

[6] [Abbott's Law Dict.]

[1] Russell v. Lathrop, 122 Mass. 302-3 (1877), cases; Attorney-General v. Young, 3 Ves. Jr. 209 (1796), cases; Rose v. Woodruff, 4 Johns. Ch. *547 (1820), cases.

[2] Thomson v. Wooster, 114 U. S. 104, 110-14, 119 (1885), cases.

[3] Frow v. De La Vega, 15 Wall. 554 (1872), Bradley, J.

[4] Re Howard, 9 Wall. 175, 182 (1869); Lyon v. Perin, 125 U. S. 702 (1888), cases.

[5] Pennington v. Gibson, 16 How. 76 (1853).

[6] Durant v. Essex Company, 7 Wall. 109 (1868), cases.

[7] Graham v. La Crosse R. Co., 3 Wall. 704 (1865); Carneal v. Banks, 10 Wheat. 181 (1825); 1 Story, Eq. §§ 28, 437, 439.

[8] Hall v. State, 16 Tex. Ap. 11 (1884), Willson, J.; Penal Code, Art. 496.

[9] L. *dedicare*, to devote: *dicare*, to declare.

1. The act of giving or devoting property to some public use.[1] Whence dedicator.

An appropriation of realty by the owner to the use of the public, and the adoption thereof by the public; as, the dedication of soil for a highway.[2]

Has respect to the possession of the land, not to the permanent estate.[3]

Express, when explicitly made by oral declaration, deed, or vote; *implied*, when there is acquiescence in a public use.[4]

Made according to the common law or in pursuance of statute. A statutory dedication operates by way of a grant; a common-law dedication, by way of estoppel *in pais*. May also be made *in præsenti* to be accepted *in futuro*.[5]

Is a conclusion of fact, from all the circumstances of each case.[6]

An appropriation of land to some public use, made by the owner of the fee, and accepted for such use by or on behalf of the public.[7]

The vital principle is the *animus dedicandi*. Time, though often a material ingredient, is not indispensable. A dedication is a conclusion of fact to be drawn by the jury from the circumstances of each case.[7]

At common law no special form of ceremony is necessary — simply assent in the owner, a public use, and acceptance by the public, which last may be evidenced by user. The assent, which must be clear, is provable by a writing, by parol, or by acts irreconcilable with any other construction; as, where a man makes a plan of lots, with streets, and sells lots by such plan. A use, from which a dedication may be presumed, may be much less than thirty years' continuance.[8]

Acceptance may be presumed where the gift is beneficial; use is evidence that it is beneficial.[9]

An act of Congress which merely "reserves" sec-

tions of public lands for school purposes does not work a dedication, in the strict sense.[1]

See EASEMENT; LICENSE, 1; SQUARE; USE, 2, User; WATER-MARK.

2. On dedicating an invention to public use, see PATENT, 2; USE, 2, Public.

3. Publishing an uncopyrighted work is a dedication of such work to the public.[2] See COPYRIGHT; DRAMA.

DEDIMUS. L. We have given. See DARE.

A commission to take testimony, the full name of which is **dedimus potestatem**, we have given power.

In English practice the writ issues out of chancery, and empowers the person named to perform designated judicial acts: as, to administer oaths, take answers in equity suits, examine witnesses.[3]

With us the term is seldom, if ever, used in any other sense than that of a commission to take testimony by deposition, *q. v.*

"In any case where it is necessary, in order to prevent a failure or delay of justice, any of the courts of the United States may grant a *dedimus potestatem* to take depositions according to common usage." [4]

"Common usage" here refers to the usage prevailing in the courts of the State in which the Federal court may be sitting.

Whether the writ is necessary to prevent a "failure or delay of justice" is for the court to determine upon the facts presented. "In any case" includes criminal as well as civil proceedings.[5]

The admissibility of the testimony will be reserved till the time of trial. The testimony may be considered by the court in imposing sentence.[6]

DEDUCTION. See DRAWBACK; REPRISES; SET-OFF.

DEED. 1. A thing done; an act; a matter of fact, as opposed to a matter of law: as, a condition, an estoppel, a seisin *in deed*. Corresponds to the French *pais*, q. v.

2. A writing sealed and delivered by the maker — the most solemn and authentic act a man can perform with relation to the disposal of property.[7]

A writing, sealed and delivered; to be duly executed, must be on paper or parchment.[8]

[1] Rees *v.* Chicago, 38 Ill. 335 (1865).

[2] [Hobbs *v.* Lowell, 19 Pick. 407–10 (1837), cases, Shaw, C. J.; Brakken *v.* Minneapolis, &c. R. Co., 29 Minn. 42 (1881).

[3] Benn *v.* Hatcher, 81 Va. 29 (1884), cases.

[4] See 30 Kan. 637–38, 642; 69 Ga. 546.

[5] City of Denver *v.* Clements, 3 Col. 479–83 (1877), cases; *ib.* 485–86.

[6] Quinn *v.* Anderson, 70 Cal. 456 (1886), cases.

[7] Ward *v.* Farwell, 6 Col. 69 (1881), Elbert, C. J.; Steele *v.* Sullivan, 70 Ala. 593–94 (1881), cases; Angell, Highw. 142.

[8] See Cincinnati *v.* White, 6 Pet. 440 (1832); Irwin *v.* Dixion, 9 How. 30–31 (1850), cases; Boston *v.* Lecraw, 17 *id.* 435–36 (1854); 1 Bond, 81; 11 Ala. 63; 4 Cal. 114; 25 Conn. 235; 12 Ga. 244; 76 Ind. 254; 21 La. An. 244; 34 *id.* 618; 124 Mass. 64; 27 N. J.; 211; 77 *id.* 561; 33 N. J. L. 13; 22 Wend. 444, 450; 6 Hill, 411; 19 Barb. 193; 26 Pa. 187; 22 Tex. 100; 9 Wis. 244; 23 *id.* 420; 3 Kent, 451; Angell, Highw. 111.

[9] Abbott *v.* Cottage City, 148 Mass. 523–26 (1887), cases.

[1] Minnesota *v.* Bachelder, 1 Wall. 114 (1863).

[2] Bartlett *v.* Crittenden, 5 McLean, 32 (1849); Pulte *v.* Derby, *ib.* 328 (1852); Thompkins *v.* Halleck, 133 Mass. 32 (1882).

[3] See 3 Bl. Com. 447; 1 *id.* 352; 2 *id.* 351.

[4] R. S. § 866: Judiciary Act, 1789, sec. 30.

[5] United States *v.* Cameron, 15 F. R. 794 (1883); Warren *v.* Younger, 18 *id.* 862 (1884); 20 Blatch. 232.

[6] United States *v.* Wilder, 4 Woods, 475 (1882): 14 F. R. 393.

[7] 2 Bl. Com. 295; Wood *v.* Owings, 1 Cranch, 251 (1803); 3 How. 645.

[8] 4 Kent, 450.

The word in itself imports a written instrument;[1] — a written instrument under seal, containing a contract of agreement which has been delivered by the party to be bound and accepted by the obligee or covenantee.[2]

An instrument or agreement under seal.[3]

This comprehensive meaning includes any writing under seal; as, a bond, lease, mortgage, agreement to convey realty, bill of sale, policy of insurance.

In common use often limited to a writing, under seal, transferring *real estate;* a deed of conveyance of realty. See CONVEYANCE, 2; TITLE, 1.

In its largest sense includes a mortgage,[4] *q. v.*

A "good deed" to land means, in a covenant, a conveyance sufficient to pass whatever right a party has in the land, without warranty or personal covenant; it does not imply the conveyance of a good title.[5]

A "good and perfect deed" to land may intend the conveyance of a perfect title clear of all incumbrances, including a right of dower.[6]

A "good and sufficient deed" may refer either to the form of the conveyance or to the interest or title.[7] A "good and sufficient deed of warranty," or "with covenant of warranty," may also refer to the kind of deed or to the quality of the title.[8]

A deed for a "sufficient title" means for a good title — with the usual covenants of warranty.[9] So as to a "good and sufficient conveyance."[10]

A "lawful deed" means a deed conveying a lawful and good title.[11]

Collateral deed. A defeasance, *q. v.*

Deed poll. A deed not indented, but cut even; a deed made by one party only: as, a sheriff's deed. See POLL, 1.

Deeds under the statute of uses. See USE, 3.

Title deed. Any sealed evidence of title, *q. v.*

Trust deed. An instrument that creates a trust, *q. v.;* also, a mortgage.

See also COMPOSITION, 3; INSPECTION, 3; SEPARATION; SETTLEMENT, 3.

At common law, the general requisites of a deed are: 1. Persons able to contract and to be contracted with for the purposes intended, and a thing or subject-matter to be contracted for,— all expressed by sufficient names. 2. A sufficient consideration. 3. Writing or printing upon paper or parchment. 4. The matter must be legally and orderly set forth: there must be words sufficient to specify the agreement and bind the parties, which sufficiency the courts decide. The formal parts of a deed conveying realty are: (a) the *premises* — the names of the parties, recitals explanatory of the transaction, the consideration, the thing granted; (b) the *habendum* and *tenedum* (to have and to hold) — defining the nature of the grant; (c) the terms of stipulation upon which the grant is made — the *reddendum* or reservation; (d) the *condition* or contingency upon the happening of which the estate will be defeated; (e) the *warranty* securing the estate; (f) the *covenants* — stipulating for the truth of facts, or that a thing will be done; (g) the *conclusion* — mentioning the execution and the time thereof. 5. Reading — when desired. 6. Sealing, and signing. 7. Delivery — absolute or conditional. 8. Attestation — for preserving evidence of the transaction.[1]

The construction of a deed must be favorable, and as near the intent of the parties as the rules of law admit; also reasonable, and agreeable to common understanding. Where the intention is clear too minute a stress is not to be laid upon the strict, precise signification of words. False English will not vitiate. The construction is to be made upon the entire deed. When all other rules fail, the language will be taken most strongly against the party who proposes it. If the words bear different senses, that is preferred which is most agreeable to law. Of two repugnant clauses the first will be received.[2]

A deed is to be so construed, when possible, as to give effect to the intention of the parties. That this may be done, the court will place itself in the situation of the grantor at the date of the transaction with his knowledge of the surrounding circumstances and of the import of the words used.[3]

See further ACKNOWLEDGMENT, 2; ALTER, 2; BOND; CANCEL; CHARTER, 1; CONDITION; CONSIDERATION, 2; COVENANT; DELIBERATION, 1; DELIVERY, 3; DESCRIPTION, 1; DURESS; ESCROW; EXCEPTION, 1; GRANT, 2; INDENTURE; INFLUENCE; INSANITY, 2(4); INSTRUMENT, 3; PARCHMENT; PARTY, 2; POSSESSION, Adverse; PREMISES; PRESENTS, (1); PROFERT; PROVIDED; READING; RECITAL; RECORDING; REGISTRY, 2; RELATION, 1; RESERVE, 4; SEAL, 1; SIGN; SPECIALTY; THENCE; WARRANTY, 1; WILL, 2; WRITING.

[1] Pierson v. Townsend, 2 Hill, 551 (1842).

[2] McMurty v. Brown, 6 Neb. 376 (1877).

[3] Master v. Miller, 4 T. R. 345 (1791). See 1 Ark. 112; 42 N. J. E. 335; 25 Hun, 224; 5 Saw. 603.

[4] Hellman v. Howard, 44 Cal. 104 (1872); People v. Caton, 25 Mich. 391 (1872).

[5] Barrow v. Bispham, 11 N. J. L. 110, 119 (1829).

[6] Greenwood v. Ligon, 18 Miss. 617 (1848); 21 *id.* 275, 532, 677.

[7] Brown v. Covilland, 6 Cal. 573 (1856); Brown v. Gammon, 14 Me. 279 (1837); Parker v. McAllister, 14 Ind. 16 (1859).

[8] Tindall v. Conover, 20 N. J. L. 215–17 (1843); Joslyn v. Taylor, 33 Vt. 474 (1860); 36 Ill. 69; 5 Mass. 494; 11 N. J. L. 119; 2 Johns. 595; 14 *id.* 224; 16 *id.* 269; 20 *id.* 130; 11 Vt. 47, 549.

[9] Ware v. Starkey, 80 Va. 196 (1885).

[10] Gates v. McLean, 70 Cal. 45, 50 (1886).

[11] Dearth v. Williamson, 2 S. & R. 499 (1816); Withers v. Baird, 7 Watts, 229 (1838). On void deeds, see McArthur v. Johnson, Phillips' Law, 317 (1867): 93 Am. Dec. 593, 596–98, cases.

[1] 2 Bl. Com. 296–309.

[2] 2 Bl. Com. 379–81; 3 Kent, 422.

[3] Cilley v. Childs, 73 Me. 133 (1882), cases; Moses v. Morse, 74 *id.* 475 (1883); Moran v. Lezotte, 54 Mich. 86 (1884), cases; 87 Ind. 179; 77 Va. 492. By corporate officers, 26 Cent. Law J. 444–45 (1888), cases.

DEEM. When by enactment certain acts are "deemed" to be a crime of a particular nature they constitute such crime, and are not a semblance or a fanciful approximation of it.[1]

"Deemed" and "adjudged," in a penal statute, have the same meaning.[2]

DEFACE. See ALTER, 2; CANCEL.

DEFALCATION.[3] 1. Reduction of a claim by allowance of a counter-claim.

Setting off another account or another contract.[4]

Defalcation was unknown at common law, according to which mutual debts were distinct and inextinguishable except by actual payment or release.[5] See RECOUP; SET-OFF.

"Defalcate" is the verb; "defalk" is obsolete.[5]

2. Misappropriation of trust funds — by a public or corporate officer.

Defaulter. One whose peculations have brought him within the cognizance of the law, to the extent, at least, of excluding him from a public trust.

To apply the epithet to a person who is free from that stigma is defamatory.[7]

DEFAMATORY. Words which produce perceptible injury to the reputation of another are described as defamatory. Whence defamation.

Defamatory words, if false, are actionable. False defamatory words, if written and published, constitute a libel; if spoken, a slander.[8]

A defamatory publication is a false publication calculated to bring the person into disrepute, but it is not necessarily malicious.[9] See FAME; LIBEL, 5; OBLOQUY; SLANDER.

DEFAULT.[10] 1, n. (1) Something wrongful; some omission to do that which ought to have been done.[11]

Non-performance of a duty; as, the non-payment of money due.[12]

In an accountable receipt executed by a person to whom property levied upon was delivered, he promising to deliver the articles whenever demanded, or "in default thereof" to pay the amount of the debt called for in the writ, *held*, that the reference was to a breach of legal duty.[1]

There can be no default where the omission to do the thing, as to make a payment on a mortgage, has the concurrence of the other party.[2]

A special promise to answer for the default of another must be in writing and signed, as see FRAUDS, Statute of.

A defaulting purchaser is one who fails to complete his purchase at a public sale. See AUCTION.

(2) An omission, neglect or failure to do something required by law, or by a court administering the law.

When a defendant omits to plead within the time allowed for that purpose, or fails to appear at the trial, he "makes default," and the judgment entered in the former case is "a judgment by default."[3]

To "suffer a default" is to let a case go by neglect or inattention, usually designed.

When the plaintiff makes default he may be nonsuited; but a default, in either party, for cause shown, may be "excused" or "saved."

A witness, a juror, and an officer of court, is said to make default when remiss in his attention to duty.

A judgment by default, for the purpose of the particular action, admits the legality of the demand in suit: it does not make the allegations of the declaration or complaint evidence in an action upon a different claim.[4] See INQUIRY, Writ of; NOTICE, 1, Judicial.

2, v. To have judgment entered against one on account of some default: as, that a defendant "shall be defaulted unless he files an affidavit of defense."

Defaulted, adj. Due, but not paid: past due: as, defaulted — interest, coupons, bonds, payment.[5]

DEFAULTER. See DEFALCATION, 2.

DEFEASANCE. A defeating: undoing, overthrow, avoidance, destruction, deprivation. See FEASANCE.

Defeasible. Capable of avoidance or destruction. **Indefeasible.** Not admitting of abolition or impairment.

Many constitutional rights are spoken of as indefeasible.

Two uses of defeasance are recognized:

1. A collateral deed, made at the same

---

[1] Commonwealth v. Pratt. 132 Mass. 247 (1882).

[2] Blaufus v. People, 69 N. Y. 111 (1877); State v. Price, 11 N. J. L. 218 (1830).

[3] A in -făl- as in fan. L. *diffalcare*, to abate, deduct, take away.

[4] Houk v. Foley, 2 P. & W. 250 (1830).

[5] Commonwealth v. Clarkson, 1 Rawle, 293 (1829); 6 Mo. 266.

[6] Webster's Dict.

[7] State v. Kountz, 12 Mo. Ap. 513 (1882).

[8] Odgers, Libel & Slander, 1.

[9] Marks v. Baker, 28 Minn. 166 (1881).

[10] F. *de-faulte*, to want, fail.

[11] Union Trust Co. v. St. Louis, &c. R. Co., 5 Dill. 22 (1878); Albert v. Grosvenor Investment Co., L. R. 3 Q. B. *128–29 (1867).

[12] Williams v. Stern, 5 Q. B. D. 413 (1879).

[1] Mason v. Aldrich, 36 Minn. 286 (1886), cases.

[2] Union Trust Co. v. St. Louis, &c. R. Co., *ante*.

[3] Page v. Sutton, 29 Ark. 306 (1874): Burrill. See also 54 Ala. 430; 5 Iowa, 265; 29 *id*. 245; 11 Neb. 398.

[4] Cromwell v. County of Sac, 94 U. S. 356 (1876). See also 3 Col. 277; 6 *id*. 485; 3 Bl. Com. 397; 24 Cent. Law J. 27 (1887), cases: as against non-residents, 21 Am. Law Rev. 715–31 (1887), cases.

[5] See Foster v. Morse, 132 Mass. 355 (1882).

time with another conveyance, containing conditions upon the performance of which the estate created may be "defeated" or totally undone.[1]

A bond for a reconveyance upon the payment of a specific sum, at a specified time, made at the same time and of the same date as a deed of conveyance.[2]

Formerly, every mortgagor enfeoffed the mortgagee who simultaneously executed a deed of defeasance, considered a part of the mortgage, whereby the feoffment was rendered void on repayment of the money at a certain day. But things that were merely executory, or to be completed by matters subsequent, could always be recalled by defeasances made subsequent to the time of their creation.[1]

It is not of the essence of a mortgage that there should be a defeasance; and there may be a defeasance of a deed of conveyance without constituting it a mortgage. The essence of a defeasance is to defeat the principal deed and make it void *ab initio*, if the condition be performed.[3]

A defeasance made subsequently to an executed contract must be part of the original transaction. At law, the instrument must be of as high a nature as the principal deed. Defeasances of deeds conveying realty are subject to the same rules as such deeds themselves, as to record and notice to purchasers; but in some States notice of the existence of a defeasance, to be binding, must be derived from the public records.[4]

When an absolute deed is shown to have been originally made as security for a loan of money, a court of equity will treat it as a *mortgage*, and allow the grantor to redeem the estate, on the ground that the defeasance was omitted from the deed by fraud or mistake.[5]

But to reduce a conveyance to a mortgage the defeasance may be required by statute to be in writing, duly acknowledged and recorded.[6]

2. A defeasance to a bond, recognizance, or judgment recovered is a condition which, when performed, defeats or undoes it, in the same manner as a defeasance to an estate.

The "condition" of a bond is always inserted in the bond or deed itself; a "defeasance" is made by a separate, and frequently by a subsequent, deed. This, like the condition of a bond, when performed, disincumbers the obligor's estate.[7] See CONDITION.

DEFEAT. See DEFEASANCE; CONDITION.

DEFECT. Under the covenant in a charter-party that the vessel is "tight, staunch, and strong," the owner is answerable for latent as well as for visible defects, whereby the cargo is damaged.[1]

See CAVEAT; CHALLENGE; CURE, 2.

DEFENCE. See DEFENSE.

DEFENDANT. One who is called upon in a court to make satisfaction for an injury done or complained of.[2]

A person sued or prosecuted; a respondent.

In the rules in admiralty, framed by the Supreme Court, "defendant" is used indifferently for a respondent in a suit *in personam* and for a claimant in a suit *in rem*.[3]

Co-defendant. A joint or fellow defendant.

Defendant above or **defendant in error.** The party against whom a writ of error is taken.

Material defendant. In equity, a defendant against whom relief is sought; opposed to *nominal* defendant.

Where a code provided that a bill in equity should be filed in the district where the defendants or a material defendant resides, it was held that the object was to discriminate between defendants whose attitude to the case does, and does not, make them real participants in the litigation, that a material defendant was one who is really interested in the suit, and against whom a decree is sought.[4]

As employed in sections of a code relating to jurisdiction, the word "defendants" was held to mean not nominal defendants merely, but parties who had a real and substantial interest adverse to the plaintiff, and against whom substantial relief was sought; and that to decide otherwise would encourage colorable practices for defeating jurisdiction in the particular class of cases.[5]

In a judgment, "defendant" may be a collective term, embracing all who by the record are liable under the judgment.[6]

A garnishee is a "defendant in the action," who, in pursuance of a statute, may be restrained from disposing of property to the injury of the attaching creditor.[7]

In the Massachusetts Gen. Sts. c. 146, § 38, providing that, if an execution has not been satisfied, the court, "upon petition of the defendant," may order a stay, if the petitioner gives the adverse party security for the prosecution of the review, refers to the party

---

[1] [2 Bl. Com. 327.

[2] [Butman v. James, 34 Minn. 550 (1885), Berry, J.; 4 Pick. 352.

[3] Flagg v. Mann, 2 Sumn. 540 (1837), Story, J.

[4] See 21 Ala. 9; 3 Mich. 482; 7 Watts, 261, 401; 13 Mass. 443; 40 Me. 381; 43 id. 206; 14 Wend. 63; 17 S. & R. 70; 2 Washb. R. P. 489.

[5] 2 Kent, 142; Butman v. James, 34 Minn. 550 (1886).

[6] See Penn. Act 8 June, 1881; Mich. R. S. 261; Minn. St. L., 1873. 34, § 23.

[7] 2 Bl. Com. 342; 43 Me. 371; 14 N. J. L. 364.

[1] Hubert v. Recknagel, 13 F. R. 912 (1882).

[2] [3 Bl. Com. 25.]

[3] Atlantic Mutual Marine Ins. Co. v. Alexander, 16 F. R. 281 (1883).

[4] Lewis v. Elrod, 38 Ala. 21 (1861), Walker, C. J.

[5] Allen v. Miller, 11 Ohio St. 378 (1860).

[6] Claggett v. Blanchard, 8 Dana, *43 (1839).

[7] Almy v. Platt, 16 Wis. *169 (1862).

against whom the judgment sought to be reversed is rendered, not to the defendant in the original action.[1]

Ordinarily, a municipal corporation is not affected by a law which speaks in general terms of defendants, unless expressly brought within the provisions.[2]

Compare LITIGANT; PARTY; PLAINTIFF; RESPONDENT; SUITOR. See DELICTUM, In pari, etc.

DEFENSE, or DEFENCE.[3] 1. Resistance of an attack; resistance with force of an attack made with force or violence.

Self-defense. Protection of person or property from injury.

The defense of one's self, or the mutual and reciprocal defense of such as stand in the relation of husband and wife, parent and child, master and servant, is a species of redress of private injury which arises from the act of the injured party. In these cases, if the party himself, or a person in one of these relations, be forcibly attacked in his person or property, it is lawful for him to repel force with force. . . The law in this case respects the passions of the human mind and makes it lawful in a man to do himself that immediate justice to which he is prompted by nature, and which no prudential motives are strong enough to restrain. It considers that the future process of the law is by no means an adequate remedy for injuries accompanied with force; since it is impossible to say to what wanton lengths of rapine or cruelty outrages of this sort might be carried unless it were permitted a man immediately to oppose one violence with another. "Self-defense," therefore, as it is justly called the primary law of nature, so it is not, neither can it be in fact, taken away by the law of society. . . Care must be taken that the resistance does not exceed the bounds of mere defense and prevention: for then the defender would himself become an aggressor.[4]

Homicide in self-defense, upon a sudden affray, is also excusable. This species of self-defense must be distinguished from such as is calculated to hinder the perpetration of a capital crime. This is that whereby a man may protect himself from an assault or the like, in the course of a sudden broil or quarrel, by killing him who assaults him. . . The right of natural defense does not imply a right of attacking: for, instead of attacking one another for injuries past or impending, men need only have recourse to the proper tribunals of justice. They cannot therefore legally exercise this right of preventive defense but in sudden and violent cases, when certain and immediate suffering would be the consequence of waiting for the assistance of the law. Wherefore, to excuse homicide by the plea of self-defense it must appear that the slayer had no other possible (or at least probable) means of escaping from his assailant.[5] . . The law requires that the person who kills another in his own defense should have retreated as far as he safely can to avoid the violence of the assault before he turns upon his assailant; . . he must flee as far as he conveniently can, by reason of some wall, ditch, or other impediment, or as far as the fierceness of the assault will permit, for it may be so fierce as not to allow him to yield a step without manifest danger of his life or enormous bodily harm, and then in his defense he may kill his assailant instantly.[1]

But no one may *revenge* himself by striking an unnecessary blow, as, when all danger is passed, nor strike when the assault is technical and trivial.[1]

The principles of the law of self-defense may be stated in three propositions: (1) A person who, in the lawful pursuit of his business, is attacked by another under circumstances which denote an intention to take his life, or to do him some enormous bodily harm, may lawfully kill the assailant, provided he uses all the means in his power, otherwise, to save his own life, or prevent the intended harm,— such as retreating as far as he can, or disabling his adversary without killing him, if it be in his power. (2) When the attack upon him is so sudden, fierce, and violent that retreat would not diminish but increase his danger, he may instantly kill his adversary without retreating at all. (3) When, from the nature of the attack, there is reasonable ground to believe that there is a design to destroy his life or commit any felony upon his person, killing the assailant will be excusable homicide, although it should afterward appear that no felony was intended.[2]

The law of self-defense is a law of necessity, real or apparently real. A party may act upon appearances, though they turn out to have been false. Whether they were real or apparently real is for the jury, in a criminal case, to decide upon consideration of all the circumstances out of which the necessity springs. If the jury should find from the evidence that the circumstances were such as to excite the fear of a reasonable man, and that the defendant, acting under the influence of such fear, killed the aggressor to prevent the commission of a felony upon his person or property, he would not be criminally responsible for his death, although the circumstances might be insufficient to prove, by a preponderance of evidence, that the aggressor was actually about to commit a felony.[3]

The right of self-defense does not imply the right of attack, and it will not avail in any case where the difficulty is sought or induced by the party himself. On the other hand, to justify killing an adversary on this ground it is not necessary that the danger apprehended should be real or actually impending. It is only necessary that the defendant should have had reasonable cause to apprehend that there was an immediate design to kill or to do him some great bodily harm, and that there should have been reasonable

---

[1] Leavitt v. Lyons, 118 Mass. 470 (1875).

[2] Schuyler County v. Mercer County, 9 Ill. 24 (1847).

[3] F. *défense*: L. *defensa*: *defendere*, to strike down or away, ward off, repel. Mid. Eng. defence.

[4] 3 Bl. Com. 3; 4 *id*. 186; 1 *id*. 130.

[5] 4 Bl. Com. 183–84.

[1] 4 Bl. Com. 184–85.

[2] Commonwealth v. Selfridge, Sup. Ct. Mass. (1806), Parker, J. Same case, Whart. Homicide, App. No. 1; Hor. & T., Cases on Self-Defense, 17; 2 Am. Cr. R. (Hawley), 259.

[3] People v. Flanagan, 60 Cal. 4 (1881), McKee, J.; 62 *id*. 208, 307; 59 *id*. 251; United States v. Wiltenberger, 3 Wash. 521 (1819).

cause to apprehend immediate danger of such design being accomplished.[1]

Adjudicated cases hold that among the slayer's acts which abrogate or abridge his right of self-defense are the following: 1. Devices to provoke the deceased to make an assault which will furnish a pretext for taking his life or inflicting serious bodily injury upon him. 2. Provocation of the deceased into a quarrel, causing the fatal affray; but mere words or libelous publications do not amount to such provocation. 3. Preconcert with the deceased to fight him with deadly weapons. 4. Commencing an attack, assault, or a battery upon the deceased. 5. Going with a deadly weapon where the deceased is, for the purpose of provoking a difficulty or bringing on an affray, and by words or acts making some demonstration of such purpose calculated to provoke them.[2]

See ARMS; ASSAULT; BATTERY; FORCE; HOMICIDE; IMMEDIATE; RETREAT; THREAT.

2. That which is offered by a defendant as sufficient to defeat a suit — by denying, justifying, or confessing and avoiding, the cause of action.

A term of art used in common-law pleading in the sense merely of "denial."[3]

When the plaintiff hath stated his case in the declaration, it is incumbent on the defendant within a reasonable time to make his "defense," and to put in a plea; else the plaintiff will recover judgment by default, q. v. . . . Defense, in its true legal sense, signifies not a justification, protection, or guard, which is its popular signification, but an opposing or denial (French, *defender*) of the truth or validity of the complaint. It is the *contestatio litis* of the civilians, a general assertion that the plaintiff hath no ground of action, which assertion is afterward extended and maintained in the plea.[4] Compare TRAVERSE.

The right possessed by a defendant, arising out of the facts alleged in his pleadings, which either partially or wholly defeats the plaintiff's claim.[5]

Defenses, in civil procedure, are stated with fullness and particularity in answers to bills and libels, and in affidavits of defense filed to affidavits of claim.

Defense, affidavit of. A sworn written statement of the facts which constitute the defense in a civil action; also called "affidavit of merits." Opposed, *affidavit of claim.*

---

[1] State v. Johnson, 76 Mo. 122, 126 (1882), Norton, J.; State v. Umfried, ib. 408 (1882); 69 id. 469.

[2] Cartwright v. State, 14 Tex. Ap. 486, 499 (1883), cases, Hart, J.; Reed v. State, 11 id. 517 (1882); 70 Ala. 7; 71 id. 336-37; 32 Conn. 83; 64 Ind. 340; 89 id. 195; 80 Ky. 36; 14 B. Mon. 103, 614; 38 Mich. 270, 732; 55 Miss. 403; 13 Johns. 12; 89 N. C. 481; 29 Ohio St. 186; 38 Pa. 267-68; 101 id. 323; 45 Vt. 308; 2 Bish. Cr. L. 877; 12 Rep. 268.

[3] United States v. Ordway, 30 F. R. 32 (1887).

[4] 3 Bl. Com. 296. See 33 Ind. 449; 8 How. Pr. 442; 10 id. 148; 24 Barb. 631.

[5] [Utah, &c. R. Co. v. Crawford, 1 Idaho, 773 (1880).

The practice which requires affidavits of claims and defense has been systemized in Pennsylvania to a degree of completeness scarcely known elsewhere. The subject is usually discussed in connection with the inquiry, What are the essentials of a "sufficient" affidavit of defense. In that State the practice originated in an agreement between members of the bar at Philadelphia, signed September 11, 1795.[1] After that, statutes extended the practice, until it became general.[2] Yet the courts, by mere rule, could have required defendants to file a statement of defense.[3]

The practice does not conflict with the right of trial by jury. If a defendant presents no defense to be tried by a jury he cannot claim that privilege is denied him. The affidavit is nothing more than a special plea under oath — by which the defendant states the facts of his case for the consideration of the court. Trial by jury in civil cases has never involved the right of the jury to decide the *law* of the case. That the defendant is obliged to state his plea, or his defense, under oath, is merely a means to prevent delay, by falsehood and fraud. Nor can it be objected, when all the facts have been stated by the defendant which he either knows or is informed of, believes and expects to be able to prove, that the court decides the law arising upon the facts as stated. This is no more than the court does upon a demurrer, a special verdict, a nonsuit or an issue in equity. The affidavit is only a modern mode of making up the issue for the jury. And when, upon a statement of all the facts a defendant can conscientiously swear to, the court finds that the law upon those facts is against him, clearly he has no right to go before a jury. The court has then done no more than it would have a right to do by instruction to the jury when all the evidence is in, with the advantage to the defendant that by his affidavit he has made the evidence to support his own case.[4]

The object is to prevent delay of justice through false defenses.[5] At the same time, the practice being in derogation of the right of trial by jury, regulations are to receive a strict construction.[6]

The procedure, being somewhat summary, the plaintiff, in his affidavit, must have complied with every requirement of the law;[7] otherwise, a judgment given him, for "insufficiency" in the matter relied upon by the defendant, will be reversed, although that matter is really insufficient.[8]

---

[1] Sellers v. Burk, 47 Pa. 344 (1864); Clark v. Dotter, 54 id. 215 (1867); Detmold v. Gate Vein Coal Co., 3 W. N. C. 567 (U. S. D. C., E. D. Pa., 1876).

[2] 2 Brightly, Purd. Dig. 1356, 1357, pl. 24, note d.

[3] Hogg v. Charlton, 25 Pa. 200 (1855); Harres v. Commonwealth, 35 id. 416 (1860).

[4] Lawrence v. Borm, 86 Pa. 226 (1878), Per Curiam; 19 id. 57; 20 id. 384; Hunt v. Lucas, 99 Mass. 409 (1868), Chapman, C. J.

[5] Wilson v. Hayes, 18 Pa. 354 (1852); Bloomer v. Reed, 22 id. 51 (1853).

[6] Yates v. Burrough of Meadville, 56 Pa. 21 (1867); Wall v. Dovey, 60 id. 212 (1869); Boas v. Nagle, 3 S. & R. 250 (1817).

[7] Knapp v. Duck Creek Valley Oil Co., 53 Pa. 185 (1866).

[8] Gottman v. Shoemaker, 86 Pa. 31 (1877).

The question of insufficiency is brought directly before the court by a rule on the defendant "to show cause why judgment should not be entered against him for want of a sufficient affidavit of defense" — the particulars of the alleged insufficiency being at the same time specified in writing and filed with the rule.

The court considers the facts set out in the affidavit and passes upon their legal sufficiency.[1] For this purpose it takes the facts as true, not to be contradicted even by a record.[2]

It is sufficient to set forth, in the affidavit — facts showing a valid defense which can properly be established;[3] — specifically, and at length, such facts as will warrant the inference of a complete legal defense;[4] — a substantially good defense;[5] — a *prima facie* good and valid defense.[6]

The defendant must state the grounds and nature of his defense, so that the court may judge how far it will avail against the plaintiff's demand, if established by proof.[7]

The facts are to be averred with reasonable precision; but the evidence by which the defendant will prove them need not be stated.[8] Nor need he meet every objection which fine critical skill may deduce.[9] While an allegation doubtfully stated or clearly evasive is to be disregarded, the defendant is not to be held to a rigor of statement so severe as to catch him in a mere net of form.[9]

The facts are to be averred with reasonable precision, and with certainty to a common intent. Toward sustaining the affidavit a reasonable intendment will be given the language.[10]

But no essential fact is to be left to inference;[11] what is not said is taken as not existing.[12] Furthermore, inasmuch as a party swearing in his own cause is presumed to swear as hard as he can with a good conscience,[13] inferences, when justifiable, are not to be pressed beyond the ordinary meaning of the terms employed.[14]

A material fact which, if it actually exists, would readily and naturally be expressly averred, must be averred.[15]

The practice which requires affidavits of defense is limited to obligations for the payment of a certain sum of *money*. Hence, it does not apply in actions for torts, nor in actions upon contracts for the payment of an uncertain sum, or where there is no standard by which to liquidate the judgment.[1]

The defendant is to make the affidavit, unless cause, such as sickness or necessary absence, is shown why he cannot make it. Then an agent, and perhaps even a stranger to the transaction, may make it.[2]

When defendant avers facts on information and belief he must add that he expects to be able to prove them or else set out specifically the source of his information or the facts themselves upon which his belief rests.[3] This affords a presumption that proof can be made.[4] Positive averment of truth is enough.[5]

The practice does not permit the filing of a *supplementary* affidavit of claim to obtain a judgment for an insufficient defense. Such affidavit may be filed for use as evidence at the trial; so, too, as to a supplemental affidavit of defense in reply to a supplemental affidavit of claim. But the court will not consider the sufficiency of either affidavit.[6]

Should the court deem the defense set out in the original affidavit to be probably good but obscurely or otherwise defectively stated, it may allow a supplemental affidavit of defense to be filed.[7] Notice thereof is to be given, to prevent surprise and delay at the time for trial.

There is no rule that such supplemental affidavit must be confined to an explanation of the original defense, and cannot set up a new and different defense; such a course, however, is suspicious, and requires that the new defense be closely scrutinized.[8]

Where judgment has been entered for want of a sufficient affidavit of defense and the record shows it to be according to law, a motion to take it off is addressed to the discretion of the court, and, in the absence of statutory provision to the contrary, is not the subject of a writ of error.[9]

It would seem that an affidavit of defense, to become part of the record, should be offered in evidence.[10]

Dilatory defense. A defense designed to dismiss, suspend, or obstruct the prosecution of a claim, without touching upon the defendant's "meritorious defense." See MERITS.

---

[1] Stitt *v.* Garrett, 3 Whart. 281 (1837); Comly *v.* Bryan, 5 *id.* 261 (1839); Marsh *v.* Marshall, 53 Pa. 396 (1866).

[2] Feust *v.* Fell, 6 W. N. C. 43 (1878); Kirkpatrick *v.* Wensell, 2 Leg. Chron. 303 (1874).

[3] Leibersperger *v.* Reading Bank, 30 Pa. 531 (1858).

[4] Bryar *v.* Harrison, 37 Pa. 233 (1860).

[5] Thompson *v.* Clark, 56 Pa. 33 (1867).

[6] Chartiers R. Co. *v.* Hodgens, 77 Pa. 187 (1874).

[7] Walker *v.* Geisse, 4 Whart. 256 (1838).

[8] Bronson *v.* Silverman, 77 Pa. 94 (1874).

[9] Lawrence *v.* Smedley, 6 W. N. C. 42 (Sup. Ct., 1878).

[10] Markley *v.* Stevens, 89 Pa. 281 (1879); 77 *id.* 283; 89 *id.* 281.

[11] Peck *v.* Jones, 70 Pa. 83 (1871).

[12] Lord *v.* Ocean Bank, 20 Pa. 384 (1853).

[13] Selden *v.* Neemes, 43 Pa. 421 (1862).

[14] Marsh *v.* Marshall, 53 Pa. 396 (1866).

[15] Markley *v.* Stevens, 89 Pa. 281 (1879).

---

[1] Borlin *v.* Commonwealth, 99 Pa. 46 (1881). See 89 *id.* 26; 90 *id.* 276.

[2] See City *v.* Devine, 1 W. N. C. 358 (1875); Clymer *v.* Fitler, *ib.* 626 (1875); Blew *v.* Schock, *ib.* 612 (1875); Crine *v.* Wallace, *ib.* 293 (1875); Burkhart *v.* Parker, 6 W. & S. 480 (1843); Hunter *v.* Reilly, 36 Pa. 509 (1860).

[3] Black *v.* Halstead, 39 Pa. 64 (1861); Thompson *v.* Clark, 56 *id.* 33 (1867).

[4] Clarion Bank *v.* Gregg, 79 Pa. 384 (1875); Renzor *v.* Supplee, 81 *id.* 180 (1876).

[5] Eyre *v.* Yohe, 67 Pa. 477 (1871); Moeck *v.* Littell, 82 *id.* 354 (1876).

[6] Anderson *v.* Nichols, 12 Pitts. Leg. J. 231 (1882).

[7] Laird *v.* Campbell, 92 Pa. 475 (1880).

[8] Callan *v.* Lukens, 89 Pa. 134 (1879), Per Curiam.

[9] White *v.* Leeds, 51 Pa. 187 (1865). See Act 18 April, 1874: P. L. 64; 2 W. N. C. 707.

[10] Maynard *v.* National Bank, 98 Pa. 250 (1881).

Equitable defense. A defense, in a common-law action, which rests upon equitable or legal and equitable grounds.

Equitable defenses, though admissible under State practice, are not admissible in the United States courts.[1] If a defendant has equitable grounds for relief he must seek to enforce them by a separate suit in equity.[2] See PROCEDURE.

Full defense. In common-law practice, a defense made by the formula he " comes and defends the force and injury when and where it shall behoove him, the damages, and whatever else he ought to defend." Shortened into he " defends the force and injury, when," etc. Opposed, **half-defense**: made by the words he " comes and defends the force and injury, and says," etc.[3]

General defense. A general denial of the material allegations of a claim.

A general denial is not equivalent to a general issue at common law. It only puts the plaintiff to proof of his substantial allegations. If the defendant has an affirmative defense in the nature of an avoidance he should plead it.[4]

Good, legal, sufficient, or valid defense. A defense which is ample or adequate in law as against the particular demand. *Legal defense* often stands opposed to *equitable defense*, q. v.

No defense. Certificates are frequently required by proposed purchasers ' of mortgages standing in the name of the mortgagee or of his transferee, that the mortgagor has no defense, in equity or law, to a demand for payment thereof.

Peremptory defense. That the plaintiff never had, or has not now, a right of action.

Sham defense. A mere pretense of a defense, set up in bad faith, and without color of fact. See further SHAM.

Whenever one is assailed in his person or property, he may defend himself, for the liability and the right are inseparable. . A sentence of a court pronounced against a party without affording him an opportunity to be heard is not a judicial determination of his rights. There must be notice of some kind, actual or constructive. The period is a matter of regulation by positive law, rule of court, or established practice.[5] See DAY, In court; ADMISSION, 2.

DEFER.[1] To postpone to a future day; as, a deferred payment of principal and interest upon account of a mortgage, or of a dividend upon account of shares of stock. See DIVIDEND, 3; STOCK, 3 (2), Deferred; POSTPONE, 1.

DEFICIENCY. That part of the debt, which a mortgage was made to secure, not realized from the subject mortgaged.[2] See ESTIMATE; MORE OR LESS.

DEFINE. To set bounds to, mark the limits of. See DEFINITIO; DEFINITION.

1. To make clear the design or scope of previous action; to remove doubt or uncertainty as to the meaning or application of; to determine authoritatively, settle officially, decide judicially.

In popular meaning, often, to make clear and certain what was before uncertain or indefinite, to render distinct; but in legislation frequently has a broader signification. Many constitutional laws have been passed conferring powers and duties which could not be considered as merely explaining or making more clear those previously conferred or sought to be, although the word " define " was used in the title. In legislation the word is frequently used in creating, enlarging, and extending the powers and duties of boards and officers, and in defining and providing punishment for offenses — thus enlarging the scope of the criminal law. It may very properly be used in the title of a statute where the object is to determine or fix boundaries, especially where a dispute has arisen concerning them, whether the extent of territory included be enlarged or lessened.[3]

2. To enumerate or prescribe what act or acts shall constitute; to declare to be an offense.

" To define piracies " is to enumerate the crimes which shall constitute piracy.[4]

Declaring that a certain act shall constitute an offense is " defining " that offense.[5]

DEFINITE. Bounded, limited, defined: determinate, precise, fixed, certain. Opposed, **indefinite**.

A " definite failure of issue " occurs when a precise time is fixed by a will for the failure of issue. An " indefinite failure of issue " is the period when the issue or descendants of the first taker shall become extinct, and when there is no longer any issue of the issue of the grantee, without reference to a particular time or event.[6] See further DIE, Without children.

---

[1] Parsons *v.* Denis, 2 McCrary, 360 (1881); Gibson *v.* Chouteau, 13 Wall. 102 (1871).

[2] Northern Pacific R. Co. *v.* Paine, 119 U. S. 561 (1887); Phillips *v.* Negley; 117 *id.* 675 (1886), cases; Herklotz *v.* Chase, 32 F. R. 433 (1887).

[3] 3 Bl. Com. 296.

[4] Walker *v.* Flint, 3 McCrary, 510 (1882).

[5] Windson *v.* McVeigh, 93 U. S. 277 (1876), Field, J.

[1] L. *dis-ferre*, to put off, delay.

[2] [Goldsmith *v.* Brown, 35 Barb. 492 (1861).

[3] People *v.* Bradley, 36 Mich. 452 (1877), Marston, J.

[4] United States *v.* Smith, 5 Wheat. 160 (1820).

[5] United States *v.* Arjona, 120 U. S. 488 (1887).

[6] Huxford *v.* Milligan, 50 Ind. 546 (1875); 14 N. H. 220; 19 *id.* 84-85; 16 Johns. 399-400; 20 Pa. 513; 40 *id.* 22; 2 Redf. Wills, 276, n.

DEFINITIO. L. A bounding, limiting: defining, definition.

Omnis definitio in jure periculosa est. All limitation in law is perilous; defining in law is dangerous. Attempts to define the meaning of words, and to limit the application of statutes, are attended with more or less difficulty.

Thus, it is difficult to frame perfectly accurate definitions of such terms as accident; general agent, special agent;[1] bailment; boarder, guest, lodger; crimen falsi;[2] cruelty; dwelling-house; fraud;[3] internal police;[4] larceny; public policy;[5] reasonable doubt; slight, ordinary, and gross negligence; regulations of commerce as distinguished from police regulations. See those terms.

Thus, also, as there are exceptions to almost every rule of law, and as circumstances alter cases infinitely, when a statute itself imposes no limitation upon its meaning or application, the courts, in construing the statute, as a rule, confine themselves to the circumstances of the case in hand.

DEFINITION. An enumeration of the particular acts included by or under a name: as, the definition of a crime.[6] See DEFINE; DEFINITIO.

Legal definitions, for the most part, are generalizations derived from judicial experience. To be complete and adequate, they must sum up the results of all of that experience.[7]

The meaning given to common words by the leading lexicographers is entitled to weight, yet regard must always be had to the circumstances under which a word (as, traveler) is used in a statute.[8]

The definitions of the standard lexicographers are authority as indicating the popular use of words.[9]

See ETYMOLOGY; INDICTMENT; WORD.

DEFINITIVE. Is generally equivalent to "final" and opposed to interlocutory or provisional. But, in some relations, as when said of a judgment, decree, or sentence, may mean being above review or contingency of reversal.[10] Compare FINAL.

DEFORCEMENT. An injury by ouster or privation of the freehold, where the entry of the present tenant or possessor was originally lawful, but his detainer has become unlawful. . . The holding of any lands or tenements to which another person hath a right.[1]

Deforciant. He who is chargeable with a deforcement.

A deforcement includes as well an abatement, an intrusion, a disseisin, or a discontinuance, or any other species of wrong whatsoever, whereby he that hath right to the freehold is kept out of possession.[1] See AMOTION.

DEFRAUD. See FRAUD.

DEGRADE. See CRIMINATE; LIBEL, 5; REINSTATE; REHABILITATE; SLANDER.

DEGREE.[2] One of a series of progressive steps upward or downward; grade.[3]

1. A remove in the line of relationship.

Levitical degrees. The degree of kinship, set forth in the eighteenth chapter of Leviticus, within which persons may not intermarry.[4]

Adopted in English and American law generally.

2. The grades of guilt or culpability attributed to the same offense committed under different circumstances: as, degrees of negligence, degrees in the law of arson or of murder, qq. v.

When a defendant is charged with an offense which includes others of an inferior degree, the law of each degree which the evidence tends to prove should be given to the jury.[5]

3. The rank to which a student who has attended a law-school is admitted among its alumni. Whence bachelor of laws, doctor of civil law, doctor of laws.

Taken in course, or conferred for supposed attainments,—the last named degree frequently so.

At the inns of court degrees were formerly conferred in the common law upon barristers. Whence the expression "take" and "receive" a degree.

DEHORNING. See CRUELTY, 3.

DEHORS.[6] From beyond; outside of: extraneous, extrinsic, foreign to, unconnected with; aliunde, q. v.

Applied to something as evidence, outside of a record, agreement, will, or other instrument.

Thus, a judgment may be falsified, reversed, or

---

[1] 1 Pars. Contr. 40.

[2] 1 Greenl. Ev. § 373.

[3] 2 Pars. Contr. 769.

[4] 11 Pet. 138.

[5] 2 Pars. Contr. 249.

[6] Marvin v. State, 19 Ind. 184 (1862), Perkins, J.

[7] [Mickle v. Miles, 31 Pa. 21 (1856), Lowrie, J.; Pardee v. Fish, 60 N. Y. 269 (1875).

[8] Pennsylvania R. Co. v. Price, 96 Pa. 267 (1880).

[9] Burnam v. Banks, 45 Mo. 351 (1870); Dole v. New England Mut. Ins. Co., 6 Allen, 386 (1863).

[10] See United States v. The Peggy, 1 Cranch, 109 (1801); 1 Watts, 257; 37 Pa. 255; 96 id. 420; 3 Bl. Com. 101.

[1] 3 Bl. Com. 172; Wildy v. Bonney, 26 Miss. 39 (1853).

[2] F. degré: L. de-gradus, a step. Cf. Pedigree.

[3] Webster's Dict.

[4] 1 Bl. Com. 435.

[5] State v. Mize, 36 Kan. 188 (1887); State v. Evans, ib. 497 (1887).

[6] De-hōrz'. A French word, equivalent to the late Latin deforis: foris, foras, out of doors.

made void for a matter *dehors* the record,-- that is, not apparent upon the face of it.[1]

A matter *dehors* a record may be shown as ground for a new trial.[2]

When doubt arises as to meaning of the words of a written contract, or difficulty as to their application, the sense may be ascertained by evidence *dehors* the instrument itself.[3]

DEL CREDERE. L. Of trust, credit.

Applied to an agent or factor who guarantees that the persons to whom he sells will perform the contracts he makes with them.[4]

When the person to whom goods or merchandise is consigned for sale undertakes, for additional compensation in case of sale, to guarantee to his principal the payment of the debt due by the buyer, he is said to receive a *del credere* commission.[5] See COMMISSION, 3; FACTOR.

DELAY. Putting off; postponement.

A conveyance may be made with intent to hinder and delay creditors without any intention to defraud them.[6] See BANKRUPTCY; CONVEYANCE, Fraudulent; HINDER.

Mere delay in enforcing equitable rights is not a defense to an action, except in cases where the statutes of limitation apply, or where the party has slept upon his rights and acquiesced for such length of time that his claim has become stale.[7] See LACHES; LIMITATION, 3, Statute of; STALE.

In the law of marine insurance, see DEMURRAGE; DEVIATION.

DELECTUS. L. Choice; selection.

Delectus personæ. Choice of person. **Delectus personarum.** Choice of persons or the persons.

The right to choose the person or persons who shall participate in a business or enterprise requiring the exercise of mutual confidence.

In particular, the absolute right which belongs to each member of a firm to decide what new partners, if any at all, shall be admitted to the firm.

In theory a partnership is a voluntary association. For this reason neither the purchaser of the interest of a member, nor his assignee, nor even his executor or heir, becomes entitled to admission into the association, except by consent of the remaining partners or by the terms of their compact.[8]

DELEGATA. See DELEGATUS.

DELEGATE, *v.* To commit power to another as agent or representative; to empower, depute. *n.* The person who is to exercise any such power; as, a Territorial delegate. See DELEGATUS.

Delegation. 1. At common law, the transfer of authority; the act of making a delegate or deputy.

2. In civil law, the substitution of one debtor for another: a species of novation.

The change of one debtor for another, when he who is indebted substitutes a third person who obligates himself in his stead to the creditor; so that the first debtor is acquitted and his obligation extinguished, and the creditor contents himself with the obligation of the second debtor.[1]

A delegation demands the consent of all three parties; any other novation demands the consent only of the two parties to the new debt.[1] See NOVATION.

DELEGATUS. L. A person chosen or commissioned: a deputy, agent, representative, trustee. **Delegata.** Deputed, empowered, intrusted.

Delegata potestas non potest delegari. Delegated authority cannot be redelegated. *Delegatus non potest delegare.* A deputy cannot deputize.

Whenever, for personal or other considerations, authority is conferred upon a particular person he cannot lawfully devolve the duties of his appointment or the functions of his office upon any other person, unless allowed so to do by express words, by acts equivalent thereto, or by the usage of trade.

Delegatus potestas, etc., as a general maxim, is correct when duly applied. For, to create a delegate by a delegate, in the sense of the maxim, implies an assignment of the whole power, which a delegate cannot make. A delegate has general powers, which he cannot transfer; but he may constitute another his servant or bailiff to do a particular act.[2]

A special authority is in the nature of a trust. It implies confidence in the ability, skill, or discretion of the party intrusted. The author of such a power may extend it if he will, as is done in ordinary powers of attorney, giving power to a person or his substitute to

---

[1] [4 Bl. Com. 390.

[2] [3 Bl. Com. 387.

[3] Sandford *v.* New York, &c. R. Co., 37 N. J. L. 4 (1874); Shore *v.* Wilson, 9 Clark & F. 566 (1842), Tindal, C. J.

[4] *Exp.* White, L. R., 6 Ch. Ap. Cas. *403 (1870), Mellish, L. J.

[5] [Story, Agency, § 33; 50 Barb. 295.

[6] Crow *v.* Beardsley, 68 Mo. 439 (1878).

[7] Williams *v.* Boston, &c. R. Co., 17 Blatch. 23 (1879).

[8] Kingman *v.* Spurr, 7 Pick. 238 (1828), cases; Mathew-

son *v.* Clarke, 6 How. 140 (1848); Crittenden *v.* Witbeck, 50 Mich. 419, 420 (1883); Story, Partn. §§ 195, 5; 3 Kent, 55; 1 Pars. Contr. 154; 17 F. R. 571.

[1] Adams *v.* Power, 48 Miss. 454 (1873), Peyton, C. J.; 1 Domat, 919, § 2318.

[2] Hunt *v.* Burrel, 5 Johns. *137 (1809), cases, Per Curiam.

do the act authorized. But when it is not so extended it is limited to the person named.[1] See DEPUTY.

The utmost relaxation of the rule, in respect to mercantile persons, is, that a consignee or agent for the sale of merchandise may employ a broker, or a sub-agent, for the purpose, when such is the usual course of business.[2]

When the principal recognizes the validity of the services rendered by the subordinate of the appointed agent he cannot repudiate the acts of his employee and escape personal liability for the want of authority to employ him.[3]

Judicial power cannot be delegated.[4] Nor can a legislature delegate its power to any commission or body except as to the functions of local self-government conferred upon municipal corporations, q. v.; and as to some matters of police regulation which the people of a locality may be permitted to accept or reject by vote, as, for example, local option laws.[5] See OPTION, Local.

DELIBERATION. Balancing, weighing: consideration; reflection; meditation, premeditation.

1. When a man passes a thing by deed, there is a determination of the mind to do it, the writing, the signing, the sealing, and the delivery; and hence his deed imports consideration, viz.: the will of the maker.[6]

2. Slander in print is graver than slander by word of mouth, because it is not only disseminated wider, but is accompanied with greater coolness and deliberation.[7]

3. In describing a crime, "deliberate" imports that the perpetrator weighs the motives for the act and its consequences, the nature of the crime, or other things connected with his intentions, with a view to decision thereon; that he carefully considers all these; that the act is not committed suddenly.[8]

If an intention to kill exists, it is willful; if this intention be accompanied by such circumstances as evidence a mind fully conscious of its own purpose and design, it is deliberate.[9]

The statutory rule of deliberation and premeditation requires that the act be "done with reflection" and "conceived beforehand."[1]

"Deliberate" is from Latin words, which mean "concerning" and "to weigh." As an adjective it means that the manner of the performance was determined upon after examination and reflection — that the consequences, chances, and means were weighed, carefully considered and estimated. "Premeditated" means, literally, planned, contrived or schemed beforehand. It is not only necessary that the accused should plan, contrive and scheme, as to the means and manner of the commission of the deed, but that he should consider different means of accomplishing the act. He must "weigh" the modes of consummation which his premeditation suggests, and determine which is the most feasible.[2]

In some States "deliberate and premeditated" are applied to the malice or intent, not to the act, and thus seem to require a purpose brooded over, formed, and matured before the occasion at which it is carried into act.[3]

See further PREMEDITATE; WILL, 1.

DELICT. 1. In civil law, the act by which a person, through fraud or malignity, causes damage to another.

In its enlarged sense includes all kinds of crimes and misdemeanors, even injuries caused voluntarily or accidentally and without evil intention; but is commonly limited to offenses punishable by a small fine or a short imprisonment.[4]

2. A *delictum*, q. v.

DELICTUM.[5] L. A wrong, whether private or public: an offense, a civil injury or tort, a crime; also, simply a failing or fault, blame, guilt, culpability.[6]

Corpus delicto. The body of the offense; the fact of a crime. See further CORPUS, Delicti.

Ex delicto. Out of fault or a fault; arising from a tort or wrong — misconduct, negligence, crime.

Said of the actions of case, replevin, trespass, and trover. Opposed, *ex contractu*. See ACTION, 2.

Flagrante delicto. The offense still burning; in the *heat* of the offense: in the very act of perpetrating a crime or the crime.[7] Compare CRIMEN, Flagrans.

[1] Sanborn v. Carleton, 15 Gray, 403 (1860), Shaw, C. J. See 2 Kent, 633.

[2] Warner v. Martin, 11 How. 223 (1850), cases, Wayne, J. See Story, Agency, § 13.

[3] Commissioners v. Lash, 89 N. C. 170 (1883), Smith, C. J. See 71 Ala. 28; 3 Dak. T. 395; 41 N. J. E. 518; 63 Pa. 85.

[4] Van Slyke v. Trempealeau Ins. Co., 39 Wis. 392 (1876), cases, Ryan, C. J.; Runkle v. United States, 122 U. S. 557 (1887),— as to the President of the United States; Cooley, Const. Lim. 116, cases.

[5] Cooley, Const. Lim. 124, cases. See also Commonwealth v. Smith, 141 Mass. 140 (1886).

See generally 21 Am. Law Rev. 936-54 (1887), cases; 26 id. 74-94 (1888), cases.

[6] Smith, Contr. 14; Williams, R. P. 143.

[7] Addison, Torts, 765.

[8] State v. Boyle, 28 Iowa, 524 (1870), Beck, J.

[9] Commonwealth v. Drum, 58 Pa. 16 (1868), Agnew, J.

[1] Summerman v. State, 14 Neb. 569 (1883), Lake, C. J.; Wharton, Homicide, 180.

[2] Craft v. State, 3 Kan. 483 (1866), Crozier, C. J.

[3] Keenan v. Commonwealth, 44 Pa. 57 (1862), Lowrie, C. J. See 71 Mo. 220; 74 id. 219, 249, 256; 76 id. 104; 23 Ind. 262.

[4] [Bouvier's Law Dict.

[5] From de-linquere, to leave a person or thing; then, to be wanting in a matter, fail in duty, offend, transgress. Compare MALUS, Malum.

[6] See 3 Bl. Com. 363; 1 Kent, 552; 2 id. 241.

[7] See 4 Bl. Com. 307; 5 Cent. Law J. 380.

In pari delicto. In equal wrong: equal in guilt: equally guilty; equally to blame.

The first part either of the maxim *in pari delicto, melior est conditio possidentis,* in equal fault, the better is the situation of the party in possession; *or else of the maxim in pari delicto, potior est conditio defendentis,* in equal fault, the stronger is the situation of the defendant. Also spoken of as the rule of *par delictum,* equal wrong: parity of unlawful conduct.

Where misconduct is mutual the law will relieve neither party, but leave them where it finds them.

While defendants derive advantage from its application, the rule was not adopted for their benefit, but solely as a principle of general policy.[1]

A court of equity will not aid parties in the consummation or perpetration of a fraud; it will not assist a party to the betrayal of a trust to derive advantage therefrom; it will not undertake to unravel a tangled web of fraud to enable one of the parties to consummate his design. A complainant must come before the court with clean hands.[2]

The court will not enforce alleged rights resting upon a prohibited contract. In the application of the rule it is necessary to give parties a right to plead and to prove the nature of the transaction.[3] Whatever is stated in a contract for an illegal purpose, as, the violation of a statute, the defendant may show as the turpitude of himself and the plaintiff to prevent its enforcement. The objection is allowed on general principles of policy.[4]

Lord Mansfield, in 1760, laid down the doctrine, which has ever since been followed, that if the act be in itself immoral, or a violation of the general laws of public policy, both parties are *in pari delicto;* but where the law is designed for the protection of the subject against oppression, extortion, and deceit, and the defendant takes advantage of the plaintiff's condition or situation, then the plaintiff shall recover.[5]

Where the illegality consists in the contract itself, and that contract is unexecuted, there is a *locus pœnitentiæ,* the *delictum* is incomplete, the contract may be rescinded by either party and money paid recovered. There is no parity where the law protects one party, or one acts under constraint, though the transaction is completed.[6]

If a contract, void as against public policy, is still executory it cannot be enforced, nor will damages be awarded for a breach thereof; but if it is executed the price paid or property delivered cannot be recovered.[1]

The rule is applied to cases of moral turpitude and to acts against public policy; not to cases of innocent mistake.[2]

One who bribes an officer of government cannot recover the money.[3]

In a few special cases, one party, less at fault than the other, has been allowed to maintain an action.[4] Compare NEGLIGENCE, Comparative, Contributory.

See ACTIO, Ex dolo, etc.; CONTRIBUTION; ESTOPPEL; INNOCENCE; LEGAL, Illegal, 2; TORT, 2; TURPITUDE; VOLO, Volenti, etc.

Propter delictum. On account of wrong — a crime or misdemeanor; as, a challenge of a juror for infamy.[5] See CHALLENGE, 4.

DELIRIUM. That state of the mind in which it acts without being directed by the power of volition, which is wholly or partially suspended.[6]

A temporary derangement of mind preceded or attended by a feverish and highly diseased state of the body.[7]

It may vary from slight wandering to violent derangement, and be accompanied, in a greater or less degree, with stupor or insensibility. A continuing insanity will not be presumed, where the malady was temporary and occasional.[7] See INSANITY; INTEMPERATE.

DELIVERY.[8] Transfer of the body or substance; surrender of physical possession or control; tradition. Opposed, **non-delivery.**

To "deliver" is to give or transfer anything to another person.

---

[1] See Holman *v.* Johnson, 1 Cowp. 343 (1775), Mansfield, C. J.; Smith, Contr. 27, 205, 263, 296.

[2] Farley *v.* St. Paul, &c. R. Co., 14 F. R. 114, 117 (1882), Treat, D. J.; Lewis *v.* Meier, *ib.* 311 (1882); 2 McCrary, 599.

[3] Funk *v.* Gallivan, 49 Conn. 128–29 (1881), cases; Heineman *v.* Newman, 55 Ga. 262 (1875), cases; Myers *v.* Meinrath, 101 Mass. 368 (1869), cases.

[4] Harris *v.* Runnels, 12 How. 86 (1851), Wayne, J.

[5] Smith *v.* Bromley, 2 Doug. 697: Thomas *v.* Richmond, *infra.*

[6] Thomas *v.* City of Richmond, 12 Wall. 355–56 (1870),

cases, Bradley, J.; Congress & Empire Spring Co. *v.* Knowlton, 103 U. S. 58–60 (1880), cases, Woods, J. See also 116 U. S. 685–86: 48 Ark. 491; 101 Mass. 150; 107 *id.* 259; 25 Pa. 441; 79 *id.* 242; 25 Barb. 341; 10 Ind. 386; 59 Iowa, 190; 6 Col. 14; 58 N. H. 249; 17 Nev. 177; 76 Va. 423; 2 Story, Contr. § 617; 3 Pars. Contr. 127, 484; 2 Greenl. Ev. § 111.

[1] Setter *v.* Alvey, 15 Kan. 160 (1875), Brewer, J.

[2] See 55 Barb. 102; 22 Mich. 427; 11 Mass. 376; 4 N. H. 455; 3 N. Y. 230.

[3] Clark *v.* United States, 102 U. S. 331 (1880).

[4] See White *v.* Franklin Bank, 22 Pick. 181–90 (1839), cases; Daniels *v.* Tearney, 102 U. S. 420 (1880). As to counter-claims, 20 Cent. Law J. 363–65 (1885), cases.

[5] See 3 Bl. Com. 363; 2 Kent, 241.

[6] Owing's Case, 1 Bland's Ch. 386 (1828). See 1 Redf. Wills, 91.

[7] [Heirs of Clark *v.* Ellis, 9 Oreg. 129, 141 (1881), Lord, Chief Justice.

[8] F. *delivrer:* L. *de-liberare,* to set free.

A law against "selling or delivering intoxicating liquor to a minor" was held not to include a delivery to a minor for his father.[1] See LIQUOR.

In the sense of release from confinement, used in "jail-delivery." See JAIL.

"Delivery," used alone, is of personal property; of letters, notices, telegrams, qq. v.; of negotiable instruments, q. v.; of sealed instruments; of opinions, charges, verdicts, qq. v.

1. In the law as to gifts, sales, and transportation of personalty, delivery is absolute or conditional, actual or constructive, and symbolical.

Absolute delivery. A transfer without any qualification, expressed or implied. **Conditional delivery.** A transfer accompanied by one or more conditions which must be fulfilled before the general property vests in the possessor.

A conditional sale may become an absolute sale by an unconditional delivery of the goods, the title then passing to the purchaser. To constitute a conditional delivery it is not necessary that the seller declare the conditions in express terms. It is sufficient if the intent of the parties, that the delivery is conditional, can be inferred from their acts and the circumstances of the case.[2]

Actual delivery. Manual or corporal transfer, made in fact or reality. **Constructive delivery.** A transfer which while not in reality made is yet viewed in law as as good as made.

"Constructive delivery" is a general term, comprehending all acts which, although not truly conferring a real possession of the thing sold on the vendee, have been held constructione juris equivalent to acts of real delivery.[3]

Symbolic or symbolical delivery. Handing over one thing as evidence of parting with ownership in another or other things.

Delivery is frequently symbolical; as, delivery of the key to a room containing goods, by marking timber on a wharf or goods in a warehouse, or by separating, measuring, or weighing them; or otherwise constructive, as by delivery of part for the whole;[4] or by delivery of a bill of lading or of a bill of sale. See GIFT, 1.

As between vendor and vendee delivery is not necessary to complete a sale of personalty, especially where impracticable;[5] but as against a third person

possession retained by the vendor is evidence of fraud — conclusive, by some authorities, by others, rebuttable.

Symbolical is a substitute for actual delivery, when the latter is impracticable, and leaves the real delivery to be made afterward. Thus, the delivery of a certificate of stock with a power of attorney in blank for making a transfer upon the proper books operates as a symbolical delivery of the stock itself, until the real delivery can be perfected.[1]

To constitute a delivery to a common carrier the latter must accept the goods as a carrier and assume exclusive control over them.[2]

What amounts to a delivery to a carrier may sometimes be a question of fact for a jury; ordinarily, a delivery at his wharf, freight or warehouse, brought to the notice of his servant, would be so considered. A delivery at a wharf may be of itself an incomplete act, to be explained by what precedes or follows.[3]

A common carrier by water must at least give notice to a consignee that the vessel has arrived or that the property has been landed.[4]

Proof of the unexplained non-delivery of property by a bailee upon demand makes a *prima facie* case of negligence, and, in the absence of evidence excusing the non-delivery, presents a question of fact as to actual negligence for the consideration of a jury.[5]

Property in a situation to be delivered to the consignee on demand may be said to be "awaiting delivery;" property on its way to a distant point to be taken thence by a connecting carrier, to be "awaiting transportation."[6]

Misdelivery. A delivery by a common carrier at such place or time as is not intended by the contract of carriage.

Opposed, a good, sufficient, or legal delivery.

A misdelivery by a carrier is equivalent to a conversion.[7]

See ACCEPT, 1; BAILMENT; CARRIER; PLACE, Of delivery; POSSESSION, Fraudulent; SALE.

As to collections on delivery, see COLLECTION.

Delivery bond. An obligation for the return of goods, or the payment of their value, taken into the possession of the law but now to be restored to the defendant; as, in seizures under revenue laws.[8]

2. Section 3892, Rev. St., is designed to

---

[1] State v. McMahon, 53 Conn. 415 (1885); Commonwealth v. Latinville, 120 Mass. 386 (1876).

[2] Fishback v. Van Dusen, 33 Minn. 116–18 (1885), cases, Mitchell, J.

[3] Bolin v. Huffnagle, 1 Rawle, *20 (1828).

[4] 1 Bouvier, 502, cases; 89 Ill. 218; 71 N. Y. 293; 2 Bl. Com. 313–15; 1 Pars. Contr. 530; 2 Kent, 508.

[5] Wyoming Nat. Bank v. Dayton, 102 U. S. 59, 62 (1880); Hare, Contr. 450.

[1] Winslow v. Fletcher, 53 Conn. 398–99 (1885); Cooke v. Hallett, 119 Mass. 148 (1875).

[2] Reed v. Philadelphia, &c. R. Co., 3 Houst. 208 (1865); O'Bannon v. Southern Express Co., 51 Ala. 484 (1874).

[3] Hobart v. Littlefield, 13 R. I. 342 (1881), cases; Hallgarten v. Oldham, 135 Mass. 3–12 (1883), cases.

[4] Ostrander v. Brown, 15 Johns. 42 (1818); 3 N. Y. 322; 11 F. R. 234.

[5] Confield v. Baltimore, &c. R. Co., 93 N. Y. 538 (1883), cases.

[6] Michigan Central R. Co. v. Mineral Springs Manuf. Co., 16 Wall. 327 (1872), cases.

[7] Forbes v. Boston, &c. R. Co., 133 Mass. 156 (1882).

[8] See R. S. § 938; 21 Wall. 98; 110 U. S. 280.

otect letters, (postal-cards, and packets),
ut by mail, from embezzlement, and from
terference, with the improper designs
erein enumerated, until they reach their
stination by actual delivery to the persons
ititled to receive them.[1]

3. As to the delivery of telegrams, see
ELEGRAPH.

4. In the law of sealed instruments, the
nal, absolute transfer to the grantee of a
omplete legal instrument sealed by the
rantor, covenantor, or obligor. As a popu-
ir word, signifies mere tradition.[2]

A deed takes effect only from its tradition or deliv-
y, which may be absolute or conditional.

Absolute delivery. A delivery to the
rantee himself. **Conditional delivery.**
o a third person to hold till some condition
s performed by the grantee.[3]

In the latter case the instrument is delivered as an
escrow " — as a scrowl or writing, not to take effect as
deed till the condition is performed.[3]

A delivery of a legal obligation made upon condi-
ion does not become a legal delivery until the condi-
ion is fulfilled.[4]

The delivery of a deed is essential to the transfer of
itle. It is the final act, without which other formal-
ies are ineffectual. The grantor must part with pos-
ession of the deed or the right to retain it; registry
nay justify a presumption of delivery.[5]

While a delivery of a deed is essential to pass an
state, and there can be no delivery without surrender
f the instrument or the right to retain it, such de-
ivery will be presumed, in the absence of direct
vidence, from the concurrent act of the parties recognizing a transfer of the title.[6]

Surrender *and* acceptance are necessary to a complete delivery.[7]

Its importance arises from the fact that the deed
las taken the place of the livery of seisin of feudal
imes, when, to give effect to the feoffment of the new
enant, the act of delivering possession in a public
manner was the essential evidence of the investiture
of title to the land. This diminished in importance
until the manual delivery of a piece of turf, and other
"symbolic" acts, became sufficient. When all this
passed away and the creation and transfer of estates
by a written instrument. called the act or "deed" of
the party, became the usual mode, the instrument was

at first delivered on the land in lieu of livery of seisin.
Finally, any delivery of the deed or any act intended
to stand for such delivery became effectual to pass the
title.[1]

Delivery in fact, by the officers of government, of recorded letters-patent for land, or of a charter, or of a
commission to an office, and the like, in which the act of
delivering is purely ministerial, may not be essential;
it is enforceable by *mandamus.*[1] Compare LIVERY.

DELUSION. "Insane delusion" and
"morbid delusion," as equivalent expressions, are common in medical jurisprudence.

If a person persistently believes supposed facts,
which have no existence except in his perverted im-
agination, and against all evidence and probability,
and conducts himself, however logically, upon the assumption of their existence, so far as these imagined
facts are concerned he is under a "morbid delusion;"
and delusion in that sense is insanity.[2]

"Insane delusion" is an unreasoning and incorrigible belief in the existence of facts which are impossible of existence, either absolutely or under the circumstances, and which, in most cases, relate to something
affecting the senses. While the delusion may concern
the relations of the party with others, generally it centers around himself, his cares, sufferings, rights and
wrongs. It comes and goes independently of the exercise of will; it is not the result of reasoning and
reflection, nor can it be dispelled by them. A conviction founded upon evidence, upon a comparison of
facts, opinions, and arguments, is not an insane delusion. Such a delusion does not relate to mere sentiments or theories or abstract questions in law, politics,
or religion: all which are subjects of opinions,— be-
liefs founded upon reasoning and reflection, and liable
to be changed by stronger external evidence or by
sounder reasoning.   . In the law of homicide the
subject is important only as it throws light upon the
question of knowledge of or capacity to know right
and wrong. If a man is under an insane delusion that
another is attempting his life and kills him in self-
defense he does not know that he is committing an
unnecessary homicide. If he insanely believes he has
a command from the Almighty to kill, it is difficult to
understand how he can know it is wrong for him to
kill.[3] See INSANITY.

---

[1] United States *v.* McCready, 11 F. R. 225, 234 (1882).

[2] Black *v.* Shreve, 13 N. J. E. 461 (1860), Whelpley, J.

[3] [2 Bl. Com. 307; 30 Wis. 646.

[4] McFarland *v.* Sikes, 54 Conn. 250 (1886).

[5] Younge *v.* Guilbeau, 3 Wall. 641 (1865), Field, J.; 5
id. 81; 79 Pa. 15; 4 Del. Ch. 311.

[6] Gould *v.* Day, 94 U. S. 412 (1876), Field, J. See Ireland *v.* Geraghty, 15 F. R. 45-46 (1883), cases,— note by
M. D. Ewell.

[7] Best *v.* Brown, 25 Hun, 224 (1881); 6 Barb. 195; 102
Ill. 287; 22 Ind. 39.

(22)

---

[1] United States *v.* Schurz, 102 U. S. 398, 397 (1880),
cases, Miller, J. See 20 Cent. Law J. 44-48 (1885), cases;
23 *id.* 8-10 (1886), cases; 26 Am. Law Reg. 451-55 (1887),
cases; 4 Kent, 466; 2 Wash. R. P. 577.

[2] Seaman's Friend Society *v.* Hopper, 33 N. Y. 624
(1865), Denio, C. J.; *Re* Forman's Will, 54 Barb. 289
(1869), cases.

[3] United States *v.* Guiteau, 10 F. R. 170-71, 182 (Jan.
25, 1882), Charge of Judge Cox. See note by Francis
Wharton, *ib.* 189; Commonwealth *v.* Rogers, 7 Metc.
502 (1844); State *v.* Pike, 49 N. H. 432 (1870); State *v.*
Jones, 50 *id.* 395 (1871); Dew *v.* Clarke, 3 Addams, 79
(1826). As to wills and deeds, Duffield *v.* Morris's Executor, 2 Harr., Del., 380 (1838); Gass's Heirs *v.* Gass's
Executor, 3 Humph. 283 (1842); Robinson *v.* Adams, 62
Me. 401 (1870); in general, Buswell, Insanity, §§ 13-16,
cases; 1 Redf. Wills, 40; 1 Whart. Cr. L. § 37.

DEMAND. 1. Any account upon which money or other thing is, or is claimed to be, due.[1]

A claim; a legal obligation.[2]

The most comprehensive word in law, except *claim*. A release of demands discharges all sorts of actions, rights, titles, conditions before or after breach, executions, appeals, rents, covenants, annuities, contracts, recognizances, etc.[3] Includes, also, a cause of action,[4] and a judgment.[5] Is more comprehensive than "debt" or "duty." [6]

The meaning may be restricted, as, to debt upon contract.[7]

Demandant. One who demands a thing as due; specifically, the plaintiff in a real action, as, partition.

Cross-demand; counter-demand. A demand set up as against another demand on which claim is or can be made; a set-off, *q. v.*

2. A request, made under claim of right, to do some specified thing.

Required, in some cases, to fasten willfulness upon a person who refuses to perform a duty. Thus it is made: for payment of rent, before re-entry; under a contract for marriage, before action can be brought for breach of promise; in cases of illegal harboring of servants, and of illegal detention of personalty; in cases of refusal to obey orders of court; in other matters of contract and of tort.[8]

Demand and refusal are never necessary, except as furnishing evidence of an unlawful taking or detention against the rights of the true owner, in an action of replevin, or of an unlawful conversion in an action of trover. When the circumstances, without these, are sufficient to prove such taking or detention, a demand and a refusal are superfluous.[9]

On demand. In a note, does not make the demand a condition precedent to a right of action; imports that the debt is due and demandable immediately, or at least that the commencement of a suit therefor is a sufficient demand.[10]

When the promise is not to pay the note at a particular place demand must be made upon the maker

personally, at his place of business or at his residence, or sufficient excuse for not making demand must be shown. Reasonable diligence must be used to find the maker, his residence and place of business.[1]

A note payable "on demand after date" is not a note "payable on time," within the meaning of the Massachusetts statute of 1874, c. 404.[2]

See CLAIM; INDORSEMENT; PAYMENT; REQUEST; STALE.

DEMENTIA. Mental derangement accompanied by general derangement of faculties.[3]

Characterized by forgetfulness, inability to follow any train of thought, and indifference to passing events.[3]

An impaired state of the mental powers, feebleness of mind caused by disease and not accompanied by delusion (*q. v.*) or uncontrollable impulse.[4]

May exist without complete prostration.

Senile dementia. That peculiar decay of the mental faculties which occurs in extreme old age, and in many cases much earlier, whereby the person is reduced to second childhood and sometimes becomes wholly incompetent to enter into a binding contract or even to execute a will. It is the recurrence of second childhood by mere decay.[5]

See further INSANITY.

DEMESNE.[6] Own, one's own; original.

Demesne land. Land reserved by the lord of a manor for the use of himself and household.[7]

Ancient demesne. Tenure of manors belonging to the crown in the days of Edward the Confessor and William the Conqueror, and referred to in Domesday book.[8]

Demesne lands of the crown. Reservations of the crown at the original distribution, or such as came to it afterward by forfeiture or other means.[9]

Comprised divers manors, the tenants of which had peculiar privileges.[8]

Seised in his demesne as of fee. Formal words expressing the highest estate a subject can have in land. It is his property or *dominicum*, since it is for him and his

[1] Stringham v. Supervisors, 24 Wis. 600 (1869), Dixon, Chief Justice.

[2] Hollen v. Davis, 59 Iowa, 447 (1882): Code, § 3591.

[3] Coke, Litt. 291 b; 8 Rep. 299; 1 Denio, 261; 6 W. & S. 226.

[4] Saddlesvene v. Arms, 32 How. Pr. 285 (1866).

[5] Henry v. Henry, 11 Ind. 237 (1858).

[6] Sands v. Codwise, 4 Johns. *558 (1808); *Re* Denny, &c. Co., 2 Hill, 223 (1842).

[7] Heacock v. Sherman, 14 Wend. 59 (1835).

[8] See 1 Bouvier, 504, cases.

[9] Edmunds v. Hill, 133 Mass. 446 (1882).

[10] Young v. Weston, 39 Me. 494 (1855) cases; Byles, Bills, 409, cases by Sharswood; 2 Pars. N. & B. 639, cases.

[1] Demond v. Burnham, 133 Mass. 341 (1882).

[2] Hitchings v. Edmands, 132 Mass. 339 (1882).

[3] [Hall v. Unger, 4 Saw. 677 (1867), Field, J.

[4] Dennett v. Dennett, 44 N. H. 537 (1863), Bell, C. J. See 2 Redf. Sur. 132; 3 Wash. 580; 4 *id.* 262; 3 Am. L. Reg. 449; 2 Abb. C. C. 511.

[5] 1 Redfield, Wills, 63, 94. Owing's Case, 1 Bland's Ch. 389 (1828).

[6] F.: L. *dominium*, ownership. Cf. DOMAIN; ASSAULT, Son, etc.

[7] 2 Bl. Com. 90.

[8] 2 Bl. Com. 99; 1 *id.* 286.

[9] 1 Bl. Com. 286.

heirs forever, not absolute, but in a qualified or feudal sense; and *as of fee*, because not purely and simply his own, since it is held of a feudal superior.[1]

The owner of an incorporeal hereditament is said to be "seised as of fee," and not "in his demesne;" since he has no property in the thing itself, but something derived out of it.[1]

"Seised in his demesne as of fee " is an allegation that the person is seised in fee-simple.[2]

DEMIJOHN. See BOTTLE.

DEMISE.[3] In a lease for years creates an implied warranty of title and a covenant for quiet enjoyment.[4]

In a lease under seal implies a covenant, and in a lease not under seal a contract, for *title* in the lessor. " Let " or an equivalent word has the same effect.[5] See LEASE.

Demise and redemise. A conveyance by mutual leases of the same land, or of something out of the same, made by one party to the other; as, in a grant of rent-charge. See next word.

DEMITTERE. L. To demise, lease, let.

Ex demissione. By demise.

Used in entitling common-law actions of ejectment. Abridged *ex dem.* and *d:* as, Doe *d.*, or *ex dem.*, Patterson *v.* Winn.[6]

Non demisit. He did not let or lease.

A plea to an action for rent on a parol agreement.

DEMONSTRATIO. L. A showing, pointing out: designation, description, demonstration, *q. v.*

Falsa demonstratio non nocet. Erroneous description does not vitiate. Spoken of as the maxim *falsa demonstratio.*

When an instrument contains an adequate description of a thing, with convenient certainty as to what was intended to be specified, a subsequent erroneous reference or addition will not vitiate the instrument. This qualification is sometimes expressed by the phrase *cum constat de corpore* or *de persona:* when it comports with the subject-matter or with the person.[7]

A false description, whether of subject-matter or parties, does not vitiate the instrument where the error appears upon its face and the writing itself supplies the means of making the correction.[1]

Applied to a devise the rule means that if there be a sufficient description, with reasonable certainty of what was meant to pass, a subsequent erroneous addition will not vitiate the devise. The characteristic of cases within the rule is that the description as far as false applies to no subject at all, and as far as true applies to one only.[2]

The maxim is of universal application as far as it means that we may reject, as surplusage, a false description not vital to the object of the controversy.[3]

Falsa demonstratione legatum non perimi. By erroneous description a legacy is not destroyed.

A bequest is not to be held void because of inaccurate language used in speaking of it.[4] See further DEMONSTRATION, 2.

DEMOCRATIC.[5] See GOVERNMENT.

DEMONSTRATION. 1. Proof which excludes possibility of error.[6]

A conclusion from a universal major premise, producing absolute certainty.[7]

Mathematical truth alone is susceptible of this high degree of evidence; matters of fact are proved by moral evidence.[6,7] See CERTAINTY; EVIDENCE, Moral.

2. Whatever is said or written to designate a person or thing; designation; description.

Demonstrative. Pointing out specifically; designating particularly: as, a legacy payable out of a particular fund. See LEGACY.

An erroneous description does not render an instrument inoperative where the thing or person intended can be identified. As far as inapplicable it will be rejected; particularly so when merely additional to another description or reference which is unambiguous: as where, in the same instrument, land is correctly described by boundaries and wrongly described by parcel or number.[8] See further DEMONSTRATIO; DESCRIPTION.

---

[1] 2 Bl. Com. 106.

[2] Butrick *v.* Tilton, 141 Mass. 94 (1886).

[3] F. *démettre*, to put away, lay down: L. *dismittere, demittere.*

[4] Stott *v.* Rutherford, 102 U. S. 109 (1875), cases, Conrad *v.* Morehead, 89 N. C. 34 (1883).

[5] Foster *v.* Peyser, 9 Cush. 246-47 (1852), cases; Metcalf, J., quoting Parker, B., in Hart *v.* Windsor, 12 M. & W. 68 (1844); Wilkinson *v.* Clauson, 29 Minn. 96 (1882); 8 Ala. 320; 50 Conn. 509; 18 Mass. 201; 9 N. H. 219; 7 Wend. 210; 26 Mo. 112; 5 Whart. 278; 105 Pa. 472.

[6] 5 Pet. 232 (1831); 7 T. R. 886.

[7] See Thomas *v.* Thomas, 6 Durnf. & E. 676 (1769), Kenyon, C. J.; Cleaveland *v.* Smith, 2 Story, 291 (1842); 71 Cal. 147; 65 Wis 270; 67 *id.* 289.

[1] Dodd *v.* Bartholomey, 44 Ohio St. 175 (1886), Minshall, J.

[2] Morrell *v.* Fisher, 4 Exch. *604 (1849), Alderson, B.; 113 U. S. 447.

[3] Broom, Max. 629; 1 Whart. Ev. § 945.

[4] Broom, Max. 645; 3 Bradf. 144, 149.

[5] In Beardsley *v.* Bridgeport, 53 Conn. 493 (1885), used in a charitable bequest.

[6] [1 Greenl. Ev. § 1.

[7] [1 Whart. Ev. § 7.

[8] 1 Greenl. Ev. § 301. See White *v.* Luning, 93 U. S. 524 (1876); Springer *v.* United States, 102 *id.* 593 (1880); Noonan *v.* Lee, 2 Black, 504 (1862); Cleaveland *v.* Smith, 2 Story, 291 (1842); Ham *v.* San Francisco, 17 F. R. 121 (1883); 105 Ill. 364; 7 Cush. 460; 45 Pa. 481; 4 C. B. 328; 11 *id.* 208; 14 *id.* 122; 2 Pars. Contr. 550, п.

DEMURRAGE.[1]   1. The delay or period of delay of a vessel in port.

2. The sum fixed by the contract of carriage as remuneration to the ship-owner for detention of his ship beyond the days allowed for loading or unloading.

It is usual to calculate this sum at so much per day, and to specify the days allowed for demurrage.

An extended freight or reward to the vessel in compensation for the earnings she is improperly caused to lose. Every improper detention may be considered a demurrage, and compensation under that name be obtained for it.[2]

Not allowed for delay caused by unloading in accordance with the custom of the port.[3] See WORKING-DAYS.

DEMURRER.[4]   A declaration that "the party will go no further, because the other has not showed sufficient matter against him;" imports that the objector will wait the judgment of the court whether he is bound to proceed.[5]

An admission of the fact, submitting the law to the court.[6]

The tender of an issue in law upon the facts established by the pleading.[7]

Also, the act of tendering such an issue; and, the writing in which the tender is made.

Demur.   To object for legal insufficiency; to interpose a demurrer.

Demurrable.   Admitting of a demurrer.

Demurrant.   One who demurs; a demurrer.

In law, or at common law, an issue upon matter of law is called a "demurrer:" it confesses the facts to be true as stated by the opposite party, but denies that, by the law arising upon those facts, any injury is done to the plaintiff, or that the defendant has made out a legitimate excuse. The party who demurs, *demoratur*, rests or abides upon the point in question. The form is by averring the declaration or plea, the replication or rejoinder, to be insufficient in law to maintain the action or defense; and, therefore, praying judgment for want of sufficient matter alleged.[8]

A demurrer in equity is nearly of the same nature as a demurrer in law, being an appeal to the judgment of the court whether the defendant shall be bound to answer the plaintiff's bill; as, for want of sufficient matter of equity therein contained; or where the plaintiff, upon his own showing, appears to have no right; or where the bill seeks discovery of a thing which may cause a forfeiture of any kind, or may convict a man of criminal misbehavior. If the defendant prevails the plaintiff's bill is dismissed; if the demurrer is overruled the defendant is ordered to answer.[1]

Demurring is incident to criminal cases when the fact alleged is admitted to be true but the prisoner joins issue upon a point of law in the indictment, by which he insists that the fact as stated is not the crime it is alleged to be. . Since the same advantage may be had upon a plea of not guilty, or by arrest of judgment when the verdict has established the fact, demurrers to indictments are seldom used.[2]

General demurrer.   An exception in general terms to the sufficiency of a pleading as a whole. **Special demurrer.**   Alleges a particular material imperfection.

In a general demurrer at law no particular cause of exception is alleged; in a special demurrer the particular imperfection is pointed out and insisted upon.[3]

In equity practice the formula for a general demurrer is that there is no equity in the bill; in the case of a special demurrer the particular defect or objection is pointed out.[4]

A general demurrer lies for defects of substance; a special demurrer lies for defects of form, and adds to the terms of the former a specification of the particular ground of exception. Thus, alleging a defective title is a fault in substance for which the party may demur generally; but if a title be defectively stated it is a fault in form which must be specifically assigned for cause of demurrer. Under statutes of 27 Eliz. (1585), c. 5, and 4 and 5 Anne (1705), c. 16, unless imperfections, omissions, defects, and other matters of like nature be specifically and particularly set down and shown for cause of demurrer, the court gives judgment according to the very right of the cause without regarding the imperfections, omissions, etc.[5]

Where the objection is to the substance of the allegation, a general demurrer is sufficient; where to a defect in form, a special demurrer is indispensable. But neither demurrer is good unless the objections are apparent upon the face of the bill, from matter inserted or omitted, or from defects in the frame or form of the pleading.[5, 4]

---

[1] L. *demorari*, to stay: *mora*, delay.

[2] Donaldson *v.* McDowell, 1 Holmes, 292 (1873), Shepley, J. See 26 N. Y. 85; 5 Phila. 112; 4 Rand. 510; L. R., 10 Exch. 135; 2 Kent, 159; 2 Pars. Contr. 304; 3 Chitt. Com. L. 426.

[3] The Elida, 31 F. R. 420 (1887).

[4] F. *demourer*, to tarry, stay, hesitate: L. *de-morari*, to delay fully, rest: *mora*, delay.

[5] Leaves *v.* Bernard, 5 Mod. *132 (1696); 2 Ark. 117; Stephen, Pl. 61; Coke, Litt. 71 *b.*

[6] [*Exp.* Vermilyea, 6 Cow. 559 (1826); Havens *v.* Hartford, &c. R. Co., 23 Conn. 89–92 (1859).

[7] Goodman *v.* Fond, 23 Miss. 595 (1852), Smith, C. J.

[8] 3 Bl. Com. 314.

[1] 3 Bl. Com. 446. See 6 Pet. 327.

[2] 4 Bl. Com. 333–34.

[3] Christmas *v.* Russell, 5 Wall. 303 (1866), Clifford, J.: 1 Chitty, Pl. 663; 2 Johns. 428.

[4] Gindrat *v.* Dane, 4 Cliff. 262 (1874); Story, Eq. Pl. § 455.

[5] Commonwealth *v.* Cross-Cut R. Co., 53 Pa. 66 (1866): Stephen, Pl. 161; 1 Saunders, Pl. & Ev. 950. See also

A demurrer admits jurisdiction and such matters of fact as are relevant and well-pleaded; but not conclusions of law drawn from the facts,[1] nor matters of inference or argument.[2]

Upon either a general or a special demurrer the opposite party must aver the matter or the form to be sufficient, which is called a "joinder in demurrer," and then the parties are at issue — which the court must determine.[3]

In England special demurrers were abolished by the procedure act of 1852, s. 51.

A party may both demur and plead. By pleading over, the right to demur may be waived.[4] The right to amend, after a demurrer has been sustained, is discretionary with the court.[5]

A demurrer cannot be good in part and bad in part; it must be sustained or fail to the whole extent to which it is interposed.[5]

The court decides for the party who, on the whole, seems best entitled to a judgment.[7] The judgment is as conclusive as a verdict.[8] That a demurrer was made cannot be used as an admission of a fact.[9]

Propositions deducible from the authorities are: (1) A judgment rendered upon a demurrer to a declaration or other material pleading setting forth the facts is as conclusive of matters admitted as a verdict would be, since the facts are established in the former case, as in the latter, by matter of record; and the rule is that facts thus established can never afterward be contested between the same parties or those in privity with them. (2) If judgment is rendered for the defendant, the plaintiff can never afterward maintain against him or his privies any similar action for the same cause upon the grounds disclosed in the declaration: the judgment determines the merits of the cause; a final judgment determining the right ends a dispute, else litigation would be endless.[10]

A demurrer to a complaint because it does not state facts sufficient to constitute a cause of action is equivalent to a general demurrer to a declaration at common law, and raises an issue which, when tried, will finally dispose of the case as stated in the complaint, on its merits, unless leave to amend or plead over is granted. The trial of such an issue is the trial of the cause as a cause, not the settlement of a mere matter of form in proceeding. There can be no other trial except at the discretion of the court.[11]

Where the demurrer goes to the form of the action, to a defect in pleading, or to the jurisdiction of the court, the judgment will not preclude future litigation on the merits of the controversy in a court of competent jurisdiction upon proper pleadings; and where it goes both to defects of form and to the merits a judgment not distinguishing between the two grounds may be presumed to rest on the former. But where the demurrer is to a pleading setting forth distinctly specific facts touching the merits of the action or defense, and final judgment is rendered thereon, it would be difficult to find any reason in principle why the facts admitted should not be considered for all purposes as fully established as if found by a jury or admitted in open court. If the party against whom a ruling is made wishes to avoid the effect of the demurrer as an admission of the facts he should seek to amend his pleading or answer, as the case may be. Leave for that purpose will seldom be refused upon a statement that he can controvert the facts by evidence. If he does not ask permission the inference may justly be drawn that he is unable to produce the evidence, and that the fact is as alleged in the pleading.[1]

Speaking demurrer. A demurrer which introduces some fact or averment, necessary to support it, not appearing distinctly upon the face of the bill.[2]

Demurrer to evidence. When a record or other matter is produced as evidence, concerning the legal effect of which there arises a doubt, and the adverse party demurs to the same as evidence.[3]

A proceeding by which the court is called upon to say what the law is upon the facts shown in evidence.[4]

The demurrant admits the truth of the testimony, and such conclusions as a jury may fairly draw; but not forced and violent inferences. The testimony is to be taken most strongly against him, and such conclusions as a jury may justifiably draw the court ought to draw.[5]

A demurrer to plaintiff's evidence admits the facts the evidence tends to prove. The court is to make every inference of fact in favor of the plaintiff which a jury might infer. If, then, the evidence is insufficient to support a verdict in his favor, the demurrer should be sustained.[6] See Nonsuit.

Coke, Litt, 72 a; 3 Bl. Com. 315; 1 Chitty, Pl. 642, 16 Am. ed., *694-95.

[1] Gindrat v. Dane, ante.

[2] United States v. Ames, 99 U. S. 45-46 (1878), cases; 14 F. R. 498, cases. See 109 U. S. 253, 550; 20 How. 125.

[3] 3 Bl. Com. 315.

[4] Stanton v. Embrey, 93 U. S. 553 (1876), cases.

[5] United States v. Atherton, 102 U. S. 375 (1880).

[6] First Nat. Bank of St. Paul v. Howe, 28 Minn. 152 (1881).

[7] See Townsend v. Jemison, 7 How. 703, 714 (1849); 16 Ill. 269; 39 Me. 426; 28 Ala. 637.

[8] Gould, Pl. 444; generally, ib. 428-46.

[9] Pease v. Phelps, 10 Conn. 68 (1834); 28 id. 92.

[10] Gould v. Evansville, &c. R. Co., 91 U. S. 533-34 (1875), cases, Clifford, J.

[11] Alley v. Nott, 111 U. S. 475 (1884), Waite, C. J.; N. Y. Code Civ. Proc. secs. 488, 497.

---

[1] Bissell v. Spring Valley Township, 124 U. S. 232 (1888), cases, Field, J.

[2] [Brooks v. Gibbons, 4 Paige, 375 (1834), Walworth, Ch. See Edsell v. Buchanan, 2 Ves. Jr. *83 (1793); 1 Sim. 5; 2 Sim. & Stu. 127; 1 Barb. Ch. Pr. 107.

[3] [3 Bl. Com. 372. See Gould, Pl. 446-58; Goodman v. Ford, 23 Miss. 595 (1852), Smith, C. J.

[4] Suydam v. Williamson, 20 How. 436 (1857), cases, Clifford. J.

[5] Pawling v. United States, 4 Cranch, 221 (1808), Marshall, C. J.; Pleasants v. Fant, 22 Wall. 121 (1874), cases; 77 Va. 212.

[6] Donohue v. St. Louis, &c. R. Co., 91 Mo. 360 (1886); 73 id. 219.

Demurrer to interrogatory. The reason a witness offers for not answering a particular question among interrogatories.

DENARIUS DEI. L. God's penny; money given to the church or to the poor; earnest-money, *q. v.*

DENIAL. See DEFENSE, 2.

DENIZEN.[1] An alien born who has obtained *ex donatione regis* letters-patent to make him a subject.[2]

Whence denizenize, denization or denization,[3] and denizenship. The crown denizenizes; parliament consents to naturalization.

A denizen is in a kind of middle state between an alien and a natural-born subject, and partakes of both. He may take lands by purchase or devise, but not by inheritance — for the parent has no inheritable blood.[4] But since 1870, in England, an alien may hold and dispose of property as a natural-born subject.

In South Carolina the status seems to have been created by law.

DENOUNCEMENT. In Mexican law, a judicial proceeding equivalent to the inquest of office at common law.[5]

DENTIST. See CARE; MECHANIC; PHYSICIAN.

DENY. See ADMISSION, 2; DEFENSE, 2; TRAVERSE.

DEODAND.[6] Any personal chattel which was the immediate cause of the death of a rational creature.[7]

The chattel, whether an animal or inanimate object, was forfeited to the king, to be applied to religious uses. Designed, originally, as an expiation for the souls of such persons as were snatched away by sudden death. If any animal killed a person, or if a cart ran over him, it was to be forfeited,—in part, also, as punishment for the supposed negligence in the owner. If the thing was in motion, as, a cart with its loading, all that moved was forfeited; if not in motion, then only the part which was the immediate cause of the death. It mattered not whether the owner was concerned in the killing or not. The right to deodands, in time, was granted to the lords of manors as a franchise.[8]

Abolished by 9 and 10 Vict. (1846) c. 62.

DEPART. See DEPARTURE.

DEPARTMENT. (*Adj.* Departmental.) The departments of government are the

legislative, the executive, and the judicial departments.

In our system, it is important that these departments be kept separate, that one be not allowed to encroach upon the domain of another.[1]

While a general separation has been observed between the different departments, so that no clear encroachment by one upon the province of the other has been sustained, the legislative department, when not restrained by constitutional provisions and a regard for certain fundamental rights of the citizen which are recognized in this country as the basis of all government, has acted upon everything within the range of civil government.[2]

The executive business of the general government, under a permission rather than a mandate of the Constitution, is distributed to seven executive "departments" of equal grade.

Administration of the duties of these respective departments is committed directly to a "secretary" or "head," who, with his principal assistants, is appointed by the President as chief executive, with the advice of the Senate.

The departments are designated as of — the interior,[3] justice,[4] the navy,[5] the post-office,[6] state,[7] the treasury,[8] and war.[9] The department of agriculture[10] is of subordinate grade.

The head of a department is required to exercise judgment and discretion in administering the concerns of his office. He exercises his own judgment in expounding the laws and resolutions of Congress under which he is to act. If he doubts, he may call on the attorney-general for counsel. If the Supreme Court should differ with him as to the construction to be placed upon any of these laws it would pronounce judgment accordingly. But the interference of the courts with the performance of the ordinary duties of the executive departments would be productive of nothing but mischief — such power was never intended to be given to them. . . The court by *mandamus* may direct the doing of a purely ministerial act, but not the exercise of a duty requiring judgment and discretion.[11]

The heads of departments are the President's authorized assistants in the performance of his "executive" duties, and their official acts, promulgated in

---

[1] F. *deinzein*, a trader "within" the privilege of a city franchise: *deinz*, within,—Skeat.

[2] 1 Bl. Com. 374; 6 Pet. 116, note.

[3] Webster's Dict.; 1 Bl. Com. 374.

[4] 1 Bl. Com. 374.

[5] [Merle *v.* Mathews, 26 Cal. 477 (1864).

[6] L. *deo-dandum*, given to God.

[7] [1 Bl. Com. 300.

[8] 1 Bl. Com. 300-2.

---

[1] See Mabry *v.* Baxter, 11 Heisk. 689-90 (1872).

[2] Maynard *v.* Hill, 125 U. S. 205 (1888). As to the independence of the departments of government, see 21 Am. Law Rev. 210-27 (1887), cases.

[3] R. S. § 437: Act 3 March, 1849.

[4] R. S. § 346: Act 24 Sept. 1789.

[5] R. S. § 415: Act 30 April, 1798.

[6] R. S. § 388: Act 8 May, 1794.

[7] R. S. § 199: Act 27 July, 1789.

[8] R. S. § 233: Act 2 Sept. 1789.

[9] R. S. § 214: Act 7 Aug. 1789.

[10] R. S. § 520: Act 15 May, 1862.

[11] Decatur *v.* Paulding, 14 Pet. 515-17 (1840), Taney, C. J.; United States *v.* Macdaniel, 7 *id.* *15 (1833); Kendall *v.* United States, 12 *id.* 610 (1838); Litchfield *v.* Register and Receiver, 9 Wall. 577 (1869); Carrick *v.* Lamar, 116 U. S. 426 (1886), cases.

the regular course of business, are presumptively his acts.[1]

When the head of a department is required by law to give information on any subject to a citizen he may ordinarily do this through subordinate officers.[2]

The supervision which the head of a department may exercise over a subordinate does not extend to a matter in which the latter is directed by statute to act judicially.[3]

See COMITY; CONSTITUTIONAL; DOCUMENT, Public; EXECUTIVE; GOVERNMENT; JUDICIARY; LEGISLATURE; MINISTERIAL, 1; PROCLAMATION, 2; REGULATION.

DEPARTURE. Parting from, separation, going away; relinquishment, dereliction.

1. "Departure from the State," said of a debtor, in a statute of limitations, does not mean temporary absence from the State, while his usual place of residence continues therein, but such absence as entirely suspends the power of the plaintiff to commence his action.[4] See ABSCOND; ABSENCE; START.

2. In marine insurance, deviation from the course prescribed.

Imports an effectual leaving of the place behind. If the vessel be detained or driven back, though she may have sailed, there is no departure.[5] See DEVIATION.

3. In pleading, the dereliction of an antecedent ground of complaint or defense for another distinct from and not fortifying the former ground.[6]

In the several stages of the process of pleading a party must not depart or vary from the title or defense he has once insisted on. For this, which is called a "departure," might occasion endless altercation. Therefore the replication must support the declaration, and the rejoinder the plea, without departing from it.[7]

When a party quits or departs from the case or defense which he has first made, and has recourse to another.[8]

Occurs when, for example, the replication or rejoinder contains matter not pursuant to the declaration or plea, not supporting and fortifying it. May arise in the replication or a subsequent pleading. If parties were permitted to wander from fact to fact, forsaking one to set up another, no issue could be

joined, nor could there be any termination of the suit. A departure may be in the substance of the action or defense, or in the law on which it is founded.[1]

Taken advantage of by a demurrer, general or special.[2] Compare VARIANCE; DUPLICITY. See ASSIGNMENT, New.

DEPENDENT. 1, *adj.* Not to be performed until a connected thing is done by another. Opposed, **independent**, completely obligatory within itself: as, a dependent, or an independent, contract or covenant, *qq. v.* Compare APPENDENT.

2, *n.* A person who is dependent for support upon another.[3]

DEPONENT; DEPOSE. See DEPOSITION.

DEPOSIT.[4] 1, *v.* (1) To give in charge to another person, to commit to the custody and care of another; to leave with for safe-keeping; to deliver to for further action, for a special or a general purpose, explained or understood.

"Deposited," in a statute prescribing the duties of an election inspector, implies that the depositary must safely keep the papers committed to his custody until he surrenders them to the board whose duty it is to canvass the returns and certify the result of the election.[5]

At an election in which a Congressman is voted for, failure to keep the election papers safely as provided by law in Indiana is an offense against the United States government.[6]

(2) Specifically, to deliver money or personalty to another for safe-keeping, without remuneration, until the owner shall request a return of the possession.

2, *n.*[7] (1) A naked bailment of goods, to be kept for the bailor without reward, and to be returned when he shall require it.[8]

A bailment of goods to be kept by the bailee without reward, and delivered according to the object or purpose of the original trust.[9]

---

[1] Runkle v. United States, 122 U. S. 557 (1887).

[2] Miller v. Mayor of New York, 109 U. S. 385, 394 (1883).

[3] Butterworth v. Hoe, 112 U. S. 50, 55 (1884), cases.

[4] Blodgett v. Utley, 4 Neb. 29 (1875), Maxwell, J.

[5] Union Ins. Co. v. Tysen, 3 Hill, 126 (1842), cases, Cowen, J. See Sloop Active v. United States, 7 Cranch, 100 (1812).

[6] Gould, Pl. 421 — Ch. VIII, sec. 65.

[7] 3 Bl. Com. 310.

[8] 1 Chitty, Pl. 674; Steph. Pl. 410; 49 Ind. 112.

[1] 1 Chitty, Pl. 674; Steph. Pl. 410; 49 Ind. 112.

[2] See 5 Ala. 344; 5 Conn. 379; 16 Mass. *2; 44 Mo. 64; 14 Nev. 239; 16 Johns. 206; 20 *id.* 160; 13 N. Y. 89.

[3] Ballou v. Gile, 50 Wis. 619 (1880); American Legion of Honor v. Perry, 140 Mass. 590 (1886).

[4] L. *de-ponere*, to lay away, place aside; intrust to.

[5] Re Coy, 31 F. R. 801 (1887), Harlan, J.; Ind. R. S. 1881, c. 56.

[6] United States v. Coy, 32 F. R. 538 (1787), Woods, J.; R. S. § 5515. Affirmed, Sup. Ct., May 14, 1888.

[7] Deposite was the old spelling,— 2 Pet. *325; 7 Conn. 495.

[8] Jones, Bailm. 36, 117: 17 Mass. 499; 40 Vt. 380.

[9] Story, Bailm. § 41; 8 Ga. 180; 42 Miss. 544; 29 N. Y. 167.

Also, the thing itself so bailed — goods, money, or other movables.

Depositor. The bailor in a contract of deposit of goods. **Depositary.** The bailee in a contract; a depositee.[1]

Depository. The place where the goods are received or kept.

General deposit. A deposit which is to be returned in kind. **Special deposit.** A deposit to be returned in the identical thing.

Quasi-deposit. Possession of another's property obtained by finding it.

A depositary is bound to take only ordinary care of the deposit. What this degree of care is varies with the circumstances of each case. . He is answerable for gross negligence, which is considered equivalent to a breach of faith. The degree of care necessary to avoid the imputation of bad faith is measured by the carefulness which he uses toward his own property of a similar kind. For although that may be so slight as to amount even to carelessness in another, yet the depositor has no reason to expect a change of character in favor of his particular interest.[2] See BAILMENT; DEPOSITUM.

(2) A delivery of money to a bank or banker upon a contract that an equal sum will be returned on demand; also, the money itself. This, by pre-eminence, is a "deposit."

Whence bank of deposit, bank-deposits, memorandum of deposit, etc.

Depositor. He who delivers money to a bank, subject to his order.

General deposit. In this the depositor parts with title to his money, — lends it to the bank which agrees to return an equivalent sum on demand. Also called an *irregular* deposit. **Special deposit.** When the depositor retains title to the thing delivered, which may be bullion, plate, securities, etc., as well as money, and the bank becomes a bailee under obligation to take ordinary care of the article and to return it to the owner when called for.

In the ordinary case of a deposit of money with a banking corporation or banker the transaction amounts to a mere loan, *mutuum*, or irregular deposit, and the bank is to restore not the same money, but an equivalent sum, when demanded. But in the case of a "special deposit" the very coin or bills are to be restored, — the transaction constitutes a genuine deposit; the banker has no authority to use the money, being bound to return it *in individuo.*[1]

Originally, a deposit of money was made by placing a sum in gold or silver with a bank or other depositary, to be returned, when called for, in the same identical coin, and without interest, the depositor paying the depositary a compensation for his care. Later, it became customary to make a deposit for a particular period, on interest, or payable at prescribed periods after notice. In time, "deposit" became a symbolical word to designate not only a deposit in its original sense, but all that class of contracts where money in any form was placed with a bank or banker, to be returned in other money on call or at a specified period, and with or without interest. The transaction, in this figurative use of the term, was in reality the same as a "loan" of money between individuals.[2]

Deposits made with bankers may be divided into two classes: that in which the bank becomes bailee of the depositor, the title to the thing remaining with the latter; and that kind of deposit of money, peculiar to banking business, in which the depositor, for his own convenience, parts with title to his money, and lends it to the banker, who, in consideration of the loan and the right to use the money for his own profit, agrees to refund the amount, or any part thereof, on demand.[3]

When the banker specially agrees to pay in bullion or coin he must do so or answer in damages for its value. But where the deposit is general, and there is no special agreement proved, the title to the money deposited passes to the bank, the transaction is unaffected by the character of the money in which the deposit was made, and the bank becomes liable for the amount as a debt, which can be discharged only by such money as is a legal tender. . When a merchant deposits money with a bank, the rule is, the title to the money passes to the bank, and the latter becomes the debtor to that amount.[4]

Deposits undoubtedly may be made with a banker under such circumstances that the conclusion would be that the title remained in the depositor; and in that case the banker would become the bailee of the depositor, and the latter might rightfully demand the identical money deposited as his property; but where the deposit is general, and there is no special agreement proven inconsistent with such theory, the title to the deposit passes to the banker, and he becomes liable for the amount as a debt which can be discharged only by a legal payment. . An agreement to refund all or part of a general deposit may be express or implied; if express, it may be to refund with or without interest. The fact that the depositary agreed to pay interest affords strong evidence that the

---

[1] 103 Pa. 534.

[2] Foster *v.* The Essex Bank, 17 Mass. 498 (1821), Parker, C. J. See 2 Bl. Com. 453.

[1] Story, Bailm. § 88; State *v.* Clark, 4 Ind. 316 (1853).

[2] Curtis *v.* Leavitt, 15 N. Y. 166 (1857), Shankland, J.

[3] Marine Bank (of Chicago) *v.* Fulton Bank (of New York), 2 Wall. 256 (1864), Miller, J. Quoted, Phœnix Bank *v.* Risley, 111 U. S. 127 (1883), cases; 92 U. S. 370, and 80 N. Y. 95, *post.* See also 34 La. An. 607; 17 Nev. 152.

[4] Thompson *v.* Riggs, 5 Wall. 678, 680 (1866), Clifford, J. Quoted, 92 U. S. 370, *post.*

title to the money passed out of the depositor by the act of making the deposit.[1]

The power to receive deposits includes all the kinds known and customary in the banking business. National banks have power to receive special deposits gratuitously or otherwise; and when received gratuitously they are liable for their loss by gross negligence. When any such bank has habitually received such deposits, this liability attaches to a deposit received in the usual way. . . . The term "special deposits" includes money, securities or other valuables delivered to banks, to be specially kept and redelivered; it is not confined to securities held as collaterals to loans. . The chief, in some cases the only, deposits received by the early banks were special deposits of money, bullion, plate, etc., for safe-keeping, to be specifically returned to the depositor. . . The definition of the business of banks of deposit, in the encyclopedias, embraces the receiving of the money or valuables of others, to keep until called for by the depositors. And although, in modern times, the business of receiving general deposits has constituted the principal business of the banks, it cannot be said that receiving special deposits is so foreign to the banking business that corporations authorized to carry on that business are incapable of binding themselves by the receipt of such deposits.[2]

Section 5228, Rev. St., which provides that it shall be lawful for a national bank after its failure to "deliver special deposits," is as effectual a recognition of its power to receive them as an express declaration to that effect would have been. The phrase "special deposits," thus used, embraces the public securities of the United States.[2]

It is now well settled that if a bank be accustomed to take special deposits, and this is known and acquiesced in by the directors, and the property deposited is lost by the gross carelessness of the bailee, a liability ensues in like manner as if the deposit had been authorized by the terms of the charter.[3]

The contract between a bank and its depositor is that of debtor and creditor. Money held by a depositor in a fiduciary capacity does not change its character by being placed to his credit.[4]

The right of the depositor is a chose in action, and his check does not transfer the debt. or give a lien upon it to a third person, without the assent of the depositary.[5]

General deposits held by a bank are part of its general fund, and loaned as other moneys. The banker agrees to discharge his indebtedness by honoring checks drawn upon the deposit. When a check on the bank itself is offered, the bank may accept or reject it or receive it conditionally. If, being genuine, it is received as a deposit, when there are no funds, the case is an executed contract, and the thing done cannot be repudiated. Depositors must comply with all reasonable regulations as to depositing and drawing.[1]

It seems to be well settled that a mere check or draft does not operate as an assignment or appropriation of the drawer's deposit in favor of the payee before acceptance by the bank, but the doctrine has not been extended beyond instruments of that character, drawn in the ordinary form; nor to a transaction not restricted to the very terms of such paper.[2]

A general deposit in a bank is so much money to the depositor's credit. It is a debt to him by the bank, payable on demand to his order; not property capable of identification and specific appropriation. A check upon a bank in the usual form, not accepted or certified by its cashier to be good, does not constitute a transfer of any money to the credit of the holder; it is simply an order which may be countermanded, and payment forbidden by the drawer, at any time before it is actually cashed. It creates no lien on the money which the holder can enforce against the bank. It does not of itself operate as an equitable assignment,[3] q. v.

A depositor in a bank who sends his pass-book to be written up and receives it back with entries of credits and debits, and his paid checks as vouchers for the latter, is bound, with due diligence, to examine the pass-book and vouchers, and to report to the bank without unreasonable delay any errors which may be discovered in them; and if he fails to do so, and the bank is thereby misled to its injury, he cannot afterward dispute the correctness of the balance shown by the pass-book.[4] See further BANK, 2; CHECK; TAX, 2.

Deposit, certificate of. A writing, issued by a bank, attesting that the person named has deposited money with it.

A negotiable security, upon the same footing as a promissory note. It is treated as money.[5] See CURRENCY.

---

[1] Scammon v. Kimball, 92 U. S. 369-70 (1875), Clifford, J.

[2] Pattison v. Syracuse Nat. Bank, 80 N. Y. 82, 89, 94 (1880), cases, Rapallo, J. Earliest case, Foster v. The Essex Bank, 17 Mass. 478, 496 (1821), Parker, C. J.,— in which the special deposit was a cask containing $53,000 in gold coin.

[3] First Nat. Bank of Carlisle v. Graham, 100 U. S. 703, 702 (1879), Swayne, J.: 79 Pa. 106. See further Prather v. Kean, 29 F. R. 498 (1887): 26 Am. Law Reg. 92; ib. 97-98 (1887), cases.

[4] Chesapeake Nat. Bank v. Connecticut Mut. Ins. Co., 104 U. S. 64-71 (1881), cases. See 37 N. J. E. 18.

[5] Nat. Bank of the Republic v. Millard, 10 Wall. 157 (1869), cases; Rosenthal v. The Mastin Bank, 17 Blatch. 322-23 (1879), cases.

[1] See Thompson v. Riggs, Scammon v. Kimball, ante; First Nat. Bank of South Bend v. Lanier, 11 Wall. 375 (1870); First Nat. Bank of Cincinnati v. Burkhardt, 100 U. S. 689 (1879); Chesapeake Nat. Bank v. Connecticut Mut. Ins. Co., 104 id. 54, 64-71 (1881), cases.

[2] Coates v. First Nat. Bank of Emporia, 91 N. Y. 26 (1883).

[3] Florence Mining Co. v. Brown, 124 U. S. 391 (1888), Field, J.

[4] Leather Manufacturers' Bank v. Morgan, 117 U. S. 106 (1886), cases, Harlan, J. See same case, ACCOUNT, 1. On relation of depositors to bank, see further Fletcher v. Sharpe. Sup. Ct. Ind. (1887); cases: 26 Am. Law Reg. 71; ib. 74-82 (1887), cases. As to fiduciary depositors, see ib. 25, 29-30 (1887), cases.

[5] Welton v. Adams, 4 Cal. 39 (1854); Gregg v. Union

By virtue of the assurance given, the credit of the bank is added to the credit of the original debtor.[1]

A certificate is a subsisting chose in action and represents the fund it describes, as in cases of notes, bonds, and other securities; so that a delivery of it as a gift constitutes an equitable assignment of the money.[2]

When in the usual form, payable to the order of the depositor, is in the nature of commercial paper, and the payee is chargeable upon his indorsement thereof. Its negotiable character is not affected by the fact that a demand is necessary before an action can be maintained thereon; nor is it changed by a provision therein by which it is made payable in current bank-notes. . . An indorser of the certificate is liable as such, until actual demand made; and the holder is not chargeable with neglect for omitting to make such a demand within any particular time.[3]

A certificate of deposit is, in effect, a negotiable promissory note; and the statute of limitations begins to run from the date of issue, without the necessity of demand of payment.[4]

If lost before it is indorsed by the depositor no title vests in the finder, and the bank cannot require of the depositor indemnity against possible future loss, although the money by the terms of the certificate is payable "on return of the certificate."[5]

By implication of law, contains a promise to repay the money, and cannot be varied by parol evidence.[6]

Deposit company. An association which, having provided a building constructed for protection against loss by theft or fire, and having furnished the same with boxes or safes for the deposit of securities, jewels, papers, etc., invites the public to lease the boxes or receptacles, the association insuring the safety of deposits against the acts of all persons except the depositors themselves.

A fuller name is "safe deposit and trust company."

Where bonds were found to be missing from a box so rented the company was held bound to explain the absence of the bonds, and, in default of evidence of negligence or guilt in the depositor, to pay him the value of the bonds.[7]

The robbery by burglars of securities deposited for safe-keeping in the vaults of a bank is not proof of negligence on the part of the bank.[8]

County Nat. Bank, 87 Ind. 239 (1882), cases; Poorman v. Woodward, 21 How. 275 (1858); 27 N. Y. 378.

[1] Downey v. Hicks, 14 How. 249 (1852).

[2] Basket v. Hassell, 107 U. S. 614 (1882).

[3] Pardee v. Fish, 60 N. Y. 265, 268-69 (1875), cases.

[4] Carran v. Witter, Sup. Ct. Wis. (1887), cases, Lyon, J.; 35 Alb. Law J. 389 (1887), cases.

[5] Citizens' Nat. Bank v. Brown, Sup. Ct. Ohio (1887), cases: 36 Alb. Law J. 26.

[6] Lang v. Straus, Sup. Ct. Ind. (1887), cases: 26 Am. Law Reg. 115. See generally 24 Cent. Law J. 196 (1887), cases.

[7] Safe Deposit Co. v. Pollock, 85 Pa. 391 (1877).

[8] Wylie v. Northampton Bank, 119 U. S. 361 (1886).

Deposit in lieu of bail. One charged with a crime or tort in some cases may make a deposit of money or valuables, instead of furnishing bail for his appearance at the hearing or trial.[1]

Deposit of title deeds. Pledging the title deeds to the owner's estate as security for the repayment of a loan.

In effect an equitable mortgage, q. v.

DEPOSITION.[2] Sometimes is synonymous with "affidavit" or "oath;" but, in its more technical and appropriate sense, is limited to the written testimony of a witness given in the course of a judicial proceeding, at law or in equity.[3]

"Deposition" is a generic expression, embracing all written evidence verified by oath, and thus includes "affidavits;" but, in legal language, a deposition is evidence given by a witness under interrogatories, oral or written, and usually written down by an official person; while an affidavit is the mere voluntary act of the party making the oath, and is generally taken without the cognizance of him against whom it is to be used. Yet the terms may be convertible, as in the rules at law of the Supreme Court.[4]

Depose. Originally, to give testimony under oath, to testify; in present usage, to give testimony which is officially written down for future use. **Deponent.** One who, being under oath, testifies in writing.

A deponent is a witness who depones (*deponit*), i. e., places his hand upon the book of the Evangelists while he is being bound by the obligation of an oath. Depose, deponent, and deposition related, originally, then, to the mode in which the oath was administered, not to the testimony itself as oral or written.[5]

Depositions are taken of witnesses out of the jurisdiction, or aged, infirm, sick, or going abroad, upon written interrogatories, the answers to be used as evidence in the event of their death or departure before trial, or of their inability to attend the trial. Testimony in equity, and much in admiralty and divorce, is thus taken, as is also testimony at preliminary examinations in criminal causes; but, in the last case, is not admissible at trial, except, perhaps, by consent of the accused.[6] See further DEDIMUS.

The testimony of any witness may be taken in any civil cause depending in a district or circuit court by deposition *de bene esse*, when the witness lives at a greater distance from the place of trial than one hundred miles, or is bound on a voyage to sea, or is about to go out of the United States, or out of the district in

[1] See Commercial Warehouse Co. v. Graber, 45 N. Y. 394 (1871); 31 Hun, 231; 18 Abb. N. Cas. 323-24 (1886), cases.

[2] L. *de-ponere*, to put, place; to lay down or aside.

[3] State v. Dayton, 23 N. J. L. 54 (1850), Green, C. J.

[4] Stimpson v. Brooks, 3 Blatch. 456-57 (1856), Betts, J.

[5] [Bliss v. Shuman, 47 Me. 252 (1859), Appleton, J.

[6] See 3 Bl. Com. 383, 438.

which the case is to be tried, or to a greater distance than one hundred miles from the place of trial, before the time of trial, or when he is ancient or infirm.[1]

Such deposition can only be read upon proof that the attendance of the witness upon the trial cannot be procured.[2]

Cases in equity are taken to the Supreme Court from the circuit courts, and the district courts sitting as circuit courts, by appeal, and are heard upon the proofs sent up with the record. "The mode of proof," by section 862, Rev. St., "shall be according to the rules now or hereafter prescribed by the supreme court, except as herein specially provided." The circuit courts are not now by law required to permit the examination of witnesses orally in open court upon the hearing of cases in equity. But if such practice is adopted, the testimony must be taken down, or its substance stated in writing and made part of the record.[3]

Formerly, in England, the mode of examining witnesses in equity was by interrogatories in writing. . . At the December term, 1861, of the Supreme Court, a new practice was introduced. Rule 67 was so amended as to make oral examination the rule, if either party desires it, and examination by written interrogatories the exception.[4]

Congress has not empowered the district and circuit courts to make rules touching the mode of taking testimony. . . Depositions taken under a State law in conflict with the provisions of the act of Congress in relation thereto are not admissible in evidence.[5]

A deposition filed is the property of the court; if the testimony is material it should be used. Some courts hold that it is as competent for one party to read a deposition filed by the other party as to introduce a witness summoned in his behalf.[6] See INTERROGATORY.

DEPOSITUM. L. A naked bailment without reward, and without any special undertaking.[7]

So called because the naked custody is given to another.[8] See DEPOSIT, 1; DEPOT, 1.

DEPOT. 1. In French law, *dépôt* is the *depositum* of the Roman and the *deposit* of the English law.

May mean a place where military stores or supplies are kept.[9]

2. A place where passengers get on and off the cars, and where goods are loaded and unloaded.

All ground necessary or convenient and actually used for these purposes is included.[1] See RAILROAD; STATION, 2.

DEPRIVE. Referring to property taken under the power of eminent domain, means the same as "take."[2]

While the Fourteenth Amendment ordains that no State shall "deprive any person of life, liberty, or property without due process of law," no definition of the word "deprive" is found in the Constitution. To determine its signification, therefore, it is necessary to ascertain the effect which usage has given it when employed in the same or a like connection.[3] See further TAKE, 8.

DEPUTY.[4] One who acts officially for another; the substitute of an officer — usually of a ministerial officer.

Deputize. To appoint another to act in one's own place or office.

General deputy. A deputy who is empowered to perform all the ordinary duties of an office. **Special deputy.** A deputy chosen to do a particular act or acts.

An attorney-general, a district-attorney, a collector of revenue, a mayor, a constable, a marshal, a sheriff, a minister or consul, and other officers, are sometimes said to act by deputy.

There are two kinds of deputies of a sheriff: a general deputy or under sheriff who by virtue of his appointment has authority to execute all the ordinary duties of the office of sheriff. He executes process without special power from the sheriff, and may even delegate authority for its execution to a special deputy, who is an officer *pro hac vice*, to execute a particular writ on some certain occasion. He acts under a specific, not a general, appointment and authority.[5]

The deputy of a ministerial officer may do whatever his principal could do under the circumstances of each case.[6] See DELEGATUS.

DERAIGN.[7] Originally, to confound, disorder; to turn out of course; to displace. In old common law, to prove by disproving,

[1] R. S. §§ 863–75.

[2] Whitford v. Clark County, 13 F. R. 837, 839 (1882), cases; Stebbins v. Duncan, 108 U. S. 45 (1883); Whitford v. Clark County, 119 id. 522 (1886).

[3] Blease v. Garlington, 92 U. S. 1, 4–8 (1875), Waite, Chief Justice.

[4] Bischoffscheim v. Baltzer, 20 Blatch. 231 (1882); s. c. 10 F. R. 3.

[5] Randall v. Venable, 17 F. R. 162 (1883).

[6] Rucker v. Reid, 36 Kan. 470 (1887). As to rules of practice, see 22 Cent. Law J. 581 (1886), cases. Taking before U. S. commissioner, 1 Kan. Law J. 245–49 (1885) — Wash. Law Rep.

[7] Foster v. Essex Bank, 17 Mass. 498 (1821), Parker, C. J.; 33 Ala. 55; 2 Bl. Com. 453.

[8] Story, Bailm. § 43.

[9] Caldwell's Case, 19 Wall. 264 (1873).

[1] Fowler v. Farmers' Loan & Trust Co., 21 Wis. 79 (1866); Pittsburgh, etc. R. Co. v. Rose, 24 Ohio St. 229 (1873); State v. New Haven, &c. R. Co., 37 Conn. 163 (1870); 34 La. An. 624; 110 U. S. 682.

[2] Sharpless v. Philadelphia, 21 Pa. 167 (1853); Grant v. Courter, 24 Barb. 238 (1857).

[3] Munn v. Illinois, 94 U. S. 123 (1876), Waite, C. J.

[4] F. député, one deputed: L. deputare, to esteem, allot, destine.

[5] Allen v. Smith, 12 N. J. L. 162 (1831), Ewing, C. J.

[6] The Confiscation Cases, 20 Wall. 111 (1873); Re Executive Communication, 12 Fla. 652 (1868).

[7] O. F. derainer, to maintain in a legal action: L. L. de rationare, to contend in law.

or simply to prove; as, to deraign a right, deraign the warranty.[1]

Also spelled darraign, darrain.

DERELICT.[2] Relinquished, deserted, abandoned.

Dereliction. The state of being abandoned or cast away; also, the thing itself of which this is predicated.

1. Land left uncovered by the receding of water from its former bed.[3] Sometimes called "reliction." See ALLUVION.

2. Anything thrown away or abandoned with intention to relinquish claim of ownership thereto.

In the civil law the voluntary abandonment of goods by the owner, without the hope or purpose of returning to the possession.[4]

Dereliction or renunciation of goods requires both the intention to abandon and external action.[5]

The right of appropriating a derelict is one of universal law. It existed in a state of nature, and is only modified by society, according to the discretion of each community.[6] See ABANDON, 1.

3. Specifically, maritime property entirely deserted.

It is sufficient that the thing is found deserted or abandoned upon the seas, whether it arose from accident or necessity, or voluntary dereliction. . . A thing was not derelict in the civil law unless the owner voluntarily abandoned it without any further claim of property in it.[7]

The abandonment must be final, without hope of recovery or intention to return. It is not sufficient that the crew have left temporarily, as, to procure assistance.[8]

A case of "quasi-derelict" occurs when the vessel is not abandoned, but those on board are physically and mentally incapable of doing anything for their safety.[9] See SALVAGE.

DERIVATIVE. See ACQUISITION; CONVEYANCE, 2.

DERIVED. See DEVOLUTION.

DEROGATION. Partial repeal or abrogation; impairment of utility and force; restriction.

Statutes in derogation of the common law or of common right are to be strictly construed.[1] In this category are: attachment laws;[2] affidavit-of-defense laws;[3] changes in commercial paper sought to be made by local statutes;[4] contracts in restraint of the taxing power;[5] summary convictions.[6]

DESCEND.[7] Sometimes, to "pass by descent or inheritance" or "be inherited by,"— thereby expressing in a single term what otherwise might require a circumlocution. When so used, in statutes, it is usually accompanied by other words which prevent ambiguity: as, "descend to his father," "to his mother," "to his next of kin;" but in these cases these terms so qualify the word "descend" as to give it the effect of "pass by inheritance" to the person named or described. In a will the word cannot be construed to include any but lineal heirs, without clear indication that it was otherwise intended by the testator.[8]

Ordinarily, for an estate to vest by operation of law in the heirs, immediately upon the death of the ancestor.[9]

In a will, does not work a descent in the strict legal sense, as inheritance is through operation of law. It indicates, presumably, a desire that property shall follow the channel into which the law would direct it.[10]

May import devolution by force of the devise made, rather than descent in the legal sense; that is, "to go down."[11]

Descendant. One who has issued from an individual, including a child, a grandchild, and their children to the remotest degree.[12] Correlative, ancestor, q. v.

Often synonymous with "heir."[13]

"Descendants" includes every person descended from the stock referred to.— is co-extensive with "issue," but not as comprehensive as "relatives;"[14]

---

[1] [Jacob's Law Dict.] "A title deraigned by a sale," Freeman, Executions, § 282.

[2] L. derelictio, complete, neglect: derelinquere, to forsake.

[3] 2 Bl. Com. 262.

[4] Jones v. Nunn, 12 Ga. 473 (1853); 2 Bl. Com. 9; 10 Johns. 356.

[5] Livermore v. White, 74 Me. 455 (1883).

[6] Hawkins v. Barney, 5 Pet. *467 (1831).

[7] Rowe v. Brig and Cargo, 1 Mas. 373, 374 (1818), Story, J.; Montgomery v. The Leathers, 1 Newb. 425 (1852); Evans v. The Charles, ib. 339 (1842); 2 Kent, 357.

[8] The Island City, 1 Black, 128 (1861), Grier, J.; The Laura, 14 Wall. 336, 342 (1871); The Hyderabad, 11 F. R. 754-55 (1882), cases.

[9] Sturtevant v. The Nicholaus, 1 Newb. 452 (1852).

[1] 1 Shars. Bl. Com. 87.

[2] Mitchell v. St. Maxent's Lessee, 4 Wall. 243 (1866); 101 U. S. 565.

[3] 56 Pa. 21.

[4] Ross v. Jones, 22 Wall. 591 (1874).

[5] Tucker v. Ferguson, 22 Wall. 575 (1874).

[6] 1 Burr. 613; 4 Bl. Com. 280; 2 Kent, 73.

[7] L. de-scendere, to pass down.

[8] Baker v. Baker, 8 Gray, 119, 120 (1857), Shaw, C. J.; McDowell v. Addams, 45 Pa. 434 (1863).

[9] [Dove v. Torr, 128 Mass. 40 (1879), Gray, C. J.

[10] Halstead v. Hall, 60 Md. 213 (1883); Dennett v. Dennett, 40 N. H. 498 (1860).

[11] Ballentine v. Wood, 42 N. J. E. 558 (1886).

[12] Jewell v. Jewell, 28 Cal. 236 (1865): Bouvier.

[13] Huston v. Read, 32 N. J. E. 599 (1880).

[14] Barstow v. Goodwin, 2 Bradf. 416 (1853).

nor does it embrace " brothers and sisters; "[1] has not the same signification that " heirs of the body " has, and may be used by a testator as synonymous with " children."[2]

Descent. Passing downward; hereditary succession.

Hereditary succession to an estate in realty. The title whereby a man on the death of his ancestor acquires his estate by right of representation as his heir at law.[3] See HEIR.

Lineal descent. Descent from father or grandfather to son or grandson; or from mother to daughter, etc. *Collateral descent.* From brother to brother, cousin to cousin, etc.

Mediate, immediate descent. A descent may be mediate or immediate in regard to the mediate or immediate descent of the estate of right, or the mediateness or immediateness of the pedigrees or degrees of consanguinity.[4]

A descent from a parent to a child cannot be construed to mean a descent through and not from a parent. When an estate is said to have descended from A to B, the obvious meaning is that it is an immediate descent from A to B. " Come by descent " means by immediate descent.[5]

Canons of descent. The rules which regulate the descent of real estates of inheritance; the rules according to which estates are transmitted from ancestor to heir.

At common law these canons are:

I. An inheritance lineally descends to the issue of the person who last died actually seised, *in infinitum,* and never lineally ascends.

II. The male issue are admitted before the female.

III. Where there are two or more males in equal degree the eldest only inherits; but females altogether.

IV. Lineal descendants, *in infinitum,* represent their ancestor.

V. On failure of the lineal descendants of the person last seised the inheritance descends to his collateral relations, being of the whole blood of the first purchaser: subject to the last three preceding rules.

VI. The collateral heir of the person last seised must be his next collateral kinsman of the whole blood.

VII. In collateral inheritances male stocks (however remote) are preferred to female (however near); unless the lands have, in fact, descended from a female.[6]

Lord Hale reduced the rules upon the subject of

descent, up to whose time they had continued the same some four hundred years, to this series of "canons." Material alteration was not again made in them till 1833,—by stat. 3 and 4 Will. IV, c. 106 (amended in 1859 by 22 and 23 Vict., c. 35, ss. 19, 20). By that act, which went into effect January 1, 1834, among other important alterations, the father is made heir to his son, the latter having no issue; all lineal ancestors are rendered capable of being heirs; and relatives of the half-blood are admitted to succeed on failure of relatives in the same degree of the whole blood.[1]

In England title by "descent" was favored by the courts, because land in the hands of the heirs at law by descent was chargeable with payment of the ancestor's debts, and because such title favored the right of escheat upon failure of heirs. On the other hand, land acquired by "purchase" was not liable for debts, and, upon the death of the owner, descended to the heirs on the paternal side, and upon failure of such heirs to the heirs on the side of the mother. Title by descent was considered the worthier, and where a will gave the devisee the same estate he would have taken as heir-at-law he was adjudged to take not under the will, but by descent or operation of law.[2]

The common-law canons of descent tended to prevent the diffusion of landed property, and to promote its accumulation in the hands of a few. The principles sprang from the martial genius of the feudal system. In the United States the English common law of descents, in its essential features, has been rejected; each State has established a law for itself.[3] So far as the British law was taken as the basis of this legislation, it was the statutes of Charles II (1671, 1678), and of James II (1685), respecting the distribution of personalty. The two systems are radically different.[4]

See BLOOD, 1; CAPUT, Per capita; DISTRIBUTION, 2; FEUD; INHERIT; PEDIGREE; PRIMOGENITURE; PURCHASE, 3.

DESCRIPTIO. L. Delineation: designation, description. Compare DEMONSTRATIO.

Descriptio personæ. Description of the person; an addition to a name or signature: as, " chairman," " president," " agent," " assignee," " executor."

An appellation thus used may not so much serve to show the capacity in which a person acts as to identify him as an individual; but circumstances may indicate an intention to qualify or limit liability.[5]

The rule is that if a person merely adds to the signature of his name the word "agent," "trustee," "treasurer," etc., without disclosing his principal, he

[1] Hamlin *v.* Osgood, 1 Redf. 411 (1862); 30 N. Y. 393; 25 Ga. 420.

[2] Schmaunz *v.* Göss, 132 Mass. 144 (1882).

[3] 2 Bl. Com. 201; 46 Miss. 395; 25 Tex. 241.

[4] Levy *v.* M'Cartee, 6 Pet. *112 (1832), Story, J.

[5] Gardner *v.* Collins, 2 Pet. *90, 91, 94 (1829), Story, J.; 3 Ohio St. 396; 35 Ind. 451.

[6] 2 Bl. Com. 208-35; Bates *v.* Brown, 5 Wall. 715-17 (1866).

[1] Williams, R. P. 93, 95, 96-106.

[2] Donnelly *v.* Turner, 60 Md. 83 (1882), Robinson, J.

[3] See 4 Kent, 412, 406, n.

[4] Bates *v.* Brown, *ante;* 2 Bl. Com. 515; McDowell *v.* Addams, 45 Pa. 434 (1863). Virginia law, 9 Va. Law J. 199-203 (1885).

[5] See Reznor *v.* Webb, 36 How. Pr. 364 (1866); DeWitt *v.* Walton, 9 N. Y. 572 (1854); Rathbon *v.* Budlong, 15 Johns. *2 (1818).

is personally bound. The appendix is regarded as a mere *descriptio personæ*. It does not of itself make third persons chargeable with notice of any representative relation of the signer. But if he is in fact a mere agent, trustee, or officer of some principal, and is in the habit of expressing in that way his representative character in his dealings with a particular party who recognizes him in that character, it would be contrary to justice and truth to construe documents thus made and used as his personal obligations, contrary to the intent of the parties.[1]

DESCRIPTION. See DESCRIPTIO.

Enumeration of characteristic qualities; designation; recital. Whence descriptive. Opposed, **misdescription**: an erroneous description.

1. A description of land is good if it identifies the land.[2]

Where the description in a deed is true in part, that which is false may be rejected. The instrument will take effect if a sufficient description remains to ascertain its application.[3]

Words clearly inconsistent with the rest of a description may be ignored.[4]

Specification of quantity, after a particular description by courses, distances, boundaries, etc., will be held subject to the controlling part of the description. If the purchaser gets the distinct thing contracted for, he cannot complain on account of a deficiency in quantity, unless deception has been practiced.[5]

A misdescription in a deed will not affect the conveyance, if the property is otherwise so described that it can be identified; especially, where the mistake is in a statement regarding the title.[6] See AT, 2; DEMONSTRATIO, FALSA, etc.; MORE OR LESS; ON; THENCE.

2. As to description of a patent, see INVENTION; PROCESS, 2.

3. Where there is a misdescription in a will, either of a person or of the subject-matter, extraneous evidence is always admissible to show who, or what property, was meant.[7] See AMBIGUITY.

4. Where words in a declaration are descriptive of the instrument sued on, the instrument, when offered in evidence, must conform strictly to that description. One bearing a different date will not be admitted. But as the same contract may be made on one day and take effect another, and as a bond may be dated

one day to become obligatory on another, either instrument may be counted on as bearing the first date.[1]

An allegation of a matter of substance may be substantially proved; an allegation of a matter of *essential* description must be proved, in cases, with literal precision. . . Allegations of time, place, quantity, quality, and allegations in aggravation of damages, are not to be strictly proved, unless descriptive. In local actions place is material, and so of the kind and boundaries of land.[2]

The strict rule of pleading which formerly required exact accuracy in the description of premises sought to be recovered, has, in modern practice, been relaxed, and a general description held to be good. The provisions of statutes as to descriptions by metes and bounds have been held to be directory only; a description by name, where the property is well known, is often sufficient, as, to enable a sheriff to execute a writ of possession, or a surveyor to ascertain the precise limits of the location of a mining claim.[3] See ALLEGATION; INDICTMENT.

DESERTION.[4] A willful abandonment of an employment or duty, in violation of a legal or moral obligation.[5]

A soldier deserts his post, a sailor his ship, an apprentice his master, when they depart from the service to which they are bound without permission or contrary to orders. The word implies a separation which is not with the assent of the person deserted.[6] See ABANDON, 2.

1. By a husband or wife — an intentional and wrongful cessation of matrimonial cohabitation.[6]

An actual abandonment of matrimonial cohabitation, with an intent to desert, willfully and maliciously persisted in, without cause. Mere separation is, then, not desertion.[7]

A breach of matrimonial duty, composed of the actual breaking off of matrimonial cohabitation and of an intent to desert.[8]

Not merely a refusal of matrimonial intercourse, which would be a breach or violation

[1] Metcalf v. Williams, 104 U. S. 98 (1881), Bradley, J.; Taylor v. Davis, 110 id. 336 (1884); Wall v. Bissell, 125 id. 393 (1888); 24 Law Reg. 781–82 (1885), cases; 102 Ind. 445.

[2] Litchfield v. County of Webster, 101 U. S. 775 (1879).

[3] White v. Luning, 93 U. S. 524 (1876); Coleman v. Manhattan Beach Improv. Co., 94 N. Y. 229 (1883); Brookman v. Kurzman, ib. 276 (1883); 10 Oreg. 88–89; 1 Greenl. Ev. § 301.

[4] Sampson v. Security Ins. Co., 133 Mass. 54–55 (1882).

[5] See 4 Kent, 466; 1 Story, Eq. § 141; 3 Washb. R. P. 630; 102 U. S. 212. Compensation for misdescription, 3 Law Quar. Rev. 54–63 (1887), Eng. cases.

[6] Sherwood v. Whiting, 54 Conn. 333–37 (1886), cases.

[7] Hawkins v. Garland, 76 Va. 153 (1882).

[1] United States v. Le Baron, 4 Wall. 642, 648 (1866).

[2] 1 Greenl. Ev. §§ 56–66, cases; Whart. Ev. §§ 942, 945, 1004, 1040, cases.

[3] Glacier Mountain Silver Mining Co. v. Willis, 127 U. S. 480 (1888), Lamar, J.

[4] L. de, apart; serere, to join: to part from.

[5] Lea v. Lea, 8 Allen, 419 (1864), Bigelow, C. J.; Ford v. Ford, 143 Mass. 580 (1887).

[6] Benkert v. Benkert, 32 Cal. 470 (1867); Bennett v. Bennett, 43 Conn. 318 (1876).

[7] Ingersoll v. Ingersoll, 49 Pa. 251 (1865); Bishop v. Bishop, 30 id. 412 (1858); Grove's Appeal, 37 id. 447 (1860); McClurg's Appeal, 66 id. 366 (1870); Sower's Appeal, 89 id. 173 (1879).

[8] Bailey v. Bailey, 21 Gratt. 47 (1871); Latham v. Latham, 30 id. 322 (1878); Burk v. Burk, 21 W. Va. 450 (1883).

of a single duty only, but a cessation of co-habitation, a refusal to live together, which involves an abrogation of all the duties resulting from the marriage contract.[1] See ABANDON, 2 (1); NECESSARIES, 1.

2. By a sailor or seaman — an unauthorized leaving or absence from the ship with an intention not to return to her service.[2]

A quitting of the ship and her service, not only without leave and against the duty of the party, but with an intent not again to return to the ship's duty.[3]

3. By a soldier — absence and an intention not to return to the service.[4]

A minor, over eighteen and under twenty-one, who enlists in the army without the consent of his parent or guardian can commit the offense, and the military tribunals may try him therefor.[5]

4. Of property, see ABANDON, 1; DERELIC-TION, 3.

DESERVING. Denotes worth or merit, without regard to condition or circumstances.[6]

DESIGN. 1. Aim, intent, purpose; object, end in view.

In an indictment for having in one's possession materials for counterfeiting, may refer to the purpose for which the materials were originally designed, and not to criminal intent in the defendant to use them.[7] See INTENT; MALICE; WILL, 1.

2. Giving a visible form to a conception of the mind, — to an invention.[8]

The acts of Congress which authorize patents for designs were intended to give encouragement to the decorative arts. They contemplate not so much utility as appearance. It is a new and original design for a manufacture, whether of metal or other material; a new and original design for a bust, statue, *bas relief*, or composition in *alto* or *basso relievo;* a new or original impression or ornament to be placed on any article of manufacture; a new and original design for the printing of woolen, silk, cotton, or other fabric; a new and useful pattern, print, or picture, to be either worked into, or on, any article of manufacture; or a new and original shape or configuration of any article of manufacture, — one or all of these the law has in view. And the thing invented or produced, for which

a patent is given, is that which gives a peculiar or distinctive appearance to the manufacture, or article to which it may be applied, or to which it gives form. The law contemplates that giving new and original appearances to a manufactured article may enhance its salable value, enlarge the demand for it, and be a meritorious service to the public. It is the appearance itself, no matter by what agency caused, that constitutes mainly, if not entirely, the contribution to the public which the law deems worthy of recompense.[1]

The test of identity of design plainly must be sameness of appearance; and mere difference of lines in the drawing or sketch, a greater or smaller number of lines, or slight variances in configuration, if sufficient to change the effect upon the eye, will not destroy the substantial identity. . . . . It is not essential that the appearance should be the same to the eye of an expert. If, in the eye of an ordinary observer, giving such attention as a purchaser usually gives, two designs are substantially the same, if the resemblance is such as to deceive such an observer, inducing him to purchase one supposing it to be the other, the first one patented is infringed by the other.[1]

The differences in designs necessary to take away their identity are such appearances as would attract the attention of an ordinary observer, giving such attention as a purchaser of the articles, for the purposes for which they were intended and purchased, would usually give. There may be an infringement of a patented design without taking the whole of it, but in such cases the part taken must be a part covered by the patent.[2]

Design patents stand on as high a plane as utility patents, and require as high a degree of the inventive or originative faculty. In patentable designs a person cannot be permitted to select an existing form, and simply put it to a new use, any more than he can be permitted to take a patent for a mere double use of a machine; but the selection and adaptation of an existing form may amount to a patentable design, as the adaptation of an existing mechanical device may amount to a patentable invention.[3] See PAINTING; PATENT, 2.

An act of Congress approved February 4, 1887 (24 St. L. 387), provides — That hereafter, during the term of letters patent for a design, it shall be unlawful for any person other than the owner of said letters patent, without the license of such owner, to apply the design secured by such letters patent, or any colorable imitation thereof, to any article of manufacture for the purpose of sale, or to sell or expose for sale any article of manufacture to which such design or colorable imitation shall, without the license of the owner, have been applied, knowing that the same has been so

---

[1] Southwick *v.* Southwick, 97 Mass. 328 (1867), Bigelow, C. J.; Magrath *v.* Magrath, 103 *id.* 579 (1870).

[2] Coffin *v.* Jenkins, 3 Story, 113 (1844), Story, J.

[3] Cloutman *v.* Tunison, 1 Sumn. 375 (1833), Story, J.; The Mary Conery, 9 F. R. 223 (1881); 3 Kent, 155.

[4] Hanson *v.* South Scituate, 115 Mass. 343 (1874).

[5] Re Zimmerman, 30 F. R. 176 (1887).

[6] Nichols *v.* Allen, 130 Mass. 218 (1881), cases, Gray, Chief Justice.

[7] Commonwealth *v.* Morse, 2 Mass. *131 (1806).

[8] [Binns *v.* Woodruff, 4 Wash. 52 (1821), Washington, J.

---

[1] Gorham Company *v.* White, 14 Wall. 524-28 (1871), cases, Strong J.: Act 29 Aug. 1842; 5 St. L. 543. See Acts 8 July, 1870, and 18 June, 1874: R. S. §§ 4929-33.

[2] Dryfoos *v.* Friedman, 18 F. R. 825 (1884), Wheeler, J.

[3] Western Electric Manuf. Co. *v.* Odell, 18 F. R. 321 (1883), Blodgett, J. For the rule as to damages for infringement, see Dobson *v.* Hartford Carpet Co., 114 U. S. 439, 445 (1885), cases, Blatchford, J.; Dobson *v.* Dornan, 118 *id.* 10, 17 (1886).

applied. Any person violating the provisions, or either of them, of this section, shall be liable in the amount of two hundred and fifty dollars; and in case the total profit made by him from the manufacture or sale, as aforesaid, of the article or articles to which the design, or colorable imitation thereof, has been applied, exceeds the sum of two hundred and fifty dollars, he shall be further liable for the excess of such profit over and above the sum of two hundred and fifty dollars; and the full amount of such liability may be recovered by the owner of the letters patent, to his own use, in any circuit court of the United States having jurisdiction of the parties, either by action at law or upon a bill in equity for an injunction to restrain such infringement.

Sec. 2. Remedies by existing law shall not be impaired; but the owner shall not twice recover the profit made from the infringement.

DESIGNATIO. L. Pointing out: designation.

Designatio personæ. Designation of the person — to a contract. Compare DE-SCRIPTIO.

Designatio unius. See EXPRESSIO, Unius, etc.

DESIGNATION. The use of an expression, instead of the name, to indicate a person or thing. Compare DEMONSTRATION, 2.

DESIRE. In a will, where the object is specified, may raise a trust.[1] See PRECA-TORY; WANT.

DESPATCH. See DISPATCH.

DESPOIL. Imports the use of violence or of clandestine means to deprive a person of something he possesses.[2]

DESTINATION. See ARRIVAL; PORT, Of destination.

DESTROY. To "destroy a vessel" is to unfit her for service beyond the hope of recovery by ordinary means.[3]

Destroyed instrument. See EVIDENCE, Secondary; LOST, 2.

Destroyed property. See MISCHIEF, Malicious; PERISHABLE; RES, Perit, etc.

DETAINER. A withholding; detention. See DETINERE.

1. Restraint of the person, unassented to. See IMPRISONMENT.

2. Withholding possession of property from the rightful owner. See CONVERSION, 2.

Forcible detainer. Keeping possession of another's realty by force and without authority of law.

The original entry may have been peaceable.[1]

Where one, who has entered peaceably upon land, afterward retains possession by force.[2]

Forcible entry and **detainer.** See EN-TRY, 1.

DETECTIVE. See DECOY; REWARD, 1.

DETENTION. See DETAINER; IMPRIS-ONMENT; REPLEVIN.

DETERIORATION. See PERISHABLE; SOUND, 2 (1).

DETERMINE.[3] To end, terminate; to close; to ascertain, settle.

1. To come to an end: as, for an estate for life to determine at death.[4]

2. To decide: as, to determine a question, a controversy. Compare DEFINE.

Determinable. Liable to come to an end: as, a determinable fee, q. v.

Determination. The ending of a thing — an action or proceeding, some right or privilege; also, the act of ascertaining a matter of fact or of law; and, again, the act of deciding, and the decision itself. Compare PREMEDITATE.

"Determined" and "has become void" both imply that the thing has in effect been brought to an end. But while the former comprehends every mode of terminating or of bringing to an end, the latter applies to termination in one specific mode.[5]

To "finally determine" refers to a final determination in the absolute sense. When a special tribunal has power to hear and determine a matter, its decision, within the scope of its authority, binds all parties. In this category, for example, are the decisions of land officers.[6] Compare SEWER; TRIBUNAL.

DETINERE. L. To hold, keep back, detain.

Detinet. He withholds. **Detinuit.** He withheld (has withheld). *Non detinet.* He does not withhold.

Technical words formerly used in actions of replevin to describe the claim, and the denial, that the property was illegally detained. See DETINUE; RE-PLEVIN. Compare DEBET, Et detinet; CAPERE, Cepit.

DETINUE. An action for depriving one of the possession of personalty acquired originally by lawful means.

Thus, if A lends B a horse, and B refuses to restore it, the injury consists in the detaining, not in the orig-

---

[1] Vandyck v. Van Beuren, 1 Caines, *84 (1803).

[2] [Suñol v. Hepburn, 1 Cal. 268 (1850).

[3] United States v. Johns, 1 Wash. 372 (1806).

[1] See 3 Bl. Com. 179.

[2] Ladd v. Dubroca, 45 Ala. 427 (1871); 71 id. 571; 1 Russ. Cr. 310; 41 Ill. 285; 4 Bl. Com. 148.

[3] L. determinare, to end, bound: terminus, limit, boundary.

[4] See 2 Bl. Com. 121, 146; 1 Washb. R. P. 380.

[5] [Sharp v. Curds, 4 Bibb, 548 (1817).

[6] Rector v. Gibbon, 2 McCrary, 286 (1881), cases; Johnson v. Towsley, 13 Wall. 83 (1871).

d taking: and possession may be recovered by an tion of detinue. To successfully maintain the action it is essential: that the defendant came lawfully to possession of the goods; that the plaintiff has a property in them; that they be of some value; and that they be identified. If the jury find for the plaintiff, they must assess the value of the several articles, and damages for the detention. The judgment is that the plaintiff recover the goods, or, if they cannot be had, then their respective values, and the damages awarded for the detention.[1]

The plea of *non detinet* raises the general issue. In some States this action has yielded to the less technical actions of trover and replevin, qq. v.

DETINUIT. See DETINERE.

DETRIMENT. See CONSIDERATION, 2; DAMAGE; DAMAGES.

DEUS. See ACTUS; DENARIUS; EX VISIATIONE.

DEVASTATION. Wasteful use of trust property; particularly, the property of a deceased person. See DEVASTAVIT.

DEVASTAVIT.[2] L. He has wasted. The technical name for waste by an executor or an administrator; occasionally, extravagance or misapplication of assets by any trustee.[3]

A wasting of assets; any act or omission, any mismanagement, by which the estate suffers loss.[4]

A waste of the estate; as, payment by an executor of his private debt with assets, the payment not being intended to replace money advanced on account of debts of the testator.[5]

One who has reasonable ground to believe that a trustee is going to misapply assets can take no advantage of his own act of connivance.[6]

The assets or their proceeds, as far as they may be traced into the hands of persons affected with notice of the misapplication, may be followed and recovered.[6] See BONA, De bonis propriis.

DEVELOP. See MINERAL; MINE; OPERATE.

DEVEST. See VEST.

DEVIATION. In marine insurance, a voluntary departure, without necessity or reasonable cause, from the usual course of the voyage.[7]

Originally, only a departure from the course of the voyage; now, a material departure from or change in the risk insured against, without just cause.[1]

Unnecessary delay may be tantamount to a deviation. It is understood as part of the contract that the voyage is to be prosecuted in the usual, ordinary route, and the business attended to with at least ordinary diligence. The shortness of the time, when delay is really intended, is immaterial.[2]

Turning aside to save the lives of persons upon a distressed vessel is not a deviation.[3]

Nor is it to touch and stay at a port out of the course of the voyage, if such departure is within the usage of the trade. When a bill of lading provides that the goods are to be carried from one port to another, *prima facie* a direct voyage is intended; but this may be controlled by usage. Established usages relating to a voyage are impliedly made part of the contract, if nothing is expressed to the contrary.[4] See TOUCH.

DEVICE. See EQUIVALENT, 2; PATENT, 3.

DEVISARE. L. To separate, divide, distribute: to dispose of property by will; to devise.

Devisavit vel non. Did he make a devise or not; did he make a will. An issue, directed by a court of probate or other court of equity, to be tried by a jury in a court of law, to test the validity of a writing purporting to be a will, when it is alleged, and by *prima facie* proof established, that there was fraud, undue influence, or incapacity in the deceased, at the time of the making of the instrument. See INFLUENCE; INSANITY, 2 (5).

The right of an executor to costs in an issue depends upon the question whether the litigation is for the benefit of those entitled to the estate.[5]

DEVISE. 1, *v.* Originally, to divide or distribute property; now, to give realty by will. See DEVISARE.

2, *n.* A disposition of real property, contained in a man's last will and testament.[6]

A testamentary disposition of land.[7]

In England, an appointment of particular lands to a particular devisee,—in the nature of a conveyance by way of appointment.[8]

---

[1] 3 Bl. Com. 151–52; Story, Eq. §§ 692–711, 906.

[2] Dĕv-as-tā'-vit.

[3] See 2 Bl. Com. 508; 3 *id.* 292; 71 Ala. 240.

[4] [Ayers *v.* Lawrence, 59 N. Y. 197 (1874); Clift *v.* White, 12 *id.* 531 (1855): 2 Williams, Exec. 1629.

[5] Smith *v.* Ayer, 101 U. S. 327–28 (1879), cases.

[6] 1 Story, Eq. §§ 580–81.

[7] [Coffin *v.* Newburyport Ins. Co., 9 Mass. *447 (1812).

[1] Wilkins *v.* Tobacco Ins. Co., 30 Ohio St. 341 (1876): 2 Pars. Mar. Ins. 1.

[2] Coffin *v.* Ins. Co., *ante;* 7 Cranch, 26; 3 Wheat. 159; 8 *id.* 294; Pet. C. C. 98; 3 Kent, 312–14.

[3] 1 Sumn. 400; 2 Wash. 80; 1 Newb. 449; Sprague, 141. See generally 15 Am. Law Rev. 108–20 (1881), cases.

[4] Hostetter *v.* Gray, 11 F. R. 181 (1882), cases.

[5] Sheetz's Appeal, 100 Pa. 197 (1882). See generally 18 Cent. Law J. 83.

[6] [2 Bl. Com. 372.

[7] Fetrow's Estate, 58 Pa. 427 (1868).

[8] Harwood *v.* Goodright, 1 Cowp. 90 (1774), Mansfield, J.; 17 E. L. & Eq. 198.

Devisor.[1] He who gives realty by will. **Devisee.** He to whom it is given.

But "devise" is often used in the sense of "bequeath" and "bequest," as referring to a legacy of personalty. In doubtful cases it is safest to adhere to the technical meaning, on the presumption that the testator used the word in that sense; but this rule will give way when it clearly appears that he understood and used the word in the popular sense.[2]

Contingent devise. When the vesting of the interest is made to depend upon the happening of some future event; in which case, if the event never occurs, or until it occurs, no estate vests. **Vested devise.** A devise which is not subject to a condition, precedent or unperformed. See VEST, 2, Vested.

Executory devise. Such a disposition of lands by will that no estate vests at the death of the devisor, but on some future contingency.[3]

A limitation by will of a future estate or interest in lands or chattels.[4]

Such a limitation of a future estate or interest in lands as the law admits in the case of a will, though contrary to the rules of limitation in conveyances at common law.[5]

Not a mere possibility, but a substantial interest, and in respect to transmissibility stands on the same footing with a contingent remainder.[6]

By it a remainder may be created contrary to the general rule, on the supposition that the testator acted without advice... An executory devise differs from a "remainder" in that it needs no particular estate to support it; by it a fee-simple or other less estate may be limited after a fee-simple; and by means of it a remainder may be limited of a chattel-interest, after a particular estate for life.[7]

A devise *in futuro* to an artificial being to be created is good as an executory devise.[8]

Although an estate may be devised to one in fee-simple or fee-tail, with a limitation over by way of an executory devise, yet, when the will shows a clear purpose to give an absolute power of disposition to the first taker, the limitation over is void.[9]

"If there be an absolute power of disposition given by the will to the first taker, as if an estate be devised to A in fee and if he dies *possessed* of the property without lawful issue, the remainder over, or the remainder over the property which he, dying without heirs, *should leave*, or without selling or devising the same,— in all such cases the remainder over is void as a remainder because of the preceding fee, and it is void as an executory devise because the limitation is inconsistent with the absolute estate or power of disposition expressly given or necessarily implied by the will."[1]

See ACCUMULATION; BEQUEST; DIE, Without children; LAPSE; LEGACY; REMAINDER; RESIDUARY; WILL, 2.

DEVOLUTION. 1. Transfer to a successor in office.

2. A passing from a person dying to a person living: as, the devolution of a title.[2]

"Devolution by law" occurs when the title is such that an heir takes under it by descent from an "ancestor" according to the rules of law applicable to the descent of heritable estates; and in all cases of descent, the estate of the successor is immediately "derived" from the "ancestor" from whom the estate descends.[3]

DI. See DIS.

DIAGRAM. See BOOK, 1.

DICE. See GAME, 2.

DICTA. See DICTUM.

DICTATE. To pronounce orally what is to be written down by another at the same time; as, to dictate a will.[4] See HOLOGRAPH.

DICTIONARY. See DEFINITION; WORD.

No meaning of a word, which has received a construction by law or uniform custom, can be adopted from the dictionaries in conflict with that construction. And where a word, as used, is reconcilable with law or established custom, a different meaning cannot be given to it upon the authority of a lexicographer.[5]

The dictionary clause of a statute is the section which defines what persons, places, things, etc., shall be included within the terms of the statute.[6]

DICTUM. L. A saying, observation, remark. Plural, *dicta*.

1. A voluntary statement; a comment. **Gratis dictum.** A gratuitous remark. A statement one is not required to make, and

---

[1] Dĕ-vīz'-or; dĕv-ĭ-zee'.

[2] Ladd *v.* Harvey, 21 N. H. 528 (1850); Fetrow's Estate, 58 Pa. 427 (1868); 21 Barb. 561; 13 *id.* 109.

[3] [2 Bl. Com. 172.

[4] Brown's Estate, 38 Pa. 294 (1861).

[5] Fearne, Cont. Rem. 386; Jarman, Wills, 864.

[6] Medley *v.* Medley, 81 Va. 268-72 (1886), cases.

[7] 2 Bl. Com. 173-75; Doe *v.* Considine, 6 Wall. 474-75 (1867); 50 Conn. 407; 2 Mich. 296; 52 N. H. 273; 11 Wend. 278; 31 Barb. 566; 2 Washb. R. P. 679.

[8] Ould *v.* Washington Hospital, 93 U. S. 313 (1877), cases; 2 Story, Eq. §§ 1146, 1160.

[9] Howard *v.* Carusi, 109 U. S. 730 (1883); Hoxsey *v.* Hoxsey, 37 N. J. E. 22 (1883); 16 S. C. 325.

---

[1] 4 Kent, 271.

[2] Parr *v.* Parr, 7 Eng. Ch. *648 (1833).

[3] Earl of Zetland *v.* Lord-Advocate, 3 Ap. Cas. 520 (1878). "Devolution of liability," 61 Wis. 380. In Louisiana an appeal may be "devolutive" or suspensive, 21 La. An. 295; 30 F. R. 538.

[4] [Prendergast *v.* Prendergast, 16 La. An. 220 (1861); Hamilton *v.* Hamilton, 6 Mart. 143 (1827).

[5] State *ex rel.* Belford *v.* Hueston, 44 Ohio St. 6 (1886), Spear, J.

[6] See R. S. §§ 1-5, 5013; 1 Shars. Bl. Com. 87.

for which he is not liable in damages for injury traceable thereto.[1]

As, an assertion by a vendor that his land is fit for a certain purpose, or is worth so much, cost so much, or that he has refused so much for it.[1] See CAVEAT, Emptor; COMMENDATIO.

2. An opinion expressed by a judge on a point not necessarily arising in a case.[2]

Dicta are opinions of a judge which do not embody the resolution or determination of the court, and, being made without argument or full consideration, are not the professed deliberate determinations of the judge himself.[3]

Obiter dicta. Such opinions, uttered "by the way," not upon the point or question pending, but as if turning aside for the time from the main topic to a collateral subject.[3] Often, simply, *obiter* or an *obiter*.

An expression of opinion upon a point in a case, argued by counsel and deliberately passed upon by the court, though not essential to the disposition of the case, if a *dictum* at all, is a "judicial" *dictum* as distinguished from a mere *obiter dictum*, i. e., an expression originating alone with the judge who writes the opinion, as an argument or illustration.[4]

To make an opinion a decision there must have been an application of the judicial mind to the precise question necessary to be determined in order to fix the rights of the parties. Therefore the Supreme Court has never held itself bound by any part of an opinion which was not needful to the ascertainment of the question between the parties.[5]

"The case called for nothing more; if more was intended by the judge who delivered the opinion, it was purely *obiter*."[6]

Dicta are not binding as precedents; at most they receive the respect due to the private opinions of the judges by whom uttered.[7] See DECISION; OPINION, 3.

DICTUS. See ALIAS.

DIE; DYING; DEATH. In several phrases, have a technical meaning:

Die by his own hand or **by suicide.** In policies of life insurance, used in a proviso exempting the company from liability.

In such case the words mean: (1) That if the assured, being in the possession of his ordinary reasoning faculties, from any cause and by any means, intentionally takes his own life, there can be no recovery;

(2) that if the death is caused by the voluntary act of the assured, he knowing and intending that death shall be the result of his act, but when his reasoning faculties are so far impaired that he is not able to understand the moral character, the general nature, consequences, and effects of the act; or when he is impelled thereto by an insane impulse, which he has no power to resist,—such death is not within the contemplation of the parties, and the insurer is liable.[1]

The proviso refers to an act of *criminal* self-destruction; it does not apply to an insane person who takes his own life intending to take it, and knowing that death would be the result.[2]

"Die by his own hand," "die by suicide," and "commit suicide," are synonymous with voluntary suicide.[2] But the addition of the condition "sane or insane" will relieve the insurer, whatever be the condition of mind of the insured.[3,2]

In 1872, when Terry's Case was decided, there was a conflict of opinion as to the interpretation to be placed upon the words "die by his own hand" or "die by suicide." All authorities agreed that the phrases did not cover every possible case of self-destruction in a blind frenzy or under an overwhelming insane impulse. Some courts held that they included every case in which a man, sane or insane, voluntarily took his own life; others, that insane self-destruction was not within the condition. . If a man's reason is so clouded or disturbed by insanity as to prevent his understanding the real nature of his act, as regards either its physical consequence or its moral aspect, the case appears to come within the forcible words uttered by the late Mr. Justice Nelson, when Chief Justice of New York, in the earliest American case upon the subject: "Self-destruction by a fellow-being, bereft of reason, can with no more propriety be ascribed to his own hand than to the deadly instrument that he may have used for the purpose;" and, whether it was by drowning, poisoning, hanging or other manner, "was no more his act, in the sense of the law, than if he had been impelled by irresistible physical power."[4]

Die in consequence of a violation of law. Expresses another condition under which a policy of life insurance will be rendered void.

In a recent case it was held that so long as there was a violation of law on the part of the assured, and death as its result, it was immaterial in what manner the death was produced, excepting that there must

[1] Medbury v. Watson, 6 Metc. 259 (1843); Gordon v. Parmelee, 2 Allen, 214 (1861).

[2] State v. Clarke, 3 Nev. 572 (1867), Beatty, C. J.

[3] Rohrback v. Germania Fire Ins. Co., 62 N. Y. 58 (1875), Folger, J.

[4] Buchner v. Chicago, &c. R. Co., 60 Wis. 267–69 (1884), Cassoday, J.

[5] Carroll v. Lessee of Carroll, 16 How. 287 (1853), Curtis, J.; 6 Wheat. 399.

[6] United States v. County of Clark, 96 U. S. 218 (1877), Strong, J.; 107 id. 179.

[7] See 17 F. R. 423, 425.

[1] Mutual Life Ins. Co. v. Terry, 15 Wall. 583 (1872), Hunt, J.; 1 Dill. 403.

[2] Bigelow v. Berkshire Life Ins. Co., 93 U. S. 286 (1876), cases; Connecticut Mut. Life Ins. Co. v. Groom, 86 Pa. 96–98 (1878), cases; Cooper v. Massachusetts Life Ins. Co., 102 Mass. 228 (1869), cases; Knights of the Golden Rule v. Ainsworth, 71 Ala. 444–49 (1882), cases.

[3] Charter Oak Life Ins. Co. v. Rodel, 95 U. S. 232 (1877), cases.

[4] Manhattan Life Ins. Co. v. Broughton, 109 U. S. 127, 131 (Nov. 5, 1883), cases, Gray, J., quoting Breasted v. Farmers' Loan & Trust Co., 4 Hill, 75 (1843).

have been a direct connection between the criminal act and the death.[1]

In such case "violation of law" means crime; and "known violation of law" indicates a voluntary criminal act. The burden of proof is upon the insurer.[2]

Death from suicide is not a death "in violation of the criminal laws" of New York.[3]

Die without children, heirs, or issue. In a will, as applied to realty, *prima facie* import an indefinite failure of issue,— total extinction of the testator's family, or the death of all his descendants to the remotest generation.

This has uniformly been the construction, when there were no expressions in the will controlling the legal meaning of the words, or pointing to a definite failure of issue.[4]

As applied to personalty, construed to mean dying without heirs living at the death of the devisee.[5]

When there is anything in a gift or limitation to show that the testator meant a failure of issue in the life-time of the first taker, instead of an indefinite failure, a limitation over is construed as an executory devise in defeasance of a fee-simple, and not as a remainder sustained by an estate-tail.[6]

Whether a presumption that a person died without issue will be indulged depends upon the circumstances shown in each case. If, for instance, circumstances are proven indicating non-marriage or childlessness, then death without issue may be presumed.[7] See further DEFINITE; ISSUE, 5.

DIES. L. A day; the day.

Ad diem. At the day; on the very day: as, the *ad diem* demand of a bill.[8]

Comperuit ad diem. He appeared at the day. A plea that the defendant in an action upon a bail bond appeared on the day designated in the bond.

---

[1] Murray *v.* N. Y. Life Ins. Co., 30 Hun, 429 (1883); Bradley *v.* Mut. Benefit Co., 45 N. Y. 422 (1871); Cluff *v.* Mut. Benefit Life Ins. Co., 95 Mass. 316 (1866).

[2] Cluff *v.* Mut. Benefit Life Ins. Co., 99 Mass. 326 (1868).

[3] Darrow *v.* Family Fund Society, 42 Hun, 245 (1886).

[4] See Williams *v.* Turner, 10 Yerg. 289 (1837); Wardell *v.* Allaire, 20 N. J. L. 9–16 (1842), cases; Davies *v.* Steele, 38 N. J. E. 170–73 (1884); 37 *id.* 81; Gray *v.* Bridgeforth, 33 Miss. 344 (1857); Wilson *v.* Wilson, 32 Barb. 332 (1860); *Re* Merceron's Trusts, 4 Ch. Div. 182 (1876): 20 Moak, 759; Snyder's Appeal, 95 Pa. 177–81 (1880), cases; Magrum *v.* Piester, 16 S. C. 323–24 (1881); Quigley *v.* Gridley, 132 Mass. 37 (1882), cases; Schmaunz *v.* Göss, *ib.* 145 (1882).

[5] Wallis *v.* Woodland, 32 Md. 104 (1869); Moffat *v.* Strong, 10 Johns. *15 (1813).

[6] Williams, R. P., 4 Rawle's ed., 207, cases; 26 Am. Law Rev. 107–15 (1888), cases.

[7] Bank of Louisville *v.* Trustees of Public Schools, 83 Ky. 231–32 (1885), cases.

[8] 101 U. S. 565.

Solvit ad diem. He paid on the day. *Solvit post diem.* He paid after the day. Pleas to actions on bonds for the payment of money.

Dies a quo. The day from which. **Dies ad quem.** The day to which. The day from which, and the day to which, to compute time.

Dies dominicus. The Lord's day — Sunday. **Dies juridicus.** A judicial or court day.

Dies dominicus non est juridicus. Sunday is a non-judicial day — is not a day for court business, except as to the issue and return of criminal process. Whence *dies non* (juridicus): a non-judicial day.

Dies non juridicus means only that process ordinarily cannot issue, be executed, or returned, and that courts do not sit, on that day. It does not mean that no judicial action can then be had.[1] See SUNDAY.

A civil process awarded or a judgment entered on a holiday is not void.[2] See HOLIDAY.

Quarto die post. On the fourth day thereafter.

On every return-day in the term the person summoned has three days of grace, beyond the day named in the writ, in which to make his appearance, and if he appears on the fourth day inclusive, *quarto die post*, it is sufficient. . . The feudal law allowed three distinct days of citation, before the defendant was adjudged contumacious for not appearing. . . At the beginning of each term, the court does not usually sit for the dispatch of business till the fourth or appearance day.[3]

DIFFERENCES. See OPTION, Contract.

DIFFICULTY. 1. As applicable to what takes place between parties, when it results in a breach of the peace or a flagrant violation of law, is in general use, and well understood.[4]

It is of constant application in legal proceedings, and in the reports of adjudicated cases. It is expressive of a group or collection of ideas that cannot, perhaps, be imparted so well by any other term.[4]

2. In the performance of a covenant, see POSSIBLE.

DIGEST. A compilation presenting the substance of many books in one, under an arrangement (usually alphabetical) intended to facilitate reference.

It reproduces the rules of the decisions by mere quotation and extract.[5]

---

[1] State *v.* Ricketts, 74 N. C. 193 (1876).

[2] Paine *v.* Fresco, 1 Co. Ct. R. 562 (Pa., 1886), cases.

[3] 3 Bl. Com. 278.

[4] Gainey *v.* People, 97 Ill. 279 (1881).

[5] [Abbott's Law Dict.

Simply a manual of reference to the original cases, which are the authority.[1]

See ABRIDGMENT; COMPILATION.

DIGGING. May mean excavating, and not be confined to removing earth as distinguished from rock.[2]

DIGNITY. In old English law, a species of incorporeal hereditament.

Dignities bear a near relation to offices. They were originally annexed to the possession of certain estates in land, and created by a grant of those estates. Although now little more than personal distinctions, they are still classed under the head of realty.[3]

DILAPIDATION. See PERISHABLE.

DILATORY. Said of a defense or a plea that resists the plaintiff's present right of recovery by interposing some temporary objection, as that the court has no jurisdiction, that the plaintiff lacks capacity to sue.[4] See PLEA.

DILIGENCE. 1. In the law of bailment and of common carriers of persons is opposed to "negligence," and synonymous with "care" in its three degrees of slight, ordinary, and extraordinary or great.[5]

Due diligence. What constitutes "due diligence," in an action to recover damages caused by negligence, is for the jury; and the burden of proof is with the plaintiff to show the negligence.[6]

Ordinary diligence. That degree of care, attention, or exertion which, under the circumstances, a man of ordinary prudence and discretion would use in reference to the particular thing were it his own property, or in doing the particular thing were it his own concern.[7]

"Common" or "ordinary" diligence is that degree of diligence which men in general exert in respect to their own concerns, and not any one man in particular.[8]

See further BAILMENT; CARE; CARRIER; NEGLIGENCE.

2. To charge the indorser of a bill or note, upon non-payment by the maker or acceptor,

the exercise of " diligence," " due diligence," or " reasonable diligence " toward notifying the indorser of the fact of non-payment, is required by the law-merchant.

Due diligence. Some effort or attempt to find the party, which the court or judge shall be satisfied is reasonable under the circumstances.[1] See PROTEST, 2.

Diligently inquire. Said of a grand jury, see INQUIRY, 2.

DIMINUTION. Omission; defect; incompleteness.

Where the whole of a record is not properly or not truly certified by an inferior court to the court of review the party injured thereby may allege or "suggest" diminution of the record, and cause it to be rectified[2] — by means of a writ of *certiorari*, q. v.

DIPLOMATIC OFFICERS. Ambassadors, envoys extraordinary, ministers plenipotentiary, ministers resident, commissioners, chargés d'affaires, agents and secretaries of legation.[3] See CONSUL; MINISTER, 3.

DIPSOMANIA. See INTEMPERATE.

DIRECT. 1, *adj.* Straight; not circuitous; immediate; the first or original.

Opposed (1) to **indirect**: as, a direct or indirect — confession, contempt, damage, docket or index, examination, interest, interrogatory or question, tax, *qq. v.*

Opposed (2) to **redirect**, the direct over again: as, an examination (*q. v.*) following a cross-examination.

Opposed (3) to *cross*: as in direct examination; to *collateral*: as, the direct line of descent; to *circumstantial*: as, direct evidence; to *contingent* or *remote*: as, a direct interest; to *consequential*: as, direct damages. See those substantives.

The "most direct route of travel" between two places, within the meaning of a statute giving a sheriff mileage for carrying prisoners to a penitentiary, is the railroad, although it is sixty-four miles long while the highway is but thirty-five.[4] See DISTANCE.

To "proceed direct" to a port is to take a direct course, without deviation or unreasonable delay; not, to leave port immediately.[5]

What cannot be done directly cannot be done indirectly.[6]

---

[1] [Bouvier's Law Dict.; 1 Bl. Com. 81.
[2] Sherman v. New York City, 1 N. Y. 320 (1848).
[3] 2 Bl. Com. 37; 1 Ld. Raym. 13; 7 Rep. 122.
[4] See 3 Bl. Com. 301.
[5] See Brand v. Troy, &c. R. Co., 8 Barb. 378 (1850); 19 How. Pr. 219; 29 Ala. 305.
[6] Haff v. Minneapolis, &c. R. Co., 14 F. R. 558 (1882).
[7] Swigert v. Graham, 7 B. Mon. 663 (1847), Marshall, Chief Justice.
[8] City of Rockford v. Hilderbrand, 61 Ill. 160 (1871), Sheldon, J.; 71 Ala. 121; 5 Kan. 180; 71 Me. 41; 6 Metc.; 25 Mich. 297; 3 Brewst. 14; 31 Pa. 572.

[1] Bixby v. Smith, 49 How. Pr. 53 (1874); Demond v. Burnham, 132 Mass. 341 (1882); Bank of Columbia v. Lawrence, 1 Am. L. C. 405; Byles, Bills, 275.
[2] [4 Bl. Com. 390; Tidd, Pr. 1109.
[3] R. S. § 1674.
[4] Maynard v. Cedar County, 51 Iowa, 431 (1879).
[5] The Onrust, 6 Blatch. 536 (1869).
[6] New York v. Louisiana, 108 U. S. 91 (1882).

2, *v.* To guide, instruct, charge. Opposed, **misdirect**, to instruct wrongly, to mislead: as, to direct, and to misdirect, a jury in the law which is to regulate its deliberations and verdict. See further CHARGE, 2 (2, c).

Directory. 1, *adj.* Containing instructions as to what may be done: as, a directory — statute, clause, trust. Opposed, *mandatory*, q. v.

"Directory," referring to a charter, means that it is to be considered as giving directions which ought to be followed, not as so limiting the power that it cannot be effectually exercised without observing them.[1] See LEGAL, Illegal; PROHIBITION, 1.

2, *n.* A board of directors, *q. v.*

DIRECTORIES. See COPYRIGHT.

Where the commercial value of two society directories depends upon the judgment of the compilers in selecting names, each is original as far as the selection is original. One compiler may not merely copy names from the other's book; but he may use it to verify the orthography of names or the correctness of addresses. The existence of the same errors in the two books raises a presumption of piracy that can be overcome only by clear evidence to the contrary.[2]

DIRECTORS. Persons legally chosen to manage the affairs of a corporation or company.

Directors, board of, or directory. The whole body of such managers, jointly considered.

The directors of a corporation are subject to the obligations imposed upon trustees and agents.[3]

They are officers and agents, and represent the interests of the abstract legal entity, and of those who own the shares of its stock.[4]

To the stockholders they are not as technical trustees, but as mandataries, bound to exercise ordinary skill and diligence. They are not liable for a mistake of judgment, within the scope of their powers; but they are responsible for losses occasioned by embezzlement, willful misconduct, breach of trust, or gross inattention by which fraud has been perpetrated by an agent, officer, or co-director.[5]

They are at least *quasi* trustees for the creditors of the corporation. When that is insolvent good faith forbids that they use their position to save themselves or one of their number at the expense of other creditors.[6]

The directors of a corporation are its exclusive executive agents, and, as it can act only through them, the powers vested in the corporation are deemed conferred upon its representatives; but they are, nevertheless, trustees for the stockholders. The law recognizes the stockholders as the ultimately controlling power in the corporation, because they may at each authorized election entirely change the organization, and may at any time keep the trustees within the line of faithful administration by an appeal to a court of equity. . . General power in a board of directors "to perform all corporate acts" refers to the ordinary business transactions of the corporation. The stockholders alone can make or authorize fundamental or organic changes.[1]

As a rule, the directors of a corporation are only required, in the management of its affairs, to keep within the limits of its powers and to exercise good faith and honesty. They undertake, by virtue of the assumption of the duties incumbent on them, to perform those duties according to the best of their judgment and with reasonable diligence, and a mere error of judgment will not subject them to personal liability for its consequences. And unless there has been some violation of the charter or the constating instruments, or unless there is shown to be a want of good faith, or a willful abuse of discretion, or negligence, there will be no personal liability. They are personally only bound, in the management of the affairs of the corporation, to use diligence and prudence, such as men usually exercise in the management of their own affairs of a similar nature. But they are personally liable if they suffer the corporate funds or property to be wasted by gross negligence and inattention to the duties of their trust.[2]

That which directors, by proper diligence, ought to have known as to the general course of business in their bank, they may be presumed to have known, in any contest between the corporation and those who are justified by the circumstances in dealing with its officers upon the basis of that course of business.[3]

See CORPORATION; DIVIDEND, 3; MEETING; MINUTES, 2; TRUST, 1.

---

[1] Town of Danville *v.* Shelton, 76 Va. 311 (1882).

[2] List Publishing Co. *v.* Keller, 30 F. R. 772 (1887), Wallace, J.

[3] Wardell *v.* Union Pacific R. Co., 103 U. S. 658 (1880), cases.

[4] Twin-Lick Oil Co. *v.* Marbury, 91 U. S. 589, 587 (1875).

[5] Spering's Appeal, 71 Pa. 20 (1872), cases, Sharswood, J.; United Society of Shakers *v.* Underwood, 9 Bush, 609 (1873), cases; First Nat. Bank of Ft. Scott *v.* Drake, 29 Kan. 326–27 (1883); Morse, Banks, 70.

[6] Coons *v.* Tome, 9 F. R. 532 (1881); s. c. 13 Rep. 136;

Drury *v.* Cross, 7 Wall. 302 (1868); Jackson *v.* Ludeling, 21 *id.* 616 (1874); Richards *v.* New Hampshire Ins. Co., 43 N. H. 263 (1861).

[1] Cass *v.* Manchester Iron, &c. Co., 9 F. R. 640 (1881); s. c. 13 Rep. 167.

[2] Ackerman *v.* Halsey, 37 N. J. E. 363 (1883), cases, Runyon, Ch. See also Williams *v.* Hilliard, 38 *id.* 374 (1884), cases; Chicago City R. Co. *v.* Allerton, 18 Wall. 233 (1873); Bradley *v.* Farwell, 1 Holmes, 440 (1874), cases.

Directors as fiduciaries, Bent *v.* Priest, 86 Mo. 476 (1885), cases: 25 Am. Reg. 125–33 (1886), cases. Liability of, of national banks, and generally, Movius *v.* Lee, 30 F. R. 306–7 (1887), cases; Witters *v.* Sowles, 31 *id.* 1 (1887), cases; 23 Cent. Law J. 172 (1886), cases. Powers of, of banks, 22 Cent. Law J. 318 (1886), cases; of corporations generally, 19 *id.* 305–10, 327–30 (1884), cases; 6 South. Law Rev. 386–413 (1880), cases. Dealing with the corporation, 1 Col. Law T. 13–95 (1888).

[3] Martin *v.* Webb, 110 U. S. 15 (1884), Harlan, J.

DIS. A prefix or inseparable preposition, used in compounds. In the Latin, corresponds to asunder, apart, in two; and denotes separation, parting from, and hence has the force of a privative or negative.

In a few words, becomes *di-*; but *di-* may be a form of *de*, as in divest.

DISABILITY. Incapacity for action under the law; incapacity to do a legal act.[1]

A personal incapacity; and may relate to power to contract or to sue, and arise from want of sufficient understanding, as in cases of lunacy and infancy; or from want of freedom of will, as in cases of coverture and duress; or from the policy of the law, as in cases of alienage, outlawry, and the like.[2]

Any incapacity of acquiring or transmitting a right, or of resisting a wrong; and arises from the act of the party, of his ancestor, of the law, or of God.[3]

Civil disability. Disqualification created by the law. **Physical disability.** An infirmity inherent in the constitution of the body or mind.

In a statute providing what shall be done in the event of the death or disability of a public officer, "disability" will cover any cause which prevents the officer from acting, as, his resignation.[4]

Where there are two or more co-existing disabilities in the same person he is not obliged to act until the last disability is removed.[5] Thus, coverture enables a wife to postpone avoidance of a deed made in infancy to a reasonable time after the coverture is ended, without regard to the statute of limitations. One under a disability to make a contract cannot confirm or disaffirm a voidable contract.[6]

Compare CAPACITY; QUALIFY. See ABATE, 5; AFFIRM, 2; RATIFICATION.

Disabling. Disqualifying; incapacitating; restricting; restraining: as, a disabling statute, *q. v.*

DISAFFIRM. See AFFIRM, 2.

DISAGREE. See JURY; VERDICT.

DISALLOW. See ALLOW.

DISAPPROVE. See ESTOPPEL; PROTEST, 1.

DISBAR. See BAR, 1.

DISBURSEMENT.[7] Paying out money; also, the money itself.

By an administrator — money or currency paid in extinguishment of the liabilities of the decedent or of the expenses of administration.[8]

Also, an expenditure of money necessarily incurred in the regular course of proceedings in an action, and allowable as costs.[1] Compare REIMBURSE. See EARNINGS.

DISCHARGE. As a verb and noun, conveys the idea of relieving of a charge, burden, weight, or of a duty, service, or responsibility.

1, *v.* (1) To empty of cargo or freight: as, to discharge a vessel; also, to remove that with which a thing is laden: as, to discharge a cargo. See DISPATCH; PORT, Of discharge.

(2) To extinguish, satisfy: as, to discharge a demand, debt, legacy, lien, judgment, incumbrance, obligation, *qq. v.*

(3) To free from the payment of indebtedness already incurred: as, to discharge a bankrupt, an insolvent, *qq. v.*

(4) To absolve from contingent pecuniary liability: as, to discharge an indorser, a surety, a guarantor, *qq. v.*

(5) To relieve from the performance of the duties of a trust: as, to discharge an assignee, administrator, executor, guardian, receiver, *qq. v.*

(6) To relieve from further service in the consideration of a cause; to dismiss: as, to discharge a jury.

(7) To set at liberty; to free from imprisonment: as, to discharge a prisoner, a convict.

(8) To decline further to entertain a proceeding; to vacate: as, to discharge a rule.

2, *n.* (1) Relief from some burden or duty: extinguishment or satisfaction of an obligation; exoneration from responsibility, accountability, liability; exemption from service or action; liberation; annulment. See CHARGE, 2.

(2) Any such action in itself considered.

(3) The certificate or document in evidence thereof.

The discharge of a guardian is any mode by which the relation of guardianship is effectually determined and brought to a close: as, by his removal, resignation, or death, by the marriage of a female ward, by the arrival of a minor ward at the age of twenty-one, or otherwise.[2]

To be construed a discharge for money, a paper need not contain the word "discharge;" every receipt for money, which is not an accountable receipt, is a discharge for money.[3]

---

[1] [Wiesner *v.* Zaun, 39 Wis. 206 (1875): Burrill.

[2] Meeks *v.* Vassault, 3 Saw. 213 (1874), Sawyer, Cir. J.

[3] See 32 Barb. 480; 108 Ind. 195; 16 Alb. L. J. 292; 3 Bl. Com. 301; Coke, Inst. l. 5, p. 21; l. 8, p. 69.

[4] State *v.* City of Newark, 27 N. J. L. 197 (1858).

[5] Mercer's Lessee *v.* Selden, 1 How. 37 (1843).

[6] Sims *v.* Everhardt, 102 U. S. 310 (1880), cases; 77 Va. 72.

[7] F. *desbourser*, to take out of a purse.

[8] Wright *v.* Wilkerson, 41 Ala. 272 (1867).

---

[1] Case *v.* Price, 9 Abb. Pr. 114 (1859). And see Hanover *v.* Reynolds, 4 Dem. 385 (1886); N. Y. Code, § 3256.

[2] Loring *v.* Alline, 9 Cush. 70 (1851), Shaw, C. J.

[3] [Commonwealth *v.* Talbot, 2 Allen, 162 (1861), cases.

DISCLAIMER. The act, declaration, or document by which a person denies, disavows, or renounces some interest or right which he formerly claimed, or which has been imputed or offered to him.[1]

1. In feudal law, when a tenant neglected to render services, and, upon an action brought to recover them, disclaimed to hold of the lord.

In a court of record, a forfeiture of the lands to the lord.[2]

When the tenant, upon a writ of assize of rent, or on a replevin, disavowed his tenure, whereby the lord lost the verdict, the lord could thereupon have a writ of right, *sur disclaimer;* and, upon proof of the tenure, recover the land as a punishment to the tenant for his false disclaimer.[3]

A disclaimer must be a renunciation by the party of his character of tenant, by setting up a title in another or by claiming title in himself.[4]

2. A formal mode of expressing a grantee's dissent to a conveyance before the title has become vested in him.[5]

Prevents the estate from passing from the grantor.[5]

It is essential that the estate disclaimed would vest but for the disclaimer, unless there be an express condition that the grantee shall elect.[6]

Filed in an action to try title to land, admits the plaintiff's title; and entitles the defendant to his costs, unless he was in possession when the suit was brought.[7]

3. Renunciation of what is or seems to be part of a patentee's claim for invention, and as to which he has no valid claim.

Wherever, through inadvertence, accident, or mistake, and without any willful default or intent to defraud or mislead the public, a patentee in his specification has claimed more than that of which he was the original and first inventor or discoverer, his patent is valid for all that part which is truly and justly his own, provided the same is a material and substantial part of the thing patented, and definitely distinguishable from the parts claimed without right; and the patentee, upon seasonably recording in the patent office a disclaimer in writing of the parts which he did not invent, or to which he has no valid claim, may maintain a suit upon that part which he is entitled to hold, although in a suit brought before the disclaimer he cannot recover costs. A reissued patent is within the letter and spirit of these provisions.[8]

Drawings cannot be used, even on an application for a reissue;[1] much less, on a disclaimer, to change the patent, and make it embrace a different invention from that described in the specification.[2] See ISSUE, 1.

4. When a defendant denies that he has or claims any right to the thing in demand by the plaintiff's bill, and disclaims, that is, renounces, all claim thereto.[3]

Where the defendant renounces all claim to the subject of the demand made by the plaintiff's bill.[4]

Distinct in substance from an answer, although sometimes confounded with it; and it can seldom be put in without an answer.[4]

DISCLOSE. 1. "Disclosing a defense upon the merits" means opening out and letting the judge see whether there really is a defense.[5]

2. An agent is said to "disclose his principal" when he makes known who his principal is; and principals are said to be "disclosed" or "undisclosed." See AGENT; AUCTIONEER.

DISCONTINUANCE. The cessation of an action or an estate.

1. (1) A chasm or gap left by neglecting to enter a continuance in an action.[6]

When a plaintiff fails to follow up his case and leaves a chasm in the proceedings by his laches.[7]

When the plaintiff leaves a chasm in the proceedings, as by not continuing the process regularly from time to time, the suit is discontinued, and the defendant need not attend.[8] See CONTINUANCE; DISMISS.

(2) At common law, the act of the plaintiff in demurring or replying to a plea which answered a part of his declaration.

By not taking judgment for the part unanswered, he was held not to have followed up his whole demand.[9]

2. When, at common law, a tenant in tail granted a larger estate than he could rightfully transfer.

Abolished in England in 1834; but prior thereto had already become obsolete.[10]

---

[1] [Abbott, Law Dict.]

[2] [2 Bl. Com. 275.

[3] 3 Bl. Com. 233.

[4] Williams *v.* Cooper, 39 E. C. L. 384 (1840), Tindal, Chief Justice.

[5] [Watson *v.* Watson, 13 Conn. 85 (1839).

[6] Jackson *v.* Richards, 6 Cow. 620 (1827).

[7] Wootters *v.* Hall, 67 Tex. 513 (1887); Prescott *v.* Hutchinson, 13 Mass. *442 (1816).

[8] Gage *v.* Herring, 107 U. S. 646 (1882), cases, Gray, J.; United States Cartridge Co. *v.* Union Cartridge Co., 112 *id.* 642 (1884); R. S. §§ 4917, 4922; 17 Blatch. 67-69.

[1] Parker & Whipple Co. *v.* Yale Lock Co., 123 U. S. 87 (1887), cases.

[2] Hailes *v.* Albany Stove Co., 123 U. S. 582 (1887).

[3] 1 Daniel, Ch. Pr. 706.

[4] Story, Eq. Pl. § 883.

[5] Whiley *v.* Whiley, 93 E. C. L. *668 (1858).

[6] Taft *v.* Northern Transportation Co., 56 N. H. 416 (1876), Cushing, C. J.

[7] Roundtree *v.* Key, 71 Ala. 215 (1883), Jackson, C. J.; *ib.* 367.

[8] [3 Bl. Com. 296.

[9] See Steph. Plead. 241; Gould, Pl. 336.

[10] See 3 Bl. Com. 172; 1 Steph. Com. 510, n.

DISCOUNT. 1. A counting off; an allowance or deduction from a gross sum on any account.[1]

A right which a debtor has to an abatement of the demand against him in consequence of a partial failure of the consideration, or on account of some equity arising out of the transaction on which the demand is founded.[2]

2. The difference between what is paid for a claim evidenced by negotiable paper and the face amount thereof.

A bank of discount furnishes loans upon drafts, promissory notes, bonds, and other securities. . . "Discounting" and "buying" a note are not identical. The latter denotes the transaction "when the seller does not indorse the note and is not accountable for it." . . Power to carry on the business of banking, by discounting evidences of debt, is merely an authority to lend money thereon, with the right to deduct the legal rate of interest in advance.[3]

In *Atlantic State Bank* v. *Savery*, 82 N. Y. 291, 302 (1880), it was decided that the purchase of a promissory note for a less sum than its face is a discount thereof within the meaning of the provision of the Banking Act of that State (Laws of 1836, c. 260, § 18), which authorizes associations organized under it to discount bills and notes. And in support of that definition of the terms the court cites the authority of McLeod on Banking, p. 43, where the author says, "The difference between the price of the debt and the amount of the debt is called discount," and "to buy or purchase a debt is always in commerce termed to discount it." In *Fleckner* v. *Bank of United States*, 8 Wheat. 350 (1823), Mr. Justice Story said, "Nothing can be clearer than that, by the language of the commercial world and the settled practice of banks, a discount by a bank means a deduction or drawback made upon its advances or loans of money, upon negotiable paper or other evidences of debt, payable at a future day, which are transferred to the bank," and added that if the transaction could properly be called a sale "it is a purchase by way of discount." Discount, then, is the difference between the price and the amount of the debt, the evidence of which is transferred, and that difference represents interest charged, being at some rate, according to which the price paid, if invested until the maturity of the debt, will just produce its amount. And the advance, therefore, upon every note discounted, without reference to its character as business or accommodation paper, is properly denominated a "loan," for interest is predicable only of loans, being the price paid for the use of money. The specific power given to national banks (Rev. St. § 5136) is "to carry on the business of banking by discounting and negotiating promissory notes, drafts,

bills of exchange, and other evidences of debt." So that the discount of negotiable paper is the form according to which they are authorized to make their loans, and the terms loans and discounts are synonymous. It was so held in *Talmage* v. *Pell*, 3 Seld. 328, 339 (1852); and in *Niagara County Bank* v. *Baker*, 15 Ohio St. 68, 87 (1864), the point decided was that "to discount paper, as understood in the business of banking, is only a mode of lending money with the right to take the interest allowed by law in advance." . . A national bank is restricted to taking no more than seven per centum for the discount of negotiable paper when the person discounting is an indorser thereon.[1] See USURY.

DISCOVERT. See COVERT.

DISCOVERY.[2] A bringing to light; making known for the first time; disclosure; also, that which is found out, revealed, disclosed.

1. Finding a previously unknown country or land. Spoken of as the "right of discovery" or of "original discovery."[3]

The English possessions in America were not claimed by right of conquest, but by right of discovery. According to the principles of international law, as then understood, the Indian tribes were regarded as the temporary occupants of the soil, and the absolute rights of property and dominion were held to belong to the European nations by which any portion of the country was first discovered.[3]

The Europeans respected the right of the natives as occupants, but asserted the ultimate dominion to be in themselves; and exercised, as a consequence, a power to grant the soil while it was yet in the possession of the natives.[4] See OCCUPANCY.

2. In the law of patent rights, refers to something that had existed unknown, until brought to light and utilized.

The Congress shall have power to secure for limited times to inventors the exclusive right to their discoveries.[5]

This does not apply to the discovery of a fundamental truth or abstract principle, in which no one can have an exclusive right; nor to a power of nature, in which the invention is in the application to a useful object. The discovery must be reduced to practice,— be embodied in some practical method for rendering it useful.[6]

In its naked, ordinary sense, a discovery is not patentable. A discovery of a new principle, force, or

---

[1] Nat. Bank of Gloversville v. Johnson, 104 U. S. 276–78 (1881). Matthews, J. See also 14 Ala. 667; 13 Conn. 259; 20 Kan. 450; 42 Md. 592; 48 Mo. 191; 7 N. Y. 343; 18 Barb. 462; 13 Bankr. Reg. 268.

[2] F. *découvrir*, to uncover.

[3] Martin v. Waddell, 16 Pet. 409 (1842), Taney, C. J.

[4] Johnson v. McIntosh, 8 Wheat. 572 (1823), Marshall, C. J.; Buttz v. Northern Pacific R. Co., 119 U. S. 67 (1886); 3 Kent, 379.

[5] [Constitution, Art. I, sec. 8, cl. 8.

[6] Burr v. Duryee, 1 Wall. 570 (1863); Le Roy v. Tatham, 14 How. 174 (1852).

---

[1] [Dunkle v. Renick, 6 Ohio St. 535 (1856).

[2] Trabue v. Harris, 1 Metc. 599 (Ky., 1858), Simpson, Chief Justice.

[3] Farmers', &c. Bank v. Baldwin, 23 Minn. 205–6 (1876), cases.

law, operating, or which can be made to operate, on matter, will not entitle the discoverer to a patent. He controls his discovery through the means by which he has brought it into practical action, or their equivalent. It is then an " invention," although it embraces a discovery. Every invention may, in a certain sense, embrace more or less of discovery, for it must always include something that is new; but it by no means follows that every discovery is an invention.[1]

See further INVENTION; PATENT, 2; PRINCIPLE, 2; PROCESS, 3; SECURE, 1; TELEPHONE.

3. In the law regulating the granting of new trials and rehearings, refers to evidence brought to light or obtainable after trial or hearing, and which, could it have been presented upon that occasion, would likely have changed the result. Whence "after-discovered" and "newly-discovered" evidence.

The unconsidered evidence must be such as reasonable diligence, on the part of the party asking for the rehearing, could not have secured at the former trial; it must be material to its object, not merely cumulative, corroborative, or collateral; and be such as ought to produce important results on its merits.[2] See AUDITA QUERELA; REVIEW, 2, Bill of.

4. In the law of limitation of actions, refers to information had of the fact that a mistake was made or fraud perpetrated.

In cases of fraud and mistake a court of equity does not allow the statute of limitations to run until the discovery thereof. This rule has been incorporated into the statute law of many of the States.[3] See further FRAUD; LIMITATION, 3; MISTAKE; RESCISSION.

5. In the law of bankruptcy, refers to the disclosure made, or to be made, by the debtor of the nature, kind, amount, situs, etc., of his assets.[4] See BANKRUPTCY.

6. In equity practice, the disclosure by the defendant of matters important to enable the plaintiff to maintain his rights. Procured by a —

Bill of discovery. Every bill in equity may be deemed such, since it seeks a disclosure from the defendant, on oath, of the truth of the circumstances constituting the plaintiff's case as propounded in his bill. But that which is emphatically called a bill of discovery is a bill which asks no relief but

simply the discovery of facts resting in the knowledge of the defendant, or the discovery of deeds, writings, or other things in his possession or power, in order to maintain a right or title of the party asking it in some suit or proceeding in another court.[1]

Not entertainable: where the subject is not cognizable in any court; where the court cannot, in this manner, aid the other court; where the plaintiff is under disability, or has no title to the character in which he sues; where the value in suit is trivial; where the plaintiff has no interest in the subject-matter or no title to the discovery required, or where an action will not lie; where some other person than the plaintiff has a right to call for the discovery; where the policy of the law exempts the defendant from discovery; where the defendant is not bound to discover his own title; where the discovery is not material to the suit; where the defendant is a mere witness; or where a discovery would criminate him.[2]

At common law, discovery could not be had before trial; hence the resort to chancery. At present it is had, in effect, by bills of particulars, by attachments in execution, by affidavits of defense, by inspection of books and documents, by examination of one's adversary before trial, and by other means specially provided by statute.

For want of the power of discovery at law, courts of equity acquired a concurrent jurisdiction with other courts in all matters of account.[3] See CREDITOR'S BILL; FISHING, 2.

DISCREDIT. See CREDIT.

DISCREPANCY. See AMBIGUITY; DESCRIPTION.

DISCRETION.[4] Discernment of what is right or proper; sound sense; deliberate judgment.

1. Capacity or understanding to discern what is right or lawful, so as to be answerable for one's actions.

Presumed to be enjoyed at fourteen — the "age of discretion;" but, really, the law has fixed no arbitrary period when the immunity of childhood ceases.[5] See AGE; CAPAX; NEGLIGENCE.

2. Foresight, wisdom, sagacity; judgment, action. Sometimes termed *personal discretion:* limited to a particular individual.

Where there is a trustee in existence, capable of acting in the exercise of a discretion vested in him by

---

[1] Morton v New York Eye Infirmary, 5 Blatch. 121 (1862), Shipman, J.

[2] Dower v. Church, 21 W. Va. 57 (1882); Codman v. Vermont, &c. R. Co., 17 Blatch. 3 (1879); Whalen v. Mayor of New York, 17 F. R. 72 (1882).

[3] West Portland Homestead Association v. Lownsdale, 17 F. R. 207, 205 (1883); Fritschler v. Koehler, 83 Ky. 82 (1885); Parker v. Kuhn, Neb., March, 1887, cases: 32 N. W. Rep. 74; 2 Story, Eq. § 1521 a.

[4] See 2 Bl. Com. 483.

[1] [2 Story, Eq. § 1486; 1 id. § 689; 1 Pomeroy, Eq. §§ 144, 191.

[2] 2 Story, Eq. § 1489; 1 Pomeroy, Eq. §§ 195-215. As against a corporation, see Post v. Toledo, &c. R. Co., 144 Mass. 347 (1887), cases; McComb v. Chicago, &c. R. Co., 19 Blatch. 69 (1881); Colgate v. Compagnie Francaise, 23 F. R. 82 (1885), cases.

[3] 3 Bl. Com. 437, 382. See 1 Bouv. 536.

[4] L. dis-cernere, to separate, distinguish, perceive.

[5] 1 Bl. Com. 453; Nagle v. Allegheny R. Co., 88 Pa. 39 (1879).

the instrument under which he is appointed, equity will not interfere to control that discretion.[1]

A devisee charged with making such provision for designated beneficiaries "as in his judgment will be best," must exercise a proper and honest judgment in determining the nature and amount of the provision, having due regard to the amount of the estate, and the condition and circumstances of the beneficiaries.[2] See BENEVOLENT; EXECUTOR; POWER, 2; TRUST, 1.

3. Applied to public functionaries — a power or right, conferred upon them by law, of acting officially in certain circumstances, according to their own judgment and conscience, uncontrolled by the judgment or conscience of others.

This discretion, to some extent, is regulated by usage, or by fixed principles. Which means merely that the same court cannot, consistently with its dignity, and with its character and duty of administering impartial justice, decide in different ways two like cases. Whether cases are alike is, of necessity, a question for the judgment of some tribunal.[3]

An officer in whom public duties are confided by law is not subject to control by a court in the exercise of a discretion reposed in him as a part of his official functions.[4] See DEPARTMENT; GRANT, 3; SEWER.

4. In legislation, the deliberate, cautious judgment of the law-making body.

The courts will not presume a detrimental exercise of judgment in the legislature. Security against abusive exercise resides in the responsibility of the law-makers to the public.[5] See POLICY, 1; PUBLIC.

5. Equitable determination by a court as to what is just, in a given case.

Judicial discretion. A discretion to be exercised in discerning the course prescribed by the law; never, the arbitrary will of the judge.[6]

According to Coke, *discernere per legem, quid sit justum:* perceiving by or through

(or according to) the law, what would be just.[1]

Arises only in the exercise of judicial authority, which presupposes the existence of some cause or controversy submitted for decision in the customary form of judicial proceedings.[2]

Judicial power, as contradistinguished from the power of the laws, has no existence. Courts are the mere instruments of the law and can will nothing. When they are said to exercise a "discretion," it is a mere legal discretion, a discretion in discerning the course prescribed by law; and when that is discerned it is the duty of the court to follow it. Judicial power is never exercised for the purpose of giving effect to the will of the judge; always for giving effect to the will of the legislature, in other words to the will of the law.[3]

Were the judges to set the law to rights as often as it differs from their ideal of excellence, their corrections would not suit those who came after them, and we should have nothing but corrections; there would be no guide in the decision of causes but the discretion of fallible judges in the court of last resort, and no rule by which the citizen might beforehand shape his actions. "The [private] discretion of a judge," said Lord Camden, "is the law of tyrants: it is always unknown; it is different in different men; it is casual, and depends upon constitution, temper and passion. In the best it is oftentimes caprice; in the worst it is every vice, folly, and passion to which human nature can be liable."[4]

The determination or disposition of many matters is committed to the sound discretion of the court; as, amendments to pleadings, and petitions; continuances, the order of introducing evidence, the amount of cumulative testimony admissible, the examination of witnesses, the granting or refusing of new trials and of the extraordinary writs, sales and resales of property; custody of children; allowances for maintenance and remuneration.

The universal rule of practice is that orders or decrees involving an exercise of judicial discretion purely are not re-examinable in a court of errors; only a plain abuse of discretion in such cases will be interfered with.[5]

Abuse of discretion, especially a "gross" and "palpable" abuse (the terms ordinarily employed), to justify an interference with the exercise of discretionary

[1] Nichols v. Eaton, 91 U. S. 724 (1875), cases; Cooper v. Cooper, 77 Va. 203 (1883); Lovett v. Thomas, 81 *id.* 255 (1885); 78 *id.* 114; 79 *id.* 640.

[2] Colton v. Colton, 127 U. S. 300 (1888). As to cases in which personal discretion was conferred upon executors and held not transmissible to the administrator *de bonis non* by such expressions in wills as think, see, or deem "advisable," "best," "fit," "prudent," "judicious," "wise," see Giberson v. Giberson, 43 N. J. E. 116–21 (1887), note, cases: 37 Alb. Law J. 7–8 (1888), cases.

[3] Judges of Oneida Common Pleas v. People, 18 Wend. 99 (1887).

[4] Gaines v. Thompson, 7 Wall. 348 (1868); County of San Mateo v. Maloney, 71 Cal. 208 (1886); 45 *id.* 639; 52 *id.* 179.

[5] Baltimore, &c. R. Co. v. Maryland, 21 Wall. 471 (1874).

[6] Tripp v. Cook, 26 Wend. 152 (1841); Platt v. Munroe, 34 Barb. 293 (1861).

[1] See Faber v. Bruner, 13 Mo. 543 (1850).

[2] States v. Judges, 34 La. An. 1116 (1882).

[3] Osborn v. United States Bank, 9 Wheat. 866 (1824), Marshall. C. J.

[4] Commonwealth v. Lesher, 17 S. & R. *164 (1827), Gibson, C. J. See also State v. Cummings, 36 Mo. 278 (1865); Rooke's Case, 3 Coke, 100 (1598); Rex v. Wilkes, 4 Burr. 2539 (1770); 1 *id.* 560, 571; 34 Ala. 235; 46 *id.* 310; 4 Iowa, 283; 25 Miss. 226; 1 Heisk. 774.

[5] Pomeroy's Lessee v. Bank of Indiana, 1 Wall. 598 (1863), cases; *Exp.* Reed, 100 U. S. 23 (1879); Wills v. Russell, *ib.* 626 (1879); United States v. Atherton, 102 *id.* 375 (1880); Tilton v. Cofield, 93 *id.* 166 (1876).

power, implies not merely error of judgment, but perversity of will, passion, prejudice, partiality, or moral delinquency.[1]

DISCRIMINATION. See CITIZEN; COMMERCE.

DISCUSSION. 1. By the Roman law, a surety was liable for the debt only after the creditor had unsuccessfully sought payment from the principal debtor. This was called the "benefit" or "right of discussion." A like rule obtains in Louisiana.[2]

2. In the sense of debate, see LIBERTY, Of press, Of speech; PRIVILEGE, 4.

DISEASE. Within the meaning of a warranty in a policy of life insurance, not a temporary ailment, unless it be such as indicates a vice in the constitution, or so serious as to have a bearing upon the general health and the continuance of life, or such as in common understanding would be called a disease.[3]

See ACCIDENT, Insurance; DISORDER, 1; EPIDEMIC; HEALTH; INSANITY; INSPECTION, 1; NUISANCE; POLICE, 2; QUARANTINE, 2; SOUND, 2 (2); SUICIDE.

DISENFRANCHISE; DISFRANCHISE. See FRANCHISE, 2.

DISENTAIL. See TAIL.

DISFIGURE. See MAIM, 2.

DISGRACE. See CRIMINATE.

DISGUISE. A man hiding behind bushes is not "in disguise," within the meaning of a statute which makes the county liable in damages to the next of kin of one murdered by persons in disguise.[4] See AMBUSH.

DISHERISON. See INHERIT.

DISHONOR. To refuse or neglect to accept or to pay negotiable paper at its maturity; also, the failure itself in this respect. Opposed, *honor*, q. v.

The law presumes that if the drawer of a bill of exchange has not had due notice of dishonor he is injured, because otherwise he might have immediately withdrawn effects from the hands of the drawee; and that if the indorser has not had timely notice the remedy against the parties liable to him is rendered more precarious. The consequence, therefore, of neglect of notice is that the party to whom it should have

been given is discharged from liability.[1] See PROTEST, 2.

DISINHERIT. See INHERIT.

DISINTEREST. See INTEREST, 2 (1).

DISJOINDER. See JOINDER.

DISJUNCTIVE. Describes a term or an allegation which expresses or charges a thing in the alternative. Opposed, *conjunctive*. See OR, 2.

DISMISS. To send away; to refuse to entertain further; to send out of court: as, to dismiss a bill in equity for defects in its structure or for insufficiency in law —

Borrowed from proceedings in a court of chancery, where the term is applied to the removal of a cause out of court without further hearing.[2]

"Dismissed" refers to the final hearing of a suit — the end of the proceeding.[3]

A bill in equity will be dismissed where (1) there is a want of certainty in the allegations to show that the plaintiff is entitled to the relief demanded; (2) where the right to relief has been barred by the statute of limitations; (3) where there has been negligence in seeking relief, unexplained by sufficient equitable reasons and circumstances.[4]

After a decree, whether final or interlocutory, has been made, by which the rights of a defendant have been adjudicated, or such proceedings have been taken as entitle him to a decree, the complainant cannot dismiss his bill without the consent of the defendant.[5]

Whenever it becomes apparent to the court that it has no authority to adjudicate the issue presented, its duty is to dismiss the cause.[6]

A dismissal for want of jurisdiction does not conclude the plaintiff's right of action.[7] See DISCONTINUANCE, 1; PREJUDICE, 2.

DISORDER. 1. Disease; physical malady.

A person suffering from a "contagious disorder" may be indicted for exposing himself in a place endangering the public health.[8] See DISEASE; HEALTH; SLANDER, 1.

2. Conduct which disturbs the community. See PEACE, 1.

Disorderly conduct. Any conduct which is contrary to law.[9]

---

[1] People v. N. Y. Central R. Co., 29 N. Y. 431 (1864); White v. Leeds, 51 Pa. 189 (1865); 21 *id.* 406; 53 *id.* 158; 67 *id.* 34; 14 Hun, 3; 78 N. Y. 56; 15 Fla. 317; 52 Ala. 87.

[2] La. Civ. Code, arts. 3014-20.

[3] Cushman v. United States Life Ins. Co., 70 N. Y. 77 (1877), cases.

[4] Dale County v. Gunter, 46 Ala. 142 (1871).

---

[1] Byles, Bills, 297; Riggs v. Hatch, 16 F. R. 838, 842-50 (1883), cases.

[2] Boscley v. Bruner, 24 Miss. 462 (1852); 3 Bl. Com. 451.

[3] Taft v. North. Transportation Co., 56 N. H. 417 (1876).

[4] Taylor v. Holmes, 14 F. R. 499 (1882).

[5] Chicago, &c. R. Co. v. Union Rolling Mill Co., 109 U. S. 713 (1883); 69 Ga. 100.

[6] Watson v. Baker, 67 Tex. 50 (1886), cases.

[7] Smith v. McNeal, 109 U. S. 429 (1883), cases.

[8] King v. Vantandillo, 4 Maule & S. 73 (1815); King v. Burnett, *ib.* 272 (1815); Boom v. City of Utica, 2 Barb. 104 (1848).

[9] State v. Jersey City, 25 N. J. L. 541 (1856).

Disorderly house. A house the inmates of which behave so badly as to become a nuisance to the neighborhood.[1]

Includes any gambling house, dance house, bawdy house, prohibited liquor saloon, or other habitation made obnoxious by the habitual recurrence of fighting, noise, or violence.[2]

The keeping may consist in allowing such disorder as disturbs the neighborhood, or in drawing together idle, vicious, dissolute or disorderly persons engaged in unlawful or immoral practices, thereby endangering the public peace and promoting immorality.[3]

A complaint will be supported by proof that one person was disturbed, if the acts are such as tend to annoy all good citizens.[4]

Disorderly person. A person amenable to police regulation, for misconduct affecting the public.[5] See BEHAVIOR.

DISPARAGEMENT. 1. Inequality in rank.

In old law, while a female infant was in ward, the guardian could tender a match "without disparagement" or inequality: lest she might marry the lord's enemy. The Great Charter provided that the next of kin should be notified of the proposed contract.[6]

2. Derogation, belittlement; impeachment.

A tenant may not disparage the title in his landlord; nor may the former owner of property disparage the title he has conveyed.

Declarations by the vendor of realty in disparagement of the grant are never admissible, nor, generally, are the assertions of the seller of a chattel.[7]

See ASSIGNMENT, 2; DECLARATION, 1; ESTOPPEL; LANDLORD.

DISPATCH. As used in charter-parties, relative to the discharge of vessels, has frequently been the subject of definition.

Customary or **usual dispatch.** In accordance or consistently with all well-established usages of the port of discharge.[8]

The usual dispatch of persons who are ready to receive a cargo.[9]

Excludes a custom by which a charterer may decline to receive a cargo, because it is advantageous to postpone.[9]

"Customary dispatch in discharging "means discharging with speed, haste, expedition, due diligence, according to the lawful, reasonable, well known customs of the port of discharge; the same as "usual dispatch," but not the same as "quick dispatch," which excludes certain usages and customs.[1]

When there is no undertaking to unload the vessel within a specified time, but she is to be discharged "with all possible dispatch," or "with usual dispatch," or "with the customary dispatch of the port," or "within reasonable time," the freighter must use reasonable diligence to do his part toward unloading according to the terms and meaning of the charter-party.[2]

DISPAUPER. See PAUPER, 2.

DISPLACE. In shipping articles, to disrate; not, to discharge.[3]

DISPOSE. 1. To alienate, direct the ownership of: as, to dispose of property.

Includes to barter, exchange, or partition; is broader than sell.[4]

Under the power "to dispose of the property of the United States," Congress may lease the public lands. The nature of the disposal is discretionary.[5]

"Dispose," said of an insolvent, in an attachment law, includes any intentional putting of property beyond reach of creditors.[6]

To convey by advancement is to dispose;[7] but to mortgage may not be, within the meaning of a statute.[8]

Disposing mind. Testamentary capacity, *q. v.* Compare JUS, Disponendi.

2. To place a dead infant upon a wall in a field is to "secretly dispose" of it.[9] See ABANDON, 2 (2).

3. To decide, determine: as, to dispose of a controversy.[10]

DISPOSSESS. See POSSESSION, Dispossession.

DISPROVE. See PROOF; REBUT.

DISPUTE. A fact alleged by one party and denied by the other, with some show of reason; not, a naked allegation without or against evidence.[11] Whence disputable,—see PRESUMPTION.

Matter in dispute. In a statute predicating appellate jurisdiction on the value of

---

[1] State *v.* Maxwell, 33 Conn. 259 (1866), Hinman, C. J.

[2] See 1 Bish. Cr. L. § 1106; 4 Bl. Com. 167.

[3] Thatcher *v.* State, 48 Ark. 63–64 (1886); 120 Mass. 356; 30 N. J. L. 104.

[4] Commonwealth *v.* Hopkins, 133 Mass. 381 (1882), cases.

[5] See 4 Bl. Com. 169.

[6] 2 Bl. Com. 70.

[7] See Roberts *v.* Medbery, 132 Mass. 101 (1882), cases; Robertson *v.* Pickrell, 109 U. S. 616 (1883).

[8] [Smith *v.* Yellow Pine Lumber, 2 F. R. 309 (1880).

[9] Lindsay *v.* Cusimano, 10 F. R. 303 (1882).

[4] Lindsay *v.* Cusimano, 12 F. R. 507 (1882).

[2] Nelson *v.* Dahl, 12 L. R., Ch. D. 568, 582–84 (1879); Williams *v.* Theobald, 15 F. R. 468, 473 (1883); Sleeper *v.* Puig, 17 Blatch. 38–39 (1879), cases; 22 F. R. 790.

[3] Potter *v.* Smith, 103 Mass. 69 (1869).

[4] Phelps *v.* Harris, 101 U. S. 380 (1879).

[5] United States *v.* Gratiot, 14 Pet. 538 (1840).

[6] Auerbach *v.* Hitchcock, 28 Minn. 74 (1881); 62 Tex. 436–37.

[7] Elston *v.* Schilling, 42 N. Y. 79 (1870).

[8] Bullene *v.* Smith, 73 Mo. 16 (1880).

[9] Queen *v.* Brown, 1 Cr. Cas. Res. *246 (1870).

[10] See *Exp.* Russell, 13 Wall. 669 (1871); 14 Blatch. 13.

[11] [Knight's Appeal, 19 Pa. 494 (1852), Black, C. J.

the "matter in dispute" — the subject of litigation, the matter for which suit is brought, on which issue is joined, and in relation to which jurors are called and witnesses examined.[1]

Until shown by the record that the sum demanded is not the matter in dispute, that sum will govern in all questions of jurisdiction. . . The amount stated in the body of the declaration is considered — the actual matter in dispute as shown by the record, and not the *ad damnum* alone.[2]

For the purpose of review the amount is fixed by the amount of the judgment below, not by the amount of the verdict.[3]

The act of March 3, 1887, excludes from the computation interest accrued up to the date of the suit.[4]

When the record is silent as to the value, it is good practice for the court below to allow affidavits and counter-affidavits of value to be filed under direction from the court.[5]

Where the value of land in controversy was necessarily involved in the determination of a case, and found by the court to be $5,000, to effect an appeal the defendant was not allowed to present affidavits showing the value to be $7,000.[6] See CONTROVERSY; REMAND, 2.

DISQUALIFY. See QUALIFY.

DISRATE. See DISPLACE.

DISSEISIN. See SEISIN.

DISSENT. See ASSENT; CONSENT; OPINION, 3.

DISSIMILAR. See SIMILAR.

DISSOLVE. 1. To put an end to, terminate: as, to dissolve a relation; *e. g.*, the marriage relation, — see DIVORCE.

The dissolution of a partnership (*q. v.*) does not affect contracts made between the partners and others.[7]

"Dissolving a corporation" is sometimes synonymous with annulling its charter or terminating its existence, and sometimes refers merely to the judicial act which alienates the property and suspends the business of the corporation, without terminating its existence.[8] See STOCK, 3 (2).

2. To discharge or relieve from a proceeding which involves a lien or seizure; to open, annul: as, to dissolve an attachment, an injunction, *qq. v.*

3. As to dissolving parliament, see PROROGUE.

DISSUADE. See JUSTICE, Offenses against.

DISTANCE. Is measured in a straight line, "as the crow flies," or on the horizontal plane.[1]

May refer to the usually traveled road.[2] See ALONG; COURSE, 1; DIRECT, 1; NEAR.

DISTILLER. Any person, firm, or corporation who distills or manufactures spirits, or who brews or makes mash, wort, or wash for distillation, or the production of spirits.[3]

One who produces alcoholic spirits by distillation.[4] Compare RECTIFIER.

Distilled spirits. The products of distillation, whether rectified or not.[5]

Unlawful distilling of spirits is sometimes termed "illicit."

The business of distilling having been made a *quasi* public employment, a distiller's books are *quasi* records.[6] See CRIMINATE.

Distillery. A place where alcoholic liquors are distilled or manufactured; not, then, every structure where the process of distillation, as of paraffine, is used.[7] See CONDITION, Repugnant.

DISTRACTED. In Illinois and New Hampshire, expresses a degree of insanity.

DISTRAIN. See DISTRESS.

DISTRESS.[8] Taking a personal chattel out of the possession of the wrong-doer into the custody of the party injured, to procure satisfaction for a wrong committed.[9]

A taking of beasts or other personal prop-

---

[1] Lee *v.* Watson, 1 Wall. 339 (1863), Field, J. See 10 La. An. 170; 12 *id.* 87; 3 Cranch, 159; 3 Dall. 405; 13 Cal. 30; 25 Gratt. 177.

[2] Hilton *v.* Dickinson, 108 U. S. 174–76 (1883), cases; The Jesse Williamson, *ib.* 309–10 (1883); Bruce *v.* Manchester, &c. R. Co., 117 *id.* 515 (1886); Gibson *v.* Shufeldt, 122 *id.* 28–40 (1887); 106 *id.* 578–80; 110 *id.* 223; 112 *id.* 227.

[3] N. Y. Elevated R. Co. *v.* Fifth Nat. Bank, 118 U. S. 608 (1886).

[4] Moore *v.* Town of Edgefield, 32 F. R. 498 (1887).

[5] Wilson *v.* Blair, 119 U. S. 387 (1886).

[5] Talkington *v.* Dumbleton, 123 U. S. 745 (1887), Waite, Chief Justice.

[7] See 3 Kent. 27.

[6] *Re* Independent Ins. Co., 1 Holmes, 109 (1872); 2

Harr., Del., 12–16; 2 Kent, 307. As to notice, see 24 Cent. Law J. 588 (1887), cases.

[1] Leigh *v.* Hind, 17 E. C. L. 774 (1829); 78 *id.* *688; 85 *id.* *92; 88 *id.* *350.

[2] Smith *v.* Ingraham, 7 Cow. 419 (1827).

[3] Revenue Act 13 July, 1866, § 9: 14 St. L. 117.

[4] R. S. § 3247; United States *v.* House No. 3, 8 Rep. 391 (1879).

[5] R. S. §§ 3248, 3289, 3299; United States *v.* Anthony, 14 Blatch. 92 (1877); Boyd *v.* United States, *ib.* 317 (1877).

[6] United States *v.* Myers, 1 Hughes, 534 (1876); R. S. § 3303.

[7] Atlantic Dock Co. *v.* Libby, 45 N. Y. 502 (1871).

[8] F. *destraindre*, to strain, press, vex extremely: L. *distringere*, to pull asunder.

[9] 3 Bl. Com. 6; 44 Barb. 488.

rty by way of pledge to enforce the performance of something due from the party distrained upon.[1]

Distrain. To take by distress.

Distrainor; distrainer. He who levies a distress.

Distraint. The act or proceeding by which a distress is made.

The more usual injury for which a distress may be taken is non-payment of rent; but it is also a remedy where another's animals are found damage-feasant (*q. v.*), and for the enforcement of some duties imposed by statute.[2]

At common law all personal chattels are distrainable, unless expressly exempted. Not distrainable are: (1) Things in which no one can have an absolute property; as, a wild animal. (2) Whatever is in personal use; as, a horse while a man is riding him. (3) Valuable things in the way of trade; as, a horse standing in a shop to be shod, or at an inn, cloth left with a tailor, grain sent to a mill or a market. These are privileged for the benefit of trade. But all chattels found upon the premises are distrainable for rent: if not, fraud could be readily practiced. A stranger to the lease may recover from the tenant. (4) The tools and utensils of one's trade or profession: taking these would prevent the owner from serving society. Beasts of the plow and sheep are privileged, dead goods and other beasts not. To deprive the debtor of the means of earning money would defeat the end for which distress is intended. (5) A thing which cannot be returned in its former good plight: a distress being only a pledge, to be restored after the debt is paid. By 2 William and Mary (1691), c. 5, grain and hay may be taken. (6) A thing fixed to the freehold. By 11 Geo. II (1729), c. 19, the landlord may distrain natural products, and harvest them when matured.[3] See CROP.

All distresses must be by day, except of animals doing damage. The distrainor must enter upon the premises; within six months after the lease ends, where the tenant continues in possession. By 8 Anne (1710), c. 14, and 11 Geo. II (1729), c. 19, the landlord may distrain goods carried off the premises clandestinely, wherever found within thirty days, unless sold to an innocent purchaser. Once inside the house, the distrainor may break open an inner door; by 11 Geo. II, he may, in the day-time, break open any place to which goods have been fraudulently removed, oath being first made, in the case of a dwelling-house, of a reasonable ground to suspect that such goods are concealed therein.[4]

A distress should be for the whole duty at once; but if mistake is made in the value of the articles, or if there is not sufficient upon the premises, a *second* distress may be taken.[5]

By 52 Hen. III (1270), c. 4, taking an unreasonable distress for rent is amercible. The remedy for an *excessive* distress is by a special action under that statute—there being, at common law, no trespass.[1]

The things distrained should be impounded. On the way they may be rescued, if the taking was unlawful. Once in the pound, they are in the custody of the law, and may be replevined.[2]

In Pennsylvania, prior to the act of March 21, 1772, a distress could be held only for enforcing payment of rent. That act provides for a sale of the goods, which makes the distress like an execution. The act is similar to that of William and Mary, *ante*—under which it was decided that a tender after an impounding availed nothing; but the later decisions are that a sale, after tender of rent and costs within five days, is illegal.[3]

In some States a lessor has no power of distress, but, instead, attachment on mesne process, an action of covenant or debt, or *assumpsit* for use and occupation. In other States the common-law right, greatly modified, is preserved.

What the power of distress was in feudal times may be inferred from the fact that the word came to signify extreme "suffering."[4] See DISTRICT, 1.

Distress infinite. A distress unlimited as to quantity, and repeatable till the delinquent does his duty.

In cases of distress for fealty or suit of court no distress could be considered unreasonable. This sort of distress was used in summoning jurors. The property was to be restored after the duty was performed.[5]

Now resorted to to compel the doing of a thing required by a court, as, to appear, when process cannot be personally served. See ATTACHMENT, Of person; DISTRINGAS; SEQUESTRATION.

See also ELOIGN; LANDLORD; POUND, 2; REPLEVIN; RESCUE, 1.

DISTRIBUTION. 1. Allotment; apportionment; division.

Specifically, division of an intestate's estate according to law.[6]

A decree distributing a fund in court will not preclude an omitted claimant from asserting, by bill or petition, his right to share in the fund.[7]

Distributee. One who receives a share or portion of the assets of an intestate's estate.[8]

Distributive. Due or received upon a legal division: as, a distributive share.

---

[1] 3 Bl. Com. 231.

[2] 3 Bl. Com. 6–7.

[3] 3 Bl. Com. 7–10. Articles exempt, 26 Am. Law Reg. 153–58 (1887), cases.

[4] 3 Bl. Com. 11.

[5] 3 Bl. Com. 11–12.

[1] 3 Bl. Com. 12. See 100 Pa. 397, 401, *infra;* 39 How. Pr. 167; 6 Kern. 299.

[2] 3 Bl. Com. 12–15.

[3] Richards v. McGrath, 100 Pa. 400 (1882); 105 E. C. L. 262; 3 Bl. Com. 14. See also Patty v. Bogle, 59 Miss. 493–94 (1882).

[4] 1 Pars. Contr. 517; Taylor, Landl. & T. §§ 558–59.

[5] 3 Bl. Com. 231.

[6] Rogers v. Gillett, 56 Iowa, 268 (1881); 102 Ind. 412.

[7] *Re* Howard, 9 Wall. 184 (1869), cases.

[8] See Henry v. Henry, 9 Ired. L. 279 (1848).

Statutes of distribution. Statutes which regulate the division of an intestate's estate among his widow and heirs or next of kin, after the debts of the estate are paid.

Title to realty vests in the heirs by the death of the ancestor; the legal title to personalty is vested in the executor or administrator, and is transferred to the distributees upon confirmation of the proceedings in distribution.[1]

In thirty or more of the States and Territories the rules for the distribution of personalty are essentially the same as the rules for the descent of realty, where no distinction is made between realty ancestral and non-ancestral, and, where such distinction is made, for the descent of realty non-ancestral.[2]

See AUDIT; DESCENT, Canons of; EQUAL, Equally; PROPERTY.

2. As applied to a publication like a newspaper or a periodical, imports a delivery to persons who have bought or otherwise become entitled to the same.[3]

DISTRICT. A division of territory.

1. Originally, the space within which a lord could coerce and punish — *distrain.*[4]

The circuit within which a man might be compelled to appear, or the place in which one hath the power of distraining.[5]

2. A division of a State or Territory for any purpose whatever: as, *collection* district, for the collection of revenue duties; *Congressional* district, for the election of representatives in Congress; *election* district, for purposes of elections, municipal, State, or United States; *judicial* district, for judicial purposes — with its district *court*, district *judge*, district *attorney*, and district *clerk*; *land* district, for regulating sales of public lands; *school* district, for purposes connected with the public schools; *tax* district, for the levying and collection of taxes.

May designate an area larger or smaller than a county; ns, the district from which the jury in a criminal case may be drawn.[6]

A "taxing" district is not necessarily a large division of a State's territory, like a county or parish, as, in the act of Congress of June 7, 1862, § 6; it may be any portion of territory solely for the assessment of taxes.[7] See D, 3; PRECINCT.

District attorney. See ATTORNEY-GENERAL.

District clerk, court, judge. See COURTS, United States.

District of Columbia. Is neither a State nor a Territory. Congress is authorized "to exercise exclusive Legislation in all Cases whatsoever over such District (not exceeding ten Miles square) as may, by Cession of particular States, and the Acceptance of Congress, become the Seat of the Government of the United States."[1]

Maryland and Virginia ceded territory on the Potomac, which Congress, by act of July 16, 1790, accepted. In December, 1800, the seat of government was removed from Philadelphia. By the act of July 11, 1846, Congress retroceded the county of Alexandria to Virginia. The District constitutes the county of Washington.

A citizen of the District of Columbia is not a citizen of a State.[2]

The laws in force December 1, 1873, were revised and republished, by direction of Congress, in a separate volume known as the Revised Statutes relating to the District of Columbia.[3] See COURTS, page 284; LEVY, 3.

DISTRINGAS. L. That you distrain.

The emphatic word in the writ of "distress infinite" (*q. v.*), when expressed in Latin. The writ enforced compliance with something required of the person (natural or artificial) named in the writ.

Referring to a defendant who neglected to appear, a process issued from the court of common pleas commanding the sheriff to distrain the defendant from time to time, by taking his goods and the profits of his lands.[4]

The process against a body corporate, which, having been served with a subpœna issued out of chancery, fails to appear in court, is by *distringas,* to distrain them by their goods and chattels, rents and profits, till they obey the summons.[5]

In detinue, after judgment, the plaintiff had a *distringas,* to compel the defendant to deliver the goods, by repeated distresses of his chattels.[6]

Distringas juratores. That you distrain the jurors. A writ commanding the sheriff to distrain jurors by their lands and goods, so that they be constrained to appear in court.[7]

Distringas nuper vice comitem. That you distrain the late sheriff. A writ to compel a sheriff who had gone out of office to bring in a defendant, or to sell goods under a *fieri facias* which he failed to do while in office.[8]

---

[1] Roorbach *v.* Lord, 4 Conn. 349 (1822).

[2] See 1 Bouvier's Law Dict. 544; 2 Kent, 420, 426.

[3] Dawley *v.* Alsdorf, 25 Hun, 227 (1881).

[4] [Webster's Dict.

[5] [Jacob's Law Dict.

[6] State *v.* Kemp, 34 Minn. 62 (1885).

[7] Keely *v.* Sanders, 99 U. S. 448–49 (1878); De Treville *v.* Smalls, 98 *id.* 517 (1878).

---

[1] Constitution, Art. I, sec. 8, par. 17.

[2] Cissel *v.* McDonald, 16 Blatch. 152–54 (1879), cases.

[3] See generally Fort Leavenworth R. Co. *v.* Lowe, 114 U. S. 528–29 (1885).

[4] 3 Bl. Com. 280.

[5] 3 Bl. Com. 445. See 37 Hun, 546; 89 N. C. 585.

[6] 3 Bl. Com. 413.

[7] 3 Bl. Com. 354; 1 Arch. Pract. 305.

[8] See 1 Tidd, Pract. 313.

DISTURBANCE. 1. Interruption of a state of peace; disquiet; disorder: as, the disturbance of a lawful public meeting.[1] See ASSEMBLY; PEACE, 1.

2. A wrong to an incorporeal hereditament, by hindering or disquieting the owner in his lawful enjoyment of it.[2] See ENJOYMENT, Quiet.

It may be of a franchise, a common, a way, or a manure.[2]

DITCH. See DRAIN.

DISUSE. See USE, 2.

DIVERS.[3] Several; sundry; more than one, yet not many.

In an indictment for the larceny of a number of articles all of one kind, the allegation may be "divers," "divers and sundry," or "a quantity," without stating a specific number, along with an averment of the aggregate value of the whole number.[4]

DIVERSION. Turning a stream, or a part of it, from its accustomed direction or natural course.[5]

DIVEST. See VEST.

DIVIDE. See DIVISION; PARTITION.

DIVIDEND. A portion of the principal or the profits of a thing divided among its several owners.[6]

1. In bankruptcy and insolvency law, assets apportioned among creditors.

2. In the administration of the estates of decedents, a distributive share.[7] See EQUAL.

3. A distribution of the funds of a corporation among its members, pursuant to a vote of the directors or managers.[8]

Corporate funds derived from the business and earnings of a corporation, appropriated by a corporate act to the use of, and to be divided among, the stockholders.[9]

Referring to a corporation engaged in business, and not being closed up and dissolved,—fund which the corporation sets apart

from its profits to be divided among its members.[1]

The dividends declared by a corporation in business are, and, except under special circumstances, always should be, from profits. Hence, the word frequently carries with it the idea of a division of profits; but that is not necessarily its only meaning. Its special signification, in a particular case, is dependent upon the character of the thing divided.[2]

Does not necessarily imply a *pro rata* distribution.[3]

Preferred dividend. A dividend paid to one class of shareholders in priority to that to be paid to another class.[4]

Preferential dividend. A preference to a limited extent in the division of the sum to be divided.[5]

Dividends on preferred stock are payable only out of net earnings applicable thereto: they are not payable absolutely and unconditionally, as is interest. Until declared, the right to a dividend is not a debt; and the obligation to declare it does not arise until there is a fund from which it can properly be made. When to declare a dividend, and the amount thereof, is, ordinarily, a matter of internal management. Unless it appears that somebody in particular will be injured, a court of equity will not interfere.[5]

A dividend declared out of earnings is not an asset of the company, but belongs to the shareholder. The corporation holds it as his trustee. Before the dividend is declared, each share of stock represents the owner's whole interest; when he transfers the share, he transfers his entire right; hence, a dividend subsequently declared belongs to the new holder.[7]

A stock dividend does not diminish or interfere with the property of a corporation. It simply dilutes the shares as they existed before. The corporation is just as capable of meeting demands upon it; the aggregate of the stockholders own the same interest they had previously. When stock has been lawfully created, a dividend may be made, provided the stock represents property. There is no statute in New York which requires dividends to be made in cash; and there is no rule or policy of law which condemns a property dividend. The stockholders can take the property divided to them and sell it for cash. But a dividend payable in cash, or payable generally, makes the corporation a debtor.[8]

See Ex, 3; STOCK, 3 (2), Preferred.

---

[1] See 4 Bl. Com. 54; State v. Oskins, 28 Ind. 364 (1867), cases; Wall v. Lee, 34 N. Y. 141 (1865), cases.

[2] [3 Bl. Com. 236.

[3] L. *diversus*, different.

[4] Commonwealth v. Butts, 124 Mass. 452 (1878), cases.

[5] [Parker v. Griswold, 17 Conn. *299 (1845).

[6] [Commonwealth v. Erie, &c. R. Co., 10 Phila. 466 (73).

[7] University v. North Carolina R. Co., 76 N. C. 105 (77).

[8] Williston v. Michigan, &c. R. Co., 13 Allen, 404 (66).

[9] [Hyatt v. Allen, 56 N. Y. 556 (1874), Andrews, J.; Chaffee v. Rutland R. Co., 55 Vt. 129 (1882); Pierce, Rlr. 120.

(24)

---

[1] Lockhart v. Van Alstyne, 31 Mich. 79 (1875), Cooley, J.; 108 U. S. 399.

[2] Eyster v. Centennial Board, 94 U. S. 504 (1876), Waite, C. J. See Cary v. Savings Union, 22 Wall. 41 (1874); 18 Barb. 657; 8 R. I. 333; 1 De G. & J. *636-37.

[3] Hall v. Kellogg, 12 N. Y. 335 (1855).

[4] Taft v. Hartford, &c. R. Co., 8 R. I. 333 (1866), Bradley, C. J. See 55 Vt. 129, *infra.*

[5] See Henry v. Great Northern Ry. Co., 1 De Gex & J. *636 (1857).

[6] Chaffee v. Rutland R. Co., 55 Vt. 126, 127, 133 (1882), cases.

[7] Jermain v. Lake Shore, &c. R. Co., 91 N. Y. 492 (1883).

[8] Williams v. Western Union Tel. Co., 93 N. Y. 189

DIVINE. See GOD; LAW; OATH; RE-
LIGION; SUNDAY; WORSHIP.

DIVISION. 1. A setting apart: separation, apportionment, partition, sharing out;
also, a separate part or portion, a share, an
allotment. See EQUAL; FENCE; WALL.

Divisible. Admitting of separation into
distinct parts; separable. **Indivisible.** Entire; inseparable.

Agreements, covenants, and considerations may or
may not be divisible into parts performed or capable
of being performed or enforced, or into parts which
are lawful and parts which are unlawful.[1] See CON-
TRACT, Divisible; UTERE, Utile, etc.

Undivided. That a tract of land, held
in common, shall remain undivided, implies
that the land is not subject to partition, is
not to be divided, set off, allotted to individuals in severalty.[2]

2. Difference of opinion; non-concurrence
in a decision. See OPINION, 3.

3. Separation of the members of a legislative body, to ascertain the vote cast.

DIVISUM. See IMPERIUM.

DIVORCE.[3] The dissolution or partial
suspension, by law, of the marital relation.
A dissolution is termed a divorce from the
bond of matrimony — *a vinculo matrimonii;*
a suspension, divorce from bed and board —
a mensa et thoro.[4]

"Divorced" imports a dissolution, in the largest
sense, of the marriage relation.[5]

In England, prior to 1857, the subject of divorce belonged to the ecclesiastical courts and to parliament.
Statutes of 20 and 21 Vict. (1857) c. 85, created the
Court of Divorce and Matrimonial Causes, with exclusive jurisdiction in all matrimonial matters. Divorce
causes are now heard in the Probate and Divorce Division of the High Court of Justice, appeal lying to the
Court of Appeal.

In this country, formerly, it was common for the
legislatures to grant divorces by special acts, but the
practice fell into disuse, and is now forbidden in some
States, by the constitution. The necessary jurisdiction is generally conferred upon courts possessing
equity powers.[6]

The inhibition upon the legislative department
against exercising judicial functions, implied from the
division of government into three departments, has
never been understood to exclude control by the legislature of a State over the marriage relation, notwithstanding that the exercise of such power may involve
investigation of a judicial nature. Hence, unless forbidden by the constitution, a legislature may grant a
divorce.[1]

Congress is not empowered to legislate upon the
subject; and the legislation of the States and Territories is far from uniform. In South Carolina divorce
is not allowed for any cause; in New York for adultery only. Elsewhere it is allowed for adultery,
cruelty, indignity, willful desertion, or sentence to a
State's prison for two years or longer period, habitual
drunkenness, pre-contract, fraud (incontinency, or
pregnancy), coercion, imbecility or impotency unknown to the other party, consanguinity, and affinity, *qq. v.*

Common defenses are: connivance, collusion, condonation, recrimination, denial of allegation of desertion or infidelity.

Some of the consequences of a divorce follow directly from the law, others may depend upon the special order of court: the law ends all rights, based upon
the marriage, not actually vested; as, dower and curtesy,[2] and the husband's power over the wife's choses
in action. The court may allow alimony, and direct
the custody of children.

A decree made in one State, being a judgment of
record, will be given its original force in every other
State. For this purpose, courts of equity, Federal,
and State, have jurisdiction.[3] But, otherwise, if the
record shows on its face that a party was a non-resident.[4]

A marriage forbidden by a decree of divorce in one
State may be contracted in another State not also
prohibiting it.[5]

The decree in nature is *in rem.* It determines the
question of the marriage relation, or of the personal
status, as against the world, and is therefore conclusive upon parties and strangers.[6]

See, further, the related topics mentioned.

DO; DONE. See ACT, 1; MAKE; FA-
CERE.

190, 192 (1883). See also Bailey v. N. Y. Central R. Co.,
22 Wall. 605, 633 (1874); generally, 19 Am. Law Rev.
571–82, 737–62 (1885), cases.

[1] See Oregon Navigation Co. *v.* Winsor, 20 Wall. 70
(1873), cases.

[2] Wellington *v.* Petitioners, 16 Pick. 98 (1834).

[3] F.: L. *divortium,* separation,—4 Mo. 142. Divorce-
ment is obsolete.

[4] 2 Bishop, Mar. & D. § 225; 1 Bl. Com. 440.

[5] Miller *v.* Miller, 33 Cal. 355 (1867).

[6] See Bishop, Mar. & D. §§ 664, 78, 85; 17 Nev. 221. In
Delaware, during the session of the legislature for
1886–87, forty-four special acts were passed.

[1] Maynard v. Hill, 125 U. S. 203–9 (1888), cases, Field,
J., deciding that the act of Dec. 22, 1852, of the Territory of Oregon, divorcing one Maynard and wife, was
constitutional.

[2] See Barrett *v.* Failing, 111 U. S. 525 (1884), cases.

[3] Barber *v.* Barber, 21 How. 591, 584 (1858); Cheever
v. Wilson, 9 Wall. 124 (1869).

[4] Hood *v.* State, 56 Ind. 263 (1877); People *v.* Baker,
76 N. Y. 78 (1879); Blackinton *v.* Blackinton, 141 Mass.
435 (1886), cases; 30 Kan. 717; 24 Iowa, 204.

[5] Van Voorhis *v.* Brintnall, 86 N. Y. 18, 24 (1881),
cases; 16 Am. Law Reg. 65–78, 193–204 (1877), cases;
Whart. Confl. Laws, § 135. Marrying again, as big-
amy, 17 Cent. Law J. 83–86 (1883), cases; 20 Am. Law
Rev. 718–26 (1886), cases. National legislation, 21 Am.
Law Rev. 675–78 (1887), cases. The new French act, 1
Law Quar. Rev. 358 (1885).

[6] McGill *v.* Deming, 44 Ohio St. 657 (1887), cases.

DOCK.[1] 1, *v.* To clip, cut off a part: to diminish.

Dock an account. To deduct something from a particular account.

Dock an entail. To curtail, destroy, defeat an estate tail.

2, *n.* (1) The space between wharves. Whence *dockage:* a charge for the use of a dock;[2] *dock-master; dock-warrant.* See WHARF.

The occupant of a dock is liable in damages to a person who, while using it, is injured in consequence of a defect permitted to exist, provided the injured person exercised due care.[3]

A dry-dock is not a subject of salvage service. The fact that it floats does not make it a "vessel," which only is a subject of salvage.[4]

(2) A space inclosed within a court room, for occupancy by an accused person while in court awaiting trial or sentence: the prisoner's dock.

DOCKET. 1, *v.* To abstract — and enter in a book.[5] See DOCK, 1.

To enter in a book called a docket.

2, *n.* A brief writing; an abstract, an epitome.

Originally, a memorandum of the substance of a document written upon the back or outside of it. In time, these memoranda, particularly those of judgments, were transcribed into books, and the name "docket" thereafter designated the books.

A brief statement in a book of the things done in court in the progress of a cause; also, the book which contains such history; and, again, a volume for the entry of all abstracts of a particular sort.

Whence docket *costs,* docket *entry,* docket *receipt,* docket *record,* docket *fee* — see FEE, 2.

Numerous terms are in use descriptive of the nature of the entries in dockets or of the persons by whom they are made. Thus, there may be a *prothonotary's,* a *clerk's* docket, a *sheriff's* or a *marshal's* docket, the docket of a *magistrate,* of an *alderman* or of a *justice of the peace,* an *attorney's* private docket; a *civil,* an *equity,* or a *criminal* docket, an *appearance* and an *issue* docket, a *recognizance* docket; a *trial* docket — often referred to as "the docket;" a *judgment* and an *execution* docket; an *ejectment,* a *mechanic's lien,* a *partition* docket; an *auditor's report* docket.

The docket of judgments is a brief writing or statement of a judgment made from the record or roll, kept with the clerk, in a book alphabetically arranged.[1]

Such docket affords purchasers and incumbrancers information as to the liens of judgments.[2]

Entries in dockets may or may not be "records." They are admissible in evidence when a formal record is not required.[3] See INDEX; JUDGMENT; MINUTES, 1; NOTICE, 1.

DOCTOR. One qualified to teach: a learned man; a person versed in one or more sciences or arts.

Doctor of laws. A title conferred by a college or university upon a person distinguished for his attainments in one or several departments of learning. Whence LL. D., from the Latin *legum* or *legibus doctor.*

Doctor of the civil law. A degree conferred upon a person who has pursued a prescribed course of study in general jurisprudence in a law school or university. Abbreviated D. C. L. See DEGREE, 3.

Doctor of medicine or **physic.** As popularly used, a practitioner of physic, irrespective of the system or school.[4] See PHYSICIAN.

DOCTRINE. The principle involved, applied, or propounded: as, the doctrine of escheat, estoppel, relation; the *cy prés* doctrine.

DOCUMENT. That which conveys information; that which furnishes evidence or proof; a written or printed instrument.

An instrument on which is recorded, by means of letters, figures, or marks, matter which may be evidentially used.[5]

Documentary. Pertaining to what is written; consisting of one or more documents: as, documentary evidence.

Ancient document. Any private writing thirty or more years old. See WRITING, Ancient.

Foreign document. Such writing as originates in or comes from another jurisdiction.

Judicial document. Any instrument emanating from a court of justice. **Legislative,** and **executive, document.** Any

---

1, *v.* Welsh *toc-, doc-,* to cut short, curtail. 2, *n.* Dutch *dokke,* a harbor: Gk. *doche,* receptacle.

City of Boston *v.* Lecrow, 17 How. 434 (1854); The Buckeye State, 1 Newb. 71 (1856).

Nickerson *v.* Tirrell, 127 Mass. 239 (1879), cases.

Cope *v.* Vallette Dry-Dock Co., 119 U. S. 627 (1887).

[3 Bl. Com. 397; 2 *id.* 511. In former times spelled "docquet."

[1] Stevenson *v.* Weisser, 1 Bradf. 344 (N. Y., 1850).

[2] Appeal of First Nat. Bank of Northumberland, 100 Pa. 427 (1882).

[3] Philadelphia, &c. R. Co. *v.* Howard, 13 How. 331 (1851), cases; *Re* Coleman, 15 Blatch. 426–27 (1879), cases.

[4] [Corsi *v.* Maretzek, 4 E. D. Sm. 5 (N. Y., 1855).

[5] 1 Whart. Ev. § 614.

instrument or record made or kept in the legislative or executive departments of government, and evidence of public business therein.

Private document. An instrument affecting the concerns of one or more individuals. **Public document.** An instrument or record concerning the business of the people at large, preserved in or emanating from any department of government; also, a publication printed or issued by order of one or both houses of Congress or of a State legislature.

Public documents include state papers, maps, charts, and like formal instruments, made under public auspices. A copy of such document, issued by public authority, is as valid as the original; as, an officially published statute. The term also embraces official records required to be kept by statute.[1]

A public statute proves its own recitals; not so, a private statute. Journals of legislatures and executive documents are *prima facie* evidence of the facts they recite.[2]

Official registers, kept as required by law, are evidence of the facts they record. They must be identified, be complete, indicate accuracy, and not be secondary.[3]

Parish records of births, baptisms, marriages, and deaths are receivable as evidence when made by the persons whose duty it was to note such facts.[4]

Family records prove family events.

A relative instrument is inadmissible without its correlative. Admission of a part involves the whole document. All the usual incidents accompany the document.[5]

A document is to be proved by him who offers it; otherwise, when produced in pursuance of notice, or by an adverse party who relies on the writing as part of his title. A document sued upon must be proved when its execution has been denied.[6]

In matters of execution the law of the place where the instrument is to have effect governs. A writing void as a contract may be valid as an admission. The identity of a signer is to be proved. An agent's power to execute must first be shown.[7]

See ALTERATION, 2; BOOK; COPY; EVIDENCE; HANDWRITING; INSPECTION, 2; INSTRUMENT, 2, 3; LOST, 2; NEWSPAPER; RECORD; SEAL, 1; STAMP; WRITING.

DOE; ROE. "John Doe" and "Richard Roe" were fictitious persons used as standing-pledges (common bail, *q. v.*) for the appearance of parties at a time when furnishing security for the prosecution of a suit by the plaintiff, and for attendance by the defendant, had become matters of form.[1]

The names may have been first used for the fictitious plaintiff and defendant in the old action of ejectment.[2] See STRAW.

Where defendants, whose real names were not known to the plaintiff, were described as "John Doe and Richard Roe, owners" of a particular vessel, and the true owners voluntarily appeared and filed answers, it was held that the plaintiff need not prove the ownership of the vessel.[3]

DOG. See ANIMAL; GAME, 2; KEEPER, 2; WORRY.

The almost unbroken current of authority is that, although dogs are property, their running at large in cities may be regulated or entirely prohibited; the requirement may be that they be classified, be registered, wear collars, and be destroyed if found running at large in violation of a statute or ordinance.[4]

A dog is a "thing of value," and may be stolen, and burglary may be committed in attempting to steal it.[5]

DOLI. See DOLUS.

DOLLAR. The unit of our currency; — money, or its equivalent.[6]

A silver coin weighing four hundred and twelve and one-half grains, or a gold coin weighing twenty-five and four-fifths grains, of nine-tenths pure to one-tenth alloy of each metal.[7]

The *coined* dollar of the United States; a certain quantity and fineness of gold or silver, authenticated as such by the stamp of the government.[8] See further COIN.

A contract to pay in "dollars" means in lawful money of the United States, and cannot be explained by parol; otherwise, of a contract made in another country, or in the late Confederate States, in which last case the reference may be to "Confederate dollars."[9]

"Dollars" will be supplied where the context shows that word omitted.[10]

---

[1] See McCall v. United States, 1 Dak. 321–28 (1876), cases; 1 Sup. R. S. pp. 154, 288.

[2] 1 Whart. Ev. §§ 639–48; Whiton v. Albany, &c. Ins. Co., 109 Mass. 30 (1871), cases.

[3] 1 Whart. Ev. §§ 639–48; 1 Greenl. Ev. §§ 493, 484, 496.

[4] 1 Whart. Ev. §§ 649–59; 1 Greenl. Ev. § 493.

[5] 1 Whart. Ev. §§ 618–20, 642.

[6] 1 Whart. Ev. §§ 689–91, 736.

[7] 1 Whart. Ev. §§ 700–2, 739 *a*.

[1] 3 Bl. Com. 274, 287, 295.

[2] 3 Steph. Com. 618.

[3] Baxter v. Doe, 142 Mass. 562 (1886); Pub. St. c. 161, § 20.

[4] State v. City of Topeka, 36 Kan. 84 (1886), cases. See generally 20 Alb. Law J. 6–10 (1879), cases.

[5] State v. Yates, C. P. of Fayette Co., Ohio: 37 Alb. Law J. 232 (1888); *ib.* 348–50, cases.

[6] United States v. Auken, 96 U. S. 368 (1878).

[7] Borie v. Trott, 5 Phila. 366, 404 (1864), Hare, J.

[8] Bank of New York v. Supervisors, 7 Wall. 30 (1868), Chase, C. J.

[9] Thornington v. Smith, 8 Wall. 12 (1868), Chase, C. J.; Cook v. Lillo, 103 U. S. 792 (1880); 35 Ill. 396, 440; 39 N. Y. 98; 1 W. N. C. 223; 33 Tex. 351.

[10] Hines v. Chambers, 29 Minn. 11 (1884); Hunt v. Smith, 9 Kan. 153 (1872).

An instrument in the form of a promissory note for e payment of "23.00 as per deed, 10 per cent. till id," is a note for twenty-five dollars.[1]

Where a jury found "for the plaintiff in the sum of irteen hundred and ninety-nine and 48-100," it was ld that the omission of the word "dollars" was not ch a defect as prevented rendering judgment ac-rding to the intent of the jury, although it would ive been more regular to have amended the verdict fore judgment.[2]

Any mark commonly employed in business trans-tions to denote the division of figures, obviously rep-senting money, into dollars and cents, is sufficient r that purpose.[3]

"One dollar" — see CONSIDERATION, 2, Nominal.

See generally CURRENCY; MONEY; TENDER, Legal; AR.

DOLUS. L. Device, artifice, guile, craft, itention to deceive, — especially when used ith *malus:* actual fraud. Evil purpose; nlawful intention, illegal ill-will; legal ialice. Compare CULPA.

Doli capax. Able to distinguish between ight and wrong; having capacity to intend rong, to commit crime. **Doli incapax.** ncapable of meditating wrong.

Capacity for guilt is measured by the strength of he understanding. Under seven years of age, an in-ant cannot be guilty of felony; under fourteen, hough he be *prima facie* adjudged *doli incapax*, yet f it appears that he was *doli capax*, and could discern etween good and evil, he may be convicted.[4]

Dolus bonus. Craftiness which falls short f fraud; as, adroitness in effecting a sale, iot amounting to false representation.

Dolus malus. Actual false representa-ion, intended to injure.

Ex dolo malo. See ACTIO.

See DECEIT; FRAUD.

DOM. As a termination — jurisdiction, iroperty, as in kingdom; or — state, condi-ion, quality, as in freedom, serfdom. Orig-nally, *doom* — judicial sentence.

Dom-bec or **-boc.** See DOME.

DOMAIN.[5] 1. Dominion, ownership, iroperty; absolute proprietorship or right of ontrol.[6]

Domain, eminent. The power to take irivate property for public uses is termed 'the right of eminent domain."[7]

"Eminent" imports having preference, being para-mount, prerogative, sovereign.

All separate interests of individuals in property are held of the government under the implied reservation that the property may be taken for the public use, upon paying a fair compensation, whenever the public interest requires it. The possession is to be resumed in the manner directed by the constitution and laws.[1]

The ultimate right of the sovereign, power to appropriate, not only the public property, but the private property of all citizens within the territorial sovereignty, to public purposes. Vattel says that the right in society or the sovereign to dispose, in case of necessity, and for the public safety, of all the wealth (prop-erty) in the state, is "eminent domain," and a prerogative of majesty.[2]

In every political sovereign community there in-heres, necessarily, the right and the duty of guarding its own existence, and of protecting and promoting the interests and welfare of the community at large. This power, denominated the "eminent domain" of the state, is, as its name imports, paramount to all private rights vested under the government, and these last are, by necessary implication, held in subordina-tion to this power, and must yield in every instance to its proper exercise. The whole policy of the country relative to roads, mills, bridges, and canals rests upon this single power, under which lands have always been condemned; without the exertion of the power no one of these improvements could be constructed. The ex-ercise of a franchise is subject to the power.[3]

The propriety of exercising the right is a political question — exclusively for the legislature to deter-mine.[4]

The mode of exercising the right, in the absence of provision in the organic law prescribing a contrary course, is within the discretion of the legislature. If the purpose be a public one, and just compensation be paid or tendered the owner of the property taken, there is no limitation upon the power of the legisla-ture.[5]

The right of eminent domain exists in the govern-ment of the United States, and may be exercised by it within the States, so far as is necessary to the en-joyment of the powers conferred by the Constitution. Such authority is essential to its independent existence and perpetuity. These cannot be preserved if the obstinacy of a private person, or if any other author-

---

[1] State *v.* Schwartz, 64 Wis. 432 (1885).

[2] Hopkins *v.* Orr, 124 U. S. 513 (1888), cases, Gray, J.

[3] Delashmutt *v.* Sellwood, 10 Oreg. 325 (1882).

[4] 4 Bl. Com. 23.

[5] F. *domaine,* a lordship: L. *dominium,* right of iwnership. Compare DEMESNE; DOMAIN.

[6] See 2 Bl. Com. 1.

[7] United States *v.* Jones, 109 U. S. 518 (1883), Field, J.

---

[1] Beekman *v.* Saratoga, &c. R. Co., 3 Paige, 72–73 (1831), Walworth, Ch.: Bloodgood *v.* Mohawk, &c. R. Co., 18 Wend. 13–18 (1837), cases.

[2] Charles River Bridge *v.* Warren Bridge, 11 Pet. *641 (1837), Story, J. Vattel is also quoted in 109 U. S. 519, *post.*

[3] West River Bridge Co. *v.* Dix, 6 How. 531–33 (1848), Daniel, J.

[4] Hyde Park *v.* Cemetery Association, 119 Ill. 149 (1886); 111 Mass. 125.

[5] Secombe *v.* Milwaukee, &c. R. Co., 23 Wall. 118 (1874); People *v.* Smith, 21 N. Y. 597-98 (1860); Holt *v.* Council of Somerville, 127 Mass. 410, 413 (1879).

ity, can prevent the acquisition of the means or instruments by which alone governmental functions can be performed. No one doubts the existence in the State governments of the right of eminent domain,—a right distinct from and paramount to the right of ultimate ownership. It grows out of the necessities of their being, not out of the tenure by which lands are held. It may be exercised, though the lands are not held by grant from the government, either mediately or immediately, and independent of the consideration whether they would escheat to the government in case of a failure of heirs. The right is the offspring of political necessity; and it is inseparable from sovereignty, unless denied to it by its fundamental law. But it is no more necessary for the exercise of the powers of a State government than for the exercise of the conceded powers of the Federal government. That government is sovereign within its sphere, as the States are within theirs. When the power to establish post-offices and to create courts within the States was conferred upon the Federal government, included in it was authority to obtain sites for such offices and for court-houses, by such means as were known and appropriate. The right of eminent domain was one of those means well known when the Constitution was adopted, and employed to obtain lands for public uses. Its existence, therefore, in the grantee of that power ought not to be questioned. The Constitution itself contains an implied recognition of it beyond what may justly be implied from the express grants. The Fifth Amendment contains a provision that "private property" shall not "be taken for public use without just compensation." What is that but an implied assertion that, on making just compensation, it may be taken. . This power of the Federal government has not heretofore been exercised adversely; but the non-user of a power does not disprove its existence. In some instances the States, by virtue of their own right of eminent domain, have condemned lands for the use of the general government, and such condemnations have been sustained by their courts, without, however, denying the right of the United States to act independently of the States. . . The proper view of the right of eminent domain seems to be that it is a right belonging to a sovereignty to take private property for its own public uses, and not for those of another. Beyond that there exists no necessity; which alone is the foundation of the right. If the United States have the power, it must be complete in itself. It can neither be enlarged nor diminished by a State. Nor can any State prescribe the manner in which it must be exercised. The consent of a State can never be a condition precedent to its enjoyment. Such consent is needed only, if at all, for the transfer of jurisdiction and of the right of exclusive legislation after the lands shall have been acquired.[1]

The right requires no constitutional recognition. When the use is public, the necessity or expediency of the appropriation is not a subject of judicial cognizance. The power may be delegated to a private corporation, to be exercised in the execution of a work in which the public is interested. Whether attached conditions have been observed is a matter for judicial cognizance.[1]

Ascertainment of the amount of compensation to be made is not an essential element of the power of appropriation. The constitutional provision for "just compensation" is merely a limitation upon the use of the power. It is no part of the power itself, but a condition upon which the power may be exercised. The proceeding for the ascertainment of the value of the property and the compensation to be made is merely an inquisition to establish a particular fact as a preliminary to the actual taking; and it may be prosecuted before commissioners, special boards, or the courts, with or without the intervention of a jury, as the legislative power may designate. All that is required is that it shall be conducted in some fair and just manner, with opportunity to the owners of the property to present evidence as to its value, and to be heard thereon. Whether the tribunal shall be created directly by an act of Congress, or one already established by the States shall be adopted for the occasion, is a matter of legislative discretion.[2]

The right over the shores and the land under the water of navigable streams resides in the State for municipal purposes, within legitimate limitations.[3]

Land taken for one purpose cannot, without special authority from the legislature, be appropriated, by proceedings *in invitum*, to a different use.[4]

The power of eminent domain expropriates, upon indemnity for public utility; the "police power" is exercised without making compensation — any loss occasioned is *damnum absque injuria*.[5] See further POLICE, 2; USE, 2, Public.

See also COMPENSATION, 3; LAND, Public; PARK, 2; TAKE, 8.

2. Territory owned and governed; lands.

Domain, public. Public lands, with any buildings thereon, held in trust by the government.

Congress has exclusive power to dispose of the public domain of the United States, and the exercise of the power is limited only by the discretion in that body.[6] See LANDS, Public.

DOME. A judgment, decree, sentence.

Dome-book. Any book of judgments.

Alfred collected the customs of the kingdom and reduced them to a system or code in his "Dom-bec,"

---

[1] Kohl v. United States, 91 U. S. 371-74 (1875), cases, Strong, J. Approved, Fort Leavenworth R. Co. v. Lowe, 114 id. 531 (1885); Roanoke City v. Berkowitz, 80 Va. 619, 623 (1885).

[1] Mississippi, &c. Boom Co. v. Patterson, 98 U. S. 406 (1878).

[2] United States v. Jones, 109 U. S. 518-19 (1883), Field, J. See Wagner v. Railway Co., 38 Ohio St. 35 (1882).

[3] Omerod v. New York, &c. R. Co., 13 F. R. 370 (1882).

[4] Prospect Park, &c. R. Co. v. Williamson, 91 N. Y. 552, 561 (1883); Anniston, &c. R. Co. v. Jacksonville, &c. R. Co., 82 Ala. 300 (1886), cases.

[5] Bass v. State, 34 La. An. 496 (1882); Davenport v. Richmond City, 81 Va. 639 (1886); 17 F. R. 114; 81 Pa. 85. See generally 3 Law Q. Rev. 314-25 (1887), cases; 2 Kent, 339; 19 Bost. Law Rep. 241, 301.

[6] West River Bridge Co. v. Dix, 6 How. 540 (1848);

for the use of his tribunals. The volume also contained the maxims of the common law, forms for judicial proceedings, and certain penalties.[1]

The book may be seen, in both Saxon and English, in "The Ancient Laws and Institutes of England," published by the Record Commissioners, Vol. 1, pp. 45-101. At the head of the book stand the Ten Commandments, followed by many Mosaic precepts. After quoting the canons of the apostolic council at Jerusalem, Alfred refers to the commandment "As ye would that men should do to you, do ye also to them," adding, "from this one doom a man may remember that he judge every one righteously: he need heed no other doom-book." [2]

The Commandments and such portions of the Law of Moses as were prefixed to the code became a part of the law of the land. Labor on Sunday was made criminal, and heavy punishments were exacted for perjury.[3]

Domesday-book. A survey of all the lands in England, with the names of their owners, their value, etc., compiled, by direction of the Conqueror, 1081-86.

The completeness of the survey made it "a day of judgment" as to the extent, value, and other qualities of every piece of land. It was practically a careful census, and became a final authority on tenures and titles. The two original volumes are preserved in the Exchequer.[4]

DOMESTIC.[5] Belonging or pertaining to one's own home, State, or country.

1. Residing in the same house with the master he serves: as, a domestic servant; or, simply, a domestic: a house servant; not, an outdoor workman, nor a person hired for a day.[6]

Living about the habitations of men; tame, domesticated: as, a domestic animal, q. v.

2. Relating to the law of the place of a person's domicil.

Having jurisdiction at one's domicil: as, the domestic court, forum, tribunal.

Appointed at the place of residence — of the person lately deceased, or of a ward: as, a domestic administrator, guardian, q. v.

3. Relating to the law, property, trade, or inhabitants of some particular State.

For the benefit of creditors within the debtor's own State: as, a domestic assignment, q. v.; whence, also, domestic creditors.

Maintainable against a resident debtor: as, a domestic attachment, q. v.

Created under the laws of the State in which it transacts business: as, a domestic corporation, q. v.

Rendered by a court of the State where it was first entered or enrolled: as, a domestic decree, or judgment, q. v.

Arising or committed within the borders of a State or among the inhabitants thereof: as, domestic violence, q. v.

4. Relating to the territorial limits or to the jurisprudence of two or more States, or of the whole United States.

Confined within the United States, or, possibly, one State: as, domestic commerce, manufactures, qq. v.

Acquired within a subdivision of a country: as, a domestic domicil, q. v.

Resident within the State or country in question: as, a domestic factor, q. v.

DOMICIL.[1] The place where a person lives or has his home; that is, where one has his true, fixed, permanent home and principal establishment, and to which, whenever he is absent, he has the intention of returning.[2]

The habitation fixed in any place, without any present intention of removing therefrom.[3]

Domiciliate, or domicile. To establish one, or oneself, in a fixed residence.

Domiciliary. Pertaining to one's permanent residence: as, a domiciliary court, the domiciliary administrator or guardian, domiciliary inspection or visitation.

There is a wide difference between domicil and mere residence. While they are usually at the same place, they may be at different places. Domicil is the established, fixed, permanent, ordinary dwelling place

---

United States v. Gratiot, 14 Pet. 536 (1840); 1 Kent, 166, 257; 37 Am. Jur. 121.

[1] 4 Bl. Com. 411; 3 id. 65.

[2] See 1 Bl. Com. 65, note by Warren.

[3] Green, Short Hist. Eng. People, 81.

[4] See 2 Bl. Com. 49, 99; 3 id. 331; Green, Short Hist. Eng. People, 114.

[5] L. domesticus, belonging to a household: domus, a house.

[6] Exp. Meason, 5 Binn. 174-84 (1812); Wakefield v. State, 41 Tex. 558 (1874); Richardson v. State, 43 id. 456 (1875); Ullman v. State, 1 Tex. Ap. 221 (1876); Waterhouse v. State, 21 id. 666 (1886). See R. S. § 4063.

[1] Spelled also domicile. F. domicile, a dwelling: L. domicilium, habitation: domus, a house; and -cilium, allied to celare, to hide.

[2] Story, Conf. Laws, § 41; Hannon v. Grizzard, 89 N. C. 120 (1883), Smith, C. J.; 75 Pa. 205.

[3] Putnam v. Johnson, 10 Mass. *501 (1813), Parker, J.; State v. Moore, 14 N. H. 454 (1843); Crawford v. Wilson, 4 Barb. 520 (1848).

or residence of a party, as distinguished from his temporary and transient though actual place of residence. One is his legal residence as distinguished from his temporary place of abode; in other words, one is his home, as distinguished from the place or places to which business or pleasure may temporarily call him.[1]

Primarily a person's domicil is his legal home; but domicil implies more than mere residence in a country.[2]

The domicil of a person may be in one place and his residence in another.[3]

Residence, with no present intention of removal, constitutes domicil.[4]

"Domicil" has a fixed and definite signification. For the ordinary purposes of citizenship there are rules of general, if not of universal, acceptation applicable to it. "Citizenship," "habitancy" and "residence" are severally words which may in the particular case mean precisely the same as "domicil," but frequently they may have other and inconsistent meanings, and while in one use of language the expressions a change of domicil, of citizenship, of habitancy, of residence, are necessarily identical or synonymous, in a different use of language they import different ideas.[5]

In international law, domicil means a residence at a particular place, accompanied with positive or presumptive proof of intending to continue there for an unlimited time.[6]

To ascertain this domicil, it is proper to take into consideration the situation, the employment, and the character of the individual; the trade in which he is engaged, the family he possesses, and the transitory or fixed character of his business are ingredients which may properly be weighed.[7]

Domicil is spoken of: as *national,* or that of a person's country, and opposed to *domestic,* or that of a subdivision of a country; as *foreign,* established in another state; as *commercial,* the place of one's trade or business; *of birth,* that of one's parents; *acquired,* vested by the law; *by choice,* selected of free will; *by law,* by operation of law.

Once existing, a domicil continues until another is acquired; when a change is alleged the burden of proof rests upon the party making the allegation. To constitute a new domicil, two things are indispen-

sable: residence in the new locality, and the intention to remain there, *facto et animo.* Mere absence from a fixed home, however long continued, cannot work the change. Among the circumstances usually relied upon to establish the *animus manendi* are: declarations, exercise of political rights, payment of personal taxes, a house of residence, a place of business.[1]

A change does not depend so much upon the intention to remain in the new place for a definite or an indefinite period, as upon its being without an intention to return to the former place of actual residence. An intention to return, however, at a remote or indefinite period, will not control, if the other facts which constitute domicil all give the new residence the character of a permanent home and place of abode. The intention and actual fact of residence must concur, when such residence is not in its nature temporary. There is a right of election by expressed intention, only when the facts are to some extent ambiguous.[2]

A domicil *of origin* is presumed to be retained until residence elsewhere has been shown.[3] A domicil of origin, or an acquired domicil, remains until a new one is acquired. A native domicil is not so easily changed as an acquired domicil, and is more easily lost. A man can have but one domicil at the same time for the same purpose.[2]

Domicil is acquired by residence and the *animûs manendi,* the intent to remain.

A wife's domicil is that of the husband; but she may acquire a separate one, whenever necessary or proper, as, for a suit in divorce,[5] *q. v.* See also CITIZEN; LEX, Domicilii; RESIDE.

DOMINANT. See EASEMENT, Dominant.

DOMINION. Complete ownership; absolute property.[6]

The right in a corporeal thing, from which arises the power of disposition and of claiming it from others.[7]

Proximate dominion. Obtaining possession by delivery of a thing sold, which,

---

[1] Town of Salem *v.* Town of Lyme, 29 Conn. 79 (1860), Hinman, J.

[2] McDonald *v.* Salem Capital Flour-Mills Co., 31 F. R. 577 (1887).

[3] Lyon *v.* Lyon, 30 Hun, 456 (1883); Foss *v.* Foss, 58 N. H. 284 (1878), cases.

[4] Lindsay *v.* Murphy, 76 Va. 430 (1882).

[5] Borland *v.* City of Boston, 132 Mass. 93 (1882), Lord, J.

[6] Guier *v.* O'Daniel, 1 Binn. *350 (1806), Rush, P. J.; State *v.* Collector, 32 N. J. L. 194 (1867); Mitchell *v.* United States, 21 Wall. 352 (1874).

[7] Livingstone *v.* Maryland Ins. Co., 7 Cranch, 542 (1813), Story, J.; The Venus, 8 Cranch, 278 (1814).

[1] Mitchell *v.* United States, 21 Wall. 353, 352 (1874), cases, Swayne, J.; Desmare *v.* United States, 93 U. S. 609 (1876); Doyle *v.* Clark, 1 Flip. 537–38 (1876), cases; Lindsay *v.* Murphy, 76 Va. 430 (1882); 21 Cent. Law J. 430–32 (1885), cases — Solicitors Journal (London).

[2] Hallet *v.* Bassett, 100 Mass. 170–71 (1868), cases, Colt, J.; Guier *v.* O'Daniel, 1 Am. Lead. Cas. 747–50, cases.

[3] Ennis *v.* Smith (Kosciusko's Case), 14 How. 423 (1852).

[4] Newton *v.* Commissioners, 100 U. S. 562 (1879), Swayne, J.

[5] Cheever *v.* Wilson, 9 Wall. 124 (1869); Cheely *v.* Clayton, 110 U. S. 705 (1884), cases; 2 Bishop, Mar. & D. 475; 23 Alb. Law J. 86 (1881), cases.

See generally 13 Am. Law Rev. 261–79 (1879), cases; 11 Cent. Law J. 421–25 (1880), cases; 1 Wall. Jr. 262; 7 Fla. 81, 152; 46 Ga. 277; 74 Ill. 314; 89 Ind. 177; 51 Iowa, 79; 20 La. 314; 26 *id.* 338; 52 Me. 165; 27 Miss. 718; 54 *id.* 310; 77 Mo. 678; 37 N. J. L. 495; 8 Wend. 142; 3 Paige, 524; 31 Barb. 476; 67 N. Y. 379; 71 Pa. 309; 42 Vt. 332.

[6] See 2 Bl. Com. Ch. I.

[7] Coles *v.* Perry, 7 Tex. 136 (1851), Hughes, S. J.

vithout anything else, being preceded by he title, vests the right in the thing — which s the dominion. **Remote dominion.** The itle which vests a right to a thing sold, and gives a cause of action against the vendor vho has not delivered the thing.[1]

Compare DEMESNE; DOMAIN; DOMINIUM.

DOMINIUM. L. Complete ownership of property.

Dominium directum. Immediate ownership, — possession.

Dominium utile. Beneficial ownership, — enjoyment.

Dominium directum et utile. Direct and beneficial ownership: complete ownership and possession in one person. Compare DROIT-DROIT.

DOMINUS. L. Lord or master; owner.

Dominus litis. The actor in a cause; the principal in a suit; the client, as distinguished from his agent or attorney.[2]

Domino perit res. The thing has perished for its owner. See further RES, Perit.

Domino volente. The owner willing.

DOMITÆ. See ANIMAL.

DOMUS. L. A house; the house.

Domus procerum. The house of lords. Abbreviated *dom. proc.*, and D. P.

Domus sua cuique est tutissimum refugium. His own dwelling is for every one the safest refuge: every man's house is his castle. See further HOUSE, 1.

DONA. See DONUM.

DONATE. See DONATION.

DONATIO. L. A giving; a gift. See DARE; GIFT.

Donatio inter vivos. A gift between living persons: when the maker of a gift is not apprehending death. See further GIFT.

Donatio mortis causa, or **causa mortis.** A gift in view of death; a death-bed disposition of personalty.

A donation *causa mortis* takes place when a person in his last sickness, apprehending dissolution near, delivers or causes to be delivered to another the possession of any personal goods to keep in case of his decease. Such a gift is to revert to the donor, if he survives, and is not valid as against creditors.[3]

There must have been a transfer of property in expectation of death from an existing illness.[1]

A gift of personal property, by a party who is in peril of death, upon condition that it shall presently belong to the donee, in case the donor shall die, but not otherwise. There must be a delivery by the donor. The gift will be defeated by revocation, or by recovery or escape from the impending peril. It is in no sense a testamentary act. There may be a good donation of anything which has a physical existence and admits of corporal or symbolical delivery. Negotiable instruments, and even bonds and mortgages, may be thus transferred.[2]

A *donatio mortis causa* must be completely executed, precisely as is required in the case of a gift *inter vivos,* subject to be devested by the happening of any of the conditions subsequent, that is, upon actual revocation by the donor, by his surviving the apprehended peril, by his outliving the donee, or by the occurrence of a deficiency of the assets necessary to pay the debts of the donor. If the gift does not take effect as a complete transfer of possession and title, legal or equitable, during the life of the donor, it is a testamentary disposition, and good only if made and proved as a will. . The instrument transferring a chose in action must be the evidence of a subsisting obligation and be delivered to the donee, so as to vest him with an equitable title to the fund it represents, and to devest the owner of all present control over it, absolutely and irrevocably, but upon the recognized conditions subsequent. A delivery which empowers the donee to control the fund only after the death of the donor, when by the instrument itself it is presently payable, is testamentary in character, and not good as a gift.[3]

Recent statutes make valid a wife's death-bed donations of personalty without her husband's assent.[4]

Donatio propter nuptias. A gift in consideration of marriage. In the civil law, the provision made by the husband as the counterpart of the *dos* or marriage portion brought by the wife.

DONATION. See DONATIO. A contract by which a person gratuitously dispossesses himself of something by transferring it to another to become the latter's property upon acceptance.[5]

---

[1] Coles *v.* Perry, 7 Tex. 136 (1851), *ante.*

[2] See 4 Hughes, 341.

[3] 2 Bl. Com. 514.

[1] Grattan *v.* Appleton, 3 Story, 755, 768 (1845).

[2] 1 Story, Eq. §§ 606–7; 3 Pomeroy, Eq. §§ 1146–51; 2 Kent, 244.

[3] Basket *v.* Hassel', 107 U. S. 609–10, 614 (1882), cases, Matthews, J.; Same *v.* Same, 108 *id.* 267 (1883), 8 Biss. 306–9 (1878), cases. See also 16 Ala. 221; 59 Cal. 665; 38 Ind. 454; 54 N. H. 37; 31 Me. 429; 77 Mo. 173; 30 Hun, 632, 635; 20 Johns. 514; 33 N. Y. 581; 23 Pa. 63; 51 *id.* 349–50; 39 Vt. 624; 4 Gratt. 479; 1 Am. Law Reg. 1–11 (1852), cases; 19 Cent. Law J. 222–26 (1884), cases; 2 Law Q. Rev. 444–52 (1886); 21 Am. Law Rev. 732–63 (1887), cases; Ward *v.* Turner, W. & T. L. C. Eq. Vol. 1, pt. 2, 1205–51, cases.

[4] Schouler, Wills, § 63, cases.

[5] See Fisk *v.* Flores, 43 Tex. 343 (1875).

Donate. To give gratuitously or without consideration.[1]

In the act of Indiana of May 9, 1869, enabling a city to aid the construction of a railroad, etc., "donation" means an absolute gift or grant of a thing without any condition or consideration.[2] See AID, 1, Municipal.

Letting the labor of convicts in consideration of their being fed, clothed, etc., by the hirer, is not a "donation" or gratuity.[3]

DONIS. See DONUM.

DONOR; DONEE. 1. The giver, and the recipient, respectively, of personalty. See DONATIO; DONATION.

2. He who confers, and he who is invested with, a power. See POWER, 2.

3. He who gives, and he who receives, lands in tail, q. v.

DONUM. L. A gift. See DARE; DONATIO.

De donis. Respecting gifts — estates-tail.

The first chapter of the statute of Westminster 2 (13 Edw. I, 1285) is called the Statute *de donis* or *de donis conditionalibus.* It took from donees the power of alienating their estates-tail, thus introducing perpetuities.

At common law an estate-tail was known as a conditional fee — limited to particular heirs; the condition being that if the donee died, without leaving an heir, the estate reverted. Upon the birth of issue the estate became absolute for three purposes: the donee could alien it, and thus bar his issue and the reversioner; he could forfeit it by an act of treason; he could encumber it. As soon as issue was born the donee aliened and immediately repurchased, thereby obtaining a fee-simple absolute for all purposes. To keep estates in the hands of the great families, the statute *de donis* was passed. It directed that the will of the donor should be observed, and forbade alienation. It abolished the conditional fee and made the estate descend *per formam doni,* or passed in reversion. The statute continued in force two centuries. In the reign of Edw. IV, it was held[4] that the entail might be destroyed by a common recovery, and the issue, the donee, and the donee's expectant, he barred, on the death of the tenant in tail "without issue." Fines and special laws subsequently effected the same end.[5] See further FEE, 1.

Dona clandestina sunt semper suspiciosa. Secret gifts are always viewed with suspicion: secret transfers of property are regarded with distrust.[1] See CONVEYANCE, Fraudulent.

DOOM. See DOME.

DOOR. See HOUSE, 1.

DORMANT. Sleeping: silent, unavowed, undisclosed: as, a dormant partner; secret, not of public record: as, a dormant judgment; in abeyance, suspended: as, a dormant execution. See those substantives.

DOS. L. A marriage portion; dowry. French *dot.*

In Roman law, property given a husband to aid him in sustaining the burdens of the marriage relation.

In English law, the portion bestowed upon a wife at marriage; also, the portion a widow is entitled to out of the estate of her deceased husband.

Dos rationalibus. A reasonable marriage portion; common-law dower,[2] q. v.

DOTAGE. See DEMENTIA, Senile.

DOTAL. Pertaining to dowry. Opposed, extra-dotal: not part of dowry. See Dos.

DOUBLE. 1. By two married persons: as, double adultery, q. v.

2. On behalf of each of two parties: as, a double agency. See BROKER.

3. For the same cause of action: as, a double arrest, q. v.; double punishment, or satisfaction, q. v.

4. Twofold: as, a contingency with a double aspect, q. v.

5. Upon the same subject-matter, twice over: as, a double assessment or taxation. See TAX, 2.

6. Twice the original: as, double costs, q. v.

7. Increased by the court, over the actual amount: as, double damages.

8. For, by, or from two persons; opposed to single: as, a double deed.

9. Additional; upon the same property, against the same risks, and for the same person: as, double insurance, q. v.

10. Second, duplicated: as, a double payment.

11. Twice the original or true amount: as, a double penalty, q. v.

12. Containing two or more distinct causes of action or defense: as, double pleading. See DUPLICITY.

---

[1] Goodhue v. City of Beloit, 21 Wis. *642 (1867).

[2] Indiana North & South R. Co. v. City of Attica, 56 Ind. 486, 476 (1877); Wilkinson v. City of Peru, 61 *id.* 9 (1878).

[3] Georgia Penitentiary Co. v. Nelms, 65 Ga. 503–5 (1880).

[4] Taltarum's Case, Year Book, 12 Edw. IV (1473), c. 19.

[5] 2 Bl. Com. 112, 360; Croxall v. Shererd, 5 Wall. 283 (1866).

[1] Broom, Max. 289, 290; 4 B. & C. 652; 1 M. & S. 253.

[2] See 2 Bl. Com. 129, 492, 516; 1 Washb. R. P. 147, 209; 132 Mass. 275; 6 Mart., La., 460.

13. Permissive and commissive: as, double waste, *q. v.*

DOUBT.[1] Fluctuation of mind arising from want of evidence or knowledge; uncertainty of mind; unsettled opinion.[2]

Equipoise of mind arising from an equality of contrary reasons.[3]

In civil cases, a doubt is to be resolved against the party who might have furnished facts to remove it, but has neglected so to do. In charges of fraud, the presumption of innocence will remove a doubt. In criminal cases, whenever a reasonable doubt exists as to the guilt of the accused he is to receive the benefit of the doubt.

Where, in a civil proceeding, proving the cause of action or the defense will also prove a crime committed by the adverse party, it is not necessary that the proof be of the degree required in a criminal proceeding for the offense, that is, beyond a reasonable doubt. The issue should be determined in accordance with the preponderance of the proof.[4]

Reasonable doubt. "That state of the case, which, after the entire comparison and consideration of all evidence, leaves the minds of jurors in that condition that they cannot say they feel an abiding conviction, to a moral certainty, of the truth of the charge." [5]

The expression is not easily defined. It does not mean mere possible doubt; because everything relating to human affairs and depending on moral evidence is open to some possible or imaginary doubt. . . All the presumptions of law independent of evidence are in favor of innocence; and every person is presumed to be innocent until proved guilty. If upon such proof there is reasonable doubt remaining, the accused is entitled to the benefit of it by an acquittal.[5]

It is not sufficient to establish a probability, though a strong one, arising from the doctrine of chances, that the fact charged is more likely to be true than the contrary; but the evidence must establish the truth of the fact to a reasonable and moral certainty; a certainty that convinces and directs the understanding, and satisfies the reason and judgment of those who are bound to act conscientiously upon it.[5]

If the law, which mostly depends upon considerations of a moral nature, should require absolute certainty, it would exclude circumstantial evidence altogether.[6]

"Proof beyond a reasonable doubt" is not beyond all possible or imaginary doubt, but such proof as precludes every reasonable hypothesis except that which tends to support. It is proof "to a moral certainty," as distinguished from an absolute certainty. As applied to a judicial trial for crime, the two phrases are synonymous and equivalent; each has been used by eminent judges to explain the other; and each signifies: Such proof as satisfies the judgment and consciences of the jury as reasonable men, and applying their reason to the evidence before them, that the crime charged has been committed by the defendant, and so satisfies them as to leave no other reasonable conclusion possible.[1] See CERTAINTY, 1, Moral.

Such doubt must be founded on something growing out of the state of the testimony, which leaves a rational uncertainty as to guilt, and which nothing else in the case removes. The degree of conviction of guilt should be something more than a bare preponderance of belief; something more than the probability of guilt merely outweighing the probability of innocence. The mind should be able to rest reasonably satisfied of the guilt of the accused before a verdict of that character is given.[2]

A doubt founded upon a consideration of all the circumstances and evidence, and not a doubt resting upon conjecture or speculation.[3]

The jury must find the facts established to such a degree of certainty as they would regard sufficient in the important affairs of life. The proof need not necessarily exclude all doubt.[4]

"A doubt which a reasonable man of sound judgment, without bias, prejudice, or interest, after calmly, conscientiously, and deliberately weighing all the testimony, would entertain as to the guilt of the prisoner." The guilt must be established to a reasonable, not an absolute, demonstrative or mathematical, certainty.[5]

An indefinable doubt which cannot be stated, with the reason upon which it rests, is not a reasonable doubt, within the rule that an accused is to be given the benefit of such doubt.[5]

Not any fanciful conjecture which an imaginative man may conjure up, but a doubt which reasonably

---

108; 3 Monta. 137, 162; 6 Nev. 340; 26 N. J. L. 615; 103 U. S. 312; 120 *id.* 440, *post,*—commented on.

[1] Commonwealth *v.* Costley, 118 Mass. 24 (1875), cases, Gray, C. J.; cited, 120 U. S. 440, *post.*

[2] United States *v.* Gleason, 1 Woolv. 137 (1867), Miller, J.

[3] United States *v.* Knowles, 4 Saw. 521 (1864), Field, J.

[4] United States *v.* Wright, 16 F. R. 114 (1883), Billings, J.

[5] State *v.* Rounds, 76 Me. 125 (1884), Peters, C. J., quoting State *v.* Reed, 62 *id.* 144, 142–45 (1874).

[6] People *v.* Guidici, 100 N. Y. 510 (1885); 3 Greenl. Ev. § 29.

---

[1] F. *douter:* L. *dubitare* (q. v.), to waiver in mind.

[2] [Webster's Dict.

[3] [Bouvier's Law Dict.

[4] Thoreson *v.* Northwestern Nat. Ins. Co., 29 Minn. 107 (1882), cases.

[5] Commonwealth *v.* Webster, 5 Cush. 320 (1850), Shaw, C. J. Frequently cited, as in 59 Cal. 395; 60 *id.*

flows from the evidence or the want of evidence; a doubt for which a sensible man could give a good reason, based upon the evidence; such a doubt as he would act upon in his own concerns.[1]

It is difficult to conceive what amount of conviction would leave the mind of a juror free from a reasonable doubt, if it be not one which is so settled and fixed as to control his action in the more weighty and important matters relating to his own affairs. Out of the domain of the exact sciences and actual observation there is no absolute certainty. The guilt of the accused, in the majority of cases, must necessarily be deduced from a variety of circumstances leading to proof of the fact. Persons of speculative minds may in almost every case suggest possibilities of the truth being different from that established by the most convincing proof. Jurors are not to be led away by speculative notions as to such possibilities.[2]

"The jury are not to go beyond the evidence to hunt up doubts, nor must they entertain such doubts as are merely chimerical or conjectural." To justify acquittal, a doubt must arise from an impartial investigation of all the evidence, and be such that, " were the same kind of doubt interposed in the graver transactions of life, it would cause a reasonable and prudent man to hesitate and pause." " If, after considering all the evidence, you can say you have an abiding conviction of the truth of the charge, you are satisfied beyond a reasonable doubt; . . you are not at liberty to disbelieve as jurors, if, from the evidence, you believe as men." [3]

An instruction which says that the doubt must be "real," substantial, well-founded, arising out of the evidence, is not reversible.[4]

As to questions relating to human affairs, a knowledge of which is derived from testimony, it is impossible to have the kind of certainty created by scientific demonstration. The only certainty we can have is a moral certainty, which depends upon the confidence placed in the integrity of witnesses, and their capacity to know the truth. If, for example, facts not improbable are attested by numerous witnesses who are credible, consistent, uncontradicted, and had every opportunity of knowing the truth, a reasonable or moral certainty would be inspired by their testimony. In such case a doubt would be unreasonable, imaginary, or speculative, which it ought not to be. It is not a doubt whether the party may not possibly be innocent in the face of strong proof of his guilt, but a sincere doubt whether he has been proved guilty, that is called "reasonable." And even where the testimony is contradictory, so much more credit may be due to one side than the other, that the same result will be produced. On the other hand, the opposing proofs may be so nearly balanced that the jury may justly doubt on which side lies the truth. In such case the accused is entitled to the benefit of the doubt. As certainty advances, doubt recedes. If one is reasonably certain, he cannot, at the same time, be reasonably doubtful, that is, have a reasonable doubt, of a fact. All that a jury can be expected to do is to be reasonably or morally certain of the fact which they declare by their verdict.[1] See also EVIDENCE; PREPONDERANCE; PROOF.

Doubtful. Where, at the date of an assignment, certain choses were reported as "doubtful," it was held that the assignee could not be charged with them unless the creditors proved that they might have been collected by due diligence.[2]

DOWER.[3] The interest which the law gives a widow in the realty of her deceased husband. Compare DOWRY.

The life estate, created by law, where a man is seised of an estate of inheritance, and dies in the life-time of his wife.[4]

In the common law, that portion of lands or tenements which the wife has for the term of her life of the lands or tenements of her husband after his decease, for the sustenance of himself and the nurture and education of her children.[5]

Tenant in dower is where the husband of a woman is seised of an estate of inheritance and dies; the wife shall then have the third part of all the lands and tenements whereof he was seised at any time during the coverture, to hold to herself for the term of her natural life.[6]

Dowable. Entitled to dower, subject to dower; endowable: as, a dowable interest in lands, dowable lands.

Dowager. A widow endowed; particularly, the widow of a person of rank. **Dowress.** A widow entitled to dower; a tenant in dower.

Endow. To assign dower to; to become invested with rights of dower. Whence endowable. See ENDOW.

The widow must have been the actual wife of the party at the time of his decease. She is endowable of all lands and tenements of which her husband was seised in fee-simple or fee-tail, at any time during the coverture, and of which any issue she might have had might by possibility have been heir. . . There was also dower *by custom:* as, that the wife should have a quarter, a half, or all of the land; dower *ad ostium*

---

[1] [United States v. Jones, 31 F. R. 724 (1887), Speer, J.; *ib.* 718, note.

[2] Hopt v. Utah, 120 U. S. 439–41 (1887), cases, Field, J.

[3] Spies *et al.* v. People, 122 Ill. 251–52 (1887), cases.

[4] State v. Blunt, 91 Mo. 506 (1887), cases.

[1] United States v. Guiteau, 10 F. R. 164 (Jan. 25, 1882), Cox, J. See Miles v. United States, 103 U. S. 312 (1880), cases; 9 Pet. *691; 18 Wall. 545; 70 Ala. 45; 37 Conn. 360; 67 Ga. 153; 39 Ill. 457; 100 *id.* 242; 104 *id.* 364; 23 Ind. 170; 64 Iowa, 90; 29 Kan. 141; 1 Duv. (Ky.) 228; 9 Bush, 593; 38 Mich. 482; 44 *id.* 230; 14 Neb. 540; 42 N. Y. 6; 4 Pa. 274; 83 *id.* 141–42; 3 Heisk. 28.

[2] Wimbish v. Blanks, 76 Va. 305, 309 (1882).

[3] F. *douaire:* L. *dotare,* to endow: *dot-,* to give.

[4] 4 Kent, 35; 71 Ala. 81.

[5] Coke, Litt. 30 b, 31 a; Sutherland v. Sutherland, 69 Ill. 485 (1873); 4 Kent, 33.

[6] 2 Bl. Com. 129–30.

ecclesiæ; when a tenant in fee-simple, at the church door (where marriages were celebrated), after affiance made, endowed the wife with a certain part of his lands; dower *ex assensu patris:* when a son, by express agreement of his father, endowed his wife with a part of the father's possessions.[1]

Dower *ad ostium ecclesiæ* and *ex assensu patris* were abolished by 3 and 4 Will. IV (1833), c. 105. Dower given by the law is the only kind which has ever obtained in this country. . . During the life of the husband the right is a mere expectancy or possibility. Not being a natural right, but being conferred by law alone, the power that gives may increase, diminish, or otherwise alter it, or even wholly take it away. Upon the death of the husband, the right of the widow becomes vested.[2]

The law of the *situs* determines rights of dower. At common law the widow has dower: in an estate in common; in incorporeal hereditaments; in mines opened by the husband. She now has dower in wild lands; in an equity of redemption; in some States only in what her husband dies seised of.

At common law she has no dower: in an inheritance of which her husband had no right of immediate seizin; in a term of years (personalty); in an estate in joint-tenancy, except as widow of the survivor; in an estate held for another's life; in a vested remainder. Nor, generally, has she dower now: in a preemption claim; in shares of a corporation; in an estate held in trust by him, but otherwise as to his equitable estates; in a mortgagee's estate, till irredeemable; in partnership lands, before the debts are paid;[3] in a contract to purchase which he could not enforce.

The right may be defeated by any claim which would have defeated the husband's seisin: at common law, by alienage,— a rule now generally changed; by foreclosure of a mortgage made by him before marriage, or made for purchase-money after marriage; in some States, by sale on an execution for a debt; by sale for taxes; by an exercise of the right of eminent domain; by dedication to a public use; not, by an assignment in insolvency or bankruptcy — as see below.

The right may be barred: by divorce *a vinculo,* she being the delinquent; by elopement and adultery; by a jointure; by a joint conveyance duly acknowledged,— the common method; by equitable estoppel; by taking what he wills her.

Dower was to be assigned or set out, by right, immediately upon his death. Magna Charta allowed her to occupy his principal " mansion-house " forty days, if on dowable lands. One mode of assigning was by " common right " — by legal process; another mode, " against common right," rested upon her agreement. The former was by metes and bounds; the latter by indenture. Procedure for assignment has been called "admeasurement." As against the heir the value at assignment is regarded; as against an alienee the value at transfer, and, according to numerous decisions, the increase from general improvement.

Two or more widows may be endowable out of the same realty. The estate is a continuation of the husband's. The widow may convey it away; and it may be levied upon.

The right, being no part of his estate, is not affected by proceedings in bankruptcy against him.[1]

A woman who is *sui juris* may, by ante-nuptial contract, relinquish the right.[2]

Writ of dower. Process to secure an " assignment " of dower.

Writ of dower *unde nihil habet* — whereof she has nothing: complains that assignment has not been made within time.[3]

See further subjects mentioned, and HUSBAND; PARAPHERNALIA; QUARANTINE, 1; SETTLE, 4; TABLE, 4.

DOWRY. That which the wife gives the husband on account of marriage,— a donation toward his maintenance and the support of the relation.[4]

In Louisiana, " the effects which the wife brings the husband to support the expenses of marriage." Being given to him to be enjoyed during the marriage, the income is his absolutely. He is to administer the property. She cannot deprive him of it. Realty is inalienable during marriage, unless the contract stipulates otherwise.[5]

"Dowry," "dowery," and "dower" are etymologically different forms of the same word. "Dowery" is obsolete. In Massachusetts, neither "dowery" nor "dowry" has ever meant "dower,"[6] *q. v.*

DRAFT.[7] 1, *n.* (1) A drawing, delineation, sketch. See COPYRIGHT.

(2) In common speech, a bill of exchange.[8] See EXCHANGE, 2.

Any order for the payment of money drawn by one person upon another.[9]

Also, money checked out of a bank by this means.

The *drawer* is he who prepares the order; the *drawee,* he to whom it is addressed.

Drafts, as used in the collection of debts, are not usually negotiable. The office of a draft is to collect for the drawer, from the drawee, residing in another

---

[1] 2 Bl. Com. 130, 131, 132.

[2] Randall *v.* Kreiger, 23 Wall. 147 (1874); 25 Minn. 464.

[3] Lenow *v.* Fones, 48 Ark. 560-67 (1886), cases.

[1] Porter *v.* Lazear, 109 U. S. 86 (1883); Lazear *v.* Porter, 87 Pa. 513 (1878).

[2] Barth *v.* Lines, 118 Ill. 382 (1886), cases; Forwood *v.* Forwood, Sup. Ct. Ky. (1887), cases.

[3] See generally 2 Bl. Com. 136-37; 3 *id.* 183, 194; 4 Kent, 35-72; Williams, R. P. 223-28; 1 Washb. R. P. 146-262; 1 Story, Eq. §§ 624-32; 3 Pomeroy, Eq., Index; 1 Bouv. 564-67, cases; Maybury *v.* Brien, 15 Pet. 21 (1841), cases.

[4] [Cutter *v.* Waddingham, 22 Mo. 254 (1855): 1 Partidas, 507.

[5] De Young *v.* De Young, 6 La. An. 787 (1851); Buard *v.* De Russy, 6 Rob. 113 (1843); Gates *v.* Legendre, 10 *id.* 78 (1845).

[6] Johnson *v.* Goss, 132 Mass. 275-76 (1882).

[7] Originally *draught,*— Webster.

[8] 2 Bl. Com. 467; 39 N. Y. 100.

[9] [Wildes *v.* Savage, 1 Story, 30 (1839).

place, money to which the former may be entitled, either on account of balances due or advances upon consignments; and although they may sometimes be used for raising money that is not the necessary or ordinary purpose for which they are employed.[1] See ASSIGNMENT, Equitable; DUPLICATE.

Overdraft. The demand against a depositor in a bank after he has drawn out more money than his balance; also, the act of drawing too much, and the state of the account thereafter.[2]

As between a banking firm and a depositor not a member of the firm, an overdraft is a loan. The payment of the latter's check when no funds stand to his credit is an advance by the firm of its own money, for the repayment of which, with lawful interest, the customer is liable. It is payable absolutely and in full, without abatement or contingency, and so constitutes a loan in all its characteristics. If more than legal interest is paid, the borrower loses the excess above the legal rate, and if the contract stands and is carried out, the loss is absolute and certain. But the situation changes when the person making the overdraft is a member of the firm which advances it.[3]

(3) An allowance to an importer, when a duty is ascertained by weight, to insure good weight.

"Tare" is allowed for the covering on the article.[4]

2, *v.* To prepare in writing. See DRAW, 3.

Draftsman. In equity practice, a person who prepares pleadings; also, one who manually writes a will.

DRAIN. 1, *n.* Any hollow space in the ground, natural or artificial, where water is collected and passes off; a ditch.[5] Compare GUTTER.

2, *v.* To rid land of its superfluous moisture, by deepening, straightening, or embanking the natural water-courses, and supplementing them, when necessary, by artificial ditches.[6]

An easement to drain water through another's land may be acquired by grant or prescription.[7]

Drainage. As a matter of legal definition it cannot be said that sewerage may not, in cases, be included in drainage; yet when the simple word "drainage" is used, as appurtenant to lands, the most obvious suggestion is drainage of water.[6]

See AQUA, Currit, etc.; MEADOW; SEWER.

DRAM. In common parlance, implies that the drink has alcohol in it — something that intoxicates.[1]

DRAMA. A public representation of an uncopyrighted play by the author, for his own advantage, is not a dedication of the play to the public.

A spectator may take notes for any fair purpose, as, for comparison with other works, or for comment as a critic. A ticket of admission is a license to witness the play, not to reproduce it, if the spectator can recollect it or stenograph it. In whatever mode a copy is obtained, a subsequent unauthorized representation, operating to deprive the author of his exclusive rights, will be enjoined.[2] See COPYRIGHT; REVIEW, 3; THEATER.

DRAW. 1. To take from a place of deposit; to call for and receive from a fund: as, to draw money from a bank or a trust, to draw a dividend or share.

2. To take names from the authorized receptacle: as, to draw a jury.

3. To write in form, prepare; to draw up: as, to draw, or draw up, a document or writing — deed, bill in equity, will, etc.

4. To produce, gain: as, for money to draw interest.

5. To drag (on a hurdle) to the place of execution: as, to draw a traitor, and to be drawn.[3] See TREASON.

Drawback. A remission of money paid as freight, taxes, or other charges. Compare REBATE. See COMMERCE, page 201, Act of 1887, sec. 2.

A refunding of duties paid upon imported merchandise which becomes an export.[4]

Drawbridge; draw. A contrivance by which a section of a bridge across a navigable water is turned upward or at right angles to itself, and parallel with the direction of the stream, so as to admit of the passage of vessels through the open space.[5] See BRIDGE.

Drawee; Drawer. See DRAFT, 1 (2).

Drawing. See COPYRIGHT.

---

[1] Evansville Nat. Bank *v.* Kaufmann, 93 N. Y. 280 (1883), Ruger, C. J.

[2] [Abbott's Law Dict.; 24 N. J. L. 484.

[3] Payne *v.* Freer, 91 N. Y. 48 (1883), Finch, J.; 2 Utah, 411.

[4] Napier *v.* Barney, 5 Blatch. 192 (1863), Nelson, J.

[5] Goldthwait *v.* East Bridgewater, 5 Gray, 64 (1855).]

[6] People *v.* Parks, 58 Cal. 639 (1881); *ib.* 648.

[7] See 3 Kent, 436.

[8] Wetmore *v.* Fiske, 15 R. I. 359 (1886).

[1] Lacy *v.* State, 32 Tex. 228 (1869). As to dram-shop keeper, see State *v.* Owen, 15 Mo. *507 (1852).

[2] Tompkins *v.* Halleck, 133 Mass. 32, 45 (1882), cases; Keene *v.* Wheatley, 9 Am. Law Reg. 33-108 (C. C., E. D. Pa., 1860).

[3] See 4 Bl. Com. 92, 377.

[4] See R. S. tit. XXXIV, Ch. 9.

[5] Hughes *v.* Northern Pacific R. Co., 18 F. R. 114 (1883). Law as to, Gates *v.* Northern Pacific R. Co., 64 Wis. 64 (1885).

DRAYMEN. See POLICE, 2.

Drayage. Where, to keep a wharf in repair, a toll was charged on coal taken from the wharf in vessels or warehoused "without drayage," it was held that the reference was to loaded conveyances, and included a tramway supported by pillars resting upon the wharf.[1]

DRED SCOTT CASE. See CITIZEN; SLAVERY.

DREDGE. Originally, a net or drag for taking oysters; now, a machine for cleansing canals and rivers,— a dredger. To dredge is to gather or take with a dredge; to remove sand, mud, etc., with a dredging machine. A dredge is not a "vessel."[2]

DRIFT-STUFF. Matters floating at random, without any discoverable owner, and which, if cast ashore, will probably never be reclaimed, but belong to the riparian proprietor.[3]

A right to "sea manure" is a right to appropriate the random drift and refuse of the ocean, but not goods washed ashore from a wrecked vessel.[3]

DRIP. See EASEMENT.

DRIVER. See LIVERY, Keeper; NEGLIGENCE.

DROIT. F. A right; law abstractly considered.

Opposed to *loi:* law in the concrete sense. Equivalent to *jus* in the Roman law. See MONSTRANS.

Autre droit. Another's right. *En autre droit.* In another's right. Applied to an administrator, executor, guardian, *prochein ami*, or other representative of another's rights or interest.[4]

Droit civil. A private right independent of citizenship.

Droit-droit. A right upon a right; a double right: rights of possession and of property joined — necessary to a complete title to land. A *jus duplicatum*.[5]

Droit international. International law.

Droit maritime. Maritime law.

Droit of admiralty. In English law, applied to a ship of the enemy taken by an uncommissioned subject; and to a vessel seized in a port, on the breaking out of war. Also spoken of as an *admiralty droit*.[6]

Droitural. Used of an action upon a writ of right, as distinguished from a *possessory* action, upon the fact of, or right to, possession merely.

DRUGGIST. In popular acceptation, one who deals in medicines, or in the materials used in the preparation of medicines — in its largest signification.[1]

Properly, one whose occupation is to buy and sell drugs, without compounding or preparation. More restricted, therefore, than "apothecary," [2] *q. v.*

Drugs. Substances used in compounding medicines, in dyeing, and in chemical operations.

"Drugs and medicines," in an insurance policy, includes saltpeter.[3] Whether benzine is a drug is a question of fact.[4] See LIQUOR; MEDICINE; OIL.

Adulterating drugs is a misdemeanor, in most of the States. In some States, competency to compound drugs must be evidenced by a certificate from a board of examiners, or from a reputable school of pharmacy.

The care required of a druggist is proportioned to the danger involved. Actual negligence must be shown before he can be made liable for the consequences of a mistake.[5]

Where a druggist informs a customer that a preparation is poisonous, and correctly instructs him as to the quantity he may take, and the purchaser dies from an overdose taken in disregard of the directions, the druggist is not liable for a failure to label the parcel "poison," as required by a statute.[6]

Nor is he liable when he has carefully compounded a physician's prescription.[7]

Criminal negligence, followed by fatal results, may convict him of involuntary manslaughter, *q. v.*[8] See POLICE, 2.

DRUMMER. A commercial agent who travels for a wholesale merchant taking orders for goods to be shipped to retail dealers.[9]

An agent, such as is usually denominated a "drummer" or "commercial traveler," who simply exhibits samples of goods kept for sale by his principal, and

---

[1] Soule *v.* San Francisco Gas Light Co., 54 Cal. 241 (1880).

[2] The Nithsdale, 15 Up. Can. Law J. 269 (1879).

[3] Watson *v.* Knowles, 13 R. I. 641 (1882).

[4] See 1 Greenl. Ev. § 179.

[5] See 2 Bl. Com. 199.

[6] See 13 Ves. 71; 3 Bos. & P. 191; 6 Wheat. 264; 8 Cranch, 110.

[1] [Mills *v.* Perkins, 120 Mass. 42 (1876), Ames, J.

[2] State *v.* Holmes, 28 La. An. 767 (1876): Webster. Hainline *v.* Commonwealth, 13 Bush, 352 (1877); 77 Mo. 128.

[3] Collins *v.* Farmville Ins. Co., 79 N. C. 281 (1878): Webster.

[4] Carrigan *v.* Lycoming Fire Ins. Co., 53 Vt. 426 (1881).

[5] Brown *v.* Marshall, 47 Mich. 583 (1882), cases; 16 Ark. 308; 32 Conn. 75; 61 Ga. 505; 13 B. Mon. 219; 15 La. An. 448; 64 Me. 120; 20 Md. 297; 106 Mass. 143; 6 N. Y. 397; 51 *id.* 746; L. R., 5 Exch. 1.

[6] Wohlfahrt *v.* Beckert, 92 N. Y. 490, 494 (1883).

[7] Ray *v.* Burbank, 61 Ga. 505 (1878).

[8] Tessymond's Case, 1 Lewin, 169 (1828).

[9] [Singleton *v.* Fritsch, 4 Lea, 96 (1879); Montana *v.* Farnsworth, 5 Monta. 303 (1885); 34 Ark. 557.

takes orders for such goods afterward to he delivered by the principal to the purchasers, payment therefor to be made to the principal, is neither a peddler nor a merchant; nor will a single sale and delivery of goods by such agent out of his samples or other lot of goods constitute him a peddler or merchant.[1] See further COMMERCE, page 199, col. 2; PEDDLER.

In common language a drummer sells goods,—by sample, by procuring orders; and the dealer sells by him as his agent. While in such cases the sale is usually consummated by a delivery at the vendor's place of business to a common carrier, and, perhaps, in another State, a legislature may say that the acts done by the drummer shall of themselves constitute a sale; as, in a statute forbidding sales of liquors by samples or by soliciting orders without first taking out a license.[2]

Article 4665, of the Revised Statutes of Texas, is unconstitutional as to a citizen of another State selling goods by sample, and having no goods in the State.[3]

DRUNKENNESS. The result of excessive drinking of intoxicating liquors; ebriety, inebriation, intoxication; the state which follows from taking into the body, by swallowing or drinking, excessive quantities of such liquors.[4]

Drunk. So far under the influence of intoxicating liquor that the passions are visibly affected or the judgment impaired.[5]

Drunkard. One whose habit is to get drunk, whose ebriety has become habitual. "Drunkard," "common drunkard" and "habitual drunkard," mean the same.[6]

While "common" imports frequency, the law does not specify the number of instances in a given time.[7]

It is impossible to lay down a rule as to when a man shall be deemed an "habitual drunkard." Occasional acts of drunkenness do not make him such: it is not necessary that he be continually intoxicated. He may become intoxicated and yet remain sober for weeks together. The test is, Has he a fixed habit of drunkenness? Is he habituated to intemperance when opportunity offers?[8]

"Habitual" imports formed or acquired by habit; customary; usual; accustomed to intemperance whenever opportunity offers.[9]

An "habitual drunkard" is a person who by frequent repetition has acquired an involuntary tendency to become intoxicated.[1]

The proceeding to determine whether a person is an habitual drunkard, and the legal consequences, are substantially the same as in a case of lunacy, q. v.

1. In civil law. A contract made by one too drunk to understand the consequence of his act is voidable, except when for necessaries or for goods kept after he becomes sober.[2]

If, without fault of his, he is unable to restore the consideration, provision for its repayment may be made in the final decree.[3]

Before a court of equity will grant relief the drunkenness must have been so excessive as to utterly deprive the complainant of the use of his reason. In that condition there can be no serious, deliberate consent.[4]

Total drunkenness in the maker of a note, known to the payee, avoids it as to him. But this defense cannot be set up against the claim of an innocent holder for value. . A drunken man is responsible to an innocent person for an act done while drunk: he voluntarily produces his disability.[5]

2. In criminal law. "A drunkard," says Lord Coke, "who is *voluntarius dæmon*, hath no privilege thereby; but what hurt or ill soever he doeth, his drunkenness doth aggravate it."[6]

No other rule would be safe for society.[7]

At common law, as a rule, voluntary intoxication affords no excuse, justification, or extenuation of a crime committed under its influence. But when a statute establishing different degrees of murder requires deliberate premeditation in order to constitute murder in the first degree, the question whether the accused is in such a state of mind, by reason of drunkenness or otherwise, as to be capable of deliberate premeditation, necessarily becomes a material subject for consideration by the jury.[8]

See INTEMPERATE; INTOXICATION; INSANITY; LIQUOR; OPTION, Local; PROHIBITION, 2.

---

[1] City of Kansas v. Collins, 34 Kan. 436-37 (1885), citing twenty-five cases.

[2] State v. Ascher, 54 Conn. 306 (1886).

[3] *Exp.* Stockton, 33 F. R. 95 (1887).

[4] [Commonwealth v. Whitney, 11 Cush. 479 (1853), Merrick, J.

[5] State v. Pierce, 65 Iowa, 85 (1886); 64 *id.* 88 (1884).

[6] Commonwealth v. Whitney, 5 Gray, 86 (1855), Thomas, J.

[7] Commonwealth v. McNamee, 112 Mass. 286 (1873).

[8] Ludwick v. Commonwealth, 18 Pa. 174 (1851), Rogers, J.

[9] Trigg v. State, 49 Tex. 676 (1878), Roberts, C. J.

[1] Murphy v. People, 90 Ill. 60 (1878), Per Curiam. See also Mahone v. Mahone, 19 Cal. 629 (1872); Wheeler v. Wheeler, 53 Iowa, 512 (1880); Walton v. Walton, 34 Kan. 198 (1885), cases; Richards v. Richards, 19 Bradw. 468 (1886), cases.

[2] Johnson v. Harmon, 94 U. S. 379-82 (1876), cases; 60 Iowa, 82; 2 Kent, 452; 1 Pars. Contr. 388.

[3] Thackrah v. Haas, 119 U. S. 499, 502 (1886): 1 Wash., Va., 164; 64 N. Y. 200.

[4] 1 Story, Eq. §§ 230-31; 2 Pomeroy, Eq. § 949.

[5] State Bank v. McCoy, 69 Pa. 207-9 (1871); McSparran v. Neeley, 91 *id.* 24 (1879); Gore v. Gibson, 13 M. & W. *626 (1845); Bush v. Breinig, 113 Pa. 316 (1886): 26 Am. Law Reg. 40-41 (1887), cases; 1 Ames, Cas. Bills & N. 558; 18 Cent. Law J. 65-68 (1884), cases; 2 Kent, 451.

[6] 1 Coke, Inst. 247; 4 Bl. Com. 25; 2 Steph. Hist. Cr. Law Eng. 165.

[7] United States v. Cornell, 2 Mas. 111 (1820); United States v. McGlue, 1 Curtis, 13 (1851).

[8] Hopt v. People, 104 U. S. 634-35 (1881), cases, Gray, J. See also Jones v. Commonwealth, 75 Pa. 406 (1874); Tidwell v. State, 70 Ala. 46 (1881); Honesty v. Commonwealth, 81 Va. 301 (1886); 24 Am. Law Reg. 507-11 (1876), cases; 27 *id.* 159-61 (1879), cases; 23 Am. Jur. 290; Bish.

DRY. See EXCHANGE, 2; RENT; TRUST, 1.

DRY-DOCK. See DOCK, 2 (1).

DRY GOODS. See PERISHABLE; SAM-
.E.

DUBITARE.[1] L. To doubt.

Dubitante. Doubting.

Affixed to the name of a judge, in a reported
se, denotes that he questions the soundness of the
cision.

Dubitantur. It is doubted.

Indicates that a proposition as sound law is open
question. Compare QUÆRE.

DUCES. See SUBPŒNA, Duces, etc.

DUE.[2] 1. Owed, or owing; payable;
mandable. See DUTY.

Applied to debts, expresses the mere state
: indebtment — is equivalent to "owed"
· "owing;" and the fact that the debt has
:come payable.[3]

A debt payable now or in the future is a "debt due."
Debt " itself implies this. But the popular accepta-
n of "due " is, payable in present time.[4]

When not qualified by a time clause, means that
e money or property is due at the time of executing
e instrument.[5]

May import indebtedness without reference to the
y of payment, or that that day has passed.[6]

May be used not in the sense of "payable," but as
porting an existing allegation.[7]

In its largest sense, covers liabilities matured and
matured.[8]

A debt which has yet to originate cannot properly
said to be a debt which is to become due.[9]

Due-bill. A written acknowledgment
at a sum of money is due.

Not payable to order, nor transferable by indorse-
ent.[10]

May be payable in specific property. When no

time or place for payment is mentioned, before a suit
to recover the amount can be maintained, a demand is
necessary.[1]

In Colorado an ordinary due-bill has the character
of a promissory note, whether it contains a promise
to pay, or words of negotiability, or not.[2] See I O U.

Overdue; past-due. Time for paying
gone by, yet not paid; matured and unpaid.

"Overdue" sometimes refers to a right of action
against a drawer or indorser: a bill is not then overdue
until presented and payment refused. Sometimes it
is used in considering whether an indorser has been
released by a failure of the holder to present the bill
for payment, and to give the indorser notice of its dishonor within time. Sometimes it is applied to a bill
which has come into the hands of an indorser so long
after its issue as to charge him with notice of its dishonor, and thus subject it in his hands to the defenses
which the drawer had against it in the hands of the
assignor.[5]

"Past-due interest" means interest which has matured, and is collectible on demand. . . Money
may be "owing" which is not "due." A man owes
the money represented by his note; but the money is
not due until the note matures.[4]

A note overdue, payable to bearer, passes, by delivery, the legal title subject to all equities between
the original parties.[5] Indorsing such a note is equivalent to making a new note payable at sight.[6]

Underdue. Not yet payable; unmatured.

In the absence of proof, the law presumes that a
note taken is underdue.[7]

See NEGOTIATE, 2; PAYMENT.

2. Required by circumstances; proper; executed by law; timely: as, due care or diligence, qq. v.

3. Regular; appropriate; usual; according
to legal form, in legal manner, conformably
to law: as, due course or process of law;
due form, notice, service, return, qq. v.

The "due execution" of a writing relates to the
manner and form of execution by a person competent
under the law of the place.[8]

Duly. In due manner; regularly; legally.

In the proper way, regularly, according
to law:[9] as, duly acknowledged, notified,
served, sworn.

: L. §§ 488-93; 1 Ben. & H. Ld. Cr. Cas. 113-24. Med-
al Jurisprudence of, 21 Am. Law Rev. 955-62 (1887),
ses. Condoning, 26 Cent. Law J. 123 (1888), cases.

[1] Literally, to waver in mind, be of two minds: *duo*,
o,—Müller, Science of Lang. 360.

[2] F. *deu; devoir:* L. *debere*, to owe.

[3] United States v. State Bank, 6 Pet. #36 (1832), Story,
stice.

[4] Leggett v. Bank of Sing Sing, 25 Barb. 332 (1857);
me v. Same, 24 N. Y. 286 (1862); People v. Arguello,
Cal. 525 (1869); Collins v. Janey, 3 Leigh, #391 (1831);
Moak, 708.

[5] Lee v. Balcom, 9 Col. 218 (1886), Beck, C. J.

[6] Scudder v. Coryell, 10 N. J. L. 345 (1829), Ewing,
J.; Allen v. Patterson, 7 N. Y. 480 (1852); Bowen v.
cum, 17 Wis. 190 (1863).

[7] Sand-Blast Co. v. Parsons, 54 Conn. 313 (1886).

[8] People v. Vail, 6 Abb. N. C. 210 (1879).

[9] Thomas v. Gibbons, 61 Iowa, 50 (1883).

See also 19 Pick. 381; 31 Mich. 215; 14 Barb. 11; 28
x. 59; Story, Bills, § 233, Prom. Notes, § 440.

[10] See Byles, Bills, #11, n. (t).

[1] Winder v. Walsh, 3 Col. 548 (1877).
[2] Lee v. Balcom, 9 Col. 218 (1886), Beck, C. J.
[3] La Due v. First Nat. Bank of Kasson, 31 Minn. 38
(1883), Mitchell, J.
[4] Coquard v. Bank of Kansas City, 12 Mo. Ap. 265
(1882).
[5] See Nat. Bank of Washington v. Texas, 20 Wall. 88
(1873).
[6] Colt v. Barnard, 18 Pick. 261 (1836); Morgan v.
United States, 113 U. S. 499-500 (1885), cases.
[7] New Orleans, &c. Co. v. Montgomery, 95 U. S. 18
(1877).
[8] Cox v. Northwestern Stage Co., 1 Idaho, 376 (1871).
[9] Gibson v. People, 5 Hun, 543 (1875).

"Duly and legally appointed," in an indictment, may be sufficient without stating by whom appointed.[1]

"Duly assigned" may require a transfer in writing.[2]

"Duly convened" means regularly convened.[3]

"Duly presented" means presented according to the custom of merchants.[4]

"Duly recorded" means recorded in compliance with the requirement of law.[5]

4. Just, lawful, legal: as, due rights.[6]

Undue. Improper, wrongful, unlawful: as, undue concealment, influence, qq. v.

DUEL.[7] In ancient law, a fight between two persons for the trial of the truth in a doubtful case.[6]

Actually fighting with weapons in pursuance of an agreement.[9]

If either participant is killed, the offense is murder in the survivor, seconds, and spectators; otherwise, the offense is a misdemeanor.[10]

Under the constitutions of several States, as of Kentucky, Pennsylvania, and Wisconsin, participation in a duel disqualifies from holding office.[11]

See AFFRAY; CHALLENGE, 1; COMBAT.

DULY. See DUE, 3.

DUM. L. While. Compare DURANTE.

Dum bene se gesserit. While he behaves well.

Dum fervet opus. While the affair is warm: while the transaction is fresh.

A party's own admission, whenever made, may be given in evidence against him; but the declaration of his agent binds him only when made during the continuance of the agency in regard to a transaction then depending et dum fervet opus.[12] See ADMISSION, 2.

Dum sola. While single, or unmarried.

DUMB. See IDIOT; WILL, 2; WITNESS.

A person who is dumb, uneducated in the use of signs, and merely able to assent or dissent to direct questions by a nod or shake of the head, may be a legal witness, but the jury should be instructed that, because it was not possible to cross-examine him, the weight of his testimony is reduced.[13]

DUNGEON. An underground apartment in a prison, for the confinement of refractory convicts.

DUPLICATE.[1] The double of anything; an original repeated; a document the same as another; a transcript equivalent to the first or original writing; a counterpart: as, a duplicate bond, certificate, check or draft, land-warrant, receipt, will. See ORIGINAL, 2.

A document essentially the same as another.[2]

A document the same in all respects as some other document, from which it is indistinguishable in its essence and operation.[3]

"Duplicate," written across the face of a draft given to replace a lost draft of the same tenor, imports that the draft is to take the place of the original, that no new liability is created by it.[4]

Each duplicate writing is complete evidence of the intention of the parties. The deliberate destruction of one, as, of a duplicate will, creates a presumption that the other was also to be destroyed.[5] See EVIDENCE, Secondary.

Duplicate United States bonds will be issued, when the originals are defaced or destroyed.[6]

DUPLICITY.[7] Double pleading. Alleging two or more distinct grounds of complaint or defense when one would be as effectual as both or all.[8]

Because it produces useless prolixity, and tends to confusion, and to the multiplication of issues, regarded as a fault in all pleading.[9]

Predicated of a plea which contains more than one matter. To avoid a multitude of issues in one dispute every plea is to be confined to a single point. "Duplicity begets confusion," that is, defeats the object of all pleading — a single issue upon the same matter.[10]

In criminal practice, joining two or more distinct offenses in one count.[11]

Not applicable to the union of several facts in one matter, nor to matters of explanation, nor where but one of the defenses is valid.

---

[1] Commonwealth v. Chase, 127 Mass. 13 (1879).

[2] Ragland v. Wood, 71 Ala. 149 (1881); ib. 335; 139 Mass. 16.

[3] People v. Walker, 3 Barb. 305 (1856).

[4] Schofield v. Bayard, 3 Wend. 491 (1831).

[5] Dunning v. Coleman, 27 La. An. 48 (1875).

[6] Ryerson v. Boorman, 8 N. J. E. 705 (1849).

[7] It. duello; L. duellum, a fight between two — duo.

[8] [Jacob's Law Dict.

[9] [Herriott v. State, 1 McMul. *130 (S. Car., 1841).

[10] 4 Bl. Com. 199, 145; 2 Bish. Cr. L. §§ 310–15; 1 Arch. Cr. Pr. 926–39; 1 Russ. Cr. 443; 2 Chitty, Cr. L. 728, 848; 3 Steph. Hist. Cr. L. Eng. 99–104.

[11] See Commonwealth v. Jones, 10 Bush, 725 (1874).

[12] 1 Greenl. Ev. § 113; Long v. Colton, 116 Mass. 415 (1875); 66 Ga. 367.

[13] Quinn v. Holbert, 55 Vt. 228 (1882).

[1] L. duplicatus, two-fold: duplicare, to double.

[2] [Toms v. Cuming, 49 E. C. L. 94 (1845).

[3] Lewis v. Roberts, 103 E. C. L. *29 (1861), Erle, C. J.

[4] Benton v. Martin, 40 N. Y. 347 (1869).

[5] 1 Whart. Ev. § 74; 1 Greenl. Ev. § 558.

[6] R. S. § 3702.

[7] F. duplicité: L. duplicitatem, doubleness.

[8] [Gould, Plead. 389. Approved,— Sprouse v. Commonwealth, infra.

[9] [Sprouse v. Commonwealth, 81 Va. 376 (1886), Lacy, J.

[10] 3 Bl. Com. 308, 311; 1 Chitty, Plead. 226; 10 Me. 53; 21 N. J. L. 344; 2 Johns. 465; 7 Cow. 452; 10 Vt. 353; 11 F. R. 238.

[11] Tucker v. State, 6 Tex. Ap. 253 (1879); State v. Gorham, 55 N. H. 163 (1875); 1 Bish. Cr. Proc. § 432.

May exist in any part of the pleadings. At common law was a fatal defect, reached by special demurrer; but not now so regarded: in the discretion of the court, tolerated for the furtherance of justice.[1]

See DISCLAIMER, 4; PLEADING; REPUGNANT.

DURANTE. L. During, while. Compare DUM.

Durante absentia. During absence. See ADMINISTRATOR.

Durante bene placito. During good pleasure. See BEHAVIOR.

Durante minore ætate. During minority. See ADMINISTRATOR.

Durante viduitate. During widowhood.

Durante vita. During life.

DURESS.[2] In its more extended sense, that degree of constraint or danger, either actually inflicted or threatened and impending, which is sufficient, in severity or in apprehension, to overcome the mind and will of a person of ordinary firmness.[3]

Actual violence is not necessary to constitute duress, even at common law, as understood in the parent country, because consent is the very essence of a contract, and, if there be compulsion, there is no actual consent, and moral compulsion, such as that produced by threats to take life or to inflict great bodily harm, as well as that produced by imprisonment, is everywhere regarded as sufficient, in law, to destroy free agency, without which there can be no contract, because, in that state of the case, there is no consent.

Text-writers divide the subject into **duress per minas** and **duress of imprisonment.** This classification was uniformly adopted in the early history of the common law, and is generally preserved in the decisions of the English courts.

Where there is an arrest for an improper purpose, without just cause, or where there is an arrest for a just cause but without lawful authority, or for a just cause but for an unlawful purpose, even though under proper process, it may be construed as "duress of imprisonment;" and if the person arrested executes a contract or pays money for his release, he may avoid the contract as one procured by duress, and recover the money in an action for money had and received.

"Duress *per minas,*" as defined at common law, is where a party enters into a contract for fear of loss of life, loss of limb, of mayhem, or imprisonment. Many modern decisions of the courts of England still restrict the operation of the rule within those limits.

Those decisions deny that contracts procured by menace of a mere battery to the person, or of trespass to lands, or loss of goods, can be avoided on that account, and the reason assigned is that such threats are not of a nature to overcome the mind and will of a prudent man, because if such an injury is inflicted adequate redress may be obtained in a suit at law.

Cases to the same effect may be found in the reports of decisions in this country, and some of our text-writers have adopted the rule that it is only where the threats uttered excite fear of death, or of great bodily harm or unlawful imprisonment, that a contract, so procured, can be avoided, because, as such courts and authors say, the person threatened with slight injury to the person, or with loss of property, ought to have sufficient resolution to resist such a threat, and to rely upon the law for his remedy.

On the other hand there are many American decisions of high authority which adopt the more liberal rule that a contract procured by threats of battery to the person, or of the destruction of property, may be avoided on the ground of duress, because in any such case there is nothing but the form of a contract.

But all cases agree that a contract procured through fear of loss of life, produced by the threats of the other party, wants the essential element of consent, and may be avoided for duress.[1]

"Duress of imprisonment" is a compulsion by an illegal restraint of liberty. This will avoid an extorted bond. But if a man is lawfully imprisoned, and to procure his discharge, or on any other fair account, seals a bond or a deed, this is not by such duress.[2]

In the law of homicide, in self-defense, "duress of imprisonment" is where a man actually loses his liberty. "Duress *per minas*" is where the hardship is only threatened and impending, and is for fear of loss of life, for fear of mayhem, or loss of limb. And this fear must be upon sufficient reason — before a man may kill in self-defense. A fear of battery is no duress; neither is fear of one's house being burned, or of one's goods being taken away and destroyed; because for these a man may have satisfaction in damages,

---

[1] See 8 Ark. 378; 8 Ind. 96; 32 Mass. 104; 32 Mo. 185; 3 N. H. 415.

[2] *Du'-ress.* Mid. Eng. *duresse;* F. *duresce;* L. *duritia,* harshness; *durus,* severe.

[3] Brown *v.* Pierce, 7 Wall. 214–16 (1868), cases, Clifford, J. Quoted or cited, Baker *v.* Morton, 12 *id.* 157 (1870); French *v.* Shoemaker, 14 *id.* 332 (1871); United States *v.* Huckabee, 16 *id.* 431–32 (1872). See also 26 Alb. Law J. 424–26 (1882), cases; 1 Chitty, Contr., 11 Am. ed., 269–73; 2 Greenl. Ev. §§ 301–2; 1 Whart. Contr. ref. iv; 2 Whart. Ev. §§ 931, 1099; 1 Story, Eq. § 239; 2 Pomeroy, Eq. § 950, cases.

---

[1] Brown *v.* Pierce, *ante.*

[2] 1 Bl. Com. 136; Heckman *v.* Swartz, 64 Wis. 55–58 (1885); 59 Pa. 444.

but no suitable atonement can be made for loss of life or limb.[1]

"Duress of goods" is by unlawfully seizing or withholding property, or threatening to do so, till some demand be acceded to.

The payment of money by the owner of goods in order to redeem them from the hands of a person who unlawfully withholds them and demands such money, may be treated as a compulsory payment, so that the amount is recoverable, as having been obtained by oppressive means. The owner of the goods may have so urgent occasion for them that the ordinary action would afford imperfect redress.[2]

Duress exists where one, by the unlawful act of another, is induced to make a contract or to perform some act under circumstances which deprive him of the exercise of free will. . . "Duress of the person" is by imprisonment, by threats, or by an exhibition of force which apparently cannot be resisted. . . "Duress of goods" may exist when one is compelled to submit to an illegal exaction in order to obtain them from one who has them in possession but refuses to surrender them unless the exaction is submitted to.[3]

To constitute coercion or duress sufficient to make a payment involuntary, there must be some actual or threatened exercise of power possessed, or believed to be possessed, by the party exacting or receiving the payment over the person or property of another, from which the latter has no other means of immediate relief than by making the payment.[4]

Excessive charges, involuntarily paid to railroad companies refusing to carry or deliver goods, have been recovered on the ground of distress.[5]

Mere vexation and annoyance do not constitute such duress as will justify setting aside a deed, unless insanity ensued and existed at the time of execution.[6]

Threats of lawful prosecution, resorted to to overcome the will through intimidation, will avoid a contract thereby obtained.[7]

Regard is had to age, sex, and condition. If the threats are such as tend to deprive a particular person of his freedom of will he will be relieved from liability, although the same threats would not produce a like effect on a firm and courageous man.[8]

Where there is no arrest made nor force used, simply threats uttered, the question as to the duress by which a promise is alleged to have been obtained

is ordinarily one of fact. It must be shown that the threats constrained the will of the promisor.[1]

See Coercion; Consent; Influence; Payment, Compulsory.

DURING. See Dum; Durante; For.

DUTCH. See Auction.

DUTY. 1. What one ought or ought not to do; legal obligation. See Due.

"Duty" and "right" are correlative terms.

Such rights as are due from the citizen are called "civil duties." All social duties are of a relative nature — due *from* one man *to* another.[2]

When a right is invaded a duty is violated. A "public duty" is one owing to the community; a "private duty" is an obligation to be observed toward one or more individuals. In an action for non-fulfillment, it is essential to show: the duty, a breach thereof, and the resulting damage. When the law "casts a duty" upon one, he is answerable for any damage consequent upon non-performance.[3]

Laws designed to enforce moral and social duties stand on the best and broadest basis. Though it is not every such duty the neglect of which is the ground of an action. For there are what are called in the civil law duties of "imperfect obligation," for the enforcing of which no action lies.[4]

See Assumpsit; Care; Charge; Demand; Knowledge, 1; Negligence; Obligation, 1; Power, 1; Presumption; Right; Undertaking.

2. An indirect tax, imposed on the importation, exportation, or consumption of goods.[5]

A "custom" is a duty imposed upon imports or exports.[5]

Duties. Things due and recoverable by law. The term, in its widest signification, is hardly less comprehensive than "taxes;" in its most restricted meaning, is applied to "customs," and in that sense is nearly the synonym of "imposts."[6]

Whence dutiable, and non-dutiable.

Ad valorem duty. A sum ascertained by a percentage on the value of the article — not necessarily the actual value. **Specific duty.** A fixed sum payable upon an article by name.[7]

---

[1] 1 Bl. Com. 131; 4 *id.* 30; United States *v.* Haskell, 4 Wash. 406 (1823).

[2] Chitty, Contr. 625. See also White *v.* Heylman, 34 Pa. 144 (1859); Miller *v.* Miller, 68 *id.* 493 (1871); Motz *v.* Mitchell, 91 *id.* 117 (1879); Block *v.* United States, 8 Ct. Cl. 461 (1872); 35 Tex. 77; 59 *id.* 478; 101 U. S. 470.

[3] Hackley *v.* Headley, 45 Mich. 574 (1881), Cooley, J.

[4] Radich *v.* Hutchins, 95 U. S. 213 (1877), cases, Field, Justice.

[5] See Garton *v.* Bristol, &c. R. Co., 28 L. J. Exch. 169 (1859).

[6] Brower *v.* Collander, 105 Ill. 100 (1882).

[7] Haynes *v.* Rudd, 30 Hun, 239 (1883); 24 Pa. 347; 31 *id.* 73.

[8] Jordan *v.* Elliott, 12 W. N. C. 56, 59 (1882). See generally 24 Cent. Law J. 75 (1887), cases.

---

[1] Dunham *v.* Griswold, 100 N. Y. 226 (1885), cases: Fisher *v.* Bishop, 36 Hun, 114 (1885), cases. As a defense in civil actions, see 9 Va. Law J. 705–17 (1885), cases.

[2] 1 Bl. Com. 123. To whom due, 21 Cent. Law J. 382 (1885), cases.

[3] See Broom, Com. Law, 109, 651 c, 655, 670–80.

[4] Pasley *v.* Freeman, 3 T. R. 63 (1789), Kenyon, C. J.

[5] Cooley, Taxation, 3.

[6] Tomlins, Law Dict.; Pacific Ins. Co. *v.* Soule, 7 Wall. 445 (1868); Hylton *v.* United States, 3 Dall. *175 (1796); 1 Story, Const. § 952.

[7] See United States *v.* Clement, 1 Crabbe, 512 (1843); 18 F. R. 394.

Laws regulating the payment of duties are for practical application to commercial operations, and to be understood in a commercial sense. It is to be presumed that Congress intended them to be so understood.[1]

The commercial will prevail over the ordinary meaning of words, where the intent is apparent.[2]

If an article is found not enumerated in the tariff laws, the first inquiry is whether it bears a similitude in material, quality, texture, or the use to which it may be applied, to any article enumerated as chargeable with duty. If it does, and the similitude is substantial, it is to be deemed the same. Though not specifically enumerated, it is provided for under the article it most resembles. If nothing is found to which it bears the requisite similitude, a duty will be assessed at the highest rates chargeable on any of its component materials. Any other construction would leave the law open to evasion.[3] See CUTLERY.

The common-law right of action to recover duties illegally collected is taken away by the statutory remedy. The time for commencing the action is within ninety days after an adverse decision by the secretary of the treasury on appeal, but if he fails to render a decision within ninety days the importer may begin suit at once, or await the decision and sue within ninety days thereafter.[4]

The plaintiff, within thirty days after notice of the appearance of the defendant, must serve a bill of the particulars of his demand, giving, among other items, the date of the appeal, and of the decision of the secretary. This requirement makes it unnecessary to state the same facts in the declaration.[5]

No recovery can be had for duties paid after the importer has received the goods, although paid under protest.[6]

When a reliquidation of duties takes place its date is the final liquidation for the purpose of protest.

A departmental regulation which has been acquiesced in for many years is not to be disregarded without the most urgent reasons.[7]

See APPRAISE; COMMERCE; CUSTOMS; DRAWBACK; ENTRY, II, 2; EXCISE; IMPOST; NEGLIGENCE; NOSCITUR; PAYMENT, Involuntary; PROTEST, 1; REFUNDS; SMUGGLE.

DWELLING. A person has his dwelling where he resides permanently, or from which he has no present intention to remove. See ABODE; DOMICIL; RESIDE.

Dwelling-house. 1. A description of realty, as a dwelling-house, in a deed, may pass a house, the buildings belonging to it, its curtilage, garden, orchard, and the close on which it is built, with reasonable limitations according to the circumstances of the case.[1] See GRANT, 2; CURTILAGE.

Includes such buildings and attachments as are for the ordinary purposes of a house.[2]

2. In a statute against pulling down dwelling-houses to alter a highway, does not include a billiard saloon.[3]

3. In a homestead exemption law, may not embrace a building adapted to purposes of business, as, a saloon, a store, or a public hall.[4]

4. In the New York statute defining arson, includes any edifice usually occupied by persons lodging therein at night; not, a warehouse, barn, shed, or other out-house, unless part of a dwelling-house.[5] See ARSON.

5. In the law of burglary, includes whatever is within the curtilage, even if not inclosed with the dwelling, if used with it for domestic purposes, — all buildings the forcible breaking of which for felonious purposes during the hours of rest would naturally cause alarm, distress and danger.[6]

Must be a habitation of man, and usually occupied by some person lodging in it at night.[7]

Not such habitation is an underground cellar, used for storing ice and beer, with no internal door communicating with the living-rooms in the upper stories, and not under the control of any occupant of the building.[8]

Whether a building is a dwelling-house depends upon the use made of it.[9] See BURGLARY.

Dwelling-place. Some permanent place of abode or residence, with intention to remain there.[10]

See HOUSE; RESIDENCE; POLICE, 3; UTERE, Sic utere, etc.

DYEING. See PROCESS, 2.

DYING. See DEATH; DECLARATION, 1, Dying.

---

[1] United States v. Casks of Sugar, 8 Pet. 279 (1831); 16 Op. Att.-Gen. 359.

[2] Newman v. Arthur, 109 U. S. 137 (1883); Arthur v. Morrison, 96 id. 110 (1877), cases; Worthington v. Abbott, 124 id. 434 (1888).

[3] Arthur v. Fox, 108 U. S. 128 (1883), Waite, C. J.; R. S. § 2499; Herrman v. Arthur, 127 id. 363 (1888).

[4] Arnson v. Murphy, 109 U. S. 238 (1883); Snyder v. Marks, ib. 193–4 (1883), cases.

[5] Beard v. Porter, 124 U. S. 437 (1888), cases.

[6] Porter v. Beard, 124 U. S. 429 (1888), cases; R. S. § 3011.

[7] Robertson v. Downing, 127 U. S. 613 (1888), cases.

[1] Marston v. Stickney, 58 N. H. 610 (1879), cases.

[2] Chase v. Hamilton Ins. Co., 20 N. Y. 55 (1859).

[3] State v. Troth, 34 N. J. L. 377 (1871); 36 id. 424.

[4] Re Lammer, 14 Bankr. Reg. 460 (1876).

[5] See 2 N. Y. Rev. St. 657, §§ 9, 10; 20 Conn. 245; 33 Me. 30; 6 Mich. 142; 13 Gratt. 763.

[6] Stearns v. Vincent, 50 Mich. 219 (1883), Cooley, J.

[7] Scott v. State, 62 Miss. 782 (1885).

[8] State v. Clark, 89 Mo. 429–30 (1886).

[9] Davis v. State, 38 Ohio St. 506 (1882). See also 2 Cranch, C. C. 21; 68 N. C. 207; 72 id. 598; 3 S. & R. 199; 16 Gratt. 543; 13 Bost. L. R. 157.

[10] Jefferson v. Washington, 19 Me. 300 (1841); 2 id. 411; 49 N. H. 553.

E.

E. 1. As an abbreviation, ordinarily denotes Easter (term), eastern (district), ecclesiastical, Edward (king), English, equity, or exchequer.

2. In *e. g.*, an abbreviation of the first word of the Latin phrase, *exempli gratia*, for (in favor of, for the sake of) an example, for instance.

3. The form of the Latin preposition, *ex*, from, before a consonant sound. See Ex, 1.

E contra. From the opposite side; on the contrary.

E converso. On the other hand; conversely.

EACH. Every one of the two or more composing the whole.

Foreign express companies being exempted, in Kentucky, from local taxation by paying a State tax, a provision in the charter of a city authorizing it to tax "each" express company was held not to apply to foreign companies.[1]

A, a testator, gave C and T "two thousand dollars each." The legatees were brother and sister, not related to the testator. C died before A. *Held*, that the legacy was of two thousand dollars to each legatee individually, and not of four thousand dollars to a class, and that the legacy to C lapsed.[2]

Compare A, 4; ALL; ANY; EVERY.

EAGLE. See COIN.

EAR. See MARK, 1 (2); MAYHEM.

EARL. See SHERIFF.

EARNEST.[3] A thing delivered to a vendor in assurance of a serious purpose to complete the contract of sale.

Giving earnest is one of the alternatives prescribed by the original Statute of Frauds (*q. v.*) for the validity of a contract for a sale of personalty of the value of £10 or more.[4]

If the purchaser accepts and pays for the goods the earnest-money counts as part of the price; if not, the amount is forfeited.

The idea was taken from the civil law. A deposit with a third person, to be forfeited if the buyer does not complete his purchase, is not earnest.[5]

Whatever may have been thought by old writers respecting the effect, in the transmission of property, of giving and receiving earnest money, it is now considered of no importance, or of the smallest importance.[6]

---

[1] Adams Express Co. *v.* Lexington, 83 Ky. 660 (1886).

[2] Claflin *v.* Tilton, 141 Mass. 343 (1886).

[3] Mid. Eng. *ernes*, a pledge.

[4] See 2 Bl. Com. 448; 2 Kent, 389.

[5] Howe *v.* Hayward, 108 Mass. 55 (1871), cases: Mass. Gen. Stat. c. 105, § 5; Benj. Sales, 2 ed., 260.

[6] The Elgee Cotton Cases, 22 Wall. 195 (1874), Strong, Justice.

EARNINGS. Money or property gained by labor or services: as, the earnings of a wife, minor, servant, insolvent debtor, corporation.

In a statute of exemptions, the gains of the debtor derived from his services or labor without the aid of capital.[1]

May embrace more than "wages," *q. v.* May apply to compensation for services rendered which involve more than mere labor, and may include expenditures;[2] or, compensation for expenditures or materials furnished, together with work done or services rendered; but will not include rents, which require no personal service by the lessor.[3]

Gross earnings; net earnings. As a general proposition, the net earnings of a railroad company are the excess of the gross earnings over the expenditures defrayed in producing them, aside from, and exclusive of, the expenditure of capital laid out in constructing and equipping the works themselves.[4] See MORTGAGE, Railroad.

"Net earnings" is often the equivalent of surplus or net profits; and may refer to the surplus for a limited period.[5]

"Gross earnings" and "receipts," in the lease of a railroad, will be taken to mean the same thing, unless other parts of the agreement require a different construction.[6] See TAX, 2.

Separate earnings. Refers to the ownership in married women of the proceeds of their own labor or services.

At common law these belonged to the husband.[7]

In some States, upon petition filed, any married woman may have a decree of court investing her with the absolute right of property in her earnings, wholly free from all claims of her husband or of his creditors, the same as if she were a single woman.

Any married woman in Pennsylvania, with or without cause, may avail herself of the act of 1872; while, to entitle her to become a *feme-sole* trader, she must bring herself within the act of 1718 or the act of 1855. The act of 1872, by securing her the earnings of her business, impliedly authorizes her to engage in business with consequent liability for her contracts.[8] See FEME-SOLE, Trader; HUSBAND.

---

[1] Brown *v.* Hebard, 20 Wis. 330 (1866).

[2] Jenks *v.* Dyer, 102 Mass. 236 (1869); Somers *v.* Keliher, 115 *id.* 167 (1874): Statute, 1865, c. 43, § 2.

[3] Kendall *v.* Kingsley, 120 Mass. 95 (1876).

[4] Union Pacific R. Co. *v.* United States, 99 U. S. 420 (1878), Bradley, J. See also St. John *v.* Erie R. Co., 22 Wall. 148 (1874); 10 Blatch. 271; 108 U. S. 279; 30 Minn. 312.

[5] Cotting *v.* New York & New England R. Co., 54 Conn. 168 (1886).

[6] Cincinnati, &c. R. Co. *v.* Indiana, &c. R. Co., 44 Ohio St. 315–16 (1886).

[7] Carter *v.* Worthington, 82 Ala. 336 (1886).

[8] Bovard *v.* Kettering, 101 Pa. 183 (1882). Compare Act June 3, 1887: P. L. 332.

Surplus earnings. An amount owned (by a company) over and above capital and actual liabilities.[1]

EARTH. Soil of all kinds, including gravel, clay, loam, and the like, in distinction from the firm rock.[2]

"Hard pan" is a "hard stratum of earth." Earth, then, includes hard-pan.[2] See ALLUVION; LAND; MINERAL.

EASEMENT.[3] A service or convenience which one neighbor has of another by charter or prescription, without profit.[4]

The right which one man has to use the land of another for a specific purpose.[5]

A liberty, privilege, or advantage in land, without profit, distinct from an ownership in the soil.[6]

Easements include all those privileges which the public, or the owner of neighboring lands or tenements, has in the lands of another, and by which the "servient owner," upon whom the burden of the privilege is imposed, is obliged to suffer, or not to do something, on his own land, for the advantage of the public, or for the "dominant owner" to whom the privilege belongs.[7]

The essential qualities of easements are: they are incorporeal; they are imposed upon corporeal property; they confer no right to participation in profits arising from such property; there must be two distinct tenements, the dominant, to which the right belongs, and the servient, upon which the obligation rests.[8]

Easements restrict the enjoyment of natural rights in land, light, air, and water. Attaching to land as incidents or appurtenances, are, among others: the rights of pasture, of way, of taking water, wood, minerals or other product of the soil, of receiving air, light, or heat, of receiving or discharging water, of support to buildings, of carrying on an offensive trade.

An easement is not a tenancy.[9]

Affirmative easement. Such right in another's land as authorizes acts actually injurious to the land; as, a right of way. **Negative easement.** Such right as is, in its exercise, consequentially injurious; as, forbidding a thing to be done, like that of obstructing light.[1]

Apparent or **continuous easement.** Depends upon some artificial structure upon, or natural formation of, the servient tenement, obvious and permanent, which constitutes the easement or is the means of enjoying it; as, the bed of a running stream, an overhanging roof. **Non-apparent** or **noncontinuous easement.** Has no means specially constructed or appropriated to its enjoyment, and is enjoyed at intervals, leaving between these intervals no visible sign of its existence; as, a right of way.[2] See CONTINUOUS, Non-continuous.

Appendant or **appurtenant easement.** When the grant of the easement is made with reference to other land whereon, or in connection wherewith, it is to be used or enjoyed.

Such easement is appendant or appurtenant to the dominant estate, and passes with it as an incident.

A right in or upon the land of another, to be used by the grantee generally, and not in connection with or dependent upon any other land or estate, is a right *in gross,*— in bulk. It belongs to, and dies with, the person.[3]

Easement of necessity. A privilege without which the dominant owner could not carry on his trade or enjoy some other property right. **Easement of convenience.** Enables such owner to prosecute his business or to enjoy some right in real property with increase of facilities or comfort.

Private easement. Exists in favor of one or more individuals. **Public easement.** Exists in favor of the people generally.

Easements originate in grant, express or implied. They do not change with the persons. Disturbances may be remedied by action on the case, by injunction, or by abatement. They are extinguished by release, merger, necessity, end of prescription, cesser of use for twenty years, renunciation or abandonment shown by decisive acts.[4]

When an easement has once been acquired, mere non-user will not defeat the right; there must be an

---

[1] People v. Commissioners, 76 N. Y. 74 (1879). See 34 N. J. L. 482.

[2] Dickinson v. Poughkeepsie, 75 N. Y. 76 (1878); Webster.

[3] F. *aise,* ease, relief: assistance, accommodation, convenience.

[4] Post v. Pearsall, 22 Wend. 438 (1839): Jacob.

[5] Jackson v. Trullinger, 9 Oreg. 397 (1881), Lord, C. J.

[6] Jamaica Pond Aqueduct Corporation v. Chandler, 9 Allen, 165 (1864), Bigelow, C. J. See also 19 Ark. 33; 74 Ill. 185; 24 Iowa, 61; 40 *id.* 456; 24 Mich. 284; 51 N. H. 330; 70 N. Y. 421; 54 Pa. 369; 44 Tex. 267; 27 Gratt. 87; 109 U. S. 255.

[7] 3 Kent, 419.

[8] Pierce v. Keator, 70 N. Y. 421 (1877). See Parsons v. Johnson, 68 *id.* 65-66 (1877); 70 *id.* 447-48; Tardy v. Creasy, 81 Va. 556-57 (1886), cases.

[9] Swift v. Goodrich, 70 Cal. 106 (1886).

---

[1] 2 Washb. R. P. 26, 56-60, 82-85, 438-56; 70 N. Y. 448.

[2] Fetters v. Humphreys, 18 N. J. E. 262 (1867), Zabriskie, Ch.

[3] Salem Capital Flour Mills Co. v. Stayton Water-Ditch & Canal Co., 33 F. R. 154 (1887); Washb. Easem. 9, cases.

[4] See Steere v. Tiffany, 13 R. I. 570 (1882); Sanderlin v. Baxter, 76 Va. 305 (1882); Washb., Easements.

adverse use by the servient estate for a period sufficient to create a prescriptive right.[1]

See Air; License, 1; Light; Nuisance; Profits, A
prendre; Servitude, 2; Support, 2; Use, 1, Non-user;
Wall; Water; Way.

EASTER. See Term, 4.

EATING-HOUSE. Compare Restaurant; Saloon.

Any place where food or refreshments of any kind,
not including spirits, wine, ale, beer, or any other malt
liquors, are provided for casual visitors, and sold for
consumption therein.[2]

A market-stall where meals are furnished to the
public is not an eating-house.[3]

EAVES-DROPPING. The nuisance of
hanging about the dwelling-house of another,
hearing tattle, and repeating it to the disturbance of the neighborhood.[4]

Eaves-droppers. Such as listen under
walls or windows, or the eaves of a house,
to hearken after discourse, and thereupon to
frame slanderous and mischievous tales.[5]

Eaves-dropping is a common nuisance, indictable at
common law, and punishable by fine and by having to
furnish sureties for good behavior.[6]

Consists in privily listening, not in looking or peep-
ing. It is a good defense that the act was authorized
by the husband of the prosecutrix.[6]

EBB AND FLOW. See Navigable.

ECCENTRICITY. See Insanity.

ECCLESIASTICAL. See Church;
Corporation.

ECLECTIC. See Medicine.

ECONOMITES. See Community, 3.

ECONOMY, PUBLIC. See Police, 2.

EDITOR. Formerly included not only
the person who wrote or selected articles for
publication, but also the person who published the paper and put it into circulation.
Now, the business of editor is separated from
that of publisher and printer.[7]

See Liberty, 1, Of the press; Newspaper.

EDUCATION. Includes proper moral,
as well as intellectual and physical, instruction.[8]

May be particularly directed to the mental,

the moral, or the physical powers and faculties, but in its broadest and best sense relates
to them all.[1]

An education acquired through the medium of the
English language is an "English education." It is the
language employed as the medium of instruction that
gives distinctive character to the education, whether
English or German, and not the branches studied. .
A "common school education" begins with the rudi-
ments of an education, whatever else it may he made
to embrace.[2]

Parents owe to their children the duty of giving
them an education suitable to their station in life. Yet
the municipal laws of most countries do not constrain
parents to bestow such education.[3]

"All persons   having children, and all the
Guardians or Trustees of Orphans, shall cause such to
be instructed in reading and writing; under a penalty
of five pounds for each child having capacity in body
and understanding."[4]

See Charity, 2; School.

-EE. See Or, 1.

EFFACE. See Alter, 2; Cancel.

EFFECT. 1. That which is produced;
result of a cause. See Cause, 1.

2. Letters-patent will not be granted for a
mere effect; they may be for a new mode or
application of machinery to produce an effect.
See Patent, 2.

3. The manner in which a contract, instrument, or law will operate, as ascertained by
construction. See Tenor.

"Take effect," "be in force," and "go into operation" are interchangeable.[5]

4. To prosecute with effect: with due diligence to a finality. See further Prosecute.

Effected. A condition in a policy of insurance
that "every person insuring in this company must
give notice .   . of any other insurance effected
in his behalf on said property," applies to all other
insurance, whether taken out before or after the execution of the policy in question.[6]

EFFECTS. A word of extensive import,
frequently used in wills as a synonym for
personal estate. In *Hogan* v. *Jackson*, 1
Cowp. 304 (1774), Lord Mansfield considered
it synonymous with "worldly substance,"
which means whatever can be turned to
value, and therefore that "real and personal
effects" means all a man's property.

---

[1] Curran v. Louisville, 83 Ky. 632 (1886), cases.

[2] Revenue Act, 13 July, 1866, § 9: 14 St. L. 118.

[3] State v. Hall, 73 N. C. 254 (1875).

[4] State v. Pennington, 3 Head, 300 (Tenn., 1859): 2
Bish. Cr. L. 274.

[5] 4 Bl. Com. 168; 1 Hawk. P. C. 132; 1 Russ. Cr. 302.

[6] Commonwealth v. Lovett, 4 Clark, 5 (Pa., 1831): 8
Haz. Pa. Reg. 305.

[7] Pennoyer v. Neff, 95 U. S. 721 (1877), Field, J.

[8] Rouhs v. Backer, 6 Heisk. 400 (1871); Tenn. Code,
§ 2521.

---

[1] Mount Hermon Boys' School v. Gill, 145 Mass. 146
(1887), Knowlton, J.

[2] Powell v. Board of Education, 97 Ill. 375 (1881).

[3] 1 Bl. Com. 450.

[4] Laws of Prov. of Penn., Ch. CXII (1682): Linn, 142.

[5] Maize v. State, 4 Ind. 348 (1853).

[6] Warwick v. Monmouth County Mut. Fire Ins. Co.,
44 N. J. L. 83 (1882).

In admiralty, includes ships.[1]

In a will, may include any personalty whatever, and even realty.[2]

Construed to include land where it can be collected from the will that such was the testator's intention.[3]

Used indefinitely in a will, but, in connection with something particular and certain, is limited by association to other things of a like kind. From the subject-matter, intention of something else may be implied; and that may be larger or less.[4]

EFFIGY. See LIBEL, 5.

EFFLUX.[5] In a lease, the ending of the contract period in the regular course of events, as distinct from an earlier termination by a subsequent agreement or by some unexpected event. "Effluxion" was formerly in use.

EGRESS. See INGRESS.

EI INCUMBIT. See PROBATIO.

EIGHT-HOUR RULE. See SERVICE, 1.

EIGN, EIGNE, or **EISNE.** Eldest, or first-born. A corruption of the French *ainé, aisné.*

Bastard eigne. A child born before the marriage of its parents. Opposed, *mulier puisné:* a legitimate child.[6]

EITHER. One *or* the other of several things; but, sometimes, one *and* the other.[7] See OR, 2.

May be used, as in a statute, in the sense of "any."[8]

EJECT. To put out or off; to dispossess, evict, oust. See EJECTIO.

Casual ejector. He who ousted the rightful lessee by making a formal entry in order to test the right to possession in court.[9] See EJECTMENT.

EJECTIO.[10] L. Dispossession; ouster.

Ejectione custodiæ. By ejectment of ward. A writ by which a guardian recovered possession of the land or person of his ward.

Ejectione firmæ. For ejectment of "farm," *q. v.* A remedy where the lessee of a term of years was deprived of possession.

The original of the later and modern action of ejectment,[1] *q. v.*

EJECTMENT. An action to recover possession of realty, with damages for the wrongful detention. See EJECTIO.

Originally devised for a lessee ousted of his term of years, and who, having but a chattel interest, could not support a real action for recovery of possession. In effect, the action was for the trespass: and the remedy was in damages for the dispossession. Later, it was decided that the lessee could also recover his *term.* This brought the action into general use; and by the formalities of lease, entry, and ouster (which see below), the action was converted into a method of trying, collaterally, the *title* of the lessor. Then, as the title was never formally and directly in issue, but the trespass for the expulsion only, the verdict was not pleadable in bar of another trespass. Thus it came that a verdict and judgment were conclusive only as regarded personalty. Afterward, when the fictions were abolished, the idea of a difference as between realty and personalty lingered in many States, a single verdict and judgment was not considered conclusive, and provision was made by statute for a second trial. Where no such provision exists a former action may be a bar.[2]

In the original action the plaintiff had to prove a *lease* from the person shown to have title, an *entry* under the lease, and an *ouster* by some third person. The modified action was brought by a fictitious person as lessee against another fictitious person (the casual ejector) alleged to have committed the ouster. Service was made upon the tenant in possession, with notice from the casual ejector to appear and defend. If the tenant failed to do this, judgment was given by default and the claimant put in possession. If he did appear, he was allowed to defend only by entering into the "consent rule," by which he confessed the fictitious lease, entry, and ouster to have been made, leaving only the *title* in question. See DOE.

These fictions were abolished in England by the common-law procedure act of 1852, and further changes were made by the judicature acts of 1873 and 1875. In some States the action has never been adopted; in others it has been materially modified by statute; in a few it still exists in its original form. The ancient form is also employed in the circuit courts of the United States sitting in States where the old form was observed when those courts were established.[3]

Ejectment is the remedy to recover a corporeal hereditament — an estate in fee-simple, fee-tail, for life, or for years; not, for rent, a right of way, or dower. The plaintiff, at the time of the institution of the suit, must have a right of entry and of possession

---

[1] The Alpena, 7 F. R. 362 (1881). Arthur *v.* Morgan, 112 U. S. 499 (1884). See also 1 Hill (S. C.), 155; 15 Ves. 507; 15 M. & W. 450; 16 East, 222.

[2] Smyth *v.* Smyth, 25 Moak, 477 (1878): 8 C. D. 561; 16 Moak, 710.

[3] Page *v.* Forest, 89 N. C. 449 (1883), cases.

[4] Ennis *v.* Smith (Kosciusko's Will), 14 How. 421 (1852), cases, Wayne, J. See also 2 Shars. Bl. Com. 284, n.; 3 Cranch, C. C. 203; 3 Minn. 389; 30 *id.* 195; 37 Tex. 19.

[5] L. *ef(ex)-fluere,* to flow out, go by.

[6] See 2 Bl. Com. 248.

[7] Chidester *v.* Springfield, &c. R. Co., 59 Ill. 89 (1871).

[8] Lafoy *v.* Campbell, 42 N. J. E. 37 (1886).

[9] 3 Bl. Com. 201.

[10] From *ejicere,* to put out: *jacere,* throw, cast.

[1] 3 Bl. Com. 199.

[2] Sturdy *v.* Jackaway. 4 Wall. 175-76 (1866), cases, Grier, J.; Miles *v.* Caldwell, 2 *id.* 40 (1864); Blanchard *v.* Brown, 3 *id.* 248 (1865); Dickerson *v.* Colgrove, 100 U. S. 583 (1879); 3 Bl. Com. 199.

[3] See 3 Bl. Com. 198-207; 3 Steph. Com. 392-94, 617-20.

under legal title. In the Federal courts of law, the strict legal title prevails. The defendant must be in actual possession, and notice be given to the terre-tenant. The action is maintainable by a joint tenant or a tenant in common against a co-tenant who has dispossessed him. Recovery is upon the strength of the plaintiff's title, not upon the weakness of the defendant's,[1] with proof of injury equivalent to a dispossession. The plea of "not guilty" raises the general issue. The judgment is, that the plaintiff recover his term, or the possession of the land, and damages, which, as a rule, are nominal.[2] See POSSESSION, Adverse; PROFITS, 1, Mesne.

Equitable ejectment. Ejectment at law, upon an equitable title; in effect, a bill in equity for the specific performance of a contract or obligation to convey land.

In Pennsylvania, whenever a court of equity will presume a trust to have arisen, compel its execution, or enforce an article of agreement, the courts of law by this means will administer the same relief.[3]

Ejectment bill. Generally, a bill in equity will not lie if it is in substance and effect an ejectment bill, and if the relief it seeks can be obtained by an action in ejectment.[4]

EJECTOR. See EJECT.

EJUSDEM GENERIS. L. Of the same kind or nature; of the same class.

In the construction of statutes, contracts, and other instruments, where an enumeration of specific things is followed by a general word or phrase, the latter is held to refer to things of the same kind as those specified.[5] See GENERAL, 6; INFERIOR, 2; OTHER; VEHICLE.

ELDEST. The eldest son is the first-born son — the *primo-genitus*.

The words "shall become the eldest son" of a person living at the date of a will cannot, without an explanatory context, be extended beyond the life-time of that person; they are connected with the heirship of, and right of succession to, a living man.[6]

ELECT.[7] To select, choose; also, selected, chosen, elected: as, a judge-elect, the President-elect.

[1] Nelson v. Triplett, 81 Va. 237 (1885), cases; Butrick v. Tilton, 141 Mass. 96 (1886); Mitchell v. Lines, 36 Kan. 380 (1887).

[2] See Gibson v. Chouteau, 13 Wall. 102 (1871); Foster v. Mora, 98 U. S. 428 (1878); Equator Co. v. Hall, 106 id. 87 (1882); Holland v. Challen, 110 id. 19 (1883); 112 id. 535; 116 id. 692; 18 Fla. 52; 55 Vt. 569; 76 Va. 288; 107 U. S. 392; Bouvier.

[3] Deitzer v. Mishler, 37 Pa. 86 (1860); 7 id. 158; 14 id. 145, 249; 22 id. 225; 87 id. 286; 1 T. & H. § 36; 2 id. § 1838.

[4] Killian v. Ebbinghaus, 110 U. S. 568, 572 (1883).

[5] See United States v. Buffalo Park, 16 Blatch. 190 (1879); Reiche v. Smythe, 13 Wall. 165 (1871); Narramore v. Clark, 63 N. H. 167 (1884), cases; Lynchburg v. Norfolk, &c. R. Co., 80 Va. 248–50 (1885), cases; 54 Conn. 467; 8 Pick. 14; 9 Metc. 258; 122 Mass. 575.

[6] Bathurst v. Errington, 2 Ap. Cas. 698 (1877); 20 Moak, 203, 213.

[7] L. *eligere*, to pick out. See ELIGIBLE.

Election. A choosing, or selecting; also, the condition of having been chosen or selected: choice, selection.

Primer election. First choice.

In England, in cases of partition, unless otherwise agreed, the eldest sister (coparcener) has the first choice of purparts.[1]

1. Selection of a person to fill an office in (1) a private corporation,— whence *corporate* election; or (2) in a department of government — national, State, county, municipal,— whence *popular* election.[2]

In its constitutional sense, a selection by the popular voice of a district, county, town, or city, or by an organized body, in contradistinction to appointment by some single person or officer.

Voting and taking the votes of citizens for members to represent them in the general assembly or other public stations.[3]

In either of the senses noted, particularly in the case of a *popular* election, whether a *general* or a *special* or *local* election, choice of persons is effected through the instrumentality of a *board* or *officers* of election, within an election *district* or *precinct*, or place of known and fixed boundaries, on an appointed election *day* and between certain election *hours*, with a prescribed mode for certifying the election *returns*, and all in conformity with the election *laws;* followed, too, in cases, by an election *contest* between opposing candidates.[4]

The doctrine at the foundation of popular government is, that in elections the will of the majority controls; mere irregularities or informalities in the conduct of an election are impotent to thwart the expressed will of the majority.[5]

All fraudulent acts affecting the purity and safety of elections are offenses at common law.[6]

But illegal votes will make void an election only when they affect the result.[7]

A statute which, in addition to the requirements of the constitution, provides that "no person hereafter naturalized shall be entitled to be registered as a voter within thirty days therefrom," is unconstitutional.[8]

[1] Littleton, § 243.

[2] Police Commissioners v. Louisville, 3 Bush, 602 (1868), William, J.

[3] Commonwealth v. Kirk, 4 B. Mon. 2 (1843), Ewing, C. J. See also 54 Ala. 205; 13 Cal. 144; 28 Mich. 341; 5 Nev. 121.

[4] See 2 Dill. 219; 41 Pa. 403; 30 Conn. 591; 44 N. H. 643.

[5] Prohibitory-Amendment Cases, 24 Kan. 720 (1881). See Commonwealth v. Smith, 132 Mass. 295 (1882).

[6] Commonwealth v. Hoxey, 16 Mass. 385 (1820); Commonwealth v. McHale, 97 Pa. 408 (1881); 91 Pa. 503.

[7] Tarbox v. Sughrue, 36 Kan. 230, 232 (1887), cases. On conducting elections, see 24 Cent. Law J. 487 (1887), cases.

[8] Kinneen v. Wells, 144 Mass. 497 (1887), cases. See also State v. Conner, Sup. Ct. Neb. (1887), cases.

Elective. (1) Pertaining to the right, in the individual, to choose agents of government: as, the elective franchise, *q. v.*

(2) Bestowed by virtue of a popular election, as opposed to being invested with by appointment: as, the elective system — for filling judicial offices. See JUDICIARY.

Elector. (1) One who has the right of a choice or vote; more particularly, one who has the right of casting a vote for a public officer.[1]

(2) One who, having a right to vote, actually votes.[2]

Electoral. Pertaining to or consisting of electors: as, the "electoral college," on which the formal legal choice of President and Vice-President is made finally to depend.

Presidential electors. Members of the electoral college.

"Each State shall appoint, in such Manner as the Legislature thereof may direct, a Number of Electors, equal to the whole Number of Senators and Representatives to which the State may be entitled in the Congress: but no Senator or Representative, or Person holding an Office of Trust or Profit under the United States, shall be appointed an Elector."[3]

"The Congress may determine the Time of choosing the Electors, and the Day on which they shall give their Votes; which Day shall be the same throughout the United States."[4]

"The Electors shall meet in their respective states, and vote by ballot for President and Vice-President, one of whom, at least, shall not be an inhabitant of the same state with themselves; they shall name in their ballots the person voted for as President, and in distinct ballots the person voted for as Vice-President, and they shall make distinct lists of all persons voted for as President, and of all persons voted for as Vice-President, and of the number of votes for each, which lists they shall sign and certify, and transmit sealed to the seat of the government of the United States, directed to the President of the Senate; — The President

of the Senate shall, in the presence of the Senate and House of Representatives, open all the certificates and the votes shall then be counted; —

The person having the greatest number of votes for President, shall be the President, if such number be a majority of the whole number of Electors appointed; and if no person have such majority, then from the persons having the highest numbers not exceeding three on the list of those voted for as President, the House of Representatives shall choose immediately, by ballot, the President. But in choosing the President, the votes shall be taken by states, the representation from each state having one vote; a quorum for this purpose shall consist of a member or members from two-thirds of the states, and a majority of all the states shall be necessary to a choice. And if the House of Representatives shall not choose a President whenever the right of choice shall devolve upon them, before the fourth day of March next following, then the Vice-President shall act as President, as in the case of the death or other constitutional disability of the President. The person having the greatest number of votes as Vice-President, shall be the Vice-President, if such number be a majority of the whole number of Electors appointed, and if no person have a majority, then from the two highest numbers on the list, the Senate shall choose the Vice-President; a quorum for the purpose shall consist of two-thirds of the whole number of Senators, and a majority of the whole number shall be necessary to a choice. But no person constitutionally ineligible to the office of President shall be eligible to that of Vice-President of the United States.[1]

The act of Congress approved February 3, 1887 (24 St. L. 373), to fix the day for the meeting of the electors of President and Vice-President, and to regulate the counting of the votes, and the decision of questions arising thereon, provides as follows:

That the electors of each State shall meet and give their votes on the second Monday in January next following their appointment, at such place in each State as the legislature of such State shall direct.

Sec. 2. That if any State shall have provided, by laws enacted prior to the day fixed for the appointment of the electors, for its final determination of any controversy or contest concerning the appointment of all or any of the electors of such State, by judicial or other methods or procedures, and such determination shall have been made at least six days before the time fixed for the meeting of the electors, such determination made pursuant to such law so existing on said day, and made at least six days prior to the said time of meeting of the electors, shall be conclusive, and shall govern in the counting of the electoral votes as provided in the Constitution, and as hereinafter regulated, so far as the ascertainment of the electors appointed by such State is concerned.

Sec. 3. That it shall be the duty of the executive of each State, as soon as practicable after the conclusion of the appointment of electors in such State, by the final ascertainment under and in pursuance of the laws of such State providing for such ascertainment,

---

[1] See Beardstown v. Virginia, 76 Ill. 39 (1875).

[2] See Taylor v. Taylor, 10 Minn. 123 (1865); State *ex rel. v.* Tuttle, 53 Wis. 49 (1881).

[3] Constitution, Art. II, sec. 1, cl. 2. See 2 Bancroft, Const. 165-85.

The electoral vote of the respective States is (1888) as follows: Alabama, 10; Arkansas, 7; California, 8; Colorado, 3; Connecticut, 6; Delaware, 3; Florida, 4; Georgia, 12; Illinois, 22; Indiana, 15; Iowa, 13; Kansas, 9; Kentucky, 13; Louisiana, 8; Maine, 6; Maryland, 8; Massachusetts, 14; Michigan, 13; Minnesota, 7; Mississippi, 9; Missouri, 16; Nebraska, 5; Nevada, 3; New Hampshire, 4; New Jersey, 9; New York, 36; North Carolina, 11; Ohio, 23; Oregon, 3; Pennsylvania, 30; Rhode Island, 4; South Carolina, 9; Tennessee, 12; Texas, 13; Vermont, 4; Virginia, 12; West Virginia, 6; Wisconsin, 11. Total, 401.

[4] Constitution, Art. II, sec. 1, cl. 3.

[1] Constitution, Amend. Art. XII. Ratified Sept. 25, 1805.

to communicate, under the seal of the State, to the secretary of state of the United States, a certificate of such ascertainment of the electors appointed, setting forth the names of such electors and the canvass or other ascertainment under the laws of such State of the number of votes given or cast for each person for whose appointment any and all votes have been given or cast; and it shall also thereupon be the duty of the executive of each State to deliver to the electors of such State, on or before the day on which they are required by the preceding section to meet, the same certificate, in triplicate, under the seal of the State; and such certificate shall be inclosed and transmitted by the electors at the same time and in the same manner as is provided by law for transmitting by such electors to the seat of government the lists of all persons voted for as President and of all persons voted for as Vice-President; and section one hundred and thirty-six of the Revised Statutes is hereby repealed; and if there shall have been any final determination in a State of a controversy or contest as provided for in section two of this act, it shall be the duty of the executive of such State, as soon as practicable after such determination, to communicate, under the seal of the State, to the secretary of state of the United States, a certificate of such determination, in form and manner as the same shall have been made; and the secretary of state of the United States, as soon as practicable after the receipt at the state department of each of the certificates hereinbefore directed to be transmitted to the secretary of state, shall publish, in such public newspaper as he shall designate, such certificates in full; and at the first meeting of Congress thereafter he shall transmit to the two Houses of Congress copies in full of each and every such certificate so received theretofore at the state department.

Sec. 4. That Congress shall be in session on the second Wednesday in February succeeding every meeting of the electors. The Senate and House of Representatives shall meet in the hall of the House of Representatives at the hour of one o'clock in the afternoon on that day, and the president of the Senate shall be their presiding officer. Two tellers shall be previously appointed on the part of the Senate and two on the part of the House of Representatives, to whom shall be handed, as they are opened by the president of the Senate, all the certificates and papers purporting to be certificates of the electoral votes, which certificates and papers shall be opened, presented, and acted upon in the alphabetical order of the States, beginning with the letter A; and said tellers, having then read the same in the presence and hearing of the two Houses, shall make a list of the votes as they shall appear from the said certificates; and the votes having been ascertained and counted in the manner and according to the rules in this act provided, the result of the same shall be delivered to the president of the Senate, who shall thereupon announce the state of the vote, which announcement shall be deemed a sufficient declaration of the persons, if any, elected President and Vice-President of the United States, and, together with a list of the votes, be entered on the journals of the two Houses. Upon such reading of any such certificate or paper, the president of the Senate shall call for objections, if any. Every objec-

tion shall be made in writing, and shall state clearly and concisely, and without argument, the ground thereof, and shall be signed by at least one Senator and one member of the House of Representatives before the same shall be received. When all objections so made to any vote or paper from a State shall have been received and read, the Senate shall thereupon withdraw, and such objections shall be submitted to the Senate for its decision; and the speaker of the House of Representatives shall, in like manner, submit such objections to the House of Representatives for its decision; and no electoral vote or votes from any State which shall have been regularly given by electors whose appointment has been lawfully certified to according to section three of this act from which but one return has been received shall be rejected, but the two Houses concurrently may reject the vote or votes when they agree that such vote or votes have not been so regularly given by electors whose appointment has been so certified. If more than one return or paper purporting to be a return from a State shall have been received by the president of the Senate, those votes, and those only, shall be counted which shall have been regularly given by the electors who are shown by the determination mentioned in section two of this act to have been appointed, if the determination in said section provided for shall have been made, or by such successors or substitutes, in case of a vacancy in the board of electors so ascertained, as have been appointed to fill such vacancy in the mode provided by the laws of the State; but in case there shall arise the question which of two or more of such State authorities determining what electors have been appointed, as mentioned in section two of this act, is the lawful tribunal of such State, the votes regularly given of those electors, and those only, of such State shall be counted whose title as electors the two Houses, acting separately, shall concurrently decide is supported by the decision of such State so authorized by its laws; and in such case of more than one return or paper purporting to be a return from a State, if there shall have been no such determination of the question in the State aforesaid, then those votes, and those only, shall be counted which the two Houses shall concurrently decide were cast by lawful electors appointed in accordance with the laws of the State, unless the two Houses, acting separately, shall concurrently decide such votes not to be the lawful votes of the legally appointed electors of such State. But if the two Houses shall disagree in respect of the counting of such votes, then, and in that case, the votes of the electors whose appointment shall have been certified by the executive of the State, under the seal thereof, shall be counted. When the two Houses have voted, they shall immediately again meet, and the presiding officer shall then announce the decision of the question submitted. No votes or papers from any other State shall be acted upon until the objections previously made to the votes or papers from any State shall have been finally disposed of.

Sec. 5. That while the two Houses shall be in meeting as provided in this act the president of the Senate shall have power to preserve order; and no debate shall be allowed and no question shall be put by the presiding officer except to either House on a motion to withdraw.

Sec. 6. That when the two Houses separate to decide upon an objection that may have been made to the counting of any electoral vote or votes from any State, or other question arising in the matter, each Senator and Representative may speak to such objection or question five minutes, and not more than once; but after such debate shall have lasted two hours it shall be the duty of the presiding officer of each House to put the main question without further debate.

Sec. 7. That at such joint meeting of the two Houses seats shall be provided as follows: For the president of the Senate, the speaker's chair; for the speaker, immediately upon his left; the Senators, in the body of the hall upon the right of the presiding officer; for the Representatives, in the body of the hall not provided for the Senators; for the tellers, secretary of the Senate, and clerk of the House of Representatives, at the clerk's desk; for the other officers of the two Houses, in front of the clerk's desk and upon each side of the speaker's platform. Such joint meeting shall not be dissolved until the count of electoral votes shall be completed and the result declared; and no recess shall be taken unless a question shall have arisen in regard to counting any such votes, or otherwise under this act, in which case it shall be competent for either House, acting separately, in the manner hereinbefore provided, to direct a recess of such House not beyond the next calendar day, Sunday excepted, at the hour of ten o'clock in the forenoon. But if the counting of the electoral votes and the declaration of the result shall not have been completed before the fifth calendar day next after such first meeting of the two Houses, no further or other recess shall be taken by either House.

See BALLOT; BRIBERY; CANDIDATE; CONGRESS; DEPOSIT, 1 (1); HOLIDAY; QUALIFIED, 1; VACANCY; VOTE.

2. The obligation imposed upon a party to choose between two inconsistent or alternative rights or claims, in cases where there is a clear intention of the person from whom he derives one that he should not enjoy both. This, technically, is "election," or the "doctrine of election," at law and equity.

In equity jurisprudence, presupposes a plurality of gifts or rights, with an intention, express or implied, of the party, who has a right to control one or both, that one should be a substitute for the other.[1]

Thus, one may have an election: to pay money or deliver goods, as a consideration; to observe a contract, or pay damages or forfeit a sum; to retain a security for a debt, or surrender it and share as a distributee in a dividend; to rescind or affirm a voidable contract; between a statutory and common-law remedy; between a joint and a several action; between suing an agent and suing his undisclosed principal; between independent grounds of defense or of action.

A very common example is the choice a widow makes between dower and a testamentary provision.

A person who is entitled to any benefit under a will or other instrument, must, if he claims that benefit, abandon every right or interest the assertion of which would defeat, even partially, any of the provisions of the instrument. But in no case is one to be put to an election unless it is clear that the provisions of the instrument in some degree would be defeated by the assertion of his other rights.[1]

The doctrine rests upon the equitable ground that no man can be permitted to claim inconsistent rights with regard to the same subject, and that any one who asserts an interest under an instrument is bound to give full effect, as far as he can, to that instrument. Or, as it is sometimes expressed, he who accepts a benefit under a deed or will must adopt the contents of the whole instrument, conforming to all its provisions and relinquishing every right inconsistent with it.[2]

An election may be implied as well as expressed. Whether there has been an election must be determined upon the circumstances of the particular case, rather than upon general principles. It may be inferred from the conduct of the party — his acts, his omissions, and his mode of dealing with the property. Unequivocal acts of ownership, with knowledge of the right to elect, and not through a mistake with respect to the condition and value of the estate, will generally be deemed an election to take under a will. It has become a maxim that no one is bound to elect in ignorance of his rights.[3] Compare SATISFY, 2 (2).

3. The right to choose, or the act of choosing, between different actions or remedies, where the plaintiff has suffered one species of wrong from the act complained of.

This right arises where he may sue in tort or upon the contract implied by law in the case; or where he may bring an action of a purely equitable nature, or such as merely seeks a money judgment.[4]

ELECTRICITY. See LIGHTNING; TELEGRAPH; TELEPHONE.

ELEEMOSYNARY. See CHARITY, 2; CORPORATION.

ELEGIT. See EXECUTION, 3, Writs of.

ELEVATED. See RAILROAD.

ELEVATOR. See NEGLIGENCE.

ELIGIBLE. Relates to capacity of holding as well as of being elected to an office.[5]

Ineligible. Refers as well to disqualification to hold, as to disqualification to be elected to, an office.[6]

[1] Gibson v. Gibson, 17 E. L. & E. 353 (1853), Kindersley, V. C.; 14 Gratt. 548; 76 Va. 123.
[2] Penn v. Guggenheimer, 76 Va. 846 (1882), Staples, J.
[3] 76 Va. 850, supra; Burroughs v. De Couts, 70 Cal. 370 (1886); Streatfield v. Streatfield (1735), 1 Lead. Cas. Eq., W. & T., 504, 510, 541; 2 Story, Eq. §§ 1076-98.
[4] See 22 Cent. Law J. 533-38 (1886), cases.
[5] [Carson v. McPhetridge, 15 Ind. 331 (1860); 15 Cal. 117; 3 Nev. 566.
[6] State v. Murray, 28 Wis. 99 (1871).

[1] 2 Story, Eq. § 1075; 1 Pomeroy, Eq. § 461 et seq.; 54 Me. 458.

Re-eligible. Capable of election, or of holding office, more than once. See ELECTION, 1; OFFICE.

ELISOR.[1] An elector chosen by a court to return a panel of jurors where the sheriff and the coroner are disqualified.[2]

If exception lies to the coroner, the *venire* is directed to two clerks of the court, or to two other persons of the county, named by the court and sworn; these two, called "elisors," or electors, indifferently name the jury, and their return is final, no challenge being allowed to their array.[2]

ELOIGN.[3] When the sheriff seeks to replevy goods distrained, and finds them carried out of the county, or concealed, he may return that they are eloigned, *elongata*, carried to a distance, to places to him unknown.[4] See CAPERE, Capias, *Withernam.*

When, under ancient practice, he sought to replevy a man and found him conveyed out of bailiwick he made return that the person was *elongatus.*[5]

Eloignment. Removal of goods distrained, to prevent a replevy.

Eloigner. He who makes an eloignment.

ELOPEMENT.[6] The act in a wife of voluntarily leaving her husband to live with another man.

She thereby forfeits her right of dower, unless the offense is condoned. The husband is not liable for her contracts for necessaries, unless, preserving her purity, she has offered to return and he has refused to receive her.[7]

The "leaving" implies a going beyond the husband's actual control.[8]

ELSEWHERE. In or at another place. Compare ALIBI.

In a will, will pass land wherever situated.[9]

In shipping articles, was construed in subordination to the principal voyage— the words being "to the Pacific ocean, or elsewhere, thence to Boston, with wages payable at Canton."[10]

EM. See EN, 3.

EMANCIPATION.[11] The act by which a person, who is under the power or control of another, is rendered free to act for himself.[1]

Filial emancipation. Enfranchisement of a minor from parental authority.

Attaining majority is, *ipso facto*, emancipation.

Emancipation proclamation. Issued, January 1, 1863, by President Lincoln as commander-in-chief of the army and navy of the United States, during the existence of armed rebellion. It purported to be "a fit and necessary war measure for suppressing said rebellion;" and declared that all persons held as slaves within designated States, and parts of States, were and henceforward should be free.[2] See CITIZEN, Amendment, XIII.

EMBARGO.[3] The detention, by a government, of ships of commerce in its ports.

A prohibition against sailing.[4]

Civil embargo. Is laid upon ships belonging to citizens of the State imposing it.

Hostile embargo. Is laid upon ships belonging to the enemy.

The effect of a hostile embargo is, that if war does not follow the vessels are restored to their owners; if otherwise, they are confiscated. Bonds for the observance of the prohibition may be required.[5] See BLOCKADE.

EMBASSADOR. See MINISTER, 3.

EMBEZZLEMENT.[6] 1. Appropriation to one's own use of anything belonging to another, whether rightfully or wrongfully in the possession of the taker; theft.

At an early date, spending, wasting, squandering. "He left an estate to an unthrift son who embezzled it."[7]

"Embezzling or vacating records . . is a felonious offense."[8]

(q. v.), purchase by imposition of hand — *manus-capere.*

[1] See Fremont *v.* Sandown, 56 N. H. 303 (1876): Bouvier.

[2] Slaughter-House Cases, 16 Wall. 68 (1882). See also 43 Ala. 592; 44 *id.* 70; 20 La. Ann. 199; 43 Miss. 102; 13 S. C. Eq. 306; 31 Tex. 504.

[3] Spanish *embargo*, putting a bar (*barra*) in the way: arrest, stoppage of ships.

[4] [The King William, 2 Wheat. 153 (1817); L. R., 8 C. P. 659.

[5] See Wheaton, Int. Law, 372: The King William, *supra;* 7 Cranch, 287; 5 Johns. 299.

[6] N. F. *embeasiler*, to filch,— Webster. Formerly, *embesile* or *-sell;* the same as *imbécill*, to weaken, diminish, subtract from. A shop-boy embezzled his master's store imperceptibly by repeated filching,— Skeat. In early statutes spelled *imbezil*,— 2 N. M. 268.

[7] Fuller, The Worthies (1662).

[8] 4 Bl. Com. 127 (1769).

---

[1] E-li'-zor. F. *eliseur;* L. *eligere*, to choose.

[2] 3 Bl. Com. 354; 91 Pa. 495.

[3] F. *éloigner*, to remove to a distance: L. L. *e-longe*, far off.

[4] 3 Bl. Com. 149.

[5] 3 Bl. Com. 129.

[6] Dutch *ontloopen*, to run away; by substituting the prefix e- for Du. *ont-*. A. S. *hleapan*, to leap, run.

[7] 2 Bl. Com. 130; 1 *id.* 442; 11 Johns. 281; 12 *id.* 293; 11 Wend. 33; 3 Pick. 289; 7 S. & R. 249; Chitty, Contr. 49; Bish. M. & D. § 625.

[8] Cogswell *v.* Tibbetts, 3 N. H. 42 (1824).

[9] 3 P. Wms. 56; 3 Atkyn, 254.

[10] Brown *v.* Jones, 2 Gall. 479 (1815).

[11] L. *e-mancipare*, to transfer ownership: *mancipium*

"Embezzlers of Charters, Grants, Records, Bonds, Bills, Wills, &c., shall make Double Satisfaction, and be publicly Disgraced as False persons." [1]

"The goods of shipwrecked vessels shall be preserved from spoil and embezzlement." [2]

"He who would embezzle a ship's furniture, would not hesitate to embezzle the cargo." [3]

Section 5467, Rev. St., creates two statutory offenses: that of embezzling a *letter* in postal custody which has a valuable thing enclosed; and that of taking and stealing such thing out of a letter which has been embezzled. A prosecution may be for one or both offenses. [4]

2. The fraudulent conversion of property by a person to whom it has been intrusted. [5]

A species of theft, consisting in the stealing of property by clerks, agents, servants — persons acting in a fiduciary capacity. [6]

Distinguishable from "larceny" in that the taker comes lawfully into possession of the property. [6]

To "embezzle" is to appropriate to one's own use property or money intrusted to him by his employer. [7]

At common law, had no definite meaning. As an offense, had its origin in efforts made to amend the law of larceny. The first statute was that of 8 Henry VIII (1517), c. 7, in which the descriptive words were "did embezzle or otherwise convert the money to his own use." Statute of 7 Geo. IV (1827) improved and superseded earlier legislation; in it the words are "shall fraudulently embezzle." [8]

Frequently termed "larceny by bailee."

Where the accused is not named as a "bailee," it may be a question of law upon the averments whether or not he was a bailee. [9] See LARCENY.

It is essential: that the accused occupy a fiduciary relation; that he received property (money) in the course of his employment; that the property belonged to his principal; that he converted it with intent to steal and embezzle it. [10]

The indictment must allege that the accused "feloniously did steal, take and carry away" the property. [11]

The details of the crime being statutory, the decisions of other States are to be read with caution. [1]

Many State statutes follow 24 and 25 Vict. (1861) c. 96, §§ 68–72. [2]

In some States the injured person may receive payment for the property embezzled or take security therefor. [3]

In the Revised Statutes, the term designates a variety of offenses having in common the idea that the person has an opportunity to commit them by reason of some office or employment; and that they include some breach of confidence or trust, some misuse of a confidential opportunity: as, conversion by a public officer to his own use of public money intrusted to him for safe-keeping, disbursement, transfer, or other purpose. [4]

See DECOY; PECULATION.

EMBLEMENTS. [5] The vegetable chattels called emblements are the corn [grain] and other growth of the earth which are produced annually, not spontaneously but by labor and industry; thence called *fructus industriales.* [6]

A growing crop of grass, even if grown from seed, and ready to be cut for hay, cannot be taken as emblements: the improvement is not distinguishable from natural product, although it may be increased by cultivation. [6]

The doctrine of emblements is founded on the uncertainty of the termination of the tenant's estate. Where that is certain there exists no title to emblements. [7]

Nursery trees more nearly resemble emblements than fixtures; emblements being the annual product or fruit of things sown or planted. Hops, berries, and the like, are such, but not the roots and bushes from which they grow. Emblements reared by a tenant entering subsequently to a mortgage pass to the purchaser at a foreclosure sale, unless gathered before the sale. [8]

The word is used both for the crops or grain and for the privilege of reaping or gathering them. See further CROP; FRUCTUS.

---

[1] Great Law of Penn., Ch. L (1682).

[2] *Ibid.,* Ch. CXXXI (1683).

[3] The Boston, 1 Sumn. 356 (1833), Story, J.

[4] United States *v.* Baugh, 4 Hughes, 508 (1880). See United States *v.* Long, 4 Woods, 454 (1881).

[5] 2 Bishop, Cr. L. § 326; Pittsburgh, &c. Pass. R'y Co. *v.* McCurdy, 114 Pa. 558 (1886).

[6] United States *v.* Lee, 12 F. R. 818 (1882), Cox, D. J.; 11 *id.* 293; State *v.* Wingo, 89 Ind. 206 (1883); 41 How. Pr. 294; 62 Wis. 63; 4 Tex. Ap. 403.

[7] State *v.* Wolff, 34 La. An. 1154 (1882), Manning, J.

[8] State *v.* Wolff, *supra;* New Mexico *v.* Maxwell, 2 N. M. 267–68 (1882); United States *v.* Conant, 9 Cent. Law J. 129 (Cir. Ct., Mass., 1879), cases: R. S. § 5209 — national bank officer or agent; 3 Steph. Hist. Cr. L. Eng. 152–53.

[9] People *v.* Johnson, 71 Cal. 392 (1886).

[10] *Exp.* Hedley, 31 Cal. 112 (1866).

[11] Commonwealth *v.* Pratt, 132 Mass. 246 (1882): Gen. Sts. c. 161, § 38.

[1] 7 Tex. Ap. 417; 4 *id.* 407–9, cases; 2 Bishop, Crim. Law, § 331.

[2] 2 Bish. Cr. L. §§ 326–70, 392–462; 2 Whart. Cr. L. §§ 1005–42, 2069–2162.

[3] Johnston Harvester Co. *v.* McLean, 57 Wis. 262 (1883); Fagnan *v.* Knox, 66 N. Y. 526 (1876). See generally Calkins *v.* State, 18 Ohio St. 366 (1868): 98 Am. Dec. 126–74, cases.

[4] United States *v.* Conant, *ante;* United States *v.* Cook, 17 Wall. 171 (1872): 6 *id.* 385. See R. S. §§ 5437, 5467, 5486, 5496.

[5] O. F. *embléer, emblader, blayer,* to sow with grain: *bled, blé,* corn, grain, "blade."

[6] Reiff *v.* Reiff, 64 Pa. 137 (1870), Read, J.; 1 Williams, Exec. 670, 672; Taylor, Landl. & T. § 543.

[7] Whitmarsh *v.* Cutting, 10 Johns. *361 (1813). See at length 2 Bl. Com. 122–23, 145–46.

[8] Hamilton *v.* Austin, 36 Hun, 142 (1885), Follett, J. See also 19 Am. Law Rev. 24–31 (1885), cases.

EMBRACERY.[1] An attempt to influence a jury corruptly to one side by promises, persuasions, entreaties, money, entertainment, and the like.[2]

Embraceer or **embracer.** One who attempts to influence a jury (or a juror) by corrupt or unlawful means.

EMERGENCY. See ACCIDENT; NEGLIGENCE.

Within the meaning of a statute against practicing medicine without a certificate, except where the services are gratuitous and "the case one of emergency," the reference is to a case in which the ordinary and qualified practitioners are not readily obtainable, not to a case in which the patient has been given up as incurable by physicians of the schools provided for by the statute.[3]

EMIGRATION. See IMMIGRATION; COMMERCE; EXIRE, Ne exeat. Compare EXPATRIATION.

EMINENT. See DOMAIN, 1.

EMIT. See CREDIT, 2, Bill of.

EMOLUMENT. Any perquisite, advantage, profit, or gain arising from the possession of an office.

Imports, then, more than "salary" or "fees."[4] See FIX, 3; OFFICE, 1.

EMOTIONAL. See INSANITY.

EMPANEL. See PANEL.

EMPHYTEUSIS.[5] An estate in land, under the Roman law, analogous to a fee-farm, or perpetual lease, in English law.

It gave the occupant, or his transferee, a perpetual lease, conditioned upon payment of rent, and, perhaps, improvement of the land.

Whence emphyteutic.[6]

EMPLOYMENT.[7] Occupation; position involving business; service.

Employ. (1), *n.* Originally, the poetical form of employment.

(2), *v.* To engage in one's service; to use as an agent or substitute in transacting business; to commission and intrust with the management of one's affairs. Used with respect to a servant or laborer, equivalent to "hire."[8]

Employed. May refer to any present occupation, but commonly to continuous occupation.[1]

"Employed" in anything imports not only the act of doing it, but also being engaged to do it, being under contract or orders to do it.[2]

Employe, or employee; employer. "Employe" is from the French, but has become naturalized in our language. Strictly and etymologically it means "a person employed;" but in practice in the French language it ordinarily denotes a person in some official employment.[3]

"Employe" is the correlative of "employer." Neither term is restricted to any particular employment or service. "To employ" is to engage or use another as an agent or substitute in transacting business, or the performance of some service, it may be skilled labor or the service of the scientist or professional man as well as servile or unskilled manual labor.[4]

"Employe" usually embraces a laborer, servant, or other person occupied in an inferior position.[5]

Applies equally to a person within or without an office, whether a servant or a clerk. An "employee in an office" is a person engaged in the performance of the proper duties of an office, whether his duties are carried on within or without the walls of the building in which the chief officer transacts his business.[6]

The English form employee, though legitimate as conforming to analogy, is not sanctioned by the usage of good writers.[7]

See BOYCOTTING; BUSINESS; CONTRACTOR; GIFT; LABOR, 1; NEGLIGENCE; SERVANT; SUNDAY; TRADE.

EMPOWER. See AGENT; AUTHORITY, 1; DELEGATUS; POWER.

EMPTY. Ordinarily, to make void, exhaust, deprive of contents.

Section 3324, Rev. St., which makes it an offense to fail to obliterate a stamp at the time of "emptying" a cask of spirits, does not mean that absolutely every particle of the spirit be drawn off. The emptying intended is such as can be conveniently done by the ordinary method.[8]

Compare OCCUPIED; VACANT.

[1] O. F. *embracer*, to clasp in the arms, embrace.

[2] 4 Bl. Com. 140. See Gibbs *v.* Dewey, 5 Cow. 505 (1826); State *v.* Sales, 2 Nev. 269 (1866); Hawk. Pl. Cr. 259.

[3] People *v.* Lee Wah, 71 Cal. 80 (1886).

[4] Apple *v.* Crawford County, 105 Pa. 303 (1884); Const. Pa. Art. III, § 13.

[5] Accent on -teu-. Gk. *emphyteuein*, to plant or improve land.

[6] See 3 Bl. Com. 232; Maine, Anc. Law, 289.

[7] F. *employer*, to involve, engage, occupy.

[8] McCluskey *v.* Cromwell, 11 N. Y. 599 (1854).

[1] Wilson *v.* Gray, 127 Mass. 99 (1879), Lord, J.

[2] United States *v.* Morris, 14 Pet. 475 (1840), Taney, C. J.; 2 Paine, C. C. 745; 22 Ohio, 194; 20 S. C. 4–5.

[3] Gurney *v.* Atlantic, &c. R. Co., 2 N. Y. Supr. Ct. 453 (1873), Talcott, J.

[4] Gurney *v.* Atlantic, &c. R. Co., 58 N. Y. 371 (1874), Allen, J.; Krauser *v.* Ruckel, 17 Hun, 465 (1879).

[5] People *v.* Board of Police, 75 N. Y. 41 (1878).

[6] Stone *v.* United States, 3 Ct. Cl. 262 (1867); Peck, J.

[7] Webster's Dict.

[8] United States *v.* Buchanan, 4 Hughes, 488 (1881).

EN. In; into.

1. The French form of the English and Latin preposition *in.* See IN, 1, 3 (2).

En autre droit. In right of another. See DROIT.

En fait. In fact; in deed.

En owel main. In equal hand. See OWELTY.

En route. On the way. See ROUTE.

En ventre. In the womb; unborn. See VENTER.

2. As a prefix, coincides with the Latin *in.*

Some English words are written indifferently *en-* or *in-*: as, encumber and incumber, endorse and indorse, enjoin and injoin. *In* seems to be preferred.

For ease of pronounciation, changes to *em-*, particularly before a labial: as, in embracery, employ, empower.

ENABLING. Describes an enactment which confers power to do a thing: as, statutes of wills, statutes permitting parties to testify; opposed to **disabling** or restraining acts or statutes.

ENACT. See ACT, 3, Enact.

ENCEINTE. See ANCIENT, 2; PREGNANCY; VENTER.

ENCHANTMENT. See WITCHCRAFT.

ENCLOSURE. Imports land enclosed with something more than the imaginary boundary line,—some visible or tangible obstruction, as, a fence, hedge, ditch, or an equivalent object, for the protection of the premises against encroachment, as by cattle.[1]

A tract of land surrounded by a fence, together with such fence: as, in a statute limiting one's right to distrain beasts to those doing damage within his enclosure.[2] See CLOSE, 3.

ENCROACH. To intrude upon, make gain upon, occupy, or use the land, right, or authority of another, as if by gradual or partial assumption of right. See PURPRESTURE.

ENCUMBER. See INCUMBER.

END. See AT, 2; FINAL; FINE; TERMINUS.

ENDORSE. See INDORSE.

ENDOW. 1. To confer rights of dower, *q. v.*

2. To make pecuniary provision for the support of a person or institution.

Endowment. The act of settling a fund upon one; also, such fund itself. Used of a policy of insurance payable at a certain age or at death.

An endowment policy is an insurance into which enters the element of life. In one respect it is a contract payable in the event of a continuance of life; in another, in the event of death before the period specified.[1]

By the endowment of a school, hospital, or chapel is commonly understood, not building or purchasing a site for the institution, but providing a fixed revenue for its support.[2]

The "endowment of a religious or educational corporation" refers to that particular fund, or part of the fund, of the institution, bestowed for its more permanent uses, and usually kept sacred for the purposes intended.[3]

ENEMY. A nation, or a citizen or subject thereof, at war with another nation.

Alien enemy. One who owes allegiance to a government at war with ours, dwelling within our territory or seeking some action from a department of our government.

Enemies of the United States. The subjects of a foreign power in a state of open hostility toward us. Does not embrace "rebels" in insurrection against their own government. An "enemy" is always the subject of a foreign power, who owes no allegiance to our government or country.[4]

"Rebels" and "enemies" may be synonymous for those who have cast off their allegiance and made war upon their own government. Who are enemies in a *civil war*, the law of nations has not defined; but, within the meaning of a confiscation act, the term may include those who are residents of the territory under the power of the parties resisting the regular government. . . In the case of a *foreign war*, applies to all who are inhabitants of the enemy's country, though not participants, and even though subjects of a neutral State, or even subjects of the government prosecuting the war against the State within which they reside.[5]

Public enemy. Referring to the undertaking of a common carrier, applies to foreign nations with whom there is open war, and to pirates, who are considered at war with all mankind; does not include robbers, thieves, rioters, insurgents, whatever be their violence, or Indians.[6]

---

[1] Brummer *v.* Cohn, 86 N. Y. 17 (1881), Andrews, J.

[2] [Edwards *v.* Hall, 6 De G. M. & G. *87, 83 (1855), Cranworth, Ld. C.

[3] State *v.* Lyon, 32 N. J. L. 361 (1867), Bedle, J.

[4] United States *v.* Greathouse, 4 Saw. 466 (1863), Field, J.

[5] Prize Cases, 2 Black, 674 (1862); Miller *v.* United States, 11 Wall. 310-12 (1870); Gates *v.* Goodloe, 101 U. S. 617 (1879); 20 How. 249; 21 W. Va. 357.

[6] Story, Contr. 752, Bailm. § 526; Southern Express Co. *v.* Womack, 1 Heisk. 269 (1870); 7 *id.* 625; State *v.* Moore, 74 Mo. 418 (1881); League *v.* Rogan, 59 Tex. 434 (1883); 4 Op. Att.-Gen. 81.

---

[1] [Porter *v.* Aldrich, 39 Vt. 331 (1866): Act 1797, R. S. 412, § 4; *ib.* 24.

[2] Taylor *v.* Wilbey, 36 Wis. 44 (1874); 34 *id.* 666.

(26)

In a policy of marine insurance, "enemies" means "public enemies," those with whom a nation is at war.[1] See CARRIER, Common; TREASON; WAR.

ENFEOFF. See FEE.

ENFORCE. See FORCE; PERFORMANCE.

ENFRANCHISE. See FRANCHISE, 2.

ENGAGEMENT. See AGREEMENT; ASSUMPSIT; CONTRACT; PROMISE; UNDERTAKING.

ENGINE. Includes a snare, which is a device or contrivance for killing game.[2]

Engineer. See ADMISSION, 2; COMMERCE.

ENGLAND; ENGLISH. See BOROUGH; CHANCERY; CHARITY, 2; CONSTITUTION; COURT; CY PRES; DESCENT, Canons of; EXTRADITION, 1; FEUD; KING; LATIN; LAW, Common; PARLIAMENT; STATUTE.

ENGRAVING. See COPYRIGHT; PRINT.

ENGROSS. 1. To write in a gross, i. e., a large, hand; to copy in a fair hand: as, to engross an instrument on parchment. Whence engrosser, engrossing.

After a proposed statute has been read and acted upon a sufficient number of times, it is ordered to be engrossed.

"A bill ordered to be engrossed is to be written in a strong gross hand."[3] See GROSS.

2. At common law the offense of **engrossing** was the getting into one's possession, or buying up, large quantities of corn [grain] or other dead victuals, with intent to sell them again.[4]

An injury to the public. If permitted, one or more men could raise the price of provisions at will. The total engrossing of any other commodity, with intent to sell it at an unreasonable price, was also an indictable offense.[4] See COMBINATION, 2; CORNER; MONOPOLY.

ENHANCED. In an unqualified sense, is equivalent to "increased," and comprehends any increase of value, however caused or arising.

In Oregon if a husband aliens dowable lands, and they become "enhanced in value" thereafter, they shall be estimated, in setting forth the dower, according to their value when aliened. *Held*, that "enhanced" included only the value caused by improvements made, and not that which arises fortuitously, or from natural causes.[5]

ENJOIN. See INJUNCTION.

ENJOYMENT. Possession; occupation; use; exercise.

Enjoyment as of right is an enjoyment had, not secretly or by stealth, or by tacit sufferance, or by permission from time to time, on each occasion, or on many occasions, of using it; but an enjoyment had openly, notoriously, without particular leave at the time, by a person claiming to use without danger of being treated as a trespasser, as a matter of right, whether strictly legal by prescription and adverse user or by deed conferring the right, or, though not strictly legal, yet lawful to the extent of excusing a trespass.[1]

Adverse enjoyment. The possession or exercise of an easement or privilege under a claim of right against the owner of land.

If open, and continued without interruption for twenty years, a conclusive prescription of grant arises, provided that during the time there was some one in possession, qualified to resist the claim.[2] Compare POSSESSION, Adverse.

Quiet enjoyment. Peaceable, undisturbed possession of land.

Covenant for quiet enjoyment. A covenant in a conveyance or lease of land, engaging that the grantee or lessee shall be permitted to use the land unmolested.[3]

Every lease implies a covenant for quiet enjoyment. But it extends only to the possession; and its breach, like that of a warranty for title, arises only from eviction by means of title. It does not protect against entry and ouster of a tort-feasor. The tenant may call his landlord into his defense; and, if eviction follows as the result of a failure to defend him, he can then refuse to pay rent, and fall back upon this covenant for quiet enjoyment to recover his damages.[4]

A lease with an express covenant for quiet enjoyment implies a covenant that the lessor has title and power and right to convey it. The implied covenant is broken if the lessor has made a prior and still outstanding lease of part of the premises. A recovery of the premises by the prior lessee is such an eviction as constitutes a breach of the covenant for quiet enjoyment; and the lessee may recoup his damages from the rent due.[5]

See DEMISE; WARRANTY, 1.

ENLARGE. To extend, increase, lengthen the time of; also, to set at liberty.

Enlarge an estate. To increase the tenant's interest.

Enlarge an order or **rule.** To extend the time for complying with it.

---

[1] Monongahela Ins. Co. *v.* Chester, 43 Pa. 493 (1862); Vattel, Law of Nations, 387.

[2] Allen *v.* Thompson, L. R., 5 Q. B. *339 (1870).

[3] 1 Bl. Com. 183.

[4] 4 Bl. Com. 158.

[5] Thornburn *v.* Doscher, 32 F. R. 812 (1887), Deady, J.; 2 Or. Laws, § 2960. The syllabus (by the court) reads "not arising from improvements."

---

[1] Tickle *v.* Brown, 31 E. C. L. 91 (1836), Denman, C. J.

[2] 2 Washb. R. P. 42, 48.

[3] 1 Washb. R. P. 325; 4 Kent, 474, *n.*

[4] Schuylkill, &c. R. Co. *v.* Schmoele, 57 Pa. 273 (1868); Mark *v.* Patchin, 42 N. Y. 171-72 (1870), cases.

[5] McAlester *v.* Landers, 70 Cal. 82-84 (1886), cases.

To " enlarge " and to " extend " the time for taking testimony may have different meanings in a particular case.[1]

Enlarging statute. Extends a right or a remedy as it exists at common law.[2]

ENLISTMENT. Either the complete act of entering into military service, or the first step taken toward that end.[3]

A technical term, derived from Great Britain. In the English Cyclopædia, defined to be " a voluntary engagement to serve as a private soldier for a certain number of years." Chambers defines it as " the means by which the English army is supplied with troops as distinguished from the conscription prevailing in many other countries." [4]

Has never included entry into service under commission as an officer.[5]

Public policy requires that a minor be at liberty to enter into a contract to serve the state, wherever such contract is not positively forbidden by the state itself. This at least is the common law of England.[6]

Rev. St., §§ 1116–17, authorizes enlistment in the army of men above the age of sixteen, no person under twenty-one to be mustered into service without the written consent of his parents or guardian.

A contract made by a minor over sixteen, without consent, can be avoided only by his parents, they claiming his custody before majority.[7]

Habeas corpus is the judicial proceeding to secure release of a minor whose parents did not consent to his enlisting.[8] See DESERTION, 3.

ENORMIA. L. Wrongs; unlawful acts.

Alia enormia. Other wrongful acts.

After a specific allegation of wrong done by a defendant, the plaintiff may further charge, generally, *alia enormia*, to the damage, etc.,— " and other wrongs then and there did against the peace," etc. Then, all matters naturally arising from the act complained of may be given in evidence.[9] See DAMAGES, Special.

ENQUIRY. See INQUIRY.

ENROLL. See ROLL; REGISTRY, Of vessels.

ENS. L. A being; a creature.

Ens legis. A creature of the law; an artificial person, a legal entity, a corporation.

---

[1] James v. McMillan, 55 Mich. 136 (1884).

[2] See 2 Bl. Com. 324; 1 *id.* 87.

[3] Tyler v. Pomeroy, 8 Allen, 485 (1864), Gray, J. See Erichson v. Beach, 40 Conn. 286 (1873); Sheffield v. Otis, 107 Mass. 282 (1871).

[4] Babbitt v. United States, 16 Ct. Cl. 213 (1880), Davis, J.

[5] Hilliard v. Stewartstown, 48 N. H. 280–81 (1869), Perley, C. J.

[6] Commonwealth v. Gamble, 11 S. & R. *94 (1824), Gibson, J.

[7] *Re* Hearn, 32 F. R. 141 (1887).

[8] *Re* Baker, 23 F R. 30 (1885), cases; R. S. § 1117.

[9] 2 Greenl. Ev. §§ 268, 273, 278; 1 Chitt. Pl. 397; 3 Mass. 222; 15 *id.* 194.

ENTAIL. See TAIL.

ENTER. See ENTRY.

ENTERPRISE. See GIFT, 1.

ENTERTAINMENT. Public reception; something connected with the enjoyment of refreshment-rooms, tables, and the like.[1] See INN.

A public aquarium is a " place of entertainment and amusement," when a band plays and the fish are fed.[2] See EXHIBITION; THEATER.

ENTICE. See ABDUCTION; HUSBAND; PERSUADE.

ENTIRE. Untouched: complete; unbroken, whole; undivided, indivisible, inseverable: as, an entire — consideration, covenant, contract,[3] *q. v.* See SEPARABLE.

An entire claim arising out of one transaction, contract or tort, cannot be divided into separate and distinct claims. A verdict for one portion will bar an action on another.[4] See DAMAGES; MULTIPLICITY.

Entirely. " Entirely satisfied " implies a firm and thorough assent of the mind and judgment to the truth of a proposition; and this may exist, notwithstanding a possibility that the fact may be otherwise.[5]

Entirety. The whole, as opposed to a moiety.

If an estate in fee be given to a man and his wife, they are neither properly joint-tenants, nor tenants in common; for, being one person in law, they cannot take the estate by moieties, but both are seized of the entirety,— the consequence of which is, that neither can dispose of any part without the assent of the other, but the whole must remain to the survivor.[6]

The right, at common law, to control the possession of the estate during their joint lives is in the husband. Subject to the limitation that neither can defeat the right of the survivor to the whole estate, the husband has such rights as are incident to his own property, and which he acquires in her realty. Having the usufruct of all her realty interests, by the weight of authority he may lease the estate during coverture. Statutes enabling married women to hold and dispose of their property as if sole do not affect this species of estate, unless expressly so stated.[7]

The survivor does not take as a new acquisition, but under the original limitation, his (or her) estate being simply freed from participation by the other; so that

---

[1] Muir v. Keay, L. R., 10 Q. B. 597–98 (1875).

[2] Terry v. Brighton Aquarium Co., L. R., 10 Q. B. 306 (1875). See Howes v. Board of Revenue, 1 Ex. Div. 385 (1876).

[3] See 2 Pars. Contr. 517.

[4] Phillips v. Berick, 16 Johns. 136 (1819).

[5] People v. Phipps, 39 Cal. 335 (1870).

[6] [2 Bl. Com. 182.

[7] Pray v. Stebbins, 141 Mass. 223–24 (1886), cases.

if, for instance, the wife survives and then dies, her heirs would take to the exclusion of the heirs of the husband. Nor can partition be made of the estate. During coverture the husband has control of the estate. Upon his death, the wife, or her heir, may enter without action against his alienee — by 32 Hen. VIII (1541), c. 28, which is in force in Kentucky, Massachusetts, Tennessee, and possibly in New York and New Jersey. Divorce of the wife from the husband restores her to her moiety. A grant or devise to them and another invests them with an entirety in one-half only. It is always competent, however, to make husband and wife tenants in common by proper words. The law of the States is not uniform on the subject.[1]

ENTITLE. See TITLE, 2.

ENTRAP. See DECOY.

ENTRY.[2] I. As relates to Property. The act of actually going upon land, or into a building.

At common law, an assertion of title by going upon the land; or, if that was hazardous, by "making continual claim."[3]

Taking possession of lands by the legal owner.[4]

1. An extrajudicial and summary remedy by the legal owner, when another person, who has no right, has previously taken possession of lands or tenements.

The party entitled may make a formal but peaceable entry thereon, declaring that thereby he takes possession, which notorious act of ownership is equivalent to a feudal investiture; or he may enter on any part of the land in the same county in the name of the whole; but if the land lies in different counties he must make different entries. If the claimant is deterred from entering by menaces he may "make claim" as near the estate as he can, with the like forms and solemnities, which claim is in force for a year and a day; and, if repeated once in the like period (called "continual claim"), has the same effect as a legal entry. Such entry puts into immediate possession him that has the right of entry, and thereby makes him complete owner, capable of conveying. But this remedy applies only in cases in which the original entry of the wrong-doer was unlawful, viz., in abatement, intrusion, and disseisin. In discontinuance and deforcement the owner of the estate cannot enter; for, the original entry being lawful, an apparent right of possession is gained, and the owner is driven to his action at law. In cases where entries are lawful, the

right of entry may be "tolled," that is, taken away, by descent. Corresponds to recaption of personalty.[1]

Re-entry. The right reserved to consider a lease forfeited and to resume possession of the premises, upon failure in the lessee to perform a covenant; also, any exercise of this right.

This being a harsh power, the courts will restrain it to the most technical limits of the terms and conditions upon which the right is to be exercised.[2]

When for rent in arrear, unless dispensed with by agreement or statute, demand of payment of the rent must first be made.[3]

2. On the subject of entry by a grantor for breach of condition by the grantee, see GRANT, 2.

3. Going upon the landed property of another for any other purpose than those above mentioned.

It is not a trespass to enter upon another's premises to abate a nuisance, retake goods, make repairs, demand rent, distrain, or capture an estray.[4] See TRESPASS, Ab initio.

Forcible entry. An entry made with violence, against the will of the lawful occupant, and without authority of law.

Such entry as is made with a strong hand, with unusual weapons, an unusual number of servants or attendants, or with menace of life or limb; not a mere trespass.[5]

"When a man enters peaceably into a house, but turns the party out of possession by force, or by threats frights him out of possession."[6]

It will be sufficient if the entry is attended with such a display of force as manifests an intention to intimidate the party in possession, or deter him from defending his rights, or to excite him to repel the invasion, and thus bring about a breach of the peace.[7]

Forcible entry and detainer. An offense against the public peace, committed by violently taking or keeping possession of lands and tenements by menaces, force, and arms, and without the authority of law.

The entry now allowed by law is a peaceable one; that forbidden is such as is carried on and maintained by force, by violence and with unusual weapons.[8]

In early days, at common law, any man who had a right of entry upon lands was authorized to enter with

---

[1] 1 Wash. R. P. 425, cases; 4 Kent, 362; Chandler v. Cheney, 37 Ind. 394–414 (1871), cases; Re Benson, 8 Biss. 118–21 (1877); Jacobs v. Miller, 50 Mich. 124 (1883); Hadlock v. Gray, 104 Ind. 598 (1885); 25 Am. Law Reg. 269–74 (1886), cases; 18 Cent. Law J. 183–88, 326–29 (1884), cases; 5 Kan. Law J. 5 (1887), cases; Thornton v. Thornton, 3 Rand. 182–90 (Va., 1825), cases; 3 Lead. Cas. R. P. 143–58 (1887), cases.

[2] F. entrer; L. in-trare, to go into.

[3] [Innerarity v. Mims, 1 Ala. 674 (1840).

[4] Guion v. Anderson, 8 Humph. 306 (1847).

[1] 3 Bl. Com. 174–79, 5; 2 id. 314.

[2] The Elevator Cases, 17 F. R. 200 (1881).

[3] Johnston v. Hargrove, 81 Va. 121–23 (1885), cases.

[4] Keifer v. Carrier, 53 Wis. 404 (1881).

[5] Willard v. Warren, 17 Wend. 261 (1837).

[6] Bacon, Abridg.: Edwick v. Hawkes, 18 Ch. Div. 211 (1881). See also 8 Ala. 87; 9 Cal. 46; 21 N. J. L. 428.

[7] Ely v. Yore, 71 Cal. 133 (1886), cases.

[8] 4 Bl. Com. 148; Reeler v. Purdy, 41 Ill. 285 (1866).

force and arms, and by force and arms retain possession — provided, possibly, that the entry was not by a breach of the public peace. The general revision of the written law upon the use of force by an individual to establish his own rights, made by statute 8 Hen. VI (1430), c. 9, is substantially the origin of existing law upon the subject of forcible entry and detainer. Prosecution under this statute is by indictment. In Massachusetts, unless the entry and detainer is accompanied by an actual breach of the peace, the process is substantially a civil proceeding. Under either procedure the court will award restitution of the premises.[1]

The purpose of statutes forbidding forcible entry and detainer is, that, without regarding the actual condition of the title to property, where a person is in the peaceable and quiet possession of it he shall not be turned out by strong hand, by force, by violence, or by terror. The party so using force and acquiring possession may have the superior title or may have the better right to the present possession, but the policy of the law is to prevent disturbances of the public peace, to forbid any person righting himself, in a case of that kind, by his own hand and by violence, and to require that the party who has in this manner obtained possession shall restore it to the party from whom it has been obtained; and that, when the parties are *in statu quo*, in the position they were in before the use of violence, the party out of possession must resort to legal means to obtain his possession, as he should have done in the first instance.[2]

If a claimant (a railroad company) of real estate, out of possession, resorts to force, amounting to a breach of the peace, to obtain possession from another claimant (also a railroad company) who is in peaceable possession, and personal injury arises therefrom, the party using the force is liable in damages, compensatory and punitive, for the injury, without regard to the legal title, or to the right of possession.[3]

4. Entrance into a dwelling-house with the whole or a part of the body, or with any implement for the purpose of committing a felony. See BURGLARY.

II. As a matter of Writing. Setting down in written characters; placing upon the record: recording.

1. Setting down in a book of accounts the particulars of a business transaction.

Original entry. The first statement made by a person in his account-books, charging another with money due upon a contract between them. Whence "book of original entries."[4] See further BOOK, Entries.

Short entry. It was a custom in London for bankers to receive bills for collection and to enter them immediately in their customers' accounts, but never to carry out the proceeds in the column to their credit until actually collected. This was called "short entry" or "entering short."[1]

2. The transaction by which an importer obtains entrance of his goods into the body of the merchandise of the country.

Until the entire transaction is closed, by a withdrawal and payment of the duties upon all the goods covered by the original paper called the entry for warehouse, the "false entry" contemplated by the act of Congress of March 3, 1863, is not completed.[2]

In the statutes in relation to duties, but one entry is referred to — the original entry provided, regulated, and defined by sections 2785-90, Rev. St. "Entry for withdrawal" is a misnomer.[3]

3. Filing or inscribing upon the records of a land-office the written proceedings required to entitle a person to a right of pre-emption or of homestead in public lands.

The act by which an individual acquires inceptive right to a portion of the unappropriated soil of the country, by filing his claim in the office of the "entry-taker," an officer who corresponds in his functions to the register of land-offices.[4] See LAND, Public; PRE-EMPTION, 2.

4. Depositing for copyright the title or description of a book or other article.

Whence "Entered according to Act of Congress," etc. See COPYRIGHT.

5. Recording in due form and order a thing done in court: as, an appearance made, a judgment rendered. Styled "docket" or "record" entries.

When a written order is signed by the judge and filed with the clerk, who enters a brief statement thereof in his "minute-book, the order, although not then recorded in the order-book, is "entered," within the meaning of a law limiting the time for appeal.[5]

In a literal sense, writing up a judgment in a docket is "entering" it; as, entering the judgment of a justice of the peace.[6]

6. In the practice of legislative bodies, the orderly inscription in a journal of any action or determination required to be preserved in writing.

The constitution of Iowa requires that a proposed amendment "shall be entered" in the journals of the two houses of Assembly "with the yeas and nays."

---

[1] Hodgkins v. Price, 132 Mass. 200 (1882), Lord, J.; Presbrey v. Presbrey, 13 Allen, 284 (1866); 10 Oreg. 485.

[2] Iron Mountain & Helena R. Co. v. Johnson, 119 U. S. 611 (1887), Miller, J.

[3] Denver & Rio Grande R. Co. v. Harris, 122 U. S. 597, 605 (1887), Harlan, J. As to civil action, see 22 Cent. Law J. 292 (1886), cases.

[4] See generally Roche v. Ware, 71 Cal. 376-77 (1886), cases; Bridgewater v. Roxbury, 54 Conn. 213 (1886).

[1] Blaine v. Bourne, 11 R. I. 121 (1875), Potter, J.

[2] [United States v. Baker, 5 Bened. 35 (1871), Blatchford, J.; 12 St. L. 737.

[3] United States v. Seidenberg, 17 F. R. 230 (1883), Pardee, J.

[4] Chotard v. Pope, 12 Wheat. 588 (1827), Johnson, J.

[5] Uren v. Walsh, 57 Wis. 102 (1883); R. S. Wis. § 3042.

[6] Conwell v. Kuykendall, 29 Kan. 707, 710 (1883); Kan. Comp. Laws, 1879, ch. 81, § 115.

This means that the amendment shall be spread at length thereon, and the yeas and nays set out in the journal in full. But instances where "to enter" and "entered" do not mean to spread at length may be cited. The object to be obtained must be considered in each case.[1] See YEAS AND NAYS.

III. As a Remedy. A "writ of entry," at common law, was a proceeding by which the possession of land, wrongfully withheld from its owner, could be recovered.

A real action, possessory in nature. In a greatly modified form, has been used in this country. In England, superseded by the action of ejectment, and, later, abolished.[2]

ENUMERATION. Separate mention.

The enumeration of particular things in an instrument may include others of the same class; there is no absolute rule that such enumeration includes things of a different class, when the general terms are broad enough to include them.[3] See EJUSDEM GENERIS; EXPRESSIO, Unius, etc.; GENERAL, 6; OTHER.

ENURE. See INURE.

ENVELOPE. See LETTER, 3; PUBLICATION, 2.

ENVOY. See MINISTER, 3.

EO. L. On that, in that; at the same. See Is.

Eo die. On the same day, at the same time; as, *eo die*, writ issued.

Eo instante. At the same moment or instant.

Eo nomine. In or under the same name; as, interest *eo nomine*.

EPIDEMIC. See DISEASE; HEALTH.

When, in a policy of insurance, it does not appear that the word "epidemics" was understood by the parties in any other than its popular sense, evidence is not admissible to change that meaning. The insurer may stipulate for exemption from liability for any disease that may by possibility prevail to an extent which could be called epidemic.[4]

EQUAL.[5] Compare EQUIVALENT.

Like or alike in quality, degree, amount, or merit; corresponding; uniform; the same: as, equal provision, equity, protection, rights.

Equal to. Not less than: as, in an agreement to keep the number of boats in a freight line "equal to" the number leased.[6]

Equally. In a will, may mean not that shares are to be held in the same manner, but as equal in quantity.[1]

A *per capita* division is intended by "divided equally," whether the devisees are children and grandchildren, brother or sisters, nephews or nieces, or strangers in blood to the testator.[2]

When a testator designates the objects of his gift by their relationship to a living ancestor, they take equal shares, *per capita*. But this rule will be controlled by the general intention of the testator.[3]

"Equality is equity," and where distribution is to be made among two or more, without anything to indicate the proportions, the presumption is that the shares are equal.[4]

An estate given to two persons, "equally to be divided" between them, is, under a *deed*, a joint tenancy; under a *will*, a tenancy in common. In the case of a deed is implied no more than the law has annexed to the estate, viz., divisibility; in the case of a will, the devisor may be presumed to have meant what is most beneficial to both devisees.[5]

Equality. Uniformity, likeness; sameness: as, of civil liberty. See CITIZEN, Amendment, XIV; EQUITY; TAX, 2.

EQUITABLE. See EQUITY, Equitable.

EQUITY.[6] 1. The point of contrast between the law of nations (*q. v.*) and the law of nature was "equity;" a term which some derive from a Greek word denoting the principle of equal distribution: but that origin is to be preferred which gives the term the sense of "leveling." The civil law of Rome recognized many arbitrary distinctions between classes of men and property. The neglect of these distinctions was that feature of the law of nature which is depicted in equity. It was first applied, without ethical meaning, to foreign litigants.[7]

2. Equality of right; exact justice between contending parties; fairness in determining conflicting claims; justice.

3. That portion of natural justice which is

---

[1] Koehler *v.* Hill, 60 Iowa, 557, 556 (1883), Seevers, J.

[2] See 3 Bl. Com. 180.

[3] Corwin *v.* Hood, 58 N. H. 402 (1878); *Re* Swigert, 119 Ill. 89 (1886).

[4] Pohalski *v.* Mutual Life Ins. Co., 36 N. Y. Super. Ct. 252 (1873); affirmed, 56 N. Y. 640 (1874).

[5] L. *æqualis: æquus*, even, level, exact; just, right, fair.

[6] Stewart *v.* Lehigh Valley R. Co., 38 N. J. L. 517 (1875).

[1] Bannister *v.* Bull, 16 S. C. 227 (1881).

[2] Purnell *v.* Culbertson, 12 Bush, 370–71 (1876), cases.

[3] Young's Appeal, 83 Pa. 63 (1876), cases; Risk's Appeal, 52 *id.* 271 (1866); Harris's Estate, 74 *id.* 453 (1873); Walker *v.* Griffin, 11 Wheat. 375 (1826).

[4] Lewis's Appeal, 89 Pa. 513 (1879). See also 37 Ala. 208; 20 Conn. 122; 120 Mass. 135; 46 Md. 186; 37 Miss. 59; 46 N. H. 439; 30 N. J. E. 595; 33 *id.* 520; 70 N. Y. 512; 33 Ohio St. 328; 104 Pa. 637; 10 Gratt. 275; 4 Ired. E. 244; 5 *id.* 324; 6 *id.* 437; 10 Ves. 166; 8 Beav. 579; 4 Kent, 375; Roper, Leg. 88, 156.

[5] 2 Bl. Com. 193; 5 Cow. 221.

[6] L. *æquitas*, the quality of being *æquus*, even, level, equal, *q. v.*

[7] Maine, Ancient Law, p. xxiv.

made up of the decisions of the judges of the English court of chancery in the exercise of their extraordinary jurisdiction. See further CHANCERY.

"In this sense, equity is wider than law, and narrower than natural justice, in the *extent* of the subject-matters within its jurisdiction: it cannot be defined in its *content* otherwise than by an enumeration of these matters."

Not the chancellor's sense of moral right nor of what is equal and just, but a complex system of established law.[1]

That portion of remedial justice exclusively administered by a court of equity, as contradistinguished from the portion exclusively administered by a court of common law.[2]

In the most general sense we are accustomed to call that equity which, in human transactions, is founded in natural justice, in honesty and right, and which properly arises *ex æquo et bono*. In this sense it answers precisely to the definition of justice, or natural law, given by Justinian in his Pandects. And the word *jus* is used in the same sense in the Roman law. . . It would be a great mistake to suppose that equity, as administered in England and America, embraced a jurisdiction as wide and extensive as that which arises from the principles of natural justice above stated. Probably the jurisprudence of no civilized nation ever attempted so wide a range of duties for any of its judicial tribunals. Even the Roman law, which has been justly thought to deal to a vast extent in matters *ex æquo et bono*, never affected so bold a design. On the contrary, it left many matters of natural justice wholly unprovided for, from the difficulty of framing general rules to meet them, and from the doubtful nature of the policy of attempting to give a legal sanction to duties of imperfect obligation, such as charity, gratitude, and kindness, or even to positive engagements of parties, where they are not founded in what constitutes a meritorious consideration. . . A still more limited sense of the term is that in which it is used in contradistinction to strict law — *strictum et summum jus*. Thus, Aristotle has defined the very nature of equity to be the correction of the law, wherein it is defective by reason of its universality. It is of this equity, as correcting, mitigating, or interpreting the law, that, not only civilians, but common-law writers, are most accustomed to speak.[3]

The general purpose of equity is to moderate the rigor of the law, supply its deficiencies, and bring it into harmony with conscience and moral justice.[4] See CONSCIENCE.

The term "equity" is also used, elliptically, for a court of equity or a court administering the principles of equity: as when it is said that equity will reform an instrument, or will afford relief or redress.

And "equities" is often employed to denote the several rights or interests, whatever they may be, belonging to one person or party, which will receive recognition and enforcement in a court of equity.[1]

"This court held that there was no equity in the bill, on the ground that, if the plaintiff had any right of action for money had and received, it was an action at law."[2] See DEMURRER, General.

Court of equity. The essential difference between a court of equity and a court of law consists in the different modes of administering justice in them, in the modes of proof, of trial, and of relief.[3]

A court of equity — (1) adapts its decrees to all the varieties of circumstances which may arise, and adjusts them to all the peculiar rights of all the parties in interest; whereas a court of common law is bound down to a fixed and invariable form of judgment in general terms, altogether absolute, for the plaintiff or the defendant. (2) It can administer remedies for rights which a court of common law does not recognize at all; or, which, if recognized, are left wholly to the conscience and good-will of the parties. Such are trusts, many cases of losses and injuries by mistake, accident, and fraud; cases of penalties and forfeitures; cases of impending irreparable injuries, or meditated mischiefs; cases of oppressive proceedings, undue advantages and impositions, betrayals of confidence, and unconscionable bargains. (3) Remedies in a court of equity are often different, in nature, mode, and degree from remedies in a court of law, even when each has jurisdiction over the subject-matter. Thus, a court of equity, if a contract is broken, will often compel specific performance; whereas a court of law can only give damages for the breach. So, a court of equity will interfere by way of injunction to prevent wrongs; whereas a court of common law can grant redress only, when the wrong is done. (4) The modes of seeking and granting relief differ. A court of law tries a contested fact by means of a jury; and the evidence is generally drawn from third persons, disinterested witnesses. But a court of equity tries causes without a jury; and, addressing itself to the conscience, requires the defendant, under oath, to give his knowledge of the facts stated in a bill in the nature of a bill of discovery,[4] *q. v.*

Perhaps the most general, if not the most precise, definition of a court of equity is, that it has jurisdiction in cases of rights, recognized and protected by the municipal juris-

---

[1] Savings Institution *v.* Makin, 23 Me. 366 (1844), Shepley, J.

[2] [1 Story, Equity Jurisprudence, § 25.

[3] 1 Story, Eq. §§ 1-3, 6, 8. See also 1 Pomeroy, Eq., pp. 36-38, 308-21.

[4] 3 Pars. Contr. 363.

[1] See 1 Pomeroy, Eq. § 146.

[2] Ætna Life Ins. Co. *v.* Middleport, 124 U. S. 547 (1888), Miller, J.

[3] 3 Bl. Com. 426.

[4] 1 Story, Eq. §§ 28-31. See also 1 Pomeroy, Eq. §§ 129-45.

prudence, where a plain, adequate, and complete remedy cannot be had in the courts of common law.[1]

In America, this branch of jurisprudence has grown up chiefly since the formation of the National government. It follows the model of the English court of chancery; except that, in some States, and in the National tribunals, it is administered by the common-law courts; in some the jurisdiction is very imperfect, in others scarcely known.[2]

The great advantage possessed by a court of equity is not so much in its enlarged jurisdiction as in the extent and adaptability of its remedial powers. Generally its jurisdiction is as well defined and limited as that of a court of law. It cannot exercise jurisdiction when there is an adequate and complete remedy at law. It cannot assume control over that large class of obligations called imperfect obligations, resting upon conscience and moral duty only, unconnected with legal obligations. Generally its jurisdiction depends upon legal obligations and its decrees can only enforce remedies to the extent and in the mode established by law. It cannot, by avowing that there is a right but no remedy known to the law, create a remedy in violation of law, or even without authority of law. It acts upon established principles not only, but through established channels.[3]

Courts of law and of equity are independent. They act upon different principles, and, except where some recognized ground of equity jurisdiction is concerned, are each alike bound to recognize the validity and conclusiveness of the record of what the other has done. Equity, in such cases, does not contradict but supplements. It does in this way what right and justice require, and what, from the inflexibility of the principles upon which a court of law proceeds, it could not do.[4]

When a court of equity has once acquired jurisdiction of a cause it may go on to a complete adjudication, even to the extent of establishing legal rights and granting legal remedies.[5]

A too severe application of the common-law rules forced the courts of chancery into existence in England. The body of the chancery law is nothing more than a system of exceptions; of principles applicable to cases falling within the letter, but not within the intention of particular rules. The exercise of equity powers, in every government of laws, is conclusive proof of a necessity that they be lodged somewhere. Every rule, from its universality, must be defective. A legislature can do little more than mark out general principles; their application, as well as the more minute details, must in general be left to the courts, as cases arise.[6]

The absence of a plain and adequate remedy at law

affords the only test of equitable jurisdiction, and the application of this principle to a particular case must depend altogether upon the character of the case as disclosed in the pleadings.[1]

Where there is plain, adequate and complete relief at law, the defendant has a right to a trial by jury.[2]

The office and jurisdiction of a court of equity, unless enlarged by express statute, are limited to the protection of rights of property. It has no jurisdiction over the prosecution, the punishment, or the pardon of crimes, or over the appointment and removal of public officers. To assume such a jurisdiction would be to invade the domain of the courts of common law, or of the administrative department of government. Any jurisdiction over criminal matters that the English court of chancery ever had became obsolete long ago, except as incidental to its peculiar jurisdiction for the protection of infants, or under its authority to issue writs of *habeas corpus* for the discharge of persons unlawfully imprisoned.[3]

Equity does not enjoin against a crime as a crime. But injunctions have often been granted against acts injurious to individuals, though they have also amounted to a crime against the public.[4]

The equity jurisdiction of the Federal courts is derived from the Constitution and laws of the United States, and is not affected by State statutes. Section 913 of the Revised Statutes, which declares that the modes of proceeding in equity causes shall be according to the principles, rules, and usages which belong to courts of equity, refers to the principles, rules, and usages by which the English court of chancery was governed at the time of the passage of the Judiciary Act in 1789.[5]

The test of equity jurisdiction in the Federal courts—namely, the inadequacy of the remedy at law—is the remedy which existed when the Judiciary Act of 1789 was adopted, unless subsequently changed by Congress.[6]

The practice in a court of equity is regulated by law or rule, and cannot be varied by the agreement of parties.[7] See PROBATE, Court of.

Bill in equity. The document by which a suit is begun in a court of equity.

Is in the style of a petition; and in the nature of a declaration at law. Sets forth the circumstances of the case at length, alleging that a trust relation exists, or that some fraud, accident, mistake, or peculiar hardship exists or has been or is attempted; avers want of adequate relief at law; asks for a subpœna

---

[1] 1 Story, Eq. § 33.

[2] 1 Story, Eq. §§ 54-58.

[3] Reese v. City of Watertown, 19 Wall. 121-22 (1873), Hunt, J.

[4] Tilton v. Cofield, 93 U. S. 167 (1876), Swayne, J.

[5] Walters v. Farmers' Bank, 76 Va. 18 (1881); 1 Story, Eq. § 65; 1 Pomeroy, Eq. § 181.

[6] Pennock v. Hart, 8 S. & R. *378 (1822), Gibson, J.

[1] Watson v. Sutherland, 5 Wall. 79 (1866), Davis, J.; Buzard v. Houston, 119 U. S. 351-52 (1886), cases.

[2] Hipp v. Babin, 19 How. 278 (1856; Parker v. Winnipiseogee, &c. Co., 2 Black, 551 (1862), cases; Smith v. Bourbon County, 127 U. S. 111 (1888).

[3] Re Sawyer, 124 U. S. 210 (1888), cases, Gray, J.

[4] Sparhawk v. Union Passenger R'y Co., 54 Pa. 413 (1867), Strong, J.

[5] Strettell v. Ballou, 3 McCrary, 47 (1881), McCrary, J.; Boyle v. Zacharie, 6 Pet. 658 (1832); 3 Wheat. 212; 4 *id.* 115; 13 How. 271; 2 Black. 551; 1 McCrary, 162.

[6] McConihay v. Wright, 121 U. S. 206 (1887).

[7] Nickerson v. Atchison, &c. R. Co., 30 F. R. 86 (1880).

to compel respondent to answer the charges, and, perhaps, for an injunction. Calls into court as parties all persons interested in the subject-matter. Should contain no scandalous or impertinent matter. Filing the bill is followed, in different suits, by service of the subpœna, sequestration, appearance, demurrer, plea to the jurisdiction or to the person, answer, amendments, supplemental bills, cross-bills, decree or reference to a master for a report as to the facts and the form of a decree, exceptions to the report, final hearing, final decree, bill of review, appeal to a higher court. See further BILL, IV.

Better equity. A claim to property superior, in contemplation of a court of equity, to another claim.

In this category is a second mortgagee who has no knowledge of the existence of a prior unrecorded mortgage.

Countervailing equity. Such equity as offsets or counteracts another equity; an adverse counter-balancing right or equity.

Equal equity. Equality of equitable right.

Exists between persons who have been equally innocent and equally diligent.[1]

Equity of a statute. The intention of the law-maker, as evinced by the spirit and reason of an enactment. See further STATUTE.

Equity of redemption. The reasonable time within which a mortgagee may redeem his estate after forfeiture. See further REDEEM.

Equity of settlement; wife's equity. See SETTLE, 3.

Secret equity. An interest or claim, cognizable in a court of equity, of which notice has been withheld from one or more interested persons or from the public generally.

Equitable. 1. According to natural right or justice; just and right in a particular case, as distinguished from the strict rule of a general, positive law. Opposed, *inequitable.*

2. That which can be sustained or made available or effective in a court of equity, or upon principles of equity jurisprudence.[2] Opposed, *legal.*

The remedies for the redress of wrongs and the enforcement of rights are: (1) those which are administered in courts of common law; and (2) those which are administered in courts of equity. Rights which are recognized and protected, and wrongs which are redressed, by the former courts are called "legal"

[1] See Boone *v.* Chiles, 10 Pet. *210 (1836).
[2] [Abbott's Law Dict.

rights and "legal" injuries. Rights which are recognized and protected, and wrongs which are redressed, by the latter courts only, are called "equitable" rights and "equitable" injuries. The former are said to be rights and wrongs at common law, and the remedies, remedies at common law; the latter, rights and wrongs in equity, and the remedies, remedies in equity.[1]

It is customary to speak of "equitable" (and legal) — action, assets, assignment, consideration, conversion, defense, estate, estoppel, execution, interest, jurisdiction, levy, lien, mortgage, owner, plaintiff, remedy, title, value, waste, *qq. v.*

In the Federal courts, the distinction between legal and equitable proceedings is strictly maintained; distinct proceedings must be instituted for the enforcement of equitable rights.[2]

Separate courts of equity exist in Alabama, Delaware, Kentucky, Maryland, Mississippi, New Jersey, and Tennessee. In Arkansas, Connecticut, Florida, Georgia, Illinois, Iowa, Maine, Massachusetts, Michigan, New Hampshire, North Carolina, Oregon, Pennsylvania, Rhode Island, Texas, Vermont, Virginia, and West Virginia, chancery powers are exercised by the judges of the common-law courts. In the other States, the distinction between actions at law and suits in equity have been abolished, but certain equitable remedies are still administered under the statutory form of the civil action.[3]

In a given case equity jurisdiction may be *exclusive* of the law, *auxiliary* to it, *remedial* of it, or *concurrent* with it — that is, executive, adjustive, or protective.[4]

Maxims embodying fundamental principles upon which equity jurisprudence rests, are: Equity, once having had, does not lose, jurisdiction; follows the law — in affording redress;[5] assists the vigilant; suffers no right to be without a remedy; suffers the law to prevail, where there is equal equity or equality; delights in equality — is equality;[6] requires that he who seeks equity must do equity — must come with clean hands;[7] as to the particular transaction in review;[8] looks on that as done which ought to be done[9] — imputes intention to fulfill obligations; delights to do justice, and that not by halves. Nothing can call forth a court of equity into activity but conscience, good faith, and reasonable diligence.[10]

See further terms in this title, and, especially, Acci-

[1] 1 Story, Eq. § 25.
[2] See Gibson *v.* Chouteau, 13 Wall. 102 (1871).
[3] See Bispham, Eq. § 15; 1 Story, Eq. §§ 56–58.
[4] Smith, Manual Eq. 33.
[5] 107 U. S. 11; 110 *id.* 284, 281.
[6] 101 U. S. 406; 109 *id.* 512.
[7] 108 U. S. 225; 109 *id.* 526.
[8] 26 Wend. 166; 1 Black, 93.
[9] 3 Wheat. 578; 50 Conn. 111.
[10] 1 How. 189, 168; 95 U. S. 160. See generally 1 Story, Eq. §§ 59–74; 1 Pomeroy, Eq., Ch. I, § 363; early English equity (uses and contracts), 1 Law Quar. Rev. 162–74 (1885), O. W. Holmes, Jr.; common law and conscience in the ancient court of chancery. *ib.* 443–54 (1885), L. Owen Pike; the administration of equity through

DENT; ADEQUATE, 2; DISCOVERY, 6; ELECTION, 2; FIC-
TION; FRAUD; HEARING; IGNORANCE; ISSUE, 4; MAS-
TER, 4; MISTAKE; PARTY, 2; PATENT, 2; PEACE, 1, Bill of;
PERFORMANCE, Specific; PREJUDICE, Without; QUIA
TIMET; RECEIVER, 2; REFORM; RELIEF, 2; RESCISSION;
SATISFACTION, (2); SEQUESTRATION, 2; SET-OFF; TRUST, 1;
USE, 2.

EQUIVALENT.[1] 1, *adj.* (1) Equal in
force or power, in effect or import: as, equivalent — terms, stipulations.

(2) Equally good: as, the equivalent chemical action of fluids.[2]

2, *n.* A device or machine operating on
the same principle and performing the same
functions, by analogous means or equivalent
combination, as another device or machine.[3]

Only those things are equivalents which perform
the same functions in substantially the same way.
Thus, celluloid is not an equivalent for hard rubber.[4]

The substantial equivalent of a thing is the same as
that thing itself. Two devices which perform the
same functions in substantially the same way, and
accomplish substantially the same result, are the
same, though they differ in name and form.[5]

A patentee is protected against equivalents for any
part of his invention. But a process is not infringed
by the use of any number of its stages less than all of
them.[6]

Equivalents may be claimed by the patentee of an
invention consisting of a combination of old elements
or ingredients, as well as of any other valid patented
improvement, provided the arrangement of the parts
comprising the invention is new, and will produce a
new and useful result. The term as applied to such
an invention is special in its signification and somewhat different from what is meant when applied to an
invention consisting of a new device or an entirely
new machine.[7]

An equivalent for an ingredient of a combination
of parts that are old must be one which was known at
the date of the original patent as a proper substitute
for the ingredient left out. An equivalent in such case
performs the same function as the other.[8] See COM-
BINATION, 1; PATENT, 2.

---

common-law forms, *ib.* 455–65 (1885), S. G. Fisher; brief
survey of equity jurisdiction, 1 Harv. Law Rev. 55–72,
111–131, 355–87 (1887), cases, C. C. Langdell.

[1] L. *æquus*, equal, *valere*, to be strong, be worth.

[2] Tyler *v.* City of Boston, 7 Wall. 330 (1868).

[6] See McCormick *v.* Talcott, 20 How. 405 (1857), Grier,
Justice.

[4] Goodyear Vulcanite Co. *v.* Davis, 102 U. S. 230, 222
(1880), Strong, J.

[5] Union Paper-Bag Machine Co. *v.* Murphy, 97 U. S.
125 (1877), Clifford, J.

[6] Goodyear Co. *v.* Davis, *supra;* Crouch *v.* Boemer,
103 U. S. 797 (1880).

[7] Imhaeuser *v.* Buerk, 101 U. S. 655 (1879), Clifford, J.

[8] Gill *v.* Wells, 22 Wall. 2, 28 (1874), cases, Clifford, J.
See Gage *v.* Herring, 107 U. S. 647 (1882); 1 Wall. 573;
2 *id.* 328.

EQUIVOCAL. See AMBIGUITY.

ER. The Teutonic form of the Latin *or*
in terminations.

Annexed to words of English origin. See OR, 1.

ERASURE. See ALTERATION, 2.

ERECT.[1] 1. To lift up, build, construct:
as, to erect — a building, a fixture.

A house cannot be said to be erected until substantially completed; before that it is a structure, not a
"building erected" for a purpose.[2]

Removing a building is not erecting it;[3] nor is ele-
vating and materially enlarging it.[4] But erecting or
repairing may include painting.[5]

An erection is a construction.[6]

A public grant conditioned on the "erection" of
buildings is satisfied by the purchase of buildings already erected.[7] See STRUCTURE.

2. To found, form, institute, establish,
create: as, to erect — a new county, a district
for election or judicial purposes, a corporation.[8]

ERIE, LAKE. See LAKES.

ERMINE. 1. The *mustela erminea*, Ar-
menian rat; the fur of which is pure white
in winter time.

2. The dignity of judges, whose state
robes, lined with the fur of the ermine,
are regarded as emblematical of purity.[9]
Whence judicial ermine, for judicial integrity. See GOWN, 2.

ERRATUM. L. Error.

In nullo est erratum. In nothing is
there error. The emphatic words of a joinder
of issue on an assignment of error, as originally expressed.

By this plea the defendant admits a fact regularly
assigned.[10] The plea is in the nature of a demurrer.[11]
See ERROR, 2 (3), Writ of.

ERRONEUS. See ERROR, 2 (2), Erroneous.

ERROR. 1. Lat. A wandering; a mistake; an error. Compare ERRATUM.

---

[1] L. *erectus*, set up, upright: *erigere*, *eregere*, to
raise or set up.

[2] McGary *v.* People, 45 N. Y. 161 (1871), Allen, J.

[3] Brown *v.* Hunn, 27 Conn. 332 (1858).

[4] Douglass *v.* Commonwealth, 2 Rawle, 264 (1830).

[6] Martine *v.* Nelson, 51 Ill. 423 (1869).

[6] Trask *v.* Searle, 121 Mass. 231 (1876); 2 Allen, 159.

[7] Kiefer *v.* German American Seminary, 46 Mich. 641
(1881).

[8] 1 Bl. Com. 469–71, 472, 474.

[9] [Webster's Dict.

[10] Burkholder *v.* Stahl, 58 Pa. 377 (1868).

[11] Bragg *v.* Danielson, 141 Mass. 195 (1886); 9 Mass.
532; 7 Wend. 55.

Communis error facit jus. A common error makes the law. Long-continued practice, though originally erroneous, establishes the rule of law.

A maxim or procedure, purely; briefly stated as the rule of *communis error*.

A received doctrine shall not be overturned or abandoned, even though its soundness in principle may be questioned. " It is more material that the law should be settled than how it is settled." [1]

" We are not inclined by a technical exposition of an act to unsettle rights honestly acquired and upon which many persons have rested for years." [2]

The executive branch of a government must necessarily construe the laws which it executes; and its construction, which has been followed for years, without interference by the law-making power, should not be departed from without the most cogent reasons. A long-continued practice under such circumstances ripens into an authoritative construction. The law, in its regard for the public good, goes so far, in some cases, as to hold that *communis error facit jus;* but courts should be slow to set up a misconception of the law as the law. [3]

Long acquiescence in repeated acts of legislation on particular matters is evidence that those matters have been generally considered by the people as properly within legislative control. Such acts are not to be set aside or treated as invalid, because upon a careful consideration of their character doubts may arise as to the competency of the legislature to pass them. [4]

See CONSENSUS, Tollit, etc.; EXPOSITIO, Contemporanea, etc.

2. Eng. (1) A mistake; an omission.

Clerical error. A failure to reduce the intent of parties to writing, not affecting the intent itself.

Attributable to carelessness or miswriting; and disregarded or corrected.

Also, a mistake of a clerk in preparing a record. See MISPRISION, 2.

(2) An unintentional deviation from the truth in a matter of fact, and from the law in a matter of opinion or decision.

Such irregularity, misconception, or wrong application of the law as directs that the proceeding should be reversed on appeal or writ of error.

---

[1] Forsythe, Hist. Lawyers, 395, quoting Lord Eldon.
[2] Kostenbader v. Spotts, 80 Pa. 437-38 (1876); 13 *id.* 561; 78 *id.* 308; Gelpcke v. Dubuque, 1 Wall. 175 (1863); Herndon v. Moore, 18 S. C. 354 (1882); 2 Whart. Ev. § 1242.
[3] Harrison v. Commonwealth, 83 Ky. 170 (1885); Robertson v. Downing, 127 U. S. 613 (1888), cases.
[4] Maynard v. Hill, 125 U. S. 204 (1888), Field, J., on the power of a legislature to grant a divorce by a special act; also, Cronise v. Cronise, 54 Pa. 261 (1867).

Applied where the practice of a colony differed from the requirements of the law of England as to a wife's acknowledging a deed,— 1 Dallas, *13, 17.

Erroneous. Deviating from the law.

What is "illegal" lacks authority of or support from law. "Erroneous rulings" always mean such as deviate from or are contrary to law. "Erroneous" alone never designates a corrupt or evil act. "Erroneous and illegal " means deviating from the law because of a mistaken construction. [1]

An "erroneous judgment" is rendered according to the course and practice of the courts, but contrary to law. An "irregular judgment" is contrary to the course and practice of the courts. [2]

(3) A writ of error: as in saying that error lies or does not lie, that a judgment may be reversed or was reversed "on error," and in speaking of the plaintiff and the defendant "in error."

Assignment of error; specification of error. The statement of the error which an inferior tribunal is alleged to have committed; also, the paper containing such statement.

Spoken of as "cross," when made upon the same matter as is alleged for error by the opposite party; as "general," when upon more matters than one; and as "specific," when upon some one matter in particular. General assignments of error are not tolerated.

Court of errors. A court for correcting errors made in administering the law in subordinate tribunals. See PAPER, 5.

Error coram nobis; error coram vobis. When a writ was had to re-examine a judgment, in a civil or criminal cause, in the court of king's bench, by that court itself, it was called " a writ of error *coram nobis*," that is, error before us — the sovereign; when to re-examine a judgment rendered in the common pleas, in a civil case only, by the king's bench, it was called " a writ of error *coram vobis*," that is, error before you — the chief justice and associates.

The writ *coram vobis* was also brought before the same court in which the error was committed to supply or rectify a mistake of fact not put in issue or passed upon by the court; such as the death of a party when the judgment was rendered, coverture of a female party, infancy and failure to appoint a guardian, error in the process, or mistake of the clerk. But if the error was in the judgment itself the writ did not lie.

The two expressions are now applied, respectively, to a writ to review proceedings, not carried to judgment, had in the same court (before us), and to a writ issued to bring up for revision a record of what was done in an inferior court.

---

[1] [Thompson v. Doty, 72 Ind. 338 (1880), Elliott, J.
[2] Wolfe v. Davis, 74 N. C. 599 (1876), Reade, J. See Koonce v. Butler, 84 *id.* 223 (1881).

What was formerly done by the writ *coram nobis* is now attained by motion and affidavit.[1]

Error in fact. Such matter of fact, not appearing on the record, as renders the judgment entered unsupportable in law; as, infancy or coverture in a party.

A fact that might have been taken advantage of in the court below is not assignable for error; nor is a fact that contradicts the record.[2]

Error in law. Any substantial defect in the proceedings not cured by the common law nor by statute, injurious to and not waived by the complainant, and made to appear on the record, is assignable for reversal; also, any incorrect decision on a right of either party, as presented by the pleadings, special verdict, bill of exceptions, or opinion filed.

Reviewable errors in law are: those apparent upon the face of the record,—available on general demurrer or in arrest of judgment; and, those brought up by a bill of exceptions,—objections to the admission or rejection of evidence and errors in the charge of the court.

Error of fact. When a fact is unknown, or is erroneously supposed to exist.

Error of law. When a person is acquainted with the existence or non-existence of a fact, but is ignorant of the legal consequence, he is under an error of law.[3] See IGNORANCE.

No error. The form of the judgment of the court of appeals of Connecticut, affirming the decision of the lower court.

Writ of error. A commission by which the judges of one court are authorized to examine a record upon which a judgment was given in another court, and, on such examination, to affirm or reverse the same according to law.[4]

An original writ, and lies only where a party is aggrieved by some error in the foundation, proceedings, judgment, or execution, of a suit in a court of record.[5]

The supervisory court is called "the court of error."

In the nature of a suit or action, when to restore one to the possession of a thing withheld from him. Submits the judgment to re-examination; operates only upon the record—which is removed into the supervisory tribunal; is the more usual mode of removing suits at common law, and the more technically proper where a single point of law, and not the whole case, is to be re-examined.[1]

Must be regular in form and duly served. To operate as a *supersedeas* and stay of execution, must be issued and returned within a given period from the date of the judgment.[2]

On review nothing is error that is not made to appear on the face of the record. Error will be inferred only when the inference is inevitable. Every error apparent is open to re-examination.[3]

A writ of error lies in all cases where a court of record has given a "final" judgment, or made an award in the nature of a judgment, or where a judgment has been arrested, or, on an appeal from a justice, has been dismissed; also, on an award of execution.[4]

Proceedings in a court of error assimilate themselves to proceedings in a court of original jurisdiction. The writ of error in a general way recites the cause of complaint, and it is left to the assignments of error to specify it as a declaration specifies the cause of action. The plea *in nullo est erratum* raises the issue. Like a declaration, therefore, each assignment must be complete in itself, that is, he self-sustaining. Whatever is part of it must be parcel of it. The burden rests upon the plaintiff to make out his assignments affirmatively.[5] See ERRATUM.

A writ of error lies from inferior criminal jurisdictions to the court of king's bench, and from the king's bench to the house of peers; and may be brought for "notorious mistake" in the judgment or other part of the record, or for an irregularity, omission, or want of form, in the process. . . To reverse a judgment in the case of a misdemeanor, allowed, not of course, but on sufficient probable cause shown to the attorney-general,—then grantable of common right and *ex debito justitiæ.* But a writ to reverse an attainder in a capital case is only allowed *ex gratia;* and not without express warrant under the king's sign-manual, or at least by consent of the attorney-general.[6]

See APPEAL, 2; CERTIORARI; EXCEPTIONS, 4, Bill of; PROSECUTE, With effect; REVIEW, 2, Bill of; SUPERSEDEAS.

ESCAPE.[7] 1, *n.* (1) Flight from custody, of a person under lawful arrest.

[1] Pickett *v.* Legerwood, 7 Pet. 147–48 (1833); *Exp.* Lange, 18 Wall. 195 (1873), cases; Bronson *v.* Schulten, 104 U. S. 410, 416–17 (1881); 1 Flip. 343; 3 Chitty, Bl. Com. 406; 4 Crim. Law Mag. 364, 371; 34 Pa. 95.

[2] Tidd, Pr. 1169; 2 Bac. Abr. 492.

[3] [Mowatt *v.* Wright, 1 Wend. 360 (1828), Savage, C. J.

[4] Cohens *v.* Virginia, 6 Wheat. 409 (1821), Marshall, Chief Justice.

[5] Suydam *v.* Williamson, 20 How. 437 (1857), Clifford, J.

[1] Cohens *v.* Virginia, *ante.*

[2] Slaughter-House Cases, 10 Wall. 290 (1869), cases; Kountz *v.* Omaha Hotel Co., 107 U. S. 381–85 (1882); Murdock *v.* City of Memphis, 20 Wall. 621 (1875).

[3] 6 Wheat. 409–11, *ante;* 20 How. 437; 16 Wall. 363, 386; 100 U. S. 690.

[4] Pontius *v.* Nesbit, 40 Pa. 310 (1861).

[5] Burkholder *v.* Stahl, 58 Pa. 376 (1868), Thompson, C. J.; Bragg *v.* Danielson, 141 Mass. 195 (1886).

[6] 4 Bl. Com. 391; 4 Burr. 2550. See also 3 Dall. 327; 7 Cranch, 111; 61 Ala. 484; 3 Col. 293; 6 Fla. 289; 13 Ga. 148; 20 *id.* 535; 1 Wash. T. 319.

[7] F. *escaper,* to slip out of one's cape: L. *ex cappa,*—Skeat. F. *escamper,* to flee: Ger. *champf,* combat,—Webster.

(2) Allowing any person lawfully in confinement to leave the place.[1]

Actual escape. Complete corporal freedom. **Constructive escape.** Any unauthorized relaxation of custody.

Negligent escape. Effected without the keeper's knowledge or consent. **Voluntary escape.** Expressly consented to by the keeper.[2]

Any liberty given for the briefest period, and not sanctioned by law, is an escape. But the court must have had jurisdiction, the process have been regular, and the place and time proper. At common law an escape is a misdemeanor in the prisoner; and, if the offense is a felony, a voluntary escape is a like felony, and a negligent escape is a misdemeanor, in the officer. An escape resulting from an act of God or of the public enemy will be excused.[3]

Formerly, when imprisonment was the only mode to enforce satisfaction of a judgment for money, to permit an escape was to lose the amount of the debt. Hence, on an escape, the sheriff was held for the whole debt.[4]

An officer of the United States who voluntarily suffers a prisoner in custody under the law of the United States to escape shall be fined not more than two thousand dollars or imprisoned not more than two years, or both.[5]

2, v. To be passed by unobserved; to be overlooked.

"To escape taxation" does not mean to be taxed insufficiently, but to have avoided notice, to be passed unobserved, to have evaded taxation.[6]

3, n. Means of retreat. See DEFENSE, 1; FIRE, Escape.

ESCHEAT.[7] In feudal law, the determination of the tenure or dissolution of the bond between lord and tenant from extinction of the blood of the latter by natural or civil means.[8]

Thus, if the tenant died without heirs of his blood, or if his blood was corrupted by commission of treason or felony, whereby the inheritable quality was blotted out, the land "fell back" to the lord of the fee — the tenure being determined by breach of the condition.[5] See ATTAINDER.

The word, originally French or Norman, signifying

chance or accident, now denotes obstruction of the course of descent, and determination of tenure, by some unforeseen contingency; in which case the land naturally results back, by a kind of reversion, to the original grantor.[1] See DESCENT.

2. In the United States, a reversion of property to the State in default of a person who can inherit it.

Depends upon positive statute, which makes the State the heir of the property. Nothing about it but the name is feudal.[2]

Escheator. An officer who takes charge of escheated estates for the government.

ESCROW.[3] An instrument delivered to a third person to hold till some condition is performed by the proposed grantee. A scrowl or writing not to take effect as a "deed" till the condition is performed.[4]

As defined by the common law, a written instrument delivered to a third person to take effect upon the happening of a contingency. Originally applied to a deed; then to written contracts generally.[5]

Nothing passes unless the condition is performed. There can be no delivery, as an escrow, to the grantee himself. When justice requires, it may take effect by relation back to the first delivery.[6] See DELIVERY, 4.

ESNECY. Eldership; the privilege of the eldest. The right in the oldest coparcener first to choose a purpart.

ESPLEES.[7] The products of the land: herbage, hay, grain; rents, services, etc.[8]

ESQUIRE.[9] 1. A title of dignity next below knight, and above gentleman.

2. A title acquired by virtue of office; as, justices of the peace, the higher officers of the courts, and others who bear any office of trust under the crown.

3. A title given to a member of the legal

---

[1] 2 Bish. Crim. L. §§ 917, 1026; 1 Russ. Cr. 416; Colby v. Sampson, 5 Mass. *312 (1809), Parsons, C. J.

[2] 3 Bl. Com. 415, 290, 165. See also 32 Ark. 126; 8 Ired. L. 151; 25 N. H. 258; 46 N. J. L. 358; 29 Pa. 446; 3 Head, 137.

[3] 4 Bl. Com. 129.

[4] Dow v. Humbert, 91 U. S. 300 (1875), cases.

[5] R. S. § 5409.

[6] Lehman v. Robinson, 59 Ala. 240 (1877).

[7] O. Eng. eschete: F. eschet, that which falls to one: eshoir, to happen. See CHEAT.

[8] 1 Bl. Com. 72.

[1] 2 Bl. Com. 244.

[2] Wallace v. Harmstad, 44 Pa. 501 (1863). See Hughes v. State, 41 Tex. 17 (1874); 4 Kent, 424; 1 Washb. R. P. 24, 27; 2 id. 443; Williams, R. P. 121.

[3] F. escrowe, scroll.

[4] [2 Bl. Com. 307.

[5] Alexander v. Wilkes, 11 Lea, 225 (1883), Cooper, J.

[6] See County of Calhoun v. American Emigrant Co., 93 U. S. 127 (1876), cases; Shoenberger v. Hackman, 37 Pa. 94 (1860); Baum's Appeal, 113 id. 58, 65 (1886), cases; Daggett v. Daggett, 143 Mass. 520 (1887), cases; 28 Am. Law Reg. 697-99 (1880), cases; 19 Cent. Law J. 127-28 (1884), cases — Solic. Jour.; 4 Cranch, 219; 14 How. 73; 4 Cal. 309, 620; 14 Conn. 270; 34 id. 92; 14 Ga. 145; 34 Ill. 29; 77 id. 480; 29 Minn. 249; 30 id. 315; 2 Johns. 253; 26 N. Y. 492; 14 Ohio St. 309; Smith, Contr. 7.

[7] Es-pleez'. L. esples; L. explere, to fill up.

[8] 8 Cranch, 249; 9 Barb. 293; 11 S. & R. *275.

[9] F. escuyer, escuier, a shield-bearer: ecu, escu: L. scutum, a shield.

profession, by virtue of length of enjoyment.[1]

4. In the United States, a title of courtesy. Abbreviated Esq., 'Squire or Squire.

ESSE. See In Esse.

ESSENCE. See Time.

ESSOIGN.[2] In old law, an excuse for non-appearance.

"Essoign-day" was for hearing such excuses,— the first day of each term.[3]

ESTABLISH.[4] To settle certainly, fix permanently, what was before uncertain, doubtful, or disputed; as, to establish a boundary line.[5]

To set or fix firmly, settle or found permanently, erect something.[6]

Authority to establish a thing contains authority to do acts which shall produce or bring into existence something; as, authority to establish a market.[6]

In a grant of power "to establish" a market, a dispensary, etc., means to permanently create or found.[7]

To establish a company for any business means to make complete and permanent provision for carrying on that business.[8]

A county seat is permanently established at a place when placed there with the intention that it shall remain.[9] See County.

The right to establish a market includes the right to shift it from place to place, as convenience demands; but gives no right to build one on the public highway.[10] Compare Permanent.

Power to establish post-offices, unless the exercise is restrained by Congress.[11]

In the Constitution the word is used in somewhat different senses: "to establish justice" seems to mean to settle firmly, fix unalterably, dispense or administer justice; "to establish a uniform rule of naturalization, and uniform laws on the subject of bankruptcy," is equivalent to to make or to form, and not to fix or settle unalterably or forever; "to establish post-offices and post-routes" means to create, found, and regulate; to "establish this Constitution" signifies to create, ratify, confirm it.[12] See further Religion.

---

[1] See 1 Bl. Com. 406.

[2] F. *essoine*, excuse.

[3] See 3 Bl. Com. 277.

[4] F. *establir*; L. *stabilis*, steady, firm: *stare*, to stand.

[5] Smith v. Forrest, 49 N. H. 237 (1870), Nesmith, J.

[6] [Ketchum v. City of Buffalo, 21 Barb. 298, 296 (1854); 27 *id*. 260; 28 *id*. 65.

[7] Ketchum v. City of Buffalo, 14 N. Y. 361 (1856).

[8] Davidson v. Lanier, 4 Wall. 455 (1866).

[9] Newton v. Mahoning County, 100 U. S. 562 (1879); Mead v. Ballard, 7 Wall. 290 (1868); Wright v. Nagle, 101 U. S. 796 (1879); 13 Ill. 463.

[10] Wartman v. Philadelphia, 33 Pa. 210 (1859).

[11] Ware v. United States, 4 Wall. 632 (1866).

[12] 1 Story, Const. § 454.

ESTATE.[1] 1. Standing: condition, category, state, *status*.

2. Position; rank in life; degree: as, an addition of estate.[2] See Addition, 2; Necessaries.

Estates of the realm. The three branches of the English legislature: the lords spiritual, the lords temporal, and the commons.[3]

3. (1) (Subjective idea.). Estate in lands, tenements, and hereditaments: such interest as the tenant has therein.[4]

In Latin *status*, the condition or circumstances in which the owner stands with regard to his property.[4]

Does not import a fee or even a freehold, but any legal interest in land.[5]

The quantity of interest which a person has, from absolute ownership down to naked possession.[6]

The condition, in respect to property, of an individual: as, in speaking of the estate of an insolvent or of a deceased person. Here, indebtedness, as well as ownership, is part of the idea. Debts and assets together constitute the estate; if an estate consisted of assets only, the expression insolvent estate would be a misnomer.[7]

(2) (Objective idea.) The thing itself of which one is owner; any species of property, real or personal. Equivalent to the more technical expression, "things real and things personal." More specifically, realty, land, "landed estate."[8]

Sometimes excludes realty; sometimes is a word of mere local description, as, "my estate at" such a place. But when it can be construed to intend all one's realty it carries a fee, as, in devises.[9]

Unless limited by some special epithet or some association, construed to mean all one's property; but "real" or "personal" puts the matter beyond cavil.[10]

---

[1] F. *estat*; L. *status; stare*, to stand.

[2] State v. Bishop, 15 Me. 124 (1838).

[3] See 1 Bl. Com. 153, 157.

[4] 2 Bl. Com. 103; 66 Ga. 711; 2 Wall. 500.

[5] Inhabitants of Sunbury v. Inhabitants of Stow, 13 Mass. *464 (1816).

[6] Jackson v. Parker, 9 Cow. 81 (1828), Savage, C. J.; Moody v. Farr, 33 Miss. 195 (1857).

[7] See Abbott's Law Dict., *Estate*, 4; Davis v. Elkins, 9 La. 142 (1835).

[8] See Sellers v. Sellers, 35 Ala. 241 (1859).

[9] See Bates v. Sparrell, 10 Mass. 334 (1813); Godfrey v. Humphrey, 18 Pick. 539 (1837); Leland v. Adams, 9 Gray, 175 (1857), cases; Canedy v. Jones, 19 S. C. 301 (1882).

[10] Hooper v. Hooper, 9 Cush. 128 (1851); Archer v. Deneale, 1 Pet. 589 (1828); Cook v. Lanning, 40 N. J. E. 372 (1885). See also 3 Cranch, 97; 2 MacA. 70; 2 Cranch, C. C. 640; 16 Conn. 1; 46 Ill. 32; 55 Me. 287; 32 Miss. 107; 14 N. J. L. 53, 68; 14 N. J. E. 51; 40 *id*. 36–37, 372; 6 Johns. 185; 11 *id*. 365; 8 R. I. 384; 26 Vt. 260.

An estate may be viewed: I. As to the quantity of interest,—measured by the duration and extent; and is 1, freehold: which is (a) for the life of the tenant, or (b) of inheritance — absolute or fee-simple, and limited or fee-tail; 2, not of freehold: which is (a) for a term of years, (b) at will, (c) at sufferance; 3, upon condition, (a) expressed, or implied, (b) in pledge — mortgage, (c) by statute merchant or staple, (d) by *elegit*.

II. As to the time the interest is to be enjoyed. This is: 1, in immediate possession; and 2, in the future, or in expectancy — (a) a remainder, preceded by a particular estate, (b) a reversion, preceded by a remainder, and executed or vested, or executory and contingent, and (c) an executory devise.

III. As to the number and connections of the tenants. An estate is held 1, in severalty, 2, in joint-tenancy, 3, in coparcenary, 4, in common.[1]

IV. As to the tribunal in which that interest or right will be recognized and enforced. When that is a court of law, the estate is *legal;* when a court of equity, *equitable.* Otherwise the same rules apply to these estates: they are alike descendible, devisable, and alienable.[2]

See CONDITION; COPARCENARY; CURTESY; DESCENT; DOWER; ENTIRETY; EXECUTION, 3; FAST, 1; FEE, 1; FREEHOLD; LIFE; MERGER, 1; PERPETUITY, 2; PRIVY, 2; PROPERTY; REMAINDER; REVERSION; SEPARATE, 2; SEVERALTY; STAPLE; SUFFERANCE; TAIL; TENANT; TRUST, 1; VEST; USE, 2; YEARS, Estate for.

ESTIMATE. Implies a computation or calculation.

The particular idea intended to be expressed by the word must be determined by the subject-matter under consideration, together with the context of any pertinent instrument. Where a redeeming mortgagee stated in his affidavit that there was unpaid on the mortgage, "as near as he could estimate," a specified sum, it was held that this was equivalent to saying that he had computed the sum.[3]

Where a tract of land, "estimated to contain 1,000 acres," was sold by written agreement, for a price in gross, it was held that acquiescence for many years would raise a presumption that the purchaser understood that the sale was in gross; also, that where land is exchanged for other land the liability of the vendor for a deficiency should not be enforced with the same strictness as in the case of a sale for money. The evidence did not disclose any fraudulent assurance calculated to deceive the purchaser.[4]

ESTOPPEL.[5] 1. A stop; obstruction, bar; hindrance, preclusion.

2. That which concludes, and "shuts a man's mouth from speaking the truth."[6]

A man shall always be estopped by his own deed, and not permitted to aver or prove anything in contradiction to what he has once solemnly and deliberately avowed.[1]

A special plea in bar — when a man has done some act or executed some deed which estops or precludes him from averring anything to the contrary.[2]

Estoppel by deed. By some matter contained in a valid sealed instrument.

Estoppel by record. By adjudication of a competent court of record.

Viewed as an admission or determination under circumstances of such solemnity that the law will not allow the fact so admitted or established to be afterward drawn in question between the same parties or their privies. To litigate the fact again would be to impeach the correctness of the former decision. The conclusion being indisputable, so are the premises.[3]

Collateral estoppel. The collateral determination of a question by a court having general jurisdiction over the matter.[4] See ADJUDICATION; RECORD.

Equitable estoppel, or estoppel in pais. An estoppel by virtue of some act or action not under seal nor of record in a court.

"Equitable" is the modern epithet,— derived from the courts of equity.

The doctrine that "what I induce my neighbor to regard as true is the truth as between us, if he has been mislead by my asseveration."[5]

Proceeds upon the ground that he who has been silent as to his alleged right when he ought in good faith to have spoken, shall not be heard to speak when he ought to be silent.[6]

Presupposes error upon one side and fault or fraud upon the other, and some defect of which it would be inequitable for the party against whom the doctrine is asserted to take advantage.[7]

The vital principle is, that he who by his language or conduct leads another to do what he would not

---

[1] 2 Bl. Com. Ch. VII–XII; 1 Ld. Cas. R. P. ix; 2 *id.* ix.

[2] Avery *v.* Durfrees, 9 Ohio, 147 (1839); 5 Wall. 281; 16 *id.* 229; 23 *id.* 125; 95 U. S. 312.

[3] Van Buskirk *v.* Clark, 37 Hun, 203 (1885).

[4] Lawson *v.* Floyd, 124 U. S. 108 (1888), Miller, J.

[5] F. *estoper,* to impede, stop.

[6] Armfield *v.* Moore, 1 Busb. L. 161 (N. C., 1852): Lord Coke; Stebbins *v.* Bruce, 80 Va. 397 (1885).

---

[1] [2 Bl. Com. 295.

[2] 3 Bl. Com. 308.

[3] Burden *v.* Shannon, 99 Mass. 203 (1868), cases; Sawyer *v.* Woodbury, 7 Gray, 502 (1856).

[4] Small *v.* Haskins, 26 Vt. 223 (1854), Redfield, C. J.

[5] Kirk *v.* Hamilton, 102 U. S. 76 (1880), Harlan, J.

[6] Morgan *v.* Chicago & Alton R. Co., 96 U. S. 720 (1877), Swayne, J.; Bank of United States *v.* Lee, 13 Pet. 119 (1839).

[7] Morgan *v.* Chicago, &c. R. Co., *supra;* Merchants' Nat. Bank *v.* State Nat. Bank, 10 Wall. 645 (1870), cases; Leather Manuf. Bank *v.* Morgan, 117 U. S. 108-9 (1886), cases; Continental Nat. Bank *v.* Bank of Commonwealth, 50 N. Y. 583 (1872).

otherwise have done, shall not subject such person to loss or injury by disappointing the expectations, upon which he acted. . . A change of position would involve fraud and falsehood. This remedy is available only for protection, and cannot be used as a weapon of assault. It accomplishes that which ought to be done between man and man, and is not permitted to go beyond this limit.[1]

The primary ground of the doctrine is, that it would be a fraud to assert what one's previous conduct had denied, when on the faith of that denial others have acted.[2]

In application there must be some intended deception in conduct or declarations, or such gross negligence as amounts to constructive fraud. But conduct founded on ignorance of one's rights seldom works such result.[3]

One should be estopped from asserting a right of property, upon which he has, by his conduct, misled another, who supposed himself to be the owner, to make expenditures. It is often applied where one owning an estate stands by and sees another erect improvements on it in the belief that he has the title or an interest in it, and does not interfere to prevent the work or inform the party of his own title. There is in such conduct a manifest intention to deceive, or such gross negligence as to amount to constructive fraud. The owner, therefore, in such a case, will not be permitted afterward to assert his title and recover the property, at least without making compensation for the improvements. But this salutary principle cannot be invoked by one who, at the time the improvements were made, was acquainted with the true character of his own title, or with the fact that he had none.[4]

It never takes place where one party did not intend to mislead, and the other party is not actually misled.[5]

An estoppel by conduct involves: a misrepresentation or a concealment of a material fact, made with knowledge of the facts, to one who is ignorant of the truth, made with intention that he should act upon it, and leading him to act upon it.[6]

The representation must be credited as true, and the thing of value be parted with, the credit be given, or the liability be incurred, in consequence thereof.[7]

Where a party gives a reason for his conduct and decision touching a thing involved in controversy, he is estopped, after litigation has begun, from changing the ground and putting his conduct upon another and different consideration.[1]

The only case in which a representation as to the future can be held to operate as an estoppel is when it relates to an intended abandonment of an existing right, and is made to influence others, and by which they have been induced to act. An estoppel cannot arise from a promise as to future action with respect to a right to be acquired upon an agreement not yet made.[2]

Binds parties and privies,[3] but not, one not *sui juris*, as, an infant,[4] nor a married woman.[5]

The principle is a means of repose; it promotes fair dealing. It cannot be made an instrument of wrong or oppression, and it often secures justice where nothing else could.[6] It is meant to prevent fraud; is invoked to hold one to facts as he alleged them, although false, and not to prove them different from the allegation.[7]

The meaning is not that equitable estoppels are cognizable only in courts of equity, for they are commonly enforced in actions at law. But it does not follow, because equitable estoppels may originate legal as distinguished from equitable rights, that it may not be necessary in particular cases to resort to a court of equity to make them available. All that can properly be said is, that to justify a resort to a court of equity, it is necessary to show some ground of equity other than the estoppel itself, whereby the party entitled to the benefit of it is prevented from making it available in a court of law. In other words, the case shown must be one where the forms of law are used to defeat that which, in equity, constitutes the right.[8]

Is not applicable to the government in a criminal prosecution.[9]

See DISPARAGE, 2; FRAUD; GRANT, 2; LACHES; LEASE; RATIFICATION, 1; SALE, Conditional; STAND BY.

---

[1] Dickerson v. Colgrove, 100 U. S. 580 (1879), Swayne, J.; Baker v. Humphrey, 101 *id.* 499 (1879), cases.

[2] Hill v. Epley, 31 Pa. 334 (1858), Strong, J.; Gregg v. Von Phul, 1 Wall. 281 (1863), cases; Dair v. United States, 16 *id.* 4 (1872).

[3] Henshaw v. Bissell, 18 Wall. 271 (1873), cases, Field, J.; Fowler v. Parsons, 143 Mass. 406 (1887).

[4] Steel v. Smelting Co., 106 U. S. 456 (1882), Field, J. See Wendell v. Van Rensselaer, 1 Johns. Ch. *354 (1815), Kent, Ch.

[5] Brown v. Bowen, 30 N. Y. 541 (1864); Jewett v. Miller, 10 *id.* 406 (1852); Catlin v. Grote, 4 E. D. Sm. 304 (1855).

[6] Stevens v. Dennett, 51 N. H. 333 (1872), Foster, J.; Denver Fire Ins. Co. v. McClelland, 9 Col. 24 (1885); Griffith v. Wright, 6 *id.* 249 (1882); 41 N. H. 385; 43 *id.* 285; 11 *id.* 81; 30 N. Y. 541.

[7] Jones v. McPhillips, 82 Ala. 116 (1886), cases, Stone, Chief Justice.

[1] Ohio & Mississippi R. Co. v. McCarthy, 96 U. S. 267 (1877), cases, Swayne, J.

[2] Union Mut. Life Ins. Co. v. Mowry, 96 U. S. 547-48 (1877), cases, Field, J.

[3] Deery v. Cray, 5 Wall. 805 (1866); Ketchum v. Duncan, 96 U. S. 666 (1877).

[4] Sims v. Everhardt, 102 U. S. 313 (1880).

[5] Jackson v. Vanderheyden, 17 Johns. 167 (1819); Keen v. Coleman, 39 Pa. 299 (1861); Bigelow, Estop. 276; 27 Am. Law Reg. 50-52 (1888), cases.

[6] Daniels v. Tearney, 102 U. S. 420 (1880).

[7] Pendleton v. Richey, 32 Pa. 63 (1858); Keating v. Orne, 77 *id.* 93 (1874).

[8] Drexel v. Berney, 122 U. S. 253 (1887), Matthews, J. See also, generally, 17 Blatch. 14; 18 *id.* 33; 6 Biss. 373; 11 *id.* 209; 2 Flip. 699; 13 F. R. 208; 16 *id.* 479; 71 Ala. 247; 3 Col. 535; 50 Conn. 86; 2 Dak. 185; 1 Idaho, 469; 105 Ill. 322; 13 Bradw. 99; 72 Ind. 480; 76 *id.* 390; 30 Kan. 640; 29 Minn. 473; 74 Mo. 67; 42 N. Y. 447; 75 *id.* 561; 100 Pa. 262, 558; 13 R. I. 265; 76 Va. 314; 10 Wis. 453; 1 Sm. L. C. 651, note; 2 Pomeroy, Eq. §§ 801-21; Herman, Estoppel ; 2 Whart. Ev., Index.

[9] Justice v. Commonwealth, 81 Va. 217 (1885), cases.

ESTOVERS.[1] Maintenance; support; necessaries. Compare BOTE.

Common of estovers; estovers. The liability of taking necessary wood from another's land for fuel, fences or other agricultural purpose.[2] See COMMON, 2, Right of.

ESTRAY.[3] An animal that has escaped from its owner, and wanders or strays about; at common law, a wandering animal whose owner is unknown.[4]

A wandering beast whose owner is unknown to the person who takes it up.[5]

Estrays are such valuable animals as are found wandering in any manor or lordship, and no man knoweth the owner of them. . Any beasts may be estrays that are by nature tame or reclaimable, and in which there is a valuable property, as, sheep, oxen, swine, and horses, which we in general call "cattle." . For animals upon which the law sets no value, as a dog or a cat, and animals *feræ naturæ*, as, a bear or a wolf, cannot be considered estrays. . The finder is bound, so long as he keeps the animal, to feed and care for it; but he may not use it at labor.[6]

By early English law, estrays were the property of the king, or of his grantee — the lord of the manor where found. Modern statutes provide that they shall be impounded, for return to the owner, on payment of expenses.[7] See USE, 2.

ESTREAT.[8] An extract or copy of an original writing or record, — especially of a fine or amercement, certified to and to be levied by an officer.

A recognizance is "estreated" when forfeited by failure of the accused to comply with the condition, as by failure to appear: it is then "extracted," that is, taken from among the other records and sent to the exchequer, the party and his sureties having become, by breach of the condition, the king's absolute debtors.[9]

ESTREPEMENT.[10] Permanent injury, destruction; waste.

Writ of estrepement. This lay at common law, *after* judgment in a "real" action, and before possession was delivered by the sheriff, to stop any waste which the vanquished party might be tempted to commit.

Now, by an equitable construction of the statute of Gloucester, 6 Edw. I (1280), c. 13, and in advancement of the remedy, a writ of estrepement, to prevent waste, may be had in every stage, as well of such actions wherein damages are recovered, as of those wherein only possession is had; for, peradventure, the tenant may not be able to satisfy the demandant his full damages. It is, then, a writ of preventive justice.[1]

The same object being attainable by injunction, the writ became obsolete in England, and was impliedly abolished by Stat. 3 and 4 Wm. IV (1834), c. 27, § 36.

In Pennsylvania, after an action in ejectment has been begun, the plaintiff may have the writ to prevent destruction of the premises: he having first given a bond, with sureties, conditioned to indemnify the defendant against damage. The court hears the parties in a summary manner, and makes such order as seems just; and it may order an inspection of the premises.[2]

ET. L. And.

The original of &, which in old books is used for *et*.[3]

Et alius. And another. *Et alii.* And others (as plaintiffs). *Et alios.* And others (as defendants). Abbreviated *et al.*, and, sometimes, for the plural, *et als.*,[4] which, strictly, should stand for *et alios*.

Et al., in every-day use in writs, pleadings, styles of cases, and entries in minutes and dockets, means "and another," or "and others," as the case may be.[5]

Et cætera. And other things; and others; and the like; and so forth; and in other relations or capacities. Also, sometimes, and other persons. Abbreviated *etc.*, *&c.*

Used in pleadings to avoid repetitions, relates to things unnecessary to be stated.[6]

A recognizance "for defendant's appearance, &c.," at a time and place, was held to mean for appearance and non-departure.[7]

Added to the reservation of a way for a particular use, as "for the purpose of carting, &c.," is, from vagueness, without meaning or effect.[8]

In a warrant for land, "&c.," in the expression "Ingersoll, &c.," without explanation, was held to have no meaning, and disregarded.[9]

---

[1] F. *estoffer*, to furnish, maintain.

[2] See 1 Bl. Com. 441; 2 *id*. 35; Van Rensselaer *v*. Radcliff, 10 Wend. 639 (1833); Livingston *v*. Ketcham, 1 Barb. 592 (1849).

[3] F. *estraier*, to wander: rove about the streets or ways: *estree:* L. *strata*, a street, way, — Skeat. L. L. *extravagare:* L. *extra*, on the outside, without; *vagare*, *vagari*, to wander, rove.

[4] Shepherd *v*. Hawley, 4 Oreg. 208 (1871), Prim, C. J.: Burrill's Law Dict.

[5] Roberts *v*. Barnes, 27 Wis. 425 (1871), Dixon, C. J.

[5] 1 Bl. Com. 297.

[7] See 1 Bl. Com. 297-98; 2 *id*. 14; 2 Kent, 359; 18 Pick. 426; 132 Mass. 29; 27 Conn. 473; 29 Iowa, 437; 60 Md. 88; 39 Mich. 451; 69 Mo. 205; 82 N. C. 175; 14 Tex. 430.

[8] F. *estrait:* L. *ex-trahere*, to draw out, extract.

[9] 4 Bl. Com. 253.

[10] Es-trēpé. F. *estreper* to destroy, strip: L. *ex-tir-pare*, to root out.

(27)

---

[1] 3 Bl. Com. 225-26

[2] 2 Brightly, Tr. & H. §§ 1857-58, cases.

[3] See 2 Ves. Sr. *153.

[4] 76 Va. 36; 77 *id*. xi; 6 Gratt.

[5] Renkert *v*. Elliott, 11 Lea, 262 (1883); Lyman *v*. Milton, 44 Cal. 633 (1872); 3 La. An. 313; 10 *id*. 164; 12 *id*. 282; 14 Pa. 161.

[6] Dano *v*. Missouri, &c. R. Co., 27 Ark. 668 (1872), McClure, C. J.

[7] Commonwealth *v*. Ross, 6 S. & R. *428 (1821).

[8] Meyers *v*. Dunn, 49 Conn. 76 (1881).

[9] Smith *v*. Walker, 93 Pa. 140 (1881).

May import other purposes of a like character to those already named.[1]

Et infra. See *Et supra.*

Et non. And not. See TRAVERSE, Absque hoc.

Et sequitur. And what follows. Plural, *et sequuntur.* Abbreviated *et seq.*

Refers to pages or paragraphs following a particular page or paragraph cited.

Et supra. And (that) above: the authority or quotation foregoing. Abbreviated *et sup.* Opposed, *et infra:* and (that or those) below, or following.

Et uxor, or uxores. And wife, or wives. Abbreviated *et ux.*

Denotes that a wife or wives are parties to a deed.

ETYMOLOGY. See DICTIONARY.

Legislative language is to be received, not necessarily according to its etymological meaning, but according to its probable acceptance, and especially in the sense in which the legislature is accustomed to use the same words. Illustrated in the expression to "connect" railroad tracks of different gauges.[2]

The courts construe words according to the common parlance of the country. Hence, a corporation engaged in removing petroleum from place to place is a "transportation" company.[3] See STATUTE.

EUNDO. See ARREST, 2.

EVANGELICAL. See CHARITY, 2; INDIGENT.

EVASION. A subtle endeavoring to set aside the truth or to escape the punishment of the law.[4]

Evasive. Tending to evade; avoiding: as, an evasive — affidavit, answer, plea, argument.

Parties are sometimes said to evade, or to seek to evade, the jurisdiction of a particular court, the operation of an obnoxious law, the payment of a tax, service of process.

EVENT. 1. That which comes to pass; result; end; final determination.

"The relator is to pay or receive costs, according to the event of the suit." [5]

2. Occurrence: as, an uncertain event. See AFTER; CONDITION; REMAINDER; WAGER, 2; WHEN.

3. Accident; casualty: as, a fortuitous event. See ACCIDENT, Inevitable.

EVERY. Originally, "everich" — ever each: each one of all.[1]

Includes all the separate individuals which constitute the whole, regarded one by one; as, in the expression, "every person not having a license shall be liable to a fine." [2]

In a statute "every railroad" may mean all railroads.[3] See ALL.

Compare A, 4; ANY; EACH.

EVICTION.[4] It is difficult to define this word with technical accuracy. Latterly, it has denoted what formerly it was not intended to express. In the language of pleading a party evicted was said to be expelled, amoved, put out. The word, which is from *evincere,* to dispossess by a judicial course, formerly denoted expulsion by the assertion of a paramount title, and by process of law. It is now popularly applied to every class of expulsion or amotion.[5]

A wrongful act by a landlord, which results in the expulsion or amotion of his tenant from the land.[6]

An act of a permanent character done by the landlord to deprive, and which has the effect of depriving, the tenant of the use of the demised thing or a part of it.[7]

To constitute an eviction which will operate as a suspension of the rent, it is not necessary that there should be an actual physical expulsion of the tenant from any part of the premises.[8]

Any act of a permanent character, done by the landlord, or by his procurement, with the intention and effect of depriving the tenant of the enjoyment of the premises demised, or a part thereof, to which he yields and abandons possession.[8]

A definition has sometimes been given by which, to constitute an eviction, there must be an amotion of the tenant from the demised premises by, or in consequence of, some act of the landlord in derogation of the rights of the tenant, and with intent to determine the tenancy, or to deprive the tenant of the enjoyment

---

[1] Schouler, Petitioner, 134 Mass. 427 (1883); Dickerson *v.* Stoll, 24 N. J. L. 553 (1854); Gray *v.* Central R. Co. of New Jersey, 11 Hun, 75 (1877). See 105´ Mass. 21; 9 Kan. 153; 1 Cow. 114; 4 Daly, 68; 4 Metc., Ky., 211; 10 Mod. R. 152; 6 E. L. & E. 238.

[2] Philadelphia, &c. R. Co. *v.* Catawissa R. Co., 53 Pa. 59 (1866).

[3] Columbia Conduit Co. *v.* Commonwealth, 90 Pa. 309 (1879); L. R., 10 Ch. Ap. 156.

[4] Jacob's Law Dict.; 1 Hawk. Pl. Cr. 81.

[5] 3 Bl. Com. 264.

[1] Brown *v.* Jarvis, 2 De Gex, F. & J. *172 (1860), Campbell, Ld. Ch.

[2] State *v.* Penny, 19 S. C. 221 (1882), Simpson, C. J.

[3] Commonwealth *v.* Richmond, &c. R. Co., 81 Va. 367 (1886).

[4] L. *evictus: evincere,* to overcome, vanquish.

[5] Upton *v.* Townend, 84 E. C. L. *64, 30 (1855), Jervis, Chief Justice.

[5] [*Ibid.* *70, Crowder, J.

[7] *Ibid.* *72, Willes, J.

[8] Royce *v.* Guggenheim. 106 Mass. 202 (1870), Gray, J.; McAlester *v.* Landers, 70 Cal. 82 (1886), cases.

of the premises, or some part thereof. The amotion may be by physical expulsion by the landlord, or by abandonment by the tenant upon some act of the landlord which amounts to an eviction at the election of the tenant. The intent with which the act is done may be an actual intent accompanying and characterizing the act, or it may be inferred from the act itself. . . . Generally the question as to what acts of the landlord, in consequence of which the tenant abandons the premises, amount to an eviction, is a question of law, and includes the question whether the acts constitute proof of the intent.[1]

Sometimes spoken of as "actual" or "constructive," and as "partial" or "total."

The idea that the ouster must be by process of law has long since been given up. The rule now is that covenants for quiet enjoyment or of warranty are broken whenever there has been an involuntary loss of possession by reason of the hostile assertion of an irresistible title. Moreover, the eviction may be "constructive"—caused by the inability of the purchaser to obtain possession by reason of the paramount title.[2]

Eviction from all or part or the premises suspends the entire rent for the time being. The tenancy is not thereby ended, but the rent and all remedy for its collection is suspended. To have the effect of suspending the rent the eviction must be effected before the rent becomes due, for rent already overdue is not forfeited. The rule is the same although the rent is payable in advance and the eviction occurs before the expiration of the period in which the rent claimed accrues.[3]

A lawful act upon an adjoining estate, done to improve that estate, is not an eviction.[4]

EVIDENCE.[5] That which demonstrates, makes clear, or ascertains the truth of the fact or point in issue.[6]

Originally, the state of being evident, that is, plain, apparent or notorious; but, by inflection, is applied to that which tends to render evident or to generate proof. Evidence is, then, any matter of fact the effect, tendency, or design of which is to produce in the mind a persuasion, affirmative or disaffirmative, of the existence of some other matter of fact.[7]

Includes all the means by which any alleged matter of fact, the truth of which is submitted to investigation, is established or disproved.[1]

In the technical sense, almost synonymous with instrument of proof. In the popular sense, conclusive testimony; that which produces full conviction.[2]

Evidence includes "testimony," which is a mode of proof; yet the two terms are often interchanged.[3]

"Proof" is applied, by accurate logicians, to the effect of evidence, not to the medium by which truth is established.[4]

"Evidence" includes the reproduction, before the determining tribunal, of the admissions of parties, and of facts relevant to the issue. "Proof," in addition, includes presumptions either of law or of fact, and citations of law. In this sense proof comprehends all the grounds on which rests assent to the truth of a specific proposition. Evidence, in this view, is adduced only by the parties, through witnesses, documents, or inspection; proof may be adduced by counsel in argument, or by the judge in summing up a case. Evidence is but a part of the proof: it is part of the material on which proof acts.[5] See PROOF; TESTIMONY.

What is required in the trial of an issue is judicial, as distinguished from moral, truth. . . . No evidence which is not admitted on the trial is to be permitted by the determining tribunal to influence its conclusions. . Absolute truth can be reached by us, from the limitation of our faculties, not objectively, as it really exists, but subjectively, as it may be made to appear to us. . . . That formal proof may express real proof is the object of jurisprudence.[6]

Evidence, to be believed, must not only proceed from the mouth of a credible witness, but it must be credible in itself—such as the common experience and observation of mankind can approve as probable under the circumstances.[7]

Evidential; evidentiary. Furnishing, or relating to evidence: as, evidentiary facts.

Evidence, v. To render clear or evident; to establish by written testimony. Whence *evidenced.*

Evidences. Bills of exchange, promissory notes, government, municipal, and corporation bonds, and other instruments for the payment of money, are spoken of as "evidences of debt" or indebtedness.[8]

Evidence is considered with reference to its nature and principles, its object, and the rules which govern

---

[1] Skally v. Shute, 132 Mass. 370–77 (1882), cases, W. Allen, J.; 113 *id.* 481; 2 Greenl. Ev. § 243.

[2] Fritz v. Pusey, 31 Minn. 870 (1884), cases, Mitchell, J.

[3] Hunter v. Reiley, 43 N. J. L. 482 (1881), cases, Scudder, J. See also 4 N. Y. 270; 3 Kent, 464.

[4] Royce v. Guggenheim, *ante.* See also 55 Ala. 71; 5 Conn. 497; 69 Ill. 212; 70 *id.* 541; 5 Ind. 393; 18 *id.* 428; 32 Iowa, 76; 15 La. An. 514; 25 Minn. 528; 31 *id.* 370; 48 Pa. 410; 91 *id.* 322; 22 Gratt. 130.

[5] L. *evidens,* visible: *evidere,* to see clearly.

[6] [3 Bl. Com. 367.

[7] 1 Best, Evidence, § 11.

[1] 1 Greenleaf, Evidence, § 1; 15 Ct. Cl. 606; 56 Ala. 93.

[2] McWilliams v. Rodgers, 56 Ala. 93 (1876), Stone, J.

[3] Coke, Litt. 283; 13 Ind. 339; 17 *id.* 272; 66 *id.* 123.

[4] 1 Greenl. Ev. § 1.

[5] 1 Wharton, Law of Evidence, § 3.

[6] 1 Whart. Ev. §§ 4–5.

[7] Daggers v. Van Dyck, 37 N. J. E. 132 (1883), Van Fleet, V. C.

[8] See R. S. § 5136.

in the production of testimony; also, with reference to the means of proof, or the instruments by which facts are established.[1] See NOTICE, Judicial.

Moral evidence. Matters of fact are proved by moral evidence alone; by which is meant, not only that kind of evidence which is employed on subjects connected with moral conduct, but all evidence not obtained from either intuition or demonstration. **Demonstrative or mathematical evidence.** Applies to mathematical truth, and excludes all possibility of error.[2] See further CERTAINTY, Moral; DEMONSTRATION; DOUBT, Reasonable.

Direct or positive evidence. Proof applied immediately to the fact to be proved, without any intervening process. **Circumstantial evidence.** Proof applied immediately to collateral facts, supposed to have a connection, near or remote, with the fact in controversy.[2]

Direct or positive evidence is evidence to the precise point in issue; as, in a case of homicide, that the accused caused the death. Circumstantial evidence is proof of a series of other facts than the fact in issue, which by experience have been found so associated with that fact, that, in the relation of cause and effect, they lead to a satisfactory and certain conclusion: as, when footprints are discovered after a recent snow, it is certain some animated being passed over the snow since it fell; and, from the form and number of the footprints, it can be determined with equal certainty whether they are those of a man, a bird, or a quadruped. Such evidence, therefore, is founded on experience and observed facts and coincidences, establishing a connection between the known and proved facts and the facts sought to be proved.[3]

Circumstantial evidence consists in reasoning from facts which are known or proved, to establish such as are conjectured to exist.[4]

The advantage of circumstantial evidence is, that, as it commonly comes from different sources, a chain of circumstances is less likely to be falsely prepared and falsehood is more likely to be detected. The disadvantage is, that the jury have not only to weigh the evidence of facts, but to draw just conclusions from them; in doing which they may be led to make hasty or false deductions: a source of error not existing in the consideration of positive evidence. Hence, each fact necessary to the inference must be distinctly and independently proved by competent evidence; and the inference must be fair and natural, not forced or artificial.[1]

Crimes are secret. Direct testimony is often wanting. The laws of nature and the relation of things to each other are so linked and combined together as to furnish a medium of proof as strong as direct testimony. . A body of facts may be proved, of so conclusive a character as to warrant a firm belief of fact, as strong as that on which discreet men are accustomed to act in relation to their most important concerns.[1]

In the abstract, circumstantial evidence is nearly, if not quite, as strong as positive evidence; in the concrete, it may be much stronger.[2]

Circumstantial evidence is often more convincing than direct testimony. A number of concurrent facts, like the rays of the sun, all converging to the center, may throw not only a clear light but produce a burning conviction. A cord of sufficient strength to suspend a man may be formed of threads.[3]

Prima facie evidence. Such evidence as in judgment of the law is sufficient to establish the fact, and, if not rebutted, remains sufficient for that purpose.[4]

Evidence which, standing alone and unexplained, would maintain the proposition and warrant the conclusion to support which it is introduced.[5]

That which suffices for the proof of a particular fact until contradicted and overcome by other evidence.[6]

Primary or best evidence. The highest evidence of which a case in its nature is susceptible. That kind of proof, which, under any possible circumstances, affords the greatest certainty of the fact in question. **Secondary evidence.** Such evidence as, in the nature of the case, supposes that better evidence exists or has existed.[7]

A written instrument is itself always regarded as the primary or best possible evidence of its existence and contents. All evidence falling short of this in its degree is secondary; as, a copy of the instrument, or a witness's recollection of the contents.[7]

That the best evidence shall be produced means that no evidence shall be received which is merely "substitutionary" in its nature, as long as the "original" can be had. The rule excludes only that evidence which itself indicates the existence of more original sources of information. But where there is

---

[1] 1 Greenl. Ev. § 3.

[2] [1 Greenl. Ev. § 13. See Chaffee v. United States, 18 Wall. 541 (1873); 58 Wis. 58.

[3] Commonwealth v. Webster, 5 Cush. 310-12 (1850), Shaw, C. J. See also People v. Cronin, 34 Cal. 202-3 (1867); People v. Morrow, 60 id. 144 (1882).

[4] People v. Kennedy, 32 N. Y. 146, 145 (1865), Denio, C. J.; 62 Wis. 63; 1 Bish. Cr. Proc. § 1069.

[1] Webster's Case, 5 Cush. 311, *ante;* Commonwealth v. Howe, 132 Mass. 259 (1882).

[2] Commonwealth v. Harman, 4 Pa. 271-73 (1846); Gibson, C. J.

[3] Thompson v. Bowie, 4 Wall. 473 (1866), Grier, J.

[4] Kelly v. Jackson, 6 Pet. *632 (1832), Story, J.; Lilienthal's Tobacco v. United States, 97 U. S. 268 (1877).

[5] Emmons v. Westfield Bank, 97 Mass. 243 (1867), Foster, J.

[6] Cal. Code Civ. Proc., § 1833; 70 Cal. 570.

[7] 1 Greenl. Ev. §§ 84, 82; 3 Bl. Com. 367.

no substitution, only a selection of weaker instead of stronger proofs, or an omission to supply all the proofs capable of being produced, the rule is not infringed.

. Until shown that the production of primary evidence is out of the party's power, no other proof of the fact is admitted. . . The distinction is one of law, and refers to the quality, not to the strength, of the proof. Evidence which carries on its face no indication that better remains behind is not secondary, but primary. If there are several distinct sources of information it is not ordinarily necessary to show that they have all been exhausted, before secondary evidence can be resorted to.[1]

The general test is immediateness, not authority. No primary testimony is rejected because of faintness.[2]

Secondary evidence is admissible when it is the best the party has it in his power to produce. The rule promotes the ends of justice and guards against fraud, surprise, and imposition. There may be degrees of secondary evidence.[3]

When the evidence is the best obtainable, it should be admitted, unless that would contravene some established rule of law. Thus, in an action against a common carrier for the loss of a pearl ring, the plaintiff was allowed to point out a pearl corresponding in size, color, and general appearance to the one lost, and an expert to testify to the value of the selected pearl.[4] See further COPY; LOST, 2; PHOTOGRAPH; PRODUCE, 1.

Presumptive evidence. Evidence afforded by circumstances from which, if unexplained, the jury may or may not infer or presume other circumstances or facts.[5] See PRESUMPTION.

Conclusive evidence. Such evidence as, being uncontradicted, controls the decision; also, such evidence as the law does not allow to be contradicted.

Parol evidence. Evidence which need not be in writing; evidence extrinsic to the language of an instrument, and brought forward to throw light upon its meaning. See further PAROL.

Hearsay evidence. The narrative of what one has heard from another, and not what he knows of his own personal knowledge. See further HEARSAY.

Relevant evidence. Such evidence as is applicable to the issue; evidence which will assist in arriving at the truth or falsity of the allegation; evidence which supports a party's theory of his case. **Irrelevant evidence.** Evidence which does not tend to support the issue; impertinent testimony.

Relevant evidence is also spoken of as *admissible*, and irrelevant as *inadmissible*, under the pleadings; that is, as proper, or improper, to be received.[1]

All evidence must have relevancy to the question in issue, and tend to prove it; if not a link in the chain of proof, it is not receivable.[2]

Where there is evidence before the jury — whether it be weak or strong — which *tends* to prove the issue on the part of either side, it is error for the court to wrest it from the exercise of their judgment. It should be submitted under instructions.[3]

But the court cannot tell the jury that *any* legal results follow from evidence which "tends" to prove the issue.[4]

If the evidence relates to the transaction under consideration, or is connected with it, and is not too remote, it is competent. "It is relevant to put in evidence any circumstance that tends to make the proposition at issue more or less improbable."[4]

The possibility of error goes to the weight of evidence, and is not a ground for rejecting it. The spirit of the law permits a resort to every reasonable source of information upon a disputed question of fact. Unless excluded by some positive exception, everything relative to the issue is admissible; and this is extended to every hypothesis pertinent to the issue.[5]

Material evidence. Evidence important to a just determination of the issue; capable of affecting the result. **Immaterial evidence.** Evidence not directly pertinent to the issue; not important enough to change the result.

Cumulative evidence. Evidence of the same kind to the same point.[7]

Additional evidence to support the same point, and of the same character with evidence already produced. From the Latin *cumulare*, to heap up.[8]

Evidence which simply repeats, in substance and effect, or adds to, what has been testified to.[9]

Evidence which merely multiplies witnesses to a fact

---

[1] 1 Greenl. Ev. §§ 82, 84, cases; Clifton v. United States, 4 How. 247 (1846).

[2] 1 Whart. Ev. Ch. III; *ib.* §§ 90, 677.

[3] Cornett v. Williams, 20 Wall. 226, 246 (1873), cases, Swayne, J.; Riggs v. Tayloe, 9 Wheat. 486 (1824); Stebbins v. Duncan, 108 U. S. 43 (1882); 12 F. R. 402; 33 Mich. 53; 38 Ohio St. 125.

[4] Berney v. Dinsmore, 141 Mass. 44 (1886).

[5] 1 Greenl. Ev. § 13.

[1] See 3 Col. 12; 43 Pa. 170; 11 S. & R. 134.

[2] Thompson v. Bowie, 4 Wall. 471 (1866).

[3] Hickman v. Jones, 9 Wall. 201 (1869), Swayne, J.

[4] City of Providence v. Babcock, 3 Wall. 244 (1865); 1 id. 368; 8 id. 268.

[5] Fee v. Taylor, 83 Ky. 264 (1885), Holt, J.; 1 Whart. Ev. § 21.

[6] Bell v. Brewster, 44 Ohio St. 696, 697 (1887), Minshall, J.; 1 Whart. Ev. § 20.

[7] Parker v. Hardy, 24 Pick. 248 (1837), cases, Morton, Justice.

[8] People v. Superior Court, 10 Wend. 294 (1833), Savage, C. J.

[9] [Parshall v. Klinck, 43 Barb. 212 (1864), E. D. Smith, Justice.

before investigated, or only adds other circumstances of the same general character.[1] See TRIAL, New.

Competent evidence. That which the nature of the fact to be proved requires as the appropriate proof in the particular case: as, the production of a writing where its contents are the subject of inquiry; that is, the best evidence.[2] **Incompetent evidence.** Inappropriate, improper evidence.

Satisfactory or sufficient evidence. That amount of proof which ordinarily satisfies an unprejudicial mind, beyond reasonable doubt.[3]

The circumstances which will amount to this degree of proof can never be previously defined; the only test of which they are susceptible is, their sufficiency to satisfy the mind and conscience of a common man, and so convince him that he would venture to act upon that conviction in matters of the highest importance to his own interests.[3]

Questions respecting the competency and admissibility of evidence are entirely distinct from those which respect its sufficiency or effect. The former are conclusively within the province of the court; the latter belong exclusively to the jury.[4]

Minor terms descriptive of species of evidence: *affirmative* as opposed to *negative* evidence; *adminicular* or *ancillary* evidence; *corroborative* evidence; *extrinsic* as opposed to *intrinsic* evidence; *inculpatory* as opposed to *exculpatory* evidence; *newly* or *after-discovered* evidence; *rebutting* evidence; *state's* evidence by an accomplice; *substitutionary* evidence, qq. v.

The object of evidence being to prove the point in issue, fundamental rules regulating its production are: 1. The evidence must correspond with the allegations, and be confined to the point in issue. 2. It is sufficient if the substance of the issue be proved. 3. The burden of proving a proposition or issue rests upon the party holding the affirmative. 4. The best evidence of which the case is susceptible must be produced.[5]

The general rules of evidence are the same in civil and criminal cases.[6]

The mode of conducting trials, the order of introducing evidence, and the time when it shall be introduced, belong largely to the practice of the court where the fact is tried.[7]

The rules of practice in jury trials are necessarily somewhat flexible as to the order of proof, the number of witnesses, and the time, manner, and extent of the cross-examination. In ordinary cases the plaintiff begins and introduces all of his substantive evidence before the defendant opens his defense; so, the defendant introduces all his substantive evidence before the plaintiff rebuts. But the judge, in the exercise of a sound discretion, may relax either rule.[1]

The order of admissibility is regulated by the court. The Federal courts, in civil cases at common law, observe as rules of decision the rules of evidence of the State in which they sit, except when otherwise provided by the Constitution or an act of Congress.[2]

A party who objects or excepts to evidence must state his reasons therefor.[3]

See further ADMISSION, 2; ANSWER, 3; BOOK; CHARACTER; CHARGE, 2 (2, c); COMPROMISE; CRIME; DECLARATION, 1; DEED: DEMURRER; DEPOSITION; DOCUMENT; DOUBT; ESTOPPEL; EXAMINATION, 9· EXCEPTION, 4; FACT; HANDWRITING; INSPECTION, 2; INSANITY; LAW; LETTER, 3; NONSUIT; NOTICE, 1, Judicial; OFFER, 2; OPINION, 1; PRACTICE; PROCEDURE; REBUT; RECORD; RES, Gestæ; SCINTILLA; STENOGRAPHER; WEIGHT, 2; WITNESS.

EVIDENT. Clear to the mind; obvious; plain; apparent; manifest; notorious; palpable.

Under the constitutional provision that bail must be taken in capital cases except where the "proof is evident," bail will be denied if the evidence adduced on the application would sustain a verdict of murder in the first degree.[4]

EVIL. See MALICE; MALUM; WRONG.

EX. 1. The Latin preposition — out of, proceeding from, from, of, by, on, on account of, by virtue of, according to; also, — beyond. See EXTRA.

In composition intensifies or else has little effect upon the signification. Before a consonant becomes simply *e*; the *x* remains before the vowels and c, p, q, s, t; assimilates with a following *f*; is dropped before other consonants.

In French *es:* as, in estreat, estrepe, escrow.

2. Prefixed to the name of an official, denotes that he formerly held the office designated: as, ex-attorney-general, ex-judge, ex-minister, ex-marshal, ex-sheriff.

Prefixed to a word denoting a civil status or condition, indicates that the person referred to formerly occupied that relation: as, ex-convict, ex-partner, ex-wife.

---

[1] Waller *v.* Graves, 20 Conn. 310-11 (1850), cases, Church, C. J. See also 2 Ark. 353; 42 Conn. 519; 27 Ga. 464; 28 Me. 383; 34 N. J. L. 156; 7 Barb. 278.

[2] [1 Greenl. Ev. §§ 2, 82; 107 U. S. 332.

[3] 1 Greenl. Ev. § 2; 30 Me. 481.

[4] 1 Greenl. Ev. § 2; 2 Pet. 44, 133, 149.

[5] 1 Greenl. Ev. § 50; Travelers' Ins. Co. *v.* Mosley, 8 Wall. 409 (1869).

[6] 4 Wheat. 472; 12 *id.* 469; 91 U. S. 438; 57 Wis. 157; 4 Bl. Com. 356.

[7] Wills *v.* Russell, 100 U. S. 623 (1879).

[1] First Unitarian Society *v.* Faulkner, 91 U. S. 417-18 (1875), Clifford, J.

[2] R. S. § 721: Act 1789; Potter *v.* Third Nat. Bank of Chicago, 102 U. S. 165 (1880), cases, Harlan, J.

[3] State *v.* Taylor, 36 Kan. 334 (1887), cases. French law of evidence, 19 Am. Law Rev. 380 (1885).

[4] *Exp.* Foster, 5 Tex. Ap. 645-47 (1879); *Exp.* Gilstrap, 14 *id.* 240, 264 (1883).

3. Prefixed to other words, denotes absence or privation of the notion conveyed by the simple word; without: as, ex-coupon, ex-dividend, ex-interest.

"Ex-dividend" is used of sales of stocks which reserve to the seller the dividend presently payable. See DIVIDEND, 3.

A sale of bonds "ex-July coupons" means a sale reserving the coupons, a sale in which the seller receives, in addition to the purchase-price, the benefit of the coupons, which benefit he may realize either by detaching them or receiving from the buyer an equivalent consideration.[1]

Ex abundantia cautela. Out of excessive care. See CAUTELA.

Ex æquo et bono. By what is fair and good: in justice and fair dealing. See ASSUMPSIT; EQUITY.

Ex antecedentibus, etc. See INTERPRETATIO.

Ex arbitrio judicis. By discretion of the magistrate or judge.

Ex colore. Under color of. See COLOR, 2.

Ex comitate. Out of courtesy. See COMITY.

Ex contractu. Out of a contract. See ACTION, 2.

Ex curia. Out of court.

Ex debito justitiæ. Out of an obligation of justice: as a matter of legal right. See DEBITUM; GRACE.

Ex delicto. Out of a fault or wrong. See ACTION, 2; DELICTUM.

Ex demissione. By demise, q. v. Abbreviated ex dem.

Ex dolo malo. Out of fraud. See DOLUS.

Ex facie. From appearance. See FACIES.

Ex facto. From a thing done. See FACTUM.

Ex gratia. Out of favor, by indulgence. See GRACE.

Ex hypothesi. Upon the supposition or theory.

Ex industria. From fixed purpose: intentionally.

Ex lege. From, or by force of, the law.

Ex maleficio. On account of misconduct: by reason of an illegal act. See MALEFICIUM.

Ex mero motu. Out of pure free-will. See MOTION, 1.

Ex mora. From delay, or default.

Ex necessitate. From necessity; necessarily.

Ex necessitate legis. From urgency of the law.

Ex necessitate rei. From urgency of the thing or case.

Ex nudo pacto. Out of an engagement without a consideration. See PACTUM.

Ex officio. By virtue of office. See OFFICIUM.

Ex parte. On behalf of. Abbreviated ex p., and exp. See PARS.

Ex post facto. After the fact. See FACTUM, Ex post facto. .

Ex proprio. Of his or its own.

Ex proprio motu. Of his own volition. See MOTION, 1.

Ex proprio vigore. Of its own inherent force. See VIGOR.

Ex relatione. On the information of. Abbreviated ex rel. See RELATION, 2.

Ex tempore. Extemporaneously.

Ex testamento. From the will. See TESTAMENTUM.

Ex turpi causa. Out of an unlawful engagement. See ACTIO, Ex turpi, etc.

Ex uno disce omnes. From one (act) learn all. Compare FALSUS, In uno, etc.

Ex vi termini. By force of the word.

Ex vi terminorum. From the very meaning of the language. See TERMINUS, 3.

Ex visceribus. From the vitals: from the inherent nature; of the essence.

Ex visceribus verborum. From the natural meaning of the words.

Ex visitatione Dei. By divine dispensation: from natural cause.

Ex voluntate. From free will.

EXACTION. A wrong done by an officer, or one in pretended authority, by taking a reward or fee for that which the law does not allow,— when he wrests a fee or reward where none is due.[1]

"Extortion" is where he extorts more than is due.[1] See EXTORTION; PAYMENT, Involuntary.

EXAMINATION.[2] A weighing, balancing: search, investigation; hearing, inquiry. Compare INSPECTION; VIEW.

Examined. Compared with the original: as, an examined copy, q. v.

---

[1] Porter v. Wormser, 94 N. Y. 445 (1884), Andrews, J.

[1] [Coke, Litt. 368; Jacob's Law Dict.

[2] L. examinare, to weigh carefully: examen, tongue of a balance.

Examining. Conducting an examination: as, the examining counsel.

Examiner. A person charged with the duty of making or conducting an examination: as, an examiner — in chancery or equity, of customs, of national banks, of patents, of titles, in divorce, lunacy, partition, qq. v.

1. Examination of a bankrupt or of a debtor. Interrogation as to the state of his property.[1]

2. Examination of an accused person. Investigation, by an authorized magistrate, of the grounds of an accusation of crime against a person, with a view to discharge him or to secure his appearance at trial, and to preserve the evidence.

Had before a justice of the peace, an alderman, or other magistrate, a United States commissioner, and, possibly, before a judge. On a *prima facie* case bail will be required, or a commitment made; otherwise, the accused is discharged. The examination may be waived. The accused has no right to the assistance of counsel; and, in many cases, he himself is not examined.

3. Examination of an invention. Of an alleged new invention, for which application for a patent has been made, to ascertain whether it is sufficiently new and useful, or whether it interferes with any other invention.[2] See PATENT, 2.

4. Examination of a long account. By a referee, of the proofs of the correctness of the items composing a long account.[3] See ACCOUNT, 1.

5. Examination of a married woman. Of a wife, separate and apart from her husband, to learn whether her acknowledgment of a mortgage, conveyance, or other deed is voluntary, without coercion of her husband. Also called her *private* or *separate* examination.[4]

Where a statute requires a "private" examination of the wife, to ascertain that she acts freely and not by compulsion of her husband, but prescribes no precise form of words to be used in the certificate of acknowledgment, it is sufficient if the words of the acknowledgment have the same meaning, and are in substance the same with those in the statute.[6]

Such statutes provide for privacy from the husband only. A certificate "privately examined apart from and out of the hearing" of the husband, can mean nothing less than that he was not present when she was examined, and satisfies a statute (of Maryland) requiring an examination "out of the presence."[1] See further ACKNOWLEDGMENT, 2.

6. Examination of a national bank. By an officer of the United States treasury, to discover whether the bank is complying with the law as to issues, reserve, etc.[2]

7. Examination of a student-at-law. This is preliminary to his admission to practice, as a test of qualification.

8. Examination of a title. A search to determine whether the title to land, proposed for conveyance or mortgage, is free from defects, and marketable, q. v.

Whence examiners of titles, and abstract or brief of title. See ABSTRACT, 2; CONVEYANCER; TITLE, 1.

9. Examination of a witness. The interrogation or questioning of a witness, to elicit his personal knowledge as to one or more facts.

Direct examination, or *examination in chief*. The first examination, on behalf of the party who calls the witness. Opposed, 1, to *examination in pais*, or on the *voir dire*: a preliminary questioning intended to test competency; 2, to *cross-examination*: by the adverse party, confined to the subject-matter elicited upon the direct examination.

Re-direct examination. Follows the cross-examination, and is confined to matters brought out under it.

Re-cross examination. Follows the re-direct examination, and is restricted to the new or additional information or answers given thereunder.

Re-examination. The re-direct or the re-cross examination in the same hearing; also, another and distinct examination in a subsequent trial.

Separate examination. Is of a witness apart from or out of the hearing of another or other witnesses.

Cross-examination, which is the right of the party against whom a witness is called, is a means of separating hearsay from knowledge, error from truth, opinion from fact, inference from recollection; of ascertaining the order of the events as narrated by the witness in his examination in chief, the time and place when and where they occurred, and the attending circumstances: and of testing the intelligence, memory, impartiality, truthfulness, and integrity of the witness.[3]

---

[1] See R. S. §§ 5086–87.

[2] R. S. § 4803.

[3] See Magown v. Sinclair, 5 Daly, 66 (1874).

[4] 1 Bl. Com. 444.

[6] Dundas v. Hitchcock, 12 How. 269 (1851).

---

[1] Deery v. Cray, 5 Wall. 807 (1866).

[2] See R. S. § 5240.

[3] The Ottawa, 3 Wall. 271 (1865), Clifford, J.

EXAMPLE						425						EXCEPTION

Cross-examination is "the crucial test" of truth. A witness may not be cross-examined as to facts and circumstances not connected with matters stated in his direct examination; if a party wishes to examine him as to such facts and circumstances he must call him as a witness in the subsequent progress of the case;[1] that is, "make him his own witness."

Greater latitude is allowed in the cross-examination of a *party* than in that of another witness. Still, this, in its course and extent, where directed to matters not inquired into in the principal examination, is largely subject to the control of the court in the exercise of a sound discretion,—as is the cross-examination of other witnesses.[2]

A party may ask questions to show bias or prejudice, or to lay a foundation to admit evidence of a prior contradictory statement.[3]

An adverse party may now generally be called in chief "as for cross-examination" whenever his testimony may be needed to make out a *prima facie* cause of action or defense.

The court may order the separate examination of a witness. Refusal to answer a proper question is a contempt of court. The court itself may examine. Prompting is not permitted. On the direct examination leading questions are generally prohibited. The extent and severity of an examination rests with the court. Examination is not allowed as to a conclusion of law, nor, in chief, as to motive, nor as to an opinion. Answers are privileged. The substance of a conversation or of an absent writing may be given. Vague impressions are inadmissible. Answers are according to recollection and belief. A witness may refresh his memory from memoranda.[4]

On cross-examination leading questions may be put. All such questioning is to be on the subject of the examination in chief. Collateral facts cannot be introduced to test memory. A witness is not compelled to criminate himself; nor to answer a question imputing disgrace, unless the question is material. May inquire as to religious belief, motive, veracity, bias, and the *res gestæ*. And may draw inferences from refusal to answer.[5]

Re-examination is permitted as to a matter requiring explanation, and as to new matters introduced by the opposition. For this reason a witness may be recalled.[6]

Re-cross examination is discretionary with the court.[6]

See CALL; CONFRONT; CRIMINATE; EVIDENCE; EXPERT; IMPEACH, 3; PREJUDICE; QUESTION, 1; REFRESH; VOIR; WITNESS.

EXAMPLE. See DAMAGES, Exemplary; PRECEDENT.

[1] Philadelphia, &c. R. Co. *v.* Stimpson, 14 Pet. 461 (1840), Story, J.; Houghton *v.* Jones, 1 Wall. 704 (1863).
[2] Rea *v.* Missouri, 17 Wall. 542 (1873), cases, Bradley, J.; Schultz *v.* Chicago, &c. R. Co., 67 Wis. 617 (1886); Knapp *v.* Schneider, 24 id. 71 (1869); 3 Dak. 78.
[3] Wills *v.* Russell, 100 U. S. 625 (1879), cases; Schuster *v.* Stout, 30 Kan. 531 (1883).
[4] 1 Whart. Ev. §§ 491–515, cases.
[5] 1 Whart. Ev. §§ 527–47, cases.
[6] 1 Whart. Ev. §§ 572–75, cases.

EXCAVATE. See DIGGING.

EXCEEDING. See MORE OR LESS.

Under an indictment for embezzlement, alleging the gross receipt of a sum "exceeding" a sum named, proof may be made of the receipt of any amount, although it exceed that sum.[1]

EXCELLENCY. "His Excellency" is the title given by the constitution of Massachusetts to the governor of that State; also, by custom, to the governors of the other States, and to the President of the United States.[2]

EXCEPTANT. See EXCEPTION.

EXCEPTIO. L. A keeping out; an exclusion; exception.

Exceptio probat regulam. The exception proves, that is, either confirms or tests, the rule: "proves," by not being within the reason; "tests" the form in which expressed, by observing whether exceptions must be allowed.

EXCEPTION. Something withheld, not granted or parted with; the exclusion of a thing, or the thing or matter itself as excluded; an objection made. Compare REGULAR.

Exceptant. One who takes or files objection to a thing done or proposed.

1. In a deed or contract, excludes from the operation of the words some part of the subject-matter then in being.

A clause in a deed whereby the donor or lessor, excepts somewhat out of that which he had granted by his deed.[3]

Always part of the thing granted, and the whole of the part excepted. A "reservation" is of a thing not in being, but newly created. The terms are often used in the same sense.[4] See RESERVE, 4.

2. In a statute, excludes from the purview a person or thing included in the words.

Exempts absolutely from the operation of the enactment. A "proviso" defeats the operation conditionally.[5]

[1] State *v.* Ring, 29 Minn. 78, 82 (1882).
[2] "The style of the Executive, as silently carried forward from the committee of detail, was still 'his Excellency;' this vanished in the committee of revision,"— 2 Bancroft, Formation of the Const. 210, 187.
[3] [Darling *v.* Crowell, 6 N. H. 423 (1833).
[4] State *v.* Wilson, 42 Me. 21 (1856); Kister *v.* Reeser, 98 Pa. 5 (1881); Green Bay, &c. Canal Co. *v.* Hewitt, 66 Wis. 465–66 (1886); 24 Am. Law Reg. 716–22 (1886), cases; 2 McLean, 301; 41 Me. 311; 51 *id.* 498; 10 N. H. 310; 37 *id.* 167; 4 Johns. 81; 3 Wend. 683; 1 Barb. 407; 19 *id.* 192; 28 Ohio St. 568; 47 Pa. 197; 5 R. I. 419; 6 Abb. N. Cas. 331; 81 Va. 28.
[5] Waffle *v.* Goble, 53 Barb. 522 (1868).

If an exception occurs in the statutory description of an offense it must be negatived, or the party will be brought within the description; but if it comes by way of *proviso* and does not alter the offense, merely states what persons are to take advantage of it, then the defense must be specially pleaded or else be given in evidence under the general issue, according to circumstances.[1]

An exception ought to be of that which otherwise would be included in the category from which it is excepted. "Where an exception is incorporated in the body of the clause, he who pleads the clause ought also to plead the exception, but when there is a clause for the benefit of the pleader, and afterward follows a *proviso* which is against him, he shall plead the clause and leave it to the adversary to show the *proviso*."[2]

See ACT, 3, Enact; GENERAL; PROVIDEN; PROVISO.

3. In equity and admiralty practice, a formal allegation that a previous adverse proceeding is insufficient in law.

4. In common-law practice, a formal notice, following the denial of a request or the overruling of an objection, made in the course of a trial, that the exceptant intends to claim the benefit of his request or objection in future proceedings; as, upon a writ of error.[3]

It is also used to signify other objections in the course of a suit. Thus, there may be exception taken to bail or security, to the ruling of a judge or master, to an appraisement, award, decree, report, or return.

Bill of exceptions. An "exception" being an objection to or a protest against a ruling or decision of the court upon a question of law,— taken or stated at the time of the ruling, unless otherwise prescribed,— a "bill of exceptions" is a written statement of the exceptions duly taken by a party to the decisions or instructions of a judge in the trial of a cause, with so much of the facts, or other matter, as is necessary to explain the rulings.[4]

Every bill must be settled, allowed, and signed by the judge, in the manner, upon the notice, and within the time pointed out by statute.[4]

Its sole office is to make matters which are extrinsic, or out of the record, part of the record.[5]

If, in his directions or decisions, the judge who tries a cause mistakes the law by ignorance, inadvertence,

or design, counsel, by statute of Westminster 2, 13 Edw. I (1286), c. 31, may require him publicly to "seal a bill of exceptions," stating the point in which he is supposed to err. Should the judge refuse to seal the bill, the party may have a writ commanding him to seal it, if the fact alleged be truly stated: and if he returns that the fact is untruly stated, when the case is otherwise, an action will lie against him for a false return. This bill of exceptions is in the nature of an appeal, examinable, after judgment entered in the court below, in the next immediate superior court, upon a writ of error.[1]

The principles of the statute of Westminster have been adopted in all of the States; in the Federal courts, bills are still drawn as at common law under the statute.[2]

The object is to secure a record which may be reviewed. In theory, the bill states what occurred while the trial was going on. Exception must be taken at the moment a ruling is made, or before verdict.[3]

A bill should present only the rulings of the court upon some matter of law, as, the admission or rejection of evidence, and should contain only so much of the testimony, or such a statement of the proofs made or offered, as may be necessary to explain the bearings of the rulings upon the issues.[4]

It is not usual to reduce the bill to form and to obtain the signature of the judge during the progress of the trial; the statute of Westminster did not require it. The exception need only be noted at the time it is made, and may be reduced to form within a reasonable time after the trial is over.[5]

It is sufficient if the judge simply signs the bill.[6]

It was early held that a bill must be signed within the term, unless by consent or special order. Otherwise the judge might be asked to sign a bill after his recollection of facts had faded, and parties might be burdened with unnecessary delay and expense. While the rule may have been established when short-hand reports were not usual, the Supreme Court considers the rule still obligatory.[7]

At common law, a writ of error might be had for an error apparent on the record or for an error in fact, but not for an error in law not appearing on the record; hence, anything alleged *ore tenus* and overruled could not be assigned for error. To remedy this evil was the object of the statute of Westminster. Under its provisions a bill of exceptions is founded on some objection in point of law to the opinion and direction of the court, either as to the competency of a witness, the admissibility or the legal effect of evidence, or

---

[1] Simpson *v.* Ready, 12 M. & W. *740 (1844), Alderson, B.

[2] United States *v.* Cook, 17 Wall. 177, 173 (1872), Clifford, J.,— quoting Treby, C. J., in Jones *v.* Axen, 1 Ld. Ray. 120 (1692), and Steel *v.* Smith, 1 B. & Al. 99 (1817).

[3] Abbott's Law Dict.

[4] Saint Croix Lumber Co. *v.* Pennington, 2 Dak. 470 (1881), Shannon, C. J.; 1 N. M. 115.

[5] Kitchell *v.* Burgwin, 21 Ill. 45 (1858); 20 *id.* 225; 3 Col. 200, 235, 251; 5 Hill, 579; 7 Baxt. 56; 77 Va. 250.

[1] 3 Bl. Com. 372.

[2] Pomeroy *v.* Bank of Indiana, 1 Wall. 599 (1863).

[3] Railway Co. *v.* Heck, 102 U. S. 120 (1880), Waite, C. J.; Hanna *v.* Maas, 122 *id.* 26 (1887), cases, Gray, J.

[4] Lincoln *v.* Claflin, 7 Wall. 136 (1868), Field, J.; Worthington *v.* Mason, 101 U. S. 149 (1879); Moulor *v.* American Life Ins. Co., 111 *id.* 337 (1884); New York, &c. R. Co. *v.* Madison, 123 *id.* 526 (1887), cases.

[5] Hunnicutt *v.* Peyton, 102 U. S. 354 (1880), cases, Strong, J.

[6] Stanton *v.* Embrey, 93 U. S. 555 (1876), cases.

[7] Marine City Stave Co. *v.* Herreshoff Manuf. Co., 32 F. R. 824 (1887), cases.

other matter of law arising from facts not denied in which either party is overruled by the court. The seal attests that the exception was taken at the trial. If the bill contains matter false or untruly stated, the judge ought to refuse to affix his seal. The substance of the bill should be reduced to writing while the thing is transacting. An exception not tendered at the trial is waived.[1]

The statute of Westminster did not apply to criminal cases. At common law, no bill of exceptions was permitted in such cases; the right depends upon enactment.[2]

See CHARGE, 2 (2, c); ERROR, 2 (3), Writ of; SEAL, 2.

EXCESSIVE. Surpassing in amount, degree, or extent that which is usual, reasonable, proper or lawful in the particular case: as, excessive — bail, damage, distress, fine, taxation, qq. v.

To constitute bail excessive it must be per se unreasonably great and clearly disproportionate to the offense involved, or the peculiar circumstances appearing must show it to be so in the particular case.[3]

EXCHANGE.[4] A reciprocal contract for the interchange of property, each party being both a vendor and a vendee.[5]

(1) Of personalty: a commutation of goods for goods.[6]

The giving of one thing and the receiving of another thing.[7]

"A contract by which the parties mutually give, or agree to give, one thing for another, neither thing, or both things, being money only."[8]

A "sale" is the giving of one thing for that which is the representative of all values — money.[9] The distinction between a "sale" and an "exchange" is rather one of shadow than of substance. In both cases the title is absolutely transferred; and the same rules of law are applicable to the transaction, whether the consideration is money or a commodity.[10] See SALE.

(2) Of realty: a mutual grant of equal interests, the one in consideration of the other.[11]

The estates exchanged must be equal in quantity; not in value, for that is immaterial, but in interest: as, a fee-simple for a fee-simple.[12]

Power to "sell and exchange" lands includes power to partition them.[1]

An exchange is as much within the statute of frauds as is a sale.[2]

At common law, the contract carried a warranty of title, with a right to re-enter one's original possession, if evicted from the later acquisition.[3]

A person seeking specific performance of a contract for an exchange of lands must prove: the contract; that the consideration has been paid or tendered; such part performance that a rescission would be a fraud on the plaintiff, and could not be compensated by a recovery of damages at law; and that delivery of possession has been made in pursuance of the contract, and acquiesced in by the other party.[2] See DEED, 2.

2. An abridgment of **bill of exchange:** an open letter of request from one man to another, desiring him to pay a sum named therein to a third person on his account. In common speech, a "draft."[4]

A written order or request from one party to another for the payment of money to a third person or his order, on account of the drawer.[5]

Originally invented among merchants in different countries, for the more easy remittance of money.

He who writes the letter is called the drawer; he to whom it is written, the drawee; he to whom it is payable, the payee.

When both drawer and drawee reside in the same country, the bill is termed an "inland" bill; when in different countries, a "foreign" bill.[6]

A foreign bill is usually drawn in three counterparts or duplicates, and numbered as the "first," "second," and "third" of exchange. The first instrument that reaches the drawee is paid. Each mentions the others, and all three together compose a "set" of exchange. The device obviates delays.[7]

Exchange is "at par" when the price of a draft is the face of it; "at a premium" or "above par," when the price is more than the face; "at a discount" or "below par," when the price is less than the face. The price paid is the "rate" of exchange.

"Arbitration of exchange:" converting the currency of one country into that of another, through the medium of an intervening currency. "Course of exchange:" the quotations for a given time. "Par of exchange:" the value of the money of one country in that of another,— either real or nominal. "Re-exchange:" the expense incurred on a bill dishonored

---

[1] Wheeler v. Winn, 53 Pa. 126 (1866), Woodward, C. J.

[2] Haines v. Commonwealth, 99 Pa. 419 (1882), Sharswood, C. J.

[3] Exp. Ryan, 44 Cal. 558 (1872), Wallace, C. J.; 6 Q. B. D. 206.

[4] F. eschanger: L. ex-cambiare, to barter, put one thing for another, change.

[5] See Bixby v. Bent, 59 Cal. 528 (1882).

[6] 2 Bl. Com. 446.

[7] 1 Pars. Contr. 521.

[8] Cal. Civil Code, § 1804; Gilbert v. Sleeper, 71 Cal. 292-93 (1886).

[9] 1 Pars. Contr. 521; 2 Bl. Com. 446.

[10] [Commonwealth v. Clark, 14 Gray, 372 (1860), Bigelow, J.

[11] 2 Bl. Com. 323.

[12] 2 Bl. Com. 323; 7 Barb. 638; 21 Wis. 123.

---

[1] Phelps v. Harris, 101 U. S. 380 (1879).

[2] Purcell v. Miner, 4 Wall. 517 (1868).

[3] 2 Bl. Com. 323.

[4] 2 Bl. Com. 466; 61 N. Y. 255; 33 Ga. 188.

[5] [Cox v. Nat. Bank of New York, 100 U. S. 709 (1879), Clifford, J.

[6] 2 Bl. Com. 466.

[7] See Bank of Pittsburgh v. Neal, 22 How. 108 (1859).

in a foreign country, where made payable, and returned to the drawer.[1]

By the act of issuing a bill the drawer agrees that, if it is not paid according to its terms, he will pay it. His liability is fixed by due presentment, demand, and notice of dishonor.[2]

A bill payable at sight, or at a date subsequent to acceptance, must be duly presented for payment, or a party conditionally liable will be discharged.[3]

The acceptor is the principal debtor; the drawer and indorsers are sureties. Discounting a bill is neither acceptance nor payment. Acceptance is an engagement to pay the bill according to its tenor and effect when due. A bill is paid only when there is an intention to discharge and satisfy it.[4]

On the question of timely presentation for payment, the law of the place where a foreign bill is payable governs.[5]

Proof of failure of consideration is a good defense as between the immediate parties — drawer and acceptor, and payee and drawee. But as between remote parties, an action will not be defeated unless there is an absence or failure of the two considerations: that which the defendant received for his liability, and that which the plaintiff gave for his title. These remote parties are the payee and acceptor, or the indorser and acceptor. The rule presupposes that the payee or indorsee became the holder of the bill before it was overdue and without knowledge of facts which impeach the title as between the immediate parties.[6]

The essential characteristic of a draft or bill of exchange is the order of one party upon another for the payment of money. . . The instruments in suit are in strictness bank-checks. They have all the particulars in which such instruments differ or may differ from regular bills of exchange. They are drawn upon a bank having funds of the drawer for their payment, and they are payable upon demand, although the time of payment is not designated. A bill of exchange may be so drawn, but it usually states the time of payment, and days of grace are allowed upon it. There are no days of grace upon checks. The instruments here are also drawn in the briefest form possible in orders for the payment of money, which is the usual characteristic of checks. A bill of exchange is generally drawn with more formality, and payment at sight, or at a specified number of days after date, is requested, and that the amount be charged to the drawer's account. When intended for transmission to another State or country they are usually drawn in duplicate or triplicate, and designated as first, second, or third of exchange. A regular bill of exchange, it is true, may be in a form similar to a bank-check, so that it may sometimes be difficult, from their form,

to distinguish between the two classes of instruments. But an instrument drawn upon a bank and simply directing payment to a party named of a specified sum of money, at the time on deposit with the drawee, without designating a future day for payment, is to be treated as a check. If the instrument designates a future day for payment, it is, according to the weight of authorities, to be deemed a bill of exchange, when, without such designation, it would be treated as a check. . . A check implies a contract on the part of the drawer that he has funds in the hands of the drawee for its payment on presentation. If it is dishonored the drawer is entitled to notice; but, unlike the drawee of a bill of exchange, he is not discharged from liability for the want of such notice, unless he has sustained damage or is prejudiced in the assertion of his rights by the omission.[1]

See further ACCEPT, 2; ASSIGNMENT, Equitable; CHECK; COLLECTION; CURRENT, Funds; FORGERY; INDORSE; DRAFT; DUE, 1; HONOR, 1; LETTER, Of credit; NEGOTIATE, 2; NOTE, Promissory; NOTING; PROTEST, 2.

3. A place where merchants and brokers meet for business, at specified hours. Contracted into 'Change.

Called "stock" exchange, "produce" exchange, "petroleum" exchange, "grain" exchange, "pork" exchange, etc., from the nature of the business in which contracts, for the purchase and sale of securities or commodities, are made. The distinctive word may designate the association itself, as well as the place where its meetings are held.

All the members of an exchange, considered together, usually constitute the board of exchange. Membership in a board may be qualified by any conditions the creators could lawfully impose. Thus, provision in the constitution of a board, whose members are limited in number and elected by ballot, that a member, upon failing to perform his contracts or becoming insolvent, may assign his seat to be sold and the proceeds be first applied for the benefit of members of the exchange to whom he is indebted, is lawful.[2]

Merchants may voluntarily associate together, and prescribe for themselves regulations to establish, define, and control the usages or customs that shall prevail in their dealings with each other. These are useful institutions, and the courts enforce their rules whenever parties deal with them, in which case the regula-

---

[1] See Adams v. Addington, 16 F. R. 91 (1883), cases.

[2] Cummings v. Kent, 44 Ohio St. 95-98 (1886), cases.

[3] Cox v. Nat. Bank of New York, ante.

[4] Swope v. Ross, 40 Pa. 188 (1861), Strong, J.

[5] Pierce v. Indseth, 106 U. S. 549 (1882).

[6] Hoffman v. Bank of Milwaukee, 12 Wall. 190-91 (1870), cases, Clifford, J. See generally Goodman v. Simonds, 20 How. 364 (1857); as to unification of the law, 2 Law Quar. Rev. 297-312 (1886).

---

[1] Bull v. Bank of Kasson, 123 U. S. 105, 109-11 (1887), cases, Field, J.

The instruments in suit read thus:

"$500. The First National Bank, Kasson, Minn., Oct. 15, 1881. Pay to the order of Mr. A. La Due five hundred dollars in current funds.

E. E. FAIRCHILD, Cashier.

To Ninth National Bank, New York City.

[Indorsed:] Pay to the order of M. Edison, Esq.

A. LA DUE.

M. EDISON.

[2] Hyde v. Woods, 94 U. S. 523 (1876), Miller, J.

tions become a part of the contract. Part of these regulations may be observed, and part discarded.[1]

See ARBITRATION; BARGAIN, Time; BROKER; CORNER; WAGES, 2.

EXCHEQUER.[2] The treasury department of the English government.

Established by William I; regulated by Edward I. Consisted of two divisions: one, for the receipt of revenue; the other, for the administration of justice in matters of revenue, and known as the *court of exchequer,* and presided over by the *chancellor* of the exchequer. This court originally had limited equity jurisdiction; then the chancellor, the Lord Chief Baron, sat apart in a hall called the exchequer *chamber.* Its present jurisdiction does not differ materially from other co-ordinate courts of common law.[3] See CHANCELLOR, 1, Of the Exchequer.

EXCISE.[4] An inland imposition, paid sometimes upon the consumption of the commodity, or frequently upon the retail trade.[5] Whence excise *duty,* excise *law.*

An inland imposition, sometimes upon the consumption of a commodity, and sometimes upon the retail trade; sometimes upon the manufacturer, and sometimes upon the vendor.[6]

A term of very general signification, meaning tribute, custom, tax, tollage, assessment.[7]

Though often synonymous with tax, may have a distinct signification. It is based on no rule of appointment or equality, as is a tax. It is a fixed, absolute and direct charge laid on merchandise, products or commodities, without regard to the amount of property belonging to those on whom it may fall, or to any supposed relation between money expended for a public object and a special benefit occasioned to those by whom the charge is to be paid.[6]

Under the constitution of Massachusetts the legislature may impose reasonable excises upon "produce, goods, wares, merchandise and commodities" within

the State; also, upon any business or calling, franchise or privilege conferred by or exercised therein.[1]

See COMMODITY; DUTY, 2; IMPOST; TAX, 2.

EXCLUSIO. See EXPRESSIO.

EXCLUSIVE. That which debars, deprives, or excepts: as, an exclusive right, privilege, or jurisdiction, which is possessed, enjoyed or exercised independently of another or others.[2] Opposed, **inclusive.**

See ENUMERATION; ONLY; POSSESSION, Adverse.

EXCULPATORY. See CULPA; FAULT.

EXCUSE. A reason for doing or not doing a thing.

Excusable. 1. Admitting of excuse; exempting from liability or responsibility: as, an excusable default, an excusable misdelivery by a carrier.

2. Done under circumstances of accident or necessity, and without legal malice: as, an excusable homicide, *q. v.*

Ignorance of a fact may excuse; ignorance of the law never excuses. Infants, lunatics, married women, and persons under duress or necessity are sometimes excused for acts done or sought to be enforced. See IGNORANCE: KNOWLEDGE, 1; NOTICE.

EXEAT. See EXIRE, Ne exeat.

EXECUTE.[3] To complete or perfect what the law directs to be done; to complete as an effective instrument.

1. Referring to a conveyance, mortgage, lease, will, contract, note, or other document, may mean, as in popular speech, to sign, or to sign and deliver; but in strict legal understanding, when said of a deed or bond, always means to sign, seal, *and* deliver.[4]

Until a promise has been performed it is termed "executory;" after performance, "executed." Obviously, one of two mutual promises may have become executed while the other yet remains executory; as where a seller pays the price, and the buyer promises delivery in the future. So, one or more of several connected promises of one party may be executed while his other engagements remain executory. What is usually meant by speaking of a contract as executory or executed is not that it is so as an entirety, but that the promise particularly under discussion is so. Thus, to speak of a sale for cash, of goods to be delivered in the future, as an executory contract, would be natural if the seller's obligation to deliver were the

---

[1] Dillard *v.* Paton, 19 F. R. 624 (1884), Hammond, J. Goddard *v.* Merchants' Exchange, 9 Mo. Ap. 290 (1880), cases; Thorne *v.* Prentiss, 83 Ill. 99 (1876); 20 Cent. Law J. 444-50 (1885), cases; 45 Ill. 113; 80 *id.* 134; 18 Abb. Pr. 271; 2 Mo. Ap. 100; 29 Wis. 48; 47 *id.* 670.

[2] F. *eschequier,* chess-board—from the cloth that originally covered the table or counter.

[3] 3 Bl. Com. 44, 56.

[4] A misspelling of Old Dutch *aksüs, aksys:* F. *assise,* a tax,—Skeat; Webster.

[5] 1 Bl. Com. 318.

[6] Pacific Ins. Co. *v.* Soule, 7 Wall. 445 (1868), Swayne, J.; Tax on Capital of Banks, 15 Op. Att.-Gen. 219 (1877); Michigan Central R. Co. *v.* Collector, 100 U. S. 595 (1879).

[7] Portland Bank *v.* Apthorp, 12 Mass. 256 (1815), Parker, C. J.

[8] Oliver *v.* Washington Mills, 11 Allen, 274 (1865), Bigelow, C. J.; Commonwealth *v.* People's Savings Bank, 5 *id.* 431 (1862).

[1] Connecticut Ins. Co. *v.* Commonwealth, 133 Mass. 161 (1882).

[2] See 3 Story, C. C. 131; 2 Dall. 211; 8 Blackf. 361; 29 Kan. 541; 36 *id.* 366; 60 Md. 80; 93 N. Y. 328.

[3] F. *executer:* L. *ex-sequi,* to follow out, follow to the end, perform.

[4] See Hepp *v.* Huefner, 61 Wis. 151 (1884); 32 Ark. 453; 9 Cal. 430; 17 Ohio, 545; 12 Ired. L. 221; 37 Mich. 459; 28 Minn. 551.

matter chiefly in question; but if the controversy related to the buyer's payment the contract would be called executed. And "executed " is (although " executory " is not) applied to contracts in a sense relating to the completion of the written instruments in which they are embodied, and not to performance of their substance. In this sense "to execute " means to complete the paper as an effective instrument; to sign it, and to seal and deliver it whenever these formalities are essential to its inception.[1]

2. Referring to a power or trust: to perform or fulfill the requirements thereof; to give effect thereto according to the intent of the creator or of the law.

3. Referring to a decree, judgment, writ or process: for the officer addressed to carry out the command therein contained.

"Executed," indorsed on a writ, means that the officer complied with the mandate.[2]

4. Referring to a criminal: to put him to death. Whence to execute the sentence, and executioner. See DEATH, Penalty.

Executed. Completed, finished, performed, perfected; vested. **Executory.** Yet to be completed, incomplete, not yet effective, finished, perfected, or vested: as, an executed or executory — agreement, consideration, contract, devise, estate, remainder, sale, trust, use, writ, qq. v.

Executive. Carrying out; pertaining to the enforcement of the laws: as, the executive department, executive business; also, the officer who superintends the enforcement of the laws. See DEPARTMENT; DOCUMENT; GOVERNMENT; OFFICER; PRESIDENT.

Execution. 1. Doing or performing a thing required.

2. Completion of the obligation of an instrument by the final act of delivering it. See *Execute*, 1.

3. Putting the sentence of the law in force.[3]

The act of carrying into effect the final judgment of the court; also, the writ which authorizes this.[4]

A writ issuing out of a court, directed to an officer thereof, and running against the body or goods of a party.[5]

Dormant execution. A writ of execution which has been delivered to the proper officer, but is held in abeyance or unexecuted; a writ as to which action has been deferred by suggestion of the creditor.

A levy for any other purpose than to realize money is fraudulent as against a subsequent execution.

Equitable execution. The appointment of a receiver to take charge of property of an equitable nature.[1]

Execution-creditor. A creditor who has prosecuted his claim to execution; in distinction from a creditor who has obtained a judgment upon which he has not issued, from a mortgage creditor, and from a general creditor, q. v.

Writ of execution. A written command or precept to the sheriff or other ministerial officer, directing him to execute the judgment of the court.[2]

Process authorizing the seizure and appropriation of the property of a defendant for the satisfaction of the judgment against him.[3]

A judicial process, issuing upon some record enrolled in court; as, at common law, to repeal a patent.[4]

Execution is " the end and fruit of the law: " it gives the successful party the fruits of his judgment.[5]

At common law, the officer may be commanded to take — the body of the defendant, his goods, his goods and the profits of his lands, his goods and the possession of his lands, or, his body, goods, and lands.[6]

Property is held by the competent authority which first actually attaches it. This is known as the rule in *Payne* v. *Drewe*.[6] See JURISDICTION, Exclusive.

At common law, all writs of execution were to be sued out within a year and a day after final judgment; otherwise, the judgment was presumed to have been satisfied. By statute, the lien of such judgment may be revived by a *scire facias*,[9] q. v.

All proceedings under a levy of execution have relation to the time of the seizure of the property.[10]

Writs of execution, named from the operative words in them when all kinds of processes were in Latin, are:

Fieri facias (abbreviated *fi. fa.*), that you

[1] Addison, Contr. *2, Am. ed., A. & W. (1883), note.

[2] Wilson v. Jackson, 10 Mo. 337 (1847); State v. Williamson, 57 id. 198 (1874).

[3] 3 Bl. Com. 412; 9 Ohio, 150.

[4] [Lockridge v. Baldwin, 20 Tex. 306 (1857).

[5] Brown v. United States, 6 Ct. Cl. 178 (1870).

[1] Davis v. Gray, 16 Wall. 217–22 (1872), cases.

[2] [Kelley v. Vincent, 8 Ohio St. 420 (1858).

[3] Lambert v. Powers, 36 Iowa, 20 (1872), Beck, C. J.

[4] [Stearns v. Barrett, 1 Mas. 164 (1816). See also Labette County Commissioners v. Moulton, 112 U. S. 223 (1884); 20 Ill. 155; 11 Wend. 635; 9 Ohio, 150.

[5] United States v. Nourse, 9 Pet. *28 (1835).

[6] 3 Bl. Com. 414. See 2 Tidd. Pr. 993.

[7] Taylor v. Carryl, 20 How. 594 (1857), cases; Covell v. Heyman, 111 U. S. 176 (1884), cases.

[8] 4 East, 547 (1804), Ellenborough, C. J.

[9] 3 Bl. Com. 421.

[10] Freeman v. Dawson, 110 U. S. 270 (1883), cases.

cause to be made out of the goods, or lands, or both, the amount of the claim.

Applies to personalty, realty, chattels real, and choses in possession. May be concurrent with an attachment in execution. A single *fieri facias* may exhaust the personalty of the debtor, and an *alias fieri facias* be issued to sell his realty. But an *alias fieri facias* may denote a second or new levy upon either personalty or realty. A sale of realty upon a single *fieri facias* may also be by express authorization from the debtor.[1]

Levari facias (abbreviated *lev. fa.*), that you cause be levied — out of the land specified. Used to collect a charge upon land: as, a mortgage, mechanic's lien, municipal claim, taxes, and the like.

May issue after a *scire facias* has been determined in favor of the creditor, as, after judgment on a *scire facias* upon a mortgage.[1]

Venditioni exponas (abbreviated *vend. ex.*), that you expose for sale — realty embraced in a levy made under a preceding *fieri facias*, and condemned under proceedings in extent, *q. v.*

Regarded as a completion of a previous execution, by which the property is appropriated, not as an original or independent proceeding.[2]

Attachment-execution. Reaches a chose in action, money and other property in the hands of a stranger, to which the defendant has no present right of possession; also called an "execution-attachment." See ATTACH, 2.

Liberari facias, that you cause to be delivered — to the creditor, such portion of the premises, not sold under a previous *levari facias,* as will satisfy the claim, according to the valuation of the inquest, to hold as his own free tenement. See EXTENT, 2.

Elegit, he has chosen. Delivers chattels to the creditor at an appraised value, and, if they are not sufficient, then one-half of the defendant's freehold, till the rents and profits pay the debt.

Then plaintiff "elected" this writ, rather than a *fieri facias,* or a *levari facias,* which last writs gave satisfaction only to the extent of chattels and present profits of lands. Authorized by statute of Westminster 2, c. 18. Prior thereto, possession of land could not be taken, the feudal principle being that service was not transferable to a stranger. The writ is still in use, enlarged or narrowed in operation.[3]

Mandamus-execution. Enforces payment of a judgment against a municipality. See further MANDARE, Mandamus.

Sequestration. Reaches the revenues of a corporation, a life-estate, or the property of an absconding debtor. See SEQUESTRATION, 2.

Capias ad satisfaciendum, that you take for satisfying. Process under which the officer arrests and detains the debtor till the judgment is satisfied. See CAPERE, Capias.

Testatum execution, certifies that the debtor has property in another county. Issues into another county than that in which the record remains. See TESTIS, Testatum.

Writs and processes of execution are: those which point out specifically the thing to be seized, and those which command the officer to make or levy certain sums of money out of the property of a party named. In the first class the officer has no discretion, but must do precisely what he is commanded. Therefore, if the court had jurisdiction to issue the writ it is a protection to the officer. In the second class the officer must determine at his own risk whether the property he proposes to seize is legally liable to be taken. For a mistake he is responsible to the extent of the injury. As to this he exercises judgment and discretion — as to who is the owner of the property, the kind that may be taken, and the quantity.[1]

If a writ be sued out of a court of competent jurisdiction, directing an officer to seize specifically described property, as in admiralty, replevin, or ejectment cases, it is a protection to the officer, when he is sued in trespass for executing it. If, however, it in general terms authorizes him to seize property, without a specific description, he acts at his own risk as regards the ownership of the property.[2]

See JURISDICTION, 2, Concurrent; LEVY, 2; MINISTERIAL, 1; WRIT.

EXECUTOR. He to whom another commits by will the execution of his last will and testament.[3] Feminine form, **executrix**. Correlative, *testator, testatrix*.

He so closely resembles an "administrator" that that term will not amount to a substantial misdescription in a deed or prosecution.[4]

Acting executor. Such executor, of two or more, as actually performs the duties of the trust.

General executor. An executor whose power is unlimited as to time, place, or subject-matter. **Special executor.** An executor who serves for a limited time, in a particular place, or as to a part of the estate.

---

[1] See 3 Bl. Com. 417.

[2] Mitchell *v.* St. Maxent's Lessee, 4 Wall. 243 (1866).

[3] 3 Bl. Com. 418; 2 *id.* 161; 4 Kent, 431, 436; Hutchinson *v.* Grubbs, 80 Va. 254 (1885); 3 Ala. 561; 10 Gratt. 582.

[1] Buck *v.* Colbath, 3 Wall. 343–44 (1865), Miller, J.

[2] Sharp *v.* Doyle, 102 U. S. 689 (1880), Miller, J.

[3] 2 Bl. Com. 503; 1 Ga. 330; 55 Md. 194; 21 Wend. 436; 60 Barb. 175; 5 Hun, 21; 5 Humph. 458.

[4] Sheldon *v.* Smith, 97 Mass. 35–36 (1867), cases; *ib.* 401.

Instituted executor. Has the option to serve before another who is named as substitute — the **substituted executor.**

Rightful executor. The executor named in the will; the lawful executor. **Executor de son tort.** An executor of his own wrong: he who, without authority, does such acts as only the rightful executor may do.

At common law an executor *de son tort* is one who, without authority from the deceased or the court of probate, does such acts as belong to the office of an executor or administrator.[1]

Not unauthorized are, acts of kindness in providing for the family of the deceased or in preserving the estate.[2]

An executor *de son tort* is liable to all the trouble of an executorship without the profits or advantages.[3]

Sole executor. The one person named to serve as executor. **Co-executor, joint-executor.** One of two or more executors.

A wife, with her husband's consent, or a minor over seventeen, or other person of sound mind, may be an executor. He takes title from the will; is a personal representative, identified in interest with the testator; holds the estate in trust for creditors and legatees. His power being founded upon the special confidence the deceased had in him, he is not ordinarily required to furnish security for the faithful performance of the duties of the trust.

He is to do the things set forth in the will: to bury the deceased, prove the will, give notice of letters issued, make an inventory, collect the money and personal effects,[4] pay the debts and legacies, and file an account or accounts.

Contract rights pass to him, but not contract duties of a purely personal nature. He can buy no part of the estate; nor let assets lie unproductive; nor use the estate for his own benefit. He may be surcharged in his accounts.

He is held to the care of a man of ordinary prudence, and to the most scrupulous good faith.

If he honestly exercises a discretion conferred upon him by the will he cannot be held liable for a loss occasioned by an honest error of judgment.[5]

The act of one co-executor is the act of all: each is liable for the other's wrong, effected through negligence or connivance. All sue and are to be sued together. Death vests all rights and duties in the survivor.

The rule is that each co-executor has complete

power to administer the estate. A payment therefore to one is payment to all.[1]

At common law executors have a joint authority and a joint interest in the property of the estate. They are esteemed in law as one person, and, as such, represent the testator, although each may be responsible only for his own acts.[2]

Whether an executor may be imprisoned for not paying over an amount due upon final account, the statutes and decisions of the States are not in accord. In Vermont and South Carolina, though refusal to pay is a contempt of court, imprisonment is not allowed under the constitutional inhibition against imprisonment for debt.[3]

See ADMINISTER, 4; ASSETS; BONA; CHARGE; COMMISSION, 3; DEVASTAVIT; DEVISAVIT; DONATIO; FUNERAL; GOODS; IMPROVIDENT; INVENTORY; LEGACY; LETTERS; PERISHABLE; POWER, 2; PROBATE; REPRESENTATIVE, (1); SETTLE, 4; TRUST, 1; VOUCHER; WITNESS.

EXEMPLARY. See DAMAGES.

EXEMPLIFICATION. An official transcript of a record, for use as evidence.

Primary evidence; in the United States courts, by act of May 26, 1790, which does not exclude other proof and is to be strictly followed. The seal of the court is essential. An exemplification of the record of the record of a deed is admissible; of a foreign will, or grant, may be proven by a certificate.[4] See further COPY; EVIDENCE, Secondary; FAITH, Full, etc.; LOST, 2; RECORD.

EXEMPTION.[5] The privilege of being excepted, excused, or freed from the operation of a law.

Used especially of goods not liable to seizure under the law of distress for rent;[6] of merchandise not subject to duties under the internal revenue laws;[7] of the property of bankrupts and insolvents excepted from sale under execution laws;[8] and of the property of a decedent not subject to administration.

Also, the property itself, in the aggregate.

---

[1] Emery *v.* Berry, 28 N. H. 481 (1854), Eastman, J.

[2] See 29 Minn. 421–22; 17 Ark. 125; 5 Heisk. 194; 26 N. H. 495; 1 Baxt. 9; 30 Conn. 329; 12 Ga. 588; 38 *id.* 264; 26 Me. 361; 8 Miss. 437; 19 Mo. 196.

[3] 2 Bl. Com. 507.

[4] See generally Wall *v.* Bissell, 125 U. S. 387, 389 (1888), cases.

[5] Cooper *v.* Cooper, 77 Va. 203 (1883); 75 *id.* 747; 24 Gratt. 225; 28 *id.* 442; 32 *id.* 262.

---

[1] Stone *v.* Union Sav. Bank, 13 R. I. 25 (1880); 8 Ga. 388; 2 Williams, Exec. 946.

[2] Caskie *v.* Harrison, 77 Va. 94 (1882); Peter *v.* Beverley, 10 Pet. *533, 564 (1836); Wilson's Appeal, 115 Pa. 95 (1887); M'Cormick *v.* Wright, 79 Va. 533 (1884), cases; 24 Cent. Law J. 147 (1887), cases.

See generally Williams, Exec.; Schouler, Ex. & Adm., and Wills; 2 Kent, 409; 1 Pars. Contr. 127; Stacy *v.* Thrasher, 6 How. 58–60 (1848); Hill *v.* Tucker, 13 *id.* 466–67 (1851); Smith *v.* Ayer, 101 U. S. 327 (1879); Colt *v.* Colt, 111 *id.* 581 (1884); Glasgow *v.* Lipse, 117 *id.* 333 (1886); 9 Gratt. 559; 21 *id.* 200, 759.

[3] *Re* Bingham, 32 Vt. 333 (1859); Golson *v.* Holman, Sup. Ct. S. C. (1888): 26 Cent. Law J. 521–22 (1883), cases.

[4] See 2 Whart. Ev. Ch. III, §§ 95–119; 1 Greenl. Ev. § 501; 7 W. Va. 413.

[5] L. *ex-imere*, to take out, remove, free.

[6] 3 Bl. Com. 6.

[7] R. S. § 3187.

[8] R. S. § 5045.

Exempt. Excepted from the burden or operation of law; also, a person so excepted, excused, or relieved.

Exemption laws. Specifically, laws which except a part of a debtor's property from seizure on execution, or other process, as not liable to the payment of his debts.

This property, in its nature and extent, varies in the different States. In some it extends only to the merest implements of household necessity; in others it includes the library of the professional man, however extensive, and the tools of mechanics; and in many it embraces the homestead in which the family resides. The creditor, when he parts with the consideration of his debt, knows that the property so exempt cannot be seized in payment.[1]

Exemption in favor of debtors is favored by liberal interpretations. The exemption law of a State bars an execution on a judgment in favor of the United States.[2]

Exemption laws seek to promote the general welfare of society by taking from the head of a family the power to deprive it of certain property by contracting debts which will enable creditors to take such property in execution. Parties ought not, therefore, to be permitted to contravene the policy of the law by contract.[3]

Waiver of the right, if permitted at all, must be in distinct and unequivocal terms, and not rest upon inference.[4]

Widow's exemption. For the benefit of the widow and children of a decedent.[5]

See AGRICULTURE; EXPRESSIO, Unius, etc.; HEIFER; HOMESTEAD; HORSE; IMMUNITY; IMPLEMENT; PRIVILEGE; TAX, 2; TEAM: TOOL; WAGON; WORKS.

EXEQUATUR. L. Let it be executed, performed, discharged.

1. In French practice, placed at the foot of a judgment obtained in another jurisdiction, authorized execution upon the judgment within the jurisdiction to which it was exemplified.

2. An order issued by the foreign department of a state to which a consul or commercial agent is accredited, that he be permitted to discharge the duties of his appointment.

Consuls on exhibiting proof of their appointment receive an *exequatur*, or permission to discharge their functions within the limits prescribed, which permission can be withdrawn for any misconduct.[1]

EXERCITOR. L. Exerciser: manager.

Exercitor maris. In civil law, he who equips a vessel; in English and American law, the managing owner of a vessel.[2]

EXHIBIT.[3] 1, *v.* To produce, offer, or expose for inspection: as, to exhibit an account, a balance, a bill in equity, a complaint or information, written interrogatories, a bill or note for payment.[4]

2, *n.* A document produced and identified for use as evidence, before a jury, referee, master, or in the course of pleading.

Where there are several such documents it is customary to identify them as "Exhibit A," "B," or A 1, A 2, etc.; and, when produced in evidence, to mark upon them also the date, and the stenographer's or commissioner's name.

A document cannot be proved as an exhibit when it requires more to substantiate it than proof of the execution or of the handwriting.[5]

"Ex. A" was held to mean "Exhibit A."[6]

EXHIBITION. Compare ENTERTAINMENT; LICENSE, 3; PRIZE-FIGHTING.

Unless skating rinks are so conducted as to be clearly shown to be "public performances or exhibitions," they cannot be brought within a statute requiring a license to be taken out for such "performances or exhibitions."[7]

EXIGENCY. Going forth; issuing: mandate; urgency. See EXIRE.

A sheriff must execute a writ addressed and delivered to him, according to its exigency, without inquiring into the regularity of the proceeding.

The "exigency of a bond" refers to the event upon the happening or not happening of which the bond is to become operative, by changing a contingent to an absolute liability.

EXIGENT. See OUTLAWRY.

EXIRE. L. To go away, go out; to issue.

Exit. It has gone forth; it has issued.

The *exit* of a writ means simply the issuing of that particular writ; and the word "exit," as a docket entry, indicates that the writ has in fact been formally issued.

Ne exeat. That he do not depart. A writ in equity practice issued to prevent a

---

[1] Nichols *v.* Eaton, 91 U. S. 726 (1875), Miller, J.

[2] Fink *v.* O'Neil, 106 U. S. 280 (1882), cases; R. S. § 916.

[3] Kneettle *v.* Newcomb, 22 N. Y. 249 (1860); Crawford *v.* Lockwood, 9 How. Pr. 547 (1854); Harper *v.* Leal, 10 *id.* 276 (1854). *Contra*, McKinney *v.* Reader, 6 Watts, 34 (1837); Case *v.* Dunmore, 23 Pa. 93 (1854); 24 *id.* 426; 31 *id.* 225.

[4] O'Nail *v.* Craig, 56 Pa. 161 (1867); Commonwealth *v.* Boyd, *ib.* 402 (1867). Exemptions of personalty, Kansas cases, 2 Kan. Law J. 146–49 (1885), cases.

[5] Hufman's Appeal, 81 Pa. 329 (1876); Nixon's Appeal, 6 W. N. C. 496 (1878).

[1] Woolsey, Intern. Law, § 100; 13 Pick. 528.

[2] See 3 Kent, 161.

[3] L. *ex-hibere*, to hold out or forth.

[4] See 3 Bl. Com. 450; Byles, Bills, 206; 2 Conn. 38.

[5] Lake *v.* Skinner, 1 Jac. & W. 9, 15 (1819); Plunkett *v.* Dillon, 4 Del. Ch. 222 (1871), cases. See generally Commercial Bank *v.* Bank of New York, 4 Hill, 519 (1842).

[6] Dugan *v.* Trisler, 69 Ind. 555 (1880).

[7] Harris *v.* Commonwealth, 81 Va. 240 (1885).

defendant from withdrawing his person and property beyond the jurisdiction of the court before a judgment and execution can be had against him.

In effect, a process to hold to bail, or to compel a party to give security to abide the decree. Not granted in the Federal courts unless a suit in equity is already commenced, and satisfactory proof is made that the defendant designs quickly to depart from the United States.[1]

The full form of the writ is *ne exeat republica;* the original in England was *ne exeat regno* or *regnum.*

The constitutions of the States declare that all persons have a natural right to emigrate from the State.[2]

EXISTING. See Creditor; Pre-existing; Previous; Prior.

"Existing laws," in the saving clause of an act, refers to laws in force at the passage of the act.[3]

EXIT. See Exire, Exit.

EXONERATION; EXONERETUR. See Onus, Exoneretur.

EXP. See Ex, Parte.

EXPATRIATION.[4] Voluntarily leaving one's native or adopted country to become a citizen in another country.

Expatriate. To leave one's country, renouncing allegiance to it, with the purpose of making a home and becoming a citizen in another country.

Includes more, then, than changing one's domicil.[5]

Act of Congress of July 27, 1868, declares that "the right of expatriation is a natural and inherent right of all people, indispensable to the enjoyment of the rights of life, liberty, and the pursuit of happiness;" disavows the claim made by foreign states that naturalized American citizens are still the subjects of such states; and enacts, further, that "any declaration, instruction, opinion, order, or decision of any officer of the United States which denies, restricts, impairs, or questions the right of expatriation, is declared inconsistent with the fundamental principles of the republic."[6]

The right is inalienable, and extends to individuals of the Indian race.[7]

The contrary is the English doctrine, expressed in the maxim *nemo potest exuere patriam.*[8]

---

[1] R. S. § 717; Lewis v. Shainwald, 7 Saw. 416–17 (1881), cases.

[2] 2 Kent, 34; 1 Bl. Com. 266; 2 Story, Eq. §§ 1465–74; 2 Daniel, Ch. Pr. 1698–1714; Adams v. Whitcomb, 46 Vt. 708 (1873).

[3] Lawrie v. State, 5 Ind. 526 (1854). See 63 Ill. 117; 38 Iowa, 215.

[4] L. *ex patria terra*, from one's fatherland.

[5] Ludlam v. Ludlam, 31 Barb. 489 (1860).

[6] R. S. §§ 1999, 2000; 9 Op. Att.-Gen. 356 (1859).

[7] United States, *ex rel.* Standing Bear v. Crook, 5 Dill. 453 (1879).

[8] 2 Kent, 36; Morse, Citizenship, § 179; 21 Am. Law Reg. 69–79 (1873); Canad. Law Times, Oct. 1883.

EXPECTANCY. A present, vested, contingent right to the future enjoyment of land. A future estate; an estate in expectancy, or, simply, an expectant estate or interest.

Expectant. Contingent as to enjoyment; also, the person entitled thereto.

An expectancy is always an estate in remainder, or a reversion. The idea is that the time of enjoyment is postponed — depends upon some subsequent circumstance or contingency. It is an executory estate, as opposed to an estate in actual, present possession — an estate executed.[1]

In New York, any present right or interest which by possibility may vest in possession at a future day.[2]

See Bargain, Catching.

EXPENDITURE. An actual payment of money.

To incur an expenditure is to make a payment, to expend money. To incur a liability and to incur an expenditure are different things.[3]

EXPENSE; EXPENSES. Vary in meaning with the intention of parties and testators, and the circumstances of particular cases.[4] See Costs.

EXPERIMENT. See Invention.

EXPERT.[5] A person instructed by experience.[6]

A skilled or experienced person; a person having skill, experience or peculiar knowledge on certain subjects or in certain professions; a scientific witness.[7]

On questions of science, skill, trade, art or others of like kind, a person of skill, sometimes called an expert, may not only testify to facts, but may give his opinion. His qualification must first be shown to the court.[8]

Whether a witness who is called as an expert has the requisite qualifications to enable him to testify is a preliminary question for the court, the decision of which is conclusive, unless it appears upon the evidence to have been erroneous or to have been founded upon some error in law.[9]

---

[1] [2 Bl. Com. 163.

[2] 1 N. Y. Rev. St. 723, § 10; *ib.* 725, § 35; 7 Paige, 76; 20 Barb. 462. See also 17 F. R. 323; 10 Ohio St. 106; 1 Story, Eq. § 334.

[3] Improvement of South Pass, 16 Op. Att.-Gen. 132 (1878).

[4] See 1 Minn. 48; 1 Cliff. 158; 8 N. J. E. 506; 12 Ct. Cl. 179; 98 E. C. L. 199.

[5] L. *expertus*, practiced, experienced, skilled.

[6] Hyde v. Woolfolk, 1 Iowa, 167, 166 (1855); 2 Best, Ev. 513; 54 Cal. 517.

[7] Heald v. Thing, 45 Me. 394 (1858); Burrill; 52 Me. 77; 41 N. H. 547; 50 *id.* 454; 48 Vt. 377.

[8] Congress, &c. Spring Co. v. Edgar, 99 U. S. 657 (1878), cases, Clifford, J.; 1 Greenl. Ev. § 440; 20 Johns. 75.

[9] Perkins v. Stickney, 132 Mass. 218 (1882).

An expert may be asked his opinion upon a case hypothetically stated, or upon a case in which the facts have been established; but he may not determine from the evidence what the facts are, to give an opinion upon them.[1]

When the subject of a proposed inquiry is not a matter of science but of common observation, upon which the ordinary mind is capable of forming a judgment, an expert may not state his opinion.[2]

An expert testifies as a specialist. He may be examined on foreign laws, and as to scientific authorities. Whether a conclusion belongs to him or not is for the court to say. He may give an opinion as to a condition known in his specialty; as, the opinion of a physician, surgeon, lawyer, scientist, practitioner in a business, artist, one familiar with a market, or with values generally, or cognizant of damage done. On sanity, friends and attendants may give their opinion. An expert may explain his opinion. His testimony is to be jealously scrutinized, particularly when given *ex parte*.[3]

The opinions of witnesses are constantly taken as to the result of their observations on a great variety of subjects. All that is required is that the witnesses should be able properly to make the observations, the result of which they give; and the confidence bestowed on their conclusions will depend upon the extent and completeness of their examination, and the ability with which it is made.[4]

The testimony of an expert has not the weight of testimony from observation. His statements are mere opinions, and entitled to such weight only as his experience justifies.[5]

The weight of authority is that he cannot be compelled to give a professional opinion without compensation.[6]

If specially feed, the jury may consider the effect on his credibility.[7]

See DESIGN, 2; HANDWRITING; INSANITY, 2 (6); INSPECTION, 2; SCIENCE.

EXPLOSION. Sudden and rapid combustion, causing violent expansion of the air, and accompanied by a report.[8]

There is no difference in common use, between "explode" and "burst." . . The ordinary idea is

that "explosion" is the cause, while "rupture" is the effect.[1]

An insurance against "loss or damage by fire" covers a loss arising in part from an explosion and in part from combustion of gunpowder.[2] See FIREWORKS.

EXPORT. To carry away: send out of a country. *Exports:* merchandise sent from one country to another.

As used in the Constitution, Art. 1, secs. 8, 10, does not include articles transported from one State into another.[3] See further IMPORT.

EXPOSE. To set out, bring into view; display, exhibit; show: as, to expose property to sale,[4] to expose the person.[5] See INDECENT.

EXPOSITIO. L. A setting out — the meaning of language; explanation; interpretation.

Contemporanea expositio optima et fortissima in lege. The explanation of the time is the fittest and strongest in law. Contemporaneous interpretation is the most satisfactory.

Words in constitutions, treaties, statutes, — old writings generally, will be given the sense and scope they had with the makers or framers. The courts will not disturb the construction put upon a doubtful law by long usage.[6]

Contemporaneous construction "can never abrogate the text, it can never fritter away its obvious sense, it can never narrow down its true limitations, it can never enlarge its natural boundaries."[7]

The contemporaneous construction of a statute by those charged with its execution, especially when it has long prevailed, is entitled to great weight, and should not be disregarded or overturned except for cogent reasons, and unless it be clear that such construction is erroneous.[8] Compare ERROR, 1, Communis, etc.

---

[1] Evans v. Columbian Ins. Co., 44 N. Y. 151–52 (1870).

[2] Scripture v. Lowell Mut. Fire Ins. Co., 10 Cush. 356 (1852). See also 56 Md. 81; 21 Wend. 367; 3 Phila. 323; 19 C. B. N. S. 126.

[3] *Exp.* Martin, 7 Nev. 142 (1871); Woodruff v. Parham, 8 Wall. 131 (1868).

[4] Adams Express Co. v. Schlessinger, 75 Pa. 256 (1874); 12 Vt. 212.

[5] 2 Bishop, Cr. L. § 318; 46 N. J. L. 16.

[6] Ames v. Kansas, 111 U. S. 464 (1884).

[7] 1 Story, Const. § 407.

[8] United States v. Johnston, 124 U. S. 253 (1888), cases, Harlan, J.; Cohens v. Virginia, 6 Wheat. 418 (1821), Marshall, C. J.; Harrison v. Commonwealth, 83 Ky. 171 (1885); United States v. Saylor, 31 F. R. 548 (1887). See also 5 Cranch, 22; 12 Wheat. 210; 99 U. S. 265; 101 *id.* 461; 107 *id.* 406; 113 *id.* 571, 733; 116 *id.* 622; 31 F. R. 268; 6 Col. 92; 9 *id.* 93; 6 Conn. 89; 119 Ill. 345; 36 Kan. 111; 83 Ky. 103; 17 Mass. *144; 44 N. J. L. 22; 16 Ohio St. 519; 70 Pa. 203; 73 *id.* 84; 94 *id.* 249; 14 S. C. 195; 66 Wis. 468.

---

[1] Dexter v. Hall, 15 Wall. 9, 26 (1872), Strong, J.

[2] Milwaukee, &c. R. Co. v. Kellogg, 94 U. S. 472 (1876), cases; Connecticut Mut. Life Ins. Co. v. Lathrop, 111 *id.* 618 (1884); Carter v. Boehm, 1 Sm. L. C. 286, cases.

[3] 1 Whart. Ev. §§ 434–56, cases.

[4] Hopt v. Utah, 120 U. S. 437–38 (1887), cases.

[5] United States v. Pendergast, 32 F. R. 198 (1887).

[6] 1 Whart. Ev. § 379, cases: Sprague, 276; 5 South. Law Rev. 793–809 (1880), cases; 6 *id.* 706–18 (1880), cases; 12 Cent. Law J. 193 (1881), cases; 21 Am. Law Rev. 571–77 (1887), cases; Medico-Leg. J., Sept., 1883; 59 Ind. 15; 13 Abb. Pr. 207, 240.

[7] 1 Whart. Ev. §§ 456, 380; Harvey v. Packet Co., 8 Biss. 99 (1877). See generally Ware v. Starkey, 80 Va. 204 (1885); 13 Bradw. 343; 70 Iowa, 432, 474; 30 Minn. 411; 2 Utah, 189; 41 N. Y. 547; 43 Pa. 12; 3 Tex. Ap. 157.

[8] United Life, &c. Ins. Co. v. Foote, 22 Ohio St. 348 (1872).

EXPRESS. 1. To declare in terms, state in words, mention distinctly, avow openly.

Express; expressed. Openly uttered and avowed; stated or mentioned in words, oral or written; made known; opposed to *implied:* left to implication or inference; as, express or an express or expressed — abrogation, *assumpsit* or undertaking, condition, consent, consideration, contract, covenant, dedication, malice, repeal, trust, warranty,[1] *qq. v.* See also EXPRESSIO.

(2) Intended for a special service; contracting for expedition in the transportation of packages: as, express — company, business, facilities, matter.

Express car. See BURGLARY, p. 141, *n.* 2.

Express companies are organized to carry small and valuable packages rapidly, in such manner as not to subject them to the danger of loss and damage which attends the transportation of heavy and bulky articles of commerce.[2] See PACKAGE.

Express companies are common carriers. Originally formed to transport money, treasure, and other valuables, they have become carriers of goods and merchandise generally.[3]

Before railroads came into use, common carriers by land delivered parcels to the consignees. Railway companies were held bound only to carry goods to their destination, and put them safely in a warehouse. To remedy this defect in the railway transportation of packages of great value in small compass, express companies were instituted. They undertake to deliver to the consignee in person.[4]

The style "express forwarders" does not necessarily make them simple forwarders.[5]

What they are is to be determined by the nature of their business, not by contracts made respecting their liability.[6]

Express business. Involves the idea of regularity, as to route or time, or both. In the act of June 30, 1864, § 104 (13 St. L. 276), does not cover what is done by a person who carries goods at special request, not running regular trips nor on regular routes.[7]

---

[1] See 2 Bl. Com. 443; 101 U. S. 670.

[2] Southern Express Co. *v.* St. Louis, &c. R. Co., 10 F. R. 213 (1882), Miller, J. See 2 Redf. Railw. 15, Carriers, 50, § 38: American Union Express Co. *v.* Robinson, 72 Pa. 278 (1872).

[3] Southern Express Co. *v.* Cook, 44 Ala. 473 (1870).

[4] 2 Redf. Railw. 21; United States Express Co. *v.* Backman, 28 Ohio St. 151 (1875).

[5] Christenson *v.* American Express Co., 15 Minn. 283 (1870).

[6] Bank of Kentucky *v.* Adams Express Co., 93 U. S. 181-85 (1876).

[7] Retzer *v.* Wood, 109 U. S. 187 (1883).

The regulation of the business of an express company upon the property of a railroad company, in the absence of legislation, is for the parties themselves to determine. . . In a few States, by recent statutes or by judicial interpretation, railroad companies are required to furnish equal facilities to all express companies desiring to use their property. . . But the reason is obvious why special contracts are necessary. The transportation required is of a kind which must, if possible, be had for the most part on passenger trains. It requires not only speed. but reasonable certainty as to the quantity that will be carried at one time. As the things carried are to be kept in the personal custody of the messenger of the express company, a certain amount of car space must be set apart, and, as far as practicable, be put in the exclusive possession of the expressman in charge. As the business to be done is "express" it implies access to the train for loading at the latest, and for unloading at the earliest, convenient moment. All this is inconsistent with the idea of an express business on trains free to all express carriers. Passenger trains are primarily for the transportation of passengers and their baggage. This must be done with reasonable promptness and comfort to the passenger. The express business is in a degree subordinate to the passenger business, and it is consequently the duty of the railroad company in arranging for the express to see that there is as little interference as possible with the wants of passengers. This implies a special understanding as to the amount of car space that will be afforded, and the conditions on which it is to be occupied, the particular trains that can be used, the places at which they shall stop, the price to be paid, etc. It by no means follows that because a railroad company can serve one express company in one way it can as well serve another company in the same way. . . As long as the public are served to their reasonable satisfaction, it is a matter of no importance who serves them. The railroad company performs its whole duty when it affords the public all reasonable express accommodations. The company may choose its own means of carriage, always provided they are such as to insure reasonable promptness and security.[1]

See CARRIER, Common.

EXPRESSIO. L. Definite statement or enumeration; expression.

Expressio unius, exclusio alterius. The statement of one thing is the exclusion of another. Sometimes put, *inclusio unius,* etc.,— "including one excludes all others."[2] Still another form is, **expressum facit cessare tacitum:** the expressed controls the

---

[1] Express Cases: Railroad Companies (Memphis & L., St. Louis, I. M. & S., and Missouri, K. & T.) *v.* Express Companies (Southern and Adams), 117 U. S. 1, 23 (1886), Waite, C. J. Commented on, Pfister *v.* Central Pacific R. Co., 70 Cal. 183 (1886). See also 57 Me. 194; 115 Mass. 416; 4 Brewst. 563. *Contra,* 2 F. R. 465; 3 *id.* 593, 775; 4 *id.* 481; 6 *id.* 427; 8 *id.* 799; 10 *id.* 213, 869; 15 *id.* 568; 18 *id.* 671, 672; 19 *id.* 21.

[2] 12 F. R. 414; 6 Col. 83, 94.

unmentioned; an unequivocal statement prevails over an implication.[1]

Express mention of one act, condition, stipulation, class or number, person or place, implies the exclusion of another or others not mentioned. The maxim restricts what is implied by what is expressed, what is general by what is particular and specific.[2]

The mode provided in a constitution for its amendment is the only mode in which it can be amended. The ordinary rule is, that where power is given to do a thing in a particular way, there affirmative words, marking out the way, by implication prohibit all other ways.[3]

It would have been impracticable for the framers of the Constitution to have enumerated all the means by the use of which the powers expressly conferred upon the government of the United States should be exercised. A sovereign must have a choice of means by which to exercise sovereign powers.[4] See NECESSITY.

Offenses not mentioned in a treaty of extradition are excluded from its operation.[5]

A special provision in an act for levying a tax of a fixed per centum excludes the levy of a higher, although necessary, tax.[6]

The creation of specific means for exercising powers of municipal government excludes all other means.[7]

The charter of a corporation is the measure of its powers, and the enumeration of those powers implies the exclusion of others.[8]

A general statement of the duties for which a bond is given will be construed to include only such other duties of the same kind as were not specifically enumerated.[9]

The expression, in a policy of insurance, that a vessel should proceed to a port in Cuba and thence to Europe, implies that she should visit no other port in Cuba.[10]

An express guaranty of a bill or note cannot be converted into an indorsement.[11]

Where a party specifies an objection to the admission of evidence it must be considered that he waives or has no ground for other objections.[12]

The maxims express the principle of the rule that excludes such parol testimony as would vary the terms of a written instrument.

They also serve to prevent fraud and perjury.[13]

They are never more applicable than when applied to the interpretation of a statute.[1]

See INCIDENT; REMEDY; SURPLUSAGE.

EXPRESSIONS, GENERAL. See CONSTRUCTION; DICTUM, 2; EXPRESSIO, Unius, etc.; OPINION, 3.

EXPULSION. See AMOTION; FRANCHISE, Disfranchise; EVICTION.

EXPUNGE. See ALTER, 2; CANCEL; SCANDAL, 2.

EXPURGATORY. See OATH.

EXTEND. To stretch or lengthen out; to continue, enlarge, expand. Compare ENLARGE; EXTENT; RENEW.

To extend a charter is to give one which now exists greater or longer time in which to operate than that to which it was originally limited.[2]

In its primary sense, when applied to a railroad track or other line, may import a continuation of the line without a break. But power to authorize a railway "to extend the location of its tracks" may be held to include the location of an additional track, not connected with existing tracks except by those of another corporation.[3]

For proper cause shown, a court will usually extend the time within which a thing was previously directed to be done; as, the taking of testimony.[4]

Extension. Imports the continuance of an existing thing.[5]

Since the act of March 2, 1861, c. 88 (12 St. L. 249), patents are granted for the term of seventeen years, and further extension is forbidden, except as to designs.[6]

In the construction of statutes a term of an inferior class will not be extended to a superior class. See GENERAL, 6.

Creditors extend, that is, increase the time of payment of their claims, by agreeing to wait a certain time after the claims become due.

EXTENT. 1. In common parlance, varies somewhat in meaning according to the subject to which it is applied, and as that changes, it may as well refer to time as to

---

[1] 71 Ala. 87; 82 *id.* 629; 62 Cal. 639; 4 Wash. C. C. 185.

[2] Broom, Max. 651, 664.

[3] *Re* Constitutional Convention, 14 R. I. 651 (1883), cases. See also Smith v. Stevens, 10 Wall. 326 (1870).

[4] 2 Story, Const, § 1243.

[5] United States v. Rauscher, 119 U. S. 420 (1886).

[6] United States v. County of Macon, 99 U. S. 590 (1878).

[7] Mayor of Nashville v. Ray, 19 Wall. 475 (1873).

[8] Thomas v. West Jersey R. Co., 101 U. S. 82 (1879).

[9] South v. Maryland, 18 How. 402 (1855).

[10] Hearne v. Marine Ins. Co., 20 Wall. 493 (1874).

[11] Central Trust Co. v. Nat. Bank of Wyandotte, 101 U. S. 70 (1879).

[12] Evanston v. Gunn, 99 U. S. 665 (1878).

[13] See Smith v. McCullough, 104 U. S. 25 (1881); 109 *id.*

628; 18 Ct. Cl. 117, 457; 31 F. R. 220; 32 *id.* 50, 554; 4 Del. Ch. 135; 66 Ga. 108; 87 Ind. 291; 59 Iowa, 77; 36 Kan. 637; 34 La. An. 225; 98 Mass. 29; 117 *id.* 448; 10 Minn. 113; 30 *id.* 297; 44 N. J. L. 45; 3 N. Mex. 56; 73 N. Y. 440; 59 Pa. 178; 71 *id.* 88, 429; 75 *id.* 63, 125, 501; 80 *id.* 412; 19 S. C. 147; 80 Va. 327, 373, 374; 60 Wis. 252; 62 *id.* 41; 66 *id.* 382, 565; 67 *id.* 89; L. R., 3 Exch. 177; 2 Pars. Cont., 6 ed., 515 (r, t).

[1] Coast-Line R. Co. v. City of Savannah, 30 F. R. 649 (1887).

[2] Moers v. City of Reading, 21 Pa. 201 (1853).

[3] South Boston R. Co. v. Middlesex R. Co., 121 Mass. 489 (1877), Morton, J. See also Volmer's Appeal, 115 Pa. 166 (1887); 19 W. N. C. 133.

[4] See James v. McMillan, 55 Mich. 136 (1884).

[5] Brooke v. Clarke, 1 B. & Al. *403 (1818).

[6] See R. S. § 4924.

space, or proportion; especially so, when applied to interests, as in patents, for a particular term of years.[1]

2. At common law, a writ of execution by which the defendant's body, lands, and goods may all be taken at once, to compel payment of a debt. At present, concerns lands only.

Originally enforced a recognizance or debt acknowledged on a statute merchant or staple. The sheriff caused the lands and tenements to be appraised to their full "extended" value that it might be known how soon the debt would be satisfied.[2] Compare STATUTE, Merchant.

Sometimes denotes a writ by which the creditor may obtain possession of the debtor's land till the debt be paid.[3] See INQUEST, Of lands.

EXTENUATION. See AGGRAVATION.

EXTINGUISH.[4] To put out or quench: to destroy, annihilate; to pay in full, satisfy: as, to extinguish a debt, an estate, a right to rent, a right of way, the rights of a corporation.

Extinguishment. Whenever a right, title or interest is destroyed or taken away by the act of God, operation of law, or act of the party.[5]

Extinguishing one debt by substituting another is always a question of intention.[6]

See RELEASE; MERGER, 1; SATISFY, 2.

EXTORTION.[7] That abuse of public justice which consists in an officer's unlawfully taking, by color of his office, from any man, any money or thing of value that is not due to him, or more than is due, or before it is due.[8] Whence extorsively.

Obtaining money or other valuable thing by compulsion, actual force, or the force of motives applied to the will.[9]

The wrongful exaction of money. The law, at the time of payment, creates an obligation to refund. Notice to refund is not necessary, therefore, unless to serve to rebut the inference that the payment was voluntary or made through mistake.[10]

---

[1] Wilson v. Rousseau, 4 How. 698 (1846).

[2] 3 Bl. Com. 420.

[3] See 1 Troub. & H. (Pa.) § 1222.

[4] L. extinguere, to quench.

[5] Moultrie v. Smiley, 16 Ga. 343 (1854): 3 Bac. Abr.; 20 Ga. 403; 4 McCord, 101; 28 N. J. L. 20.

[6] Potter v. McCoy, 26 Pa. 452, 460 (1856). See 3 W. & S. 277; 4 Watts, 379; 6 Fla. 25; 35 N. H. 421; 12 Barb. 128; 29 Vt. 488.

[7] L. extorquere, to twist or wring out.

[8] 4 Bl. Com. 141; 6 Cow. 663.

[9] [Commonwealth v. O'Brien, 12 Cush. 90 (1853), Shaw, Chief Justice.

[10] United States Bank v. Bank of Washington, 6 Pet. *19 (1832). See also 3 Saw. 474; 14 F. R. 597; 35 Ark.

No public officer may take other fees or rewards than such as are given by virtue of some statute.[1]

The taking or obtaining of anything from another by a public officer by means of illegal compulsion or oppressive exaction. The offense, by § 3169, Rev. St., is the same as extortion at common law.[2]

Compare EXACTION; BLACKMAIL; OPPRESSION. See PAYMENT, Involuntary; PROTEST, 1.

EXTRA. A Latin preposition and adverb, contracted from extera (parte): exter, or exterus, outward: ex, out.

1. On the outside: outside; without; beyond.

2. Except; besides.

3. In extra costs, extra services, extra wages, and the noun extras, supposed to be an abbreviation of "extraordinary:" beyond what is common, additional to what is due or expected.

See Dermott v. Jones, under CONTRACT, Executed.

Extra-dotal. Beyond dower. See DOTAL.

Extra-hazardous. Specially risky. See HAZARD.

Extra-judicial. Beyond the jurisdiction; not judicial; outside of, or out of, court: as, an extra-judicial — act, admission, decision, oath. See JUDGE; JUDICIAL.

Extra-official. Outside the duties of an office, q. v.

Extra-territorial. Beyond the territory, q. v.

EXTRACT. See COPY; ESTREAT; EVIDENCE, Secondary; REVIEW, 3.

EXTRADITION.[3] Surrender, by one government to another, of a person who has fled to the territory of the former to escape arrest and punishment under the criminal laws of the latter. Whence extradite, extraditable, non-extraditable.

International or **foreign extradition.** Exists between independent nations. **Inter-State extradition.** Exists between individual States of the same nation or union.

For a crime committed against the law of a State, extradition of the offender from a foreign country must be negotiated through the Federal government, conformably to the existing treaty.

1. As between nations, the surrender of a fugitive is a matter of conventional arrange-

---

442: 2 Bish. Cr. L. § 390; 4 Conn. 480; 2 Sneed, 162; 7 Pick. 287.

[1] R. S. §§ 3169, 5481: United States v. Waitz, 3 Saw. 474 (1875).

[2] United States v. Deaver, 14 F. R. 597 (1882), Dick, District Judge.

[3] L. ex-tradere, to deliver over.

ment, not a matter of right. The obligation is not imposed by the law of nations. Deliveries not provided for by treaty stipulation have been made in many cases, but always upon the principle of comity.[1]

The trespass of a kidnaper, unauthorized by either government, is not a case provided for in the treaties hitherto made, and the remedy for the trespass is by a proceeding by the government whose law he may have violated, or by the party injured. How far a forcible transfer, made with no reference to the existing treaty, may be set up against the right to try the accused, is for the State court to decide: it presents no question upon which the Supreme Court can review the decision.[2]

Treaties have been made between the United States and the following foreign states, for crimes specified and defined in the treaties themselves respectively:

Great Britain, Aug. 9, 1842 (8 St. L. 576).

France, Nov. 9, 1843 (8 St. L. 582); Feb. 24, 1845 (*ib.* 617); Feb. 10, 1858 (11 *id.* 741).

Hawaiian Islands, Dec. 20, 1849 (9 St. L. 981).

Swiss Confederation, Nov. 25, 1850 (11 St. L. 587).

Prussia and Germanic Confederation, June 16, 1852 (10 St. L. 964); Nov. 16, 1852 (*ib.* 964).

Bavaria, Sept. 12, 1853 (10 St. L. 1022).

Hanover, Jan. 18, 1855 (10 St. L. 1138).

Two Sicilies, Oct. 1, 1855 (11 St. L. 651).

Austria, July 3, 1856 (11 St. L. 691); re-declared Sept. 20, 1870 (17 *id.* 835).

Baden, Jan. 30, 1857 (11 St. L. 713); re-declared July 19, 1868 (16 *id.* 733).

Sweden and Norway, March 21, 1860 (12 St. L. 1125).

Venezuela, Aug. 27, 1860 (12 St. L. 1143).

Mexico, Dec. 11, 1861 (12 St. L. 1199); re-declared July 10, 1868 (15 *id.* 688).

Hayti, Nov. 3, 1864 (13 St. L. 711).

Dominican Republic, Feb. 8, 1867 (15 St. L. 473).

Italy, March 23, 1868 (11 St. L. 629); Jan. 21, 1869 (16 *id.* 767); June 11, 1884 (24 *id.* 1001).

Salvador, May 23, 1870 (18 St. L. 693, 796).

Nicaragua, June 25, 1870 (17 St. L. 815).

Peru, Sept. 12, 1870 (18 St. L. 719).

Orange Free State, Dec. 22, 1871 (18 St. L. 751).

Ecuador, June 28, 1872 (18 St. L. 756).

Belgium, March 19, 1874 (18 St. L. 804); June 13, 1882 (22 *id.* 972).

Ottoman Empire, Aug. 11, 1874 (19 St. L. 572).

Spain, Jan. 5, 1877 (19 St. L. 650); Aug. 7, 1882 (22 *id.* 991).

Netherlands, May 22, 1880 (21 St. L. 709).

Luxemburg, Oct. 29, 1883 (23 St. L. 808).

Japan, April 29, 1886 (24 St. L. 1015).[1]

Treaties have also been made with Indian tribes by which they stipulate to surrender persons accused of crime against the laws of the United States; and some provide for the mutual extradition of offenders.[2]

Treaties also provide for the mutual surrender of deserting seamen.

Most of the treaties prescribe the evidence required to authorize an order of extradition.

. All hearings under treaty stipulation or convention shall be held on land, publicly, and in a room or office easily accessible to the public.[3] . . On the hearing of any case, upon affidavit being filed by the person charged, that he cannot safely go to trial without certain witnesses, what he expects to prove by each of them, that he is not possessed of sufficient means and is actually unable to pay the fees of such witnesses, the judge or commissioner before whom the hearing is had may order that they be subpœnæd; the costs to be paid as similar fees are paid in the case of witnesses subpœnæd in behalf of the United States.[4] . . Fees and costs shall be certified to the secretary of state of the United States, who shall authorize payment of the same out of the appropriation to defray the expenses of the judiciary, and shall cause the amount to be reimbursed by the foreign government by whom the proceeding may have been instituted.[5] . Where any depositions, warrants, or other papers or copies thereof shall be offered in evidence upon the hearing of any case, the same shall be received as evidence for all the purposes of such hearing if they shall be legally authenticated so as to entitle them to be received for similar purposes by the tribunals of the foreign country from which the accused shall have escaped, and the certificate of the principal diplomatic or consular officer of the United States resident in such foreign country shall be proof that any deposition, warrant, or other paper or copies thereof, so offered, are authenticated in the manner required by this act.[6]

The complaint made before the United States commissioner should show on its face that he who makes it is a representative of the foreign government.[7]

---

[1] *Re* Metzgar, 5 How. 188 (1847); United States *v.* Davis, 2 Sumn. 482 (1837); United States *v.* Rauscher, 119 U. S. 411 (1886); 12 Blatch. 391; 59 N. H. 110; 14 How. 112; 16 Alb. Law J. 444; 1 Kent, 36; Woolsey, Int. Law, §§ 77–80.

[2] Ker *v.* Illinois, 119 U. S. 436 (Dec. 6, 1886), Miller, J. Ker, who was charged with larceny in Cook county, Illinois, fled to South America. He was apprehended in Peru by one Julian (who had proper extradition papers), forcibly placed on board the United States vessel Essex, transferred at Honolulu to the City of Sydney, carried to San Francisco, and thence taken to Cook county, where he was convicted and sentenced. Same case, 110 Ill. 627; 51 Am. R. 706; 35 Alb. Law J. 69.

As to abducting an escaped criminal from another State, see Mahon *v.* Justice, Jailer, etc., 127 U. S. 700 (1888), in which case Mahon, residing in West Virginia, was, by persons acting as private citizens, forcibly and without process conveyed back to Kentucky, to be tried for murder. The circuit court of Kentucky, and, later, the Supreme Court of the United States, refused to discharge the accused upon a writ of *habeas corpus*.

[1] See generally R. S. §§ 5270–80; 23 Cent. Law J. 247 (1886) — London Times.

[2] See 11 St. L. 612, 703.

[3] Act 3 August, 1882, sec. 1: 22 St. L. 215.

[4] *Ibid.*, sec. 3.

[5] *Ibid.*, sec. 4.

[6] *Ibid.*, sec. 5. Sec. 2 prescribes the fees to be paid to commissioners. Sec. 6 repeals Act 19 June, 1876: R. S. § 5271.

[7] *Re* Herris, 32 F. R. 583 (1887).

Most of the treaties exclude "political offenses" from their operation, that is, offenses incidental to and forming part of a political disturbance.[1]

Some treaties also provide that a citizen or subject of the country on which the demand is made shall not be surrendered.

Under the Ashburton Treaty of 1842, between Great Britain and the United States, a fugitive who has been surrendered to this country cannot lawfully be tried for any other offense than that for which he was extradited — at least until he has had an opportunity to return to the country from which he was taken. National honor requires that good faith be kept in this regard.[2]

Act of 33 and 34 Vict. (1870) c. 52, sec. 3, provides that a fugitive shall not be surrendered to a foreign state unless provision is made "by the law of that state, or by arrangement," that, "until he has been restored or had an opportunity of returning to her Majesty's dominions," he shall not "be detained or tried in that foreign state for any offense committed prior to his surrender, other than the extradition crime."[3]

2. Extradition as between the States, Territories, and the District of Columbia, is regulated by the Constitution and by statutes. The former provides that "A Person charged in any State with Treason, Felony, or other Crime, who shall flee from Justice, and be found in another State, shall on Demand of the executive Authority of the State from which he fled, be delivered up, to be removed to the State having Jurisdiction of the Crime."[4]

The words "treason, felony, or other crime" embrace every act forbidden and made punishable by a law of the State. The words "treason and felony" were introduced to guard against any restriction of the word "crime," and to prevent the provision from being construed by the rules and usages of independent nations in compacts for delivering up fugitives from justice. According to these usages, even where the obligation to deliver the fugitive was admitted, persons who fled on account of "political offenses" were almost always excepted; and the nation upon

which the demand is made also uniformly exercises a discretion in weighing the evidence of the crime, and the character of the offense. . . And as the States, although united as one nation for certain specified purposes, are yet, as far as concerns their internal government, separate sovereignties, independent of each other, it was deemed necessary to show, by the terms used, that this compact was not to be regarded as an ordinary treaty for extradition between nations altogether independent of each other, but was intended to embrace political offenses against the sovereignty of the State, as well as all other crimes. And as treason was "felony" it was necessary to insert those words, to show, in language that could not be mistaken, that political offenders were included in it. For this was a compact binding the States to aid each other in executing their laws and preserving order within their respective confines. . . As early as 1643, certain plantations in New England pledged themselves to deliver up fugitives from justice found within their borders. The advantages derived from this compact doubtless suggested the introduction into the Articles of Confederation of the provision that "If any person guilty of, or charged with treason, felony, or other high misdemeanor in any State, shall flee from justice, and be found in any of the United States, he shall upon demand of the Governor or Executive power, of the State from which he fled, be delivered up and removed to the State having jurisdiction of the offense. Full faith and credit shall be given in each of these States to the records, acts and judicial proceedings of the courts and magistrates of every other State." (Art. IV, sec. 2-3.) The colonies, having learned from experience the necessity of this provision for the internal safety of each of them, and to promote concord and harmony among all their members, incorporated it in the Constitution substantially in the same words, but substituting the word "crime" for "high misdemeanor," thereby showing the deliberate purpose to include every offense known to the law of the State from which the party charged had fled. . . The compact gives the right to the executive authority of the State to demand the fugitive from the executive authority of the State in which he is found. The right to "demand" implies that it is an absolute right; and it follows that there must be a correlative obligation to deliver, without reference to the character of the crime charged, or to the policy or laws of the State to which the fugitive has fled. This is the construction put upon this Article in the act of Congress of 1793, a statute passed by many who had been framers of the Constitution.

If the duty of providing by law the regulations necessary to carry the compact into execution had been left to the States, each State might have required different proof to authenticate the judicial proceeding upon which its demand was to be founded; and as the duty of the governor of the State in which the fugitive is found is merely ministerial, without the right to exercise either executive or judicial discretion, he could not lawfully issue a warrant to arrest an individual without a law of the State or of Congress to authorize it. These difficulties presented themselves in 1791, in a demand by the governor of Pennsylvania upon the governor of Virginia, and both of them

[1] 2 Steph. Hist. Cr. L. Eng. 70; 2 Law Quar. Rev. 177–87 (1886), cases; Kentucky v. Dennison, post.

[2] United States v. Rauscher, 119 U. S. 411–33 (Dec. 6, 1886), cases, Miller, J.; Waite, C. J., dissenting. Same case, 26 Am. Law Reg. 241–46 (1887), cases; 25 Cent. Law J. 267 (1887); 35 Alb. Law J. 204–8 (1887), cases, S. T. Spear. See also 19 Cent. Law J. 22–24 (1884), cases. Evidence under treaty with Great Britain, Exp. McPhun, 30 F. R. 57 (1887). Our state department and extradition, 20 Am. Law Rev. 540 (1886).

[3] See also Exp. Coy, 32 F. R. 911 (1887), Turner, J.; ib. 917, cases; Re Miller, 23 id. 32 (1885), cases. Clarke, Extrad. XXXVI; Spear, Inten. Extrad. 158–59; 14 Alb. Law J. 85–99 (1876); 6 Can. Law J. 227; 8 Blatch. 131. See generally 10 Am. Law Rev. 617 (1876); 17 id. 315–49 (1883).

[4] Constitution, Art. IV, sec. 2, cl. 2.

brought the subject before the President, who immediately submitted the matter to the consideration of Congress. This led to the act of February 12, 1793. Difficulty as to authenticating the judicial proceeding was removed by the Article in the Constitution which declares that "Full Faith and Credit shall be given in each State to the public Acts, Records, and judicial Proceedings of every other State. And the Congress may by general Laws prescribe the Manner in which such Acts, Records, and Proceedings shall be proved, and the Effect thereof." (Art. IV, sec. 1.) The provision for the delivery of fugitives was doubtless in mind when this power was given to Congress.

The act of 1793, as re-enacted in the Revised Statutes, reads as follows: "Sec. 5278. Whenever the executive authority of any State or Territory demands any person as a fugitive from justice of the executive authority of any State or Territory to which such person has fled, and produces a copy of the indictment found or an affidavit made before a magistrate of any State or Territory, charging the person demanded with having committed treason, felony, or other crime, certified as authentic by the governor or chief magistrate of the State or Territory from whence the person so charged has fled, it shall be the duty of the executive authority of the State or Territory to which such person has fled to cause him to be arrested and secured, and to cause notice of the arrest to be given to the executive authority making such demand, or to the agent of such authority appointed to receive the fugitive, and to cause the fugitive to be delivered to such agent when he shall appear. If no such agent appears within six months from the time of the arrest, the prisoner may be discharged. All costs or expenses incurred in apprehending, securing, and transmitting such fugitive to the State or Territory making such demand shall be paid by such State or Territory." "Sec. 5279. Any agent, so appointed, who receives the fugitive into his custody, shall be empowered to transport him to the State or Territory from which he fled. And every person who, by force, sets at liberty or rescues the fugitive from such agent while so transporting him, shall be fined not more than five hundred dollars, or imprisoned not more than one year." (1 St. L. 302, ch. 7, §§ 1, 2.)

The judicial acts which are necessary to authorize the demand are plainly specified in the foregoing enactment; and the certificate of the executive authority is made conclusive as to their verity when presented to the executive of the State where the fugitive is found. He has no right to look behind them, or to question them, or to look into the character of the crime specified in the judicial proceeding. His duty is merely ministerial — to cause the party to be arrested and delivered to the agent of the State where the crime was committed. The words "it shall be the duty" were not used as mandatory and compulsory, but as declaratory of the moral duty which the compact between the United States and each State created, when Congress had provided the mode of carrying it into execution. There is no power delegated to the general government to use coercive means to compel the governor of a State to discharge his duty in this respect.[1]

<hr>

[1] Commonwealth of Kentucky v. Dennison, Gov-

It is within the power of each State, except as her authority may be limited by the Constitution, to declare what shall be offenses against her laws, and citizens of other States, when within her jurisdiction, are subject to those laws. In recognition of this right, the words of the clause in reference to fugitives from justice were made sufficiently comprehensive to include every offense against the demanding State, without exception as to the nature of the crime. The demand may be made upon the governor of a Territory. Upon the executive of the State in which the accused is found, rests the responsibility of determining, in some legal mode, whether he is a fugitive from the justice of the demanding State. He does not fail in his duty if he makes it a condition precedent to surrender that it be shown by competent proof that the accused is in fact a fugitive from such State.[1]

The accused is entitled to have the lawfulness of his arrest inquired into, by a court of the State or of the United States, by a writ of *habeas corpus*. . . It must appear to the governor of the State on whom the demand is made that the person demanded is substantially charged with a crime against the laws of the demanding State, by an indictment or an affidavit, certified as authentic by the governor of the latter State; and that the person is really a fugitive from the justice of that State. The first of these prerequisites is a question of law, always open upon the face of the papers to judicial inquiry, on an application for a discharge. The second is a question of fact, which the governor upon whom the demand is made must decide, upon such evidence as he may deem satisfactory. A certified copy of the law alleged to have been broken need not be furnished. The courts of the United States take judicial notice of the laws of all the States. To be a "fugitive from justice" it is not necessary that the accused should have left the State after an indictment found, or to avoid a prosecution anticipated or begun, but simply that, having within a State committed that which by its laws constitutes a crime, when he is sought to be subjected to its criminal process to answer for his offense, he has left its jurisdiction and is found within the territory of another.[2]

<hr>

ernor of Ohio, 24 How. 66, 99–110 (1860), Taney, C. J. This was a motion for a rule on Dennison to show cause why a *mandamus* should not be issued by the Supreme Court, commanding him to cause one Lago to be surrendered to the authorities of Kentucky. Lago, a free man of color, after being indicted for assisting a slave to escape, fled to Ohio. The governor of that State, on the advice of the attorney-general, refused to deliver up the fugitive, on the ground that the act for which Lago was indicted was neither "treason," nor "felony" nor any "other crime," either at common law or under the laws of Ohio.

[1] *Exp.* Reggel, 114 U. S. 642, 650, 652 (1885), Harlan, J. Reggel was indicted in Pennsylvania for obtaining goods by false pretenses, and fled to Utah.

[2] Roberts v. Reilly, 116 U. S. 80, 94–97 (1885), Matthews, J. Roberts petitioned the District Court for the Southern District of Georgia for a discharge, alleging that he was illegally restrained of his liberty by Reilly, agent of the State of New York, in which

A State may legislate in aid of the enactments of Congress.[1] And, as seen above, the courts of a State may pass upon the legality of an arrest.[2]

The provision is a national police regulation.[3]

See FUGITIVE; REQUISITION; EXPRESSIO, Unius, etc.

EXTRAORDINARY. 1. The utmost; the highest under the circumstances: as, extraordinary care or diligence. See CARE; NEGLIGENCE.

2. Out of the common order; not usual or regular: as, extraordinary jurisdiction, remedies. See CHANCERY, 1; MINISTER, 3.

Poverty or financial embarrassment is not an "extraordinary circumstance," within the meaning of a statute excusing laches in proceeding with a cause.[4]

As between ship-owner and insurer, the former is bound to provide against *ordinary*, while the latter insures against *extraordinary* perils. By "extraordinary" is not meant what has never been previously heard of, or is within former experience, but what is beyond the ordinary, usual, or common.[5]

EXTRAVAGANT. See IMPROVIDENT; SPENDTHRIFT.

EXTREME. See CRUELTY; PENALTY.

EXTREMIS. See IN EXTREMIS.

EXTRINSIC. See EVIDENCE.

EYE. See MAYHEM; SECURITY, Personal.

F.

F. 1. Was anciently branded upon the ear or face of a person guilty of falsity, fighting, or of a felony admitted to clergy.

Abolished by 7 and 8 Geo. IV (1827), c. 28, s. 6.

2. Stands for words sometimes abbreviated: as, first, French.

F. F. *Fieri facias.* See EXECUTION, 3, Writs of.

F. J. First judge or justice.

Roberts stood indicted for the larceny of railroad bonds.

[1] *Exp.* Ammons, 34 Ohio St. 518 (1878); Wilcox v. Nolz, *ib.* 520 (1878), cases.

[2] Robb v. Connolly, 111 U. S. 624, 637 (1884).

[3] See generally *Re* Leary, 10 Bened. 203, 205–22 (1879); 18 Blatch. 430; 8 Law. 370; 2 Flip. 183; 16 F. R. 93; 7 Op. Att.-Gen. 6; 8 *id.* 306, 396, 521; 63 Ind. 344; 50 Iowa, 106; 34 Ohio St. 71–79; 4 Tex. Ap. 662; 60 Wis. 594; 18 Alb. Law J. 146–51; 2 West Coast Rep. 599.

Rules proposed by Inter-State Conference, 36 Alb. Law J. 220 (Sept. 10, 1887). The new extradition bill, 37 *id.* 88–93 (1888), A. T. Spear.

[4] Whalen *v.* Sheridan, 10 F. R. 662 (1880); Müller *v.* Ehlers, 91 U. S. 251 (1875).

[5] Moses *v.* Sun Mut. Ins. Co., 1 Duer, 170 (1852); The Titania, 19 F. R. 105 (1883).

FABRICATE. In a statute against "fabricating" a voting paper, imports an act done with criminal intent; implies fraud or falsehood, a false or fraudulent concoction, by one knowing that it is wrong and contrary to law.[1] Compare FORGE, 2.

FAC. See FACERE.

FACE. 1. As a thing is made: impression; expression; appearance, *q. v.:* as, the face of a bill, bond, note, check, draft, judgment, record.

A purchaser must look at the face of a bond,[2] *q. v.*

A contract, on its face, may be *ultra vires.*[3]

2. The sum, less interest, which appears to be due by an instrument or record: as, the face of a judgment.[4]

3. Presence; sight; front; view: as, for parties or witnesses to meet face to face; that is, front to front, and, perhaps, facing the court or jury. See CONFRONT; CONTEMPT.

4. Mere appearance or aspect; phase; semblance, likeness: as, an act intended to give an honest face to a transaction. See INTENTION.

FACERE. L. To make, do, perform. Compare FIERI.

Fac simile. Made like in appearance; a copy.

Said of counterfeits, designs, signatures, trademarks, *qq. v.*

Facias. That you make or cause to be made. See EXECUTION, 3, Writs of.

Facies. Appearance; view. See PRIMUS, Prima, etc.

Factum. A thing done; a fact. See FACTUM.

Qui facit per alium, facit per se. He who acts through another acts by himself. The act of the agent is the act of the principal — within the scope of the employment.

The authorized act of an agent is imputed to his employer.

An act done by one under the command and direction of the owner of a vessel, with his approbation and for his benefit, is as much his own act in contemplation of law as if done by himself. To this extent at least the maxim applies. And it is not material whether the act is done in his absence from, or his presence in, the scene.[5] See AGENT; CONTRACTOR.

[1] Aberdare v. Hammett, L. R., 10 Q. B. 165–66 (1875).

[2] 1 Wall. 93; 5 *id.* 734.

[3] 96 U. S. 267.

[4] See Osgood v. Bringolf, 32 Iowa, 270 (1871).

[5] United States v. Gooding, 12 Wheat. 472 (1827), Story, J. See also 1 Bl. Com. 474; 91 U. S. 312; 48 Ark.

FACT. Anything done, or said; an act or action; an actual occurrence; a circumstance; whatever comes to pass; an event. See FACTUM.

Subjects of jurisprudence are facts and laws: facts are the source and cause of laws. From facts proceed rights and wrongs. By fact is meant anything the subject of testimony. Perception is a fact. If any emotion is felt, as joy, grief, anger, the feeling is a fact. If the operation of the mind is productive of an effect, as intention, knowledge, skill, the possession of this effect is a fact. If any proposition be true, whatever is affirmed or denied in it is a fact.[1]

"Fact" and "truth" are often used in common parlance as synonymous; as employed in pleadings they are widely different. A fact in pleading is a circumstance, act, event or incident; a truth is a legal principle which declares or governs the facts and their operative effect.[2]

An act, deed, circumstance, or event is none the less a fact because reached as a conclusion of law.[3] See CIRCUMSTANCES, 1.

After the fact; before the fact. See ACCESSARY; FACTUM, Ex post, etc.

Collateral fact. A fact not directly connected with the matter under consideration.

Material fact. Such a fact as influences action in favor of or against a thing about to be done; such a fact as is essential to the right of action or defense. **Immaterial fact.** A fact not important to a determination; not essential to a conclusion; not necessary to be alleged, nor to be proved if alleged.

In fire insurance any fact is material, the knowledge or ignorance of which would naturally influence an insurer in making the contract, in estimating the degree and character of the risk, or in fixing the rate of insurance.[4] See CONCEAL, 5.

Verbal fact. (1) A fact which, if stricken out, would have the effect produced by striking out the controlling member (*verb*) of a sentence, or the controlling sentence from its context.

(2) A declaration accompanying a thing done, explanatory of it, unfolding its nature and quality; as, what is said about sickness or affection, where either is the subject of inquiry.[5]

In fact. In reality; in a matter of fact. Opposed, *in law*: in a matter of law; empowered by law; imputed in law: as, an attorney in fact and an attorney at-law; error or fraud in fact and in law. See ATTORNEY; ERROR, 2 (2); FRAUD; PAIS.

"Fact" is contrasted with "law." Law is a principle, fact is an event; law is conceived, fact is actual; law is a rule of duty, fact is that which accords with or contravenes the rule.[1]

Questions, issues, conclusions, and errors are of law or of fact, or of mixed law and fact.

Facts, not evidence, are to be pleaded; and are proven by moral evidence. Questions of fact are said to be solved by the jury, questions of law by the court.

See DEMURRER; IGNORANCE; INQUIRY; JURY; KNOWLEDGE, 1; LAW; MISTAKE; NOTICE, 1; PRESUMPTION; RES, Gestæ; ULTIMATE.

FACTOR.[2] An agent who is commissioned by a merchant or other person to sell goods for him and receive the proceeds.[3]

A commercial agent, transacting the mercantile affairs of other men, in consideration of a fixed salary or certain commission, and, principally, though not exclusively, in the buying and selling of goods.[4]

An agent employed to sell goods or merchandise, consigned or delivered to him, by or for his principal, for a compensation called his "factorage" or commission.[5]

Often called a "commission merchant" or "consignee;" and the goods received by him a "consignment." When, for an additional compensation in case of sale, he undertakes to guarantee the payment of the debt due by the buyer, he is said to receive a *del credere* commission; that is, a commission of trust or credit.[5]

A factor or commission merchant may buy and sell in his own name, and he has the goods in his possession. A "broker" cannot ordinarily buy and sell in his own name and has no possession of the goods.[5]

Domestic factor. A factor who resides in the same country with his principal. A **foreign factor** resides in a different country.

A factor may sell sufficient of the merchandise to reimburse himself for advances, or to meet liabilities incurred, unless he has agreed not to do so, or the consignor is ready to reimburse him. He must obey the orders of his principal.[7]

320; 22 Ind. 471; 15 La. An. 456; 1 Pick. 476; 10 Mass. 155; 3 Gray, 361; 11 Metc. 71; 18 Me. 127; 58 N. H. 53; 9 Pa. 13; 98 *id.* 9; Story, Ag. § 440; Whart. Max. 165.

[1] Ram on Facts, Ch. I.

[2] Drake *v.* Cockroft, 4 E. D. Smith, 37 (1855), Woodruff, J. See Lawrence *v.* Wright, 2 Duer, 674-75 (1853).

[3] Levins *v.* Rovegno, 71 Cal. 277 (1886).

[4] Boggs *v.* American Ins. Co., 30 Mo. 68 (1860); Clark *v.* Union Mut. Fire Ins. Co., 40 N. H. 338 (1860).

[5] See Beaver *v.* Taylor, 1 Wall. 642 (1863); Travelers' Ins. Co. *v.* Mosley, 8 *id.* 404-5 (1869), Swayne, J.

[1] Abbott's Law Dict.

[2] L. *facere*, q. v.

[3] Cotton *v.* Hiller, 52 Miss. 13 (1876), Simrall, C. J.

[4] Lawrence *v.* Stonington Bank, 6 Conn. 527 (1827), Hosmer, C. J.

[5] Story, Agency, §§ 33, 357; Duquid *v.* Edwards, 50 Barb. 295 (1867); Whart. Ag. § 784; *Exp.* White, L. R., 6 C. Ap. 403 (1871); 1 Pars. Contr. 78; 1 Bl. Com. 427.

[5] Slack *v.* Tucker, 23 Wall. 330 (1874), Bradley, J. See also Perkins *v.* State, 50 Ala. 156 (1873).

[7] Brown *v.* M'Gran, 14 Pet. 494 (1840).

To the extent of advances and charges, he has a lien, a special property, in the merchandise; and he may pledge articles to the amount of that lien. He may protect his possession by a suit against a trespasser. He cannot sell to his own creditor in payment of his debt; nor can he delegate his authority without assent of the principal. Before he has effected a sale, the principal may reclaim possession by paying advances, interest thereon, and expenses.[1] The principal may sue and be sued on a contract made by the factor in his own name.[2]

If guilty of gross negligence in conducting the business, he forfeits all claim to compensation for his services.[3] See further AGENT.

Factor's Act. Statute of 6 Geo. IV (1826), c. 94. Empowered a factor to pledge the goods, and protected persons who believed him to be the real owner.

Statute of 5 and 6 Vict. (1842) further enabled him, as if the true owner, to enter into any agreement respecting the goods by way of "pledge, lien or security," excepting as to antecedent debts; and this, notwithstanding the lender is aware that the borrower is a factor only. Similar legislation exists in the States.

Factorizing process. Trustee process; garnishment,[4] q. v.

FACTORY. A contraction of "manufactory,—a building, or collection of buildings, appropriated to the manufacture of goods."

Includes the building, the machinery necessary to produce the particular goods, and the engine or other power requisite to propel such machinery.[5] See CONTAINED.

FACTUM. L. A thing done; a deed; a fact. Compare FAIT.

De facto. In point of fact: actual. Opposed, *de jure*: by right, rightful.

Said of a blockade (q. v.) actually maintained;[6] of actual duress;[7] of a wife or husband whose marriage may be annulled;[8] of a person in office under apparent right or under color of right — as by an appointment or election not strictly legal;[9] and of a vacancy (q. v.) in an office; of a government (q. v.) actually in power in place of the lawful government;[1] of increase of stock.[2]

Ex facto jus oritur. Out of the fact the law arises: the law attaches to facts.

Ex post facto. From an after fact — a subsequent matter; after the fact or act.

"No State shall . . pass any . . ex post facto Law."[3]

That is, a law concerning, and after, a fact, or thing done, or action committed.[4]

Relates to penal and criminal proceedings, which impose punishments or forfeitures, not to civil proceedings which affect private rights retrospectively.[5]

Embraces only such laws as impose or affect penalties or forfeitures. A retrospective act is not therefore necessarily such a law.[6] See RETROSPECTIVE.

Includes every law: (1) That makes an action done before the passing of the law, and which was innocent when done, criminal, and punishes such action. (2) That aggravates a crime, or makes it greater than it was when committed. (3) That changes the punishment, and inflicts a greater punishment than the law annexed to the crime when committed. (4) That alters the rule of evidence, and receives less or different testimony than the law required at the time of the commission of the offense, to convict the offender.[7]

A law which imposes a punishment for an act not punishable at the time it was committed; or imposes additional punishment to that then prescribed; or changes the rules of evidence by which less or different testimony is sufficient to convict than was then required.[8]

The term necessarily implies a fact or act done, "after" which the law in question is passed. Whether it is *ex post facto* or not relates, in criminal cases, to which alone the phrase applies, to the time at which the offense charged was committed. If the law complained of was passed after the commission of the offense, it is as to that *ex post facto*, though whether of the class forbidden by the Constitution may depend on other matters. But so far as this depends on the *time* of its enactment, it has reference solely to the

---

[1] Warner v. Martin, 11 How. 223 (1850), cases; United States v. Villalonga, 23 Wall. 42 (1874); Mechanics', &c. Ins. Co. v. Kiger, 103 U. S. 355 (1880); Steiger v. Third Nat. Bank, 2 McCrary, 503 (1881); Goodenow v. Tyler, 1 Am. L. C. 788, 797; Laussatt v. Lippincott, *ib.* 805, 812; 73 Ill. 103; 5 S. & R. 540; 70 E. C. L. 418; 2 Kent, 622.

[2] Higgins v. McCrea, 116 U. S. 680 (1886), cases.

[3] Fordyce v. Pepper, 16 F. R. 516, 520-21 (1883), cases.

[4] See Drake, Attach. § 451.

[5] Schott v. Harvey, 105 Pa. 227 (1884). See 76 Va. 1012; 8 Md. 495.

[6] 1 Kent, 44.

[7] 15 Gray, 471.

[8] 1 Bl. Com. 435; 4 Kent, 36.

[9] 2 Kent, 295; 1 Bl. Com. 371; 27 Minn. 293; 3 Mont. 430; 55 Pa. 468.

---

[1] 92 U. S. 133; 96 *id.* 185; 97 *id.* 616; 43 Ala. 213; 42 Miss. 703; 47 Pa. 170.

[2] 95 U. S. 668.

[3] Constitution, Art. I, sec. 10. See 2 Bancroft, Const. 213.

[4] Calder v. Bull, 3 Dall. 390-91 (1798), Chase, J.

[5] Watson v. Mercer, 8 Pet. 110 (1834), cases, Story, J.

[6] Locke v. New Orleans, 4 Wall. 172 (1866).

[7] Calder v. Bull, *supra;* State v. Hoyt, 47 Conn. 532 (1880).

[8] Cummings v. Missouri, 4 Wall. 326 (1866), Field, J.; 9 Wall. 38.

date at which the offense was committed to which the new law was sought to be applied. . . Any law passed after the commission of an offense which "in relation to that offense or its consequences, alters the situation of a party to his disadvantage," is an *ex post facto* law, and forbidden.[1]

Does not involve a change of place of trial.[2]

Illustration: a State may not disqualify from further employment as such, teachers and clergymen who took part in the late rebellion.[3]

A statute which simply enlarges the class of persons who may be competent to testify is not *ex post facto* as to offenses previously committed. Such alteration in the law relates to the mode of procedure only, in which no one can be said to have a vested right, and which the State, upon grounds of public policy, may regulate at pleasure.[4]

Factum probandum. The fact to be proved.[5]

Ipso facto. By the fact itself; by the mere fact; from the effect of the fact or act.

The mere fact of a collision between trains is evidence *ipso facto* of negligence.[6] Attaining twenty-one years of age *ipso facto* emancipates from the disabilities of infancy.

Non est factum. It is not his deed. The name of the issue joined in an action on a specialty, by a defendant who denies that he executed the instrument.[7]

FACULTY. A special privilege or license granted to a person permitting him to do something which otherwise the law would not allow.

FAILURE. 1. The state or condition of being wanting; a falling short; deficiency or lack; defect, want, absence; default; defeat.

Failure of consideration. Want or absence of a legal consideration.

This may be either partial or total.[8] See CONSIDERATION.

Failure of evidence. Absence of legal evidence.

Total failure of evidence. Not only the utter absence of all evidence, but also failure to offer proof, either positive or inferential, to establish one or more of the many facts, the establishment of all of which is indispensable to the finding of the issue for the plaintiff.[1]

Failure of issue. Want or non-existence of descendants; more particularly, lack of issue who may take an estate limited over by an executory devise.

This may be *definite* or *indefinite*. See further DIE, Without children.

Failure of justice. Defeat of right and justice from want of legal remedy.

Failure of record. Neglect to produce a record relied upon in a plea.

Failure of title. Defect or want of title.

When discovered before the money has been paid, the purchaser may deduct an amount equal to the value of the land of which he is deprived.

Failure of trust. Defeat of a proposed trust from want of constituting facts or elements or of law to effectuate the object.

2. Default; omission; neglect; non-performance, *q. v.*; as, failure to perform a contract, *q. v.*

3. Inability to pay debts, from insolvency; suspension of payment: as, failure in business, a failing debtor.

Failing circumstances. In a statute, may imply that the insolvent is about failing and closing his affairs, knowing his inability to continue in business and meet his payments.[2] See BANKRUPTCY; INSOLVENCY.

FAIR. 1, *adj.* Equal; just; proper; reasonable; equitable. See EQUITY.

Fair abridgment. A real substantial condensation of copyrighted materials, as the result of labor and judgment. See ABRIDGE.

Fair average crop. Takes into account the nature of the season and unforeseen events beyond the control of a prudent, faithful overseer.[3]

Fair criticism. See REVIEW, 3.

Fair knowledge or **skill.** A reasonable degree of knowledge or measure of skill.[4]

Fair preponderance. Of evidence — a preponderance perceptible upon fair consideration.[5]

Fair sale. A sale conducted with fairness as respects the rights of the parties affected.[6]

---

[1] Kring *v.* Missouri, 107 U. S. 225, 227, 235, 238, 250 (1882), Miller, J. Approved, Hopt *v.* Utah, *infra.*

[2] Gut *v.* Minnesota, 9 Wall. 37 (1869).

[3] Locke *v.* New Orleans, *ante.*

[4] Hopt *v.* Utah, 110 U. S. 589-90 (1884), Harlan, J. See Pacific Coast Law J., May 26, 1883; 25 Am. Law Reg. 680-95 (1886), cases.

[5] 1 Greenl. Ev. § 13.

[6] 91 U. S. 492.

[7] See 3 Bl. Com. 305; 1 Litt. 158; 6 Rand. 86; Gould, Pl. 300-2.

[8] See Torinus *v.* Buckham, 29 Minn. 131 (1882).

[1] Cole *v.* Hebb, 7 Gill & J. 28 (Md., 1835).

[2] Utley *v.* Smith, 24 Conn. 310 (1855); Bloodgood *v.* Beecher, 35 *id.* 482 (1868).

[3] Wright *v.* Morris, 15 Ark. 450 (1855).

[4] Jones *v.* Angell, 95 Ind. 382 (1883).

[5] [State *v.* Grear, 29 Minn. 225 (1882); Bryan *v.* Chicago, &c. R. Co., 63 Iowa, 466 (1884); City Bank's Appeal, 54 Conn. 274 (1886); 86 Pa. 268.

[6] [Lalor *v.* M'Carthy, 24 Minn. 419 (1878).

Fairly. Equitably; reasonably.

In "fairly merchantable," conveys the idea of mediocrity in quality, or something just above that.[1]

May be deemed synonymous with "equitably."[2]

But is not synonymous with "truly:" language may be truly yet unfairly reported.[3] See FAITHFULLY.

Fairness. In speaking of a sale, "fairness and good faith" refers to the fair dealing which usually characterizes business transactions.[4]

2, *n.* In English law, a species of market held by grant from the crown.[5]

In the United States, "fairs" are governed by the law as to partnerships and sales. See MARKET.

FAIT. F. A fact. Compare FACTUM.

Before or at full age an infant may avoid a matter *in fait;* and a matter of record, during majority.[6]

Wife *de fait:* a wife *de facto.*

FAITH. Belief; confidence; reliance; credence; trust, *q. v.* Fair intent of purpose; honesty, openness, uprightness; sincerity; fidelity to a representation, promise, or duty.

Good faith. Honest, lawful intent; the condition of acting without knowledge of fraud and without intent to assist in a fraudulent or otherwise unlawful scheme. **Bad faith.** Guilty knowledge or willful ignorance.

The corresponding Latin expressions are *bona fides,* and *mala fides.* See FIDES.

A creditor,[7] holder, possessor,[8] purchaser,[9] or transferee in good faith is one who has loaned money or purchased property fairly, in the usual course of business, and without being cognizant of, or implicated in, any intent which the borrower or seller may have had to evade the claims of his creditors or to defraud some person interested in the matter.[10]

The title of a person who takes negotiable paper before it is due, for a valuable consideration, can only be defeated by showing bad faith in him, which implies guilty knowledge or willful ignorance of the facts impairing the title of the party from whom he received it. The burden of proof lies on the assailant of the taker's title.[11]

A purchaser in good faith of negotiable paper for value, before maturity, takes it freed from all infirmities in its origin, unless it is absolutely void for want of power in the maker to issue it, or its circulation is by law prohibited by reason of the illegality of the consideration. His transferee, with notice of the infirmities, may equally recover.[1]

A party who, before its maturity and for a valuable consideration, purchases mercantile paper from the apparent owner thereof, acquires a right thereto which can only be defeated by proof of bad faith or of actual notice of such facts as impeach the validity of the transaction.[2]

A holder in good faith is a purchaser for value without notice, or his successor.[3]

The bad faith in the taker of negotiable paper which will defeat a recovery by him must be something more than a failure to inquire into the consideration upon which it was made or accepted, because of rumors or general reputation as to the bad character of the maker or drawer.[4] See further NEGOTIATE, 2; NOTICE, 1; LOST, 2.

One who buys at a voluntary sale from his debtor, crediting the consideration on a pre-existing debt, is not a *bona fide* purchaser for value: he advances nothing, and, if the title fails, loses nothing.[5]

The highest good faith is exacted of a person dealing with a trustee respecting the trust property. See TRUST, 1; FIDUCIARY.

Full faith and credit. "Full Faith and Credit shall be given in each State to the public Acts, Records, and judicial Proceedings of every other State. And the Congress may by general Laws prescribe the Manner in which such Acts, Records and Proceedings shall be proved, and the Effect thereof."[6]

For the history of this provision, see EXTRADITION, page 441.

A record must be authenticated as prescribed by act of May 26, 1790.[7] The records and judicial proceedings of the courts of any State (authenticated as herein prescribed) "shall have such faith and credit given to them, in every court within the United States, as they have by law or usage in the courts of the State from which they are taken."[8]

The judgments of the courts of the United States have invariably been recognized as upon the same

[1] Warner v. Arctic Ice Co., 74 Me. 479 (1883).

[2] Satcher v. Satcher, 41 Ala. 40 (1867).

[3] Lawrence v. Finch, 17 N. J. E. 239 (1865).

[4] Morgan v. Hazlehurst Lodge, 53 Miss. 683 (1876).

[5] See 1 Bl. Com. 274.

[6] 1 Pars. Contr. 333.

[7] See 66 Ga. 722; 30 Minn. 272.

[8] See 31 Md. 454; 8 Wheat. 79; 12 Tex. 222; 24 *id.* 379.

[9] See 71 Ala. 231; 44 Conn. 459; 65 Barb. 231; 7 Johns. Ch. 65; 2 Utah, 52.

[10] [1 Abbott's Law Dict. 536; 111 U. S. 80.

[11] Hotchkiss v. Tradesmen's, &c. Nat. Banks, 21 Wall. 359 (1874), cases; Dresser v. Missouri, &c. Co., 93 U. S. 94–95 (1876), cases; Collins v. Gilbert, 94 *id.* 754 (1876), cases.

[1] Cromwell v. County of Sac, 96 U. S. 51, 59 (1877), cases, Field, J.; Bowditch v. New England Life Ins. Co., 141 Mass. 296 (1886).

[2] Swift v. Smith, 102 U. S. 444 (1880), Strong, J.

[3] McClure v. Township of Oxford, 94 U. S. 432 (1876), Waite, C. J.

[4] Goetz v. Bank of Kansas City, 119 U. S. 560 (1887), Field, J. See, in general, 22 Cent. Law J. 437–42 (1886), cases.

[5] Overstreet v. Manning, 67 Tex. 661 (1887); 61 *id.* 648.

[6] Constitution, Art. IV, sec. 1.

[7] Caperton v. Ballard, 14 Wall. 241 (1871).

[8] Act 26 May, 1790, c. 11; Act 27 March, 1804, c. 56: R. S. § 905.

footing, so far as concerns the obligation created by them, with domestic judgments of the States.[1]

A judgment duly rendered in one State is conclusive as to the merits of the case in every other State.[2]

But want of jurisdiction over the party, or matter, may be shown *dehors*, and even in contradiction of the record.[3]

The Federal courts give the judgment of a State court the force and effect to which it is entitled in the courts of the State.

No greater effect can be given to any judgment of a court of one State in another State than is given to it in the State where rendered. Any other rule would contravene the policy of the provision of the Constitution and laws of the United States on that subject.[4]

The evils which would result from a general system of re-examination of the judicial proceedings of other States are apparent. The framers of the Constitution intended to attribute to the "public acts, records, and judicial proceedings" of each of the States positive and absolute verity, so that they cannot be contradicted, or the truth of them denied, any more than in the State where they originated.[5]

The duty to follow the courts of a State, upon questions arising upon the construction of its own statutes, rests upon comity. . . The provision relates only to the conclusiveness of judgments as between parties and privies.[6] See COMITY; LAW, Foreign.

The Federal courts, exercising their *original* jurisdiction, take notice, without proof, of the laws of the several States; but, as no State court is charged with a knowledge of the laws of another State, in the Supreme Court, when acting under its appellate jurisdiction, whatever was matter of fact in the court whose judgment is under review, continues matter of fact.[7]

Faithfully. When a public officer gives a bond conditioned faithfully to discharge his official duties, "faithfully" implies that he has assumed the measure of responsibility laid on him by law had no bond been given. Everything is unfaithfulness which the law does not excuse.[8]

"Fairly and impartially," in the expression "faithfully, fairly, and impartially," add something to the force of the word "faithfully," and should not be omitted from a statutory form of an oath of office.[1]

A bond that one will "well, truly, firmly, and impartially" perform the duties of an office, is not invalid as varying from the statutory form "for the faithful performance of his duties."[2]

FALCIDIAN LAW, or PORTION. In the reign of Augustus, on motion of Publius Falcidius, it was enacted (40 B. C.) that a testator could not bequeath away from his heir more than three-fourths of his estate.[3]

In principle, adopted in Louisiana, and perhaps elsewhere.

FALL. A life estate is sometimes said to "fall into," that is, to merge with, the fee.

FALSA. See FALSUS.

FALSE. Somewhat more than erroneous, untrue, or illegal: distinctively characterizes a wrongful act known to involve an error or untruth.[4]

As, false or a false — action, answer, claim, date, imprisonment, oath, swearing, testimony or witness, personation, pretenses, representation, return, token, signature, weights and measures, writing, *qq. v.* Compare SHAM.

Falsehood. Any untrue assertion or proposition; a willful act or declaration contrary to the truth.[5]

Does not necessarily imply a lie or willful untruth.[6]

See COMMENDATIO, Simplex; CONCEAL; CRIMEN, Falsi; DECEIT; ESTOPPEL; FALSUS, In uno; FRAUD; OATH; PERJURY.

Falsely. Applied to forging an instrument, implies that the writing is false, not genuine, fictitious, not true, — without regard to the truth or falsehood of the statement it contains, — the counterfeit of something which is or has been genuine, which purports to be a genuine instrument when it is not such.[6] See further COUNTERFEIT; FORGERY.

Falsify. 1. To represent a fact falsely.

2. To tamper with a document by interlineation, obliteration, or otherwise. See ALTERATION, 2; RECORD.

3. To prove a thing to be false, particularly an item of debit in an account.

---

[1] Embry v. Palmer, 107 U. S. 10-11 (1882), cases.

[2] M'Elmoyle v. Cohen, 13 Pet. 326 (1839).

[3] Thompson v. Whitman, 18 Wall. 462-64 (1873), cases; Pennoyer v. Neff, 95 U. S. 729 (1877); 30 Gratt. 266.

[4] Board of Public Works v. Columbia College, 17 Wall. 529 (1873); Robertson v. Pickrell, 111 U. S. 611 (1883); Chicago, &c. R. Co. v. Wiggins Ferry Co., 119 *id.* 622 (1887).

[5] 2 Story, Const., 3 ed., § 1310.

[6] Wiggins Ferry Co. v. Chicago, &c. R. Co., 3 McCrary, 609, 613 (1882), cases; 11 F. R. 381, 384.

[7] Chicago, &c. R. Co. v. Wiggins Ferry Co., 119 U. S. 622 (1887).

[8] State v. Chadwick, 10 Oreg. 468 (1881); 16 Op. Att.-Gen. 318.

---

[1] Perry v. Thompson, 16 N. J. L. 73 (1837).

[2] Mayor of Hoboken v. Evans, 31 N. J. L. 342 (1865).

[3] See Hadley, Rom. Law, 322.

[4] See People v. Gates, 13 Wend. 320-21 (1835).

[5] Putnam v. Osgood, 51 N. H. 207 (1871); Rosc. Cr. Ev. 362.

[6] [State v. Young, 46 N. H. 270 (1865).

Falsification. Applied to some item among debts which is wholly false or in some part erroneous.[1] See further SURCHARGE.

FALSUS; FALSA. L. Deceptive; erroneous; false.

Crimen falsi. The offense of deceiving or falsifying. See further CRIMEN, Falsi.

Falsa demonstratio non nocet. An erroneous designation does not impair. See further DEMONSTRATIO.

Falsa grammatica non vitiat chartam. Bad grammar does not invalidate an instrument. See further GRAMMAR.

Falsus in uno, falsus in omnibus. False in one (particular), false in all. Deliberate falsehood in one matter will be imputed to related matters.

If the circumstances respecting which testimony is discordant be immaterial, and of such a nature that mistakes may easily exist, and be accounted for in a manner consistent with the utmost good faith and probability, there is much reason for indulging the belief that the discrepancies arise from the infirmity of the human mind, rather than from deliberate error. But where the party speaks to a fact in respect to which he cannot be presumed liable to mistake, as in relation to the country of his birth, or his being in a vessel on a particular voyage, or living in a particular place, if the fact turn out otherwise, it is extremely difficult to exempt him from the charge of deliberate falsehood; and courts of justice, under such circumstances, are bound upon principles of law, morality, and justice, to apply the maxim *falsus in uno, falsus in omnibus.*[2]

The maxim is applied to discredit the testimony of witnesses; it is the foundation of the old rule which excluded the testimony of infamous persons. Holds good where the party calling the witness is cognizant of the falsehood, or where the falsehood affects the credibility of the witness's testimony. Never applied to misstatements which are wholly inadvertent, or attributable to the ordinary fluctuations of memory. Proper where the special falsity is of a nature to imply falsity as to the whole case; and where contradictions are so numerous as to show imbecility of memory.[3]

He who would embezzle a ship's furniture would not hesitate to embezzle the cargo.[4]

FAME. Report or opinion generally diffused; repute, reputation; public estimation; name.

Defame. To maliciously injure a name; to slander. Whence defamation, *q. v.*

Good fame. Favorable reputation. **Ill-fame.** Evil fame or name; ill-repute.

"Ill-fame" distinctly describes a person who visits gaming houses, bawdy-houses, and other forbidden resorts, as well as the resorts themselves. While in popular parlance the term designates bawdy-houses, with no reference to their "fame," some courts allow proof of the fact to be aided by proof of the fame.[1] See further HOUSE, Of ill-fame.

Infamous. Not of good repute; incompetent to testify by reason of conviction of crime. Whence infamy, *q. v.*

FAMILY.[2] Originally, servants; in its modern comprehensive meaning, a collective body of persons living together in one house, or within the curtilage.[3]

In popular acceptance includes parents, children, servants — all whose domicil or home is ordinarily in the same house and under the same management and head.[4]

In its limited sense signifies father, mother, and children; in its ordinary acceptation, all the relatives who descend from a common root; in its most extensive scope, all the individuals who live together under the authority of another, including even servants.[5]

The most comprehensive definition is, a number of persons who live in one house and under one management or head.[6]

No specific number of persons is required; nor that they eat where they live, nor that they be employed in or about the house.[6]

Children, wife and children, blood relatives, or the members of the domestic circle; according to the connection.[7]

Includes children over age, if they have no home elsewhere.[8]

Family arrangement. An arrangement between members of a family as to the disposition of their property.

---

[1] [Bailey *v.* Westcott, 6 Phila. 527 (1868), Sharswood, J.; 2 Barb. 592; 2 Edw. Ch. 23.

[2] The Santissima Trinidad, 7 Wheat. 339 (1822), Story, J.

[3] See 1 Whart. Ev. § 412; 36 F. R. 577; 18 Fla. 462; 97 Mass. 406; 62 Miss. 26; 91 Mo. 439; 14 Neb. 101; 44 N. Y. 172; 15 Wend. 602; 81 Va. 154; 3 Wis. 645.

[4] The Boston, 1 Sumn. 356 (1833).

[1] See 1 Bish. Cr. L. § 1088; 2 Greenl. Ev. § 44; 38 Conn. 467; 132 Mass. 2; 74 Me. 153; 29 Minn. 193, 195.

[2] L. *familia*, household: domestics: *famulus*, a servant.

[3] Wilson *v.* Cochran, 31 Tex. 680 (1869); Roco *v.* Green, 50 *id.* 483 (1878).

[4] Cheshire *v.* Burlington, 31 Conn. 329 (1863); 51 Mich. 494.

[5] Galligar *v.* Payne, 34 La. An. 1058 (1882), Bermudez, C. J.: 15 Rep. 464.

[6] Poor *v.* Hudson Ins. Co., 2 F. R. 436 (1880).

[7] Spencer *v.* Spencer, 11 Paige, 160 (1844), Walworth, Ch. See also Muir *v.* Howell, 37 N. J. L. 39 (1883), cases; Race *v.* Oldridge, 90 Ill. 252 (1878); 3 Woods, 494; 53 Iowa, 707; 56 *id.* 389; 125 Mass. 377; 128 *id.* 334; 137 *id.* 55.

[8] Stilson *v.* Gibbs, 53 Mich. 280 (1884): Exemp. Law.

Family Bible. Containing entries of family incidents,—births, marriages, and deaths, made by a parent, since deceased, will be received in evidence.[1] See PEDIGREE.

Family council, or meeting. In Louisiana, a meeting of the relatives or friends of a minor or other person incompetent to act for himself, may be held, by judicial appointment, to advise upon the interests of such person.[2]

Family physician. The physician who usually attends and is consulted by the members of a family as their physician.[3]

It is not necessary that he should invariably attend and be consulted by each and all the members of the family.[3]

Family use. Such use as is appropriate to the individual needs of the members of a household, and to the needs of the household in its collective capacity.[4]

To supply water for family use in a city includes supplying city buildings, such as a jail, and hospitals, poorhouses, schools, and other institutions.[4]

Groceries kept by a merchant as part of his stock are not "provisions found on hand for family use," within the meaning of an exemption law.[5]

Head of a family. The person who controls, supervises or manages the affairs about a house.

Where there is a husband or father, he is ordinarily the head; but there may be a head where there is no marriage relation.[6] Compare HOUSEHOLDER; PATER.

FARE. See BRIDGE; CARRIER; FERRY; PASSENGER; RAILROAD; TOLL, 2.

FARM.[7] 1. Provision; rent; tenure by rent. 2. Land rented; land devoted to purposes of agriculture.

Farm, or *feorme,* is an old Saxon word signifying provision. It came to be used instead of rent or render, because anciently the greater part of rents were reserved in provisions — corn [grain], poultry, etc., till the use of money became more frequent. So that a farmer, *firmarius,* was one who held his lands upon payment of rent or *feorme;* though at present, by a gradual departure from the original sense, the word "farm" signifies the very estate or lands so held upon farm or rent.[1]

That which is held by a person who stands in the relation of a tenant to a landlord.[2]

An indefinite quantity of land, some of which is cultivated.[3]

"Farm" and "homestead farm" are words of large import. In England, farm commonly implies an estate leased. The word is collective, consisting of divers things gathered into one, as a messuage, land, meadow, pasture, wood, common, etc. In the United States, it is a parcel of land used, occupied, managed, and controlled by one proprietor.[4] See CROP.

"To farm," in a lease of mineral lands, means to bring the minerals up to light for purposes of commerce, and make them profitable to lessor and lessee.[5]

See AGRICULTURE; EXEMPTION; IMPLEMENT; PLANTATION; TOOL.

Fee-farm. To let lands to farm in fee-simple, instead of for life or years; also, the land itself so held on perpetual rent.

Fee-farm rent. A rent-charge issuing out of an estate in fee.[6] Compare, FEUD, To feu.

To farm let. A technical expression in a lease creating a term for years.

Usual, but not essential.[7]

To farm out. To rent for a term of years; also, to give over something to another for a share of the income or profit: as, to farm out revenues, or taxes.

FARO. See GAME, 2.

FASHIONS. See PERISHABLE.

FAST. 1. As descriptive of days, see HOLIDAY.

2. Referring to an estate — real, of the nature of realty.[8]

3. Moving more than a specified number of miles, as eight, per hour.[9]

---

[1] See 1 Whart. Ev. § 219; 1 Greenl. Ev. § 104; 53 Ga. 535; 30 Iowa, 301.

[2] See La. Civ. Code, Art. 305-11; 6 Mart. 455.

[3] [Price *v.* Phœnix Ins. Co., 17 Minn. 519 (1871); Reid *v.* Piedmont, &c. Ins. Co., 58 Mo. 424 (1874).

[4] Spring Valley Water Works *v.* San Francisco, 52 Cal. 120 (1877).

[5] State *v.* Conner, 73 Mo. 575 (1881).

[6] See 17 Ala. 486; 41 Ga. 153; 90 Ill. 250; 110 *id.* 533; 11 Iowa, 266; 48 *id.* 180; 52 *id.* 431; 53 *id.* 706; 20 Mo. 75; 45 *id.* 483; 69 *id.* 415; 51 N. H. 253; 9 Wend. 476; 5 S. C. 493; 32 Gratt. 18.

[7] A. S. *feorm,* food, property, use: L. L. *firma,* a feast, tribute: *firmus,* durable. From the "fixed" rent,—Skeat. L. *firmus: firmare,* to make fast. Farms were at first enclosed or fortified with walls; or, the leases were made more certain by signature,—Webster.

[1] 2 Bl. Com. 318, 57.

[3] [Lane *v.* Stanhope, 6 T. R. 353 (1795), Kenyon, C. J.; 4 Best & S., Q. B. 931.

[3] Commonwealth *v.* Carmatt, 2 Binn. *238 (1810), Tilghman, C. J.

[4] Aldrich *v.* Gaskill, 10 Cush. 158 (1852), Shaw, C. J.; Black *v.* Hill, 32 Ohio St. 318 (1877): Shep. Touch. 93.

[5] [Price *v.* Nicholas, 4 Hughes, 619 (1878).

[6] 2 Bl. Com. 43; De Peyster *v.* Michael, 6 N. Y. 497 (1852); 2 Washb. R. P., 4 ed., 274.

[7] 2 Bl. Com. 317.

[8] See 6 Johns. 185; 9 N. Y. 502.

[9] Indianapolis, &c. R. Co. *v.* Peyton, 76 Ill. 340 (1875).

4. In Georgia, describes a bill of exceptions by which the proceedings in an injunction case, or other case in equity of an extraordinary nature, may be reviewed by the supreme court without the delay incident to ordinary cases.[1]

FAT CATTLE. See PERISHABLE; PROVISIONS.

FATHER. See ANCESTOR; BASTARD; CHILD; CONSANGUINITY; DESCENT; MOTHER; NAME, 1; PARENT. Compare PATER; PARTUS.

FAUCES TERRÆ. L. The jaws of the land: projecting headlands inclosing an arm of the sea.[2] See SEA.

FAULT. 1. An improper act due to ignorance, negligence or willfulness,[3] *qq. v.* Compare CULPA; DELICTUM.

In averments in pleadings, has substantially the same meaning as "negligence."[4]

Attributed to a carrier, may mean actual negligence.[5]

2. Defect; blemish.

With all faults. In the absence of fraud in the vendor, a sale "with all faults" covers such defects as are not inconsistent with the identity of the goods as those described.

Parol evidence is admissible to show the meaning in trade.[6]

FAVOR. See CHALLENGE, 3; PREFER, 2; PREJUDICE.

FEALTY.[7] The oath or obligation of a vassal, under the feudal system, to be faithful to his lord and defend him against all enemies.[8]

The original of the oath of allegiance, *q. v.* See also FEUD.

FEAR. See AFFRAY; DEFENSE, 1; DURESS; INFLUENCE; QUIA TIMET; ROBBERY.

FEASANCE.[9] A doing; a performing or performance.

Gratuitous feasance. A voluntary service — rendered or undertaken.

The essence of bailment by mandate, *q. v.*

---

[1] See Sewell v. Edmonston, 66 Ga. 353 (1881).

[2] 5 Wheat. 106; 1 Story, 259; 1 Kent, 367.

[3] See 5 Ct. Cl. 489.

[4] Rogers v. Overton, 87 Ind. 411 (1882).

[5] School District v. Boston, &c. R. Co., 102 Mass. 555 (1869).

[6] Whitney v. Boardman, 118 Mass. 247-48 (1875), cases; 1 Pars. Contr. 590.

[7] L. *fidelitas: fides*, confidence, trust, faith.

[8] 1 Bl. Com. 367; 2 *id.* 45, 53; 44 Pa. 499.

[9] F. *faire:* L. *facere*, to make, do.

Malfeasance. The doing of an act wholly wrongful and unlawful. **Misfeasance.** A default in not doing a lawful act in the proper manner — omitting to do it as it should be done. **Non-feasance.** Any omission to perform a required duty at all, or a total neglect of duty.[1]

Misfeasance may amount to non-feasance; as, in cases of gross negligence.[2] See TRUSTEE.

See DAMAGE, Feasant; DEFEASANCE; TORT, 2, Feasor.

FEBRUARY. See HOLIDAY; YEAR, Leap-year.

FEDERAL.[3] 1. Pertaining to a league or compact between independent sovereignties. 2. Composed of states which retain only a portion of their original sovereignty; relating to the constitution, treaties, or laws, or the power or government of the organization thereby formed.

Appropriate to our General Government, the government of the United States, considered as a Union of States or local governments. The word "National" recognizes the State governments and the government of the Union as distinct systems.[4]

In the second sense are the common expressions Federal or federal — amendments, Constitution, courts, elections, decisions, judges, laws and statutes, question, government, officer. In these phrases the word of contrast is "State:" as, State constitutions, courts, laws, etc. See those titles.

FEDERALIST. A publication issued from 1787 to 1789, and consisting of papers, written by Hamilton, Madison, and Jay, intended to prepare the people for accepting the Constitution.

Of its eighty-five numbers, Jay wrote five, Madison twenty-nine, and Hamilton fifty-one. "They form a work of enduring interest, because they are the earliest commentary on the new experiment of mankind in establishing a republican form of government for a country of boundless dimensions."[5]

In itself a complete commentary on the Constitution. The opinions expressed in it have always been considered as of great authority. Its intrinsic merit entitles it to high rank; and the part which two of its authors [Madison, the chief author, and Hamilton] performed in framing the Constitution, put it very much in their power to explain the views with which it was framed. These essays, published while the

---

[1] Coite v. Lynes, 33 Conn. 114-15 (1865), Butler, J.

[2] Story, Agency, § 218; 1 Woolw. 374-75; 3 Pet. 283.

[3] L. *fœdus*, a league, treaty, compact.

[4] See United States v. Cruikshank, 92 U. S. 542 (1875).

[5] 2 Bancroft, Formation Const. 336.

Constitution was before the nation for adoption or rejection, and written in answer to objections founded upon the extent of its powers, and on its diminution of State sovereignty, are entitled to more consideration where they frankly avow that the power objected to is given, and defend it.[1]

FEE. 1. (1) In feudal law, an allotment of land in consideration of military service; land held of a superior, on condition of rendering him service, the ultimate property remaining in him. Opposed to *allodium*. See ALLODIAL.

The districts of land allotted by the conquering general to his superior officers, and by them dealt out again in smaller parcels, were called *feoda*, feuds, fiefs, or fees — a conditional stipend or reward.[2] See, at length, FEUD.

"Fee," at its origin, related to the quality of the estate. It now denotes the quantity of interest the owner has in land.[3]

(2) An estate of inheritance — the highest and most extensive interest a man can have in a feud.

Fee-simple. An absolute inheritance, clear of any condition, limitation or restriction to particular heirs, but descendible to the heirs general, whether male or female, lineal or collateral.[4]

"Fee," with or without the adjunct "simple," is used in contradistinction to the fee-conditional of the common law, and to fee-tail created by statute.

Tenant in fee-simple, or tenant in fee, is he that has lands, tenements, or hereditaments, to hold to him and his heirs forever — generally, absolutely and simply; without mentioning what heirs, but referring that to his own pleasure or to the disposition of the law.[4]

The term "fee" alone implies an inheritable estate. "Simple" or "absolute" adds nothing to the comprehensiveness of the original term. In modern estates, fee, fee-simple, and fee-simple absolute are synonymous.[5]

"An estate in fee-simple is where a man has an estate in land or tenements to him and his heirs forever."

Limitation of the power of sale for a limited period, as for five years, is not inconsistent with a fee-simple estate.[6]

Called a "fee-simple" because it signifies a pure inheritance, clear of any qualification or condition. It is an estate of perpetuity, and confers an unlimited power of alienation.[1]

That "heirs" or other appropriate word of perpetuity in a deed conveying land is essential to pass a fee simple estate is not a rule admitting of no exception. When, for example, a mortgage evidences an intention to pass the entire estate as security, and express provisions cannot otherwise be carried into effect, the instrument will pass such an estate, although no formal word of perpetuity is employed.[2]

A "fee limited" is an estate of inheritance clogged or confined with a condition or qualification of some sort. This may be one of the following estates:

Base, qualified, or determinable fee. Has a qualification subjoined thereto, and terminates whenever the qualification is at an end.[3]

As, a grant "to A and his heirs, tenants of the manor of Dale," that is, as long as they continue tenants. This estate is a fee, because it may endure forever, yet the duration depends upon a circumstance, and this debases the purity of the donation.[3]

Conditional fee. At common law, a fee restrained to particular heirs, exclusive of others; as, to the heirs "of a man's body," by which only his lineal descendants were admitted, in exclusion of collateral heirs; or to the "heirs-male of his body," in exclusion of collaterals, and of lineal females.

Called "conditional" from the condition, expressed or implied in the donation, that if the donee died without such particular heirs, the land should revert to the owner. Such fees were strictly agreeable to the nature of feuds, when they first ceased to be mere estates for life, and had not yet become absolute estates in fee-simple. . . As soon as the grantee had issue born, his estate was supposed to become absolute; at least to enable him to alien the land, and thereby bar not only his own issue, but also the donor of his reversion; to subject the land to forfeiture for treason; and to charge the land with incumbrances, so as to bind the issue. If the tenant did not in fact alien the land, the course of descent was not altered by fulfillment of the condition; the land, by the terms of the donation, could descend to none but the heirs "of his body," and, therefore, in default of them, reverted to the donor. Hence, to subject the land to the ordinary course of descent, the donees of these conditional fee-simples aliened as soon as issue was born, and afterward repurchased the lands, which gave them a fee-simple absolute that would descend to the heirs in

---

[1] Cohens v. Virginia, 6 Wheat. 418 (1881), Marshall, Chief Justice.

[2] 2 Bl. Com. 45, 104-6.

[3] Wendell v. Crandall, 1 N. Y. 495 (1848); Taul v. Campbell, 7 Yerg. 325 (1835).

[4] 2 Bl. Com. 106, 105.

[5] Jecko v. Taussig, 45 Mo. 169 (1869).

[6] Libby v. Clark, 118 U. S. 255 (1886), Miller, J., quoting 4 Com. Dig., Estates, 1.

[1] 4 Kent, 5; 1 Barb. 575; 11 Wend. 277; 12 Johns. 177; 52 Me. 261; 54 *id.* 426; 2 Oreg. 32; 42 Vt. 690; 23 N. J. E. 308.

[2] Brown v. National Bank, 44 Ohio St. 273 (1886), cases, Owen, C. J.

[3] [2 Bl. Com. 109. See also 3 Law Quar. Rev. 799 (1887); 5 Dill. 411; 94 Ill. 93; 19 Allen, 168; 1 Whart. 427; 1 Barb. 575; 11 *id.* 28; 35 Wis. 36.

general, according to the course of the common law. The courts favored "this subtle finesse of construction," to shorten the duration of these conditional estates. But the nobility, to perpetuate possessions in their own families, procured the enactment of the statute *de donis conditionalibus*, 13 Edw. I (1286), c. 1. This statute revived, in some sort. the ancient feudal restraints, by enacting that the will of the donor should be observed, and that the tenements should go to the issue, if any; if none, should revert to the donor.[1] See further Donum, De donis.

A "fee-simple" is the largest estate a man can have in lands, being an absolute estate in perpetuity. The essential matter is that such an estate is so brought into existence that it *may* continue forever. Where an estate is granted subject to some condition in the instrument creating it, or to some condition implied by law to be thereafter performed, it is called a "conditional fee." A "determinable fee" embraces all fees which are determined by some act or event expressed, in their limitation, to circumscribe their continuance, or inferred by law as bounding their extent. In its broader sense, a determinable fee embraces what is known as a conditional fee. When it becomes an established fact that the event which may terminate. the estate will never occur, a determinable fee enlarges into a fee-simple absolute. So, when the condition upon which a conditional fee rests has been performed, the estate becomes an absolute fee.[2]

Fee-tail. Upon the construction of the statute of *de donis*, the judges held that the donee had no longer a conditional fee-simple, but a particular estate, which they denominated a "fee-tail;" and the donor had the ultimate fee-simple, expectant on the failure of issue; *i. e.*, the reversion.[3]

The term "fee-tail" was borrowed from the feudists, among whom it signified any mutilated or truncated inheritance, from which the heirs general were "cut" off; being from a verb *tailare,* to cut.[3]

Estates tail general. Where lands and tenements are given to one and the "heirs of his body begotten." *Estate tail-special.* Where the gift is restricted to certain heirs of the donee's body; as, to the "heirs of his body, to be begotten by his present wife."

An estate in general or special tail given to a man and the heirs-male of his body begotten is an "estate in tail-male general;" given to a man and the heirs female of his body begotten, is an "estate tail-female."[4]

Estate tail after possibility of issue extinct. Where one is tenant in special tail, and a person, from whose body the issue was

to spring, dies without issue, or, having left issue, that issue becomes extinct.[1]

As the word "heirs" is necessary to create a fee, "body," or some other word of procreation, is necessary to make a fee-tail.[2]

"Issue forever," and "posterity," have been held not less extensive than "heirs of the body." "Children," or equivalent words, will not create the estate. Where such estates are forbidden, estates which formerly would have been deemed such are now held to be estates in fee-simple, and words will be given this construction if possible.[3]

Growth of the estate tail: (1) Permission was granted the heirs of the tenant to succeed him as their deceased ancestor. (2) "Heirs" acquired a breadth of meaning sufficient to admit collaterals. (3) Collaterals were excluded by limiting the estate to a man and the "heirs of his body." (4) This limitation was construed to be a conditional gift — the condition being "issue;" and, a child being born, the estate became a fee-simple, alienable, etc. (5) The statute *de donis* created the estate tail as it at present exists.

See Feud; Recovery, Common; Shelley's Case; Tail. See also Abeyance; Demesne; Descent; Escheat; Farm, Fee-farm; Felony; Heir.

2. Compensation for services,[4] paid to an attorney, an officer of the law, a physician, or an expert.

A sum of money paid to a person for a service done by him to another.[5]

A recompense allowed by law to an officer for his labor and trouble.[6]

Contingent fee. Compensation payable upon an event more or less uncertain, as, upon success in a lawsuit.

An attorney may contract with his client for a contingent fee, but the law will see that the transaction is fair, and that no undue advantage has been taken of the necessities or the ignorance of the client.[7]

County commissioners may employ counsel to collect a claim due the county, for a reasonable compensation only.[7]

An agreement to pay for services of a legitimate character in prosecuting a claim against the United States, in an executive department, violates neither law nor public policy. When the amount of compensation is not agreed upon, evidence of what is ordinarily charged in cases of the same character is admissible.[5]

---

[1] 2 Bl. Com. 110–11; Pierson *v.* Lane, 70 Iowa, 62 (1882); 3 Kent, 11.

[2] Fletcher *v.* Fletcher, 88 Ind. 420 (1882), Niblack, J.

[3] 2 Bl. Com. 112; 11 Wend. 278.

[4] 2 Bl. Com. 113–14.

[1] 2 Bl. Com. 124.

[2] 2 Bl. Com. 114.

[3] Brann *v.* Elzey, 83 Ky. 442–43 (1885), Holt, J.

[4] 3 Bl. Com. 28.

[5] Bloor *v.* Huston, 28 E. L. & E. 360 (1854). Maule, J.

[6] Harbor Master *v.* Southerland, 47 Ala. 517 (1872): 2 Bac. Abr. 463; Musser *v.* Good, 11 S. & R. 248 (1824); Camp *v.* Bates, 13 Conn. *9 (1838); Williams *v.* State, 2 Sneed, 162 (1854).

[7] County of Chester *v.* Barber, 97 Pa. 455, 463 (1881), cases.

[5] Stanton *v.* Embrey, 93 U. S. 557 (1876), cases; Taylor *v.* Bemiss, 110 *id.* 45 (1883).

But a contract for lobbying services stands upon a different footing.[1]

Docket fee. A fee payable to counsel, as part of the costs of record, usually for the use of the successful party.

In Federal practice, "docket fees" in civil cases are a lump sum substituted for the small "fees" formerly allowed attorneys and solicitors, chargeable to and collectible from their clients. This sum is only taxable as costs against the losing party "in cases where by law costs are recoverable in favor of the prevailing party."[2]

In a law case where there is a final trial before a jury, the attorney's fee of twenty dollars, allowed by Rev. St. §§ 823-24, is always to be taxed; and it is for the court to determine who is the prevailing party.[3]

A solicitor for an intervenor in an equity case who prevails is not entitled to the fee; the termination not being such "a final hearing in equity" as is meant by the statute. A special master in chancery is not a referee within the statute.[4] See MARSHAL, 1 (2); PREVAIL.

At common law, an attorney's fee was not recoverable by an action. The reason was, fees were originally given as a gratuity, an *honorarium*, expressive of gratitude. The rule is traceable to the relation between patron and client in ancient Rome: the patron practiced for honor and influence. See HONORARIUM.

Fee-bill. A schedule prescribing the charges to be paid by litigants for the various orders, notices, pleadings, writs, depositions, hearings, transcriptions, etc., had or procured in the conduct of causes.

Some of these charges are payable in advance; others abide (q. v.) the event of the suit. The schedule is prepared by or in pursuance of legislative enactment, or by order of the particular court. See FOLIO.

The term is also used to designate the maximum charges the members of a bar association may make.

See ATTORNEY; COSTS; EXPERT; RETAINER; SALARY.

FEED. Referring to cattle and hogs, may mean to make fit for market by feeding.[5]

FEEDER. See RAILROAD.

FEIGNED. See ISSUE, 2.

FELLOW. See PARTNER; SERVANT.

FELO DE SE. L. 1. A felon (q. v.) of himself. He that deliberately puts an end to his own existence, or commits any unlawful malicious act, the consequence of which is his own death; a self-murderer.[1] See further SUICIDE.

2. A destroyer of itself; a thing that defeats its own purpose.

In this category are: a construction of a proclamation,[2] or instrument,[3] in effect nugatory of the purpose thereof; a bill for peace which makes litigation;[4] a decree which, instead of removing a cloud from a title, places another upon it; unauthorized action by a court.[5]

FELONY.[6] An offense which, at common law, occasioned a total forfeiture of lands or goods, or both, and to which capital or other punishment could be added, according to the degree of guilt. . . In general acceptation, comprises every species of crime which occasioned at common law the forfeiture of lands and goods.[7]

The term is incapable of definition, and descriptive of no offense. It conveys no distinct idea. Its origin has puzzled law-writers. It comprehended two descriptions of punishment, the one capital, with the forfeiture of lands and chattels; the other not capital, with forfeiture of chattels only, and burning in the hand, to which imprisonment could be added.[8]

A vague term, definable by the statutes and decisions of each State for itself.[9]

In general, includes capital and State's prison offenses.[10]

The laws of the United States contain no definition.[11]

Tested by the common law, the term has no determinate meaning, and can apply to no case in this country except treason, where limited forfeiture of estate is allowed. But, technically, that is a crime of a higher grade than felony, although it imports also felony. If it be conceded that capital punishment imports a felony, there can be no felonies, at common law, except capital crimes. But that test is untechnical and founded in error. The notion of "moral degradation" by confinement in a penitentiary has grown into a general understanding that that constitutes any offense a felony. This modern idea has come into general use by force of State legislation on the subject.[12]

---

[1] Trist v. Child, 21 Wall. 450 (1874).

[2] Goodyear v. Sawyer, 17 F. R. 2 (1883); R. S. §§ 823, 824, 983. See generally Coy v. Perkins, 13 F. R. 111, 113-16 (1882), cases; Re Rand, 18 id. 99 (1883).

[3] Williams v. Morrison, 32 F. R. 682 (1887), Thayer, J.

[4] Central Trust Co. v. Wabash, &c. R. Co., 32 F. R. 684 (1887), Thayer, J.

[5] Brockway v. Rowley, 66 Ill. 102 (1872).

[1] 4 Bl. Com. 189; 2 id. 499; 3 C. B. 461.

[2] 2 Black, 678.

[3] 9 Mo. 152; 36 Pa. 136.

[4] 18 How. 266.

[5] 30 Minn. 204.

[6] *Fee*, feud; and *lon*, price or value,—4 Bl. Com. 95. L. L. *felonem*, from *felo, fello*, a traitor, rebel,—Skeat.

[7] 4 Bl. Com. 94-98; 3 Col. 68; 10 Mich. 182; 23 N. Y. 257; 99 id. 216.

[8] Lynch v. Commonwealth, 88 Pa. 192 (1878), Agnew, Chief Justice.

[9] Bruguier v. United States, 1 Dak. 7 (1867).

[10] See State v. Felch, 58 N. H. 2 (1876), cases; 20 Cal. 117; 48 Me. 218; 94 Ill. 501; 55 Ala. 241; 4 Ohio St. 542.

[11] See R. S. § 4090.

[12] United States v. Coppersmith, 2 Flip. 551-58 (1880),

From an early day, and as a necessity, the State legislatures have passed laws defining and enumerating felonies as those crimes punishable by confinement in the penitentiary; and such confinement has come to be the test in nearly every State.[1]

The term as used in acts of Congress is not susceptible of definition.[1]

As a rule, the grade of the offense is determined by the nature of the punishment prescribed. A crime which might be punished by imprisonment in a State's prison was a felony, in New York, prior to the adoption of the Penal Code.[2]

Offenses made felonies by statute are called *statutory felonies*, in contradistinction to *common-law felonies* — murder, manslaughter, rape, arson, burglary, theft, and robbery.

The common-law procedure in the prosecution and punishment, without forfeiture, continues as the characteristic by which felony is distinguished from treason on the one hand and from misdemeanor on the other.

Felon. One who has committed a felony.

Felonious; feloniously. Generally, so indispensable in an indictment for felony, that no other word will be recognized as equivalent.[3]

See ASSAULT; CRIME; DAMAGES; HOMICIDE; INFAMY; MISPRISION.

FEMALE. See FEME; GENDER; VENTER; WOMAN.

FEME; or FEMME. F. A woman; a wife.

Feme is the older form: L. *femella*, *femina*, a young woman. Plural, *femes*, *femmes*.

Feme covert, or feme-covert. A married woman.

By marriage, husband and wife are one person in law. Under his protection and "cover," she does everything; and is therefore called in law-French a *feme-covert;* while her condition is called "coverture,"[4] *q. v.*

Feme sole, or feme-sole. A single woman: one who has never been married, who has been judicially separated from her husband, or whose marriage has been dissolved by divorce from, or by the death of, the husband.

Feme-sole trader. A married woman who trades on her own account as if unmarried.

Originated in a custom of London. Recognized in several States by statutes which enable the wives of mariners at sea, and wives whose husbands from any cause, as, drunkenness or profligacy, desert them, or refuse or neglect to provide for them.

A judicial decree is not a prerequisite. The statutes being designed to suspend the marital rights of the husband in consequence of the acts enumerated, and to relieve the wife from her marital obligations, the establishment of those acts is all that is required of her. The statutes are remedial, and to be interpreted benignly.[1] Compare EARNINGS, Separate.

Her privileges extend no further than to contracts connected with her trade.[2]

A married woman who, in matters of property, is independent of her husband, is a *feme sole* as to such property, and may deal with it as if she were unmarried.[3] See HUSBAND.

FENCE. A line of obstacle, composed of any material that will present the desired obstruction.[4]

Partition fence. As contemplated in a statute, a fence on the line between two proprietors, where there is no road, alley, or other thing which would prevent the erection of such a fence.[5] See WALL.

Fences are regulated by local laws. Boundary fences are to be built on the line, and, when made as intended by law, the cost is borne equally between the parties. A partition fence is presumed to be the common property of both owners.[6]

In some States, steam railway companies are required by statute to protect their tracks by fences. Failure to comply with its contract to fence renders a company liable for injuries to children and animals, consequent thereon.[7]

A statute requiring a railroad to maintain fences and cattle-guards on the sides of its road, and, if it does not, making it liable in double the amount of

---

cases, Hammond, J. See United States v. Staats, 8 How. 44–45 (1850); United States v. Watkids, 7 Saw. 90–94 (1881), cases; People v. Lyon, 99 N. Y. 210 (1885).

[1] United States v. Coppersmith, *ante.*

[2] People v. Lyon, 99 N. Y. 216 (1885).

[3] See Reed v. State, 14 Tex. Ap. 664 (1883); State v. Yates, 21 W. Va. 763 (1883); 64 N. C. 273; 31 N. H. 510; 2 Utah, 457.

[4] 1 Bl. Com. 442; 2 *id.* 292, 433, 497; 32 Barb. 258; 63 Ill. 162; 21 How. 589.

[1] Black v. Tricker, 59 Pa. 13, 16 (1868), Thompson, C. J.; 2 S. & R. 189; 6 W. & S. 346; 14 W. N. C. 191.

[2] McDowall v. Wood, 2 N. & Mc. *242 (S. C., 1820); Newbiggin v. Pillans, 2 Bay, 165 (S. C., 1798); *ib.* 113.

[3] Taylor v. Meads, 34 L. J. Ch. 207 (1865); 21 Cent. Law J. 47–49 (1885), cases; 24 Am. Law Reg. 353–68, 659–62 (1885), cases; 1 Story, Eq. § 243; 2 Kent, 150.

[4] [Allen v. Tobias, 77 Ill. 171 (1875), Breese, J.

[5] Hewit v. Jewell, 59 Iowa, 33 (1882), Seevers, C. J.: Iowa Code, § 1495; 58 Iowa, 256; Jacobs v. Moseley, 91 Mo. 462 (1886).

[6] See 15 Conn. 526; 50 Iowa, 237; 59 *id.* 38; 2 Me. 72; 11 Mass. 294; 2 Metc., Mass., 180; 28 Mo. 556; 12 Mo. Ap. 558; 3 Wend. 142; 32 Pa. 65; 2 Greenl. Ev. § 617; 2 Washb. R. P. 79; 3 Kent, 438.

[7] See Hayes v. Michigan Central R. Co., 111 U. S. 228 (1884); 50 Conn. 128; 62 Ga. 679; 68 Ind. 297; 22 Kan. 359; 63 Me. 308; 24 Minn. 394; 25 *id.* 328; 31 Miss. 157; 46 *id.* 573; 69 Mo. 91, 215; 6 Mo. Ap. 397; 18 Hun, 108; 15 Pa. 290; 1 Thomp. Neg. 501, cases.

damages occasioned thereby to animals, does not deprive it of its property without due process of law or deny it the equal protection of the laws. The additional damages are by way of punishment for negligence; and the sufferer may receive them, rather than the State.[1]

In California, fences erected upon the line between the roadway of a railroad and the land of coterminous properties are not part of the "roadway" to be included by the State board in its valuation of the property of the corporation, but are "improvements" assessable by the local authorities of the proper county.[2]

At common law, the owner of land was not bound to fence it. In Massachusetts, prior to the statute of 1841, c. 125, there was no provision for fences along railroads, and the common law as to the owners and occupiers of adjoining lands applied. Neither had a right to trespass, himself or by his servants or cattle, on the land of the other, and neither could require the other to prevent trespasses by maintaining a fence.[3]

Constructing a barbed-wire fence along a highway is not in itself an actionable wrong, in the absence of statutory inhibition, although animals may attempt to enter the enclosure. If the land owner keeps in good order such fences as are usually built, there is no liability for injury to animals. He is not bound to use boards in constructing a wire fence. But he must not let a fence of any kind become a trap for passing animals, which may be allured from the road to the inadequately fenced enclosure, by the presence of other animals or by the sight of pasture.[4]

See APPENDAGE; CLOSE, 3; ENCLOSURE; OBSTRUCT, 1; TIMBER.

FEOD. See FEUD.

FEOFFMENT. 1. The gift of a feud; infeudation. See FEUD.

Enfeoff. To give a feud.

Feoffor. The grantor of a feud.

Feoffee. The grantee of a feud.

2. The gift of any corporeal hereditament,[5] by delivery of possession upon or within view of the land.[6]

The most ancient method of conveyance. The aptest word was "*do*" or "*dedi*," I give or have given. As the personal abilities of the feoffee were the inducement, his estate was confined to his person, and subsisted for life. By a feoffment, later, a fee-simple was frequently created. With livery of seisin (*q. v.*), the feoffee had an estate at will.[6] At present, land is transferred only by deed or will.

---

[1] Missouri Pacific R. Co. *v.* Humes, 115 U. S. 512 (1885).

[2] Santa Clara County *v.* Southern Pacific R. Co., 118 U. S. 414 (1886).

[3] Boston, &c. R. Co. *v.* Briggs, 132 Mass. 26 (1882), cases.

[4] Sisk *v.* Crump, 112 Ind. 504 (1887); also Haughey *v.* Hart, 62 Iowa, 96 (1883). In general, 22 Cent. Law J. 196 (1886), cases.

[5] 2 Bl. Com. 310.

[6] 3 N. H. 260.

FERÆ NATURÆ. See ANIMAL.

FERMENTED. See LIQUOR.

FEROCIOUS. See ANIMAL.

FERRY.[1] A place where persons and things are taken across a stream or body of water, in boats, for hire.[2]

May refer to the water traversed or to the landing-place or places.[3]

Ferry franchise. A right conferred to land at a particular point upon a stream, and to secure toll for the transportation of passengers and property from that point across the stream.[4]

The essential element is the exclusive right to transport persons, their horses, vehicles, and personal goods, from one shore to the other, over the intervening water, for the toll.[5]

Ferriage. The price or fare to be paid for crossing a ferry; also, the transportation itself.[6]

Ferryman. At common law, one who had the exclusive right of transporting passengers over rivers or other water-courses, for hire, at an established rate.[7]

The grant of a ferry franchise in its nature implies the taking of toll. The only ferries known in some places, as in Massachusetts, are *toll* ferries.[8]

The ordinary ferry is a substitute for the ordinary bridge, for the accommodation of the public generally. The *railroad* ferry is a substitute for the railroad bridge, being the continuation of the railroad tracks across a stream of water; it is not a grant of an exclusive ferry franchise.[9]

One may lawfully transport his own goods in his own boat where another has an exclusive right of ferry.[10]

A State may impose a license fee, directly or through a municipal corporation, upon the ferry-

---

[1] A. S. *ferian*, to convey across, carry, go.

[2] [Akin *v.* Western R. Co., 30 Barb. 310 (1857); Same *v.* Same, 20 N. Y. 376 (1859); Newton *v.* Cubitt, 12 C. B. *58 (1862); 14 Bradw. 381.

[3] Schuylkill Bridge Co. *v.* Frailey, 13 S. & R. *424 (1825); State *v.* Hudson, 23 N. J. L. 209 (1851).

[4] [Mississippi Bridge Co. *v.* Lonergan, 91 Ill. 513 (1879); 23 *id.* 369; 2 Gilm. 169.

[5] [Broadnax *v.* Baker, 94 N. C. 678 (1886), cases, Smith, C. J.; s. c. 55 Am. R. 633. Approved, Mayor of New York *v.* Starin, 106 N. Y. 11 (1887).

[6] [People *v.* San Francisco, &c. R. Co., 35 Cal. 619 (1868).

[7] Clarke *v.* State, 2 McCord, 48 (S. C., 1822).

[8] Attorney-General *v.* Boston, 123 Mass. 468 (1877), cases.

[9] Mayor of New York *v.* New England Transfer Co., 14 Blatch. 168 (1877), cases.

[10] Alexandria, &c. Ferry Co. *v.* Wisch, 73 Mo. 655 (1881). See also 3 Bl. Com. 219; 2 *id.* 37; 5 Cal. 470; 20 Geo. 529; 42 Me. 20; 11 Mich. 53; 58 Miss. 796; 20 N. Y. 370; 77 Va. 218–19; 2 Dill. 332.

keepers living in the State, for boats which they use in conveying, from a landing in the State, passengers and goods across a navigable river to a landing in another State.[1]

Any person who invades the rights of the owner of a ferry franchise by running a ferry himself, is liable for any damages he causes the owner, and may be restrained from a continuance. But, probably, the courts would not restrain the operation of a ferry demanded by public convenience simply because the rightful owner of the franchise neglects or refuses to use it. Such franchise does not include the carrying of merchandise without the presence of the owners; this is the business of a common carrier, and may be done without interference with such franchise. The grant of a franchise may be perpetual.[2]

See BRIDGE; CARRIER, Common; COMMERCE; FRANCHISE, 1; LICENSE, 3; NUISANCE; TOLL, 2; TONNAGE; VEHICLE.

FEU. See FEUD.

FEUD.[3] Land held of a superior, on condition of rendering him service. Opposed to *allodium*, the absolute or ultimate property, which continued to reside in the superior.[4] See ALLODIAL.

A tract of land held by a voluntary and gratuitous donation, on condition of fidelity and certain services.[5]

The constitution of feuds originated in the military policy of the Celtic nations, a policy which was continued in their acquisitions after the fall of the Roman empire. To secure those acquisitions, large districts of land were allotted by the conquering general to his superior officers, and by them, in smaller parcels, to the inferior officers and most deserving soldiers. These allotments were called *feods, feoda, feoffs, feus, fiefs. fieus,* and *fees* — conditional stipends or rewards. The condition annexed was, that the possessor should do service faithfully, at home and in war, to him by whom they were given; for which purpose he took the oath of fealty (*q. v.*), and for a breach of this condition and oath, by not performing the stipulated service or by deserting the lord in battle, the lands were to revert to him who granted them.[6]

Allotments, thus acquired, mutually engaged such as accepted them to defend them; and, as they all sprang from the same right of conquest, no part could subsist independently of the whole; wherefore, all givers as well as all receivers were mutually bound to defend each other's possessions. But as that could not be done effectually in a tumultuous, irregular way, government, and, to that purpose, subordination, was

necessary. Every receiver of lands was therefore bound, when called upon by his benefactor, or the immediate lord of his feud or fee, to do all in his power to defend him. Such benefactor or lord was likewise . subordinate to and under command of his immediate benefactor or superior; and so upward to the prince or general himself; and the several lords were also reciprocally bound, in their respective gradations, to protect the possessions they had given.[1]

Feudal; feodal. Relating to a feud or feuds: as, feudal services or tenures, the feudal law or system.

Feudalism. The feudal system; the principles and constitution of feuds.

Feudalize. To reduce to feudal tenure.

Feudary. Held by or concerning feudal tenure: also, the tenant of a feud.

Feudatory; feudatary. A feudal proprietor, or person who received a feud.

Feudist. One versed in feudal law.

Feudal system. A system of military tenure of landed property, adopted by the general assembly of the principal landholders of the realm (Brittany) for self-protection.

Prevailed from the ninth to the thirteenth centuries, attaining maturity under the Conqueror — 1066-1087. Something similar had been in use among the Saxons. The fundamental maxim was. all lands were originally granted by the sovereign, and are, therefore, held mediately or immediately of the crown.

The grantor was the proprietor or lord; the king was "lord paramount;" his immediate tenants were "lords mesne" — tenants *in capite*, in chief; their tenants were "tenants paravail:" they made profit (avail) out of the land.

At first, grants were held at the will of the lord; then, for a certain period; next, by the grantee and one or more sons; about 1000 A. D., they became hereditary.

Ceremonies observed were: presentation of the prospective tenant; the grant — *dedi et concessi*, I have given and granted; corporal investiture — putting a robe on the tenant, before witnesses; homage or manhood — professing to "become his (the lord's) man . . . of life, and limb and earthly honor." The service to be rendered was called the rent. See DELIVERY, 1.

The grant was made upon the personal ability of the grantee to serve in war, and do suit at court. Hence, he could not alien, nor exchange, nor devise, nor encumber, without consent of the lord. For those reasons, also, women and monks were never made grantees.

The grantor assumed to protect the grantee in his . enjoyment of the land, and was to supply other land of equal value if the tenant was deprived of the grant.

The services were: *free* — such as a freeman or soldier might perform; or *base* — fit for one of servile rank. In quantity and time they were also certain or uncertain.

[1] Wiggins Ferry Co. *v.* East St. Louis, 107 U. S. 365, 370 (1882), Woods, J.

[2] Mayor of New York *v.* Starin, 106 N. Y. 1, 9 (1887), cases.

[3] L. *fides*, faith, and Teut. *ead, odh,* or *od,* property, estate in land, — or, *vieh,* cattle, property; *i. e.,* land held on pecuniary consideration: A. S. *feah,* cattle.

[4] [2 Bl. Com. 105.

[5] Wallace *v.* Harmstad, 44 Pa. 499 (1863).

[6] 2 Bl. Com. 45-46.

[1] 2 Bl. Com. 45-46.

The tenure was: 1. *Frank-tenure:* on consideration of military service and homage. When such service was free but uncertain, the tenure was termed "knight-service," or "tenure in chivalry"—the most honorable of all. When the service was both free and certain, as fealty, or fealty and rent. the tenure was termed "free-socage." 2. *Villeinage:* "pure," when the service was base and uncertain; and "privileged," when the service was base but certain. The last species was called "villain socage." See SOCAGE.

Inseparably incident to tenure in chivalry were: aids, relief, primer seisin, wardship, marriage, fines for alienation, and escheat, *qq. v.*

Under the great survey, made in 1086, the realm was divided into sixty thousand knight's fees, corresponding to the number of men in the army.

Personal service was gradually changed into pecuniary assessments; and, finally, by statute of 12 Chas. II (1661), military tenures were abolished.[1]

In the United States, while lands are generally declared to be allodial, feudal principles, adopted as part of the common law of England, continue to be recognized.

The feudal system, to perpetuate estates in the same family, favored the heir-at-law. Hence, English courts have placed the narrowest construction on the words of wills.[2]

The Revolution threw off the dominion of the mother country, and established the independent sovereignty of the colonies or States. In Pennsylvania, for example, an act was passed, November 27, 1779, for vesting the estates of the late proprietaries in the Commonwealth. The manors and lands which had been surveyed for them were excepted, and a pecuniary compensation provided. The "province" had been a fief, held immediately of the crown. The Revolution, and subsequent legislation, emancipated the soil from the chief characteristic of the feudal system. After this change, the proprietaries held their lands as other citizens — under the Commonwealth, by a title purely allodial. Lands are now held mediately or immediately of the State, but by titles cleared of the rubbish of the dark ages, excepting only the feudal names of things no longer feudal. . . The State sold her lands for the best price she could get, and conferred upon the purchasers the same absolute estate she held, excepting the fifth part of any gold or silver found, and six acres in the hundred for roads; and these have been reserved, as everything else has been granted, by *contract.* Her patents acknowledge a pecuniary consideration, and stipulate for no fealty, escheat, rent-service, or other feudal incident. The State is the lord paramount as to no man's land. When any of it is wanted for public purposes, the State, in virtue of her political sovereignty, takes it, but she compels herself, or those who claim under her, to make full compensation to the owner.[3]

---

[1] See 2 Bl. Com. 43-102; 4 *id.* 418-39; 1 *id.* 410; 1 Washb. R. P. 18.

[2] Bosley *v.* Bosley's Executrix, 14 How. 397 (1852).

[3] Wallace *v.* Harmstad, 44 Pa. 500 (1863), Woodward, J.: Huhley *v.* Vanhorne, 7 S. & R. 188 (1821), Gibson, J.; 3 *id.* 447; 9 *id.* 333. See Green, Short Hist. Eng. Peop. 112-14.

Subinfeudation. Subletting part of a feud; carving smaller holdings out of a feudal estate.

Since this deprived the superior lord of his profits of wardship, marriage, and escheat, which fell into the hands of the middle lord, it was restricted by Magna Charta, c. 32 (9 Hen. 3, 1225), and by Quia Emptores (18 Edw. 1, 1290) entirely suppressed, and alienation, in the modern sense, introduced.[1]

To feu; a feu. A right to the use of lands, houses, and other heritable subjects, in perpetuity, in consideration of an annual payment in grain or money, called *feu-duty,* and certain other contingent burdens. Whence, also, *feu farm, feu holding.*

Practically, a sale for a stipulated annual payment equivalent to chief rent. Modern feu-duties are generally paid in money. On this footing almost all the house property in towns, and suburban-villa property, in Scotland, is held.[2] Compare FARM, Fee farm.

See also ABEYANCE; ATTAINDER; ATTORNMENT; DEMESNE; DESCENT, Canons of; ESCHEAT; FEE, 1; FEOFFMENT; PRIMOGENITURE; PUEBLO; RELIEF, 1; TENURE, 1; VILLAIN; WARD, 3.

FI. FA. See EXECUTION, 3, Writs of.

FIAT. See FIERI.

FICTION.[3] That which is feigned, assumed, pretended. The legal assumption that something is true which is or may be false; an assumption of an innocent and beneficial character, made to advance the ends of justice. Compare ESTOPPEL; PRESUMPTION.

An allegation in legal proceedings that does not accord with the actual facts; and which may therefore be contradicted for every purpose except to defeat the beneficial end for which the fiction is allowed.[4]

Fictions of law are highly beneficial and useful; especially as "no fiction extends to work an injury:" the proper operation being to prevent mischief or remedy an inconvenience that might result from a general rule. The maxim is, *in fictione juris semper subsistit æquitas* — in a fiction of law equity always subsists; a legal fiction is consistent with justice.[5]

But not admitted, where life, liberty, or personal safety is in jeopardy.[6]

Illustrative examples: that the king was the original proprietor of all lands.[7] That an original *capias* had been granted, when a *testatum capias* issued into

---

[1] 2 Bl. Com. 91; 44 Pa. 498.

[2] Chamber's Encyclopedia.

[3] L. *fictio; fingere,* to invent.

[4] [Strafford Bank *v.* Cornell, 2 N. H. 327 (1821).

[5] 3 Bl. Com. 43, 283. See Best, Presump., 27; 2 Burr *962.

[6] 4 Bl. Com. 280.

[7] 4 Bl. Com. 418.

another county.[1] That a summons issues in an amicable action. That a person bailed is in the custody of his bail. That a feigned issue is based upon a wager made. That what ought to be done is done, and relates back to the time when it was to be done.[2] The doctrine of abeyance.[3] That a term of court consists of a single day.[4] That a writ of error actually removes the record, instead of a transcript of the record.[5] That every person knows what is passing in the courts.[6] That the possession of one who has a right of lien is the possession of the law.[7] That the law takes no notice of a fraction of a day.[8] The doctrine of equitable conversion.[9] The doctrine of representation in an agent, and in a decedent; and some features of the early action of ejectment.

Fiction makes several corporations out of what is really one, in order to give each State control over the charters it grants.[10]

Fictio, in old Roman law, is properly a term of pleading, and signifies a false averment which the defendant was not allowed to traverse; as, that the plaintiff was a Roman citizen, when in truth he was a foreigner. The object was to give jurisdiction. . . Legal fiction may be used to signify an assumption which conceals, or affects to conceal, the fact that a rule of law has undergone alteration, its letter remaining unchanged while its operation is modified. The "fact" is that the law has been wholly changed; the "fiction" is that it remains what it always was. . . Fictions are particularly congenial to the infancy of society. They satisfy the desire for improvement, while they do not offend the disrelish for change. Thus they become invaluable expedients for overcoming the rigidity of law.[11]

Fictitious. 1. Not real; feigned: as, a fictitious — action, case, issue, name, party, payee.

A fictitious case is a suit brought upon facts with respect to which no real controversy exists.

Any attempt, by a mere colorable dispute, or where the appellant has become the sole party in interest, to get up a case for the opinion of the court, where there is no real and substantial controversy, is an abuse reprehended by all courts, and punishable as a contempt.[12]

2. Imaginary; unsubstantial: as, fictitious bail, *q. v.*

3. Not made in good faith: as, a fictitious bid, *q. v.*

---

[1] 3 Bl. Com. 283.
[2] 3 Bl. Com. 433.
[3] 2 Bl. Com. 107.
[4] Newhall *v.* Sanger, 92 U. S. 766 (1875).
[5] Hunnicutt *v.* Peyton, 102 U. S. 356 (1880).
[6] 3 Pars. Contr. 282.
[7] 3 Pars. Contr. 234.
[8] 3 Pars. Contr. 504 (g).
[9] 1 Pars. Contr. 134.
[10] Horne *v.* Boston, &c. R. Co., 18 F. R. 50 (1883).
[11] Maine, Ancient Law, 24–25.
[12] Lord *v.* Veazie, 8 How. 255 (1850), Taney, C. J ; Cleveland *v.* Chamberlain, 1 Black, 426 (1861); Bartmeyer *v.* Iowa, 18 Wall. 134–35 (1873).

FIDES. L. Trust, confidence, reliance; credence, belief, faith.

Bona fides. Good faith. *Bona fide.* In, with, or by good faith. **Mala fides.** Bad faith. *Mala fide.* In, with, or by bad faith. **Uberrima fides.** The best faith, the severest good faith. *Uberrima fide.* With the strictest good faith. See FAITH, Good, Bad.

Fidei commissum (pl. **commissa**). A thing committed to one's faithfulness; a bequest or devise in trust; a trust.

Fidei commissarius. The beneficiary under a donation in trust; a *fidei* or *fide* commissary; a *cestui que trust*.

A *fidei commissum* (usually created by a will) was the disposal of an inheritance, in confidence that the transferee would convey it or dispose of the profits at the will of another. It was made the business of a particular magistrate, the *prætor fidei commissarius*, to enforce observance of this confidence. The right thereby given was looked upon as vested, and entitled to a remedy. These *fidei commissa* were the originals of modern uses and trusts.[1] See USE, 2.

Fide-jussio or **fidejussio.** A giving or being surety; suretyship; bail.

Fidejussor. A surety; bail in admiralty.

He is absolutely bound to pay the costs and condemnation at all events.[2]

Admiralty may take a fidejussory caution or stipulation in cases *in rem*, and in a summary manner award execution to the prevailing party. Delivery of property on bail being given, is implied.[3]

Fides servanda. Faith must be kept; the good faith of a transaction will be given effect.

A maxim with regard to sales of personalty. If there is no express warranty, general rules of implication should be adopted with this maxim in view. A warranty will be implied only when good faith requires it.[4]

FIDELITY. See FAITH; FIDES; INSURANCE; TRUST, 1.

FIDUCIARY.[5] Held, founded, resting upon an actual trust: as, a fiduciary — capacity or character, contract or relation, debt, debtor, creditor.

Fiducial. Of the nature of a trust.

---

[1] 2 Bl. Com. 327; 1 Story, Eq. § 321; 2 *id.* §§ 965–67; 1 Pomeroy, Eq. § 151. See 3 La. An. 432; 2 How. 619; 15 *id.* 357.
[2] 3 Bl. Com. 291, 108.
[3] Brig Alligator, 1 Gall. 149 (1812); United States *v.* Ames, 99 U. S. 40 (1878).
[4] McCoy *v.* Artcher, 3 Barb. 330 (1848); 23 *id.* 524; 1 Metc., Mass., 551.
[5] L. *fiduciarius: fiducia*, confidence: *fides*, q. v.

A fiduciary debt is founded or arises upon some confidence or trust, as distinguished from a debt founded simply upon contract.[1]

A fiduciary relationship is one in which, if a wrong arises, the same remedy exists against the wrong-doer on behalf of the principal as would exist against a trustee on behalf of the *cestui que trust*.[2]

In the New York laws allowing arrest as a remedy for debts incurred in a fiduciary capacity, "fiduciary" imports trust, confidence; refers to integrity or fidelity rather than to credit or ability; contemplates good faith rather than legal obligation.[3]

A debt contracted in a fiduciary capacity was not released by a discharge in bankruptcy.[4] This applied to technical trusts only, not to trusts implied from contracts of agency or bailment.[5]

"Fiduciary" and "confidential" relation seem to be used by the courts and law-writers as convertible expressions. It is a peculiar relation which exists between client and attorney, principal and agent, principal and surety, landlord and tenant, parent and child, guardian and ward, ancestor and heir, husband and wife, trustee and *cestui que trust*, executors or administrators and creditors, legatees, or distributees, appointer and appointee under powers, partner and part-owners. In these and like cases the law, to prevent undue advantage from the unlimited confidence, affection, or sense of duty which the relation creates, requires the utmost of good faith in all transactions between the parties.[6]

See FRAUD; INFLUENCE; TRUST, 1.

FIEF. See FEUD.

FIELD. 1. A lot in a town may be a field.[7] But a one-acre lot used for cultivating vegetables is a "garden."[8] See AGRICULTURE.

2. "In the field," said of a soldier, means in the military service for the purpose of carrying on a particular war.[9]

FIERI. L. To be done; to be made. Compare FACERE.

---

[1] Crisfield v. State, &c., 55 Md. 194 (1880), Robinson, J.

[2] Re West of England Bank, *Exp.* Dale, 11 Ch. D. 778 (1879), Fry, J.; Connecticut Mut. Ins. Co. v. Central Nat. Bank, 104 U. S. 68 (1881).

[3] Stoll v. King, 8 How. Pr. 299 (1853), cases; Frost v. M'Carger, 14 *id.* 137 (1857); Sutton v. De Camp, 4 Abb. Pr. 484 (1868); 1 Code R. 86, 87; 5 Duer, 86.

[4] R. S. § 5117.

[5] Chapman v. Forsyth, 2 How. 208 (1844); Hennequin v. Clews, 111 U. S. 681 (1884); Woodward v. Towne, 127 Mass. 42 (1879), cases; 104 *id.* 248; 15 Gray, 547–49; 16 Conn. 223; 77 N. Y. 427; 13 Rep. 468; 9 Bened. 495–97, cases; 5 Biss. 324.

[6] Robins v. Hope, 57 Cal. 497 (1881); 1 Story, Eq. § 218. As to fiduciary depositors in banks, see Naltner v. Dolan, 108 Ind. 500 (1886); 26 Am. Law Reg. 29–30 (1887), cases.

[7] State v. McMinn, 81 N. C. 587 (1879); Commonwealth v. Josselyn, 97 Mass. 412 (1867).

[8] Simons v. Lovell, 7 Heisk. 510 (1872).

[9] Sargent v. Ludlow, 42 Vt. 720 (1870).

Fiat. Let it be done. An order or allowance by a judge or court.

Fiat justitia. Let justice be done.

Fieri facias. Cause to be made. See EXECUTION, 3, Writs of.

In fieri. In course of being done; not yet completed. Opposed, *in esse*, q. v.

FIFTEENTH AMENDMENT. See CITIZEN.

FIGHT. Does not necessarily imply that both parties should give and take blows. It is sufficient that they voluntarily put their bodies in position with that intent.[1] See COMBAT; DUEL; MAYHEM; PRIZE-FIGHTING.

FIGURES. Numerals.

Arabic, 1888; Roman, MDCCCLXXXVIII.

The objection to using Arabic figures in formal documents is that they may be readily altered. In some States they are not allowed in complaints and indictments, except in setting forth copies. It is considered better to date formal instruments by writing the day and year in words; and to write in words in the body of a bill, note, or receipt the sum for which it is given. See DESCRIPTION, 4; FOLIO, 2; FORGERY; WORDS.

FILE.[2] 1. At common law, a thread, string or wire, upon which writs or other exhibits are fastened for safe-keeping and ready reference.[3]

2. To exhibit or present to a court in the regular way: as, to file a bill in equity, a libel in admiralty or divorce, a petition, answer, exception, writ of error.

Also, to leave a paper with an officer for action or preservation; and, to indorse a paper, as received into custody, and give it its place among other papers, — to file away.

Files. Collections of papers, orderly arranged; also, papers under official custody.

On file. Kept in an orderly collection; in its proper place.

Filing a paper consists in placing it in the proper official custody, by the party charged with this duty, and the making of the proper indorsement by the officer.[4]

A paper is filed when delivered to the proper officer, and by him received, to be kept on file.[5]

---

[1] State v. Gladden, 73 N. C. 155 (1875); Tate v. State, 46 Ga. 148 (1872).

[2] L. *filum*, a thread.

[3] [Gorham v. Summers, 25 Minn. 86 (1878); 27 *id.* 18, 23; 16 Ohio St. 548; 14 Tex. 339.

[4] Phillips v. Beene, 38 Ala. 251 (1862).

[5] Peterson v. Taylor, 15 Ga. 484 (1854); Powers v. State, 87 Ind. 148 (1882); Amy v. Shelby County, 1 Flip. 104 (1872); 6 Ind. 309; 2 Blackf. 247; 2 Iowa, 91; 29 *id.*

An allegation that "no certificate has been filed" in the office of the register, is equivalent to "has not been left for record." [1]

An affidavit of claim is "filed with" a declaration when both are filed at the same time. And this is not affected by their being detached, or by the place of deposit in the office. [2] See LODGE, 1 (2).

In modern practice, "the file" is the manner adopted for preserving papers; the mode is immaterial. Such papers as are not for transcription into records are folded similarly, indorsed with a note or index of their contents, and tied up in a bundle — "a file."

FILIAL. See EMANCIPATION; PARENT.

FILIATION. The relation or tie between a child and its parent, especially its father; also, ascertainment of paternity, affiliation.

Affiliation. Judicial determination of paternity — that a man is the father of a bastard. See FILIUS.

The mother's testimony must be corroborated. [3]

FILIUS. L. A child; a son.

Filius nullius. The child of nobody.

Filius populi. The child of the people. A bastard, q. v.

FILUM. L. A thread; a line — the middle line of a stream or road.

The imaginary line drawn through a stream or highway at which the titles of the opposite owners presumably meet. [4]

Filum aquæ. The line of the water; water-line.

Ad filum aquæ. To the line of the water.

Medium filum aquæ. The middle line of the water. See RIPARIAN.

Filum viæ. The line of the way.

Medium filum viæ. The middle line of the road.

FINAL. [5] 1. Pertaining to the end; to be paid at the close of a cause: as, final costs. Opposed, *interlocutory,* q. v.

2. The last: as, a final account, balance, settlement, qq. v.

3. Putting an end to; conclusively determined in a particular court: as, a final — adjudication, decree, disposition, judgment, order, sentence, qq. v. Opposed, *interlocu-*

---

tory: ending or concerning some intermediate matter or issue; also opposed to *preliminary,* as in final injunction, q. v. Compare DEFINITIVE.

A final judgment or decree puts an end to the action by declaring that the plaintiff has or has not entitled himself to recover the remedy for which he sues. [1]

A judgment or decree which determines the particular case is final. [2]

A decree is final when the court has completed its adjudication of the cause. [3]

It has long been well settled that a judgment or decree, to be final, must terminate the litigation between the parties on the merits of the case, so that if there should be an affirmance in the appellate court, the court below would have nothing to do but to execute the judgment or decree it had already rendered. It has not always been easy to decide when decrees in equity are final within this rule, and there may be some apparent conflict in the cases on that subject, but in the common-law courts the question has never been a difficult one. If the judgment is not one which disposes of the whole case on its merits, it is not final. Consequently it has been uniformly held that a judgment of reversal with leave for further proceedings in the court below cannot be brought before the Supreme Court on a writ of error. [4]

Thus, a decree of sale in a foreclosure suit, which settles all the rights of the parties and leaves nothing to be done but to make the sale and pay out the proceeds, is final for purposes of appeal. [5]

FIND. 1. To come lawfully into the possession of lost or abandoned personalty.

The finder has a clear title against all the world except the true owner, who has not shown any intention to abandon. [6] He stands in the place of the owner, is a trustee for the owner. The place of finding creates no exception. After the original owner is known and accessible, any keeping with intention to appropriate is larceny. Reasonable diligence to learn who the rightful owner is should be used. Necessary expenses incurred in preserving the property or in discovering the owner are a lien. [7]

Thus, as between the finder and the owner of a paper-sack in which bank-notes are found, the notes are the property of the finder; [8] so, also, as between

---

468; 135 Mass. 580; 138 *id.* 196; 55 Mo. 301; 65 *id.* 500; 13 Barb. 326; 2 Caldw. 488; 14 Tex. 339.

[1] Wood *v.* Union Gospel Church Association, 63 Wis. 13 (1885).

[2] Hossler *v.* Hartman, 82 Pa. 53 (1876).

[3] 1 Whart. Ev. § 414.

[4] See 3 Kent, 427, 428, 432, 434.

[5] L. *finalis: finis,* limit, end.

---

[1] 3 Bl. Com. 398, 452.

[2] Weston *v.* Council of Charleston, 2 Pet. 464 (1829), Marshall, C. J.

[3] Green *v.* Fisk, 103 U. S. 519 (1880), Waite, C. J.

[4] Bostwick *v.* Brinkerhoff, 106 U. S. 3 (1882), cases, Waite, C. J.; Dainese *v.* Kendall, 119 *id.* 54 (1886), cases.

[5] Grant *v.* Phœnix Ins. Co., 106 U. S. 431 (1882). See St. Louis R. Co. *v.* Southern Express Co., 108 *id.* 28 (18..3); 17 Johns. 548; 50 Cal. 557; 50 Me. 401; 14 Blatch. 130.

[6] 2 Bl. Com. 9; 2 Kent, 290.

[7] Durfee *v.* Jones, 11 R. I. 588 (1877), cases; Griggs *v.* State, 58 Ala. 425 (1877), cases; N. Y. & Harlem R. Co. *v* Haws, 56 N. Y. 178 (1874); Armory *v.* Delamirie, 1 Sm. L. C. 636-66, cases.

[8] Bowen *v.* Sullivan, 62 Ind. 288-91 (1878), cases.

the finder and the keeper of a hotel in which money or other thing of value is found.[1]

The owner of a tannery neglected to remove all of the hides he had placed in the vats. The land was sold, and, forty years later, a laborer discovered the hides. *Held*, that the representative of the owner was entitled to them.[2]

Property is not lost, in the sense of the rule, if it was intentionally laid on a table, counter, or other place, by the owner, who forgot to take it away. In such case the proprietor of the premises is entitled to the custody. Whenever the surroundings show that the article was deposited in its place, the finder has no right of possession against the owner of the building. An article casually dropped is also within the rule.[1]

See ABANDON, 1; ESTRAY; REWARD, 2; TREASURE-TROVE; TROVER.

2. A corporation engaged in business within a State is said to be " found " doing business there.[3]

To give the Federal courts jurisdiction *in personam* over a foreign corporation, in the absence of a voluntary appearance, it must appear, as a fact, that the corporation is carrying on business in such foreign State or district; that such business is transacted or managed by some agent or officer representing the corporation, and some local law must make the corporation amenable to suit there.[4]

The presence of the chief officers of a corporation in a State other than that of its creation does not change its residence, nor does the fact that the officers take into such State corporate property for exhibition and advertisement, bring the corporation into the State as an " inhabitant," or so that it can be " found " there.[5]

Corporations are citizens of the State under whose laws they are created. They cannot, by engaging in business in another State, acquire a residence there.[6]

3. " Find " and " found," said of a defendant as to whom a summons or other process has been issued, have a technical meaning, the equivalent of the Latin *inventus*, come upon, met.[7]

Opposed, "not found:" *non est inventus*, he has not been found; abbreviated *n. e. i.*

---

[1] Hamaker *v.* Blanchard, 90 Pa. 379 (1879), cases, Trunkey, J.

[2] Livermore *v.* White, 74 Me. 452 (1883), cases.

[3] R. S. § 739; *Exp.* Schollenberger, 96 U. S. 378 (1877); Blackburn *v.* Selma, &c. R. Co., 2 Flip. 525 (1879); Robinson *v.* Nat. Stock-Yard Co., 12 F. R. 361 (1882); Mohr Distilling Co. *v.* Insurance Cos., *ib.* 474, 476 (1882), cases; Merchants' Manuf. Co. *v.* Grand Trunk R. Co., 13 *id.* 358, 360 (1882), cases.

[4] United States *v.* American Bell Telephone Co., 29 F. R. 17 (1886), cases, Jackson, J.; 32 *id.* 437.

[5] Carpenter *v.* Westinghouse Air Brake Co., 32 F. R. 434 (1887), Brewer, J.

[6] Fales *v.* Chicago, &c. R. Co., 32 F. R. 678-79 (1887), cases.

[7] Carter *v.* Youngs, 42 N. Y. Supr. Ct. 172 (1877), Sanford, J.

" Not found " is an abridged form of return which usage sanctions. It imports that the defendant was not found within the meaning of the precept, that is, after proper effort to find him in the due execution of the precept.[1] See RESIDE.

4. To arrive at as a conclusion: to conclude or terminate formally: as, to find an indictment, a verdict.

If the grand jury are satisfied of the truth of an accusation, they indorse upon it "a true bill." The indictment is then said to be " found." To this at least twelve jurors must agree. Opposed, "not found."[2]

Finding. The decision of a judge, arbitrator, jury, or referee.

Finding against evidence. A finding which negatives the existence of a fact admitted by the pleadings; also, a finding not sustained by the evidence.[3]

General finding; special finding. Issues of fact in civil cases in any circuit court may be tried and determined by the court, without the intervention of a jury, whenever the parties, or their attorneys of record, file with the clerk a stipulation in writing waiving a jury. The finding of the court upon the facts, which may be either general or special, shall have the same effect as the verdict of a jury.[4]

The parties are concluded by the propositions of fact which the evidence, in the opinion of the court, establishes. Whether general or special, the finding has the same effect as the verdict of a jury; and its sufficiency to sustain the judgment is the only matter for review,[5] — the "sufficiency " of the finding, not of the facts, is meant.[6]

Special finding. A statement of the ultimate facts on which the law must determine the rights of the parties.[7]

The finding of a referee should have the precision of a special verdict; it should specify with distinctness the facts found, and not leave them to be inferred.[8] See VERDICT, Special.

FINE.[9] 1. An amicable composition or agreement of a suit, actual or fictitious, by leave of the king or of his justices, whereby

---

[1] International Grain Ceiling Co. *v.* Dill, 10 Bened. 95 (1878), Choate, J.

[2] 4 Bl. Com. 305.

[3] Silvey *v.* Neary, 59 Cal. 98 (1881); Harris *v.* Harris, *ib.* 620 (1881).

[4] R. S. § 649.

[5] R. S. § 700; Ryan *v.* Carter, 93 U. S. 81 (1876), cases; Tyng *v.* Grinnell, 92 U. S. 469 (1875), cases; 18 Wall. 254; 103 U. S. 556; 112 *id.* 604.

[6] Walnut *v.* Wade, 103 U. S. 688 (1880).

[7] Norris *v.* Jackson, 9 Wall. 127 (1869), cases.

[8] Mason Lumber Co. *v.* Buchtel, 101 U. S. 637 (1879).

[9] L. *finis*, end.

lands in question become, or are acknowledged to be, the right of one of the parties.[1]

It put an "end" to controversies concerning the matter. The plaintiff began an action of covenant upon a supposed agreement to convey to him. The defendant (the deforciant) then applied to the court for leave to settle the matter; which he did by acknowledging that the lands were the right of the complainant. The "note" of the fine was an abstract of the writ of covenant, and the concord; it named the parties, the land, and the agreement. The "foot" or conclusion recited the parties, day, year, place, and before whom acknowledged or levied. The party levying the fine was called the "cognizor;" he to whom it was levied, the "cognizee." The proceeding was a solemn conveyance on record, and bound parties, privies, and strangers — after five years.[1]

The object oftenest sought by "levying a fine" was the barring of an estate tail. The statute of fines, 11 Hen. VII (1496), c. 1, and 32 Hen. VIII (1541), c. 36, were abolished by 3 and 4 Wm. IV (1833), c. 74, which substituted a disentailing deed by the tenant in tail.[2]

The object of a fine was to quiet titles more speedily than by the ordinary limitation of twenty and twenty-five years. One of two contesting claimants could compel an assertion or abandonment of the pretensions of his adversary in one-fifth the usual period of delay. . . In use in New York down to 1830.[3]

Compare RECOVERY, Common. See ACKNOWLEDGMENT, 2.

2. A pecuniary punishment for an offense, inflicted by sentence of a criminal court. A penalty; a forfeiture.[4]

A sum of money imposed by a court according to law, as a punishment for the breach of some penal statute. Never applied to damages or compensation for loss.[5]

A pecuniary penalty.[6]

A "fine" is an amercement imposed upon a person for a past violation of law; "exemplary damages" have reference rather to the future than the past conduct of the offender, and are given as an admonition not to repeat the offense.[7]

Excessive fines shall not be imposed.[8]

This applies to national, not to State, legislation.

---

[1] 2 Bl. Com. 349–57.

[2] Williams, Real Prop. 47–49.

[3] McGregor v. Comstock, 17 N. Y. 162, 166 (1858); 6 id. 495. See also Guthrie v. Owen, 10 Yerg. 341 (1837).

[4] Hanscomb v. Russell, 11 Gray, 374 (1858), Metcalf, J.

[5] Atchison, &c. R. Co. v. State, 22 Kan. 15 (1879), Valentine, J.; Jockers v. Borgman, 29 id. 122 (1883), cases, Horton, C. J.

[6] New Mexico v. Baca, 2 N. M. 190 (1882). See also 1 Ind. 315; 4 Iowa, 300; 6 Neb. 37; 4 Lans. 140; 15 Rich. 20; 14 Tex. 398.

[7] Schafer v. Smith, Sup. Ct. Ind. (1877): 4 Cent. Law J. 272.

[8] Constitution, Amd. Art. VIII.

The Supreme Court cannot, on *habeas corpus*, revise a sentence on the ground that the fine is excessive.[1]

See AMERCE; PARDON; PUNISH.

FINGER. See MAYHEM.

FINIS. See FINAL; FINE.

FINISHED. See FINAL; PERFECT.

Moving into a house may not estop the owner to deny that it was finished, within the meaning of his acceptance of an order "to be paid when the house is finished."[2]

FIRE. A policy of insurance against fire includes every loss necessarily following directly from the occurrence of a fire.[3] See CAUSE, 1, Proximate; EXPLOSION; INSURANCE; LIGHTNING.

Fire-arm. A weapon acting by the force of gunpowder.[4] See ARMS, 2; LOADED; WEAPON.

Fire department. A city which is authorized to maintain water-works and a fire department, and which collects taxes for those purposes, is not responsible for the negligence of its fire department in permitting private property to be burned.[5]

Fire-escape. An act which directs that certain buildings shall be provided with fire-escapes by the "owners," does not apply to an owner in fee, not in possession, who has leased the premises, but to the tenant. Being a penal statute, it cannot be extended by implication to parties who do not clearly come within its terms.[6]

Fire ordeal. See ORDEAL.

Fireworks. Percussion caps, designed for signaling railway trains are "explosive preparations," within the meaning of a statute regulating the keeping of such articles, although they may not be "fireworks" as the latter term is known to commerce.[7]

Set on fire. A statute giving damages against any one who shall "set on fire" the woods of another, does not apply to an accidental firing by a locomotive engine, without negligence.[8]

See ARSON; NECESSITY; RES, Perit, etc.; SALVAGE; TAKE, 8.

---

[1] *Exp.* Watkins, 7 Pet. *574 (1833); Pervear v. Massachusetts, 5 Wall. 480 (1866). As to the power in associations to impose fines upon members, see 27 Am. Law Reg. 370–74 (1888), cases.

[2] Robbins v. Blodgett, 121 Mass. 584 (1877).

[3] Brady v. North Western Fire Ins. Co., 11 Mich. 445 (1863).

[4] Atwood v. State, 53 Ala. 509 (1875); Evins v. State, 46 id. 88 (1871); Hutchinson v. State, 62 id. 3 (1878); Williams v. State, 61 Ga. 417 (1878).

[5] Robinson v. Evansville, 87 Ind. 334, 336–37 (1882): 85 id. 130; 17 B. Mon. 720; 19 Ohio St. 19; 16 Gray, 297; 104 Mass. 87; 123 id. 311; 69 Pa. 420; 38 Conn. 368; 53 Mo. 159; 18 Wis. 83; 33 id. 314; 39 Iowa, 575; 51 Ala. 139; Dill. Munic. Corp. § 774.

[6] Schott v. Harvey, 105 Pa. 222 (1884); Lea v. Kirby, 10 Cin. Law Bul. 449.

[7] Bliss v. Lilley, 113 E. C. L. 133 (1862).

[8] Missouri, &c. R. Co. v. Davidson, 14 Kan. 349 (1875). Liability of railroad companies for causing fires, 4 South. Law Rev. 703–69 (1878), cases.

FIRM. See PARTNERSHIP; SIGNATURE; TRADE-MARK.

FIRST. 1. Preceding all others; foremost, earliest, preferred: as, first — mortgage, occupant, purchaser, taker, term; first of exchange, *qq. v.*

2. In a will, may not import precedence of one bequest over another.[1]

Compare PRIMA; PRIMARY.

FISCAL. See CONFISCATE; FORFEITURE.

FISH; FISHERY. 1. The right to take fish at a certain place or in particular waters is a "fishery."

Common of fishery or **piscary.**[2] A liberty of fishing in another's waters. **Free fishery.** The exclusive right of fishing in a public river. **Several fishery.** The owner of this is also owner of the soil, or derives his right from such owner; a separate fishery.[3]

A *common of fishery* is not an exclusive right, but is enjoyed in common with certain other persons. A *free fishery* is a franchise, obtained by grant or prescription, and is distinct from ownership in the soil.[4]

The right to take fish in waters upon the soil of a private proprietor, for one's own use, is not an easement, but a right of profit in lands. It can be acquired only by grant or prescription. But neither prescription, nor custom, nor dedication raises a general right in the public to enter upon private land to fish in the waters thereon.[5]

Each State owns the bed of all tide-waters within its jurisdiction, unless it has granted them away; also, the tide-waters themselves, and the fish in them, as far as capable of ownership while running. The ownership is that of the people in their united sovereignty. The title thus held is subject to the paramount right of regulating navigation, granted to the United States. The fisheries remain under the exclusive control of the State. The State has the right, in its discretion, to appropriate its tide-waters and the beds to be used by its people as a common for taking and cultivating fish [oysters], so far as may be done without obstructing navigation. Such appropriation is a regulation of the use by the people of their common property. The right in the people comes from citizenship and property combined. It is a property right, not a mere privilege or immunity of citizenship. As the State may grant the exclusive use of any part of its common property to one of its citizens, so it may confine the use to its own citizens.[6]

Oysters are fish, within the meaning of a covenant not to retail fish.[1]

Oysters which have been taken, and thus become private property, may be planted in a place subject to the flow of the tide and where there are none naturally, and remain private property.[2]

The owner has the same absolute property in oysters that he has in inanimate things or in domestic animals. Oysters planted in public waters will not be considered abandoned to the public unless planted where oysters naturally grow. If they interfere with the rights of navigation, they may be removed as a nuisance; but a private person, not the owner, may not convert them to his own use.[3]

In the exercise of its police power, a State may grant to individual citizens the exclusive right to plant and to remove oysters under the public waters.[4] See AQUA, Currit, etc.

Fish commissioner. An act of Congress approved February 9, 1871, provides for the appointment of a commissioner of fish and fisheries, with power to preserve and increase food fishes throughout the United States.[5] Some of the States have a board of commissioners, with like powers.

An act approved January 20, 1888, amends the foregoing act so that it reads: There shall be appointed by the President, by and with the advice and consent of the Senate, a person of scientific and practical acquaintance with the fish and fisheries to be a commissioner of fish and fisheries; that he shall receive a salary at the rate of five thousand dollars a year, be removable at the pleasure of the President, and shall not hold any other office or employment under the authority of the United States or any State.[6]

Fish laws. See GAME, 1; SEA.

2. Referring to a bill in equity or to interrogatories, "fishing" imports seeking to pry into the title or individual affairs of an adverse party.

A "fishing bill" is a bill in which the plaintiff shows no cause of action, and endeavors to compel the defendant to disclose a cause in the plaintiff's favor.[7]

A bill in equity that seeks a discovery upon general, loose, and vague allegations is styled a "fishing

---

Waite, C. J. See also Boggs v. Commonwealth, 76 Va. 989 (1882); M'Candlish v. Commonwealth, *ib.* 1004 (1882).

[1] Caswell v. Johnson, 58 Me. 166 (1870).

[2] Fleet v. Hegeman, 14 Wend. 42 (1835); State v. Sutton, 2 R. I. 434 (1853); Lowndes v. Dickerson, 34 Barb. 586 (1861).

[3] State v. Taylor, 27 N. J. L. 119 (1858), Green, C. J. See also Johnson v. Loper, 46 *id.* 321 (1884).

[4] People v. Thompson, 30 Hun, 457 (1883).

[5] R. S. § 4395.

[6] 25 St. L. 1.

[7] [Carroll v. Carroll, 11 Barb. 298 (1851), Mitchell, J.

---

[1] Everett v. Carr, 59 Me. 330 (1871): 57 *id.* 523.

[2] L. *piscarius*, relating to fishes or fishery: *piscis*, a fish.

[3] [2 Bl. Com. 34, 39–40; 15 Op. Att.-Gen. 663.

[4] 3 Kent, 329. See 1 Whart. 132.

[5] Cobb v. Davenport, 33 N. J. L. 225–26 (1868), Depue, J. See also Cole v. Eastman, 133 Mass. 67 (1882), Devens, Justice.

[6] McCready v. Virginia, 94 U. S. 394–97 (1876), cases,

bill;" any such bill will be at once dismissed upon that ground alone.[1]

A party has no right to any discovery except of facts, deeds, and other writings necessary to the title under which he claims.[2] See DISCOVERY, 6.

FIT. See CULTIVATION; DISCRETION, 2.

FIX.[3] 1. To render finally liable: as, to fix bail, *q. v.*

2. To set for trial or hearing: as, to fix a case on a list.

3. To prescribe the rule by which a thing is to be determined: as, a constitutional direction that the general assembly shall fix the compensation of all officers.[4]

A salary is "fixed" when it consists of a stipulated rate for a definite period. Pay or emolument is fixed when the amount is agreed upon and the service defined.[5]

A salary, pay or emolument is fixed by law when the amount is named in a statute; and, by regulation, when named in a general order, promulgated under provision of law, and applicable to a class or classes of persons.[6]

FIXTURE. A thing fixed or affixed to another thing.

A thing fixed in a greater or less degree to realty.[6]

Anything annexed to the freehold; that is, fastened to or connected with it.[7]

A chattel annexed to the freehold, but removable at the will of the person who annexed it.[8]

Does not necessarily import a thing affixed to the freehold. The word is modern, and generally understood to comprehend any article which a tenant has the power of removing.[9]

As a rule, articles, to become fixtures, must either be fastened to the realty or to what is clearly a part of it, or they must be placed upon the land with a manifest intent that they shall permanently remain there,

and should be peculiarly fitted to something that is actually fastened upon it, and essential to its profitable enjoyment.[1]

If the building, or permanent fixture, is erected upon or attached to the realty by the owner of the realty, it is not the subject of conveyance as personalty, even by the owner of the freehold. . . If a building is erected without the assent of the land-owner, it becomes at once a part of the realty, and is the property of the owner of the freehold. A building, resting upon blocks and not firmly attached to the freehold, placed upon another's land by his assent, continues to be personalty even though there is no express agreement that the owner shall remove it.[2]

Articles that may assume the character of realty or personalty, according to circumstances, are "fixtures"—things substantially and permanently affixed to the soil, though in their nature removable. The old notion of physical attachment is, by some courts, regarded as exploded. Whether a structure is a fixture depends upon the nature and character of the act by which the structure is put in its place, the policy of the law connected with its purpose, and the intent of those concerned in the act. Other courts still hold that it is essential that the article should not only be annexed to the freehold, but that it should clearly appear that a permanent accession was intended.[3]

A thing is deemed to be affixed to land when attached by the roots, imbedded in it, permanently resting upon it, or permanently attached to what is thus permanent.[4]

The persons between whom questions ordinarily arise in relation to fixtures are: vendor and vendee, including mortgagor and mortgagee; heir and executor; landlord and tenant; executor of tenant for life, and reversioner or remainder-man.

The rule of the common law is that whatever is once annexed to the freehold becomes part of it, and cannot afterward be removed, except by him who is entitled to the inheritance. The rule, however, was never inflexible or without exceptions. It was construed most strictly between executor and heir, in favor of the latter; more liberally between tenant for life or in tail and remainder-man or reversioner, in favor of the former; and with much greater latitude between landlord and tenant, in favor of the tenant. But an exception of a much broader cast, and almost as ancient as the rule itself, is of fixtures erected for purposes of *trade*. Upon principles of public policy, and to encourage trade and manufactures, fixtures erected to carry on a business have been allowed to be removed by the tenant during his term, and are deemed personalty for many other purposes.[5]

---

[1] *Re* Pacific Railway Commission, 32 F. R. 263 (1887), Sawyer, Cir. J.; 1 Story, Eq. Pl. § 325, cases.

[2] 2 Story, Eq. § 1490; Lewis *v.* Shainwald, 7 Saw. 413 (1881), cases.

[3] L. *fixum: figuere,* to fasten, attach.

[4] Cricket *v.* State, 18 Ohio St. 21 (1868).

[5] [Hedrick *v.* United States, 16 Ct. Cl. 101 (1880), Davis, J.

[6] [2 Kent, 343.

[7] Elwes *v.* Mawe, 2 Sm. L. C. 177, 187, cases.

[8] [Hallen *v.* Runder, 1 Crom., M. & R. 276 (1834), Parke, B.

[9] Sheen *v.* Rickie, 5 M. & W. *182 (1839), Parke, B. See also Rogers *v.* Gilinger, 30 Pa. 189 (1858); 2 W. & S. 116.

---

[1] Farmer's Loan, &c. Co. *v.* Hendrickson, 25 Barb. 489 (1857), Strong, P. J.

[2] Washburn, Real Prop. 3.

[3] Washb. R. P. 6 (18); Hill *v.* Sewald, 53 Pa. 273-75 (1866); Meigs's-Appeal, 62 *id.* 33 (1869); Capen *v.* Peckham, 35 Conn. 93-94 (1868); Voorhees *v.* McGinnis, 48 N. Y. 282 (1872); Stout *v.* Stoppel, 30 Minn. 58 (1882), cases.

[4] Cal. Civil Code, § 660.

[5] Van Ness *v.* Pacard, 2 Pet. *143, 147 (1829), Story, J. As between vendor and vendee, see Fratt *v.* Whittier,

As between mortgagor and mortgagee, the mortgagor may remove that which is not a fixture, and which was placed upon the ground after the mortgage was executed.[1]

The law imposes no obligation on a landlord to pay the tenant for buildings erected on the demised premises. The common-law rule is that all buildings become part of the freehold. The innovation on this rule has extended no further than the right of removal while the tenant is in possession.[2]

Rolling-stock is inseparably connected with its railroad in its entire length, and is part of the security of lienholders.[3]

Trees reared in nursery grounds for sale as merchandise possess none of the legal characteristics of fixtures. Fixtures are articles which have an existence independent of the freehold, and are afterward annexed to and become part of it.[4] See EMBLEMENTS.

But there is no universal test for determining whether an article, personal in nature, has acquired the character of realty. In each case regard is to be had to the nature of the chattel itself, the injury that would result from its removal, and the intention in placing it upon the premises with reference to trade, agriculture, or ornament.[5] See MACHINERY; STORE.

FLAG. See LAW, Of the flag.

The act of April 4, 1818, as re-enacted in Rev. St. §§ 1791-92, directs that the flag of the United States shall be thirteen horizontal stripes, alternate red and white; that the union thereon shall be thirty-seven stars, white in a blue field; that on the admission of a new State one star shall be added, such addition to take effect on the fourth of July next succeeding such admission.

FLAGGING. See PAVE.

FLAGRANS. L. Burning, flaming up: in actual execution or commission. Whence flagrant, flagrancy.

---

58 Cal. 126, 128-33 (1881), cases; 23 Cent. Law J. 485 (1886), cases. See also Carpenter v. Walker, 140 Mass. 419 (1886); Hedderick v. Smith, 103 Ind. 203 (1885), cases; 25 Am. Law Reg. 24-28, 664-66 (1886), cases.

[1] Cope v. Romeyne, 4 McLean, 384 (1848).

[2] Kutter v. Smith, 2 Wall. 497, 499 (1864), Miller, J.

[3] Milwaukee, &c. R. Co. v. St. Paul R. Co., 2 Wall. 644 (1864); ib. 645-49, Mr. Carpenter's brief. See also Freeman v. Dawson, 110 U. S. 270 (1883), cases.

[4] Hamilton v. Austin, 36 Hun, 141-42 (1885), Follett, J.

[5] Coburn v. Litchfield, 132 Mass. 448 (1882), cases, Morton, C. J.; Thomas v. Davis, 76 Mo. 76 (1882); 6 Am. Law Rev. 412-26 (1872), cases; 2 Flip. 200; 70 Ala. 230; 9 Cal. 119; 9 Conn. 67; 16 Ill. 421, 482; 18 Ind. 231; 35 id. 387; 8 Iowa, 544; 21 id. 177; 44 id. 60; 10 Kan. 314; 54 Me. 266; 14 Mass. 352; 30 Minn. 58; 16 Miss. 444; 42 id. 71, 732; 43 id. 349; 32 Mo. 206; 76 id. 119; 5 Mo. Ap. 293; 3 Neb. 131; 8 id. 192; 3 Nev. 82; 6 id. 248; 7 id. 37; 41 N. H. 503; 57 id. 514; 14 N. J. L. 395; 24 id. 287; 38 id. 457; 24 N. J. E. 260; 20 Wend. 656; 10 Barb. 157, 496; 11 id. 43; 35 id. 58; 51 id. 45; 12 N. Y. 170; 20 id. 344; 35 id. 279; 48 id. 278; 66 id. 489; 93 id. 311; 1 Ohio St. 524; 22 id. 563; 2 R. I. 15; 26 Gratt. 752; 17 Vt. 403; 28 id. 428; 24 Wis. 571; 6 Am. L. Rev. 412; 17 Am. Dec. 686, 690.

Flagrante bello. War raging: during hostilities. See WAR.

Flagrante crimine or **delicto.** While the offense is being perpetrated: in the very act. See DELICTUM, Flagrante.

FLAT. A place within a river, cove, creek, or harbor, more or less under water; "a shallow or shoal water."[1]

FLEE. See FUGITIVE.

Flee to the wall. Signifies that a person must use every reasonable means of escape before he may kill a man who assails him with apparently felonious intent.

To excuse homicide on the plea of self-defense it must appear that the slayer had no other possible (or at least probable) means of escaping from his assailant.[2] See DEFENSE, 1; RETREAT.

FLEET. A celebrated prison in London.

Named from a river or ditch near by. Used chiefly for debtors and bankrupts, and for persons charged with contempt of the courts of chancery, exchequer, and common pleas. Abolished in 1842; and torn down in 1845.[3]

FLOAT. A certificate authorizing the holder to enter a certain amount of land.[4]

Floating debt. That mass of valid claims against a corporation, for the payment of which there is no money in the treasury specifically designated, nor any taxation or other means of raising money particularly provided.[5] Compare FUNDING.

FLOGGING. Beating with lashes; whipping, q. v.

Abolished in the army by act of August 5, 1861;[6] in the navy by act of June 6, 1872.[7]

FLOOD. See ACT, 1, Of God; ALLUVION.

FLOOR. A section of a building between horizontal planes.

The words, used in a lease, the "first floor" are equivalent to the "first story" of the building, and naturally include the walls, unless other words control such meaning. A covenant by a lessee not to underlet any part of the premises is not broken by his allowing a third person, in consideration of an annual payment, to place a sign upon the outside wall, for a stated time.[8]

FLOTSAM. Floating. Goods lost by shipwreck which continue to float on the

---

[1] Stannard v. Hubbard, 34 Conn. 376 (1867).

[2] 4 Bl. Com. 184; 3 id. 3-4.

[3] Cowell; Tomlins; Hayden, Dict. Dates.

[4] Marks v. Dickson, 20 How. 504 (1857).

[5] [People v. Wood, 71 N. Y. 374 (1877), Folger, J. See Cook v. Saratoga Springs, 23 Hun, 59 (1880).

[6] R. S. § 1342, art. 98.

[7] R. S. § 1642, art. 49.

[8] Lowell v. Straban, 145 Mass. 8 (1887), W. Allen, J.

water. Compare JETSAM. See DRIFT-STUFF; WRECK.

FLOWERS. See LARCENY; PERISHABLE;

FOAL. See PARTUS.

FOEDAL. See FEUD.

FŒDUS. See FEDERAL; CONFEDERATION.

FŒNUS NAUTICUM. L. Marine interest.

Sometimes designates a loan of money to be employed in an adventure by sea, upon condition to be repaid with extraordinary interest, in case the voyage is safely performed.[1] See INSURANCE, Marine.

FŒTICIDE. See HOMICIDE.

FOLIO.[2] 1. A leaf.

References to old law-books are by the folio, instead of the page. See A, 1, par. 2.

2. A certain number of words, established by usage or law, as a unit of measurement for estimating the length of a document.

Originated in some estimate of the number of words that a folio ought to contain.

The number has varied, in different jurisdictions, from seventy-two, to ninety, and one hundred.

By the act of February 26, 1853, § 3, a folio is one hundred words, counting each figure a word.[3]

FOLLOW. See PROSECUTE; PROSEQUI; PURSUE; SUIT.

Follow copy. See TELEGRAPH.

Follow a fund or property. See IDENTITY, 2.

Follows the person. See PROPERTY, Personal.

FOOT. See POSSESSIO, Pedis.

Foot-way. See BRIDGE; SIDEWALK.

FOR. 1. On account of, by reason of, because of; in behalf of; as agent for.[4] See AGENT.

2. May mean "during."

As, in Neb. code, § 947, which requires public notice of the time and place of the sale of realty upon execution to be given "for at least thirty days" before the day of sale, by advertisement in some newspaper. One publication thirty days before the sale would not, therefore, be sufficient.[5]

For account. See CONCERN.

For collection. See COLLECTION, 2.

For cause. See CAUSE, 2.

For that. Introduces a positive allegation. *For that whereas* introduces a recital.

For use. A, "for use, etc.," for the benefit of some other, the assignor. See USE, 2.

For whom it may concern. In an insurance policy, for all persons who may have an insurable interest. See further AUCTION; CONCERN.

FORBEARANCE. Suspension of an existing demand.[1]

Delay in enforcing a right.

In statutes against usury, giving additional time, after the time originally limited for the return of a loan has passed.[2]

An agreement to forbear bringing a suit for a debt due, although for an indefinite time, and even although it cannot be construed to be an agreement for perpetual forbearance if followed by actual forbearance for a reasonable time, is a good consideration for a promise.[3] See CONSIDERATION, 2; SURETY.

FORCE.[4] Compare VIGOR; VIS.

Strength; power.

1. Strength applied or exerted; power in action or motion; active power; compulsion; resistance; also, unlawful violence,—violence, *q. v.*

Actual force. Force applied in point of fact. **Implied force.** Force inferred from the doing of an unlawful act. See BATTERY; CASE, 3; KIDNAPING; RAPE; ROBBERY.

Enforce. To constrain, or compel; to give effect to: as, to enforce an order of court; Congress may enforce constitutional prohibitions by appropriate legislation; to enforce a contract.

Power to enforce the collection of a fine implies power to give a receipt which will discharge the party.[5]

Enforcement Act of 1870. See RIGHT, 2, Civil (2).

Force and arms. Charges violence in declarations and indictments for trespasses; as, in trespass for entering a close.[6] See HAND, 2; TRESPASS.

Force and fear. Is ground for annulling a contract, when the fear would affect a mind of ordinary firmness. See DURESS.

---

[1] [2 Bl. Com. 458.

[2] L. *in folio: folium,* a leaf, sheet.

[3] 10 St. L. 168: R. S. § 828. See Amy v. Shelby County, 1 Flip. 104 (1872); Cavender v. Cavender, 3 McCrary, 384 (1882); Jerman v. Stewart, 12 F. R. 275 (1882); 38 Mich. 639.

[4] Strong v. Sun Mut. Ins. Co., 31 N. Y. 105 (1865).

[5] Lawson v. Gibson, 18 Neb. 139 (1885). See also Whitaker v. Beach, 12 Kan. 493 (1874); 16 Ohio, 563.

---

[1] Goodman v. Simonds, 20 How. 370 (1857), cases.

[2] [Dry Dock Bank v. American Life Ins., &c. Co., 3 N. Y. 355 (1850).

[3] Howe v. Taggart, 133 Mass. 287 (1882), cases.

[4] F. *force;* L. *fortis,* strong, powerful.

[5] People v. Charisterson, 59 Ill. 158 (1871).

[6] 2 Chitty, Pl. 846, 850; 2 Steph. Com. 364; 4 *id.* 372.

Force to force. Resistance to unlawful violence,— allowed to the extent of the violence. See ASSAULT; BATTERY; DEFENSE, 1.

Irresistible force. Human agency in its nature and power absolutely uncontrollable.[1] See ACCIDENT; ACT, 1, Of God; CARRIER, Common; ENEMY, Public.

Forced; forcible; forcibly. (1) Against the will or consent: as, a forcible abduction, dispossession, entry and detainer, sale, qq. v.

(2) Against the will and under express protest: as, a forced payment, q. v.

"Forcibly" doing an act is merely doing the act with force.[2]

"Violently" may not be equivalent to "by force," in an indictment for rape.[3]

All civil injuries are either without force or violence, as in cases of slander and breach of contract; or else are coupled with force and violence, as in cases of battery and false imprisonment.[4]

The government of the United States may, by means of physical force, exerted through its official agents, execute on every foot of American soil the powers and functions that belong to it. This power does not derogate from a State the right to execute its laws at the same time and place. The one does not exclude the other, except where both cannot be exercised at the same time; then the Federal authority prevails.[5] See WAR.

(3) Arrived at by violence done to language; strained; unnatural: as, a forced construction, q. v.

2. Power to persuade or convince, or impose an obligation; legal effect or operation; binding effect; validity; efficacy. See VOID.

By force of. By virtue of; by reason of; in consequence of.[6]

FORECLOSURE. A closing up, shutting out, barring, preclusion.

1. Specifically, the extinguishment of a mortgagor's equity of redemption beyond possibility of recall.[7]

A mortgage is foreclosed in the sense that no one has the right to redeem it, or to call the mortgagee to account under it.[8]

In no sense can the term be applied to a mortgage until *sale* of the property has been effected.[9]

---

[1] Story, Bailm. § 25.

[2] United States v. Bachelder, 2 Gall. 19 (1814), Story, J. See 115 Mass. 563.

[3] State v. Blake, 39 Me. 324 (1855).

[4] 3 Bl. Com. 118.

[5] *Exp.* Siebold, 100 U. S. 395 (1879), Bradley, J.

[6] Fischer v. Hope, &c. Ins. Co., 40 N. Y. Super. 299 (1876).

[7] [2 Bl. Com. 159.

[8] Puffer v. Clark, 7 Allen, 85 (1863), Hoar, J.

[9] Duncan v. Cobb, 32 Minn. 464 (1884).

Foreclosure takes place where a mortgagor has forfeited his estate by non-payment of money due upon the mortgage, but still retains his equity of redemption. In that case, the mortgagee may file a bill of foreclosure to compel the debtor to redeem his estate presently (as, within six months), or, in default, to be forever closed or barred from the right. This is known as strict foreclosure. In Indiana, Kentucky, Maryland, New York, South Carolina, Tennessee, Virginia, and other States, the mortgagee obtains a decree for a sale of the land, the proceeds to be applied to satisfying incumbrances in the order of their priority.[1]

A suit to foreclose a mortgage, not seeking a personal judgment, is essentially a proceeding *in rem.*[2] See MORTGAGE; REDEMPTION.

2. Also applied to the suit by a pledgee to extinguish the pledgor's right to redeem the personalty, after default made; and to proceedings to collect charges or liens upon other specific property, as, a foreclosure of a mechanic's lien.

FOREIGN.[3] 1. That which belongs or pertains to another country, nation, or sovereignty; or to another State, or division of a State.[4]

As, foreign or a foreign — administrator, allegiance, assignment, attachment, charity, coin, commerce or trade, corporation, county, court, creditor, decree, divorce, document, domicil, exchange or bill of exchange, factor, guardian, judgment or sentence, law, minister, patent, port, vessel, voyage, qq. v.

Foreigner. A citizen or subject of another country or nation; an alien, q. v.

A naturalized citizen is no longer a foreigner.[5]

See BANKRUPTCY; CITIZENSHIP; COPYRIGHT; PATENT, 3.

2. Irrelevant; impertinent; extrinsic; not germane: as, matter or testimony foreign to the issue. Compare ALIUNDE; DEHORS.

FOREMAN. The presiding member of a jury, grand or petit.

From the persons summoned and accepted as grand jurors, the court appoints the foreman, who has power to administer oaths to witnesses.[6] The first

---

[1] See Hatch v. White, 2 Gall. 154 (1814), Story, J.; Sprague v. Martin, 29 Minn. 229 (1882); Du Val v. Johnson, 39 Ark. 188 (1832); 44 Ohio St. 275; 4 Kent, 180; 2 Washburn, R. P. 261, note; Williams, R. P. 409; Daniel, Ch. Pr. 1204.

[2] Martin v. Pond, 30 F. R. 18 (1887), cases.

[3] F. *forain*, alien, strange: L. *foras*, out of doors, abroad.

[4] See Cherokee Nation v. Georgia, 5 Pet. *56 (1831).

[5] Spratt v. Spratt, 1 Pet. *349 (1828).

[6] [R. S. § 809; United States v. Plumer, 3 Cliff. 71 (1867).

person drawn and accepted upon a petit jury becomes its foreman. A jury speaks through its foreman.

FOREST. Forests were waste grounds, belonging to the king, replenished with beasts of chase, which are under his protection.[1]

For the preservation of the king's game there were particular laws, privileges, courts, and offices belonging to the king's forests. Part of the king's ordinary revenue consisted of fines levied for offenses against the forest laws.[1] See GAME, 1.

FORESTALLING. Buying or contracting for merchandise or victual on its way to market; dissuading persons from bringing their goods or provisions there; or persuading them to enhance the price when there: any of which practices makes the market dear to the fair dealer.[2]

So described in statute 5 and 6 Edw. VI (1552), c. 14.

At common law, such practices were an offense against public trade; otherwise, since 7 and 8 Vict. (1844) c. 24. Compare ENGROSS, 2; MONOPOLY; REGRATING.

FOREVER. Compare PERMANENT.

Used of the location of a county seat, may mean until changed by law.[3]

In a conveyance, was held not to impart inheritable quality.[4]

FORFEIT.[5] 1. To divest or to suffer divestiture of property, without compensation, in consequence of a default or offense. 2. To pay money as a mulct, or for a default or wrong.

To take away all right from one person and transfer it to another.[6]

In a contract that a party shall "forfeit" a specified sum on a breach, equivalent to "penalty."[7]

Forfeitable. Admitting of divestiture or loss by way of punishment or for neglect; opposed to **non-forfeitable**: as, a forfeitable or non-forfeitable policy of insurance.

Forfeiture. Lands or goods whereof the property is gone away or departed from the owner.[8]

A punishment annexed by law to some illegal act or negligence in the owner of lands, tenements, or hereditaments, whereby he loses all his interest therein, and they go to the party injured, as a recompense for the wrong which either he alone or the public together with himself has sustained.[1]

Forfeitures were called *bona confiscata* by the civilians, because they belonged to the *fiscus* or imperial treasury; and now, by us, *foris facta*, that is, such whereof the property is gone away or departed from the owner.[2] Compare CONFISCATE.

Forfeitures of estates were for breaches of the condition that the tenant should not do any act incompatible with the estate.[3]

A penalty by which one loses his rights and interest in his property.[4]

Property rights are forfeitable: by commission of crime; by alienation contrary to law (as, in mortmain, to an alien); by non-performance of a condition; by waste; and by bankruptcy.[5]

Goods and chattels were totally forfeited by conviction of treason, misprision of treason, felony, petit larceny, flight upon charge of treason, etc.[6]

In theory, the guilty person wholly abandoned his connection with society.[7]

At common law, a forfeiture transferred title to the sovereign. In a statute, may mean that the State by indictment shall recover a sum to be levied of the person's property as a "fine."[8]

"Forfeiture" has frequently been spoken of as equivalent to conveyance or grant.[9]

Forfeitures are not favored. They are often the means of oppression and injustice. Hence, the courts are prompt to seize upon any circumstances that indicate an election to waive a forfeiture; as, the course of action of an insurance company. Where adequate compensation can be made, the law in many cases, and equity in all cases, discharges the forfeiture, upon such compensation being made.[10]

Equity never lends its aid to enforce a forfeiture or penalty.[11]

A clause of forfeiture in a law is construed differently from a similar clause in an engagement between individuals. A legislature always imposes a forfeiture

---

[1] 1 Bl. Com. 289; 2 *id.* 38, 414-16; 3 *id.* 73; 4 *id.* 415, 420, 423, 432, 437.

[2] [4 Bl. Com. 158; 10 Phila. 361.

[3] Casey *v.* Harned, 5 Iowa, 14 (1857); 1 La. An. 315.

[4] Dennis *v.* Wilson, 107 Mass. 593 (1871), cases.

[5] F. *forfait,* a crime punishable by fine, a fine: L. L. *foris-facere,* to trespass. lit. "to do beyond:" *foris,* out of doors, abroad, beyond; *facere,* to do,—Skeat; 1 Bl. Com. 299.

[6] [Walter *v.* Smith, 5 B. & Ald. 157 (1822), Best, J.

[7] Taylor *v.* The Marcella, 1 Woods, 304 (1873); 17 Barb. 260; 15 Abb. Pr. 273.

[8] [1 Bl. Com. 299.

[1] 2 Bl. Com. 267.

[2] 1 Bl. Com. 299. See 1 Kent, 67; 1 Story, 134; 13 Pet. 157.

[3] 2 Bl. Com. 153.

[4] Gosselink *v.* Campbell, 4 Iowa, 300 (1856).

[5] See 2 Bl. Com. 267; 20 How. Pr. 370.

[6] 2 Bl. Com. 421.

[7] 3 Bl. Com. 299; 4 *id.* 381.

[8] Commonwealth *v.* Avery, 14 Bush, 638 (1879).

[9] Wallach *v.* Van Riswick, 92 U. S. 211 (1875), cases, Strong, J.

[10] Knickerbocker Life Ins. Co. *v.* Norton, 96 U. S. 239, 242 (1877), cases, Bradley, J.; Ins. Co. *v.* Eggleston, *ib.* 577 (1877); Olmstead *v.* Farmers' Mut. Fire Ins. Co., 50 Mich. 206 (1883).

[11] Marshall *v.* Vicksburgh, 15 Wall. 149 (1872), cases; McCormick *v.* Rossi, 70 Cal. 474 (1886); Manhattan Life Ins. Co. *v.* Smith, 44 Ohio St. 167 (1886).

as a punishment inflicted for a violation of some duty enjoined by law; whereas individuals can only make it a matter of contract.[1]

Provisions for forfeiture are regarded with disfavor and construed with strictness — when applied to contracts, and the forfeiture relates to a matter admitting of compensation or restoration; but there is no leaning against a forfeiture intended to secure the construction of public works where compensation cannot be made for the default, nor where the forfeiture is imposed by positive law.[2]

Where an act works a forfeiture of goods, the government may at once seize them.[3] Where an absolute forfeiture is the penalty, title accrues in the government when the penal act is committed. But where the forfeiture is in the alternative (property, or its value), title does not vest till an election is made.[4]

Where property is seized for condemnation for forfeiture, some notification of the proceedings, beyond the mere seizure, may be necessary.[5]

Failure to pay a premium of life insurance (*q. v.*) at the time specified involves an absolute forfeiture, for which, unless waived by the company, relief cannot be had.[6] See WAR.

Forfeitures for common-law offenses have been generally abolished.

See ATTAINDER; BOND; CHARTER, 2; CONDITION; DOWER; FELONY; LAND, Public; PARDON; PENALTY; RECOGNIZANCE; SEARCH-WARRANT.

FORGE.[7] 1. A mechanical contrivance by which iron is made or manufactured from the ore.

But a blacksmith's forge is not a "forge or furnace for manufacturing iron."[8]

2. To make in the likeness of something else.[9] Compare FABRICATE.

Forger. A person guilty of forgery.

Forgery. At common law, the fraudulent making or alteration of a writing to the prejudice of another man's right.[10]

"The word is taken metaphorically from the smith, who beateth upon his anvil and forgeth what fashion and shape he will."[11]

In common speech, also, the altered instrument itself.

The fraudulent making of a false writing, which, if genuine, would be apparently of some legal efficacy.[1]

May be committed as to any writing, which, if genuine, would operate as the foundation of another man's liability, or the evidence of his right.[2]

Imports a false making (which includes every alteration of or addition to a true instrument) — a making *malo animo*, of any written instrument for the purpose of fraud and deceit: with intent to deceive.[3]

In general terms, forgery is the false making or material alteration of, or addition to, a written instrument for the purpose of fraud and deceit. It may be — the making of a false writing purporting to be that of another; the alteration in some material particular of a genuine instrument by a change of its words or figures; the addition of some material provision to an instrument otherwise genuine; the appending of a genuine signature to an instrument for which it was not intended. The false writing may purport to be the instrument of a person or firm existing or fictitious; or of a person having the same name as the accused. As a rule, it must purport to be the writing of another than the person who made it.[4]

May be committed by making a note in the name of a fictitious person, in an assumed name, or in the name of a bank which does not exist. It is not necessary that the note be one which, if genuine, would be a valid and binding obligation. It is sufficient that the instrument purports to be good. To relieve from the character of forgery, the want of validity must appear upon the face of the paper itself.[5]

It is immaterial whether the forgery is committed by means of printing, stamping, an engraved plate, or by writing with a pen.[6]

---

[1] Maryland v. Baltimore, &c. R. Co., 3 How. 552 (1845), Taney, C. J.

[2] Farnesworth v. Minnesota, &c. R. Co., 92 U. S. 68 (1875), Field, J.; 2 Story, Eq. § 1326.

[3] Henderson's Spirits, 14 Wall. 56 (1871), cases; Thatcher's Spirits, 103 U. S. 682 (1880).

[4] The Mary Celeste, 2 Low. 356 (1874), cases.

[5] Windsor v. McVeigh, 93 U. S. 274 (1876).

[6] New York Life Ins. Co. v. Statham, 93 U. S. 24, 30 (1876); 100 Pa. 180. As to fire insurance, see Smith v. St. Paul Fire & Mar. Ins. Co., 3 Dak. T. 80 (1882).

[7] F. *forge*; L. *fabrica*, a workshop; *faber*, a workman, smith: *fa-*, to make.

[8] [Rogers v. Danforth, 9 N. J. E. 296 (1853).

[9] State v. McKenzie, 42 Me. 394 (1856).

[10] 4 Bl. Com. 247; L. R., 1 C. C. R. *203.

[11] 3 Coke, Inst. 169.

[1] 2 Bishop, Cr. L. §§ 624, 523, note.

[2] 3 Greenl. Ev. § 103, cases.

[3] Rex v. Coogan, 2 East, P. C. 852-53 (1803): Commonwealth v. Ayer, 3 Cush. 152 (1849); Garner v. State, 5 Lea, 215 (1880); State v. McKiernan, 17 Nev. 228 (1882).

[4] Commonwealth v. Baldwin, 11 Gray, 198 (1858), Thomas, J.

[5] United States v. Turner, 7 Pet. *134 (1833); United States v. Mitchell, Baldw. 366 (1831); 11 F. R. 55.

[6] Benson v. McMahon, 127 U. S. 467-71 (1888), cases. Benson, by falsely representing himself in the City of Mexico as Marcus Meyer, agent for Henry E. Abbey, under whom Adelina Patti was to appear at the Teatro Nacional, in December, 1886, sold $25,000 to $30,000 worth of tickets of admission. In February, 1888, Benson was arrested in the city of New York, and committed for his return to Mexico, in accordance with the extradition treaty of 1861, the circuit court having refused to release him upon a writ of *habeas corpus.* "About the only contest" made by him before the Supreme Court was that the tickets were not forgeries, mainly because the name of Mr. Abbey, who was represented as having authorized their issue and sale, was not "in writing," *i. e.*, made in script, by the use of a pen. *Ib.* 464-65.

The crime is generally defined to be "the fraudulent making or alteration of a writing to the prejudice of another man's rights." The intent to defraud is its essence. There must be a possibility of some person being defrauded. Where the effect, if successful, would be to defraud a particular person, he should be named in the indictment, if known; if otherwise, a general allegation of the intent should be made. The question of intent is for the jury; but such intent, to be proved, must be alleged. The nature of the offense is a species of false pretenses or fraud; hence the importance of setting forth the intent, and the name of the person, if known.[1]

It is sufficient if the forgery would have the effect of defrauding a particular person. A person may not fraudulently sign his own name (in this case to a money-order) although identical with the name of the person who should have signed.[2]

Forgery of a bill or note is by counterfeiting a signature, or by filling up a paper with a genuine signature, so as to make it appear to be signed as maker, or indorser, or other party.[3]

"False, forged, and counterfeit," in the act of February 25, 1862 (12 St. L. 347), necessarily implies that the instrument so characterized is not genuine, but only purports to be, or is in the similitude of, such instrument.[4]

"False or forged," applied to an instrument in writing, means that the instrument is counterfeit or not genuine,— that some one has attempted to imitate another's personal act, and, by means of such imitation, to cheat and defraud.[5]

To falsely make an affidavit is one thing; to make a false affidavit is another. It is the false making that is forgery.[6]

Making and uttering an instrument as agent, under a false assumption of authority, is not forgery.[6]

In charging forgery, the variance or the omission of a letter, to be material, must change the word attempted to be written into another word having a different meaning. The rigor of the old English law in this respect was due to the barbarous punishments imposed. The insertion or omission of a word or words will not create a variance unless the sense is thereby altered. Illustrations of harmless changes are: "to H. C. P. or order," "B. A. or bearer," "pay to bearer," "undertood" for understood, "Fayelville" for Fayetville, "Jna." for Jno.[7]

Money paid under a mistake of fact can be recovered. Hence, where one pays money on forged paper by discounting or cashing it, he can always recover it, provided: that he has not himself contributed materially to the mistake by his own fault or negligence; and that by an immediate or sufficiently early notice he enables the party to whom he paid it to indemnify himself as far as possible. The doctrine is favored that even negligence in making the mistake is no bar to a recovery.[1]

See ALTER, 2; COUNTERFEIT; FAITH, Good; GENUINE; MISTAKE; OBLIGATION, 2; ORDER.

FORGIVE. See CONDONE; MERCY; PARDON.

FORGOTTEN PROPERTY. See FIND, 1.

FORM. 1. Established method of expression or practice; a fixed way of proceeding. Compare COURSE, 2.

2. The model of an instrument or legal proceeding; a formula.[2] See BLANKS.

Opposed to *substance*. That without which the right sufficiently appears to the court is "form." Whatever is wanting or imperfect, by reason whereof the right appears not, is a defect of substance.[3]

Matter of form is whatever relates, not to the purpose or object of an instrument, or to a right involved in, or affected by, it, but merely to the language or expression, without affecting the issue presented, the evidence requisite, the right of a party, or a step necessary in furtherance of legal proceedings.

Formal. Belonging or essential to the form or frame of a thing; not of the substance: as, a formal defect or irregularity, a formal party, q. v.; also, according to regular method of procedure. Opposed, *substantial, real.* See DEMURRER.

Form of action. The peculiar technical mode of framing the writ and pleadings appropriate to the particular injury which the action is intended to redress.[4]

Forms of action. The classes into which actions at law are divided. Distinguishable, by peculiarities in the writs and pleadings, at common law, as account, annuity, *assumpsit*, covenant, debt, detinue, ejectment, replevin, trespass on the case; in some juris-

---

[1] State v. Gavigan, 36 Kan. 326 (1887), Horton, C. J.

[2] United States v. Long, 30 F. R. 679 (1887).

[3] 2 Daniel, Neg. Inst., 2 ed., § 1344; 11 Gratt. 822.

[4] United States v. Howell, 11 Wall. 432, 437 (1870).

[5] State v. Wilson, 28 Minn. 54 (1881), Mitchell, J.; State v. Young, 46 N. H. 270 (1865); Mann v. People, 15 Hun, 155 (1878), cases; State v. McKiernan, 17 Nev. 228 (1882), cases.

[6] United States v. Cameron, 3 Dak. T. 140 (1882).

[7] People v. Phillips, 70 Cal. 64–66 (1886), cases.

[1] 2 Daniel, Neg. Inst., 2 ed., § 1369, cases; Collins v. Gilbert, 94 U. S. 754 (1876), cases; Frank v. Lanier, 91 N. Y. 116 (1883), cases.

See also 4 Wash. 726; 66 Ga. 53; 19 Iowa, 299; 29 *id.* 493, 495; 52 *id.* 68; 2 Me. 365; 50 *id.* 409; 3 Gray, 441; 114 Mass. 318; 16 Minn. 473; 46 N. H. 267; 1 Wend. 200; 9 *id.* 141; 17 *id.* 229; 91 N. Y. 113; 15 Ohio, 721; 1 Ohio St. 187; 2 Binn. 529; 3 Phila. 351; 32 Pa. 529; 89 *id.* 432; 37 Tex. 592; 2 Bish. Cr. L. § 495, 2 Cr. Pr. § 398; 3 Chitty, Cr. L. 1022; 2 Whart. Cr. L. § 1418; 2 Arch. Cr. Pr. 797; 4 Cr. L. Mag. 545, 865.

[2] See Webster's Dict.

[3] [Heard v. Baskerville, 1 Hob. *233; 109 U. S. 274.

[4] Broom, Com. Law, 118 (m).

dictions are or have also been included, injunction, *mandamus, scire facias.*

In Kansas there is but one form of action, called a civil action. The plaintiff, for cause of action, states the actual facts, without common-law forms or fictions.[1]

In Pennsylvania, by an act approved May 25, 1887 (P. L. 271), the forms of action are *assumpsit,* to which the plea of the general issue is "non assumpsit," with the privilege of pleading payment, set off, and the statute of limitation; and trespass, in which the only plea is "not guilty."

Where the common-law forms have been abolished, the principles governing them at common law are frequently invoked.

Where the formal distinctions between actions are abolished, the declaration states the facts which constitute the cause of action. . . When the facts are plainly and distinctly stated, the action will be regarded as either in tort or in contract; having regard, first, to the character of the remedy such facts indicate; and, second, to the most complete and ample redress which, upon the facts stated, the law can afford.[2] See ACTION, 2; CODE.

Form of the statute. The provision or enactment, the prohibition or direction, of a statute.

Against the form of the statute. A technical phrase used in an indictment for a statutory offense; the "conclusion against the statute."

"Against the form of the statute in such case made and provided" is the usual expression, but any equivalent expression will be sufficient — any phrase which shows that the offense charged is founded on some statute.[3]

Formality. Established order or method, rule of proceeding or expression. Opposed, informality.[4]

Compare REFORM; UNIFORM. See MANNER; SUBSTANCE; TECHNICAL.

FORMA. L. Form; formality; character. Occurs in the phrases *in forma pauperis,* and *pro forma,* qq. v.

Formaliter. In form; formally.

FORMEDON. A writ which lay for a person who, being interested in an estate-tail, was liable to be defeated of his right by a discontinuance of the estate.

He claimed *per formam doni.* It was in the remainder, reverter, or descender. Abolished by 3 and 4 Wm. IV (1834), c. 37.[5]

FORMER. See ACQUITTAL; ADJUDICATION; CONVICTION; RECOVERY.

FORNICATION.[1] Illicit carnal intercourse by an unmarried person with a person of the opposite sex.[2]

Sexual intercourse between a man, married or single, and an unmarried woman, as to the unmarried party.[3]

Illicit carnal connection is called by different names, according to the circumstances which attend it. Unaccompanied with any facts which tend to aggravate it, it is "simple fornication." When it causes the birth of an illegitimate child, it is "fornication and bastardy." When the person who commits it is married, it is "adultery." When the parties are related within certain degrees of consanguinity or affinity, it becomes "incest." Where it is preceded by fraudulent arts (including a promise of marriage) to gain the consent of the female, who is under the age of consent, and of good repute, it is "seduction." But the body of all these offenses is the illicit intercourse; in each case, the essential fact which constitutes the crime is fornication. On an indictment for any offense, below the grade of felony, of which illicit connection forms an essential part, the defendant may be found guilty of fornication.[4]

In a few States, fornication is not punishable by statute.

To charge another with fornication is actionable *per se.*[5] See SLANDER.

See ADULTERY; BAD, 1; BAWD; MERETRICIOUS; POLYGAMY; PROSTITUTION, 2.

FORNIX. L. Fornication. Originally, a vault, an arch, — a brothel.

Fornix et cætera. Fornication and the rest: fornication and bastardy, qq. v.

FORO. See FORUM.

FORSWEAR. To swear falsely.

Does not necessarily import perjury, q. v. One may swear to what is not true before an officer not qualified to administer an oath.[6]

FORT. Implies something more than a mere military camp, post, or station; a fortification or a place protected from attack by some such means as a moat, wall, stockade, or parapet.[7] See LAND, Public.

FORTE ET DURE. See PEINE.

---

[1] St. Louis, &c. R. Co. *v.* Chenault, 36 Kan. 55 (1886); Losch *v.* Pickett, *ib.* 222 (1887); Kansas, &c. R. Co. *v.* Rice, *ib.* 599 (1887): Civ. Code, § 10.

[2] New Orleans, &c. R. Co. *v.* Hurst, 36 Miss. 667 (1859); Gulf, &c. R. Co. *v.* Levy, 59 Tex. 548 (1883).

[3] United States *v.* Smith, 2 Mas. 150 (1820), Story, J.

[4] 16 S. & R. *118.

[5] See 2 Bl. Com. 193; 3 *id.* 191.

---

[1] From *fornix,* q. v.

[2] [Montana *v.* Whitcomb, 1 Monta. 362 (1871), Wade, Chief Justice.

[3] Hood *v.* State, 56 Ind. 271 (1877), Perkins, C. J. See also 3 Monta. 54; 51 Wis. 461; 4 Bl. Com. 65.

[4] Dinkey *v.* Commonwealth, 17 Pa. 129-30 (1851), Black, C. J.

[5] Page *v.* Merwin, 54 Conn. 434 (1886).

[6] See Heard, Libel & Sl. §§ 16, 34; 1 Johns. 505; 2 *id.* 10; 13 *id.* 48, 80: 12 Mass. 496; 2 Har. & J. (Md.) 363.

[7] United States *v.* Tichenor, 8 Saw. 153 (1882), Deady, J.; s. c. 12 F. R. 424.

FORTHCOMING. Describes a bond given to a sheriff, conditioned that property seized by him shall be produced or forthcoming when lawfully required.[1]

Also said of a person released on bail, *q. v.*

FORTHWITH. Has a relative meaning, and will imply a longer or a shorter period, according to the nature of the thing to be done.[2]

1. Immediately; without delay; directly.[3]

2. Within reasonable time; with convenient celerity; with reasonable diligence.[4]

With due diligence, under the circumstances.[5]

As soon as, by reasonable exertion confined to the object, an act may be done.[6]

In some matters of practice, within twenty-four hours.[7]

See Immediately; Instanter; Possible; Time, Reasonable.

FORTUITOUS. Resulting from chance, or unavoidable cause; casual; inevitable: as, a fortuitous collision or event.[8] See Accident.

FORTUNE-TELLING. See Witchcraft.

FORTY DAYS. See Quarantine, 1.

FORUM. The place where court was held in cities of the Roman empire; the place where redress is to be sought; place of jurisdiction; jurisdiction; a judicial tribunal, *q. v.*; a court; the bar of a court.

From *fero*, to lead out of doors: what is outside; an outside space; a public place, a market place. Compare Curia; Locus.

Foro. In the court of. Whence *foro cœli, foro conscientiæ*, etc.

Forum cœli. The court of heaven.

Forum conscientiæ. The bar of conscience, *q. v.*

Forum contractus. The court of the place where a contract is made.

Forum domesticum. The home tribunal.

Forum domicilii. The court of one's domicil, *q. v.*

Forum rei. 1. The court of the defendant — of the place where he resides.

2. The court of the thing — of the locality where a thing in controversy is or is found.

Forum rei gestæ. The court of the thing done — at the place of the transaction.

Forum rei sitæ. The court of the place where a thing is situated. See Place, 1; Res.

Forum seculare. A secular court.

FORWARDER. A person who receives and transports merchandise at his own expense of time and money, in consideration of a compensation paid him by the owner or consignee; and who has no concern in the means of transportation, nor any interest in the freight; a "forwarding merchant."[1]

He is a warehouseman and agent for a compensation to forward goods.[2]

An agreement "to forward" goods may still amount to a contract for carrying.[3] See Carrier, Common.

FOSSIL. See Mineral.

FOUND. See Find; Office; Trover.

FOUR. Has no technical meaning.

Four corners. All parts; the whole.

Take by the four corners: construe an instrument as a whole.

Four seas. The waters surrounding England.

Within the four seas: within her territorial jurisdiction.

On all-fours. Said of cases precisely alike. See All-Fours.

FOURTEENTH AMENDMENT. See Citizen.

FOURTH OF JULY. See Holiday.

FOWL. See Animal; Cruelty, 3; Damage, Feasant; Nuisance; Trespass; Worry.

FOX HUNTING. See Cruelty, 3.

FRACTION. See Day.

FRAIS. F. Cost, price; expense.

Frais jusqu'a bord. Expenses to the board (vessel); free on board.

In an invoice of imported goods, excludes cartage and commissions paid to the shipping merchant who receives and places the goods on board ship for exportation. Such charges are not dutiable.[4] See Free, On board.

FRANCE. See Law, Civil; Salic.

---

[1] See 61 Ga. 520; 11 Gratt. 522.

[2] Moffat *v.* Dickson, 3 Col. 314 (1877), Elbert, J.

[3] See Inman *v.* Western Ins. Co., 12 Wend. 460 (1834); Whitemore *v.* Smith, 50 Conn. 379 (1882); Hull *v.* Mallory; 56 Wis. 356 (1882); 22 E. C. L. 527; L. R., 4 Q. B. D. 471.

[4] See Burgess *v.* Bœtefeur, 7 Mar. & G. *494 (1844); Bennett *v.* Lycoming Ins. Co., 67 N. Y. 277 (1876), cases; 44 Ohio St. 437.

[5] Edwards *v.* Lycoming Ins. Co., 75 Pa. 378 (1874).

[6] [8 Chitty, Gen. Pr. 112.

[7] Champlin *v.* Champlin, 2 Edw. *329 (N. Y., 1834).

[8] See Story, Bailm. § 25.

[1] See Story, Bailm. § 502, cases.

[2] Bush *v.* Miller, 13 Barb. 488 (1852); Angell, Car. § 44.

[3] Blossom *v.* Griffin, 13 N. Y. 575 (1856).

[4] Bartels *v.* Redfield, 16 F. R. 337 (1883); *ib.* 341; Robertson *v.* Downing, 127 U. S. 607 (1888).

FRANCHISE.[1] 1. A royal privilege, or branch of the king's prerogative, subsisting in the hands of a subject.[2]

A special privilege conferred by government upon individuals, and which does not belong to citizens of the country generally, of common right.[3]

A generic term covering all rights granted to a corporation by the legislature. Whence "corporate franchises."[4]

A corporate franchise is a legal estate vested in the corporation as soon as it is *in esse*. Not a mere naked power, but a power coupled with an interest.[5]

A privilege conferred by the immediate or antecedent legislation of an act of incorporation, with conditions expressed or necessarily inferential from its language, as to the manner of its exercise and for its enjoyment.[6]

To ascertain how it is brought into existence, the whole charter must be consulted.[6]

Generalized, and divested of the special form which it assumes under a monarchical government based on feudal traditions, a franchise is a right, privilege or power of public concern, which ought not to be exercised by private individuals at their mere will and pleasure, but should be reserved for public control and administration, either by the government or directly, or by public agents, acting under such conditions and regulations as the government may impose in the public interest, and for the public security.[7]

Such rights and powers must exist under every form of society. They are always educed by the laws and customs of the community. Under our system, their existence and disposal are under the legislative department, and they cannot be assumed or exercised without legislative authority. Thus, no private person can establish a public highway, or a public ferry, or railroad, or charge tolls for the use of the same, or

exercise the right of eminent domain or corporate capacity, without authority from the legislature, direct or derived.[1]

The word is used as synonymous with privilege and immunity of a personal character; but in law imports something which the citizen cannot enjoy without legislative grant. What members obtain in a religious, benevolent, or scientific association incorporated under general or special laws, is membership.[2]

A corporation is itself a franchise belonging to the members of the corporation, and the corporation, itself a franchise, may hold other franchises. The different powers of the corporation are franchises.[3]

The essential properties of corporate existence are quite distinct from the franchises of the corporation. The franchise of being a corporation belongs to the corporators, while the powers and privileges vested in, and to be exercised by, the corporate body as such, are the franchises of the corporation. The latter has no power to dispose of the franchise of its members, which may survive in the mere fact of corporate existence, after the corporation has parted with all its property and all its franchises. The franchise to be a corporation is not a subject of sale and transfer, unless made so by a statute, which provides a mode for exercising it.[4]

Often synonymous with rights, privileges, and immunities, though of a personal and temporary character; so that, if any one of these exists, it is loosely termed a "franchise." But the term must always be considered in connection with the corporation or property to which it is alleged to appertain. The franchises of a railroad corporation are the rights or privileges which are essential to the operations of the corporation, and without which its road and works would be of little value; such as the franchise to run cars, to take tolls, to appropriate earth for the bed of its road, or water for its engines, and the like. These are positive rights or privileges without the possession of which the road could not be successfully worked. But immunity from taxation is not a franchise.[5]

The franchises of a railroad company are in a large measure designed to be exercised for the public good, which exercise is the consideration for granting them. The company cannot, therefore, render itself incapable of performing its duties, or absolve itself from the obligation, without the consent of the State.[5]

A franchise is property and nothing more;[7] it is in-

---

[1] Frăn'-chĭz. F. *franchise*, privileged liberty: *franc*, free.

[2] 2 Bl. Com. 37; 127 U. S. 40.

[3] Bank of Augusta v. Earle, 13 Pet. 595 (1839), Taney, Chief Justice.

[4] Atlantic & Gulf R. Co. v. Georgia, 98 U. S. 365 (1878), Strong, J.

[5] Dartmouth College v. Woodward, 4 Wheat. 700 (1819), Story, J.; Society for Savings v. Coite, 6 Wall. 606 (1867). See also 3 Kent, 458; 73 Ill. 547; 45 Mo. 20; 15 Johns. 387.

[6] Woods v. Lawrence County, 1 Black, 409 (1861), Wayne, J.

[7] California v. Pacific R. Co., 127 U. S. 40 (1888), Bradley, J.

[1] California v. Pacific R. Co., *ante*.

[2] Board of Trade v. People, 91 Ill. 82 (1878), cases, Scott, J.

[3] Pierce v. Emery, 32 N. H. 507 (1856), Perley, C. J.

[4] Memphis R. Co. v. Commissioners, 112 U. S. 619 (1884), cases, Matthews, J.; Willamette Manuf. Co. v. Bank of British Columbia, 119 *id.* 191 (1886).

[5] Morgan v. Louisiana, 93 U. S. 223 (1876), cases, Field, J.; East Tennessee, &c. R. Co. v. County of Hamblen, 102 U. S. 275-77 (1880), cases; State v. Maine Central R. Co., 66 Me. 512 (1877).

[6] Thomas v. West Jersey R. Co., 101 U. S. 83-84 (1879), cases, Miller, J.; Balsley v. St. Louis, &c. R. Co., 119 Ill. 72-73 (1886).

[7] West River Bridge Co. v. Dix, 6 How. 534 (1848); 22 Cal. 422; 17 Conn. 40; 25 *id.* 36.

corporeal property. As such it is liable for debts and subject to the right of eminent domain.[1]

The ordinary franchise of a railway company is to condemn, take, and use lands for the purpose of a public highway, and to take tolls from those who use it as such. Land, in itself, is not a franchise. A franchise is an incorporeal hereditament; a liberty proceeding from the commonwealth.[2]

A grant of a corporate franchise by an act of legislation, accepted by the grantee, is a *contract* between the State and the grantee, the obligation of which a subsequent legislature cannot impair.[8]

Exclusive rights to public franchises are not favored; if granted they will be protected, but they are never presumed.[4]

A corporation cannot dispose of its franchises to another corporation without legislative authority.[5]

A grant of corporate franchises is necessarily subject to the condition that the privileges conferred shall not be abused, or be employed to defeat the ends for which they were conferred; and that when abused or misemployed, they may be withdrawn by proceedings consistent with law. . . . A corporation is subject to such reasonable regulations as the legislature may from time to time prescribe, as to the general conduct of its affairs, serving only to secure the ends for which it was created, and not materially interfering with the privileges granted to it.[6]

See BONUS; GRANT, 3; MONOPOLY; RAILROAD; TAX, 2; TOLL, 2; WARRANTUM.

2. In a popular sense, the political rights of subjects and citizens are called franchises: as, the electoral franchise — the right of suffrage.[7]

The right of voting for a member to serve in parliament is called the "parliamentary franchise;" the right of voting for an alderman or town councilor, the "municipal franchise."[8]

Elective franchise. The right of choosing governmental agents.[9]

Enfranchise. 1. To make free of a city or state. 2. To invest with political freedom and capacity.

Disfranchise. To deprive of a franchise conferred; to suspend or withdraw the exer-

cise of a corporate or political right or privilege.[1]

FRANK.[2] Free.

Frankalmoign. Tenure in consideration of religious services (alms).[3]

Frankpledge. Surety for general good behavior, anciently required of freeborn persons.

Franktenement. A freehold. See FEUD.

To frank. To send free.

Franking privilege. The liberty of sending postal matter through the mails free of charge.

Has existed, in theory, for the public good. The act of January 31, 1873, repealed former laws, from and after July 1, 1873.[4] The act of March 3, 1875, secs. 3, 5, 7, permits members of Congress, and certain executive officials, to send free, public documents (*q. v.*), acts of Congress, and seeds supplied by the commissioner of agriculture.[5] The acts of March 3, 1877, sec. 7, and of March 3, 1879, sec. 1, provide that the privilege shall be enjoyed until the first Monday of December following the expiration of the individual's term of office[6] — the fourth of March.

The privilege is also spoken of as the member's "frank."

FRATERNITY. See ASSOCIATION; COMMUNITY, 3.

FRATRICIDE. See HOMICIDE.

FRAUD.[7] Craft, cunning; cheating, imposition, circumvention.

An artifice to deceive or injure.[8]

An intention to deceive.[9]

Defraud. To cheat; to deceive; to deprive of a right by an act of fraud.

To withhold from another what is justly due him, or to deprive him of a right, by deception or artifice.[10]

Fraud, in the Roman civil law, meant any cunning, deception, or artifice, used to circumvent, cheat, or deceive another. This corresponds to "positive fraud" in modern law.[11]

---

[1] 2 Washb. R. P. 24; 1 Redf. Ry. §§ 1, 4, 10, cases.

[2] Shamokin Valley R. Co. *v.* Livermore, 47 Pa. 468 (1864), Agnew, J.

[3] Chincleclamonche Lumber, &c. Co. *v.* Commonwealth, 100 Pa. 444 (1882); The Binghamton Bridge, 3 Wall. 51 (1865).

[4] Wright *v.* Nagle, 101 U. S. 796 (1879).

[6] Branch *v.* Jesup, 106 U. S. 484, 478 (1882).

[5] Chicago Life Ins. Co. *v.* Needles, 113 U. S. 574, 580 (1885), Harlan, J. See also 66 Cal. 106-7; 36 Conn. 206; 47 *id.* 602; 21 Ill. 69; 37 *id.* 547; 95 *id.* 575; 30 Kan. 657; 13 Bush, 185; 28 La. An. 493; 45 Md. 379; 15 N. Y. 170; 27 *id.* 619; 68 *id.* 555; 1 Oreg. 37; 39 Tex. 478; 77 Va. 212.

[7] Pierce *v.* Emery, 32 N. H. 507 (1856), Perley, C. J.

[8] Mozley & Whiteley's Law Dict.

[9] See State *v.* Staten, 6 Coldw. 255 (1869).

[1] See People *v.* Medical Society, 24 Barb. 577-78 (1857).

[2] F. *franc*, free.

[3] See 2 Bl. Com. 101; 2 Kent, 281.

[4] 17 St. L. 421.

[5] 1 Sup. R. S. 154.

[6] 1 Sup. R. S. 288, 454.

[7] From *fraus*, q. v.

[8] Byles, Bills, 133.

[9] Lord *v.* Goddard, 13 How. 211 (1851), Catron, J. On definitions of, see 3 Law Quar. Rev. 419-28 (1887), cases.

[10] Burdick *v.* Post, 12 Barb. 186 (1851); People *v.* Kelley, 35 *id.* 452 (1862).

[11] [1 Story, Eq. § 186. See 2 Steph. Hist. Cr. Law Eng. 121.

The common law asserts as a general principle that there shall be no definition of fraud.[1]

The courts have never laid down as a general proposition what shall constitute fraud, or any rule, beyond which they will not go, lest other means of avoiding equity should be found.[2]

In the sense of a court of equity, fraud properly includes all acts, omissions, and concealments which involve a breach of legal or equitable duty, trust, or confidence, justly reposed, and are injurious to another, or by which an undue and unconscientious advantage is taken of another.[3]

Consists in deception practiced, in order to induce another to part with property or surrender some legal right, and which accomplishes the end desired.[4]

Consists in the suppression of the truth — *suppressio veri*, or in the assertion of what is false — *suggestio falsi.*

No one can be permitted to say, in respect to his own statements upon a material matter, that he did not expect to be believed; and if they are knowingly false, and willfully made, the fact that they are material is proof of an attempted fraud, because their materiality, in the eye of the law, consists in their tendency to influence the conduct of the party who has an interest in them, and to whom they are addressed.[5]

Fraud is sometimes said to consist of "any kind of artifice employed by one person to deceive another." But the term admits of no positive definition, and cannot be controlled in its application by fixed rules. It is to be inferred or not, according to the special circumstances of every case.[6]

Actual, positive, moral fraud; fraud in fact. Fraud as a matter of fact, involving moral turpitude and intentional wrong. **Implied, constructive, legal fraud; fraud in law.** Fraud as a conclusion of law, and may exist without imputation of bad faith or immorality.[7]

When a party intentionally misrepresents a material fact, or produces a false impression, in order to mislead another, or to entrap or cheat him, or to obtain an undue advantage over him, there is a "positive fraud" in the truest sense. There is an evil act with an evil intent. And the misrepresentation may be as well by deeds or acts, as by words; by artifice to mislead, as well as by positive assertions.[5]

By "constructive frauds" are meant such acts or contracts, as, although not originating in any actual evil design, or contrivance to perpetrate a positive fraud or injury upon other persons, are yet, by their tendency to deceive or mislead other persons, or to violate private or public confidence, or to impair or injure the public interests, deemed equally reprehensible with positive fraud, and, therefore, are prohibited by law, as within the same reason and mischief, as acts and contracts done *malo animo.* The doctrine is founded in an anxious desire of the law to apply the principle of preventive justice, so as to shut out the inducements to perpetrate a wrong, rather than to rely on mere remedial justice, after a wrong has been committed.[1]

An "actual fraud" is something said, done, or omitted by a person with the design of perpetrating what he must have known to be a positive fraud. "Constructive frauds" are acts, statements, or omissions which operate as virtual frauds on individuals, or which, if generally permitted, would be prejudicial to the public welfare, and yet may have been unconnected with any selfish or evil design.[2]

A breach of duty is a constructive fraud.[3]

In the sense of bankrupt acts, "a debt fraudulently contracted by a person occupying a fiduciary relation" involves positive fraud, involving moral turpitude or intentional wrong.[4]

Fraud in fact in the transfer of chattels consists in the intention to prevent creditors from recovering their just debts, by an act that withdraws the debtor's property from their reach. And an act that, though not fraudulently intended, yet has a tendency to defraud creditors, if it vests the property of the debtor in his grantee, is void for legal fraud. Legal fraud is tantamount to actual fraud. Actual fraud is for the jury; legal fraud, where the facts are undisputed or are ascertained, is for the court.[5]

Fraudulent. Infected with fraud, actual or legal; as, a fraudulent — bankruptcy, claim, concealment, conveyance or gift, possession, representation, *qq. v.* Compare VOID.

When an act charged in an indictment is fraudulent, it is not necessary to use the word "fraudulent" in the indictment itself.[6]

---

man, 44 N. J. L. 175 (1882), Depue, J.; 29 Conn. 588, note.

[1] 1 Story, Eq. § 258. See People v. Kelly, 35 Barb. 457 (1862).

[2] Smith, Manual of Equity, 71.

[3] Baker v. Humphrey, 101 U. S. 502 (1879).

[4] Neal v. Clark, 95 U. S. 704 (1877); Hennequin v. Clews, 111 id. 676, 679–81 (1884), cases; Strang v. Bradner, 114 id. 559 (1885).

[5] McKibbin v. Martin, 64 Pa. 356 (1870), Sharswood, J.; Hanson v. Eustace, 2 How. 688 (1844).

See generally Bigelow, Law of Fraud, 137, *et seq.,* cases; Willink v. Vanderveer, 1 Barb. 607 (1847); Birchell v. Strauss, 28 id. 293 (1858); People v. Kelly, 35 id. 456 (1862); Vulcan Oil Co. v. Simons, 6 Phila. 564 (1868); 2 Pomeroy, Eq. § 858; 2 Ala. 593; 5 id. 601; 7 Ark. 171; 6 Ga. 614; 47 id. 109; 27 Me. 308; 29 N. H. 354; 3 Den. 236.

[6] United States v. Caruthers, 15 F. R. 309 (1882).

---

[1] 2 Pars. Contr. 769.

[2] [1 Story, Eq. § 186.

[3] [1 Story, Eq. § 187.

[4] Alexander v. Church, 53 Conn. 562 (1885), Park, C. J., quoting Cooley, Torts, 474; Judd v. Weber, 55 Conn. 277 (1887), Loomis J.

[5] Claflin v. Commonwealth Ins. Co., 110 U. S. 95 (1884), Matthews, J.; 27 Me. 308; 7 Bing. 105; 56 N. H. 401; 58 id. 245; 3 B. & Ad. 114.

[6] Fenner v. Dickey, 1 Flip. 36 (1861), Wilson, J.

[7] [Neal v. Clark, 95 U. S. 709 (1877), Harlan, J.

[8] [1 Story, Eq. § 192. See also Ackerman v. Acker-

Fraudulently. With a deliberately planned purpose and intent to deceive and thereby gain an unlawful advantage.[1]

The ordinary means of fraud are false representations and concealments. The more numerous is the implied or constructive class—which includes all frauds on public policy: agreements to influence testators, to facilitate or restrain marriages, in restraint of trade, for public offices, to suppress criminal proceedings, champertous and other corrupt considerations; all frauds by persons in confidential relations: as, by a guardian, adviser, minister of religion, attorney, doctor, agent, trustee, executor, administrator, debtor, creditor, surety; all frauds upon persons peculiarly liable to be imposed upon: as, bargains with expectant heirs, remaindermen, reversioners, common sailors; and all virtual frauds on individuals irrespective of any confidential relation or liability to imposition: as, forbidden practices at auctions, misuse of the Statute of Frauds, clandestine marriages, frauds on marital rights, frauds under 13 Eliz. c. 5, 96, fraudulent dealing with trustees, appointments, etc.[2]

The fraud must relate directly and distinctly to the contract, if a contract and must affect its very essence. If the fraud be such that had it not been practiced the contract would not have been made, the fraud is *material*. Whether it is or is not material, in a given case, is a question for a jury, possibly under instructions.[3]

The length of time that the intent to defraud precedes the act is not material, provided there is the relation of design and its consummation. Concealment by mere silence is not enough. There must be some trick or contrivance intended to exclude suspicion and prevent inquiry. There must be reasonable diligence; and the means of knowledge are the same thing in effect as knowledge itself. The circumstances of the discovery must be fully stated and proved, and the delay which had occurred shown to be consistent with the requisite diligence.[4]

Fraud binds the injured person, as a cause of action, only from the time of discovery.[5]

The bar of the statute of limitations does not begin to run until the fraud is discovered. Where ignorance has been produced by affirmative acts of the guilty party in concealing the facts, the statute will not bar relief, provided that suit is brought within proper time after the discovery. Nor is relief barred where the party injured has remained in ignorance without fault or want of diligence on his part.[6]

The weight of authority is, that, *in equity*, where the injured person remains in ignorance of fraud without want of care on his part, the bar does not begin to run until the fraud is discovered, though there be no special circumstances or efforts in the guilty party to conceal knowledge. On the question as it arises in actions *at law*, there is a decided conflict of authority. Some courts make concealed fraud an exception on purely equitable principles. The English courts, and the courts of Connecticut, Massachusetts, Pennsylvania, and other States, hold that the doctrine is equally applicable to cases at law.[1] See LIMITATIONS, Statute of.

A court of equity has an undoubted jurisdiction to relieve against every species of fraud. 1. The fraud, which is *dolus malus*, may be actual, arising from facts and circumstances of imposition. 2. It may be apparent from the intrinsic nature and subject of the bargain itself; such as no man in his senses and not under delusion would make on the one hand, and as no honest and fair man would accept on the other. 3. It may be presumed from the circumstances and condition of the parties contracting,—from weakness or necessity. 4. It may be inferred from the nature and circumstances of the transaction, as being an imposition and deceit on persons not parties to the agreement.[2]

There is no fraud *in law* without some moral delinquency; there is no actual legal fraud which is not also a moral fraud. This immoral element consists in the necessary guilty knowledge and consequent intent to deceive—sometimes designated by the technical term the "scienter." The very essence of the legal conception is the fraudulent intention flowing from the guilty knowledge. . . There may be actual fraud *in equity* without any feature or incident of moral culpability. A person making an untrue statement, without knowing or believing it to be untrue, and without any intent to deceive, may be chargeable with actual fraud in equity. . . Forms of fraudulent misrepresentations in equity are: 1. Where a party makes a statement which is untrue, and has at the time actual knowledge of its untruth. 2. Where he makes an untrue statement and has neither knowledge nor belief as to the truth. 3. Where he makes an untrue statement and has no knowledge of the truth, and there are no reasonable grounds for his believing it to be true. 4. But where he makes a statement of fact which is untrue, honestly believing it to be true, and this belief is based upon reasonable grounds which actually exist, there is no fraud. Yet, 5, in that case, if he afterward discovers the truth, and suffers the other party to continue in error, and to act upon the belief that no mistake has been made, this, from the time of discovery, becomes a fraudulent representation. 6. If a statement of fact actually untrue is made by a person who honestly believes it to be true, but under such circumstances that the *duty* of knowing the truth rests upon him, which, if fulfilled, would have prevented him from making the statement, such misrepresentation may be fraudulent in equity.[3]

---

[1] Bank of Montreal *v.* Thayer, 2 McCrary, 5 (1881), McCrary, Cir. J.

[2] See 1 Story, Eq. Ch. VI; Smith, Man. Eq. Ch. IV; 2 Pars. Contr. Ch. XII.

[3] 2 Pars. Contr. 770; Bishop, Contr. §§ 641, 652.

[4] Wood *v.* Carpenter, 101 U. S. 143, 140 (1879), cases, Swayne, J.

[5] Dresser *v.* Missouri, &c. R. Co., Construction Co., 93 U. S. 94–96 (1876), cases.

[6] Bailey *v.* Glover, 21 Wall. 347–50 (1874), cases, Miller, J.; Fritschler *v.* Koehler, 83 Ky. 82 (1885).

[1] Tyler *v.* Angevine, 15 Blatch. 541–42 (1879), cases, Blatchford, J.

[2] Chesterfield *v.* Janssen, 2 Ves. Sr. *155 (1750), Hardwicke, L. C. Same case, 1 L. C. Eq., 4 Am. ed., 773.

[3] 2 Pomeroy, Equity, §§ 884–89, cases.

Fraud avoids a contract *ab initió* — vitiates all contracts whether intended to operate against a party, a stranger, or the public generally. The guilty party cannot allege his own fraud in order to avoid his own act; and he may be liable in damages where real injury is done. The agreement cannot be adopted in part: all must be disaffirmed or none.[1]

Fraud is never presumed. The burden of proving it rests upon him who alleges it. It is a question of fact to be determined from all the circumstances in each case.[2]

Allegations of fraud must be specific in time, place, persons, etc., so that the defendant may meet the charge, and the court see whether ordinary diligence to discover the fraud has been used.[3]

Being a term which the law applies to certain facts, where, upon the facts, the law adjudges fraud, it need not be expressly alleged.[4]

Gross negligence tends to show fraud.[5]

All avenues that facilitate the detection of fraud are to be kept open and free from bars and estoppels.[6]

The presence of fraud is a fact, the evidence of which must satisfy an unprejudiced mind beyond a reasonable doubt.[7]

Circumstantial evidence is, in most cases, the only proof that can be adduced.[8]

While the common law affords reasonable protection against fraud in dealing, it does not go to the romantic length of giving indemnity against the consequences of indolence and folly, or of careless indifference to the ordinary and accessible means of knowledge.[9]

A court of equity will not grant relief when the complainant has a complete, effectual, direct, certain and adequate remedy in a court of common law.[10]

Statutes make many different acts frauds, and provide for punishment by criminal proceedings. Remedies available at law are: an action on the case in the nature of a writ of deceit for damages; and an action for money received, by which the tort is waived. Remedies in equity: rescission of the contract; specific performance; injunction; declaration of trust *ex maleficio*.[1] See those titles.

See particularly CAVEAT, Emptor; CONCEAL, 5; COVIN; DECEIT; EQUITY; ESTOPPEL; FORGERY; GUILTY; IDENTITY, 2; INFLUENCE; INNOCENCE; INSOLVENCY; MISTAKE; RATIFICATION; REFORM; REPRESENTATION, 1; RESCISSION; TRUST, 1.

Statute of Frauds. Statute of 29 Charles II (1678), c. 3 — "An Act for the Prevention of Frauds and Perjuries."

It object was to prevent the facility to perpetrate frauds and the temptation to commit perjury, held out by the enforcement of obligations depending for their evidence upon the unassisted memory of witnesses, by requiring certain transfers of land and certain cases of contracts to be reduced to writing and signed by the parties to be charged therewith, or by their agents thereunto lawfully authorized in writing.

Its policy is to impose such requisites upon private transfers of property, as, without being hinderances to fair transactions, may be either totally inconsistent with dishonest practices, or tend to multiply the chances of detection.[2]

Every day's experience more fully demonstrates that the statute was founded in wisdom, and absolutely necessary to preserve the title to real property from the chances, the uncertainty, and the fraud attending the admission of parol testimony. When courts of equity have relaxed the rigid requirements of the statute, it has always been for the purpose of hindering the statute, made to prevent frauds, from becoming the instrument of fraud.[3]

The substance of the statute has been re-enacted in the States; and other points, coming within its general policy, have been added.[4]

I. As applying to Realty. The statute enacts that all leases, estates, and interest in lands, made without writing signed by the parties or their agents lawfully authorized in writing, shall have the force and effect of estates at will only (sec. 1); except leases not exceeding three years from the making, which reserve at least two-thirds of the improved value of the land (sec. 2); and that no lease, estate, or interest shall be assigned, granted, or surrendered unless by writing signed by the assignor, grantor, etc., or his agent authorized in writing, except assignments, etc., by operation of law (sec. 3).[5] See under FRUCTUS.

II. As applying to Equity. Enacts that all declarations or creations of trusts of land shall be in writing signed by the declarant or creator (sec. 7), except trusts arising by construction of law, or transferred by act of law (sec. 8); that all grants or assignments of trusts

---

[1] Foreman *v.* Bigelow, 4 Cliff. 543–49 (1878), cases, Clifford, J. See also Feltz *v.* Walker, 49 Conn. 98 (1881), cases, Carpenter, J.

[2] Hager *v.* Thompson, 1 Black, 91 (1861); Humes *v.* Scruggs, 94 U. S. 28 (1876); 2 Pars. Cont. 784.

[3] See Stearns *v.* Page, 7 How. 829 (1849); Moore *v.* Greene, 19 *id.* 70 (1856); Badger *v.* Badger, 2 Wall. 95 (1864); Ambler *v.* Choteau, 107 U. S. 591 (1882).

[4] Stimson *v.* Helps, 9 Col. 36 (1885); Kerr, Fraud, &c. 366, cases.

[5] First Nat. Bank of Carlisle *v.* Graham, 100 U. S. 702 (1879), cases.

[6] Pendleton *v.* Richey, 32 Pa. 63 (1858); 11 Wend. 117; 4 Kent, 269.

[7] Young *v.* Edwards, 72 Pa. 267 (1872).

[8] Rea *v.* Missouri, 17 Wall. 543 (1873); Craig *v.* Fowler, 59 Iowa, 203 (1882); Moore *v.* Ullman, 80 Va. 311 (1885), cases.

[9] 2 Kent, 484, cases; Senter *v.* Senter, 70 Cal. 622–24 (1886), cases.

[10] Green *v.* Spaulding, 76 Va. 411, 417 (1882): 1 Story, Eq. § 33.

---

[1] See Pasley *v.* Freeman, 2 Sm. L. C. 93–113, cases.

[2] 1 Greenl. Ev. § 262; 2 Whart. Ev. § 853; 3 Pars. Contr. 3.

[3] Purcell *v.* Miner, 4 Wall. 517 (1866), Grier, J.

[4] Browne, Stat. Fr., Appendix.

[5] 2 Bl. Com. 297; 2 Whart. Ev. §§ 854–68, 883.

shall also be in writing, signed by the grantor or assignor (sec. 9); and that estates *pur autre vie* may be taken in execution for debt, or be deemed assets by descent for the payment of debts (sec. 10).[1]

III. As applying to Common Law. Enacts that no action shall be brought whereby: (1) To charge an executor or administrator upon any special promise to answer for damages out of his own estate.[2] (2) To charge the defendant upon any special promise to answer for the debt, default, or miscarriage of another. See Promise, Original; Guaranty, 2. (3) To charge any person upon any agreement made upon consideration of marriage. See Settlement, Marriage. (4) To charge any person upon any contract or sale of lands, or any interest in or concerning them. See Land. (5) To charge any person upon any agreement that is not to be performed within one year from the making thereof,—*unless*, in each case (1–5), the agreement or some note or memorandum thereof is in writing and signed by the party to be charged therewith or by his agent thereunto lawfully authorized in writing (sec. 4).[3]

If the performance of the contract depends upon a contingency which may happen within a year, the contract need not be in writing. It is sufficient if the possibility of performance exists.[4]

(6) That in a contract for the sale of goods, wares, or merchandise, for the price of ten pounds or upward, the buyer must actually receive and accept part of the goods, etc., or give something in earnest or in part payment, or the parties, or their agents, sign some note or memorandum of the bargain (sec. 17).[5] See Earnest; Payment, Part.

(7) That judgments against lands shall bind purchasers from the day of signing, and against goods when the writ of execution is delivered to the sheriff (secs. 14, 15).

(8) Provides for additional solemnities in the execution of wills.[6] See Will, 2, Statute of wills.

The provisions as to the transfer of interests in land, and to promises, which at common law could be effected by *parol*, that is, without writing, comprise all that in professional use is meant by the statute.

The theory is that the writing required in any case will secure an exact statement and the best evidence of the terms and conditions of a promise made.[7] See Agreement; Parol, Evidence.

See also Performance, Part; Verbum, Verba illata.

Statute of 9 Geo. IV (1829), c. 14, called *Lord Tenterden's Act*, enlarged the application of the Statute of Frauds, by rendering a written memorandum necessary in cases of a promise: to bar the Statute of Limitations; by an adult to pay a debt contracted during his infancy; as to a representation of ability in trade,

upon the strength of which credit is to be given; and as to contracts for the sale of goods, not yet made or finished, amounting to ten pounds or upward.[1]

FRAUS. L. A cheating; deceit; imposition; fraud. Compare Dolus.

Fraus est celare fraudem. It is a fraud to conceal a fraud. Concealment (*q. v.*) may amount to fraud.

Fraus latet in generalibus. Fraud lurks in general expressions.

Pia fraus. Pious fraud: evasion of law to advance the interests of a religious institution. See Mortmain.

FREE. Not subject to restraint or control; having freedom of will; at liberty; also, that on which no charge is made. Compare Frank.

1. Liberated from control of parent, guardian, or master; *sui juris:* said of a child, ward, apprentice.

2. Individual; exclusive; privileged; independent; opposed to common: said of a fishery, a warren, and formerly of a city or town, *qq. v.* See also Municipium.

3. Clear of offense, guiltless, innocent; also, released from arrest, liberated: used of persons acquitted or released from imprisonment.

4. Open to all citizens alike: as, a free school, *q. v.*

5. Not arbitrary or despotic; assuring liberty; defending individual rights against encroachment by any person or class: as, a free government, free institutions.[2]

6. Certain; honorable; becoming a freeman; opposed to base: as, free-socage, *q. v.*

7. That for which no charge is made for use; opposed to toll: as, a free bridge, *q. v.*

Not gained by purchase: as, free admission, free passage.

Free on board. In a contract for the sale and delivery of goods "free on board" vessel, the seller is under no obligation to act until the buyer names the ship to which the delivery is to be made: until he knows that he could not put the articles on board.[3] Compare Frais.

8. Neutral: as in saying that "free ships make free goods."

Freely. Without constraint, coercion, or compulsion.[4] See Duress; Will, 1.

---

[1] 2 Bl. Com. 337, 259; 2 Whart. Ev. § 903.

[2] 2 Bl. Com. 466; 3 Pars. Contr. 19.

[3] 3 Bl. Com. 159; 3 Pars. Contr. 19, 29, 31, 35; 2 Whart. Ev. §§ 878–80; Mahan *v.* United States, 16 Wall. 146 (1872); Becker *v.* Mason, 30 Kan. 700–2 (1883), cases.

[4] Stowers *v.* Hollis, 83 Ky. 548–49 (1886), cases; Doyle *v.* Dixon, 97 Mass. 211 (1867): 93 Am. Dec. 85–90, cases.

[5] 2 Bl. Com. 448; 3 Pars. Contr. 39; 2 Whart. Ev. § 869; 1 Law Q. Rev. 1–24 (1884); 37 Alb. L. J. 492 (1888).

[6] 2 Bl. Com. 376, 500, 515; 2 Whart. Ev. §§ 884–900.

[7] Browne, Stat. Fr. § 346.

[1] Smith, Contr. 95; Reed, St. Frauds.

[2] Webster's Dict.

[3] Dwight *v.* Eckert, 117 Pa. 508 (1888), cases.

[4] Dennis *v.* Tarpenny, 20 Barb. 374 (1855); Meriam *v.* Harsen, 2 Barb. Ch. 269 (1847).

Freedman. One made free; a manumitted slave. See CITIZEN, Amendments; LIBERTY, 1.

Freeman. One born or made free as to civil rights.

In the constitutions of Pennsylvania of 1776 and 1790, "freemen" described citizens who were capable of electing or being elected representatives of the people in the Provincial Council or General Assembly. The term with this meaning was brought by William Penn from England. A freeman is one in possession of the civil rights enjoyed by the people generally. This freedom of civil rights was termed his "free-law," and was liable to forfeiture for disloyalty and infamy. . . The language of the amended constitution of 1838 was " white freeman." [1]

In those constitutions, referring to the right of suffrage, does not include females. [2]

Freehold. The possession of soil by a freeman. Such estate as requires actual possession of the land. Such estate in lands as is conveyed by livery of seisin, or, in tenements of an incorporeal nature, by what is equivalent thereto; as, by receipt of rent. [3]

An estate in real property, of inheritance or for life; or, the term by which it is held. [4]

Any estate of inheritance or for life, in real property, whether it be a corporeal or incorporeal hereditament. [5]

Also, the land itself. See ABATEMENT, 1; WASTE, 1.

Freeholder. The actual owner of land.

He was originally a suitor of the courts, a juror, voted for members of parliament, and could defend his title to land. [6]

Such as holds a freehold estate, that is, lands or tenements, in fee-simple, fee-tail, or for term of life. [7]

One who owns land in fee, or for life, or for some indeterminate period. The estate may be legal or equitable. [8]

One who has title to real estate, irrespective of the amount or value thereof. [9]

A freeholder whose estate is worth a specified sum, clear of incumbrances, is, by the law of some localities, privileged from arrest in civil actions; and he may not be required to furnish security for the performance of a legal obligation. See further ARREST, 2.

Freehold estates are: 1. Of inheritance — (a) absolute, as tenancy in fee-simple; (b) limited: qualified or base, and conditional — later, fees-tail. 2. Not of inheritance. These are chattel interests in lands. They are for life, and either conventional or legal; the lowest species is the estate for the life of another. [1] See CONDITION; FEE, 1; FEUD; SHELLEY'S CASE.

FREIGHT. Merchandise transported or to be transported; also, compensation for that service.

In its widest sense, may include fare, for it is that " with which anything is *fraught* or laden for transportation;" and, by a figure of speech, the price paid for the transportation. [2]

The burden or loading of a ship, or the cargo which she has on board; likewise, the hire agreed upon between the owner or master of a vessel for the carriage of goods from one port or place to another. [3]

Goods carried; and the price to be paid for the carriage, or for the hire of a vessel under a charter-party or otherwise. [4]

Compensation for the carriage of goods. [5]

In policies of marine insurance, freight means the earnings or profit derived by the ship-owner or the hirer from the use of the ship himself, or from letting it to others, or from carrying goods for others. Does not include cargo or goods laden on board, which are insured under the term goods, cargo, merchandise, or word of like import; nor profit which the owner of the cargo expects to derive from the transportation. [6]

Affreightment. The contract for the use of a vessel.

Dead freight. Money paid or due for unoccupied capacity in a vessel. [7]

The amount of freight to be paid rests upon contract expressed in the charter-party or bill of lading, or else is implied in law — for a reasonable sum. [8]

In the absence of a different stipulation, freight is only payable when the merchandise is in readiness

[1] McCafferty v. Guyer, 59 Pa. 115–18 (1868), Agnew, J.

[2] Burnham v. Luning, 9 Phila. 241 (1871).

[3] [2 Bl. Com. 104, 209.

[4] Gage v. Scales, 100 Ill. 221 (1881), Craig, C. J.

[5] 4 Kent, 24.

[6] 2 Bl. Com. 120.

[7] Bradford v. State, 15 Ind. 353 (1860): Jacob.

[8] State v. Ragland, 75 N. C. 13 (1876), Rodman, J.

[9] [People v. Scott, 8 Hun, 567 (1876), Talcott, J.

[1] 2 Bl. Com. 120; 80 Va. 844.

[2] Pennsylvania R. Co. v. Sly, 65 Pa. 211 (1870), Sharswood, J.

[3] [Brittan v. Barnaby, 21 How. 533 (1858), Wayne, J.

[4] [Lord v. Neptune Ins. Co., 10 Gray, 112 (1857), Shaw, C. J. See also 1 Mas. 12; 3 *id.* 314; 1 Sprague, 219; 1 Ware, 188; 13 East, 325; L. R., 7 C. P. 348.

[5] Palmer v. Gracie, 4 Wash. 123 (1821).

[6] [Minturn v. Warren Ins. Co., 2 Allen, 91 (1861), Bigelow, C. J.

[7] See Gray v. Carr, L. R., 6 Q. B. *528 (1871); Phillips v. Rodie, 15 East, 264 (1812).

[8] Palmer v. Gracie, 4 Wash. 123 (1821).

to be delivered to the person having the right to receive it.[1]

Freight *pro rata itineris* not being earned where, from necessity, cargo is accepted before arrival at the port of destination, in a case of average, there can be no contribution on it.[2]

Freighter. He who loads a vessel, under a contract of hire or of affreightment.[3]

The ship-owners undertake that they will carry the goods to the place of destination, unless prevented by the dangers of the seas, or other unavoidable casualty; and the freighter undertakes that, if the goods be delivered at the place of destination, he will pay the stipulated freight. . If the ship be disabled from completing her voyage, the owner may still entitle himself to the whole freight by forwarding the goods by some other means to their destination; but he has no right to any freight if they be not so forwarded, unless the forwarding be dispensed with, or there be a new bargain made. If the ship-owner will not forward them, the freighter is entitled to them without paying anything. The general property in the goods is in the freighter; the ship-owner has no right to withhold the possession from him, unless he has either earned his freight or is going on to earn it.[4]

See AVERAGE; CHARTER, 1, Party; COMMERCE; DISPATCH; FRAIS; INSURANCE, Marine; LADING, Bill of; RESTITUTIO; SEAWORTHY.

FRENCH. Law-French, which is used in old law-books and legal proceedings, exhibits many terms and idioms not employed in classic French.

Under William the Norman and his sons, all the public proceedings of the courts, including arguments and decisions, were expressed in Norman law-French. In the thirty-sixth year of Edward III (1363), it was enacted that all pleas should be shown, answered, debated, and judged in the English tongue, but be entered and enrolled in Latin, which, being a dead language, was immutable. However, the practitioners and reporters continued to take notes in the customary law-French. This law-French differs as much from modern French as the diction of Chaucer differs from the diction of Addison. English and Norman being concurrently used for several centuries, the two idioms assimilated and borrowed from each other.[5]

"The constitution of the *aula regis*, and the judges themselves, were fetched from Normandy; in consequence, proceedings in the king's courts were carried on in Norman."[6]

Norman-French, as employed about the courts, was often intermixed with scraps of Latin and pure English.[7] See LATIN.

FREQUENT, *v.* A single visit to a place, or once passing through a street, cannot be said to be a "frequenting" that place or street.

May be used in contradistinction to "found," which applies to the case of a person apprehended in a building or inclosed ground, where the necessary inference would be that the purpose was unlawful, in which case it would be enough to show that the party was in the place only once.[1]

Webster's definition "visiting often, resorting to often or habitually," expresses the popular understanding. What amounts to "frequenting" a street must depend upon circumstances.[2]

FRESH. See SUIT, 1.

FRESHET. See ACT, 1, OF GOD; BED, 2; WATER-COURSE.

FRIDAY, GOOD. See HOLIDAY.

FRIEND. Compare AMI; AMICUS.

One favorably disposed to another person.

Friend of the court. A disinterested by-stander who furnishes information to the judge trying a cause, or to a court, on a matter of law or fact of which notice may be taken without proof. Usually, a member of the bar of the court. See AMICUS, Curiæ.

Next friend. One who acts for another who is not *sui juris:* a representative for the special office of carrying on a suit in court.

An infant sues by his "next friend," and defends by his guardian *ad litem.* Similarly, a married woman, who has an interest which conflicts with the interest of her husband, may sue him by her "next friend" — any acquaintance. The next friend may be held for the costs of unsuccessful litigation; and he may be required to file his authority to appear.[3]

FRIVOLOUS. Is applied to an answer, plea, or objection which upon its face is clearly insufficient in law, and apparently made for purposes of delay or to embarrass an adversary.

An answer is frivolous when it controverts no material allegation in the complaint, and presents no tenable defense;[4] when it sets up a matter which may be true in fact, but forms no defense. A *sham* or *false* answer may be good in form, but false in fact.[5] See SHAM.

To constitute a pleading frivolous, it must be ap-

---

[1] Brittain *v.* Barnaby, 21 How. 533 (1858).

[2] The Joseph Farwell, 31 F. R. 844 (1887).

[3] See 3 Kent, 173; 3 Johns. 105.

[4] Hunter *v.* Prinsep, 10 East, 394 (1808), Ellenborough, C. J. Approved, The Tornado, 108 U. S. 347, 349 (1883), Blatchford, J.

[5] [3 Bl. Com. 317-18.]

[6] 4 Bl. Com. 416.

[7] 2 Hume, Hist. Engl. 115.

[1] Clark *v.* The Queen, 14 Q. B. D. 98 (1884), Grove, J.; Vagrant Act, 5 Geo. IV (1825), c. 83.

[2] *Ibid.* 101-2, Hawkins, J.

[3] See 3 Bl. Com. 300; Herzberg *v.* Sachse, 60 Md. 432 (1883).

[4] Lefferts *v.* Snediker, 1 Abb. Pr. o. s. 42 (1854); Brown *v.* Jennison, 3 Sandf. L. 732 (1851); Lerdall *v.* Charter Oak Ins. Co., 51 Wis. 430 (1881): 7 *id.* 383.

[5] People *v.* McCumber, 18 N. Y. 321 (1858).

parent on mere inspection, without examination or research, that it is utterly invalid.[1]

When it needs argument to prove that an answer or demurrer is frivolous, it is not frivolous.[2]

A pleading seen to be frivolous, upon bare inspection, will be stricken off by the court.[3]

FROM. Compare AFTER; AT; TO.

1. Is taken inclusively according to the subject-matter; as, in a grant of power to construct a railroad "from" a place.[4]

"From" a street may mean from any part of the street; not, necessarily, from its inner or nearest line.[5]

"From the city" was held to mean from any point within the city.[6]

2. In computing time "from" a day, the rule is to exclude that day.[7] See DAY.

3. Descent "from" a parent means by act of the parent.[8] See DESCENT.

4. An indictment that charges stealing corn "in" the field may be fatally defective under a statute which makes stealing "from" a field a felony.[9]

FRUCTUS. L. Fruit, fruits; increase; profit.

Fructus industriales. Cultivated fruits. **Fructus industriæ.** Fruit of labor, or industry; emblements, the products of planting and cultivation. **Fructus naturales.** Nature's growths; natural fruits: increase by the unassisted powers of nature; as, the fruits of uncultivated trees, the young of animals, and wool.

Although the cases are not uniform, there is abundant authority for holding that crops, such as corn, wheat, rye, potatoes, and the like, called *fructus industriales*, are regarded as the representatives of the labor and expense bestowed upon them, and as chattels, while yet growing; and, hence, as such, go to the executor, may be seized upon execution as chattels, and be sold or bargained by parol; while growing grass and trees and the fruit on them, called *fructus naturales*, are a part of the soil of which they are the natural growth, descend with it to the heir, and, until severed, cannot be seized upon execution, and, under the statute of frauds, cannot be sold or conveyed by

parol. But if the owner of the fee, by a conveyance in writing, sells these natural products of the earth, which grow spontaneously without cultivation, to be taken from the land, or sells the land reserving them to be cut and removed by himself, the law regards this action as equivalent to an actual severance.[1] See CROP; EMBLEMENTS; FRUIT.

Fructus legis. The fruit of the law — execution.

Fructus pendentes. Hanging fruits. **Fructus stantes.** Standing fruits; fruits united to the thing which produces them.

See USUS, FRUCTUS.

FRUIT. Increase; profit; product; enjoyment.

Natural fruits. The natural product of trees, bushes, and other plants. **Artificial fruits.** Such things as interest on money, loaned or due.

Figurative expressions are: fruits of crime; that execution is the fruit of a judgment.

See FRUCTUS; EMBLEMENTS; LARCENY; PERISHABLE.

FUGITIVE. Used only in the sense of a "fugitive from justice:" a person who commits a crime within a State, and withdraws himself from its jurisdiction without waiting to abide the consequences of his act.[2]

Acts of limitation of criminal prosecution do not apply to persons "fleeing from justice."[3]

"Fleeing from justice" (act of 1790) is, leaving one's home or residence or known place of abode, with intent to avoid detection or punishment for some public offense against the United States. An offender may flee by secreting himself, or by not being usually and publicly known as being within the district.[4]

"A Person charged in any State with Treason, Felony, or other Crime, who shall flee from Justice," etc., are the words of the Constitution relating to extradition of offenders.[5]

There must be an actual fleeing. "Who shall flee" does not include a person who was never in the place from which he is said to have fled.[6]

Defendant may plead either specially or generally; if specially, the government may reply "He fled," etc. Defendant may not demur.[7] See at length EXTRADITION.

---

[1] Cahoon v. Wisconsin R. Co., 10 Wis. *293 (1860), cases.

[2] Cottrill v. Cramer, 40 Wis. 559 (1876), Ryan, C. J.

[3] Taylor v. Nyce, 3 W. N. C. 433 (Pa., 1877).

[4] Union Pacific R. Co. v. Hall, 91 U. S. 348 (1875), cases.

[5] City of Pittsburgh v. Cluley, 74 Pa. 261 (1873).

[6] Appeal of West Penn. R. Co., 99 Pa. 161 (1881). See also 33 Me. 67; 52 id. 252; 7 Allen, 487; 7 Barb. 416; 9 Wend. 346; 3 Head, 596; 2 Mas. 137.

[7] Sheets v. Selden, 2 Wall. 190 (1864); Best v. Polk, 18 id. 119 (1873). See also 19 Conn. 376; 52 Ga. 244; 24 Ind. 194; 13 B. Mon. 460; 13 Me. 198; 9 N. H. 304; 24 Barb. 9; 9 Cranch, 104; 1 Gall. 248.

[8] Gardner v. Collins, 2 Pet. *91 (1829); Case v. Wildridge, 4 Ind. 54 (1853).

[9] State v. Shuler, 19 S. C. 140 (1883).

---

[1] Kimball v. Sattley, 55 Vt. 291 (1883), cases, Veazey, J.; ib. 540; 118 Mass. 125; 40 Md. 212.

[2] [Re Voorhees, 32 N. J. L. 150 (1867), Beasley, C. J.

[3] See Act of 1790, § 32; R. S. § 1043; Act of 1804, § 3; R. S. § 1046.

[4] United States v. O'Brian, 3 Dill. 383 (1874), Dillon, Cir. J.

[5] Constitution, Art. IV, sec. 2, cl. 2.

[6] Jones v. Leonard, 50 Iowa, 108 (1878). See also United States v. Smith, 4 Day, 125 (1809); United States v. White, 5 Cranch, C. C. 44 (1836).

[7] United States v. Cook, 17 Wall. 168 (1872); United States v. Norton, 91 U. S. 566 (1875); 3 Crim. Law Mag. 787-810 (1882), cases on points of practice.

FULFILL. See PERFORM.

FULL. Not wanting in any essential quality; complete; entire; whole; perfect; adequate.

Full age. The age of twenty-one years; majority. See AGE.

Full blood. Whole blood. See BLOOD.

Full court. All the members of a court sitting together.

Full defense. A general defense. See DEFENSE, 2.

Full faith and credit. Entire confidence and efficacy. See further FAITH, Full.

Full price. A price which is fair or reasonable. See PRICE.

Full proof. Proof to the exclusion of a reasonable doubt. See PROOF.

Fully. See ADMINISTER, 4.

In full. 1. Completed, filled up, not blank; as, an indorsement (q. v.) which names the indorsee.

2. For all that is due, and not on account: as, a receipt in full, satisfaction in full, qq. v.

FUNCTUS. See OFFICIUM, Functus, etc.

FUND; FUNDS.[1] A deposit of resources; stock or capital; money invested for a specific object; revenue: as, the fund of a bank, or of a trust.[2]

"Funds," as employed in commercial transactions, usually signifies money.[3]

A "fund" is merely a name for a collection or an appropriation of money.[4]

While the restricted meaning of "funds" is cash on hand, the broader meaning includes property of every kind, when such property is specially contemplated as something to be used or applied in the payment of debts. Thus, for example, as employed in a statute, may comprehend all the resources of a corporation.[5]

Current funds. Current money; currency, q. v.

Funded debt. The term "fund" was originally applied to a portion of the national revenues set apart or pledged to the payment of a particular debt. And a "funded debt"

was a debt for the payment of the principal or interest of which some fund was appropriated.[1]

Funding. Has been applied to the process of collecting together a variety of outstanding debts against corporations, the principal of which was payable at short periods, and borrowing money upon the bonds or stocks of the corporation to pay them off; the principal of such bonds or stocks being made payable at periods comparatively remote. The word is never used to describe an ordinary debt growing out of a transaction with an individual and represented by a single instrument.[1]

Fundholder. A person to whose custody money is committed, or into whose care trust funds come. Compare STAKEHOLDER.

No funds. No resources or assets, as when it is said that a trustee has "no funds;" also no money on deposit to one's credit, as when a draft drawn upon a bank is returned "no funds."

If a formal demand is made, during banking hours, by the holder of a note, at the bank where it is payable, and there are no funds, it is the duty of the bank to say that there are "no funds;" and there is then a breach of the contract on the part of the maker, and notice thereof would bind the indorsers. There is no necessity for a personal demand upon the maker elsewhere. But if no such demand is made, and the note is only sent or placed in the bank for collection, then the maker has till the close of business hours to make payment. Sending a note through the clearing-house is not a formal demand for immediate payment made during business hours, but is equivalent to leaving the note at the bank for collection from the maker on or before the close of banking hours.[2] See ASSIGNMENT, Equitable.

Public funds. The stock of a public debt; securities of government.[3]

Sinking fund. Money, arising from particular taxes or duties, appropriated toward the payment of the principal and interest of a public loan.[4]

See IDENTITY, 2; MARSHAL, 2.

FUNDAMENTAL. See CONSTITUTION.

Alterations in a charter which are not "fundamental," and are authorized by the legislature, may be effectually accepted by a majority of the stockholders — a majority per capita or of the shares voted, as the case may require. Alterations which actually

[1] F. fond, a merchant's stock: L. fundus, bottom. Whence "fundamental."

[2] See Webster's Dict.

[3] Galena Ins. Co. v. Kupfer, 28 Ill. 335 (1862). See 91 N. Y. 65; 24 N. J. E. 358.

[4] People v. N. Y. Central R. Co., 34 Barb. 135 (1861).

[5] Miller v. Bradish, 69 Iowa, 280 (1886), Seevers, J.

[1] Ketchum v. City of Buffalo, 14 N. Y. 367, 379 (1865), Selden, J.

[2] Nat. Exchange Bank v. Nat. Bank of North America, 132 Mass. 148 (1882).

[3] See 1 Bl. Com. 331.

[4] See Ketchum v. City of Buffalo, 14 N. Y. 367 (1865); Union Pacific R. Co. v. Buffalo County, 9 Neb. 453 (1880); Bank for Savings v. Mayor of New York, 102 N. Y. 313, 325 (1886).

change the nature and purposes of the corporation, or of the enterprise for the prosecution of which it was created, are "fundamental."[1]

FUNERAL. See BURIAL.

"Funeral expenses" may include the cost of carriage-hire, vault, and tombstone, besides the cost of shroud, coffin, grave, etc.[2]

But not, charges for dinner and horse-feed furnished to persons attending the funeral. See EXECUTOR.[3]

FURNITURE. That which furnishes, or with which anything is furnished or supplied. Whatever may be supplied to a house, a room, or the like, to make it habitable, convenient, or agreeable. Goods, vessels, utensils and other appendages, necessary or convenient for housekeeping. Whatever is added to the interior of a house or apartment for use or convenience.[4]

Relates, ordinarily, to movable personal chattels; but is very general, in meaning and application, and the meaning changes, so as to take the color of, or to accord with, the subject to which it is applied.[5]

Household furniture. Those vessels, utensils, or goods, which, not becoming fixtures, are designed, in their manufacture, originally and chiefly for use in the family, as instruments of the household and for conducting and managing household affairs. Does not include a trunk or a cabinet box.[6]

Embraces everything about a house that has been usually enjoyed therewith, including plate, linen, china, and pictures.[7]

A bequest of household furniture ordinarily comprises everything that contributes to the convenience of the householder or to the ornament of the house. Does not include the furniture of a school-room in a boarding-school.[8]

As used in a bequest, includes bronzes, statuary, and pictures placed in various parts of the house to render it more agreeable as a place of residence, if comporting with the testator's means and the general style of furnishing the house.[9] See CONTAINED; IMPLEMENTS.

Furniture of a ship. Includes everything with which a ship requires to be furnished or equipped to make her seaworthy.[1] See APPURTENANCE.

FURS. See PERISHABLE.

FURTHER. Additional: as, further — assurance, compensation, proof, qq. v.; also, subsequent or later: as, a further hearing, q. v.

"Any further tax," used with relation to some other tax, must mean any additional tax besides that referred to, and not any further like tax.[2]

FUTURE. That which may or will be hereafter: as, future — advances, damage, earnings, estate, qq. v. See also DEVISE, Executory; EXPECTANCY; REMAINDER; SALE; TIME; USE, 2.

Futures. The expression "dealing in futures" has grown out of those purely speculative transactions in which there is a nominal contract of sale for future delivery, but where in fact none is ever intended or executed. The nominal seller does not have or expect to have the stock or merchandise he purports to sell, nor does the nominal buyer expect to receive it or to pay the price. Instead, a percentage or "margin" is paid, which is increased or diminished as the market rates go up or down, and accounted for to the buyer. This is simply speculation and gambling; mere wagering on prices within a given time.[3]

"One person says: I will sell you cotton (for example) at a certain time in the future for a certain price. You agree to pay that price, knowing that he has no cotton to deliver at the time, but with the understanding that, when the time for delivery arrives, you are to pay him the difference between the market value of the cotton and the price you agreed to pay, if cotton declines, and, if it advances, he is to pay you the difference between what you promised to give and the advanced market price."[4]

There is no gambling unless both sides gamble; and from the intent or belief of one party it is not fair to presume a like intent or belief as to the other party.[5] See further WAGER, 2.

[1] Mower v. Staples, 32 Minn. 286 (1884), cases, Berry, Judge.

[2] Donald v. McWhorter, 44 Miss. 29 (1870); Matter of Luckey, 4 Redf. 95 (1879); 14 S. & R. 64.

[3] Shaeffer v. Shaeffer, 54 Md. 683 (1880). See, in general, McClellan v. Filson, 44 Ohio St. 188–89 (1886), cases.

[4] Bell v. Golding, 27 Ind. 179 (1866), Ray, C. J. See also Crossman v. Baldwin, 49 Conn. 491 (1882).

[5] [Fore v. Hibbard, 63 Ala. 412 (1879), Manning, J.

[6] Towns v. Pratt, 33 N. H. 350 (1856), Sawyer, J.

[7] Endicott v. Endicott, 41 N. J. E. 96 (1896); M'Micken v. M'Micken University, 2 Am. Law Reg. 489 (1863); 2 Jarm. Wills, 352; 63 N. H. 295.

[8] Hoopes's Appeal, 60 Pa. 227 (1869), cases, Sharswood, J.

[9] Richardson v. Hall, 124 Mass. 237 (1878), Colt, J. See also 33 Me. 535; 14 Mich. 506; 1 Johns. Ch. 329, 1 Robt.

21; 13 R. I. 20; 30 Vt. 224; 2 Munf. 234; 5 id. 272; 18 Wis. 163; 1 Ves. Sr. 97; 1 Jarman, Wills, 501, 506, note; 2 Williams, Ex. 1017.

[1] Weaver v. The S. G. Owens, 1 Wall. Jr. 360, 359 (1849), Grier, J.

[2] Gordon v. Appeal Tax Court, 3 How. 147 (1845).

[3] King v. Quidnick Company, 14 R. I. 138 (1883), Stiness, J. See also Hatch v. Douglas, 48 Conn. 127 (1880), Carpenter, J.

[4] Cunningham v. Nat. Bank of Augusta, 71 Ga. 408 (1883), cases, Blanford, J.; Mutual Life Ins. Co. v. Watson, 30 F. R. 653 (1887).

[5] Bangs v. Hornick, 30 F. R. 98 (1887), cases. See generally Marshall v. Thurston, 3 Lea, 740 (1879), cases; Bartlett v. Smith, 13 F. R. 263 (1882); Irwin v. Millar, 110 U. S. 499, 508–11 (1884), cases; Kirkpatrick v. Adams, 20 F. R. 287, 293 (1884); Beadles v. McElrath, Sup. Ct. Ky. (1887); 3 S. W. Rep. 152, note.

G.

G. In a few words, originally beginning with *u* or *w*, prefixed to the form which comes through the French, as, in guard for ward; in law-French, equivalent to our *w*.

Whence, also, the doublets gage and wage, guaranty and warranty, guardian and ward, garnish and warn; also seen in warden, warren, and award.[1]

G. S. General statutes.

GAGE. See G; MORTGAGE.

GAIN. See BET; EARNINGS; INCOME; LUCRUM; PROFIT.

GALLON. The gallon of our commerce conforms to the old wine-measure of two hundred and thirty-one cubic inches.[2]

GALLOWS.[3] A beam laid over and fastened to one or two posts, from which a criminal, condemned to death, is suspended. See DEATH, Penalty.

GAMBLE. To play a game of chance or skill for stakes, or to bet on the result of the game; to game or play for money.

Gambler. One who follows or practices games of chance or skill with the expectation and purpose of thereby winning money or other property.[4]

Common gambler. Applied to a person who furnishes facilities for gambling,— one who, for gambling purposes, keeps or exhibits any gambling table, establishment, device or apparatus.[5]

Gambling. Anything which induces men to risk their money or property without other hope of return than to get for nothing a given amount from another person.[6]

Gambling device. An invention to determine who wins and who loses among those that risk their money on a contest or chance of any kind.[7]

Gambling house. Keeping a structure of any kind for purposes of gambling, is an indictable offense at common law.[1]

Gambling policy. A policy of life insurance issued to a person who has no pecuniary interest in the life insured.[2]

See further GAME, 2; HOUSE, 1.

GAME. 1. Wild animals pursued for amusement or profit. In its most comprehensive sense includes beasts, birds or fowl, and fishes.

Game laws. Statutes regulating the taking or killing of animals of a wild nature. Another designation is *Game and Fish Laws.* See FISH, 1.

Game laws are designed to preserve insectivorous birds, and the breeds of fowl and quadrupeds valuable to man for food and for sport. The details of these regulations must be sought for in the statutes of the several States.[3] See PROPERTY, Qualified.

In English law, a "chase" is the liberty of keeping beasts of chase or royal game in an uninclosed space, protected even from the owner of the land, with right to hunt them thereon. A "park" is an inclosed chase, extending over a man's own grounds. A "forest," in the hands of a subject, is the same as a chase. At common law, it was once unlawful to kill beasts of park or chase, except as to such persons as possessed one of these franchises.[4]

In 1831 the law was modified to enable any one to obtain a license to kill game, on the payment of a fee.[5] See CRUELTY, 3; WARREN.

Game; games; gaming; gambling. A device or play the terms of which are that the winner shall receive something of value from the loser. The act of playing a game for stakes.

"Gaming," without the prefix "unlawful," seems usually to imply something of an unlawful nature, by betting on the sport. "Persons may play at a game which is not in itself unlawful, without gaming; but if money is staked it becomes gaming."[6]

"Gaming" is the risking of money, between two or more persons, on a contest or chance of any kind, where one must be the loser and the other the gainer.[7]

Implies something which in its nature de-

---

[1] See Ayers *v.* Findley, 1 Pa. 501 (1845), Gibson, C. J.; Webster's Dict.

[2] Duty on Ale, &c., 16 Op. Att.-Gen. 359 (1879); R. S. § 2504, Sch. D.

[3] Gäl'-lus. Mid. Eng. *galwes*, pl. of A. S. *galga*, cross, gibbet.

[4] Buckley *v.* O'Niel, 113 Mass. 193 (1873), Ames, J.

[5] People *v.* Sponsler, 1 Dak. 291–95 (1876), cases.

[6] Brua's Appeal, 55 Pa. 296 (1867), cases; Smith *v.* Bouvier, 70 *id.* 325 (1872); 14 Bush, 741; 49 Mich. 387; 73 E. C. L. 525.

[7] [Portis *v.* State, 27 Ark. 362 (1872); State *v.* Bryant, Mo. Sup. Ct. (1887): 2 S. W. Rep. 836; 2 Whart. Cr. L. § 1465.

[1] People *v.* Sponsler, *ante;* 2 Whart. Cr. Law, § 1466.

[2] Gambs *v.* Covenant Life Ins. Co., 50 Mo. 47 (1872).

[3] See 19 Kan. 127; 128 Mass. 410; 7 Mo. Ap. 553; 60 N. Y. 10; 95 U. S. 465; L. R. 2 C. P. 553.

[4] 2 Bl. Com. 38, 416.

[5] See Appleton's New Am. Cyc. VIII; Wharton's Law Dict.

[6] Bishop, Stat. Crimes, § 860, quoting Campbell, C. J., in Regina *v.* Ashton, 16 E. L. & E. 316 (1852). See Ansley *v.* State, 36 Ark. 67 (1880); *Re* Lee Tong, 18 F. R. 253 (1883).

[7] Portis *v.* State, 27 Ark. 362 (1872), Bennett, J.

ends upon chance, or in which chance is an element.[1]

"Gaming" is an offense against the public police or economy. It tends to promote idleness, theft, and debauchery among those of the lower class; and among persons of a superior rank it has frequently been attended with the sudden ruin and desolation of families, and an abandoned prostitution of every principle of honor and virtue, and often has ended in self-murder itself.[2]

Playing at a game of chance for mere recreation is lawful.[3]

"Illegal gaming" implies gain and loss between the parties by betting, such as would excite a spirit of cupidity.[4]

A "game of chance" is such a game as is determined entirely or in part by lot or mere luck, and in which judgment, practice, skill, adroitness, and honesty have no office at all, or are thwarted by chance. In a "game of skill" nothing is left to chance.[5]

A "gaming table" is any table kept and used for playing games of chance. It need not be necessary to the game, nor made in any particular way.[6]

"Gaming" implies games. "To game" is to play at any sport or diversion; to play for a stake or prize; to use cards, dice, billiards, or any other instrument according to certain rules with a view to win money or any other thing waged upon the issue of the contest; to practice playing for money or any other stake; to gamble. "Game" embraces every contrivance or institution intended to furnish sport, recreation, or amusement. When a stake is laid upon the chances, the game becomes "gaming." "Games" become unlawful by being prohibited by statute.[7]

In common usage, "betting" and "gaming" are employed interchangeably; yet not always so. If two persons play at cards for money, they are said to be gambling or gaming. They are gambling because they lay a wager or make a bet on the result of the game. To say that they are betting is equally appropriate. If two persons lay a wager upon the result of a pending election, it will be said that they are betting, not gaming. There is no gaming in which the element of the wager is wanting, but there is betting which the term gaming does not commonly embrace. It is so common to apply gaming or gambling to any species of immoral betting that the precise meaning intended in a given case can be learned only from the connection. The terms are often applied to transactions which are illegal in the sense only of being immoral, but which involve the element of wager, as in the case of option contracts. But while such contracts are probably not gaming in the sense of any criminal law, there could be nothing to prevent their being legislated against under that head,

when they are of the nature of gaming and embody its evils. . . . Base-ball and horse-races are games, and any "pooling" scheme in betting thereon is gaming, and the place where the pools are sold is a pooling room or place.[1]

The means or device for either gaming or gambling may be — backgammon,[2] bagatelle,[3] billiards,[4] candy prize-packages,[5] cards,[6] cock-fighting,[7] dog-fights,[8] faro,[9] gift-enterprises [10] (q. v.), horse-racing,[11] keno,[12] loto,[13] poker or draw-poker,[14] pool,[15] raffle with dice,[16] rondo,[17] stocks,[18] tan, tantan,[19] ten-pins.[20]

A discharge will not be granted to an insolvent debtor who has spent property in gaming: his is fraudulent insolvency.[21] Property so acquired is an asset, which may not be spent in gaming; and the mode of acquisition cannot be inquired into.[22]

Money lost by gaming is not recoverable.[23]

Statutes which allow gaming are to be strictly construed.[24]

See BET; LICENSE, 3; LOTTERY; MORALS; OR, 2; POOLING-TABLE; SPECULATION; STAKEHOLDER; WAGER, 2.

GANANICAL. "Gananical property," in Spanish law, is the community of *gains*, acquisitions, profits, made during marriage out of the property of either husband or wife or of both.[25]

[1] People v. Weithoff, *ante.*

[2] 55 Ala. 198.

[3] 22 Gratt. 23.

[4] 22 Ala. 54; 49 *id.* 37; 40 Ill. 294; 15 Ind. 474; 50 *id.* 181; 60 *id.* 457; 75 *id.* 586; 39 Iowa, 42; 41 *id.* 550; 34 Miss. 606; 8 Cow. 139; 28 How. Pr. 247; 17 Ohio St. 32.

[5] 3 Heisk. 488.

[6] 36 Ark. 67.

[7] 8 Metc. 232; 11 *id.* 79; 1 Humph. 486; 4 Sneed, 614; 3 Keb. 465; 3 Camp. 140.

[8] 1 Carr. & P. 613.

[9] 4 Cranch, C. C. 707, 719; 5 *id.* 378, 390; 53 Cal. 246.

[10] 5 Sneed, 507; 3 Heisk. 488.

[11] 23 Ark. 726; 30 *id.* 428; 9 Col. 214; 4 Harr., Del., 554; 69 Ga. 609; 23 Ill. 493; 51 *id.* 184, 473; 9 Ind. 35; 1 Allen, 563; 51 Mich. 212; 18 Me. 337; 16 Minn. 299; 4 Mo. 536, 599; 31 *id.* 35; 1 N. M. 621; 13 Johns. 88; 8 Gratt. 592; L. R., 6 Q. B. 514, 130.

[12] 48 Ala. 122; 27 Ark. 355, 360; 7 La. An. 651.

[13] 1 Mo. 722.

[14] 2 Monta. 437; 32 Gratt. 884.

[15] 39 Mo. 420; 51 Mich. 203, 214; 120 Mass. 273; 8 Lea, 411; L. R., 6 Q. B. 514.

[16] 26 Ala. 155; 15 Ark. 71; 5 Rand. 652; 14 Gray, 26, 390; 21 Tex. 692.

[17] 15 Ark. 259.

[18] 70 Pa. 325.

[19] 70 Cal. 516; 18 F. R. 253.

[20] 29 Ala. 32; 32 N. J. L. 158; 11 Ired. L. 273. See generally 2 Whart. Cr. L. § 1465; Cooley, Const. Lim. 749; 29 Me. 457; 8 Gray, 488; 38 N. H. 426.

[21] R. S. §§ 5132, 5110.

[22] *Re* Marshall, 1 Low. 462 (1870).

[23] 2 Bish. Cr. L. § 507.

[24] Alcardi v. Alabama, 19 Wall 639 (1873).

[25] [Cutter v. Waddingham, 22 Mo. 256, 255 (1855), Leonard, J.

[1] Bew v. Harston, L. R., 3 Q. B. 456 (1878), Cockburn, C. J. See also Bell v. State, 5 Sneed, 509 (1858).

[2] 4 Bl. Com. 171.

[3] 4 Chitty, Bl. Com. 171.

[4] People v. Sergeant, 8 Cow. 141 (1828).

[5] State v. Gupton, 8 Ired. L. 273 (1848), Ruffin, C. J.

[6] Toney v. State, 61 Ala. 3 (1878); Whitney v. State, 10 Tex. Ap. 377 (1881); Walz v. State, 33 Tex. 335 (1870).

[7] People v. Weithoff, 51 Mich. 203, 210 (1883), Cooley, J.

"The right to *gananicas* is founded in the partner-ship which is supposed to exist between husband and wife, because. she bringing her fortune in *dote*, gift and paraphernalia, and he his in the estate and prop-erty which he possesses, it is directed that the gains, which result from the joint employment of this mass, be equally divided." [1]

That property which husband and wife, living to-gether, acquire during matrimony by a common title, lucrative or onerous; or that acquired by either or both, by purchase or industry; also, the fruits of the separate property which each brings to the matri-mony or acquires by lucrative title during the contin-uance of the partnership. The gain is common to both. [2]

GAOL. See JAIL.

GARDEN. See CURTILAGE; FIELD, 1; MESSUAGE.

GARDENING. See AGRICULTURE.

GARNISH. [3] 1. To warn, make aware, notify. 2. To attach property or a debt due or belonging to a defendant.

Garnishee. One warned by legal process in respect to the interest of a third party in property held by him. [4]

One in whose hands money or goods have been attached: he is "warned" not to pay the money nor to deliver the property to the defendant. [5]

The best reporters do not use garnishee as the verb. [6] The person warned is garnish*eed;* the fund or property is garnish*ed.*

Garnishment. The process of warning or citation. [4]

Originally, a notice to a person not a party to a suit, to appear in court and explain his interest in the subject-matter of the litiga-tion or to furnish other information.

Now, the act or proceeding of attaching money or property belonging to a judgment debtor but in the possession of a third per-son. Otherwise known as "factorizing," "garnishee," or "trustee process."

In the nature of an equitable attachment of the debt or assets of the principal defendant in the hands of a third person. Its object is to reach such assets and apply them in discharge of the principal debt. [7]

The office of a garnishment is to apply the debt due by a third person to the defendant in a judgment to the extinguishment of that judgment, or to appropri-ate effects belonging to a defendant in the hands of a third person to its payment. [1]

There must be a debt due from the garnishee to the defendant in the judgment, payable at the time of the service of the writ, or to become payable. The debt must be at least a cause of action. [2]

The person warned becomes a mere stakeholder, with a right to such defense against the new claimant as he has against the judgment-debtor. The proceed-ing is substantially an attachment, q. v. It arrests the property in the hands of the garnishee, interferes with the owner's or creditor's control over it, subjects it to the judgment of the court, and thus operates as a seizure. It is effected by serving notice as directed by statute. [3]

GAS COMPANIES. See MONOPOLY; POLICE, 2.

GASOLINE. See OIL.

GATES. See WAY, Right of.

GAVELKIND. [4] A particular custom in vogue in Kent (though perhaps general till the Conquest) which ordained that all sons alike should succeed to their father's estate.

The estate was not subject to escheat for attainder; the tenant could alien by enfeoffment at fifteen, and could devise by will. It was a species of socage tenure modified by custom. [5]

GAZETTE. Originally, a piece of money current at Venice; next the price at which sheets of news were sold; then the sheets themselves. [6]

The official publication of the English gov-ernment; also called the "London Gazette."

It is evidence of acts of state, and of all political acts performed by the Queen; orders of adjudica-tion in bankruptcy are also published in it.

"When the defendant cannot be found to be served with a subpœna in chancery, a day for him to appear, being first appointed, is inserted in the Lon-

---

[1] [Cutter *v.* Waddingham, *ante.*

[2] [Cartwright *v.* Cartwright, 18 Tex. 634 (1857), Hemp-hill, C. J.

[3] F. *garnir:* A. S. *warnian.* See G.

[4] [Smith *v.* Miln, 1 Abb. Adm. 280 (1848), Betts, J.

[5] [Welsh *v.* Blackwell, 14 N. J. L. 348 (1834): 3 Jacob, 175; Pennsylvania R. Co. *v.* Pennock, 51 Pa. 254 (1865).

[6] 22 Alb. Law J. 181 (1880).

[7] Bethel *v.* Judge of Superior Court, 57 Mich. 381 (1885), Champlin, J.

[1] Strickland *v.* Maddox, 4 Ga. 394 (1848); Western R. Co. *v.* Thornton, 60 *id.* 306 (1878); Curry *v.* Woodward, 50 Ala. 260 (1873); Harris *v.* Miller, 71 *id.* 32 (1881); Rose *v.* Whaley, 14 La. An. 374 (1859); Schindler *v.* Smith, 18 *id.* 479 (1866); Perkins *v.* Guy, 2 Monta. 20 (1873); Oregon R. & Nav. Co. *v.* Gates, 10 Oreg. 515 (1882); Godding *v.* Pierce, 13 R. I. 533 (1882); Steen *v.* Norton, 45 Wis. 414 (1878); Bickle *v.* Chrisman, 76 Va. 691 (1882).

[2] Lane's Appeal, 105 Pa. 65 (1884).

[3] Miller *v.* United States, 11 Wall. 297 (1870), Strong, J.; Schuler *v.* Israel, 120 *id.* 506 (1887); 24 Am. Law Reg. 625–34 (1885), cases. Inter-State exemptions, 21 Cent. Law J. 425–28 (1885), cases.

[4] "Gave all kinde,"—1 Coke, Litt. 140 *a.*

[5] See 1 Bl. Com. 75; 2 *id.* 84; Williams, R. P. 124–26.

[6] Trench, Glossary.

don Gazette. In default of appearance, the bill will be taken *pro confesso.*" [1]

GENDER. See MAN.

In the Revised Statutes, and in acts and resolutions of Congress, passed subsequently to February 25, 1871, words imparting the masculine gender may be applied to females. [2]

GENEALOGY. See AFFINITY; CONSANGUINITY; PEDIGREE.

GENERAL. 1. Relating to a whole *genus* (q. v.) or kind, to a whole class or order; [3] whether of persons, relations, things, or places.

Opposed (1) to *local, private,* or *special* (see 6, below): as, general or a general — custom, jurisdiction, law, practice, restraint, statute, usage, *qq. v.*

Opposed (2) to *partial:* as, a general assignment, *q. v.*

Opposed (3) to *particular:* as, general average, a general challenge, a general lien, *qq. v.*

Opposed (4) to *private* or *individual:* as, a general ship, *q. v.*

Opposed (5) to *specific:* as, a general — intent, legacy, malice, *qq. v.*

Opposed (6), and chiefly, to *special:* as, general or a general — agent, appearance, appointment, charge, covenant, damage, demurrer, deposit, deputy, issue, executor, finding, guaranty, guardian, monition, occupant, order, owner, property, return, return-day, rule, session, sessions, tail, traverse, verdict, warranty, *qq. v.*

2. Belonging to, concerning, or affecting two or more persons or classes of persons, or persons in the same category; and opposed to *individual:* as, general — assets, creditors, meeting, partners, *qq. v.*

3. Common; obtaining among acquaintances or in the community at large: as, general — credit, reputation, *qq. v.*

4. Representing or pertaining to the public at large, whether constituting a State or the United States; State, or National: as, the general assembly, a general election, the general government, *qq. v.*

5. Over all others; chief, superior, head: as, in attorney-general, postmaster-general, solicitor-general. Contradistinguished from *deputy, district, local, special.*

6. Inclusive of many species or individuals; comprehensive; generic: as, a general — term, word, expression.

Maxims: general words are taken in their general sense; general expressions are restrained within the subject-matter; special provisions derogate from general provisions; a general clause does not extend to things included in a prior special clause.

Deceivers deal in general expressions; fraud lurks in general expressions; error attends upon general expressions.

"Where general words follow an enumeration of particular cases, such words apply only to cases of the same kind as those expressly mentioned." Thus, a land-warrant is not to be included in an act punishing forgery of "an indenture, certificate of public stock, or debt, treasury note, or other public security." [1] See NOSCITUR, A sociis.

The meaning of general words will be restricted to carry out the legislative intent. [2]

Where particular words, in a statute, are followed by words of a general character, the latter are to be restricted to the objects particularly mentioned. If the act begins with words which speak of things or persons of an inferior degree and concludes with general words, the latter are not to be extended to a thing or person of a higher degree. If a particular class is mentioned and general words follow, they must be treated as referring to matters of the same kind, thus subordinating general terms to the preceding particulars. [3]

"General words in any instrument or statute are strengthened by exceptions, and weakened by enumeration." [4]

See further EJUSDEM GENERIS; VIDERE, Videlicet.

GENERIC. See GENERAL; GENUS.

GENTLE. Imports that a horse is docile, tractable, and quiet; not, that he has received special training. [5]

GENTLEMAN. "One who bears court armor, the grant of which adds gentility to a man's family." [6]

Originally, a man of gentle blood; now, a person of any rank from the upper to the lowest verge of the middle classes. [7]

A journeyman butcher may be described as a gentleman. [8]

On a jury list, as, "A. B., gent.," implies that the person has either no occupation or no occupation known to the officials who made out the list. See ADDITION, 2.

---

[1] 3 Bl. Com. 445.

[2] R. S. § 1. See also Atchison, County Judge v. Lucas, 83 Ky. 464 (1885).

[3] Brooks v. Hyde, 37 Cal. 376 (1869).

[1] United States v. Irwin, 5 McLean, 183–84 (1851).

[2] Reiche v. Smythe, 13 Wall. 165 (1871).

[3] Barbour v. Louisville, 83 Ky. 100 (1885), Holt, J.

[4] Sharpless v. Philadelphia, 21 Pa. 161 (1853), Black, C. J.; 66 Wis. 395.

[5] Bodurtha v. Phelon, 2 Allen, 348 (1861).

[6] 1 Bl. Com. 406: Coke, 2 Inst. 668.

[7] [Smith v. Cheese, 1 C. P. D. 61 (1875), Grove, J.

[8] Re European Bank, L. R., 7 Ch. Ap. 300 (1872).

GENUINE. Belonging to the original kind or stock; native; hence, not false, fictitious, simulated, spurious, or counterfeit: as, a genuine note.[1]

Genuineness. Of an instrument — predicates that it is the act of the party as represented; that the signature is not spurious, that nothing has been added to or taken away from it that would lay the party changing the instrument or signing the name liable to forgery.[2]

See COUNTERFEIT; FALSE; FORGE, 2; SPURIOUS.

GENUS. L. Kind; class; nature.

Used in the phrases *alieni generis*, *ejusdem generis*, *in genere*, *sui generis*, qq. v. See also GENERAL.

GEOGRAPHICAL NAMES. See TRADE-MARK.

GESTÆ. See RES, Gestæ.

GIFT. See GIVE.

The gratuitous transfer of personalty.[3]

The transfer of property without consideration.[4]

The thing itself so transferred.

An immediate, voluntary and gratuitous transfer of his personal property by one to another, the transfer being executed by delivery.[5]

A word of the largest signification, applied to either realty or personalty.[6]

As a general rule, delivery is essential.[7]

A true and proper gift is always accompanied with delivery of possession — after which the gift is executed in the donee; and it is not in the donor's power to retract it, unless it be prejudicial to creditors, or the donor was under some legal incapacity, as, infancy, coverture, duress, or was imposed upon. If the gift does not take effect by immediate possession it is not properly a gift, but a contract.[8]

A gift may be to a charity not in existence. See CHARITY, 2.

To complete a gift of money in trust, it is not necessary that the beneficiary should be informed of the fact of the gift.[9]

Where the local law does not forbid, the United States government may take property by gift.[1]

A naked promise to give, without some act sufficient to pass title, is not a gift,— a *locus pœnitentiæ* exists.[2]

See ADVANCEMENT; DONATIO; DONUM; INFLUENCE; ONEROUS; POSSESSION; PRESENTS, 2; SERVICE, 3, Civil Service.

Gift enterprise. In common parlance, a scheme for the division or distribution of certain articles of property, to be determined by chance, among those who have taken shares in the scheme.[3] See GAME, 2.

2. At common law, also, the creation of an estate-tail.[4]

GIRARD WILL CASE. See CHARITY, 2; ORPHAN.

GIST.[5] The ground upon which a thing rests; the essence of an obligation or proposition.

The "gist of an action" is the cause for which an action will lie,— the ground or foundation of a suit, without which it would not be maintainable,— the essential ground or object of a suit, and without which there is not a cause of action.[6]

That without which there is no cause of action; comprehends, therefore, whatever is indispensable in law to a right of recovery. Hence, if anything of this kind be omitted, the defect is incurable.[7]

GIVE. 1. To transfer gratuitously, without an equivalent.[8] See GIFT.

2. To furnish or supply: as, to give liquor to a minor.[9]

3. To find, furnish, supply: as, to give bail or security.

4. To forbear to sue; to extend time: as, to give time to a debtor. See FORBEARANCE.

5. To admit an apparent right in another: as, to give color. See COLOR, 2.

---

[1] [Baldwin *v.* Van Deusen, 37 N. Y. 492 (1868).

[2] [Cox *v.* North Western Stage Co., 1 Idaho, 380 (1871), Whitson, J.

[3] 2 Bl. Com. 441.

[4] Kehr *v.* Smith, 20 Wall. 34 (1873), Davis, J. See also Gray *v.* Barton, 55 N. Y. 72 (1873); Chadsey, Administrator *v.* Lewis, 6 Ill. 155 (1844); Hynson *v.* Terry, 1 Ark. 87 (1833). As to the difference, in a liquor law, between "gift" and "sale," see Parkinson *v.* State, 14 Md. 194, 197 (1859); Holley *v.* State, 14 Tex. Ap. 512 (1883).

[5] [Flanders *v.* Blandy, 45 Ohio St. 113 (1887), cases, Dickman, J.: 26 Am. Law Reg. 587–92 (1887), cases. In general, 19 Cent. Law J. 422–26 (1884), cases.

[6] See Allen *v.* White, 97 Mass. 507 (1867).

[7] Adams *v.* Adams, 21 Wall. 191 (1874).

[8] Martin *v.* Funk, 75 N. Y. 187–43 (1878), cases.

[1] Dickson *v.* United States, 125 Mass. 313–16 (1878), cases; 52 N. Y. 530; 94 U. S. 315, 321.

[2] Pearson *v.* Pearson, 7 Johns. 28 (1810). Delivery, when not essential, 31 Alb. Law J. 426–29, 445–48 (1885), cases.

[3] Lohman *v.* State, 81 Ind. 17 (1881), Niblack, J; Act of Congress 13 July, 1866: 14 St. L. 120.

[4] 2 Bl. Com. 315.

[5] Jist. O. F. *gist*, it lies: the point wherein the matter lies.

[6] First Nat. Bank of Flora *v.* Burkett, 101 Ill. 394 (1882), Walker, J. See also *Re* Murphy, 109 *id.* 33 (1884).

[7] Gould, Plead. 162: Ch. IV, § 12.

[8] See 1 Iowa, 282; 2 N. Y. 153; 33 Conn. 297; 2 Ala. 555; 23 Me. 219; 8 Cow. 38; 14 Wend. 38.

[9] Commonwealth *v.* Davis, 12 Bush, 240 (1876); Halley *v.* State, 14 Tex. Ap. 512 (1883); Parkinson *v.* State, 14 Md. 194 (1856).

6. To expound; to administer, apply: as, to give law.

7. To surrender voluntarily to an officer of the law: as, to give one's self up.

GLANDERS. See HEALTH, Boards of.

GLOUCESTER, STATUTE OF. See COSTS.

GO. The first word of a few idiomatic or technical expressions. See GOING.

Go bail. To become surety on a bail-bond, *q. v.*

Go to. 1. To be given to, to descend to.[1]

2. A circumstance which concerns or affects one's competency or credibility as a witness, or the jurisdiction of the court, is sometimes said to "go to" the competency, to the jurisdiction, to the question, etc.

"When mutual covenants go to the whole consideration on both sides, they are mutual conditions."[2]

"A demurrer may go to the form of the action, to a defect in pleading, or to the jurisdiction of the court."[3]

Go to prison. To be committed or sentenced to a jail, penitentiary, or other place of confinement for persons accused or convicted of a criminal offense. See PRISON.

Go to protest. Said of commercial paper which becomes protested for non-payment or non-acceptance: to become dishonored. See PROTEST, 2.

Go without day. For an acquitted person to be dismissed from court with no day set for reappearing — *sine die;* also, the record entry in such a case.

GOD. In the generally received sense, occurs in a few expressions:

Act of God. See ACT, 1, Of God.

God and my country. A prisoner, upon arraignment, answered (or answers) that he would be tried " By God and my country."

The practice arose when he elected a trial by ordeal or by a jury. The original form was, likely, By God or by my country: the answer was meant to assert innocence by a readiness to be tried by either mode.[4] See further ARRAIGN.

God's penny. Earnest-money; originally, a small coin given to the church or to the poor.

So help you God. See OATH.

See CHRISTIANITY; LAW, Divine; RELIGION.

GOING. See CROP; GO; RATE, 1.

Going concern. A corporation which, although it may be insolvent, still continues to transact its ordinary business.[1]

Going witness. A witness who is about to go out of the jurisdiction of the court in which his testimony will be desired. See DEPOSITION.

GOLD. See COIN; MINE; MONEY; TENDER, 2.

GOOD. Generally speaking, preserves its popular, untechnical meanings. Compare BAD; BONUS.

1. Orderly, lawful: as, good behavior *q. v.*

2. Fair, honorable: as, good fame, or character, *q. v.*

3. Valid, valuable: as, a good consideration, *q. v.*

4. Legally sufficient: as, a good — count, deed, defense, ground, *qq. v.*

5. With lawful intent: as, good faith, *q. v.*

6. Genuine, not spurious; also, collectible: as, a good note.[2]

7. Responsible; able to pay a money obligation.

In this sense bondsmen, indorsers, partners, and wrong-doers are spoken of as "good."

In this sense, also, is "good" written upon the face of a check. See CHECK, Certified.

8. Welfare, prosperity, happiness: as, the public good; also whatever promotes the general welfare of society: as, good morals, "the greatest good." See MORALS; POLICE, 2; WELFARE.

GOOD FRIDAY. See HOLIDAY.

GOODS. Has a very extensive meaning.

In *penal statutes,* is limited to movables which have intrinsic value, and does not include securities, which merely represent value. In *wills,* when there is nothing to restrain its operation, includes all the personal estate.[3]

In a limited sense, articles of merchandise; not fixtures, nor chattels real; but may include animals.

In a merchant's store, refers to the merchandise and commodities kept for sale.[4]

---

[1] Ivin's Appeal, 106 Pa. 181 (1884).

[2] Lowber v. Bangs, 2 Wall. 736 (1864).

[3] Bissell v. Spring Valley Township, 124 U. S. 232 (1888).

[4] See 1 Chitty, Cr. Law, 416; 4 Bl. Com. 323.

[1] White, &c. Manuf. Co. v. Pettes Importing Co., 30 F. R. 865 (1887).

[2] See Polk v. Frash, 61 Ind. 206 (1878); Corbet v. Evans, 25 Pa. 310 (1855); 16 Barb. 342; 14 Wend. 231; 1 Cush. 473; 18 Pick. 321; 4 Metc. 48; 26 Vt. 406.

[3] Keyser v. School District, 35 N. H. 483 (1857), Perley, C. J.; United States v. Moulton, 5 Mas. 545 (1830), Story, J.; Jarman, Wills, 692; 44 N. Y. 310.

[4] Curtis v. Phillips, 5 Mich. 113 (1858).

Goods and chattels. Includes only personal property which is visible, tangible, and movable; not, a right of action;[1] nor, a thing real.

The expression is equivalent to goods, wares, and merchandise.[2]

The precise import depends upon the subject-matter and the context.[3] See CHATTEL.

Goods and merchandise. In the business of commerce, commodities bought and sold by merchants and traders.[4]

Goods, wares, and merchandise. In duty-laws, the word "merchandise" may include goods, wares, and chattels of every description capable of being imported.[5]

In the Statute of Frauds, the expression does not include fixtures, but does include growing crops. Promissory notes and shares in an unincorporated company, and even money, have been held to be within it;[6] also, cattle.[7]

The words of the Statute have never been extended beyond securities which are subjects of common sale and barter, and which have a visible and palpable form. They do not, therefore, include an interest in an unpatented invention.[8] See MERCHANDISE.

See BONA, 2; CONFUSION, 1; DISTRESS; DURESS; EXECUTION, 3; PERISHABLE; PROPERTY, Personal.

GOOD-WILL. Favorable reputation.

The probability that the old customers will resort to the old place.[9]

The advantage or benefit which is acquired by an establishment beyond the mere value of the capital, stock, funds, or property employed therein, in consequence of the general public patronage and encouragement which it receives from constant or habitual customers, on account of its local position or common celebrity, or reputation for skill or affluence, or punctuality, or from other accidental circumstances or necessities, or even from ancient partialities or prejudices.[1]

The benefit or advantage which accrues to the firm, in addition to the value of their property, derived from their reputation for promptness, fidelity and integrity in their transactions, from their mode of doing business, and other incidental circumstances, in consequence of which they acquire general patronage from constant and habitual customers.[2]

Every positive advantage that has been acquired by a proprietor, in carrying on his business, whether connected with the premises in which the business is conducted, or with the name under which it is managed, or with any other matter carrying with it the benefit of the business.[3]

Good-will is a firm asset; whether it survives to a partner has not been uniformly decided; after a voluntary dissolution, each partner has a right to use the old firm name, unless otherwise agreed; it is the subject of sale like other personalty.[4]

GOSPELS. See BLASPHEMY; CHARITY, 2; CHRISTIANITY; INDIGENT; OATH, Corporal.

GOVERNMENT.[5] 1. The controlling power in society.[6]

The aggregate of authorities which rule a society.[7]

That form of fundamental rules by which the members of a body politic regulate their social action, and the administration of public affairs, according to established constitutions, laws, and usages.[8]

2. The state, the commonwealth, the people; as, in criminal practice.

3. In a commercial sense "governments" signifies securities of government, State or United States.

[1] Kirkland v. Brune, 31 Gratt. 131 (1878).

[2] Passaic Manuf. Co. v. Hoffman, 3 Daly, 512 (1871).

[3] Gibbs v. Usher, 1 Holmes, 351 (1874); Jarman, Wills, 731; Addison, Contr. 31, 201, 912.

[4] Chamberlain v. Western Transp. Co., 45 Barb. 223 (1866); 44 N. Y. 310 (1871); The Marine City, 6 F. R. 415 (1881), cases. See also Tisdale v. Harris, 20 Pick. 9, 13 (1838).

[5] R. S. § 2766. See The Elizabeth & Jane, 2 Mas. 407 (1822); 2 Sumn. 362; 4 Blatch. 136.

[6] 2 Pars. Cont. 330-32; 2 Kent, 510, note; Benj. Sales, § 111.

[7] Weston v. McDowell, 20 Mich. 357 (1870).

[8] Somerby v. Buntin, 118 Mass. 285 (1875), Gray, C. J.; 1 Woolw. 217; 3 Daly, 512; 6 Wend. 355; 40 Ind. 593; 55 Iowa, 520; 2 Bl. Com. 387.

[9] Crultwell v. Lye, 17 Ves. *346 (1810). Eldon, Ld. C.; Bradford v. Peckham, 9 R. I. 252 (1869); Chittenden v. Witbeck, 50 Mich. 420 (1883); Myers v. Kalamazoo Buggy Co., 54 id. 222 (1884); 128 U. S. 522.

[1] Story, Partnership, § 99. See also 33 Cal. 624; 65 Ga. 14; 1 Mo. Ap. 601; 44 N. H. 343; 70 N. Y. 473; 36 Ohio St. 522; 60 Pa. 121; 19 How. Pr. 26.

[2] [Angier v. Webber, 14 Allen, 215 (1867), Bigelow, C. J.; Munsey v. Butterfield, 133 Mass. 494 (1882).

[3] Glen & Hall Manuf. Co. v. Hall, 61 N. Y. 230 (1874), Dwight, C.

[4] See Barber v. Connecticut Mut. Life Ins. Co., 15 F. R. 312, 315-22 (1883), cases; 14 Am. Law Reg. 1-11, 329-41, 649-59, 713-25 (1885), cases; 13 Cent. Law J. 162-65 (1881), cases; 19 id. 362-68 (1884), cases; 19 Alb. Law J. 502-3 (1879), Eng. cases; 3 Kent, 64; 1 Pars. Cont. 153; 62 Pa. 81; 5 Ves. 539; 15 id. 218, 237.

[5] O. F. govener: L. gubernare, to steer a ship, to rule. Whence "ship of state."

[6] 1 Sharswood, Bl. Com. 48.

[7] Francis Lieber: 1 Bouv. 715.

[8] Winspear v. Township of Holman, 37 Iowa, 544 (1873); Young, Science Gov., p. 13.

The government of a state being the most prominent feature, or that most readily perceived, "government" is frequently used for "state." Similarly, government is also used for "administration."[1]

The object of government is to secure to the governed the right to pursue their own happiness; that is, the happiness of the individuals who compose the mass. In this consists civil liberty.[2] See HAPPINESS; LIBERTY, 1, Civil.

Government is formed by depriving all persons of a portion of their natural rights. The rights they enjoy under government are not conferred by it, but are those of which they have not been deprived. It is only by a deprivation of all persons of a portion of their rights that it is possible to form and maintain government. . Its organization means a surrender by each of a portion and the control of his reserved rights, and the power of the government to control all persons in the exercise of these reserved rights must be conceded. *Salus populi suprema lex.* In the maintenance of the government and the general welfare, individual rights, whether of natural persons or corporate bodies, must yield to the public good, and the General Assembly is invested with the sole power of determining under what restraints all persons, whether natural or artificial, shall pursue their various vocations, unless restricted by constitutional limitation.[3]

Government is a moral relation, necessarily resulting from the nature of man. . The wants and fears of individuals in society tend to government. Blackstone supposes that sovereignty resides in the hands of the law-makers. Our idea is that government is a mere agency established by the people for the exercise of those powers which reside in them. The powers of government are, in strictness, delegated powers, and, as such, trust powers, capable of revocation. A written constitution is but the letter of attorney.[4] See COMPACT, Social.

Government is an abstract entity. It speaks and acts through agents; these hold offices under law, constitutional or statutory, with prescribed duties and limited authority.[5]

The theory of our government is that all public stations are trusts, and that those clothed with them are to be animated in the discharge of their duties solely by considerations of right, justice, and the public good. The correlative duty resting upon the citizen is to exhibit truth, frankness, and integrity.[6]

Constitutional government. Applies to a state whose fundamental rules and maxims not only define how those shall be chosen or designated to whom the exercise of sovereign powers shall be confided, but

also impose efficient restraints on the exercise for the purpose of protecting individual rights and privileges, and shielding them against any assumption of arbitrary power.[1] See CONSTITUTION.

Government de facto. A government that unlawfully gets possession and control of the rightful legal government, and maintains itself there, by force and arms, against the will of the rightful government, and claims to exercise the powers thereof. Government de juro. The rightful, legal government.[2]

A government *de facto*, in firm possession of any country, is clothed with the same rights, powers, and duties as a government *de jure*. . . In all cases where the United States have been called upon to recognize the government or independence of any other country, they have looked only to the "fact," and not to the right.[3]

A government *de facto* is (1) such as exists after it has expelled the regularly constituted authorities from the seat of power and the public offices, and set its own functionaries in their places, so as to represent in fact the sovereignty of the nation; or (2) such as exists where a portion of the inhabitants of a country have separated themselves from the parent state and established an independent government. As far as other nations are concerned, the former is treated in most respects as possessing rightful authority; its contracts and duties are enforced; its acquisitions are retained; its legislation is in general recognized; and the rights acquired under it are, with few exceptions, respected after the restoration of the authorities which were expelled. The validity of the acts of the latter depends entirely upon its ultimate success. If it fails to establish itself permanently, all such acts perish with it; if it succeeds and becomes recognized, its acts are upheld as those of an independent nation.

The late Confederate government was distinguished from each of those. It was simply the military representative of the insurrection against the authority of the United States. When its military forces were overthrown, it perished, and with it all enactments and other acts. Legislative acts of the several States, so far as they did not tend to impair Federal supremacy, or the rights of citizens under the Constitution, are valid and binding.[4] See MONEY, Lawful; OATH, Of office.

Local government; municipal government. See CORPORATION, Municipal.

[1] Francis Lieber: 1 Bouv. 715.

[2] 1 Sharswood, Bl. Com. 128, 127.

[3] Wiggins Ferry Co. *v.* East St. Louis, 102 Ill. 569 (1882), Walker, J.

[4] 1 Sharswood, Bl. Com. 48–49. See also Virginia Coupon Cases, 114 U. S. 290 (1885).

[5] The Floyd Acceptances, 7 Wall. 676 (1868), Miller, J.

[6] Trist *v.* Child, 21 Wall. 450 (1874), Swayne, J.; Stone *v.* Mississippi, 101 U. S. 820 (1879).

[1] Calhoun, Works, 1, II; Cooley, Principles Const. Law, 22.

[2] Chisholm *v.* Coleman, 43 Ala. 213 (1869), Peck, C. J.

[3] Phillips *v.* Payne, 92 U. S. 133 (1875), Swayne, J.

[4] Williams *v.* Bruffy, 96 U. S. 185 (1877), Field, J. See also Thornington *v.* Smith, 8 Wall. 8–9 (1868), Chase, C. J.; Ford *v.* Surget, 97 U. S. 616, 610 (1879), cases, Clifford, J.; Fifield *v.* Ins. Co. of Pennsylvania, 47 Pa. 170–88 (1884).

Federal, General, National, United States Government; States governments. In the United States, powers of government are of four classes: (1) Those which belong exclusively to the States. (2) Those which belong exclusively to the National Government. (3) Those which may be exercised concurrently and independently by both. (4) Those which may be exercised by the States, but only until Congress shall see fit to act upon the subject.[1]

When the government of the United States was formed, some of the attributes of State sovereignty were partially, and others wholly, surrendered and vested in the United States.[2] The special powers delegated to it are principally such as concern the foreign relations of the country, the rights of war and peace, the regulation of foreign and domestic commerce, and other subjects of general importance.[3] Its peculiar duty is to protect one part of the country from encroachments by another upon the national rights which belong to all.[4] Its authority extends over the whole territory of the Union; it acts upon the States and the people of the States. It is, so far as its sovereignty extends. supreme. No State can exclude it from exercising its powers, obstruct its authorized officers against its will, or withhold cognizance of any subject which the Constitution has committed to it,—otherwise it would cease to exist.[5] Congress may make all laws necessary (*q. v.*) and proper for carrying into execution the powers delegated to it.[5] The powers not delegated, nor prohibited to the States, in the Constitution, are reserved to the States respectively, or to the people.[6] Every addition to its power is a corresponding diminution of the powers of the States.[7] The rights of each sovereignty are to be equally respected. Both are essential to the preservation of our liberties and the perpetuity of our institutions.[8] See CONSTITUTION.

The departments of government are the legislative, which deals mainly with the future; the executive, which deals with the present; and the judicial, which is retrospective, dealing with acts done or threatened, promises made, and injuries suffered.[9]

The theory of government, State and National, is opposed to the deposit of unlimited power anywhere.[1] The Constitution reposes unlimited power in no department of the National government. The lines of separation are to be closely followed to avoid encroachment.[2] A co-ordinate branch will be decided to have transcended its powers only when that is so plain that the duty cannot be avoided.[3] See DEPARTMENT.

The power of governing being a trust committed by the people to the government, no part of the power can be granted away, as, the power to tax. The several agencies can govern according to their discretion, but cannot give away or sell the discretion of their successors.[4]

Republican form of government. See REPUBLIC, Republican, etc.

See further ALLEGIANCE; ANARCHY; APPRAISER; CITIZEN; COURT; DOMAIN; ELECTION, 1; FAITH, Full, etc.; FRANCHISE; GIFT, 1; INDEPENDENCE; INDIAN; JUDICIARY; JURISDICTION; KING; LACHES; LAW, Common; LEGISLATION; LIBERTY, 1; LIMITATIONS, Statute of; MAGNA CHARTA; MAY; MINISTER, 3; OFFICE; PEOPLE; POLICE, 2; POLICY, 1; PRIVILEGE, 1; RELIGION; REVENUE; SEDITION; SERVICE, 3; SOVEREIGNTY; STATE, 3; SUIT; TAX, 2; TORT; TREASON.

GOVERNOR. See GOVERNMENT; VETO.

GOWN. 1. That worn by the justices of the Supreme Court of the United States has always been a long robe of *black* silk.

A portrait of the first chief justice, John Jay, represents him in a borrowed robe, with broad scarlet facings and collar and sleeves of the same color. This gave rise to the tradition that the justices wore *red* gowns in the early days of the court.

In the higher tribunals of the States, *scarlet* gowns were worn, in some instances, as late as 1815.[5]

2. In England, the *silk* gown is the professional robe worn by those barristers who have been appointed of the number of her Majesty's counsel, and is the distinctive badge of Queen's counsel, as the *stuff* gown is of the juniors who have not obtained that dignity.

Accordingly, when a barrister is raised to the degree of Queen's counsel, he is said to "get a silk gown." The right to confer this dignity resides with the Lord Chancellor, who disposes of this branch of his patronage according to the talents, the practice, the seniority, and the general merits of the junior counsel.[6]

"The rules as to the robes worn by British judges have been transmitted orally. Scarlet is the color for the judges sitting in banc on the first day of the term; also in banc on such days as appear with red letters in

---

[1] Chicago, &c. R. Co. *v.* Fuller, 17 Wall. 568 (1873), Swayne, J.; 100 U. S. 386, 390.

[2] United States *v.* Cruikshank, 92 U. S. 549 (1875); Tennessee *v.* Davis, 100 *id.* 263 (1879); Tarble's Case, 13 Wall. 456 (1871).

[3] 1 Sharswood, Bl. Com. 49.

[4] Pensacola Telegraph Co. *v.* Western Union Telegraph Co., 96 U. S. 10 (1877).

[5] Constitution, Art. I, sec. 8, cl. 18.

[6] Constitution, Amd. Art. X.

[7] *Exp.* Virginia, 100 U. S. 346 (1879).

[8] *Exp.* Siebold, 100 U. S. 394 (1879).

[9] See Wayman *v.* Southard, 10 Wheat. 46 (1825); 21 Am. Law Rev. 399–417 (1887), cases; 1 Law Quar. Rev. 80–99 (1885); 4 R. I. 324; 11 Pa. 489; 29 Mich. 451; 58 N. H. 453.

---

[1] Loan Association *v.* Topeka, 20 Wall. 663 (1874).

[2] Kilbourn *v.* Thompson, 103 U. S. 190 (1880).

[3] Trade-Mark Cases, 100 U. S. 96 (1879).

[4] Stone *v.* Mississippi, 101 U. S. 820 (1879).

[5] See The Century, Dec. 1882.

[6] See 5 Alb. Law J. 225 (1872); Jeaffreson, Courts & Lawyers, 180; Brown, Law Dict.

the calendar. On circuit, at the opening of the commission, scarlet robes are worn by both judges, should two be present. After the commission is opened, the judge who sits in the crown court and tries prisoners continues to wear scarlet until all the prisoners are dealt with. He is hence termed by criminals 'the red-gown judge.' The judge who tries *nisi prius* cases removes his scarlet, puts on black, and is called 'the black-gown judge.' The scarlet robes worn in winter in town, and on circuit, whether in summer or winter, are trimmed with ermine, but in town in summer these robes are trimmed with gray silk. When on circuit, the senior or 'red-gown judge' sits in the crown court at the first town in the circuit, while the junior judge takes *nisi prius* cases, but at the next place 'the red gown judge' becomes 'the black-gown judge,' and so they alternate throughout the circuit. On ordinary days the judges sitting in banc wear dark blue or purple robes, which in winter are trimmed with ermine, and in summer with bronze silk."

GRACE. Favor, indulgence, toleration; opposed to right, strict right: as, that a thing done in court is allowed as a matter of grace.

Act of grace. An act of pardon or amnesty, *qq. v.*

Days of grace. Certain days, in addition to the time specified in a bill or note, in which payment may be made, before it can be lawfully protested.

In common speech this period is termed "grace;" as in saying that "grace" is or is not allowed on a particular instrument.

Originally allowed by the custom of merchants as a matter of favor or indulgence. This custom received the sanction of the courts, and so grew into law. The statute of 3 and 4 Anne (1705), which made promissory notes negotiable, also conferred this right to days of grace. That statute has been generally adopted in our States.

In the absence of an express contract to the contrary, the allowance now enters into every bill or note of a mercantile character, and forms a part of it, so that the paper, in fact and in law, is usually due on the last day of grace.

Demand is made on the last day, and interest is charged on all the days. If the last day is Sunday or a legal holiday, the paper is due the preceding day.

Checks are not entitled to the favor; nor are sight drafts, nor judgment notes.[1]

The number of days varies from three to thirty. Three is the limit in the United States; except in Vermont, where, it seems, no grace at all is allowed. In Louisiana, an inland bill or note is due without grace for purposes of set-off. In New York, bills on bank corporations are not entitled to the favor.

In Great Britain and Ireland, Berlin, and Vienna, the number of days is three; in Frankfort-on-the-main,

four; in Sweden, six; in Bremen, and Denmark, eight; in Hamburg, twelve; in Spain, fourteen on foreign bills. No grace is recognized in Amsterdam, Antwerp, France, Genoa, Germany (generally, since 1871), Leghorn, Leipsic, or Naples.[1]

The law of the place of payment is regarded. He who claims the benefit of a foreign law or usage must prove the existence of the law.[2] See PLACE, Of payment; MATURITY, 2.

Grace widow. A widow by a decree of a court of divorce.

Corrupted into *grass*-widow.

GRADE. 1, *v.* To reduce to a certain degree of ascent or descent.

The power to grade a street is co-extensive with the duty.[3] See OVER, 1; PAVE.

2, *n.* Degree, order, rank. See DEGREE.

Grades of crime. These are higher or lower according to the measure of punishment, and the consequences resulting to the convicted party.[4]

Grade and rank. Navy officers are classified — 1, according to duty, office, or title; 2, according to relative importance or honor; 3, according to compensation. All of these classes come within the normal meaning of the words "grade or rank." The law designates some of them as grades or ranks by name, others only by description.[5] See RANK; TITLE, 5.

GRADUATE. In the universities, a student who has honorably passed through the prescribed course of study and received a certificate to that effect.

A cadet-engineer who has successfully completed his academic course, passed the closing examination, and received from the Academic Board a certificate to that effect, has hitherto been called a "graduate." The act of August 5, 1882 (22 St. L. 285), did not make such graduates "naval cadets."[6] See CADET; TITLE, 5; ALCOHOL.

GRAFT. In equity, describes the right in a creditor, who holds a mortgage upon property to which the mortgagor had an imperfect title, to a lien upon the premises, after the debtor has acquired a good title.[7]

GRAIN. See CROP.

Includes or may include: flax-seed,[8] millet and sugar-cane seed,[9] oats,[10] peas.[11]

[1] See Byles, Bills, 209, 210; Bank of Washington *v.* Triplett, 1 Pet. *31–55 (1828), cases, Marshall, C. J.; Cookendorfer *v.* Preston, 4 How. 326 (1846); Bell *v.* First Nat. Bank of Chicago, 115 U. S. 379–83 (1885), cases.

[1] See Byles, Bills, 205; Chitty, Bills, 11 ed. (1878); Pierce *v.* Indseth, 106 U. S. 550 (1882).

[2] See Story. Prom. Notes, §§ 216, 247.

[3] Smith *v.* Washington City, 20 How. 148 (1857).

[4] People *v.* Rawson, 61 Barb. 631 (1872).

[5] Rutherford *v.* United States, 18 Ct. Cl. 343 (1883); McClure *v.* United States, *ib.* 347 (1883).

[6] Leopold *v.* United States, 18 Ct. Cl. 546, 557 (1883), Schofield, J.

[7] See La. Civ. Code, art. 3271; 9 Mass. *36.

[8] Hewitt *v.* Watertown Ins. Co., 55 Iowa, 324 (1880).

[9] Holland *v.* State, 34 Ga. 457 (1866).

[10] Smith *v.* Clayton, 29 N. J. L. 361 (1862).

[11] State *v.* Williams, 2 Strob. L. 477 (S. C., 1848). See Park, Ins. 112; 1 Marsh. Ins. 223, n.

"Corn" in the text of Blackstone's commentaries means grain.[1] "Corn-laws" regulated trade in breadstuffs.

In this country, in statutes of modern date, corn means Indian corn, maize;[2] and either shelled or in the ear.[3]

See also AGRICULTURE; EMBLEMENTS; PERISHABLE; PROVISIONS; SEED.

GRAMMAR. False grammar (syntax) alone never invalidates written instruments: *false, or mala, grammatica non vitiat chartam.*[4]

See BLANK, 2; PUNCTUATION.

GRAND. Great; greatest; chief; advanced in rank; opposed to *common, petit* or *petty,* q. v.

As, in grand jury or inquest, grand larceny; and, also, as in grandchild and grandparent, *qq. v.*

GRANGER CASES. See *Munn v. Illinois,* CHARTER, 2, Private; POLICY, 1, Public.[5]

GRANT. 1. At common law, the method of transferring the property of incorporeal hereditaments, or such things whereof no livery can be had.[6]

An incorporeal hereditament was said to lie *in grant;* and a corporeal hereditament, *in livery.* A grant differed little from a feoffment (*q. v.*), except in the subject-matter; the same words were used.[6]

2. A generic term applicable to all transfers of realty.[7]

Any conveyance of realty.[8]

"Hereby granted" imports an immediate transfer of interest.[9]

To constitute a grant, it is not indispensable that technical words be used; any words that manifest the same intention will suffice.[10]

Statute of 8 and 9 Vict. (1845) c. 106, made all corporeal rights, as regards the conveyance of the immediate freehold, to be deemed to lie in grant as well as in livery.

---

[1] 3 Bl. Com. 10, 152, 156, 218; 4 *id.* 159.

[2] Kerrick *v.* Van Dusen, 32 Minn. 318 (1884); Commonwealth *v.* Pine, 2 Pa. Law J. R. *412 (1844); Sullins *v.* State, 53 Ala. 475 (1875); Wood *v.* State, 18 Fla. 969 (1882); 46 Tex. 402.

[3] State *v.* Nipper, 95 N. C. 655 (1886).

[4] 2 Bl. Com. 379; State *v.* Shaw, 58 N. H. 74 (1877); 112 U. S. 216; 63 Iowa, 65; 70 Pa. 237; 80 Va. 599; 1 Whart. Cr. 199; Broom, Max. 535.

[5] See also 19 F. R. 698.

[6] 2 Bl. Com. 317; Williams, R. P. 147; 5 Mass. 471; 16 N. Y. 75; 1 Black, 358.

[7] 3 Washb. R. P. 181, 353, 378; Durant *v.* Ritchie, 4 Mas. 69 (1825).

[8] McVey *v.* Green Bay R. Co., 42 Wis. 535-36 (1877); Lambert *v.* Smith, 9 Oreg. 193 (1881).

[9] Wright *v.* Roseberry, 121 U. S. 496, 500 (1887).

[10] East Jersey Iron Co. *v.* Wright, 32 N. J. E. 252 (1880); Barksdale *v.* Hairston, 81 Va. 765 (1886), cases.

Grant and demise. In a lease for years, create an implied warranty of title and a covenant for quiet enjoyment.[1] See DEMISE.

Grant, bargain, and sell. In a deed, do not import a general covenant of seisin or against incumbrances, but a covenant that the grantor has done nothing whereby the estate granted may be defeated, — for quiet enjoyment, at least.[2]

They imply a covenant against incumbrances, including taxes.[2] See COVENANT, Implied; SUFFER.

A grant of personalty is termed an assignment or a bill of sale. See ASSIGNMENT, 2; GIFT, 1; SALE, Bill of; TITLE, 1.

3. Any concession by the public, being evidenced by an enactment or record; in particular, a transfer of public land, or the creation of a franchise by charter, or of a monopoly by letters patent, or of an exclusive privilege by certificate of copyright.

Described as a legislative, government, official, public, State, or United States grant.

Grantor. He who makes a grant.

Grantee. 1. He to whom a grant is made.

2. One who has transferred to him, in writing, the exclusive right, under a patent, to make and use, and to grant to others to make and use, the thing patented, within and throughout some specified portion of the United States.[4] See ASSIGNEE; LICENSEE.

The king's grants are matter of public record. Whether of lands, honors, liberties, franchises, or aught besides, they are contained in charters, or letters patent. The manner of granting by him does not differ from that by a subject more than the construction of his grants, when made. (1) A grant by the king, at the suit of the grantee, shall be taken most beneficially for the king; whereas the grant of a subject is construed most strongly against the grantor. (2) A subject's grant shall be construed to include many things, besides what are expressed, if necessary for the operation of the grant. Therefore, in a private grant of the profits of land for one year, free ingress, egress, and regress, to cut and carry away those profits, are inclusively granted. But the king's grant shall not enure to any other intent than that which is previously expressed in the grant. (3) When it appears, from the face of the grant, that the king is mistaken or deceived in a matter of fact or of law, or if his own title be different from what he supposes, or if the

---

[1] Scott *v.* Rutherford, 92 U. S. 109 (1875), cases.

[2] 4 Kent, 460; 2 Ala. 535; 5 *id.* 586; 12 *id.* 159; 7 Ill. 148; 19 *id.* 235; 21 *id.* 220; 50 Pa. 480.

[3] Blossom *v.* Van Court, 34 Mo. 390 (1864). See further 4 Oreg. 235; 1 Conn. 79; 1 T. B. Mon. 30; 32 Me. 329; 8 Barb. 463; 5 Tenn. 124; 25 Cal. 175; 32 Ill. 348; 60 Mo. 138; Rawle, Cov. Tit. 481-97, cases.

[4] Act 4 July, 1836, §§ 13, 14; Potter *v.* Holland, 4 Blatch. 211 (1858).

grant be informal, or if he grants an estate contrary to the rules of law,— the grant is absolutely void.[1]

By a grant everything passes which is necessary to the full enjoyment of the right, title, or estate which is included in the words. A grant of a mere way carries an easement only — the ownership of the soil not being essential to the free use of the right. But a grant of an estate designated only by the particular use for which the land is appropriated will pass the fee; as, a grant of "a house." "a wharf," "a mill," "a well," "a barn," and the like.[2]

With respect to "public grants," the rule is, that rights, privileges, and immunities not expressly granted are reserved. Nothing can be presumed against the State. There would be no safety to public interests in any other rule. The rule applies with special force where the claim would abridge or restrain a power of government, as, the power of taxation.[3]

Where a statute operates as a grant of public property to an individual, or the relinquishment of a public interest, and there is a doubt as to the meaning of its terms, or as to its general purpose, that construction should be adopted which will support the claim of the government rather than that of the individual. Nothing can be inferred against the State. Such acts are usually drawn by interested parties; and they are presumed to claim all they are entitled to. The rule serves to defeat any purpose concealed by the skilful use of terms, to accomplish something not apparent upon the face of the act, and thus sanctions only open dealing with legislative bodies.[4]

A more liberal rule of construction is allowable in interpreting a grant from one State or political community to another, than is permitted in interpreting a private grant.[5]

Where power or jurisdiction is delegated to any public officer or tribunal, and its exercise is confided to his or their discretion, acts done are binding as to the subject-matter; and individual rights will not be disturbed collaterally for anything so done. The only questions which can arise between an individual claiming a right under the acts and the public, or a person denying its validity, are power in the officer and fraud in the party. All other questions are settled by the decision made by the tribunal or officer, whether executive, legislative, judicial, or special, unless an appeal is provided for, or other revision, by some appellate or supervisory tribunal, is prescribed. In no case have documents of title, executed by officers of the government, been held sufficient where the fact in issue was whether the government had any title to convey, to establish the fact in dispute, as against parties claiming a pre-existing, adverse, and paramount title themselves.[1]

No one can grant what he does not own.[2] See DARE, Nemo, etc.

See CHARTER, 2; CONDITION; DEED, 2; DELIVERY; DISCLAIMER, 2; DISPARAGEMENT, 2; INCIDENT; LAND, Public; PATENT 1 (1), 2.

4. To confer, bestow, allow, permit, award, issue: as, to grant a rule to show cause, letters testamentary or of administration, a writ of *certiorari*, *habeas corpus*, or *mandamus*.

GRASS. See CROP.

GRASS WIDOW. See GRACE.

GRATIA. See E, 2; GRACE.

GRATIS. See DICTUM, Gratis.

GRATUITOUS CONTRACT or SERVICE. See CONSIDERATION, 2; DEPOSIT, 1; SUBSCRIBE, 2.

GRATUITY. See BONUS, 2; BOUNTY; CHARITY, 2; DEPOSIT, 1; TRUST, 1.

GRAVAMEN. L. Burden, weight.

That part of a charge which weighs most heavily against the accused; the essence of an accusation.

The grievance complained of; the substantial cause of an action.[3]

GRAVE. See BURIAL; SEPULCHRE.

GREAT. See CARE; CHARTER, 1; SEAL, 1. Compare GRAND; GROSS; MAGNUS.

Greater. Larger; superior; chief; principal.

The greater includes the less.

The greater power of making wholly new legislation includes the lesser power of altering old legislation.[4]

The withdrawal or extinguishment of the greater carries the less; thus, the withdrawal or extinguishment of a franchise authorizes the withdrawal or extinguishment of every right which is a part of the franchise.[5]

---

[1] 2 Bl. Com. 346–48, 121, 380.

[2] Jamaica Pond Aqueduct Corporation v. Chandler, 9 Allen, 164 (1864), Bigelow, C. J.; Johnson v. Rayner, 6 Gray, 110 (1856), cases; United States v. Appleton, 1 Sumn. 500 (1823); Bank of British North America v. Miller, 7 Saw. 163 (1881), cases; Green Bay, &c. Canal Co. v. Hewitt, 66 Wis. 464–65 (1886); Lowell v. Strahan, 145 Mass. 1, 11 (1887), cases; 26 Am. Law Reg. 722–26 (1887), cases; 19 Cent. Law J. 446 (1884) — Solic. Journ.

[3] The Delaware Railroad Tax, 18 Wall. 225 (1873), Field, J. See also Schulenberg v. Harriman, 21 id. 62 (1874); Heydenfeldt v. Daney Gold, &c. Co., 93 U. S. 638 (1876); Wiggins Ferry Co. v. East St. Louis, 107 id. 371 (1882), cases; Ruggles v. Illinois, 108 id. 531 (1883), cases; Hannibal, &c. R. Co. v. Missouri River Packet Co., 125 id. 271 (1888), cases; Swann v. Jenkins, 82 Ala. 482 (1886); Omaha Horse R. Co. v. Cable Co., 30 F. R. 328 (1887), cases. Limitation on legislative grants, 26 Am. Law Reg. 65–71 (1887), cases.

[4] Slidell v. Grandjean, 111 U. S. 437 (1884), Field, J.

[5] Indiana v. Milk, 11 Biss. 205 (1882), Gresham, J.

[1] Sabariego v. Maverick, 124 U. S. 280 (1888), cases, Matthews, J., quoting United States v. Arredondo, 6 Pet. *727 (1832), cases.

[2] 23 How. 175; 1 Wall. 254; 11 id. 459; 94 U. S. 382; 95 id. 10; 34 La. An. 791.

[3] See 1 Greenl. Ev. § 66.

[4] *Exp.* Siebold, 100 U. S. 384 (1879).

[5] Atlantic & Gulf R. Co. v. Georgia, 98 U. S. 365 (1878); 54 Ga. 401; Branch v. Jesup, 106 U. S. 478 (1882); 21 Wall. 175; 111 U. S. 270.

Upon indictment for a particular crime, the accused may be convicted of a less offense included in the crime charged. But at common law, under an indictment for felony, there cannot be conviction for a misdemeanor.[1] See ACQUITTAL, Former.

See MAJOR, In se; MERGER.

GREEN. See BAG.

GREENBACK. A popular name applied exclusively to United States treasury notes.

When an indictment charges larceny of treasury notes, the proof may be that the notes were "greenbacks."[2]

Originally, a nick-name or slang word, derived from the color of the engraving on the back of the currency. The fact that the word, from its convenience, has come into common use, does not make it of itself a proper designation in an indictment.[3] See TENDER, Legal.

GRETNA-GREEN. A "Gretna-Green marriage" was a marriage solemnized in Scotland by parties who went there to avoid the delay and formalities required in England.

Gretna-Green, being the nearest place across the boundary line, was the more generally resorted to. Statute of 19 and 20 Vict. (1856), c. 96, requires that at least one of the parties shall have his or her usual place of residence in Scotland, or shall have lived there twenty-one days preceding the marriage.[4]

In the United States, the term describes marriages celebrated between residents of a State who go to a place beyond and yet near to the boundary line of an adjoining State, on account of some advantage afforded by the law of that State.

GRIEVOUS. See ASSAULT; INJURY.

GROCERIES. See PROVISIONS.

Whether wines and liquors are groceries is a question of fact.[5]

Shovels, pails, baskets, and the like, are not, although usually kept in a country grocery store.[6] See FAMILY, Use.

GROSS. Great, large; entire, undiminished, whole; general; extreme. See ENGROSS.

Gross average. General average upon ship, cargo, and freight. See AVERAGE.

Gross earnings. The whole amount of earnings received. See EARNINGS; PROFIT, Net.

Gross neglect or **negligence.** Extreme want of care; the absence of ordinary or reasonable care and skill. See CARE; NEGLIGENCE.

Gross receipts. All receipts had, undiminished by expenses or other deductions. Compare EARNINGS, Gross.

In gross. 1. In the entirety; as, a sale in gross, q. v.

2. Independent of; not annexed to another: as, a common, a power, a right in gross. See COMMON, 2; EASEMENT, Appendant; POWER, 2.

GROUND. 1. Land; soil; earth. See LAND.

May include an improved town lot.[1]

Ground-rent. A rent reserved as the consideration of a conveyance of land in fee-simple.

Ground-landlord. The grantor of such an estate.

Rent payable to the grantee, who erects and leases houses upon the land, is called the "builder's rent." See further, RENT, Ground-rent.

2. "Good ground" to believe or to act means simply good cause.[2]

Ground of action. The foundation, basis, or data, upon which a cause of action rests.

GROWING. See CROP.

GRUDGE. See MALICE; PREJUDICE.

GUARANTEE.[3] 1, v. (1) To engage to do a thing; to assure, stipulate, or covenant solemnly.

"The United States shall guarantee to every State . . a Republican (q. v.) Form of Government."[4]

(2) To engage that another will do as he has promised.

2, n. The person with whom such engagement is made.

Guarantor. He from whom the engagement proceeds.

To guarantee may be equivalent to to promise.[5]

Guaranteed. Warranted, preferred: as, guaranteed stock.[6] See STOCK, 3 (2).

Guaranty. (1) Solemn assurance, covenant, or stipulation that something shall be

---

[1] Hunter v. Commonwealth, 79 Pa. 505 (1875), cases.

[2] Hickey v. State, 23 Ind. 23 (1864), Davison, J.

[3] Wesley v. State, 61 Ala. 287 (1878), Manning J. See Grant v. State, 55 id. 209 (1876).

[4] See 2 Steph. Com. 259, note; Brook v. Brook, 9 H. L. 193 (1861).

[5] Niagara Ins. Co. v. De Graff, 12 Mich. 125 (1863).

[6] Fletcher v. Powers, 131 Mass. 335 (1881).

[1] Ferree v. School District, 76 Pa. 378 (1874).

[2] Supervisors v. Pabst, 64 Wis. 244 (1885).

[3] F. garantir, to warrant, lit., to guard, keep. See G.

[4] Constitution, Art. IV, sec. 4.

[5] Thayer v. Wild, 107 Mass. 452 (1871); McNaughton v. Conklings, 9 Wis. *320 (1859).

[6] Taft v. Hartford, &c. R. Co., 8 R. I. 333 (1866).

or be done: as, the guaranties in the Constitution and Amendments thereto.

Guaranty clause. Specifically, section four of article four of the Constitution, guaranteeing a republican form of government to each State. See GUARANTEE, 1.

(2) Distinctively, a promise "to answer for the debt, default or miscarriage" of another person.

This by the statute of frauds (*q. v.*) must be in writing and be signed by the guarantor.

The contract by which one person is bound to another, for the fulfillment of the promise or engagement of a third party.[1]

Usually, a collateral undertaking to pay the debt of another in case he does not pay it.[2]

An undertaking by one person that another shall perform his contract or fulfill his obligation, or that, if he does not, the guarantor will do it for him.[3]

May also mean security or lien; as, in an agreement that lumber should be held as guaranty for the payment of a debt.[4]

An engagement to pay in default of solvency in the debtor, provided due diligence be used to obtain payment from him. A contract of "suretyship" is a direct liability to the creditor for the act to be performed by the debtor; whereas a "guaranty" is a liability only for his ability to perform this act. A "surety" assumes to perform the contract for the principal debtor if he should not; a "guarantor" undertakes that his principal can perform, that he is able to perform. The undertaking of a "surety" is immediate and direct, that the act shall be done, and, if not done, then he is to be responsible at once; but from the nature of the undertaking of a "guarantor," non-ability (insolvency) must be shown.[5]

A "guarantor" insures the solvency of the debtor; a "surety" insures the debt itself. A surety must demand proceedings, with notice that he will not continue bound unless they are instituted; whereas a guarantor may rely upon the obligation of the creditor to use due diligence to secure satisfaction of his claim.[6]

To enable a creditor to enforce a contract of guaranty, he must exercise "due diligence" to enforce payment from the principal. That is, the creditor must bring suit within a reasonable time after the maturity of the claim, and duly prosecute the same to judgment and execution, unless it appears that such proceedings can produce no beneficial results.[1]

Absolute guaranty; conditional guaranty. A guaranty that a note is collectible is a conditional promise binding upon the guarantor only in case of diligence. To perfect the obligation so as to render him liable thereon, the guarantee must use diligence in the endeavor to collect his note, for it is a condition precedent. The inchoate obligation does not become absolute until the guarantee has performed the condition on his part.[2]

Continuing guaranty. An undertaking to be responsible for moneys to be advanced or goods to be sold to another from time to time.[3]

General guaranty; special guaranty. A special guaranty operates only in favor of the person to whom it is addressed; a general guaranty is open for acceptance by the public generally.

Guaranties are sometimes further classified as such as are limited to a single transaction, and such as embrace continuous or successive dealings.

A guaranty is a contract in and of itself: but it also has relation to some other contract or obligation with reference to which it is collateral; and it always requires a consideration. When executed at or about the time of the execution of the main contract, as part of one transaction, one consideration may support both contracts; so also where the guaranty is executed in pursuance of the assignment of the main contract.[4]

The real party in interest is now entitled to maintain an action for damages arising from a breach of such contract in his own name, although he was not originally privy to it. That is, both equitable and legal assignments now are equally cognizable in a court of law.

A special guaranty contemplates a trust in the addressee, and no cause of action arises thereon, except upon compliance with its conditions by such person. Until a right of action has arisen, the guaranty is not assignable.

A consideration is necessary; if it is not acknowledged, it must be proved.

Guaranties are construed so as to accord with the apparent intention of the parties. Where the lan-

---

[1] 2 Pars. Contr. 3, 26; Story, Prom. Notes, § 457; 3 Kent, 121.

[2] See Dole *v.* Young, 24 Pick. 252 (1837), Shaw, C. J.; Parker *v.* Culvertson, 1 Wall. Jr. 160 (1846); Hill *v.* Smith, 24 How. 286 (1858).

[3] Gridley *v.* Capen, 72 Ill. 13 (1874), Breese, C. J.

[4] Wilkie *v.* Day, 141 Mass. 72 (1886).

[5] Reigart *v.* White, 52 Pa. 440 (1866), Agnew, J.

[6] Kramph *v.* Hatz, 52 Pa. 529 (1866), Woodward, C. J. See also 21 Cent. Law J. 6-9 (1885), cases.

[1] National Loan, &c. Society *v.* Lichtenwalner, 100 Pa. 103 (1883), cases, Paxson, J.; 26 Am. Law Reg. 129-47, 201-218 (1887), cases; 18 F. R. 126; 27 Conn. 37; 2 N. Y. 549; 60 *id.* 444; 11 Ohio St. 168; 13 R. I. 119; 7 Humph. 539; 20 Vt. 503.

[2] Edwards, Bills, 238; 2 Daniel, Neg. Inst. § 1769; Allen *v.* Rundle, 50 Conn. 20-22 (1882), cases.

[3] Buck *v.* Burk, 18 N. Y. 343 (1858), Selden, J.; Addison, Contr. 668.

[4] Briggs *v.* Latham, 36 Kan. 209 (1887), Valentine, J.

(32)

guage is ambiguous, the surrounding circumstances may be looked at. When the meaning is ascertained, the guarantor is entitled to the application of the strict rule governing the contracts of sureties, and cannot be held beyond the plain terms of the contract.[1] See further CONSTRUCTION, Liberal.

As a principle, a guaranty is not negotiable; it may, perhaps, be made so by negotiable language.[2]

The negotiation of a bill or note is not a guaranty.[3]

The rule requiring notice of the acceptance of a guaranty applies only where the instrument is merely an offer or proposal, acceptance of which is necessary to mutual assent. Made at the request of the guarantee, its delivery constitutes the contract. The same result follows where the agreement to accept is contemporaneous with the guaranty, and is its consideration. An unconditional guaranty of advances is a waiver of demand of payment, and notice of the debtor's default to the amount of the advances, etc. Delay in giving notice, when required, is a defense to an action to the extent of the loss or damage proved. Notwithstanding that the contract is the obligation of a surety, it is to be construed as a mercantile instrument in furtherance of its spirit, and, literally, to promote the convenience of commercial intercourse.[4]

See FRAUDS, Statute of, III (2); LETTER, 3, Of credit; PROMISE, Collateral; SURETY; WARRANTY.

GUARDIAN.[5] 1. A keeper, protector, conservator; a warden.

Guardian of the peace. A person charged with the duty of securing or protecting the public peace; a conservator of the peace. See PEACE, 1.

Guardian of the poor. A person specially elected or appointed to administer the poor-laws. See POOR.

2. One that legally has the care and management of the person or the estate, or both, during his minority, of a child whose father has died.[6] Correlative, *ward.*

The authorized agent, appointed by law, to take care of the ward's estate and manage his affairs.[7]

Domestic guardian. A guardian appointed at the place of the infant's domicil. **Foreign guardian.** A guardian appointed under the law of another State than that of the infant's domicil.

Their rights and powers are local. By comity only is anything conceded in another State to the claims of the guardian of the domicil. It is usual, however, to appoint in a foreign State the guardian of the domiciliary court.[1]

Guardian ad litem. A person appointed by a court to look after the interests of an infant when his property is involved in litigation.[2]

He manages the defense of an infant defendant, where there is no parent, or other guardian. The power of appointing such a guardian is incident to every court.[3]

He is a species of attorney, whose duty is to prosecute for the infant's rights, and to bring those rights directly under the notice of the court. He can do nothing to the injury of the infant. His duty ends when the suit ends, when it is prosecuted to final judgment. Since he may be required to pay the costs of the action, a person cannot be compelled to serve against his consent. Anciently the custom was to appoint an officer of the court. He may have reimbursement for costs and expenses out of the infant's estate.[4] See FRIEND, Next.

General guardian. A guardian who has general charge of the person and property of a fatherless minor. **Special guardian.** A guardian charged with the management of some particular interest; as, a guardian *ad litem,* or a guardian of the estate or of the person only.[5]

Guardian of the estate. A guardian who has been lawfully invested with the power of taking care and managing the estate of an infant. **Guardian of the person.** A guardian lawfully invested with the care of an infant, whose father is dead.[6]

At common law, a general guardian performs the office of *tutor* of the person and *curator* of the estate as distinguished in the Roman law.[7]

Statute or **statutory guardian.** A guardian appointed by last will; also, a guardian appointed by a court in pursuance of a statute.

---

[1] Evansville Nat. Bank v. Kaufmann, 93 N. Y. 276–81 (1883), cases, Ruger, C. J.; How v. Kemball, 2 McLean, 103 (1840), cases; 2 How. 449; 62 Barb. 355.

[2] Story, Prom. Notes, § 481; 36 Kan. 211.

[3] Central Trust Co. v. Cook County. Nat. Bank, 101 U. S. 70 (1879), cases.

[4] Davis v. Wells, 104 U. S. 159, 163–66 (1881), cases, Matthews, J.

[5] F. *garder:* A. S. *weard-*; Ger. *warten,* to watch, have ward. See G.

[6] Bass v. Cook, 4 Port., Ala., 392: Reeves, Dom. Rel. *311.

[7] Waldrip v. Tulley, 48 Ark. 300 (1886), Smith, J.

[1] Hoyt v. Sprague. 103 U. S. 631–32 (1880), Bradley, J.

[2] See N. Y. Life Ins. Co. v. Bangs, 103 U. S. 438 (1880); Colt v. Colt, 111 *id.* 578 (1884).

[3] 3 Bl. Com. 427.

[4] Leopold v. Meyer, 10 Abb. Pr. o. s. 40 (N. Y. Com. Pleas, 1860), cases; Tucker v. Dabbs, 12 Heisk. 20 (1873); Simmons v. Baynard, 30 F. R. 533 (1887): 2 Story, Eq. § 1352:, Turrentine v. Daly, 82 Ala. 208 (1886),— final account; Cates v. Pickett, 97 N. C. 26 (1887),— selling land (local); Hinton v. Bland, 81 Va. 592–93 (1886),— of lunatic; Story, Eq. Pl. § 70.

[5] See Colt v. Colt, 111 U. S. 578 (1884).

[6] Nicholson v. Spencer, 11 Ga. 609 (1852).

[7] 1 Bl. Com. 460.

Testamentary guardian. A person named for the office of guardian in the will of the father of the minor.

Instituted by Statute 12 Charles II (1660), c. 24.[1]

Guardian by chancery. A guardian appointed by a court of equity or of probate.

Guardian in chivalry. The lord of the heir of a tenant in capite, and of body and lands, with no duty to account for profits.

Guardian by common law, or *in socage.* Where a minor was entitled to an estate in lands, his next of kin, to whom the estate could not descend, became such guardian until the minor attained fourteen.

Guardian by nature. The father, and, after his decease, the mother. Has charge of person and estate, and is controlled by a court of equity or probate.

Guardian for nurture. Either of the parents till the child is fourteen, but relates to the care of the person solely.

Guardian ad interim or *interim.* Serves while another guardian is out of the jurisdiction.[2]

In general, guardians exist either by nature or by appointment of a court. At common law, a person became such by relation to the minor, without judicial appointment. In the province of York, on failure of the father to name a guardian by will, the ordinary made the appointment. The power to appoint and to pass upon accounts has been generally conferred by statutes upon the probate courts.

At fourteen, the child may choose a guardian.

A guardian is a temporary parent. The lord chancellor is the general guardian of all infants in England; in the States, the court of probate is the general guardian, the nominal guardian being but an agent or officer of the court.[3]

The reciprocal duties of the persons depend upon the nature of the guardianship. A guardian of the person has a right to the obedience of the ward, but not to his services; and owes the ward protection, but not support. The guardian of the estate is to support and educate the ward in a manner suited to the ward's station in life.

Ordinary skill, prudence, and caution are all that are required of a guardian. Many of his duties are regulated by statute. He may lease the ward's realty; and he receives the rents and profits thereof. He may sell personalty without an order of court, but not realty; nor may he so convert personalty into realty. If he uses money, or neglects to invest it for an unrea-

sonable period, he is chargeable with interest; and if he trades with the money, the ward may demand the principal with either interest or the profits. He is liable for waste as to realty, and for negligence as to personalty. He cannot waive the ward's rights.[1]

The relation ceases at twenty-one. As to the person of a female ward, ceases with marriage to a minor; and as to both person and estate, upon marriage to an adult. Continues, as to his estate, after the marriage of a male ward. But neither may marry without the consent of the guardian.

The court will remove a guardian for misconduct; may require a change in his sureties; may compel him to file an account; may appoint an interim guardian; will regulate the maintenance and education (*q. v.*) of the ward; and may even control the actions of a testamentary guardian.[2]

After the ward becomes of age the guardian is bound to exercise proper care of his property until he has duly accounted for it, and delivered up possession.[3]

See COMMITTEE, 1; CURATOR; DISCHARGE, 1; INVEST; TUTOR; WARD, 3; WITNESS.

GUBERNATORIAL. See GOVERNMENT.

GUEST. A traveler, wayfarer, or a transient comer to an inn for lodging and entertainment. It is not now deemed essential that the person should have come from a distance.[4]

As inns are instituted for travelers, a neighbor or friend who lodges in an inn is not deemed a guest. A traveler who is accepted becomes instantly a guest. The length of time a man is at an inn makes no difference; so, although he is not strictly transient, he retains his character as a traveler. He may, by special contract to board and sojourn, make himself a "boarder." Numerous late cases hold that a special agreement as to time and price does not absolutely disturb the relationship of innkeeper and guest. These cases indicate a tendency to conform the old rule to the changes made in hotel keeping in modern times.[5]

See further BOARDER; INN, 1; LODGER; RESIDENCE.

GUILTY.[6] 1. The state or condition of one who has committed a crime, a civil in-

---

[1] See 2 Kent, 224–25; Schouler, Dom. R. 400; 4 Johns. Ch. 380; 12 Ill. 431; 37 Cal. 661.

[2] See 1 Bl. Com. 461–63; 2 *id.* 67, 88; 2 Kent, 220; Reeves, Dom. R. 311; 1 Pars. Contr. 133; De Krafft *v.* Barney, 2 Black, 710 (1862); Lamar *v.* Micou, 112 U. S. 452 (1884); 6 Conn. 500; 33 *id.* 327.

[3] 1 Bl. Com. 463; 3 *id.* 141; 2 *id.* 461.

---

[1] See Lamar *v.* Micou, 112 U. S. 463–70 (1884), cases; Boaz *v.* Milliken, 83 Ky. 638 (1886); Eyster's Appeal, 16 Pa. 372 (1851).

[2] See Reeves, Dom. R. 311; Schouler, Dom. R. § 283; 1 Pars. Contr. 134–37; Lord *v.* Hough, 37 Cal. 660–69 (1869); 1 Johns. Ch. 109.

[3] Hudson *v.* Bishop, 32 F. R. 521 (1887).

[4] Curtis *v.* Murphy, 63 Wis. 6 (1885), cases, Cole, C. J. See also Russell *v.* Ryan, Sup. Ct. Del. (1886), Comegys, Chief Justice.

[5] See Story, Bailm. § 477; 2 Pars. Contr. 150; Hancock (Mrs. Gen.) *v.* Rand, 94 N. Y. 5, 10 (1883), cases; McDaniels *v.* Robinson, 26 Vt. 330–44 (1854), cases; Calye's Case, 1 Sm. L. C. 211–47, cases; Coggs *v.* Bernard, *ib.* 401–6, cases; 16 Ala. 666; 26 *id.* 377; 33 Cal. 557; 35 Conn. 183; 25 Iowa, 553; 53 Me. 163; 100 Mass. 495; 145 *id.* 244; 12 Mich. 52; 53 Mo. 547; 33 N. Y. 577; 61 *id.* 34; 36 Pa. 452; 62 *id.* 92; 41 Vt. 5; 35 Wis. 118.

[6] A. S. *gylt,* a fine for an offense; an offense.

jury, or a contempt of court. 2. As a plea, the judicial confession of a crime charged.

Not guilty. A plea denying the commission of a crime or a tort.

The plea of "not guilty" raises the general issue; it denies the whole indictment or declaration. In civil law, applicable in delicts sounding in trespass or case, for misfeasance or non-feasance, in ejectment, in garnishment, and in interpleader.[1]

When an accused person is arraigned (*q. v.*), the clerk inquires: "How say you, A. B., are you guilty or not guilty?" His answer, which is recorded, constitutes his plea. If "not guilty," the trial proceeds.

The plea waives objection to the complaint for misnomer or for neglect to add a place of residence.[2]

Where guilty knowledge is an ingredient of a crime, evidence of the commission of other kindred offenses about the same time is admissible as tending to prove that ingredient. Many cases of fraud require the application of the same principle,— as fraud involves intent, and intent can be deduced only from a variety of circumstances. Collateral facts, each insufficient in itself, whose joint operation tends to support the charge, or to disprove it, are then receivable.[3]

Where a statute prohibits an act being done, or being done under certain circumstances, without making knowledge or intent an ingredient in the offense, the person doing the act is bound at his peril to see that the circumstances are such as do not make it unlawful.[4]

Jurors are not called to pass upon a defendant's innocence, but solely whether or not the State has proven beyond reasonable doubt an affirmative proposition, to wit, his guilt.[5]

See CONFESSION, 2; CONVICT; CRIME; DOUBT; INTENT; NEGLIGENCE; WILL, 1. Compare CULPA.

GUITEAU'S CASE.[6] See DELUSION; DOUBT, Reasonable; INSANITY, 2 (6).

GUN. See BAGGAGE; SHOOTING-MARK; TOOL; WEAPON.

GUNPOWDER. See EXPLOSION; POLICE, 2.

GUTTER. See DRAIN.

An ordinance requiring lot-owners to keep the "gutters" opposite their premises in good repair, and free from obstructions, was held to refer to the ordinary open gutters along the streets, and not to a blind ditch or culvert covered with planks and soil.[7]

---

[1] See 3 Bl. Com. 305; 4 *id.* 338; Gould, Pl. 284.

[2] State *v.* Drury, 13 R. I. 540 (1882); 41 N. H. 407; 1 Bish. Cr. Proc. § 791. On withdrawal of plea, see 23 Cent. Law J. 75 (1886), cases.

[3] United States *v.* Clapboards, 4 Cliff. 303-5 (1874), cases, Clifford, J.; Commonwealth *v.* Jackson, 132 Mass. 18-21 (1882), cases; People *v.* Gibbs, 93 N. Y. 473 (1883); 19 Cent. Law J. 408 (1884).

[4] United States *v.* Curtis, 16 F. R. 187 (1883), cases, Brown, J.; Halstead *v.* State, 41 N. J. L. 589-96, 577-84 (1879), cases, Beasley, C. J.

[5] McNair *v.* State, 14 Tex. Ap. 84 (1883).

[6] Reported in 10 F. R. 161. See also 18 Rep. 138, 717.

[7] Gilluly *v.* City of Madison, 63 Wis. 518 (1885).

H.

H. As an initial, may denote *habeas,* Henry (king), Hilary, *hoc,* house.

H. B. House bill.

H. C. *Habeas corpus;* House of Commons.

H. L. House of Lords.

H. R. House of Representatives.

Abbreviations of the Latin *hoc,* this, formerly more in use than at present, are: *h. a.* for *hoc anno,* this year; *h. t.* for *hoc titulo,* this title; *h. v.* for *hoc verbo* or *his verbis,* this word or these words;— the last two being employed as references.

HABENDUM. See HABERE, Habendum.

HABERE. L. To grasp, lay hold of: to have, hold.

Habeas corpus. That you have the body. The emphatic words of several common-law writs issued to bring persons into court for a designated purpose. See particularly, 6, below.

1. *Habeas corpus ad faciendum et recipiendum.* That you have the body for doing and receiving. Removes an action into a superior court: commands the judge of the inferior court to produce the body of the defendant, with a statement of the cause of his detention (whence called, also, *habeas corpus cum causa*), to do and to receive whatever the higher court shall decree.

Applicable where the simpler writ of *habeas corpus ad subjiciendum* is inadequate; and grantable of right, without motion. Operates as a *supersedeas.*

2. *Habeas corpus ad prosequendum.* That you have the person for prosecuting. Removes a prisoner to the jurisdiction wherein it is alleged he committed a crime.

3. *Habeas corpus ad respondendum.* That you have the person for answering. Removes a prisoner that he may be charged with a new action in a higher court.

4. *Habeas corpus ad satisfaciendum.* That you have the person for satisfaction. Removes a prisoner into a superior court that he may there be charged with process of execution.

5. *Habeas corpus ad testificandum.* That you have the person for testifying. Removes a person from a place of detention that he may give testimony before a court.[1]

6. *Habeas corpus ad subjiciendum.* That

---

[1] See generally *Exp.* Marmaduke, 91 Mo. 228, 251 (1886), cases.

you have the body for submitting to and receiving. Commands the person who has another in detention to produce the body of the prisoner, with the day and cause of his caption and detention, to do, submit to, and receive whatever the judge or court awarding the writ shall consider (*q. v.*) in that behalf.[1]

This last, the great and efficacious prerogative writ, is commonly called The Writ of Habeas Corpus. It is the best and only sufficient defense of personal freedom.[2]

It is the remedy which the law gives for the enforcement of the civil right of personal liberty. . . The judicial proceeding under it is not to inquire into the criminal act complained of, but into the right to liberty notwithstanding the act. The prosecution against the prisoner is a criminal proceeding, but the writ of *habeas corpus*, which he may obtain, is not a proceeding in that prosecution. On the contrary, it is a new suit brought by him to enforce a right, which he claims, as against those who are holding him in custody under the criminal process. If he fails to establish his right to his liberty, he may be detained for trial for the offense; but if he succeeds, he must be discharged from custody. The proceeding is one instituted by himself for his liberty, not by the government to punish him for his crime. It is of a wholly civil nature.[3]

The writ was likely used at first to effect relief from private restraint. Trace of early use is found in Year Book 48 Edw. III, 22 (1375); was well understood in the time of Henry VI (1422–61); became available against the crown in the reign of Henry VII (1485–1509); in the time of Charles I (1625–49), was adjudged a constitutional remedy.[4]

The availability of the writ, as it obtained at common law, has been facilitated by statutes, particularly by 31 Charles II (1680), c. 2, called the *Habeas Corpus Act*, another Magna Charta, and by 56 Geo. III (1816), c. 100.[5] Acts having the same general nature and object exist in the various States. A case outside of a statute is governed by the common law.[6]

The general principles were settled long before our national independence, and were in mind when the power was given to the Federal courts and judges.[7]

The Constitution provides that "The Privilege of the Writ of Habeas Corpus shall not be suspended, unless when in Cases of Rebellion or Invasion the public Safety may require it." [8]

This provision has been copied into the constitutions of the States.

Congress, by act of March 3, 1863, authorized the President to suspend the privilege of the writ whenever, during the rebellion, in his judgment, the public safety might require it.[1]

Suspension of the writ simply denies to the person arrested the privilege of its use, to obtain his liberty.[2]

Not a writ of error, though in some cases, in which the court issuing it has appellate power over the court by whose authority the petitioner is held in custody, it may be used with the writ of *certiorari* for that purpose. Used alone, its purpose is to enable the court to inquire, first, if the petitioner is restrained of his liberty. If he is not, the court can do nothing but discharge the writ. If there is such restraint, the court can then inquire into the cause of it, and, if the alleged cause be unlawful, it must discharge the prisoner. Wives restrained by husbands, children withheld from the proper parent or guardian, persons held under arbitrary custody by private individuals, as in a madhouse, as well as those under military control, may become subjects of relief by the writ. But something more than moral restraint is necessary: there must be actual confinement or the present means of enforcing it.[3]

The writ is of right, in the nature of a writ of error, grantable on cause shown. The usual course is for the court on application to issue the writ, and, on its return, to hear and dispose of the case: but where the cause of imprisonment is fully shown by the petition, the court may determine that the prisoner, if produced, would or would not be entitled to a discharge.[4]

The writ affords relief only where the proceedings below are entirely void, for any cause, as for want of jurisdiction,[5] or because of the unconstitutionality of a statute.[6]

The reviewing power of the Supreme Court, in a criminal case, is confined to determining whether the lower court had jurisdiction to try and sentence for the offense.[7]

Ordinarily, the Supreme Court can issue the writ only under its appellate jurisdiction,— except in cases affecting public ministers or consuls, or those in which a State is a party.[8]

The act of March 27, 1868 (15 St. L. 44), took from the Supreme Court jurisdiction to review on appeal the decision of a circuit court upon a writ of *habeas corpus;* and it has no jurisdiction to review such decision on a

---

[1] 3 Bl. Com. 130; *Exp.* Bollman, 4 Cranch, 97–99 (1807), Marshall, C. J.; Tidd, Pr. 296–301, 739.

[2] *Exp.* Yerger, 8 Wall. 95 (1868).

[3] *Exp.* Tom Tong, 108 U. S. 559 (1883), Waite, C. J.; *Exp.* Bollman, 4 Cranch, 101 (1807).

[4] See Hurd, Habeas Corpus, 145.

[5] 3 Bl. Com. 130; 8 Wall. 95; 3 Hallam, Const. Hist. 19.

[6] 3 Bl. Com. 137.

[7] *Exp.* Parks, 93 U. S. 21 (1876); *Exp.* Yeager, 8 Wall. 95 (1868).

[8] Constitution, Art. I, sec. 9, cl. 2.

---

[1] 12 St. L. 755. See generally R. S. §§ 751–66, cases.

[2] *Exp.* Milligan, 4 Wall. 2, 3, 115 (1866); *Exp.* Merryman, 9 Am. Law Reg. 524 (1861), Taney, C. J.; *Exp.* Field, 5 Blatch. 67 (1862); 21 Ind. 370, 472; 44 Barb. 98; 16 Wis. 360; 1 Pac. Law Mag. 360.

[3] Wales *v.* Whitney, 114 U. S. 571–72 (1885), Miller, J.

[4] *Exp.* Milligan, *supra.*

[5] *Exp.* Parks, 93 U. S. 21 (1876).

[6] *Exp.* Rollins, 80 Va. 316 (1885), cases.

[7] *Exp.* Curtis, 106 U. S. 375 (1882); *Exp.* Carll, *ib.* 522 (1882), cases, Waite, C. J.

[8] *Exp.* Hung Hang, 108 U. S. 552 (1883), cases; State *v.* Neel, 48 Ark. 289 (1886), cases; 2 Kan. Law J. 225–32 (1885), cases.

writ of error. It may still issue its own writ of *habeas corpus*.[1]

A circuit court may discharge a person restrained of his liberty in violation of the Constitution, although held on an indictment for an offense against a State.[2]

Congress has prescribed the jurisdiction of the Federal courts under the writ; but as it has never particularly prescribed the mode of procedure, they have followed in substance the rules of the common law. The legislatures of the States not only provide what courts or officers may issue the writ, but, to a considerable extent, have regulated the practice under it.[3]

See EXTRADITION; INDIAN.

Habendum. To have; for having. *Habendum et tenendum:* to have and to hold.

The initial, emphatic word in that clause of a deed which follows the granting part. Determines what estate or interest is granted; may lessen, enlarge, explain, or qualify, but not totally contradict or be repugnant to, the estate granted in the premises, *q. v.*[4]

Habere facias possessionem. That you cause to have possession. **Habere facias seisinam.** That you cause to have seisin.

If the plaintiff recovers in any action whereby the seisin or possession of land is awarded him, the writ of execution is an *habere facias seisinam*, or writ of seisin, of a freehold; or an *habere facias possessionem*, or writ of possession, of a chattel interest. These are writs commanding the sheriff to give actual possession to the plaintiff of the land recovered.[5]

At present, an *habere facias possessionem* puts into possession of the land a plaintiff who has been successful in an action of ejectment; and the writ of *habere facias seisinam* is in vogue in some States in connection with the action of dower.[6]

Habere facias visum. That you cause to have a view. A writ, and the characteristic phrase in the same, which directed the sheriff to have land viewed by a jury.

Habilis. Having: capable, suitable; fit.

By the canon law, if the parties are *habiles ad matrimonium*, it is a good marriage, whatever their ages.[7]

HABIT.[8] A person's habits refer to his customary conduct, to pursue which he has acquired a tendency, from frequent repetition of the same acts.[9]

It would be incorrect to say that a man has a habit of anything from a single act.[9]

Habitual. According to or by force of habit or frequent use; originating in a fixed habit; habituated.

See CHARACTER; DRUNKARD; INTEMPERATE.

HABITANCY. Embraces the fact of residence at a place, together with the intent to regard it and make it a home.

It is difficult to give an exact definition.[1] See INHABITANT.

HABITATION. See DWELLING.

HÆRES. L. Heir. In Roman law, resembled an executor in English law. See HEIR, 2.

Hæreditas. Inheritance. See DAMNUM, Damnosa, etc.

Hæres natus. An heir born; an heir by descent. **Hæres factus.** An heir by appointment; a devisee.[2]

Nemo est hæres viventis. No one can be the heir of a living person.

No person can be the actual complete heir of another till that other is dead. Before that time the person next in the line of succession is called the "heir apparent," or "heir presumptive."[3]

HÆRET IN CORTICE. See LITERA QUI hæret, etc.

HAIR. May not include bristles.[4]

Hair clippers. See CUTLERY.

HALF. See BLOOD; COIN; DEFENSE, 2; MOIETY; ORPHAN; SISTER.

HALLOWEEN. See NIGHTWALKERS; WANTONNESS.

HALLUCINATION. See INSANITY.

HAMMER. "Under the hammer" refers to public sales by a sheriff or auctioneer.

In Rome, auctioneers stood beside a spear fixed upright in the forum; and the goods were said to be sold *sub hasta*, under the spear.

HANAPER.[5] A bag or basket, kept in offices of the court of chancery to receive dues paid for the seals of charters, patents, commissions, and writs; then, the exchequer of chancery.

Writs issuing out of the ordinary court of chancery (relating to the business of the subject) and the returns thereto were, according to the simplicity of ancient times, originally kept *in hanaperio;* and others (relating to affairs of the crown) were preserved in a little sack or bag; and thence has arisen the distinction of "hanaper office" and "petty-bag office," both

---

[1] *Exp.* Royall, 112 U. S. 181 (1884); *Exp.* Yerger, 8 Wall. 103 (1868).

[2] *Exp.* Royall, 117 U. S. 241 (1886).

[3] See generally People *ex rel.* Tweed *v.* Liscomb, 60 N. Y. 559 (1875); 18 Cent. Law J. 368–70 (1884), cases.

[4] 2 Bl. Com. 298; 4 Kent, 468; 3 Washb. R. P. 436.

[5] 3 Bl. Com. 412; Tidd, Pr. 1081; 2 Arch. Pr. 58.

[6] See Brightly, T. & H. (Pa.) §§ 1802, 1807.

[7] 1 Bl. Com. 436.

[8] L. *habitus; habere*, to have oneself, be in a condition.

[9] Knickerbocker Life Ins. Co. *v.* Foley, 105 U. S. 354 (1881), Field, J.

[1] Lyman *v.* Fiske, 17 Pick. 234 (1835), Shaw, C. J.

[2] See Borland *v.* Nichols, 18 Pa. 43 (1849).

[3] 2 Bl. Com. 208.

[4] Von Stade *v.* Arthur, 13 Blatch. 251 (1876).

[5] L. L. *hanaperium*, a large vase; a vessel to keep cups in; *hanapus*, a cup, bowl. Whence hamper.

of which belong to the common-law court in chancery.[1]
See PETIT, Petty Bag.

HAND. 1. As the member of the body with which a thing is held, an instrument used, force or action originated or exerted, or a deed done, is in frequent use. See AR-RAIGN; BURN; DEATH; MAYHEM. Compare MAIN; MANUS.

Handbill. A written or printed public notice of something to be done; as, of a judicial sale of property.

The number, time, and manner of posting such bills is regulated by local statute or rule of court.

Hand-money. The price or earnest given to bind a bargain, after shaking hands, or instead thereof; the consideration of a hand-sale. See EARNEST.

Hand-sale. Anciently, among northern nations, shaking of hands was necessary to bind a bargain; a custom retained in verbal contracts.[2]

Uplifted hand. Refers to an oath taken by raising the right hand toward Heaven.

Whip-hand. The right hand; the side of a road toward the right hand. See ROAD, 1, Law of.

2. Force; violence.

Strong hand. "With strong hand" implies a degree of criminal force, more than "with force and arms." Statutes relating to forcible entry (q. v.) use the words in describing the degree of force which makes an entry or detainer criminal, and entitles the prosecutor, under some circumstances, to restitution and damages.[3]

"With force and arms" are merely formal words in the action of trespass, and if issue be taken upon them, the plaintiff is not bound to prove any actual force.[3]

3. Chirography; penmanship; handwriting.

Whatever one has written with his hand; not merely his usual style of chirography.[4]

Comparison of hands, or of handwriting. Proving penmanship by its likeness to other writing, admitted or proven to be genuine.

The rule of the common law is to disallow a comparison of hands as proof of signature. An exception is, that if a paper, admitted to be in the hands of a party or to be subscribed by him, is in evidence for some other purpose, the signature or paper in question may be compared with it by the jury.[1]

A paper, otherwise irrelevant, may not be put in evidence merely to enable the jury to make a comparison.[2]

When a witness is called to prove a signature from his knowledge of the signer's writing, he should be first cross-examined as to his means of knowledge.[3]

Handwriting is proved by the writer, by his admission, by his writing in court, or by a witness who has either seen him write or is familiar with his hand. The witness may be tested by other writings. In England, comparison is permitted only as to test paper already in court. In some States, comparison with other papers is allowed. Test papers made for the purpose are inadmissible. An expert in handwriting may say whether in his opinion a hand is feigned or natural.[4]

All evidence of handwriting, except in the single instance where the witness saw the document written, is in its nature comparison of hands. It is the belief which the witness entertains upon comparing the writing in question with the exemplar in his mind derived from previous knowledge. Any witness, otherwise disinterested, who has had the opportunity of acquiring such an exemplar, is competent to speak of his belief. It is one of the few instances in which the law accepts from witnesses belief in facts, instead of facts themselves. If, from having seen the party write or from correspondence with him, the witness has become familiar with his hand, he may testify his belief as to the genuineness of the writing in question. Technically, comparison of handwriting means a "comparison by the juxtaposition of two writings, to ascertain whether both were written by the same person." . . (1) Evidence as to the genuineness of a paper may be corroborated by a comparison, to be made by the jury, between that paper and other well authenticated writings. (2) A mere expert may not make the comparison. (3) Witnesses having knowledge of the party's handwriting may testify as to the paper; but they are not to make the comparison. (4) Test documents should be established by the most satisfactory evidence. (5) An expert may be examined to prove forged or simulated writings, and to give conclusions of skill; but not to compare a writing, as, a note, in suit, with other test papers, and express his opinion, when he had no knowledge of the defendant's handwriting.[5]

The rule is that a witness who is introduced to prove

[1] 3 Bl. Com. 49; Yates v. People, 6 Johns. *363 (1810).
[2] 2 Bl. Com. 448.
[3] King v. Wilson, 8 T. R. 362 (1799), Lawrence, J.; Harvey v. Brydges, 14 M. & W. *443 (1845), Parke, B.; Lawe v. King, 1 Saund. 81 (1668).
[4] Commonwealth v. Webster, 5 Cush. 301 (1850), Shaw, C. J.

[1] Moore v. United States, 91 U. S. 274 (1875); Strother v. Lucas, 6 Pet. *767 (1832); 1 Greenl. Ev. § 578.
[2] United States v. Jones, 20 Blatch. 236 (1882).
[3] Frew v. Clark, 80 Pa. 181 (1875).
[4] 1 Whart. Ev. §§ 705-40, cases; Commonwealth v. Webster, 5 Cush. 301 (1850).
[5] Travis v. Brown, 43 Pa. 12, 13, 17 (1862), cases, Woodward, J. See also Ballentine v. White, 77 id. 26 (1874); Aurnick v. Mitchell, 82 id. 213 (1876); Reese v. Reese, 90 id. 94 (1879); Berryhill v. Kirchner, 96 id. 492 (1880); Lessee of Clark v. Courtney, 5 Pet. *344 (1831); Winn v. Patterson, 9 id. 674-75 (1835); Williams v. Conger, 125 U. S. 413, 397 (1888), cases.

the handwriting of a person must have personal knowledge of it, either by having seen him write, or by having seen writing admitted by him to be his or, with his knowledge, acted upon as his, or so adopted into the ordinary business of life as to create a reasonable presumption of its genuineness. Exceptions are, first, where the paper is not old enough to prove itself, and yet is so old that living witnesses cannot be had: then, other writings proven to be genuine, or to have been acted upon as such by all parties, may be offered, and experts, by comparison, may give their opinion as to the genuineness; or, second, where other writings admitted to be genuine are already in the case, when the jury may make the comparison without expert aid. The civil and ecclesiastical law permitted the testimony of experts as to handwriting by comparison. The rule varies in the different States. In some, comparison is allowed between the writing in question and any other writing shown to be genuine, whether already in the case or not, or relevant or not; while in others, it is only permitted as between the disputed paper and one already in the case and relevant to it.[1] See FORGERY; SUBSCRIBE.

Under hand and seal, or witness my hand, etc. Said of an instrument of writing, and refers, specifically, to the name or signature thereto. See SEAL, 1.

4. Condition or attitude before the law; as, in the expression —

Clean hands. Upright before the law; free from fault; in a position to ask the intervention of a court of equity.

Hand down. To decide, declare, announce.

Hand down an opinion. When a member of a court of errors and appeals has written an opinion in a case and delivered it to the clerk for transmission to the court whose decision has been under review, the opinion is said to be "handed down."

HANGING. The judgment in a capital case is, that the prisoner "be hanged by the neck till dead."[2]

Hanged is preferred to *hung*, as the past participle.

Hangman. One who executes a prisoner condemned to death by suspension by the neck; also, he who holds the office of public executioner. See DEATH, Penalty.

HAPPEN. See CONTINGENCY; OCCUR.

HAPPINESS. The foundation of ethics or natural law is "that every man should

pursue his own true and substantial happiness."[1]

But as *utility* contradicts the common sense and feeling of mankind, utility is not the standard of right and wrong.[2]

The object of all government is to promote the happiness and prosperity of the community by which it is established.[3]

Happiness is an inalienable right. In its pursuit all avocations, honors, positions, are alike open to every one.[4]

The right of men to pursue their happiness means the right to pursue any lawful business or vocation, in any manner not inconsistent with the equal rights of others, which may increase their prosperity or develop their faculties, so as to give them their highest enjoyment.[5]

The right to follow any of the common occupations of life is an inalienable right; it was formulated as such under the phrase "pursuit of happiness" in the Declaration of Independence. This right is a large ingredient in the civil liberty (*q. v.*) of the citizen. No legislature may deny the right to all but a few favored individuals, by investing the latter with a monopoly.[6] See PRIVILEGE, 2.

HARBOR. 1, *v.* To receive and conceal clandestinely; to secrete, so that another who has the right of custody shall be deprived thereof: as, to harbor a wife, child, apprentice, fugitive slave.[7]

2, *n.* A haven or port. See COMMERCE; LADING; PORT; WHARF.

HARD. See HARDSHIP; LABOR, 1.

HARDPAN. See EARTH.

HARDSHIP. Refers to an argument why a thing should or should not be allowed because of the severity of the law as applied to the particular case.

Where a statute is clear and imperative, of no avail.[8]

Settled principles cannot, with safety to the public, be disregarded to remedy the hardship of a special case.[9]

---

[1] Fee v. Taylor, 83 Ky. 262–63 (1885), Holt, J. See also Rose v. First Nat. Bank of Springfield, 91 Mo. 401–3 (1886), cases; Bell v. Brewster, 44 Ohio St. 696, 698 (1887), cases; Smyth v. Caswell, 67 Tex. 573 (1887); as to evidence of identity. 22 Cent. Law J. 316 (1886), cases.

[2] 4 Bl. Com. 403.

[1] 1 Bl. Com. 41.

[2] 1 Shars. Bl. Com. 41.

[3] Charles River Bridge v. Warren Bridge, 11 Pet. 547 (1837), Taney, C. J.

[4] Cummings v. Missouri, 4 Wall. 321 (1866), Field, J.

[5] Butchers' Union Co. v. Crescent City Co., 111 U. S. 757 (1884), Field, J.

[6] Butchers' Union Co., &c., *supra*, 111 U. S. 762: Bradley, Harlan, Woods, JJ.

[7] See Driskill v. Parrish, 3 McLean, 643 (1847); Jones v. Van Zandt, 5 How. 227 (1847); Van Metre v. Mitchell, 2 Wall. Jr. 317 (1853); 24 Ga. 71; 26 *id.* 593; 5 N. H. 498; 10 *id.* 247; 1 Abb. Pr. 259; 2 N. Car. Law R. 249.

[8] The Cherokee Tobacco, 11 Wall. 620 (1870).

[9] Buchanan v. Litchfield, 102 U. S. 293 (1880); *ib.* 404.

The certainty of the law is of more importance than individual convenience. Inconvenience and hardship are considerations for the legislature.[1]

See POLICY, 1, Public; POSSIBILITY. '

HARDWARE. See CUTLERY.

HARVEST. Referring to a season of the year, the time when crops of grain and grass are gathered; does not apply to second crops cut out of harvest time.[2] See CROP; EMBLEMENTS.

HAUL. See CARRY, 1.

HAVE. See MAY, May have.

"To have and to hold," in a deed, defines the extent of ownership in the matter granted.

Rejected, if repugnant to the rest of the deed.[5] See further HABERE, Habendum.

HAWKER. The primary idea of a "hawker and peddler" is that of an itinerant or traveling trader, who carries goods about for sale, and actually sells them, in contradistinction to a trader who sells goods in a fixed place of business. Superadded to this (though perhaps not essential), by a "hawker" is generally understood one who not only carries goods for sale, but who seeks for purchasers, either by *outcry* or by attracting attention to them, as goods for sale, by an actual exhibition or exposure of them, by placards or labels, or by a conventional signal, like the sound of a horn for the sale of fish.[4]

A "hawker and peddler" is an itinerant trader, who goes from place to place, or from house to house, carrying for sale and exposing to sale the goods, wares or merchandise which he carries.[5]

He generally deals in small and cheap articles, such as he can conveniently carry in a cart or on his person. He may be required to take out a license.[6]

Hawking. Embraces the business of one who sells, or offers goods for sale, on the streets by outcry, or by attracting the attention of persons by exposing his goods in a public place, or by placards, labels, or signals.[6]

HAZARD.[1] Danger, peril, risk, but not necessarily the greatest degree.[2]

Hazardous. Involving danger; accompanied with risk; perilous: as, a hazardous contract.

"Hazardous," "extra hazardous," "special hazardous," and "not hazardous," have distinct meanings in the business of fire insurance. What goods are included under any one designation may not be so well known as to dispense with proof.[3] See INSURANCE; RISK.

Games of hazard. See GAME, 2.

HEAD. 1. He who provides for a family, *q. v.*

2. The responsible person; the chief; the principal: as, the head of a department of government, *q. v.*

3. Compare CAPUT; POLL.

Headnote. A statement of the points decided in a case, and preceding the printed report thereof. See SYLLABUS.

HEALTH. Exemption from disease; freedom from sickness or pain; exemption from prevailing or unusual disease or contagion.

A person is "healthy" who is free from disease or bodily ailment, or that state of the system peculiarly susceptible or liable to disease or bodily ailment.[4]

The degree of health ordinarily enjoyed by men in health, and the physical ability which men of sound bodies ordinarily possess, places one in the class of the "healthy and able-bodied," within the meaning of poor-laws, although there may be casual or temporary illness, or bodily unsoundness.[5]

"Sound health," as used in contracts for life insurance, does not mean absolute freedom from bodily infirmity or tendency to disease.[6] See INTEMPERATE.

Public health. The wholesome sanitary condition of the community at large; the exemption of a municipality or region from any prevailing and unusual disease or mortality; general health: health of the people.

Laws to secure the general health of the people at large are called "public-health laws;" and the officers charged with administering them, the "public-health board," or "public-health officers," or, briefly, the "health-board" or "health-officers."

---

[1] Silliman *v.* United States, 101 U. S. 471 (1879); Stewart *v.* Platt, *ib.* 738 (1879); 3 How. 61; 21 Wall. 178; 102 Ill. 221.

[2] Wendall *v.* Osborne, 63 Iowa, 102, 103 (1884), Beck, J.

[3] Jamaica Pond Aqueduct Corporation *v.* Chandler, 9 Allen, 168 (1864), Bigelow, C. J.

[4] [Commonwealth *v.* Ober, 12 Cush. 495 (1853), Shaw, Chief Justice.

[5] Commonwealth *v.* Farnum, 114 Mass. 270 (1873), Endicott, J.; Morrill *v.* State, 38 Wis. 437 (1875)

[6] Graffty *v.* Rushville, 107 Ind. 505 (1886), Mitchell, J.

[1] F. *hazard,* accident; unfortunate throw of dice: *zar,* a die.

[2] Butterfoss *v.* State, 40 N. J. E. 330 (1885).

[3] See Pindar *v.* Continental Fire Ins. Co., 38 N. Y. 364 (1868).

[4] Bell *v.* Jeffreys, 13 Ired. L. 357 (1852), Pearson, J.

[5] Starksboro *v.* Hinesburgh, 15 Vt. 209 (1843), Royce, Judge.

[6] Morrison *v.* Wisconsin Odd Fellows' Mut. Life Ins. Co., 59 Wis. 170 (1884), Lyon, J. See Moulor *v.* American Life Ins. Co., 111 U. S. 335 (1884); May, Ins. § 295, cases.

Bill of health. A certificate given by the authorities of the port from which a vessel clears, showing the state of the public health at the port.

Clean bill of health. A certificate that no infectious disease exists; opposed to a *touched* or *suspected* bill, or a bill actually *foul*.

Board of health. A board of officials specially charged with the preservation of the general health of the people at large.

Their jurisdiction is, ordinarily, a municipality, or a State.

National Board of Health. Established by act of Congress of March 3, 1879, ch. 202, § 1 (20 St. L. 484). Consists of seven members appointed by the President, and four members detailed from the departments. Their duties are to obtain information upon all matters affecting the public health, to advise the heads of departments and State executives, to make necessary investigations at any place in the United States, or at foreign ports, and to make rules guarding against the introduction of contagious diseases into the country and their spread from State to State.[1]

The preservation of the public health is one of the chief purposes of local government. Hence, municipal corporations are liberally endowed with power to prevent and abate nuisances. Public policy requires that health-officers be not disturbed in the exercise of their powers, unless clearly transcending their authority.[2]

All sanitary cordons and preventive regulations come under the right of preventing more serious injuries by stifling the sources of evil. In doing this, health-officers must not interfere with the natural rights of individuals.[3]

Power in boards of health to abate nuisances and the causes of them, and to enforce sanitary regulations, are very great. The courts have excused an excessive exercise of power in cases where there was great peril to the public health. But an exercise which is clearly unlawful, and has no great public necessity to excuse it, will be restrained, however praiseworthy the motive. The people " shall be secure in their persons and houses from unreasonable searches and seizures." [4]

By statute of 1 James I (1603), c. 31, a person infected with the plague, or dwelling in an infected house, could be compelled to keep his house. If he went into company, he could be punished by whipping, be bound

to good behavior, or be adjudged guilty of felony. By 26 Geo. II (1753), c. 26, quarantine of ships from infected countries was regulated.[1]

In England the public health is secured by various statutes, principally by the Public Health Act, 11 and 12 Vict. (1848), c. 63, the Local Government Acts of 1858, and amendments thereto. These statutes give large powers to the local authorities for removing nuisances, regulating burials, checking the sale of injurious food and drink, and otherwise preventing disease.

The preservation of health is an absolute right of personal security.[2]

Injuries to a man's health occur when, by any unwholesome practices of another, a man sustains any apparent damage in his vigor or constitution: as, by the sale of bad provisions, by the exercise of a noisome trade, or by the neglect or unskillful management of his physician, surgeon, or apothecary. For such, a special action of trespass on the case for damages lies.[3]

An act (supplementary) of New Jersey, approved March 12, 1880, makes animals with contagious diseases common nuisances; another act (also supplementary), approved March 12, 1884, makes horses affected with glanders common nuisances; and both acts authorize destruction of the animals under prescribed conditions. *Held*, that the acts are within the police powers of the State; that they are not within the prohibition of the Fourteenth Amendment, because, although they authorize the abatement of nuisances in advance of a judicial adjudication of the fact of nuisance, yet they do not make the determination as to that fact conclusive, and only permit acts, in abating a particular nuisance, to be justified by proof of its actual existence; thirdly, that the conditions under which the officials may act, by the statute of 1880, are mere limitations upon their power for the benefit of the owners of animals, and their adjudication that such conditions exist will not protect them, unless the existence of the common nuisance is shown.[4]

See ADULTERATE; DISEASE; POLICE, 2; QUARANTINE, 2; SOUND, 2 (2).

HEARING. 1. The trial of a suit in equity. 2. The session of any court, or of an adjunct thereof, for considering the proofs in a cause. 3. An examination of the testimony offered against a person charged with crime.

As applied to equity cases, " hearing " means the same as " trial " at law.[5]

Final hearing. The trial of an equity case upon its merits; as distinguished from

[1] R. S , 1 Sup. p. 480.

[2] Hart *v.* Mayor of Albany, 3 Paige, 218 (1832); 1 Dillon, Munic. Corp. §§ 369, 374.

[3] Spalding *v.* Preston, 21 Vt. 13-14 (1848).

[4] Eddy *v.* Board of Health, 10 Phila. 94 (1873), cases, Peirce, J. See also Butterfoss *v.* State, 40 N. J. E. 325 (1885).

[1] 4 Bl. Com. 161; King *v.* Vantandillo, 4 M. & S. 73 (1815); King *v.* Burnett, *ib.* 272 (1815).

[2] 1 Bl. Com. 129, 131.

[3] 3 Bl. Com. 122.

[4] Newark & South Orange Horse Ry. Co. *v.* Hunt, Sup. Ct. N. J. (Feb. 27, 1888), cases, Magie, J. Same case, 37 Alb. Law J. 356.

[5] Vannevar *v.* Bryant, 21 Wall. 43 (1874); Jones *v.* Foster, 61 Wis. 29 (1884); 19 Wall. 225; 3 Dill. 463; 40 Ind. 179.

the hearing of any preliminary question aris-ing in the cause, termed "interlocutory." [1]

Further hearing. An adjourned or con-tinued hearing.

Re-hearing. A new hearing in a mat-ter once decided; consideration under a re-examination or re-argument.[2]

A petition for the re-hearing of a case may be re-quired to be made at the term when the cause was first decided.

See NOTICE, 1; JURISDICTION, 2; PROCESS, 1, Due; REMAND, 1; TERM, 4; TRIAL; WAIVER. Compare AU-DIAE; OYER; PRESENCE.

HEARSAY. What is heard as rumored; testimony not a matter of personal knowl-edge with the witness.

That kind of evidence which does not de-rive its value solely from the credit to be given to the witness himself, but rests also, in part, on the veracity and competency of some other person.[3]

In the largest sense, interchangeable with non-original evidence. This is generally inadmissible, be-cause of the depreciation of truth from passage through fallible media; because of non-discrimination by juries between primary and secondary evidence; and because it is irresponsible in its first exhibition.[4]

Because it wants the sanction of an oath, and affords no opportunity for cross-examination, is ex-cluded.[5]

Supposes that better testimony may be had; is in-trinsically too weak to satisfy the mind; under its color fraud might be practiced.[6]

Admissible in the following cases: 1. As to a wit-ness — what was said in a former trial by a person now dead, out of the jurisdiction, subsequently incom-petent, insane, or sick.[7]

2. As to depositions in perpetuam. But the testi-mony must be ephemeral; taken conformably to the rules of evidence; be deposited in court; and the cause be not delayed.[6]

3. As to matters of general interest, and ancient possession. But the witnesses must be disinterested. Includes declarations of deceased persons as to bound-aries.[9] Ancient documents, in proper custody, prove ancient possessions.[10]

4. As to pedigree and relationship: birth, marriage, and death. Common family tradition is receivable; also, statements of deceased relatives made before a dispute arose; also, family records, epitaphs, armorial bearings, and the like.[1] See PEDIGREE.

5. As to declarations against interest by deceased persons. This means against pecuniary or proprietary interest; not as to incidental matters, and although better evidence may be had. But must be brought home to an imputed declarant.[2]

6. As to business entries. By a deceased or absent partner or clerk, and made in the regular course of business, admitted. So of notes by surveyor, counsel, bank messenger, notaries, and others. But the entry must have been made contemporaneously with the transaction, confined to the matter it was the person's duty to record. and, in its nature, original.[3] See fur-ther ENTRY, II, 1.

7. As to general reputation when material.[4] See CHARACTER; REPUTATION.

8. To refresh memory, as to extrinsic incidents of testimony; as, dates, places, etc.[5] See REFRESH.

9. As to res gestæ. Includes declarations coincident with business acts, and torts; not, if the acts are in themselves inadmissible, or there exists opportunity for concoction.[6] See RES, Gestæ.

10. As to declarations concerning a party's own health and state of mind. These chiefly regard state-ments as to injuries and motives.[7]

See further DECLARATION, 2; EVIDENCE; HISTORIES.

HEARSE. See WAGON.

HEATHEN. See OATH; RELIGION.

HEAVY. As applied to different articles, is a comparative term.

Whether a bale of cotton is a "heavy article" or "an article of measurement," within the meaning of a railroad charter, is a question of fact, to be deter-mined by a jury, and regulated by proof of custom.[8]

HEIFER. A female calf of the bovine species, from the end of the first year until she has had a calf.[9]

"Heifer" and "steer" describe animals of the bo-vine species advanced to an age beyond that of a calf. A more definite description is "yearling heifer," and "yearling steer." [10] See COW.

---

[1] Akerly v. Vilas, 24 Wis. 171 (1869), Paine, J.; Jones v. Foster, 61 id. 29 (1884); Galpin v. Critchlow, 112 Mass. 343 (1873).

[2] [3 Bl. Com. 453.

[3] 1 Greenl. Ev. § 99; [1 Phill. Ev. 169.

[4] 1 Whart. Ev. §§ 170–75, cases.

[5] 1 Greenl. Ev. §§ 163, 98, 124.

[6] Mima Queen v. Hepburn, 7 Cranch, 295 (1813), Marshall, C. J.; Hopt v. Utah, 110 U. S. 581 (1884); 1 Wheat. 8; 8 Wall. 409.

[7] 1 Whart. Ev. §§ 177–80, cases.

[8] 1 Whart. Ev. §§ 181–84, cases.

[9] See Clement v. Packer, 125 U. S. 321 (1888), cases.

[10] 1 Whart. Ev. §§ 185–200, cases; 1 Greenl. Ev. §§ 127–40.

[1] 1 Whart. Ev. §§ 201–25, cases; 1 Greenl. Ev. §§ 103–7, cases.

[2] 1 Whart. Ev. §§ 226–37, cases.

[3] 1 Whart. Ev. §§ 238–51, cases; 1 Greenl. Ev. §§ 115–23, cases.

[4] 1 Whart. Ev. §§ 252–56, cases.

[5] 1 Whart. Ev. § 257, cases.

[6] 1 Whart. Ev. §§ 258–67, cases; 1 Greenl. Ev. §§ 108, 112–14, cases.

[7] 1 Whart. Ev. §§ 268–69, cases; 1 Greenl. Ev. §§ 102, 110, cases.

[8] Elder v. Charlotte, &c. R. Co., 13 S. C. 281 (1879); Bonham v. Same, ib. 276 (1879).

[9] Freeman v. Carpenter, 10 Vt. 435 (1838).

[10] Milligan v. Jefferson County, 2 Monta. 546 (1877). See also 7 Vt. 465; 40 id. 641; 11 Gray, 211; 8 Allen, 583; 16 Kan. 294.

HEIR. See HÆRES. 1. At common law, he upon whom the law casts the estate immediately on the death of the ancestor.[1] Correlative, *ancestor*, q. v.

Uncontrolled by the context, the person appointed by law to succeed to the real estate in case of intestacy.[2]

Simply one who succeeds to the estate of a deceased person.[3]

Whoever succeeds to property of an intestate.[4]

In a will, unexplained and uncontrolled by the context, construed according to its strict technical import,— the person who, by the statute of descent, would succeed to the real estate in case of intestacy. A term of description of a class of persons who, in the prescribed contingency, take the estate.[5]

He upon whom the law casts an estate of inheritance immediately on the death of the owner.[6]

The primary meaning is, the person related to one by blood, who would take the latter's real estate if he died intestate. The proper primary meaning of "next of kin" is, the person related by blood, who takes personal estate of one who dies intestate.

In New York "heirs," applied to the successors of personality, means next of kin, and does not therefore include a widow or a husband of an intestate. In a few cases in other States "heirs," applied to personalty, has been held to mean those who by the statute of distributions take the personalty in case of intestacy. There is much confusion in the English cases upon the subject.[7]

No rule can be stated under which all the decisions can be classified. In general, where there is a gift to a person or his heirs, the word "heirs" denotes succession or substitution; the gift being primarily to the person named, or, if he is dead, then to his heirs in his place. In such cases, it has often been held that the word should be construed to mean the persons who would legally succeed to the property according to its nature or quality; and that the heirs at law would take the realty, and the next of kin or persons entitled to inherit personalty would take the personal estate. But where the gift is directly to the heirs of a person, as a substantive gift to them of something which their ancestor was in no event to take, this element of succession or substitution is wanting, and the heirs take as the persons designated in the instrument to take in their own right; and in such cases the courts have usually held that the word "heirs" must receive its common-law meaning —the persons entitled to succeed to real estate in a case of intestacy.[1]

"Heir" is a word of law; "son," "child," and the like, are words of nature.

"Heirs" may be used in deeds,[2] as it is often used in wills, for "children" or "issue,"[3] or grandchildren.[4] May mean "devisee," "legatee," or "distributee."[5] May be used where there is no subject to be inherited.[6]

A "widow" is an heir in a special, limited sense only.[7]

A "husband" is neither the heir nor next of kin of his wife, in any technical sense.[8]

In a devise, "heir" is a word of limitation.[9] See SHELLEY'S CASE.

Collateral heir. A relative not of the direct line of descent, but of a collateral line.

Heir apparent. He whose right of inheriting is indefeasible, provided he outlives the ancestor.[10]

In this sense, "heir" is in popular use.

Heir at law; heir at common law, or **heir general.** He upon whom the law casts the realty of an intestate.[11]

Heir of the body or **natural heir.** An heir begotten of the body; a lineal descendant.[12]

---

[1] 2 Bl. Com. 201; Bailey v. Bailey, 25 Mich. 188 (1872).

[2] Gauch v. St. Louis M. L. Ins. Co., 88 Ill. 256 (1878), Schoefield, C. J.; Fahens v. Fahens, 141 Mass. 399 (1886).

[3] McKinney v. Stewart, 3 Kan. 392 (1869), Valentine, J.; Cushman v. Horton, 59 N. Y. 151–52 (1874); Fountain County Coal, &c. Co. v. Beckleheimer, 102 Ind. 76 (1884).

[4] [Eckford v. Knox, 67 Tex. 203 (1886), Willie, C. J.

[5] Clark v. Cordis, 4 Allen, 480 (1862), Bigelow, C. J. See also Lombard v. Boyden, 5 id. 254 (1862); Loring v. Thorndike, ib. 269 (1862); Rand v. Sanger, 115 Mass. 128 (1874); Minot v. Harris, 132 id. 530–31 (1882), cases; Rand v. Butler, 48 Conn. 298 (1880); 101 Ind. 194; 65 Iowa, 80; 18 B. Mon. 329; 40 Miss. 758; 15 N. J. L. 404.

[6] Lavery v. Egan, 143 Mass. 392 (1887), Field, J.

[7] [Tillman v. Davis, 95 N. Y. 24–29 (1884), cases, Earl, J.

[1] Fahens v. Fahens, 141 Mass. 399–400 (1886), cases, C. Allen, J.

[2] Heard v. Horton, 1 Denio, 167–70 (1845), cases; See v. Derr, 57 Mich. 373 (1885).

[3] Haly v. Boston, 108 Mass. 579 (1871); Taggart v. Murray, 53 N. Y. 233 (1873); Jones v. Lloyd, 33 Ohio St. 578–80 (1878), cases; Eldridge v. Eldridge, 41 N. J. E. 91 (1886), cases; 42 id. 559; Myrick v. Heard, 31 F. R. 244 (1887).

[4] Woodruff v. Pleasants, 81 Va. 40 (1885).

[5] Sweet v. Dutton, 109 Mass. 591 (1872); Cushman v. Horton, 59 N. Y. 151 (1874); Elsey v. Odd Fellows Relief Society, 142 Mass. 226 (1886).

[6] Aspden's Estate, 2 Wall. Jr. 445 (1853).

[7] Unfried v. Heberer, 63 Ind. 72 (1878); Rusing v. Rusing, 25 id. 63 (1865); Eisman v. Poindexter, 52 id. 401 (1876); Clark v. Scott, 67 Pa. 452–53 (1871), cases.

[8] Ivins's Appeal, 106 Pa. 184 (1884).

[9] Daly v. James, 8 Wheat. 534 (1823); 99 Ind. 190.

[10] 2 Bl. Com. 208; 8 Bush, 115; 51 Barb. 137; 22 Me. 257.

[11] Aspden's Estate, 2 Wall. Jr. 433–38 (1853).

[12] Smith v. Pendell, 19 Conn. 111 (1848); Williams v. Allen, 17 Ga. 84 (1855); Roberts v. Ogbourne, 37 Ala. 178 (1861); Sewall v. Roberts, 115 Mass. 276–77 (1874).

Heir presumptive. He who, if the ancestor should die immediately, would, in the present circumstances of things, be his heir; but whose right of inheritance may be defeated by the contingency of some nearer heir being born.[1]

Heiress. A female heir; but, in law-language, " heir" includes both sexes.

At common law, "heir" is a word of inheritance, necessary to the *grant* of an estate larger than a life interest.[2] This nicety is a relic of feudal strictness.[3] Unless changed by statute, the rule requiring the use of the word is imperative: no synonym will supply its place; nor will any word of perpetuity.[4]

To bind his heirs, an *obligor* must use the word "heir" or its equivalent; not so, to bind an administrator or an executor.[5]

See ADOPT, 3; DESCENT; HEIRLOOM; HEREDITAMENT; INHERIT; PURCHASE, 2; RIGHT, 1.

2. In civil law, he who is called to the "succession" (*q. v.*), whether by the act of the deceased or by operation of law.

The universal successor is the "testamentary heir;" and, in cases of intestacy, the next of kin by blood is the "heir by intestacy" or "heir-at-law." The former corresponds to the executor, the latter to the administrator, of the common law. The "heir" administers both the real and the personal estate.[6] See HÆRES.

Heirloom. Such personalty as, contrary to the nature of chattels, goes by special custom to the heir along with the inheritance, and not to the executor of the last proprietor.[7]

"Loom" is in Saxon *geloma, leoma:* limb, member; so that "heirloom" is a limb or member of the inheritance · Heirlooms are generally such things as cannot be taken away without damaging or dismembering the freehold: as, charters, deeds, and other evidences of title to land. with the chests containing them; chimney-pieces, pumps, old fixed or dormant tables, benches and the like; also, the ancient jewels of the crown. Of the same nature is a monument or tombstone, a pew in a church, and like articles which, by special custom, cannot be devised away from the heir.[7]

Or, again, "loom" meant, at first, an implement for weaving, and, later, any household article—a table, cupboard, bedstead, wainscot, and the like. These came to be called "heir-looms" because, by special custom, they went to the heir of the owner at his decease, with the house in which they were used.[1]

Heirlooms are properly portraits, coats of arms, paintings, and such like, of the former owners of an inheritance.[2]

A bill in equity will lie for the specific delivery of an heirloom to the rightful owner.[3]

Heirlooms do not seem to be recognized by the law of this country.[4]

HELD. See HOLD, 1.

HELP. See AID, 1.

In an action by A to recover money promised him if he would " help " B to effect the sale of land, it was admitted that A had rendered the required services, and the parties in their pleadings construed the agreement to be that A should use his best effort to bring about the sale. *Held,* that parol evidence was not admissible to explain the word.[5]

HENCE. Compare So.

HEREAFTER. Will of itself make a statute prospective, and save pending suits.[6]

HEREBY. See GRANT, 2.

HEREDITAMENT. Anything that may be inherited, be it corporeal or incorporeal, real, personal, or mixed.[7]

The word is almost as comprehensive as property.[8]

Corporeal hereditament. Such thing as affects the senses, as may be seen and handled. **Incorporeal hereditament.** Is not the object of sensation, can neither be seen nor handled; is a creature of the mind, exists only in contemplation.[9] See CORPOREAL.

Corporeal hereditaments consist wholly of substantial and permanent objects; all which may be comprehended under the general denomination of "land."[9]

An incorporeal hereditament is a right issuing out of a thing corporate (whether real or personal), or concerning, annexed to, or exercisable within the same. Its effects and profits may be objects of the senses: as, an annuity to a man and his heirs, rents, commons, ways, offices, franchises; and, formerly, advowsons, tithes, dignities, and corodies or pensions,[10] *qq. v.*

The right to a seat in a board of exchange is an incorporeal hereditament.[11]

---

[1] 2 Bl. Com. 208.

[2] St. Clair County Turnpike Co. *v.* Illinois, 96 U. S. 68 (1877).

[3] 2 Bl. Com. 107.

[4] 1 Washb. R. P. 56.

[5] Shep. Touch. 369; Coke, Litt. 209, *a*.
See also 44 Cal. 253; 40 Ga. 562; 45 Me. 250; 63 *id*. 379; 45 Pa. 201; 5 *id*. 461; 69 *id*. 190; 10 R. I. 509; 9 Ired. L. 370.

[6] 1 Brown, Civ. Law, 344; Story, Confl. Laws, § 508.

[7] [2 Bl. Com. 427–29, 17.

[1] Cowell; Coke, Litt. 18 *b*; Shep. Touch. 432.

[2] Brown's Law Dict.

[3] Pusey *v.* Pusey, 1 White & T., L. C. *1109–11; 1 Story, Eq. § 709.

[4] 1 Washb. R. P., 4 ed., 20. See Moseley's Estate, 5 W. N. C. 102 (1877).

[5] Hooker *v.* Hyde, 61 Wis. 209 (1884).

[6] State *v.* Hicks, 48 Ark. 520 (1886).

[7] 1 Coke, Inst. 6; 5 Conn. 518; 13 N. Y. 159; 28 Barb. 338; 5 Wend. 453.

[8] 3 Kent, 401.

[9] [2 Bl. Com. 17–18; 28 Barb. 340.

[10] 2 Bl. Com. 20–21.

[11] Hyde *v.* Woods, 94 U. S. 524 (1876).

In principle there is no difference, as to the acquisition of rights, between corporeal and incorporeal objects. But, with regard to possession alone, as affecting title, a difference is introduced by reason of the statute of limitations. A grant of land, conferring an entire title, is not presumed from mere possession short of the statutory period. The statute makes all the provisions deemed necessary for quieting possessions of a corporeal nature, thereby removing these cases from the operation of the common law. Conclusive presumption of title to an incorporeal hereditament is afforded by twenty years' adverse, exclusive, undisturbed possession.[1]

See DEMESNE, Seized, etc.; DISTURBANCE; EJECTMENT; GRANT, 1.

HEREDITARY. 1. Subject to inheritance, q. v.

2. Transmitted to descendants: as, hereditary insanity, q. v.

HEREIN. May refer to the section, the chapter, or the entire enactment in which it is used.[2]

HEREINBEFORE. Compare ANTE.

In the clause, in a will, "I give . . to the persons, societies and corporations to whom I have hereinbefore made bequests . . . " means, as the same now is or exists.[3]

HERESY. See RELIGION.

HERETOFORE. In time past,[4] See JURY, Trial by.

HERIOT.[5] A render of the best beast or other good (as the custom may be) to the lord on the death of the tenant of a copyhold estate.[6]

Also called "heriot-custom." "Heriot-service" was, substantially, a rent due upon a special reservation in a grant or lease of lands.[7]

HERITABLE. See INHERITANCE.

HERMENEUTICS. "Legal hermeneutics" are the rules, as a system, for discovering the meaning of written language.[8]

HIDALGO. See PUEBLO.

HIDE. See ABSCOND; CONCEAL.

HIDES. See FUR.

HIGH. Elevated above another; superior; supreme.

In some connections, the use is pleonastic.

1. Having authority to preserve the peace within a district larger than some other's; opposed to petty: as, a high constable, q. v.

2. Supreme: above others: as, high court.

3. The more heinous: as, high crimes and misdemeanors, q. v.

4. Uninclosed; below low water-mark: as, the high sea, q. v. See also WATER-MARK.

5. Charged with the largest executive functions: as, high sheriff, q. v.

6. Directed against the government: as, high treason; opposed to petty treason. See TREASON.

7. Belonging to, or for use by, the public at large: as, in highway. See WAY.

Highest. 1. Superior to any other: as, the highest bid, q. v.

2. The most scrupulous: as, the highest good faith, q. v.

HILARY. See TERM, 4.

HINDER. To "hinder and delay" creditors is to do something which is an attempt to defraud them; to put some obstacle in the path, or interpose some time, unjustifiably, before the creditor can realize what is owed him out of the debtor's property.[1]

The hindering and delaying which vitiates an assignment is such as is sought through covin or malice on the part of the debtor for his benefit. The fraudulent intent is a question of fact.[2] See CONVEYANCE, Fraudulent; DELAY.

HIRING. A contract for the use of personalty, or for services. A species of bailment for a price or recompense.

1. As to things. A contract whereby the possession and a transient property is transferred for a particular time or use, on condition to restore the goods as soon as the time is expired or the use performed, together with the price, expressly agreed upon or left to he implied by law according to the value of the service.[3]

The hirer acquires a temporary property in the thing, accompanied with an implied condition to use it with moderation; while the owner or lender retains a reversionary interest in the thing, and acquires a new property in the price or reward. Of such is the loan of money on interest.[3]

2. As to services. The contracts classed under this head are contracts for work, for

---

[1] Cornett v. Rhudy, 80 Va. 712–14 (1885), cases.

[2] See State ex rel. Smiley v. Glenn, 7 Heisk. 485, 475, 480 (1872).

[3] Wetmore v. Parker, 52 N. Y. 464 (1873).

[4] Andrews v. Thayer, 40 Conn. 157 (1873); 13 N. Y. 427, 458; 1 N. J. L. 272.

[5] A. S. heregeatu, military apparel.

[6] 2 Bl. Com. 97.

[7] 2 Bl. Com. 421–25.

[8] See Lieber, Leg. & Pol. Herm.

---

[1] Burnham v. Brennan, 42 N. Y. Super. 63 (1877), Curtis, C. J.: 74 N. Y. 597 (1878).

[2] Burr v. Clement, 9 Col. 8–10 (1885), cases.

[3] [2 Bl. Com. 453. See 2 Kent, 456; Story, Bailm. § 359; 24 Am. Law Reg. 238–43 (1886), cases.

the safe-keeping of personalty, and for the carriage of persons or personalty.

"Storage" and "carriage" are in more common use than any inflections of hire, to designate a contract for the custody of ordinary merchandise, or for the transportation of persons or property.[1]

The idea of "hiring" may be involved in "employment," but its application is not restricted to any particular mode of use.[2]

See BAILMENT; DEPOSIT, 1; LOCATIO.

HISTORIES. See BOOK.

Historical facts, of general and public notoriety, may be proved by reputation; and that reputation may be established by historical works of known character and accuracy. But evidence of this sort is confined in a great measure to ancient facts, which do not presuppose better evidence in existence; and where, from the nature of the transaction, or the remoteness of the period, or the public and general reception of the facts, a just foundation is laid for general confidence. The work of a living author who is within reach of process is not of this nature. He may be called as a witness, and examined as to the sources and accuracy of his information. If the facts are of recent date, and within the knowledge of many persons living, from whom he derived his materials, his book is not the best evidence.[3]

HITHERTO. Restrains the meaning of a phrase to a period of time then elapsed.[4]

HOC. See under H.

HODGE-PODGE. See HOTCHPOT.

HOE. See WEAPON, Deadly.

HOG. Hogs are "cattle," within the meaning of a guaranty of drafts against shipments of "cattle."[5]

And also within a statute requiring fencing to protect lands from "straying cattle."[6]

Hogs are "swine;" and the word "hog" will also include a "sow."[7]

In a statute punishing larceny, the live animal or its carcass may be meant;[8] and the word will describe a pig four or five months old.[9]

See ANIMAL; CATTLE.

HOLD. 1. To decide, adjudge, decree.

Whence *held*, decided, ruled, adjudged: as, the court "held" the evidence admissible, or the defendant not liable. In head-notes to reports of cases, follows the statement of the facts and introduces the decision of the court thereon.

2. To deduce as a rule or principle; to maintain on the strength of decided cases: as, the authorities "hold" so and so.

3. To assert, declare, maintain; to occupy the position of propounding as a fact or as law: as, the plaintiff "holds" the affirmative of the issue. See BURDEN, Of proof.

4. To cause to be bound or obligated; to confine or restrain: as, "to hold him to his contract," "the obligor is held and firmly bound," "persons held to service;" "hold" and "held to bail," or "for court," or "for trial." Compare BIND.

5. To sit for a specified purpose; to sit to administer justice: as, to "hold court," "hold pleas;" to "hold an election;" to "hold a hearing" or "session."

6. To possess by virtue of a lawful title: as, "hold a note" or "bond;" "hold lands" or "property," "to have and to hold" described premises; "hold office;" "hold" a fund, or lien, a policy of insurance, a share, stakes, stocks, etc. Compare TENURE.

Whence also free*hold*, lease*hold*.

"Holding," relating to ownership in property, embraces two ideas: actual possession of some subject of property, and being invested with the legal title. It may be applied to anything the subject of property, in law or in equity.[1]

Under an act forbidding a foreign corporation to "acquire and hold" land, a conveyance is not necessarily void. The holding may be subject to the right of escheat.[2]

Holder. One who has possession of anything. One who possesses by virtue of a lawful title:

As, a bondholder, fundholder, lienholder, officeholder, property holder, policy-holder, shareholder, stakeholder, stockholder, qq. v.

Holder in good faith; holder for value; innocent holder. He is a holder of negotiable paper or bonds for value, who pays real, in contradistinction from apparent, value, without notice of any fraud or illegality affecting the instrument.[3]

---

[1] [1 Abbott's Law Dict. 565.

[2] Hightower v. State, 72 Ga. 484 (1884).

[3] Morris v. Lessee of Harmer's Heirs, 7 Pet. *558 (1833), Story, J. See 1 Greenl. Ev. § 497; 1 Whart. Ev. §§ 664, 338.

[4] Mason v. Jones, 13 Barb. 479 (1852).

[5] First Nat. Bank of Decatur v. Home Savings Bank of St. Louis, 21 Wall. 299 (1874).

[6] Child v. Hearn, L. R., 9 Ex. 181 (1874).

[7] Rivers v. State, 10 Tex. Ap. 179 (1881).

[8] Whitson v. Culbertson, 7 Ind. 195 (1855); Hunt v. State, 55 Ala. 140 (1876); Reed v. State, 16 Fla. 564 (1878).

[9] Lavender v. State, 60 Ala. 60 (1877).

---

[1] Witsell v. Charleston, 7 S. C. 99 (1875). See also Godfrey v. Godfrey, 17 Ind. 9 (1861); Hurst v. Hurst, 7 W. Va. 297 (1874); Runyan v. Coster, 14 Pet. 120 (1840); 39 N. J. E. 547.

[2] Hickory Farm Oil Co. v. Buffalo, &c. R. Co., 32 F. R. 22 (1887); Runyan v. Lessee of Coster, 14 Pet. 128 (1840).

[3] Montclair Township v. Ramsdell, 107 U. S. 161, 159 (1882), Harlan, J.; Story, Prom. Notes, § 195; Byles, Bills, 117, 119, 124.

If any previous holder of bonds in suit was a *bona fide* holder for value, the plaintiff, without showing that he himself paid value, can avail himself of the position of such previous holder.[1]

See further BEARER; CHECK; FAITH, Good; NEGOTIATE, 2.

Holding over; hold over. (1) Retaining possession of premises after a lease has expired, and without fresh leave from the owner.

Such tenant holds "at sufferance," and his estate is destroyed when the owner makes actual entry, or gives notice to quit. Being once in possession, the law supposes a continuance authorized. The tenant may be required to account for profits made.[2] See DETAINER, 2; ENTRY, I, 1; QUIT, 2.

(2) Continuing to exercise the functions of an office after the end of one's term, and before a successor is qualified.

In many cases statutes, and in others common-law rules, to prevent an interregnum in an office, authorize the incumbent to continue to serve until a successor has been regularly qualified. See VACANCY.

HOLIDAY. A secular day on which the law exempts all persons from the performance of contracts for labor or other personal service, from attendance at court, and from attention to legal proceedings.

Legal or **public holidays** are appointed by statute law, or are authorized by custom having the force of law. These are New Year's day, Washington's birthday, Decoration day, Independence day, Thanksgiving day, Christmas day; in some States good Friday; general election days; and other days appointed by the President or the governor of the State for thanksgiving, fasting, or other observance.

On these days public business is suspended, and the presentment and protest of paper is excused, as on Sunday. Falling on Sunday, the Monday succeeding is generally observed; paper becoming due on such Monday is payable on the Saturday preceding. Paper due on Decoration day or Good Friday is generally payable on the secular day next previous thereto.[3]

The observance of a holiday binds no man's conscience. It is his privilege to labor or not, as he prefers.[4]

The expression "legal holiday" of itself imports a *dies non juridicus*[5] See SUNDAY.

HOLOGRAPH.[1] An instrument written entirely in the hand of one person, as, by a grantor, or testator. Spelled also **olograph.** Whence holographic, and olographic.[2]

An olographic will being "one that is entirely written, dated, and signed by the hand of the deceased," a will partly written upon a printed form is not such.[3] Opposed, *dictated* will.

Generally speaking, holograph wills require no attestation.[4]

HOMAGE. See ALLEGIANCE; FEUD.

HOME. While children "remain at home," in a will, may refer to the household of which the testator was head.[5] See HOUSEHOLD.

Where a person takes up his abode, without any present intention to remove therefrom permanently.[6] See further ABODE; DOMICIL; HOUSE; RESIDENCE.

Homestall. In ancient law, a mansion house.[7]

"Stall" and "stead" were Anglo-Saxon for place, seat, fixed spot, station.

Homestead. The home-stall, home-place.

The dwelling-house, at which the family resides, with the usual and customary appurtenances, including outbuildings of every kind necessary and convenient for family use, and lands used for the purposes thereof.[8] Whence *homesteader.*

In its popular sense, whatever is used, being either necessary or convenient, as a place of residence for the family, as contradistinguished from a place of business.[9]

Sometimes used as a verb; as, he "homesteaded his pre-emption."[10]

Homestead laws. Constitutional or stat-

---

[1] Montclair Township v. Ramsdell, *ante.*

[2] See 2 Bl. Com. 150; 3 *id.* 210; Pickard v. Kleis, 56 Mich. 604 (1885).

[3] See Penn. Acts 25 May, 1874, 12 April, 1869, 2 April, 1873; N. Y. Stat. 1873, c. 577.

[4] Richardson v. Goddard, 23 How. 43, 41 (1859).

[5] Lampe v. Manning, 38 Wis. 676 (1875); 14 Bank. Reg. 388.

[1] Gk. *holo-graphos,* wholly written.

[2] See La. Civ. Code, art. 1581; Code Civ. 970.

[3] Cal. Civ. Code, § 1277; *Re* Estate of Rand, 61 Cal. 468 (1882); 14 Rep. 716; 3 Woods, 77.

[4] See 3 Jarman, Wills (R. & T.), 767, note.

[5] Manning v. Woff, 2 Dev. & B., Eq. 12 (N. C. 1838).

[6] Warren v. Thomaston, 43 Me. 418 (1857); 3 *id.* 229; 15 *id.* 58; 19 *id.* 293; 35 Vt. 232.

[7] Dickinson v. Mayer, 11 Heisk. 521 (1872); 4 Bl. Com. 225.

[8] Gregg v. Bostwick, 33 Cal. 227 (1867), Sanderson, J.; Estate of Delaney, 37 *id.* 179 (1869); 4 *id.* 23; 16 *id.* 181.

See also 63 Ala. 238; 31 Ark. 468; 48 *id.* 236; 54 Ill. 175; 12 Kan. 257; 77 N. C. 384; 7 N. H. 245; 36 *id.* 166; 46 *id.* 52; 51 *id.* 266; 63 *id.* 428; 6 Tex. 102; 23 *id.* 498; 48 *id.* 37; 28 Vt. 672; 46 *id.* 292; 1 Wash. R. P. 352.

[9] Gregg v. Bostwick, 33 Cal. 228, 226–27 (1867); *Re* Crowey, 71 *id.* 303 (1886).

[10] Timber Cases, 11 F. R. 81 (1881).

utory provisions for the exemption of a certain amount or value of realty, occupied by a person as his homestead, from a forced sale for the payment of his debts. In some States restraints are placed upon alienation by the owner, and in some the property descends to the widow and minor children free from liability for his debts. The estate is like an estate for life.[1]

It is settled: 1. That the object of the homestead law is to protect the family of the owner in the possession and enjoyment of the property. 2. That that construction must be given such laws which will best advance and secure their object. 3. To divest a homestead estate, there must be a literal compliance with the mode of alienation prescribed by statutes.[2]

While a very limited estate in the land, perhaps even a leasehold, may support a claim, some estate is essential.[3]

Where the "joint consent" of a husband and wife is essential to the alienation of a homestead, the better rule is to have it evidenced by their signatures to the same instrument, before the same officer, and in the presence of each other.[4]

The act of May 20, 1862, is the first homestead law of the general government. By it a quantity of land not exceeding 160 acres is given to any person who is the head of a family, or who is twenty-one, and a citizen or intends to become such, on condition of settlement, cultivation, and continuous occupancy as a home for the period of five years.[5] See ABANDON; OWNER.

HOMICIDE.[6] The killing of any human creature.[7]

A generic term, embracing every mode by which the life of one man is taken by the act of another.[8]

Criminal homicide consists in the unlawful taking by one human being of the life of another in such a manner that he dies within a year and a day from the time of the giving of the mortal wound.[1]

If committed with malice, express or implied, it is murder; if without malice, manslaughter. The injury must continue to affect the body of the victim till death. If death ensues from another cause, no murder or manslaughter has been committed. The person who unlawfully sets the means of death in motion, whether through an irresponsible instrument or agent, or in the body of the victim, is the guilty cause of the death at the time and place at which his unlawful act produces its fatal result.[1]

Homicidal. Involving or directed toward the killing of a fellow man: as, homicidal intent, or monomania.

"Homicide," as a term, does not necessarily import crime: it includes acts which are crimes. The distinctions denoted by "fratricide," "matricide," "parricide," "patricide," "regicide," "sororicide," are not observed in law. But "prolicide," destroying offspring, "fœticide," killing an unborn child, "infanticide," killing an infant soon after its birth, and "suicide," killing one's self, are employed in senses which involve, more or less, commission of crime.

Killing is justifiable, excusable, or felonious.

Justifiable homicide. When a life is taken in the performance of a duty or the exercise of a right.

This is (1) owing to some unavoidable necessity, without any will, intention, or design, and without any inadvertence or negligence in the party killing, and is, therefore, without blame. Or, it is (2) for the advancement of public justice — by permission: as, where an officer kills a person who resists lawful arrest; where one kills a person charged with felony; killing in dispersing a riot, or by a jailer to prevent an escape. In these cases there must be an apparent necessity. Of this character, also, is killing in war; and so were deaths in trials by battle. To this grade likewise belong killings to prevent forcible or atrocious crimes: as, robbery, murder, burglary, arson; but not mere larceny from the person, nor house-breaking in the day-time. A husband or father may kill for attempted rape,[2] — *flagrante crimine.*

Where one in defense of his person, habitation, or property kills another, who manifestly intends and endeavors by violence or surprise to commit a forcible or atrocious felony, such killing is justifiable homicide. In that case, also, the justification must depend upon the circumstances as they appear to the prisoner.[3]

Excusable homicide. When a life is lost by an accident in the lawful doing of a proper act, or is taken to prevent death or grievous injury to another person.

---

[1] See Barney v. Leeds, 51 N. H. 261 (1871); Fink v. O'Neil, 106 U. S. 275 (1882); 10 Am. Law Reg. 641-56, 705-17 (1862), cases; 20 id. 1-17, 137-50 (1871), cases,— as to the Southern States; Thompson, Homest, &c. § 1; 4 Cal. 26, 33; 33 id. 226; 11 Ga. 89; 1 Iowa, 439; 18 Tex. 415; 34 Wis. 657; 61 id. 374; 102 U. S. 321; 1 Bouvier, Law Dict. 754.

[2] Howell v. McCrie, 36 Kan. 644 (1887), cases, Simpson, Commissioner.

[3] Myrick v. Bill, 3 Dak. 292 (1884), cases.

[4] Howell v. McCrie, 36 Kan. 645 (1887).

[5] R. S. §§ 2289-2317; Seymour v. Sanders, 3 Dill. 441 (1874). Waiving the right, Linkenhoker's Heirs v. Detrick, 81 Va. 44, 56 (1885), cases.

[6] F. *homicide,* manslaughter: L. *homicidium;* or, a man-killer: L. *homicida: homo,* a man; *cædere,* to kill.

[7] 4 Bl. Comm. 177.

[8] Commonwealth v. Webster, 5 Cush. 303 (1850), Shaw, C. J.

---

[1] Commonwealth v. Macloon, 101 Mass. 6-8 (1869), cases, Gray, J.

[2] 4 Bl. Com. 178-82.

[3] Parrish v. Commonwealth, 81 Va. 1, 14-16 (1884), cases. See in general, 26 Am. Law Reg. 706-8 (1887), cases; committed from necessity, 1 Law Quar. Rev. 51-61 (1885).

This is (1) by misadventure, where a man doing a lawful act without intention to hurt, unfortunately kills another: as, where the head of a hatchet flies off and kills a by-stander; where a parent, teacher, or officer causes death from moderate punishment of a child, or of a criminal. The act is in itself lawful; the effect is accidental. This species of homicide is to be distinguished from manslaughter. Or, it is (2) in self-defense, upon a sudden affray, and with no avenue of escape from manifest danger to life or great bodily harm.[1]

Felonious homicide. Killing a human creature, of any age or sex, without justification or excuse.[2]

The killing may be of one's self or of another person. When without malice, the crime is manslaughter; when with malice, murder.[2]

See further DEFENSE, 1; INSANITY, 2 (6); MALICE; MANSLAUGHTER; MURDER; PROVOCATION; RETREAT; SUICIDE; THREAT.

HOMO. L. A human being; man, a man; a person.

Literally, a creature of the earth — *humus*. Derivatives: homage, homicide.

De homine replegiando. For replevying a man. See REPLEVIN, 2.

Liber homo. A free man; also, in Roman law, a freedman.

Liber et legalis homo. A free (good) and lawful person: a juror, who was to be neither a bondsman nor infamous.[3]

Novus homo. A new man; a man pardoned of crime.

HOMOLOGATE.[4] To say the like.[5]

Homologation. Approbation; confirmation; ratification, whether by a party or a court.

In use in civil and Scotch law.

HONESTE VIVERE. See LAW.

HONESTY. When a transaction is as compatible with honesty as with dishonesty, the former is always presumed.[6]

A person who keeps in his employ a servant found to be dishonest cannot have recourse to the guarantor of the servant's integrity for a loss occurring during subsequent service.[7] See CONSCIENCE; EQUITY; FAITH; TRUST, 1.

HONOR. *v,* 1. To accept a bill of exchange, or to pay a promissory note, according to its tenor.

Dishonor. To neglect or refuse to accept or pay commercial paper when due. See further DISHONOR.

Act of honor. An instrument drawn by a notary, after a bill has been protested, or on behalf of a friend of the maker, who wishes to protect the maker's credit, by an acceptance. See PROTEST, 2, Supra, etc.

2, *n.* A term of respect given, in the course of address, to persons occupying the higher judicial positions: as, "his honor," "your honor," "their honors;" also, "honorable court."

HONORARIUM. L. A gift for services rendered.

A voluntary donation, in consideration of services which admit of no compensation in money; in particular, a donation to an advocate at law, who was deemed to practice for honor and influence, and not for fees.[1] See FEE, 2.

HOOK. "To hook" may not be equivalent to "to steal."[2]

HORN-BOOK. A name formerly given to an elementary treatise upon any subject.

Horn-book law. Elementary or rudimentary law.

A "horn-book" was originally a sheet containing the alphabet, mounted on wood and protected with transparent horn, or simply pasted on a slice of horn.[3]

HORSE. A generic term, including, ordinarily, the different species of the animal, however diversified by age, sex, or artificial means.[4]

In a given connection may not include a "gelding, mare, or colt."[4]

In an action against a railroad company for damages for killing a "horse," an amendment of the complaint describing the animal as a "mare" does not introduce a new cause of action.[5]

An "ass" or "jackass" may be considered as a horse, within the meaning of an exemption law.[6]

So may a "mule" be, within a statute giving a remedy for injuries to "horses and cattle" by a railroad company.[7]

---

[1] 4 Bl. Com. 182–88.

[2] 4 Bl. Com. 188–201.

[3] 3 Bl. Com. 340, 362.

[4] Gk. *homologein*, to assent, agree; *homos*, the same; *log-, leg-,* to speak.

[5] Syndics *v.* Gardenier, 9 Mart. o. s. 546 (1821).

[6] Chapman *v.* McIlwrath, 77 Mo. 44 (1882).

[7] Roberts *v.* Donovan, 70 Cal. 110 (1886); Brandt, Sure. § 368.

---

[1] McDonald *v.* Napier, 14 Ga. 105 (1853); 3 Bl. Com. 28; 19 Pa. 95; Weeks. Atty's, 536.

[2] Hays *v.* Mitchell, 7 Blackf. *117 (1844).

[3] See Ency. Britannica.

[4] Banks *v.* State, 28 Tex. 647 (1866); Taylor *v.* State, 44 Ga. 264 (1871); Owens *v.* State, 38 Tex. 557 (1873); Turley *v.* State, 3 Humph. 324 (1842); State *v.* Dunnavant, 3 Brev. 10 (S. C., 1811).

[5] South & North Ala. R. Co. *v.* Bees, 82 Ala. 342 (1886), cases.

[6] Richardson *v.* Duncan, 2 Heisk. 222 (1870); Ohio, &c. R. Co. *v.* Brubaker, 47 Ill. 463 (1868).

[7] Toledo, &c. R. Co. *v.* Cole, 50 Ill. 186 (1869); Brown *v.* Bailey, 4 Ala. 413 (1842).

A colt may be exempt as a "horse" or as a "work-beast," if the debtor has nothing more nearly answering the description of a horse.[1]

A "span of horses" means two horses which may be connected together or united for the purposes of a team. A colt four months old is not exempt from sale on execution, as forming with its dam a "span of horses," within the meaning of a statute.[2]

But an uncastrated colt two years old is not a "stallion."[3]

A stallion, not kept for farm work, is not a "horse" exempt from execution.[4]

A horse not broken to harness may still be a "work-horse" — an animal of the horse kind fit for service.[5]

The exemption of a horse from execution may include everything essential to its beneficial use, as, a bridle, a saddle, etc.[6]

See ANIMAL; BATTERY; CATTLE; DECEIT; GENTLE; HEALTH, Boards of; HIRING; IMPLEMENTS; LIVERY-STABLE; MANAGEABLE; SOUND, 2 (2); TEAM; WARRANTY, 2.

Horse-racing. See GAME, 2.

Horse-railway. See RAILROAD.

HORTICULTURE. See AGRICULTURE.

HOSPITAL. See CHARITY, 2.

HOSTELER. See HOTEL; INN.

HOSTILE. See EMBARGO; ENEMY; POSSESSION. Adverse.

HOTCHPOT.[7] Blending properties belonging to two or more persons in order to make an equal division.

Also spelled hodge-podge, hotch-potch, hotspot.

As, where advancements (*q. v.*) are treated as returned, and the estate as a whole divided anew.

"Hotch-pot meant, originally, a pudding: for in a pudding is put one thing with other things."[8]

By this metaphor our ancestors meant that lands in partition among co-parceners, given in frank-marriage, and lands descending in fee-simple, should be mixed or blended together, and then divided in equal portions among all the daughters of their ancestor.

. . An incident to an estate is co-parcenary. If, to advance a daughter in marriage, an estate-tail in lands was given her, and afterward lands descended from the donor to her and her sisters in fee-simple, she had no share in the latter unless she agreed to divide her advancement in equal proportion with the lands so

descended. Hereby two sorts of lands were mixed and then divided equally.[1]

HOTEL. What in France was known as a *hotelerie*,[2] and in England as a common "inn" of the superior class found in cities and large towns.[3] See INN; TAVERN.

HOUMAS GRANTS. Certain grants of land in Louisiana; as to the history of which see the case cited hereto.[4]

HOUR. See BUSINESS; DAY; SERVICE, 1; TIME.

HOUSE. 1. A dwelling-house; a building divided into floors and apartments, with four walls, a roof, doors, and chimneys.

But not necessarily precisely this.[5]

Involves the ideas of an edifice or structure, and the abode or residence of human beings.

Criminal statutes constantly use "house" as equivalent to "building." A term indicating the particular purpose to which a building is applied may be prefixed; as in state-house, court-house, school-house. In "out-house," buildings that are not dwellings, but merely appendages to some dwelling, are included. When a dwelling is meant, "dwelling-house" or "mansion-house" is usually and properly employed.[6]

While "house" is broader than "dwelling-house," it is narrower than "building."[7]

Does not necessarily mean a whole building; is often applied to a separate apartment.[8,7]

May mean "messuage" — land and structure; as in a will, and in statutes exempting property from taxation.[9]

The law of England has so particular and tender a regard to the immunity of a man's house that it styles it his "castle" and will not suffer it to be violated with impunity. Whence the aphorism, "every man's house is his castle." For this reason, no outside door can, in general, be broken open to execute civil process; though, in criminal causes, the public safety supersedes private. Hence, also, in part, arises the

---

[1] Winfrey v. Zimmerman, 8 Bush, 588 (1871); Mallory v. Berry, 16 Kan. 295 (1876). Compare Carruth v. Grassie, 11 Gray, 211 (1858); Johnson v. Babcock, 8 Allen, 583 (1864).

[2] Ames v. Martin, 6 Wis. *362 (1858).

[3] Aylesworth v. Chicago, &c. R. Co., 30 Iowa, 460 (1870).

[4] Robert v. Adams, 38 Cal. 383 (1869); Allman v. Gann, 29 Ala. 242 (1856).

[5] Noland v. Wickham, 9 Ala. 171 (1846); Winfrey v. Zimmerman, 8 Bush, 588 (1871).

[6] Cobbs v. Coleman, 14 Tex. 598 (1855); Dearborn v. Phillips, 21 *id.* 451 (1858).

[7] F. *hochepot*, shake-pot; a medley,— Skeat.

[8] Littleton, §§ 267, 55; 3 Coke, Litt. ch. 12.

[1] 2 Bl. Com. 190-91, 517. See Comer v. Comer, 119 Ill. 179 (1886).

[2] From *hostel*, Latin *hospes*, a stranger who lodged at the house of another; also, the master of a house who entertains travelers or guests.

[3] Cromwell v. Stephens, 2 Daly, 21 (1867), Daly, F. J.; *ib.* 200; 54 Barb. 316; 4 Duer, 116; 33 Cal. 557.

[4] Slidell v. Grandjean, 111 U. S. 412 (1884).

[5] Daniel v. Coulsting, 49 E. C. L. *125 (1845), Tindal, C. J.; Surman v. Darley, 14 Me. & W. 185 (1845); 2 Man. & R. 514; 8 Barn. & C. 461; 1 Car. & K. 533.

[5] State v. Powers, 36 Conn. 79 (1869), Parke, J.; 4 Bl. Com. 221, 224; 7 Biss. 271.

[7] State v. Garity, 46 N. H. 62 (1865).

[8] Quinn v. People, 71 N. Y. 563-74 (1878), cases; Commonwealth v. Bulman, 118 Mass. 456 (1875).

[9] Rogers v. Smith, 4 Pa. 101 (1846); McMillan v. Solomon, 42 Ala. 358 (1868); Council of Richmond v. State, 5 Ind. 337 (1854); Trinity Church v. Boston, 118 Mass. 165 (1875).

animadversion of the law upon eavesdropping, nuisances, incendiaries; and for this reason a man may assemble people together lawfully, to protect and defend his house.[1]

A man may defend his house even to the taking of life, if apparently necessary to prevent persons from forcibly entering it against his will, and when warned not to enter and to desist from the use of force. But the law does not sanction taking life to prevent a mere trespass upon real estate.[2] See DOMUS, SUA, etc.

A landlord might not formerly break open a house to make a distress; that would be a breach of the peace. But when he was once in the house, he might break open an inner door.[3] See *Mansion-house.*

Ancient house. A house which has stood for twenty years.

In England, such house acquires a prescriptive right to support from the adjoining soil. In the United States, as a rule, each land-owner has a right to the support of his ground in its natural state from the adjoining land, but not for buildings.[4] See SUPPORT, 2.

House-breaking. Breaking and entering the dwelling-house of another with intent to commit a felony therein, irrespective of the time of day. Compare BURGLARY.

Household. A family; also, pertaining or appropriate to a house or family: as, household furniture, goods, stuff. See FURNITURE.

Persons who dwell together as a family.[5]

Household goods. Articles of a permanent nature, not consumed in their enjoyment, that are used, purchased or otherwise acquired by a person for his house.[6]

Not then, such articles as potatoes, bacon, vinegar, and salt, especially when held for sale or barter.[6]

Householder. The head of a household; the person who has charge of, and provides for, a family or household.[7] See EXEMPTION; FAMILY.

In a statute requiring jurors to be householders, means something more than occupant of a room or house; implies the idea of a domestic establishment, of the management of a household.[1]

House of correction. A prison for the confinement, after conviction, of paupers who refused to work, and vagrants.

Established in the reign of Elizabeth.[2]

For idle and disorderly persons, parents of bastards, beggars, servants who run away, trespassers, rogues, vagabonds, spendthrifts, and the like.[3]

House of ill-fame. A brothel or bawdy-house.

A synonym for "bawdy-house." Has no reference to the fame of the place, but denotes the fact; proof of the fact may be aided by proof of the fame.[4]

Such resorts are public nuisances: they draw lewd persons, endanger the peace, and corrupt the manners.[5]

A flat-boat may be kept as such a house.[6]

A house of prostitution is a constant menace to the good order of the community. It is a nuisance and the keeping of it a misdemeanor at common law. Its suppression, with punishment, are proper subjects of police regulation. In one form or another the authority to prohibit and suppress is given to cities and towns.[7]

See further FAME, Ill-fame; BAWDY-HOUSE; LEWD; PATRONIZE.

House of refuge. A public institution for the confinement of incorrigible youth.

Mansion-house. In the law of burglary, a dwelling-house.

If a house, stable, or warehouse be parcel of the mansion-house, and within the same common fence, though not under the same roof or contiguous, a burglary may be committed therein; for the capital house protects and privileges all its branches or appurtenances, if within the curtilage or home-stall. A chamber in a college is the mansion-house of the owner. So also is a room or lodging in any private house the mansion, for the time being, of the lodger, if the owner does not dwell in the house, or if he and the lodger enter by different doors. But a tent or booth is not a mansion-house: the law regards thus highly nothing but permanent edifices.[8]

Public-house. (1) "Public" may be applied to a house, either on account of the proprietorship, as, a court-house, which belongs

---

[1] 4 Bl. Com. 223. See also 3 Kan. Law J. 294, 314 (1886) — Chic. Leg. Adv.

[2] Davison v. People, 90 Ill. 229 (1878).

[3] 3 Bl. Com. 11. See particularly Semayne's Case, 5 Rep. 91 (1605): 1 Sm. L. C. (H. & W.) 228; Curtis v. Hubbard, 4 Hill, 437 (1842); Nash v. Lucas, L. R., 2 Q. B. *593 (1867).

[4] See 2 Kent, 437.

[5] Arthur v. Morgan, 112 U. S. 499 (1884), Blatchford, J., defining household effects subject to duty under R. S. § 2505.

[6] [Smith v. Findley, 34 Kan. 316, 328 (1885), Horton, Chief Justice.

[7] Griffin v. Sutherland, 14 Barb. 458 (1852); Bowne v. Witt, 19 Wend. 475 (1838); Woodward v. Murray, 18 Johns. *402 (1820); 52 Ala. 161; 6 Bush, 429; 15 B. Mon. 447; 110 Ill. 533; 57 Miss. 288; 2 Tex. Ap. 448.

[1] Aaron v. State, 37 Ala. 113 (1861); 21 *id.* 261; 17 *id.* 482; 6 Baxt. 522.

[2] 3 Steph. Com. 225; 4 Bl. Com. 370, 377.

[3] Tomlin; Laws, Prov. of Penn. (1682).

[4] State v. Smith, 29 Minn. 195 (1882); 28 Mich. 213; 29 Wis. 435; 38 Tex. 603; 1 Bish. Cr. L. § 1088; 2 Whart. Cr. L. § 1451.

[5] Cadwell v. State, 17 Conn. 471 (1846); State v. Main, 31 *id.* 574 (1863); McAlister v. Clark, 33 *id.* 92 (1865); State v. Garing, 74 Me. 153 (1882); Commonwealth v. Lavonsair, 132 Mass. 3 (1882).

[6] State v. Mullen, 35 Iowa, 207 (1872).

[7] Rogers v. People, 9 Col. 452 (1886), Helm, J.

[8] 4 Bl. Com. 224–26.

to the county, or from the purposes for which it is used, as, a tavern, a store-house, or a house for retailing liquors.[1]

Statutes against gaming in "public-houses" have particularly in view houses that are public on account of the uses to which they are put. Whether any specified house is public is a question of law, although the general question whether a place is public may be a question of fact.[1] Compare PLACE, Public.

(2) An hotel or inn, qq. v.

See BAY-WINDOW; CLEARING; CURTILAGE; DISORDERLY; DOMICIL; DWELLING; FAMILY; FINISHED; FLOOR; GRANT, 2; HEALTH; HEIRLOOM; INCIDENT; LAND; MESSUAGE; NUISANCE; SEARCH; SERVANT, 1. Compare DOMUS.

2. A body of persons organized for the performance of business or duties of a public nature; in particular, a legislative assembly, or a branch thereof.

May mean the entire number of members;[2] or merely the members present doing business.[3]

House of Commons, or of Lords. See PARLIAMENT.

House of Representatives. See ASSEMBLY; CONGRESS.

Lower House. The popular branch of a legislature; the house of representatives. *Upper House.* The Senate.

HUCKSTER. Compare HAWKER.

HUE-AND-CRY.[4] In old common law, pursuing, with horn and voice, felons and such as dangerously wounded another.

Statute of 13 Edw. I (1286), c. 1-4, directed that every county should be so well kept, that immediately upon felonies being committed, fresh suit should be made from town to town and from county to county, and that *hue and cry* should be raised upon the felons, and that they that kept the town should follow with hue and cry with all the town and the towns near, until the fugitives were taken. . By statute of 27 Eliz. (1585), c. 13, no hue and cry was sufficient unless made with both horsemen and footmen. . . The whole district was liable to be amerced, according to the law of Alfred, if a felon escaped. Hue and cry could be raised either by the precept of a justice, or by a peace-officer, or by any private man who knew that a felony had been committed. The party raising it

communicated all the circumstances he knew as to the crime and the person of the felon.[1]

HUMANE SOCIETIES. See CRUELTY.

HUNDRED. A civil division of a county.

Consisted of ten tithings. So called, because it was equal to a hundred hides of land; or because it furnished one hundred men in time of war.[2]

Hundredor. An inhabitant of a hundred; also, a qualified juryman within a hundred; and, also, the executive officer of a hundred.[2]

HUNG. Is sometimes applied to a jury which fails to agree upon a verdict.

HURDLE. In old English law, a species of sledge, on which traitors were drawn to the place of execution.[3] See TREASON.

HURON. See LAKES.

HUSBAND. A man who has a wife; a man legally bound in wedlock to a wife.

"Husband and wife" describes persons connected by the marriage tie, and the relation signifies those mutual rights and obligations which flow from the marriage contract.[4]

At *common law*, husband and wife are one person in law, and he is that person; that is, the legal existence of the woman is suspended or at least incorporated into that of the husband, under whose protection she performs everything. Hence, he cannot grant her anything, nor contract with her; but she can be his agent, and take a bequest from him. He must provide her with necessaries, or she can contract for them on his credit. He pays her ante-nuptial debts; such of her personalty as is in her possession, or as he reduces to possession, is his; likewise, the profits of her lands. Her estate is liable for his debts. She is sued and sues with him, unless he is civilly dead. They cannot give evidence for or against each other. He may chastise her moderately. Either one may have security of the peace against the other. For any crime, committed in his presence, except treason and murder, she is presumed to act by his coercion. The injuries to his rights are abduction, adultery, and beating.[5]

By the common law, her money and earnings belonged to him absolutely. The idea was that as he was bound to support the wife and the family, he was entitled to whatever she possessed or acquired. Such property then being absolutely his own, was subject to his disposal without regard to the necessities of the family, and might be taken in execution by his creditors.[6]

As, at common law, the personal property of the wife

[1] Shihagan v. State, 9 Tex. 431 (1853); 10 *id.* 275, 545; 12 Ala. 492; 19 *id.* 528; 20 *id.* 51; 27 *id.* 31, 47; 25 *id.* 78; 29 *id.* 40, 46; 30 *id.* 19, 524, 532, 550; 31 *id.* 371; 32 *id.* 596; 35 *id.* 390.

[2] *Re* Executive Communication, 12 Fla. 656 (1868).

[3] Southworth v. Palmyra, &c. R. Co., 2 Mich. 288 (1851); Green v. Weller, 32 Miss. 669 (1856); Frellsen v. Mahan, 21 La. An. 103 (1869).

[4] Hue: F. *huer*, to hoot, shout; or, to foot, *i. e.*, up foot and cry: run and cry after the felon, — Wood, Inst. 370. F. *cry de pais.*

[1] 4 Bl. Com. 293-94; 1 Steph. Hist. Cr. Law Eng. 187.

[2] 1 Bl. Com. 116; 3 *id.* 34, 161, 350; 4 *id.* 245, 294, 352, 411.

[3] 4 Bl. Com. 92, 376.

[4] People v. Hovey, 5 Barb. 118 (1849). See Hardy v. Smith, 136 Mass. 330 (1884).

[5] 1 Bl. Com. 442; 2 *id.* 433; 3 *id.* 139; 4 *id.* 28; Bank of America v. Banks, 101 U. S. 243 (1879).

[6] Jackson v. Jackson, 91 U. S. 124 (1875), Field, J.

passed to the husband upon marriage, she was deprived of this means of supporting her children, and all legal duties growing out of the marriage were imposed upon him. . . Even where the wife possesses separate property, it has been held, independently of statutory obligation, that she is not compelled to support the children of the marriage. See EARNINGS, Separate.[1]

She is always under his power. Hence, the disabilities and safeguards the law places around her. He is liable for her frauds, torts, and breaches of trust.[2] He, she, or both, may have a remedy for an injury to her person or reputation,[3]—the right of action in herself alone being given by statute.

Unless the existing claims of creditors are thereby impaired, his settlement of property upon her is valid. And he may now make the transfer directly to her, instead of through a third person.[4]

An ante-nuptial settlement upon her is valid, if the consideration is legal, and she is not a participant in a fraud intended upon creditors.[5] See SETTLE, 4.

A gift between them is invalid as against creditors.[6]

She is now the owner of her separate estate, as if a *feme sole*, in most of the States, the common-law rule having been greatly relaxed.[7]

But if she allows her money to go into his business, and be mixed with his property, and he uses it for purposes of credit, the property all becomes his and he cannot convey it back in fraud of creditors.[8] See SEPARATE, 2.

And her separate estate may be held for improvements which she permits him, being insolvent, to make to it.[9]

Either may act as agent for the other, with or without compensation; and the husband's creditors, where he so uses his skill without an agreement for remuneration, are not thereby defrauded.[10]

He has an action for enticing her away, even as against a parent. Proof of something done tending to prevent or dissuade her from living with him is necessary.[1]

She may sue a person who maliciously induces him to abandon her, for damages for the loss of support and of his society.[2] See CONSORTIUM.

Either person may prove the marriage collaterally. She cannot be compelled to incriminate him. In bigamy, the lawful wife cannot prove the marriage. Neither can testify as to a confidential communication, except by consent. Under enabling statutes, either may testify for or against the other. In suits by or against a stranger, they may contradict each other. In divorce proceedings, their testimony is closely scrutinized.[3]

In the Federal courts she is not a competent witness for or against him in a criminal case, on the score of public policy.[4]

See also ABANDON, 2 (1); ABDUCTION; ACKNOWLEDGMENT, 2; ADULTERY; BIGAMY; COERCION; COHABITATION; COMMUNICATION, Privileged, 1; CONDONATION; COVERT; CRUELTY, 1; CURTESY; DESERTION, 1; DISABILITY; DIVORCE; DOWER; DOWRY; ELOPEMENT; ENTIRETY; FAMILY; FEME; HEIR, 1; JOINTURE; KIN, Next of; MARRIAGE; NECESSARIES, 1; PARAPHERNALIA; PIN-MONEY; QUARANTINE, 1; RELATION, 3; RELICT; UNITY, 2; WHIPPING-POST; WIDOW; WIFE; WITNESS; WOMAN.

HUSBANDRY. See AGRICULTURE.

HUSH-MONEY. See BLACKMAIL.

HUSTINGS.[5] 1. A temporary court held for the election of members of parliament; also a court held in London before the lord mayor, recorder, and sheriffs, with jurisdiction over actions for the recovery of land within the city, except by ejectment.[6]

"Hustings (*hustengum*) is a court of common pleas held before the mayor and aldermen of London, and it is the highest court they have, for error or attaint lies there of a judgment or false verdict in the sheriff's court. . . Other cities and towns have had a court of the same name."[7]

2. A local court in Virginia.

The Hustings Court of the city of Richmond has exclusive original jurisdiction of all presentments, indictments and informations for offenses committed within the city (except prosecutions against convicts in the penitentiary), and concurrent jurisdiction of

---

[1] Gleason *v.* City of Boston, 144 Mass. 27 (1887).

[2] Trust Co. *v.* Sedgwick, 97 U. S. 308 (1877); 2 Kent, 149; 4 Saw. 603.

[3] Shaddock *v.* Clifton, 22 Wis. 110 (1867): 94 Am. Dec. 591–94 (1888), cases.

[4] Jones *v.* Clifton, 101 U. S. 225 (1879), cases; Clark *v.* Killian, 103 *id.* 766 (1880).

[5] Prewit *v.* Wilson, 103 U. S. 24 (1880), cases.

[6] Spelman *v.* Aldrich, 126 Mass. 117 (1879), cases.

[7] Radford *v.* Carwile, 13 W. Va. 576, 85 (1878), cases; Vail *v.* Vail, 49 Conn. 52 (1881), cases; McClellan *v.* Filson, 44 Ohio St. 190 (1886); 30 Am. Law Rev. 356 (1886).

[8] Humes *v.* Scruggs, 94 U. S. 27 (1876), cases. Her contracts, under statutes, 19 Am. Law Rev. 359–79 (1885), cases.

[9] 23 Cent. L. J. 293 (1886), cases.

[10] See generally, wife as husband's agent, 31 Alb. Law J. 206–7 (1885), cases; he as her agent, with compensation, 30 *id.* 444–45 (1885), cases; without compensation, King *v.* Voos, Sup. Ct. Oreg. (1887), cases; 26 Am. Law Reg. 246, 250–53 (1887), cases: 26 Cent. Law J. 259–62 (1888), cases. As to his carrying on business in her name, after she pays some bills, 26 Am. Law Reg. 781–84 (1887), cases.

---

[1] Bennett *v.* Smith, 21 Barb. 441 (1856); Modisett *v.* McPike, 74 Mo. 639 (1881). .

[2] Westlake *v.* Westlake, 34 Ohio St. 626–34 (1878), cases. Effect of abandonment on her power to contract, 20 Am. Law Reg. 745–53 (1887), cases.

[3] 1 Whart. Ev. §§ 421–33, cases; 1 Greenl. Ev. §§ 333–47, cases.

[4] United States *v.* Jones, 32 F. R. 569 (1887); *id.* 571, note. See generally 25 Am. Law Reg. 353–65, 417–31 (1886), cases.

[5] A. S. *husting*, a place of council: *hus*, house; *thing*, cause, council.

[6] See 3 Bl. Com. 80; 3 Steph. Com. 293, note.

[7] Termes de la Ley (1721).

cases with n a space of one mile around the city on the north of James river. Also exclusive jurisdiction of all appeals allowed by any State law, or ordinance of the city, from the judgments of the police justices courts, and of all causes removable from them; of proceedings for the condemnation, for public use, of lands, and of motions to correct erroneous assessments on realty; also, concurrent jurisdiction of actions for unlawful or forcible entry or detainer.[1]

HYDRAULIC MINING. See AQUA, Currit, etc.

HYGIENE. See ALCOHOL.

HYPOTHECATION.[2] In Roman law, a pledge without possession by the pledgee,—the possession remaining in the pledgor.[3]

A security whereby realty or personalty is appropriated or pledged for the discharge of a debt or engagement, with no transfer of property or of possession, the debt being viewed as tacked to and following the thing.[4]

There is no pure *hypotheca* in our law. Approaches to it are, bottomry bonds, maritime liens of material-men, and seaman's wages.[5]

Hypothecary; hypothecator. One who proposes and makes a contract of hypothecation.

Hypothecation bond. A bottomry or respondentia bond.

Evidences a marine hypothecation of a vessel or its cargo, for necessary repairs or supplies.[6]

The hypothecation of a vessel is authorized by the necessity of obtaining the means to prosecute the voyage, and inability to get the required funds in any other way.[7]

Established rules as to marine hypothecation are: 1. Liens for repairs and supplies, or for funds to pay for the same, are enforceable only upon proof that the same were necessary, or believed to be necessary. 2. Where proof is made of the necessity, and of credit given to the ship, a presumption arises of a necessity for the credit. 3. Necessity is proven when such circumstances of urgency are shown as would induce a prudent owner, if present, to order the repairs or supplies, or to provide funds for the cost on the security of the ship. 4. An order by the master is sufficient proof of such necessity to support an implied hypoth-

ecation in favor of a material-man or lender of money who acts in good faith. 5. To support an hypothecation by bottomry, evidence of actual necessity is required. If the fact of necessity is left unproved, evidence is required of due inquiry and of reasonable ground of belief that the necessity was real and exigent.[1]

If communication with the owner is practicable, that must first be had.[2]

Hypothecation bonds must be recorded by collectors of customs.[3] See BOTTOMRY; RESPONDENTIA.

HYPOTHESIS.[4] In criminal practice, a theory proposed in explanation of the facts in a case, and to establish either guilt or innocence.

Hypothetical. Assumed for the purpose of inference or of opinion.

An hypothetical case consists of a statement of assumed facts intended to be propounded to an expert, in order to elicit his opinion. Thus, an expert in insanity may say whether a person, under indictment for murder, would be likely to be predisposed to emotional insanity, upon a statement of facts, admitted or assumed, supposed to exhibit his individual and family history. See *Dexter* v. *Hall*, EXPERT.

I.

I. As an abbreviation, is used for institutes, internal, Irish.

I. C. C. Inter-State commerce commission (reports).

I. e. (Usually *i. e.*) *Id est*, that is (to say).

I O U. "I owe you." A popular designation of a due-bill or memorandum of debt.

Consists of those letters, a sum of money, and the debtor's signature. As it contains no direct promise to pay, it is not a promissory note, but a mere acknowledgment of indebtedness.[5]

IB. See IDEM.

IBI. See RATIO, Ibi, est, etc.

IBID; IBIDEM. See IDEM.

ICE. Uncut, is an accession or increment to the land.[6]

A riparian proprietor upon an *unnavigable* stream, having title to the middle of the stream, owns the ice that forms over his half of the water.[6]

---

[1] See Code, 1887, § 3072.

[2] L. *hypotheca*: Gk. *hypo*, under; *tith-*, to place; to obligate, charge.

[3] See 2 Bl. Com. 159.

[4] See Herman, Mortgages, §§ 3, 1; Taylor *v.* Hudgins, 42 Tex. 247 (1875).

[5] [Story, Bailm., 9 ed., § 288; The Young Mechanic, 2 Curtis, 410 (1855).

[6] The Grapeshot, 9 Wall. 140–41 (1869), Chase, C. J.; The Julia Blake, 107 U. S. 418 (1882), cases, Waite, C. J.; 16 Blatch. 472.

[7] Delaware Mut. Safety Ins. Co. *v.* Gossler, 96 U. S. 648 (1877), cases; The Emily Souder, 17 Wall. 671, 669 (1873), cases.

[1] The Grapeshot, 9 Wall. 141–42 (1869), Chase, C. J.

[2] The Julia Blake, 16 Blatch. 484–85, 490–94 (1879), cases: 107 U. S. 432, *ante*.

[3] R. S. §§ 4192, 4382.

[4] Gk. *hypothesis*, a placing under: supposition.

[5] See 1 Daniel, Neg. Inst. § 36, cases; 1 Parsons, Notes, &c. 25; Story, Prom. Notes, 14; Smith *v.* Shelden, 35 Mich. 47 (1876).

[6] Washington Ice. Co. *v.* Shortall, 101 Ill. 54 (1881), See also Bigelow *v.* Shaw, Sup. Ct. Mich. (1887), cases; 34 Conn. 462; 33 Ind. 402; 8 Mich. 18; 30 N. Y. 519; 15 How. Pr. 376.

But he has no proprietary interest in ice that forms upon the water of a *navigable* stream adjacent to his own shore, unless he first takes and secures it.[1]

Since the owner of land bordering upon a flowing stream may use a reasonable quantity of the water, he may detain a reasonable portion until it freezes, and cut and sell the ice. But he may not interfere with the beneficial enjoyment of the water by owners below him.[2]

Ice *upon* a pond or stream is of such an ephemeral nature as to be more like personal than real property. It may be sold by parol as personalty.[3] See CAR-LOAD.

To thaw a neighbor's ice is an unlawful conversion of it.[4]

Ice fields upon navigable rivers must be so guarded that pedestrians will be protected against accident.[5]

As to the duty of removing ice from pavements, see SIDEWALK.

Ice-cream. See MANUFACTURER; SUNDAY.

ID. See IDEM; CERTUM; Is.

IDAHO. See TERRITORY, 2.

IDEM. L. The same.

Referring to a volume, the same series or set; also, the same book or page. Abbreviated *id.* Compare Is.

Ibidem. In the very same place: the same section, page, or book. Abbreviated *ibid., ib.*

Idem sonans. Sounding the same; substantially identical in sound.[6] Plural *idem sonantia.*

Applies to the names of persons substantially the same in sound, though different in spelling. In searches for liens, all spellings of a name which are pronounced alike are to be noted; and in pleadings, substantial identity in sound is generally sufficient.

Difference of meaning in the original language, as in the German, is not material. Appearance and sound, alone, are important. The initial being the same, allowance must be made for slight differences in the spelling — to which the eye will be directed. Then, a slight difference should put one on inquiry. But the rule does not apply to judgments entered in different initials from those which are usual in English: as, in Yoest for Joest.[7]

Examples of not fatal variances: Bupp and Bopp;[1] Charleston and Charlestown;[2] Heckman and Hackman;[3] Hutson and Hudsou;[4] Japheth and Japhath;[5] Jeffers and Jeffries;[6] Lewis and Louis;[7] Penryn and Pennyrine;[8] Ricketts, Rickets, and Ricket;[9] Shaffer and Shafer;[10] Woolley and Wolley.[11] Examples of fatal variances: Hanthorn and Hawthorn;[12] Spintz and Sprinz;[13] Whortman and Workman.[14]

A name need not be correctly spelled in an indictment. When substantially the same sound is preserved, variant orthography makes no difference.[15]

Whether one name sounds like another may be a question for a jury.[16]

If the two names, spelled differently, do not necessarily sound alike, the question whether they are *idem sonans* is one of fact for the jury.[17] See NAME, 1.

IDENTITY. Sameness.

1. In larceny, trover, detinue, and replevin, the thing in question must be identified; so in torts, for damage done to specific property; and so in all indictments where the taking of property is the gist. Identity of person must be proven in all criminal prosecutions.[18]

In the ordinary case of buying and selling for cash, the identity of the parties is entirely immaterial; and in many cases where that matter is material, a party is estopped by his dealing with the other from saying that he was mistaken as to the person.[19] See ARRAIGN; CONFUSION, Of goods; DESCRIPTION; NAME.

2. Property transferred in fraud of creditors may be subjected to the payment of their claims upon identification of the property; as, in the case of personalty given to a wife.[20]

One who obtains property by fraud acquires no title to it, but he and all transferees with notice are trustees for the original owner, who may recover the property as long as it can be traced and identified in its

---

[1] Wood *v.* Fowler, 26 Kan. 690 (1882), cases: 14 Rep. 267.

[2] Myer *v.* Whitaker, 15 Abb. N. C. 176 (1878), cases; Stevens *v.* Kelley, 78 Me. 450 (1886), cases: 35 Alb. Law J. 42–3 (1887), cases.

[3] Higgins *v.* Kusterer, 41 Mich. 322 (1879): 32 Am. Rep. 164–68 (1880), cases.

[4] Aschermann *v.* Best Brewing Co., 45 Wis. 266 (1878). As to value, when unlawfully replevied, see Washington Ice Co. *v.* Webster, 125 U. S. 426 (1888), cases.

[5] Woodman *v.* Pitman, 79 Me. 456 (1887).

[6] Commonwealth *v.* Stone, 103 Mass. 421 (1869).

[7] Bergman's Appeal, 88 Pa. 123 (1878); Heil's Appeal, 40 *id.* 453 (1861).

[1] Myer *v.* Fegaley, 39 Pa. 429 (1861).

[2] Alvord *v.* Moffatt, 10 Ind. 366 (1858).

[3] Bergman's Appeal, 88 Pa. 120 (1878).

[4] Cato *v.* Hutson, 7 Mo. 142 (1841).

[5] Morton *v.* McClure, 22 Ill. 257 (1859).

[6] Jeffries *v.* Bartlett, 75 Ga. 232 (1885).

[7] Marr *v.* Wetzel, 3 Col. 5 (1876).

[8] Elliott *v.* Knott, 14 Md. 121 (1859).

[9] Stanley *v.* Noble, 59 Iowa, 410 (1882).

[10] Rowe *v.* Palmer, 29 Kan. 337 (1883).

[11] Power *v.* Woolley, 21 Ark. 462 (1860).

[12] Marx *v.* Hanthorn, 30 F. R. 586 (1887).

[13] United States *v.* Spintz, 18 F. R. 377 (1883).

[14] City of Lafayette *v.* Wortman, 107 Ind. 404 (1886).

[15] Smurr *v.* State, 88 Ind. 506 (1883), cases; 107 *id.* 410.

[16] Siebert *v.* State, 95 Ind. 471 (1884). See 1 Bish. Cr. Pr. § 688; 1 Whart. Cr. L. 309.

[17] Commonwealth *v.* Warren, 143 Mass. 569 (1887), in which "Celestia" and "Celeste" were found to be the same name; other cases cited.

[18] See 4 Bl. Com. 396; 2 Crim. Law Mag. 287; 34 La. An. 1082.

[19] Clement *v.* British American Assurance Co., 141 Mass. 303 (1886), Morton, C. J.

[20] Phipps *v.* Sedgwick, 95 U. S. 9 (1877).

original or substituted form.[1] See *ad fin.* TRUST, 1; CONCEAL, 1.

2. Of literary composition, consists in the sentiment and the language: the same conception clothed in the same words must necessarily be the same composition.[2]

3. Identity of designs, etc. See DESIGN, 2; PATENT, 2.

IDEO. See CONSIDERATION, 1.

IDIOCY. Not the condition of a deranged mind, but the total absence of all mind.[3]

A congenital disorder, consisting in a defect or sterility of the intellectual powers.[4]

Idiot. One that hath had no understanding from his nativity.[5]

A person who has been defective in intellectual powers from birth, or from a period before the mind received the impression of any idea.[6]

He is presumed never likely to attain any understanding. But a man is not an idiot if he hath any glimmering of reason, so that he can tell his parents, his age, or like common matters. One born deaf, dumb, and blind is looked upon by the law as in the same state with an idiot.[7]

See INSANITY; LUNACY.

IDLENESS. See VAGRANCY.

IF. Implies a condition precedent, unless controlled by other words.[8]

A word of condition, or of conditional limitation.[9]

To sell property "if it be thought best" means, if in the course of the administration of the estate it should be found necessary or advisable to take that course.[10] See BEST.

"If," in a judge's charge, may not save it from assuming the existence of a fact.[11]

See CONDITION; PROVIDED; WHEN.

-IFF. See PLAINTIFF; SHERIFF.

IGNOMINY. Shame, disgrace, dishonor: as, in a statute excusing a witness from answering to save himself from ignominy.[1] See CRIMINATE.

IGNORAMUS. See IGNORARI.

IGNORANCE. Want of knowledge or information, whether of a matter of fact or of a matter of law. See ILLITERATE.

Ignorance of a particular fact consists in this, that the mind, capable of healthy action, has never acted upon the fact, because the subject has never been brought to the notice of the perceptive faculties.[2]

Voluntary ignorance. Exists when one by reasonable exertion might have acquired knowledge. **Involuntary ignorance** does not proceed from choice; could not be overcome by the use of any known means.

Ignorance of a fact sometimes excuses; ignorance of law, never. In the law of crimes, ignorance of a fact is regarded as a defect of will. It occurs where a man intending to do a lawful act does that which is unlawful: the deed and the will do not concur.[3] See GUILTY.

If ignorance of what one might know were admitted as an excuse, the laws would become of no effect.[4] See PRESCRIBE.

"If ignorance of the law was admitted as a ground of exemption, the courts would be involved in questions which it were scarcely possible to solve, and which would render the administration of justice next to impossible; for in almost every case ignorance would be alleged, and, for the purpose of determining the point, the court would be compelled to enter upon questions of facts insoluble and indeterminable." So, if a person will not read or does not know what he signs, or is misinformed as to the effect, he alone is responsible.[5]

The maxim that "ignorance of the law excuses no one" is not universally applicable, but only when damages have been inflicted or crimes committed.[6]

When parties have acted under a mutual mistake of law, and the party jeopardized can be relieved without substantial injustice to the other side, a court of equity will afford redress, especially if the one to be benefited by the mistake invokes the aid of equity to put him in a position where the mistake will become advantageous to him.[7]

---

[1] Third Nat. Bank of St. Paul *v.* Stillwater Gas Co., 36 Minn. 78 (1886), cases: 26 Am. Law Reg. 253 (1887); *ib.* 256–60, cases; Fletcher *v.* Sharpe, 108 Ind. 279 (1886), cases: 26 Am. Law Reg. 71; *ib.* 74–82 (1887), cases; 25 Cent. Law J. 315–21 (1887), cases; 2 Harv. Law Rev. 28–39 (1888), cases.

[2] 2 Bl. Com. 405.

[3] Owings' Case, 1 Bland. Ch. 386 (Md., 1828).

[4] Stewart *v.* Lispenard, 26 Wend. 314 (N. Y., 1841); 1 Redf. Wills, 59, 61, 64.

[5] 1 Bl. Com. 303; 88 Ill. 502.

[6] [Crosswell *v.* People, 13 Mich. 435 (1865), Cooley, J.; Chitty, Med. Jur.

[7] 1 Bl. Com. 303–4. See 4 Johns. Ch. 441; 3 Ired. Ch. 535; Ray, Med. Jur. Ins. 86, 743; 1 Whart. & St. Med. J. § 1; Taylor, Med. J. 789–91.

[8] Crabbe, R. P. § 2152.

[9] Sutton *v.* West, 77 N. C. 431 (1877); Owen *v.* Field, 102 Mass. 105 (1869); 18 N. J. L. 36.

[10] Chandler *v.* Rider, 102 Mass. 271 (1869).

[11] Chambers *v.* People, 105 Ill. 418 (1883).

[1] Brown *v.* Kingsley, 38 Iowa, 221 (1874).

[2] Boylan *v.* Meeker, 28 N. J. L. 279 (1860).

[3] 4 Bl. Com. 27.

[4] 1 Bl. Com. 46.

[5] Upton *v.* Tribilcock, 91 U. S. 50–51 (1875), cases, Hunt, J. See also Hunt *v.* Rhodes, 1 Pet. 1, 13–15 (1828); 17 Cent. Law J. 422–27 (1883), cases; 18 *id.* 7–10 (1884), cases; 2 Flip. 116; 3 Col. 555; 13 Ill. 395; 60 Md. 355; 50 Mich. 551, 594; 23 Miss. 134; 76 Va. 315; 62 Wis. 332; 1 Johns. Ch. 515; 2 *id.* 60; 6 *id.* 170; Bisp. Eq. § 187; 1 Story, Eq. Ch. V; 2 Pomeroy, Eq. §§ 838–71.

[6] Brock *v.* Weiss, 44 N. J. L. 244 (1882), cases.

[7] Freichnecht *v.* Meyer, 39 N. J. E. 551, 558–60 (1885), cases.

When a party in one State makes a contract with direct reference to the law of another State, he will be held to know the law of the latter State.[1] See LAW, Foreign.

See also ESTOPPEL; IGNORARI; INQUIRY, 1; KNOWLEDGE, 1; MISTAKE; REFORM.

IGNORANTIA. See IGNORARI.

IGNORARI. Not to know or know of; to have no knowledge of.

Ignoramus. We do not know it; we ignore it.

If the grand jury think an accusation groundless, they endorse on the back of the bill "*ignoramus*:" we know nothing of it — the truth does not appear.[2]

Modern expressions are: "not a true bill;" "no bill;" "not found." A fresh bill may be referred to a subsequent jury.[3]

Ignorantia. Non-information: ignorance.

Ignorantia facti excusat; ignorantia juris non excusat. Ignorance of fact excuses; ignorance of the law does not excuse.

Ignorantia legis neminem excusat. Ignorance of the law excuses no one. See IGNORANCE.

IGNORE. To refuse to find a bill of indictment. See IGNORARI.

IL-. A prefix from the Latin *in*, not; negatives the sense of the simple word. See IN, 3.

ILL. 1. Contracted from *evil:* as in ill-fame.

2. Contrary to rule or practice: as in ill-pleading; ill for want of certainty. Compare BAD, 2; WELL, 2.

ILLEGAL. See LEGAL; ERROR, 2 (2), Erroneous.

ILLEGITIMATE. See LEGITIMATE.

ILLEVIABLE. See LEVY.

ILL-FAME. See HOUSE, Of ill-fame.

ILLICIT.[4] Disallowed: forbidden by law; unlawful; illegal: as, illicit intercourse, trade, distilling.

Illicit intercourse. Fornication, or adultery.

Illicit trade. In marine insurance, trade made unlawful by the law of the country to which the object or vessel is bound.[5]

ILLITERATE. Without knowledge of written language; ignorant.

To induce an illiterate person, by false reading, to subscribe an agreement, may be a fraud upon his rights, and may even amount to an indictable deceit.[1] See INFLUENCE; READING.

ILLNESS. See BENEFITS; DISEASE; HEALTH; LANGUIDUS.

ILL-PLEADING. See ILL, 2.

ILL-TREATMENT. See CRUELTY; MALTREATMENT.

ILLUSION. See INSANITY. Compare DELUSION.

ILLUSORY. See APPOINTMENT, 2.

ILL-WILL. See MALICE; PREJUDICE.

IM-. A prefix from the Latin *in*, not; in, into, upon. See IN, 3.

IMAGINE. See TREASON.

IMBECILITY. Without strength, impotent.

In a petition for divorce by a wife for corporal imbecility in the husband, it is necessary to show a permanent, incurable impotency to consummate the marriage. "Corporal imbecility" does not, *ex vi termini*, import such impotency.[2] See DIVORCE.

On mental imbecility, see [3] INSANITY.

IMMATERIAL. See MATERIAL.

IMMATURE. See MATURE.

IMMEDIATE. Direct; present; near — in time, or kinship.

That which is produced directly by the act to which it is ascribed, without the intervention or agency of any distinct, intermediate cause: as, immediate interest.[4]

In the law of self-defense, "immediate" generally signifies present in time and place. Thus "immediate danger" of losing life or of sustaining great bodily injury, means that the danger is then and there present and the injury apparently about to be inflicted.[5]

"Immediate delivery," among dealers in coal, means a delivery within the present or, in cases, within the succeeding month.[6]

An action is said to be prosecuted for the immediate (direct) benefit of a person;[7] and devises are made to immediate issue.[8]

---

[1] Huthsing *v.* Bosquet, 3 McCrary, 575, 576 (1882), cases; Storrs *v.* Barker, 10 Am. Dec. 316, 323-28, cases; Story, Confl. L. §§ 76, 233, 274.

[2] 4 Bl. Com. 305.

[3] United States *v.* Watkins, 3 Cranch, C. C. 506 (1829).

[4] L. *illicitus*, not allowed: *in-licere*.

[5] 1 Pars. Mar. Ins. 614; 2 La. 337, 338; 3 S. & R. 73; 4 *id.* 29; 5 Binn. 403.

---

[1] See 2 Bl. Com. 304; 2 Whart. Ev. § 1243, cases; 2 Bish. Cr. L. § 156.

[2] Ferris *v.* Ferris, 8 Conn. 167 (1830). See generally 1 Bish. Mar. & Div. §§ 321-39, cases.

[3] Delafield *v.* Parish, 5 N. Y. Sur. 115 (1857). See generally 1 Wharton & St. Med. J. § 691; Taylor, Med. J. 789.

[4] Fitch *v.* Bates, 11 Barb. 473 (1851): Bouvier.

[5] Bailey *v.* Commonwealth, 11 Bush, 691 (1876), Cofer, J.; United States *v.* Baldridge, 11 F. R. 558 (1882): R. S. § 5515; s. c. 3 Cr. Law Mag. 850.

[6] Neldon *v.* Smith, 36 N. J. L. 153 (1873).

[7] Butler *v.* Patterson, 13 N. Y. 293 (1855).

[8] Turley *v.* Turley, 11 Ohio St. 179 (1860).

Immediately. Within reasonable time. Never, or very rarely, employed to designate an exact portion of time.[1] Compare FORTHWITH.

IMMEMORIAL. See CUSTOM; MEMORY.

IMMIGRATION. Moving into a country, usually to acquire citizenship.

The act of Congress of August 3, 1882 (22 St. L. 214), which levies a duty of fifty cents for every foreign passenger coming by vessel to the United States, to be paid to the collector of customs of the port, by the owner or agent of the vessel, is a valid regulation of commerce with foreign nations. The duty is a license fee, a tax on the owner of the vessel, and on the business of bringing in alien passengers. It is not a capitation tax. The contribution is designed to mitigate the evils incident to immigration from abroad, by raising a fund for that purpose.[2]

See COMMERCE; EXPATRIATION; CHINESE.

IMMORAL. See MORALS.

IMMORTALITY. See CORPORATION.

IMMOVABLES. See MOVABLE.

IMMUNITY.[3] Exemption from a duty, obligation, penalty, or service, which the law requires of citizens in general.

Freedom from what otherwise would be a duty or burden.[4]

The Fourteenth Amendment secures immunity from inequality of legal protection, as to life, liberty, or property.[5]

Immunity from taxation, as of the property of a railroad corporation, not being a franchise, but a personal privilege, is not transferable even under a decree of foreclosure.[6]

See further PRIVILEGE, 1; PROHIBITION, 1; TAX, 2.

IMPAIR. To make worse: to diminish in quantity, value, excellence, strength; to lessen in power; to deteriorate.[7] To relax, weaken, injure.

Impair health. See INTEMPERATE.

"No State shall . . . pass any . . Law impairing the Obligation of Contracts."[8]

To relieve the distress which followed the war of the Revolution, paper money was issued, worthless lands, and other property of no use to the creditor, were made a tender in payment of debts, and the time of payment stipulated in contracts was extended by law. These were the peculiar evils of the day. So much mischief was done and so much more apprehended, that general distrust prevailed, and confidence between man and man was destroyed. . To restore public confidence, the framers of the Constitution prohibited the use of any means by which the same mischief might again be produced: they established the principle that contracts should be inviolable.[1]

The reference is to contracts respecting *property*, under which an individual may claim a right to something beneficial to himself.[2] The contracts protected are such as relate to property rights, not governmental. It may not be easy to tell on which side of the line a particular case is to be put.[3] There was no intention to restrain the States in the regulation of their civil institutions, adopted for internal government.[2]

The prohibition does not include grants for public purposes, which are in effect mere regulations of internal police.[4] See further MONOPOLY; POLICY, 1, Public.

"Obligation" means the law which binds the parties to perform their undertaking.[5] See OBLIGATION, 3.

The prohibition applies to implied as well as to express, and to executory as well as to executed, contracts: as, a grant of lands by a State to an individual;[6] or, a compact between States;[7] or, a grant of corporate powers[8] — unless a right of revocation or alteration is reserved in the grant or by a general law.[9]

But it does not include all contracts by a State with its public officers or municipal corporations.[10] After a public officer has rendered the services required of

the committee on style, resolute not "to countenance the issue of paper money, and the consequent violation of contracts," of himself added "No State shall pass laws altering or impairing the obligation of contracts." In the shorter form adopted by the convention, "an end was designed to be made to barren land laws, laws for the installment of debts, and laws closing the courts against suitors,"— 2 Bancroft, Hist. Const. 214 (1882).

[1] Sturges *v.* Crowninshield, 4 Wheat. 204, 206, 199 (1819), Marshall, C. J.

[2] Dartmouth College *v.* Woodward, 4 Wheat. 628 (1819), Marshall, C. J.; Butler *v.* Pennsylvania, 10 How. 416 (1850); Newton *v.* Commissioners, 100 U. S. 557 (1879); Charles River Bridge *v.* Warren Bridge, 11 Pet. *572 (1837); 2 Bancroft, Hist. Const. 213; Federalist, No. 44.

[3] Stone *v.* Mississippi, 101 U. S. 820, 816 (1879).

[4] East Hartford *v.* Hartford Bridge Co., 10 How. 535 (1850).

[5] Sturges *v.* Crowninshield, 4 Wheat. 197 (1819), *supra.*

[6] Fletcher *v.* Peck, 6 Cranch, 137 (1810).

[7] Green *v.* Biddle, 8 Wheat. 1, 84 (1823).

[8] Dartmouth College *v.* Woodward, 4 Wheat. 628 (1819); Home of the Friendless *v.* Rouse, 8 Wall. 437 (1869).

[9] Holyoke Company *v.* Lyman, 15 Wall. 522 (1872).

[10] Butler *v.* Pennsylvania, 10 How. 416-17 (1850).

[1] See Thompson *v.* Gibson. 8 M. & W. *286–89 (1841); McLure *v.* Colclough, 17 Ala. 100 (1849); Gaddis *ads.* Howell, 31 N. J. L. 316 (1865); Lockwood *v.* Middlesex Mut. Assur. Co., 47 Conn. 566–68 (1880), cases; 11 F. R. 555; 44 Ind. 460; 51 Md. 512; 14 Neb. 151-52; 20 Barb. 468; 29 Pa. 198; 40 *id.* 289; 75 *id.* 378; 43 Wis. 318, 479; 62 *id.* 244; 5 Biss. 476; 43 Ill. 155; 13 N. J. L. 313; L. R., 4 Q. B. 471; 20 Moak, 466, 463.

[2] The Head-Money Cases, 18 F. R. 135 (1883), Blatchford, J.: s. c. 112 U. S. 580 (1884), Miller, J.

[3] L. *immunis*, free from public service: *in*, not; *munus*, duty.

[4] Lonas *v.* State, 3 Heisk. 306 (1871).

[5] Strauder *v.* West Virginia, 100 U. S. 310 (1879).

[6] Morgan *v.* Louisiana, 93 U. S. 223 (1876), cases.

[7] Webster's Dict.; Edwards *v.* Kearzey, 96 U. S. 600 (1877).

[8] Constitution, Art. I, sec. 10. Gouverneur Morris, of

him under an enactment which fixes the rate of compensation (*q. v.*), the obligation to pay for the services at that rate is perfected and rests on the remedies which the law then gives for its enforcement.[1]

A charter granted to a private corporation, which in effect is a mere license, may be withdrawn;[2] so may any other engagement which is a mere gratuity;[3] but not, without consent of the *bona fide* bondholder, power given a municipality to levy a tax with which to pay its bonds.[4] And a State may not tax mortgage bonds, secured on property within it, held by non-residents.[5]

Liability for a tort, created by statute, although reduced to judgment, is not such a debt by contract as is contemplated.[6]

Imprisonment for debt, not being regarded as a part of a contract, may be abolished.[7]

The prohibition extends to provisions of a State constitution, as well as to ordinary legislation.[8]

The existing laws of the place where, or in reference to which, the contract is made, affecting its validity, construction, discharge, or enforcement, form part of the contract. The remedy, or means of enforcing the contract, is part of the obligation.[9]

Judicial construction, being a part of a statute, a change of decision is the same in effect as a new enactment.[10]

The Constitution intended to prohibit a law interpolating a new term or condition foreign to the original agreement.[11]

In short, any deviation from the terms of the contract, by postponing or accelerating the period of performance which it prescribes, by imposing conditions not expressed in the contract, or by dispensing with the performance of those which are expressed, however minute or apparently immaterial in their effect upon the contract, impairs its obligation.[12]

Diminishing value by legislation is impairment.[13]

But it is not necessarily impaired by a reasonable change in the mode of enforcing it;[14] unless it substantially lessens the rights of the creditor;[15] nor is it

impaired, necessarily, by a new statute of limitations.[1] In modes of proceeding and forms to enforce a contract, the legislature has control, and may enlarge, limit, or otherwise alter them, provided it does not deny a remedy or so embarrass it with conditions or restrictions as seriously to impair the value of the right.[2,3] See REMEDY; BOUNTY.

The prohibition in the Constitution refers to enactments to which the State gives the force of law; it does not apply to decisions of the courts, or acts of executive or administrative boards or officers, or doings of corporations or individuals. . . . " When the State court decides against a right claimed under a contract, and there was no law subsequent to the contract, this (the Supreme) court clearly has no jurisdiction. When the existence and the construction of a contract are undisputed, and the State court upholds a subsequent law, on the ground that it did not impair the obligation of the admitted contract, it is equally clear that this court has jurisdiction. When the State court holds that there was a contract conferring certain rights, and that a subsequent law did not impair those rights, this court has jurisdiction to consider the true construction of the supposed contract, and, if it is of opinion that it did not confer the rights affirmed by the State court, and therefore its obligation was not impaired by the subsequent law, may on that ground affirm the judgment. So, when the State court upholds the subsequent law, on the ground that the contract did not confer the right claimed, this court may inquire whether the supposed contract did give the right, because, if it did, the subsequent law cannot be upheld. But when the State court gives no effect to the subsequent law, but decides, on grounds independent of that law, that the right claimed was not conferred by the contract, the case stands just as if the subsequent law had not been passed, and this court has no jurisdiction." [4]

IMPANEL. See PANEL.

IMPARLANCE.[5] Opportunity for a conference.

1. An indulgence granted a defendant to defer pleading to the action until a subsequent term.

---

[1] Fisk *v.* Jefferson Police Jury, 116 U. S. 131, 134 (1885).

[2] Stone *v.* Mississippi, 101 U. S. 820, 816 (1879).

[3] West Wisconsin R. Co. *v.* Supervisors, 93 U. S. 595 (1876).

[4] Von Hoffman *v.* City of Quincy, 4 Wall. 535, 544 (1866); Wolff *v.* New Orleans, 103 U. S. 358 (1880).

[5] State Tax on Foreign-Held Bonds, 15 Wall. 325 (1872).

[6] Louisiana *v.* New Orleans, 109 U. S. 285 (1883); Chase *v.* Curtis, 113 *id.* 464 (1885).

[7] Penniman's Case, 103 U. S. 717, 720 (1880), cases.

[8] Dodge *v.* Woolsey, 18 How. 331 (1855); New Orleans Gas Co. *v.* Louisiana Light Co., 115 U. S. 650, 672 (1885), cases; Fisk *v.* Jefferson Police Jury, 116 *id.* 131 (1885).

[9] Walker *v.* Whitehead, 16 Wall. 317 (1872); Edwards *v.* Kearzey, 96 U. S. 600 (1877), cases; 102 *id.* 532.

[10] Douglass *v.* County of Pike, 101 U. S. 687 (1879).

[11] West River Bridge Co. *v.* Dix, 6 How. 533 (1848).

[12] Green *v.* Biddle, 8 Wheat. 84 (1823), Washington, J.

[13] Planters' Bank *v.* Sharp, 6 How. 327 (1848).

[14] Mason *v.* Haile, 12 Wheat. 378 (1827).

[15] Bronson *v.* Kinzie, 1 How. 311 (1843); Woodruff *v.*

Trapnall, 10 How. 190 (1850); Hawthorne *v.* Calef, 2 Wall. 23 (1864); Gunn *v.* Barry, 15 *id.* 623 (1872); Walker *v.* Whitehead, 16 *id.* 318 (1872); Antoni *v.* Greenhow, 107 U. S. 774, 778 (1882); 101 *id.* 339.

[1] Koshkonong *v.* Burton, 104 U. S. 675 (1881), cases; Gilfillan *v.* Union Canal Co., 109 *id.* 401 (1883); Mitchell *v.* Clark, 110 *id.* 642 (1883).

[2] Penniman's Case, 103 U. S. 717, 720 (1880), cases.

[3] See also Kring *v.* Missouri, 107 U. S. 233 (1882), cases; Civil Rights Cases, 109 *id.* 12 (1883); Louisville, &c. R. Co. *v.* Palmes, *ib.* 256 (1883); Louisiana *v.* Mayor of New Orleans, *ib.* 285 (1883); Nelson *v.* St. Martin's Parish, 110 *id.* 720 (1884); Parker *v.* Buckner, 67 Tex. 23 (1885); 25 Am. Law Reg. 81-97 (1885), cases; 2 Story, Const. §§ 1368-91.

[4] New Orleans Water-works Co. *v.* Louisiana Sugar Co., 125 U. S. 18, 30, 38 (1888), cases, Gray, J.; Kreiger *v.* Shelby R. Co., *ib.* 39 (1888).

[5] F. *parler*, to speak.

Before the defendant puts in his defense he is entitled to demand one imparlance, or *licentia loquendi*, to see if he can end the matter amicably without further suit, by talking with the plaintiff; a practice supposed to have arisen in obedience to the precept " Agree with thine adversary quickly, whilst thou art in the way," Matt. v. 25. The Roman law of the Twelve Tables likewise directed the parties to make up the matter while going to the prætor.[1]

General imparlance. That just defined, and grantable of course. **Special imparlance.** Saved all exceptions to the writ or count, and was granted by the prothonotary. *More special imparlance.* Saved all exceptions whatsoever, and granted at the discretion of the court.[2]

Imparlances are no longer recognized in this country, where, after appearance by the defendant, the cause stands continued until the end of the time within which the plea is to be filed. See CONTINUANCE.

2. Stay of execution.[3]

IMPARTIAL.[4] 1. Applied to a juror, indifferent as he stands unsworn;[5] has not formed an opinion as to the issue.[6]

"In all criminal prosecutions, the accused shall enjoy the right to a speedy and public trial, by an impartial jury of the State and district wherein the crime shall have been committed," etc.[7] Compare INDIFFERENT; PREJUDICE, 1.

The courts are not agreed as to the knowledge upon which an opinion must rest to render a juror incompetent, or whether the opinion must be accompanied by malice or ill-will; but all unite in holding that it must be founded on some evidence, and be more than a mere impression. Some say it must be positive; others, that it must be decided and substantial; others, that it must be fixed; others again, that it must be deliberate and settled. All concede, however, that if hypothetical only, the partiality is not so manifest as to necessitate setting the juror aside.[8]

2. As understood in conditions annexed to bonds, see FAITHFULLY.

IMPEACH.[9] 1. To call to account: as, to impeach a tenant for waste.[10]

---

[1] 3 Bl. Com. 299.

[2] 3 Bl. Com. 301.

[3] Act 19 May, 1828, § 2: R. S. § 988.

[4] L. *im-pars*, not of a part or party.

[5] Littleton, 155 *b.*

[6] Reynolds *v.* United States, 98 U. S. 154 (1878): Coke, Litt. 155 *b.*

[7] Constitution, Amd. Art. VI.

[8] Reynolds *v.* United States, 98 U. S. 155 (1878), Waite, C. J., citing 11 Leigh, 659; 10 Gratt. 658; 13 Ill. 685; 2 Dev. & B. L. (N. Car.) 196; 74 Pa. 458; 84 *id.* 151. See also Northern Pacific R. Co. *v.* Herbert, 116 U. S. 646 (1886), cases.

[9] F. *empeecher,* to prevent, hinder, bar: L. *impedicare,* to impede; or *impingere,* to thrust against.

[10] 2 Bl. Com. 283; 6 Fla. 480.

2. To impugn, call in question, seek to disparage: as, to impeach the authenticity of a document, the irregularity or legality of a judgment or sale, one's title to negotiable paper or to property. See DISPARAGE, 2; FACIES, Prima; JUDGMENT.

3. To seek to prove unworthy of belief; to discredit: as, to impeach the veracity of a witness.

To charge or accuse of want of veracity; and, to establish such charge.[1]

To accuse, blame, censure. Thus, to impeach one's official report or conduct is to show that it was occasioned by some partiality, bias, prejudice, inattention to or unfaithfulness in the discharge of that duty; or, that it was based upon such error that the existence of those influences may justly be inferred from the extraordinary character or grossness of that error.[2]

Unimpeached. Not discredited, undiscredited; not shaken in character or worth, professed or attributed. **Unimpeachable.** Not to be questioned as to credit; irreproachable; blameless.

After a witness has been examined in chief, his credit may be impeached in various modes besides that of exhibiting the improbabilities of his story by a cross-examination: (1) By disproving the facts stated by him, by other witnesses. (2) By general evidence affecting his credit for veracity. (3) By proof that he has made statements out of court contrary to what he has testified at the trial. But this is only in matters relevant to the issue; and, beforehand, he must be asked as to the time, place, and persons involved in the supposed contradiction: upon the general question he may not remember whether he has said so or not; and justice requires that his attention be first called to the subject. Then he may correct or explain the former statement.[3]

By calling, the party represents his witness as worthy of credit or at least as not so infamous as to be wholly unworthy of credit. For him to attack the witness's veracity would be bad faith to the court, and give the power to destroy if the witness spoke unfavorably, and to make good if he spoke favorably. Hence, at common law, while a party may contradict, and to that extent discredit, he cannot ordinarily " impeach " his own witness.[4]

An adverse witness who contradicts his former statement, thereby surprising the party calling him, may be examined as to his former statement, when

---

[1] [White *v.* McLean, 47 How. Pr. 199 (1874).

[2] Bryant *v.* Glidden, 36 Me. 47 (1853), Shepley, C. J.

[3] 1 Greenl. Ev. §§ 461–62. See Becker *v.* Koch, 104 N. Y. 401 (1887), cases; Conrad *v.* Griffey, 16 How. 46–47 (1853), cases.

[4] United States *v.* Watkins, 3 Cranch, C. C. 442 (1829); Commonwealth *v.* Donahoe, 133 Mass. 408 (1882); Sheppard *v.* Yocum, 10 Oreg. 410 (1882); Stearns *v.* Merchants' Bank, 53 Pa. 492–99 (1866), cases.

it would appear that deception has been practiced, the examiner being guilty of no laches.[1]

May impeach an opposing witness by ·· former statement contradicting that made in his examination in chief;[2] but cannot contradict on a collateral matter. May contradict answers as to motive; question veracity; show bias or conviction of infamous crime.[1] May attack the impeaching witness, and sustain the impeached, but not by proof of former consistent statements. Corroboration is discretionary in the court.[3]

To impair his credibility, a witness may be cross-examined as to specific facts tending to disgrace or degrade him, although irrelevant to the main issue. The range of cross-examination depends upon the appearance and conduct of the witness and other circumstances. It is only where the discretion in the court has been abused, to the prejudice of a party, that error will lie.[4] See CHARACTER; CREDIT, 1; EXAMINATION, 9; REPUTATION.

4. To convict of such misconduct as justifies removal from office.

Articles of impeachment. The formal statement of charges of misconduct preferred against an officer.

Like an indictment for crime, must be sufficiently certain in averment to admit of a defense being framed, and to be used in bar of another accusation upon the same subject-matter in case of acquittal.

Court of impeachment. The tribunal before which articles of impeachment are presented and the charges tried.

Charges which will warrant an impeachment may not sustain an indictment. The prosecution is conducted before some branch of the political power, or before a *quasi* political tribunal.

"The President, Vice President and all civil Officers of the United States, shall be removed from Office on Impeachment for, and Conviction of, Treason, Bribery, or other high Crimes and Misdemeanors."[5]

"The House of Representatives . . . shall have the sole Power of Impeachment."[6]

"The Senate shall have the sole Power to try all Impeachments. When sitting for that Purpose, they shall be on Oath or Affirmation. When the President of the United States is tried, the Chief Justice shall preside: and no Person shall be convicted without the Concurrence of two-thirds of the Members present." "Judgment in Cases of Impeachment shall not extend further than to removal from Office, and disqualification to hold and enjoy any Office of Honor, Trust or Profit under the United States: but the Party convicted

shall nevertheless be liable and subject to Indictment, Trial, Judgment and Punishment, according to Law."[1]

The Senate has sat as a court of impeachment in the cases of Judge Chase, in 1804; Judge Peck, in 1831; Judge Humphreys, in 1862; and of President Johnson, in 1868.[2]

Proceedings under the constitutions of the States, for the trial of State officials, are similar to the foregoing. See JUDGE; PARDON.

IMPEDE. See OBSTRUCT.

IMPERFECT. See DUTY, 1; PERFECT.

IMPERIUM. L. Dominion; authority; jurisdiction.

Divisum imperium. A divided jurisdiction; jurisdiction belonging to more than one tribunal, or exercised alternately between powers.

As, the jurisdiction of common-law and admiralty courts exercised between high and low water-mark; the jurisdiction exercised concurrently by common-law and equity courts.

Imperium in imperio. A power within a power; a sovereignty within a sovereignty; a jurisdiction within a jurisdiction.[3]

IMPERTINENCE. The introduction of any matter in a bill, answer, or other pleading or proceeding in a suit, which is not properly before the court for decision at any particular stage of the suit.[4]

The court will not strike out the matter unless its impertinence clearly appears; for if erroneously stricken out, the error is irremediable; if left to stand, the court may set the matter right in taxing the costs. Matter which is scandalous (*q. v.*) is also impertinent.[4]

The test is, would the matter, if put in issue, be proper to be given in evidence.[5]

Impertinent. See PERTINENT.

IMPLEAD. See PLEA, 2.

IMPLEMENTS. Things necessary in any trade, without which the work cannot be performed; also, the furniture of a house. Implements of household are tables, presses, cupboards, bedsteads, wainscot, and the like.[6]

Rarely, if ever, includes an animal.[6]

As used in a statute of exemptions, does not include a horse and cart.[7]

---

[1] 1 Whart. Ev. §§ 549–67, cases.

[2] Ferry v. Breed, 117 Mass. 165 (1875); 35 Vt. 68.

[3] 1 Whart. Ev. §§ 568–71, cases. See generally Seller v. Jenkins, 97 Ind. 433–39 (1884), cases.

[4] State v. Pfefferle, 36 Kan. 92–96 (1886), cases, Johnston, J. See also Pullen v. Pullen, 43 N. J. E. 136 (1887), cases; State v. Thomas, Sup. Ct. N, C. (Dec. 21, 1887), cases.

[5] Constitution, Art. II. sec. 4.

[6] Constitution, Art. I. sec. 2, cl. 5.

[1] Constitution, Art. I. sec. 8, cl. 6–7. See 2 Bancroft, Const. 193.

[2] See Story, Const. § 791; 2 Am. Law Rev. 547–67 (1868); 6 Am. Law Reg. 257–83 (1867), T. W. Dwight; ib. 641–80 (1867), W. Lawrence; 4 Bl. Com. 259–61.

[3] 17 Wall. 328; 106 U. S. 562; 37 Pa. 292.

[4] Story, Eq. Pl. §§ 266–70; Wood v. Mann, 1 Sumn. 588–89 (1834), Story, J.; 3 Story R. 13; 15 F. R. 561.

[5] Woods v. Morrell, 1 Johns. Ch. *106 (1814), Kent, Ch. See also Hood v. Inman, 4 id. *438 (1820).

[6] Coolidge v. Choate, 11 Metc. 82 (1846).

[7] Enscoe v. Dunn, 44 Conn. 99 (1876); Wallace v. Collins, 5 Ark. 46 (1843).

A music teacher's piano is an "implement of business."[1] Compare Tools.

IMPLICATION. An inference of something, not directly declared, but arising from what is admitted or expressed.[2]

Implied. Infolded: involved in language or intention; resting upon inference; imputed in law.[3] Opposed, *expressed, constructive*, qq. v.

Where it is the duty of a defendant to do an act, the law imputes a promise to fulfill that obligation.[4] See Assumpsit.

What is clearly implied in a statute, pleading, contract, will, or other instrument, is as much a part of it as what is expressed.[5] See Incident.

IMPORT. 1, *v.* To bring from a foreign jurisdiction or country merchandise not the product of this country.[6]

n. Most commonly *imports:* the goods or other articles brought into this country from abroad — from another country.[7] Opposed, *export, exports*, q. v.

"No State shall, without the Consent of the Congress, lay any Imposts or Duties on Imports or Exports, except what may he absolutely necessary for executing its inspection Laws . . and all such Laws shall be subject to the Revision and Controul of the Congress."[8]

This does not relate to articles imported from one State into another; only to articles imported from foreign countries.[9]

Nothing is imported till it comes within the limits of a port. The term "imports" covers nothing not actually brought into our limits.[10]

Imposing a license tax on importers is an indirect tax on imports.[11]

See Commerce; Duty, 2; Entry, II, 2; Impost; Inspection, 1.

2. As to import of language, see Purport.

IMPOSE. See Term, 2.

IMPOSITION. See Deceit; Extortion; Fraud; Mistake; Reform.

IMPOSSIBILITY. See Possibility.

IMPOST. A custom or tax levied on articles brought into a country.[1]

A duty on imported goods and merchandise. In a larger sense, any tax or imposition. Synonymous with duty; comprehends every species of tax or contribution not included under the ordinary terms "taxes and excises."[2]

IMPOTENCE. See Imbecility; Inspection, Of person.

IMPOUND. See Pound, 2.

IMPRESSION. 1. A cause in which a question arises for the first time is termed a "case of the first impression."[3]

2. Effect produced upon the mind of a juror.[4] See Opinion, 2.

IMPRIMUS. See Primus; First, 2.

IMPRISONMENT. Detention of another against his will, depriving him of the power of locomotion.[5] Compare Prison.

Confinement of the person in anywise; as, keeping a man against his will in a private house, arresting or forcibly detaining him in the street.[6]

In the penal legislation of Arkansas, the word "imprisonment," used alone, means imprisonment in a county jail or local prison. Confinement in a penitentiary is not meant, unless expressly so stated.[7]

In Louisiana, "imprisonment," unqualified, in penal statutes, is used in contradistinction to "imprisonment at hard labor."[8]

Duress of imprisonment. A compulsion by an illegal restraint of liberty, until one does some act, as, seal a bond.[9] See further Duress.

False, or **unlawful, imprisonment.** Any confinement or detention of the person without sufficient authority.[10]

---

[1] Amend *v.* Murphy, 69 Ill. 338 (1873). See also 23 Iowa, 359; 124 Mass. 418; 6 Gray, 298; 45 N. H. 552.

[2] Re City of Buffalo, 68 N. Y. 173 (1877), Folger, J.

[3] See Homan *v.* Earle, 53 N. Y. 271 (1873); 13 Abb. Pr. 413.

[4] Bailey *v.* N. Y. Central R. Co., 22 Wall. 639 (1874), cases.

[5] United States *v.* Babbit, 1 Black, 61 (1861), cases; 20 Wall. 493; 101 U. S. 82, 202; 110 *id.* 658.

[9] [United States *v.* The Forrester, 1 Newb. 94 (1856).

[7] [Brown *v.* Maryland, 12 Wheat. 437 (1827), Marshall, C. J.

[8] Constitution, Art. I, sec. 10, cl. 2.

[9] Woodruff *v.* Parham, 8 Wall. 131 (1868), cases; Brown *v.* Houston, 113 U. S. 628 (1885).

[10] Marriott *v.* Brune, 9 How. 632 (1850); Arnold *v.* United States, 9 Cranch, 120 (1815); 4 Metc., Mass., 282.

[11] Brown *v.* Maryland, 12 Wheat. 419 (1827); Waring *v.* Mayor of Mobile, 8 Wall. 110 (1868).

---

[1] Brown *v.* Maryland, 12 Wheat. 437 (1827), Marshall, Chief Justice.

[2] Pacific Ins. Co. *v.* Soule, 7 Wall. 445 (1868), cases, Swayne, J.; 1 Story, Const. § 669. See also 8 Wall. 131; 14 Mo. 335; 9 Rob., La., 324; 1 Story, Const. § 949; Federalist, No. 30.

[3] 103 U. S. 168; 21 Pa. 175; 98 *id.* 104.

[4] See Greenfield *v.* People, 74 N. Y. 283 (1878).

[5] United States *v.* Benner, Baldw. 239 (1830).

[6] 1 Bl. Com. 136; 3 *id.* 127.

[7] Cleaney *v.* State, 36 Ark. 80 (1880).

[8] State *v.* Hyland, 36 La. An. 710 (1884).

[9] [1 Bl. Com. 136, 131.

[10] 3 Bl. Com. 127.

May consist in detaining another by threats of violence, thereby preventing him from going where he wishes by a reasonable apprehension of personal danger.[1]

A violation of the right of personal liberty. May arise by executing a lawful process at an unlawful time, as, on Sunday. Remedies: *habeas corpus*, and an action for damages,[2] *qq. v.*

An action will lie for the misuse or abuse of process, beyond the fact of arrest and detention.[3]

Imprisonment for debt. No person shall be imprisoned for debt in any State . . on Federal process . . where imprisonment for debt is abolished. The State course of proceeding is to be followed.[4]

"No crime known to the law brought so many to the jails and prisons (one hundred years ago) as the crime of debt, and the class most likely to get into debt was the most defenseless and dependent, the great body of servants, of artisans, of laborers."[5]

See ARREST, 2; COMMITMENT; FELONY; LABOR, 1; PROSECUTION, Malicious.

IMPROVE. To cultivate, as, land.

"Improved land" is such as has been reclaimed, is used for purposes of husbandry, and is cultivated as such,— whether the appropriation is for tillage, meadow or pasture.[6]

Improvement. 1. Amelioration in the condition of property by the outlay of labor or money.

Includes repairs or additions to buildings, the erection of fences, the annexation of fixtures, etc.[7] See BETTERMENT; ESTOPPEL.

As used in a will, relative to property, construed according to the subject-matter. A gift of the improvement of land may constitute a freehold estate, for the devisee's life; of plate, pictures, furniture, it would be the possession and use; of money, securities, or stocks, it would be the income.[8]

Bedding oysters is not an "improvement," within the meaning of a statute authorizing riparian owners to make improvements on navigable streams. The mere depositing of the oysters in the water implies no essential union or relation between the main land and the soil under the water contiguous; and there-

fore does not effect an improvement of the land implied in something created or constructed, attached to the shore.[1]

Internal improvements. Works within the State, by which the public are supposed to be benefited; such as the improvement of highways and channels of travel and commerce.[2] See AID, 1, Municipal.

Under improvement. Used, occupied, employed, turned to profitable account.[3]

2. An addition of some useful thing to a patentable object. See further INVENTION; PATENT, 2; PROCESS, 3.

IMPROVIDENT. In a statute excluding from an administratorship or executorship a person improvident in habits, the reference is to such habits of mind and conduct as render a man unfit for the duties of the trust.[4] Compare INCAPABLE; SUITABLE, 1.

Improvidently. Designates a rule, order, or decree, had or made prematurely or inconsiderately.

IMPULSE. A sudden impelling.

An irresistible impulse to commit an act known to be wrong does not constitute the insanity which is a legal defense. The law does not recognize an impulse as uncontrollable which yet leaves the reasoning powers — including the capacity to appreciate the nature and quality of the particular act — unaffected by mental disease.[5] See INSANITY.

IMPUNITY. Applies to something which may be done without penalty or punishment.[6]

IMPUTE. See KNOWLEDGE, 1; IMPLICATION.

IN. Introduces English, French, and Latin phrases:

1. English. (1) The preposition: within, inside of, surrounded by.[7]

Under a statute requiring notices to be posted "in" public places, a posting "at" such places may not be sufficient.[8]

---

[1] [Pike v. Hanson, 9 N. H. 493 (1838); Smith v. State, 7 Humph. 43 (1846). See also 35 Ind. 15, 286; 43 *id.* 65; Baldw. 600; 12 Ark. 43; 133 Mass. 399; 81 N. C. 528; 9 Johns. 117; 5 Vt. 588; 1 Bish. Cr. L. § 553.

[2] 3 Bl. Com. 127, 138; 4 *id.* 218; Castro v. De Uriarte, 12 F. R. 253 (1882).

[3] Wood v. Graves, 144 Mass. 367-68 (1887), cases.

[4] R. S. § 990; The Blanche Page, 16 Blatch. 8 (1879).

[5] 1 McMaster, Hist. Peop. U. S. 98 (1883).

[6] [Clark v. Phelps, 4 Cow. 203 (1825). See also 40 Cal. 83; 8 Allen, 213; 68 Pa. 396.

[7] See Schenley's Appeal, 70 Pa. 102 (1871); Schmidt v. Armstrong, 72 *id.* 356 (1872); French v. Mayor of New York. 16 How. Pr. 222 (1858); 32 Iowa, 254; 34 *id.* 559; 1 Cush. 93; 22 Barb. 260; 78 N. Y. 1, 581; 18 N. J. L. 424.

[8] Lamb v. Lamb, 11 Pick. *375 (1831), Shaw, C. J.

---

[1] Hess v. Muir, 65 Md. 586, 598 (1886).

[2] Union Pacific R. Co. v. Commissioners, 4 Neb. 456 (1876); Dawson County v. McNamar, 10 *id.* 281 (1880); Traver v. Merrick County, 14 *id.* 333 (1883); Blair v. Cuming County, 111 U. S. 370-73 (1884), cases.

[3] Chase v. Jefts, 58 N. H. 281 (1878).

[4] [Emerson v. Bowers, 14 N. Y. 454 (1856): s. c. 14 Barb. 660; Coope v. Lowerre, 1 Barb. Ch. 47 (1845).

[5] People v. Hain, 62 Cal. 123. (1882).

[6] Dillon v. Rogers, 36 Tex. 153 (1871).

[7] See Mayor of New York v. Second Avenue R. Co., 31 Hun, 245 (1883).

[8] Hilgers v. Quinney, 51 Wis. 71 (1881)

In a bond payable " in twenty-five years " means, at the end of that period, not within nor at any time during the period.[1]

" The city of Wichita claims that when the act was passed there was no Gilbert's addition *in* the city, upon which the act could operate. Such addition may have been in the town or city, considering the collective body of people in that vicinity as the town or city, and not merely the corporate limits." [2]

In action. See ACTION, 2; CHOSE.

In banc or bank. See BANK, 2 (1).

In blank. See BLANK.

In case. See CASE, 1.

In chief. See CHIEF.

In court. See OUT, Of court.

In equity. See EQUITY; LAW.

In evidence. See EVIDENCE.

In fact. See FACT.

In full. See INDORSEMENT, 2; RECEIPT, 2.

In gross. See GROSS.

In kind. See KIND.

In law. See FACT; LAW.

In like manner. See LIKEWISE.

In mercy. See MERCY.

In possession. See POSSESSION.

In that case or event. See THEN; UPON, 2.

In the peace. See PEACE, 1.

In the presence. See PRESENCE.

In the same manner. See MANNER.

(2) The adverb: not out, within; invested with title or possession: as, " in " by descent, " in " by purchase.

2. French. Used for *en* — equivalent to the English and Latin *in*.

In autre droit. In another's right. See DROIT.

In pais or pays. In the country : in deed. See PAIS.

In ventre. In the womb. See ABORTION; VENTER.

3. Latin. (1) An inseparable particle, meaning not. Like the English *un*, negatives the sense of the simple word.

Before *l*, changes to *il*, as in illegal; before *b, m, p,* (labials), changes to *im*, as in imbecile, immaterials; before *r*, changes to *ir*, as in irregular, irrelevant. Compare EN, 2; NON.

(2) A preposition, denoting rest or motion within or into a place or thing. Opposed to *ex*, coming out from within. May be translated in, into, within, among; to, toward, at; on, upon; against. Compare EN, 1.

[1] Allentown School District *v.* Derr, 115 Pa. 446 (1887).
[2] City of Wichita *v.* Burleigh, 36 Kan. 41 (1886).

(34)

In adversum. Against a resisting party. Compare *In invitum.*

In æquali jure. In equal right. See JUS.

In articulo mortis. At point of death. See ARTICLE, 3.

In banco. In bank. See BANK, 2 (1).

In bonis. In property. See BONA.

In capita. Among the persons. See CAPUT.

In capite. In chief. See CHIEF.

In cujus rei testimonium. In testimony of which thing; in testimony whereof.

In consimili casu. In like cause. See CASUS, Consimili.

In custodia legis. In possession of the law. See CUSTODY.

In dubiis. In matters of doubt.

In esse. In existence; opposed to *in posse*, q. v. See REMAINDER; SALE.

In extenso. At length; fully. See AT LARGE, 1.

In extremis. (*a*) At the end, the last. See ARTICLE, 3; NUNCUPATIVE.

(*b*) Under stress of apparent necessity.

A movement *in extremis* by a vessel is not chargeable as a fault in the master or pilot, though erroneous and useless.[1]

In facie ecclesiæ. Before the church. See DOWER.

In favorem libertatis. In favor of liberty.

In favorem vitæ. In favor of life.

In fictione. See FICTION.

In fieri. In the to be made : in the making; in process of being made, created, completed : not completed.

During the term of a court, proceedings are said to be *in fieri*.[2]

In fine. At the end — of the page, title, etc. Abridged *in fin., in f.*

In forma pauperis. As a poor person. See PAUPER, 1.

In foro conscientiæ. Before the bar of conscience. **In foro domestico.** Before the home tribunal. **In foro seculari.** Before the civil court. See FORUM.

In fraudem legis. In evasion of the law.

In futuro. At a future time.

[1] The Alabama, 17 F. R. 864 (1883), cases; 11 *id.* 922; 112 U. S. 526.
[2] 18 Wall. 193; 109 U. S. 499; 70 Ala. 402; 87 Ind. 26; 3 Bl. Com. 407.

In genere. In kind; opposed to *in specie*, q. v.

In gremio legis. In the bosom, protection, of law. See LEX.

In hac parte. On this side.

In hæc verba. In these words. See VERBUM.

In hoc. In this; as to this.

In individuo. In the undivided state: entire.

In infinitum. To infinity; indefinitely.

In initio. In the beginning; from the first.

In integrum. In the unbroken state: whole, entire.

In invitum. Against one not assenting: unwillingly; as, a tax levied *in invitum*. See INVITUS.

In judicio. By judicial procedure; in court.

In jure. In right: rightfully.

In limine. At the threshold: at first inception; at first opportunity.

An objection to testimony must be offered *in limine*.[1]

In litem. In the suit. See OATH, In litem.

In loco parentis. In the place of the parent.

Guardians and teachers are said to stand *in loco parentis*. See further PARENS.

In misericordia. In mercy. Abridged *in m'ia*. See MERCY.

In mitiori sensu. In the milder meaning. See SLANDER; SENSUS.

In mortua manu. In dead hand — mortmain, q. v.

In nubibus. In the clouds: in abeyance.

In nullo erratum. In nothing is there error. See ERRATUM.

In odium spoliatoris. In hatred of a despoiler. See ALTERATION, 2; SPOLIATION.

In pari causa. In an equal cause: equal right. **In pari delicto.** In equal wrong-doing. See DELICTUM.

In pari materia. On like subject. See MATERIA; REPEAL.

In perpetuam rei memoriam. For preserving evidence of the matter.

In personam. Against the person; opposed to *in rem*, q. v. See PERSONA.

In pios usus. For religious purposes. See USE, 3, Pious.

In posse. In possibility; opposed to *in esse*, q. v.

In præparatorio. In preparation: being fitted out.[1]

In præsenti. At present time. See MARRIAGE.

In propria persona. In his own person. See PERSONA.

In propria causa. In his own suit. See CAUSA.

In quo. In which. See LOCUS.

In re. In the matter of: in regard to. See RES.

In rem. Against a thing — property; opposed to *in personam*, q. v. See RES.

In rerum natura. In the nature of things; in existence.

In se. In itself.

In solido; in solidum. For the whole; as an entire thing; exclusive of another.

In the case of a joint and several obligation, each obligor is liable for the whole amount; so, possession by a partner accrues to all copartners.

In specie. In the very thing; also, according to the precise terms; opposed to *in genere*, in kind. See DEPOSIT, 2; DISTRESS (4); GENUS; LOSS, 2; SPECIES.

In statu quo. In the condition in which — a person or thing was formerly. See STATUS; RESCISSION.

In terrorem. For a warning: as a threat.

In testimonium. In witness whereof.

In thesi. For a proposition: in statement.

In totidem verbis. In the very words: word for word. See VERBUM.

In toto. In the whole: entirely; absolutely.

In transitu. In passage; on the way. See STOPPAGE.

INABILITY. See ABILITY; DISABILITY.

INACCURACY. See AMBIGUITY.

INADEQUATE. See ADEQUATE.

INADMISSIBLE. See ADMISSION, 1.

INALIENABLE. See ALIEN, 2.

INAUGURATION. See OATH, Of office.

In order to vest official authority in a President or governor elect, it is only necessary that he take the oath of office.

INCAPABLE. Referring to a person disqualified from administering upon an estate, is not limited to mere mental or phys-

[1] 109 U. S. 70, 71; 121 *id.* 400.

[1] 107 U. S. 71.

ical incapacity; includes the idea of unfitness, unsuitableness.[1] Compare IMPROVIDENT.

INCAPACITY. See CAPACITY.

INCENDIARY. See ARSON.

INCERTA. See CERTUM.

INCEST.[2] Illicit intercourse between persons within those degrees of consanguinity as to which marriage is forbidden by law.[3]

There may be a certain power exerted, resulting from age, relationship, or other circumstance, which overcomes the objections of the female, without amounting to that violence which would constitute rape.[4]

Incestuous adultery or **fornication.** The crime of adultery or fornication aggravated by the additional crime of incest.

While cognizable as an offense under the canon law, incest does not seem to have been punishable by indictment at common law. It is now punishable by statutes, which also prescribe the prohibited degrees of kinship.[5]

Where a defendant in an action for libel alleged that the plaintiff had committed incest from which she was pregnant, and did not attempt to prove the latter act, the plaintiff was held entitled to a verdict.[6] See IGNORANCE; POLYGAMY.

INCHASTITY. See CHASTITY; INCEST.

INCHOATE.[7] Commenced, but not completed; not fully in existence or operation; inceptive; incomplete; imperfect. Opposed, *consummate*, q. v.

Designates a right, title, or claim, not yet complete.[8] Thus, a marriage between minors is inchoate and incomplete.[9] Before the husband's death, right to dower is inchoate.[10] The right of an unborn child to take by descent is inchoate.[11] A legacy transfers an inchoate property to the legatee, perfected by assent of the executor.[12]

The right to a copyright may be inchoate.[13] From the moment of his invention, an inventor has an in-

choate property in his invention, which he may complete by taking out a patent.

A purchaser at a judicial sale acquires an inchoate right to the property.[1] An informer, by commencing suit, obtains an inchoate property in the penalty, consummated by judgment.[2] The law forbids the inchoate step to an illegal act.[3] See PERFECT.

INCIDENT.[4] Whatever inseparably belongs to, is connected with, or inheres in another thing as *principal;* less properly, a thing connected with another, even separably.[5]

Incident; incidental. Connected with something of more worth or importance; occupying a subordinate relation; accessory; collateral.

The "incidental" labor for which a mechanic's lien may be filed in Colorado must be directly done for, connected with, or actually incorporated into the building or improvement, and not indirectly and remotely associated with the construction.[6]

Customary incidents. Such incidents as originate in usage or custom.[7]

Annex incidents. Show what things are to be treated as incidental to another thing the subject of a contract.[8]

Parol evidence is admissible to annex incidents.

The rule is that the incident follows the principal. "When the law doth give anything to one, it giveth impliedly, whatever is necessary for enjoying the same."[9]

When the use of a thing is granted, everything is granted by which the grantee may enjoy such use. The grantor is presumed to intend to make the grant effectual.[10]

Thus, whatever is part and parcel of a house, mill, or factory is conveyed *eo nomine.*[11] Land covered by the eaves of a house goes with a grant of the house.[12] The use of a front-door, entry, windows, closets, pumps, etc., is incident to the tenancy of a room in a house, unless otherwise agreed. The key is an incident to a building; so are the title-deeds to the land; so is rent to the reversion;[13] and so is a remainder to the particular estate. The right of alienation is necessarily incident to a fee-simple at common law.[14]

---

[1] Drews' Appeals, 58 N. H. 320 (1878), cases.

[2] F. *inceste;* L. *incestus: in,* not; *castus,* pure.

[3] Daniels v. People, 6 Mich. 386 (1859); Territory v. Corbett, 3 Monta. 55 (1877); Commonwealth v. Lane, 113 Mass. 463 (1873); 39 Mich. 124; 44 Pa. 310.

[4] Raiford v. State, 68 Ga. 672 (1882).

[5] See 4 Bl. Com. 64; 1 Bishop, Cr. L. § 502, 1 Mar. & D. § 312, St. Cr. § 727; 2 Kent, 83; State v. Fritts, 48 Ark. 68–70 (1886), cases.

[6] Edwards v. Kansas City Times Co., 32 F. R. 813 (1887).

[7] In'-cō-āte. L. *inchoare,* to begin.

[8] Trenier v. Stewart, 101 U. S. 802 (1879).

[9] 1 Bl. Com. 436.

[10] 2 Bl. Com. 130.

[11] Marsellis v. Thalhimer, 2 Paige, Ch. 35 (1830).

[12] 2 Bl. Com. 512.

[13] Lawrence v. Dana, 4 Cliff. 66 (1869).

[1] Delaplaine v. Lawrence, 10 Paige, 602 (1844).

[2] 2 Bl. Com. 437.

[3] Trist v. Child, 21 Wall. 451 (1874).

[4] L. *incidere,* to fall upon or into.

[5] See Neal v. East Tennessee College, 6 Yerg. 206 (1834).

[6] Rara Avis Mining Co. v. Bouscher, 9 Col. 388 (1886).

[7] 1 Whart. Ev. § 969.

[8] 1 Greenl. Ev. § 294.

[9] 2 Bl. Com. 36.

[10] Steam Stone Cutter Co. v. Shortsleeves, 16 Blatch. 382 (1879), cases.

[11] 1 Greenl. Ev. §§ 286, 294, cases.

[12] Sherman v. Williams, 113 Mass. 484 (1873).

[13] 2 Bl. Com. 111, 176.

[14] 1 Washb. R. P. 54.

A vessel is incident to its keel; the frame to a picture; the halter to a horse sold; wool upon a pelt to the pelt; wages to freight; interest to its principal; the subscription list to a newspaper establishment; the custody of goods by an innkeeper to the contract for entertainment; such subordinate acts by a special agent as are usually done in connection with the principal act.[1]

Some writs are incidents to the other writs. Power to make rules of court is incidental to the general power invested in every court of record.[2] Power to call for proofs, to compel the attendance of witnesses, and to fine or imprison for non-attendance or non-production, is incidental to the power to hear and determine causes.[3] Costs follow a judgment as an incident thereto.

Power to make by-laws is incident to general corporate powers.

See further ACCESSORY; APPENDAGE; APPENDANT; APPURTENANT; CESSION; COMMAND; GRANT, 2, 3; JOINDER; MACHINERY; MESSUAGE; PRINCIPAL, 1; PROHIBITION, 1; RAILROAD.

INCIPITUR. L. It is begun: the beginning.

Formerly, when parties came to an issue, the plaintiff entered it, with all prior pleadings, on an issue-roll; later, only the commencement of the pleadings was entered. This was termed entering the *incipitur* — the beginning.[4]

INCLOSE. "Inclose" and "include" are of the same derivation. One of their common significations is, to confine within.[5] See INCLUDE.

Inclosure. A tract of land surrounded by an actual fence, and such fence.[6] See CLOSE, 3.

A testator directed his executors "to inclose with an iron fence the Friends' meeting-house grounds, the school-house grounds, and the Friends' burial-ground." These three grounds were adjoining. *Held*, that there was no latent ambiguity as to his intention to inclose each of the grounds on all sides.[7]

INCLUDE.[8] To confine within; to comprise, embrace, comprehend. See INCLOSE.

Including. A legacy of "one hundred dollars, including money trusteed" at a bank, was held to intend a gift of one hundred dollars only.[9]

Inclusive. Embraced; comprehended; opposed to *exclusive*. See DAY; CONSISTING.

[1] 2 Pars. Contr. 57.

[2] 25 Pa. 516; 3 Binn. 417, 277.

[3] 1 Greenl. Ev. § 309.

[4] See 3 Steph. Com. 566, n.; 1 Arch. Pr. 350.

[5] [Campbell *v.* Gilbert, 57 Ala. 571 (1877), Brickell, Chief Justice.

[6] Taylor *v.* Welbey, 36 Wis. 44 (1874); Pettit *v.* May, 34 *id.* 672 (1874); Porter *v.* Aldrich, 39 Vt. 321 (1866); Gundy *v.* State, 63 Ind. 530 (1878); 8 Hun, 269.

[7] Appeal of Hall, 112 Pa. 52 (1886).

[8] L. *in-claudere*, to shut in, keep within.

[9] Brainard *v.* Darling, 132 Mass. 218 (1882).

INCLUSIO. See EXPRESSIO.

INCOME. That which comes in, or is received from any business or investment of capital, without reference to the outgoing expenditures. Applied to the affairs of an individual, conveys the same idea that "revenue" expresses when applied to the affairs of a state or nation. Sometimes, is synonymous with "profits," the gain as between receipts and payments.[1] See PROFIT, 1. Compare EARNINGS.

The "income of an estate" is the profit it will yield after deducting the charges of management, or the rent which may be obtained for the use of it. "Rent and profits," "income," and "net income" of the estate, are equivalent expressions.[2]

The income from a profession, trade, or employment, which may be taxed, is the result of the business for a given period, the net result of many combined influences: the creation of capital, industry, and skill.[3]

In the ordinary commercial sense, "income," especially when connected with the word "rent," may mean net or clear income. But one may say that his "income" from a certain property amounts to a particular sum, and yet be speaking merely of the accruing rent, without regard to insurance, taxes, or repairs. Outside of business circles we can never know whether net or gross income is meant without further inquiry. "Produce" or "product," as a substituted word, may relieve a will from obscurity.[4]

"Income" is the gain which accrues from property, labor, or business. It is applicable to the periodical payments, in the nature of rent, usually made under mineral leases.[5]

May mean "money," and not the expectation of receiving or the right to receive money at a future time. A note is ground for expecting income, and, in the sense of a statute taxing incomes, the amount thereof is to be returned when paid.[6] See BOND.

An absolute gift of all of the income of property, without limitation as to time, is a gift of the property itself.[7]

INCOMMUTABLE. See COMMUTATION.

INCOMPATIBLE. Offices are said to be "incompatible and inconsistent" when,

[1] [People *v.* Supervisors of Niagara, 4 Hill, 23 (1842), Bronson, J.

[2] Andrews *v.* Boyd, 5 Me. *203 (1828), Weston, J. Compare Scott *v.* West, 63 Wis. 582, 590 (1885).

[3] Wilcox *v.* County Commissioners, 103 Mass. 546 (1870), Ames, J.

[4] Thompson's Appeal, 100 Pa. 481-82 (1882), Gordon, J.; Sim's Appeal, 44 *id.* 347 (1863).

[5] Eley's Appeal, 103 Pa. 306 (1883), Sterrett, J.

[6] United States *v.* Schillinger, 14 Blatch. 71 (1876); Gray *v.* Darlington, 15 Wall. 63 (1872).

See also 14 La. An. 815; 9 Mass. 372; 8 Duer, 426; 30 Barb. 637; 4 Abb. N. C. 400; 1 Wil. (Ind.) 219; 16 F. R. 14.

[7] Bristol *v.* Bristol, 53 Conn. 259 (1885); Sproul's Appeal, 105 Pa. 441 (1884); 2 Roper, Leg. 371.

from the multiplicity of business, they cannot be executed by the same person with care and ability; or, when their being subordinate and interfering with each other induces a presumption that they cannot both be executed with impartiality and honesty.[1]

Incompatibility. See DIVORCE.

INCOMPETENT. See COMPETENT.

INCOMPLETE. See INCHOATE; PERFECT.

INCONCLUSIVE. See CONCLUDE, 2.

INCONSISTENT. See CONDITION; INCOMPATIBLE; REPUGNANT.

INCONTESTABLE. See CONTEST.

INCONVENIENCE. See HARDSHIP.

INCORPORATE. See CORPORATE.

INCORPOREAL. See CORPOREAL.

INCORRIGIBLE. See REFORMATORY.

INCREASE. That which grows out of land or is produced by the cultivation of it.[2] Compare ACCRETION; EARNINGS; INCOME; PROFIT.

Increased costs. See COSTS.

INCREDIBLE. See CREDIT.

INCREMENT. See ACCESSORY; INCIDENT; ICE.

INCRIMINATE. See CRIMINATE.

INCULPATE. See CULPA.

INCUMBENT. 1. Resting as a duty or obligation.

2. One who is legally authorized to discharge the duties of an office.[3] See VACANCY.

INCUMBIT. See PROBARE, Probatio.

INCUMBRANCE.[4] A burden, an obstruction, impediment.

Whatever charges, burdens, obstructs, or impairs the use of an estate in land, or prevents or impairs its transfer.[5]

An estate or interest in or a right to land, to the diminution of its value.[6]

Every right to or interest in land which

may subsist in a third person to the diminution of the value of the land, but consistent with the passing of the fee by the conveyance.[1]

An outstanding lease is such an incumbrance.[2]

So is a subsisting lien of a mechanic or material-man.[3]

Incumber. To charge or burden with a lien, or an estate. **Disincumber.** To relieve of such charge or burden.

Incumbrancer. He who places a charge upon his interest in realty, as, by a mortgage, or a judgment confessed.

"Incumbrance" is broader than "lien." An "incumbrancer" is one who has a legal claim upon an estate. An absolute conveyance is an incumbrance, in the fullest sense of the term.[4]

Unincumbered. Not bound by or subject to anything in the nature of a lien or burden: as, an unincumbered title.[5]

Incumbrances are spoken of as prior, subsequent; first, second, etc.

Covenant against incumbrances. A stipulation that there are no charges against land which will diminish its value.

The mere existence of any such charge constitutes a breach of the covenant. If in the present tense, does not run with the land. The covenantee may extinguish the claim, and recover therefor.[6]

But in a policy of fire insurance a warranty concerning "incumbrances of all kinds" includes only such as are created by the act or consent of the parties, not those created by law.[7]

See BURDEN; CHARGE; LIEN; ONUS, Cum onere; UNDER AND SUBJECT.

INCUR. See EXPENDITURE.

Men contract debts affirmatively; they incur liabilities — the liability is cast upon them by act or operation of law. "Incur" implies, then, something not embraced in the words "debts and contracts."[8]

INCURABLE. See CURE, 2.

INDEBITATUS. See ASSUMPSIT.

INDEBTED. See DEBT.

---

[1] People v. Green, 46 How. Pr. 170 (1873): 4 Inst. 100; Bac. Abr. See also Commonwealth v. The Sheriff, 4 S. & R. *277 (1818); Commonwealth v. Binns, 17 id. *220 (1828); State v. Buttz, 9 S. C. 179 (1877); Constitution, Art. I, sec. 6, cl. 2.

[2] De Blane v. Lynch, 23 Tex. 27 (1859).

[3] State v. McCollister, 11 Ohio, 50 (1841); County of Scott v. Ring, 29 Minn. 403 (1882).

[4] F. encumbrer, to load: combrer, to hinder; L. cumbrus: L. cumulus, a heap. Also spelled encumbrance; encumber, disencumber.

[5] Anonymous, 2 Abb. N. C. 63 (1876).

[6] Newcomb v. Fiedler, 24 Ohio St. 466 (1873).

[1] Rawle, Cov. Tit. 94; Kelsey v. Remer, 43 Conn. 138 (1875); Alling v. Burlock, 46 id. 510 (1878); Fritz v. Pusey, 21 Minn. 369 (1884), cases. See also 51 Me. 72; 4 Mass. 627; 2 Greenl. Ev. § 242.

[2] Fritz v. Pusey, 31 Minn. 369 (1884), cases.

[3] Redmon v. Phœnix Fire Ins. Co., 51 Wis. 300 (1881).

[4] Warden v. Sabins, 36 Kan. 169 (1887), Horton, C. J.

[5] Gillespie v. Broas, 23 Barb. 376 (1856); 5 Abb. Pr. 28.

[6] See 20 Ala. 137, 156; 6 Conn. 249; 4 Ind. 533; 8 id. 171; 10 id. 424; 19 Mo. 480; 20 N. H. 369; 25 id. 229; 10 Ohio, 317; 5 Wis. 17; 27 Vt. 739; Rawle, Cov. Tit. 89; 2 Washb. R. P. 658; 2 Greenl. Ev. § 242; Tud. L. C. 60.

[7] Hosford v. Hartford Fire Ins. Co., 127 U. S. 404 (1888).

[8] [Crandall v. Bryan, 15 How. Pr. 56 (1857): 5 Abb. Pr. 169. See also 14 Barb. 202; 4 Duer, 101.

INDECENT. Whatever shocks the sense of decency in people generally.

At common law, indictable as a misdemeanor. Examples: Exposure of the person in public, exhibiting pictures of nude persons. What are acts of indecency is generally to be decided by a jury.

Indecent assault; indecent exposure; indecent prints or publications. These offenses (largely self-defining) are punishable, in England, under statute 24 & 25 Vict. (1861) c. 100, s. 52; in the United States, by statute in each State; in Pennsylvania, by the Crimes Act of March 31, 1860, § 44.[1]

In Rev. St. § 3893, which forbids mailing indecent matter, "indecent" means immodest, impure, not simply coarse, nor even profane.[2]

But a sealed letter is not within the prohibition.[3]

Public indecency. Has no fixed legal meaning; is too vague to imply, of itself, a definite offense. The courts, by a kind of judicial legislation, have usually limited the operation of the expression to public displays of the naked person, the publication, sale, or exhibition of obscene books and prints, or the exhibition of a monster,—acts which have a direct bearing on the public morals, and affect the body of society.[4]

The place is "public" if the exposure is such that it is likely to be seen by a number of casual observers.[5]

Where the bodily injury from an indecent assault is trifling, the gravamen of an action for damages must be the mental suffering. In such case evidence is always admissible to show that the plaintiff was a woman of unchaste character.[6]

In an action for defamation, words which in their common acceptation charge the crime of public indecency are actionable per se.[7]

See LEWD; MORALS; OBSCENE.

INDEFEASIBLE. See DEFEASANCE.

INDEFINITE. See DEFINITE.

INDEMNITY.[8] 1. Compensation for a loss sustained. 2. An engagement to make good loss that may be sustained: a bond of indemnity.[9]

Indemnify. To compensate for loss, sustained or anticipated.

Indemnitor. He who undertakes to protect another from loss that may be incurred on account of an act or action by the latter in behalf of the former. Opposed, indemnitee.[1]

Property insurance is a contract for indemnity. Officers selling personalty, under executions, require bonds of indemnity against damages recoverable for trespass.[2] Persons who distribute trust moneys require bonds for pro rata repayment in the event of unexpected claims arising; and settlements and wills may contain clauses of indemnity for the protection of executants.

There is difference between an agreement to indemnify and an agreement to pay.[3]

See DAMNUM, Damnificatus; INJUNCTION; INSURANCE; SURETY.

3. Statutes designed to relieve the occupant of an office who has failed to do some act necessary fully to qualify him for the discharge of the duties of the office, or to exempt from punishment persons guilty of offenses, have been called "acts of indemnity." See AMNESTY.

INDENTURE.[4] A deed: a writing sealed and delivered.[5]

A deed *inter partes*, or a mutual deed.[6]

Named from being indented or cut on the top or the side by a waving line or a line of indenture so as to fit the counterpart from which it is supposed to have been separated.[5]

Formerly, when there were more parties than one to a sealed instrument, a copy for each was made, and cut or indented (in acute angles *instar dentium:* like the teeth of a saw, but, later, in a waving line) on the top or side, to tally with the other; which deed, so made, was called an "indenture." Both parts were written on the same piece of parchment, with some word or letters between them and through which the parchment was cut so as to leave half on each part. Later, the indenting was not through any word at all; and, in time, the term "indenture" served merely to give name to the species of deed. The part executed by the grantor was the original, the others counterparts. Where all the parties executed every part, each part was an original. Opposed, *deed-poll.*[7]

By 8 and 9 Vict. (1845), c. 106, the necessity for indenting was abolished in the case of ordinary deeds, and by 24 Vict. (1861), c. 9, as a requisite in gifts of land to charities.[7]

---

[1] See Cooley, Const. Lim. 748; 2 Whart. Cr. L. §§ 2385, 2544; 2 Chitty, Cr. L. 42; 1 Russ. Cr. 326; 2 S. & R. *91; 128 Mass. 52; 2 C. & K. 933.

[2] United States v. Smith, 11 F. R. 663, 665 (1882), Barr, District Judge.

[3] United States v. Loftis, 12 F. R. 671 (1882), Deady, J.

[4] McJunkins v. State, 10 Ind. 145 (1858), Hanna, J. See Jennings v. State, 16 id. 335 (1861); Ardery v. State, 56 id. 328 (1877).

[5] Van Houten v. State, 46 N. J. L. 17 (1884), Beasley, Chief Justice.

[6] Mitchell v. Work, 13 R. I. 646 (1882), cases.

[7] Seller v. Jenkins, 97 Ind. 430 (1884), cases.

[8] L. *indemnitas: in-demnis*, unharmed, free from *damnum*, hurt, loss.

[9] See Weller v. Eames, 15 Minn. 467 (1870); 2 McCord, 283.

---

[1] 30 Minn. 321; 15 id. 461.

[2] 87 Ill. 243.

[3] Wicker v. Hoppock, 6 Wall. 99 (1867).

[4] L. L. *indentare*, to notch: L. *dens*, a tooth.

[5] Overseers of Hopewell v. Overseers of Amwell, 6 N. J. L. 175 (1822).

[6] Bowen v. Beck, 94 N. Y. 89 (1883).

[7] 2 Bl. Com. 295; 2 Washb. R. P. 587; Williams, R. P. 146-47; 1 Reeve. Hist. Eng. Law, 89.

Indent. *n.* Any contract or obligation in writing; but may have a narrower signification.[1]

INDEPENDENCE. The Declaration of Independence, the state paper issued July 4, 1776, by the "Representatives of the United States of America," was, "that these United Colonies, are and of Right ought to be, Free and Independent States; that they are Absolved from Allegiance to the British Crown, and that all political connection between them and the State of Great Britain is and ought to be totally dissolved; . . . and that as Free and Independent States they have full Power to levy War, conclude Peace, contract Alliances, establish Commerce, and to do all other Acts and Things which Independent States may of right do."[2]

The inherent rights which lie at the foundation of all action between fellow-men are happily expressed in the preamble, viz.: "We hold these truths to be self-evident "— that is, so plain that their truth is recognized upon their mere statement,—"that all men are endowed "— not by edicts of emperors, or decrees of Parliament, or acts of Congress, but "by their Creator with certain inalienable rights "—that is, rights which cannot be bartered, given, or taken away except in punishment of crime,—"and that among these are life, liberty, and the pursuit of happiness, and to secure these "—not grant them —" governments are instituted among men, deriving their just powers from the consent of the governed."[3] See CONFEDERATION; HAPPINESS.

Independence Day. See HOLIDAY.

INDEPENDENT. See DEPENDENT; COVENANT.

INDEX. A portion of a book exhibiting, in alphabetical order, and in more or less detail, the contents of the whole volume; or, a book in itself containing, in like order, references to the contents of a series of volumes. Latin plural, *indices;* English plural, indexes.

Direct index. Exhibits the names of grantors, lessors, mortgagors, and other parties of the first part to recorded instruments. **Indirect** or **reverse index.** Gives the names of grantees, lessees, mortgagees, and other like parties to whom recorded instruments were executed; also called *ad sectam* index: literally, at the suit of, that is, orig-

inally, containing instruments made or delivered to plaintiffs.

Indexes, directed by statute to be made, are designed to facilitate the examination of records, not to protect the interests of persons whose conveyances are recorded. In such case the failure of the officer to make the index will not prejudice the title of a grantee or mortgagee.[1] See IDEM, Sonans.

INDIAN. Includes descendants of Indians who have an admixture of white or negro blood, provided they retain their distinctive character as members of the tribe from which they trace descent.[2]

The United States adopted the principle originally established by European nations, that the aboriginal tribes were to be regarded as the owners of the territories they respectively occupied.[3] See DISCOVERY, 1.

Indians who maintain their tribal relations are the subjects of independent governments, and as such not in the jurisdiction of the United States, because the Indian nations have always been regarded as distinct political communities between which and our government certain international relations were to be maintained. These relations are established by treaties to the same extent as with foreign powers. They are treated as sovereign communities, possessing and exercising the right of free deliberation and action, but, in consideration of protection, owing a qualified subjection to the United States.[4]

If the tribal organization of Indian bands is recognized by the political department of the National government as existing; that is to say, if the government makes treaties with and has its agent among them, paying annuities, and dealing otherwise with "head men " in its behalf, the fact that the primitive habits and customs of the tribe have been largely broken into by intercourse with the whites, does not authorize a State government to regard the tribal organization as gone, and the Indians as citizens of the State where they are and subject to its laws.[5]

When members leave their tribe and become merged into the mass of the people they owe complete

---

[1] United States *v.* Irwin, 5 McLean, 183–84 (1851).

[2] See Rev. Stat., 2 ed., pp. 3–6.

[3] Butchers' Union Co. *v.* Cresent City Co., 111 U. S. 756 (1884), Field, J.

[1] Nichol *v.* Henry, 89 Ind. 54, 58–59 (1883); Bedford *v.* Tupper, 30 Hun, 176 (1883). See also 35 Ala. 23; 50 Ga. 327; 19 Ill. 486; 29 La. An. 116; 31 *id* 33; 44 Mich. 123; 46 Mo. 472; 87 N. Y. 257; 16 Ohio St. 543; 76 Pa. 398; 82 *id.* 116; 11 W. N. C. 567; 24 Vt. 327, 338; 4 Biss. 437, 445; Cooley, Torts, p. 387, cases.

[2] Wall *v.* Williams, 11 Ala. 836 (1847). See Relation of Indians to Citizenship, 7 Op. Att.-Gen. 746, 750 (1856); Campan *v.* Dewey, 9 Mich. 435 (1861).

[3] United States *v.* Rogers, 4 How. 567 (1846); Johnson *v.* M'Intosh, 8 Wheat. 574, 584 (1823); United States *v.* Kagama, 118 U. S. 381–82 (1886); 3 Kent, 378; 2 Washb. R. P. 521.

[4] *Exp.* Reynolds, 18 Alb. Law J. 8 (U. S. D. C., W. D. Ark., 1878), Parker, J. See also Cherokee Nation *v.* Georgia, 5 Pet. *16 (1831); Worcester *v.* Georgia, 6 *id.* 515, 584 (1832); Dred Scott *v.* Sandford, 19 How. 403 (1856); Cherokee Trust Funds, 117 U. S. 288 (1886); 2 Story, Const. §§ 1097–1100; 3 Kent, 308–18; 50 Mich. 585.

[5] The Kansas Indians, 5 Wall. 737, 756 (1866), Davis, J.

allegiance to the government of the United States and are subject to its courts.[1]

A white man who is incorporated with a tribe by adoption does not thereby become an Indian, so as to cease to be amenable to the laws of the United States or to lose the right to trial in their courts.[2]

Under the Constitution "Indians not taxed" are not counted in apportioning representatives and direct taxes among the States; and Congress has power to regulate commerce with the Indian tribes. The tribes are alien nations, distinct political communities, with whom the United States have habitually dealt either through treaties or acts of Congress. The members owe immediate allegiance to their several tribes, and are not part of the people of the United States. They are in a dependent condition, a state of pupilage, resembling that of a ward to his guardian. Indians and their property, exempt from taxation by treaty or statute of the United States, cannot be taxed by any State. General acts of Congress do not apply to Indians, unless so expressed as to clearly manifest an intention to include them. The alien and dependent condition of the members of the tribes cannot be put off at their own will, without the assent of the United States. They have never been deemed citizens, except under explicit provisions of treaty or statute to that effect; nor were they made citizens by the Fourteenth Amendment.[3]

While the government has recognized in the Indian tribes heretofore a state of semi-independence and pupilage, it has the right and authority, instead of controlling them by treaties, to govern them by acts of Congress: they being within the geographical limits of the United States, and necessarily subject to the laws which Congress may enact for their protection and that of the people with whom they came in contact. A State has no power over them as long as they maintain their tribal relations: the Indians then owe no allegiance to the State, and receive from it no protection.[4]

In construing a treaty, if words be used which are susceptible of a more extended meaning than their plain import, as connected with the tenor of the treaty, they should be considered as used in the latter sense. How the words were understood by the unlettered people, rather than their critical meaning, should form the rule of construction.[5]

The relations between the United States and the different tribes being those of a superior toward an inferior who is under its care and control, its acts touching them and its promises to them, in the execution of its own policy and in the furtherance of its own interests, are to be interpreted as justice and reason demand in all cases where power is exerted by the strong over those to whom they owe care and

protection. The inequality between the parties is to be made good by the superior justice which looks only to the substance of the right, without regard to technical rules framed under a system of municipal jurisprudence, formulating the rights and obligations of private persons, equally subject to the same laws. . . A treaty is not to be read as rigidly as a document between private persons governed by a system of technical law, but in the light of that larger reason which constitutes the spirit of the law of nations.[1]

Indian country. That portion of the United States declared such by act of Congress; not, a country owned or inhabited by Indians in whole or in part.

As, in the act declaring it a crime to introduce spirituous liquors in such country.[2]

Applies to all the country to which the Indian title has not been extinguished, whether within a reservation or not, and whenever acquired.[3]

Indian Territory. An act approved February 15, 1888 (25 St. L. 33), provides that any person hereafter convicted in the United States courts having jurisdiction over the Indian Terrritory or parts thereof, of stealing any horse, mare, gelding, filly, foal, ass or mule, when said theft is committed in the Territory, shall be punished by a fine of not more than one thousand dollars, or by imprisonment not more than fifteen years, or by both, at the discretion of the court.

SEC. 2. That any person convicted of any robbery or burglary in the Territory shall be punished by a fine not exceeding one thousand dollars, or imprisonment not exceeding fifteen years, or both, at the discretion of the court; *Provided,* That the act shall not be construed to apply to any offense committed by one Indian upon the person or property of another Indian, or so as to repeal any former act in relation to robbing the mails or robbing any person or property belonging to the United States; nor shall the act affect or apply to any prosecution now pending, or the prosecution of any offense already committed.

SEC. 3. That all acts inconsistent with this act are hereby repealed: *Provided, however,* That such acts shall remain in force for the punishment of persons who have heretofore been guilty of the crime of larceny in the Territory.

See COMMERCE; EXPATRIATION; EXTRADITION, 1; GRAIN; PARTUS; PUEBLO.

INDICATE. See SHOW.

INDICIA. L. Marks; signs; appearances; color.

In civil law, circumstantial evidence — facts which give rise to inferences. In common law, indications

---

[1] *Exp.* Reynolds, *ante.*

[2] United States v. Rogers, 4 How. 567 (1846); 2 Op. Att.-Gen. 693; 4 *id.* 258; 7 *id.* 174.

[3] Elk v. Wilkins, 112 U. S. 99-100, 132 (1884), cases, Gray, J.

[4] United States v. Kagama, 118 U. S. 375, 381-82 (1886), cases, Miller, J. Act 3 March, 1871: R. S. § 2079; 119 U. S. 27.

[5] Worcester v. Georgia, 6 Pet. *582 (1832), M'Lean, J.

---

[1] Choctaw Nation v. United States, 119 U. S. 28 (1886), Matthews, J. On Indian citizenship, see 20 Am. Law Rev. 183-93 (1886), cases.

[2] United States v. Seveloff, 2 Saw. 311 (1872); Pelcher v. United States, 3 McCrary, 510, 515 (1882), cases; United States v. Martin, 8 Saw. 473 (1883), cases; Forty-Three Cases of Brandy, 14 F. R. 539-42 (1882), cases; United States v. Earl, 17 *id.* 75 (1883), cases; United States v. Holliday, 3 Wall. 407, 415-19 (1865).

[3] *Exp.* Crow Dog, 109 U. S. 556, 561 (1883). See also United States v. Le Bris, 121 *id.* 287 (1887); R. S. § 2139.

of character: as, *indicia* of authority, of fraud, of title.[1] See BADGE, 2.

INDICTMENT.[2] A written accusation of one or more persons of a crime or misdemeanor, preferred to and presented upon oath by a grand jury.[3]

Indict. To charge with crime by means of an indictment. **Indicted.** Charged by indictment. *Indictor* and *indictee* are not now in use. **Indictable.** Admitting of prosecution by indictment.

Bill of indictment. The written accusation presented to the grand jury, and found by them to be a "true bill" or "not a true bill."

The indictment intended by the Vth Amendment is the presentation to the proper court, under oath, by a grand jury, duly impaneled, of a charge describing an offense against the law for which the party may be punished.[4]

No change can be made in the body of such instrument without a re-submission to the grand jury — except where statutes prescribe otherwise. But changes may be made in the "caption."[4]

The object of indictment is, first, to furnish the accused with such a description of the charge against him as will enable him to make his defense, and avail himself of his conviction or acquittal for protection against a further prosecution for the same offense; and, second, to inform the court of the facts alleged, so that it may decide whether they are sufficient in law to support a conviction if one should be had.[5]

The object is, that the defendant may know what to meet; that he may plead a former acquittal or conviction; and that he may take the opinion of the court before which he is indicted, by demurrer or motion in arrest of judgment, or, the opinion of a court of error on the sufficiency of the statements in the indictment.[6]

Facts are to be stated, not conclusions of law alone. A crime is made up of acts and intent; and these must be set forth with reasonable particularity of time, place, and circumstances. Every ingredient of the offense must be clearly alleged. Where the definition of an offense includes generic terms, the indictment must state the species.[7]

Where the offense is a common-law offense, the technical words of the common law must be used; where the offense is statutory, the substance of the words may be followed.[1]

For a statutory offense, the charge must be so laid as to bring the case within the description of the offense given in the statute, alleging distinctly the essential requisites. Nothing is to be left to implication or intendment. It is sufficient to pursue the words of the act, or, if that would leave an ambiguity, then the substance and legal effect of the words.[2]

The rule that a statutory offense need not be charged in the words of the statute does not apply to technical terms and words of art which have acquired a conventional meaning and cannot be dispensed with, such as "murdered," "feloniously," and the like. But every material ingredient, constituting the description of the offense in the statute, whether an act done, knowledge had, an intent or purpose entertained, or the existence of any collateral fact, must be affirmatively stated in plain, direct, intelligible language.[3]

Where the statute simply designates the offense, and does not in express terms name its constituent elements, the information must sometimes be expanded beyond the statutory terms.[4]

When a statute contains provisos and exceptions in distinct clauses, it is not necessary to state that the defendant does not come within the exceptions, or to negative the provisos. But if the exceptions are contained in the enacting clause, it will be necessary to negative them, that the description of the crime may in all respects correspond with the statute.[5]

Where an offense may be committed by doing any one of several things, the indictment may, in a single count, group them together, and charge the defendant with having committed them all, and a conviction may be had of any one of the things, without proof of the commission of the others.[6]

Several offenses of the same class or kind, growing out of the same transaction, though committed at different times, may be joined in the same indictment in separate counts.[7]

Where the same offense is charged in different

---

[1] 60 Mo. 420; 1 Pars. Contr. 45.

[2] F. *indicter*, to accuse: L. L. *indicare*, to point out: L. *indicere*, to proclaim.

[3] 4 Bl. Com. 302. See also 4 Col. 202; 12 Conn. 452; 4 Mich. 424; 72 Mo. 106; 13 Wend. 317; 24 *id.* 570; 11 Ohio, 71; 19 Ohio St. 255.

[4] *Exp.* Bain, 120 U. S. 1, 6–9 (1887), cases, Miller, J. And see 26 Am. Law Reg. 446–47 (1887), cases.

[5] United States *v.* Cruikshank, 92 U. S. 558 (1875), Waite, C. J.

[6] United States *v.* Bennett, 16 Blatch. 350–51 (1879), Blatchford, J.; Bradlaugh *v.* The Queen, L. R., 3 Q. B. 616 (1878).

[7] United States *v.* Cruikshank, *supra;* United States

v. Cook, 17 Wall. 173–77 (1872), cases; United States *v.* Hess, 124 U. S. 483 (1888), cases.

[1] United States *v.* Bachelder, 2 Gall. *18 (1814), Story, J.; Cannon *v.* United States, 116 U. S. 78 (1885), cases.

[2] United States *v.* Staats, 8 How. 44 (1850), Nelson, J.

[3] Edwards *v.* Commonwealth, 19 Pick. 125 (1837), Shaw, C. J. See 4 Bl. Com. 307, 227; 11 F. R. 240; 2 Flip. 319; 87 Ind. 70; 30 Kan. 365, 612; 17 Nev. 286; 50 Pa. 249; 77 Va. 54.

[4] State *v.* Gavigan, 36 Kan. 327 (1887); 30 *id.* 365. See generally State *v.* Campbell, 29 Tex. 46 (1867), cases: 94 Am. Dec. 252–58 (1888), cases.

[5] 1 Chitty, Cr. L. 283 *b*, 284: United States *v.* Britton, 107 U. S. 670 (1882); United States *v.* Cook, 17 Wall. 173–74 (1872), cases.

[6] Bork *v.* People, 91 N. Y. 13 (1883); State *v.* Gray, 29 Minn. 144 (1882), cases.

[7] United States *v.* Wentworth, 11 F. R. 52 (1882); *Exp.* Peters, 12 *id.* 461 (1880); *ib.* 464, cases: R. S. § 1024.

counts, the whole indictment may be submitted to the jury, with instructions, if they find the defendant guilty upon any count, to return a general verdict of guilty; otherwise, where one count is had, and the evidence thereon is submitted with the rest, against objection.[1] See BAD, 2.

For a common-law offense, the conclusion of an indictment is "against the peace and dignity" of the commonwealth or State; for a statutory offense, "against the form of the statute in such case made and provided."[2] See AMENDMENT, 1; FORM, 2, Of statute.

An indictment is to be distinguished from a presentment and an information, qq. v.

See also ABBREVIATIONS; CAPTION, 2; CHALLENGE. 2; COMMENCEMENT; CONFESSION, 2; COPY; CRIME; DEMURRER; DIVERS; EVIDENCE; EXCEEDING; IDEM, Sonans; IDENTITY, 1; IGNORE; INDORSE, 1; INFAMY; JEOFAIL; JOINT; JURY; NEGATIVE; OR, 2; NOLLE PROSEQUI; NOLO CONTENDERE; PLACE, 1; QUASH; SENTENCE; THEN AND THERE; VERBUM, In hæc.

INDIFFERENT. 1. Said of an appraiser, where property has been taken in execution: impartial, free from bias.[3]

2. Said of a juror: that the mind is in a state of neutrality as respects the person and the matter to be tried; that there exists no bias, for or against either party, calculated to operate upon him; that he comes to the trial with a mind uncommitted and prepared to weigh the evidence in impartial scales.[4] Compare IMPARTIAL.

INDIGENT. See PAUPER; POOR.

A gift "to aid indigent young men" of a certain town or State "in fitting themselves for the evangelical ministry," is not void for uncertainty. The words "indigent" and "evangelical" are sufficiently definite, within ordinary intelligence. "They describe a man who is without sufficient means of his own, and whom no person is bound and able to supply, to enable him to prepare himself for preaching the Gospel."[5]

INDIGNITY. What acts or course of conduct will amount to such indignities as constitute a cause for divorce seems to be nowhere defined, and they are perhaps incapable of exact specification.

In Pennsylvania, a single act of indignity is not enough: there must be such a course of conduct, or continued treatment, as renders the wife's condition

intolerable and her life burdensome. Indignities to the person need not be such as would endanger life or health; they may be such as would render life too humiliating to be borne.[1]

In North Carolina, the indignity must be such as may be expected seriously to annoy a woman of ordinary good sense and temper, and must be continued in, so that it may appear to have been done willfully or at least consciously.[2]

That condition which renders life burdensome must be shown to exist in fact, and not be merely inferred from facts.[3] Compare CRUELTY, 1.

INDIRECT. See DIRECT.

INDISPUTABLE. See PRESUMPTION.

INDIVIDUAL. Pertaining or belonging to a single or distinct person, considered apart from a number of persons jointly associated or involved; personal; private: as, individual — assets, liability. See LIABILITY; PARTNERSHIP; CONTRIBUTION.

Individuals. See POLICE, 2; WELFARE.

INDIVISIBLE. See DIVISION, 1.

INDORSE.[4] 1. To write upon the back of any instrument or paper: as, to indorse a deed with the day or book of its record; to indorse a pleading filed with the time of receipt, payment of costs, etc.; to indorse a warrant of arrest prior to action under it in another county.[5]

In many cases, simply to write upon. In this sense words may be indorsed upon the *face* of a paper, even upon the face of a bill of exchange or promissory note.[6]

While the word has no definite technical meaning, other than that of some writing "upon the back," its particular meaning is always determined by the context, if in writing, and by its connection, if in spoken words.[7]

Indorsement. Has its primitive and popular sense of something written on the outside or back of a paper, on the opposite side from which something else had been previously written, when the context shows that that sense is necessary to give effect to

[1] Commonwealth v. Boston, &c. R. Co., 133 Mass. 391-92 (1882); 16 Gray, 11, 17; 120 Mass. 372.

[2] See Insall v. State, 14 Tex. Ap. 144 (1883); Holden v. State, 1 id. 234 (1876), cases.

[3] Fox v. Hills, 1 Conn. 307 (1815); Mitchell v. Kirtland, 7 id. *231 (1828); Fitch v. Smith, 9 id. *45 (1831).

[4] People v. Vermilyea, 7 Cow. 122 (1827).

[5] Storr's Agricultural School v. Whitney, 54 Conn. 352 (1887), cases, Pardee, J.: 35 Alb. Law J. 387, cases. Compare Hunt v. Fowler, 121 Ill. 269 (1887), cases: 36 Alb. Law J. 113; ib. 115, cases.

[1] May v. May, 62 Pa. 210 (1869).

[2] Miller v. Miller, 78 N. C. 106 (1878).

[3] Cline v. Cline, 10 Nev. 474-77 (1881), cases.

[4] F. endosser, to put on the back of: en, L. in, on; dos, L. dorsum, the back. Indorse seems to be preferred to endorse.

[5] See 2 Bl. Com. 468; Hartwell v. Hemmenway, 7 Pick. 119 (1828); Marian, etc. Gravel Road Co. v. Kessinger, 66 Ind. 553 (1879).

[6] Commonwealth v. Butterick, 100 Mass. 16 (1868); 2 Bish. Cr. L. § 570 a.

[7] Commonwealth v. Spilman, 124 Mass. 329 (1878); Davis v. Town of Fulton, 52 Wis. 662 (1881).

the pleading or other instrument in which it occurs.[1]

2. For the person to whom or to whose order a bill of exchange or a promissory note is payable, to write his name on the *back* of such bill or note in order to assign over his property therein.[2]

That is the common meaning, but it is not impossible to indorse by placing the name upon the face of the bill or note.[3]

Indorser. He who writes his name upon a negotiable instrument prior to transferring it by delivery. **Indorsee.** He to whom the instrument is delivered; the transferee.

Indorsement. The act by which a bill or note payable to order is transferred; the transfer of the legal title to any such instrument.

As far as it operates as a transfer of the instrument, it is an executed contract; and also, since it imports, unless restricted, future liability in the indorser, it is an executory contract. But every contract, whether executed or executory, evidenced by a written instrument, must be delivered and accepted. Hence, to complete a contract of indorsement, in addition to writing the name of the payee on the back, the further act of delivering the instrument to the person to whom title is to be transferred is necessary. Indorsing, then, imports delivery.[4]

Accommodation indorsement. In effect, a loan of the indorser's credit without consideration.

Blank indorsement. The form in which the indorser does not name the transferee. *Indorsement in full.* Contains the name of the transferee.[5]

Irregular indorsement. An indorsement which departs from common practice as to the place where the name should be written.[6]

Qualified indorsement. By this form the indorser limits or modifies his liability as ordinarily understood.

The words used are "without recourse;" without liability in case of non-acceptance or non-payment. They are written after the indorser's signature.[7]

Evidence that an indorsement in blank was "without recourse" is inadmissible.[1] See further RE-COURSE.

Restrictive indorsement. Restrains negotiability to a particular person, or for a special purpose.[2]

"Unqualified" and "unrestricted" designate that form of indorsement which is most common — the wholly unmodified form. And this, the ordinary contract, imports: as to a *bill*, that the indorser will pay it at maturity, if, on presentment for acceptance, it is not accepted, and he is duly notified of the dishonor; and as to a *bill* or *note*, that the indorser will pay it if it is not duly paid by the acceptor or maker, and he is duly notified; that it is genuine; that the signatures of the immediate parties, and, in the better opinion, of prior indorsers, are genuine; that it is a valid and subsisting obligation according to the ostensible relations of the parties; that the original parties, and, in the better opinion, prior indorsers, could bind themselves as they have assumed to do; and that the indorser has a lawful title and the right to transfer it.[3]

An indorser's contract is a new one, as compared with the maker's. He is not a surety, as is sometimes said, for a surety is a joint promisor with the principal.[4]

The maker is liable without demand of payment — his undertaking being conditional; but the indorser undertakes to pay only if the maker does not pay, which makes it necessary for the holder to take proper steps to obtain payment from the maker, from which it follows that his contract is that due diligence shall be used to that end.[5]

An indorser is only conditionally liable. His responsibility is a contingent one, and, ordinarily, performance of the condition to make demand of the maker and give notice of his default in due time is an essential part of the title of one who asserts an indorser's liability. The reason is, that the indorser, if looked to for payment, may have the earliest opportunity to take steps for his own protection. There is much inconsistency in the decisions whether demand and notice is necessary when they by no possibility could have enabled him to protect himself. The best considered cases hold that he is entitled to notice although he has taken indemnity from the maker — since that may prove insufficient. In general, every indorser ought to have notice whenever he has a remedy over against the maker. Where, by agreement with the maker, the indorser has become the principal debtor, no notice is needed — for the indorser then has no remedy over.[6]

---

[1] Powell *v.* Commonwealth, 11 Gratt. 830 (1854).

[2] 2 Bl. Com. 468.

[3] Haines *v.* Dubois, 30 N. J. L. 262 (1863), cases; Commonwealth *v.* Butterick, *ante;* Clark *v.* Sigourney, *infra.*

[4] Clark *v.* Sigourney, 17 Conn. *519 (1846).

[5] See Byles, Bills, 150–51, by Sharswood.

[6] See 24 Cent. Law J. 3–6 (1887), cases.

[7] Story. Prom. Notes, §§ 138, 146; Hailey *v.* Falconer, 32 Ala. 539 (1858).

[1] Martin *v.* Cole, 104 U. S. 30, 36–39 (1881), cases. See generally, as to parol explanations of indorsements, 18 Cent. Law J. 382–86 (1884), cases.

[2] See Armour Banking Co. *v.* Riley County Bank, 30 Kan. 165 (1883); 11 R. I. 119. Suffixes as *descriptio personæ*, Falk *v.* Moebs, 127 U. S. 597, 602–7 (1888), cases.

[3] See 1 Daniel, Neg. Inst. 498.

[4] Ross *v.* Jones, 22 Wall. 588 (1874), cases.

[5] Cox *v.* Nat. Bank of New York, 100 U. S. 713 (1879), cases.

[6] Ray *v.* Smith, 17 Wall. 415 (1873), Strong, J.

An indorser may sue all prior parties concurrently or successively, but can have only one satisfaction.[1]

Contracts of indorsement are to be construed according to the law of the place where made, unless it appears that they are to be performed according to the laws of another State.[2]

See further ACCEPT, 2; ACCOMMODATION; ASSIGN, 2; BEARER; BLANK; DESCRIPTIO PERSONAE; EXCHANGE, 3, Bill of; FAITH, Good; GUARANTY; NEGOTIATE, 2; NOTE, 2; PROTEST, 2.

INDUCEMENT. 1. In pleading, matter merely introductory to the essential ground or substance of the complaint or defense, or explanatory of it or of the manner in which it originated or took place.[3]

Being explanatory, it does not, in general, require exact certainty. Matter unnecessarily stated may be stricken out, or need not be proved.[4]

Thus, in trover, the loss and the finding of the goods, and, in nuisances, the possession of the subject injured, are alleged by way of inducement.[5]

Thus, also, in a suit upon a negotiable coupon, explanation of the relation the bond and the coupon have held, is by way of inducement: in the nature of a preamble, stating the circumstances under which the contract to pay interest was made.[4]

Commonly commences with the word "whereas." The importance of stating matter of inducement has been much relaxed by legislation. See AMENDMENT, 1.

2. In the sense of motive, see CONFESSION, 2; CONSIDERATION.

INDULGENCE. See FORBEARANCE; FAVOR; SURETY.

INEBRIATE. See INTEMPERATE.

INELIGIBLE. See ELIGIBLE.

INEQUITABLE. See EQUITY, Equitable.

INEVITABLE. See ACCIDENT; NECESSITY.

INFAMY. The condition of being without repute, honor, or character: disqualification to testify as a witness or to sit as a juror, on account of conviction of a heinous offense. Whence infamous.

"No person shall be held to answer for a capital or otherwise infamous crime unless on a presentment or indictment of a Grand Jury, except in cases arising in the land or naval forces, or in the Militia, when in actual service in time of War or public danger. . . ."[5]

"Infamous crime" is descriptive of an offense that subjects a person to infamous punishment or prevents his being a witness. The fact that an offense may be or must be punished by imprisonment in the penitentiary does not necessarily make it, in law, infamous.[1]

The Fifth Amendment had in view the rule of the common law, governing the mode of prosecuting those accused of crime, by which an information by the attorney-general, without the intervention of a grand jury, was not allowed for a capital crime, nor for any felony; rather than the rule of evidence, by which those convicted of crimes of a certain character were disqualified to testify as witnesses. In other words, of the two kinds of infamy known to the law of England before the Declaration of Independence, the Constitutional Amendment looked to the one founded on the opinions of the people respecting the mode of punishment, rather than to that founded in the construction of law respecting the future credibility of the delinquent. The leading word "capital" describing the crime by its punishment only, the associated words "or other infamous crime" must, by an elementary rule of construction, be held to include any crime subject to infamous punishment, even if they should be held to include also crimes infamous in their nature, independently of the punishment affixed to them. Having regard to the object and the terms of the Amendment, as well as to the history of its proposal and adoption, and to the early understanding and practice under it, no person can be held to answer, without presentment or indictment by a grand jury, for any crime for which an infamous punishment may be lawfully imposed by the court. The test is whether the crime is one for which the statutes authorize the court to award an infamous punishment, not whether the punishment ultimately awarded be an infamous one; when the accused is in danger of being subjected to an infamous punishment if convicted, he has the right to insist that he shall not be put upon his trial except on the accusation of a grand jury. What punishments shall be considered as infamous may be affected by the changes of public opinion from one age to another. For more than a century, imprisonment at hard labor in the State prison or penitentiary has been considered an infamous punishment, in England and America. Such imprisonment with or without hard labor is at present considered infamous punishment.[2]

The term "infamous" — without fame or good report — was applied at common law to certain crimes, upon conviction of which a person became incompetent to testify as a witness. This was upon the theory that a person would not commit a crime of such heinous character, unless so depraved as to be wholly insensible to the obligation of an oath, and, therefore, unworthy of credit. These crimes are treason, felony, and the *crimen falsi*. As to what or whether all species of the last are infamous, there is

[1] Brooklyn City, &c. R. Co. v. Nat. Bank of the Republic, 102 U. S. 35-37 (1880), cases.

[2] Briggs v. Latham, 36 Kan. 259-61 (1887), cases.

[3] [Gould, Plead. 42.

[4] City of Kenosha v. Lamson, 9 Wall. 482 (1869); 1 Chitty, Pl. 290.

[5] Constitution, Amd. V.

[1] United States v. Maxwell, 3 Dill. 276 (1875), cases, Dillon, Cir. J.; People v. Sponsler, 1 Dak. 297 (1876); Jones v. Robbins, 8 Gray, 348-49 (1857)

[2] Mackin v. United States, 117 U. S. 350-52 (1886), Gray, J.; Exp. Wilson, 114 id. 429, 423-29 (1885), cases, Gray, J.; Parkinson v. United States, 121 id. 281 (1887). See also Star-Route Cases (United States v. Brady), 3 Cr. Law Mag. 69 (1881).

disagreement among the authorities. . . A crime is not infamous, within the Fifth Amendment, unless it not only involves the charge of falsehood, but may also injuriously affect the public administration of justice by the introduction therein of falsehood and fraud.[1]

Under the Constitution and statutes there are no infamous crimes except those therein denounced as capital, or as felonies, or punished with disqualification as witnesses or jurors. If Congress makes a crime non-infamous, it can be pursued through information. . Stealing from the mails has not been made infamous.[2]

In early times the character of the crime was determined by the punishment inflicted, but in modern times the act itself, its nature, purpose, and effect, are looked at in determining whether it is infamous or not. Passing counterfeit money is not an infamous crime.[3]

Infamous persons are such as may be challenged as jurors *propter delictum;* and, therefore, they shall never be admitted to give evidence to inform that jury with whom they are too scandalous to associate.[4]

See CRIMEN, Falsi; TURPITUDE.

INFANT.[5] A person under the age of legal capacity; a minor.

Infancy. The status of one who has not attained his majority; minority; non-age.

An infant has a mind, but it is immature, insufficient to justify his assuming a binding obligation.[6]

He can do no legal act that will bind him, except enter into an apprenticeship, contract for necessaries and teaching,[7] and, perhaps, enlist in the army or navy.[8] He may deny or avoid any other contract during his majority or after he comes of age. At common law, also, a male under fourteen, and a female under twelve, cannot make a will.[9] But an infant may serve as agent. He sues by his guardian or next friend, and he defends by his guardian, perhaps by a special guardian *ad litem.*[10]

Under the age of discretion he is not punishable criminally.[11]

If he understands the nature of an oath, he may give evidence.[12]

At common law, the father is liable for torts committed by an infant.[1]

His disabilities are really privileges: to secure him from loss by improvident acts.[2]

In England, the lord chancellor is the general guardian of all infants. The origin of the jurisdiction of the court of chancery is in the crown as *parens patriæ.*[3]

See further ABANDON, 2 (2); AFFIRM, 2; AGE; DISABILTY; CAPAX; CHILD; DISCRETION, 1; FRIEND, Next; GUARDIAN; LACHES; NECESSARIES, 1; NEGLIGENCE; OATH; ORPHAN; PARENT; RATIFICATION; VOID; WARD, 3.

INFANTICIDE. See HOMICIDE.

INFEOFFMENT. See FEOFFMENT.

INFER. To bring a result or conclusion from something back of it, that is, from some evidence or data from which it may logically be deduced.[4]

To " presume " is to take or assume a matter beforehand, without proof — to take for granted.[4]

Inference. A deduction or conclusion from facts or propositions known to be true.[5] See PRESUMPTION.

INFERIOR. 1. The lower of two grades of authority or jurisdiction; subordinate: as, an inferior court or tribunal, an inferior officer. Opposed, *superior.* See COURT; OFFICER.

2. Of less worth or importance; the less significant: as, when it is said that terms of a lower class cannot be extended by construction to include terms or members of a higher class.

Thus, the term "animals," meaning quadrupeds, will not be held to include "birds."[6] See GENERAL; SUPERIOR.

INFIDEL. One who does not recognize the inspiration or obligation of the Holy Scriptures, or the generally recognized features of the Christian religion.[7] See ATHEIST; OATH.

Infidelity. See CHARITY, p. 170, col. 2.

INFINITE. See DISTRESS.

INFIRM. 1. Legally insufficient; lacking legal efficacy; incomplete; invalid. See FAITH, Good; NEGOTIABLE.

2. As to physical and mental infirmity, see INFLUENCE; INSANITY.

---

[1] United States *v.* Block, 4 Saw. 212 (1877), Deady, J.; Sylvester *v.* State, 71 Ala. 25 (1881).

[2] United States *v.* Wynn, 3 McCrary, 276 (1882), Treat, Judge.

[3] United States *v.* Yates, 6 F. R. 866 (1881), Benedict, J.; United States *v.* Petit, 11 *id.* 58 (1882); United States *v.* Field, 16 *id.* 778 (1883); *ib.* 779–82, cases.

[4] 3 Bl. Com. 370. See also 59 Pa. 116; 17 Fla. 185; 1 Greenl. Ev. § 373; 1 Bish. Cr. L. § 972.

[5] L. *in,* not; *fans,* speaking: *fari,* to speak.

[6] Dexter *v.* Hall, 15 Wall. 21 (1872).

[7] 1 Bl. Com. 465.

[8] 4 Binn. 487; 5 *id.* 423; 30 Vt. 357.

[9] 2 Bl. Com. 497; 1 *id.* 463.

[10] 1 Bl. Com 464.

[11] 4 Bl. Com. 22.

[12] See Commonwealth *v.* Lynes, 142 Mass. 570–80 (1833), cases.

[1] 18 Cent. Law. J. 3–7 (1884), cases.

[2] 1 Bl. Com. 464.

[3] 3 Bl. Com. 141; L. R., 10 Eq. 530.

[4] Morford *v.* Peck, 46 Conn. 385 (1878), Loomis, J.

[5] Gates *v.* Hughes, 44 Wis. 336 (1878).

[6] Reiche *v.* Smythe, 13 Wall. 164 (1871); United States *v.* Mattock, 2 Saw. 149–51 (1872).

[7] Gibson *v.* American Mut. Life Ins. Co., 37 N. Y. 584 (1868), Hunt, C. J.; Hale *v.* Everett, 53 N. H. 55 (1868); Omichund *v.* Barker, 1 Sm. L. C. 799–54, cases.

INFLUENCE. Most frequently used in connection with "undue," and refers to persuasion, machination, or constraint of will presented or exerted to procure a disposition of property — by gift, conveyance, or will.

The influence which is undue in cases of gifts *inter vivos* differs from that which is required to set aside a will. In testamentary cases, undue influence is always defined as coercion or fraud, but, *inter vivos*, no such definition is applied. Where parties occupy positions in which one is more or less dependent upon the other, courts of equity hold that the weaker party must be protected, and they set aside his gifts if he had not proper advice independently of the other.[1]

Influence, to vitiate an act, must amount to force and coercion destroying free agency; it must not be the influence of affection or attachment; not the mere desire of gratifying the wishes of another. There must be proof that the act was obtained by coercion, by importunity which could not be resisted; that it was done merely for the sake of peace; so that the motive was tantamount to force or fear.[2]

Undue influence is often defined by the courts to be a "fraudulent and controlling influence." In any application, the phrase savors of what is meant by fraud.[3]

When a person, from infirmity and mental weakness, is likely to be easily influenced by others, a transaction entered into by him, without independent advice, will be set aside, if there is any unfairness in it. Thus, where there is great weakness of mind in a grantor, arising from age, sickness, or other cause, though not amounting to absolute disqualification, and the consideration is grossly inadequate, a court of equity, upon proper and seasonable application of the person injured, his representatives or heirs, will set the conveyance aside. In such case, it is sufficient to show: great mental weakness — not amounting to insanity or extreme imbecility; and, inadequacy of consideration.[4]

Influence obtained by modest persuasion and arguments addressed to the understanding or by mere appeal to the affections, cannot be termed "undue;" but influence obtained by flattery, importunity, superiority of will, mind, or character, or by what art soever that human thought, ingenuity, or cunning may employ, which would give dominion over the will of the testator to such an extent as to destroy free agency or constrain him to do, against his will, what he is unable to refuse, is "undue."[5]

The undue influence for which a deed or will will

be annulled must be such that the party making it has no free will but stands *in vinculis*. "It must amount to force or coercion, destroying free agency." The ground upon which courts of equity grant relief is that one party by improper means has gained an unconscionable advantage over another. Each case must be decided on its own merits.[1]

Where a testator embraced spiritualism as practiced by his beneficiary, and became possessed by it, and this belief was used by the beneficiary to alienate him from his only child, his will was set aside.[2]

See DURESS; FRAUD; INSANITY, 2 (5); READING; SPIRITUALISM.

INFORMALITY. See FORMALITY.

INFORMATION.[3] Knowledge imparted or obtained. See BELIEF; COMMUNICATION.

In a statute intended to prevent physicians from disclosing "information" acquired from patients, comprehends knowledge acquired in any way while attending a patient, whether by the physician's own insight, or by verbal statement from the patient, from members of his household, or from nurses or strangers, given to aid the physician in the performance of his duty. Knowledge, however communicated, is information.[4]

An answer to a decoy letter written in a fictitious name, giving "information" of an article reputed to prevent conception, was held not to be within the meaning of a statute prohibiting the mailing of obscene matter.[5]

2. A complaint preferred on behalf of the government in a civil cause.

Bill of information. A bill in equity filed by the attorney-general, or other proper officer, in behalf of the state or of those

---

[1] Haydock v. Haydock, 34 N. J. E. 575 (1881); Huguenin v. Baseley, 2 L. C. Eq., 4 Am. ed., 1271, 1192–1290, cases.

[2] Goodwin v. Goodwin, 59 Cal. 561 (1881): Jarm. Wills, Perk. Notes, 41; Layman v. Conrey, 60 Md. 232 (1883).

[3] Wessell v. Rathjohn, 89 N. C. 383 (1883).

[4] Allore v. Jewell, 94 U. S. 511–12 (1876), Field, J. Approved, Griffith v. Godey, 113 id. 95 (1885); Crebs v. Jones, 79 Va. 382 (1884). See also Harding v. Wheaton, 2 Mas. 386 (1821), Story, J.; Harding v. Handy, 11 Wheat. 103, 119 (1826), Marshall, C. J.

[5] Schofield v. Walker, 58 Mich. 106 (1885), quoting probate court of Kent county.

---

[1] Conley v. Nailor, 118 U. S. 127, 133, 134–35 (1886), cases, Woods, J.

See further, as to gifts or conveyances, Nichols v. McCarthy, 53 Conn. 314–21 (1885), cases; Woodbury v. Woodbury, 141 Mass. 331–33 (1886), cases; Dunn v. Dunn, 42 N. J. E. 431 (1886); Davis v. Dean, 66 Wis. 110–11 (1886), cases; Bingham v. Fayerweather, 144 Mass. 51 (1887), cases; June v. Willis, 30 F. R. 11, 14 (1887), cases; Hall v. Knappenberger, Sup. Ct. Mo. (1888): 26 Cent. Law J. 317; ib. 319–22 (1888), cases; 3 McCrary, 650; 59 Cal. 560; 12 Mo. Ap. 293, 314; 34 N. J. E. 570; 1 Story, Eq. §§ 237–38; — as to wills, 22 Cent. Law J. 173 (1886), cases; 28 Ala. 107; 69 Ga. 89; 22 Kan. 79; 99 Mass. 112; 58 Mich. 106; 63 N. Y. 504; 88 id. 357; 41 Pa. 317; 43 id. 46; 76 id. 114.

[2] Thompson v. Hawks, 14 F. R. 902 (1883), Gresham, D. J.; ib. 905, note. See Lyon v. Home, L. R., 6 Eq. *655 (1868); Robinson v. Adams, 62 Me. 369 (1874); Smith's Will, 52 Wis. 543 (1881); 26 Am. Law Reg. 523–31 (1887), cases.

[3] L. *in-formare*, to put into shape: *forma*, form. See INFORMATUS.

[4] Edington v. Mut. Life Ins. Co., 5 Hun, 8 (1875): 2 N. Y. R. S. 406, § 73.

[5] United States v. Whittier, 5 Dill. 42 (1878).

whose rights are the objects of its protection.[1]

One method of redressing such injuries as the crown may receive from the subject is by an information filed in the exchequer by the king's attorney-general. This is a suit for recovering money or other chattel, or for obtaining satisfaction in damages for any personal wrong committed in the lands or other possessions of the crown. It differs from an information filed in the court of king's bench, in that this is instituted to redress a private wrong by which the property of the crown is affected; that is, is calculated to punish some public wrong, or heinous misdemeanor. It is grounded on no writ under seal, but merely on the intimation of the king's officer, who " gives the court to understand and be informed of " the matter in question; upon which the party is put to answer, and trial is had, as in suits between subject and subject. The most usual informations are those of intrusion or trespass committed on the lands of the crown; and debt upon any contract for moneys due to the king, or for forfeiture upon breach of a penal statute. There is also an information *in rem*, when any goods are supposed to become the property of the crown, and no man appears to claim them.[2]

In the United States, the more familiar informations are informations in the nature of a *quo warranto*, proceedings against persons alleged to be usurping a franchise or office; and *qui tam* informations — actions upon penal statutes, part of the penalty being for the use of the plaintiff; and proceedings to recover forfeitures under the revenue laws. See further QUI TAM; WARRANTUM; REVENUE.

3. A complaint lodged with a magistrate clothed with power to commit to prison, that a person named is guilty of a criminal offense.

The purpose is to effect a summary conviction of the accused, or a holding to bail for indictment and trial. In the latter case, a paper, called the " information," containing the details of the complaint, the names of the witnesses, the hearing or hearings had, the judgment, items of costs, etc., is transmitted to the grand jury for use in finding their bill of indictment, and perhaps accompanies the indictment into court before the trial jury.[3]

4. A criminal proceeding at the suit of the king, without a previous indictment or presentment by a grand jury.[4]

An " indictment " is an accusation found by the oath of a grand jury; an " information " is the allegation of a law-officer.[5]

An information was filed in the king's bench at the mere discretion of the proper law-officer of the government, and *ex officio*. It is sometimes called a " criminal " information.[1]

Prosecution by criminal information as at common law having been used for oppression, the statute of 4 and 5 William & Mary (1693), c. 18, was passed, requiring express leave of court to institute the proceeding.[2]

Under the laws of the United States, informations are resorted to in cases of illegal exportation of goods,[3] of smuggling,[4] and for offenses, not infamous, against the elective franchise.[5] See further INFAMY.

Informer. He who prefers a charge against another person by way of an information in a court exercising penal or criminal jurisdiction.

Common informer. A person who sues for forfeitures created by penal statutes.[6]

Whether the information he gives applies to customs, internal revenue, criminal matters, or forfeitures for any reason, an informer is one who gives the information which leads directly to the seizure and condemnation, regardless of the questions of evidence furnished, or interest taken in the prosecution.[7] See ACTION, 2, Popular; QUI TAM; MOIETY; PARDON.

INFORMATUS. L. Instructed; informed.

Non sum informatus. I am not informed. A judgment by default, when a defendant's attorney declares he has no instruction to say anything by way of answer or defense.[8]

INFRA. L. Below, beneath, under; within; during. Opposed, *supra.*

Used alone, refers to a citation or other matter further on, as in the text or at the foot of the particular page. Whence also *ut infra,* as (see) below.

Infra ætatem. Under age.

Infra annos nubiles. Within marriageable years.

Infra annum luctus. Within the year of mourning. See ANNUS, Luctus.

Infra corpus comitatus. Within the body of the county. See COUNTY, Body of.

Infra hospitium. Within the inn, — said of property in charge of an innkeeper.

Infra sex annos. Within six years. See ANNUS.

---

[1] [1 Bouvier's Law Dict. 245.

[2] 3 Bl. Com. 261; 4 *id.* 308. See also 3 Pick. 224; 6 Leigh, 588; 15 Johns. *387.

[3] See Goddard *v.* State, 12 Conn. *451 (1838).

[4] [4 Bl. Com. 308.

[5] United States *v.* Borger, 19 Blatch. 253 (1881); 4 Tex. 246.

[1] See 2 Story, Const. § 1786; 3 *id.* § 659; 1 Bish. Cr. Proc. § 141; Edwards *v.* Brown, 67 Mo. 379 (1878); State *v.* Concord, 20 N. H. 296 (1850).

[2] See 4 Bl. Com. 311.

[3] 1 Gall. 3.

[4] 1 Mass. 482, 500; 1 Wheat. 9; 9 *id.* 381.

[5] Act 31 May, 1870: R. S. § 1022.

[6] 3 Bl. Com. 161; 2 *id.* 437.

[7] The City of Mexico, 32 F. R. 106 (1887), cases, Locke, Judge.

[8] [3 Bl. Com. 397.

INFRINGEMENT.[1]
Breaking, infraction, violation; a trespass, transgression, invasion.

Infringer. One who invades or violates another's right.

Infringement, with its inflections is used of a violation of a law, regulation, contract, or common right; more often of the usurpation of an exclusive right. Thus it has acquired a use almost technical in reference to the law of copyrights, patents, and trade-marks: an infringement of any one of which consisting in violating the exclusive right another person has secured to make, sell, or use the thing in question.

In determining the question of the infringement of a patent right, the court or jury, as the case may be, are not to judge about similarities or differences by the names of things, but are to look at the machines or their several devices or elements in the light of what they do, or what office or function they perform, and how they perform it, and to find that one thing is substantially the same as another, if it performs substantially the same function in substantially the same way to obtain the same result, always bearing in mind that devices in a patented machine are different in the sense of the patent law when they perform different functions or in a different way, or produce a substantially different result.[2]

Where a defendant, who had been enjoined from using an invention, asked that he might give bond so that he could continue to use the invention and fill contracts therefor, it was held that a bond would not be adequate protection to the complainant's rights. The defendant also asked that the life of the injunction be limited to a day when, it was alleged, the patent would expire; but the court held that the time being in litigation the question could be disposed of on a motion to dissolve when that time arrived. It was further decided that the court had no authority to restrain the complainant from publishing the fact that the injunction had been issued.[3]

A right of action for the infringement of a patent survives to the personal representative of the patentee, and he may transfer the right to another person.

There is no Federal statute of limitations in force respecting infringements committed since June 22, 1874. State statutes of limitations have no application.[4]

See COPYRIGHT; DESIGN, 2; PATENT, 2; PROFIT, 2; TRADE-MARK. Compare INTERFERENCE.

INGRESS.
The right of entry upon land in a prescribed way.

"Egress" is the right of going off the premises to other points in any lawful way. "Regress" is the right of returning in any of these ways.

A grant of a right of "ingress, egress, and regress" is of a right of way from the *locus a quo* to the *locus ad quem*, and from the latter forth to any other spot to which the grantee may lawfully go, or back to the *locus a quo*.[1]

INHABITANT.[2]
Implies a more fixed and permanent abode than "resident;" frequently imports many privileges and duties to which a mere resident could not lay claim or be subject.[3]

One domiciled: one who has his domicil or fixed residence in a place, in opposition to a mere "sojourner."[4]

A person may be an inhabitant without being a citizen; and a citizen may not be an inhabitant, though he retains his citizenship.[5]

A legal voter; as, in a statute requiring that a subscription in aid of a railroad must be approved by the inhabitants of a town.[6]

In a figurative sense, a corporation may be said to inhabit the place where its members reside; and since, in a legal sense, it may be an occupier of land, any such corporation in England has been called an inhabitant. But an ordinary business corporation, keeping an office merely as a place for transacting business, cannot be said to inhabit the town where such office happens to be.[7]

Inhabitancy. A fixed and permanent abode or dwelling-place for the time being, as contradistinguished from a mere temporary locality of existence. Not the same as "domicil," when applied to successions to personalty.[8] See HABITANCY.

See BELONG; CITIZEN; DOMICIL; RESIDENCE.

INHERIT.
To take property by descent as an heir.

As used by a testator, may refer to lands devised or conveyed by an ancestor.[9]

---

[1] L. *in-fringere*, to break into, in upon.

[2] Union Paper-Bag Machine Co. *v.* Murphy, 97 U. S. 125 (1877), Clifford, J. Approved, Cantrell *v.* Wallick, 117 *id.* 695 (1886), Woods, J.

[6] Westinghouse Air Brake Co. *v.* Carpenter, 32 F. R. 545 (1887), Shiras, J.

[4] May *v.* County of Logan, 30 F. R. 250 (1887), cases, Jackson, J.

[1] Somerset *v.* Great Western Ry. Co., 46 L. T. 884 (1882).

[2] L. *in-habitare*, to dwell in: *habitare*, to have (oneself) often: *habere*, to have.

[3] Supervisors of Tazewell County *v.* Davenport, 40 Ill. 206 (1866); 19 Wend. 13.

[4] Barnet's Case, 1 Dall. *153 (1785); Borland *v.* Boston, 132 Mass. 98-99 (1882).

[5] Picquet *v.* Swan, 5 Mas. 46 (1828), Story, J.

[6] Walnut *v.* Wade, 103 U. S. 694 (1880).

[7] Hartford Fire Ins. Co. *v.* Hartford, 3 Conn. 25 (1819). See also 1 Dall. 480; 2 Pet. Adm. 450; 3 Ala. 547; 4 *id.* 630; 2 Conn. 20; 32 *id.* 47; 28 Ga. 121; 3 Ill. 403; 6 Ind. 83; 87 Me. 369; 2 Gray, 484; 132 Mass. 98-99; 45 N. H. 87; 23 N. J. L. 527; 36 *id.* 368; 8 Wend. 141; 10 *id.* 186; 4 Barb. 521; 48 *id.* 51; 1 Bradf. 83; Cooley, Const. Lim. 755.

[8] *Re* Wrigley, 8 Wend. 140 (1831); 132 Mass. 98; 9 F. R. 229.

[9] De Kay *v.* Irving, 5 Denio, 646, 654 (1846); 113 U. S. 380.

May refer to a distributive share of the proceeds arising from the sale of land.[1]

Disinherit. To direct by will that an heir shall receive no part of the testator's estate. See INOFFICIOUS.

Heritable. Capable of taking, or of passing, by descent.

Inheritance. An estate which descends, or may descend, to the heir upon the death of the ancestor;[2] also, the fact of receiving an estate as heir.

Estates of freehold are estates of inheritance, absolute or limited; and estates not of inheritance, or for life only.[3]

In its popular acceptation, "inheritance" includes all the methods by which a child or relative takes property from another at his death, except by devise, and includes as well succession as descent. As applied to personalty, signifies succession.[4]

An estate acquired by inheritance is one that has descended to the heir, and been cast upon him by the single operation of law.[5]

Shifting inheritance. An inheritance liable to be defeated by the birth of a nearer heir.

Does not prevail in the United States, where change of title from the living person is made by deed, rather than by the statute of descent, as in England where the canons of descent are designed to accumulate property in the hands of a few. By the rule of shifting inheritances, "If an estate is given to an only child, who dies, it may descend to an aunt, who may be stripped of it by an after-born uncle, on whom a subsequent sister of the deceased may enter, and who again will be deprived of the estate by the birth of a brother."[6]

See DESCENT; FREEHOLD; HEIR, 1; SUCCESSION, 1; WASTE, 1.

INHIBITION.[7] Forbidding; interdiction; prohibition.

A writ to forbid a judge from proceeding in a cause, or an individual from doing some act. Nearly the same as "prohibition" (*q. v.*) at common law, and "injunction" in equity.[8]

INITIALS. See IDEM, Sonans; NAME, 1.

INJUNCTION.[9] A remedial writ, formerly issued almost exclusively by a court of chancery, to restrain the commission of a threatened act, or the continuance of an act.

A judicial process operating *in personam,* and requiring the person to whom it is directed to do or to refrain from doing some particular thing.[1]

Enjoin. To prohibit by an injunction.[2]

Preliminary injunction. An injunction granted at the outset of a suit brought to restrain the doing of a threatened act, until the rights of the disputants have been determined. Called also an *interlocutory* or *provisional* injunction, or an injunction *pendente lite;* and, also, a *mandatory* or *preventive* injunction, according as the order is to do or refrain from doing the particular act. Opposed, **final injunction**: issued upon final adjudication of the rights in question. Being designed to effect permanent relief, is frequently termed the *perpetual* injunction.

The object of a preliminary or interlocutory injunction is, in general, simply preventive — to maintain things in the condition they are in at the time, until the rights and equities of the parties can be considered and determined after a full examination. Such injunction is never awarded, except when the right or equity of the plaintiff is clear, at least supposing the facts of which he gives *prima facie* evidence to be ultimately established. All injunctions are generally processes of mere restraint; yet final injunctions may certainly go beyond this and command acts to be done or undone. They are then called "mandatory;" and often are necessary to do complete justice. But the authorities are clear that an interlocutory or preliminary injunction cannot be mandatory. . . Injunction as a measure of mere temporary restraint is a mighty power to be wielded by one man. . . An interlocutory injunction may be granted on an *ex parte* application; when it is upon notice it is upon *ex parte* affidavits.[3]

As a preliminary injunction is in its operation somewhat like judgment and execution before trial, it is only to be resorted to from a pressing necessity to avoid injurious consequences which cannot be repaired under any standard of compensation.[4]

As it is, in fact, the result of an interlocutory decree in advance of a regular hearing and plenary proofs, it should never be granted except where irreparable injury is threatened; and the court should be

---

[1] Ridgeway *v.* Underwood, 67 Ill. 426 (1873).

[2] [2 Bl. Com. 201.

[3] 2 Bl. Com. 104, 120.

[4] Horner *v.* Webster, 33 N. J. L. 413 (1867).

[5] Estate of Donahue, 36 Cal. 332 (1868).

[6] 2 Christ. Bl. Com. 208 n; Bates *v.* Brown, 5 Wall. 713–19 (1866), cases.

[7] L. *in-hibere,* not to have: to keep in, hold in, check.

[8] See Termes de la Ley; Wharton's Law Dict.; 6 Q. B. D. 420.

[9] L. *injunctio: injungere,* to bid, command.

[1] High, Injunctions, § 1.

[2] See 31 Alb. Law J. 181, 220, 240, 279 (1885).

[3] Audenried *v.* Philadelphia & Reading R. Co., 68 Pa. 375–78 (1871), cases, Sharswood, J. See generally 18 Cent. Law J. 323–26, 343–46 (1884), cases.

[4] Mammoth Vein Coal Co.'s Appeal, 54 Pa. 188 (1867), Thompson, J. See also Ballantine *v.* Harrison, 37 N. J. E. 561 (1883); Stanford *v.* Lyon, *ib.* 113 (1883).

satisfied that in attempting to prevent such injury as to one party it will not bring like injury upon the adverse party.[1]

An injunction is generally a preventive, not an affirmative, remedy. But it is sometimes used in the latter character to carry into effect a court's own decree; as, to put into possession the purchaser under a decree of foreclosure of a mortgage.[2] Where granted without a trial at law, it is upon the principle of preserving the property until a trial at law can be had. A strong *prima facie* case of right must be shown, and there must have been no improper delay. In granting or refusing the writ, the court exercises a careful discrimination.[3]

A court of equity may substitute a bond of indemnity for an injunction, if the ends of justice will thereby be promoted: especially if a public interest may suffer by the continuance of an injunction.[4]

An injunction is available to stay proceedings at law; to restrain the transfer of stocks, notes, bills, and other evidences of debt; to restrain the transfer of the possession or title to property; to restrain one from setting up an inequitable defense at law; to restrain the infringement of a patent, a copyright, a trade-mark; to prevent the removal of property or the evidence of title to property or of indebtedness out of the jurisdiction; to restrain the commencement of proceedings in a foreign court; to restrain an illegal act by municipal officers; to prevent the creation or the continuance of a nuisance; to restrain acts of waste.

A court of equity has no power to enjoin the prosecution of an offense in a court of common law.[5]

But there must be no plain, adequate, and complete remedy at law. The writ will not be granted at all while the rights between the parties are undetermined, except, as seen, where irreparable injury will be done. The petition or bill must sufficiently appraise the respondent as to what duty is required of him.[6]

An injunction must be respected while in force, although improperly granted; but it cannot affect the rights of a person who is not a party or privy to the proceeding.[7]

In England, a *common* injunction has been issued as of course when the defendant failed to enter his appearance or to answer the bill within the prescribed time; and a *special* injunction, by leave of court, upon proof of the charges and notice to the adverse parties. At present, it seems, that any court of that country may issue injunctions of all kinds.[8]

See ADEQUATE, 2; EQUITY; INJURY, Irreparable.

[1] Wagner v. Drake, 31 F. R. 853 (1887); High, Inj. §§ 7-10, cases.

[2] Walkley v. City of Muscatine, 6 Wall. 483 (1867).

[3] Parker v. Winnipiseogee, &c. Co., 2 Black, 552 (1862), cases.

[4] Northern Pacific R. Co. v. St. Paul, &c. Co., 4 F. R. 688 (1880).

[5] Suess v. Noble, 31 F. R. 855 (1887); *Re* Sawyer, 124 U. S. 210 (1888), cases.

[6] See R. S. §§ 718-20; 1 Hughes, 607; 3 F. R. 507; 4 Dill. 600; 2 Woods, 621.

[7] Roberts v. Davidson, 83 Ky. 282 (1885).

[8] 1 Story, Eq. § 892.

INJURIA. L. Wrong; injury. A tortious act, whether willful and malicious, or accidental.[1] Compare DELICTUM.

Ab assuetis non fit injuria. From matters of long standing no injury arises.

Acquiescence with a state of things as it has long existed, operates as a waiver or abandonment of one's right therein. See ESTOPPEL.

Damnum absque injuria. Loss without such injury as the law recognizes. See further DAMNUM.

De injuria. Of (his own) wrong. See REPLICATION.

Volenti non fit injuria. To him who wills a thing there can be no injury. See further VOLO, Volenti.

INJURY. A privation of legal right; a wrong; a tort. See INJURIA.

A wrong done to a person; a violation of his right.[2]

"Injury" is the wrongful act or tort which causes harm or injury to another. "Damages" are allowed as an indemnity to the person who suffers loss or harm from injury. "Injury" denotes the illegal act; "damages," the sum recoverable as amends for the wrong.[3]

Civil injury. A private wrong; an infringement or privation of the private or civil rights belonging to an individual considered as an individual.

It affects an absolute or relative right, and is committed with force and violence, as in battery and false imprisonment; or without force, as in slander and breach of contract. *Public injuries* are public wrongs or crimes,[4] *q. v.*

Results from non-feasance, misfeasance, or malfeasance; and affects the person, personalty, or realty. See TAKE, 8.

Irreparable injury. Injury of such nature that the party wronged cannot be adequately compensated in damages, or when the damages which may result cannot be measured by any certain pecuniary standard.[5]

All that is meant is, that the injury would be a grievous one, or at least a material one, and not adequately reparable in damages. The term does not mean that there must be no physical possibility of repairing the injury.[6]

[1] Wright v. Chicago, &c. R. Co., 7 Bradw. 446 (1880).

[2] Parker v. Griswold, 17 Conn. *302 (1845).

[3] North Vernon v. Veegler, 103 Ind. 319 (1885), Elliott, J.; 25 Am. Law Reg. 101, 112-15 (1886), cases.

[4] 3 Bl. Com. 2, 118.

[5] [Wilson v. Mineral Point, 39 Wis. 164 (1875): High, Injunc. § 460.

[6] Sanderlin v. Baxter, 76 Va. 306 (1882): Kerr, Injunc. 199; Moore v. Steelman, 80 Va. 340 (1885), cases; Wahle v. Reinbach, 76 Ill. 326 (1875).

The word "irreparable" is unhappily chosen to express the rule that an injunction may issue to prevent wrongs of a repeated and continuing character, or which occasion damages estimable only by conjecture and not by any accurate standard.[1]

In the sense in which used in conferring jurisdiction upon courts of equity, does not necessarily mean that the injury complained of is incapable of being measured by a pecuniary standard.[2]

Literally, anything is irreparable injury which cannot be restored *in specie*. In law nothing is irreparable which can be fully compensated in damages. To entitle a party to an injunction, he must show that the injury complained of is irreparable because the law affords no adequate remedy.[3]

Injuriously affect. See TAKE, 8.

See further ADMISSION, 2; CASE, 3; CAUSE, 1; CONTINUOUS, 2; CONTINUANDO; DECLARATION, 1; INSPECTION, 2, Of person. Compare DAMAGE; REDRESS; RELIEF; TORT; WRONG.

INJUSTICE. See JUSTICE, 1.

INK. See WRITING.

INLAND. See COMMERCE; EXCHANGE, Bill of; NAVIGATION.

In the act of July 2, 1864, §7, that no property seized upon "any of the inland waters of the United States," by the naval forces, shall be regarded as maritime prize, "inland" applies to all waters upon which a naval force could go, other than bays and harbors on the sea-coast.[4]

INN. A house where the traveler is furnished with everything which he hath occasion for whilst upon his way.[5]

A public house of entertainment for all who choose to visit it.[6]

A house kept open publicly for the lodging and entertainment of travelers in general, for a reasonable compensation.[7]

The leading ideas of all the definitions are, that an inn is a house for the entertainment of travelers and wayfarers, at all times and seasons, who properly apply and behave with decency, and this as guests for a brief period, not as lodgers or boarders, by contract, for the season.[1]

Synonymous with "tavern" and "hotel;" not with "boarding-house," "restaurant," or "lodging-house."[2]

Innkeeper. A person who makes it his business to entertain travelers and passengers, and provide lodging and necessaries for them, their horses and attendants.[3]

He is a guest at an inn or hotel who is away from home and receives accommodations at the house as a traveler. See further GUEST.

An innkeeper's liability for a loss to his guest is the same in character and extent as the liability of a common carrier. In the absence of proof that the loss was occasioned by the hand or through the negligence of the hotel keeper, or by a clerk or servant employed by him, the guest cannot recover the amount of the loss from the keeper.[4]

His responsibility approximates to insurance when an article (a valise) is entrusted by a guest to his keeping.[5]

An innkeeper impliedly engages to entertain all persons who apply; and an action on the case will lie against him for damages, if, without good reason, he refuses to admit a traveler. To frustrate, in that way, the end of the institution, was held to be disorderly behavior. Indeed, for an unreasonable refusal to receive travelers, the proprietor could even be indicted and his inn suppressed.[6]

The common-law liability of an innkeeper has been generally changed by statute. He is not now liable for money, jewelry, or other valuables, lost or stolen, if he provides a safe for their keeping and duly notifies guests thereof. Nor should he be held liable for goods stolen from a room furnished for the display of samples of merchandise.[7]

He is not liable as an innkeeper for the loss of

---

[1] Commonwealth v. Pittsburgh, &c. R. Co., 24 Pa. 160 (1854), cases.

[2] Wilmarth v. Woodcock, 58 Mich. 485 (1885), Champlin, J.

[3] Brace Brothers v. Evans et al., C. P. No. 1, Allegheny Co., Pa. (April 21, 1888), Slagle, J.: 35 Pitts. Leg. J. 406, cases. A boycotting case. "The business lost, and which will be destroyed by defendants' acts, cannot be restored. If permitted, plaintiffs may build up a new business, but the old one cannot be replaced. It is gone irreparably." See also Breuschke v. The Furniture Makers' Union, Sup. Ct. Cook Co., Ill. (188–); Western Union Tel. Co. v. Rogers, 42 N. J. E. 314 (1886); Emack v. Kane, 3 Ry. Corp. Law J. 317 (1888).

[4] Porter v. United States, 106 U. S. 612 (1882).

[5] Thompson v. Lacy, 3 B. & A. 285 (1820), Bayley, J.

[6] Wintermute v. Clarke, 5 Sandf. 247 (1851), Oakley, C. J.; Walling v. Potter, 35 Conn. 185 (1868); 36 Barb. 462.

[7] 2 Kent, 595.

[1] Bonner v. Welborn, 7 Ga. 307 (1849).

[2] People v. Jones, 54 Barb. 316–17 (1863), cases; Pinkerton v. Woodward, 33 Cal. 596 (1867), cases.

[3] Bacon, Abr., Inn. B.; Carter v. Hobbs, 12 Mich. 56 (1863); Howth v. Franklin, 20 Tex. 801 (1858).

[4] Elcox v. Hill, 98 U. S. 224 (1878), cases; 66 Ga. 206; 1 Bl. Com. 430; 2 Kent, 592; Story, Bailm. § 470.

[5] Murray v. Marshall, 9 Col. 482 (1886), cases.

[6] 3 Bl. Com. 166; 4 id. 167.

[7] Fisher v. Kelsey, 121 U. S. 383, 385–86 (1887), cases. The plaintiff, a traveling salesman, engaged a room in the Planters' House, city of St. Louis, for the exhibition of articles of jewelry. During his occupancy of the room, articles valued at $12,600 were stolen, without neglect in him or in the proprietor of the hotel. Held, that the relation of innkeeper and guest did not exist as to the use made of the sample room; also, that knowledge in the proprietor that the articles were brought into his hotel to be exhibited for sale, did not relieve the owner from serving written notice upon the proprietor, as required by statute in Missouri, that he had such merchandise in his possession.

money deposited with him for safe-keeping by a person not a guest.[1]

The owner of a steamship is not an innkeeper.[2]

See BOARD, 1; HOTEL; LIEN, Common-law; LODGER; RESIDE; RESTAURANT; RIGHT, 2, Civil Rights Acts; TAVERN.

Inns of court. Originally, town-houses in which the nobility and gentry resided when in attendance at court; later, schools for the study of law.

The name was given to law societies which occupied certain "Inns," as Lincoln's Inn, Gray's Inn. The buildings were originally private residences, or *hospitia* — town-houses. They retained, in their new use, their former names; in them lectures were read, and degrees conferred in the common law.[3] See BENCHER.

INNER. See BARRISTER.

INNOCENCE. Being free from the guilt of crime, fraud, or negligence.

Innocent. Not chargeable with fault, fraud, or wrong: as, an innocent purchaser or holder.

1. Where one of two innocent parties must suffer through the fraud or wrong of a third party, the loss falls upon him who gave the credit; as, where one signs his name to blank paper which is afterward fraudulently made a promissory note.[4]

If one of two innocent parties must suffer for a deceit, it is more consonant to reason that he who "puts the trust and confidence in the deceiver (agent, cashier, etc.) should be the loser, rather than the stranger."[5]

The loss should fall on him who by reasonable diligence could have protected himself.[6]

He who gave the power to do the wrong must bear the burden of the consequences.[7]

In the negotiation of commercial paper, a holder is not innocent where there is any circumstance to excite the suspicion of a man of ordinary caution as to a defect or irregularity in the paper, or a want of power in any party thereto.[8] See FAITH, Good; KNOWLEDGE, 1.

2. In the law of criminal procedure, innocence is presumed until the contrary is proven. That is, a reasonable doubt of guilt is a ground of acquittal, where, if the probative force of the presumption were excluded, there might be a conviction. This presump-

tion or probative evidence is not applicable in civil cases or in revenue seizures — where the issue depends upon the evidence, but the defendant is not put to his defense until a *prima facie* case is made out by the plaintiff.[1]

Innocence is always presumed, except as against the publisher of a libel.[2]

See DOUBT, Reasonable; INTENT; LIBEL, 5.

INNUENDO. L. With the meaning; thereby meaning. A clause in a pleading explanatory of a preceding word or averment.

The same in effect as "that is to say." While used almost exclusively in actions for defamation, it may be inserted in declarations in other actions, to explain the meaning of a written instrument.[3]

In a declaration for slander or libel, explains the words uttered; annexes to them their proper meaning. It cannot enlarge or extend the sense of expressions beyond their usual, natural import, unless something is put upon the record by way of introductory matter with which they can be connected. Then, words which are equivocal or ambiguous, or fall short in their natural sense of importing any defamatory charge, may have fixed to them a meaning certain and defamatory, extending beyond their ordinary import.[4]

If the words impute an infamous crime punishable by law, an *innuendo*, undertaking to state the same in other words, is superfluous; if they do not, an *innuendo* cannot aid the averment, as it is a clear rule of law that an *innuendo* cannot introduce a meaning broader than that the words naturally bear, unless connected with proper introductory averments.[5]

See COLLOQUIUM; LIBEL, 5; SLANDER.

INOFFICIOUS. An inofficious will is one in which natural affection and the claims of near relationship have been disregarded.[6]

The civil law defines an inofficious or undutiful will to be such as substantially departs from the disposition of the estate which would be made in case of intestacy.

In America, authority to make a will implies the power to discriminate between, or to disinherit, next of kin; and the fact of such discrimination raises no presumption of undue influence.[7]

See TESTAMENTUM, Inofficiosum.

INOPERATIVE. See OPERATIVE, 2.

INOPS CONSILII. L. Without legal counsel.

Devises by will are more favored in construction than formal deeds, which are presumed to be made

[1] Arcade Hotel Co. *v.* Wiatt, 44 Ohio St. 45-46 (1886). As to lien, see 21 Am. Law Rev. 679-95 (1887), cases.

[2] Clark *v.* Burns, 118 Mass. 277 (1875), cases. See, in general, 25 Am. Law Reg. 904-6 (1886), cases; 1 Sm. Ld. Cas. 401-6, cases.

[3] See 1 Bl. Com. 23-25; 3 *id.* 39.

[4] Bank of Pittsburgh *v.* Neal, 22 How. 111 (1859), cases.

[5] Carpenter *v.* Longan 16 Wall. 273 (1872).

[6] Nat. Savings Bank *v.* Creswell, 100 U. S. 643 (1879).

[7] People's Bank *v.* Manufacturers' Nat. Bank, 101 U. S. 183 (1879).

[8] Merchants' Bank *v.* State Bank, 10 Wall. 604, 646 (1870); 34 La. An. 180; 34 N. Y. 30.

[1] Lilienthal's Tobacco *v.* United States, 97 U. S. 267 (1877); 15 Gray, 415; 2 Whart. Ev. § 1245.

[2] 1 Greenl. Ev. § 36; 1 Cr. Law Mag. 1; 4 *id.* 643, 845.

[3] See Whitsett *v.* Womack, 8 Ala. 482 (1845).

[4] Beardsley *v.* Tappan, 1 Blatch. 591 (1850), cases, Nelson, J.; Young *v.* Cook, 144 Mass. 41-42 (1887), cases.

[5] Pollard *v.* Lyon, 91 U. S. 233 (1875), cases, Clifford, J. See also 8 Biss. 268; 29 Kan. 518; 50 Mich. 640; 5 Johns. *438; 53 Pa. 418; 59 *id.* 488; 114 *id.* 558.

[6] Banks *v.* Goodfellow, 39 L. J. R., Q. B. 248, 244 (1870), Cockburn, C. J.

[7] Stein *v.* Wilzinski, 4 Redf. 450 (1880).

with great caution, forethought, and advice. In this principle originated executory devises.[1]

INQUEST. An inquiry by a jury, duly impaneled by the proper officer, into any cause, civil or criminal; also, such jury itself. Compare INQUIRY, 2, 3.

Coroner's inquest. An inquiry by a coroner, assisted by a jury, into the manner of death of one who has been killed, or died suddenly or in prison. See CORONER.

Grand inquest. The grand jury, *q. v.*

Inquest of lands; sheriff's inquisition. In Pennsylvania, after a sheriff has levied upon a debtor's realty, he summons a jury of at least six men who ascertain whether the rents and profits of the estate, beyond all reprises, will be sufficient, within seven years, to satisfy the judgment and costs of suit. The right to the proceeding is frequently waived.[2]

Inquest of office. A method of redressing an injury which the crown (state) receives from a subject.

An inquiry made by a sheriff, coroner, escheator, or commissioners specially appointed, concerning any matter that entitles the king to the possession of lands or tenements, goods or chattels; as, reversions accruing to the crown, escheats, forfeitures, whether one is a lunatic and what property he has, the fact of a wreck, of treasure-trove, etc. Also known as "office found,"[3] *q. v.*

INQUIRY. A seeking: search, investigation. Compare INQUEST.

1. When there are facts sufficient to put a man of ordinary caution upon inquiry, the means of knowing and knowledge itself are, in legal effect, the same thing. See further KNOWLEDGE, 1; NOTICE, 1.

2. In the oath of grand jurors "diligently inquire" means diligently inquire into the circumstances of the charges, the credibility of the witnesses, and, from the whole, judge whether the accused ought to be put upon trial.[4]

3. A writ by which the sheriff is directed to summon a jury to ascertain the damages due from a defendant against whom there has been an interlocutory judgment, entered either by default or by confession, the amount not being ascertainable by mere calculation.[5]

INQUISITION. See INQUEST; INQUIRY.

INSANITY.[1] Disorder of mind from disease or defect in the brain; disease of the mind.

1. In pathology. A condition in which the intellectual faculties, or the moral sentiments, or the animal propensities,— any one or all of them,— have their free action destroyed by disease, whether congenital or acquired. . . A disease of the brain, affecting one or more of the mental faculties — intellectual or emotional.[2]

A manifestation of disease of the brain, characterized by a general or partial derangement of one or more faculties of the mind, and in which, while consciousness is not abolished, mental freedom is perverted, weakened, or destroyed.[3]

By "disease" is here meant structural change due to injury, malformation, malnutrition, non-development, or other cause.[3]

Insanity is due: I. To defective development of faculties; called *idiocy* or *imbecility*, resulting from congenital defect, or from an obstacle to development, supervening in infancy. II. To lesion of faculties subsequent to development; called *mania*, intellectual or affective, and either general or partial, or *dementia*, consecutive to mania, or to injury to the brain, or else senile.[4]

Most of the definitions, so called, are merely sententious descriptions of the disease. It is impossible to frame a perfectly consistent definition. No words can comprise the different forms and characters the malady may assume. The more common forms are *mania*, *monomania*, and *dementia*; each of which implies a derangement of the faculties of the mind from their normal or natural condition. *Idiocy* (q. v.) is more properly the absence of mind than derangement of its faculties; it is congenital, and consists not in the loss or derangement of the powers, but in the destitution of powers never possessed. *Mania* is derangement accompanied with more or less excitement, amounting, in cases, to a fury. The individual is subject to hallucinations and illusions; is impressed with the reality

---

[1] 2 Bl. Com. 381, 172, 115, 108.

[2] See 1 Bright. T. & H. Pr. §§ 1222–36.

[3] 3 Bl. Com. 258; 2 Kent, 16, 23.

[4] Respublica *v.* Shaffer, 1 Dall. *237 (1788).

[5] See 3 Bl. Com. 398; Hanley *v.* Sutherland, 74 Me. 213 (1882), cases; McHenry *v.* Union Passenger Ry. Co., 14 W. N. C. 404 (Pa., 1884).

---

[1] L. *insanitas*, unsoundness of mind: *in*, not; *sanus*, healthy, whole, sound.

[2] Tuke (Bucknill & T.), Insanity, ed. 1858, p. 88.

[3] Hammond, Treatise on Insanity, 265 (1881). See also Ray, Med. Jurisp. of Ins. § 54; Elwell, Malpr. &c. 338.

[4] Ray, Med. Jurisp. of Ins. (1871), § 56. See further 25 Cent. Law J. 195–218 (1887), cases.

of events which have never occurred, and of things which do not exist; and acts more or less in conformity with these particulars. The mania may be general, and affect all or most of the operations of the mind; or partial, and be confined to particular subjects — which last constitutes *monomania*. An absence of reason on one matter, indeed on many matters, may exist, and at the same time the patient exhibit a high degree of intelligence and wisdom on other matters. The cases show a want of entire soundness of mind or partial insanity. This form does not necessarily unfit the patient for transacting business on all subjects. *Dementia* is derangement accompanied with general enfeeblement of the faculties. It is characterized by forgetfulness, inability to follow any train of thought, and indifference to passing events. There is not usually equal weakness exhibited on all subjects, nor in all the faculties. Matters which, previously to the existence of the malady, the patient frequently thought of, are generally retained with greater clearness than less familiar subjects. One faculty, as, the memory, will be greatly impaired, while other faculties retain some portion of their original vigor. The disease is of all degrees, from slight weakness to absolute loss of reason. These three forms of insanity,— mania, monomania, dementia,— present themselves in an infinite variety of ways, seldom exhibiting themselves in any two cases exactly in the same manner.[1]

Emotional insanity. The condition of one, in possession of his ordinary reasoning faculties, whose passions convert him into a maniac, and, while in this condition, he commits an act in question.

Impulsive insanity. Exists when one is irresistibly impelled to the commission of an act.[2]

To be distinguished from the case where, being in possession of his reasoning faculties, the person is impelled by passion merely.[2] See IMPULSE.

Moral insanity. Describes a mind which, while undisturbed by hallucination or illusion, and qualified to judge between right and wrong, is yet powerless to control conduct according to knowledge; as, in *kleptomania.*

---

[1] Hall *v.* Unger, 2 Abb. U. S. 510-15 (1867), Field, J., Cir. Ct., 9th Cir., Dist. Cal.

[2] Mut. Life Ins. Co. *v.* Terry, 15 Wall. 590 (1872).

Consists in a morbid perversion of the feelings, affections or active powers, without any illusion or erroneous conviction impressed upon the understanding.[1]

2. In medical jurisprudence. The law, being neither a medical nor a metaphysical science, has no theory on the subject of diseases of the brain. It seeks practical rules which may be administered, without inhumanity, for the security of society, by protecting it from crime. It holds every man responsible who is a free agent. "Insanity" is really not a legal term.

Questions involving sanity arise in determining what degree of unsoundness will make void a marriage, disqualify for the duties of an office or trust, render incompetent or discredit as a witness, advise commitment to an asylum, or negative consent in the commission of certain crimes. On these and kindred subjects, no uniform test has been established; each case is to be decided from a consideration of its own circumstances.[2]

In the Revised Statutes and in any act or resolution of Congress passed subsequently to February 1, 1871, the words "insane person" and "lunatic" include every idiot, *non compos*, lunatic, and insane person.[3]

In particular, questions as to legal capacity arise in connection with the receiving of testimony, with the right to exercise the elective franchise; in proceedings to place a person or his property in charge of a committee or trustee; in discussions as to the validity of contracts, and deeds; upon contests as to the validity of wills; and with regard to punishment for crime.

(1) As to giving testimony. A person affected with insanity is admissible as a witness, if it appears to the court, upon examining him and competent witnesses, that he has sufficient understanding to apprehend the obligation of an oath, and to be capable of giving a correct account of the matters he has seen or heard in reference to the questions at issue.[4]

(2) As to exercising the elective franchise. A person who is capable of doing ordinary work, and transacting business, who knows what money is and its value, makes his own contracts and does his own trading, or a person vacillating and easily persuaded, or a person who has been laboring under some kind of illusion or hallucination, but not so as to incapacitate him for the general management of business, which illusion or hallucination is not shown to extend to political matters, cannot be denied the privilege of the elective franchise on the ground of a want of mental capacity.[5]

(3) As to proceedings *de lunatico.* The inquiry is as

---

[1] Forman's Will, 54 Barb. 291 (1869); Prichard, Ins. 16, 19, 30. See Taylor *v.* Commonwealth, 109 Pa. 270 (1885). Moral mania, 3 Law Quar. Rev. 339 (1887).

[2] People *v.* Finley, 38 Mich. 483 (1878); United States *v.* McGue, 8 Curtis, 13 (1851).

[3] R. S. § 1.

[4] District of Columbia *v.* Armes, 107 U. S. 521 (1882), Field, J.; Regina *v.* Hill, 5 Cox, Cr. C. 266 (1850).

[5] Clark *v.* Robinson, 88 Ill. 499, 502 (1878), Sheldon, J.

to the individual's fitness to manage his own affairs, and to conduct himself with safety to himself and others. See further LUNACY.

(4) As to contracts and deeds. The inquiry is, what degree of mental capacity is essential to the proper execution of the act; and was that capacity possessed at the time of the execution. Different degrees are requisite for contracts of a complicated character, and for a single transaction of a simple nature.

The law presumes every adult sane, his will standing as the reason for his conduct. Whoever denies his sanity must establish the position. Testimony as to previous or subsequent insanity will not answer, unless the insanity be shown to be habitual, that is, continuous and chronic. Habitual insanity, once shown, is presumed to continue.[1]

The burden of proof is upon him who alleges incapacity, unless it is shown that he was insane prior to the date of the contract; then the burden shifts, and the person claiming under the contract must show that it was executed during a lucid interval. Partial insanity, in the absence of fraud or imposition, will not avoid a contract, unless it exists with reference to the subject of it at the time of its execution; but in cases of fraud it may be considered in determining whether a party has been imposed upon.[2]

In a policy of insurance, "sane or insane" refers to intended self-destruction, whether the insured was of sound mind or in a state of insanity. To avoid the policy, the insured must have been conscious of the physical nature of his act, and intended by it to cause his death, although at the time he was incapable of judging between right and wrong, and of understanding the moral consequences of what he was doing.[3] See further SUICIDE.

(5) As to testamentary capacity. A testator must have a sound and disposing mind and memory: he ought to be capable of making his will with an understanding of the nature of the business in which he is engaged, a recollection of the property he means to dispose of, of the persons who are the objects of his bounty, and the manner in which it is to be distributed between them. It is sufficient if he has such a mind and memory as will enable him to understand the elements of which the matter is composed — the disposition of his property in its simple forms. Bodily health may be in a state of extreme infirmity, and he yet have sufficient understanding to direct how his property shall be disposed of. His capacity may be perfect to dispose of his property by will, and yet be inadequate to the transaction of other business, as, the making of a contract. . He expresses the previously formed deliberations of his own mind. Soundness is to be judged from his conversation and actions at the time the will is made.[4]

The mere fact that a testator is subject to insane delusions is no sufficient reason why he should be held to have lost his right to make a will, if the jury are satisfied that the delusions have not affected the general faculties of his mind and cannot have influenced him in any particular disposition of his property.[1]

Want of the requisite soundness is incapable of definition suited to all cases. Each case is largely to be tested by its own facts.[2]

The best considered cases put the question upon the basis of knowing and comprehending the nature of the transaction.[3]

Old age, failure of memory, eccentricity, ignorance, credulity, vacillation of purpose, irritability, passion, prejudice, meanness, and even degrees of idiocy, may all exist along with adequate capacity.[4]

When the due execution of a paper, rational in its provisions and consistent in its details, language, and structure, has been proven, the propounder has made out a *prima facie* case. The burden of showing that the testator was not of disposing mind then shifts to to the contestant.[5] See further INFLUENCE.

(6) As to responsibility for crime. The decisions show "a steady amelioration, in the light of advancing medical knowledge." They have regard to the possession of the faculty of understanding right from wrong. But some, in addition, regard the power of choosing between acts.

All well considered cases, since 1843, in both England and America, are founded upon the doctrine laid down by the fourteen judges in *M'Naghten's Case*,[6] that "the jurors ought to be told in all cases that every man is presumed to be sane, and to possess a sufficient degree of reason to be responsible for his crimes, until the contrary be proved to their satisfaction; and that, to establish a defense on the ground of insanity, it must be clearly proved that, at the time of the commitment of the act, the party accused was laboring under such a defect of reason, from disease of the mind, as not to know the nature and quality of the act he was doing; or, if he did not know it, that he did not know he was doing what was wrong."

That rule, however, is not universal. In some States the question is left to the jury, in a general way, whether insanity caused the act; in others, knowledge of right and wrong is the test; and in others, to that test is coupled an inquiry as to the power to control action.

[1] Hall *v.* Unger, 2 Abb. U. S. 513–15 (1867); 8 Conn. 39; 7 Ga. 484; 32 Ind. 126; 56 Me. 246; 58 *id.* 453; 33 Md. 23; 4 Neb. 115; 23 N. J. E. 509; 9 Gratt. 704.

[2] McNett *v.* Cooper, 13 F. R. 586, 590 (1882), cases; Dexter *v.* Hall, 15 Wall. 9, 20 (1872), cases; Griffith *v.* Godey, 113 U. S. 95 (1885).

[3] Bigelow *v.* Berkshire Life Ins. Co., 93 U. S. 287 (1876), cases, Davis, J.

[4] Harrison *v.* Rowan, 3 Wash. 585–86 (1820), Washing-

ton, J. Approved, 1 Redf. Wills, 30; 29 Pa. 302,— in many cases.

[1] Banks *v.* Goodfellow, 39 L. J. R., Q. B. 237, 243 (1870), Cockburn, C. J.

[2] Thompson *v.* Kyner, 65 Pa. 378 (1870).

[3] 1 Redfield, Wills, *124; 18 Cent. L. J. 282–86 (1884), cases; 26 Alb. L. J. 384–86 (1882), cases.

[4] See generally 2 N. J. E. 11; 3 *id.* 581; 5 John. Ch. 158; 87 Ind. 18; 50 Mich. 456; 9 Oreg. 129; 33 Pa. 469; 65 *id.* 377; 8 W. N. C. 203.

[5] Fee *v.* Taylor, 83 Ky. 261 (1885), Holt, J.; 18 Cent. Law J. 282–87 (1884), cases.

[6] M'Naghten's Case, 10 Cl. & F. 210, 200 (House of Lords), per Tindal, Ld. C. J.; United States *v.* Holmes, 1 Cliff. 120 (1858), Clifford, J.; 2 Steph. Hist. Cr. L. Eng. 158.

The right and wrong test seems to prevail in Alabama, California, Connecticut, Delaware, Georgia, Louisiana, Maine, Mississippi, Missouri, Nebraska, New Jersey, New York, North Carolina, Tennessee, Texas, Virginia, Wisconsin, and in the Federal courts.[1] To that test seems to be added the power to control acts, in Indiana, Iowa, Kentucky, Massachusetts, Minnesota, Ohio, and Pennsylvania.[2] While in Illinois, Kansas, Michigan, and New Hampshire, responsibility would seem to be left in broad terms to the jury.[3]

The required proof of insanity is either preponderance of testimony, or satisfaction beyond a reasonable doubt. The burden to establish a *prima facie* case rests upon the accused; after which the prosecution may rebut.

The defendant is not entitled to the benefit of a reasonable doubt whether he was or was not insane.[4] See DOUBT, Reasonable.

That the accused is more ignorant and stupid than common men, of bad education, and of bad passions and bad habits, does not excuse. Those qualities are but the common causes of crime.[5]

To constitute the crime of murder, the assassin must have a reasonably sane mind. " Sound memory and discretion," in the old common-law definition of murder, means that. The condition of mind of an irresponsibly insane man cannot be separated from his act. If he is laboring under disease of his mental faculties to such extent that he does not know what he is doing, or does not know that it is wrong, he is wanting in that sound memory and discretion which make a part of the definition of murder. As insanity is the exception, the law presumes sanity. It is for the defendant to prove insanity in the first instance, to show that the presumption is a mistake as far as it relates to him. Mind can only be known by its outward manifestations,— the language and conduct of the man. By these his thoughts and emotions are read, and according as they conform to the practice of people of sound mind, who form the large majority of mankind, or contrast harshly with it, we form our judgment as to his soundness of mind. . . Was the accused's ordinary, permanent, chronic condition of

mind such, in consequence of disease, that he was unable to understand the nature of his actions, or to distinguish between right and wrong in his conduct? Was he subject to insane delusions that destroyed his power of so understanding? And did this continue down to and embrace the act for which he is tried? If so, he was simply an irresponsible lunatic. The answer of the judges in *M'Naghten's Case* has not been deemed entirely satisfactory, and the courts have settled down upon the question of knowledge of right and wrong as to the particular act, or rather the capacity to know it, as the test of responsibility. . . Distinction must be made between mental and moral obliquity; between a mental incapacity to understand the distinctions between right and wrong, and a moral indifference and insensibility to those distinctions. Indifference to what is right is not ignorance of it, and depravity is not insanity.[1]

The opinion of a non-professional witness as to the mental condition of a person, in connection with a statement of the facts and circumstances, within his personal knowledge, upon which that opinion is formed, is competent evidence. In a substantial sense, and for every purpose essential to a safe conclusion, the mental condition of an individual, as sane or insane, is a fact, and the expressed opinion of one who has had adequate opportunities to observe his conduct and appearance is but the statement of a fact. Insanity is a condition, which impresses itself as an aggregate on the observer.[2]

See DELIRIUM; DELUSION; INTELLIGENCE; LUCID INTERVAL; WILL, 1.

INSCRIPTIONS. See EVIDENCE, Secondary.

INSENSIBLE. See SENSE.

INSIMUL. See COMPUTARE, Insimul.

INSINUATION. Suggestion; information communicated: as, at the insinuation of the plaintiff, the court made a particular order.

INSOLVENCY. Sometimes, the insufficiency of the entire property and assets of an individual to pay his debts — the general and popular meaning. In a more restricted sense, inability to pay debts as they become due in the ordinary course of business.

The term is used in the latter sense when traders and merchants are said to be insolvent, also in bankrupt laws. With reference to persons not engaged in trade and commerce, the term may have a less restricted meaning.[3] Opposed, *solvency*, q. v.

In the sense of the Bankrupt Act, means that a party, whose business affairs are in question, is unable

[1] 25 Ala. 21; 71 *id*. 393; 24 Cal. 230; 62 *id*. 54, 120; 10 Conn. 136; 46 *id*. 330; 1 Houst. Cr. 249; 42 Ga. 9; 45 *id*. 57; 25 La. An. 302; 34 *id*. 186; 57 Me. 574; 3 S. & M. 518; 64 Mo. 591; 4 Neb. 407; 21 N. J. L. 196; 52 N. Y. 467; 75 *id*. 159; Phil. L. R. 376; 3 Heisk. 348; 40 Tex. 60; 20 Gratt. 860; 40 Wis. 304; 57 *id*. 56; 1 Cliff. 118.

[2] 31 Ind. 492; 88 *id*. 27; 25 Iowa, 67; 41 *id*. 232; 1 Duv. 224; 7 Met. 500; 13 Minn. 341; 23 Ohio, 146; 4 Pa. 264; 76 *id*. 414; 78 *id*. 128; 88 *id*. 291; 100 *id*. 573.

[3] 31 Ill. 385; 11 Kan. 32; 17 Mich. 9; 19 *id*. 401; 43 N. H. 224; 50 *id*. 369. See generally 16 Cent. L. J. 282-86 (1883), cases; 17 *id*. 408-10 (1883), cases; 36 Alb. Law J. 326-31 (1887), cases.

[4] State *v*. Johnson, 91 Mo. 443 (1886); United States *v*. Ridgeway, 31 F. R. 144 (1887). As to "reasonable doubt," see also 18 Cent. Law J. 402-5 (1884), cases.

[5] United States *v*. Cornell, 2 Mas. 109 (1820), Story, J.; Goodwin *v*. State, 96 Ind. 550 (1883). See also 16 Cent. Law J. 282-86 (1883), cases; 4 Crim. Law Mag. 512-14 (1883), cases; Med. Leg. J., Sept. 1883; Wash. Law R., May, 1883.

[1] United States *v*. Guiteau, 10 F. R. 163, 166, 167-68, 182-83 (Jan. 25, 1882), Cox, J.; note and cases to same, pp. 189-203, by Dr. Wharton.

[2] Connecticut Mut. Life Ins. Co. *v*. Lathrop, 111 U. S. 618-20 (1884), Harlan, J.; 1 Whart. & S. Med. J. § 257.

[3] Toof *v*. Martin, 13 Wall. 47 (1871), Field, J. See Clarion Bank *v*. Jones, 21 *id*. 338 (1874); Cunningham *v*. Norton, 125 U. S. 90 (1888).

to pay his debts as they become due in the ordinary course of his daily business.[1]

Insolvency is owing debts in excess of the value of one's tangible property. Without debts there can be no insolvency. Poverty and insolvency are not synonymous terms within the meaning of a statute conferring the right to administer upon an estate.[2]

Insolvent. 1, *adj.* Not possessing the means with which to pay debts in full; concerning one so involved. In the last sense "insolvency" is frequently used. Thus we have insolvent debtor, trader, criminal, circumstances; and insolvent or insolvency laws.

2, *n.* A person who is not pecuniarily able to pay his debts as they fall due; also, a person whose property, if distributed *pro rata* among his creditors, would not be sufficient to pay their claims in full.

Insolvency or **insolvent laws.** Laws passed by the individual States for the distribution, among creditors, of the property of persons who are unable to pay their debts in the ordinary course of business.

In strictness, "bankrupt" laws apply only to traders or merchants, and "insolvent" laws to all other persons. Insolvent laws are bankrupt laws passed by the States. Bankrupt laws discharge absolutely; insolvent laws leave future acquisitions liable. State laws are suspended while a national law is in operation.[3]

See BANKRUPTCY; CAUSE, 1 (2), Probable; CIRCUMSTANCES, 2; CONTEMPLATION; PREFERENCE.

INSPECTION. A looking at: examination; view. Whence inspector, inspectorship.

1. An official examination of articles of food or of merchandise, to determine whether they are suitable for market or commerce.[4]

"No State shall, without the Consent of the Congress, lay any Imposts or Duties on Imports or Exports, except what may be absolutely necessary for executing its inspection Laws." [5]

The object of inspection laws is to improve the quality of articles produced by the labor of a country; to fit them for exportation, or, it may be, for domestic use. They act upon the subject before it becomes an article of foreign commerce, or of commerce among the States, and prepare it for that purpose. They form a portion of that immense mass of legislation which embraces everything within the territory of a State, not surrendered to the general government: all of which can be most advantageously exercised by the States themselves.[1]

The scope of inspection laws is not confined to articles of domestic produce or manufacture, or to articles intended for exportation, but applies to articles imported, and to those intended for domestic use as well.[2]

Recognized elements of inspection laws have always been quality of the article, form, capacity, dimensions, and weight of package, mode of putting up, and marking and branding of various kinds; all these matters being supervised by a public officer having authority to pass or not pass as lawful merchandise, as it did or did not answer the prescribed requirements. It is not necessary that all these elements should co-exist to make a valid inspection law. Quality alone may be the subject of inspection, or the inspection may be made to extend to all of the above matters. These laws are none the less inspection laws because they may have a remote and considerable influence upon commerce. Congress may interpose if a statute, under the guise of an inspection law, goes beyond the limit prescribed by the Constitution.[3]

A State may not require the payment of an assessment or fee for each passenger upon an ocean vessel who is inspected to ascertain if he has leprosy, and impose a fine upon the owners of the vessel for non-payment.[4] See POLICE, 2.

Inspection laws have exclusive reference to personal property; they never apply to free human beings. A State cannot make a law designed to raise money to support paupers, to detect or prevent crime, to guard against disease, and to cure the sick, an inspection law, within the constitutional meaning of that word, by calling it so in the title. . . An inspection is something which can be accomplished by looking at or weighing or measuring the thing to be inspected, or applying to it at once some crucial test. When testimony is to be taken and examined, it is not inspection in any sense whatever.[5]

2. In the reception of evidence, a substitution of the eye for the ear.

---

[1] Buchanan *v.* Smith, 16 Wall. 308 (1872), Clifford, J.; Wager *v.* Hall, *ib.* 599 (1872); Dutcher *v.* Wright, 94 U. S. 557 (1876); May *v.* Le Claire, 18 F. R. 166 (1882); *Re* Bininger, 7 Blatch. 264, 273 (1870), cases.

[2] Bowersox's Appeal, 100 Pa. 438 (1882); Daniels *v.* Palmer, 35 Minn. 347–50 (1886), cases.

See also 1 Dill. 195; 2 Low. 401; 1 Woods, 434; 2 *id.* 401; 9 Cal. 45; 33 *id.* 625; 20 Conn. 69; 2 Ind. 57; 88 *id.* 573; 19 La. An. 183, 197; 4 Cush. 134; 3 Gray, 600; 3 Allen, 114; 123 Mass. 13; 9 N. Y. 594; 15 *id.* 9, 199; 43 *id.* 73; 25 Hun, 169; 4 Hill, 652; 57 N. H. 458; 2 N. J. E. 173; 9 *id.* 457; 12 Ohio, 336; 13 Gratt. 683; 116 E. C. L. 1090; 2 Bl. Com. 285, 481; 2 Kent, 389.

[3] Sturges *v.* Crowninshield, 4 Wheat. 195 (1819), Marshall, C. J.; 2 Mas. 160; 12 Wheat. 230.

[4] See 2 Woods, 290; 20 Blatch. 303.

[5] Constitution, Art. I, sec. 10, cl. 2.

[1] Gibbons *v.* Ogden, 9 Wheat. 203 (1824), Marshall, C. J.; 8 Cow. 46; 64 Pa. 105.

[2] Neilson *v.* Garza, 2 Woods, 290 (1876), Bradley, J.; Brown *v.* Maryland, 12 Wheat. 438 (1827), Marshall, C. J.

[3] Turner *c.* Maryland, 107 U. S. 55, 54, 51–54, note (1882), cases, Blatchford, J.

[4] People *v.* Pacific Mail Steamship Co., 8 Saw. 640 (1883), Sawyer, Cir. J.

[5] People *v.* Compagnie Générale Transatlantique, 107 U. S. 61–63 (1882), Miller, J.: 20 Blatch. 296; 10 F. R. 357; Story, Const. § 1017; Cooley, Const. Lim. 730.

Inspection of documents, or of records. Refers to the right of a party to a suit to inspect and take copies of writings or records, in the possession of his opponent or of a public officer, which are material to the maintenance of his case.

In civil practice, independently of the old doctrine of profert and oyer, a rule may be granted to compel the production and permit the copying of such papers as are essential to the maintenance of a contested right. But surrender of the documents will not be ordered. The doctrine applies to public, corporation, and private documents, in which the petitioner has an interest, and which are not of an incriminating nature. Previous demand must have been made, and the documents must be under respondent's exclusive control.[1] See Discovery, 6, Bill of; Produce, 2; Record, Nul tiel.

Inspection of the person. In an action for damages for personal injuries, the plaintiff may be required by the court, upon application, to submit his person to an examination for the purpose of ascertaining the character and extent of his injuries.

The courts have held in divorce cases, that an examination may be ordered of a defendant alleged to be impotent.[2]

Trial by inspection. When, for the greater expedition of a cause, in some point or issue the object of the senses, the judge, upon the testimony of his own sense, decides the point in dispute.[3]

When the fact, from its nature, must be evident to the court either from ocular demonstration or other irrefragable proof, there the law departs from its usual custom, the verdict of twelve men, and relies upon the judgment of the court alone; as, in allegations of non-age, that plaintiff is dead when one calling himself plaintiff appears, that a man is an idiot; and in references to the almanac. But in all these cases, the judges, if they conceive a doubt, may order it to be tried by jury.[3]

Inspection is to be regarded rather as a means of dispensing with evidence than as evidence itself. That which the court or jury sees need not be proved. It is valuable as an ingredient of circumstantial evidence. A common illustration is where juries are taken to view the scene where the events of litigation occurred. . . All materials and objects in any way part of the *res gestæ* may be produced at the trial of

the case. But inspection alone is not relied upon when more exact proof can be produced.[1]

3. Supervision; trusteeship.

Deed of inspectorship. An assignment by a debtor of his property, by which he is allowed to manage the property for a specified time, under the inspection of certain individuals, appointed by the body of the creditors, whose duty is to see that the property is disposed of in the manner most conducive to the interests of the creditors.[2] See Composition; Liquidator.

INSTALLMENT.[3] One of the several portions of a debt, payable at different periods.

Where, for the purpose of collection, an assessment for benefits accruing from a public improvement is divided into installments, each one may be regarded as an assessment, and a statute of limitations run against it as a distinct claim.[4]

Buying or selling personalty upon the installment plan is upon the scheme of different portions of the price at stipulated intervals. When the seller, at his option, may remove the property for breach of contract, replevin will not lie, until after demand and refusal to surrender.[5] See Sale, Conditional; Lien, Secret.

INSTANCE. Application to set aside a proceeding for irregularity must be made as early as possible — "in the first instance."[6]

Instance court. That branch of the English court of admiralty which has cognizance of all matters pertaining to intercourse upon the high seas except prizes.[7]

INSTANTER. L. Without delay: within twenty-four hours.[8] See Immediately.

INSTAR. L. Like; resembling; equivalent to.

Instar omnium. Representative of all.

Money is said to be *instar omnium* as to values;[9] one act, as to the purpose of all acts;[10] and one case, as to the reasoning in all cases of its class.[11]

---

[1] 1 Whart. Ev. §§ 742–56, cases; 1 Greenl. Ev. §§ 471–78, 559–62, cases; Brewer *v.* Watson, 71 Ala. 304–6 (1882), cases; Commonwealth, *ex rel.* Sellers *v.* Phœnix Iron Co., 105 Pa. 115–19 (1884), cases; 23 Am. Law Reg. 395–400 (1884), cases; 22 Cent. Law J. 341 (1886), cases.

[2] See generally Schroeder *v.* Chicago, &c. R. Co., 47 Iowa, 376–83 (1877); Atchison, &c. R. Co. *v.* Thul, 29 Kan. 466, 474 (1883); 19 Cent. Law J. 144–48 (1884), cases; 2 Bish. M. & D. § 590, cases.

[3] 3 Bl. Com. 332–33.

[1] 1 Whart. Ev. §§ 345–47, cases; 25 Law J. 3–7 (1887), cases.

[2] [4 South. Law Rev. 639 (1878), cases.

[3] Spelled, also, instalment.

[4] Pelton *v.* Bemis, 44 Ohio St. 57 (1886); Ryall *v.* Prince, 82 Ala. 266 (1886).

[5] Cushman *v.* Jewell, 7 Hun, 525 (1876); Smith *v.* Newland, 9 *id.* 553 (1877); 89 Ill. 233; 20 Kan. 137; 27 Mich. 209, 463; 33 *id.* 94; 41 N. Y. 155; 70 *id.* 466; 13 Rep. 511.

[6] 3 Chitty, Bl. Com. 287.

[7] See 3 Kent, 355, 378; 18 Johns. 292.

[8] Moffat *v.* Dickson, 3 Col. 315 (1877).

[9] 1 Bl. Com. 266; 2 *id.* 466; 3 *id.* 231.

[10] 4 Bl. Com. 155.

[11] 4 W. N. C. (Pa.) 500.

INSTITUTE. 1. To commence: as, to institute an action, proceeding, suit.

2. To appoint: an instituted executor is one chosen by the testator.

3. To establish upon a permanent basis. Whence institutional.

Institutes. Text-books exhibiting the established principles of jurisprudence; comprehensive treatises upon elementary law; commentaries upon law.

Institution. A permanent establishment, as contradistinguished from an enterprise of a temporary character.[1] See PERMANENT.

Sometimes describes the establishment or place where the business or operations of a society or association are carried on; at other times, designates the organized body.[2]

INSTRUCT. 1. To give orders to an agent in relation to the duties of his employment.

Section 251, Rev. St., empowering the secretary of the treasury to issue regulations for the government of collectors of revenue, makes a distinction between "instructions" and "regulations," which is inherent in the nature of the two things. An instruction is a direction to govern the conduct of the particular officer to whom it is addressed; a regulation affects a class or classes of officers.[3]

2. To direct a jury as to their duties under the law in a cause about to be submitted to them for a verdict.

Binding or **peremptory instruction.** Directs the kind of verdict the jury should return.

The jury may be instructed to find for the defendant, where, if the verdict were against him, the court would set it aside.[4]

The practice saves time and costs; gives the certainty of applied science to the results of judicial investigation; draws clearly the line which separates the provinces of the judge and the jury, and fixes where it belongs the responsibility which should be assumed by the court.[5]

Misinstruct. To charge a jury erroneously with respect to the law in the case pending before them.

See ADVISE; CHARGE, 2 (2, c); JURY, Trial by.

---

[1] Indianapolis v. Sturdevant, 24 Ind. 395 (1865).

[2] Gerke v. Purcell, 25 Ohio St. 244 (1874); Appeal Tax Court v. St. Peter's Academy, 50 Md. 345 (1878).

[3] Landram v. United States, 16 Ct. Cl. 86 (1880).

[4] Griggs v. Houston, 104 U. S. 553 (1881); Montclair v. Dana, 107 id. 162 (1882); 93 id. 143; 106 id. 30; 122 id. 411; 2 McCrary, 268; 17 F. R. 133.

[5] Merchants' Nat. Bank v. State Nat. Bank, 10 Wall. 637 (1870), Swayne, J.

INSTRUMENT. 1. An implement or tool, qq. v.

2. Whatever may be presented as evidence to the senses of an adjudicating tribunal,—a document, witness, or even a living thing produced for inspection.[1]

A means of proof; the means by which the truth is in fact established, and whether written or unwritten.[2]

3. Anything reduced to writing: a "written instrument" or "instrument of writing;" more particularly, a document of a formal or solemn character.

Common descriptive epithets: commercial, negotiable, sealed and unsealed instruments.

"Instruments in writing," associated in a statute with "bonds," "laws," "deeds," and "records," has a restrictive connotation. Independently of such surroundings, the expression, by itself, does not comprehend all written papers, but only written papers of a class. An instrument is "something reduced to writing as a means of evidence." Returns of births, marriages, and deaths, to a department of government, are not "instruments."[3]

A generic term for bills, bonds, conveyances, leases, mortgages, promissory notes, wills, and like formal or solemn writings. Scarcely includes accounts, letters in ordinary correspondence, memoranda, and similar writings, with respect to which the creation of evidence to bind the party, or the establishment of an obligation or title, is not the primary motive.[4]

Instruments will be so construed as to carry into effect the intention of the parties, but there must always be sufficient words to enable the courts to ascertain what this intention was. The rule that courts will so construe an instrument as to make it effective, does not mean that they will inject into it new and distinct provisions. Thus, that an instrument may have effect as a conveyance, it must contain words importing a grant.[5]

See ALTERATION, 2; CAPTION, 2; CANCEL; DATE; DESCRIPTION; FORGERY; LOST, 2; PAPER; PRESENTS (1); PROFERT; REDUNDANCY; REFORM; REPUGNANT; SEAL, 1; SIGN; SPECIALTY; SPOLIATION; SUBSCRIBE; WRITING.

INSUFFICIENT. See SUFFICIENT.

INSULT. See ASSAULT; PROVOCATION.

INSURANCE. Making sure, secure, safe: indemnity against loss; a contract to pay money in the event of pecuniary loss from a specified cause.

Assurance. Formerly used in the sense of insurance; is sometimes limited to risks upon lives. Whence "assurer" and "assured."

---

[1] [1 Whart. Ev. § 615.

[2] 1 Greenl. Ev. §§ 3, 306–8.

[3] State v. Kelsey, 44 N. J. L. 34 (1882), Beasley, C. J.

[4] [Abbott's Law Dict.; Hankinson v. Page, 31 F. R. 186 (1887).

[5] Hummelman v. Mounts, 87 Ind. 180 (1882).

There are instances in which "the assured" refers to the person for whose benefit the contract is effected, and "the insured" to the person whose life is insured. The application of either term to the party for whose benefit the insurance is effected, or to the party whose life is insured, has generally depended upon its collocation and context in the policy.[1]

Insurer. The party who engages to make the indemnity. **Insured,** *n.* He who is to receive the indemnity: also, the person the continuance of whose life has been made the subject of a contract.

The subjects of insurance are property, life, and health. In *fire* and *marine* insurance, the subject is property; in *life* and *accident* insurance, the lives, and health or freedom from physical injuries, of human beings. Contracts are also made upon the *fidelity* of agents and trustees, and upon the *honesty* of customers as debtors; upon *titles* to realty; upon valuables against *theft;* upon *plate-glass* windows against breakage; upon *steam-boilers* against explosion; upon the lives and good condition of domestic *animals.* There are also other species. The commonest kinds are *accident, fire, life,* and *marine* insurance. In general, insurance is applicable to protect men against uncertain events which may in any wise be of disadvantage to them.[2]

Insurance is a contract whereby one, for a consideration, undertakes to compensate another if he shall suffer loss.[3]

A contract of insurance is an agreement, by which one party, for a consideration (usually paid in money, either in one sum or at different times during the continuance of the risk), promises to make a certain payment of money upon the destruction or injury of something in which the other party has an interest.[4]

A contract between A and B, that, upon A's paying a premium equivalent to the hazard run, B will indemnify him against a particular event.[5]

Policies of insurance against *fire* and *marine* risks are contracts of indemnity,—the insurer engaging to make good, within limited amounts, the losses sustained by the assured in their buildings, ships, and effects. The contract called *life* assurance is a mere contract to pay a certain sum of money on the death of a person, in consideration of the due payment of a certain annuity for his life. This last species in no way resembles a contract of indemnity.[1]

Guaranty insurance is instituted as a substitute for private suretyship, to aid persons in obtaining places of trust and responsibility, and to protect employers from the unfaithfulness of their employes.[2]

The word "insurance," in common speech and with propriety, is used quite as often in the sense of *contract* of insurance, or *act* of insuring, as in that expressing the abstract idea of *indemnity* or security against loss.[3]

A contract of *life* assurance is not an assurance for a single year, with a privilege of renewal from year to year by paying the annual premium, but an entire contract of assurance for life, subject to discontinuance and forfeiture for non-payment of any of the stipulated premiums. The payment of each premium is not, as in fire policies, the consideration for insurance during the next following year. It often happens that the assured pays the entire premium in advance, or in five, ten, or twenty annual installments. Each installment is, in fact, part consideration of the entire insurance for life. The annual premiums are an annuity, the present value of which is calculated to correspond with the present value of the amount insured, a reasonable percentage being added to the premiums to cover expenses and contingencies. The whole premiums are balanced against the whole insurance. . . All the calculations of the insurance company are based on the hypothesis of prompt payments. Forfeiture for non-payment is a necessary means of protecting itself from embarrassment. The insured parties are associates in a great scheme. This associated relation exists whether the company be a mutual one or not. Each is interested in the engagements of all; for out of the co-existence of many risks arises the law of average, which underlies the whole business. An essential feature of the scheme is the mathematical calculations referred to, on which the premiums and amounts assured are based. And these calculations, again, are based on the assumption of average mortality, and of prompt payments and compound interest thereon.[4]

---

[1] Connecticut Mut. Life Ins. Co. *v.* Luchs, 108 U. S. 504 (1883), Field, J.

[2] See May, Ins. § 73.

[3] May, Ins. § 1.

[4] Commonwealth *v.* Wetherbee, 105 Mass. 160 (1870), Gray, J. Approved, 71 Ala. 443; 30 Kan. 587; 72 Mo. 159.

[5] 2 Bl. Com. 458; Cummings *v.* Cheshire County Fire Ins. Co., 55 N. H. 458 (1875), Foster, C. J.

[1] Dalby *v.* The Indian & London Life Assur. Co., 80 E. C. L. *387 (1854), Parke, B. See also Mutual Life Ins. Co. *v.* Girard Life Ins. Co., 100 Pa. 180 (1882).

[2] May, Ins. §§ 73, 540.

[3] Funke *v.* Minnesota Farmers' Mut. Fire Ins. Association, 29 Minn. 354 (1882), cases; 44 N. J. L. 87.

[4] New York Life Ins. Co. *v.* Statham, 93 U. S. 30-31 (1876), Bradley, J.; Klein *v.* New York Life Ins. Co., 104 *id.* 88 (1881); Thompson *v.* Knickerbocker Life Ins.

A policy of *marine* insurance is a contract of indemnity against all losses accruing to the subject-matter of the policy from certain perils during the adventure. This subject-matter need not be strictly a property in the ship, goods, or freight.[1]

The contract of insurance sprang from the law maritime, and derives all its material rules and incidents therefrom. It was unknown to the common law. Its first appearance in any code or system of laws was in the law maritime as promulgated by the various maritime states and cities of Europe. It grew out of the doctrine of contribution and general average, which is found in the maritime laws of the ancient Rhodians. By this law, if ship, freight, or cargo was sacrificed to save the others, all had to contribute their proportionate share of the loss. This division of loss suggested a previsional division of risk; first, among those engaged in the same enterprise; and, next, among associations of ship-owners and shipping merchants. Hence, too, the earliest form of the contract was that of mutual insurance. The next step was that of insurance upon premium. Capitalists, familiar with the risks of navigation, were found willing to guarantee against them for a small consideration or premium paid. This, the final form, was in use as early as the beginning of the fourteenth century.[2]

Insurable interest. (1) In life insurance. Any reasonable expectation of pecuniary benefit or advantage from the continued life of another creates an insurable interest in such life. Examples are, the interest of a man in his own life, in the life of his wife or child; the interest of a woman in her husband; a creditor's interest in the life of his debtor; interest in one's own life for a relative or friend; the interest of two or more in their joint lives for the survivor. The essential thing is, that the policy is obtained in good faith, and not for the purpose of speculating upon the hazard of a life in which the insured has no interest.[3]

It is not easy to define with precision what will in all cases constitute an insurable interest, so as to take the contract out of the class of wager policies. It may be stated generally, however, to be such an interest, arising from the relations of the party obtaining the insurance, either as creditor of or surety for

the assured, or from the ties of blood or marriage to him, as will justify a reasonable expectation of advantage or benefits from the continuance of his life. It is not necessary that the expectation of advantage or benefit should be always capable of pecuniary estimation; for a parent has an insurable interest in the life of his child, and a child in the life of his parent, a husband in the life of his wife, and a wife in the life of her husband. The natural affection in cases of this kind is considered as more powerful, as operating more efficaciously, to protect the life of the insured than any other consideration. But in all cases there must be a reasonable ground, founded upon the relations of the parties to each other, either pecuniary or of blood or affinity, to expect some benefit or advantage from the continuance of the life of the assured.[1]

Otherwise, the contract is a mere wager, by which the party taking the policy is directly interested in the death of the assured. Such policies have a tendency to create a desire for the event. They are, therefore, independently of any statute on the subject, condemned as being against public policy. For which reasons, a person who has procured a policy upon his own life cannot *assign* it to a party who has no insurable interest in his life.[1]

(2) In fire and marine insurance. These being contracts of indemnity, the insured must have some interest in the property at the time of injury.[2]

But he need not have either a legal or equitable title. If he has a right in or against the property, which some court will enforce, a right so dependent for value upon the continued existence of the property alone as that a loss of the property will cause him pecuniary damage, he has an insurable interest.[3]

A right of property is not indispensable. Injury from its loss or benefit from its preservation may be

---

Co., *ib.* 252 (1881); Connecticut Mut. Life Ins. Co. v. Home Ins. Co., 17 Blatch. 146–47 (1879); 100 Pa. 180.

[1] Lloyd v. Fleming, L. R., 7 Q. B. 302 (1872), Blackburn, J.; 3 Kent, 253.

[2] New England Mut. Marine Ins. Co. v. Dunham, 11 Wall. 31–33 (1870), Bradley, J.

[3] Connecticut Mut. Life Ins. Co. v. Schaefer, 94 U. S. 460, 457 (1876), Bradley, J.

[1] Warnock v. Davis, 104 U. S. 779, 782 (1881), Field, J. Approved, Connecticut Mut. Life Ins. Co. v. Luchs, 108 *id.* 505 (1883). See also 32 Alb. Law J. 385–88, 403–6 (1885), cases; 25 Cent. Law J. 27 (1887), cases; 22 How. 388; 13 Wall. 619; 15 *id.* 643; 8 Saw. 620; 16 F. R. 652; 41 Ind. 116; 101 Mass. 564; 13 N. Y. 31; 20 *id.* 32. On assigning life policies, see McCrum v. Missouri Life Ins. Co., 36 Kan. 148 (1887), cases; 18 Cent. L. J. 346–49 (1884), cases; 24 Am. Law Reg. 753–69 (1885), cases. Rights in policy for the benefit of a wife after the death of her husband, 27 *id.* 377–81 (1888), cases.

[2] Connecticut Mut. Life Ins. Co. v. Schaefer, *ante.*

[3] [Rohrback v. Germania Fire Ins. Co., 62 N. Y. 54 (1875), Folger, J. See also Buck v. Chesapeake Ins. Co., 1 Pet. 151 (1828); 12 Iowa, 287; 42 *id.* 13.

sufficient. Hence, an agent, factor, bailee, carrier, trustee, consignee, mortgagee, or other lien-holder, may insure to the extent of his interest; and by the clause " on account of whom it may concern," for all others to the extent of their interests, where there is previous authority or subsequent ratification.[1]

The owner of an equity of redemption (an equitable interest) has an insurable interest equal to the value of the buildings, whether personally liable for the mortgage debt or not. And so has the holder of a mechanic's lien.[2]

From the nature of the contract of insurance as a contract of indemnity, the insurer, when he has paid the assured the amount of the indemnity agreed upon, is entitled, by way of salvage, to the benefit of anything that may be received, either from the remnants of the goods or from damages paid by third persons for the loss.[3]

The insurance which a person has on property is not an interest in the property itself, but is a collateral interest, personal to the insured.[4]

Insurance agent. An insurance company is responsible for the acts of its agent within the general scope of the business intrusted to his care, and no limitation on his power, unknown to strangers, will bind them.[5]

Insurance broker. If the insured employs an insurance broker to place insurance for him, he is his agent, and not that of the company. But if, acting on behalf of an agent of the company, the broker solicits the insurance, he is the agent of the company.[6]

Insurance company. An association, usually incorporated, which makes a business of entering into contracts of insurance.

Mutual insurance company. This is composed of the persons insured, in their lives or property. They contribute *pro rata* upon the amount they have insured (and, possibly, a sum *per capita*, annually or otherwise) to a fund, out of which losses and expenses are paid.

The theory is that the premiums paid, or to be paid, constitute a fund for the liquidation of losses. They may be paid by note or cash.[1]

Mutuality exists when the members contribute cash or assessable notes, or both, to a common fund, out of which each is entitled to indemnity in case of loss.[2]

Stock insurance company. In this the members contribute a capital which is liable for losses and expenses, and the insured pay premiums.

There are companies which combine both schemes.

Insurance loss. The occurrence of a casualty insured against — the loss of a life or lives, the impairment of health, or the destruction of property, with consequent damage.

Insurance policy. A contract for insurance reduced to writing. Called, briefly, " a policy;" practically, a bond of indemnity.

Implies a contract in writing, the usual mode among prudent persons.[3]

But, unless prohibited by positive regulations, may be by parol.[4]

The contract may be either made or changed by parol.[5]

Blanket or *floating policy.* Is issued to a factor or warehouseman, and intended to cover margins uninsured by other policies, or to cover the limited interest of the factor or warehouseman.[6]

Endowment policy. In one respect, a contract payable in the event of a continuance of life; in another respect, in the event of death before the period specified.[7]

Interest policy. States or intends that the insured has a real and substantial interest in the thing insured. Opposed, *wager policy.*[8]

Open or *running policy.* Enables a merchant to insure goods shipped at a distant port when it is impossible for him to be advised of the particular ship upon which they

[1] Hooper *v.* Robinson, 98 U. S. 538 (1878), cases, Swayne, J.; Home Ins. Co. *v.* Baltimore Warehouse Co., 93 *id.* 543 (1876), cases.

[2] Insurance Co. *v.* Stinson, 103 U. S. 29 (1880).

[3] Phœnix Ins. Co. *v.* Erie Transportation Co., 117 U. S. 321 (1886), cases, Gray, J.

[4] The City of Norwich, 118 U. S. 494 (1886), cases. Contracts as effected by changes of title, 19 Am. Law Rev. 895-915 (1885), cases. After-acquired titles, 21 Cent. Law J. 500-3 (1885), cases. On assigning fire and marine policies, see 1 Harv. Law Rev. 388-98 (1888), cases.

[5] Union Mut. Ins. Co. *v.* Wilkinson, 13 Wall. 222, 235 (1871), cases. See also 25 Conn. 53, 465, 542; 26 *id.* 42; 37 N. H. 35; 19 N. Y. 305; 23 Pa. 50, 72; 26 *id.* 50; 2 Phill. Ins. § 1848; May, Ins. §§ 118-55.

[6] Mohr Distilling Co. *v.* Ohio Fire Ins. Co., 13 F. R. 74 (1882); May, Ins. § 123. See also Haden *v.* Farmers', &c. Fire Association, 80 Va. 683 (1885); Kyte *v.* Commercial Union Assurance Co., 144 Mass. 46 (1887).

[1] State *v.* Manufacturers' Mut. Fire Ins. Co., 91 Mo. 318 (1886), cases.

[2] Spruance *v.* Farmers', &c. Ins. Co., 9 Col. 77 (1885), cases.

[3] Manny *v.* Dunlap, 1 Woolw. 374 (1869); 11 Paige, 556.

[4] Humphry *v.* Hartfield Fire Ins. Co., 15 Blatch. 511 (1879), cases; Relief Fire Ins. Co. *v.* Shaw, 94 U. S. 574 (1876), cases.

[5] Cohen *v.* Continental Fire Ins. Co., 67 Tex. 328 (1887), cases.

[6] Howe Ins. Co. *v.* Baltimore Warehouse Co., 93 U. S. 541 (1876).

[7] Brummer *v.* Cohn, 86 N. Y. 17 (1881).

[8] See Sawyer *v.* Dodge County Ins. Co., 37 Wis. 539 (1875); May, Ins. § 33.

are laden, and when, therefore, he cannot name the ship in the policy.

The usual words are the cargo "on board ship or ships," with a condition that the particular ship, as soon as known, shall be declared to the underwriter, whose agreement is that the policy shall attach if the vessel is seaworthy. From the uncertainty attending the unknown condition of the vessel, a high rate of premium is demanded.[1]

Paid-up policy. A policy upon which all the annual premiums are paid, or considered as paid, at one time.

A policy of life insurance containing a provision that a default in payment of premiums shall not work a forfeiture, but that the sum insured shall then be reduced and commuted to the annual premiums paid, confers the right on the assured to convert the policy at any time, by notice to the insurer, into a paid-up policy for the amount of premiums paid.[2]

Time policy. In this the duration of the risk is fixed by definite periods. In a *voyage policy* the duration is determined by geographical limits.[3]

Valued policy. When the parties, having agreed upon the value of the interest insured, to save the necessity of further proof, insert the valuation in the policy in the nature of liquidated damages.[4] See VALUE, Equitable.

Wager policy. In this the insured party has no interest in the matter insured, only an interest in its loss or destruction.

Void, as against public policy or positive law. But precisely what interest is necessary to take a policy out of this category has been the subject of much discussion. In life insurance it is at least essential that the policy be obtained in good faith, and not for speculation upon the hazard of a life in which the insured has no interest. In marine and fire insurance, where the insurance is strictly an indemnity, the difference is not so great.[5] See further *Insurable Interest;* WAGER, 2.

Insurance risk or **peril.** The event or casualty insured against. See PERIL; RISK.

Double insurance. A second insurance upon the same interest, against the same perils, in favor of the same person.[6]

In such case the policies are considered as one; the insurers are liable *pro rata*, and are entitled to contribution to equalize payments made on account of losses.[1]

Over insurance. Insurance upon property in an amount exceeding the value. See VALUATION, Over.

Premium of insurance. The consideration in a contract of insurance.

Usually paid in money, in one sum, or at different times during the continuance of the risk. The amount may be secured by a *premium note.* See PREMIUM.

Re-insurance. Insurance upon an underwriter's contracts of insurance.[2]

Contracts of re-insurance, by which one insurer causes the sum which he has insured to be re-assured to him by a distinct contract with another insurer, with the object of indemnifying himself against his own responsibility, though prohibited for a time in England by statute, are valid by the common law, and have always been lawful in this country; and in a suit upon such a contract, the subject at risk and the loss thereof must be proved in the same manner as if the original assured were the plaintiff.[3]

When a policy of insurance contains contradictory provisions, or has been so framed as to leave room for construction, rendering it doubtful whether the parties intended the exact truth of the applicant's statements to be a condition precedent to a binding contract, the court should lean against that construction which imposes upon the assured the obligations of a warranty. It is the language of the company which the court is invited to interpret, and it is both reasonable and just that its own words should be construed most strongly against itself.[4]

As to fire and marine insurance, see ABANDON, 1; ACCIDENT; AVERAGE; CAPTURE; CONCEAL, 5; CONTAINED; CONTRIBUTION; DEPARTURE, 2; DEVIATION; FREIGHT; HAZARDOUS; LOSS, 2; OCCUPIED; PREMISES, 3; REFORM; REPRESENTATION, 1; SEIZURE, 2; UNDERWRITER; VALUATION.

As to life insurance, see DECLARE, 4; DISEASE; EPIDEMIC; FORFEITURE; INTEMPERATE; REPRESENTATION, 1; SUICIDE; TRUE.

INSURRECTION. A rising against civil or political authority; the open and active opposition of a number of persons to the

---

[1] Orient Mut. Ins. Co. v. Wright, 23 How. 405–6 (1859), cases, Nelson, J.; 38 Ohio St. 134; 3 Kent, 258, 272; May, Ins. § 31.

[2] Lovell v. St. Louis Mut. Life Ins. Co., 111 U. S. 264, 272 (1884), Bradley, J.

[3] May, Ins. § 34.

[4] See 3 Kent, 272; May, Ins. § 30; Wood, Ins. § 41; 38 Ohio St. 134; 100 Mass. 475.

[5] Connecticut Mut. Life Ins. Co. v. Schaefer, 94 U. S. 460 (1876), Bradley, J.; 2 Bl. Com. 460; 3 Kent, 275; May, Ins. § 33.

[6] See Turner v. Meridan Fire Ins. Co., 16 F. R. 454, 460–65 (1883), cases; May, Ins. § 440.

[1] Sloat v. Royal Ins. Co., 49 Pa. 14, 18 (1865); 2 Wood, Fire Ins. §§ 372–407.

[2] See Commercial Ins. Co. v. Detroit Fire & Mar. Ins. Co., 38 Ohio St. 15–16 (1882); May, Ins. § 11; Phillips, Ins. § 374.

[3] Phœnix Ins. Co. v. Erie Transp. Co., 117 U. S. 323 (1886), cases, Gray, J.; Sun Mut. Ins. Co. v. Ocean Ins. Co., 107 id. 485, 510 (1882); 2 Kent, 278–79.

[4] First Nat. Bank of Kansas City v. Hartford Ins. Co., 95 U. S. 678 (1877), Harlan, J.; Grace v. American Central Ins. Co., 109 id. 282 (1883); Moulor v. American Ins. Co., 111 id. 341–42 (1884); Dwight v. Germania Life Ins. Co., 103 N. Y. 347–48 (1886), cases; Travelers' Ins. Co. v. McConkey, 127 U. S. 666 (1888), cases.

execution of law in a city or a state; a rebellion; a revolt.[1] See MOB; WAR.

INTELLIGENCE. Discernment; understanding; knowledge.

The possession of intelligence is not a test of sanity; for with it there may be an absence of power to determine the nature of the act, and its effect upon the subject.[2]

INTEMPERATE. If the rule or habit is to drink to intoxication when occasion offers, and sobriety or abstinence is the exception, then the charge of "intemperate habits" is established. It is not necessary that the custom be an every-day rule.[3]

"Sober and temperate" does not imply total abstinence from intoxicating liquor. The moderate, temperate use of intoxicating liquors is consistent with sobriety.[4]

While in a very clear case a court may assume that certain facts disclose a case of habitual intemperance, or that they warrant the opposite conclusion, in the main these are questions to be submitted to the jury.[5]

A life policy provided that it should be void if the insured "became so far intemperate as to impair health, or induce delirium tremens." The trial court charged that the "impairment of health" was not the indisposition arising from a drunken debauch, but that arising from such frequency of use as indicated an injurious addiction to the practice. *Held*, that it was for the jury to decide whether death was caused by an excessive use of stimulants.[6]

See DRUNKENNESS; HABIT; INTOXICATE.

INTENDMENT. The correct understanding or intention of the law; the true meaning or correct policy of a law.

INTENT; INTENTION. Design; determination; purpose.

"Intent" implies purpose only — refers to the quality of the mind with which an act is done. "Attempt" (*q. v.*) implies an effort to carry intent into execution.[7]

Common intent. The ordinary meaning of words.

Criminal intent. Evil, malicious will expressed in a criminal act.

While crime proceeds from a criminal mind, ignorance of the law is not a defense.

General intent. A purpose to do something in general: as 1, to benefit a class of persons or objects by a charitable devise; 2, to violate law. Opposed, 1, **particular intent:** an intent, expressed in a will, which cannot be given effect,— see CY PRES; and, 2, **specific intent:** applied to an act done with a particular design.

When an act, in general terms, is indictable, a criminal intent need not be shown, unless, from the language or effect of the law, a purpose to require the existence of such intent can be discovered. To introduce into the law the requisite of a guilty mind it must appear that such was the intent of the law-maker.[1]

Neglect to discharge a duty, or indifference to consequences, is, in cases, equivalent to a specific criminal intent.[2]

"Act" and "intention," in the phrase "die by his own act or intention," mean the same as "act" alone, for act implies intention.[3]

A criminal intent and a criminal act make a crime. But here a "specific intent" and a "criminal intent" are not to be confounded: they have nothing in common except as mental operations. The former determines the object toward which the act shall be directed; the latter that the act so directed shall be done. The former, as part of the criminal act, must be alleged and proved as any other portion of the act; the latter is neither alleged nor proved, but inferred from the commission of the act. Thus, a criminal act presumes criminal intent, though the accused was intoxicated; but where the existence of a specific intent is necessary to the act, a degree of drunkenness incompatible with the formation of that intent negatives the act and disproves the crime.[4] See further CRIME; INDICTMENT; MALICE; PREMEDITATE.

Intention is judged of with reference to voluntary action.[5]

When guilty knowledge is an ingredient of an offense, evidence may be given of the commission of other acts of a like character where they are necessarily connected in time or place or as furnishing a clue to the motive.[6] See further GUILTY.

Intention may be proved inductively by collateral facts; as, in trespass, slander, libel, fraud, adultery, questions of good faith, of prudence, etc.[7]

---

[1] County of Allegheny *v.* Gibson, 90 Pa. 417 (1879): Worcester's Dict.

[2] Ortwein *v.* Commonwealth, 76 Pa. 421 (1874); Bennett *v.* State, 57 Wis. 86 (1883).

[3] Tatum *v.* State, 63 Ala. 152 (1879), Stone, J.

[4] Brockway *v.* Mutual Benefit Life Ins. Co., 9 F. R. 253 (1881). See Knickerbocker Life Ins. Co. *v.* Foley, 105 U. S. 354 (1881); 122 *id.* 512; Union Mut. Life Ins. Co. *v.* Reif, 36 Ohio St. 599 (1881); 62 Cal. 178; 34 Iowa, 222; 70 N. Y. 605; 9 R. I. 346; 1 F. & F. 735.

[5] Northwestern Mut. Life Ins. Co. *v.* Muskegon Bank, 122 U. S. 506 (1887), Miller, J.

[6] Ætna Life Ins. Co. *v.* Davey, 123 U. S. 743-44 (1887); N. W. Life Ins. Co. *v.* Muskegon Bank, 122 *id.* 505 (1887), distinguished.

[7] Prince *v.* State, 35 Ala. 369 (1860), cases.

[1] Halsted *v.* State, 41 N. J. L. 552, 589-91 (1879), cases, Beasley, C. J. See also United States *v.* Bayaud, 16 F. R. 383 (1883).

[2] United States *v.* Thomson, 12 F. R. 245 (1882).

[3] Chapman *v.* Republic Ins. Co., 6 Biss. 240 (1874).

[4] See 3 Greenl. Ev. §§ 13-19; 1 Bish. Cr. L. §§ 488-93; Broom, Com. 876, 887-88; 2 Steph. Hist. Cr. Law Eng. 110-13; Commonwealth *v.* Hersey, 2 Allen, 179-81 (1861), cases.

[5] *Re* Bininger, 7 Blatch. 267 (1870).

[6] People *v.* Gibbs, 93 N. Y. 473 (1883); 58 *id.* 555.

[7] 1 Whart. Ev. §§ 31-37, cases.

At common law, an intention to commit a felony does not amount to the felony, though it did, by statute, where the intention was to commit treason.[1]

An intention to commit a fraud has been given the force and effect of fraud.[2]

"Intent to injure and defraud" charges embezzlement, forgery, and like offenses.[3]

As men seldom do unlawful acts with innocent intentions, the law presumes a wicked intent from any such act; but the *prima facie* case thus made out may be rebutted by showing the contrary. Thus, in murder, malice is presumed from the fact of killing.[4]

Every person of sound mind is presumed to intend the necessary, natural, or legal consequences of his deliberate act.[5] This presumption may be conclusive, as when the consequences must necessarily follow the act; or be disputable, rebuttable by evidence of want of intention, where the consequences do not necessarily follow the act. Thus, where one voluntarily points a loaded pistol at a vital part, the law declares that the natural, inevitable consequence of that act is to kill, provided the pistol be fired; and the individual cannot be heard to say that he had no intent to kill. So, when a debtor procures his property to be taken on legal process, the effect being to defeat or delay the operation of a bankrupt act, he is held to have intended that effect.[6] The intention is the turning point in an issue to decide whether a judgment against an insolvent was obtained with a view to give a preference.[7]

Persons of sound mind and discretion are understood to intend, in the ordinary transactions of life, that which is the necessary and unavoidable consequences of their acts, as they are supposed to know what the consequences of their acts will be in such transactions. This rule applies in civil and criminal cases. Exceptions may arise; as, where the consequences likely to flow from the act are not matters of common knowledge, or where the act or the consequence is attended by circumstances tending to rebut the ordinary probative force of the act or to exculpate the intent of the agent — as, that the holder of a warrant to confess judgment could enter judgment to get a preference.[8] See further CONSEQUENCES.

Intention is gathered from all the things done, said, written; in ordinary documents, any words expressing it may be used. In wills it is "the pole-star of interpretation," when no rule of law is violated. In construing writings generally, the courts strive after the intention, putting themselves in the place of the party or parties.[9]

See ABANDON; CONTRACT; DOMICIL; GRANT; IGNORANCE; STATUTE; WILL.

[1] 4 Bl. Com. 221.
[2] 2 Pars. Contr. 772.
[3] United States v. Taintor, 11 Blatch. 378 (1873).
[4] 1 Greenl. Ev. § 34.
[5] Reynolds v. United States, 98 U. S. 167 (1878).
[6] *Re* Bininger, 7 Blatch. 268, 277 (1870), cases.
[7] Little v. Alexander, 21 Wall. 500 (1874).
[8] Clarion Bank v. Jones, 21 Wall. 337 (1874), Clifford, Justice.
[9] 1 Greenl. Ev. §§ 287-89. As to presumptions, see 30 Alb. Law J. 66-70 (1884), cases; evidence of, 22 Cent. Law J. 271 (1886), cases.

(36)

INTER. L. In the midst; among; between.

Used in Latin phrases, and in compound words; in the latter, the simple words are sometimes separated by a hyphen.

Inter alia. Among other things.

Inter alios. Among other persons — as to strangers. See RES, Inter, etc.

Inter.com. See INTERIM, Committitur.

Inter conjuges. Between husband and wife.

Inter pares. Between equals — in capacity or opportunity.

Inter partes. Between persons — the immediate parties to an instrument. See PARS, Inter, etc.

Inter rusticos. Among the unlearned.

Inter se, or **sese.** Between themselves.

Inter vivos. Between living persons. See GIFT.

INTERCOMMON. See COMMON, Right of.

INTERCOURSE. Between nations and the States, see COMMERCE. Between persons, see ACCESS; COHABIT.

INTERESSE. L. To be of interest to: interest. See INTEREST, 1.

Interesse termini. Interest in a term.

"A bare lease does not vest any estate in the lessee, but only gives a right of entry, which right is his interest in the term, or *interesse termini*."[1]

The right to the possession of a term at a future time.[2] See TERMINUS, 2.

Pro interesse suo. To the extent of his interest.

A party may intervene in litigation instituted by others, *pro interesse suo*.[3]

INTEREST. I. Lat. It interests, concerns, is of importance to.

Interest reipublicæ ut sit finis litium. It concerns the commonwealth that there be an end to lawsuits. The general welfare requires that litigation be not interminable.

No maxim is more firmly established or of more value in the administration of justice. It prevents repeated litigation between the same parties in regard to the same subject.[4]

It prevents multiplicity of suits.[5]

In it originates the rule against circuity of action;

[1] 2 Bl. Com. 144, 314.
[2] 4 Kent, 106; 72 Mo. 542.
[3] 106 U. S. 565.
[4] United States v. Throckmorton, 98 U. S. 65 (1878); Miles v. Caldwell, 2 Wall. 39 (1864); 3 Bl. Com. 308.
[5] Stark v. Starr, 94 U. S. 485 (1876); 71 Pa. 177; 2 Pars. Contr. 620.

and it states the principle upon which rest statutes of set-off and of limitations.

For this reason, the prevention of litigation is a valid consideration.[1]

For this reason, also, but one action lies for all the articles converted by one act.[2]

It is the policy of the law to settle in one suit the interests of all parties in the subject-matter, leaving as little room as possible for multiplicity of actions.[3]

2. **Eng.** (1) Concern, advantage, good; share, portion, part, participation.[4]

Concern, advantage, benefit. Such relation to the matter in issue as creates a liability to pecuniary gain or loss from the event of the suit.[5] Opposed, *disinterest.*

In this sense a witness is said to be incompetent, and a judge or juror disqualified, from interest.

At common law, a party could testify for himself only when he alone knew the matter to be proved. This was to prevent absolute failure of justice, where his right to relief was shown by other evidence.[6]

An interest disqualifying a witness, at common law, must be legal, real, substantial, present, certain, vested, and *ex parte.* Interest in the question is not meant, nor inclination arising from relationship, friendship, or other motive.

The meaning is that parties legally interested in the result are incompetent. This interest is to be real, not merely apprehended, and in the event of the cause. The true test regards gain or loss by the judgment. The degree is not regarded. A remote, contingent, uncertain interest does not disqualify. One may testify against his interest; and an offer to release an interest qualifies. Equal interest on both sides does not disqualify. Objection for interest must be made before examination. Precisely what interest disqualifies is largely a question for the court.[7]

But the common-law rule has been generally abrogated. The effect of interest upon credibility is now left to the jury to determine.[8] See further PARTY, 2; WITNESS.

(2) Right of property in a thing.

May denote the property itself, objectively considered.[9]

A claim to advantage or benefit; any right, in the nature of property, less than title; title to a share.[1]

Spoken of as present or vested, contingent or future, chattel or landed, beneficial, reversionary, undivided, legal, equitable, etc.

The quantum depends upon the title in the possessor. As respects realty, this may be freehold or less; as respects chattels, it is *joint,*—shared with other persons; or *several* or *sole,* — possessed by one person exclusively, or by more than one, their interests then not being in common.

The chief use of the word is to designate some right which cannot or need not be defined with precision. In some connections it includes title; in others, advantages less than title. Sometimes it is added to words of more definite meaning by way of precaution that no conceivable claim shall be omitted; sometimes it signifies an undefined share.[1] Compare CLAIM; DEMAND.

Community of interest. See COMMUNITY, 1.

Coupled with an interest. Said of an agency in which the agent has a business interest, along with his principal.

A power coupled with an interest is where the grantee has an interest in the estate as well as in the exercise of the power.

It is determined to exist or not according as the agent is found to have such estate or not before the execution of the power. If his interest is only a right to share the proceeds which result from the execution of the power, he has no such power.[2]

Such a power survives the person giving it, and may be executed after his death. This refers to an interest in the thing itself, a power which accompanies, or is connected with, an interest.[3]

Equitable interest. Such interest as is cognizable in a court of equity. **Legal interest.** An interest cognizable in a court of common law.

Immediate interest. See IMMEDIATE.

Interest or no interest. Refers to a policy of insurance which is to be valid whether the insured has or does not have an insurable interest,[4] *q. v.*

Opposing interest. At the meeting of the creditors of a bankrupt to elect an assignee, if no choice was made, the judge, or, if there was "no opposing interest," the register, appointed a person. This meant, not merely an interest contending by vote for the election of a particular person, but an interest in

---

[1] 1 Pars. Contr. 438; Smith, Contr. 179.

[2] Phillips v. Berick, 16 Johns. 140 (1819). See also 105 Ill. 108.

[3] Eckford v. Knox, 67 Tex. 205 (1886); 2 Kan. Law J. 280 (1885); 6 Tex. 446; 30 F. R. 911; 41 N. J. E. 443; 7 Mass. 432; 99 *id.* 203; 4 Allen, 473; 16 Gray, 27; 5 *id.* 197; 1 *id.* 302; 24 Pick. 61; 22 *id.* 83; 21 *id.* 253; 20 *id.* 290; 15 *id.* 286.

[4] Fitch v. Bates, 11 Barb. 473 (1851).

[5] Bouvier, Law Dict.; Inhabitants of Northampton v. Smith, 11 Metc. 394-96 (1846), cases, Shaw, C. J.

[6] United States v. Clark, 96 U. S. 41 (1877); 3 Bl. Com. 370; 1 Greenl. Ev. § 348.

[7] 1 Greenl. Ev. §§ 386-430, cases.

[8] 1 Whart. Ev. § 419; 30 Hun, 557; 63 Pa. 156; 64 *id.* 29; 65 *id.* 126; 82 Tex. 141.

[9] Pierce v. Pierce, 14 R. I. 517 (1884).

[1] [Abbott's Law Dict.

[2] Flanagan v. Brown, 70 Cal. 259 (1886); Brown v. Pforr, 38 *id.* 550 (1869); Hartley's Appeal, 53 Pa. 212 (1866); Frink v. Roe, 70 Cal. 310 (1886).

[3] Hunt v. Rousmanier, 8 Wheat. 203 (1823), Marshall, C. J.; Walker v. Walker, 125 U. S. 842 (1888); 59 Tex. 399.

[4] See 2 Bl. Com. 460.

opposition to the power of appointment by the register.[1]

(3) Increase by way of compensation for the use of money; price or reward for the loan of money; a premium for the hire of money; a reasonable equivalent for the temporary inconvenience the lender of money may feel by the want of it.[2]

Compensation allowed by law, or fixed by the parties, for the use or forbearance of money, or as damages for it detention.[3]

A compensation for the loan or use of money.[4]

The measure of damages for money withheld upon contract.[5]

Though interest, *eo nomine*, may be a creation of statute law, it is allowed as mulct or punishment for some fraud, delinquency, or injustice of the debtor, or from some injury done by him to the creditor.[6]

Simple interest. Interest computed solely upon the principal of the loan. **Compound interest.** Is reckoned upon the principal for the first period, and thereafter upon both principal and accrued interest; interest upon interest.

"Compound interest" signifies the adding of the growing interest of any sum to the sum itself, and then the taking of interest upon this accumulation.[7]

At interest. In ordinary parlance "money at interest" refers more to money loaned than to interest-bearing notes and accounts received for property sold.[8]

Ex-interest. Said of a sale of stocks or bonds without interest already or soon payable. See Ex, 3.

With interest. When a note is made payable at a future day, "with interest" at a prescribed rate *per annum*, such interest does not become due or payable before the principal, unless there is a special provision to that effect.[1]

The rate, or sum, depends upon the usual or general inconvenience of parting with the loan, and the hazard of losing it entirely. Where the hazard is peculiarly great, as in contracts of bottomry and respondentia, policies of insurance, and annuities upon lives, the rates are high. Charging an exorbitant rate, in an ordinary case, is usury,[2] *q. v.*

As compensation for the use or detention of money, has its origin in the usages of trade, by contract, or by statute. Hence, the rules in regard to it are as diversified as the trade, habits of the people, and their peculiar laws may be.[3]

Spoken of as lawful or legal, and unlawful or illegal, excessive or usurious, as marine or maritime, etc.

Follows the principal as an incident.

Not chargeable upon claims against the assets of an insolvent from the date of the assignment, or against the estate of a decedent from the day of death; nor upon an advancement; nor upon costs.

Where not stipulated as part of a contract, given as damages for detaining money, property, or services, and from the day of default.[4]

In torts, allowance as damages rests in the discretion of the jury. Has been allowed upon money obtained by fraud or detained by an officer.[5]

The practice of the treasury department of the United States has always been not to pay interest upon claims against the government, without express statutory authorization; and Congress has repeatedly refused to pass any general law for the allowance of interest.[6]

Compound interest is not recoverable, unless there has been a settlement, or a judgment whereby the aggregate amount of principal and interest due is turned into a new principal; or where there is a specific agreement to do so.[7]

If interest upon interest were allowed in all cases, debts would increase beyond all ordinary calculation and endurance; common business could not stand the overwhelming accumulation.[8]

See BONUS; COUPON, Bond; DAMAGES; DEPOSIT, 2; DISCOUNT, 2; WAR.

INTERFERENCE. Is used in the Revised Statutes prescribing proceedings when an application is made for a patent which

---

[1] R. S. § 5034; *Re* Jackson, 7 Biss. 287 (1876).

[2] [2 Bl. Com. 454.

[3] Brown *v.* Hiatts, 15 Wall. 185 (1872), Field, J.; Insurance Co. *v.* Piaggio, 16 *id.* 386 (1872), cases; Aurora City *v.* West, 7 *id.* 105 (1868), cases; Redfield *v.* Ystalyfera Iron Co., 110 U. S. 176 (1884); 12 F. R. 864; 2 McCrary, 394; 8 Saw. 189.

[4] Turner *v.* Turner, 80 Va. 381 (1885).

[5] Loudon *v.* Taxing District, 104 U. S. 774 (1881). See also 2 Cal. 568; 28 Conn. 20; 42 *id.* 528; 3 Dak. 460; 66 Ga. 501; 3 N. Y. 355; 87 *id.* 437; 13 Barb. 76; 30 Pa. 341; 34 *id.* 211.

[6] Rensselaer Glass Factory *v.* Reid, 5 Cow. 609-18 (1825), cases; Heidenheimer *v.* Ellis, 67 Tex. 428 (1887), cases.

[7] Camp *v.* Bates, 11 Conn. 501 (1836); Koshkonong *v.* Burton, 104 U. S. 677 (1881), cases; 105 Ill. 553; 34 Pa. 212.

[8] Wasson *v.* First Nat. Bank of Indianapolis, 107 Ind. 212 (1886).

[1] Tanner *v.* Dundee Land Investment Co., 12 F. R. 648 (1882).

[2] 2 Bl. Com. 454.

[3] Stokely *v.* Thompson, 34 Pa. 211 (1859).

[4] United States *v.* Hills, 4 Cliff. 621-22 (1878), cases.

[5] Lincoln *v.* Claflin, 7 Wall. 139 (1868); Frazer *v.* Bigelow Carpet Co., 141 Mass. 127-28 (1886), cases.

[6] Angarica *v.* Bayard, 127 U. S. 260 (1888), cases.

[7] Stokely *v.* Thompson, Camp *v.* Bates, *supra.*

[8] Connecticut *v.* Jackson, 1 Johns. Ch. *14 (1814), Kent, Ch. See generally Selleck *v.* French, 1 Conn. 32 (1814): 1 Am. L. C. 500-35, cases; 25 Cent. Law J. 293 (1887), cases.

may interfere with a pending application or with an unexpired patent.[1] See. PATENT, 2.

INTERIM. L. *Inter ipsum (tempus),* within that time: in the meantime, meanwhile; provisionally.

Ad interim. For the time intervening.

Interim committitur. In the meantime, let him be committed; meanwhile he will be kept in prison.

Abridged to "inter. com.," has been used for the docket entry in cases where, until some further action can be taken or proceeding be had, a prisoner is remanded to jail; as, in a case of conviction for murder, when sentence of death is pronounced, to be carried into execution at a distant day.

Interim officer. One appointed when another, the principal, is absent, is incapable of acting, or has not yet been chosen or fully qualified.

Sometimes termed the *ad interim* officer. Such is a provisional assignee, trustee, curator, guardian.

Interim order. An order taking effect provisionally, or until further direction; in particular, an order made pending an appeal.

Interim receipt. A deposit or protection receipt for money paid on a proposed contract of insurance; also, *ad interim* receipt.

Holds the applicant secure until his proposal is accepted or rejected. If the risk is not approved, the money is returned, less the premium for the time being.[2]

INTERLINEATION. See ALTERATION, 2; BLANK, 2.

INTERLOCUTORY.[3] Intervening — happening, accruing, or imposed between the commencement and the termination of proceedings — during the progress of an action at law or of a suit in equity: as, interlocutory — costs, decree, judgment, order, report, *qq. v.* Compare FINAL.

INTERMARRIAGE. See MARRIAGE.

INTERMIXTURE. See ACCESSION.

INTERN.[4] To imprison by restricting to a limited territory: as, to intern a political prisoner within a city or upon an island.

INTERNAL. See IMPROVEMENT; REVENUE.

INTERNATIONAL. See EXTRADITION; LAW; NATION.

INTERNUNCIO. See MINISTER, 3.

INTERPLEAD. To become parties litigant; to determine a dispute by judicial action.

Interpleader; bill of interpleader. Where a person, who owes a debt to one of the parties in a suit, but, till the determination of it, he knows not to which one, desires that they may interplead, that he may be protected in making the payment.[1]

The stakeholder prays that the court judge between the claimants, to whom the thing belongs, and that he be indemnified. He alleges that the persons have preferred a claim against him, and for the same thing, that he has no beneficial interest in the matter, and that he cannot determine, without hazard, to which of them the thing or right belongs.[2]

The plaintiff must have no interest in the thing, no adequate remedy at law, and be ignorant of the rights of the claimants.[3]

If the thing claimed is a sum of money, the holder may pay it into court.

The bill will not lie if the complainant sets up an interest in the subject-matter of the suit, and the relief sought relates to that interest. The relief sought, in a bill in the nature of a bill of interpleader, must be equitable.[4]

In cases of adverse independent legal titles, the party holding the property must defend himself as well as he can at law.[5]

INTERPRETATIO. L. Expounding, explanation: construction, interpretation, *q. v.*

Ex antecedentibus et consequentibus, fit optima interpretatio. From what things go before and come after, the best explanation is had. A doubtful word or passage may be best understood by reference to the whole instrument — deed, will, contract, statute. Intention may be read in the light of surrounding circumstances.[6] Compare NOSCITUR, A sociis.

INTERPRETATION. Is used interchangeably with "construction." Opposed, *misinterpretation.*

The act of finding out the true sense of any form of words, that is, the sense their

---

[1] See R. S. § 4904; Gold Separating Co. *v.* Disintegrating Co., 6 Blatch. 310 (1869).

[2] See May, Ins. §§ 57–59.

[3] L. *inter-loqui,* to speak in between.

[4] L. *internus: intra,* within.

[1] [3 Bl. Com. 448.

[2] Atkinson *v.* Marks, 1 Cow. 703 (1823).

[3] Howe Machine Co. *v.* Gifford, 66 Barb. 599 (1872). See also 2 Paige, Ch. 200; 2 Story, Eq. Ch. XX.

[4] Killian *v.* Ebbinghaus, 110 U. S. 571 (1884), cases.

[5] 2 Story, Eq. § 820; Third Nat. Bank *v.* Lumber Co., 132 Mass. 410 (1882), cases. See generally McMunn *v.* Carothers, 4 Clarke, Pa., 134–36 (1848); 3 Pomeroy, Eq. §§ 1319–29.

[6] 2 Bl. Com. 379; 1 Greenl. Ev. §§ 201, 437; 71 Pa. 301; 76 Va. 714.

author intended; and of enabling others to derive from them the same idea.[1]

Properly precedes construction, but does not go beyond the written text.[2] See further CONSTRUCTION; INTERPRETATIO.

INTERPRETER. One who translates the testimony of witnesses speaking a foreign tongue, for the benefit of the court and jury.

His re-statement is not hearsay; it may be impeached for inaccuracy.[3]

INTERROGATORY. One of a series or set of written questions prepared by counsel for the examination of a party to a suit in equity.

A formal question, in writing, for the judicial examination of a party or a witness.[4]

Direct or **original interrogatory.** An interrogatory exhibited by the party who calls a witness in the first instance. **Counter** or **cross interrogatory:** is exhibited by the adverse party.

Fishing interrogatory. Inquiries after a matter as to which proponent has no right to a discovery.

Suggestive interrogatory. Indicates the answer desired.

Interrogatories accompany bills in the nature of discovery, proceedings for contempt, attachment in execution against garnishees, commissions to take testimony out of court. They are subject to the same rules as examinations in court.[5]

See CHANCERY, Bill in; DEPOSITION; DISCOVERY, 6; EXAMINATION, 9; QUESTION, 1.

INTERSECT. Ordinarily, to cross.[6]

A railroad which runs along a turnpike so as to require a change in the traveled path, does not intersect the turnpike.[6]

Roads intersect at their middle lines.[7]

INTER-STATE. See COMMERCE; EXTRADITION, 2; STATE, 3 (2).

INTERVAL. See LUCID INTERVAL.

INTERVENE.[8] To file a claim or a defense in a suit instituted by or against others.

Intervener; intervenor. One who applies to be heard as an original party in another's suit, he being interested in the result of the suit.

Intervention. The act or proceeding by which one, on his own motion, becomes a party to a suit pending between others: as, in a case in equity or in admiralty. Opposed, non-intervention.

INTESTATE. 1, *adj.* Without a will; the status of a person who dies without having disposed of his property by means of a will, and the condition in which the property itself stands before the law: as, intestate — estate, property, laws. Opposed, *testate.*

2, *n.* A person who has died without leaving a valid will: as, an intestate, an intestate's estate or property.[1] Opposed, *testator.*

Intestacy. Dying without a will; the state or condition of one who dies without having made a valid testamentary disposition of his property. Opposed, *testacy.*

Intestable. Without capacity to make a valid will; also, incapable of transfer by will. Opposed, *testable.* See further TESTACY; DISTRIBUTION, 2; DESCENT.

INTIMATE. Compare ACQUAINTED.

That a man has been "intimate" with another's wife, does not of necessity import criminalty.[2]

INTIMIDATION. See BOYCOTTING; DURESS; ELECTION, 1; FEAR; STRIKE, 2.

INTOXICATE. To become inebriated or drunk.[3]

Intoxicated. Drunk, from use of spirituous liquor.[4]

Whenever any other idea is intended other words are used; as, in saying that a person is intoxicated or drunk with opium, ether, or laughing gas.[4]

Intoxicating liquor. "Intoxicating liquors or mixtures thereof" are liquors which will intoxicate and which are commonly used as beverages for such purpose; also, any mixture of such liquors as, retaining their intoxicating qualities, it may fairly be presumed may be used as a beverage and become a substitute for the ordinary intoxicating drinks.[5]

In the absence of evidence to the contrary, beer will always be presumed to be an intoxicating liquor.[6]

But "intoxicating" and "spirituous" not being

---

[1] Lieber, Herm. 23; 14 How. Pr. 272; 36 N. J. L. 209; 1 Bl. Com. 59.

[2] 2 Pars. Contr., 7 ed., 491 (*a*).

[3] 1 Whart. Ev. § 493.

[4] See 3 Bl. Com. 438; 4 *id.* 287; 5 N. J. L. 772.

[5] See Bischoffsheim *v.* Baltzer, 20 Blatch. 231 (1882).

[6] State *v.* New Haven, &c. R. Co., 45 Conn. 344 (1877).

[7] Springfield Road, 73 Pa. 129 (1873); 74 *id.* 259.

[8] L. *inter-venire*, to come in between.

[1] See 2 Bl. Com. 294.

[2] Adams *v.* Stone, 131 Mass. 433 (1881).

[3] Mullinix *v.* People, 76 Ill. 213 (1875).

[4] State *v.* Kelley, 47 Vt. 296 (1875).

[5] Intoxicating-Liquor Cases, 25 Kan. 767 (1881), Brewer, J.; State *v.* McGinnis, 30 Minn. 52 (1882).

[6] State *v.* Teissedre, 30 Kan. 484 (1883); Briffitt *v.* State, 58 Wis. 41 (1883), cases; 6 Kan. 371; 16 Mo. 380; 14 Ohio, 586; 12 Gray, 29; 63 N. Y. 277; 11 R. I. 592.

synonymous, an indictment for unlawful sales of "spirituous *and* intoxicating" liquors is not supported by proof of sales of liquors which are intoxicating but not spirituous.[1]

See further CONDITION; DRUNKENNESS; LIQUOR; POLICY, Public.

INTRA. See INFRA; ULTRA.

INTRINSIC. See VALUE.

INTROMISSION. Dealings in stock, goods, or cash of a principal, coming into the hands of his agent, to be accounted for by the agent.[2]

INTRUDER. A person who enters upon land when he has no right.[3] Compare SQUATTER. See LAND, Public.

Intrusion. Injury by ouster, or amotion of possession from the freehold: the entry of a stranger, after a particular estate of freehold is determined, before him in remainder or reversion.[4]

INUNDATION. See ACT, 1, Of God; WATERCOURSE.

INURE.[5] To serve to the use, benefit, or advantage of some one; to take or have effect; to operate.

As, that discharge of the principal inures to the benefit of the surety; that confirmation of a title inures to the grantee; that a grant by the state inures to the intent expressed.[6]

Inurement. Use, user, usage.

Passage of title by inurement and estoppel is the work of the common law and legislation.[7]

INVALID, *adj.* See VALID.

INVALID, *n.* See WITNESS.

INVASION. See WAR.

INVEIGLE. See KIDNAPING; PERSUADE.

INVENTION.[8] Finding out, by some effort of the understanding; not merely putting two things together, although never done before.[9]

The process of thought and experiment by which some new machine, composition, design, improvement or other article or thing is brought into existence; also, the thing itself thus produced.

[1] Commonwealth v. Livermore, 4 Gray, 20 (1855).

[2] Stewart v. M'Kean, 29 E. L. & Eq. 391 (1855), Alderson, B.

[3] [O'Donnell v. McIntyre, 16 Abb. N. Cas. 88 (1885).

[4] 3 Bl. Com. 169; 9 Ill. 170.

[5] L. *in ure*, in operation, work, use. Preferred to enure.

[6] See 2 Bl. Com. 347.

[7] Dickerson v. Colgrove, 100 U. S. 583, 584 (1879).

[8] F. *inventer*, to devise: L. *in venire*, to come upon, find out.

[9] Earle v. Sawyer, 4 Mas. 5 (1825), Story, J.

The applicant for a patent must be the first as well as the original inventor; and a subsequent inventor, although an original inventor, is not entitled to a patent, if the invention is perfected and put into actual use by the first and original inventor. Until an invention is perfected and adapted to use, it is not patentable. An invention resting in mere theory, or in intellectual notion, or in uncertain experiments, and not actually reduced to practice and embodied in some distinct machinery, apparatus, manufacture, or composition of matter, is not patentable.[1]

The patent law requires a thing to be new as well as useful. To be new, it must be the product of original thought or inventive skill, and not a mere formal and mechanical change of what was old and well-known. But the effect produced by change is often an appropriate, though not a controlling, consideration in determining the character of the change itself.[2]

Merely turning down and cementing the edges of celluloid collars in the form of a hem is not invention.[3]

It is becoming more and more difficult to distinguish between skill and invention. As the standard of skill in mechanics is raised, the standard of invention is also raised.[4]

Useful invention. Such invention as may be applied to some beneficial use in society, in contradistinction to an invention which is injurious to the morals, the health, or the good order of society.[5]

All improvement is not invention; to entitle it to protection it must be the product of some exercise of the inventive faculties, and involve something more than what is obvious to persons skilled in the art.[6]

The improvement must be distinct from the conception which originated the original article or product. A mere carrying forward or new or more extended application of the original thought, a change only in form, proportion, or degree, the substitution of equivalents, doing substantially the same thing in the same way by substantially the same means with better results, is not such invention as will sustain a patent.[7]

[1] Reed v. Cutter, 1 Story, 596, 599 (1841), Story, J.

[2] The Stanley Works v. Sargent & Co., 8 Blatch. 346 (1871), Shipman, J. See also Smith v. Goodyear Co., 93 U. S. 495 (1876); Washburn & Moen Manuf. Co. v. Haish, 10 Biss. 72–75 (1880); Western Electric Light Co. v. Chicago Electric Light Manuf. Co., 11 *id.* 427 (1882); Gardner v. Herz, 118 U. S. 180 (1886), cases, Blatchford, J.; Pomace Holder Co v. Ferguson, 119 *id.* 338 (1886), cases.

[3] Celluloid Manuf. Co. v. Zylonite Novelty Co., 30 F. R. 617 (1887).

[4] Wilcox v. Bookwalter, 31 F. R. 229 (1887).

[5] Bedford v. Hunt, 1 Mas. 303 (1817), Story, J.; 18 Wis. 442; 13 N. H. 318.

[6] Pearce v. Mulford, 102 U. S. 118 (1880), Strong, J.

[7] Smith v. Nichols, 21 Wall. 119 (1874), Swayne, J. See also Stephenson v. Brooklyn R. Co., 114 U. S. 154 (1885), cases.

Inventor. He who originally contrives or devises a new article or thing.

Inventors are a meritorious class generally, and favored in law.[1] Acts intended to determine the value, utility, or success of an invention are liberally construed.[2] But inventors must comply with statutory conditions. They cannot, without cause, hold an application pending more than two years.[2]

Exact description is requisite: that the government may know what it has granted, and what will become public property when the patent expires; that licensees may know how to use the invention; and that subsequent inventors may know what portion of the field has been occupied.[4]

While an agreement to assign in gross a man's future labors does not address itself favorably to the courts, an inventor may dispose of his invention and bind himself to assign to the purchaser any improvements he may thereafter make; and a pecuniary interest in the sale of the patent does not seem to be necessary to the validity of such a bargain.[5]

See further ORIGINALITY; PATENT, 2; TELEPHONE CASE; USE, 2, Useful.

INVENTORY.[6] A list or schedule of articles of property.

A list or schedule, or enumeration of the articles of property, setting out the names of the different articles, either singly or in classes.[7]

Accounts of the items of property levied upon are called inventories; and insolvents file inventories of assets. A more common use is in the administration of the estates of decedents. The representative, at the outset, files an inventory of the assets. This is made by two or more fair-minded persons as sworn appraisers. The representative is then charged with the amount of the inventory. Articles not converted into money, and disbursements, may afterward be allowed as credits. The inventory exhibits to creditors, legatees, and distributees, the nature and amount of the estate.

The inventory made by a landlord who distrains for rent should be full enough to inform the tenant of the articles distrained, for which he may have a writ of replevin.[8]

INVENTUS. See FIND, 3.

INVEST. 1. To clothe with power or authority. See VEST.

2. In common parlance, to put out money on interest.

To place money so that it will yield a profit; as commonly understood, to give money for other property.[1]

Includes, but is not restricted to, "loan."[2]

Does not universally import preservation or a permanent keeping for the purpose of collecting income. "It is not uncommon to have it said that the best investment of money is in paying debts."[3]

Invested. A sum represented by anything but money is invested.[4]

Money loaned is invested in a debt against the borrower, regardless of the evidence.[5]

Investment. Laying out money in such manner that it may produce a revenue, whether the particular method be a loan or the purchase of stocks, securities, or other property. In common parlance, putting out money on interest, either by way of loan or by the purchase of income-producing property.[6]

An investment of money in the business of another is more than a loan: it is a contribution to the capital.[7]

Neglect by a trustee to invest moneys in his hands is a breach of trust, and ground for removal.[8]

The rule is everywhere recognized that a trustee, when investing property in his hands, is bound to act honestly and faithfully, and to exercise a sound discretion, such as men of ordinary prudence and intelligence use in their own affairs. In some jurisdictions, no attempt has been made to establish a more definite rule; in others, the discretion has been confined, by the legislature or the courts, within strict limits.[9]

INVESTIGATION. Inquiry by observation, experiment, or discussion.[10]

The Penal Code of New York, § 79, makes it compulsory upon persons concerned in bribery to testify "upon any trial . . . or investigation" thereof, their testimony not to be used against them in any subsequent proceeding. This does not refer to an "investigation" in the course of a criminal prosecution, but to any inquiry in the conduct of which persons may be called by authority to testify, and hence includes an inquiry directed by the legislature, and conducted by any of its committees.[11]

---

[1] Wilson v. Rousseau, 4 How. 674 (1846).

[2] Jennings v. Pierce, 15 Blatch. 45–46 (1878), cases; Lyman v. Maypole, 19 F. R. 735, 737–44 (1884), cases.

[3] Planing-Machine Co. v. Keith, 101 U. S. 485 (1879).

[4] Tucker v. Tucker Manuf. Co., 4 Cliff. 400 (1876), Clifford, J.; Parker v. Stiles, 5 McLean, 55 (1849).

[5] Aspinwall Manuf. Co. v. Gill, 32 F. R. 700 (1887), Bradley, J.

[6] L. in-venire, to find.

[7] [Silver Bow Mining Co. v. Lowry, 5 Monta. 621 (1885).

[8] Richards v. McGrath, 100 Pa. 400 (1882); 59 Wis. 403,

[1] Neel v. Beach, 92 Pa. 226 (1879).

[2] Shoemaker v. Smith, 37 Ind. 127 (1871).

[3] New England Life Ins. Co. v. Phillips, 141 Mass. 540, 543 (1886).

[4] Parker Mills v. Commissioners, 23 N. Y. 244 (1861).

[5] Jennings v. Davis, 31 Conn. 140 (1862). See also 2 Cow. 678; 1 Edw. 513; 10 Gill. & J. 299.

[6] Una v. Dodd, 39 N. J. E. 186 (1884), Van Fleet, V. C. See also People v. Utica Ins. Co., 15 Johns. *392 (1818).

[7] Lyon v. Zimmer, 30 F. R. 410 (1887).

[8] Cavender v. Cavender, 114 U. S. 473 (1885), cases.

[9] Lamar v. Micou, 112 U. S. 465–70 (1884), cases, Gray, J.; New England Trust Co. v. Eaton, 140 Mass. 535 (1886), cases; 25 Am. Law Reg. 217–34 (1886), cases.

[10] Wright v. Chicago, 48 Ill. 290 (1868).

[11] People v. Sharp, 107 N. Y. 427 (1887).

INVESTITURE. A grant of land in feudal ages was perfected by the ceremony of corporal investiture: open and notorious delivery of possession in the presence of other vassals.

Made by putting a *vestis*, a robe, upon the tenant. Perpetuated memory of the transaction at a time when writing was little known.[1] See DELIVERY, 1.

INVIOLABLE. See IMPAIR.

INVIOLATE. See JURY, Trial by.

INVITATION. See NEGLIGENCE.

INVITUS. L. Against the will; unwilling.

Ab invito. From an unwilling person.

In invito. Against a resisting party.

Frequently applied to proceedings against a party who opposes the demand made upon him, and also to the judgment or decree made in such case. Taxes are said to be levied *in invitum*.

Invito domino. The owner being unwilling.

Said of the "taking" in larceny.

INVOICE.[2] A document transmitted from the shipper to his factor or consignee, containing the particulars and prices of the goods shipped.[3]

A written account of the particulars of merchandise shipped to a purchaser, factor or consignee, with the value or prices and charges annexed.[4]

Invoice cost or price. Sometimes, the prime price or cost of goods, whether there is an invoice in fact or not.[5]

An invoice is not a bill of sale, nor is it evidence of a sale. It is a mere detailed statement of the nature, quality, and cost or price of things invoiced, and is as appropriate to a bailment as to a sale. It does not of itself necessarily indicate to whom the things are sent, or even that they have been sent at all. Hence, standing alone, it is never regarded as evidence of title.[6] See BOOK-ENTRIES.

INVOLUNTARY. See VOLUNTARY.

IPSE. L. He himself. *Ipsud*, it itself; the very same.

Ipsissimis verbis. In the identical words. See VERBUM.

Ipso facto. By the mere fact.

Ipso jure. By the law itself.

IRON CLAD OATH. See OATH, Of office.

IRREGULAR. See ERRONEOUS; REGULAR.

IRRELEVANT. See RELEVANT.

IRREPARABLE. See INJURY.

IRRESISTIBLE. See ACCIDENT; FORCE.

IRRESPONSIBLE. See RESPONSIBLE.

IRREVOCABLE. See REVOKE.

IRRIGATION. See AQUA, Currit, etc.; RIPARIAN.

IS. L. That one; he.

Inflections: *id, ei, ejus, eo*, qq. v.

ISSINT.[1] Introduced a statement that special matter amounted to a denial — "the general issue with an *issint*."[2]

ISSUABLE. See ISSUE, 3.

ISSUE.[3] 1, *v.* To send out: as, to issue a writ or process.

A process is "issued" when made out and placed in the hands of a person authorized to serve it, with a *bona fide* intent to have it served.[4]

n. A causing to go forth: as, the issue of an order or writ, the issue of letters patent or letters testamentary. Compare EXIRE, Exit.

Re-issue; re-issued. Refer, in particular, to a continuation of an original patent. Whence re-issuable.

Whenever a patent is inoperative or defective, by reason of a defective or insufficient specification or claim of more than the applicant has a right to as new, if the error has arisen by inadvertence, accident, or mistake, and without deceptive intention, the commissioner of patents, on the surrender of such patent, shall cause a new patent to issue in accordance with the corrected specification. The surrender takes effect from the issue of the amended patent, and runs for the unexpired term of the original patent. But new matter may not be introduced.[6]

The surrender of valid patents, and the granting of re-issued patents thereon, with expanded or equivocal claims, where the original was clearly neither "inoperative nor invalid,"[7] and whose specification is neither "defective or insufficient," is a great abuse of the privilege granted, and productive of great injury to the public.[6]

A re-issue must be for the same invention, and, in

---

[1] 3 Bl. Com. 53, 311.

[2] A corruption of *envois*, Eng. plural of F. *envoi*, a sending.

[3] Le Roy *v.* United Ins. Co., 7 Johns. *354 (1811).

[4] Pipes *v.* Norton, 47 Miss. 76 (1872), Tarbell, J.; 16 Op. Att.-Gen. 160.

[5] Sturm *v.* Williams, 6 Jones & S. 342 (1874); 7 Johns. *354.

[6] Dows *v.* Nat. Exch. Bank of Milwaukee, 91 U. S. 630 (1875), Strong, J. See 2 Wash. 124, 155; 4 Abb. Ap. Dec. 78.

---

[1] Norm. F., thus, so.

[2] Gould, Pl. 313; 4 Rawle, 83.

[3] F. *issir:* L. *ex-ire*, to go out.

[4] Mills *v.* Corbett, 8 How. Pr. 502 (1853); Bragg *v.* Thompson, 17 S. C. 378 (1882).

[5] R. S. §§ 4916, 4895.

[6] Burr *v.* Duryee, 1 Wall. 577 (1863), Grier, J.; James *v.* Campbell, 104 U. S. 371 (1881).

judgment of law, is only a continuation of the original patent.[1]

If, on comparing a re-issue with its original, the former appears on its face to be for a different invention from that described or indicated in the latter, it must be declared invalid.[2]

A re-issue can only be granted for the same invention which was originally patented. If it were otherwise, a door would be opened to the admission of the greatest frauds. Claims and pretensions shown to be unfounded at the time, might, after the lapse of a few years, a change of officers in the patent office, the death of witnesses, and the dispersion of documents, be set up anew, and a reversal of the first decision be obtained without an appeal, and without any knowledge of the previous investigations on the subject. New light breaking in upon the patentee as the progress of improvement goes on, and as other inventors enter the field, and his monopoly becomes less and less necessary to the public, might easily generate in his own mind an idea that his invention was really broader than had been set forth in the specification of his patent. It is easy to see how such new light would naturally be reflected in a re-issue of the patent, and how unjust it might be to third parties who had kept pace with the march of improvement.[3]

By a curious misapplication of the law it has come to be principally resorted to for the purpose of enlarging and expanding patent claims. And the evils which have grown from the practice have assumed large proportions. Patents have been so expanded and idealized, years after their first issue, that thousands of mechanics and manufacturers, who had just reason to suppose that the field of action was open, have been obliged to discontinue their employments, or to pay an enormous tax for continuing them.[4]

The patentee has no rights except such as grow out of the re-issued patent. No damages can be recovered for any acts of infringement committed prior to the re-issue. The reason is, the original patent, which is surrendered, becomes extinguished by a re-issue.[5]

Whether there was an "inadvertent" mistake in the specification is, in general, a matter of fact for the commissioner of patents to decide; but whether the application for re-issue is made within a reasonable time is a matter of law, which the courts may determine by comparing the re-issued patent with the original, and, if necessary, with the records in the patent office when presented by the record.[6]

A patentee who imposes words of limitation upon his claim, especially so when required by the patent office in taking out his re-issue, is bound by such limitations in subsequent suits on the re-issued patents.[1] See PATENT, 2.

2, v. To put into circulation; to emit, q. v.: as, to issue bank notes, bonds, script.

n. All of a class or series of like securities or instruments for the payment of money put forth at one time.[2]

3, n. The disputed point or question.[3]

A single, certain, and material point, arising out of the allegations or pleadings of the parties, and generally made by an affirmative and a negative.[4]

When the parties come to a point which is affirmed on one side, and denied on the other, they are said to be "at issue." All debate is then contracted into a single point, which must be determined in favor of one of the parties.[5]

Issuable. Permitting an issue to be framed: as, issuable matter, or plea; to plead issuably.

Issue, *exitus*, is the end of all pleadings. It is upon a matter of law or of fact. An issue upon a matter of law is called a demurrer, q. v. An issue of fact is where the fact only, and not the law, is disputed.[5]

When either side denies the facts pleaded by his antagonist, he usually "tenders an issue." If the denial comes from the defendant, the form is "And of this he puts himself upon the country;" if from the plaintiff, the form is "And this he prays may be inquired of by the country"—a jury. Thereupon the other party subjoins "And the said A does the like." Which done, the issue is said to be "joined," both parties agreeing to rest the fate of the cause upon the truth of the fact in question.[7]

Thus also in equity, the plaintiff may aver, in reply, that his bill is true, certain, and sufficient, and defendant's answer the reverse, which he is ready to prove as the court shall award; upon which the defendant rejoins, averring the like on his side.[8]

Collateral issue. An issue upon an incidental matter.[9]

Feigned issue. As no jury is summoned to attend a court of equity, a matter of fact, strongly controverted, is directed to be tried at the bar of a court of law, upon a "feigned" issue. This is an action wherein the plaint-

[1] Read v. Bowman, 2 Wall. 604 (1864), Clifford, J.

[2] Ball v. Langles, 102 U. S. 130 (1880), cases, Strong, J.

[3] Swain Turbine & Manuf. Co. v. Ladd, 102 U. S. 413 (1880), Bradley, J.; Parker & Whipple Co. v. Yale Lock Co., 123 *id.* 87, 97 (1887).

[4] Miller v. Bridgeport Brass Co., 104 U. S. 353 (1881), Bradley, J.

[5] Peck v. Collins, 103 U. S. 664 (1880), Bradley, J. See also *ib.* 791; Heald v. Rice, 104 *id.* 749 (1881); Wing v. Anthony, 106 *id.* 147 (1882); Moffitt v. Rogers, *ib.* 423, 428 (1882), cases; 18 Blatch. 534; 17 F. R. 235.

[6] Mahn v. Harwood, 112 U. S. 359-60 (1884), cases, Bradley, J.; Hoskin v. Fisher, 125 *id.* 223 (1888), cases.

[1] Crawford v. Heysinger, 123 U. S. 606 (1887), cases, Blatchford, J.

[2] See 8 Mich. 104; 2 McCrary, 449; 17 Barb. 341.

[3] Seller v. Jenkins, 97 Ind. 438 (1884).

[4] Simonton v. Winter, 5 Pet. *149 (1831); Gould, Pl. 279.

[5] 3 Bl. Com. 313. See 2 Ark. 104; 30 Conn. 488; 55 Ga. 61; 9 Gill, 258; 2 N. J. E. 157; 51 Wis. 77.

[6] 3 Bl. Com. 314-15; 2 N. J. E. 157; 51 Wis. 76.

[7] 3 Bl. Com. 313, 315; 57 N. H. 164.

[8] 3 Bl. Com. 448.

[9] See 4 Bl. Com. 396.

iff, by a fiction, declares that he laid a wager with the defendant, and then re-avers the truth of the fact, and therefore demands the amount of the wager. The defendant admits the wager, but denies the truth of the fact; whereupon the issue is joined, which is directed to be tried out of chancery. This issue is also used in the courts of law by consent, to determine some disputed right without the formality of pleading, and to save time and expense.[1]

A frequent use is in the trial of issues *devisavit vel non*, q. v.

A feigned issue is a mode of procedure adopted from the civil law by courts of law as well as courts of equity as a means of having some question of fact arising incidentally, and to be made the foundation of an order or decree, determined by the verdict of a jury. It is called a "feigned" issue for the reason that its object is not the establishment of a legal right on which a judgment shall regularly follow, but the ascertainment by a formal issue of some issue of fact arising in another cause, and material to the decision of the latter. For convenience of trial the issue must be given the form of a common-law action, with appropriate pleadings, and an issue thereon; but, nevertheless, the nature and purpose of the issue give it character as a feigned issue or otherwise, and not the form in which the issue is expressed.[2]

Formal issue. Framed according to rule; opposed to *informal* issue.

General issue. Traverses and denies the whole declaration, without offering any special matter whereby to evade it. Leaves everything open — the fact, the law, and the equity of the case.

Special issue. Denies some one substantial point as decisive of the whole cause.[3]

Common general issues: *nil* or *nihil debet; non assumpsit; non cepit; non detinet; non est factum; not guilty; nul tiel record; nulla bona; plene administravit; rein en arreare*, qq. v.[4]

Material issue. Framed upon a matter decisive of the question in dispute. **Immaterial issue.** Framed upon a point not decisive of the right.[5]

In equity practice, a material issue is an issue upon a fact which has some bearing upon the equity sought to be established.[6]

Matter in issue. That matter upon which the plaintiff proceeds by his action,

and which the defendant controverts by his pleadings.[1]

4, *n*. **Issues:** rents and profits of realty: as, in the expression, "rents, issues, and profits."[2]

5, *n*. Heirs of the body; all ones lineal descendants indefinitely: as, in the expressions, issue of body, failure of issue, die without issue.[3]

In wills and deeds of settlement, while "issue" is construed to include grandchildren, "child" or "children" is not, unless a contrary intent is clear.[4]

"Issue" necessarily includes children; but "children" does not include more remote issue.[5]

In a will, "issue" means, *prima facie*, the same as "heirs of the body," and in general is to be construed as a word of limitation. But this construction will give way if there be on the face of the instrument sufficient to show that the word was intended to have less extended meaning, and to be applied only to children or to descendents of a particular class or at a particular time.[6]

In a devise, "issue" is a word of purchase or of limitation, as best answers the intention; in a deed, it is always a word of purchase.[7]

Issue of body. Is more flexible than "heirs of the body;" courts more readily interpret the former as synonymous with "children" and a mere description of persons.[8]

See CHILD; DESCEND; DIE, Without issue; FAILURE; HEIR; SHELLEY'S CASE; TAIL; WILL, 2.

ITA. See LEX, Ita, etc.

ITEM.[9] 1. In like manner; after the same manner; likewise; also; again.

2. A particular in an account or bill. See ACCOUNT, 1; BALANCE.

Formerly used in wills to mark a new paragraph or division after the first paragraph — which was the *imprimis*.[10] See ALSO; FIRST.

ITINERANT. See CIRCUIT.

---

[1] [3 Bl. Com. 452.

[2] American Dock, &c. Co. *v.* Trustees of Public Schools, 37 N. J. E. 269 (1883), Depue, J.

[3] See 3 Bl. Com. 305; 4 *id.* 340; 55 Vt. 97; Gould, Pl. 282-315.

[4] See 3 Bl. Com. 305; Gould, Pl. 284.

[5] [Wooden *v.* Waffle, 6 How. Pr. 151 (1851).

[1] King *v.* Chase, 15 N. H. 16 (1844), Parker, C. J.; 55 *id.* 592; 58 *id.* 117, 471; 4 F. R. 390; 18 Blatch. 457.

[2] 3 Bl. Com. 280; Perot's Appeal, 102 Pa. 256 (1883).

[3] Holland *v.* Adams, 3 Gray, 193 (1855), Shaw, C. J.; 140 Mass. 267; 60 N. H. 451.

[4] Ingraham *v.* Meade, 3 Wall. Jr. 42 (1855); Adams *v.* Law, 17 How. 421 (1854).

[5] Bigelow *v.* Morong, 103 Mass. 289 (1869).

[6] Taylor *v.* Taylor, 63 Pa. 483 (1870), Sharswood, J.; Kleppner *v.* Laverty, 70 *id.* 72 (1871); Robins *v.* Quinliven, 79 *id.* 335 (1875); Wister *v.* Scott, 105 *id.* 200, 214-16 (1884), cases; Reinoehl *v.* Shirk, *id.* (1885), cases; Palmer *v.* Horn, 84 N. Y. 519 (1881), cases; Magnum *v.* Piester, 16 S. C. 324 (1881); Atkinson *v.* M'Cormick, 76 Va. 799 (1882).

[7] 2 Washb. R. P., 4 ed., 604: 4 T. R. 299; 13 N. J. 177; 63 Pa. 483; 28 *id.* 102; 40 *id.* 65; 100 *id.* 540.

[8] Daniel *v.* Whartenby, 17 Wall. 643 (1873).

[9] L. *ita*, so; or, *is, id*, that same.

[10] See Hopewell *v.* Ackland, 1 Salk. *239 (1710).

Made in the USA
Las Vegas, NV
19 September 2024

95473763R00319